JAN 2 4 2018

Beginning Java 9 Fundamentals

Arrays, Objects, Modules, JShell, and Regular Expressions

Second Edition

Kishori Sharan

Apress®

Beginning Java 9 Fundamentals: Arrays, Objects, Modules, JShell, and Regular Expressions

Kishori Sharan
Montgomery, Alabama, USA

ISBN-13 (pbk): 978-1-4842-2843-2
https://doi.org/10.1007/978-1-4842-2902-6

ISBN-13 (electronic): 978-1-4842-2902-6

Library of Congress Control Number: 2017958824

Cover image by Freepik (www.freepik.com)

Managing Director: Welmoed Spahr
Editorial Director: Todd Green
Acquisitions Editor: Steve Anglin
Development Editor: Matthew Moodie
Technical Reviewer: Wallace Jackson
Coordinating Editor: Mark Powers
Copy Editor: Kezia Endsley

Distributed to the book trade worldwide by Springer Science+Business Media New York, 233 Spring Street, 6th Floor, New York, NY 10013. Phone 1-800-SPRINGER, fax (201) 348-4505, e-mail orders-ny@springer-sbm.com, or visit www.springeronline.com. Apress Media, LLC is a California LLC and the sole member (owner) is Springer Science + Business Media Finance Inc (SSBM Finance Inc). SSBM Finance Inc is a **Delaware** corporation.

For information on translations, please e-mail rights@apress.com, or visit http://www.apress.com/rights-permissions.

Apress titles may be purchased in bulk for academic, corporate, or promotional use. eBook versions and licenses are also available for most titles. For more information, reference our Print and eBook Bulk Sales web page at http://www.apress.com/bulk-sales.

Any source code or other supplementary material referenced by the author in this book is available to readers on GitHub via the book's product page, located at www.apress.com/9781484228432. For more detailed information, please visit http://www.apress.com/source-code.

Printed on acid-free paper

Contents at a Glance

Contents

About the Author

Kishori Sharan works as a senior software engineer lead at IndraSoft, Inc. He earned a master's of science degree in computer information systems from Troy State University, Alabama. He is a Sun-certified Java 2 programmer and has over 20 years of experience in developing enterprise applications and providing training to professional developers using the Java platform.

About the Technical Reviewer

Wallace Jackson has been writing for leading multimedia publications about his work in new media content development since the advent of *Multimedia Producer Magazine* nearly two decades ago. He has authored a half-dozen Android book titles for Apress, including four titles in the popular Pro Android series. Wallace received his undergraduate degree in business economics from the University of California at Los Angeles and a graduate degree in MIS design and implementation from the University of Southern California. He is currently the CEO of Mind Taffy Design, a new media content production and digital campaign design and development agency.

Acknowledgments

I would like to thank my family members and friends for their encouragement and support: my mom Pratima Devi; my elder brothers, Janki Sharan and Dr. Sita Sharan; my nephews, Gaurav and Saurav; my sister Ratna; my friends Karthikeya Venkatesan, Rahul Nagpal, Ravi Datla, Mahbub Choudhury, Richard Castillo; and many more friends not mentioned here.

My wife, Ellen, was always patient when I spent long hours at my computer desk working on this book. I want to thank her for all of her support in writing this book.

My special thanks to my friend Preethi Vasudev for offering her valuable time for providing solutions to the exercises in this book. She likes programming challenges—particularly Google Code Jam. I bet she enjoyed solving the exercises in each chapter of this book.

My sincere thanks are due to the wonderful team at Apress for their support during the publication of this book. Thanks to Mark Powers, the Editorial Operations Manager, for providing excellent support. Last but not least, my sincere thanks to Steve Anglin, the Lead Editor at Apress, for taking the initiative for the publication of this book.

Introduction

How This Book Came About

My first encounter with the Java programming language was during a one-week Java training session in 1997. I did not get a chance to use Java in a project until 1999. I read two Java books and took a Java 2 Programmer certification examination. I did very well on the test, scoring 95 percent. The three questions that I missed on the test made me realize that the books that I had read did not adequately cover details of all the topics necessary about Java. I made up my mind to write a book on the Java programming language. So, I formulated a plan to cover most of the topics that a Java developer needs to use the Java programming language effectively in a project, as well as to get a certification. I initially planned to cover all essential topics in Java in 700 to 800 pages.

As I progressed, I realized that a book covering most of the Java topics in detail could not be written in 700 to 800 pages. One chapter alone that covered data types, operators, and statements spanned 90 pages. I was then faced with the question, "Should I shorten the content of the book or include all the details that I think a Java developer needs?" I opted for including all the details in the book, rather than shortening its content to keep the number of pages low. It has never been my intent to make lots of money from this book. I was never in a hurry to finish this book because that rush could have compromised the quality and the coverage of its contents. In short, I wrote this book to help the Java community understand and use the Java programming language effectively, without having to read many books on the same subject. I wrote this book with the plan that it would be a comprehensive one-stop reference for everyone who wants to learn and grasp the intricacies of the Java programming language.

One of my high school teachers used to tell us that if one wanted to understand a building, one must first understand the bricks, steel, and mortar that make up the building. The same logic applies to most of the things that we want to understand in our lives. It certainly applies to an understanding of the Java programming language. If you want to master the Java programming language, you must start by understanding its basic building blocks. I have used this approach throughout this book, endeavoring to build each topic by describing the basics first. In the book, you will rarely find a topic described without first learning its background. Wherever possible, I have tried to correlate the programming practices with activities in our daily life. Most of the books about the Java programming language available in the market either do not include any pictures at all or have only a few. I believe in the adage, "A picture is worth a thousand words." To a reader, a picture makes a topic easier to understand and remember. I have included plenty of illustrations in the book to aid readers in understanding and visualizing the contents. Developers who have little or no programming experience have difficulty in putting things together to make it a complete program. Keeping them in mind, the book contains over 290 complete Java programs that are ready to be compiled and run.

I spent countless hours doing research for writing this book. My main source of research was the Java Language Specification, whitepapers, and articles on Java topics, and Java Specification Requests (JSRs). I also spent quite a bit of time reading the Java source code to learn more about some of the Java topics. Sometimes, it took a few months researching a topic before I could write the first sentence on the topic. Finally, it was always fun to play with Java programs, sometimes for hours, to add them to the book.

Introduction to the Second Edition

I am pleased to present the second edition of the *Beginning Java 9 Fundamentals* book. It is the first book in the three-volume "Beginning Java 9" series. It was not possible to include all JDK 9 changes in this volume. I have included JDK9-specific changes at appropriate places in three volumes. If you are interested in learning only JDK9-specific topics, I suggest you read my *Java 9 Revealed* book (ISBN: 978-1484225912), which contains only JDK9-specific topics. There are several changes in this edition and they are as follows.

I have added a separate chapter (Chapter 2) on setting up your environment, such as downloading and installing JDK and verifying the JDK version, etc.

The most notable change is the introduction to the Module System, which is a new topic in JDK 9. Chapter 3 provides a comprehensive introduction to the Module System. I provide a step-by-step process on how to write, compile, package, and run your first Java program using a command prompt and the NetBeans Integrated Development Environment (NetBeans IDE). Chapter 10 contains an in-depth coverage of the Module System. The second volume in this series delves deeper into the Module System to cover the Module API, Module Layers, etc.

JDK 9 ships with a very valuable and exciting tool call the JShell tool (short for Java Shell). It lets you explore the Java programming language interactively by entering chunks for code, rather than writing a full-fledged program. I strongly encourage you to use this tool to play with snippets of Java code when you are writing a Java program. I introduced this tool in Chapter 2 and I have covered it extensively in Chapter 23. The reason I did not cover it in one of the first few chapters of the book is because, as a beginner, you need to know the basics of Java programming first.

The first edition contained a chapter entitled "Classes and Objects", which was over 120 pages long. This edition has divided this chapter into three chapters titled "Classes," "Methods," and "Constructors" (Chapters 7-9).

I have added a new section in Chapter 19 that deals with performing operations on arrays. They include how to sort, search, compare, etc., arrays. This section contains all new API changes in JDK 9 dealing with arrays.

The previous edition of this book had three appendixes. This edition retains the first two appendixes. I have updated Appendix B to cover new Javadoc features in JDK 9. In the previous edition, Appendix C covered compact profiles, which were introduced in JDK 8. Now you can create a custom runtime image in JDK 9, which makes compact profiles kind of redundant. This made me drop Appendix C in this edition. I cover creating custom runtime uimages in JDK 9 in the third volume of this series.

I received several emails from the readers about the fact that the books in this series do not include questions and exercises, which are needed mainly for students and beginners. Students use this book in their Java classes as a Java text book and many beginners use it to learn Java. Based on this popular demand, I spent over 60 hours preparing questions and exercises at the end of each chapter of this book. I still needed a lot more hours to provide the solutions to these exercises. My friend Preethi offered her help and provided the solutions.

Apart from these changes, I have updated all chapters, which were part of the first edition. I have edited the contents to make them flow better, changed or added new examples, and updated the contents to include JDK9-specific features.

It is my sincere hope that this edition of the book will help you learn Java better.

Structure of the Book

This book contains 23 chapters and two appendixes. The chapters contain fundamental topics of Java such as syntax, data types, operators, classes, objects, etc. The chapters are arranged in an order that aids learning the Java programming language faster. The first chapter, "Programming Concepts," explains basic concepts related to programming in general, without going into too many technical details; it introduces Java and its features.

The third chapter, "Writing Java Programs," introduces the first program using Java; this chapter is especially written for those learning Java for the first time. Subsequent chapters introduce Java topics in an increasing order of complexity. The new features of Java 9 are included wherever they fit in the chapter.

After finishing this book, to take your Java knowledge to the next level, two companion books are available by the author: *Beginning Java 9 Language Features* and *Beginning Java 9 APIs, Extensions, and Libraries*.

At the end of each chapter, you can find questions and exercises that challenge you with the knowledge you gain in the chapter. Questions and exercises are geared toward students taking Java classes and beginners. Answers to all questions and solution to all exercises are available at www.apress.com.

Audience

This book is designed to be useful to anyone who wants to learn the Java programming language. If you are a beginner, with little or no programming background, you need to read the first chapter to the last, in order. The book contains topics of various degrees of complexity. As a beginner, if you find yourself overwhelmed while reading a section in a chapter, you can skip to the next section or the next chapter and revisit it later when you gain more experience.

If you are a Java developer with an intermediate or advanced level of experience, you can jump to a chapter or to a section in a chapter directly. If a section uses an unfamiliar topic, you need to visit that topic before continuing the current one.

If you are reading this book to get a certification in the Java programming language, you need to read almost all of the chapters, paying attention to all the detailed descriptions and rules. Most of the certification programs test your fundamental knowledge of the language, not the advanced knowledge. You need to read only those topics that are part of your certification test. Compiling and running over 290 complete Java programs will help you prepare for your certification.

If you are a student who is attending a class in the Java programming language, you need to read the first 10 chapters of this book thoroughly. These chapters cover the basics of the Java programming languages in detail. You cannot do well in a Java class unless you first master the basics. After covering the basics, you need to read only those chapters that are covered in your class syllabus. I am sure, you, as a Java student, do not need to read the entire book page-by-page.

How to Use This Book

This book is the beginning, not the end, for you to gain the knowledge of the Java programming language. If you are reading this book, it means you are heading in the right direction to learn the Java programming language that will enable you to excel in your academic and professional career. However, there is always a higher goal for you to achieve and you must constantly work harder to achieve it. The following quotations from some great thinkers may help you understand the importance of working hard and constantly looking for knowledge with both your eyes and mind open.

> *The learning and knowledge that we have, is, at the most, but little compared with that of which we are ignorant.*

—Plato

> *True knowledge exists in knowing that you know nothing. And in knowing that you know nothing, that makes you the smartest of all.*

—Socrates

Readers are advised to use the API documentation for the Java programming language, as much as possible, while using this book. The Java API documentation is the place where you will find a complete list of documentation for everything available in the Java class library. You can download (or view) the Java API documentation from the official web site of Oracle Corporation at www.oracle.com. While you read this book, you need to practice writing Java programs yourself. You can also practice by tweaking the programs provided in the book. It does not help much in your learning process if you just read this book and do not practice by writing your own programs. Remember that "practice makes perfect," which is also true in learning how to program in Java.

Source Code

Source code for this book can be accessed by clicking the Download Source Code button located at www.apress.com/9781484228432.

Questions and Comments

Please direct all your questions and comments for the author to ksharan@jdojo.com.

CHAPTER 1

■ ■ ■

Programming Concepts

In this chapter, you will learn:

- The general concept of programming

- Different components of programming

- Major programming paradigms

- What the object-oriented paradigm is and how it is used in Java

What Is Programming?

The term "programming" is used in many contexts. We discuss its meaning in the context of human-to-computer interaction. In the simplest terms, programming is the way of writing a sequence of instructions to tell a computer to perform a specific task. The sequence of instructions for a computer is known as a *program*. A set of well-defined notations is used to write a program. The set of notations used to write a program is called a *programming language*. The person who writes a program is called a *programmer*. A programmer uses a programming language to write a program.

How does a person tell a computer to perform a task? Can a person tell a computer to perform any task or does a computer have a predefined set of tasks that it can perform? Before we look at human-to-computer communication, let's look at human-to-human communication. How does a human communicate with another human? You would say that human-to-human communication is accomplished using a spoken language, for example, English, German, Hindi, etc. However, spoken language is not the only means of communication between humans. We also communicate using written languages or using gestures without uttering any words. Some people can even communicate sitting miles away from each other without using any words or gestures; they can communicate at the thought level.

To have a successful communication, it is not enough just to use a medium of communication like a spoken or written language. The main requirement for a successful communication between two parties is the ability of both parties to understand what is communicated from the other party. For example, suppose there are two people. One person knows how to speak English and the other one knows how to speak German. Can they communicate with each other? The answer is no, because they cannot understand each other's language. What happens if we add an English-German translator between them? We would agree that they would be able to communicate with the help of a translator even though they do not understand each other directly?

Computers understand instructions only in binary format, which is a sequence of 0s and 1s. The sequence of 0s and 1s, which all computers understand, is called machine language or machine code. A computer has a fixed set of basic instructions that it understands. Each computer has its own set of instructions. For example, one computer may use 0010 as an instruction to add two numbers, whereas another computer may use 0101 for the same purpose. Therefore, programs written in machine language

© Kishori Sharan 2017
K. Sharan, *Beginning Java 9 Fundamentals*, https://doi.org/10.1007/978-1-4842-2902-6_1

are machine-dependent. Sometimes machine code is referred to as native code as it is native to the machine for which it is written. Programs written in machine language are very difficult, if not impossible, to write, read, understand, and modify. Suppose you want to write a program that adds two numbers, 15 and 12. The program to add two numbers in machine language will look similar to the one shown here. You do not need to understand the sample code written in this section. It is only for the purpose of discussion and illustration.

```
0010010010    10010100000100110
0001000100    01010010001001010
```

These instructions are to add two numbers. How difficult will it be to write a program in machine language to perform a complex task? Based on this code, you may now realize that it is very difficult to write, read, and understand a program written in a machine language. But aren't computers supposed to make our jobs easier, not more difficult? We needed to represent the instructions for computers in some notations that were easier to write, read, and understand, so computer scientists came up with another language called an assembly language. An assembly language provides different notations to write instructions. It is little easier to write, read, and understand than its predecessor, machine language. An assembly language uses mnemonics to represent instructions as opposed to the binary (0s and 1s) used in machine language. A program written in an assembly language to add two numbers looks similar to the following:

```
li $t1, 15
add $t0, $t1, 12
```

If you compare the two programs written in the two different languages to perform the same task, you can see that assembly language is easier to write, read, and understand than machine code. There is one-to-one correspondence between an instruction in machine language and assembly language for a given computer architecture. Recall that a computer understands instructions only in machine language. The instructions that are written in an assembly language must be translated into machine language before the computer can execute them. A program that translates the instructions written in an assembly language into machine language is called an *assembler*. Figure 1-1 shows the relationship between assembly code, an assembler, and machine code.

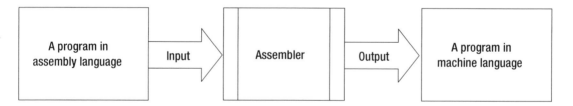

Figure 1-1. *The relationship between assembly code, assembler, and machine code*

Machine and assembly languages are also known as low-level languages because a programmer must understand the low-level details of the computer to write a program using these languages. For example, if you were writing programs in these languages, you would need to know what memory location you are writing to or reading from, which register to use to store a specific value, etc. Soon programmers realized a need for a higher-level programming language that could hide the low-level details of computers from them. The need gave rise to the development of high-level programming languages like COBOL, Pascal, FORTRAN, C, C++, Java, C#, etc. The high-level programming languages use English-like words, mathematical notation, and punctuation to write programs. A program written in a high-level programming language is also called *source code.* They are closer to the written languages that humans are familiar with. The instructions to add two numbers can be written in a high-level programming language, for example, Java looks similar to the following:

```
int x = 15 + 12;
```

You may notice that the programs written in a high-level language are easier and more intuitive to write, read, understand, and modify than the programs written in machine and assembly languages. You might have realized that computers do not understand programs written in high-level languages, as they understand only sequences of 0s and 1s. So there's a need for a way to translate a program written in a high-level language to machine language. The translation is accomplished by a compiler, an interpreter, or a combination of both. A compiler is a program that translates programs written in a high-level programming language into machine language. Compiling a program is an overloaded phrase. Typically, it means translating a program written in a high-level language into machine language. Sometimes it is used to mean translating a program written in a high-level programming language into a lower-level programming language, which is not necessarily the machine language. The code that is generated by a compiler is called *compiled code.* The compiled program is executed by the computer.

Another way to execute a program written in high-level programming language is to use an interpreter. An interpreter does not translate the whole program into machine language at once. Rather, it reads one instruction written in a high-level programming language at a time, translates it into machine language, and executes it. You can view an interpreter as a simulator. Sometimes a combination of a compiler and an interpreter may be used to compile and run a program written in a high-level language. For example, a program written in Java is compiled into an intermediate language called bytecode. An interpreter, specifically called a Java Virtual Machine (JVM) for the Java platform, is used to interpret the bytecode and execute it. An interpreted program runs slower than a compiled program. Most of the JVMs today use just-in-time compilers (JIT), which compile the entire Java program into machine language as needed. Sometimes another kind of compiler, which is called an ahead-of-time (AOT) compiler, is used to compile a program in an intermediate language (e.g., Java bytecode) to machine language. Figure 1-2 shows the relationship between the source code, a compiler, and the machine code.

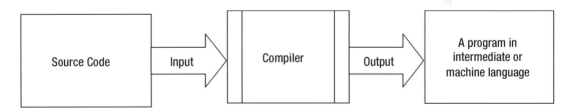

Figure 1-2. *The relationship between source code, a compiler, and machine code*

Programming languages are also categorized as first, second, third, and fourth generation languages. The higher the generation of the language, the closer it gets to the plain spoken human language to write programs in that language. The machine language is also known as first generation programming language or 1GL. The assembly language is also known as second generation programming language or 2GL. High-level procedural programming languages such as C, C++, Java, and C#, in which you have to write the algorithm to solve the problem using the language syntax, are also known as third generation programming languages or 3GL. High-level non-procedural programming languages, in which you do not need to write the algorithm to solve a program, are known as fourth generation programming languages or 4GL. Structured Query Language (SQL) is the most widely used 4GL programming language, which is used to communicate with databases.

Components of a Programming Language

A programming language is a system of notations used to write instructions for computers. It can be described using three components:

- Syntax

- Semantics

- Pragmatics

The syntax part deals with forming valid programming constructs using available notations. The semantics part deals with the meaning of the programming constructs. The pragmatics part deals with the use of the programming language in practice.

Like a written language (e.g., English), a programming language has vocabulary and grammar. The vocabulary of a programming language consists of a set of words, symbols, and punctuation marks. The grammar of a programming language defines rules on how to use the vocabulary of the language to form valid programming constructs. You can think of a valid programming construct in a programming language like a sentence in a written language, which is formed using the vocabulary and grammar of the language. Similarly, a programming construct is formed using the vocabulary and the grammar of the programming language. The vocabulary and the rules to use that vocabulary to form valid programming constructs are known as the *syntax* of the programming language.

In a written language, you may form a grammatically correct sentence, which may not have any valid meaning. For example, "The stone is laughing." is a grammatically correct sentence. However, it does not make any sense. In a written language, this kind of ambiguity is allowed. A programming language is meant to communicate instructions to computers, which have no room for any ambiguity. We cannot communicate with computers using ambiguous instructions. There is another component of a programming language, which is called *semantics*, which explain the meaning of the syntactically valid programming constructs. The semantics of a programming language answer the question, "What does this program do when it is run on a computer?" Note that a syntactically valid programming construct may not also be semantically valid. A program must be syntactically and semantically correct before it can be executed by a computer.

The pragmatics of a programming language describe its uses and its effects on the users. A program written in a programming language may be syntactically and semantically correct. However, it may not be easily understood by other programmers. This aspect is related to the pragmatics of the programming language. The pragmatics are concerned with the practical aspect of a programming language. It answers questions about a programming language like its ease of implementation, suitability for a particular application, efficiency, portability, support for programming methodologies, etc.

Programming Paradigms

The online Merriam-Webster's Learner's dictionary defines the word "paradigm" as follows:

> *"A paradigm is a theory or a group of ideas about how something should be done, made, or thought about."*

In the beginning, it is a little hard to understand the word "paradigm" in a programming context. Programming is about providing a solution to a real-world problem using computational models supported by the programming language. The solution is called a program. Before we provide a solution to a problem in the form of a program, we always have a mental view of the problem and its solution. Before I discuss how to solve a real-world problem using a computational model, let's take an example of a real-world social problem, one that has nothing to do with computers.

Suppose there is a place on Earth that has a shortage of food. People in that place do not have enough food to eat. The problem is "shortage of food." Let's ask three people to provide a solution to this problem. The three people are a politician, a philanthropist, and a monk. A politician will have a political view about the problem and its solution. He may think about it as an opportunity to serve his countrymen by enacting some laws to provide food to the hungry people. A philanthropist will offer some money/food to help those hungry people because he feels compassion for all humans and so for those hungry people. A monk will try to solve this problem using his spiritual views. He may preach to them to work and make livings for themselves; he may appeal to rich people to donate food to the hungry; or he may teach them yoga to conquer their hunger! Did you see how three people have different views about the same reality, which is "shortage of food"? The ways they look at the reality are their paradigms. You can think of a paradigm as a mindset with which a reality is viewed in a particular context. It is usual to have multiple paradigms, which let one view the same reality differently. For example, a person who is a philanthropist and politician will have his ability to view the "shortage of food" problem and its solution differently, once with his political mindset and once with his philanthropist mindset. Three people were given the same problem. All of them provided a solution to the problem. However, their perceptions about the problem and its solution were not the same. We can define the term paradigm as a set of concepts and ideas that constitutes a way of viewing a reality.

Why do we need to bother about a paradigm anyway? Does it matter if a person used his political, philanthropical, or spiritual paradigm to arrive at the solution? Eventually we get a solution to our problem. Don't we?

It is not enough just to have a solution to a problem. The solution must be practical and effective. Since the solution to a problem is always related to the way the problem and the solution are thought about, the paradigm becomes paramount. You can see that the solution provided by the monk may kill the hungry people before they can get any help. The philanthropist's solution may be a good short-term solution. The politician's solution seems to be a long-term solution and the best one. It is always important to use the right paradigm to solve a problem to arrive at a practical and the most effective solution. Note that one paradigm cannot be the right paradigm to solve every kind of problem. For example, if a person is seeking eternal happiness, he needs to consult a monk, not a politician or a philanthropist.

Here is a definition of the term "programming paradigm" by Robert W. Floyd, who was a prominent computer scientist. He gave this definition in his 1978 ACM Turing Award lecture titled "The Paradigms of Programming."

"A programming paradigm is a way of conceptualizing what it means to perform computation, and how tasks that are to be carried out on a computer should be structured and organized."

You can observe that the word "paradigm" in a programming context has a similar meaning to that used in the context of daily life. Programming is used to solve a real-world problem using computational models provided by a computer. The programming paradigm is the way you think and conceptualize about the real-world problem and its solution in the underlying computational models. The programming paradigm comes into the picture well before you start writing a program using a programming language. It is in the analysis phase when you use a particular paradigm to analyze a problem and its solution in a particular way. A programming language provides a means to implement a particular programming paradigm suitably. A programming language may provide features that make it suitable for programming using one programming paradigm and not the other.

A program has two components—data and algorithm. Data is used to represent pieces of information. An algorithm is a set of steps that operates on data to arrive at a solution to a problem. Different programming paradigms involve viewing the solution to a problem by combining data and algorithms in different ways. Many paradigms are used in programming. The following are some commonly used programming paradigms:

- Imperative paradigm

- Procedural paradigm

- Declarative paradigm

- Functional paradigm

- Logic paradigm

- Object-oriented paradigm

Imperative Paradigm

The imperative paradigm is also known as an algorithmic paradigm. In the imperative paradigm, a program consists of data and an algorithm (sequence of commands) that manipulates the data. The data at a particular point in time defines the state of the program. The state of the program changes as the commands are executed in a specific sequence. The data is stored in memory. Imperative programming languages provide variables to refer to the memory locations, an assignment operation to change the value of a variable, and other constructs to control the flow of a program. In imperative programming, you need to specify the steps to solve a problem.

Suppose you have an integer, say 15, and you want to add 10 to it. Your approach would be to add 1 to 15 10 times and you get the result, 25. You can write a program using an imperative language to add 10 to 15, as follows. Note that you do not need to understand the syntax of the following code; just try to get the feeling of it.

```
int num = 15;          // num holds 15 at this point
int counter = 0;       // counter holds 0 at this point

while (counter < 10) {
    num = num + 1;          // Modifying data in num
    counter = counter + 1; // Modifying data in counter
}

// num holds 25 at this point
```

The first two lines are variable declarations that represent the data part of the program. The while loop represents the algorithm part of the program that operates on the data. The code inside the while loop is executed 10 times. The loop increments the data stored in the num variable by 1 in its each iteration. When the loop ends, it has incremented the value of num by 10. Note that data in imperative programming is transient and the algorithm is permanent. FORTRAN, COBOL, and C are a few examples of programming languages that support the imperative paradigm.

Procedural Paradigm

The procedural paradigm is similar to the imperative paradigm with one difference: it combines multiple commands in a unit called a *procedure*. A procedure is executed as a unit. Executing the commands contained in a procedure is known as calling or invoking the procedure. A program in a procedural language consists of data and a sequence of procedure calls that manipulate the data. The following piece of code is typical for a procedure named addTen:

```
void addTen(int num) {
    int counter = 0;

    while (counter < 10) {
        num = num + 1;           // Modifying data in num
        counter = counter + 1;   // Modifying data in counter
    }

    // num has been incremented by 10
}
```

The addTen procedure uses a placeholder (also known as parameter) num, which is supplied at the time of its execution. The code ignores the actual value of num. It simply adds 10 to the current value of num. Let's use the following piece of code to add 10 to 15. Note that the code for addTen procedure and the following code are not written using any specific programming language. They are provided here only for the purpose of illustration.

```
int x = 15; // x holds 15 at this point
addTen(x);  // Call addTen procedure that will increment x by 10

// x holds 25 at this point
```

You may observe that the code in imperative paradigm and procedural paradigm are similar in structure. Using procedures results in modular code and increases reusability of algorithms. Some people ignore this difference and treat the two paradigms, imperative and procedural, as the same. Note that even if they are different, a procedural paradigm always involves the imperative paradigm. In the procedural paradigm, the unit of programming is not a sequence of commands. Rather, you abstract a sequence of commands into a procedure and your program consists of a sequence of procedures instead. A procedure has side effects. It modifies the data part of the program as it executes its logic. C, C++, Java, and COBOL are a few examples of programming languages that support the procedural paradigm.

Declarative Paradigm

In the declarative paradigm, a program consists of the description of a problem and the computer finds the solution. The program does not specify how to arrive at the solution to the problem. It is the computer's job to arrive at a solution when a problem is described to it. Contrast the declarative paradigm with the imperative paradigm. In the imperative paradigm, we are concerned about the "how" part of the problem. In the declarative paradigm, we are concerned about the "what" part of the problem. We are concerned about what the problem is, rather than how to solve it. The functional paradigm and the logic paradigm, which are described next, are subtypes of the declarative paradigm.

Writing a database query using a structured query language (SQL) falls under programming based on the declarative paradigm, where you specify what data you want and the database engine figures out how to retrieve the data for you. Unlike the imperative paradigm, the data is permanent and the algorithm is transient in the declarative paradigm. In the imperative paradigm, the data is modified as the algorithm is executed. In the declarative paradigm, data is supplied to the algorithm as input and the input data remains unchanged as the algorithm is executed. The algorithm produces new data rather than modifying the input data. In other words, in the declarative paradigm, execution of an algorithm does not produce side effects.

Functional Paradigm

The functional paradigm is based on the concept of mathematical functions. You can think of a function as an algorithm that computes a value from some given inputs. Unlike a procedure in procedural programming, a function does not have a side effect. In functional programming, values are immutable. A new value is derived by applying a function to the input value. The input value does not change. Functional programming languages do not use variables and assignments, which are used for modifying data. In imperative programming, a repeated task is performed using a loop construct, for example, a while loop. In functional programming, a repeated task is performed using recursion, which is a way in which a function is defined in terms of itself. In other words, a recursive function does some work, then calls itself.

A function always produces the same output when it is applied to the same input. A function, say add, that can be applied to an integer x to add an integer n to it may be defined as follows:

```
int add(x, n) {
    if (n == 0) {
        return x;
    } else {
        return 1 + add(x, n-1); // Apply the add function recursively
    }
}
```

Note that the add function does not use any variable and does not modify any data. It uses recursion. You can call the add function to add 10 to 15, as follows:

```
add(15, 10); // Results in 25
```

Haskell, Erlang, and Scala are a few examples of programming languages that support the functional paradigm.

▓ **Tip**   Java SE 8 added a new language construct called *lambda expressions*, which can be used to write functional programming style code in Java.

Logic Paradigm

Unlike the imperative paradigm, the logic paradigm focuses on the "what" part of the problem rather than how to solve it. All you need to specify is what needs to be solved. The program will figure out the algorithm to solve it. The algorithm is of less importance to the programmer. The primary task of the programmer is to describe the problem as closely as possible. In the logic paradigm, a program consists of a set of axioms and a goal statement. The set of axioms is the collection of facts and inference rules that make up a theory. The goal statement is a theorem. The program uses deductions to prove the theorem within the theory. Logic programming uses a mathematical concept called a relation from set theory. A relation in set theory is defined as a subset of the Cartesian product of two or more sets. Suppose there are two sets, Persons and Nationality, defined as follows:

```
Person = {John, Li, Ravi}
Nationality = {American, Chinese, Indian}
```

The Cartesian product of the two sets, denoted as `Person x Nationality`, would be another set, as shown:

```
Person x Nationality = {{John, American}, {John, Chinese}, {John, Indian},
                        {Li, American}, {Li, Chinese}, {Li, Indian},
                        {Ravi, American}, {Ravi, Chinese}, {Ravi, Indian}}
```

Every subset of `Person x Nationality` is another set that defines a mathematical relation. Each element of a relation is called a *tuple*. Let `PersonNationality` be a relation defined as follows:

```
PersonNationality = {{John, American}, {Li, Chinese}, {Ravi, Indian}}
```

In logic programming, you can use the `PersonNationality` relation as the collection of facts that is known to be true. You can state the goal statement (or the problem) like so

```
PersonNationality(?, Chinese)
```

which means "give me all names of people who are Chinese." The program will search through the `PersonNationality` relation and extract the matching tuples, which will be the answer (or the solution) to your problem. In this case, the answer will be `Li`.

Prolog is an example of a programming language that supports the logic paradigm.

Object-Oriented Paradigm

In the object-oriented (OO) paradigm, a program consists of interacting objects. An object encapsulates data and algorithms. Data defines the state of an object. Algorithms define the behavior of an object. An object communicates with other objects by sending messages to them. When an object receives a message, it responds by executing one of its algorithms, which may modify its state. Contrast the object-oriented paradigm with the imperative and functional paradigms. In the imperative and functional paradigms, data and algorithms are separated, whereas in the object-oriented paradigm, data and algorithms are not separate; they are combined in one entity, which is called an object.

Classes are the basic units of programming in the object-oriented paradigm. Similar objects are grouped into one definition called a class. A class' definition is used to create an object. An object is also known as an instance of the class. A class consists of instance variables and methods. The values of instance variables of an object define the state of the object. Different objects of a class maintain their states separately. That is, each object of a class has its own copy of the instance variables. The state of an object is kept private to that object. That is, the state of an object cannot be accessed or modified directly from outside the object. Methods in a class define the behavior of its objects. A method is like a procedure (or subroutine) in the procedural paradigm. Methods can access/modify the state of the object. A message is sent to an object by invoking one of its methods.

Suppose you want to represent real-world people in your program. You will create a `Person` class and its instances will represent people in your program. The `Person` class can be defined as shown in Listing 1-1. This example uses the syntax of the Java programming language. You do not need to understand the syntax used in the programs that you are writing at this point; I discuss the syntax to define classes and create objects in subsequent chapters.

Listing 1-1. The Definition of a Person Class Whose Instances Represent Real-World Persons in a Program

```
package com.jdojo.concepts;

public class Person {
    private String name;
    private String gender;

    public Person(String initialName, String initialGender) {
        name = initialName;
        gender = initialGender;
    }

    public String getName() {
        return name;
    }

    public void setName(String newName) {
        name = newName;
    }

    public String getGender() {
        return gender;
    }
}
```

The Person class includes three things:

- Two instance variables: name and gender

- One constructor: Person(String initialName, String initialGender)

- Three methods: getName(), setName(String newName), and getGender()

Instance variables store internal data for an object. The value of each instance variable represents the value of a corresponding property of the object. Each instance of the Person class will have a copy of name and gender data. The values of all properties of an object at a point in time (stored in instance variables) collectively define the state of the object at that time. In the real world, a person possesses many properties, for example, name, gender, height, weight, hair color, addresses, phone numbers, etc. However, when you model the real-world person as a class, you include only those properties of the person that are relevant to the system being modeled. For this current demonstration, let's model only two properties—name and gender—of a real-world person as two instance variables in the Person class.

A class contains the definition (or blueprint) of objects. There needs to be a way to construct (to create or to instantiate) objects of a class. An object also needs to have the initial values for its properties that will determine its initial state at the time of its creation. A constructor of a class is used to create an object of that class. A class can have many constructors to facilitate the creation of its objects with different initial states. The Person class provides one constructor, which lets you create its object by specifying the initial values for name and gender. The following snippet of code creates two objects of the Person class:

```
Person john = new Person("John Jacobs", "Male");
Person donna = new Person("Donna Duncan", "Female");
```

The first object is called john with "John Jacobs" and "Male" as the initial values for its name and gender properties, respectively. The second object is called donna with "Donna Duncan" and "Female" as the initial values for its name and gender properties, respectively.

Methods of a class represent behaviors of its objects. For example, in the real world, a person has a name and his ability to respond when he is asked for his name is one of his behaviors. Objects of the Person class have abilities to respond to three different messages: getName, setName, and getGender. The ability of an object to respond to a message is implemented using methods. You can send a message, say getName, to a Person object and it will respond by returning its name. It is the same as asking "What is your name?" and having the person respond by telling you his name.

```
String johnName = john.getName();   // Send getName message to john
String donnaName = donna.getName(); // Send getName message to donna
```

The setName message to the Person object asks him to change his current name to a new name. The following snippet of code changes the name of the donna object from "Donna Duncan" to "Donna Jacobs":

```
donna.setName("Donna Jacobs");
```

If you send the getName message to donna object at this point, it will return "Donna Jacobs", not "Donna Duncan".

You may notice that your Person objects do not have the ability to respond to a message, such as setGender. The gender of Person object is set when the object is created and it cannot be changed afterwards. However, you can query the gender of a Person object by sending the getGender message to it. What messages an object may (or may not) respond to is decided at design-time based on the need of the system being modeled. In the case of the Person objects, we decided that they would not have the ability to respond to the setGender message by not including a setGender(String newGender) method in the Person class. Figure 1-3 shows the state and interface of the Person object called john.

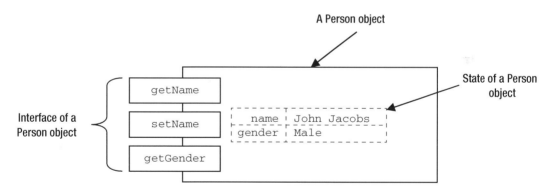

Figure 1-3. *The state and the interface for a Person object*

The object-oriented paradigm is a very powerful paradigm for modeling real-world phenomena in a computational model. We are used to working with objects all around us in our daily life. The object-oriented paradigm is natural and intuitive, as it lets you think in terms of objects. However, it does not give you the ability to think in terms of objects correctly. Sometimes, the solution to a problem does not fall into the domain of an object-oriented paradigm. In such cases, you need to use the paradigm that suits the problem domain the most. The object-oriented paradigm has a learning curve. It is much more than just creating and using objects in your program. Abstraction, encapsulation, polymorphism, and inheritance are some of the important features of the object-oriented paradigm. You must understand and be able to use these features to take full advantage of the object-oriented paradigm. I discuss these features in the sections to follow. In subsequent chapters, I discuss these features and how to implement them in programs in detail.

To name a few, C++, Java and C# (pronounced "C sharp") are programming languages that support the object-oriented paradigm. Note that a programming language itself is not object-oriented. It is the paradigm that is object-oriented. A programming language may or may not have features to support the object-oriented paradigm.

What Is Java?

Java is a general purpose programming language. It has features to support programming based on the object-oriented, procedural, and functional paradigms. You often read a phrase like "Java is an object-oriented programming language." What is meant is that the Java language has features that support the object-oriented paradigm. A programming language is not object-oriented. It is the paradigm that is object-oriented, and a programming language may have features that make it easy to implement the object-oriented paradigm. Sometimes, programmers have misconceptions that all programs written in Java are always object-oriented. Java also has features that support the procedural and functional paradigms. You can write a program in Java that is a 100% procedural program without an iota of object-orientedness in it.

The initial version of the Java platform was released by Sun Microsystems (part of Oracle Corporation since January 2010) in 1995. Development of the Java programming language was started in 1991. Initially, the language was called Oak and it was meant to be used in set-top boxes for televisions.

Soon after its release, Java became a very popular programming language. One of the most important features for its popularity was its "write once, run anywhere" (WORA) feature. This feature lets you write a Java program once and run it on any platform. For example, you can write and compile a Java program on UNIX and run it on Microsoft Windows, Macintosh, or UNIX machine without any modifications to the source code. WORA is achieved by compiling a Java program into an intermediate language called bytecode. The format of bytecode is platform-independent. A virtual machine, called the Java Virtual Machine (JVM), is used to run the bytecode on each platform. Note that JVM is a program implemented in software. It is not a physical machine and this is the reason it is called a "virtual" machine. The job of a JVM is to transform the bytecode into executable code according to the platform it is running on. This feature makes Java programs platform-independent. That is, the same Java program can be run on multiple platforms without any modifications.

The following are a few characteristics behind Java's popularity and acceptance in the software industry:

- Simplicity

- Wide variety of usage environments

- Robustness

Simplicity may be a subjective word in this context. C++ was the popular and powerful programming language widely used in the software industry at the time Java was released. If you were a C++ programmer, Java would provide simplicity for you in its learning and use over the C++ experience you had. Java retained most of the syntax of C/C++, which was helpful for C/C++ programmers trying to learn this new language. Even better, it excluded some of the most confusing and hard-to-use-correctly features (though powerful) of C++. For example, Java does not have pointers and multiple inheritance, which are present in C++.

If you are learning Java as your first programming language, whether it is a simple language to learn may not be true for you. This is the reason why I said that the simplicity of Java or any programming language is very subjective. The Java language and its libraries (a set of packages containing Java classes) have been growing ever since its first release. You will need to put in some serious effort in order to become a serious Java developer.

Java can be used to develop programs that can be used in different environments. You can write programs in Java that can be used in a client-server environment. The most popular use of Java programs in its early days was to develop applets, which have been deprecated in Java SE 9. An applet is a Java program that is embedded in a web page, which uses the HyperText Markup Language (HTML), and is displayed in a web browser such as Microsoft Internet Explorer, Google Chrome, etc. An applet's code is stored on a web server, downloaded to the client machine when the HTML page containing the reference to the applet is loaded by the browser, and run on the client machine.

Java includes features that make it easy to develop distributed applications. A distributed application consists of programs running on different machines connected through a network. Java has features that make it easy to develop concurrent applications. A concurrent application has multiple interacting threads of execution running in parallel. I discuss these features of the Java platform in detail in subsequent chapters in this book.

Robustness of a program refers to its ability to handle unexpected situations reasonably. The unexpected situation in a program is also known as an error. Java provides robustness by providing many features for error checking at different points during a program's lifetime. The following are three different types of errors that may occur in a Java program:

- Compile-time errors

- Runtime errors

- Logic errors

Compile-time errors are also known as syntax errors. They are caused by incorrect use of the Java language syntax. They are detected by the Java compiler. A program with compile-time errors does not compile into bytecode until the errors are corrected. Missing a semicolon at the end of a statement, assigning a decimal value such as 10.23 to a variable of integer type, etc., are examples of compile-time errors.

Runtime errors occur when a Java program is run. This kind of error is not detected by the compiler because a compiler does not have all of the runtime information available to it. Java is a strongly typed language and it has a robust type checking at compile time as well as runtime. Java provides a neat exception handling mechanism to handle runtime errors. When a runtime error occurs in a Java program, the JVM throws an exception, which the program may catch and deal with. For example, dividing an integer by zero (e.g., 17/0) generates a runtime error. Java avoids critical runtime errors, such as memory overrun and memory leaks, by providing a built-in mechanism for automatic memory allocation and deallocation. The feature of automatic memory deallocation is known as garbage collection.

Logic errors are the most critical errors in a program, and they are hard to find. They are introduced by the programmer by implementing the functional requirements incorrectly. This kind of error cannot be detected by a Java compiler or Java runtime. They are detected by application testers or users when they compare the actual behavior of a program with its expected behavior. Sometimes, a few logic errors can sneak into the production environment and they go unnoticed even after the application is decommissioned.

An error in a program is known as a *bug*. The process of finding and fixing bugs in a program is known as *debugging*. All modern integrated development environments (IDEs) such as NetBeans, Eclipse, JDeveloper, and IntelliJ IDEA provide programmers with a tool called a *debugger*, which lets them run the program step-by-step and inspect the program's state at every step to detect the bug. Debugging is a reality of programmer's daily activities. If you want to be a good programmer, you must learn and be good at using the debuggers that come with the development tools that you use to develop your Java programs.

The Object-Oriented Paradigm and Java

The object-oriented paradigm supports four major principles: *abstraction, encapsulation, inheritance,* and *polymorphism*. They are also known as four pillars of the object-oriented paradigm. Abstraction is the process of exposing the essential details of an entity, while ignoring the irrelevant details, to reduce the complexity for the users. Encapsulation is the process of bundling data and operations on the data together in an entity. Inheritance is used to derive a new type from an existing type, thereby establishing a parent-child relationship. Polymorphism lets an entity take on different meanings in different contexts. The four principles are discussed in detail in the sections to follow.

Abstraction

A program provides a solution to a real-world problem. The size of the program may range from a few lines to a few million lines. It may be written as a monolithic structure running from the first line to the millionth line in one place. A monolithic program becomes harder to write, understand, and maintain if its size is over 25 to 50 lines. For easier maintenance, a big monolithic program must be decomposed into smaller subprograms. The subprograms are then assembled together to solve the original problem. Care must be taken when a program is being decomposed. All subprograms must be simple and small enough to be understood by themselves, and when assembled, they must solve the original problem. Let's consider the following requirement for a device:

Design and develop a device that will let the users type text using all English letters, digits, and symbols.

One way to design such a device is to provide a keyboard that has keys for all possible combinations of all letters, digits, and symbols. This solution is not reasonable as the size of the device will be huge. You may realize that we are talking about designing a keyboard. Look at your keyboard and see how it has been designed. It has broken down the problem of typing text into typing a letter, a digit, or a symbol one at a time, which represents the smaller part of the original problem. If you can type all letters, all digits, and all symbols one at a time, you can type text of any length.

Another decomposition of the original problem may include two keys: one to type a horizontal line and another to type a vertical line, which a user can use to type in E, T, I, F, H, and L because these letters consist of only horizontal and vertical lines. With this solution, a user can type six letters using the combination of just two keys. However, with your experience using keyboards, you may realize that decomposing the keys so that a key can be used to type in only part of a letter is not a reasonable solution, although it is a solution.

Why is providing two keys to type six letters not a reasonable solution? Aren't we saving space and number of keys on the keyboard? The use of the phrase "reasonable" is relative in this context. From a purist point of view, it may be a reasonable solution. My reasoning behind calling it "not reasonable" is that it is not easily understood by users. It exposes more details to the users than needed. A user would have to remember that the horizontal line is placed at the top for T and at bottom for L. When a user gets a separate key for each letter, he does not have to deal with these details. It is important that the subprograms that provide solutions to parts of the original problem must be simplified to have the same level of detail to work together seamlessly. At the same time, a subprogram should not expose details that are not necessary for someone to know in order to use it.

Finally, all keys are mounted on a keyboard and they can be replaced separately. If a key is broken, it can be replaced without worrying about other keys. Similarly, when a program is decomposed into subprograms, a modification in a subprogram should not affect other subprograms. Subprograms can also be further decomposed by focusing on a different level of detail and ignoring other details. A good decomposition of a program aims at providing the following characteristics:

- Simplicity
- Isolation
- Maintainability

Each subprogram should be simple enough to be understood by itself. Simplicity is achieved by focusing on the relevant pieces of information and ignoring the irrelevant ones. What pieces of information are relevant and what are irrelevant depends on the context.

Each subprogram should be isolated from other subprograms so that any changes in a subprogram should have localized effects. A change in one subprogram should not affect any other subprograms. A subprogram defines an interface to interact with other subprograms. The inner details about the subprogram are hidden from the outside world. As long as the interface for a subprogram remains unchanged, the changes in its inner details should not affect the other subprograms that interact with it.

Each subprogram should be small enough to be written, understood, and maintained easily.

All of these characteristics are achieved during decomposition of a problem (or program that solves a problem) using a process called abstraction. Abstraction is a way to perform decomposition of a problem by focusing on relevant details and ignoring the irrelevant details about it in a particular context. Note that no details about a problem are irrelevant. In other words, every detail about a problem is relevant. However, some details may be relevant in one context and some in another. It is important to note that it is the "context" that decides what details are relevant and what are irrelevant. For example, consider the problem of designing and developing a keyboard. For a user's perspective, a keyboard consists of keys that can be pressed and released to type text. Number, type, size, and position of keys are the only details that are relevant to the users of a keyboard. However, keys are not the only details about a keyboard. A keyboard has an electronic circuit and it is connected to a computer. A lot of things occur inside the keyboard and the computer when a user presses a key. The internal workings of a keyboard are relevant to keyboard designers and manufacturers. However, they are irrelevant to the users of a keyboard. You can say that different users have different views of the same thing in different contexts. What details about the thing are relevant and what are irrelevant depends on the user and the context.

Abstraction is about considering details that are necessary to view the problem in the way that is appropriate in a particular context and ignoring (hiding or suppressing or forgetting) the details that are unnecessary. Terms like "hiding" and "suppressing" in the context of abstraction may be misleading. These terms may mean hiding some details of a problem. Abstraction is concerned with which details of a thing should be considered and which should not for a particular purpose. It does imply hiding of the details. How things are hidden is another concept called information hiding, which is discussed in the following section.

The term "abstraction" is used to mean one of the two things: a process or an entity. As a process, it is a technique to extract relevant details about a problem and ignore the irrelevant details. As an entity, it is a particular view of a problem that considers some relevant details and ignores the irrelevant details.

Abstraction for Hiding Complexities

Let's discuss the application of abstraction in real-world programming. Suppose you want to write a program that will compute the sum of all integers between two integers. Suppose you want to compute the sum of all integers between 10 and 20. You can write the program as follows. Do not worry if you do not understand the syntax used in programs in this section; just try to grasp the big picture of how abstraction is used to decompose a program.

```
int sum = 0;
int counter = 10;

while (counter <= 20) {
    sum = sum + counter;
    counter = counter + 1;
}

System.out.println(sum);
```

This snippet of code will add 10 + 11 + 12 + … + 20 and print 165. Suppose you want to compute sum of all integers between 40 and 60. Here is the program to achieve just that:

```
int sum = 0;
int counter = 40;

while (counter <= 60) {
    sum = sum + counter;
    counter = counter + 1;
}

System.out.println(sum);
```

15

This snippet of code will perform the sum of all integers between 40 and 60, and it will print 1050. Note the similarities and differences between the two snippets of code. The logic is the same in both. However, the lower and upper limits of the range are different. If you can ignore the differences that exist between the two snippets of code, you will be able to avoid the duplicating of logic in two places. Let's consider the following snippet of code:

```
int sum = 0;
int counter = lowerLimit;

while (counter <= upperLimit) {
    sum = sum + counter;
    counter = counter + 1;
}

System.out.println(sum);
```

This time, you did not use any actual values for the lower and upper limits of any range. Rather, you used lowerLimit and upperLimit placeholders that are not known at the time the code is written. By using two placeholders in your code, you are hiding the identity of the lower and upper limits of the range. In other words, you are ignoring their actual values when writing this piece of code. You have applied the process of abstraction in the code by ignoring the actual values of the lower and upper limits of the range.

When this piece of code is executed, the actual values must be substituted for lowerLimit and upperLimit placeholders. This is achieved in a programming language by packaging the snippet of code inside a module (subroutine or subprogram) called a *procedure*. The placeholders are defined as formal parameters of that procedure. Listing 1-2 has the code for such a procedure.

Listing 1-2. A Procedure Named getRangeSum to Compute the Sum of All Integers Between Two Integers

```
int getRangeSum(int lowerLimit, int upperLimit) {
    int sum = 0;
    int counter = lowerLimit;

    while (counter <= upperLimit) {
        sum = sum + counter;
        counter = counter + 1;
    }

    return sum;
}
```

A procedure has a name, which is getRangeSum in this case. A procedure has a return type, which is specified just before its name. The return type indicates the type of value that it will return to its caller. The return type is int in this case, which indicates that the result of the computation will be an integer. A procedure has formal parameters (possibly zero), which are specified within parentheses following its name. A formal parameter consists of data type and a name. In this case, the formal parameters are named as lowerLimit and upperLimit, and both are of the data type int. It has a body, which is placed within braces. The body of the procedure contains the logic.

When you want to execute the code for a procedure, you must pass the actual values for its formal parameters. You can compute and print the sum of all integers between 10 and 20 as follows:

```
int s1 = getRangeSum(10, 20);
System.out.println(s1);
```

This snippet of code will print 165. To compute the sum all integers between 40 and 60, you can execute the following snippet of code:

```
int s2 = getRangeSum(40, 60);
System.out.println(s2);
```

This snippet of code will print 1050, which is exactly the same result you achieved before.

The abstraction method that you used in defining the getRangeSum procedure is called *abstraction by parameterization*. The formal parameters in a procedure are used to hide the identity of the actual data on which the procedure's body operates. The two parameters in the getRangeSum procedure hide the identity of the lower and upper limits of the range of integers. Now you have seen the first concrete example of abstraction. Abstraction is a vast topic. I cover some more basics about abstraction in this section.

Suppose a programmer writes the code for the getRangeSum procedure, as shown in Listing 1-2, and another programmer wants to use it. The first programmer is the designer and writer of the procedure; the second one is the user of the procedure. What pieces of information does the user of the getRangeSum procedure need to know in order to use it?

Before you answer this question, let's consider a real-world example of designing and using a DVD (Digital Versatile Disc) player. A DVD player is designed and developed by electronic engineers. How do you use a DVD player? Before you use a DVD player, you do not open it to study all the details about its parts that are based on electronics engineering theories. When you buy it, it comes with a manual on how to use it. A DVD player is wrapped in a box. The box hides the details of the player inside. At the same time, the box exposes some of the details about the player in the form of an interface to the outside world. The interface for a DVD player consists of the following items:

- Input and output connection ports to connect to a power outlet, a TV set, etc.

- A panel to insert a DVD

- A set of buttons to perform operations such as eject, play, pause, fast forward, etc.

The manual that comes with the DVD player describes the usage of the player's interface meant for its users. A DVD user need not worry about the details of how it works internally. The manual also describes some conditions to operate it. For example, you must plug the power cord to a power outlet and switch on the power before you can use it.

A program is designed, developed, and used in the same way as a DVD player. The user of the program, shown in Listing 1-2, need not worry about the internal logic that is used to implement the program. A user of the program needs to know only its usage, which includes the interface to use it, and conditions that must be met before and after using it. In other words, you need to provide a manual for the getRangeSum procedure that will describe its usage. The user of the getRangeSum procedure will need to read its manual to use it. The "manual" for a program is known as its specification. Sometimes it is also known as documentation or comments. It provides another method of abstraction, which is called abstraction by specification. It describes (or exposes or focuses) the "what" part of the program and hides (or ignores or suppresses) the "how" part of the program from its users.

Listing 1-3 shows the same getRangeSum procedure code with its specification.

Listing 1-3. The getRangeSum Procedure with its Specification for Javadoc Tool

```
/**
 * Computes and returns the sum of all integers between two
 * integers specified by lowerLimit and upperLimit parameters.
 *
 * The lowerLimit parameter must be less than or equal to the
 * upperLimit parameter. If the sum of all integers between the
```

```
 * lowerLimit and the upperLimit exceeds the range of the int data
 * type then result is not defined.
 *
 * @param lowerLimit The lower limit of the integer range
 * @param upperLimit The upper limit of the integer range
 * @return The sum of all integers between lowerLimit (inclusive)
 *          and upperLimit (inclusive)
 */
public static int getRangeSum(int lowerLimit, int upperLimit) {
    int sum = 0;
    int counter = lowerLimit;
    while (counter <= upperLimit) {
        sum = sum + counter;
        counter = counter + 1;
    }
    return sum;
}
```

It uses Javadoc standards to write a specification for a Java program that can be processed by the Javadoc tool to generate HTML pages. In Java, the specification for a program element is placed between /** and */ immediately before the element. The specification is meant for the users of the getRangeSum procedure. The Javadoc tool will generate the specification for the getRangeSum procedure, as shown in Figure 1-4.

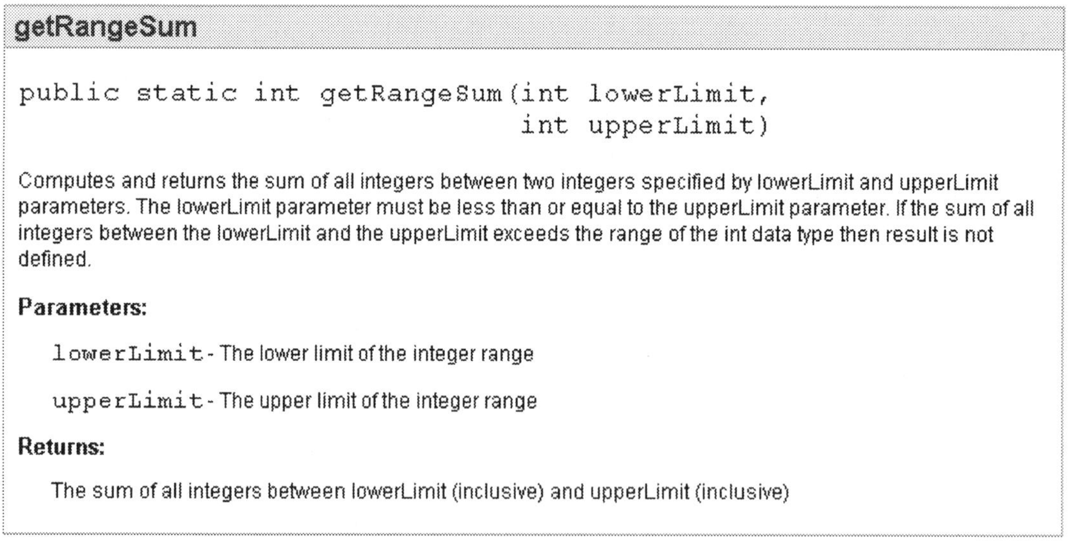

getRangeSum

```
public static int getRangeSum(int lowerLimit,
                              int upperLimit)
```

Computes and returns the sum of all integers between two integers specified by lowerLimit and upperLimit parameters. The lowerLimit parameter must be less than or equal to the upperLimit parameter. If the sum of all integers between the lowerLimit and the upperLimit exceeds the range of the int data type then result is not defined.

Parameters:

lowerLimit - The lower limit of the integer range

upperLimit - The upper limit of the integer range

Returns:

The sum of all integers between lowerLimit (inclusive) and upperLimit (inclusive)

Figure 1-4. *The specification for the getRangeSum procedure*

This specification provides the description (the "what" part) of the getRangeSum procedure. It also specifies two conditions, known as pre-conditions, which must be true when the procedure is called. The first pre-condition is that the lower limit must be less than or equal to the upper limit. The second pre-condition is that the value for lower and upper limits must be small enough so that the sum of all integers between them fits in the size of the int data type. It specifies another condition that is called post-condition, which is specified in the "Returns" clause. The post-condition holds as long as pre-conditions hold.

The pre-conditions and post-conditions are like a contract (or an agreement) between the program and its user. It states that as long as the user of the program makes sure that the pre-condition holds true, the program guarantees that the post-condition will hold true. Note that the specification never tells the user about how the program fulfills (implementation details) the post-condition. It only tells "what" it is going to do rather than "how" it is going to do it. The user of the getRangeSum program, who has the specification, need not look at the body of the getRangeSum procedure to figure out the logic that it uses. In other words, you have hidden the details of the implementation of the getRangeSum procedure from its users by providing this specification to them. That is, users of the getRangeSum procedure can ignore its implementation details for the purpose of using it. This is another concrete example of abstraction. The method of hiding implementation details of a subprogram (the "how" part) and exposing its usage (the "what" part) by using specification is called *abstraction by specification*.

Abstraction by parameterization and abstraction by specification let the users of a program view the program as a black box, where they are concerned only about the effects that program produces rather than how the program produces those effects. Figure 1-5 depicts the user's view of the getRangeSum procedure. Note that a user does not see (and need not see) the body of the procedure that has the details. The details are relevant only to the writer of the program, not its users.

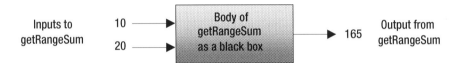

Figure 1-5. *User's view of the getRangeSum procedure as a black box using abstraction*

What advantages did you achieve by applying the abstraction to define the getRangeSum procedure? One of the most important advantages is isolation. It is isolated from other programs. If you modify the logic inside its body, other programs, including the ones that are using it, need not be modified. To print the sum of integers between 10 and 20, you use the following program:

```
int s1 = getRangeSum(10, 20);
System.out.println(s1);
```

The body of the procedure uses a while loop, which is executed as many times as the number of integers between lower and upper limits. The while loop inside the getRangeSum procedure executes n times where n is equal to (upperLimit - lowerLimit + 1). The number of instructions that needs to be executed depends on the input values. There is a better way to compute the sum of all integers between two integers, lowerLimit and upperLimit, using the following formula:

```
n = upperLimit - lowerLimit + 1;
sum = n * (2 * lowerLimit + (n-1))/2;
```

If you use this formula, the number of instructions that are executed to compute the sum of all integers between two integers is always the same. You can rewrite the body of the getRangeSum procedure, as shown in Listing 1-4. The specification of getRangeSum procedure is not shown here.

Listing 1-4. Another Version of the getRangeSum Procedure with the Logic Changed Inside its Body

```
public int getRangeSum(int lowerLimit, int upperLimit) {
    int n = upperLimit - lowerLimit + 1;
    int sum = n * (2 * lowerLimit + (n-1))/2;
    return sum;
}
```

Note that the body (implementation or the "how" part) of the getRangeSum procedure has changed between Listing 1-3 and Listing 1-4. However, the users of the getRangeSum procedure are not affected by this change because the details of the implementation of this procedure were kept hidden from its users by using abstraction. If you want to compute the sum of all integers between 10 and 20 using the version of the getRangeSum procedure, as shown in Listing 1-4, your old code is still valid.

```
int s1 = getRangeSum(10, 20);
System.out.println(s1);
```

You have just seen one of the greatest benefits of abstraction, in which the implementation details of a program (in this case, a procedure) can be changed without warranting any changes in the code that uses the program. This benefit also gives you a chance to rewrite your program logic to improve performance in the future without affecting other parts of the application.

I consider two types of abstraction in this section:

- Procedural abstraction

- Data abstraction

Procedural abstraction lets you define a procedure, for example, getRangeSum, that you can use as an action or a task. So far, I have been discussing procedural abstraction. Abstraction by parameterization and abstraction by specification are two methods to achieve procedural abstraction as well as data abstraction. The next section discusses data abstraction in detail.

Data Abstraction

Object-oriented programming is based on data abstraction. However, I need to discuss data type briefly before I discuss data abstraction. A data type (or simply a type) is defined in terms of three components:

- A set of values (or data objects)

- A set of operations that can be applied to all values in the set

- A data representation, which determines how the values are stored

Programming languages provide some predefined data types, which are known as built-in data types. They also let programmers define their own data types, which are known as user-defined data types. A data type that consists of an atomic and indivisible value, and that is defined without the help of any other data types, is known as a primitive data type. For example, Java has built-in primitive data types such as int, float, boolean, char, etc. Three components that define the int primitive data type in Java are as follows:

- An int data type consists of a set of all integers between -2147483648 and 2147483647.

- Operations such as addition, subtraction, multiplication, division, comparison, and many more are defined for the int data type.

- A value of int data type is represented in 32-bit memory in 2's complement form.

All three components of the int data type are predefined by Java language. You cannot extend or redefine the definition of the int data type. You can give a name to a value of the int data type as

```
int n1;
```

This statement says that n1 is a name (technically called an identifier) that can be associated with one value from the set of values that defines values for int data type. For example, you can associate integer 26 to the name n1 using an assignment statement as follows:

```
n1 = 26;
```

At this stage, you may be asking, "Where is the value 26, which is associated with the name n1, stored in memory?" You know from the definition of int data type that n1 will take 32-bit memory. However, you do not know, cannot know, and do not need to know where in the memory that 32-bit is allocated for n1. Do you see an example of abstraction here? If you see an example of abstraction in this case, you are right. This is an example of abstraction, which is built into the Java language. In this instance, the pieces of information about the data representation of the data value for int data type are hidden from the users (programmers) of the data type. In other words, a programmer ignores the memory location of n1 and focuses on its value and the operations that can be performed on it. A programmer does not care if the memory for n1 is allocated in a register, RAM, or the hard disk.

Object-oriented programming languages such as Java let you create new data types using an abstraction mechanism called data abstraction. The new data types are known as abstract data types (ADT). The data objects in ADT may consist of a combination of primitive data types and other ADTs. An ADT defines a set of operations that can be applied to all its data objects. The data representation is always hidden in ADT. For users of an ADT, it consists of operations only. Its data elements may only be accessed and manipulated using its operations. The advantage of using data abstraction is that its data representation can be changed without affecting any code that uses the ADT.

▓ **Tip**   Data abstraction lets programmers create a new data type called an abstract data type, where the storage representation of the data objects is hidden from the users of the data type. In other words, ADT is defined solely in terms of operations that can be applied to the data objects of its type without knowing the internal representation of the data. The reason this kind of data type is called abstract is that users of ADT never see the representation of the data values. Users view the data objects of an ADT in an abstract way, by applying operations on them without knowing the details about representation of the data objects. Note that an ADT does not mean absence of data representation. Data representation is always present in an ADT. It only means hiding of the data representation from its users.

Java has constructs, for example, class, interface, annotation, and enum, that let you define new ADTs. When you use a class to define a new ADT, you need to be careful to hide the data representation, so your new data type is really abstract. If the data representation in a Java class is not hidden, that class creates a new data type, but not an ADT. A class in Java gives you features that you can use to expose the data representation or hide it. In Java, the set of values of a class data type are called *objects*. Operations on the objects are called *methods*. Instance variables (also known as fields) of objects are the data representation for the class type.

A class in Java lets you implement operations that operate on the data representation. An interface in Java lets you create a pure ADT. An interface lets you provide only the specification for operations that can be applied to the data objects of its type. No implementation for operations or data representation can be mentioned in an interface. Listing 1-1 shows the definition of the Person class using Java language syntax. By defining a class named Person, you have created a new ADT. Its internal data representation for name and gender uses String data type (String is a built-in ADT provided by Java class library). Note that the definition of the Person class uses the private keyword in the name and gender declarations to hide it from the outside world. Users of the Person class cannot access the name and gender data elements. It provides four operations: a constructor and three methods (getName, setName, and getGender).

A constructor operation is used to initialize a newly constructed data object of the Person type. The getName and setName operations are used to access and modify the name data element, respectively. The getGender operation is used to access the value of the gender data element.

Users of the Person class must use only these four operations to work with data objects of the Person type. Users of the Person type are oblivious to the type of data storage being used to store name and gender data elements. I am using three terms, "type," "class," and "interface," interchangeably because they mean the same thing in the context of a data type. It gives the developer of the Person type freedom to change the data representation for the name and gender data elements without affecting any users of Person type. Suppose one of the users of Person type has the following snippet of code:

```
Person john = new Person("John Jacobs", "Male");
String intialName = john.getName();
john.setName("Wally Jacobs");
String changedName = john.getName();
```

This snippet of code has been written only in terms of the operations provided by the Person type. It does not (and could not) refer to the name and gender instance variables directly. Let's see how to change the data representation of the Person type without affecting the snippet of code. Listing 1-5 shows the code for a newer version for the Person class.

Listing 1-5. Another Version of the Person Class That Uses a String Array of Two Elements to Store Name and Gender Values as Opposed to Two String Variables

```
package com.jdojo.concepts;

public class Person {
    private String[] data = new String[2];

    public Person(String initialName, String initialGender) {
        data[0] = initialName;
        data[1] = initialGender;
    }

    public String getName() {
        return data[0];
    }

    public void setName(String newName) {
        data[0] = newName;
    }

    public String getGender() {
        return data[1];
    }
}
```

Compare the code in Listing 1-1 and Listing 1-5. This time, you have replaced the two instance variables (name and gender), which were the data representation for the Person type in Listing 1-1, with a String array of two elements. Since operations (or methods) in a class operate on the data representation, you had to change the implementations for all four operations in the Person type. The client code in Listing 1-5 was written in terms of the specifications of the four operations and not their implementation. Since you have not changed the specification of any of the operations, you do not need to change the snippet of code that uses the Person class; it is still valid with the newer definition of the Person type, as shown in Listing 1-5. Some methods in the Person class use the abstraction by parameterization and all of them use the abstraction by specification. I have not shown the specification for the methods here, which would be Javadoc comments.

You have seen two major benefits of data abstraction in this section.

- It lets you extend the programming language by letting you define new data types. The new data types you create depend on the application domain. For example, for a banking system, Person, Currency, and Account may be good choices for new data types, whereas for an auto insurance application, Person, Vehicle, and Claim may be good choices. The operations included in a new data type depend on the need of the application.

- The data type created using data abstraction may change the representation of the data without affecting the client code using the data type.

Encapsulation and Information Hiding

The term encapsulation is used to mean two different things: a process or an entity. As a process, it is an act of bundling one or more items into a container. The container could be physical or logical. As an entity, it is a container that holds one or more items.

Programming languages support encapsulations in many ways. A procedure is an encapsulation of steps to perform a task; an array is an encapsulation of several elements of the same type, etc. In object-oriented programming, encapsulation is bundling of data and operations on the data into an entity called a class. Java supports encapsulation in various ways.

- It lets you bundle data and methods that operate on the data in an entity called a *class*.

- It lets you bundle one or more logically related classes in an entity called a *package*. A package in Java is a logical collection of one or more related classes. A package creates a new naming scope in which all classes must have unique names. Two classes may have the same name in Java as long as they are bundled (or encapsulated) in two different packages.

- It lets you bundle packages into a *module*, which was introduced in Java SE 9. A module can export its packages. Types defined in exported packages are accessible to other modules, whereas types in non-exported packages are inaccessible to other modules.

- It lets you bundle one or more related classes in an entity called a *compilation unit*. All classes in a compilation unit can be compiled separately from other compilation units.

While discussing the concepts of object-oriented programming, the two terms—*encapsulation* and *information hiding*—are often used interchangeably. However, they are different concepts in object-oriented programming, and they should not be used interchangeably as such. Encapsulation is simply the bundling of items together into one entity. Information hiding is the process of hiding implementation details that are likely to change. Encapsulation is not concerned with whether the items that are bundled in an entity are hidden from other modules in the application or not. What should be hidden (or ignored) and what should not be hidden is the concern of abstraction. Abstraction is only concerned about which item should be hidden. Abstraction is not concerned about how the item should be hidden. Information hiding is concerned with how an item is hidden.

Encapsulation, abstraction, and information hiding are three separate concepts. They are very closely related, though. One concept facilitates the workings of the others. It is important to understand the subtle differences in roles they play in object-oriented programming.

▓ **Tip**   In Java SE 9, you will often come across a phrase like "a module provides strong encapsulation". Here, the term *encapsulation* is used in the sense of information hiding. It means that types in non-exported packages in a module are hidden from (or inaccessible to) other modules.

It is possible to use encapsulation with or without hiding any information. For example, the Person class in Listing 1-1 shows an example of encapsulation and information hiding. The data elements (name and gender) and methods (getName(), setName(), and getGender()) are bundled together in a class called Person. This is encapsulation. In other words, the Person class is an encapsulation of the data elements name and gender, plus the methods getName(), setName(), and getGender(). The same Person class uses information hiding by hiding the data elements from the outside world. Note that name and gender data elements use the Java keyword private, which essentially hides them from the outside world. Listing 1-6 shows the code for a Person2 class.

Listing 1-6. The Definition of the Person2 Class in Which Data Elements Are Not Hidden by Declaring Them Public

```java
package com.jdojo.concepts;

public class Person2 {
    public String name;    // Not hidden from its users
    public String gender; // Not hidden from its users

    public Person2(String initialName, String initialGender) {
        name = initialName;
        gender = initialGender;
    }

    public String getName() {
        return name;
    }

    public void setName(String newName) {
        name = newName;
    }

    public String getGender() {
        return gender;
    }
}
```

The code in Listing 1-1 and Listing 1-6 is essentially the same except for two small differences. The Person2 class uses the keyword public to declare the name and gender data elements. The Person2 class uses encapsulation the same way the Person class uses it. However, the name and gender data elements are not hidden. That is, the Person2 class does not use data hiding (data hiding is an example of information hiding). If you look at the constructor and methods of Person and Person2 classes, their bodies use information hiding because the logic written inside their bodies is hidden from their users.

▓ **Tip**   Encapsulation and information hiding are two distinct concepts of object-oriented programming. The existence of one does not imply the existence of the other.

Inheritance

Inheritance is another important concept in object-oriented programming. It lets you use abstraction in a new way. You have seen how a class represents an abstraction in previous sections. The Person class shown in Listing 1-1 represents an abstraction for a real-world person. The inheritance mechanism lets you define a new abstraction by extending an existing abstraction. The existing abstraction is called a supertype, a superclass, a parent class, or a base class. The new abstraction is called a subtype, a subclass, a child class, or a derived class. It is said that a subtype is derived (or inherited) from a supertype; a supertype is a generalization of a subtype; and a subtype is a specialization of a supertype. The inheritance can be used to define new abstractions at more than one level. A subtype can be used as a supertype to define another subtype and so on. Inheritance gives rise to a family of types arranged in a hierarchical form.

Inheritance allows you to use varying degrees of abstraction at different levels of hierarchy. In Figure 1-6, the Person class is at the top (highest level) of the inheritance hierarchy. Customer and Employee classes are at the second level of inheritance hierarchy. As you move up the inheritance level, you focus on more important pieces information. In other words, at a higher level of inheritance, you are concerned about the bigger picture; and at lower levels of inheritance, you are concerned about more and more details. There is another way to look at inheritance hierarchy from abstraction point of view. At the Person level in Figure 1-6, you focus on the common characteristics of Customer and Employee, ignoring the differences between them. At the Employee level, you focus on common characteristics of Clerk, Programmer, and Cashier, ignoring the differences between them.

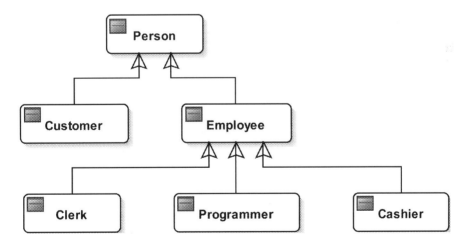

Figure 1-6. *Inheritance hierarchy for the Person class*

In inheritance hierarchy, a supertype and its subtype represent an "is-a" relationship. That is, an Employee is a Person; a Programmer is an Employee, etc. Since the lower level of inheritance means more pieces of information, a subtype always includes what its supertype has and maybe some more. This characteristic of inheritance leads to another feature in object-oriented programming, which is known as *the principle of substitutivity*. It means that a supertype can always be substituted with its subtype. For example, you have considered only name and gender information for a person in your Person abstraction. If you inherit Employee from Person, Employee includes name and gender information, which it inherits from Person. Employee may include some more pieces of information such as employee ID, hire date, salary, etc. If a Person is expected in a context, it implies that only name and gender information are relevant in that context. You can always replace a Person in that context with an Employee, a Customer, a Clerk, or a Programmer because being a subtype (direct or indirect) of the Person these abstractions guarantee that they have the ability to deal with at least name and gender information.

At programming level, inheritance provides a code reuse mechanism. The code written in supertype may be reused by its subtype. A subtype may extend the functionality of its supertype by adding more functionalities or by redefining existing functionalities of its supertype.

▓ **Tip** Inheritance is also used as a technique to implement polymorphism, which is discussed in the next section. Inheritance lets you write polymorphic code. The code is written in terms of the supertype and the same code works for subtypes.

Inheritance is a vast topic. This book devotes a complete chapter on how to use inheritance in Java.

Polymorphism

The word "polymorphism" has its root in two Greek words: "poly" (means many) and "morphos" (means form). In programming, polymorphism is the ability of an entity (e.g., variable, class, method, object, code, parameter, etc.) to take on different meanings in different contexts. The entity that takes on different meanings is known as a polymorphic entity. Various types of polymorphism exist. Each type of polymorphism has a name that usually indicates how that type of polymorphism is achieved in practice. The proper use of polymorphism results in generic and reusable code. The purpose of polymorphism is writing reusable and maintainable code by writing code in terms of a generic type that works for many types (or ideally all types). Polymorphism can be categorized in the following two categories:

- Ad hoc polymorphism

- Universal polymorphism

If a piece of code works for a finite number of types and all those types must be known when the code is written, it is known as *ad hoc polymorphism*. Ad hoc polymorphism is also known as *apparent polymorphism* because it is not polymorphism in a true sense. Some computer science purists do not consider ad hoc polymorphism to be polymorphism at all.

Ad hoc polymorphism is further divided into two categories:

- Overloading polymorphism

- Coercion polymorphism

If a piece of code is written in such a way that it works for an infinite number of types (will also work for new types not known at the time the code is written), it is called *universal polymorphism*. In universal polymorphism, the same code works on many types, whereas in ad hoc polymorphism, different implementations of code are provided for different types, giving an apparent impression of polymorphism.

Universal polymorphism is further divided into two categories:

- Inclusion polymorphism

- Parametric polymorphism

In the subsequent sections, I describe these types of polymorphism in detail with examples.

Overloading Polymorphism

Overloading is an ad hoc polymorphism. Overloading results when a method (called a method in Java and a function in other languages) or an operator has at least two definitions that work on different types. In such cases, the same name (for the method or operator) is used for their different definitions. That is, the same name exhibits many behaviors and hence the polymorphism. Such methods and operators are called overloaded methods and overloaded operators. Java lets you define overloaded methods. Java has some overloaded operators, but it does not let you overload an operator for an ADT. That is, you cannot provide a new definition for an operator in Java. Listing 1-7 shows code for a class named MathUtil.

Listing 1-7. An Example of an Overloaded Method in Java

```java
// MathUtil.java
package com.jdojo.concepts;

public class MathUtil {
    public static int max(int n1, int n2) {
        /* Code to determine the maximum of two integers goes here */
    }

    public static double max(double n1, double n2) {
        /* Code to determine the maximum of two floating-point numbers goes here */
    }

    public static int max(int[] num) {
        /* Code to determine the maximum in an array of int goes here */
    }
}
```

The max() method of the MathUtil class is overloaded. It has three definitions and each of its definitions performs the same task of computing maximum, but on different types. The first definition computes a maximum of two numbers of int data type, the second one computes a maximum of two floating-point numbers of double data type, and the third one computes a maximum of an array of numbers of int data type. The following snippet of code uses all three definitions of the overloaded max() method:

```java
int max1 = MathUtil.max(10, 23);           // Uses max(int, int)
double max2 = MathUtil.max(10.34, 2.89);   // Uses max(double, double)
int max3 = MathUtil.max(new int[]{1, 89, 8, 3}); // Uses max(int[])
```

Note that method overloading gives you only sharing of the method name. It does not result in the sharing of the methods' definitions. In Listing 1-7, the method name, max, is shared by all three methods, but they all have their own definition of computing maximum of different types. In method overloading, the definitions of methods do not have to be related. They may perform entirely different things and share the same name.

The following snippet of code shows an example of operator overloading in Java. The operator is +. In the following three statements, it performs three different things:

```
int n1 = 10 + 20;              // Adds two integers
double n2 = 10.20 + 2.18;      // Adds two floating-point numbers
String str = "Hi " + "there";  // Concatenates two strings
```

In the first statement, the + operator performs addition on two integers, 10 and 20, and returns 30. In the second statement, it performs addition on two floating-point numbers, 10.20 and 2.18, and returns 12.38. In the third statement, it performs concatenation of two strings, "Hi" and "there", and returns "Hi there".

In overloading, the types of the actual parameters of methods (the types of operands in case of operators) are used to determine which definition of the code to use. Method overloading provides only the reuse of the method name. You can remove method overloading by simply supplying a unique name to all versions of an overloaded method. For example, you could rename the three versions of the max() method as max2Int(), max2Double(), and maxNInt(). Note that all versions of an overloaded method or operator do not have to perform related or similar tasks. In Java, the only requirement to overload a method name is that all versions of the method must differ in number and/or type of their formal parameters.

Coercion Polymorphism

Coercion is an ad hoc polymorphism. Coercion occurs when a type is implicitly converted (coerced) to another type automatically even if it was not intended explicitly. Consider the following statements in Java:

```
int num = 707;
double d1 = (double)num; // Explicit conversion of int to double
double d2 = num;         // Implicit conversion of int to double (coercion)
```

In the first statement, the variable num has been declared to be of int data type, and it's assigned a value of 707. The second statement uses cast, (double), to convert the int value stored in num to double, and it assigns the converted value to a variable named d1. This is the case of explicit conversion from int to double. In this case, the programmer makes his intention explicit by using the cast. The third statement has exactly the same effect as the second one; however, it relies on implicit conversion (called widening conversion in Java) provided by the Java language that converts an int to double automatically when needed. The third statement is an example of coercion. A programming language (including Java) performs different types of coercion in different contexts: assignment (shown previously), method parameters, etc.

Consider the following snippet of code that shows a definition of a square() method, which accepts a parameter of double data type:

```
double square(double num) {
    return num * num;
}
```

The square() method can be called with actual parameter of double data type, as follows:

```
double d1 = 20.23;
double result = square(d1);
```

The same square() method may also be called with actual parameter of int data type, as follows:

```
int k = 20;
double result = square(k);
```

You have just seen that the square() method works on parameters of the double as well as int data type, although you have defined it only once in terms of a formal parameter of double data type. This is exactly what polymorphism means. In this case, the square() method is called a polymorphic method with respect to double and int data types. Thus, the square() method is exhibiting polymorphic behavior even though the programmer who wrote the code did not intend it. The square() method is polymorphic because of the implicit type conversion (coercion from int to double) provided by the Java language. Here is a more formal definition of a polymorphic method:

> *Suppose m is a method that declares a formal parameter of type T. If S is a type that can be implicitly converted to T, the method m is said to be polymorphic with respect to S and T.*

Inclusion Polymorphism

Inclusion is a universal polymorphism. It is also known as *subtype (or subclass) polymorphism* because it is achieved using subtyping or subclassing. This is the most common type of polymorphism supported by object-oriented programming languages. Java supports it.

Inclusion polymorphism occurs when a piece of code that is written using a type works for all its subtypes. This type of polymorphism is possible based on the subtyping rule that a value that belongs to a subtype also belongs to the supertype. Suppose T is a type and S1, S2, S3... are subtypes of T. A value that belongs to S1, S2, S3... also belongs to T. This subtyping rule makes it possible to write code as follows:

```
T t;
S1 s1;
S2 s2;
...
t = s1; // A value of type s1 can be assigned to a variable of type T
t = s2; // A value of type s2 can be assigned to a variable of type T
```

Java supports inclusion polymorphism using inheritance, which is a subclassing mechanism. You can define a method in Java using a formal parameter of a type, for example, Person, and that method can be called on all its subtypes, for example, Employee, Student, Customer, etc. Suppose you have a method processDetails() as follows:

```
void processDetails(Person p) {
    /* Write code using the formal parameter p, which is of type Person. The same code will
       work if an object of any of the subclass of Person is passed to this method.
    */
}
```

The processDetails() method declares a formal parameter of the Person type. You can define any number of classes that are subclasses of the Person class. This method will work for such subclasses. Assume that Employee and Customer are subclasses of the Person class. You can write code like this:

```
Person p1 = create a Person object;
Employee e1 = create an Employee object;
Customer c1 = create a Customer object;
processDetails(p1); // Use the Person type
processDetails(e1); // Use the Employee type, which is a subclass of Person
processDetails(c1); // Use the Customer type, which is a subclass of Person
```

The effect of the subtyping rule is that the supertype includes (hence the name inclusion) all values that belong to its subtypes. A piece of code is called universally polymorphic only if it works on an infinite number of types. In the case of inclusion polymorphism, the number of types for which the code works is constrained but infinite. The constraint is that all types must be the subtype of the type in whose term the code is written. If there is no restriction on how many subtypes a type can have, the number of subtypes is infinite (at least in theory). Note that inclusion polymorphism not only lets you write reusable code, it also lets you write extensible and flexible code. The processDetails() method works on all subclasses of the Person class. It will keep working for all subclasses of the Person class, which will be defined in the future, without any modifications. Java uses other mechanisms, like method overriding and dynamic dispatch (also called late binding), along with subclassing rules to make the inclusion polymorphism more effective and useful.

Parametric Polymorphism

Parametric is a universal polymorphism. It is also called "true" polymorphism because it lets you write true generic code that works for any types (related or unrelated). Sometimes, it is also referred to as *generics*. In parametric polymorphism, a piece of code is written in such a way that it works on any type. Contrast parametric polymorphism with inclusion polymorphism. In inclusion polymorphism, code is written for one type and it works for all of its subtypes. It means all types for which the code works in inclusion polymorphism are related by a supertype-subtype relationship. However, in parametric polymorphism, the same code works for all types, which are not necessarily related. Parametric polymorphism is achieved by using a type variable when writing the code, rather than using any specific type. The type variable assumes a specific type for which the code needs to be executed. Java supports parametric polymorphism since Java 5 through generics. Java supports polymorphic entities (e.g., parameterized classes) as well as polymorphic methods (parameterized methods) that use parametric polymorphism.

In Java, parametric polymorphism is achieved in using generics. All collection types in Java use generics. You can write code using generics as follows:

```
/* Example #1 */
// Create a List of String
List<String> sList = new ArrayList<String>();

// Add two Strings to the List
sList.add("string 1");
sList.add("string 2");

// Get the first String from the List
String s1 = sList.get(0);

/* Example #2 */
// Create a List of Integer
List<Integer> iList = new ArrayList<Integer>();

// Add two Integers to the list
iList.add(10);
iList.add(20);

// Get the first Integer from the List
int k1 = iList.get(0);
```

This code uses a List object as a list of String type and a List object as a list of Integer type. Using generics, you can treat a List object as a list of any type in Java. Note the use of <Xxx> in these examples to specify the type for which you want to instantiate the List object.

Summary

Writing a set of instructions for a computer to accomplish a task is known as programming. The set of instructions is known as a program. Different types of programming languages exist. They differ in their closeness to the instructions that the hardware can understand or the paradigm. A machine language lets you write programs using 0s and 1s, and it is the lowest level programming language. A program written in machine language is known as machine code. An assembly language lets you write programs using mnemonics. A program written using an assembly language is known as assembly code. Later, higher-level programming languages were developed, using an English-like language.

Several types of programming paradigms are in practice. A programming paradigm is a thinking cap for viewing and analyzing real-world problems in a particular way. Imperative, procedural, functional, and object-oriented are some widely used paradigms in software development. Java is a programming language that supports procedural, functional, and object-oriented programming paradigms.

Abstraction, encapsulation, inheritance, and polymorphism are the four pillars of object-oriented paradigms. Abstraction is the process of hiding details of a program that are irrelevant to the users of that program. Encapsulation is the process of bundling multiple items into one entity. Inheritance is the process of arranging classes in a hierarchical manner to build supertype-subtype relationships. Inheritance promotes reusability of code by allowing programmers to write the code in terms of a supertype that also works for all of the subtypes. Polymorphism is the way of writing a piece of code once that can operate on multiple types. Method overloading, method overriding, subtyping, and generics are some of the ways to implement polymorphism.

EXERCISES

Answers to all of the following questions can be found in the different sections of this chapter.

1. What is programming and what is a program?

2. What is the difference between an assembler and a compiler?

3. What is machine language and what does a program written in machine language consist of?

4. What is assembly language and what does a program written in assembly language consist of?

5. Name three higher-level programming languages.

6. Based on the generation of a programming language (1GL, 2GL, etc.), in what categories do Java and SQL fall?

7. What is a programming paradigm? Describe procedural, functional, and object-oriented paradigms with examples.

8. Name the four pillars of object-oriented programming and describe each of them with examples.

9. What is "true" polymorphism and how does Java support it?

10. What is an abstract data type? How does Java support the abstract data type?

CHAPTER 2

■ ■ ■

Setting Up the Environment

In this chapter, you will learn:

- What software you need to write, compile, and run Java programs

- From where to download the required software

- How to verify the installation of the Java Development Kit 9 (JDK 9)

- How to start the `jshell` command-line tool that lets you run snippets of Java code

- From where to download, install, and configure the NetBeans IDE (Integrated Development Environment) used to write, compile, package, and run Java programs

System Requirements

You need to have the following software installed on your computer to follow the examples in this book:

- JDK 9

- A Java editor, preferably NetBeans 9.0 or later

Installing JDK 9

You will need JDK 9 to compile and run the Java programs. You can download JDK 9 for your operating system from `http://www.oracle.com/technetwork/java/javase/downloads/index.html`. Follow the instructions on this web page to install the JDK on your operating system. The web page at `https://docs.oracle.com/javase/9/install/toc.htm` contains a detailed explanation of the JDK installation.

Throughout this book, I assume that you have installed the JDK in the `C:\java9` directory on Windows. If you have installed it in a different directory or you are using a different operating system, you need to use the path for the JDK installation on your system. For example, if you have installed it in the `/home/ksharan/jdk9` directory on a UNIX-like operating system, use `/home/ksharan/jdk9` whenever I use `C:\java9` in this book.

When you work with Java, you will frequently hear three terms:

- `JDK_HOME`

- `JRE_HOME`

- `JAVA_HOME`

JDK_HOME refers to the directory on your computer in which the JDK is installed. If you have installed the JDK in C:\java9, JDK_HOME refers to the C:\java9 directory.

There is a subset of the JDK, which is called the JRE (Java Runtime Environment). If you have compiled Java code and just want to run it, you need to install only the JRE. The JDK contains the JRE with several tools, such as the Java compiler. JRE_HOME refers to the directory on your computer in which you have installed the JRE. You can always use the JDK installation directory as the value for the JRE_HOME because JDK includes JRE.

Typically, JAVA_HOME refers to the JRE_HOME. Depending on the context, it may also refer to the JDK_HOME.

I use the term JDK_HOME in this book to refer to the directory where the JDK 9 is installed. In the next two sections, I explain the directory structure of the JDK and how to verify the JDK installation.

The JDK Directory Structure

In this section, I explain the directory structure of the JDK installation. There are a few significant changes in the way JDK's directories and their contents are organized in JDK 9. I also compare the JDK 8 and JDK 9 directory structure. If you want to migrate your JDK 8 application to JDK 9, the new JDK 9 structure may break your application and you need to pay close attention to the changes described in this section.

Before JDK 9, the JDK build system used to produce two types of runtime images—A Java Runtime Environment (JRE) and a Java Development Kit (JDK). The JRE was a complete implementation of the Java SE Platform and the JDK had an embedded JRE and development tools and libraries. You had a choice to install only JRE or a JDK, which had an embedded JRE. Figure 2-1 shows the main directories in JDK installation prior to Java SE 9. The JDK_HOME is the directory in which the JDK was installed. If you installed JRE only, you will have only directories under the jre directory.

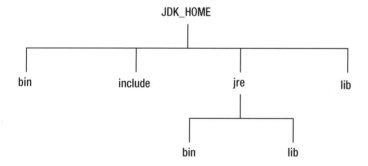

Figure 2-1. *JDK and JRE installation directory arrangements before Java SE 9*

The installation directories in JDK 8 are arranged as follows:

- The bin directory contains the command-line development and debugging tools such as javac, jar, and javadoc. It also contains the java command to launch Java applications.

- The include directory contains C/C++ header files to be used while compiling the native code.

- The lib directory contains several JARs and other types of files for the JDK's tools. It had a tools.jar file, which contains the Java classes for the javac compiler.

- The jre\bin directory contains essential commands such as the java command. On the Windows platform, it contains the system's runtime dynamically linked libraries (DLLs).

- The jre\lib directory contains user-editable configuration files such as .properties and .policy files.

- The jre\lib\endorsed directory contains JARs that allow the Endorsed Standards Override Mechanism, which allows the later versions of classes and interfaces that implement Endorsed Standards or Standalone Technology, which are created outside the Java Community Process, to be incorporated into the Java Platform. These JARs were prepended to the JVM's bootstrap class path, thus overriding any definition of these classes and interfaces present in the Java runtime.

- The jre\lib\ext directory contains JARs that allow the extension mechanism. This mechanism loads all JARs in this directory by an extension class loader, which is the child of the bootstrap class loader and parent of the system class loader, which loads all application classes. By placing JARs in this directory, you can extend the Java SE Platform. The contents of these JARs are visible to all applications that compile with or run on this runtime image.

- The jre\lib directory contains several JARs. The rt.jar file contains the Java classes and resource files for the runtime. Many tools depend on the location of the rt.jar file.

- The jre\lib directory contains dynamically linked native libraries for non-Windows platforms.

- The jre\lib directory contains several other sub-directories, which contain runtime files such as fonts and images.

The root directory of the JDK and of the JRE that is not embedded in a JDK used to contain several files such as COPYRIGHT, LICENSE, and README. A release file in the root directory contains a key-value pair describing the runtime image, such as the Java version, OS version, and architecture. The following is a sample release file from JDK 8, whose partial contents are shown:

```
JAVA_VERSION="1.8.0_66"
OS_NAME="Windows"
OS_VERSION="5.2"
OS_ARCH="amd64"
BUILD_TYPE="commercial"
```

The Java SE 9 has flattened the directory hierarchy for the JDK and removed the distinction between a JDK and a JRE. Figure 2-2 shows the directories for a JDK installation in JDK 9. The JRE 8 installation does not contain the include and jmods directories.

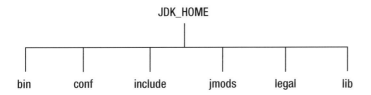

Figure 2-2. *JDK directory arrangements in Java SE 9*

The installation directories in JDK 9 are arranged as follows:

- There is no subdirectory named `jre`.

- The `bin` directory contains all commands. On the Windows platform, it continues to contain the system's runtime dynamically linked libraries.

- The `conf` directory contains the user-editable configuration files such as `.properties` and `.policy` files that used to be in the `jre\lib` directory before.

- The `include` directory contains C/C++ header files to be used while compiling the native code as before. It exists only in the JDK.

- The `jmods` directory contains the platform modules in JMOD format. You need it when creating a custom runtime image. It exists only in the JDK, not in the JRE.

- The `legal` directory contains legal notices.

- The `lib` directory contains the dynamically linked native libraries on the non-Windows platform. Its subdirectories and files are not supposed to be directly edited or used by developers. It contains a file named `modules` that contains the Java SE platform modules in an internal format named JIMAGE.

▓ **Tip**   The JDK 9 is much bigger than JDK 8 because JDK 9 contains two copies of the platform modules—one in the `jmods` directory in the JMOD format and one in the `lib\modules` file in the JIMAGE format.

The root directory of the JDK 9 continues to have files such as COPYRIGHT, LICENSE, and README. The `release` file in JDK 9 contains a new entry with a MODULES key whose value is a list of modules included in the image. Partial contents of a `release` file in JDK 9 image are as follows:

```
MODULES=java.rmi,jdk.jdi,jdk.policytool
OS_VERSION="5.2"
OS_ARCH="amd64"
OS_NAME="Windows"
JAVA_VERSION="9"
JAVA_FULL_VERSION="9-ea+133"
```

I have shown only three modules in the list. In a full JDK install, this list will include all platform modules. In a custom runtime image, this list will contain only the modules that you included in the image.

▓ **Tip**   The `lib\tools.jar` in the JDK and the `lib\rt.jar` in the JRE have been removed from Java SE 9. Classes and resources that were available in these JARs are now stored in the `lib` directory in internal format. A new scheme called `jrt` may be used to retrieve those classes and resources from the runtime image. Applications dependent on the locations of these JARs will stop working.

Verifying the JDK Installation

The JDK_HOME\bin directory contains a command named java, which is used to launch a Java application. When the java command is run with one of the following options, it prints the JDK version information:

- -version
- --version
- -showversion
- --show-version

All four options print the same JDK version information. The options starting with one hyphen are UNIX-style options, whereas the options starting with two hyphens are GNU-style options. JDK 9 introduced GNU-style options. The UNIX-style options print the JDK version on the standard error stream, whereas the GNU-style options print it on the standard output stream. The -version and --version options exit after printing the information, whereas the -showversion and --show-version options continue to execute other options after printing the information. The following command shows how to print the JDK version:

```
C:\>java --version
java 9
Java(TM) SE Runtime Environment (build 9+181)
Java HotSpot(TM) 64-Bit Server VM (build 9+181, mixed mode)
```

If the first line of the output prints "java 9", your JDK installation is fine. You might get an output similar to the one shown:

```
'java' is not recognized as an internal or external command, operable program or batch file.
```

This output indicates that the JDK_HOME\bin directory is not included in the PATH environment variable on your computer. In that case, you can use the full path of the java command to print its version and everywhere else you need it. My JDK_HOME is C:\java9 on Windows. The following commands show you how to use the full path and how to set the PATH environment variable on the command prompt:

```
C:\>C:\java9\bin\java --version
java 9
Java(TM) SE Runtime Environment (build 9+181)
Java HotSpot(TM) 64-Bit Server VM (build 9+181, mixed mode)

C:\>SET PATH=C:\java9\bin;%PATH%

C:\>java --version
java 9
Java(TM) SE Runtime Environment (build 9+181)
Java HotSpot(TM) 64-Bit Server VM (build 9+181, mixed mode)
```

You can also set the PATH environment variable permanently on Windows using the following:

```
 Control Panel > System and Security > System > Advanced system settings > Environment
 Variables
```

If you have more than one JDK installed on your computer, it is easier to create a batch (or a shell) script to open a command prompt and set the PATH environment variable in the script. This way, you can work with multiple JDKs without setting the PATH environment variable at the system level.

Starting the JShell Tool

JDK 9 includes a jshell tool in the JDK_HOME\bin directory. The tool lets you execute a snippet of Java code instead of writing a full Java program. This is very helpful for beginners. Chapter 23 covers the jshell tool in detail. The following commands shows you how to start the jshell tool, execute a few Java snippets of code, and then exit the jshell tool:

```
C:\>jshell
|  Welcome to JShell -- Version 9
|  For an introduction type: /help intro

jshell> System.out.println("Hello JDK 9!")
Hello JDK 9!

jshell> 2 + 2
$2 ==> 4

jshell> /exit
|  Goodbye

C:\>
```

While you are reading subsequent chapters, you can start the jshell tool on a command prompt and enter a snippet of code to see the results.

Installing NetBeans 9

You need a Java editor to write, package, compile, and run your Java application and NetBeans is one such Java editor. The source code for this book contains NetBeans projects. However, it is not necessary to use NetBeans. You can use another Java editor such as Eclipse, IntelliJ IDEA, or JDeveloper. To follow the examples in this book, you need to copy the source code (the .java files) to the projects that you create using another Java editor.

You can download NetBeans from *https://netbeans.org/*. NetBeans 9.0 runs on JDK 8 and JDK 9. When you install NetBeans, it will ask you to select the JDK home directory. If you install NetBeans on JDK 8, you can select JDK 9 as the Java platform to use JDK 9 inside NetBeans. If you install it on JDK 9, JDK 9 will be the default Java platform inside NetBeans. In the next section, I show you how to select a Java platform inside the NetBeans IDE.

Configuring NetBeans

Start the NetBeans IDE. If you open the IDE for the first time, it shows a pane titled Start Page, as shown in Figure 2-3. If you do not want this to show again, you can uncheck the checkbox labeled Show On Startup, which is on the upper-right corner of the pane. You can close the Start Page pane by clicking the X in the pane's header. If you want to show this page at any time, you can use the Help --> Start Page menu item.

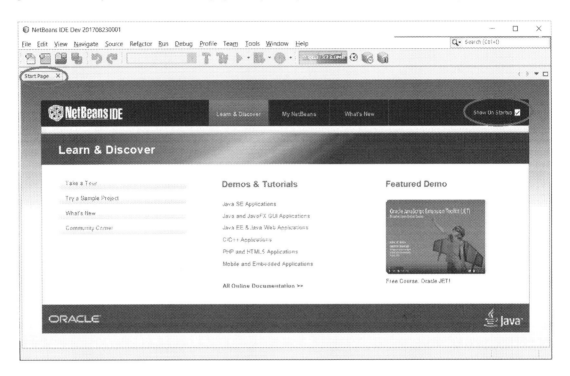

Figure 2-3. *The Initial NetBeans IDE screen*

Select Tools ➤ Java Platform to display the Java Platform Manager dialog box, as shown in Figure 2-4. I am running the NetBeans IDE on JDK 1.8, which is shown in the Platforms list. If you are running it on JDK 9, the JDK 9 will be shown in the Platforms list and you do not need any further configuration.

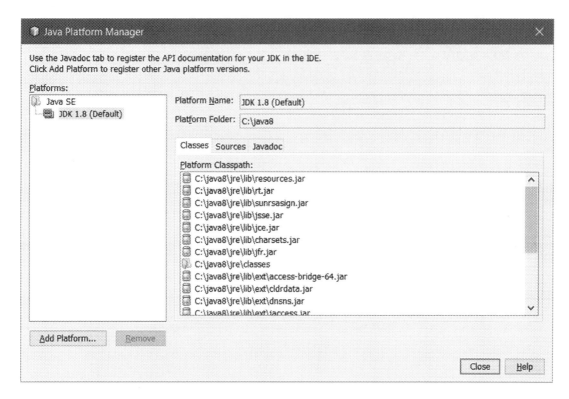

Figure 2-4. *The Java Platform Manager dialog box*

If you see JDK 9 in the Platforms list, your IDE has been configured to use JDK 9 and you can close the dialog box by clicking the Close button. If you do not see JDK 9 in the Platforms list, click the Add Platform... button to open the Add Java Platform dialog box, as shown on in Figure 2-5. Make sure that the Java Standard Edition radio button is selected. Click the Next ➤ button to display the Add Java Platform dialog box, as shown in Figure 2-6.

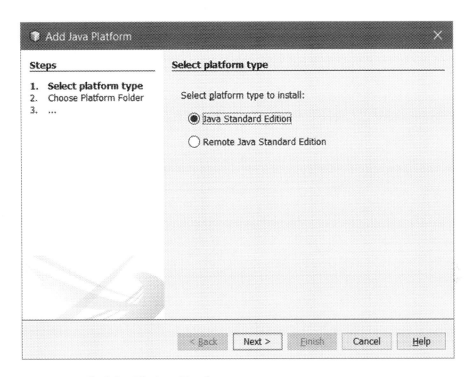

Figure 2-5. *The Select Platform Type box*

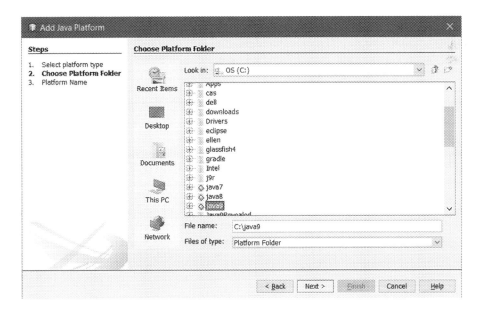

Figure 2-6. *The Add Java Platform dialog box*

On the Add Java Platform dialog box, select the directory in which the JDK 9 is installed. I installed the JDK 9 in C:\java9, so I selected the C:\java9 directory on this dialog box. Click the Next ➤ button. The Add Java Platform dialog box, as shown in Figure 2-7, is displayed. The Platform Name and Platform Sources fields are prefilled.

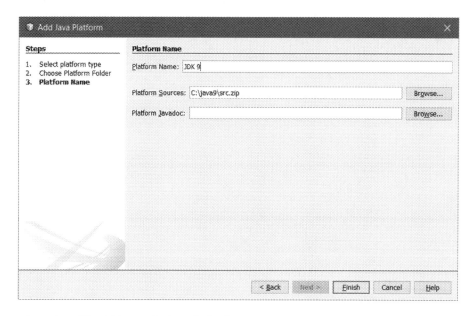

Figure 2-7. *The Add Java Platform dialog box*

Click the Finish button, which will bring you back to the Java Platform Manager dialog box showing JDK 9 as an item in the Platforms list, as shown in Figure 2-8. Click the Close button to close the dialog box. You are done with configuring the NetBeans IDE to use the JDK 9.

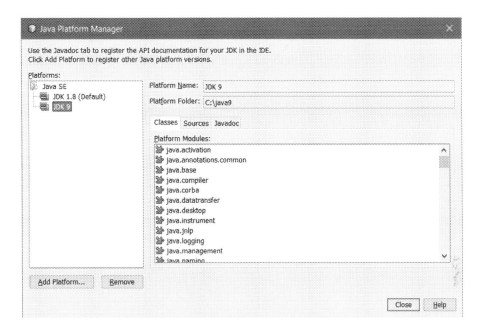

Figure 2-8. *The Java Platform Manager showing JDK 1.8 and JDK 9 as Java platforms*

Summary

To work with Java programs, you need to install JDK 9 and a Java editor such as NetBeans. The directory in which the JDK is installed is typically referred to as JDK_HOME. JDK installation copies many Java tools/commands in the JDK_HOME\bin directory, such as the javac command to compile a Java program, the java command to run a Java program, and the jshell tool to run snippets of Java code.

The NetBeans IDE can be installed on top of JDK 8 or JDK 9. When you install it on top of JDK 8, you need to configure the IDE to use JDK 9 as one of the Java platforms.

CHAPTER 3

Writing Java Programs

In this chapter, you will learn:

- About the structure of a Java program
- How to organize the source code of a Java program
- How to write, compile, and run a Java program using the Java Shell, a command prompt, and the NetBeans integrated development environment (IDE)
- What observable and resolved modules are
- What a module graph is
- What the module path and the class path are and how to use them
- Briefly about the Java Platform and the Java Virtual Machine (JVM)

This chapter and the rest of the chapters in this book assume that you have installed JDK 9 and NetBeans IDE 9, as described in Chapter 2.

The Goal Statement

The main goal of this chapter is simple—write a Java program to print the following message on the console:

```
Welcome to Java 9!
```

You might think—how hard would it be to print a message in Java? In fact, it is not hard to print a message in Java. The following one line of code will print this message:

```
System.out.println("Welcome to Java 9!");
```

However, you have to do a lot of plumbing work to print this message in a full-fledged Java program. I will show you how to print a message in Java using three methods:

- Using the Java Shell, which is also known as the JShell tool
- Using a command prompt or a terminal
- Using the NetBeans IDE

Using the JShell tool requires no plumbing work and is the easiest of all. It will let you print a message without knowing anything else about the Java programming language.

Using a command prompt requires the most plumbing work and makes you learn the basics of the Java program's structure before you can print a message as the stated goal in this section.

Using the NetBeans IDE requires a little plumbing work and provides the most help you would need as a developer. After this chapter, you will use only NetBeans to write all programs unless the other two methods are required to show their special features. The following sections show you how to achieve the stated goal using the three methods.

Using the JShell Tool

Chapter 2 has a quick introduction to the JShell tool. You need to enter the following line of code to print the message:

```
System.out.println("Welcome to Java9!");
```

I explain each part of this code in the next section. The following JShell session shows you all the steps in a Windows command prompt:

```
c:\>jshell
|  Welcome to JShell -- Version 9-ea
|  For an introduction type: /help intro

jshell> System.out.println("Welcome to Java 9!");
Welcome to Java 9!

jshell> /exit
|  Goodbye

c:\>
```

You have seen how to execute a Java statement using JShell. You have not seen a full Java program yet. JShell is a very powerful tool and you can use it to learn the Java language quickly. For the next few chapters, it will be a handy tool to experiment with code snippets used in examples. I cover all its details in a chapter later in this book.

What Is a Java Program?

A Java program, which is written using the rules and grammar of the Java programming language, is a set of instructions to be executed by a computer to perform a task. In the next few sections, I explain only the basics involved in writing a Java program. I cover a detailed explanation of all aspects of a Java program in subsequent chapters. Developing a Java application involves four steps:

- Writing the source code

- Compiling the source code

- Packaging the compiled code

- Running the compiled code

You can write Java programs using a text editor of your choice, such as Notepad on Windows and the vi editor on UNIX. The source code is compiled into object code, also known as *bytecode*, using a Java compiler. The compiled code is packaged into a JAR file (**J**ava **Ar**chive). The packaged compiled code is run by a JVM.

When you are using an IDE such as NetBeans, the IDE provides you with a built-in editor to write the source code. The IDE also provides you simple ways to compile, package, and run the application.

Writing the Source Code

This section covers the details of writing the source code. I demonstrate this by using Notepad on Windows. You can use a text editor of your choice that is available on your operating system.

▒ **Note**   I cover using the NetBeans IDE later in this chapter. I first want to cover using a text editor because the process reveals a lot about Java programs that you need to know.

When you finish writing the source code, you must save the file with the extension .java. You are going to name your source code file Welcome.java. Note that any extension to the file other than .java is not acceptable. For example, the names like Welcome.txt and Welcome.doc are not valid source code file names.

Whenever you use a language to write something (in your case, Java source code), you need to follow the grammar of that language, and use a specific syntax depending on the thing you are writing. Let's take an example of writing a letter to your friend. The letter will have several parts: a heading, a greeting, a body, closing statements, and your signature. In a letter, it is not just important to put all five parts together; rather, they should also be placed in a specific order. For example, the closing needs to follow the body. Some parts in a letter may be optional and others mandatory. For example, it is fine to exclude the return address in a letter to your friend, whereas it is mandatory in a business letter. In the beginning, you can think of writing a Java program similar to writing a letter.

A Java program consists of one or more modules. A module contains zero or more packages. A package contains one or more types. The term *type* is a generic term that refers to a user-defined data type. You can have four types of user-defined data types—classes, interfaces, enums, and annotations. Broadly speaking, enums and annotations are specialized types of classes and interfaces, respectively. In the next several chapters, you will be working with only classes. Figure 3-1 shows the arrangement of a module.

Module

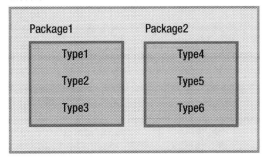

Figure 3-1. *The structure of a Java program*

▓ **Note** Modules were introduced in JDK 9. Up to JDK 8, you had packages and types, but no modules.

Pure Java programs are operating system agnostic. You write the same Java code on all operating systems. Operating systems use different syntax to refer to files and separate file paths. While working with Java programs, you have to refer to files and directories and you will need to use the syntax for your operating system. Windows uses a backslash (\) as a directory separator in a file path, for example, `C:\bj9f\src`, whereas UNIX-like operating systems use a forward slash (/), for example, `/home/ksharan/bj9f`. Windows uses a semicolon (;) as a path separator, for example, `C:\java9\bin;C:\bj9r`, whereas UNIX-like operating systems use a colon (:), for example, `/home/ksharan/java9/bin:/home/ksharan/bj9f`. I use Windows to work with examples in this book. I also explain the differences while using different operating systems whenever they exist.

I use the following directory structure to work with the example in this section.

- `bj9f`
- `bj9f\src`
- `bj9f\mod`
- `bj9f\lib`

I named the top-level directory `bj9f`, which is short for Beginning Java 9 Fundamentals. You can create this directory inside any other directory on your computer. For example, you can have it as `C:\bj9f` on Windows and `/home/ksharan/bj9f` on UNIX. You will store the source code in the `bj9f\src` directory, the compiled code in the `bj9f\mod` directory, and the packaged code in the `bj9f\lib` directory. Go ahead and create these directories on your computer. You need them in the sections that follow.

Writing Comments

Comments are non-executable code that is used to document the code. The Java compiler ignores them. They are included in source code to document the program's functionality and logic. Java supports three types of comments:

- Single-line comment
- Multi-line comment
- Documentation comment or Javadoc comment

A single-line comment starts with two forward slashes (//) followed by text. For example:

```
// This is a single-line comment
package com.jdojo.intro; // This is also a single-line comment
```

A single-line comment may start at any position in a line. The part of the line starting from two forward slashes to the end of the line is considered a comment. As shown previously, you can also mix Java source code, for example, a package declaration and a comment in one line. Note that this type of comment cannot be inserted in the middle of the Java code. The following package declaration, which is discussed shortly in detail, is incorrect because the package name and the semicolon are also considered as part of the comment:

```
package // An incorrect single-line comment com.jdojo.intro;
```

The following line is a single-line comment. It has a valid package declaration as the comment's text. It will be treated as a comment, not as a package declaration.

```
// package com.jdojo.intro;
```

The second type of comment is called a multi-line comment. A multi-line comment may span multiple lines. It starts with a forward slash immediately followed by an asterisk (/*) and ends with an asterisk immediately followed by a forward slash (*/). An example of a multi-line comment in a Java source code is as follows:

```
/*
    This is a multi-line comment.
    It can span more than one line.
*/
```

This comment can also be written using two single-line comments, as follows:

```
// This is a multi-line comment.
// It can span more than one line
```

The style of comment that you use in the source code is your personal choice. A multi-line comment may be inserted in the middle of Java code, as shown here. The compiler ignores all text starting from /* to */.

```
package /* A correct comment */ com.jdojo.intro;
```

The third type of comment is called documentation (or Javadoc) comment, which is also a multi-line comment. It is used to generate documentation for Java programs. This kind of comment begins with a forward slash immediately followed by two asterisks (/**) and ends with an asterisk that is immediately followed by a forward slash (*/).The following is a simple example of a documentation comment:

```
/**
    This is a documentation comment. javadoc generates documentation from such comments.
*/
```

Writing Javadoc comments is a vast topic. It is covered in Appendix B in detail. I start all source code in this book with a single-line comment that contains the name of the file that contains the source code, for example:

```
// Welcome.java
```

Declaring a Module

A module acts as a container for packages. A module may contain packages that may be used internally within the module or by other modules. A module controls the accessibility of its packages. A module exports its packages for other modules to use them. If a module needs to use packages from another module,

49

the first module needs to declare dependency on the second module and the second module needs to export the packages used by the first module. The following is the simplified syntax to declare a module:

```
module <module-name> {
    <module-statement-1>
    <module-statement-2>
}
```

A module's declaration starts with a keyword module, which is followed with a module name. Within braces, you place the body of the module's declaration, which contains zero or more module statements. Listing 3-1 contains the complete code for a module named jdojo.intro.

Listing 3-1. The Declaration of a Module Named jdojo.intro

```
// module-info.java
module jdojo.intro {
    // An empty module body
}
```

The jdojo.intro module contains no module statements. That is, it does not export any packages for other modules to use and does not depend on any other modules. JDK 9 consists of several modules; one of those modules is named java.base. The java.base module is known as the primordial module. It depends on no other modules and all other modules—built-in and user-defined—implicitly depend on it.

▓ **Tip**   In Java, three terms—"depends on," "reads," and "requires"—are used interchangeably to indicate dependency of one module on another module. If module P depends on module Q, you can also state it as "Module P reads module Q" or "Module P requires module Q".

The dependency of a module is declared inside its body using a requires statement. Its simplest syntax is as follows:

```
requires <module-name>;
```

You have not declared any dependencies for the jdojo.intro module. However, as every module in Java implicitly depends on the java.base module, the compiler will add a dependency to the java.base module in your java.intro module. The compiler-modified declaration of the module is shown in Listing 3-2.

Listing 3-2. The Compiler-Modified Declaration of the jdojo.intro Module

```
// module-info.java
module jdojo.intro {
    requires java.base;
}
```

If you wish, you can always include a "requires java.base" statement in your module declaration. If you do not do so, the compiler always adds it for you. I do not include it in module declarations in this book.

Why does every module depend on the java.base module? The java.base module contains several Java packages that are required to provide basic functionalities in all Java programs. For example, you want to print a message on the console and the printing functionality is contained in the java.base module in a package named java.lang.

Typically, a module declaration is saved in a module-info.java file in the root directory of the source for the module. Create a subdirectory named jdojo.intro inside the bj9f\src directory in which you place all source for the jdojo.intro module. Save the code shown in Listing 3-1 in a file called bj9f\src\jdojo.intro\module-info.java. This completes your module declaration.

Is it mandatory to save the module declaration in a root directory named the same as the module name? No. This is not mandatory. You could have saved the module-info.java file inside the bj9f\src directory and everything would have worked. Saving all source code of a module in a directory named after the module name makes compiling the module's code easier. JDK 9 also supports saving a module's code in different root directories.

Declaring Types

A package is divided into several compilation units. A compilation unit contains the source code for these types. For the most part, you can think of a compilation unit as a .java file that contains source code for types such as classes and interfaces. When you compile a Java program, you compile the compilation units that program comprises. Typically, a compilation unit contains the declaration of one type. For example, you are going to declare a class named Welcome and you will place the source code for the Welcome class in a compilation unit (or a file) named Welcome.java. A compilation unit consists of three parts:

- One package declaration
- Zero or more import declarations
- Zero or more type declarations: class, interface, enum, or annotation declarations

All three parts, if present, must be specified in the mentioned order. Figure 3-2 shows the three parts of a compilation unit, which contains one type declaration. The type is a class named Welcome. Subsequent sections describe each part of a compilation unit in detail.

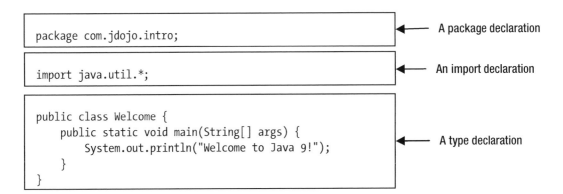

Figure 3-2. Parts of a compilation unit

Package Declaration

The general syntax for a package declaration is as follows:

```
package <your-package-name>;
```

A package declaration starts with the keyword package followed with a user-supplied package name. Whitespace (spaces, tabs, new lines, carriage returns, tabs, and form-feeds) separate the keyword package and the package name. A semicolon (;) ends the package declaration. For example, the following is the package declaration for a package named com.jdojo.intro:

```
package com.jdojo.intro;
```

Figure 3-3 shows the parts of a package declaration.

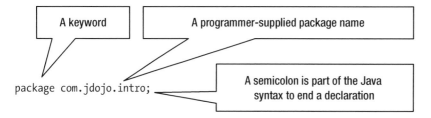

Figure 3-3. *Parts of a package declaration in a compilation unit*

You supply the package name. A package name may consist of one or more parts separated by a dot (.). In this example, the package name consists of three parts: com, jdojo, and intro. There is no limit to the number of parts in a package name. You can have maximum of one package declaration in a compilation unit. All types declared in a compilation unit become a member of that package. The following are some examples of valid package declarations:

```
package intro;
package com.jdojo.intro.common;
package com.ksharan;
package com.jdojo.intro;
```

How do you choose a good package name? It is important to keep your package names unique, so they do not conflict with other package names used in the same application. It is recommended to use the reverse domain name notation for the leading part of a package such as com.yahoo for Yahoo, com.google for Google, etc. Using the reverse domain name of the company as the leading part of the package name guarantees that a package name will not conflict with package names used by other companies, provided they follow the same guidelines. If you do not own a domain name, make up one that is likely to be unique. This is just a guideline. There is nothing in practice that guarantees a unique package name for all Java programs written in the world. For example, I own a domain named jdojo.com and I start all my package names with com.jdojo to keep them unique. In this book, I start a package named com.jdojo followed by the topic name.

Why do we use a package declaration? A package is a logical repository for types. In other words, it provides a logical grouping for related types. A package can be stored in a host-specific file system or a network location. In a file system, each part of a package name denotes a directory on the host system. For example, the package name com.jdojo.intro indicates the existence of a directory named com, which contains a subdirectory named jdojo, which contains a subdirectory named intro. That is, the package name com.jdojo.intro indicates existence of a com\jdojo\intro directory on Windows and a com/jdojo/intro directory on UNIX-like operating systems. The intro directory will contain the compiled Java code for all types in the com.jdojo.intro package. A dot, which is used to separate parts in a package name, is treated as a file-separator character on the host system. Note that a backslash (\) is the file-separator character on Windows, and a forward slash (/) is used on UNIX-like operating systems.

The package name specifies only the partial directory structure in which the compiled Java program (class files) must exist. It does not specify the full path of the class files. In this example, the package declaration com.jdojo.intro does not specify where the com directory is placed. It may be placed under the C:\ directory, or the C:\myprograms directory, or under any other directory in the file system. Knowing just the package name is not enough to locate a class file, because it specifies only a partial path to the class file. The leading part of the class file path on the file system is obtained from *module path*, which you need to specify when you compile and run Java programs. Before JDK 9, class files in a package were located using class path, which is still supported in JDK 9 for backward compatibility. I discuss both approaches later in this chapter.

Java source code is case sensitive. The keyword package has to be written as is—in all lowercase. The word Package or packAge cannot replace the keyword package. The package name is also case sensitive. On some operating systems, the names of files and directories are case sensitive. On those systems, the package names will be case sensitive, as you have seen: the package name is treated as a directory name on the host system. The package names com.jdojo.intro and Com.jdojo.intro may not be the same depending on the host system that you are working on. It is recommended to use package names in all lowercase.

Before JDK 9, the package declaration in a compilation unit was optional. If a compilation unit does not contain a package declaration, the types declared in that compilation unit belong to a package called *unnamed package*. JDK 9 does not allow an unnamed package in a module. If you are placing your types in modules, your compilation unit must contain a package declaration.

Import Declarations

Import declarations in a compilation unit are optional. You may develop a Java application without using even a single import declaration. Why is an import declaration needed at all? Using import declarations makes your life easier. It saves you some typing and makes your code cleaner and easier to read. In an import declaration, you tell the Java compiler that you may use one or more types from a particular package. Whenever a type is used in a compilation unit, it must be referred to by its fully qualified name. Using an import declaration for a type lets you refer to a type using its simple name. I will discuss simple and fully qualified names of a type shortly.

Unlike a package declaration, there is no restriction on the number of import declarations in the source code. The following are two import declarations:

```
import com.jdojo.intro.Account;
import com.jdojo.util.*;
```

I discuss import declarations in detail later in this book. In this section, I discuss only the meanings of all parts of an import declaration.

An import declaration starts with the keyword import. The second part in an import declaration consists of two parts:

- A package name from which you want to use types in the current compilation unit

- A type name or an asterisk (*) to indicate that you may use one or more of the types stored in the package

Finally, an import declaration ends with a semicolon. The previous two import declarations state the following:

- We may use a type named `Account` by its simple name from the `com.jdojo.intro` package.

- We may use any types by their simple names from the `com.jdojo.util` package.

If you want to use a class named `Person` from the `com.jdojo.common` package, you need to include one of the following two import declarations in your compilation unit:

```
import com.jdojo.common.Person;
```

or

```
import com.jdojo.common.*;
```

The following import declarations do not include classes in the package `com` or `com.jdojo`:

```
import com.jdojo.intro.Account;
import com.jdojo.intro.*;
```

You might think that an import declaration like this

```
import com.*.*;
```

would let you use the simple names of all types whose first part of package declaration is `com`. Java does not support this type of wildcard use in an import declaration. You are allowed only to name one type in a package (`com.jdojo.intro.Account`) or all types in a package (`com.jdojo.intro.*`); any other syntax to import types is invalid.

The third part in a Java source code contains type declarations, which may contain zero or more declarations for types: class, interface, enum, and annotation. According to the Java Language Specification, type declaration is also optional. However, if you omit this part, your Java program does not do anything. To make your Java program meaningful, you must include at least one type declaration in a compilation unit. I will defer the discussion of interfaces, enums, and annotations until later chapters in this book. Let's discuss how to declare a class in a compilation unit.

Class Declaration

In the simplest form, a class declaration looks as follows:

```
class Welcome {
    // Code for the class body goes here
};
```

Figure 3-4 shows parts of this class declaration.

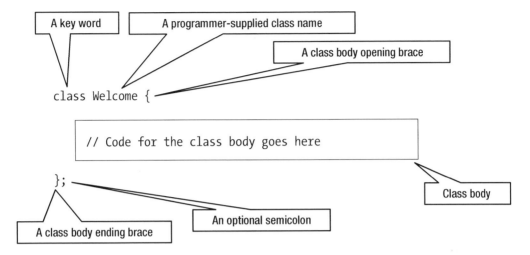

Figure 3-4. *Parts of a class declaration in a compilation unit*

A class is declared by using the keyword class, which is followed by the name of the class. In this example, the name of the class is Welcome.

The body of the class is placed between an opening brace and a closing brace. The body may be empty. However, you must include the two braces to mark the beginning and the end of the body.

Optionally, a class declaration may end with a semicolon. This book will not use the optional semicolon to end a class declaration.

The simplest class declaration in a Java program may look as follows:

```
class Welcome { }
```

This time, I placed the whole class declaration on one line. You can place the keyword class, the name of the class Welcome, and the two braces in any position you want, except that you must include at least one whitespace character (space, newline, tab, etc.) between the keyword class and class name Welcome. Java allows you to write source code in a freeform text format. All of the following three class declarations are the same:

```
// Class Declaration #1
class
Welcome { }

// Class Declaration #2
class
        Welcome {
}

// Class Declaration #3
class Welcome {
}
```

This book uses the following class declaration format: the opening brace is placed on the same line following the class name, and the closing brace is placed on a separate line and is aligned with the first character of the first line of the class declaration, like so:

```java
class Welcome {
}
```

The body of a class consists of four parts. All parts are optional, may appear in any order, and can be split into multiple sections.

- Field declarations

- Initializers: Static initializers and instance initializers

- Constructors

- Method declarations

Java does not impose any order in which the four parts of the body of a class may appear. I start with method declarations and confine the discussion only to simple method declarations in this chapter. I discuss advanced aspects of method declarations and other parts of class body declarations in a later chapter.

Let's discuss how to declare a method in a class. You might guess that the method declaration would begin with a keyword method, as package and class declarations began with the keywords package and class, respectively. However, a method declaration does not begin with a keyword method. In fact, method is not a keyword in Java language. You begin a class declaration with the keyword class indicating that you are going to declare a class. However, in case of a method declaration, the first thing you specify is the type of value that a method will return to its caller. If a method does not return anything to its caller, you must mention that fact at the beginning of the method declaration using the keyword void. The name of the method follows the return type of the method. The method name is followed with a left and a right parenthesis. Like a class, a method has a body, which is enclosed in braces. The simplest method declaration in Java looks like the following:

```java
<method-return-type> <method-name> (<arguments-list>) {
    // Body of the method goes here
}
```

The following is an example of a method declaration:

```java
void main() {
    // Empty body of the main method
}
```

This method declaration contains four things:

- The method does not return anything, as indicated by the keyword void.

- The name of the method is main.

- The method requires no arguments.

- The method does not do anything, as its body is empty.

The return value of a method is something that the method returns to its caller. The caller of the method may also want to pass some values to the method. If a method requires its caller to pass values to it, this fact must be indicated in the method's declaration. The fact that you want to pass values to a method is specified within the parentheses that follow the method name. You need to specify two things about the values you want to pass to a method:

- The type of the value you want to pass. Suppose you want to pass an integer (say 10) to the method. You need to indicate this by using a keyword int, which is used to indicate an integer value like 10.

- The identifier, which will hold the value you pass to the method. Identifier is a user-defined name. It is called a parameter name.

If you want the main method to accept one integer value from its caller, its declaration will change to the following one:

```
void main(int num) {
}
```

Here, num is an identifier, which will hold the value passed to this method. Instead of num, you may choose to use another identifier, for example, num1, num2, num3, myNumber, etc. The declaration of the main method is read as follows:

The main method accepts one parameter of the type int and it does not return any value to its caller.

If you want to pass two integers to the main method, its declaration will change to the following:

```
void main(int num1, int num2) {

}
```

It is clear from this declaration that you need to separate the parameters passed to a method by a comma (,). What will you do if you want to pass 50 integers to this method? You will end up with a method declaration like this:

```
void main(int num1, int num2, ..., int num50) {

}
```

I have shown only three parameter declarations. However, when you write a Java program, you will have to type all 50 parameter declarations. Let's look for a better way to pass 50 parameters to this method. There is one similarity among all 50 parameters—that they are all of the same type—an integer. No values will contain fractions like 20.11 or 45.09. This similarity among all parameters allows you to use a magical creature in the Java language called an *array*. What is required to use an array to pass 50 integer parameters to this method? When you write

```
int num
```

it means that num is an identifier of the type int and it can hold one integer value. If you place two magic brackets ([]) after int, as in

```
int[] num
```

it means that num is an array of int and it can hold as many integer values as you want. There is a limit to the number of integers that num can hold. However, that limit is very high and I discuss that limit when I discuss arrays in detail. The values stored in num can be accessed using subscripts: num[0], num[1], num[2], etc. Note that in declaring an array of the type int, you have not mentioned the fact that you want num to represent 50 integers. Your modified declaration for the main method, which can accept 50 integers, would be as follows:

```
void main(int[] num) {

}
```

How will you declare the main method, which will let you pass names of 50 persons? Since int can only be used for integers, you must look for some other type that represents text in Java language because the name of a person will be text, not an integer. There is a type String (note the uppercase S in String) that represents text in the Java language. Therefore, to pass 50 names to the method main, you can change its declaration as follows:

```
void main(String[] name) {

}
```

In this declaration, you need not necessarily change the parameter name from num to name. You changed it just to make the meaning of the parameter clear and intuitive. Now let's add some Java code to the body of the main method, which will print a message on the console.

```
System.out.println("The message you want to print");
```

This is not the appropriate place to discuss what System, out, and println are all about. For now, just type in System (note the uppercase S in System), a dot, out, a dot, println followed by two parentheses that contain the message you want to print within double quotes. You want to print a message "Welcome to Java 9!" so your main method declaration will be as follows:

```
void main(String[] name) {
    System.out.println("Welcome to Java 9!");
}
```

This is a valid method declaration that will print a message on the console. Your next step is to compile the source code, which contains the Welcome class declaration, and run the compiled code. When you run a class, the Java runtime looks for a method named main in that class and the declaration of the method must be as follows, though name could be any identifier.

```
public static void main(String[] name) {
}
```

Apart from two keywords, public and static, you should be able to understand this method declaration, which states: "main is a method that accepts an array of String as a parameter and returns nothing."

For now, you can think of public and static just as two keywords, which must be present to declare the main method. Note that the Java runtime also requires that the name of the method be main. This is the reason that I chose main as the name of the method from the very beginning. The final version of the source code is shown in Listing 3-3. I made two changes:

- I declared the Welcome class as public.

- I named the parameter to the main method as args.

Save the source code in a file named Welcome.java in the bj9f\src\jdojo.intro\com\jdojo\intro directory.

Listing 3-3. The Source Code for the Welcome Class

```
// Welcome.java
package com.jdojo.intro;

public class Welcome {
    public static void main(String[] args) {
        System.out.println("Welcome to Java 9!");
    }
}
```

The Java compiler imposes a restriction on the file name of the source code. If you have declared a public type (e.g., a class or interface) in a compilation unit, the file name of the compilation unit must be the same as the name of the public type. In this example, you have declared the Welcome class public, which requires you to name the file as Welcome.java. This also means that you cannot declare more than one public type in a compilation unit. You can have maximum one public type and any number of non-public types in a compilation.

At this point, the source directory and files for this example look as follows:

- bj9f\src\jdojo.intro\module-info.java

- bj9f\src\jdojo.intro\com\jdojo\intro\Welcome.java

Types Have Two Names

Every class (in fact, every type) in Java has two names

- A simple name

- A fully qualified name

The simple name of a class is the name that appears after the class keyword in the class declaration. In this example, Welcome is the simple name of the class. The fully qualified name of a class is its package name followed by a dot and its simple name. In this example, com.jdojo.intro.Welcome is the fully qualified name of the class.

```
Simple-Name = "Name appearing in the type declaration"
Fully-Qualified-Name = "package name" + "." + "Simple-Name"
```

The next question that might arise in your mind is, "What is the fully qualified name of a class that does not have a package declaration?" The answer is simple. In such a case, the simple name and the fully qualified name of the class are the same. If you remove the package declaration from the source code, Welcome will be both names for your class.

Compiling the Source Code

Compiling is the process of translating the source code into a special binary format called *bytecode*. This is accomplished using a program (usually called a compiler) called javac, which ships with the JDK. The process of compiling Java source code is shown in Figure 3-5.

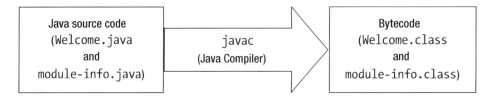

Figure 3-5. *The process of compiling Java source code into bytecode*

You supply the source code (in your case, Welcome.java and module-info.java) as input to the Java compiler and it generates two files with the extension .class. The file with the extension .class is called a class file. A class file is in a special format called bytecode. Bytecode is a machine language for Java virtual machine (JVM). I discuss the JVM and bytecode later in this chapter.

Now, I walk through the steps that are needed to compile the source code on Windows. For other platforms, for example, UNIX and MacOS X, you need to use the file path syntax specific to those platforms. I assume that you have saved the two source files on Windows as follows:

- C:\bj9f\src\jdojo.intro\module-info.java

- C:\bj9f\src\jdojo.intro\com\jdojo\intro\Welcome.java

Open a command prompt and change the current directory to the C:\bj9f. The prompt should look as follows:

C:\bj9f>

The syntax to use the javac command is as follows:

javac –d <output-directory> <source-file1> <source-file2>...<source-fileN>

The -d option specifies the output directory where the compiled class files will be placed. You can specify one or more source code files. If the –d option is not specified, the compiled class files are placed in the same location as the source file.

Your output directory will be bj9r\mod\jdojo.intro because you want to place all class files in this directory. You will specify two source files, which will be module-info.java and Welcome.java. The following command will compile your source code. The command is entered on one line, not on two as shown:

C:\bj9f>javac -d mod\jdojo.intro src\jdojo.intro\module-info.java src\jdojo.intro\com\jdojo\intro\Welcome.java

Note that the command uses relative paths such as mod and src, which are relative to the current directory C:\bj9f. If you wish, you can use absolute paths such as C:\bj9f\mod\jdojo.intro.

60

If you do not get an error message, it means your source files were compiled successfully and the compiler generated two files named `module-info.class` and `Welcome.class` as follows:

- `C:\bj9f\mod\jdojo.intro\module-info.class`

- `C:\bj9f\mod\jdojo.intro\com\jdojo\intro\Welcome.class`

Note that the compiler placed the `Welcome.class` file by creating a directory hierarchy that mirrors the package declaration in the `Welcome.java` file. Recall that a package name mirrors a directory hierarchy. For example, a package named `com.jdojo.intro` corresponds to a directory named `com\jdojo\intro`. You had placed the `Welcome.java` file by creating a directory hierarchy mirroring the package name. The Java compiler is smart enough to read the package name and create a directory hierarchy in the output directory to place the generated class files.

If you get any error while compiling the source code, there could be one of three reasons:

- You have not saved the `module-info.java` and `Welcome.java` file in the directories as specified at the beginning of this section.

- You may not have installed the JDK 9 on your machine.

- If you have already installed the JDK 9, you have not added the `JDK_HOME\bin` directory to the `PATH` environment variable, where `JDK_HOME` refers to the directory where you installed the JDK 9 on your machine. If you installed JDK 9 in the directory `C:\java9`, you need to add `C:\java9\bin` to the `PATH` environment variable on your machine.

If the discussion about setting the `PATH` environment variable did not help, you can use the following command. This command assumes that you have installed JDK in the directory `C:\java9`.

```
C:\bj9f> C:\java9\bin\javac -d mod\jdojo.intro src\jdojo.intro\module-info.java src\jdojo.
intro\com\jdojo\intro\Welcome.java
```

If you get the following error message while compiling your source code, it means you are using an older version of the JDK, for example, JDK 8 or JDK 7.

```
src\jdojo.intro\module-info.java:1: error: class, interface, or enum expected
module jdojo.intro {
```

Modules are supported starting JDK 9. Compiling the `module-info.java` source file on older JDKs will cause this error. The fix is to use the `javac` command from JDK 9 to compile your source files.

The name of the bytecode file (the `.class` file) is `Welcome.class`. Why did the compiler choose to name the class file `Welcome.class`? You have used the word "Welcome" at three places when you wrote the source code and compiled it.

- First, you declared a class named `Welcome`.

- Second, you saved the source code in a file named `Welcome.java`.

- And third, you passed the `Welcome.java` file name to the compiler as an input.

Which one of your three steps prompted the compiler to name the generated bytecode file as `Welcome.class`? As a first guess, it appears to be the third step, which is passing `Welcome.java` as an input file name to the Java compiler. However, the guess is wrong. It is the first step, which is declaring a class named `Welcome` in the file `Welcome.java`, which prompted the compiler to name the output bytecode file `Welcome.class`. You can declare as many classes as you want in one compilation unit. Suppose you declare two classes, `Welcome` and `Bye`, in a compilation unit named `Welcome.java`. What file name will the compiler choose to name the output class file? The compiler scans the whole compilation unit. It creates one class file for each class (in fact, for each type) declared in the compilation unit. If the Welcome.java file had three classes—Welcome, Thanks, and Bye—the compiler would have generated three class files, Welcome.class, Thanks.class, and Bye.class.

To run a Java program, you can arrange class files:

- In exploded directories, as you have them at this point

- In one or more JAR files

- Or a combination of the two—exploded directories and JAR files

You can run your program now using the class files in the bj9f\mod\java.intro directory. I will defer running it for now. First I show you how to package your compiled code into a JAR file in the next section.

Packaging the Compiled Code

The JDK ships with a tool named jar, which is used to package Java compiled code in JAR files. The JAR file format uses the ZIP format. A JAR file is simply a ZIP file with a .jar extension and a MANIFEST.MF file in its META-INF directory. The MANIFEST.MF file is a text file that contains information about the JAR file and its contents that is used by different Java tools. The JDK also contains APIs to programmatically work with JAR files. I cover JAR files in detail in the second volume of this *Beginning Java 9* series. In this section, I explain briefly how to use the jar tool to create a JAR file. The syntax to use the jar command is as follows:

```
jar [options] [-C <dir-to-change>] <file-list>
```

The --create option creates a new JAR file. The --file option is used to specify the name of the JAR file to be created. The –C option is used to specify a directory, which will be used as the current directory and all the files specified following this option will be included to the JAR file. If you want to include files from several directories, you can specify the –C option multiple times.

The following command creates a JAR file named com.jdojo.intro.jar in the C:\bj9f\lib directory. Make sure that the C:\bj9f\lib directory exists before you run the command.

```
C:\bj9f>jar --create --file lib/com.jdojo.intro.jar -C mod/jdojo.intro .
```

Here,

- The --create option specifies that you want to create a new JAR file.

- The --file lib/com.jdojo.intro.jar option specifies the path and the name of the new file. Note that the file path starts with lib, which is relative to the C:\bj9f directory. You are free to use an absolute path such as C:\bj9f\lib\com.jdojo.intro.jar.

- The -C mod/jdojo.intro option specifies that the jar command should change to the mod/jdojo.intro directory.

- Note that the -C option is followed by a space, which in turn is followed with a dot or the command ends with a dot. A dot means the current directory, which is the directory specified with the -C option. It says to change to the mod/jdojo.intro directory and include all files in that directory recursively.

This command creates the following file:

```
C:\bj9f\lib\com.jdojo.intro.jar
```

You can use the --list option with the jar command to list the contents of a JAR file. Use the following command to list the contents of the com.jdojo.intro.jar file, which was created by the previous command:

```
C:\bj9f>jar --list --file lib/com.jdojo.intro.jar
```

```
META-INF/
META-INF/MANIFEST.MF
module-info.class
com/
com/jdojo/
com/jdojo/intro/
com/jdojo/intro/Welcome.class
```

The output shows all directories and files in the JAR file. You did not have a file named MANIFEST.MF in the input directory. The jar command creates a MANIFEST.MF file for you. You can also see that the root directory of the JAR file contains the module-info.class file and the Welcome.class file has been placed in a directory, mirroring the directory it was placed in the mod\jdojo.intro directory, which in turn mirrored the directory hierarchy specified in its package name.

If a JAR file contains a module-info.class file, which is also known as a module descriptor, the file is called a *modular* JAR. Otherwise, the file is simply known as a JAR. In this example, the com.jdojo.intro.jar file is a modular JAR. If you remove the module-info.class file from it, it will become a JAR.

▓ **Tip**   A JAR file that contains a module descriptor (module-info.class) in its root directory is known as a modular JAR. There were no modules before JDK 9 and so there were no modular JARs.

You can use the jar tool to describe a module using the --describe-module option and by specifying the modular JAR using the --file option. The following command describes the module packaged in the com.jdojo.intro.jar file:

```
C:\bj9f>jar --describe-module --file lib/com.jdojo.intro.jar
```

```
jdojo.intro jar:file:///C:/bj9f/lib/com.jdojo.intro.jar/!module-info.class
requires java.base mandated
contains com.jdojo.intro
```

Consider the output of this command:

- The first line starts with the module name, which is `jdojo.intro`. The name is followed with the path to the module description. The path uses a `jar` scheme and points to the file system.

- The second line mentions a `requires` statement indicating that the `jdojo.intro` module requires the `java.base` module. Recall that every module implicitly depends on the `java.base` module. The compiler added this for you. The last word, `mandated`, indicates that the dependency on the `java.base` module is mandated by the Java module system.

- The third line indicates that the `jdojo.intro` module contains a package named `com.jdojo.intro`. The phrase `contains` is used to indicate that the package is in the module, but it is not exported by the module, so other modules cannot use this package. For every exported package, this command will print the following:

  ```
  exports <package-name>.
  ```

The last line in the output needs a bit of explanation. Figure 3-1 shows that a module contains one or more packages. The output shows that the `jdojo.intro` module contains a `com.jdojo.intro` package. However, you never specified a link between the module and the package—not when writing the source code nor during the compilation or packaging. So, how do modules know the packages they contain? The answer is simple. Placing the `module-info.class` file in the root directory makes the module contain all packages underneath. In your case, the `com/jdojo/intro` directory that mirrors the `com.jdojo.intro` package for the `Welcome` class is underneath the root directory in the module JAR. This is the reason that it became part of the module.

▓ **Tip** A modular JAR contains code for only one module. All packages under the root directory are part of that module.

Running a Java Program

A Java program is run by a JVM. A JVM is invoked using a command called `java`, which is located in the `JDK_HOME\bin` directory. The `java` command is also known as a Java launcher. The syntax to run it is as follows:

```
java [options] --module <module-name>[/<main-class-name>] [arguments]
```

Here,

- `[options]` indicate zero or more options passed to the `java` command.

- The `--module` option specifies the module name and the main class name inside the module. `<module-name>` is the module name. For example, `jdojo.intro` and `<main-class-name>` is the *fully qualified name* of the main class, for example, `com.jdojo.intro.Welcome`. When you package a module in a modular JAR, you can specify the main class name for the module, which is stored in the module descriptor—the `module-info.class` file. You have not specified the main class name when you created the `com.jdojo.intro.jar` modular JAR in the last section. Passing the `<main-class-name>` is optional. If it is not specified, the `java` command will use the main class name from the module descriptor. The command calls the `main()` method of the `<main-class-name>`.

- [arguments] is a space-separated list of arguments passed to the main() method of the main class. Note that [options] are passed to the java command (or JVM), whereas [arguments] are passed to the main() method of the main class being run. [arguments] must be specified after the --module option.

Let's try to run the Welcome class using the following command:

```
C:\bj9f>java --module jdojo.intro/com.jdojo.intro.Welcome
```

```
Error occurred during initialization of boot layer
java.lang.module.FindException: Module jdojo.intro not found
```

Oops! You got an error. I used this command intentionally, so you can understand the behind-the-scene process that takes place when you run a Java program. There are two messages in the output:

- The first message states that an error occurred when the JVM was trying to initialize the boot layer.

- The second message states that the JVM was not able to find the jdojo.intro module.

At startup, JVM resolves modules' dependencies. If all required modules are not resolved at startup, the program fails to start. This is a significant improvement in Java 9, where all dependencies are verified at startup. Before Java 9, the runtime would attempt to resolve the dependencies (the types) as the program needed them, not at startup, which led to many runtime surprises.

All modules that are accessible to the module system in a phase (compile-time or runtime) are called *observable modules*. Module resolution starts with a set of initial modules called *root modules* and follows the dependency chain until the java.base module is reached. The set of resolved modules is called a *module graph*. In a module graph, each module is represented as a node. A directed edge from a module to another module exists if the first module depends on the second module.

Figure 3-6 shows a module graph with two root modules named A and B. Module A depends on module P, which in turn depends on the java.base module. Module B depends on module Q, which in turn depends on the java.base module. Java runtime will use only resolved modules at runtime. That is, Java runtime knows only about the modules in the module graph.

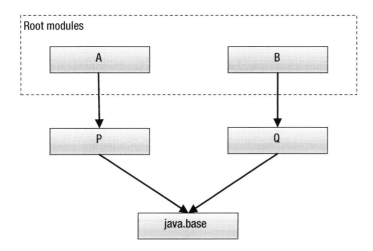

Figure 3-6. *A module graph*

Typically, you have only one root module. How is the set of root modules determined? When you run a Java program from a module, the module containing the main class is the only default root module.

▓ **Tip**   If you need to resolve additional modules, which otherwise won't be resolved by default, you can add them to the default set of root modules using the `--add-modules` command-line option. I will defer discussion of adding root modules to later a chapter because it is an advanced topic.

Let's get back to resolving our error. The previous command tried to run the `Welcome` class, which is in the `jdojo.intro` module. Therefore, the `jdojo.intro` module is the only root module. If everything was fine, the JVM would have created a module graph as shown in Figure 3-7.

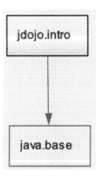

Figure 3-7.   *The module graph created at startup when the Welcome class is run*

To construct this module graph, the JVM needed to locate the root module `jdojo.intro`. The JVM will look for a module only in the set of observable modules. The second line in the error indicates that the JVM could not find the root module `jdojo.intro`. To fix the error, you need to include the `jdojo.intro` module in the set of observable modules. You know that the module's code exists at two locations:

- `bj9f\mod\jdojo.intro` directory
- `bj9f\lib\com.jdojo.intro.jar` file

There are two types of modules: built-in modules that are shipped with the JDK and the user-defined modules that you create. The JVM knows about all built-in modules and includes them in the set of observable modules. You need to specify the locations of the user-defined modules using the `--module-path` option. Modules found on the module path will be included in the set of observable modules and they will be resolved during the module resolution process. The syntax to use this option is as follows:

`--module-path <your-module-path>`

Module-path is a sequence of pathnames where a pathname may be a path to a directory, a modular JAR, or a JMOD file. The path can be absolute or relative. I discuss JMOD files later in this book. Pathnames are separated by a platform-specific path-separator character, which is a colon (`:`) on the UNIX-like platforms and a semicolon (`;`) on Windows. The following are valid module paths on windows:

- `C:\bj9f\lib`
- `C:\bj9f\lib;C:\bj9f\mod\jdojo.contact\com.jdojo.contact.jar`
- `C:\bj9f\lib;C:\bj9f\extlib`

The first module path contains the path to a directory named `C:\bj9f\lib`. The second one contains the path to a `C:\bj9f\lib` directory and a modular JAR at `C:\bj9f\mod\jdojo.contact\com.jdojo.contact.jar`. The third one contains paths to two directories—`C:\bj9f\lib` and `C:\bj9f\extlib`. The equivalent of these module paths on a UNIX-like platform will look similar to these:

- `/home/ksharan/bj9f/lib`

- `/home/ksharan/bj9f/lib:/home/ksharan/bj9f/mod/jdojo.contact/com.jdojo.contact.jar`

- `/home/ksharan/bj9f/lib:/home/ksharan/bj9f/extlib`

How does the JVM find modules using the module path? The JVM scans all modules present in the module paths using the following rules:

- If the pathname is a directory, three places are scanned for `module-info.class` files containing modules: the directory itself, all immediate subdirectories, and the root directories of all modular JARs in the directory. If a `module-info.class` file is found in any of these places, that module is included in the set of observable modules. Note that subdirectories are not scanned recursively.

- If the pathname is a modular JAR or a JMOD file, the modular JAR or the JMOD file is considered to contain a module, which is included in the set of observable modules.

Using the first rule, if you place `N` modular JARs in a `C:\bj9f\lib` directory, specifying this directory in the module path will include all `N` modules in the set of observable modules. You can use the second form, the path to a modular JAR or JMOD file, if you have multiple modules in a directory, but you want to include only a few of them in the set of observable modules.

You have placed the modular JAR named `com.jdojo.intro.jar` for this example into the `C:\bj9f\lib` directory. Therefore, specifying `C:\bj9f\lib` as the module path will enable the JVM to find the `jdojo.intro` module. Let's use the following command to run the `Welcome` class:

```
C:\bj9f>java --module-path C:\bj9f\lib --module jdojo.intro/com.jdojo.intro.Welcome
```

```
Welcome to Java 9!
```

This command assumes that `C:\bj9f` is the current directory. You could have used a relative path in the module path, which would be `lib` instead of `C:\bj9f\lib` as shown:

```
C:\bj9f>java --module-path lib --module jdojo.intro/com.jdojo.intro.Welcome
```

```
Welcome to Java 9!
```

This time, the JVM was able to find the `jdojo.intro` module. It found a modular JAR, the `com.jdojo.intro.jar` file, in the module inside the `C:\bj9f\lib` directory, which contained the `jdojo.intro` module.

You saved the compiled classes for the module in the `C:\bj9f\mod\jdojo.intro` directory. The module code exists in exploded directories inside this directory. The root directory contains the `module-info.class` file. You can also run a class inside a module whose code is saved inside an exploded directory structure like the one in the C:\bj9f\mod\jdojo.intro directory. The following command runs the Welcome class inside the jdojo.intro module whose code is in the C:\bj9f\mod\jdojo.intro directory:

```
C:\bj9f>java --module-path C:\bj9f\mod\jdojo.intro --module jdojo.intro/com.jdojo.intro.
Welcome
```

Welcome to Java 9!

This time, the NVM scanned the C:\bj9f\mod\jdojo.intro directory and found a module-info.class file that contains the jdojo.intro module's descriptor.

You can run the same command using the C:\bj9f\mod directory as part of the module path as follows:

```
C:\bj9f>java --module-path C:\bj9f\mod --module jdojo.intro/com.jdojo.intro.Welcome
```

Welcome to Java 9!

How did the JVM find the jdojo.intro module this time? Recall the rules for finding module descriptors in a directory. The JVM looked in the C:\bj9f\mod directory for a module-info.class file, which does not exist. It looked for any modular JARS in the directory and found none. Now it looked for immediate subdirectories of the C:\bj9f\mod directory. It found one subdirectory named jdojo.intro. It scanned the jdojo.intro subdirectory for a module-info.class file and it found one having the module descriptor for the jdojo.intro module. This is how the jdojo.intro module was found.

Many GNU-style options also have shorter names. For example, you can use the shorter names –p and –m for the --module-path and --module options, respectively. The previous command can also be written as follows:

```
C:\bj9f>java -p C:\bj9f\mod -m jdojo.intro/com.jdojo.intro.Welcome
```

Resolving a module does not load all classes in that module. It would be inefficient to load all classes in all modules at once. Classes are loaded as and when they are referenced for the first time in the program. JVM only locates the module and does some housekeeping to have more pieces of information about the modules. For example, it keeps track of all packages that the module contains. How did the JVM load the Welcome class? The JVM used three pieces of information of a class: the module path, the module name, and the fully qualified name of the class. You specified two pieces of information when you ran the Welcome class:

- The main module name, which is jdojo.intro. This made the JVM to locate this module and know that this module contains the com.jdojo.intro package. Recall that a package corresponds to a directory structure. In this case, the JVM knows that inside the module contents, a modular JAR or a directory containing the module descriptor, there exists a package com/jdojo/intro, which holds the contents in the com.jdojo.intro package.

- Along with the main module, you specified the fully qualified name of the main class, which was com.jdojo.intro.Welcome. To locate the Welcome class, the JVM first finds the module that contains the com.jdojo.intro package. It finds the jdojo. intro module to contain this package. It converts the package name into a directory hierarchy, appends a .class extension to the class name, and tries to locate the class at com/jdojo/intro/Welcome.class.

With these two rules, let's locate the Welcome class file. If you have specified the bj9f\lib directory as the module path, the com.jdojo.intro.jar file contains the contents of the jdojo.intro module and this file also contains the com/jdojo/intro/Welcome.class file. This is how the Welcome class file will be located and then loaded. If you specified the bj9f\mod directory as the module path, the bj9f\mod\jdojo. intro directory contains the contents of the jdojo.intro module and this directory also contains the com/ jdojo/intro/Welcome.class file. Figure 3-8 depicts the process of finding the Welcome.class file when the Welcome class needs to be loaded. The figure uses the C:\bj9f\mod\jdojo.intro as the location of the module and Windows path separator, which is a backslash. The path separator will be a forward slash on UNIX-like operating systems. JAR files also uses a forward slash as a path separator.

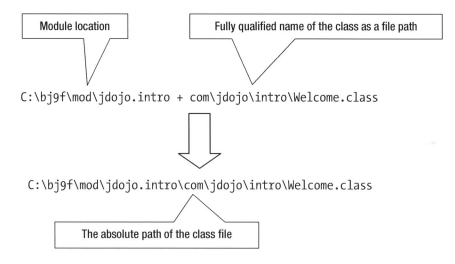

Figure 3-8. *The process of finding a class file in a module using the module path*

This example was simple. It involved only two modules—java.base and java.intro. If you followed the discussion, you know how these modules were resolved when you ran the Welcome class. There are several command-line options that help you understand what goes on behind the scenes when you use modules. The following section explores such command-line options.

Playing with Module Options

There are command-line options that let you obtain more information about which modules are used and how those modules are resolved. These options are useful for debugging or reducing the number of resolved modules. In this section, I show you a few examples of using a few of those options.

Listing Observable Modules

Using the --list-modules option with the java command, you can print a list of observable modules. The option does not take any arguments. The following command will print a list of all platform modules that are included in the set of observable modules. The command prints approximately 100 modules. A partial output is shown.

```
C:\bj9f>java --list-modules
```

```
java.activation@9-ea
java.base@9-ea
java.desktop@9-ea
java.se@9-ea
java.se.ee@9-ea
...
```

In the output, the module name is followed by a string "@9-ea". If a module descriptor contain a module version, the version is displayed after the @ sign. I am using the Early Access build of JDK 9, so the versions of the built-in modules are shown as "9-ea". If you are using the final release of JDK 9, the version number will be "9".

To include your modules in the set of observable modules, you need to specify the module path where your modules are placed. The following command will include the `jdojo.intro` module in the set of observable modules. Partial output is shown.

```
C:\bj9f>java --module-path C:\bj9f\lib --list-modules
```

```
java.activation@9-ea
java.base@9-ea
java.desktop@9-ea
java.se@9-ea
java.se.ee@9-ea
...
jdojo.intro file:///C:/bj9f/lib/com.jdojo.intro.jar
```

Note the last entry in the output:

- It did not print a module version of the `jdojo.intro` module. This is because you had not specified a module version when you created the modular JAR, `com.jdojo.intro.jar`. I will show you in the next section how to specify a version of your module.

- It printed the path of the modular JAR in which the `jdojo.intro` module was found. This is very helpful in debugging when your modules are not correctly being resolved.

Limiting the Observable Modules

You can reduce the number of observable modules using `--limit-modules`. It accepts a comma-separated list of module names:

```
--limit-modules <module-name>[,<module-name>...]
```

The observable modules are limited to the list of the specified modules along with the modules they depend on recursively, plus the main module specified using the `--module` option, plus any modules specified using the `--add-modules` option. This option is useful when you run a Java program in legacy mode by placing the JARs on the class path, in which case all platform modules are included in the set of root modules.

Let's see the effect of this option by using it while running the Welcome class. The Welcome class uses only the java.base module. To limit the observable modules to the java.base and jdojo.intro modules, you can specify java.base as the value for the --limit-modules option, as shown:

```
C:\bj9f>java --module-path C:\bj9f\lib --limit-modules java.base --module jdojo.intro/com.
jdojo.intro.Welcome
```

```
Welcome to Java 9!
```

Note that even though you have specified only the java.base module to the --limit-modulus option, the jdojo.intro module is also included in the observable module because it is the main module you are running.

You can use the -verbose:module option to print the loaded module. The following command runs the Welcome class with the --limit-module option and loads only two modules:

```
C:\bj9f>java --module-path C:\bj9f\lib --limit-modules java.base -verbose:module --module
jdojo.intro/com.jdojo.intro.Welcome
```

```
[0.079s][info][module,load] java.base location: jrt:/java.base
[0.135s][info][module,load] jdojo.intro location: file:///C:/bj9f/lib/com.jdojo.intro.jar
Welcome to Java 9!
```

The following command runs the Welcome class without the --limit-module option and loads about 40 modules. A partial output is shown.

```
C:\bj9f>java --module-path C:\bj9f\lib -verbose:module --module jdojo.intro/com.jdojo.intro.
Welcome
```

```
[0.082s][info][module,load] java.base location: jrt:/java.base
[0.142s][info][module,load] jdk.naming.rmi location: jrt:/jdk.naming.rmi
[0.144s][info][module,load] jdk.scripting.nashorn location: jrt:/jdk.scripting.nashorn
[0.144s][info][module,load] java.logging location: jrt:/java.logging
[0.144s][info][module,load] jdojo.intro location: file:///C:/bj9f/lib/com.jdojo.intro.jar
[0.156s][info][module,load] java.management location: jrt:/java.management
...
Welcome to Java 9!
```

Describing a Module

You can describe a module using the --describe-module option with the java command. Recall that you can also use this option with the jar command (see the "Packaging the Compiled Code" section for an example) to describe a module in a modular JAR. Make sure to specify the module path when you describe your module. To describe the platform modules, you do not need to specify the module path. The following commands show a few examples:

```
C:\bj9f>java --module-path C:\bj9f\lib --describe-module jdojo.intro
```

```
jdojo.intro file:///C:/bj9f/lib/com.jdojo.intro.jar
requires java.base mandated
contains com.jdojo.intro
```

```
C:\bj9f>java --describe-module java.sql
```

```
java.sql@9-ea
exports java.sql
exports javax.sql
exports javax.transaction.xa
requires java.xml transitive
requires java.base mandated
requires java.logging transitive
uses java.sql.Driver
```

Printing Module Resolution Details

Using the --show-module-resolution option with the java command, you can print the details of the module resolution process that occurs at startup. The following command uses this option when the Welcome class is run. A partial output is shown.

```
C:\bj9f>java --module-path C:\bj9f\lib --show-module-resolution --module jdojo.intro/com.
jdojo.intro.Welcome
```

```
root jdojo.intro file:///C:/bj9f/lib/com.jdojo.intro.jar
java.base binds jdk.zipfs jrt:/jdk.zipfs
java.base binds jdk.jdeps jrt:/jdk.jdeps
java.base binds java.desktop jrt:/java.desktop
java.desktop requires java.xml jrt:/java.xml
java.desktop requires java.datatransfer jrt:/java.datatransfer
java.desktop requires java.prefs jrt:/java.prefs
...
Welcome to Java 9!
```

The first line in the output shows the root module that is resolved and the location of the root module. The java.base module does not require any other modules. However, it uses many service providers if they are present. The "java.base binds ..." text in the output indicates that the service providers used by the java.base module are present in the set of observable modules and they are resolved. A service provider module may require other modules, which will be resolved as well. The resolution of the java.desktop module is one such case. The java.desktop module is resolved because it provides a service used by the java.base module, which triggers resolving the java.xml, java.datatransfer, and java.prefs modules because the java.desktop module requires these three modules.

■ **Tip**   Even though your program uses only the `java.base` module, which does not require any other modules, other platform modules will be resolved because they provide services used by the `java.base` module. The best way to limit the platform modules to the `java.base` module is to use the `--limit-modules` option with `java.base` as its value.

Dry Running Your Program

You can dry run a class using the `--dry-run` option. It creates the JVM and loads the main class, but does not execute the `main()` method of the main class. This option is useful for verifying the module configuration and for debugging purposes. The following command shows its use. The output does not contain a welcome message because the `main()` method of the `Welcome` class is not executed. A partial output is shown:

```
C:\bj9f>java --module-path C:\bj9f\lib --dry-run --show-module-resolution --module jdojo.
intro/com.jdojo.intro.Welcome
```

```
root jdojo.intro file:///C:/bj9f/lib/com.jdojo.intro.jar
java.base binds jdk.zipfs jrt:/jdk.zipfs
java.base binds java.logging jrt:/java.logging
java.base binds jdk.localedata jrt:/jdk.localedata
...
```

Enhancing a Module Descriptor

You declare a module in a `module-info.java` file. A module declaration is compiled into a class file named `module-info.class`. The module's designer could have used XML or JSON format to declare a module. Why did they choose the class file format to store the module declaration? There are several reasons for this:

- The class file format was already well known to the Java community.

- The class file format is extensible. That is, tools can augment the `module-info.class` file after it is compiled.

- JDK already supported a similar file named `package-info.java`, which is compiled into a `package-info.class` file to store package information.

The `jar` tool contains a few options to augment a module descriptor, two of which are module version and main class name. You cannot specify the version of a module in its declaration. The JDK 9 designer stayed away from dealing with a module's version in its declaration, stating that managing a module's version is the job of a build tool such as Maven and Gradle, not of the module system provider. Given the extensible nature of the module descriptor, you can store a module's version in the `module-info.class` file as an attribute of the class file. As a developer, it is not easy to add class file attributes. You can use the `--module-version` option of the `jar` tool to add a module version to the `module-info.class` file. You have already created a `com.jdojo.intro.jar` file, which contains the module descriptor for the `jdojo.intro` module. Let's rerun the command that describes the jdojo.intro module in the existing com.jdojo.intro. jar file as follows:

```
C:\bj9f>jar --describe-module --file lib/com.jdojo.intro.jar
```

```
jdojo.intro jar:file:///C:/bj9f/lib/com.jdojo.intro.jar/!module-info.class
requires java.base mandated
contains com.jdojo.intro
```

There is no module version in the output. The following command recreates the com.jdojo.intro.jar file by specifying the module version as 1.0:

```
C:\bj9f>jar --create --module-version 1.0 --file lib/com.jdojo.intro.jar -C mod/jdojo.intro.
```

▓ **Tip**   Typically, you should append the module version to the module JAR name. In the previous example, you should name the file com.jdojo.intro-1.0.jar, so its owner will know what version of the module is stored in this modular JAR. I chose the same name (com.jdojo.intro.jar) to keep things simple for this example.

The following command re-describes the module and the output shows the module name and its version. If a version is present, a module name is printed in the form of <module-name>@<module-version>.

```
C:\bj9f>jar --describe-module --file lib/com.jdojo.intro.jar
```

```
jdojo.intro@1.0 jar:file:///C:/bj9f/lib/com.jdojo.intro.jar/!module-info.class
requires java.base mandated
contains com.jdojo.intro
```

In a typical application, you will have one main module, which is a module containing a main class. You can store the name of the main class in the module descriptor. All you need to do is use the --main-class option with the jar tool when you create or update the modular JAR. The main class name is the fully qualified name of the class that contains the main() method that you want to use as an entry-point for the application. The following command updates the existing modular JAR to add a main class name:

```
C:\bj9f>jar --update --main-class com.jdojo.intro.Welcome --file lib\com.jdojo.intro.jar
```

The following command recreates the modular JAR with a module version and a main class name:

```
C:\bj9f>jar --create --module-version 1.0 --main-class com.jdojo.intro.Welcome --file lib/
com.jdojo.intro.jar -C mod/jdojo.intro .
```

What do you do with the module version and main class in the module descriptor? The module version is meant to be used by build tools such as Maven and Gradle. You need to include correct versions of a module in your application when multiple versions of the module exist. If your module descriptor contains a main-class attribute, you can use the name of the module to run the application. The JVM will read the main class name from the module descriptor. Now your module descriptor for the `jdojo.intro` module contains the main class name. The following command will run the `Welcome` class:

```
C:\bj9f>java --module-path C:\bj9f\lib --module jdojo.intro
```

```
Welcome to Java 9!
```

Running Java Programs in Legacy Mode

The module system was introduced in JDK 9. How were Java programs written, compiled, packaged, and run before? Take the module system out and you will find that Java programs were almost written the same way before. However, the mechanism to run them was different. The `Welcome` class that you have written in this chapter will also compile and run in JDK 8. Barring a few exceptions, Java has always been backward compatible. Programs that you wrote in JDK 8 will also work in JDK 9. Before JDK 9, you will not have a `module-info.class` file in your program. You also did not have a module path, which is used to locate modules.

Before JDK 9, classes were located using the class path. The class path is a sequence of directories, JAR files, and ZIP files. Each entry in the class path is separated by a platform-specific path-separator character, which is a semicolon (`;`) on Windows and a colon (`:`) on UNIX-like operating systems. If you compare the definition of the class path and the module path, they look the same. The difference between them is that the class path is used to locate classes (more specifically types), whereas the module path is used to locate modules.

░ **Tip** You will encounter two terms "loading classes" and "loading modules". When a class is loaded, its class file is read—either from module path or class path—and the class is represented as an object at runtime. When a module is loaded, the module descriptor (the `module-info.class` file) is read along with some other housekeeping processing; the module is represented as an object representation at runtime. Loading a module does not mean loading all classes in that module, which would be very inefficient. Classes in a module are loaded when they are referenced in the program for the first time at runtime.

JDK 9 allows you to use only the module path, only the class path, or a combination of both. Using only the module path means your program consists of only modules. Using only class path means your programs does not consist of modules. Using a combination of both means some part of your program consists of some modules and some part does not. JDK 9 has modularized the JDK code. For example, whether you run a program from a module or not, the `java.base` module is always used. JDK 9 supports three modes:

- Module mode
- Legacy mode
- Mixed mode

Using only modules in your program is called *module mode* and only the module path is used. Using only the class path is called *legacy mode* and only the class path is used. Using a combination of both is called *mixed mode*. JDK 9 supports these modes for backward compatibility. For example, you should be able to run your JDK 8 programs "as-is" in JDK 9 using the legacy mode in which you will place all your existing JARs on the class path. If you are developing a new Java application using modules in JDK 9, but still have a few JARs from JDK 8, you can use the mixed mode by placing your modular JARs on the module path and the existing JARs on the class path.

A class can be specified using three synonymous options: `--class-path`, `-classpath`, and `-cp`. The first option was added in JDK 9 and the other two existed before. The general syntax to run a Java program in legacy mode is as follows:

```
java [options] <main-class-name> [arguments]
```

Here, `[options]` and `[arguments]` have the same meanings as discussed in the previous section, "Running a Java Program". Since there are no user-defined modules in legacy mode, you simply specify the fully qualified name of the main class that you want to run as `<main-class-name>`. As you had specified the module path in module mode, you must specify the class path in legacy mode.

The following command runs the `Welcome` class in legacy mode. You do not need to recompile the `Welcome` class. You can keep the `module-info.class` file or delete it because it will not be used in legacy mode.

```
C:\bj9f>java --class-path C:\bj9f\mod\jdojo.intro com.jdojo.intro.Welcome
```

```
Welcome to Java 9!
```

The JVM used the following steps to run the `Welcome` class:

- It detected that you were trying to run the `com.jdojo.intro.Welcome` class.

- It converted the main class name into a file path, `com\jdojo\intro\Welcome.class`.

- It took the first entry in the class path and looked for the existence of the path for the `Welcome.class` file computed in the previous step. There was only one entry in the class path and it found the `Welcome.class` file using that entry. The JVM tries to find the class file using all entries in the class path until it find the class file. If it does not find the class file using all entries, it throws a `ClassNotFoundException`.

There are a few differences in how the class path and the module path work. The entries in the class path are used "as-is". That is, if you specify a directory path in the class path, that directory path is prepended to the class file path to look for the class file. Contrast this with the module path that contained a directory path where the directory itself, all modular JARS in the directory, and all immediate subdirectories were searched for module descriptors. Using this rule, if you want to run the `Welcome` class in legacy mode from a JAR file, you need to specify the full path of the JAR in the class path.

The following commands are not able to find the `Welcome` class because the `com\jdojo\intro\Welcome.class` file is not found in the `C:\bj9f\mod` or the `C:\bj9f\lib` directories:

```
C:\bj9f>java --class-path C:\bj9f\mod com.jdojo.intro.Welcome
```

```
Error: Could not find or load main class com.jdojo.intro.Welcome
Caused by: java.lang.ClassNotFoundException: com.jdojo.intro.Welcome
```

```
C:\bj9f>java --class-path C:\bj9f\lib com.jdojo.intro.Welcome
```

```
Error: Could not find or load main class com.jdojo.intro.Welcome
Caused by: java.lang.ClassNotFoundException: com.jdojo.intro.Welcome
```

The following command finds the Welcome class because you specified the JAR path in the class path:

```
C:\bj9f>java --class-path C:\bj9f\lib\com.jdojo.intro.jar com.jdojo.intro.Welcome
```

```
Welcome to Java 9!
```

It is typical of a non-trivial Java application to have multiple JARs. Adding the full path of all JARs to the class path is simply inconvenient. To support this use case, the class path syntax supports an asterisk (*) in an entry as the last character, which is expanded to all JAR and ZIP files in the directory represented by that entry. Suppose you have a directory named cdir that contains two JARs—x.jar and y.jar. To include these two JARs in the class path, you can use one of the following sequences of paths on Windows:

- cdir\x.jar;cdir\y.jar

- cdir*

The asterisk in the second case will be expanded to one entry per JAR/ZIP file in the cdir directory. This expansion happens before the JVM starts. The following command shows how to use an asterisk in the class path:

```
C:\bj9f>java -cp C:\bj9f\lib\* com.jdojo.intro.Welcome
```

```
Welcome to Java 9!
```

You must use an asterisk in a class path entry in the end or by itself. If you use an asterisk by itself, the asterisk will be expanded to include all JAR/ZIP files in the current directory. The following command uses the C:\bj9f\lib directory as the current directory and an asterisk as the class path to the run the Welcome class:

```
C:\bj9f\lib>java -cp * com.jdojo.intro.Welcome
```

```
Welcome to Java 9!
```

In mixed mode, you can use both the module path and the class path like so:

```
java --module-path <module-path> --class-path <class-path> <other-arguments>
```

There may be a situation when you may have duplicate classes—one copy in the module path and another in the class path. In this case, the version on the module path is used, effectively ignoring the class path copy. If duplicate classes exist on the class path, the class found first in the class path is used. Duplicate packages and hence duplicate classes are not allowed between modules. That is, if you have a package named com.jdojo.intro, all classes in this package must be available through one module. Otherwise, your application won't compile/run.

JDK 9 works only with modules. How are non-modular types loaded from the class path used? Types are loaded by class loaders. Every class loader has a module called *unnamed* modules. All types loaded from the class path become members of the unnamed module of their class loader. All modules loaded from the module path are members of the module in which they are declared. I revisit unnamed modules in later chapters.

Duplicate Modules on Module Path

Sometimes, you may have multiple versions of the same modules on the module path. How does the module system choose which module copy to use from the module path? It is always a mistake to have two modules with the same name on the module path. The module system safeguards you against such mistakes in a limited way.

Let's start with an example to understand the rule in resolving the duplicate modules. You have two versions of the jdojo.intro module—one in the com.jdojo.intro.jar file inside the C:\bj9f\lib directory and another in the C:\bj9f\mod\jdojo.intro directory. Run the Welcome class and include both directories in the module path:

```
C:\bj9f>java --module-path C:\bj9f\lib;C:\bj9f\mod\jdojo.intro --module jdojo.intro/com.
jdojo.intro.Welcome
```

```
Welcome to Java 9!
```

You might have expected this command to fail because it does not make sense to run a program having two versions of the same module accessible to the runtime system. Which copy of the module was used by this command? It is hard to tell by looking at the output, because both copies of the module contain the same code. You can use the --show-module-resolution option to see the location from where the module was loaded. The following command does this. A partial output is shown.

```
C:\bj9f>java --module-path C:\bj9f\lib;C:\bj9f\mod\jdojo.intro --show-module-resolution
--module jdojo.intro/com.jdojo.intro.Welcome
```

```
root jdojo.intro file:///C:/bj9f/lib/com.jdojo.intro.jar
...
Welcome to Java 9!
```

The output indicates that the jdojo.intro module, which is a root module in this case, was loaded from the modular JAR com.jdojo.intro.jar, from the C:\bj9f\lib directory. Let's switch the order of entries in the module path and rerun the command:

```
C:\bj9f>java --module-path C:\bj9f\mod\jdojo.intro;C:\bj9f\lib --show-module-resolution
--module jdojo.intro/com.jdojo.intro.Welcome
```

```
root jdojo.intro file:///C:/bj9f/mod/jdojo.intro/
...
Welcome to Java 9!
```

This time, the output indicates that the jdojo.intro module was loaded from the C:\bj9f\mod\jdojo.intro directory. Here is the rule:

If there are multiple copies of a module with the same name accessible through different entries in the module path, the module's copy that is found first on the module path is used.

Using this rule, when you had the lib directory listed first in the module path, the jdojo.intro module was used from the lib directory and the module's copy in the mod\jdojo.intro directory was ignored. When you reversed the order of these entries in the module path, the module in the mod\jdojo.intro directory was used.

Notice the *"accessible through different entries in the module path"* phrase in the rule. This rule applies as long as multiple copies of a module exist in different module path entries. If, however, multiple copies of a module are accessible through the same entry in the module path, an error occurs. How can you get into this situation? Here are a few possibilities:

- Multiple modular JARs with different file names, but having the code for a module with the same name, may exist in the same directory. If such a directory is an entry in the module path, multiple copies of a module are accessible through this single module path entry.

- When a directory is used as a module path entry, all modular JARs in that directory and all immediate subdirectories containing a module descriptor locate modules through that module path entry. This opens up the possibility of having multiple modules with the same name accessible through a single module path entry.

In our example, the two copies of the jdojo.intro module are not accessible through a single module path entry. Let's simulate the error using the following steps:

- Create a directory called C:\bj9f\temp.

- Copy the C:\lib\com.jdojo.intro.jar file to the C:\bj9f\temp directory.

- Copy the C:\mod\jdojo.intro directory to the C:\bj9f\temp directory.

At this point, you have the following files:

- C:\bj9f\temp\com.jdojo.intro.jar

- C:\bj9f\temp\jdojo.intro\module-info.class

- C:\bj9f\temp\jdojo.intro\com\jdojo\intro\Welcome.class

If you include the C:\bj9f\temp directory in the module path, two copies the jdojo.intro module are accessible—one in the module JAR and one in the subdirectory. The following command fails with a clear message indicating the problem:

```
C:\bj9f>java --module-path C:\lib;C:\bj9f\temp --module jdojo.intro/com.jdojo.intro.Welcome
```

```
Error occurred during initialization of boot layer
java.lang.module.FindException: Error reading module: C:\lib\com.jdojo.intro-1.0.jar
Caused by: java.lang.module.InvalidModuleDescriptorException: this_class should be module-info
```

The following command includes the C:\bj9f\lib directory as the first entry in the module path, where only one copy of the module will be found. It includes the C:\bj9f\temp directory as the second entry in the module path. You still get the same error:

```
C:\bj9f>java --module-path C:\bj9f\lib;C:\bj9f\temp --module jdojo.intro/com.jdojo.intro.Welcome
```

```
Error occurred during initialization of boot layer
java.lang.module.FindException: Two versions of module jdojo.intro found in C:\bj9f\temp
(jdojo.intro and com.jdojo.intro.jar)
```

Syntax for Command-Line Options

JDK 9 supports two styles for specifying command-line options:

- UNIX style

- GNU style

A UNIX-style option starts with a hyphen (-) followed by the option name as one word, for example, -p, -m, and -cp. A GNU-style option starts with two hyphens (--) followed by the option name, where each word in the option name is hyphenated, for example, --module-path, --module, and --class-path.

JDK designers were running out of short names for options that were also meaningful to developers. Therefore, JDK 9 started using GNU-style options. Most options are available in both styles. You are encouraged to use the GNU-style options if available because they are easier to remember and intuitive to readers.

▓ **Tip** To print a list of all standard options supported by a JDK tool, run the tool with the --help or -h option and, for all non-standard options, run the tool with the --help-extra or -X option. For example, the java --help and java --help-extra commands print a list of standard and non-standard options for the java command, respectively.

An option may take a value as its argument. The value for an option follows the option name. The option name and the value must be separated by one or more spaces. The following examples show you how to specify the module path with the java command using both options:

```
// Using the UNIX-style option
C:\bj9f>java -p C:\applib;C:\extlib <other-args-go-here>

// Using the GNU-style option
C:\bj9f>java --module-path C:\applib;C:\lib <other-args-go-here>
```

When you use the GNU-style option, you can specify the value for the option in one of two forms:

- --<name> <value>

- --<name>=<value>

The previous command can also be written as follows:

```
// Using the GNU-style option
C:\>java --module-path=C:\applib;C:\lib <other-args-go-here>
```

When using spaces as the name-value separator, you need to use at least one space. When using a = as a name-value separator, you must not include any spaces around it. This option

```
--module-path=C:\applib
```

is valid, whereas this option

```
--module-path =C:\applib
```

is invalid because " =C:\applib" will be interpreted as a module path, which is an invalid path.

Writing Java Programs Using the NetBeans IDE

You can use the NetBeans IDE to write, compile, and run Java programs. In this section, I walk you through the steps of working with NetBeans. First, you will learn how to create a new Java project, write a simple Java program, compile, and run it. At the end, you will learn how to open the NetBeans project for this book and use the source code supplied with this book. Refer to Chapter 2 on how to download, install, and configure the NetBeans IDE.

░ **Note** At the time of this writing, NetBeans IDE 9.0 has not been released. It will be released with JDK 9. By the time you read this chapter, the final release version 9.0 should be available. In this section, I use the nightly build of NetBeans 9.0 beta version.

Creating a Java Project

When you start the NetBeans IDE, the startup page is displayed, as shown in Figure 3-9. The startup page contains useful links for developers, such as links for tutorials for Java, JavaFX, C++, etc. If you don't want the startup page to display every time you start the IDE, you need to uncheck the Show on Startup checkbox in the upper-right corner of the startup page. You can close the startup page by clicking the X icon displayed in the Start Page tab. Use Help ➤ Start Page to open the Start Page at any time.

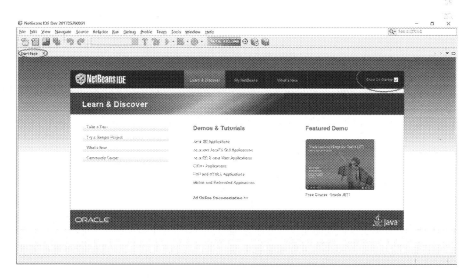

Figure 3-9. The NetBeans IDE with the startup page

To create a new Java project, follow these steps:

1. Select File ➤ New Project or press Ctrl+Shift+N. The New Project dialog is displayed, as shown in Figure 3-10.

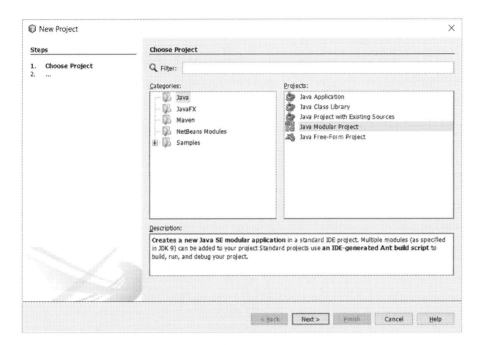

Figure 3-10. *A New Project dialog*

2. In the New Project dialog, select Java in the Categories list. In the Projects list, you can select Java Application, Java Class Library, or Java Modular Project. When you select a category, its description is displayed at the bottom. In the first two categories, you can have only one Java module, whereas the third one lets you have multiple Java modules. Select the Java Modular Project option and click the Next button. The New Java Modular Application dialog, as shown in Figure 3-11, is displayed.

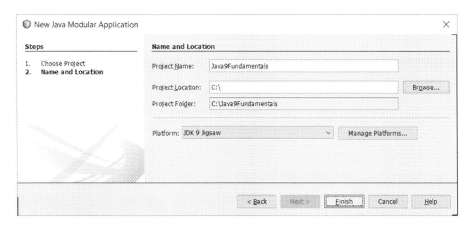

Figure 3-11. *The New Java Modular Application dialog*

3.   In the New Java Modular Application dialog, enter Java9Fundamentals as the project name. In the Project Location field, enter or browse to a location where you want to save the project files. I entered C:\ as the project location. NetBeans will create a C:\Java9Fundamentals directory where all files for the Java9Fundamentals project will be stored. Select JDK 9 as the Java platform from the Platform dropdown. If JDK 9 is not available for selection, click the Manage Platforms... button and create a new Java platform. Creating a new Java platform is simply adding a location where a JDK is stored in the file system and giving that location a name. Click the Finish button when you are done. The new Java9Fundamentals project is displayed in the IDE, as shown in Figure 3-12.

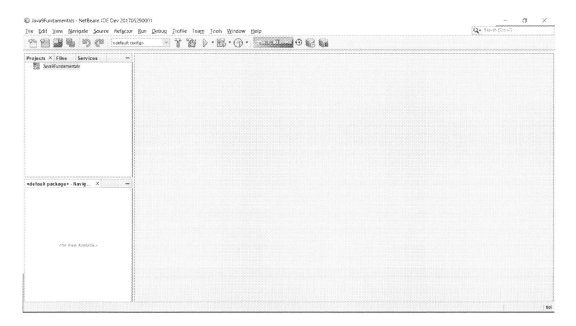

Figure 3-12. *The NetBeans IDE with the Java9Fundamentals Java Project*

At the top left, you see three tabs: Projects, Files, and Services. The Projects tab shows you all the project related files. The Files tab lets you view all system files on your computer. The Services tab lets you work with services such as databases and web servers. If you close these tabs, you can re-open them using the submenus with the same name as these tabs under the Window menu.

At this point, you have created a modular Java application project that contains no modules. You need to add modules to your project. To create a new module, select the project name, Java9Fundamentals, in the Projects tab and right-click to select New ➤ Module, as shown Figure 3-13. A New Module dialog is displayed, as shown in Figure 3-14. Enter jdojo.intro as the module name and click the Finish button.

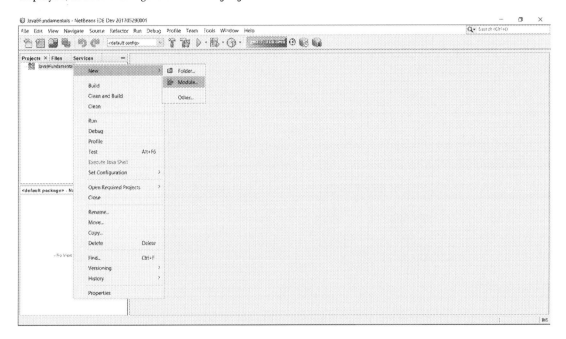

Figure 3-13. *Selecting the Module menu item to create a menu module*

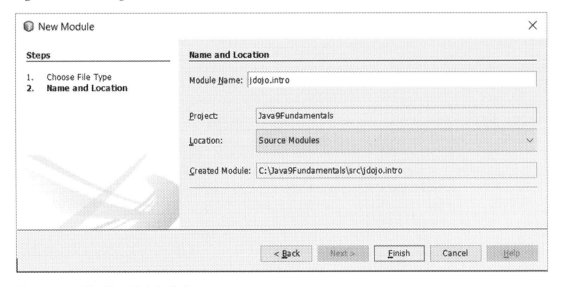

Figure 3-14. *The New Module dialog*

Figure 3-15 shows the editor with the `module-info.java` file open. I have removed the comments added by the NetBeans IDE and add a comment at the top. You might have to expand the file-tree in the Project tab to see all files. Creating a `jdojo.intro` module created a `module-info.java` file with a module declaration for the `jdojo.intro` module. When a `module-info.java` file is open in the editor, the NetBeans IDE displays three tabs—Source, History, and Graph. Selecting the Graph tab displays the module graph, as shown in Figure 3-16. Right-click on the empty area in the module graph to see options to customize the graph. Using the Layouts options, you can arrange the nodes in the graph in different ways. I prefer viewing the graph by arranging nodes hierarchically. Use the Export As Image right-click option to export the image as a PNG image. Selecting a node highlights all edges coming to and going out of the selected node, which easily lets you visualize a module's roles in a graph. Select the Source tab under the `module-info.java` tab to see the source code for the module.

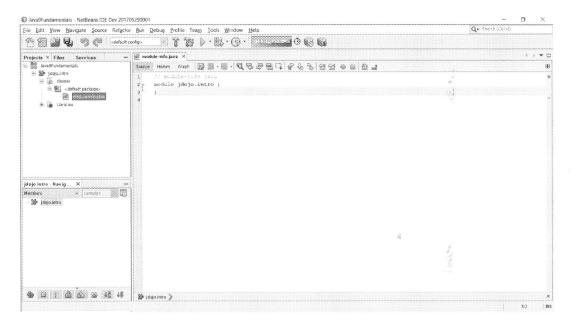

Figure 3-15. *The jdojo.intro module with its module-info.java file open in the editor*

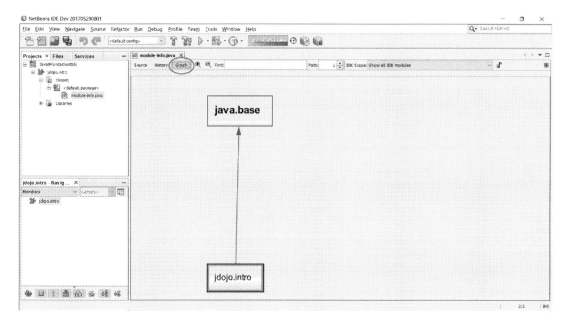

Figure 3-16. *The module graph created by the NetBeans IDE*

Now you are ready to add the Welcome class to the jdojo.intro module. Select the jdojo.intro module node in the Projects tab and right-click. Then choose New ➤ Java Class…, which displays the New Java Class dialog shown in Figure 3-17. Enter Welcome as the class name and com.jdojo.intro as the package name. Then click the Finish button.

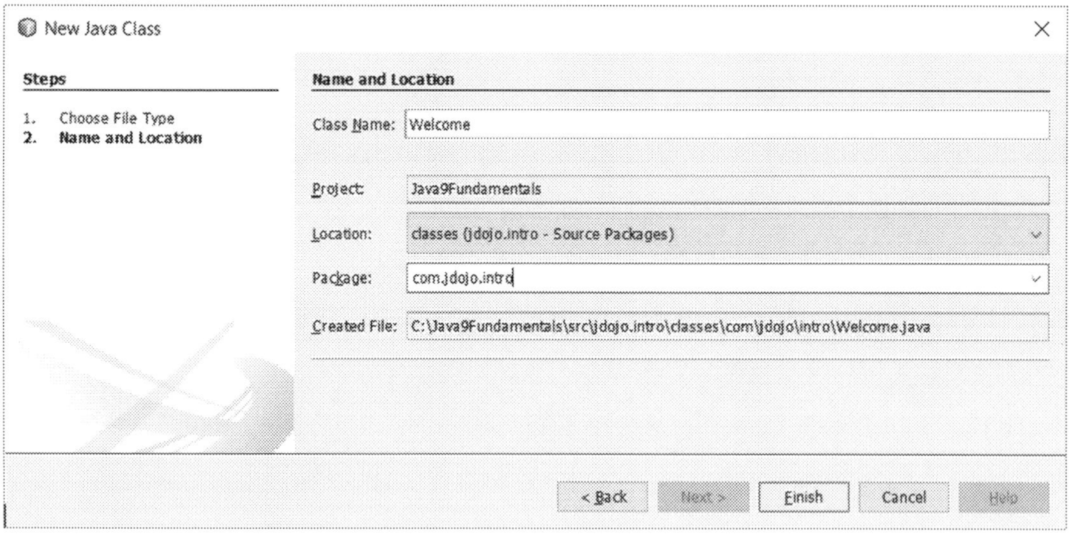

Figure 3-17. *Entering the class details in the New Java Class dialog*

Figure 3-18 shows the source code that was created for the Welcome class. I have cleaned up the comments that are added by NetBeans when you create a new class. You need to add a main() method to the Welcome class, as shown in Listing 3-3. Figure 3-19 shows the Welcome class with a main() method. You can save all your changes by pressing Ctrl+Shift+S or you can save the changes in the active file using Ctrl+S. Alternatively, you can use the File ➤ Save All and File ➤ Save menus or the toolbar buttons.

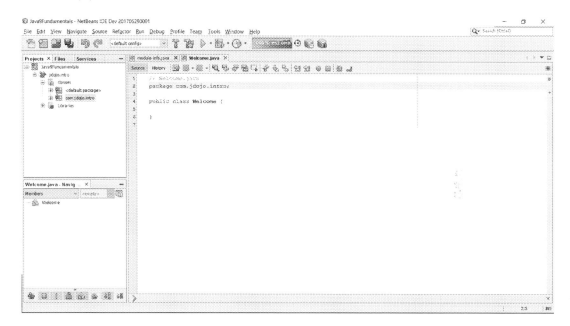

Figure 3-18. *The Welcome class created by NetBeans*

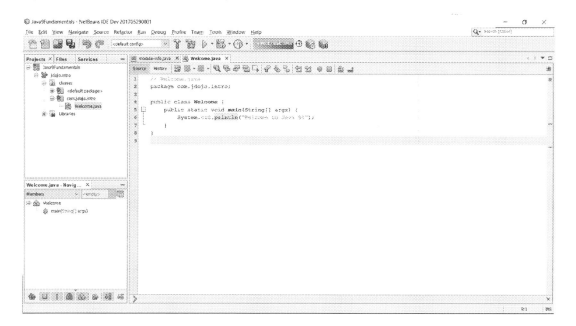

Figure 3-19. *The Welcome class code with a main() method*

You do not need to compile the code when you use NetBeans. By default, NetBeans compiles your code when you save it. Now you are ready to run the Welcome class. NetBeans lets you run a project or a single Java class. You can run a Java file if it contains a main class. To run the Welcome class, you will need to run the Welcome.java file in NetBeans. You can run the Welcome class in one of the following ways:

- Open the Welcome.java file in the editor and press Shift+F6. Alternatively, you can right-click in the editor while the Welcome.java file is open and select Run File.

- Select the Welcome.java file in the Projects tab and press Shift+F6. Alternatively, select the Welcome.java file in the Projects tab and select Run File.

- Select the Welcome.java file in the Projects tab and choose Run ➤ Run File.

When you run the Welcome class, the output appears in an Output tab, as shown in Figure 3-20.

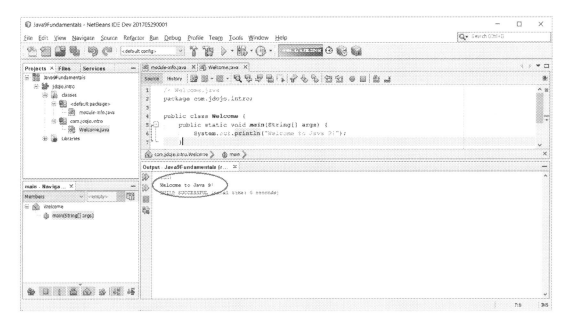

Figure 3-20. *The output when the Welcome class is run*

Creating Modular JARs in NetBeans

You can build a modular JAR from inside the NetBeans IDE. Press F11 to build the project, which will create a modular JAR for each module you have added to your NetBeans project. You can press Shift+F11 to clean and build, which deletes all existing compiled class files and modular JARs and recompiles all classes before creating new modular JARs. Alternatively, you can select the Run ➤ Build Project (<Your Project Name>) menu item to build your project.

Where are the modular JARs created when you build a project? NetBeans creates a dist directory under the project directory. Recall that you have saved your NetBeans project in C:\Java9Fundamentals, so NetBeans will create a C:\Java9Fundamentals\dist directory when you build the project in the IDE. Suppose you have two modules in your projects—jdojo.intro and jdojo.test. Building the project will create the following two modular JARs:

- C:\Java9Fundamentals\dist\jdojo.intro.jar

- C:\Java9Fundamentals\dist\jdojo.test.jar

NetBeans Project Directory Structure

NetBeans uses a default directory structure to store the source code, compiled code, and packaged code. The following directories are created under the NetBeans project directory:

- `src\<module-name>\classes`

- `build\modules\<module-name>`

- `dist`

Here, `<module-name>` is your module name such as `jdojo.intro`. The `src\<module-name>\classes` directory stores the source code for a specific module. The `module-info.java` file for the module is stored in the `classes` subdirectory. The `classes` subdirectory may have several subdirectories mirroring the directory structure required by the package of types stored in the module.

The `build\modules\<module-name>` directory stores the compiled code for a module. For example, the `module-info.class` file for the `jdojo.intro` module will be stored at `build\modules\jdojo.intro\module-info.class`. The `build\modules\<module-name>` directory mirrors the package of types stored in the module. For example, the `Welcome.class` file in our example will be stored at `build\modules\jdojo.intro\com\jdojo\intro\Welcome.class`. When you clean a project (right-click and choose Clean) or clean and build a project, the entire `build` directory is deleted and recreated.

The `dist` directory stores a modular JAR for each module in the project. The `Clean` or `Clean+Build` action on the project deletes all modular JARs and recreates them.

I will refer to this NetBeans directory structure in subsequent chapters when I need to show you examples using the same modules on the command-line. You can use NetBeans to write the module's code and build a modular JAR for the module. You can add the `dist` directory of your NetBeans project to the module path to use the modular JARs on the command-line.

Adding Classes to a Module

Typically, you have several classes in a module. To add a new class to your module, right-click the module in the Projects tab and select New ➤ Java Class.... Fill out the class name and the package name on the New Java Class dialog.

Customizing NetBeans Project Properties

NetBeans lets you customize several properties for your Java project using the Project Properties dialog. To open the projects Properties dialog, right-click the project name in the Projects tab and select Properties. The Project Properties dialog for the `Java9Fundamentals` project is shown in Figure 3-21.

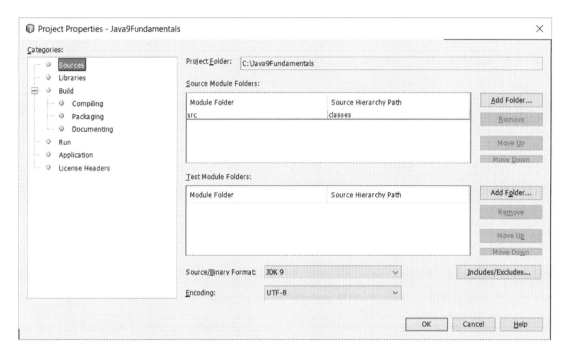

Figure 3-21. *The Project Properties dialog for the Java9Fundamentals project*

On the left side of the dialog is the list of categories of properties. When you select a property category, the details are displayed on the right side. The following are brief descriptions of each property category:

- *Sources*: It is used to set source code-related properties, for example, source folder, format, JDK, encoding, etc. When you select a JDK from the Source/Binary Format dropdown, the NetBeans IDE will restrict you from using the API outside of that JDK version. The Includes/Excludes button lets you include and exclude fields from the project. Use this button when you want to keep some files in the project, but do not want to compile them, for example, the files may not be compiled as they are not complete.

- *Libraries*: Among several properties, it lets you set three important properties: the Java platform, the module path and the class path. Clicking the Manage Platforms button opens the Java Platform Manager dialog where you can select an existing platform or add a new platform. Use the + sign on the right of the `Modulepath` and `Classpath` to use the Add Project, Add Library, and Add JAR/Folder buttons to add projects, predefined sets of JAR files, and JAR/Folder to the module path and class path. The module path and class path set here are used to compile and run your Java project. Note that all the modules you add to your project are automatically added to your module path. If you have modular JARs outside the current NetBeans project, you can add them to the module path using this dialog.

- *Build*: It lets you set properties for several subcategories. Under the Compiling subcategory, you can set compiler-related options. You can choose to compile the source code when it is saved or you can choose to compile the source code yourself using the menu options in the IDE. Under the Packaging subcategory, you can set options for packaging your modules. The Documenting subcategory lets you set options for generating Java documentation for the project.

- • *Run*: This category lets you set properties that are used to run the project. You can set the Java platform and JVM arguments. Using the category, you can set main class for your project. Typically, when you are learning, you run a Java file as you did in the previous sections, not a modular Java project.

Opening an Existing NetBeans Project

It is assumed that you have downloaded the source code for this book. The source code contains a NetBeans 9.0 project. To open the project, follow these steps.

1. Press Ctrl+Shift+O or select File ➤ Open Project. The Open Project dialog is displayed.

2. Navigate to the folder that contains the unzipped downloaded source code. The project Java9Fundamentals is displayed, as shown in Figure 3-22.

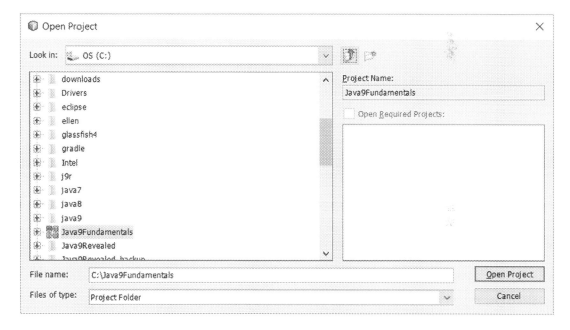

Figure 3-22. *Opening the NetBeans Java project for the source code for this book*

3. Select the project and click the Open Project button. The project is opened in the IDE. Use the Project or Files tabs on the left to browse the source code for all chapters in this book. Refer to the previous sections on how to compile, build, and run classes in the source code.

Behind the Scenes

This section answers some general questions related to compiling and running Java programs. For example, why do we compile Java source code to bytecode format before running it? What is the Java platform? What is a JVM and how does it work? The detailed discussion of these topics is beyond the scope of this book. Refer to the JVM specification for detailed discussions on any topic related to the JVM functionality. The JVM specification is available online at http://docs.oracle.com/javase/specs.

Let's look at a simple daily life example. Suppose there is a Frenchman who can understand and speak only French and he has to communicate with three other persons—an American, a German, and a Russian—and these three only know one language (English, German, and Russian, respectively). How will the Frenchman communicate with the other three? There are many ways to solve this problem.

- The Frenchman may learn all three languages.

- The Frenchman may hire a translator who knows all four languages.

- The Frenchman may hire three translators who know French-English, French-German, and French-Russian.

There are numerous other possible solutions to this problem. Let's consider the similar problem in the context of running a Java program. The Java source code is compiled into bytecode. The same bytecode needs to be run without any modification to all operating systems. Designers of the Java language chose the third option, which is to have a translator for each operating system. The job of the translator is to translate the bytecode into machine code, which is native to the operating system running the translated code. The translator is called a Java Virtual Machine (JVM). You need to have a JVM for each operating system. Figure 3-23 is a pictorial view of how the JVM acts as a translator between the bytecode (class file) and different operating systems.

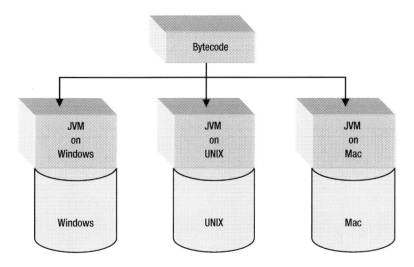

Figure 3-23. *A JVM as a translator between bytecode and an operating system*

A Java program compiled into bytecode format has two advantages:

- You do not need to recompile your source code if you want to run it on another machine with a different operating system. It is also called platform independence in Java. It is also known as "write once, run anywhere" for Java code.

- If you are running a Java program over a network, the program runs faster because of the compact size of the bytecode format, which results in less loading time over the network.

In order to run a Java program over the network, the size of the Java code must be compact enough to be transported over the network faster. The class file, which is generated by a Java compiler in bytecode format, is very compact. This is one of the advantages of compiling the Java source code in bytecode format.

The second important advantage of using bytecode format is that it is architecture-neutral. By bytecode format being architecture-neutral, it means if you compile the Java source code on a specific host system, say, Windows, the generated class file does not have any mention or effects that it was generated on Windows. If you compile the same Java source code on two different host systems, for example, Windows and UNIX, both class files will be the same.

The class file in bytecode format cannot be directly executed on a host system because it does not have any host system-specific direct instructions. In other words, we can say that bytecode is not a machine language for any specific host system. Now, the question is, who understands the bytecode and who translates it into underlying host system specific machine code? The JVM performs this job. The bytecode is the machine language for the JVM. If you compile Java source code to generate a class file on Windows, you can run the same class file on UNIX if you have a Java platform (JVM and Java API collectively are known as the Java platform) available on the machine running on UNIX. You do not need to recompile your source code to generate a new class file for UNIX, because the JVM running on UNIX can understand the bytecode you generated on Windows. This is how the concept of "write once, run anywhere" is implemented for a Java program.

The Java platform, also called Java runtime system, consists of two things:

- The Java virtual machine (JVM)

- The Java Application Programming Interface (Java API)

The term "JVM" is used in three contexts:

- *The JVM specification*: It is the specification or standard of an abstract machine for which a Java compiler can generate bytecode.

- *The concrete realization of the JVM specification*: If you want to run your Java program, you need to have a real JVM, which is developed using the abstract specification for a JVM. To run the Java program in the previous section, you used the java command, which a concrete implementation of the abstract JVM specification. The java command (or the JVM) has been implemented completely in software. However, a JVM can be implemented in software or hardware, or a combination of both.

- *A running JVM instance*: You have a running JVM instance when you invoke the java command.

This book uses the term JVM for all three cases. Its actual meaning should be understood by the context of its use.

One of the jobs a JVM performs is to execute the bytecode and generate a machine-specific instruction set for the host system. A JVM has class loaders and an execution engine. A class loader reads the content of a class file when required and loads it into memory. The job of the execution engine is to execute the bytecode.

A JVM is also called a Java Interpreter. Often, the term "Java Interpreter" is misleading, particularly to those who have just started learning the Java language. By the term "Java Interpreter," they conclude that the execution engine of a JVM interprets the bytecodes one at a time, and so Java must be very slow. The name "Java Interpreter" for a JVM has nothing to do with the technique the execution engine uses to execute the bytecode. The actual technique, which the execution engine may opt to execute the bytecode, depends on the specific implementation of the JVM. Some execution engines types are interpreter, just-in-time compiler, and adaptive optimizer. In its simplest kind, which is interpreter, the execution engine interprets the bytecodes one at a time, and therefore, it is slower. In its second kind, which is the just-in-time compiler, it compiles the whole code for a method in the underlying host machine language for the first time that method is called. Then it reuses the compiled code the next time the same method is called. This kind of execution engine is faster compared with the first kind, but requires more memory to cache the compiled code. In adaptive optimizer technique, it does not compile and cache the whole bytecode; rather it does so only for the most heavily used part of the bytecode.

What is an API (application programming interface)? An API is a specific set of methods made available by an operating system or by an application to the programmers for direct use. In the previous sections, you created the Welcome class in the com.jdojo.intro package, which declared a method main, which accepts an array of String as an argument and returns nothing (indicated by keyword void). If you expose all these pieces of information about the created package, class, and method, and make it available to other programmers for use, your method main in the Welcome class is a typical, though trivial, example of an API. Generally, when we use the term "API," we mean a set of methods that are available to the programmer for use. Now it is easy to understand what the Java API means. The Java API is the set of all classes and other components that are available to programmers for use while writing Java source code. In your Welcome class example, you have already used one Java API. You used it inside the body of the main method to print the message on the console. The code, which used the Java API, is

```
System.out.println("Welcome to Java 9!");
```

You did not declare any method named println in your code. This method was made available to the JVM at runtime through the Java API, which is the part of Java Platform. Broadly speaking, Java API can be classified in two categories: Core API and Extension API. Every JDK must support the Core API. Examples of Core Java APIs are Java runtimes (e.g., Applets, AWT, I/O, etc.), JFC, JDBC, etc. Java Extension APIs are JavaMail, JNDI (Java Naming and Directory Interface), etc. Java 9 includes JavaFX API as an extension API. The process of compiling and running a Java program is depicted in Figure 3-24.

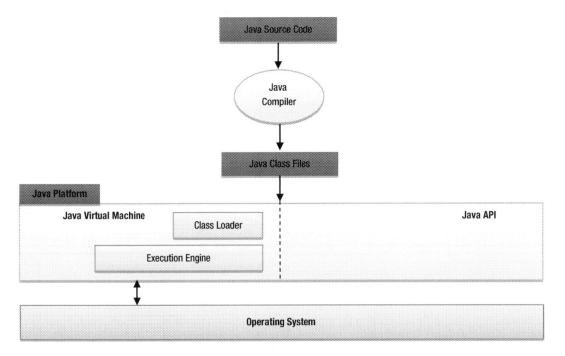

Figure 3-24. *Components involved in compiling and running a Java program*

Summary

Java programs are written in plain text format using a text editor or IDE. The Java source code is also known as a compilation unit and it is stored in a file with a `.java` extension. Several integrated development environments (IDEs) for Java, such as NetBeans, are freely available in the market. Using an IDE to develop Java applications reduces the time and effort involved in developing a Java application.

JDK 9 introduced the module system to the Java platform. A Java application consists of modules. A module contains packages, which in turn consists of types. A type could be a class, an interface, an enum, or an annotation. A module is declared in a source file named `module-info.java` and it is compiled into a class file named `module-info.class`. A compilation unit contains the source code for one or more types. When a compilation unit is compiled, a class file is generated for each type declared in the compilation unit.

Java source code is compiled into class files using a Java compiler. The class files contain bytecode. The Java compiler that ships with the JDK is called `javac`. The compiled code is packaged into JAR files using a tool called `jar`. When a JAR file contains a `module-info.class` file, which is a module descriptor, at its root directory, the JAR file is called a modular JAR. The compiled code is run by a JVM. The JDK installs a JVM that can be run as a `java` command. Both `javac` and `java` commands are located in the `JDK_HOME\bin` directory, where `JDK_HOME` is the installation directory for the JDK.

A module may contain packages for external and external use. If a module exports a package, the public types contained in that package may be used by other modules. If a module wants to use packages exported by another module, the first module must declare a dependency on the second module. JDK 9 consists of several modules, known as platform modules. The `java.base` module is a primordial module and all other modules implicitly depend on it.

The module path is a sequence of pathnames where a pathname may be a path to a directory, a modular JAR, or a JMOD file. Each entry in the module path is separated by a platform-specific path-separator character, which is a semicolon (`;`) on Windows and a colon (:) on UNIX-like operating systems. User-defined modules are located by the module system using the module path. The module path is set using the `--module-path` (or the shorter version `-p`) command-line option.

Before JDK 9, classes were located using the class path. The class path is a sequence of directories, JAR files, and ZIP files. Each entry in the class path is separated by a platform-specific path=separator character, which is a semicolon (`;`) on Windows and a colon (:) on UNIX-like operating systems. You can specify the class path using the `--class-path` (or `-cp` or `-classpath`) command-line option.

Values for the class path and the module path may look the same, but they are used for different purposes. The class path is used to locate classes (more specifically types), whereas the module path is used to locate modules.

You can print the description of a module using the `--describe-module` (or the shorter version `-d`) option with the `jar` and `java` commands. If you have a modular JAR, use the `jar` command. If you have a module in a modular JAR or exploded directory on the module path, use the `java` command.

All modules accessible to the module system in any phase (compile-time or runtime) are known as observable modules. You can print the list of observable modules using the `--list-modules` command-line option. The module system creates a module graph by reclusively resolving the dependencies of a set of modules known as *root modules* with respect to the set of observable modules. At compile-time, all modules being compiled make up the set of root modules. The main module whose main class is run makes up the set of root modules at runtime. If the main class is on the class path, all system modules are root modules. You can add modules to the set of root modules using the `--add-modules` command-line option. You can limit the number of observable modules using the `--limit-modules` command-line option.

JDK 9 works with only modules where your code is inside a module or not. Each class loader has an unnamed module. If a class loader loads a type from the module path, the type is a member of a named module. If a class loader load a type from the class path, the type becomes the member of the unnamed module of that class loader.

Before JDK 9, JDK tools supported only UNIX-style options. JDK 9 has added GNU-style options to all tools. A UNIX-style option name starts with a hyphen (-) and it is specified in the form "`<name> <value>`" where `<name>` and `<value>` are separated by one or more spaces. A GNU-style option starts with two hyphens (--) and it can be specified in "`<name> <value>`" or "`<name>=<value>`" forms. Most options are available in both styles.

EXERCISES

1. What is the extension of the file that contains the source code for a Java program?

2. What is a compilation unit?

3. How many types can you declare in a compilation unit?

4. How many public types can you declare in a compilation unit?

5. What is the restriction on naming a compilation unit if it contains a public type? What would be the name of the compilation unit if it contains the declaration of a public class named `HelloWorld`?

6. In what order are the following constructs specified in a compilation unit: type declaration, packages, and import statements?

7. How many package statements can you have in one compilation unit?

8. What is the extension of a file that contains Java compiled code?

9. What are the names of files that contain the source code and the compiled code for a Java module?

10. What keyword do you use to declare a module?

11. How many modules can you declare in one `module-info.java` file?

12. What is an unnamed module? How many unnamed modules can a class loader have? When does a type (e.g., a class) become a member of an unnamed module?

13. What is a JAR? What is the difference between a JAR file and a ZIP file?

14. What is a modular JAR and how does it differ from a JAR? Can you use a modular JAR as a JAR and vice versa?

    Hint: A modular JAR is also a JAR and it can be used as such. A JAR placed on the module path acts as a modular JAR and, in that case, the module definition is automatically derived by the module system; such a module is known as an *automatic* module.

15. What command do you use to start the JShell tool and where is the command located?

16. What command do you use to compile Java source code?

17. What command do you use to package Java compiled code into a JAR or a modular JAR?

18. Where is the module descriptor (`module-info.class` file) placed in a modular JAR?

19. You have a modular JAR saved at `C:\lib\com.jdojo.test.jar`. It contains a module named `jdojo.test` and a main class named `com.jdojo.test.Test`. Write the commands to run this class in module mode and in legacy mode.

20. You have a modular JAR saved at `C:\lib\com.jdojo.test.jar`. Write the command using the `jar` command to describe the module packaged in this modular JAR.

21. What is a module descriptor? Can you specify the version for a module when you declare the module? How do you specify a module version?

22. What are observable modules? What are root modules and how are they used in a constructing a module graph?

23. Write the name of a command-line option that is used to add modules to the set of root modules.

24. What command-line option do you use to print the list of observable modules?

25. What command-line option do you use to limit the set of observable modules?

26. The GNU-style option name for specifying the module path is `--module-path`. What is its equivalent UNIX-style option?

27. What are the options to print the help on a command? How do you print extra help for non-standard options available for a command?

CHAPTER 4

▦ ▦ ▦

Data Types

In this chapter, you will learn:

- What identifiers are and the detailed rules to declare them

- What data types are

- The difference between primitive and reference data types

- How to declare variables of a data type

- How to assign a value to a variable

- Detailed descriptions of all primitive data types in Java

- What literals of a data type are

- What casting is and when it is needed

- Binary representation of integers and floating-point numbers

- Different rounding modes for floating-point numbers

- How Java implements IEEE floating-point standards

I use a lot of snippets of code in this chapter. The quickest way to evaluate those snippets and see the results is to use the JShell tool. Refer to Chapter 2 on how to start the JShell tool on a command prompt and inside the NetBeans IDE.

What Is a Data Type?

A data type (or simply a type) is defined in terms of three components:

- A set of values (or data objects)

- A set of operations that can be applied to all values in the set

- A data representation, which determines how the values are stored

A programming language provides some predefined data types, which are known as built-in data types. A programming language may also let programmers define their own data types, which are known as user-defined data types.

A data type that consists of an atomic, indivisible value, and that is defined without the help of any other data types, is known as a *primitive* data type. User-defined data types are defined in terms of primitive data types and other user-defined data types. Typically, a programming language does not let the programmers extend or redefine primitive data types.

© Kishori Sharan 2017
K. Sharan, *Beginning Java 9 Fundamentals*, https://doi.org/10.1007/978-1-4842-2902-6_4

Java provides many built-in primitive data types, such as int, float, boolean, char, etc. For example, the three components that define the int primitive data type in Java are as follows:

- An int data type consists of a set of all integers between -2147483648 and 2147483647.

- Operations such as addition, subtraction, multiplication, division, comparison, and many more are defined for the int data type.

- A value of the int data type is represented in 32-bit memory in 2's complement form.

All three components of the int data type are predefined by the Java language. Developers cannot extend or redefine the definition of the int data type. You can give a name to a value of the int data type as follows:

```
int employeeId;
```

This statement states that employeeId is a name (technically called an identifier) that can be associated with one value from the set of values that defines values for the int data type. For example, you can associate integer 1969 to the name employeeId using an assignment statement like this:

```
employeeId = 1969;
```

What Is an Identifier?

An *identifier* in Java is a sequence of characters of unlimited length. The sequence of characters includes all Java letters and Java digits, the first of which must be a Java letter. Java uses the Unicode character set. A Java letter is a letter from any language that is represented by Unicode character set. For example, A-Z, a-z, _ (underscore), and $ are considered Java letters from the ASCII character set range of Unicode. Java digits include 0-9 ASCII digits and any Unicode character that denotes a digit in a language. Spaces are not allowed in an identifier.

░ **Tip**   An identifier in Java is a sequence of one or more Unicode letters and digits and it must start with a letter.

Identifier is a technical term for "name". Therefore, an identifier is simply the name given to an entity in a Java program such as a module, a package, a class, a method, a variable, etc. in a Java program. In the previous chapter, you declared a module named jdojo.intro, a package named com.jdojo.intro, a class named Welcome, a method named main, and an argument to the main method named args. All these names are identifiers.

You have seen names in two forms: a name that consists of only one part such as Welcome and a name that consists of multiple parts separated by dots such as jdojo.intro and com.jdojo.intro. Names that consist of only one part without using any dots are known as *simple names*; names that can consists of parts separated by dots are known as *qualified names*. There are rules regarding what kind of entities in Java can have simple names and qualified names. For example, modules and packages can have qualified names, whereas classes, methods, and variables can have only simple names. An entity that can have a qualified name does not mean that the name of such an entity must consist of at least two parts such as x.y; it simply means that such an entity's name may consists of parts separated by dots. For example, the module name ComJdojoIntro is as valid as the module name com.jdojo.intro or jdojo.intro.

Why do we have two types of names—simple and qualified? To understand the reason behind it, consider the following two questions:

- John and his friend Anna live in the UK. John tells Anna that he will go to *Birmingham* tomorrow.

- Thomas and his friend Wanda live in the USA. Thomas tell Wanda that he will go to *Birmingham* tomorrow.

Are John and Thomas talking about the same Birmingham city? The answer is no. Both the UK and the USA have a city named Birmingham. John is talking about the city in the UK and Thomas is talking about the city in the USA. When you use a name in a daily conversation or a Java program, the name has a space (an area, a region, or a scope) in which is it is valid and must be unique. Such a space is called a namespace. In our example, UK and USA are serving as namespaces in which the Birmingham city name is unique. A qualified name lets you use namespaces for the name. For example, John and Thomas might have used `UK.Birmingham` and `USA.Birmingham` as city names, which would be qualified names in Java terminology.

When a Java entity can occur as a standalone, for example, modules and packages, qualified names for such entities are allowed to prevent name collision. Suppose I have a module named `jdojo.intro` and someone else also creates a module named `jdojo.intro`. These modules cannot be used (or referred to) in the same Java application because of their name collision. However, these names are fine if these modules will be used standalone. A class always occurs (or, is declared) inside a package; therefore, a class name must be a simple name as long as that simple name is unique within the package.

A simple rule of thumb in naming your reusable and published modules and packages is to use Internet reverse-domain naming convention. If you own `jdojo.com`, use `com.jdojo` as a prefix to the names of all your modules and packages. I use only `jdojo` as a prefix for all module names in this book because these modules are not for public use; they are only used in examples of this book and they are only for learning purposes; a shorter module name is also easy for me and you to type and read!

The Java programming language is case-sensitive. All characters used in an identifier are important, as is their case. The names `welcome`, `Welcome`, and `WELCOME` are three different identifiers. It helps the readers of your code if you use intuitive names in your Java programs that convey the purpose of the entity. Suppose you need to store an employee's ID in a variable. You can name the variable `n1` and `id` and Java won't complain. However, if you name it `employeeId` or `empId`, your code becomes more readable. Anybody reading your code will get the right context and the purpose for that variable. Table 4-1 contains examples of a few valid and invalid identifiers in Java.

Table 4-1. *Examples of Valid and Invalid Identifiers in Java*

Identifier	Valid	Description
Welcome	Yes	Consists of all letters.
num1	Yes	Consists of three letters and a digit.
_myId	Yes	Can start with an underscore.
sum_of_two_numbers	Yes	Can have letters and underscores.
Outer$Inner	Yes	Can have letters and a $.
$var	Yes	Can start with a $.
$	Yes	Can be only a $.
_	No	Starting JDK 9, an underscore cannot be used as an identifier by itself. However, an underscore can be part of a multi-character identifier name.
2num	No	An identifier cannot start with a digit.
my name	No	An identifier cannot contain spaces.
num1+num2	No	An identifier cannot contain symbols like +, -, *, /, etc.

Keywords

Keywords are words that have predefined meanings in the Java programming language. They can only be used in contexts defined by the Java programming language. Keywords cannot be used as identifiers. Table 4-2 contains a complete list of keywords in Java.

Table 4-2. *List of Keywords and Reserved Words in Java*

abstract	continue	for	new	switch
assert	default	if	package	synchronized
boolean	do	goto	private	this
break	double	implements	protected	throw
byte	else	import	public	throws
case	enum	instanceof	return	transient
catch	extends	int	short	try
char	final	interface	static	void
class	finally	long	strictfp	volatile
const	float	native	super	while
_ (underscore)				

The two keywords, const and goto, are not currently used in Java. They are reserved keywords and they cannot be used as identifiers.

With the introduction of the module system, Java SE 9 has introduced 10 new restricted keywords, which cannot be used as identifiers. Those restricted keywords are open, module, requires, transitive, exports, opens, to, uses, provides, and with. They are restricted keywords because they are treated as keywords only in the context of module declaration; everywhere else in a program, they can be used as identifiers. They were not keywords in Java SE 8. If they were declared keywords in Java SE 9, many programs written in Java SE which used them as identifiers would have broken.

▨ **Tip**   You will encounter three words—true, false, and null—in Java programs. They appear to be keywords, but they are not. Rather, true and false are boolean literals and null is a null literal. You cannot use true, false, or null as identifiers in Java, even though they are not keywords.

Data Types in Java

Before we start discussing all data types available in Java, let's look at a simple example of adding two numbers. Suppose your friend asks you to add two numbers. The procedure to add two numbers goes as follows.

1.   Your friend tells you the first number, you listen to him, and your brain records the number at a particular location in your memory. Of course, you do not know where the number is exactly stored in your brain's memory.

2.   Your friend tells you the second number, you listen to him, and again, your brain records it at a particular location in your memory.

3. Now, your friend asks you to add the two numbers. Your brain comes into action again. It recalls (or reads) the two numbers and adds them, and you tell your friend the sum of the two numbers.

Now, if your friend wants you to tell him the difference between the same two numbers, he does not need to tell you those two numbers again. This is because these two numbers are stored in your memory, and your brain can recall and use them again. However, whether your brain can perform addition of those two numbers depends on many factors, for example, how big those two numbers are; whether your brain can memorize (or store) those big numbers; whether your brain is trained to do addition, etc. The process of adding two numbers also depends on the type of these two numbers. Your brain will use different logic to add them depending on whether two numbers are whole numbers (e.g., 10 and 20), real numbers (e.g., 12.4 and 19.1), or the mix of whole and real numbers (e.g., 10 and 69.9). The entire process takes place in your brain without you noticing it (maybe because you are so accustomed to doing these additions). However, when you want to do any kind of manipulation on numbers or any other types of values in a Java program, you need to specify the details about the values you want to manipulate and the procedure for manipulating those values.

Let's discuss the same example of adding two numbers in a Java program. The first thing you need to tell Java is the type of the two numbers you want to add. Let's assume that you want to add two integers, 50 and 70. When you added two numbers by yourself, your brain gave each number a name (maybe as the first number and the second number). You did not notice the naming of those numbers by your brain. However, in a Java program, you have to explicitly give names (also known as identifiers) to both numbers. Let's name the two numbers as num1 and num2, respectively. The following two lines in a Java program indicate the fact that there are two integers, num1 and num2:

```
int num1;
int num2;
```

The int keyword is used to indicate that the name that follows represents an integer value, for example, 10, 15, 70, 1000, etc. When these two lines of code are executed, Java allocates two memory locations and associates the name num1 with the first memory location and the name num2 with the second memory location. The memory state at this point is depicted in Figure 4-1.

Figure 4-1. *Memory state when two int type variables are declared*

These memory locations are called variables which have been named num1 and num2. Strictly speaking, num1 and num2 are two names associated with two memory locations. However, roughly speaking, you say

- num1 and num2 are two variables, or

- num1 and num2 are two variables of int data type, or

- num1 and num2 are two int variables.

Because you have declared num1 and num2 variables of the int data type, you cannot store a real number, such as 10.51, at these memory locations. The following piece of code stores 50 in num1 and 70 in num2:

```
num1 = 50;
num2 = 70;
```

Memory state after these two lines of code are executed has been depicted in Figure 4-2.

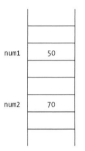

Figure 4-2. *Memory state after two int type variables are assigned a value*

Now, you want to add the two numbers. Before you add them, you must allocate another memory location, which will hold the result. You name this memory location as num3 and the following piece of code performs these tasks:

```
int num3;            // Allocates the memory location num3
num3 = num1 + num2;  // Computes sum and store the result in num3
```

Memory state after these two lines of code are executed has been depicted in Figure 4-3.

Figure 4-3. *Memory states in the process of adding two numbers*

The two previous lines can be combined into one:

```
int num3 = num1 + num2;
```

A variable has three properties:

- A memory location to hold the value

- The type of the data stored at the memory location

- A name (also called an *identifier*) to refer to the memory location

104

The data type of the variable also determines the range of the values that the memory location can hold. Therefore, the amount of memory allocated for a variable depends on its data type. For example, 32 bits of memory is allocated for a variable of the int data type. In this example, each variable (num1, num2, and num3) uses 32 bits of memory.

Java supports two kinds of data types:

- Primitive data type

- Reference data type

A variable of the primitive data type holds a value, whereas a variable of the reference data type holds the reference to an object in memory. I discuss one of the reference data types available in Java, String, in this section. String is a class defined in the Java library and you can use it to manipulate text (sequence of characters). You declare a reference variable named str of String type as follows:

```
String str;
```

Before you assign the reference of an object to a reference variable, you need to create an object. You create an object using the new operator. You can create an object of the String class with "Hello" as its contents as follows:

```
// Creates a String object and assigns the reference of the object to str
str = new String("Hello");
```

What happens when this code is executed? First, memory is allocated and the name of the variable str is associated with that memory location, as shown in Figure 4-4. This process is the same as declaring a primitive data type variable. The second piece of code creates a String object in memory with the text "Hello" and stores the reference (or memory address) of the String object into the variable str. This fact is shown in the second half of Figure 4-4 by using an arrow pointing from the variable str to the object in memory.

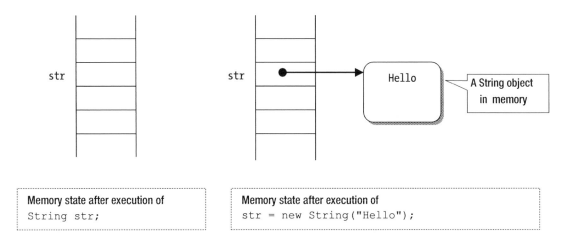

Memory state after execution of
`String str;`

Memory state after execution of
`str = new String("Hello");`

Figure 4-4. *Memory states using reference variables*

You can also assign the reference of an object stored in one reference variable to another reference variable. In such cases, both reference variables refer to the same object in memory. This can be achieved as follows:

```
// Declares String reference variable str1 and str2
String str1;
String str2;

// Assigns the reference of a String object "Hello" to str1
str1 = new String("Hello");

// Assigns the reference stored in str1 to str2
str2 = str1;
```

There is a reference constant (also known as a reference literal) null, which can be assigned to any reference variable. If null is assigned to a reference variable, it means that the reference variable is not referring to any object in memory. The null reference literal can be assigned to str2.

```
str2 = null;
```

Memory states after execution of all of these statements are depicted in Figure 4-5.

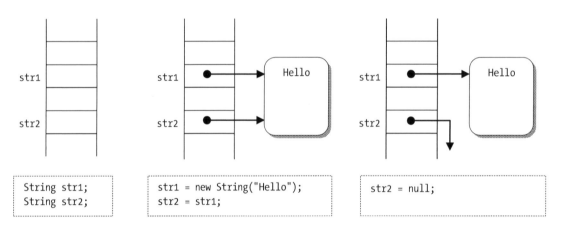

Figure 4-5. *Memory states using null in the reference variables assignments*

A String object is created using the new operator. However, strings are used so often that there is a shortcut to create a string object. All string literals, a sequence of characters enclosed in double quotes, are treated as String objects. Therefore, instead of using the new operator to create a String object, you can use string literals like so:

```
// Assigns the reference of a String object with text "Hello" to str1
String str1 = "Hello";

// Assigns the reference of a String object with text "Hello" to str1
String str1 = new String ("Hello");
```

There is a subtle difference between these two statements, which assign a String object to str1 with the same text "Hello". I discuss the difference when I cover the String class in a separate chapter.

Primitive Data Types in Java

Java has eight primitive data types. Table 4-3 lists their names, sizes, whether they are signed or unsigned, their range, and a few examples. The following sections describe them in detail.

Table 4-3. *List of Primitive Data Types, Their Size, Range, and Examples*

Data Type	Size in Bits	Signed/Unsigned	Range	Example
byte	8	Signed	-2^7 to $+2^7 - 1$	-2, 8, 10
short	16	Signed	-2^{15} to $+2^{15} - 1$	-2, 8, 10
int	32	Signed	-2^{31} to $+2^{31} - 1$	1990, -90, 23
long	64	Signed	-2^{63} to $+2^{63} - 1$	1990L, -90L, 23L
char	16	Unsigned	0 to 65535	'A', '8', '\u0000'
float	32	Signed	-3.4×10^{38} to $+3.4 \times 10^{38}$	12.89F, -89.78F
double	64	Signed	-1.7×10^{308} to $+1.7 \times 10^{308}$	12.78, -78.89
boolean	Unspecified	N/A	true and false	true, false

The eight primitive data types are divided into two categories:

- boolean data type
- Numeric data type

The numeric data type can be further subdivided into integral and floating-point types. All primitive data types and their categories are shown in Figure 4-6. The subsequent sections describe all primitive data types in detail.

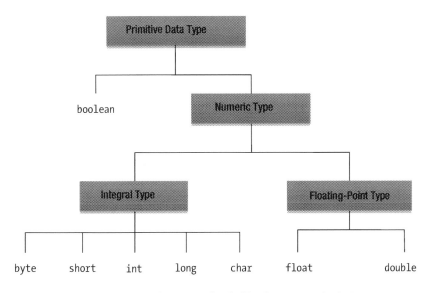

Figure 4-6. *List of primitive data types divided by their categories in Java*

░ **Alert**   I have received several emails from readers of the first edition of this book that it is an error to list the char data type under the numeric data type category. However, that is not true. The char data type is a numeric data type by all means. You can assign an integer to a char variable and you can also perform arithmetic operations such as addition and subtraction on char variables. The Java Language Specification also categories char as a numeric data type. Many Java books either list char as a separate data type or describe it as a non-numeric data type; both are wrong.

You will come across the term "literal" several times while reading this book and while working with Java. A literal of type X means a value of type X that can be directly represented in the source code without requiring any computations. For example, 10 is an int literal, which means whenever you need a value 10 of int type in a Java program, you can simply type 10. Java defines literals for all primitive types and for two reference types, the String type and null type.

Integral Data Types

An integral data type is a numeric data type whose values are whole numbers (i.e., integers). Java offers five integral data types: byte, short, int, long, and char. All integral data types are described in detail in the sections to follow.

The int Data Type

The int data type is a 32-bit signed Java primitive data type. A variable of the int data type takes 32 bits of memory. Its valid range is -2,147,483,648 to 2,147,483,647 (-231 to 231 - 1). All whole numbers in this range are known as integer literals (or integer constants). For example, 10, -200, 0, 30, 19, etc. are integer literals of int type. An integer literal can be assigned to an int variable, say num1, like so:

```
int num1 = 21;
```

Integer literals can be expressed in the following formats:

- Decimal number format

- Octal number format

- Hexadecimal number format

- Binary number format

When an integer literal starts with a zero and has at least two digits, it is considered to be in the octal number format. The following line of code assigns a decimal value of 17 (021 in octal) to num1:

```
// 021 is in octal number format, not in decimal
int num1 = 021;
```

The following two lines of code have the same effect of assigning a value of 17 to the variable num1:

```
// No leading zero - decimal number format
int num1 = 17;

// Leading zero - octal number format. 021 in octal is the same as 17 in decimal
int num1 = 021;
```

Be careful when using int literals with a leading zero, because Java will treat these literals as in octal number format. Note that an int literal in octal format must have at least two digits and must start with a zero to be treated as an octal number. The number 0 is treated as zero in decimal number format, and 00 is treated as zero in octal number format.

```
// Assigns zero to num1, 0 is in the decimal number format
int num1 = 0;

// Assigns zero to num1, 00 is in the octal number format
int num1 = 00;
```

Note that 0 and 00 represent the same value, zero. Both have the same effect of assigning a value of zero to the variable num1.

All int literals in the hexadecimal number format start with 0x or 0X, that is, zero immediately followed by an uppercase or lowercase X, and they must contain at least one hexadecimal digit. Hexadecimal number format uses 16 digits, 0-9 and A-F (or a-f). The case of the letters A to F does not matter. The following are the examples of using int literals in hexadecimal format:

```
int num1 = 0x123;
int num2 = 0xdecafe;
int num3 = 0x1A2B;
int num4 = 0X0123;
```

An int literal can also be represented using the binary number format. All int literals in the binary number format start with 0b or 0B, that is, zero immediately followed by an uppercase or lowercase B. The following are examples of using int literals in the binary number format:

```
int num1 = 0b10101;
int num2 = 0b00011;
int num3 = 0b10;
int num4 = 0b00000010;
```

The following assignments assign the same decimal number 51966 to an int variable named num1 in all four different formats:

```
num1 = 51966;                  // Decimal format
num1 = 0145376;                // Octal format, starts with a zero
num1 = 0xCAFE;                 // Hexadecimal format, starts with 0x
num1 = 0b1100101011111110;     // Binary format starts with 0b
```

Java has a class named Integer (note the uppercase I in Integer) that defines two constants to represent maximum and minimum values for the int data type, Integer.MAX_VALUE and Integer.MIN_VALUE. For example,

```
int max = Integer.MAX_VALUE; // Assigns maximum int value to max
int min = Integer.MIN_VALUE; // Assigns minimum int value to min
```

The long Data Type

The long data type is a 64-bit signed Java primitive data type. It is used when the result of calculations on whole numbers may exceed the range of the int data type. Its range is -9,223,372,036,854,775,808 to 9,223,372,036,854,775,807 (-2^{63} to 2^{63} - 1). All whole numbers in the range of long are called integer literals of long type.

51 is an integer literal. What is its data type: int or long? An integer literal of type long always ends with L (or lowercase l). This book uses L to mark the end of an integer literal of the long type, because l (lowercase L) is often confused with 1 (digit one) in print. The following are examples of using an integer literal of long type:

```
long num1 = 0L;
long num2 = 401L;
long mum3 = -3556L;
long num4 = 89898L;
long num5 = -105L;
```

▨ **Tip**   25L is an integer literal of long type, whereas 25 is an integer literal of int type.

Integer literals of long type can also be expressed in octal, hexadecimal, and binary formats. For example,

```
long num1;
num1 = 25L;       // Decimal format
num1 = 031L;      // Octal format
num1 = 0X19L;     // Hexadecimal format
num1 = 0b11001L;  // Binary format
```

When a long literal is assigned to a variable of type long, the Java compiler checks the value being assigned and makes sure that it is in the range of the long data type; otherwise it generates a compile-time error. For example

```
// One more than maximum positive value for long. This will generate a compile-time error
long num1 = 9223372036854775808L;
```

Because the int data type has a lower range than the long data type, the value stored in an int variable can always be assigned to a long variable.

```
int num1 = 10;
long num2 = 20;   // OK to assign int literal 20 to a long variable num2
num2 = num1;      // OK to assign an int to a long
```

▨ **Tip**   When you assign a value of a smaller type to a variable of bigger type (e.g., int to long), Java performs an automatic widening conversion to fill the higher order bits in the destination with zero, preserving the sign bit of the source. For example, assigning an int literal to a variable of a long variable, Java performs the widening conversion.

The assignment from int to long is valid, because all values that can be stored in an int variable can also be stored in a long variable. However, the reverse is not true. You cannot simply assign the value stored in a long variable to an int variable. There is a possibility of value overflow (or loss of value). Consider the following two variables:

```
int num1 = 10;
long num2 = 2147483655L;
```

If you assign the value of num2 to num1 as

```
num1 = num2;
```

the value stored in num2 cannot be stored in num1, because the data type of num1 is int and the value of num2 falls outside the range that the int data type can handle. To guard against inadvertently making such errors, Java does not allow you to write code like this:

```
// A compile-time error. long to int assignment is not allowed in Java
num1 = num2;
```

Even if the value stored in a long variable is well within the range of the int data type, the assignment from long to int is not allowed, as shown in the following example:

```
int num1 = 5;
long num2 = 25L;
```

```
// A compile-time error. Even if num2's value 25 which is within the range of int
num1 = num2;
```

If you want to assign the value of a long variable to an int variable, you have to explicitly mention this fact in your code, so that Java makes sure you are aware that there may be loss of value. You do this using "cast" in Java, like so:

```
num1 = (int)num2; // Now it is fine because of the "(int)" cast
```

By writing (int)num2, you are instructing Java to treat the value stored in num2 as an int. At runtime, Java will use only the 32 least significant bits of num2 and assign the value stored in those 32 bits to num1. If num2 has a value that is outside the range of the int data type, you would not get the same value in num1.

Java has a class Long (note the uppercase L in Long) that defines two constants to represent maximum and minimum values of long data type, Long.MAX_VALUE and Long.MIN_VALUE.

```
long max = Long.MAX_VALUE;
long min = Long.MIN_VALUE;
```

The byte Data Type

The byte data type is an 8-bit signed Java primitive integer data type. Its range is -128 to 127 (-2^7 to 2^7 - 1). This is the smallest integer data type available in Java. Generally, byte variables are used when a program uses a large number of variables whose values fall in the range -128 to 127 or when dealing with binary data in a file or over the network. Unlike int and long literals, there are no byte literals. However, you can assign any int literal that falls in the range of byte to a byte variable. For example,

```
byte b1 = 125;
byte b2 = -11;
```

Java generates a compiler error if you assign a value outside the range -128 to 127 to a byte variable. The following assignment produces a compile-time error:

```
// An error. 150 is an int literal outside -128 to 127
byte b3 = 150;
```

Note that you can only assign an int literal between -128 and 127 to a byte variable. However, this does not imply that you can also assign the value stored in an int variable, which is in the range of -128 to 127, to a byte variable. The following piece of code will generate a compile-time error, because it assigns the value of an int variable, num1, to a byte variable, b1:

```
int num1 = 15;
```

```
// OK. Assignment of int literal (-128 to 127) to byte.
byte b1 = 15;
```

```
// A compile-time error. Even though num1 has a value of 15, which is in the range -128 and 127.
b1 = num1;
```

Why did the compiler complain when num1 is assigned to b1? The compiler does not try to read the value stored in num1 because num1 is a variable and its value is known only at runtime. It sees num1 as an int type, which is 32-bit big, whereas it sees b1 as byte type, which is 8-bit big. Based on their size, the compiler sees that you are assigning a bigger variable to a smaller variable and there is a potential of loss of data. When you assign 15 to b1, 15 is an int literal and its value is known at compile-time; the compiler can make sure that 15 is within the range of a byte (-128 to 127). If you declare num1 as a compile-time constant in the previous snippet of code, the compiler will not generate an error. A compile-time constant is a variable declared using the final keyword and whose value is known at compile-time. The following snippet of code does this:

```
// Using final makes the num1 variable a compile-time constant
final int num1 = 15;
```

```
// OK. Assignment of int literal (-128 to 127) to byte.
byte b1 = 15;
```

```
// Now, the compiler knows the value of num1 as 15 and it is fine.
b1 = num1;
```

112

You can also fix this error by using a cast, as you did in the case of the long-to-int assignment. The assignment of num1 to b1 can be rewritten as follows:

```
int num1 = 15;
byte b1 = 15;
b1 = (byte)num1; // Ok. Using a cast
```

After this cast from int to byte, the Java compiler would not complain about the int-to-byte assignment. If num1 holds a value that cannot be correctly represented in the 8-bit byte variable b1, the higher order bits (9th to 32nd) of num1 are ignored and the value represented in the lower 8 bits is assigned to b1. In such a case of int-to-byte assignment, the value assigned to the destination byte variable may not be the same as the value of the source int variable if the value of the source variable falls outside the range of byte data type.

However, irrespective of the value in the source int variable, the destination byte variable will always have a value between -128 and 127. Like int, since long is also a bigger data type than byte, you need to use explicit cast if you want to assign the value of a long variable to a byte variable. For example,

```
byte b4 = 10;
long num3 = 19L;

b4 = (byte)num3;  // OK because of cast
b4 = 19L;         // Error. Cannot assign long literal to byte
b4 = (byte)19L;   // OK because of cast
```

It is true that both 19 and 19L represent the same number. However, to the Java compiler, they are different. 19 is an int literal, that is, its data type is int, whereas 19L is a long literal, that is, its data type is long.

Java has a class named Byte (note the uppercase B in Byte) that defines two constants to represent maximum and minimum values of the byte data type, Byte.MAX_VALUE and Byte.MIN_VALUE.

```
byte max = Byte.MAX_VALUE; // Same as byte max = 127;
byte min = Byte.MIN_VALUE; // Same as byte min = -128;
```

The short Data Type

The short data type is a 16-bit signed Java primitive integer data type. Its range is -32768 to 32767 (or -2^{15} to $2^{15} - 1$). Generally, short variables are used when a program uses a large number of variables whose values fall in the range of the short data type or when dealing with data in a file, which can be easily handled using short data type. Unlike int and long literals, there are no short literals. However, you can assign any int literal that falls in the range of short (-32768 to 32767) to a short variable. For example,

```
short s1 = 12905;   // ok
short s2 = -11890;  // ok
```

The value of a byte variable can always be assigned to a short variable because the range of the byte data type falls within the range of the short data type. All other rules for assignment of a value from an int or long variable to a short variable are the same as that for the byte variable. The following snippet of code illustrates the assignment of byte, int, and long values to short variables:

```
short s1 = 15;  // OK
byte b1 = 10;   // OK
s1 = b1;        // OK
```

```
int num1 = 10;      // OK
s1 = num1;          // A compile-time error
s1 = (short)num1;   // OK because of cast from int to short
s1 = 35000;         // A compile-time error of an int literal outside the short range

long num2 = 555L; // OK
s1 = num2;          // A compile-time error
s1 = (short)num2;   // OK because of the cast from long to short
s1 = 555L;          // A compile-time error
s = (short)555L;    // OK because of the cast from long to short
```

Java has a class called Short (note the uppercase S in Short) that defines two constants to represent maximum and minimum values of the short data type, Short.MAX_VALUE and Short.MIN_VALUE.

```
short max = Short.MAX_VALUE;
short min = Short.MIN_VALUE;
```

The char Data Type

The char data type is a 16-bit *unsigned* Java primitive data type. Its value represents a Unicode character. Note that char is an unsigned data type. Therefore, a char variable cannot have a negative value. The range of the char data type is 0 to 65535, which is the same as the range of the Unicode character set. A character literal represents a value of the char data type. A character literal can be expressed in the following formats:

- As a character enclosed in single quotes

- As a character escape sequence

- As a Unicode escape sequence

- As an octal escape sequence

Character Literals in Single Quotes

A character literal can be expressed by enclosing it in single quotes. The following are a few examples:

```
char c1 = 'A';
char c2 = 'L';
char c3 = '5';
char c4 = '/';
```

Recall that a sequence of characters enclosed in double quotes is a String literal. A String literal cannot be assigned to a char variable, even if the String literal consists of only one character. This restriction is because Java does not allow you to mix values of primitive and reference data types. String is a reference data type, whereas char is a primitive data type. The following are a few examples:

```
char c1 = 'A';      // OK
String s1 = 'A';    // An error. Cannot assign a char 'A' to a String s1
String s2 = "A";    // OK. "A" is a String literal assigned to a String variable
String s3 = "ABC"; // OK. "ABC" is a String literal
char c2 = "A";      // An error. Cannot assign a String "A" to char c2
char c4 = 'AB';     // An error. A character literal must contain only one character
```

114

Character Escape Sequence

A character literal can also be expressed as a character escape sequence. A character escape sequence starts with a backslash immediately followed by a character, and both are enclosed in single quotes. There are eight predefined character escape sequences, as listed in Table 4-4. You cannot define your own character escape sequence in Java.

Table 4-4. *List of Character Escape Sequences*

Character Escape Sequence	Description
'\n'	A linefeed
'\r'	A carriage return
'\f'	A form feed
'\b'	A backspace
'\t'	A tab
'\\'	A backslash
'\"'	A double quote
'\''	A single quote

A character literal expressed in the form of a character escape sequence consists of two characters—a backslash and a character following the backslash. However, they represent only one character. The following are a few examples of using character sequences:

```
char c1 = '\n'; // Assigns a linefeed to c1
char c2 = '\"'; // Assigns double quote to c2
char c3 = '\a'; // A compile-time error. Invalid character escape sequence
```

Unicode Character Escape Sequence

A character literal can also be expressed as a Unicode escape sequence in the form '\uxxxx', Here, \u (a backslash immediately followed by a lowercase u) denotes the start of the Unicode escape sequence, and xxxx represents exactly four hexadecimal digits. The value represented by xxxx is the Unicode value for the character. The character 'A' has the Unicode value of 65. The value 65 in decimal can be represented in hexadecimal as 41. So, the character 'A' can be expressed in Unicode escape sequence as '\u0041'.The following snippet of code assigns the same character 'A' to the char variables c1 and c2:

```
char c1 = 'A';
char c2 = '\u0041';  // Same as c2 = 'A';
```

Octal Character Escape Sequence

A character literal can also be expressed as an octal escape sequence in the form '\nnn'. Here, n is an octal digit (0-7). The range for the octal escape sequence is '\000' to '\377'. The octal number 377 is the same as the decimal number 255. Therefore, using an octal escape sequence, you can represent characters whose Unicode code range from 0 to 255 decimal integers.

A Unicode character set (code range 0 to 65535) can be represented as a Unicode escape sequence (`'\uxxxx'`). Why does Java have another octal escape sequence, which is a subset of the Unicode escape sequence? The octal escape sequences exist to represent characters for compatibility with other languages that use 8-bit unsigned chars to represent a character. Unlike a Unicode escape sequence, where you are always required to use four hexadecimal digits, in an octal escape sequence you can use one, two, or three octal digits. Therefore, an octal escape sequence may take on the form `'\n'`, `'\nn'`, or `'\nnn'`, where n is one of the octal digits 0, 1, 2, 3, 4, 5, 6, and 7. Some examples of octal escape sequences are as follows:

```
char c1 = '\52';
char c2 = '\141';
char c3 = '\400'; // A compile-time error. Octal 400 is out of range
char c4 = '\42';
char c5 = '\10';  // Same as '\n'
```

You can also assign an `int` literal to a `char` variable if the `int` literal falls in the range 0-65535. When you assign an `int` literal to a `char` variable, the `char` variable represents the character whose Unicode code is equal to the value represented by that `int` literal. The Unicode code for the character `'a'` (lowercase A) is 97. The decimal value 97 is represented as 141 in octal and 61 in hexadecimal. You can represent the Unicode character `'a'` in different forms in Java: `'a'`, `'\141'` and `'\u0061'`. You can also use `int` literal 97 to represent the Unicode character `'a'`. The following four assignments have the same meanings in Java:

```
char c1 = 97;         // Assign 'a' to c1
char c2 = 'a';        // Assign 'a' to c2
char c3 = '\141';     // Assign 'a' to c3
char c4 = '\u0061';   // Assign 'a' to c4
```

A byte variable takes 8 bits and a char variable takes 16 bits. Even if the byte data type has a smaller range than the char data type, you cannot assign a value stored in a byte variable to a char variable. The reason is that byte is a signed data type, whereas char is an unsigned data type. If the byte variable has a negative value, say -15, it cannot be stored in a char variable without losing the precision. For such an assignment to succeed, you need to use an explicit cast. The following snippet of code illustrates possible cases of assignments from char to other integral data types and vice versa:

```
byte b1 = 10;
short s1 = 15;
int num1 = 150;
long num2 = 20L;
char c1 = 'A';

// byte and char
b1 = c1;          // An error
b1 = (byte)c1;    // OK
c1 = b1;          // An error
c1 = (char)b1;    // OK
```

```
// short and char
s1 = c1;        // An error
s1 = (short)c1; // OK
c1 = s1;        // An error
c1 = (char)s1;  // OK

// int and char
num1 = c1;        // OK
num1 = (int)c1;   // OK. But cast is not required. Use num1 = c1
c1 = num1;        // An error
c1 = (char)num1;  // OK
c1 = 255;         // OK. 255 is in the range of 0-65535
c1 = 70000;       // An error. 70000 is out of range 0-65535
c1 = (char)70000; // OK. But will lose the original value

// long and char
num2 = c1;        // OK
num2 = (long)c1;  // OK. But cast is not required. Use num2 = c1
c1 = num2;        // An Error
c1 = (char)num2;  // OK
c1 = 255L;        // An error. 255L is a long literal
c1 = (char)255L;  // OK. But use c1 = 255 instead
```

The boolean Data Type

The boolean data type has only two valid values: true and false. These two values are called boolean literals. You can use boolean literals as follows:

```
// Declares a boolean variable named done
boolean done;

// Assigns true to done
done = true;
```

░ **Tip**   In Java, 1 and 0 are not treated as boolean values true and false, respectively. This is a change for you if you are coming from a C/C++ background. Java defines only two boolean values, known as boolean literals, which are true and false. You cannot assign any other values to a boolean variable other than true and false.

One important point to note is that a boolean variable cannot be cast to any other data type and vice versa. Java does not specify the size of the boolean data type. Its size is left up to the JVM implementation. Typically, a value of a boolean data type is mapped by the compiler to int and boolean arrays are encoded as byte arrays.

Floating-Point Data Types

A number that contains a fractional part is known as a real number, for example, 3.25, 0.49, -9.19, 19.0, etc. A computer stores every number, real or integral, in binary format, which consists of only 0s and 1s. Therefore, it is necessary to convert a real number to its binary representation before it can be stored. It must be converted back to a real number after its binary representation is read. When a real number is converted to its binary representation, the computer must also store the position of the decimal point within the number. There are two strategies to store a real number in computer memory.

- Store only the binary representation of the number assuming that there is always a fixed number of digits before and after the point. A point is called a decimal point in the decimal representation of a number and a binary point in the binary representation. The type of representation in which the position of the point is always fixed in a number is known as *fixed-point number format*.

- Store the binary representation of the real number and the position of the point in the real number. Since the number of digits before and after the point can vary in this kind of representation of the real number, we say that the point can float. This kind of representation is called a *floating-point format*.

Floating-point representations are slower and less accurate compared to fixed-point representations. However, floating-point representations can handle a larger range of numbers with the same amount memory as compared to fixed-point representations.

Java supports the floating-point number format. It is important to note that not all real numbers have exact binary representations, and therefore, they are represented as floating-point approximations. Java uses the IEEE 754 floating-point standard to store real numbers. IEEE is an acronym for the Institute of Electrical and Electronic Engineers. Java has two floating-point numeric data types:

- float

- double

The float Data Type

The float data type uses 32 bits to store a floating-point number in the IEEE 754 standard format. A floating-point number represented in 32 bits according to the IEEE 754 standard is also known as a single-precision floating-point number. It can represent a real number as small as 1.4×10^{-45} and as big as 3.4×10^{38} (approx.) in magnitude. The range includes only the magnitude. It could be positive or negative. Here, 1.4×10^{-45} is the smallest positive number greater than zero that can be stored in a float variable.

All real numbers that end with f or F are called float literals. A float literal can be expressed in the following two formats:

- Decimal number format

- Scientific notation

A few examples of float literals in decimal number format are as follows:

```
float f1 = 8F;
float f2 = 8.F;
float f3 = 8.0F;
float f4 = 3.51F;
float f5 = 0.0F;
float f6 = 16.78f;
```

The real number 3.25 is also written using exponential forms such as 32.5 x 10⁻¹ or 0.325 x 10¹. In Java, such real numbers can be represented as float literals using scientific notation. In scientific notation, the number 32.5 x 10⁻¹ is written as 32.5E-1. As a float literal, it can be written as 32.5E-1F or 32.5E-1f. All of the following float literals denote the same real number 32.5:

- 3.25F
- 32.5E-1F
- 0.325E+1F
- 0.325E1F
- 0.0325E2F
- 0.0325e2F
- 3.25E0F

The float data type defines two zeros: +0.0F (or 0.0F) and -0.0F. However, for the comparison purposes, +0.0F and -0.0F are considered equal.

The float data type defines two infinities: positive infinity and negative infinity. For example, the result of the dividing 2.5F by 0.0F is a float positive infinity, whereas the result of dividing 2.5F by -0.0F is a float negative infinity.

Results of some operations on float are not defined. For example, dividing 0.0F by 0.0F is indeterminate. Indeterminate results are represented by a special value of the float data type called NaN (Not-a-Number). Java has a Float class (note the uppercase F in Float) that defines three constants that represent positive infinity, negative infinity, and NaN of the float data type. Table 4-5 lists these float constants and their meanings. The table also lists two constants, which represent the maximum and minimum (greater than zero) float values that can be stored in a float variable.

Table 4-5. *Constants Defined in the Float Class*

float Constants	Meaning
Float.POSITIVE_INFINITY	Positive infinity of type float.
Float.NEGATIVE_INFINITY	Negative infinity of type float.
Float.NaN	Not a Number of type float.
Float.MAX_VALUE	The largest positive value that can be represented in a float variable. This is equal to 3.4×10^{38} (approx.).
Float.MIN_VALUE	The smallest positive value greater than zero that can be represented in a float variable. This is equal to 1.4×10^{-45}.

The value of all integral types (int, long, byte, short, and char) can be assigned to a variable of the float data type without using an explicit cast. The following are a few examples:

```
int num1 = 15000;
float salary = num1;       // OK. int variable to float
salary = 12455;            // OK. int literal to float
float bigNum = Float.MAX_VALUE; // Assigns maximum float value
bigNum = 1226L;            // OK, a long literal to float
float justAChar = 'A';     // OK. Assigns 65.0F to justAChar
```

```
// OK. Assigns positive infinity to the fInf variable
float fInf = Float.POSITIVE_INFINITY;

// OK. Assigns Not-a-Number to fNan variable
float fNan = Float.NaN;
// A compile-time error. Cannot assign a float literal to a float variable
// greater than the maximum value of float(3.4E38F approx)
float fTooBig = 3.5E38F;

// A compile-time error. Cannot assign a float literal to a float variable less
// than the minimum value (greater than zero) of float 1.4E-45F
float fTooSmall = 1.4E-46F;
```

A float value must be cast before it is assigned to a variable of any integral data type int, long, byte, short, or char. The reason behind this rule is that an integral data type cannot store the fraction part stored in a float value, so Java warns you of a loss of precision when you convert a float value to an integer. Here are a few examples:

```
int num1 = 10;
float salary = 10.6F;
num1 = salary;        // A a compile-time error. Cannot assign float to int
num1 = (int)salary;   // OK. num1 will store 10
```

Most floating-point numbers are approximations of their corresponding real numbers. The assignment of int and long to float may result in loss of precision. Consider the following piece of code:

```
int num1 = 1029989998; // Stores an integer in num1
float num2 = num1;      // Assigns the value stored in num1 to num2
int num3 = (int)num2;   // Assigns the value stored in num2 to num3
```

You expect that the value stored in num1 and num3 should be the same. However, they are not because the value stored in num1 cannot be stored exactly in a floating-point format in the float variable num2. Not all floating-point numbers have an exact representation in binary format. This is the reason that num1 and num3 are not equal. Refer to the section "Binary Representation of Floating-Point Numbers" described later in this chapter for more details. The following JShell session shows you that num3 is 18 more than num1.

```
jshell> int num1 = 1029989998;
num1 ==> 1029989998

jshell> float num2 = num1;
num2 ==> 1.02999002E9

jshell> int num3 = (int)num2;
num3 ==> 1029990016

jshell> num1 - num3
$4 ==> -18
```

▦ **Tip**   Assigning an int to a float may result in loss of precision. However, such assignments do not result in errors in Java.

The double Data Type

The double data type uses 64 bits to store a floating-point number in the IEEE 754 standard format. A floating-point number represented in 64 bits according to IEEE 754 standard is also known as a double-precision floating-point number. It can represent a number as small as 4.9×10^{-324} and as big as 1.7×10^{308} (approx.) in magnitude. The range includes only magnitude. It could be positive or negative. Here, 4.9×10^{-324} is the smallest positive number greater than zero that can be stored in a double variable.

All real numbers are called double literals. A double literal may optionally end with d or D, for example, 19.27d. That is, both 19.27 and 19.27d represent the same double literal. This book uses double literals without the suffix d or D. A double literal can be expressed in the following two formats:

- Decimal number format
- Scientific notation

A few examples of double literals in decimal number format are as follows:

```
double d1 = 8D
double d2 = 8.;
double d3 = 8.0;
double d4 = 8.D;
double d5 = 78.9867;
double d6 = 45.0;
```

░ **Tip**   8 is an int literal whereas 8D, 8., and 8.0, are double literals.

Like a float literal, you can also use scientific notation to express double literals like so:

```
double d1 = 32.5E-1;
double d2 = 0.325E+1;
double d3 = 0.325E1;
double d4 = 0.0325E2;
double d5 = 0.0325e2;
double d6 = 32.5E-1D;
double d7 = 0.325E+1d;
double d8 = 0.325E1d;
double d9 = 0.0325E2d;
```

Like the float data type, the double data type defines two zeros, two infinities, and a NaN. They are represented by constants in the Double class. Table 4-6 lists these constants and their meanings. Table 4-6 also lists two constants, which represent the maximum and minimum (greater than zero) double values that can be represented in a double variable.

Table 4-6. *Constants in the Double Class*

double Constants	Meaning
Double.POSITIVE_INFINITY	Positive infinity of type double.
Double.NEGATIVE_INFINITY	Negative infinity of type double.
Double.NaN	Not a Number of type double.
Double.MAX_VALUE	The largest positive value that can be represented in a double variable. This is equal to 1.7×10^{308} (approx.).
Double.MIN_VALUE	The smallest positive value greater than zero that can be represented in a double variable. This is equal to 4.9×10^{-324}.

The value of all integral types (int, long, byte, short, char) and float can be assigned to a variable of the double data type without using a cast.

```
int num1 = 15000;
double salary = num1;          // OK. An int to double assignment
salary = 12455;                // OK. An int literal to double
double bigNum = Double.MAX_VALUE; // Assigns the maximum double value to bigNum
bigNum = 1226L;                // OK. A long literal to double
double justAChar = 'A';        // OK. Assigns 65.0 to justAChar

// Assigns positive infinity to dInf variable
double dInf = Double.POSITIVE_INFINITY;

// Assigns Not-a-Number to dNan variable
double dNan = Double.NaN;

// A compile-time error. Cannot assign a double literal to a double variable
// greater than the maximum value of double (1.7E308 approx)
double dTooBig = 1.8E308;

// A compile-time error. Cannot assign a double literal to a double variable
// less than the minimum value (greater than zero) of double 4.9E-324
double dTooSmall = 4.9E-325;
```

A double value must be cast to the integral type before it is assigned to a variable of any integral data type (int, long, byte, short, or char).

```
int num1 = 10;
double salary = 10.0;
num1 = salary;     // A compile-time Error. Cannot assign double to int
num1 = (int)salary; // Now Ok.
```

Underscores in Numeric Literals

Beginning with Java 7, you can use any number of underscores between two digits in numeric literals. For example, an int literal 1969 can be written as 1_969, 19_69, 196_9, 1___969, or any other forms using underscores between two digits. The use of underscores is also allowed in octal, hexadecimal, and binary formats. Big numbers are harder to read without any punctuation marks (e.g., a comma as a thousand-separator). Use of underscores in big numbers makes them easier to read. The following examples show the valid uses of underscores in numeric literals:

```
int x1 = 1_969;   // Underscore in decimal format
int x2 = 1__969; // Multiple consecutive underscores
int x3 = 03_661; // Underscore in octal literal
int x4 = 0b0111_1011_0001; // Underscores in binary literal
int x5 = 0x7_B_1;        // Underscores in hexadecimal literal
byte b1 = 1_2_7;         // Underscores in decimal format
double d1  = 1_969.09_19; // Underscores in double literal
```

Underscores are allowed in numeric literals only between digits. This means that you cannot use underscores in the beginning or end of a numeric literal. You cannot use underscores with prefixes such as 0x for hexadecimal format and 0b for binary format, and suffixes such as L for long literal and F for float literal. The following examples show the invalid uses of underscores in numeric literals:

```
int y1 = _1969;       // An error. Underscore in the beginning
int y2 = 1969_;       // An error. Underscore in the end
int y3 = 0x_7B1;      // An error. Underscore after prefix 0x
int y4 = 0_x7B1;      // An error. Underscore inside prefix 0x
long z1 = 1969_L;     // An error. Underscore with suffix L
double d1 = 1969_.0919; // An error. Underscore before decimal
double d1 = 1969._0919; // An error. Underscore after decimal
```

░ **Tip**   You can write the int literal 1969 in octal format as 03661. The zero at the beginning of an int literal in the octal format is considered a digit, not a prefix. It is allowed to use underscores after the first zero in an int literal in octal format. You can write 03661 as 0_3661.

Java Compiler and Unicode Escape Sequence

Recall that any Unicode character in a Java program can be expressed in the form of a Unicode escape sequence. For example, the character 'A' can be replaced with '\u0041'. The Java compiler first converts every occurrence of a Unicode escape sequence to a Unicode character. A Unicode escape sequence starts with \u followed by four hexadecimal digits. '\\u0041' is not a Unicode escape sequence. To make uxxxx a valid part of a Unicode escape sequence, it must be preceded by an odd number of backslashes, because two contiguous backslashes (\\) represent one backslash character. Therefore, "\\u0041" represents a 6-character string composed of '\', 'u', '0', '0', '4', and '1'. However, "\\\u0041" represents a two-character string "\A".

Sometimes, inappropriate use of Unicode escape sequence in Java source code may result in a compile-time error. Consider the following declaration of a char variable:

```
char c = '\u000A'; // Incorrect
```

The programmer intends to initialize the variable c with a linefeed character whose Unicode escape sequence is \u000A. When this piece of code is compiled, the compiler will convert \u000A into an actual Unicode character and this piece of code will be split into two lines as follows:

```
// After the actual linefeed is inserted
char c = '
          ';
```

Since a character literal cannot continue in two lines, this piece of code generates a compile-time error. The correct way to initialize the variable c is to use the character escape sequence \n as shown:

```
char c = '\n'; // Correct
```

In character literals and String literals, linefeed and carriage return should always be written as \n and \r, respectively, not as \u000A and \u000D. Even a line of comment may generate a compile-time error if you do not use the linefeed and carriage return characters correctly. Suppose you commented the wrong declaration of the char variable, as shown:

```
// char c = '\u000A';
```

Even if this line is a comment line, it will generate a compile-time error. The comment will be split into two lines before compilation, like so:

```
// char c = '
';
```

The second line, which contains, ';, causes the error. The multi-line comment syntax would not generate a compiler error in such a case.

```
/* char c = '\u000A'; */
```

would be converted to

```
/* char c = '
'; */
```

which is still a valid multi-line comment.

A Short Break

I have finished discussing all primitive data types in Java. In the following section, I discuss the general concepts of binary numbers and their use in representing different types of values in Java. If you have a computer science background, you may skip the following section.

Classes in this chapter are members of the `jdojo.datatype` module declared in Listing 4-1. The program in Listing 4-2 shows how to declare variables of different data types and use different types of literals. It also prints the values for some constants in the Double class. Java 8 has added the `Double.BYTES` constant, which contains the number of bytes used by a double variable.

Listing 4-1. The Declaration of a Module Named jdojo.datatype

```
// module-info.java
module jodjo.datatype {
    // No module statement needed at this time
}
```

Listing 4-2. Using Primitive Data Types

```
// NumberTest.java
package com.jdojo.datatype;

public class NumberTest {
    public static void main(String[] args) {
        int anInt = 100;
        long aLong = 200L;
        byte aByte = 65;
        short aShort = -902;
        char aChar = 'A';
        float aFloat = 10.98F;
        double aDouble = 899.89;

        // Print values of the variables
        System.out.println("anInt = " + anInt);
        System.out.println("aLong = " + aLong);
        System.out.println("aByte = " + aByte);
        System.out.println("aShort = " + aShort);
        System.out.println("aChar = " + aChar);
        System.out.println("aFloat = " + aFloat);
        System.out.println("aDouble = " + aDouble);

        // Print some double constants
        System.out.println("Max double = " + Double.MAX_VALUE);
        System.out.println("Min double = " + Double.MIN_VALUE);
        System.out.println("Double.POSITIVE_INFINITY = " + Double.POSITIVE_INFINITY);
        System.out.println("Double.NEGATIVE_INFINITY = " + Double.NEGATIVE_INFINITY);
        System.out.println("Not-a-Number for double = " + Double.NaN);
        System.out.println("Double takes " + Double.BYTES + " bytes");
    }
}
```

```
anInt = 100
aLong = 200
aByte = 65
aShort = -902
aChar = A
aFloat = 10.98
aDouble = 899.89
Max double = 1.7976931348623157E308
Min double = 4.9E-324
Double.POSITIVE_INFINITY = Infinity
Double.NEGATIVE_INFINITY = -Infinity
Not-a-Number for double = NaN
Double takes 8 bytes
```

Binary Representation of Integers

Computers use the binary number system to work with data. All data in a binary system is stored using 1s and 0s. Characters 1 and 0 are called bits (short for binary digit). They are the smallest units of information a computer can work with. A group of 8 bits is called a byte or octet. Half a byte (i.e., a group of four bits) is called a nibble. A computer uses data bus, a pathway, to send data from one part of the computer system to another. How much information can be moved from one part to another at one time depends on the bit-width of the data bus. The bit-width of the data bus on a particular computer is also known as word-size, and information contained in one word-size is simply referred to as a word. Therefore, a word may refer to 16-bit or 32-bit or another bit-width depending on computer's architecture. The long and double data types in Java take 64 bits. On a computer with a word-size of 32 bits, these two data types are not treated atomically. For example, to write a value in a long variable, two write actions are performed—one for each 32-bit half.

A decimal number can be converted to binary format using the following steps:

1. Divide the decimal number successively by 2.

2. After each division, record the remainder. This will be 1 or 0.

3. Continue Steps 1 and 2 until the result of the division is 0.

4. The binary number is formed by writing digits in the remainder column from bottom to top.

For example, the binary representation of decimal number 13 can be computed as shown in Table 4-7.

Table 4-7. *Decimal-to-Binary Conversion*

Number	Divided by 2	Result	Remainder
13	13/2	6	1
6	6/2	3	0
3	3/2	1	1
1	1/2	0	1

The binary representation of decimal number 13 is 1101. A byte variable in Java occupies one byte. The value 13 in a byte variable is stored as 00001101. Note that four zeros are added in front of the binary representation 1101 because a byte variable always occupies 8 bits irrespective of the value that it contains. The rightmost bit in a byte or a word is known as the least significant bit (LSB) and the leftmost bit as the most significant bit (MSB). The MSB and LSB for the binary representation of 13 are shown in Figure 4-7.

Figure 4-7. *MSB and LSB in a binary number*

Each bit in a binary number is assigned a weight, which is a power of 2. A binary number can be converted to its decimal equivalent by multiplying each bit in the binary number by its weight and adding them. For example, 1101 in binary can be converted to its decimal equivalent as follows:

$$\left(1101\right)_2 \ = 1 \ \times \ 2^0 \ + \ 0 \ \times \ 2^1 \ + \ 1 \ \times \ 2^2 \ + \ 1 \ \times \ 2^3$$
$$= 1 \ + \ 0 \ + \ 4 \ + \ 8$$
$$= \ \left(13\right)_{10}$$

Java stores the negative integral numbers in 2's complement form. Let's discuss the complement of a number in a given number system. Every number system has a base, also known as radix. For example, 10 is the radix for the decimal number system, 2 for the binary number system, and 8 for the octal number system. We will use the symbol R for radix. Every number system defines two types of complements:

- Diminished radix complement, which is also known as the (R-1)'s complement.

- Radix complement, which is also known as the R's complement.

Therefore, for the decimal number system, we have 9's complement and 10's complement; for the octal number system, we have 7's and 8's complements, and for the binary number system, we have 1's and 2's complements.

Diminished Radix Complement

Let N be a number in a number system with radix R and n is the total number of digits in N. The diminished radix complement or (R-1)'s complement of the number N is defined as

$$\left(R^n-1\right) \ - \ N$$

In the decimal number system, the 9's complement of the number N is

$$\left(10^n \ -1\right) \ - \ N$$

Since 10^n consists of a 1 followed by n zeros, $\left(10^n \ -1\right)$ consists of n 9s. Therefore, 9's complement of a number can be computed simply by subtracting each digit in the number from 9. For example, the 9's complement of 5678 is 4321 and the 9's complement of 894542 is 105457.

In the binary number system, the 1's complement of a binary number is

$$\left(2^n-1\right) \ - \ N$$

Since 2^n in binary number system consists of a 1 followed by n zeros, $(2^n -1)$ consists of n 1s. For example, the 1's complement of 10110 (here, n is 5) can be computed as $(2^5 -1)$ - 10110, which is 11111 - 10110 ($2^5 -1$) is 31, which is 11111 in binary.

The 1's complement of a binary number can be computed simply by subtracting each digit in the number from 1. A binary number consists of 0s and 1s. When you subtract 1 from 1, you get 0, and when you subtract 0 from 1, you get 1. Therefore, the 1's complement of a binary number can be computed just by inverting the bits of the number, that is, by changing 1 to 0 and 0 to 1. For example, the 1's complement of 10110 is 01001 and the 1's complement of 0110001 is 1001110.

In a number system, the (R-1)'s complement of a number is computed by subtracting each digit of the number from the maximum digit value of that number system. For example, the maximum digit value in an octal number system is 7, and therefore, the 7's complement of an octal number is computed by subtracting each digit of that number from 7. For a hexadecimal number system, the maximum digit value is 15, represented by F. For example, the 7's complement of an octal number 56072 is 21705 and the 15's complement of a hexadecimal number 6A910F is 956EF0.

Radix Complement

Let N be a number in a number system of radix R, and n is the total number of digits in the number N. The radix complement or the R's complement of the number N is defined as follows:

R^n - N

For N = 0, the R's complement is defined as zero. It is evident from the definition of the R's and (R-1)'s complements that the R's complement of a number is computed by adding 1 to the (R-1)'s complement of that number. Therefore, the 10's complement of a decimal number is obtained by adding 1 to its 9's complement, and the 2's complement of a binary number is obtained by adding 1 to its 1's complement. For example, the 2's complement of 10110 is 01001 + 1, which is 01010. By carefully looking at the procedure to compute the 2's complement of a binary number, you can observe that it can be computed just by looking at the binary number. The simple procedure to compute the 2's complement of a binary number can be described as follows:

1. Start from the right end of the binary number.

2. Write down all digits unchanged up to the first 1 bit.

3. Subsequently invert the bits to get the 2's complement of the binary number.

For example, let's compute the 2's complement of 10011000. Start from the right end and write down all the digits unchanged up to the first 1 bit. Since the fourth digit from the right is 1, you will write first four digits unchanged, which is 1000. Now, invert the bits starting from the fifth bit from the right, which will give you 01101000. This procedure is illustrated in Figure 4-8.

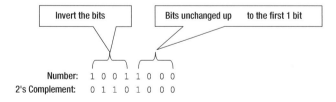

Figure 4-8. *Computing 2's complement of a binary number*

All negative integers (byte, short, int, and long) are stored as their 2's complements in memory. Let's consider two byte variables in Java.

```
byte bPos = 13;
byte bNeg = -13;
```

The bPos is stored in memory as 00001101. The 2's complement of 00001101 is computed as 11110011. Therefore, bNeg, which is -13, is stored as 11110011, as shown in Figure 4-9.

bPos   00001101
          ↑
          Sign bit 0 denotes a positive number

bNeg   11110011
          ↑
          Sign bit 1 denotes a negative number

Figure 4-9. *Storing the number 13 in 2's complement forms*

Binary Representation of Floating-Point Numbers

A binary floating-point system can represent only a finite number of floating-point values in exact form. All other values must be approximated by the closest representable value. The IEEE 754-1985 is the most widely accepted floating-point standard in the computer industry, and it specifies the format and the method to represent binary floating-point numbers. The goal of the IEEE standard, which is designed for engineering calculations, is to maximize accuracy (to get as close as possible to the actual number). Precision refers to the number of digits that you can represent. The IEEE standard attempts to balance the number of bits dedicated to the exponent with the number of bits used for the fractional part of the number, to keep both accuracy and precision within acceptable limits. This section describes IEEE 754-1985 standard for binary floating-point format in general and points out how Java supports this standard. A floating-point number has four parts:

- Sign
- Significand (also known as a mantissa)
- Base (also known as a radix)
- Exponent

The floating-point number 19.25 can be represented with all its four parts as

$$+19.25 \times 10^0$$

Here, the sign is + (positive), the significand is 19.25, the base is 10, and the exponent is 0.

The number 19.25 can also be represented in many other forms, as shown here. I omit the positive sign of the number by writing +19.25 as 19.25.

- 19.25×10^0
- 1.925×10^1
- 0.1925×10^2
- 192.5×10^{-1}
- 1925×10^{-2}

A floating-point number can be represented in an infinite number of ways. A floating-point number represented in base 10 is said to be in normalized form if its significand satisfies the following rule:

```
0.1 <= significand < 1
```

According to this rule, the representation 0.1925×10^2 is the normalized form of 19.25. The floating-point number 19.25 (base 10) can be written as 10011.01 in binary form (base 2). The floating-point number 19.25 can be rewritten in many different binary forms. Some of the alternate binary representations of decimal 19.25 are as follows:

- 10011.01×2^0
- 1001.101×2^1
- 100.1101×2^2
- 1.001101×2^4
- 100110.1×2^{-1}
- 1001101×2^{-2}

Note that in binary form, the base is 2. When the binary point is shifted to the left by one digit, the exponent is incremented by one. When the binary point is shifted to the right by one digit, the exponent is decremented by one. A floating-point number in a binary form is normalized if its significand satisfies the following condition:

```
1 <= significand < 2
```

If the significand of a binary floating-point number is of the form `1.bbbbbbb...,` where b is a bit (0 or 1), the binary floating-point number is said to be in normalized form. Therefore, 1.001101×2^4 is the normalized form of binary floating-point number 10011.01. In other words, a normalized binary floating-point number starts with a bit 1, immediately followed by a binary point.

The floating-point numbers, which are not normalized, are called denormalized floating-point numbers. A denormalized floating-point number is also called denormal or subnormal. All floating-point numbers cannot be represented in a normalized form. There could be two reasons for this.

- The number does not contain any bit as 1. An example of this is 0.0. Since 0.0 does not have any bit set as 1, it cannot be represented in the normalized form.

- Computers use a fixed number of bits to store the sign, significand, and exponent of a binary floating-point number. If the exponent of a binary floating-point number is the minimum exponent allowed by the computer storage format and the significand is less than 1, such a binary floating-point number cannot be normalized. For example, suppose that -126 is the minimum exponent value that can be stored in a given storage format for a binary floating-point number. If the binary floating-point number is 0.01101×2^{-126}, this number cannot be normalized. The normalized form of this number will be 1.101×2^{-128}. However, the given storage format allows minimum exponent as -126 (I have assumed number -126 for this example). Therefore, the exponent -128 (-128 < -126) cannot be stored in the given storage format and that is why 0.01101×2^{-126} cannot be stored in the normalized form.

Why do we need to normalize a binary floating-point number before storing it in memory? The following are the advantages of doing this:

- The normalized representation is unique.

- Because the binary point in a binary floating-point number can be placed anywhere in the number, you must store the position of the binary point along with the number. By normalizing the number, you always place the binary point after the first 1 bit, and therefore, you need not store the position of the binary point. This saves memory and time to store one extra piece of information.

- Two normalized binary floating-point numbers can be compared easily by comparing their signs, significands, and exponents.

- In a normalized form, the significand can use all its storage bits to store significant digits (bits). For example, if you allocate only five bits to store the significand, for the number 0.0010110×2^{10} only 0.00101 part of the significand will be stored. However, if you normalize this number as 1.0110×2^7, the significand can be stored fully in five bits.

- In a normalized form, the significand always starts with a 1 bit, which can be omitted while storing the significand. When reading back, you can add the leading 1 bit. This omitted bit is called the "hidden bit' and it provides one extra bit of precision.

The IEEE 754 -1985 standard defines the four floating-point formats as follows:

- 32-bit single-precision floating-point format

- 64-bit double-precision floating-point format

- Single-extended floating-point format

- Double-extended floating-point format

Java uses IEEE 32-bit single-precision floating-point format to store the values of `float` data type. It uses 64-bit double-precision floating-point format to store the values of `double` data type.

I discuss only IEEE 32-bit single-precision floating-point format. The difference between single-precision floating-point format and other formats are the total number of bits used to store the binary floating-point numbers and the distribution of number of bits among sign, exponent, and significand. The difference among different IEEE formats is shown at the end of the discussion.

32-bit Single-Precision Floating-Point Format

The 32-bit single-precision floating-point format uses 32 bits to store a binary floating-point number. A binary floating-point number is of the following form:

```
Sign * Significand * 2^Exponent
```

Since the base is always 2, this format does not store the value of the base. The 32 bits are distributed as follows:

- 1 bit to store the sign

- 8 bits to store the exponent

- 23 bits to store the significand

The layout for the single-precision floating-point format is shown in Table 4-8.

Table 4-8. *IEEE Single-Precision Format Layout*

1-Bit Sign	8-Bit Exponent	23-Bit Significand
s	eeeeeeee	fffffffffffffffffffffff

Sign

IEEE single-precision floating-point format uses 1 bit to store the sign of the number. A 0 sign bit indicates a positive number and 1 sign bit indicates a negative number.

Exponent

The exponent takes 8 bits. The exponent can be positive or negative. The range of the exponent value that can be stored in 8 bits is -127 to 128. There must be a mechanism to represent the sign of the exponent. Note that the 1-bit sign field in the layout shown in Table 4-8 stores the sign of the floating-point number, not the sign of the exponent. To store the sign of the exponent, you can use the sign-magnitude method, where 1 bit is used to store the sign and the remaining 7 bits store the magnitude of the exponent. You can also use the 2's complement method to store the negative exponent as is used to store integers. However, IEEE does not use either of these two methods for storing the exponent. IEEE uses the biased representation of the exponent to store the exponent value.

What are a bias and a biased exponent? A bias is a constant value, which is 127 for IEEE 32-bit single-precision format. The bias value is added to the exponent before storing it in memory. This new exponent, after adding a bias, is called a biased exponent. The biased exponent is computed as follows:

```
Biased Exponent = Exponent + Bias
```

For example, 19.25 can be written in normalized binary floating-point format as 1.001101×2^4. Here, the exponent value is 4. However, the exponent value stored in memory will be a biased exponent, which will be computed as follows:

```
Biased Exponent = Exponent + Bias
                = 4 + 127 (Single-precision format)
                = 131
```

For 1.001101×2^4, 131 will be stored as the exponent. When reading back the exponent of a binary floating-point number, you must subtract the bias value for that format to get the actual exponent value.

Why does IEEE use a biased exponent? The advantage of using a biased exponent is that positive floating-point numbers can be treated as integers for comparison purposes.

Suppose E is the number of bits used to store the exponent value in a given floating-point format. The value of the bias for that format can be computed as follows:

```
Bias = 2^(E - 1) - 1
```

The exponent ranges from -127 to 128 for the single-precision format. Therefore, the biased exponent ranges from 0 to 255. Two extreme exponent values (-127 and 128 for unbiased, and 0 and 255 for biased) are used to represent special floating-point numbers, such as zero, infinities, NaNs, and denormalized numbers. The exponent range of -126 to 127 (biased 1 to 254) is used to represent normalized binary floating-point numbers.

Significand

IEEE single-precision floating-point format uses 23 bits to store the significand. The number of bits used to store the significand is called the precision of that floating-point format. Therefore, you might have guessed that the precision of floating-point numbers stored in the single-precision format is 23. However, this is not true. But first I need to discuss the format in which the significand is stored before I conclude about the precision of this format.

The significand of a floating-point number is normalized before it is stored in memory. The normalized significand is always of the form 1.fffffffffffffffffffffff. Here, an f denotes a bit 0 or 1 for the fractional part of significand. Because the leading 1 bit is always present in the normalized form of the significand, you need not store the leading 1 bit. Therefore, while storing the normalized significand, you can use all 23 bits to store the fractional part of the significand. In fact, not storing the leading 1 bit of a normalized significand gives you one extra bit of precision. This way, you represent 24 digits (1 leading bit + 23 fraction bits) in just 23 bits. Thus, for a normalized significand, the precision of a floating-point number in IEEE single-precision format is 24.

```
Actual Significand: 1.fffffffffffffffffffffff (24 digits)
Stored Significand:   fffffffffffffffffffffff (23 digits)
```

If you always represent the significand of a binary floating-point number in normalized form, there is a gap around zero on the number line. The minimum number in magnitude that can be represented in IEEE single-precision format can be computed as follows:

- *Sign*: It can be 0 or 1, denoting a positive or negative number. For this example, let's assume the sign bit is 0 to indicate a positive number.

- *Exponent*: The minimum exponent value is -126. Recall that the exponent values -127 and 128 are reserved to represent special floating-point numbers. The minimum biased exponent will be -126 + 127 = 1. The binary representation of the biased exponent 1 in 8-bit is 00000001.

- *Significand*: The minimum value of a significand in the normalized form will consist of the leading 1 bit and all 23 fraction bits set to 0, as 1.00000000000000000000000.

If you combine the binary representation of a normalized floating-point number with the minimum possible values for the exponent and significand, the actual number stored in the computer will look like the one shown in Table 4-9.

Table 4-9. *Minimum Possible Normalized Number*

Sign	Exponent	Significand
0	00000001	00000000000000000000000
1-bit	8-bit	23-bit

The value of the minimum floating-point number in decimal is 1.0×2^{-126}. Therefore, 1.0×2^{-126} is the first representable normalized number after zero, leaving a gap around zero on the number line.

If you store only normalized floating-point numbers using IEEE single-precision format, all numbers less than 1.0×2^{-126} in magnitude must be rounded to zero. This will cause a serious problem when dealing with tiny numbers in a program. In order to store numbers smaller than 1.0×2^{-126}, the numbers must be denormalized.

Special Floating-Point Numbers

This section describes special floating-point numbers and their representations in the IEEE single-precision format.

Signed Zeros

The IEEE floating-point format allows for two zeros, +0.0 (or 0.0) and -0.0. Zero is represented by the minimum exponent value -127 for the single-precision format. The significand is 0.0 for zero. Since the sign bit can be 0 or 1, there are two zeros: +0.0 and -0.0. The binary representations of zeros in the single-precision format are shown in Table 4-10.

Table 4-10. *Binary Representations of Positive and Negative Zeros in the Single-Precision Format*

Number	Sign	Exponent	Significand
0.0	0	00000000	00000000000000000000000
-0.0	1	00000000	00000000000000000000000

For comparison purposes, +0.0 and -0.0 are considered equal. Therefore, the expression 0.0 == -0.0 always returns true.

Why does IEEE define two zeros if they are considered equal? The sign of zero is used to determine the result of an arithmetic expression involving multiplication and division. The result of 3.0 * 0.0 is a positive zero (0.0), whereas the result of 3.0 * (-0.0) is a negative zero (-0.0). For a floating-point number num with the values ±Infinity, the relation 1/(1/num) = num holds true only because of two signed zeros.

Signed Infinities

The IEEE floating-point format allows for two infinities: positive infinity and negative infinity. The sign bit represents the sign of infinity. The maximum exponent value 128 (the biased exponent 255) for the single-precision format and zero significand represents infinity. The maximum biased value 255 can be represented in 8-bit with all bits set to 1 as 11111111. The binary representations of infinities in single-precision format are shown in Table 4-11.

Table 4-11. *Binary Representations of Positive and Negative Infinities in the Single-Precision Format*

Number	Sign	Exponent	Significand
+Infinity	0	11111111	00000000000000000000000
-Infinity	1	11111111	00000000000000000000000

NaN

NaN stands for "Not-a-Number." NaN is the result of arithmetic operations that do not have meaningful results, such as dividing zero by zero, the square root of a negative number, adding -Infinity to +Infinity, etc.

NaN is represented by a maximum exponent value (128 for single-precision format) and a non-zero significand. The sign bit is not interpreted for NaN. What happens when NaN is one of the operands in an arithmetic expression? For example, what is the result of NaN + 100? Should the execution of an arithmetic expression involving NaNs be stopped or continued? There are two types of NaNs:

- Quiet NaN

- Signaling NaN

A quiet NaN, when encountered as an operand in an arithmetic expression, quietly (i.e., without raising any trap or exception) produces another quiet NaN as the result. In case of a quiet NaN, the expression NaN + 100 will result in another quiet NaN. The most significant bit in the significand is set to 1 for a quiet NaN. Table 4-12 shows a binary representation of a quiet NaN. In the table, s and b indicate a 0 or 1 bit.

Table 4-12. *A Binary Representation of a Quiet NaN*

Number	Sign	Exponent	Significand
Quiet NaN	s	11111111	1bbbbbbbbbbbbbbbbbbbbbbb

When a signaling NaN is encountered as an operand in an arithmetic expression, an invalid operation exception is signaled and a quiet NaN is delivered as the result. Signaling NaNs are generally used to initialize the uninitialized variables in a program, so when variables are not initialized before they are used, errors can be signaled. The most significant bit of the significand is set to 0 for a signaling NaN. Table 4-13 shows a binary representation of a signaling NaN. In the table, s and b indicate a 0 or 1 bit.

Table 4-13. *A Binary Representation of a Quiet NaN*

Number	Sign	Exponent	Significand
Signaling NaN	s	11111111	0bbbbbbbbbbbbbbbbbbbbbbb

▓ **Tip** IEEE defines 2^{24} - 2 distinct NaNs for the single-precision format and 2^{53} - 2 distinct NaNs for the double-precision format. However, Java has only one NaN for the float data type and one NaN for the double data type. Java always uses a quiet NaN.

Denormals

When the biased exponent is 0 and the significand is non-zero, it denotes a denormalized number. Table 4-14 shows the bits pattern to represent denormalized numbers in the single-precision format.

Table 4-14. *The Bits Pattern for a Denormalized Single-Precision Floating-Point Number*

Sign	Exponent	Significand
s	000000000	fffffffffffffffffffffff

In Table 4-14, s denotes a sign bit, which can be 0 for a positive number and 1 for a negative number. The exponent bits are all zeros. At least one of the bits in the significand is denoted 1. The decimal value of the denormalized number is computed as shown:

$(-1)^s$ * 0.fffffffffffffffffffffff * 2^{-126}

Suppose you want to store a number 0.25×2^{-128} in the single-precision format. If you write this number in normalized form after converting 0.25 in binary, it will be 1.0×2^{-130}. However, the minimum exponent allowed for single-precision format is -126. Therefore, this number cannot be stored in normalized form in single-precision format. The exponent is kept as -126 and the binary point is shifted to the left, resulting in denormalized form as 0.0001×2^{-126}. The number is stored, as shown in Table 4-15.

Table 4-15. *Bits Pattern for a Denormalized Number $1.0 * 2^{-130}$*

Number	Sign	Exponent	Significand
0.0001 x 2-126	0	00000000	00010000000000000000000

It seems that for the number 0.0001×2^{-126}, the biased exponent should be computed as -126 + 127 = 1 and the exponent bits should be 00000001. However, this is not true. For denormalized numbers, the exponent is stored as all 0 bits; when reading it back, it is interpreted as -126. This is because you need to distinguish between normalized and denormalized numbers when reading back floating-point numbers, and for all denormalized numbers, there is no leading 1-bit in their significands. The denormalized numbers fill the gap around zero on the number line, which would have been there if you had stored only normalized numbers.

Rounding Modes

Not all real numbers can be exactly represented in binary floating-point format in a finite number of bits. Therefore, real numbers that cannot be exactly represented in a binary floating-point format must be rounded. There are four rounding modes:

- Round toward zero
- Round toward positive infinity
- Round toward negative infinity
- Round toward nearest

Rounding Toward Zero

This rounding mode is also called truncation or chop mode. In this rounding mode, the total number of bits (or digits) retained from the original number is the same as the number of bits available to store the floating-point number in the given format. The rest of the bits are ignored. This rounding mode is called "rounding toward zero' because it has the effect of making the rounded result closer to zero. Some examples of rounding toward zero are shown in Table 4-16.

Table 4-16. *Examples of Rounding Toward Zero*

Original Number	Available Number of Binary Points	Rounded Number
1.1101	2	1.11
-0.1011	2	-0.10
0.1010	2	0.10
0.0011	2	0.00

Rounding Toward Positive Infinity

In this rounding mode, numbers are rounded to a value closer to the positive infinity. Some examples of rounding toward positive infinity are shown in Table 4-17.

Table 4-17. *Examples of Rounding Toward Positive Infinity*

Original Number	Available Number of Binary Points	Rounded Number
1.1101	2	10.00
-0.1011	2	-0.10
0.1010	2	0.11
0.0011	2	0.01

Rounding Toward Negative Infinity

In this rounding mode, numbers are rounded to a value closer to the negative infinity. Some examples of rounding toward negative infinity are shown in Table 4-18.

Table 4-18. *Examples of Rounding Toward Negative Infinity*

Original Number	Available Number of Binary Points	Rounded Number
1.1101	2	1.11
-0.1011	2	-0.11
0.1010	2	0.10
0.0011	2	0.00

Rounding Toward Nearest

In this rounding mode, the rounded result is the nearest representable floating-point number. In case of a tie, that is, if there are two representable floating-point numbers that are equally near to the original number, the result is the one that has its least significant bit as zero. In other words, in case of a tie, the rounded result is the even number. The system, which implements IEEE floating-point standards, has this mode as the default rounding mode. The IEEE standard states that the system should also allow users to select one of the other three rounding modes. Java uses this mode as the default rounding mode for floating-point numbers. Java does not allow users (that is, programmers) to select any other rounding modes. Some examples of rounding toward nearest are shown in Table 4-19.

Table 4-19. *Examples of Rounding Toward Nearest*

Original Number	Available Number of Binary Points	Rounded Number
1.1101	2	1.11
-0.1011	2	-0.11
0.1010	2	0.10
0.0011	2	0.01

IEEE Floating-Point Exceptions

The IEEE floating-point standard defines several exceptions that occur when the result of a floating-point operation is unacceptable. Exceptions can be ignored, in which case some default action is taken, such as returning a special value. When trapping is enabled for an exception, an error is signaled whenever that exception occurs. Floating-point operations can lead to any of the following five types of floating point exceptions:

- Division by zero exception
- Invalid operation exception
- Overflow exception
- Underflow exception
- Inexact exception

Division by Zero Exception

A division by zero exception occurs when a non-zero number is divided by a floating-point zero. If no trap handler is installed, infinity of the appropriate sign is delivered as the result.

Invalid Operation Exception

An invalid operation exception occurs when the operand is invalid for an operation being performed. If no trap handler is installed, a quiet NaN is delivered as the result. The following are some of the operations that raise an invalid exception:

- Square root of a negative number
- Division of zero by zero or of infinity by infinity

- Multiplication of zero and infinity

- Any operation on a signaling NaN

- Subtracting infinity from infinity

- When a quiet NaN is compared with the > or < relational operators

Overflow Exception

An overflow exception occurs when the result of a floating-point operation is too large in magnitude to fit in the intended destination format. For example, this will occur when you multiply Float.MAX_VALUE by 2 and try to store the result in a float variable. If no trap handler is installed, the result to be delivered depends on the rounding mode and the sign of the intermediate result.

- If the rounding mode is rounding toward zero, the result of overflow is the largest finite number that can be represented in that format. The sign of the result is the same as the sign of the intermediate result.

- If the rounding mode is rounding toward positive infinity, the negative overflow results in the most negative finite number for that format and the positive overflow results in the most positive finite number for that format.

- If the rounding mode is rounding toward negative infinity, the negative overflow results in negative infinity and the positive overflow results in the most positive finite number for that format.

- If the rounding mode is rounding toward nearest, the overflow results in infinity. The sign of the result is the same as the sign of the intermediate result.

However, if a trap handler is installed, the result delivered to the trap handler in case of an overflow is determined as follows: the infinitely precise result is divided by 2^t and rounded before delivering it to the trap handler. The value of t is 192 for single-precision format, 1536 for double-precision format, and $3 \times 2^{n-1}$ for extended format, where n is the number of bits used to represent the exponent.

Underflow Exception

The underflow exception occurs when the result of an operation is too small to be represented as a normalized float in its format. If trapping is enabled, the floating-point-underflow exception is signaled. Otherwise, the operation results in a denormalized float or zero. Underflow can be abrupt or gradual. If the result of an operation is less than the minimum value that can be represented in normalized form in the format, the result could be delivered as zero or a denormalized number. In case of an abrupt underflow, the result is zero. In case of a gradual underflow, the result is a denormalized number. The IEEE default is gradual underflow (denormalized numbers). Java supports gradual underflow.

Inexact Exception

The inexact exception is signaled if the rounded result of an operation is not identical to the infinitely precise result. Inexact exceptions are quite common. 1.0/3.0 is an inexact operation. Inexact exceptions also occur when the operation overflows without an overflow trap.

Java and IEEE Floating-Point Standards

Java follows a subset of the IEEE-754 standard. The following are some of the differences between the IEEE floating-point standard and their Java implementations:

- Java does not signal the IEEE exceptions.

- Java has no signaling NaN.

- Java uses the rounding toward nearest mode to round the inexact results. However, Java rounds toward zero when converting a floating value to an integer. Java does not provide the user-selectable rounding modes for floating-point computations: up, down, or toward zero.

- IEEE defines (2^{24} - 2) NaNs for single-precision format and (2^{53} - 2) NaNs for double-precision format. However, Java defines only one NaN for each of these two formats.

Table 4-20 lists the parameters for different IEEE formats.

Table 4-20. *Parameters for the IEEE Formats*

	Width in Bits	Exponent Width in Bits	Precision	Maximum Exponent	Minimum Exponent	Exponent Bias
Single-precision	32	8	24	127	-126	127
Double-precision	64	11	53	1023	-1022	1023
Single-extended	>= 43	>= 11	>= 32	>= 1023	<= -1022	Unspecified
Double-extended	>= 79	>= 15	>= 64	>= 16383	<= -16382	Unspecified

Little-Endian and Big-Endian

These two terms are related to the direction of bytes in a word within the CPU architecture. Computer memory is referenced by addresses that are positive integers. It is "natural" to store numbers with the least significant byte coming before the most significant byte in the computer memory. Sometimes computer designers prefer to use a reversed order version of this representation. The "natural" order, where the less significant byte comes before more a significant byte in memory, is called little-endian. Many vendors, like IBM, CRAY, and Sun, prefer the reverse order that, of course, is called big-endian. For example, the 32-bit hex value 0x45679812 would be stored in memory as follows:

```
Address        00  01  02  03
------------------------------
Little-endian  12  98  67  45
Big-endian     45  67  98  12
```

Difference in endian-ness can be a problem when transferring data between two machines. Table 4-21 lists some vendors, their float types, and the endian-ness on their machines.

Table 4-21. *Vendors, Float Types, and Endian-Ness*

Vendor	Float Type	Endian-ness
ALPHA	DEC/IEEE	Little-endian
IBM	IBM	Big-endian
MAC	IEEE	Big-endian
SUN	IEEE	Big-endian
VAX	DEC	Little-endian
PC	IEEE	Little-endian

Everything in Java binary format files is stored in big-endian order. This is sometimes called network order. This means that if you use only Java, all files are done the same way on all platforms: Mac, PC, UNIX, etc. You can freely exchange binary data electronically without any concerns about endian-ness. The problem comes when you must exchange data files with some program not written in Java that uses little-endian order, most commonly a program written in C. Some platforms use big-endian order internally (Mac, IBM 390); some uses little-endian order (Intel). Java hides that internal endian-ness from you.

Summary

Everything in a program, such as values and entities, that needs to be referred to is given a name. A name in Java is called an identifier. An identifier in Java is a sequence of characters of unlimited length. The sequence of characters includes all Java letters and Java digits, the first of which must be a Java letter. Java uses the Unicode character set. A Java letter is a letter from any language that is represented by Unicode character set. For example, A-Z, a-z, _ (underscore), and $ are considered Java letters from the ASCII character set range of Unicode. Java digits include 0-9 ASCII digits and any Unicode character that denotes a digit in a language. Spaces are not allowed in an identifier.

Keywords are words that have predefined meanings in the Java programming language. The Java programming language defines several keywords. Beginning Java SE 9, underscore (_) is a keyword. A few examples of keywords in Java are class, if, do, while, int, long, and for. Keywords cannot be used as identifiers. Reserved keywords are keywords that have been reserved for future use, for example, goto and const. A restricted keyword is a keyword that has special meaning when used in specific places and in other places they are not treated as keywords. Examples of restricted keywords are module, exports, open, opens, requires, etc.

Every value in Java has a data type. Java supports two kinds of data types: primitive data types and reference data types. Primitive data types represent atomic, indivisible values. Java has eight primitive data types: byte, short, int, long, float, double, char, and boolean. Literals of primitive data types are constants that can be represented directly in source code. Reference data types represent references of objects in memory. Java is a statically typed programming language. That is, it checks the data types of all values at compile-time.

The byte data type is an 8-bit signed Java primitive integer data type. Its range is -128 to 127 (-2^7 to $2^7 - 1$). This is the smallest integer data type available in Java.

The short data type is a 16-bit signed Java primitive integer data type. Its range is -32768 to 32767 (or -2^{15} to $2^{15} - 1$).

The int data type is a 32-bit signed Java primitive data type. A variable of the int data type takes 32 bits of memory. Its valid range is -2,147,483,648 to 2,147,483,647 (-2^{31} to $2^{31} - 1$). All whole numbers in this range are known as integer literals (or integer constants). For example, 10, -200, 0, 30, 19, etc. are integer literals of int type.

The long data type is a 64-bit signed Java primitive data type. It is used when the result of calculations on whole numbers may exceed the range of the int data type. Its range is -9,223,372,036,854,775,808 to 9,223,372,036,854,775,807 (-2^{63} to $2^{63} - 1$). All whole numbers in the range of long are called integer literals of long type. An integer literal of long type must end with L or l, for example, 10L and 897L.

The char data type is a 16-bit *unsigned* Java primitive data type. Its value represents a Unicode character. The range of the char data type is 0 to 65535, which is the same as the range of the Unicode character set. A character literal represents a value of the char data type and it can be represented in four formats: a character enclosed in single quotes, a character as escape sequence enclosed in single quotes, as Unicode escape sequence, and as an octal escape sequence. 'A', 'X', and '8' are examples of char literals.

The float data type uses 32 bits to store a floating-point number in the IEEE 754 standard format. A floating-point number represented in 32 bits according to the IEEE 754 standard is also known as a single-precision floating-point number. It can represent a real number as small as 1.4×10^{-45} and as big as 3.4 x 1038 (approx.) in magnitude. The range includes only the magnitude. It could be positive or negative. Here, 1.4×10^{-45} is the smallest positive number greater than zero that can be stored in a float variable. A float literal must end with an F or f. A few examples of float literals are 2.0f, 56F, 0.78F.

The double data type uses 64 bits to store a floating-point number in the IEEE 754 standard format. A floating-point number represented in 64 bits according to IEEE 754 standard is also known as a double-precision floating-point number. It can represent a number as small as 4.9×10^{-324} and as big as 1.7×10^{308} (approx.) in magnitude. The range includes only magnitude. It could be positive or negative. A real number. All real numbers are called double literals. A double literal may optionally end with d or D, for example, 19.27d. That is, both 19.27 and 19.27d represent the same double literal.

The boolean data type has only two valid values: true and false. These two values are called boolean literals.

To make big numeric values expressed as numeric literal more readable, Java allows you to use any number of underscores between two digits in numeric literals. For example, an int literal 1969 can be written as 1_969, 19_69, 196_9, 1___969, or any other forms using underscores between two digits. The use of underscores is also allowed in octal, hexadecimal, and binary formats.

EXERCISES

1. What is an identifier in Java? What can an identifier consist of? List five valid and five invalid identifiers in Java.

2. What are keywords, reserved keywords, and restricted keywords in Java? Is an underscore a keyword in Java?

3. What is a data type? What is the difference between a primitive data type and a reference data type?

4. List the names of all eight primitive data types supported by the Java programming language. List their size in bytes.

5. What are literals? List two literals of each primitive type in Java.

6. What is the shortest numeric primitive type in Java? What is the range of its values?

7. Consider the following two variable declarations:

```
byte small = 10;
int big = 99;
```

How will you assign the value in the big variable to the small variable?

8. Why do you need to use a cast when you assign a variable of a bigger size to a variable of smaller size, for example, assigning an `int` variable to a `byte` variable?

9. Name two primitive data types in Java whose values can be floating-point numbers.

10. If you declare a variable of the `boolean` type, what are the two possible values it can have?

11. Can you cast a `boolean` value to an `int` type, as shown in the following statement?

    ```
    boolean done = true;
    int x = (int) done;
    ```

    What happens when you compile this snippet of code?

12. Are the `boolean` literals `true` and `false` the same as integers 1 and 0?

13. Name an unsigned numeric data type in Java.

14. Name the four different formats of writing the literals of `char` data types. Give two examples of each.

15. How do you represent a backslash (\) and a double quote (") as `char` literals in Java? Write code to declare two `char` variables named `c1` and `c2`. Assign a backslash character to `c1` and a double quote character to `c2`.

16. What are 1's and 2's complements of binary numbers? Compute the 1's and 2's complements of the binary number 10111011.

17. Why does the following line of comment in a Java program not compile? \u000A is a Unicode code value for linefeed.

    ```
    char c = '\u000A';
    ```

18. How many zeros are supported by `float` and `double` data types?

19. What is NaN? How many NaNs are supported by `float` and `double` types in Java? Differentiate between a quiet NaN and a signaling NaN. What types of NaNs are supported by Java—quiet NaNs, signaling NaNs, or both?

20. What are denormals or denormalized floating-point numbers?

21. What are the different rounding modes for floating-point numbers? What rounding modes are supported by Java?

22. What are little-endian order and big-endian order? What endian-order does Java use to encode the multi-byte binary data in class files?

CHAPTER 5

Operators

In this chapter, you will learn:

- What operators are

- The different types of operators available in Java

- Operator precedence, which determines the order in which operators are evaluated when multiple operators are used in the same expression

I use a lot of snippets of code in this chapter. The quickest way to evaluate those snippets and see the results is to use the JShell tool. Refer to Chapter 2 on how to start the JShell tool on a command prompt and inside the NetBeans IDE.

All classes in this chapter are a member of a module named `jdojo.operator` whose declaration is shown in Listing 5-1.

Listing 5-1. Declaration of a Module Named jdojo.operator

```
// module-info.java
module jdojo.operator {
    // No module statements
}
```

What Is an Operator?

An *operator* is a symbol that performs a specific kind of operation on one, two, or three operands, and produces a result. The type of the operator and its operands determine the kind of operation performed and the type of the result produced. Operators in Java can be categorized based on two criteria:

- The number of operands they operate on

- The type of operation they perform on the operands

There are three types of operators based on the number of operands:

- Unary operator

- Binary operator

- Ternary operator

If an operator takes one operand, it's called a unary operator; if it takes two operands, it's called a binary operator; if it takes three operands, it's called a ternary operator.

A unary operator can use postfix or prefix notation. In the postfix notation, the operator appears after its operand.

```
<operand> <postfix-unary-operator>
```

The following is an example of using a postfix unary operator:

```
// num is an operand and ++ is a Java unary operator
num++
```

In a prefix notation, the unary operator appears before its operand.

```
<prefix-unary-operator> <operand>
```

The following is an example of using a prefix unary operator. Note that the ++ operator in Java can be used as a prefix as well as postfix operator.

```
// ++ is a Java unary operator and num is an operand
++num
```

A binary operator uses infix notation. The operator appears in between the two operands. The syntax to use an infix binary operator is as follows:

```
<first-operand> <infix-binary-operator> <second-operand>
```

The following is an example of using + as an infix binary operator:

```
// 10 is the first operand, + is a binary operator, and 15 is the second operand
10 + 15
```

Like a binary operator, a ternary operator uses infix notation. The syntax to use an infix ternary operator is as follows:

```
<first-operand> <operator1> <second-operand> <operator2> <third-operand>
```

Here, both <operator1> and <operator2> make a ternary operator.
The following is an example of using a ternary operator in Java:

```
// isSunday is the first operand, ? is the first part of ternary operator,
// holiday is the second operand,: is the second part of ternary operator, noHoliday is the
// third operand
isSunday ? holiday : noHoliday
```

Depending on the type of operation an operator performs, you can categorize them in the following categories:

- Arithmetic operators

- Relational operators

- Logical operators

- Bitwise operators

Java has a big list of operators. This chapter discusses most of the Java operators. I discuss a few of them in later chapters when the context is appropriate. Enjoy the long journey of learning operators in Java in subsequent sections!

Assignment Operator

An assignment operator (=) is used to assign a value to a variable. It is a binary operator. It takes two operands. The value of the right-hand operand is assigned to the left-hand operand. The left-hand operand must be a variable. For example,

```
int num;
num = 25;
```

Here, num = 25 uses the assignment operator =. In this example, 25 is the right-hand operand and num is the left-hand operand, which is a variable.

Java ensures that the value of the right-hand operand of the assignment operator is assignment-compatible to the data type of the left-hand operand; otherwise, a compile-time error occurs. In the case of reference variables, you may be able to compile the source code and get a runtime error if the object represented by the right-hand operand is not assignment compatible to the reference variable specified as the left-hand operand. For example, the value of type byte, short, and char are assignment-compatible to the int data type, and hence the following snippet of code is valid.

```
byte b = 5;
char c = 'a';
short s = -200;
int i = 10;
i = b; // OK. byte b is assignment compatible to int i
i = c; // OK. char c is assignment compatible to int i
i = s; // OK. short s is assignment compatible to int i
```

However, long to int and float to int assignments are not compatible and hence the following snippet of code generates compile-time errors.

```
long big = 524L;
float f = 1.19F;
int i = 15;
i = big; // A compile-time error. long to int, assignment incompatible
i = f;   // A compile-time error. float to int, assignment incompatible
```

In cases where the right-hand operand's value is not assignment-compatible with the left-hand variable's data type, the value of the right-hand operand must be cast to the appropriate type. The previous piece of code, which uses assignment operators, can be rewritten with a cast as follows.

```
i = (int)big; // OK
i = (int)f;   // OK
```

An *expression* is a series of variables, operators, and method calls, constructed according to the syntax of the Java programming language that evaluates to a single value. For example, num = 25 is an expression. The expression, which uses the assignment operator, also has a value. The value of the expression is equal to the value of the right-hand operand. Consider the following piece of code, assuming that num is an int variable.

```
num = 25;
```

Here, num = 25 is called an expression and num = 25; is called a statement. The expression num = 25 does two things.

- Assigns the value 25 to the variable num.

- Produces a value 25, which is equal to the value of the right-hand operand of the assignment operator.

The second effect (producing a value) of using the assignment operator in an expression may seem strange at this point. You may wonder what happens to the value 25 produced by the expression num = 25. Do we ever use the value returned by an expression? The answer is yes. We do use the value returned by an expression. Consider the following expression, which uses chained assignment operators, assuming that num1, and num2, are int variables.

```
num1 = num2 = 25;
```

What happens when this code is executed? First, the part of the expression num2 = 25 is executed. As mentioned earlier, there will be two effects of this execution:

- It will assign a value of 25 to num2.

- It will produce a value of 25. In other words, you can say that after assigning the value 25 to num2, the expression num2 = 25 is replaced by a value 25, which changes the main expression num1 = num2 = 25 to num1 = 25.

Now, the expression num1 = 25 is executed and the value 25 is assigned to num1 and the value produced, which is 25, is ignored. This way, you can assign the same value to more than one variable in a single expression. There can be any number of variables used in such a chained assignment expression. For example:

```
num1 = num2 = num3 = num4 = num5 = num6 = 219;
```

Suppose that there are two int variables num1 and num2. The following assignment, num1 = num2, assigns the value 200 stored in num2 to num1.

```
int num1 = 100; // num1 is 100
int num2 = 200; // num2 is 200
num1 = num2; // num1 is 200. num2 is 200
num2 = 500;  // num2 is 500. num1 is still 200
```

When you say num1 = num2, the value stored in num2 is copied to num1 and both num1 and num2 maintain their own copy of the same value, 200. Later on, when num2 = 500 is executed, the value of only num2 changes to 500. But the value of num1 remains the same, 200. Now, suppose there are two reference variable, ref1 and ref2, which refer to two different objects of the same class. If we write:

```
ref1 = ref2;
```

The effect of the expression, ref1 = ref2, is that both reference variables, ref1 and ref2, now refer to the same object in memory—the object that was being referred to by ref2. After this assignment, both reference variables, ref1 and ref2, are equally capable of manipulating the object. The changes made to the object in memory by reference variable ref1 will be observed by ref2 also and vice versa. Chapter 7 covers more on reference variable assignments.

Declaration, Initialization, and Assignment

Before a variable of any type is used in a Java program, it must be declared and have a value assigned to it. Suppose you want to use an int variable named num1. First, you must declare it as follows:

```
// Declaration of a variable num1
int num1;
```

A value can be assigned to a variable after it is declared or at the time of declaration itself. When a value is assigned to a variable after it has been declared, it is known as assignment. The following piece of code declares an int variable num2 and assigns 50 to it.

```
int num2;    // Declaration of a variable num2
num2 = 50;   // Assignment
```

When a value is assigned to a variable at the time of declaration itself, it is known as initialization. The following code declares an int variable num3 and initializes it to a value 100.

```
// Declaration of variable num3 and its initialization
int num3 = 100;
```

You can declare more than one variable of the same type in one declaration by separating each variable's name by a comma.

```
// Declaration of three variables num1, num2 and num3 of type int
int num1, num2, num3;
```

You can also declare more than one variable in one declaration, and initialize some or all.

```
// Declaration of variables num1, num2 and num3. Initialization of only num1 and num3
int num1 = 10, num2, num3 = 200;
```

```
// Declaration and initialization of variables num1, num2 and num3
int num1 = 10, num2 = 20, num3 = 30;
```

Java will not let you use a variable unless it has been assigned a value either through the process of initialization or assignment. Java implicitly initializes variables declared in a few contexts. Variables declared in other contexts must be initialized, or assigned a value, before they are used, if Java does not initialize them implicitly. I discuss the implicit initialization of a variable by Java in the Chapter 7. It is good practice to initialize a variable at the time of its declaration.

Arithmetic Operators

An arithmetic operator is an operator that takes numeric values as its operands and performs an arithmetic operation, for example, addition and subtraction, to compute another numeric value. Table 5-1 lists all arithmetic operators in Java. All operators listed in Table 5-1 can only be used with numeric type operands. That is, both operands to arithmetic operators must be one of types byte, short, char, int, long, float, or double. These operators cannot have operands of boolean primitive type and reference type. The following sections describe arithmetic operators in detail.

Table 5-1. *List of Arithmetic Operators in Java*

Operators	Description	Type	Usage	Result
+	Addition	Binary	2 + 5	7
-	Subtraction	Binary	5 - 2	3
+	Unary plus	Unary	+5	Positive five. Same as 5.
-	Unary minus	Unary	-5	Negative of five.
*	Multiplication	Binary	5 * 3	15
/	Division	Binary	5 / 2	2
			6 / 2	3
			5.0 / 2.0	2.5
			6.0 / 2.0	3.0
%	Modulus	Binary	5 % 3	2
++	Increment	Unary	num++	Evaluates to the value of num, increment num by 1.
--	Decrement	Unary	num--	Evaluates to the value of num, decrement num by 1.
+=	Arithmetic *compound-assignment*	Binary	num += 5	Adds 5 to the value of num and assigns the result to num. If num is 10, the new value of num will be 15.
-=	Arithmetic *compound assignment*	Binary	num -= 3	Subtracts 3 from the value of num and assigns the result to num. If num is 10, the new value of num will be 7.
*=	Arithmetic *compound assignment*	Binary	num *= 15	Multiplies 15 to the value of num and assigns the result to num. If num is 10, the new value of num will be 150.
/=	Arithmetic *compound assignment*	Binary	num /= 5	Divides the value of num by 5 and assigns the result to num. If num is 10, the new value of num will be 2.
%=	Arithmetic *compound assignment*	Binary	num %= 5	Calculates the remainder of num divided by 5 and assigns the result to num. If num is 12, the new value of num will be 2.

Addition Operator (+)

The addition operator (+) is an arithmetic operator and it is used in the following form:

```
operand1 + operand2
```

The addition operator is used to add two numeric values represented by the two operands, for example, 5 + 3 results in 8. The operands may be any numeric literals, numeric variables, numeric expressions, or method calls. Every expression involving the addition operator (+) has a data type. The data type of the expression is determined according to one of four rules:

- If one of the operands is double, the other operand is converted to double and the whole expression is of type double. Otherwise,

- If one of the operands is float, the other operand is converted to float and the whole expression is of type float. Otherwise,

- If one of the operands is of long, the other operand is converted to long and the whole expression is of type long. Otherwise,

- If none of the previous three rules applies, all operands are converted to int, provided they are not already of int type, and the whole expression is of type int.

These rules have some important implications. Consider a byte variable b1, which is assigned a value of 5, as shown in the following piece of code.

```
byte b1;
b1 = 5;
```

You get a compile-time error when you try to assign the same value 5 to a byte variable b1, as shown in the following snippet of code.

```
byte b1;
byte b2 = 2;
byte b3 = 3;
b1 = b2 + b3; // A compile-time error. Trying to assign 5 to b1
```

Why does this snippet of code result in a compile-time error? Do the expressions b1 = 5 and b1 = b2 + b3 not have the same effect of assigning 5 to the variable b1? Yes, the effect would be the same. However, the rules that govern the assignment operation are different in two cases. In the expression, b1 = 5, the assignment is governed by the rule that any int literal between -128 and 127 can be assigned to a byte variable. Because 5 is between -128 and 127, the assignment b1 = 5 is valid. The second assignment, b1 = b2 + b3, is governed by the fourth rule for the determination of the data type of an arithmetic expression, which uses addition operator (+). Because both operands in the expression b2 + b3 are of byte types, the operands b2 and b3 are first converted to int, and then the expression, b2 + b3, becomes of the int type. Because the data type of b1 is byte, which is smaller than the int data type of the expression b2 + b3, the assignment b1 = b2 + b3, that is, int to byte, is not compatible, and that is the reason it generates an error. In such a case, you need to cast the result of the right-hand expression to the data type of the left-hand operand.

```
b1 = (byte)(b2 + b3); // OK now
```

Beginners may try to write this statement of code as follows:

```
b1 = (byte) b2 + b3; // A compile-time error again
```

The two expressions, (byte)(b2 + b3) and (byte)b2 + b3, are not the same. In the expression (byte) (b2 + b3), first, b2 and b3 are promoted to int, and then, an addition is performed, which results in a value 5 of the int type. Then, the int value 5 is cast to byte and assigned to b1.

In the expression (byte)b2 + b3, first, b2 is cast to byte. Note that this cast is redundant since b2 is already of type byte; both b2 and b3 are promoted to int; the whole expression (byte)b2 + b3 is of type int. Since int to byte assignment is not permitted, the expression would not compile.

The error produced by the second expression (byte)(b2 + b3) raises an interesting question. Why did Java not first compute b2 + b3 in (byte)b2 + b3 and then applied (byte) to the result? Because there were two operations to be done, one being the cast to byte and another being the addition of b2 and b3, Java did cast on b2 first and the addition second. The decision to perform the cast first followed by the addition was not arbitrary. Each operator in Java has a precedence order. The operator that has higher precedence is evaluated first, before the operators having lower precedence order. The cast operator has higher precedence than the addition operator. This is the reason that (byte)b2 was evaluated first in (byte)b2 + b3. You can always override the precedence of operators using parentheses. We overrode the precedence of the cast operator by using parentheses in expression (byte)(b2 + b3). Consider another example.

```
byte b1;
b1 = 3 + 2; // Will this line of code compile?
```

Will the expression, b1 = 3 + 2, compile? If we apply the fourth rule for determining the data type of this expression, it should not compile because 3 and 2 are int literals. The expression 3 + 2 is of type int. Because int is not assignment compatible to byte, the expression b1 = 3 + 2 should give an error. However, our assumption is wrong and the expression b1 = 3 + 2 will compile fine. In this case, the assignment proceeds as follows.

The operands 3 and 2 are constants, so their values are known at compile time. Therefore, the compiler computes the result of the expression 3 + 2 at the time of compilation and replaces 3 + 2 by its result 5. The expression b1 = 3 + 2 is replaced by b1 = 5 by the compiler. Now, you can see why Java didn't give any errors for this expression. Because the int literal 5 is in the range -128 to 127, b1 = 5 is a valid assignment, according to the rule of assignment of int literal to a byte variable. However, if you try to write an expression as b1 = 127 + 10, certainly it would not compile because the result of 127 + 10, which is 137, is out of range for a byte data type. Here are the final words on the data type conversion of the operands and the determination of the type of the expression involving the addition operator.

```
var = operand1 + operand2;
```

If operand1 and operand2 are compile-time constants, the result of operand1 + operand2 determines whether this assignment is valid. If the result of operand1 + operand2 is in the range for the data type of the variable var, the expression will compile. Otherwise, a compiler error is generated. If either operand1 or operand2 is a variable (that is, the value of either operand1 or operand2 cannot be ascertained at compile-time), the data type of the expression is determined according to one of the four rules discussed at the beginning of this section. The following are examples of correct and incorrect uses of the addition operator. The comments along with the code indicate whether the use is correct.

```
byte b1 = 2;
byte b2 = 3;
short s1 = 100;
int i = 10;
int j = 12;
```

```
float f1 = 2.5F;
double d1 = 20.0;

// OK. 125 is in the range -128 and 127
b1 = 15 + 110;

// An error. Data type of i + 5 is int and int to byte assignment is not permitted
b1 = i + 5;

b1 = (byte)(i + 5); // OK

// An error. s1 is promoted to int and s1 + 2 is of the data type int.
// int to byte assignment is not permitted
b1 = s1 + 2;

// An error. b2 is promoted to float and f1 + b2 is of the data type float.
// float to byte assignment is not permitted
b1 = f1 + b2;

// An error. f1 is promoted to double and f1 + d1 is of the data type double
b1 = f1 + d1;

// OK. i is promoted to float and i + f1 is of the data type float
f1 = i + f1;

// An error. i is promoted to double and i + d1 is of data type double.
// double to float assignment is not permitted
f1 = i + d1;

f1 = (float)(i + d1); // OK

// An error. 2.0 and 3.0 are of the type double. The result of 2.0 + 3.2 is 5.2,
// which is also of the type double. double to float assignment is not permitted.
f1 = 2.0 + 3.2;

// OK. 2.0F and 3.2F are of the type float. The result of 2.0F + 3.2F,
// which is 5.2F is of the type float.
f1 = 2.0F + 3.2F;

// OK. j is promoted to float and f1 + j is of the data type float.
// float to double assignment is permitted.
d1 = f1 + j;
```

Subtraction Operator (-)

The subtraction operator (-) is an arithmetic operator and it is used in the following form:

```
operand1 - operand2
```

The subtraction operator is used to compute the difference of two numbers, for example 5 - 3 results in 2. All rules that I discussed about the numeric data conversion of the operands and the determination of the data type of the expression involving the addition operator are also applicable to an expression involving subtraction operator. Following are a few examples of using the subtraction operator.

```
byte b1 = 5;
int i = 100;
float f1 = 2.5F;
double d1 = 15.45;

// OK. 200 - 173 will be replaced by 27.
// b1 = 27 is OK because 27 is in the range -128 and 127
b1 = 200 - 173;

// An error.  i - 27 is of the type int. int to byte assignment is not allowed
b1 = i - 27;

b1 = (byte)(i - 27);   // OK. Assigns 73 to b1
d1 = f1 - i;           // OK. Assigns -97.5 to d1
```

Multiplication Operator (*)

The multiplication operator (*) is an arithmetic operator and it is used in the following form:

```
operand1 * operand2
```

The multiplication operator (*) is used to compute the product of two numbers, for example, 7 * 3 results in 21. All rules that I discussed about the numeric data conversion of the operands and the determination of the data type of the expression involving the addition operator are also applicable to an expression involving the multiplication operator. The following are some examples of using the multiplication operator.

```
byte b1 = 5;
int i = 10;
float f1 = 2.5F;
double d1 = 15.45;

// OK. 20 * 6 will be replaced by 120
// b1 = 120 is OK because 120 is in the range -128 and 127
b1 = 20 * 6;

// An error. i * 12 is of the type int. int to byte assignment is not allowed
b1 = i * 12;

b1 = (byte)(i * 12); // OK. Assigns 120 to b1

// OK. i * b1 is of the type int. int to float assignment is allowed
f1 = i * b1;

// An error. d1 * i is of type double. double to float assignment is not allowed
f1 = d1 * i;

f1 = (float)(d1 * i); // OK. Assigns 154.5 to f1
```

154

Division Operator (/)

The division operator (/) is an arithmetic operator and it is used in the following form:

```
operand1 / operand2
```

The division operator (/) is used to compute the quotient of two numbers, for example 5.0/2.0 results in 2.5. All rules I discussed about the numeric data conversion of the operands and the determination of the data type of the expression involving the addition operator (+) are also valid for expression involving the division operator. There are two types of division:

- Integer division
- Floating-point division

If both the operands of the division operator are integers, that is, byte, short, char, int, or long, the usual division operation is carried out and the result is truncated toward zero to represent an integer. For example, if you write an expression 5/2 the division yields 2.5; the fractional part 0.5 is ignored; the result is 2. The following examples illustrate the integer division:

```
int num;
num = 5/2; // Assigns 2 to num
num = 5/3; // Assigns 1 to num
num = 5/4; // Assigns 1 to num
num = 5/5; // Assigns 1 to num
num = 5/6; // Assigns 0 to num
num = 5/7; // Assigns 0 to num
```

In all these examples, the value assigned to the variable num is an integer. The result is an integer in all cases not because the data type of variable num is int. The result is integer because both the operands of the division operator are integers. Because the data types of both operands are int the whole expression 5/3 is of type int. Because the fractional portion (e.g., 0.5, 0.034) cannot be stored in an int, the fractional portion is ignored and the result is always an integer. Using the JShell tool is a great way to experiment with these operators. The following jshell session shows you the results of these expressions:

```
jshell> int num;
num ==> 0

jshell> num = 5/2;
num ==> 2

jshell> num = 5/3;
num ==> 1

jshell> num = 5/4;
num ==> 1

jshell> num = 5/5;
num ==> 1

jshell> num = 5/6;
num ==> 0

jshell> num = 5/7;
num ==> 0
```

If either or both operands of the division operator are float or double, a floating-point division is performed and the result is not truncated. Here are a few examples:

```
float f1;

// 15.0F and 4.0F are of float type. So, the expression 15.0F/4.0F is of the type float.
// The result 3.75F is assigned to f1.
f1 = 15.0F/4.0F;

// 15 is of type int and 4.0F is of type float. The expression 15/4.0F is of type float.
// The result 3.75F is assigned to f1.
f1 = 15/4.0F;

// An error. 15.0 is of the type double and 4.0F is of the type float. The expression
// 15.0/4.0F is of type double. The result 3.75 is of the type double and cannot be
// assigned to f1 because double to float assignment is not allowed.
f1 = 15.0/4.0F;

// OK. 3.75F is assigned to f1
f1 = (float)(15.0/4.0F);

// 15 and 4 are of type int. The expression 15/4 is of type int. An integer division
// is performed. The result 3 is assigned to f1 because int to float assignment is allowed.
f1 = 15/4;
```

What happens when you try to divide a number (integer or floating-point) by zero? The result of dividing a number by zero depends on the type of division. If an integer division is performed on the number, dividing by zero results in a runtime error. If you write an expression 3/0 in a Java program, it compiles fine, but it gives an error when this expression is executed at runtime. For example:

```
int i = 2;
int j = 5;
int k = 0;
i = j/k;  // A runtime error. Divide by zero
i = 0/0;  // A runtime error. Divide by zero
```

If either operand of the division operator is a floating-point number, a floating-point division is performed and the result of dividing the number by zero is not an error. If the dividend (in 7/2, 7 is the dividend and 2 is the divisor) is a non-zero number in a floating-point divide-by-zero operation, the result is a positive infinity or a negative infinity. If the dividend is a floating-point zero (e.g., 0.0 or 0,0F), the result is a NaN. For example:

```
float  f1 = 2.5F;
double d1 = 5.6;

f1 = 5.0F/0.0F;    // Float.POSITIVE_INFINITY is assigned to f1
f1 = -5.0F/0.0F;   // Float.NEGATIVE_INFINITY is assigned to f1
f1 = -5.0F/-0.0F;  // Float.POSITIVE_INFINITY is assigned to f1
f1 = 5.0F/-0.0F;   // Float.NEGATIVE_INFINITY is assigned to f1
d1 = 5.0/0.0;      // Double.POSITIVE_INFINITY is assigned to d1
d1 = -5.0/0.0;     // Double.NEGATIVE_INFINITY is assigned to d1
```

```
d1 = -5.0/-0.0;     // Double.POSITIVE_INFINITY is assigned to d1
d1 = 5.0/-0.0;      // Double.NEGATIVE_INFINITY is assigned to d1

// 5.0F is of the type float and 0 is of the type int. 5.0F/0 is of type float.
// Float.POSITIVE_INFINITY is assigned to f1
f1 = 5.0F/0;

// A compile-time error. 5.0F is of the type float and 0.0 is of the type double
// 5.0F/0.0 is of the type double. double to float assignment is not allowed.
f1 = 5.0F/0.0;

f1 = (float)(5.0F/0.0); // f1 is assigned Float.POSITIVE_INFINITY
f1 = 0.0F/0.0F;         // Assigns Float.NaN to f1
d1 = 0.0/0.0;           // Assigns Double.NaN to d1
d1 = -0.0/0.0;          // Assigns Double.NaN to d1
```

Modulus Operator (%)

The modulus operator (%) is an arithmetic operator and it is used in the following form:

```
operand1 % operand2
```

The modulus operator (%) is also known as the remainder operator. The modulus operator performs a division on the left-hand operand by its right-hand operand and returns the remainder of the division, for example, 7%5 evaluates to 2. All rules about the numeric data conversion of the operands and the determination of the data type of the expression involving the addition operator (+) are also applicable to expressions involving the modulus operator. Because the use of the modulus operator involves a division operation, there are a few special rules to determine the result of a modulus operation.

If both operands of the modulus operator are integers, the following rules are applied to compute the result.

Rule #1

It is a runtime error if the right-hand operand is zero. For example,

```
int num;
num = 15 % 0; // A runtime error
```

Rule #2

If the right-hand operand is not zero, the sign of the result is the same as the sign of the left-hand operand. For example,

```
int num;
num = 15 % 6;   // Assigns 3 to num
num = -15 % 6;  // Assigns -3 to num
num = 15 % -6;  // Assigns 3 to num
num = -15 % -6; // Assigns -3 to num because left-hand operand is -15, which is negative
num = 5 % 7;    // Assigns 5 to num
num = 0 % 7;    // Assigns 0 to num
```

If either operand of the modulus operator is a floating-point number, the following rules are applied to compute the result.

Rule #1

The operation never results in an error even if the right-hand operand is a floating-point zero.

Rule #2

The result is NaN if either operand is NaN. For example,

```
float f1;
double d1;
f1 = Float.NaN % 10.5F;     // Assigns Float.NaN to f1
f1 = 20.0F % Float.NaN;     // Assigns Float.NaN to f1
f1 = Float.NaN % Float.NaN; // Assigns Float.NaN to f1

// A compile-time error. The expression is of the type double.
// double to float assignment is not allowed.
f1 = Float.NaN % Double.NaN;

d1 = Float.NaN % Double.NaN; // Assigns Double.NaN to d1
```

Rule #3

If the right-hand operand is zero, the result is NaN. For example,

```
float f1;
f1 = 15.0F % 0.0F; // Assigns Float.NaN to f1
```

Rule #4

If the left-hand operand is infinity, the result is NaN. For example,

```
float f1;
f1 = Float.POSITIVE_INFINITY % 2.1F; // Assigns Float.NaN to f1
```

Rule #5

If none of the previous rules apply, the modulus operator returns the remainder of the division of the left-hand operand and the right-hand operand. The sign of the result is the same as the sign of the left-hand operand. For example,

```
float f1;
double d1;
f1 = 15.5F % 6.5F; // Assigns 2.5F to f1
d1 = 5.5 % 15.65;  // Assigns 5.5 to d1
d1 = 0.0 % 3.78;   // Assigns 0.0 to d1
```

```
d1 = 85.0 % Double.POSITIVE_INFINITY;   // Assigns 85.0 to d1
d1 = -85.0 % Double.POSITIVE_INFINITY; // Assigns -85.0 to d1
d1 = 85.0 % Double.NEGATIVE_INFINITY;   // Assigns 85.0 to d1
d1 = -85.0 % Double.NEGATIVE_INFINITY; // Assigns -85.0 to d1
```

Unary Plus Operator (+)

The unary plus operator (+) is an arithmetic operator and it is used in the following form:

```
+operand
```

The operand must be a primitive numeric type. If the operand is a byte, short, or char, the unary plus operator promotes it to an int. Otherwise, there is no effect of using this operator. For example, if there is an int variable num that has a value of 5, +num still has the same value 5. The following examples illustrate the use of this operator:

```
byte b1 = 10;
byte b2 = 5;

b1 = b2;  // OK. byte to byte assignment

// A compile-time error. b2 is of the type byte. But, use of the unary plus operator on
// b2 promoted its type to int. Therefore, +b2 is of the type int.
// int (+b2) to byte (b1) assignment is not allowed.
b1 = +b2;

b1 = (byte) +b2; // OK
```

Unary Minus Operator (-)

The unary minus operator (-) is an arithmetic operator and it is used in the following form:

```
-operand
```

The unary minus operator arithmetically negates the value of its operand. The operand must be a primitive numeric type. If the operand is a byte, short, or char, it is promoted to an int. The following examples illustrate its use:

```
byte b1 = 10;
byte b2 = 5;

b1 = b2;  // OK. byte to byte assignment

// A compile-time error. b2 is of the type byte. But, use of unary minus operator (-) on
// b2 promoted its type to int. Therefore, -b2 is of type int.
// int (-b2) to byte (b1) assignment is not allowed.
b1 = -b2;

b1 = (byte) -b2; // OK
```

159

Compound Arithmetic Assignment Operators

Each of the five basic arithmetic operators (+, -, *, /, and %) has a corresponding compound arithmetic assignment operator. These operators can be explained better with an example. Suppose you have two variables, num1 and num2:

```
int num1 = 100;
byte num2 = 15;
```

If you want to add the value of num1 to num2, you would write the code as follows:

```
num2 = (byte)(num2 + num1);
```

You need to cast the result of num2 + num1 to byte because the data type of the expression is int. The same effect can be rewritten using a compound arithmetic operator (+=), as follows.

```
num2 += num1; // Adds the value of num1 to num2
```

A compound arithmetic assignment operator is used in the following form:

```
operand1 op= operand2
```

Here, op is one of the arithmetic operators +, -, *, /, and %. operand1 and operand2 are of primitive numeric data types, where operand1 must be a variable. The previous expression is equivalent to the following expression.

```
operand1 = (Type of operand1) (operand1 op operand2)
```

For example,

```
int i = 100;
i += 5.5;      // Assigns 105 to i
```

is equivalent to

```
i = (int)(i + 5.5); // Assigns 105 to i
```

There are two advantages of using the compound arithmetic assignment operators.

- The operand1 is evaluated only once. For example, in i += 5.5, the variable i is evaluated only once, whereas in i = (int) (i + 5.5), the variable i is evaluated twice.

- The result is automatically cast to the type of operand1 before assignment. The cast may result in a narrowing conversion or an identity conversion. In the previous example, the cast is a narrowing conversion. The expression i + 5.5 is of the type double and the result of this expression is cast to int. So, the result double 105.5 is converted to int 105. If you write an expression like i += 5, the equivalent expression will be i = (int)(i + 5). Because the type of the expression i + 5 is already int, casting the result to int again is an identity conversion.

The compound assignment operator += can also be applied to String variables. In such cases, operand1 must be of type String and operand2 may be of any type including boolean. For example,

```
String str1 = "Hello";
str1 = str1 + 100;     // Assigns "Hello100" to str1
```

can be rewritten as:

```
str1 += 100; // Assigns "Hello100" to str1
```

░░ **Tip**   Only the += operator can be used with a String left-hand operand.

The following are examples of using the compound assignment operators. In the examples, each use of a compound assignment operator is independent of the effects of its previous uses. In all cases, it has been assumed that the values of the variables remain the same, as the values assigned to them at the time of their declarations.

```
int i = 110;
float f = 120.2F;
byte b = 5;
String str = "Hello";
boolean b1 = true;

i += 10;       // Assigns 120 to i

// A compile-time error. boolean type cannot be used with +=
// unless left-hand operand (here i) is a String variable
i += b1;

i -= 15;  // Assigns 95 to i. Assuming i was 110
i *= 2;   // Assigns 220 to i. Assuming i was 110
i /= 2;   // Assigns 55 to i. Assuming i was 110
i /= 0;   // Run-time error. Divide by zero error
f /= 0.0; // Assigns Float.POSITIVE_INFINITY to f
i %= 3;   // Assigns 2 to i. Assuming i is 110

str += " How are you"; // Assigns "Hello How are you" to str
str += f; // Assigns "Hello120.2" to str. Assuming  str was "Hello"
b += f;   // Assigns 125 to b. Assuming b was 5, f was 120.2
str += b1; // Assigns "Hellotrue" to str. Assuming str was "Hello"
```

Increment (++) and Decrement (--) Operators

The increment operator (++) is used with a variable of numeric data type to increment the variable's value by 1, whereas the decrement operator (--) is used to decrement the value by 1. In this section, I discuss only the increment operator. The same discussion applies to the decrement operator with the only difference being that it will decrement the value of 1 instead of increment it by 1. Suppose there is an int variable i declared as follows:

```
int i = 100;
```

To increment the value of i by 1, you can use one of the three following expressions.

```
i = i + 1; // Assigns 101 to i
i += 1;    // Assigns 101 to i
i++;       // Assigns 101 to i
```

The increment operator ++ can also be used in a more complex expression such as:

```
int i = 100;
int j = 50;
j = i++ + 15;  // Assigns 115 to j and i becomes 101
```

The expression, i++ + 15, is evaluated as follows:

- The value of i is evaluated and the right-hand expression becomes 100 + 15.

- The value of i in memory is incremented by 1. So, at this stage the value of the variable i in memory is 101.

- The expression 100 + 15 is evaluated and the result 115 is assigned to j.

There are two kinds of increment operator:

- Post-fix increment operator, for example, i++

- Pre-fix increment operator, for example, ++i

When ++ appears after its operand, it is called a post-fix increment operator. When ++ appears before its operand, it is called a pre-fix increment operator. The only difference in post-fix and pre-fix increment operators is the order in which they use the current value of its operand and the increment in its operand's value. The post-fix increment uses the current value of its operand first, and then, increments the operand's value, as you saw in the expression j = i++ + 15. Because i++ uses a post-fix increment operator, first, the current value of i is used to compute the value of expression i++ + 15 (e.g., 100 + 15). The value assigned to j is 115. And, then, the value of i is incremented by 1. The result would be different if this expression is rewritten using a pre-fix increment operator:

```
int i = 100;
int j = 50;
j = ++i + 15;   // Assigns 116 to j and i becomes 101
```

In this case, the expression, ++i + 15, is evaluated as follows:

- Because ++i uses a pre-fix increment operator, first the value of i is incremented in memory by 1. Therefore, the value of i is 101.

- The current value of i, which is 101, is used in the expression and the expression becomes 101 + 15.

- The expression 101 + 15 is evaluated and the result 116 is assigned to j.

Note that after evaluation of both expressions i++ + 15 and ++i + 15, the value of i is the same, which is 101. However, the values assigned to j differ. If you are using the increment operator ++ in a simple expression as in i++ or ++i, you cannot observe any difference in using a post-fix or pre-fix operator.

There is a puzzle for Java beginners. The puzzle includes the use of the increment operator as follows:

```
int i = 15;
i = i++; // What will be the value of i after this assignment?
```

Guess what the value of i will be after i = i++ is executed? If your guess is 16, you are wrong. Here is the explanation of how the expression is evaluated:

- i++ is evaluated. Because i++ uses a post-fix increment operator, the current value of i is used in the expression. The current value of i is 15. The expression becomes i = 15.

- The value of i is incremented by 1 in memory as the second effect of i++. At this point, the value of i is 16 in memory.

- The expression i = 15 is evaluated and the value 15 is assigned to i. The value of the variable i in memory is 15 and that is the final value. In fact, variable i observed a value 16 in the previous step, but this step overwrote that value with 15. Therefore, the final value of the variable i after i = i++ is executed will be 15, not 16.

In this example, the order of operations is important. It is important to note that in case of i++ the value of the variable i is incremented as soon as the current value of i is used in the expression. To make this point clearer, consider the following example:

```
int i = 10;
i = i++ + i;   // Assigns 21 to i
i = 10;
i = ++i + i++; // Assigns 22 to i
```

There are also post-fix and pre-fix decrement operators, e.g., i--, --i. The following are a few examples of using post-fix and pre-fix decrement operators:

```
int i = 15;
int j = 16;
i--;
--i;
i = 10;
i = i--;  // Assigns 10 to i
i = 10;
j = i-- + 10;  // Assigns 20 to j and 9 to i
i = 10;
j = --i + 10;  // Assigns 19 to j and 9 to i
```

There are two important points to remember about the use of increment and decrement operators:

- The operand of the increment and decrement operators must be a variable. For example, the expression 5++ is incorrect, because ++ is being used with a constant.

- The result of the expression using the ++ or -- operator is a value, not a variable. For example, i++ evaluates to a value, so we cannot use i++ as the left-hand of an assignment operator or where a variable is required.

String Concatenation Operator (+)

The + operator is overloaded in Java. An operator is said to be overloaded if it is used to perform more than one function. So far, you have seen its use as an arithmetic addition operator to add two numbers. It can also be used to concatenate two strings. Two strings, for example, "abc" and "xyz", can be concatenated using the + operator as "abc" + "xyz" to produce a new string "abcxyz". Another example of a string concatenation is as follows:

```
String str1 = "Hello";
String str2 = " Alekhya";
String str3 = str1 + str2; // Assigns "Hello Alekhya" to str3
```

The string concatenation operator is also used to concatenate a primitive and a reference data type value to a string. I discuss only concatenation of string and primitive data types in this section. When either operand of the + operator is a string, it performs a string concatenation. When both operands of + are numeric, it performs a number addition. Consider the following snippet of code:

```
int num = 26;
String str1 = "Alphabets";
String str2 = num + str1; // Assigns "26Alphabets" to str2
```

When the expression num + str1 is executed, the + operator acts as a string concatenation operator, because its right-hand operand str1 is a String. Before num and str1 are concatenated, num is replaced by its string representation, which is "26". Now, the expression becomes "26" + str1, which results in "26Alphabets". Table 5-2 lists the string representation of the values of the primitive data types.

Table 5-2. *String Representations of the Values of Primitive Data Types*

Data Type	Value	String Representation
int, short, byte, long	1678	"1678"
	0	"0"
char	'A'	"A"
	'\u0041' (Unicode escape sequence)	"A"
boolean	true	"true"
	false	"false"
float	2.5	"2.5"
	0.0F	"0.0"
	-0.0F	"-0.0"
	Float.POSITIVE_INFINITY	"Infinity"
	Float.NEGATIVE_INFINITY	"-Infinity"
	Float.NaN	"NaN"
double	89.12	"89.12"
	0.0	"0.0"
	-0.0	"-0.0"
	Double.POSITIVE_INFINITY	"Infinity"
	Double.NEGATIVE_INFINITY	"-Infinity"
	Double.NaN	"NaN"

If a String variable contains the null reference, the concatenation operator uses a string "null". The following examples illustrate the use of string representations of the values of primitive data types in string concatenation:

```
boolean b1 = true;
boolean b2 = false;
int num = 365;
double d = -0.0;
char c = 'A';
String str1;
String str2 = null;

str1 = b1 + " friends";  // Assigns "true friends" to str1
str1 = b2 + " identity"; // Assigns "false identity" to str1

// Assigns "null and void" to str1. Because str2 is null, it is replaced
// by a string "null" by the string concatenation operator
str1 = str2 + " and void";

str1 = num + " days"; // Assigns "365 days" to str1
str1 = d + " zero";   // Assigns "-0.0 zero" to str1
```

```
str1 = Double.NaN + " is absurd"; // Assigns "NaN is absurd" to str1

str1 = c + " is a letter"; // Assigns "A is a letter" to str1
str1 = "This is " + b1;     // Assigns "This is true" to str1

// Assigns "Beyond Infinity" to str1
str1 = "Beyond " + Float.POSITIVE_INFINITY
```

It may sometimes be confusing to determine the result of an expression that uses more than one + operator and strings. What will be the result of the following expression?

```
12 + 15 + " men"
```

Will the result be "1215 men" or "27 men"? The key to finding the correct answer is to find which + is an arithmetic operator and which + is a string concatenation operator.

If both the operands are numeric, the + operator performs addition. If either operand is a string, the + operator performs string concatenation. The execution of an expression proceeds from left to right unless overridden by using parentheses. In the expression 12 + 15 + " men", the first + from the left performs addition on 12 and 15, which results in 27. After that, the expression reduces to 27 + " men". Now, the + operator performs a string concatenation because the right-hand operand, " men", is a string and it results in "27 men". Consider the following piece of code.

```
int num1 = 12;
int num2 = 15;
String str1 = " men";
String str2;
```

We want to create a string "1215 men" using the three variables num1, num2, and str1, and the + operator. We want to assign the result to str2. Here is the first attempt.

```
str2 = num1 + num2 + str1;
```

This statement will assign "27 men" to str2. Another solution is to place num2 + str1 in parentheses.

```
str2 = num1 + (num2 + str1); // Assigns "1215 men" to str2
```

The expression in parentheses is evaluated first. The expression (num2 + str1) is evaluated first to reduce the expression to num1 + "15 men", which in turn will evaluate to "1215 men". Another option is to place an empty string at the beginning of the expression.

```
str2 = "" + num1 + num2 + str1; // Assigns "1215 men" to str1
```

In this case, "" + num1 is evaluated first, and it results in "12", which reduces the expression to "12" + num2 + str1. Now, "12" + num2 is evaluated, which results in "1215". Now, the expression is reduced to "1215" + " men", which results in a string "1215 men". You may also place an empty string between num1 and num2 in the expression to get the same result.

```
str2 = num1 + "" + num2 + str1; // Assigns "1215 men" to str2
```

Sometimes, the string concatenation is trickier than you think. Consider the following piece of code.

```
boolean b = false;
int num = 15;
String str1 = "faces";
String str2 = b + num + str1; // A compile-time error
```

The last statement generates a compile-time error. What is wrong with this statement? You were expecting a string "false15faces" to be assigned to str2. Weren't you? Let's analyze the expression b + num + str1. Is the first + operator from the left an arithmetic operator or a string concatenation operator? For a + operator to be a string concatenation operator, it is necessary that at least one of its operands is a string. Since neither b nor num is a string, the first + operator from the left in b + num + str1 is not a string concatenation operator.

Is it an arithmetic addition operator? Its operands are of type boolean (b) and int (num). You have already learned that an arithmetic addition operator (+) cannot have a boolean operand. The presence of a boolean operand in the expression b + num caused the compile-time error. A boolean cannot be added to a number. However, the + operator works on a boolean as a string concatenation operator if another operand is a string. To correct this error, you can rewrite the expression in a number of ways as follows:

```
str2 = b + (num + str1);      // OK. Assigns "false15faces" to str2
str2 = "" + b + num + str1;   // OK. Assigns "false15faces" to str2
str2 = b + "" + num + str1;   // OK. Assigns "false15faces" to str2
```

You use the println() or print() method to print a message on the standard output as follows.

```
System.out.println("Prints a new line at the end of text");
System.out.print("Does not print a new line at the end of text");
```

If you use the System.out.println() method to print text on the console, after printing the text, it also prints a new line character at the end of the text. The only difference between using println() and print() is that the former prints a new line at the end of the text, whereas the latter does not. The println() and print() methods are overloaded. Until now, you have seen their use only with string arguments. You can pass any Java data type argument to these two methods. The following snippet of code illustrates how to pass Java primitive types as arguments to these methods.

```
int num = 156;

// Prints 156 on the console
System.out.println(num);

// Prints, Value of num = 156, on the console
System.out.println("Value of num = " + num);

// Prints a new line character on the console
System.out.println();
```

Listing 5-2 contains a complete program to demonstrate the use of arithmetic operators and the string concatenation operator.

Listing 5-2. An Example of Using Java Operators

```java
// ArithOperator.java
package com.jdojo.operator;

class ArithOperator {
    public static void main(String[] args) {
        int num = 120;
        double realNum = 25.5F;
        double veryBigNum = 25.8 / 0.0;
        double garbage = 0.0 / 0.0;
        boolean test = true;

        // Print the value of num
        System.out.println("num = " + num);

        // Print the value of realNum
        System.out.println("realNum = " + realNum);

        // Print the value of veryBigNum
        System.out.println("veryBigNum = " + veryBigNum);

        // Print the value of garbage
        System.out.println("garbage = " + garbage);

        // Print the value of test
        System.out.println("test = " + test);

        // Print the maximum value of int type
        System.out.println("Maximum int = " + Integer.MAX_VALUE);

        // Print the maximum value of double type
        System.out.println("Maximum double = " + Double.MAX_VALUE);

        // Print the sum of two numbers
        System.out.println("12.5 + 100 = " + (12.5 + 100));

        // Print the difference of two numbers
        System.out.println("12.5 - 100 = " + (12.5 - 100));

        // Print the multiplication of two numbers
        System.out.println("12.5 * 100 = " + (12.5 * 100));

        // Print the result of division
        System.out.println("12.5 / 100 = " + (12.5 / 100));

        // Print the result of modulus
        System.out.println("12.5 % 100 = " + (12.5 % 100));
```

```
        // Print the result of string concatenation
        System.out.println("\"abc\" + \"xyz\" = " + "\"" + ("abc" + "xyz") + "\"");
    }
}
```

```
num = 120
realNum = 25.5
veryBigNum = Infinity
garbage = NaN
test = true
Maximum int = 2147483647
Maximum double = 1.7976931348623157E308
12.5 + 100 = 112.5
12.5 - 100 = -87.5
12.5 * 100 = 1250.0
12.5 / 100 = 0.125
12.5 % 100 = 12.5
"abc" + "xyz" = "abcxyz"
```

Relational Operators

A relational operator compares values of its operands. A few examples of such comparisons are comparison for equality, inequality, greater than, less than, etc. Java supports seven relational operators, six of which are listed in Table 5-3. The seventh one is the `instanceof` operator, which I discuss later in this book.

Table 5-3. *List of Relational Operators in Java*

Operators	Meaning	Type	Usage	Result
==	Equal to	Binary	3 == 2	false
!=	Not equal to	Binary	3 != 2	true
>	Greater than	Binary	3 > 2	true
>=	Greater than or equal to	Binary	3 >= 2	true
<	Less than	Binary	3 < 2	false
<=	Less than or equal to	Binary	3 <= 2	false

All relational operators are binary operators. That is, they take two operands. The result produced by a relational operator is always a `boolean` value: `true` or `false`.

Equality Operator (==)

The equality operator (==) is used in this form:

```
operand1 == operand2
```

The equality operator is used to test two operands for equality. It uses the following rules.

- Both operands must be either primitive type or reference type. Mixed operands types are not allowed.

- For primitive operands, it returns true if the both operands represent the same value; otherwise it returns false. Both operands must be either numeric or boolean. A mix of numeric and boolean types is not allowed.

- For reference operands, it returns true if both operands refer to the same object in memory; otherwise it returns false.

Suppose there is an int variable named i declared as follows:

```
int i = 10;
```

Now, i == 10 will test whether i is equal to 10 or not. Because i is equal to 10, the expression i == 10 will evaluate to true. Consider another example:

```
int i;
int j;
int k;
boolean b;

i = j = k = 15;    // Assign 15 to i, j and k
b = (i == j == k); // A compile-time error
```

In this example, you tried to test whether the three variables i, j, and k have the same value and the expression (i == j == k) resulted in an error. Why did you get the error? The expression (i == j == k) is evaluated as follows:

- First, i == j is evaluated in expression i == j == k. Since both i and j have the same value, which is 15, the expression i == j returns true.

- The first step reduced the expression i == j == k to true == k. This is an error because the operands of the == operator are of boolean and int types. You cannot mix boolean and numeric types operands with the equality operator.

The following rules apply when the operands of the equality operator are floating-point types.

Rule #1

Both negative zero (-0.0) and positive zero (0.0) are considered equal. Recall that -0.0 and 0.0 are stored differently in memory.

```
double d1 = 0.0;
double d2 = -0.0;
boolean b = (d1 == d2); // Assigns true to b
```

Rule #2

Positive and negative infinities are considered unequal.

```
double d1 = Double.POSITIVE_INFINITY;
double d2 = Double.NEGATIVE_INFINITY;
boolean b = (d1 == d2); // Assigns false to b
```

Rule #3

If either operand is NaN, the equality test returns false.

```
double d1 = Double.NaN;
double d2 = 5.5;
boolean b = (d1 == d2); // Assigns false to b
```

Note that even if both operands are NaN, the equality operator will return false.

```
d1 = Double.NaN;
d2 = Double.NaN;
b = (d1 == d2); // Assigns false to b
```

How do you test whether the value stored in a float or double variable is NaN? If you write the following piece of code to test for the value of a double variable d1 being NaN, it will always return false.

```
double d1 = Double.NaN;
boolean b = (d1 == Double.NaN); // Assigns false to b. Incorrect way of testing
```

Float and Double classes have an isNaN() method, which accepts a float and a double argument, respectively. It returns true if the argument is NaN; otherwise, it returns false. For example, to test if d1 is NaN, the previous expression can be rewritten as follows:

```
double d1 = Double.NaN;

// Assigns true to b. Correct way to test for a NaN value
b = Double.isNaN(d1);
```

You should not use the == operator to test two strings for equality. For example,

```
String str1 = new String("Hello");
String str2 = new String("Hello");
boolean b;

b = (str1 == str2); // Assigns false to b
```

The new operator in Java always creates a new object in memory. Therefore, str1 and str2 refer to two different objects in memory and this is the reason that str1 == str2 evaluates to false. It is true that both String objects in memory have the same contents. Whenever the == operator is used with reference variables, it always compares the references of the objects its operands are referring to. To compare the text represented by two String variables str1 and str2, you should use the equals() method of the String class, as shown:

```
// Assigns true to b because str1 and str2 have the same text "Hello"
b = str1.equals(str2);

// Assigns true to b because str1 and str2 have the same text "Hello"
b = str2.equals(str1);
```

I discuss more about string comparison in Chapter 15, covering Strings.

Inequality Operator (!=)

The inequality operator (!=) is used in the form:

```
operand1 != operand2
```

The inequality operator returns true if operand1 and operand2 are not equal. Otherwise, it returns false. The rules for the data types of the operands of the inequality (!=) operator are the same that of the equality operator (==). Here are a few examples of using the inequality operator:

```
int i = 15;
int j = 10;
int k = 15;
boolean b;
b = (i != j);      // Assigns true to b
b = (i != k);      // Assigns false to b
b = (true != true);  // Assigns false to b
b = (true != false); // Assigns true to b
```

If either operand is NaN (float or double), the inequality operator returns true. If d1 is a floating-point variable (double or float), d1 == d1 returns false and d1 != d1 returns true if and only if d1 is NaN.

Greater Than Operator (>)

The greater than operator (>) is used in the form:

```
operand1 > operand2
```

The greater than operator returns true if the value of operand1 is greater than the value of operand2. Otherwise, it returns false. The greater than operator can be used only with primitive numeric data types. If either of the operands is NaN (float or double), it returns false. The following are a few examples of using this operator:

```
int i = 10;
int j = 15;
double d1 = Double.NaN;
boolean b;
```

```
b = (i > j); // Assigns false to b
b = (j > i); // Assigns true to b

// A compile-time error. > cannot be used with boolean operands
b = (true > false);

b = (d1 > Double.NaN); // Assigns false to b

String str1 = "Hello";
String str2 = "How is Java?";

// A compile-time error. > cannot be used with reference type operands str1 and str2
b = (str1 > str2);
```

If you want to test if the number of characters in String str1 is greater than that of str2, you should use the length() method of the String class. The length() method of the String class returns the number of characters in the string. For example,

```
i = str1.length(); // Assigns 5 to i. "Hello" has 5 characters
b = (str1.length() > str2.length()); // Assigns false to b
b = (str2.length() > str1.length()); // Assigns true to b
```

Greater Than or Equal to Operator (>=)

The greater than or equal to operator (>=) is used in this form:

```
operand1 >= operand2
```

The greater than or equal to operator returns true if the value of operand1 is greater than or equal to the value of operand2. Otherwise, it returns false. The greater than or equal to operator can be used only with primitive numeric data types. If either of the operands is NaN (float or double), greater than or equal to operator returns false. The following are a few examples of using this operator:

```
int i = 10;
int j = 10;
boolean b;

b = (i >= j);  // Assigns true to b
b = (j >= i);  // Assigns true to b
```

Less Than Operator (<)

The less than operator (<) is used in the form:

```
operand1 < operand2
```

The less than operator returns `true` if operand1 is less than operand2. Otherwise, it returns `false`. The operator can be used only with primitive numeric data types. If either operand is NaN (`float` or `double`), the less than operator returns `false`. The following are a few examples of using this operator:

```
int i = 10;
int j = 15;
double d1 = Double.NaN;
boolean b;
b = (i < j);  // Assigns true to b
b = (j < i);  // Assigns false to b

// A compile-time error. < cannot be used with boolean operands
b = (true < false);

b = (d1 < Double.NaN); // Assigns false to b
```

Less Than or Equal to Operator (<=)

The less than or equal to operator (`<=`) is used in the form:

```
operand1 <= operand2
```

The less than or equal to operator returns `true` if the value of operand1 is less than or equal to the value of operand2. Otherwise, it returns `false`. The operator can be used only with primitive numeric data types. If either of the operands is NaN (`float` or `double`), the less than or equal to operator returns `false`. The following are a few examples of using this operator:

```
int i = 10;
int j = 10;
int k = 15;
boolean b;

b = (i <= j);  // Assigns true to b
b = (j <= i);  // Assigns true to b
b = (j <= k);  // Assigns true to b
b = (k <= j);  // Assigns false to b
```

Boolean Logical Operators

A boolean logical operator takes `boolean` operands, applies a boolean logic to them, and produces a `boolean` value. Table 5-4 lists `boolean` logical operators available in Java. All `boolean` logical operators can be used only with `boolean` operands. Subsequent sections explain the use of these operators in detail.

Table 5-4. *List of Boolean Logical Operators*

Operators	Meaning	Type	Usage	Result
!	Logical NOT	Unary	`!true`	`false`
&&	Short-circuit AND	Binary	`true && true`	`true`
&	Logical AND	Binary	`true & true`	`true`
||	Short-circuit OR	Binary	`true || false`	`true`
|	Logical OR	Binary	`true | false`	`true`
^	Logical XOR (Exclusive OR)	Binary	`true ^ true`	`false`
&=	AND assignment	Binary	`test &= true`	
|=	OR assignment	Binary	`test |= true`	
^=	XOR assignment	Binary	`test ^= true`	

Logical NOT Operator (!)

The logical NOT operator (!) is used in the form:

`!operand`

The operator returns `true` if operand is `false`, and `false` if operand is `true`.

```
boolean b;
b = !true;      // Assigns false to b
b = !false;     // Assigns true to b

int i = 10;
int j = 15;
boolean b1 = true;
b = !b1;        // Assigns false to b
b = !(i > j);   // Assigns true to b, because i > j returns false
```

Suppose you want to change the value of a boolean variable b to `true` if its current value is `false`, and to `false` if its current value is `true`. This can be achieved as follows.

```
b = !b; // Assigns true to b if it was false and false if it was true
```

Logical Short-Circuit AND Operator (&&)

The logical short-circuit AND operator (&&) is used in the form:

`operand1 && operand2`

The && operator returns true if both operands are true. If either operand is false, it returns false. It is called a short-circuit AND operator because if operand1 (the left-hand operand) evaluates to false, it returns false without evaluating operand2 (the right-hand operand).

```
int i = 10;
int j = 15;
boolean b = (i > 5 && j > 10);  // Assigns true to b
```

In this expression, i > 5 is evaluated first and it returns true. Because the left-hand operand evaluated to true, the right-hand operand was also evaluated. The right-hand operand j > 10 is evaluated, which also returns true. Now, the expression is reduced to true && true. Because both operands are true, the final result is true. Consider another example:

```
int i = 10;
int j = 15;
boolean b = (i > 20 && j > 10);  // Assigns false to b
```

The expression i > 20 returns false. The expression reduces to false && j > 10. Because the left-hand operand is false, the right-hand operand j > 10 is not evaluated and && returns false. However, there is no way to prove in this example that the right-hand operand, which is j > 10, was not evaluated. Consider another example to prove this point. We have already discussed the assignment operator (=). If num is a variable of type int, num = 10 returns a value 10.

```
int num = 10;
boolean b = ((num = 50) > 5); // Assigns true to b
```

Note the use of parentheses in this example. In the expression ((num = 50) > 5), the (num = 50) expression is evaluated first. It assigns 50 to num and returns 50, reducing the expression to (50 > 5), which in turn returns true. If you use the value of num after the num = 50 expression is executed, its value will be 50. Keeping this point in mind, consider the following snippet of code.

```
int i = 10;
int j = 10;
boolean b = (i > 5 && ((j = 20) > 15));

System.out.println("b = " + b);
System.out.println("i = " + i);
System.out.println("j = " + j);
```

```
b = true
i = 10
j = 20
```

Because the left-hand operand, which is i > 5, evaluated to true, the right-hand operand ((j = 20) > 15) was evaluated and the variable j was assigned a value 20. If we change this code so the left-hand operand evaluates to false, the right-hand operand would not be evaluated and the value of j will remain 10. The changed piece of code is as follows:

```
int i = 10;
int j = 10;

// ((j = 20) > 5) is not evaluated because i > 25 returns false
boolean b = (i > 25 && ((j = 20) > 15));

System.out.println ("b = " + b);
System.out.println ("i = " + i);
System.out.println ("j = " + j); // Will print j = 10
```

```
b = false
i = 10
j = 10
```

Logical AND Operator (&)

The logical AND operator (&) is used in the form:

```
operand1 & operand2
```

The logical AND operator returns true if both operands are true. If either operand is false, it returns false. The logical AND operator (&) works the same way as the logical short-circuit AND operator (&&), except for one difference—the logical AND operator (&) evaluates its right-hand operand even if its left-hand operand evaluates to false.

```
int i = 10;
int j = 15;
boolean b;

b = (i > 5 & j > 10);              // Assigns true to b
b = (i > 25 & ((j = 20) > 15));   // ((j = 20) > 5) is evaluated even if i > 25 returns false
System.out.println ("b = " + b);
System.out.println ("i = " + i);
System.out.println ("j = " + j); // Will print j = 20
```

```
b = false
i = 10
j = 20
```

Logical Short-Circuit OR Operator (||)

The logical short-circuit OR operator (||) is used in the form:

```
operand1 || operand2
```

The logical short-circuit OR operator returns true if either operand is true. If both operands are false, it returns false. It is called a short-circuit OR operator, because if operand1 evaluates to true, it returns true without evaluating operand2.

```
int i = 10;
int j = 15;
boolean b = (i > 5 || j > 10); // Assigns true to b
```

In this expression, i > 5 is evaluated first, and it returns true. Because the left-hand operand evaluated to true, the right-hand operand is not evaluated, and the expression (i > 5 || j > 10) returns true. Consider another example:

```
int i = 10;
int j = 15;
boolean b = (i > 20 || j > 10); // Assigns true to b
```

The expression i > 20 returns false. The expression reduces to false || j > 10. Because the left-hand operand to || is false, the right-hand operand j > 10 is evaluated, which returns true and the entire expression returns true.

Logical OR Operator (|)

The logical OR operator (|) is used in the form:

```
operand1 | operand2
```

The logical OR operator returns true if either operand is true. If both operands are false, it returns false. The logical OR operator works the same way as the logical short-circuit OR operator, except for one difference—the logical OR operator evaluates its right-hand operand even if its left-hand operand evaluates to true.

```
int i = 10;
int j = 15;
boolean b = (i > 5 | j > 10); // Assigns true to b
```

In this expression, i > 5 is evaluated first and it returns true. Even if the left-hand operand i > 5 evaluates to true, the right-hand operand, j > 15, is still evaluated, and the whole expression (i > 5 | j > 10) returns true.

Logical XOR Operator (^)

The logical XOR operator (^) is used in the form:

```
operand1 ^ operand2
```

The logical XOR operator returns `true` if operand1 and operand2 are different. That is, it returns `true` if one of the operands is `true`, but not both. If both operands are the same, it returns `false`.

```
int i = 10;
boolean b;

b = true ^ true;      // Assigns false to b
b = true ^ false;     // Assigns true to b
b = false ^ true;     // Assigns true to b
b = false ^ false;    // Assigns false to b
b = (i > 5 ^ i < 15); // Assigns false to b
```

Compound Boolean Logical Assignment Operators

There are three compound `boolean` logical assignment operators. Note that Java does not have any operators like &&= and ||=. These operators are used in the form:

```
operand1 op= operand2
```

operand1 must be a `boolean` variable and op may be &, |, or ^. This form is equivalent to writing:

```
operand1 = operand1 op operand2
```

Table 5-5 shows the compound logical assignment operators and their equivalents.

Table 5-5. *Compound Logical Assignment Operators and Their Equivalents*

Expression	Is Equivalent To
operand1 &= operand2	operand1 = operand1 & operand2
operand1 |= operand2	operand1 = operand1 | operand2
operand1 ^= operand2	operand1 = operand1 ^ operand2

If both operands evaluate to `true`, &= returns `true`. Otherwise, it returns `false`.

```
boolean b = true;
b &= true;  // Assigns true to b
b &= false; // Assigns false to b
```

If either operand evaluates to `true`, |= returns `true`. Otherwise, it returns `false`.

```
boolean b = false;
b |= true;  // Assigns true to b
b |= false; // Assigns false to b
```

If both operands evaluate to different values, that is, one of the operands is `true` but not both, ^= returns `true`. Otherwise, it returns `false`.

```
boolean b = true;
b ^= true;  // Assigns false to b
b ^= false; // Assigns true to b
```

Ternary Operator (? :)

Java has one conditional operator. It is called a ternary operator. It takes three operands. It is used in the form:

```
boolean-expression ? true-expression : false-expression
```

Two symbols ? and : make the ternary operator. If the boolean-expression evaluates to true, it evaluates the true-expression; otherwise, it evaluates false-expression.

Suppose you have three integer variables num1, num2, and minNum. You want to assign minNum the minimum of num1 and num2. You can use ternary operator to accomplish this:

```
int num1 = 50;
int num2 = 25;

// Assigns num2 to minNum, because num2 is less than num1
int minNum = (num1 < num2 ? num1 : num2);
```

Bitwise Operators

A bitwise operator is an operator that performs an action on its integer operands using their bit patterns. Bitwise operators in Java are listed in Table 5-6.

Table 5-6. *List of Bitwise Operators*

Operators	Meaning	Type	Usage	Result
&	Bitwise AND	Binary	25 & 24	24
|	Bitwise OR	Binary	25 | 2	27
^	Bitwise XOR	Binary	25 ^ 2	27
~	Bitwise NOT (1's complement)	Unary	~25	-26
<<	Left shift	Binary	25 << 2	100
>>	Signed right shift	Binary	25 >> 2	6
>>>	Unsigned right shift	Binary	25 >>> 2	6
&=, !=, ^=, <<=, >>=, >>>=	Compound assignment bitwise operators	Binary		

All bitwise operators work with only integers. The bitwise AND (&) operator operates on corresponding bits of its two operands and returns 1 if both bits are 1, and 0 otherwise. Note that the bitwise AND (&) operates on each bit of the respective operands, not on the operands as a whole. Following is the result of all bit combination using the bitwise AND (&) operator.

```
1 & 1 = 1
1 & 0 = 0
0 & 1 = 0
0 & 0 = 0
```

Consider the following piece of code in Java.

```
int i = 13 & 3;
```

The value of 13 & 3 is computed as follows. The 32 bits have been shown in 8-bit chunks for clarity. In memory, all 32 bits are contiguous.

```
13          00000000 00000000 00000000 00001101
 3          00000000 00000000 00000000 00000011
----------------------------------------------
13 & 3 -    00000000 00000000 00000000 00000001 (Equal to decimal 1)
```

Therefore, 13 & 3 is 1, which is assigned to i in the previous piece of code.

The bitwise OR (|) operates on corresponding bits of its operands and returns 1 if either bit is 1, and 0 otherwise. The following is the result of all bit combination using the bitwise OR (|) operator.

```
1 | 1 = 1
1 | 0 = 1
0 | 1 = 1
0 | 0 = 0
```

The value of 13 | 3 can be computed as follows. The result of 13 | 3 is 15.

```
13          00000000 00000000 00000000 00001101
 3          00000000 00000000 00000000 00000011
----------------------------------------------
13 | 3      00000000 00000000 00000000 00001111 (Equal to decimal 15)
```

The bitwise XOR (^) operates on corresponding bits of its operands and returns 1 if only one of the bits is 1. Otherwise, it returns 0. The following is the result of all bit combinations using the bitwise XOR (^) operator.

```
1 ^ 1 = 0
1 ^ 0 = 1
0 ^ 1 = 1
0 ^ 0 = 0
```

The value of 13 ^ 3 can be computed as follows. The result of 13 ^ 3 is 14.

```
13          00000000 00000000 00000000 00001101
 3          00000000 00000000 00000000 00000011
----------------------------------------------
13 ^ 3      00000000 00000000 00000000 00001110 (Equal to decimal 14)
```

The bitwise NOT (~) operates on each bit of its operand. It inverts the bits, that is, 1 is changed to 0 and 0 is changed to 1. It is also called a *bitwise complement operator*. It computes 1's complement of its operand. Following is the result of all bit combinations using the bitwise NOT (~) operator.

```
~1 = 0
~0 = 1
```

The value of ~13 can be computed as follows. The result of ~13 is -14.

```
13      00000000 00000000 00000000 00001101
------------------------------------------
~13     11111111 11111111 11111111 11110010  (Equal to decimal -14)
```

The bitwise left shift operator (<<) shifts all the bits to the left by the number of bits specified as its right-hand operand. It inserts zeros at the lower order bits. The effect of shifting 1 bit to the right is the same as multiplying the number by 2. Therefore, 9 << 1 will produce 18, whereas 9 << 2 produces 36. The procedure to compute 13 << 4 is shown in Figure 5-1.

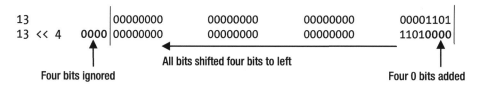

Figure 5-1. *Computing 13 << 4*

What is the result of 13 << 35? You might have guessed zero. However, this is not true. In fact, only 32 bits are used to represent 13, because 13 is considered as int literal and int occupies 32 bits. You can shift all bits to the left only by 31 bits in an int. If the left-hand operand of bitwise left shift operator (<<) is int, only five lower order bits' value of the right-hand operand is used as the number of bits to shift. For example, in 13 << 35, the right-hand operand (35) can be represented in binary as follows.

```
00000000000000000000000000100011
```

The five lower order bits in 35 is 00011, which is equal to 3. Therefore, when you write 13 << 35, it is equivalent to writing 13 << 3. For all positive right-hand operand of bitwise left shift operator, you can take modulus of the right-hand operand with 32, which would be the final number of bits to shift. Therefore, 13 << 35 can be considered as 13 << (35 % 32), which is the same as 13 << 3. If the left-hand operand is long, the first six lower order bits' value of the right-hand operand is used as the number of bits to shift.

```
long  val = 13;
long result;
result = val << 35;
```

Since val is a long, six lower order bits of 35, which is 100011, will be used as the number to shift. Figure 5-2 shows the steps used to compute 13 >> 4 and -13 >> 4.

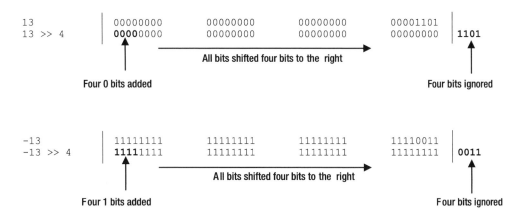

Figure 5-2. *Computing 13 >> 4 and -13 >> 4*

The bitwise signed right shift operator (>>) shifts all the bits to the right by the number specified as its right-hand operand. If the most significant digit of the left-hand operand is 1 (for negative numbers), all higher order bits are filled with 1s after the shift operation. If the most significant bit is 0 (for positive numbers), all higher order bits are filled with 0s. Because the sign bit after the right shift operation (>>) remains the same, it is called signed right shift operator. For example, 13 >> 4 results in zero, as depicted in Figure 5-2. Also note that in case of -13 >> 4, all four higher order bits are filled with 1s, because, in -13, the most significant digit is 1. The result of -13 >> 4 is -1.

The unsigned right shift operator (>>>) works the same way as the signed right shift operator (>>), except for one difference—it always fills the higher order bits with zero. The result of 13 >>> 4 is zero, whereas the result of -13 >>> 4 is 268435455 as shown. There is no unsigned left shift operator.

```
13        00000000 00000000 00000000  00001101
13 >>> 4  00000000 00000000 00000000  00000000 1101

-13        11111111 11111111 11111111  11110011
-13 >>> 4  00001111 11111111 11111111  11111111 0011
```

A compound bitwise assignment operator is used in the following form:

```
operand1 op= operand2
```

Here, op is one of the bitwise operators &, |, ^, <<, >>, and >>>. operand1 and operand2 are of primitive integral data type, where operand1 must be a variable. The previous expression is equivalent to the following one.

```
operand1 = (Type of operand1) (operand1 op operand2)
```

Assuming that there are two int variables: i and j, Table 5-7 lists the equivalent expressions for compound bitwise assignment operators.

Table 5-7. *List of Compound Bitwise Assignment Operators*

Expression	Is Equivalent To
i &= j	i = i & j
i |= j	i = i | j
i ^= j	i = i ^ j
i <<= j	i = i << j
i >>= j	i = i >> j
i >>>= j	i = i >>> j

Operators Precedence

Consider the following piece of code.

```
int result;

// What will be the value assigned to result?
result = 10 + 8 / 2;
```

What will be the value assigned to the variable result after the last statement is executed? Will it be 9 or 14? It depends on the operation that is done first. It will be 9 if the addition 10 + 8 is performed first. It will be 14 if the division 8/2 is performed first. All expressions in Java are evaluated according to operator precedence hierarchy, which establishes the rules that govern the order in which expressions are evaluated. Operators with higher precedence are evaluated before the operators with lower precedence. If operators have the same precedence, the expression is evaluated from left to right. Multiplication, division and remainder operators have higher precedence than addition and subtraction operators. Therefore, in the previous expression, 8/2 is evaluated first, which reduces the expression to 10 + 4, which in turn results in 14. Consider another expression:

```
result = 10 * 5 / 2;
```

The expression, 10 * 5 / 2, uses two operators: a multiplication operator and a division operator. Both operators have the same precedence. The expression is evaluated from left to right. First, the expression 10 * 5 is evaluated, and then the expression 50 / 2 is evaluated. The whole expression evaluates to 25. If you wanted to perform division first, you must use parentheses. Parentheses have the highest precedence, and therefore, the expression within parentheses is evaluated first. You can rewrite the previous piece of code using parentheses:

```
result = 10 * (5 / 2); // Assigns 20 to result. Why?
```

You can also use nested parentheses. In nested parentheses, the innermost parentheses' expression is evaluated first. Table 5-8 lists Java operators in their precedence order. Operators in the same level have the same precedence. Table 5-8 lists some of the operators I have not discussed yet. I discuss them later in this chapter or in other chapters. In the table, a lower value in the level column indicates a higher precedence.

Table 5-8. *Java Operators and Their Precedence*

Level	Operator Symbol	Action Performed
1	++	Pre-or-post increment
	--	Pre-or-post decrement
	+, -	Unary plus, unary minus
	~	Bitwise complement
	!	Logical NOT
	(type)	Cast
2	*, /, %	Multiplication, division, remainder
3	+, -	Addition, subtraction
	+	String concatenation
4	<<	Left shift
	>>	Signed right shift
	>>>	Unsigned right shift
5	<	Less than
	<=	Less than or equal
	>	Greater than
	>=	Greater than or equal
	instanceof	Type comparison
6	==	Equal in value
	!=	Not equal to
7	&	Bitwise AND
	&	Logical AND
8	^	Bitwise XOR
	^	Logical XOR
9	|	Bitwise OR
	|	Logical OR
10	&&	Logical short-circuit AND
11	||	Logical short-circuit OR
12	?:	Ternary operator
13	=	Assignment
	+=, -=, *=, /=, %=, <<=, >>=, >>>=, &=, |=, ^=	Compound assignment

Summary

An operator is a symbol that is used to perform some type of computation on its operands. Java contains a rich set of operators. Operators are categorized as unary, binary, or ternary based on the number of operands they take. They are categorized as arithmetic, relational, logical, and bitwise based on the operands types and the operation they perform on their operands.

An arithmetic operator is an operator that takes numeric values as its operands and performs an arithmetic operation, for example, addition and subtraction, to compute another numeric value. A few examples of arithmetic operators in Java are +, -, *, and /.

In Java, the + operator is overloaded. When one of its operands is a String, it performs a string concatenation. For example, an expression 50 + " States" produces another string, "50 States".

A relational operator compares values of its operands returning a boolean value—true or false. A few examples of relational operators are ==, !=, >, >=, <, and <=.

A boolean logical operator takes boolean operands, applies a boolean logic to them, and produces a boolean value. A few examples of boolean logical operators in Java are &&, ||, and &.

Java supports a ternary operator (?:), which takes three operands. It is also known as conditional operator. If the first operand evaluates to true, the second operand is evaluated and returned; otherwise, the third operand is evaluated and returned.

A bitwise operator is an operator that performs an action on its integer operands using their bit patterns. A few examples of bitwise operators in Java are & and |.

An operator is called overloaded if it can be used in multiple contexts to perform different types of computations. Java contains a + operator that is overloaded. It is used as an arithmetic addition operator as well as a string concatenation operator. Unlike C++, Java does not let developers overload operators.

Every operator in Java has a precedence order with respect to other operators. If multiple operators appear in a single expression, the operands of operators with higher precedence are evaluated before the operands of operators with lower precedence.

EXERCISES

1. What is an operator? What are unary, binary, and ternary operator? Give an example of each type of operator in Java.

2. What is the difference between prefix, postfix, and infix operators? Give an example of such operators in Java.

3. What are arithmetic operators, what types of operands do they take, and what type of results do they produce?

4. Name two operators in Java that take only boolean operands and produce a boolean value.

5. What is the difference between the two operators: = and ==?

6. Consider the following snippet of code:

```
boolean done;
/* Some code goes here */
your-code-goes-here;
```

Using a `boolean` logical operator, invert the current value stored in the done variable. That is, write a statement that will assign `true` to the done variable if its current value is `false` and `false` if its current value is `true`.

7. Consider the following snippet of code:

```
int x = 23;
int y = ++x % 3;
```

What will be the value of y after this snippet of code is executed?

8. Consider the following snippet of code:

```
int x = 23;
x = x++ % x;
```

What will be the value of x after this snippet of code is executed? Explain your answer with steps performed explaining how the value of x changes during the execution of the second statement.

9. Explain why the following snippet of code does not compile.

```
int x = 10;
boolean yes = (x = 20);
```

10. What will be the value assigned to the variable named yes when the following snippet of code is executed:

```
int x = 10;
boolean yes = (x == 20);
```

11. What will be the value of y when the following snippet of code is executed:

```
int x = 19;
int y = x > 10 ? 69 : 68;
```

12. You have a short variable named x, which is declared and initialized as follows:

```
short x = -19;
```

You want to assign 19 to x using the following statements, both of which do not compile:

```
x = -x;
x = -1 * x;
```

How will you rewrite these two statements to make them compile? What is wrong with the following statement that attempts to fix the compile-time error in these statements, but fails to assign 19 to x?

```
x -= x;
```

13. What will be the output when the following snippet of code is executed:

```
boolean b = true;
String str = !b +" is not " + b;
System.out.println(str);
```

14. What will be the output when the following snippet of code is executed:

```
boolean b = true;
String str = (b ^= b) + " is " + b;
System.out.println(str);
```

15. What will be the output when you execute the following snippet of code:

```
int x = 10;
int y = x++;
int z = ++x;
System.out.println("x = " + x + ", y = " + y + ", z = " + z);
```

16. Complete the second statement using the ternary operator (?:) and the bitwise AND operator (&) that will make a message "x is odd". Your code must contain of the following tokens in any order: x, &,==, ?, :, "odd", and "even". You may use additional tokens as needed.

```
int x = 19;
String msg = your-code-goes-here ;
System.out.println("x is " + msg);
```

17. Which of the following assignments will fail to compile and why?

```
int i1 = 100;
int i2 = 10.6;
byte b1 = 90;
byte b2 = 3L;
short s1 = -90;
float f1 = 12.67;
float f2 = 0.00f;
double d1 = 12.56;
double d2 = 12.78d;
boolean bn1 = true;
boolean bn2 = 0;
char c1 = 'A';
char c2 = "A";
char c3 = 0;
char c4 = '\u0000';
```

18. Write down the value assigned to the declared variable in each of the following statements. If a statement generates a compile-time error, explain the reason behind the error and, if possible, provide a solution to fix the error.

```
int i1 = 10/4;
int i2 = 10.0/4.0;
int i3 = 0/0;
long l1 = 10/4;
long l2 = 10.0/4.0;
float f1 = 10/4;
float f2 = 10.0/4.0;
double d1 = 10/4;
double d2 = 10.0/4.0;
double d3 = 0/0;
double d4 = 0/0.0;
double d5 = 2.9/0.0;
```

19. Complete the following snippet of code that will assign a 2's complement of x to y. You must use the bitwise operator.

```
int x = 19;
int y = your-code-goes-here;
```

20. What will be the output of the following snippet of code:

```
int x = 19;
int y = (~x + 1) + x;
System.out.println(y);
```

CHAPTER 6

Statements

In this chapter, you will learn:

- What statements are

- What declaration statements are

- What expressions in Java are and how to convert them into expression statements

- What a block statement is and what the scope of variables declared inside a block is

- What control-flow statements are and how to use if-else, for-loop, while-loop, and do-while loop statements

- How to use the break statement to exit a loop or a block

- How to use the continue statement to ignore the rest of the body of a loop statement and continue the next iteration

- What an empty statement is and where to use it

All examples in this chapter are in the jdojo.statement module, whose declaration is shown in Listing 6-1.

Listing 6-1. The Declaration of a Module Named jdojo.statement

```
// module-info.java
module jdojo.statememnt {
    // No module statements
}
```

What Is a Statement?

A statement specifies an action in a Java program, such as assigning the sum of x and y to z, printing a message to the standard output, writing data to a file, looping through a list of values, conditionally executing a piece of code, etc. Statements are written using keywords, operators, and expressions.

Types of Statements

Depending on the action performed by a statement, statements in Java can be broadly classified into three categories:

- Declaration statements

- Expression statements

- Control flow statements

Subsequent sections describe all statement types in detail.

Declaration Statement

A declaration statement is used to declare a variable. You have already been using this type of statement. The following are a few examples of declaration statements in Java:

```
int num;
int num2 = 100;
String str;
```

Expression Statement

Expressions in Java consist of literals, variables, operators, and method invocation and they are the building blocks of a Java program. An expression is evaluated and the evaluation may produce a variable, a value, or nothing. An expression always has a type, which many be void if it is a method invocation to a method whose return type is void. The following are a few examples of expressions in Java:

- `19 + 69`

- `num + 2`

- `num++`

- `System.out.println("Hello")`

- `new String("Hello")`

An expression with a semicolon at the end is called an *expression statement*. However, not all Java expressions can be converted to expression statements by appending a semicolon to them. Assuming x and y as two int variables, the following is an arithmetic expression that evaluates to an int value:

```
x + y
```

However, the following is not a valid expression statement in Java:

```
x + y;
```

Allowing a statement like this does not make sense. It adds the values of x and y and does nothing with the value. Only the following four kinds of expressions can be converted to expression statements by appending a semicolon to them:

- Increment and decrement expressions

- Assignment expressions

- Object creation expressions

- Method invocation expressions

A few examples of increment and decrement expression statements are as follows:

```
num++;
++num;
num--;
--num;
```

A few examples of assignment expression statements are as follows:

```
num = 100;
num *= 10;
```

An example of an object creation expression statement is as follows:

```
new String("This is a text");
```

Note that this statement creates a new object of the String class. However, the new object's reference is not stored in any reference variable. Therefore, this statement is not very useful. In some cases, however, you can use such an object creation statement in a useful way, for example, JDBC drivers register themselves with the driver manager when the driver class is loaded and one way to load the driver class is to create its object and discard the created object.

You invoke the method println() to print a message on the console. When you use the println() method without a semicolon at the end, it is an expression. When you add a semicolon to the end of the method call, it becomes a statement. The following is an example of a method invocation expression statement:

```
System.out.println("This is a statement");
```

Control Flow Statement

By default, all statements in a Java program are executed in the order they appear in the program. However, you can change the order of execution using control flow statements. Sometimes you may want to execute a statement or a set of statements only if a particular condition is true. Sometimes you may want to execute a set of statements repeatedly for a number of times or as long as a particular condition is true. All of these are possible in Java using control flow statements; the if and for statements are examples of control flow statements. I discuss control flow statements shortly.

A Block Statement

A block statement is a sequence of zero or more statements enclosed in braces. A block statement is generally used to group together several statements, so they can be used in a situation that requires you to use a single statement. In some situations, you can use only one statement. If you want to use more than one statement in those situations, you can create a block statement by placing all your statements inside braces, which would be treated as a single statement. You can think of a block statement as a compound statement that is treated as one statement. The following are examples of block statements:

```
{ /* Start of a block statement. A block statement starts with { */
    int num1 = 20;
    num1++;

} /* End of the block statement. A block statement ends with } */

{
  // Another valid block statement with no statements inside
}
```

All the variables declared in a block statement can only be used within that block. In other words, you can say that all variables declared in a block have local scope. Consider the following snippet of code:

```
// Declare a variable num1
int num1;

{ // Start of a block statement
    // Declares a variable num2, which is a local variable for this block
    int num2;

    // num2 is local to this block, so it can be used here
    num2 = 200;

    // We can use num1 here because it is declared outside and before this block
    num1 = 100;
} // End of the block statement

// A compile-time error. num2 has been declared inside a block and
// so it cannot be used outside that block
num2 = 50;
```

You can also nest a block statement inside another block statement. All the variables declared in the enclosing blocks (outer blocks) are available to the enclosed blocks (inner blocks). However, the variables declared in the enclosed inner blocks are not available in enclosing outer blocks. For example,

```
// Start of the outer block
{
    int num1 = 10;

    // Start of the inner block
    {
```

```
        // num1 is available here because we are in an inner block
        num1 = 100;
        int num2 = 200; // Declared inside the inner block
        num2 = 678;     // OK. num2 is local to inner block
    }
    // End of the inner block

    // A compile-time error. num2 is local to the inner block.
    // So, it cannot be used outside the inner block.
    num2 = 200;
}
// End of the outer block
```

One important point to remember about nested block statements is that you cannot define a variable with the same name inside an inner block if a variable with the same name has already been defined in the outer block. This is because the variables declared in the outer block can always be used inside the inner block and if you declare a variable with the same name inside the inner block, there is no way for Java to differentiate between these two variables inside the inner block. The following snippet of code won't compile:

```
int num1 = 10;
{
    // A Compile-time error. num1 is already in scope. Cannot redeclare num1
    float num1 = 10.5F;

    float num2 = 12.98F; // OK

    {
        // A compile-time error. num2 is already in scope.
        // You can use num2 already defined in the outer
        // block, but cannot redeclare it.
        float num2;
    }
}
```

The if-else Statement

The format of an if-else statement is as follows:

```
if (condition)
    statement1
else
    statement2
```

The condition must be a boolean expression. That is, it must evaluate to true or false. If the condition evaluates to true, statement1 is executed. Otherwise, statement2 is executed. The flow diagram for an if-else statement is shown in Figure 6-1.

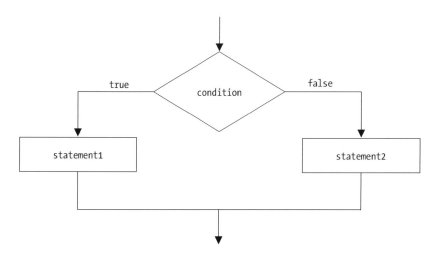

Figure 6-1. *The flow diagram for an if-else statement*

The else part in an if-else statement is optional. If the else part is missing, the statement, sometimes, is simply called an if statement. You may write an if statement as follows:

```
if (condition)
    statement
```

The flow diagram for an if statement is shown in Figure 6-2.

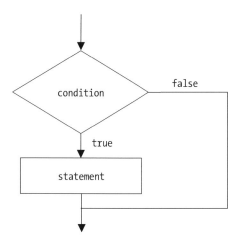

Figure 6-2. *The flow diagram for an if statement*

Suppose there are two int variables named num1 and num2. Suppose you want to add 10 to num2 if num1 is greater than 50. Otherwise, you want to subtract 10 from num2. You can write this logic using an if-else statement:

```
if (num1 > 50)
    num2 = num2 + 10;
else
    num2 = num2 - 10;
```

Suppose you have three int variables named num1, num2, and num3. You want to add 10 to num2 and num3 if num1 is greater than 50. Otherwise, you want to subtract 10 from num2 and num3. You may try the following snippet of code, which is incorrect:

```
if (num1 > 50)
    num2 = num2 + 10;
    num3 = num3 + 10;
else
    num2 = num2 - 10;
    num3 = num3 - 10;
```

This code generates a compile-time error. What is wrong with this code? You can place only one statement between if and else in an if-else statement. This is the reason that the statement num3 = num3 + 10; caused a compile-time error. In fact, you can always associate only one statement with the if part in an if-else statement or in a simple if statement. This is also true for the else part. In this example, only num2 = num2 - 10; is associated with the else part; the last statement, num3 = num3 - 10;, is not associated with the else part. You want to execute two statements when num1 is greater than 50 or not. In this case, you need to bundle two statements into one block statement, like so:

```
if (num1 > 50) {
    num2 = num2 + 10;
    num3 = num3 + 10;
} else {
    num2 = num2 - 10;
    num3 = num3 - 10;
}
```

The if-else statement can be nested, as shown:

```
if (num1 > 50) {
    if (num2 < 30) {
        num3 = num3 + 130;
    } else {
        num3 = num3 - 130;
    }
} else {
    num3 = num3 = 200;
}
```

Sometimes, it is confusing to determine which else goes with which if in nested if-else statements. Consider the following piece of code:

```
int i = 10;
int j = 15;

if (i > 15)
if (j == 15)
    System.out.println("Thanks");
else
    System.out.println("Sorry");
```

What will be the output of this snippet of code? Will it print "Thanks" or "Sorry" or does not print anything? If you guessed that it would not print anything, you already understand if-else association.

You can apply a simple rule to figure out which else goes with which if in an if-else statement. Start with the else and move up. If you do not find any other else statements, the first if you find goes with the else you started with. If you find one else in moving up before you find any if, the second if goes with the else you started with, and so on. In this example, starting with else, the first if you find is if (j == 15) and so the else goes with this if. The previous piece of code can be rewritten using indentation and block statements as follows:

```
int i = 10;
int j = 15;

if (i > 15) {
    if (j == 15) {
        System.out.println("Thanks");
    } else {
        System.out.println("Sorry");
    }
}
```

Because i is equal to 10, the expression i > 15 will return false and hence the control would not enter the if statement at all. Therefore, there would not be any output.

Note that the condition expression in an if statement must be of the boolean type. Therefore, if you want to compare two int variables, i and j, for equality, your if statement must look like the following:

```
if (i == j)
    statement
```

You cannot write an if statement like this:

```
if (i = 5) /* A compile-time error */
    statement
```

This if statement will not compile because i = 5 is an assignment expression and it evaluates to an int value 5. The condition expression must return a boolean value: true or false. Therefore, an assignment expression cannot be used as a condition expression in an if statement, except when you are assigning a boolean value to a boolean variable, like so:

```
boolean b;
if (b = true) /* Always returns true */
    statement
```

Here, the assignment expression b = true always returns true after assigning true to b. In this case, the use of the assignment expression in the if statement is allowed because the data type of expression b = true is boolean.

You can use the ternary operator in place of simple if-else statement. Suppose, if a person is male, you want to set the title to Mr. and if not, to Ms. You can accomplish this using an if-else statement and also using a ternary operator, like so:

```
String title;
boolean isMale = true;

// Using an if-else statement
if (isMale)
    title = "Mr.";
else
    title = "Ms.";

// Using a ternary operator
title = (isMale ? "Mr." : "Ms.");
```

You can see the difference in using the if-else statement and the ternary operator. The code is compact using the ternary operator. However, you cannot use a ternary operator to replace all if-else statements. You can use the ternary operator in place of the if-else statement only when the if and else parts in the if-else statement contain only one statement and both statements return the same type of values. Because the ternary operator is an operator, it can be used in expressions. Suppose you want to assign the minimum of i and j to k. You can do this in the following declaration statement of the variable k:

```
int i = 10;
int j = 20;
int k = (i < j ? i : j); // Using a ternary operator in initialization
```

The same can be achieved using an if-else statement, as shown:

```
int i = 10;
int j = 20;
int k;

if (i < j)
    k = i;
else
    k = j;
```

Another difference in using a ternary operator and an if-else statement is that you can use an expression, which uses a ternary operator as an argument to a method. However, you cannot use an if-else statement as an argument to a method. Suppose you have a calc() method that accepts an int as an argument. You have two integers, num1 and num2. If you want to pass the minimum of the two integers to the calc() method, you would write the code as shown:

```
// Use an if-else statement
if (num1 < num2)
    calc(num1);
else
    calc(num2);

// Use a ternary operator
calc(num1 < num2 ? num1 : num2);
```

Suppose you want to print the message "k is 15" if the value of an int variable k is equal to 15. Otherwise, you want to print the message "k is not 15". You can print the message using a ternary operator and writing one line of code as follows:

```
System.out.println(k == 15 ? "k is 15" : "k is not 15");
```

The switch Statement

The general form of a switch statement is

```
switch (switch-expression) {
    case label1:
        statements

    case label2:
        statements

    case label3:
        statements

    default:
        statements
}
```

The switch-expression must evaluate to a type: byte, short, char, int, enum, or String. Refer to Chapter 22 on enums for details on how to use an enum type in a switch statement. Refer to Chapter 15 on strings for details on how to use strings in a switch statement. The label1, label2, etc. are compile-time constant expressions whose values must be in the range of the type of the switch-expression. A switch statement is evaluated as follows:

- The switch-expression is evaluated.

- If the value of the switch-expression matches a case label, the execution starts from the matched case label and executes all statements until the end of the switch statement.

- If the value of the switch-expression does not match a case label, execution starts at the statement following the optional default label and continues until the end of the switch statement.

The following snippet of code is an example of using a switch statement:

```
int i = 10;
switch (i) {
```

```
    case 10: // Found the match
        System.out.println("Ten"); // Execution starts here
    case 20:
        System.out.println("Twenty"); // Also executes this statement
    default:
        System.out.println ("No-match"); // Also executes this statement
}
```

```
Ten
Twenty
No-match
```

The value of i is 10. The execution starts at the first statement following case 10: and falls through case 20: and default labels executing the statements under these labels. If you change the value of i to 50, there would not be any match in case labels and the execution would start at the first statement after the default label, which will print "No-match". The following example illustrates this logic:

```
int i = 50;
switch (i) {
    case 10:
        System.out.println("Ten");
    case 20:
        System.out.println("Twenty");
    default:
        System.out.println("No-match"); // Execution starts here
}
```

```
No-match
```

The default label does not have to be the last label to appear in a switch statement and is optional. The following is an example of a default label, which is not the last label:

```
int i = 50;
switch (i) {
    case 10:
        System.out.println("Ten");
    default:
        System.out.println("No-match"); // Execution starts here
    case 20:
        System.out.println("Twenty");
}
```

```
No-match
Twenty
```

Because the value of i is 50, which does not match any of the case labels, the execution starts at the first statement after the default label. The control falls through the subsequent label case 20: and executes the statement following this case label, which prints Twenty. Generally, you want to print Ten if the value of i is 10 and Twenty if the value of i is 20. If the value of i is not 10 or 20, you want to print No-match. This is possible using a break statement inside the switch statement. When a break statement is executed inside a switch statement, the control is transferred outside the switch statement. The following is an example of using break statements inside a switch statement:

```
int i = 10;
switch (i) {
    case 10:
        System.out.println("Ten");
        break; // Transfers control outside the switch statement
    case 20:
        System.out.println("Twenty");
        break; // Transfers control outside the switch statement
    default:
        System.out.println("No-match");
        break; // Transfers control outside the switch statement. It is not necessary.
}
```

Ten

Note the use of the break statement in the previous snippet of code. In fact, the execution of a break statement inside a switch statement stops the execution of the switch statement and transfers control to the first statement, if any, following the switch statement. In the previous snippet of code, the use of a break statement inside the default label is not necessary because the default label is the last label in the switch statement and the execution of the switch statement will stop after that anyway. However, I recommend using a break statement even inside the last label to avoid errors if additional labels are added later.

The value of the constant expressions used as the case labels must be in the range of the data type of switch-expression. Keeping in mind that the range of the byte data type in Java is -128 to 127, the following code would not compile because the second case label is 150, which is outside the range of the byte data type:

```
byte b = 10;
switch (b) {
    case 5:
        b++;
    case 150: // A compile-time error. 150 is outside the range -128 to 127
        b--;
    default:
        b = 0;
}
```

Two case labels in a switch statement cannot be the same. The following piece of code would not compile because the case label 10 is repeated:

```
int num = 10;
switch (num) {
    case 10:
        num++;
    case 10: // A compile-time error. Duplicate label 10
        num--;
```

```
    default:
        num = 100;
}
```

It is important to note that the label for each `case` in a `switch` statement must be a compile-time constant. That is, the value of the labels must be known at compile-time. Otherwise, a compile-time error occurs. For example, the following code would not compile:

```
int num1 = 10;
int num2 = 10;
switch (num1) {
    case 20:
        System.out.println("num1 is 20");
    case num2: // A Compile-time error. num2 is a variable and cannot be used as a label
        System.out.println("num1 is 10");
}
```

You might say that you know the value of num2 is 10 when the `switch` statement will be executed. However, all variables are evaluated at runtime. The values of variables are not known at compile-time. Therefore, the `case num2:` causes the compiler error. This is necessary because Java makes sure at compile-time itself that all `case` labels are within the range of the data type of the `switch-expression`. If they are not, the statements following those case labels will never get executed at runtime.

▓ **Tip**   The `default` label is optional. There can be at most one `default` label in a `switch` statement.

A `switch` statement is a clearer way of writing an `if-else` statement when the condition-expression in an `if-else` statement compares the value of the same variable for equality. For example, the following `if-else` and `switch` statements accomplish the same thing:

```
// Using an if-else statement
if (i == 10)
    System.out.println("i is 10");
else if (i == 20)
    System.out.println("i is 20");
else
    System.out.println("i is neither 10 nor 20");

// Using a switch statement
switch (i) {
    case 10:
        System.out.println("i is 10");
        break;
    case 20:
        System.out.println("i is 20");
        break;
    default:
        System.out.println("i is neither 10 nor 20");
}
```

The for Statement

A for statement is an iteration statement, which is used to loop through a statement a number of times based on some conditions. It is also called a for-loop statement or simply a for loop. The general form of a for-loop statement is

```
for (initialization; condition-expression; expression-list)
    statement
```

The initialization, condition-expression, and expression-list are separated by semicolons. A for-loop statement consists of four parts:

- Initialization

- Condition-expression

- Statement

- Expression-list

First, the initialization part is executed; then, the condition-expression is evaluated. If the condition-expression evaluates to true, the statement associated with the for-loop statement is executed. After that, all expressions in the expression-list are evaluated. The condition-expression is evaluated again, and if it evaluates to true, the statement associated with the for-loop statement is executed and then the expression-list, and so on. This loop of execution is repeated until the condition-expression evaluates to false. Figure 6-3 shows the flow diagram for a for-loop statement.

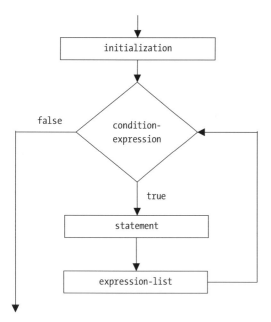

Figure 6-3. *The flow diagram for a for-loop statement*

For example, the following for-loop statement will print all integers between 1 and 10, inclusive:

```
for(int num = 1; num <= 10; num++)
    System.out.println(num);
```

First, int num = 1 is executed, which declares an int variable named num and initializes it to 1. It is important to note that variables declared in the initialization part of the for-loop statement can only be used within that for-loop statement. Then, condition-expression num <= 10 is evaluated, which is 1 <= 10; it evaluates to true for the first time. Now, the statement associated with the for-loop statement is executed, which prints the current value of num. Finally, the expression in the expression-list, num++, is evaluated, which increments the value of num by 1. At this point, the value of num becomes 2. The condition-expression 2 <= 10 is evaluated, which returns true, and the current value of num is printed. This process continues until the value of num becomes 10 and it is printed. After that, num++ sets the value of num to 11, and the condition-expression 11 <= 10 returns false, which stops the execution of the for-loop statement.

All three parts (initialization, condition-expression, and expression-list) in a for-loop statement are optional. Note that the fourth part, the statement, is not optional. Therefore, if you do not have a statement to execute in a for-loop statement, you must use an empty block statement or a semicolon in place of a statement. A semicolon that is treated as a statement is called an *empty statement* or a *null statement*. An infinite loop using a for-loop statement can be written as follows:

```
for( ; ; ) {
    // An infinite loop
}
```

The previous for-loop statement can be rewritten using an empty statement, which is a semicolon, as follows:

```
// An infinite loop. Note a semicolon as a statement
for( ; ; );
```

A detailed discussion of each part of a for-loop statement follows.

Initialization

The initialization part of a for-loop statement can have a variable declaration statement, which may declare one or more variables of the same type, or it can have a list of expression statements separated by a comma. Note that the statements used in the initialization part do not end with a semicolon. The following snippet of code shows the initialization part in a for-loop statement:

```
// Declares two variables i and j of the same type int
for(int i = 10, j = 20; ; );

// Declares one double variable salary
for(double salary = 3455.78F; ; );

// Attempts to declare two variables of different types
for(int i = 10, double d1 = 20.5; ; ); /* A compile-time error */

// Uses an expression i++
int i = 100;
for(i++; ; ); // OK
```

```
// Uses an expression to print a message on the console
for(System.out.println("Hello"); ; );   // OK

// Uses two expressions: to print a message and to increment num
int num = 100;
for(System.out.println("Hello"), num++; ; );
```

▓ **Tip**   The initialization part of a for loop is executed only once when the for loop is executed.

You can declare a new variable in the initialization part of a for-loop statement. However, you cannot re-declare a variable that is already in scope.

```
int i = 10;
for (int i = 0; ; ); // An error. Cannot re-declare i
```

You can reinitialize the variable i in the for-loop statement, as shown:

```
int i = 10; // Initialize i to 10
i = 500;    // Value of i changes here to 500

/* Other statements go here... */

for (i = 0; ; ); // Reinitialize i to zero inside the for-loop loop
```

Condition-Expression

The condition-expression must evaluate to a boolean value of true or false. Otherwise, a compile-time error occurs. The condition-expression is optional. If it is omitted, a boolean value of true is assumed as a condition-expression, which results in an infinite loop unless a break statement is used to stop the loop. The following two for-loop statements result in infinite loops and they are the same:

```
// An infinite loop - Implicitly condition-expression is true
for( ; ; );

// An infinite loop - An explicit true is used as the condition-expression
for( ; true; );
```

A break statement is used to stop the execution of a for-loop statement. When a break statement is executed, the control is transferred to the next statement, if any, after the for-loop statement. You can rewrite the for-loop statement to print all integers between 1 and 10 using a break statement.

```
// A for-loop with no condition-expression
for(int num = 1;  ; num++) {
    System.out.println(num); // Print the number

    if (num == 10) {
        break; // Break out of loop when i is 10
    }
}
```

This for-loop statement prints the same integers as the previous for-loop statement did. However, the latter is not recommended because you are using a break statement instead of using the condition-expression to break out of the loop. It is good programming practice to use a condition-expression to break out of a for loop, whenever possible.

Expression-List

The expression-list part is optional. It may contain one or more expressions separated by a comma. You can use only expressions that can be converted to a statement by appending a semicolon at the end. Refer to the discussion on the expression statement at the beginning of this chapter for more details. You can rewrite the same example of printing all integers between 1 and 10 as follows:

```
for(int num = 1; num <= 10; System.out.println(num), num++);
```

Note that this for-loop statement uses two expressions in the expression-list, which are separated by a comma. A for-loop statement gives you more power to write compact code.

You can rewrite the previous for-loop statement as follows to make it more compact and accomplish the same task:

```
for(int num = 1; num <= 10; System.out.println(num++));
```

Note that you combined the two expressions in the expression-list into one. You used num++ as the argument to the println() method, so it prints the value of num first, and then increments its value by 1. Can you predict the output of the previous for-loop statement if you replace num++ with ++num?

You can also use nested for-loop statements, that is, for-loop statements inside another for-loop statement. Suppose you want to print a 3x3 (read as three by three) matrix as follows:

```
11      12      13
21      22      23
31      32      33
```

The code to print the 3x3 matrix can be written as follows:

```
// Outer for-loop statement
for(int i = 1; i <= 3; i++) {
    // Inner for-loop statement
    for(int j = 1; j <= 3; j++) {
        System.out.print(i + "" + j);

        // Prints a tab after each column value
        System.out.print("\t");
    }

    System.out.println(); // Prints a new line
}
```

The previous piece of code can be explained using the following steps.

1. The execution starts in the initialization part (int i = 1) of the outer for-loop statement, where i is initialized to 1.

2. The condition-expression for the outer for-loop statement (i <= 3) is evaluated for i equal to 1, which is true.

3. The statement part of the outer for loop starts with an inner for-loop statement.

4. Now j is initialized to 1.

5. The condition-expression for the inner for-loop statement (j <= 3) is evaluated for j equal to 1, which is true.

6. The block statement associated with the inner for-loop statement is executed, which prints 11 and a tab.

7. The expression-list of the inner for-loop statement (j++) is executed, which increments the value of j to 2.

8. The condition expression for the inner for-loop statement (j <= 3) is evaluated for j equal to 2, which is true.

9. The block statement associated with the inner for-loop statement is executed, which prints 12 and a tab. At this stage, the printed text looks like this:

    11   12

10. The expression-list of the inner for-loop statement (j++) is executed, which increments the value of j to 3.

11. The condition-expression for the inner for-loop statement (j <= 3) is evaluated for j equal to 3, which is true.

12. The block statement associated with the inner for-loop statement is executed, which prints 13 and a tab. At this stage the printed text looks like this:

    11   12   13

13. The expression-list of the inner for-loop statement (j++) is executed, which increments the value of j to 4.

14. The condition expression for the inner for-loop statement (j <= 3) is evaluated for j equal to 4, which is false. At this point, the inner for loop is finished.

15. The last statement of the block statement for the outer for-loop statement, which is System.out.println(), is executed. It prints a system-dependent line separator.

16. The expression-list of the outer for-loop statement (i++) is executed, which increments the value of i to 2.

17. Now, the inner for-loop statement is started afresh with the value of i equal to 2. This sequence of steps is also executed for i equal to 3. When i becomes 4, the outer for-loop statement exits, and at this point, the printed matrix will look like this:

    11 12 13

    21 22 23

    31 32 33

Note that this snippet of code also prints a tab character at the end of every row and a new line after the last row, which are not necessary. One important point to note is that the variable j is created every time the inner for-loop statement is started and it is destroyed when the inner for-loop statement exits. Therefore, the variable j is created and destroyed three times. You cannot use the variable j outside the inner for-loop statement because it has been declared inside the inner for-loop statement and its scope is local to that inner for-loop statement. Listing 6-2 contains the complete code for the discussion in this section. The program makes sure not to print extra tabs and new line characters.

Listing 6-2. Using a for Loop to Print a 3x3 Matrix

```java
// PrintMatrix.java
package com.jdojo.statement;

public class PrintMatrix {
    public static void main(String[] args) {
        for (int i = 1; i <= 3; i++) {
            for (int j = 1; j <= 3; j++) {
                System.out.print(i + "" + j);

                // Print a tab, except for the last number in a row
                if (j < 3) {
                    System.out.print("\t");
                }
            }

            // Print a new line, except after the last line
            if (i < 3) {
                System.out.println();
            }
        }
    }
}
```

```
11      12      13
21      22      23
31      32      33
```

The for-each Statement

Java 5 introduced an enhanced for loop, which is called a for-each loop. It is used for iterating over elements of arrays and collections. This section is included here to complete the list of statements that lets you loop through a collections of values. Refer to the chapters on arrays and collections for a detailed explanation of the for-each loop. The general syntax for a for-each loop is as follows:

```java
for(Type element : a_collection_or_an_array) {
    // This code will be executed once for each element in
    // the collection/array.
    // Each time this code is executed, the element
    // variable holds the reference
    // of the current element in the collection/array
}
```

The following snippet of code prints all elements of an `int` array `numList`:

```
// Create an array with 4 elements
int[] numList = {10, 20, 30, 40};

// Print each element of the array in a separate line
for(int num : numList) {
    System.out.println(num);
}
```

```
10
20
30
40
```

The while Statement

A while statement is another iteration (or loop) statement, which is used to execute a statement repeatedly as long as a condition is true. A while statement is also known as a while-loop statement. The general form of a while-loop statement is

```
while (condition-expression)
    statement
```

The condition-expression must be a `boolean` expression and the statement can be a simple statement or a block statement. The condition-expression is evaluated first. If it returns `true`, the statement is executed. Again, the condition-expression is evaluated. If it returns `true`, the statement is executed. This loop continues until the condition-expression returns `false`. Figure 6-4 shows the flow diagram for a while statement.

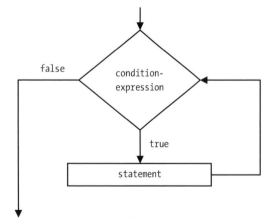

Figure 6-4. *The flow diagram for a while statement*

Unlike the for-loop statement, the condition-expression in a while-loop statement is not optional. For example, to make a while statement an infinite loop, you need to use the boolean literal true as the condition-expression.

```
while (true)
    System.out.println ("This is an infinite loop");
```

In general, a for-loop statement can be converted to a while-loop statement. However, not all for-loop statements can be converted to while-loop statements. The conversion between a for-loop and a while-loop statement is shown here:

```
// A for-loop statement
for (initialization; condition-expression; expression-list)
    statement

// Equivalent while-loop Statements
initialization
while (condition-expression) {
    statement
    expression-list
}
```

You can print all integers between 1 and 10 using a while-loop as shown:

```
int i = 1;
while (i <= 10) {
    System.out.println(i);
    i++;
}
```

This while-loop can be rewritten in three different ways as follows:

```
// #1
int i = 0;
while (++i <= 10) {
    System.out.println(i);
}

// #2
int i = 1;
while (i <= 10) {
    System.out.println(i++);
}

// #3
int i = 1;
while (i <= 10) {
    System.out.println(i);
    i++;
}
```

A break statement is used to exit the loop in a while-loop statement. You can rewrite the previous example using a break statement as follows. Note that the following piece of code is written only to illustrate the use of a break statement in a while-loop; it is not a good example of using a break statement.

```
int i = 1;
while (true) { /* Cannot exit the loop from here because it is true */
    if (i <= 10) {
        System.out.println(i);
        i++;
    } else {
        break; // Exit the loop
    }
}
```

The do-while Statement

The do-while statement is another loop statement. It is similar to the while-loop statement with one difference. The statement associated with a while loop statement may not be executed even once if the condition-expression evaluates to false for the first time. However, the statement associated with a do-while statement is executed at least once. The general form of a do-while statement is

```
do
    statement
while (condition-expression);
```

Note that the do-while statement ends with a semicolon. The condition-expression must be a boolean expression. The statement can be a simple statement or a block statement. The statement is executed first. Then the condition-expression is evaluated. If it evaluates to true, the statement is executed again. This loop continues until the condition-expression evaluates to false. Figure 6-5 shows the flow diagram for a do-while statement.

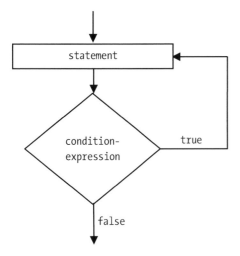

Figure 6-5. *The flow diagram for a do-while statement*

Like in a for loop and a while loop, a break statement may be used to exit a do-while loop. A do-while loop can compute the sum of integers between 1 and 10 as shown:

```
int i = 1;
int sum = 0;
do {
    sum = sum + i; // Better to use sum += i
    i++;
}
while (i <= 10);

// Print the result
System.out.println("Sum = " + sum);
```

```
Sum = 55
```

When do you use a do-while statement instead of a while statement? You can rewrite every do-while statement as a while statement and vice versa. However, using the do-while statement in some use cases makes your code more readable. Consider the following snippet of code:

```
String filePath = "C:\\kishori\\poem.txt";
BufferedReader reader = new BufferedReader(new FileReader(filePath));

String line;
while((line = reader.readLine()) != null) {
    System.out.println(line);
}
```

The code reads the contents of a file one line at a time and prints it on the standard output. I have left out the details of error checking and import statements for this snippet of code. It uses a while loop. The following snippet of code use a do-while statement to do the same:

```
String filePath = "C:\\kishori\\poem.txt";
BufferedReader reader = new BufferedReader(new FileReader(filePath));

String line;
do {
    line = reader.readLine();
    if (line != null) {
        System.out.println(line);
    }
} while (line != null);
```

You can see that the logic does not flow smoothly when you used the do-while statement. Before printing, you had to use an additional if statement to check if a line was read before. In this case, using a while statement is a better choice.

When the condition expression for the loop depends on values computed inside the loop, you need to use the do-while statement. Suppose you need to ask the user to enter a value for a month that must be between 1 and 12. The program keeps asking the user until a valid value is entered. A do-while statement is more suitable in this scenario. Listing 6-3 contains the complete program. I have left out error checks such as when the user enters text instead of an integer.

Listing 6-3. Using a do-while Statement to Accept a Valid User Input

```java
// UserInput.java
package com.jdojo.statement;

import java.util.Scanner;

public class UserInput {
    public static void main(String[] args) {
        Scanner input = new Scanner(System.in);

        int month;
        do {
            System.out.print("Enter a month[1-12]: ");

            // Read an input from the user
            month = input.nextInt();
        } while (month < 1 || month > 12);

        System.out.println("You entered " + month);
    }
}
```

```
Enter a month[1-12]: 20
Enter a month[1-12]: -1
Enter a month[1-12]: 0
Enter a month[1-12]: 9
You entered 9
```

The Scanner class is used to read inputs from the standard input. In this case, the keyboard is the standard input. The nextInt() method of the Scanner class reads the next integer from the keyboard. The program runs in a loop until users enter an integer between 1 and 12. If users enter a non-integer value, the program is aborted with an error.

The break Statement

A break statement is used to exit from a block. There are two forms of the break statement:

- Unlabeled break statement
- Labeled break statement

An example of an unlabeled break statement is

```
break;
```

An example of a labeled break statement is

```
break label;
```

You have already seen the use of the unlabeled break statement inside switch, for-loop, while-loop, and do-while statements. It transfers control out of the switch, for-loop, while-loop, and do-while statement in which it appears. In the case of nested statements of these four kinds, if an unlabeled break statement is used inside the inner statement, it transfers control only out of the inner statement, not out of the outer statement. Suppose you want to print the lower half of the 3x3 matrix as shown:

```
11
21      22
31      32      33
```

To print only the lower half of the 3x3 matrix, you can write the following snippet of code:

```java
for(int i = 1; i <= 3; i++) {
    for(int j = 1; j <= 3; j++) {
        System.out.print ( i + "" + j);
        if (i == j) {
            break; // Exit the inner for loop
        }
        System.out.print("\t");
    }
    System.out.println();
}
```

```
11
21      22
31      32      33
```

The break statement has been used inside the inner for-loop statement. When the value of the outer loop counter (i) becomes equal to the value of the inner loop counter (j), the break statement is executed, and the inner loop exits. If you want to exit from the outer for-loop statement from inside the inner for-loop statement, you have to use a labeled break statement. A label in Java is any valid Java identifier followed by a colon. The following are some valid labels in Java:

- label1:

- alabel:

- Outer:

- Hello:

- IamALabel:

Now use a labeled break statement in the previous example and see the result.

```java
outer:  // Defines a label named outer
for(int i = 1; i <= 3; i++ ) {
    for(int j = 1; j <= 3; j++ ) {
        System.out.print(i + "" + j);
        if (i == j) {
            break outer;  // Exit the outer for loop
        }
```

```
        System.out.print("\t");
    }
    System.out.println();
}  // The outer label ends here
```

The output of the previous snippet of code will be as follows:

11

Why did it print only one element of the 3x3 matrix? This time you have used a labeled break statement inside the inner for-loop statement. When i == j evaluates to true for the first time, the labeled break statement is executed. It transfers control out of the block, which has been labeled as outer. Note that the outer label appears just before the outer for-loop statement. Therefore, the block associated with the label outer is the outer for-loop statement. A labeled statement can be used not only inside switch, for-loop, while-loop, and do-while statements; rather, it can be used with any type of a block statement. The following is a trivial example of a labeled break statement:

```
blockLabel:
{
    int i = 10;
    if (i == 5) {
        break blockLabel; // Exits the block
    }

    if (i == 10) {
        System.out.println("i is not five");
    }
}
```

An important point to remember about a labeled break statement is that the label used with the break statement must be the label for the block in which that labeled break statement is used. The following snippet of code illustrates an incorrect use of a labeled break statement:

```
lab1:
{
    int i = 10;
    if (i == 10)
        break lab1; // Ok. lab1 can be used here
}

lab2:
{
    int i = 10;
    if (i == 10)
        // A compile-time error. lab1 cannot be used here
        // because this block is not associated with
        // lab1 label. We can use only lab2 in this block.
        break lab1;
}
```

The continue Statement

A continue statement can only be used inside the for-loop, while-loop, and do-while statements. There are two forms of continue statements:

- Unlabeled continue statement

- Labeled continue statement

An example of an unlabeled continue statement is

```
continue;
```

An example of a labeled continue statement is

```
continue label;
```

When a continue statement is executed inside a for loop, the rest of the statements in the body of the loop are skipped and the expressions in the expression-list are executed. You can print all odd integers between 1 and 10 using a for-loop statement, as shown:

```
for (int i = 1; i < 10; i += 2) {
    System.out.println(i);
}
```

In this for-loop statement, you increment the value of i by 2 in the expression-list. You can rewrite the previous for-loop statement using a continue statement, as shown in Figure 6-6.

```
for (int i = 1; i < 10; i++) {
    if (i % 2 == 0) {
        continue;
    }

    System.out.println(i);
}
```

Figure 6-6. *Using a continue statement inside a for-loop statement*

The expression i % 2 returns 0 for the values of i that are multiples of 2, and the expression i % 2 == 0 returns true. In such cases, the continue statement is executed and the last statement, System.out.println(i), is skipped. The increment statement i++ is executed after the continue statement is executed. The previous snippet of code is certainly not the best example of using a continue statement; however, it serves the purpose of illustrating its use.

When an unlabeled continue statement is executed inside a while loop or do-while loop, the remaining statements in the loop are skipped and the condition-expression is evaluated for the next iteration. For example, the snippet of code in Figure 6-7 will print all odd integers between 1 and 10, using a continue statement inside a while loop.

```
int i = 1;
while (i < 10) {
    if (i % 2 == 0) {
        i++;
        continue;
    }

    System.out.println(i);
    i++;
}
```

Figure 6-7. *Using a continue statement inside a while-loop statement*

The main difference in using a `continue` statement inside a `for` loop and a `while` loop is the place where the control is transferred. Inside a `for` loop, control is transferred to the expression-list, and in a `while` loop, the control is transferred to the condition-expression. This is why a `for`-loop statement cannot always be converted to a `while`-loop statement without modifying some logic.

An unlabeled `continue` statement always continues the innermost `for` loop, `while` loop, and `do-while` loop. If you are using nested loop statements, you need to use a labeled `continue` statement to continue in the outer loop. For example, you can rewrite the snippet of code that prints the lower half of the 3x3 matrix using a `continue` statement as shown:

```
outer: // The label "outer" starts here
for(int i = 1; i <= 3; i++) {
    for(int j = 1; j <= 3; j++) {
        System.out.print(i + "" + j);
        System.out.print("\t");
        if (i == j) {
            System.out.println(); // Print a new line
            continue outer;    // Continue the outer loop
        }

    }
}   // The label "outer" ends here
```

An Empty Statement

An empty statement is a semicolon by itself. An empty statement does nothing. If an empty statement does not do anything, why do we have it? Sometimes a statement is necessary as part of the syntax of a construct. However, you may not need to do anything meaningful. In such cases, an empty statement is used. A `for`-loop must have a statement associated with it. However, to print all integers between 1 and 10 you can only use initialization, condition-expression, and expression-list parts of a `for`-loop statement. In this case, you do not have a statement to associate with the `for`-loop statement. Therefore, you use an empty statement in this case, as shown:

```
for(int i = 1; i <= 10; System.out.println(i++))
; // This semicolon is an empty statement for the for loop
```

Sometimes, an empty statement is used to avoid double negative logic in the code. Suppose noDataFound is a boolean variable. You may write a snippet of code as shown:

```
if (noDataFound)
    ; // An empty statement
else {
    // Do some processing
}
```

The previous if-else statement can be written without using an empty statement, like so:

```
if (!noDataFound) {
    // Do some processing
}
```

It is a personal choice, which code to use. Finally, note that if you type two or more semicolons where only one is required, it will not cause any errors, because each extra semicolon is considered as an empty statement. For example,

```
i++;  // Ok. Here, semicolon is part of statement
i++;; // Still Ok. The second semicolon is considered as empty statement.
```

You cannot use an empty statement where a statement is not allowed. For example, when only one statement is allowed, adding an extra empty statement will cause an error, as shown in the following snippet of code. It associates two statements, i++; and an empty statement (;), to an if statement, where only one statement is allowed.

```
if (i == 10)
    i++;; // A compile-time error. Cannot use two statements before an else statement
else
    i--;
```

Summary

A statement in a Java program specifies an action. Statements in Java can be broadly classified in three categories: declaration statements, expression statements, and control flow statements. A declaration statement is used to declare variables. An expression statement is used to evaluate an expression. A control flow statement controls the order in which other statements are executed. Control flow statements include if, if-else, and looping statements. A looping statement executes a block of statements repeatedly until some condition becomes false. Java provides four looping statements: the for loop, for-each loop, while loop, and do-while loop. A break statement is used to transfer control outside of a block statement or a loop. A continue statement is used to ignore executing the remaining code for a loop and continue with the next iteration. Java has an empty statement, too, which is simply a semicolon by itself.

EXERCISES

1. What is a statement?

2. What is an expression? How do you convert an expression into an expression statement in Java? Can you convert all types of expressions in Java into expression statements?

3. What are control statements and why do you use them?

4. What is a block statement and how to you create a block statement?

5. What is an empty statement?

6. What is the difference between `while`-loop and `do-while` statements?

7. A `switch` statement contains a `switch-expression`. List all the types that a `switch-expression` must evaluate to.

8. When can you use a `switch` statement in place of an `if-else` statement?

9. Consider the following snippet of code. The valid value of the `count` variable must be in the range 11 (inclusive) and 20 (inclusive). Write the condition for the `if-else` statement, so a correct message is printed.

    ```
    int count = 20;
    if(<your-code-goes-here>)
        System.out.println("Count is valid.");
    else
        System.out.println("Count is invalid");
    ```

10. Fix the compile-time errors in the following snippet of code. Make sure the fixed code prints the value of `y`.

    ```
    int x = 10;
    int y = 20;
    if (x = 10)
        y++;
        System.out.println("y = " + y);
    else
        y--;
        System.out.println("y = " + y);
    ```

11. Rewrite the following snippet of code using an `if-else` statement. Make sure that the `switch` and `if-else` statements both have the same output when you initialize the variable `x` to another value. (Hint: This is a tricky question because there are no `break` statements in any `case` labels.)

    ```
    int x = 50;
    switch (x) {
        case 10:
    ```

```
            System.out.println("Ten");
        default:
            System.out.println("No-match");
        case 20:
            System.out.println("Twenty");
    }
```

12. The following snippet of code is a modified version of the previous one. Rewrite it using an `if-else` statement. Make sure that the `switch` and `if-else` statements both have the same output when you initialize the variable x to another value.

```
int x = 50;
switch (x) {
    case 10:
        System.out.println("Ten");
        break;
    default:
        System.out.println("No-match");
        break;
    case 20:
        System.out.println("Twenty");
        break;
}
```

13. A programmer was learning about the `switch` statement and he tried to use it everywhere he could. The following snippet of code is an example of such a forced use where it is not needed. Rewrite the following snippet of code using no control flow statements. That is, you need to get rid of the `switch` statement and leave the program logic intact.

```
int x = 10;

// Some logic goes here...

switch(x) {
    default:
    x++;
}
```

14. How do you write an infinite loop using the `for`, `while`, and `do-while` statements? Give an example of each.

15. The intent of the following `for` statement is to print integers from 1 to 10 in reverse order. The code does not print the numbers as intended. Identify the logical error and fix the code, so it prints 10, 9, 8, ...1.

```
for(byte b = 10; b >= 1; b++)
    System.out.println(b);
```

16. Write a `for` statement that prints all odd numbers from 13 to 1 in reverse order. The body of the `for` statement must be an empty statement. That is, you can use only the initialization, condition-expression, and expression-list of the `for` statement to write all your logic. The template of your `for` statement is as follows:

```
for(<your-code>; <your-code>; <your-code>);
```

17. Write a snippet of code using a `for` statement that calculates the sum of all integers from 1 to 10 and prints it on the standard output. The template for your code is as follows:

```
int sum = 0;
for(<your-code>; <your-code>; <your-code>);
System.out.println("Sum = " + sum);
```

18. Use a nested `for` statement to print the following pyramid.

```
   *
  ***
 *****
*******
```

19. Write a nested `for` statement that will print the following:

```
     1
    22
   333
  4444
 55555
666666
```

20. Complete the following snippet of code. It is supposed to print a comma-separated list of all integers from `lower` to `upper`. For example, if `lower` is 1 and `upper` is 4, it should print `1, 2, 3, 4`. (Hint: Use `System.out.print()` to print a message without a new line.)

```
int lower = 1;
int upper = 4;

for(<your-code-goes-here>) {
    <your-code-goes-here>
}
```

CHAPTER 7

Classes

In this chapter, you will learn:

- What classes are in Java

- How to declare classes in Java

- How to declare class members such as fields

- How to create objects of a class

- How to declare import statements in a compilation unit

What Is a Class?

Classes are the basic units of programming in the object-oriented paradigm. In Chapter 3, you looked at some elementary aspects of a class in Java, for example, using the class keyword to declare a class, declaring the main() method to run a class, etc. This chapter explains how to declare and use a class in detail.

Let's start with a simple example of a class in the real world to build the technical concept of a class in Java. When you look around, you see a number of objects, such as books, computers, keyboards, tables, chairs, humans, etc. Each object that you see belongs to a class. Ask yourself a simple question, "Who am I?" Your obvious answer would be: I am a human. What do you mean by saying that you are a human? You mean that a human class exists in the world and you are one of the instances ("being") of that class. You also understand that other humans (other instances of the human class) also exist, who are similar, but not the same, to you. Both you and your friend, being instances of the same human class, have the same properties, such as name, gender, height, weight, and behaviors, such as the ability to think, talk, walk, etc. However, the properties and behaviors differ for you and your friend in value, quality, or both. For example, both have a name and the ability to talk. However, your name may be Richard and your friend's name may be Greg. You may talk slowly whereas your friend may talk fast. If you want to prepare a model for you and your friend to examine your behaviors, there are two choices.

- You can list all properties and behaviors for you and your friend separately and examine them separately as if there is no connection between you and your friend.

- You can list the properties and behaviors for you and your friend that are in common and then examine them as properties and behavior for an entity without naming you and your friend. This model assumes that all listed properties and behaviors will be present in an entity (without naming it), though they may vary from entity to entity. You may want to list all properties and behaviors for you and your friend as properties and behaviors of a class, say human, and treat you and your friend as two different instances of that human class. Essentially, you have grouped together entities (e.g., you and your friend) with similar properties and behaviors and called that group a class. Then you will treat all objects (again, you and your friend) as instances of that class.

© Kishori Sharan 2017

K. Sharan, *Beginning Java 9 Fundamentals*, https://doi.org/10.1007/978-1-4842-2902-6_7

223

The first approach treats each object as a separate entity. In the second approach, objects are classified based on similarity of properties and behaviors where an object always belongs to a class; the class becomes the essential part of programming. To determine any property or behavior of an object, you need to look up its class definition. For example, you are an object of the human class. Can you fly? This question can be answered by going through a series of steps. First, you need to answer the question "What class do you belong to?" The answer is that you belong to the human class. Does the human class define a flying behavior? The answer is no. Because you are an instance of the human class that does not define the flying behavior, you cannot fly. If you look carefully at the way you arrived at the answer, you would find that the question is asked on an object (you), but the answer was provided by the class (human) to which the object belongs.

Classes are essential, and they are basic parts of programs in object-oriented programming. They are used as templates to create objects. How do you define a class in Java? A class in Java may consist of five components:

- Fields

- Methods

- Constructors

- Static initializers

- Instance initializers

Fields and methods are also known as members of the class. Classes and interfaces can also be members of a class. This chapter focuses only on fields. I discuss classes and interfaces as class members in the second volume of the *Beginning Java 9* series. A class can have zero or more class members. A class member of a class is also known as a *nested class*.

Similar to giving the initial characteristics of a human like a name, a gender, height, and weight when a baby is born, properties of a newly created object are initialized at the time when the objects are created. In Java, giving initial values to the properties of an object is called *initializing* an object. Constructors are used to initialize objects of a class. You must have at least one constructor for a class.

Initializers are used to initialize fields of a class. You can have zero or more initializers of static or instance types. Initializers perform the same task as constructors. Initializers can also be used to initialize class-level fields, whereas constructors can initialize only object-level fields.

The rest of this chapter discusses how to declare and use the fields of a class.

Declaring a Class

The general syntax for declaring a class in Java is as follows:

```
[modifiers] class <class-name> {
    // Body of the class goes here
}
```

Here,

- `modifiers` are optional; they are keywords that associate special meanings to the class declaration. A class declaration may have zero or more modifiers.

- The keyword `class` is used to declare a class.

- The `class-name` is a user-defined name of the class, which should be a valid Java identifier.

- Each class has a body, which is specified inside a pair of braces ({}). The body of a class contains its different components, for example, fields, methods, etc.

The following snippet of code defines a class named Human with an empty body. Note that the Human class does not use any modifiers.

```
// Human.java
class Human {
    // An empty body for now
}
```

The following snippet of code defines a public class named Human with an empty body. Note that this declaration uses a public modifier.

```
// Human.java
public class Human {
    // An empty body for now
}
```

I explain the differences between a public and other types of classes in detail later in this chapter.

Declaring Fields in a Class

Fields of a class represent properties (also called attributes) of objects of that class. Suppose every object of a Human class has two properties: a name and a gender. The Human class should include declarations of two fields: one to represent the name and one to represent the gender.

The fields are declared inside the body of the class. The general syntax to declare a field in a class is

```
[modifiers] class <class-name> {
    // A field declaration
    [modifiers] <data-type> <field-name> [= <initial-value>];
}
```

A field declaration can use zero or more modifiers. The data type of the field precedes its name. Optionally, you can also initialize each field with a value. If you do not want to initialize a field, its declaration should end with a semicolon after its name.

With two fields, name and gender, the declaration of the Human class will look as shown:

```
// Human.java
class Human {
    String name;
    String gender;
}
```

▓ **Tip**   It is a convention (not a rule or a requirement) in Java to start a class name with an uppercase letter and capitalize the subsequent words, for example, Human, Table, ColorMonitor, etc. The name of fields and methods should start with a lowercase letter and the subsequent words should be capitalized, for example, name, firstName, maxDebitAmount, etc.

The Human class declares two fields: name and gender. Both fields are of the String type. Every instance (or object) of the Human class will have a copy of these two fields.

Sometimes a property belongs to the class itself, not to any particular instance of that class. For example, the count of all humans is not a property of any specific human. Rather, it belongs to the human class itself. The existence of the count of humans is not tied to any specific instance of the human class, even though each instance of the human class contributes to the value of the count property. Only one copy of the class property exists irrespective of the number of instances that exist for the class. However, a separate copy of the instance property exists for each instance of a class. For example, a separate copy of the name and the gender properties exist for each instance of the Human class. You always specify name and gender of a human. However, even if there is no instance of the Human class, you can say that the count of the Human class instances is zero.

Java lets you declare two types of fields for a class:

- Class fields

- Instance fields

Class fields are also known as *class variables*. Instance fields are also known as *instance variables*. In the previous snippet of code, name and gender are two instance variables of the Human class. Java has a different way to declare class variables. All class variables must be declared using the static keyword as a modifier. The declaration of the Human class in Listing 7-1 adds a count class variable.

Listing 7-1. Declaration of a Human Class with One Class Variable and Two Instance Variables

```java
// Human.java
package com.jdojo.cls;

class Human {
    String name;        // An instance variable
    String gender;      // An instance variable
    static long count;  // A class variable because of the static modifier
}
```

░ **Tip** A class variable is also known as a *static variable*. An instance variable is also known as a *non-static variable*.

Creating Instances of a Class

The following is the general syntax to create an instance of a class:

```
new <Call-to-Class-Constructor>;
```

The new operator is followed by a call to the constructor of the class whose instance is being created. The new operator creates an instance of a class by allocating the memory on heap. The following statement creates an instance of the Human class:

```
new Human();
```

Here, Human() is a call to the constructor of the Human class. Did you add any constructor to your Human class? No. You have not added any constructor to your Human class. You have added only three fields to it. How can you use a constructor for a class that you have not added? When you do not add a constructor to a class, the Java compiler adds one for you. The constructor that is added by the Java compiler is called a default constructor. The default constructor accepts no arguments. The name of the constructor of a class is the same as the class name. I discuss constructors in detail in Chapter 9.

What happens when an instance of a class is created? The new operator allocates memory for each instance field of the class. Recall that class variables are not allocated memory when an instance of the class is created. Figure 7-1 depicts an instance of the Human class in memory.

Figure 7-1. *An instance of the Human class in memory created by the new Human() instance creation expression*

Figure 7-1 shows that memory is allocated for the instance variables name and gender. You can create as many instances of the Human class as you want. Each time you create an instance of the Human class, Java runtime allocates memory for the name and gender instance variables. How much memory is allocated for an instance of the Human class? The simple answer is that you do not know exactly how much memory is used by an instance of a class and, in fact, you do not need to know this. The Java runtime takes care of memory allocation as well as deallocation automatically for you.

Now, you want to move a step forward and assign values to the name and gender instance variables for the newly created instance of the Human class. Can you assign values to the name and gender instance variables of the newly created instance of the Human class? The answer is no. You cannot access the name and gender instance variables, even though they exist in memory. To access instance variables of an instance of a class, you must have its reference (or handle). The expression new Human() creates a new instance of the Human class in memory. The newly created instance is like a balloon filled with Helium gas left in the air. When you release a Helium-filled balloon in the air, you lose control of the balloon. If you attach a string to the balloon before releasing it in the air, you can control the balloon using the string. Similarly, if you want to have control of (or access) an instance of a class, you must store the reference of that instance in a reference variable. You control a balloon with a string; you control a television with a remote control. The type of controlling device depends on the type of the object that you want to control. Similarly, you need to use different types of reference variables to refer to (or to handle, or to work with) instances of different classes.

The name of a class defines a new reference type in Java. A variable of a specific reference type can store the reference of an instance of the same reference type in memory. Suppose you want to declare a reference variable, which will store a reference of an instance of the Human class. You will declare the variable as shown:

```
Human jack;
```

Here, Human is the class name, which is also a reference type, and jack is a variable of that type. In other words, jack is a reference variable of Human type. The jack variable can be used to store a reference of an instance of the Human class.

The new operator allocates the memory for a new instance of a class and returns the reference (or the indirect pointer) to that instance. You need to store the reference returned by the new operator in a reference variable.

```
jack = new Human();
```

Note that jack itself is a variable and it will be allocated memory separately. The memory location for the jack variable will store the reference of the memory location of the newly created instance of the Human class. Figure 7-1 depicts the memory state when the reference variable jack is declared and when an instance of the Human class is created and its reference is assigned to the jack variable.

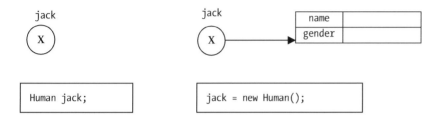

Figure 7-2. *Memory states when a reference variable is declared and when a reference variable is assigned the reference of an instance of a class*

You can think of the jack variable as a remote controller for a Human instance in memory. You can refer to the Human instance in memory using the jack variable. I discuss how to use a reference variable in the next section. You can also combine the two statements into one.

```
Human jack = new Human();
```

The null Reference Type

Every class in Java defines a new reference type. Java has a special reference type called a null type. It has no name. Therefore, you cannot define a variable of the null reference type. The null reference type has only one value defined by Java, which is the null literal. It is simply null. The null reference type is assignment-compatible with all the other reference types. That is, you can assign null to a variable of any reference type. Practically, null stored in a reference variable means that the reference variable is referring to no object. You can think of storing null in a reference variable as a string with no balloon attached to it, where the balloon is a valid object and the string is a reference variable. For example, you can write code like the following:

```
// Assign null to john
Human john = null;  // john is not referring to any object
john = new Human(); // Now, john is referring to a valid Human object
```

You can use null with comparison operators to check for equality and inequality.

```
if (john == null) {
    // john is referring to null. Cannot use john for anything
} else {
    // Do something with john
}
```

If you perform an operation on a null reference, a NullPointerException is thrown.

```
Human john = null;

// The following statement throws a NullPointerException because john is null and you
// cannot use any operation on a null reference variable
String name = john.name;
```

Note that null is a literal of the null type. Java does not let you mix reference types and primitive types. You cannot assign null to a primitive type variable. The following assignment statement will generate a compile-time error:

```
// A compile-time error. A reference type value, null, cannot be assigned to
// a primitive type variable num
int num = null;
```

Because null (or any reference type value) cannot be assigned to a primitive type variable, Java compiler does not allow you to compare a primitive value to a null value. The following comparison will generate a compile-time error. In other words, you can compare a reference type with other reference types, and a primitive type with other primitive types.

```
int num = 0;

// A compile-time error. Cannot compare a primitive type to a reference type
if (num == null) {
}
```

▒ **Tip**   Java has a special reference type that is called *null* type. The null type does not have a name. The null type has a literal value, which is represented by null. The null type is assignment-compatible with all the other reference types. You can assign any reference type variable a null value. You can cast a null value to any reference type. It is to be emphasized that null is a literal value of "null reference type", not a keyword.

Using Dot Notation to Access Fields of a Class

Dot notation is used to refer to instance variables. The general form of the dot notation syntax is as follows:

```
<reference-variable-name>.<instance-variable-name>
```

For example, you use jack.name to refer to the name instance variable of the instance to which the jack reference variable is referring. If you want to assign a value to the name instance variable, you can use the following:

```
jack.name = "Jack Parker";
```

The following statement assigns the value of the name instance variable to a String variable aName:

```
String aName = jack.name;
```

How do you refer to class variables? You have two ways to refer to a class variable using dot notation:

- Using the name of the class
- Using a reference of an instance of the class

You can refer to a class variable using the name of the class.

```
<class-name>.<class-variable-name>
```

For example, you can use Human.count to refer to the count class variable of the Human class. To assign a new value, say 101, to the count class variable, you can write this:

```
Human.count = 101;
```

To read the value of the count class variable into a variable called population, you can use this:

```
long population = Human.count;
```

You can also use a reference variable to refer to the class variable of a class. For example, you can use jack.count to refer to the count class variable of the Human class. You can use the following statement to assign value, say 101, to the count class variable:

```
jack.count = 101;
```

The following statement reads the value of the count class variable into a variable called population:

```
long population = jack.count;
```

Both of these statements assume that jack is a reference variable of Human type and that it refers to a valid Human instance.

⬛ **Tip** You can use the class name or a reference variable of the class type to refer to a class variable. Since the class variable belongs to the class and it is shared by all instances of the class, it is logical to refer to it using the class name. However, you must always use a reference variable of a class type to refer to the instance variables.

It is time to see fields in the Human class in action. Most classes in this chapter are part of the jdojo.cls module, as declared in Listing 7-2. The cls in the module name is short for class. You cannot use jdojo.class as a module name because class is a keyword. The module exports a com.jdojo.cls package. You have not learned about the exports statement in a module declaration yet. I explain it in this chapter.

Listing 7-2. Declaration of the jdojo.cls Module

```
// module-info.class
module jdojo.cls {
    exports com.jdojo.cls;
}
```

Listing 7-3 has a complete program that demonstrates how to access class variables and instance variables of a class.

Listing 7-3. Using Fields in a Class Declaration

```java
// FieldAccessTest.java
package com.jdojo.cls;

class FieldAccessTest {
    public static void main(String[] args) {
        // Create an instance of the Human class
        Human jack = new Human();

        // Increase count by one
        Human.count++;

        // Assign values to name and gender
        jack.name = "Jack Parker";
        jack.gender = "Male";

        // Read and print the values of name, gender and count
        String jackName = jack.name;
        String jackGender = jack.gender;
        long population = Human.count;

        System.out.println("Name: " + jackName);
        System.out.println("Gender: " + jackGender);
        System.out.println("Population: " + population);

        // Change the name
        jack.name = "Jackie Parker";

        // Read and print the changed name
        String changedName = jack.name;
        System.out.println("Changed Name: " + changedName);
    }
}
```

```
Name: Jack Parker
Gender: Male
Population: 1
Changed Name: Jackie Parker
```

The following statement in this program needs some explanation:

```java
// Increase count by one
Human.count++;
```

It uses the increment operator (++) on the count class variable. After the count class variable is incremented by 1, you read and print its value. The output shows that after incrementing its value by 1, its value becomes 1. It means that its value was zero before the Human.count++ statement was executed. However, you have never set its value to zero. Its declaration was as follows:

```java
static long count;
```

When the count class variable was declared as shown previously, it was initialized to zero by default. All fields of a class (class variables and instance variables) are initialized to a default value, if you do not assign an initial value to them. The next section describes the rules used to initialize fields of a class.

Default Initialization of Fields

All fields of a class, static as well as non-static, are initialized to a default value. The default value of a field depends on its data type.

- A numeric field (byte, short, char, int, long, float, and double) is initialized to zero.

- A boolean field is initialized to false.

- A reference type field is initialized to null.

According to these rules, the fields of the Human class will be initialized as follows:

- The count class variable is initialized to zero because it is of numeric type. This is the reason that Human.count++ evaluated to 1 (0 + 1 = 1), as shown in the output of Listing 7-3.

- The name and gender instance variables are of String type. String is a reference type. They are initialized to null. Recall that a copy of the name and gender fields exists for every object of the Human class, and each copy of name and gender is initialized to null.

If you consider the default initialization of the fields of the Human class, it behaves as if you have declared the Human class as follows. This declaration of the Human class and the one shown in Listing 7-1 are the same.

```
class Human {
    String name = null;
    String gender = null;
    static long count = 0;
}
```

Listing 7-4 demonstrates the default initialization of fields. The DefaultInit class includes only instance variables. The class fields are initialized with the same default value as the instance fields. If you declare all fields of the DefaultInit class as static, the output will be the same. The class includes two reference type instance variables, str and jack, which are of String and Human types. Note that both String and Human are reference types and null is assigned to their references by default.

Listing 7-4. Default Initialization of Class Fields

```
// DefaultInit.java
package com.jdojo.cls;

class DefaultInit {
    byte b;
    short s;
    int i;
    long l;
    float f;
    double d;
    boolean bool;
```

```
    String str;
    Human jack;

    public static void main(String[] args) {
        // Create an object of DefaultInit class
        DefaultInit obj = new DefaultInit();

        // Print the default values for all instance variables
        System.out.println("byte is initialized to " + obj.b);
        System.out.println("short is initialized to " + obj.s);
        System.out.println("int is initialized to " + obj.i);
        System.out.println("long is initialized to " + obj.l);
        System.out.println("float is initialized to " + obj.f);
        System.out.println("double is initialized to " + obj.d);
        System.out.println("boolean is initialized to " + obj.bool);
        System.out.println("String is initialized to " + obj.str);
        System.out.println("Human is initialized to " + obj.jack);
    }
}
```

```
byte is initialized to 0
short is initialized to 0
int is initialized to 0
long is initialized to 0
float is initialized to 0.0
double is initialized to 0.0
boolean is initialized to false
String is initialized to null
Human is initialized to null
```

Access Level Modifiers for a Class

In Listing 7-1, you created the Human class in the com.jdojo.cls package. You used the Human class in Listing 7-3 to create its object in the FieldAccessTest class, which is in the same module and the same package as the Human class. You had no problem compiling and running the following statement in Listing 7-3:

```
Human jack = new Human();
```

Let's create a class called ClassAccessTest in the com.jdojo.common package in the jdojo.cls module. Note that the ClassAccessTest and Human classes are in different packages. The ClassAccessTest class declaration is as follows:

```
// ClassAccessTest.java
package com.jdojo.common;

public class ClassAccessTest {
    public static void main(String[] args) {
        Human jack;
    }
}
```

The code for the ClassAccessTest class is very simple. It does only one thing—declares a reference variable of the Human type in its main() method. Compile the ClassAccessTest class. Oops! You got a compile-time error:

```
ClassAccessTest.java:6: error: cannot find symbol
        Human jack;
        ^
  symbol:   class Human
  location: class ClassAccessTest
1 error
```

If you read the error carefully, the compiler is complaining about the type Human in the following variable declaration:

```
Human jack;
```

The compiler is stating that it could not find the definition of the term Human. What is wrong in the ClassAccessTest class with the jack variable declaration? When you refer to a class by its simple name, the compiler looks for that class declaration in the same package where the referring class is. In your case, the referring class ClassAccessTest is in the com.jdojo.common package and it uses the simple name, Human, to refer to the Human class. Therefore, the compiler looks for the Human class in the com.jdojo.common package. The compiler is looking for a com.jdojo.common.Human class, which does not exist. This is the reason you received the error.

By using the simple name Human in ClassAccessTest, you meant to refer to the Human class in the com.jdojo.cls package, not in the com.jdojo.common package. If you had the Human class in the com.jdojo.common package, your code for ClassAccessTest would have compiled. Let's assume that you do not have a com.jdojo.common.Human class and you want to fix this error. You can fix it by using the fully qualified name of the Human class, like so:

```
// ClassAccessTest.java
package com.jdojo.common;

public class ClassAccessTest {
    public static void main(String[] args) {
        com.jdojo.cls.Human jack;
    }
}
```

Now compile the ClassAccessTest class. Oops! You got a compilation time error again. However, this time, the error is different.

```
ClassAccessTest.java:6: error: Human is not public in com.jdojo.cls; cannot be accessed from
outside package
        com.jdojo.cls.Human jack;
                     ^
1 error
```

This time, the compiler is not saying that it does not understand the Human type. It is saying that it knows what com.jdojo.cls.Human type is; however, it is accessible only inside the com.jdojo.cls package in which it has been declared. In other words, the Human type is not accessible inside the com.jdojo.common package. Here comes the concept of the access level for a class.

When you declare a class, you can also specify whether the class can be accessed (or used, or referred to) from any package or only from within the package in which it has been declared. For example, you can specify in the declaration of the Human class whether it can be accessed only from within the com.jdojo.cls package or from any package, including the com.jdojo.common package. The general syntax specifying access level for a class is as follows:

```
[access-level-modifier] class <class-name> {
    // Body of the class goes here
}
```

There are only two valid values for an access-level modifier in a class declaration: no value and public.

- *No value*: It is the same as the absence of an access level modifier. It is also known as package-level access. If a class has package-level access, it can be accessed only within the package in which it has been declared. The Human class in Listing 7-1 has package-level access. This is the reason that you were able to use (or access) the Human class in the FieldAccessTest class in Listing 7-3. Note that the Human class and the FieldAccessTest class are in the same package and both have package-level access. Therefore, they can refer to each other. The Human class is in the com.jdojo.cls package and it has package-level access. Therefore, it cannot be accessed from any other package, for example, com.jdojo.common. This is the reason that you received an error when you tried to compile the ClassAccessTest class.

- *public*: A class with a public access-level modifier can be accessed from any package in the same module. If you want the Human class to be accessible from any package (e.g., com.jdojo.common), you need to declare it as public.

Can a class C declared in module M be accessed in module N? The answer to this question depends on the access level modifier of class C and declaration of modules M and N. For class C to be accessible in a package in module N, the following criteria must be met:

- Class C in module M must be declared public.

- Module M must export the package of class C to all other modules or to at least module N. By exporting a package, a module states that the public classes (or any type) in the package can be used by all or some other modules.

- The declaration of module N must require module M.

Module dependency is a vast topic. I discuss it in detail in Chapter 10. In this chapter, I limit the discussion of accessibility of a type in the same module unless module dependency must be mentioned.

Let's redefine the Human class, as shown in Listing 7-5. This time, you have specified its access level as public, so it is accessible from any package.

Listing 7-5. Redefined Human Class with the Public Access Level Modifier

```
// Human.java
package com.jdojo.cls;

public class Human {
    String name;          // Instance variable
    String gender;        // Instance variable
    static long count;    // Class variable
}
```

Recompile the Human class and then compile the ClassAccessTest class. This time, the ClassAccessTest class compiles without any errors.

▓ **Tip**   What does it mean when I state that a class is accessible from a package? A class defines a new reference type. A reference type can be used to declare a variable. When a class is accessible in a package, the class name can be used as a reference type, for example, to declare a variable, in the code that resides in that package.

Import Declarations

You learned two rules in the previous section:

- You must declare a class public to use it in a package other than the package in which it is declared. If the other package is in another module, additional work is needed in both module declarations for the public class to be accessible.

- You need to use the fully qualified name of a class to use it in a package other than the one in which it is declared. A class can be referred to using its simple name in the package in which it is declared.

There is no alternative to the first rule. That is, a class must be declared public if it needs to be accessible from outside its package.

There is another way to deal with the second rule. You can refer to a class by its simple name outside its package by using an import declaration. An import declaration is used to import a class into a compilation unit from outside the package of the compilation unit. Technically speaking, an import declaration is used to import any type into a compilation unit, not just a class. Import declarations appear just after the package declaration and before the first type declaration. Figure 7-3 shows the place where import declarations appear. You can have zero or more import declarations in a compilation unit.

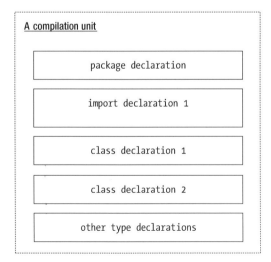

Figure 7-3. *The structure of a compilation unit in Java*

This section mentions importing only classes. However, the same rules apply for importing any other types, for example, interfaces, annotations, or enums. Because I have covered only class types up to this point, I do not mention any other types in this discussion.

There are two types of import declarations:

- Single-type import declaration

- Import-on-demand declaration

Single-Type Import Declaration

A single-type import declaration is used to import a single type (e.g., one class) from a package. It takes the following form:

```
import <fully-qualified-name-of-a-type>;
```

The following import declaration imports the Human class from the com.jdojo.cls package:

```
import com.jdojo.cls.Human;
```

A single-type import declaration imports only one type from a package. If you want to import more than one type (e.g., three classes) from a package, you need to use a separate import declaration for each type. The following import declarations import Class11 from the pkg1 package, Class21 and Class22 from the pkg2 package, and Class33 from the pkg3 package:

```
import pkg1.Class11;
import pkg2.Class21;
import pkg2.Class22;
import pkg3.Class33;
```

Let's revisit the com.jdojo.common.ClassAccessTest class, which had a compile-time error.

```
// ClassAccessTest.java
package com.jdojo.common;

public class ClassAccessTest {
    public static void main(String[] args) {
        Human jack;
    }
}
```

You received a compile-time error when you used the simple name of the Human class because the compiler could not find a Human class in the com.jdojo.common package. You resolved this error by using the fully qualified name of the Human class, like so:

```
// ClassAccessTest.java
package com.jdojo.common;
```

```
public class ClassAccessTest {
    public static void main(String[] args) {
        com.jdojo.cls.Human jack; // Uses full qualified name for the Human class
    }
}
```

You have another way to resolve this error, which is by using a single-type-import declaration. You can import the com.jdojo.cls.Human class to use its simple name. The modified ClassAccessTest class declaration is as follows:

```
// ClassAccessTest.java - Modified version
package com.jdojo.common;

import com.jdojo.cls.Human; // Import the Human class

public class ClassAccessTest {
    public static void main(String[] args) {
        Human jack; // Use simple name of the Human class
    }
}
```

The modified version of the ClassAccessTest class compiles fine. When the compiler comes across the simple name of the Human class in the statement, like

```
Human jack;
```

it goes through all import declarations to resolve the simple name to a fully qualified name. When it tries to resolve the simple name Human, it finds the import declaration, import com.jdojo.cls.Human, which imports the Human class. It assumes that you intended to use the com.jdojo.cls.Human class when you used the simple name Human in the previous statement. The compiler replaces the previous statement with the following statement:

```
com.jdojo.cls.Human jack;
```

■ **Tip**   Import declarations let you use the simple name of a type in your code, thus making your code more readable. When you compile your code, the compiler replaces the simple name of a type with its fully qualified name. It uses import declarations for converting simple names of the types to their fully qualified names. It is to be emphasized that using import declarations in your Java program does not affect the size of your compiled code or runtime performance. Using import declarations is just a way to use the simple names of classes in your source code.

There are many subtle points to remember while using import declarations. I discuss them shortly.

Import-on-Demand Declaration

Sometimes you may need to import multiple types from the same package. You need to use as many single-type-import declarations as the number of types you need to import from the package. An import-on-demand declaration is used to import multiple types from a package using one import declaration. The syntax for an import-on-demand declaration is

```
import <package-name>.*;
```

Here, the package name is followed by a dot and an asterisk (*). For example, the following import-on-demand declaration imports all types from the com.jdojo.cls package:

```
import com.jdojo.cls.*;
```

Sometimes, the use of an asterisk in an import-on-demand declaration leads to the wrong assumption about the types that are imported. Suppose there are two classes, C1 and C2. They are in packages p1 and p1.p2, respectively. That is, their fully qualified names are p1.C1 and p1.p2.C2. You may write an import-on-demand declaration as

```
import p1.*;
```

thinking that it will import both classes, p1.C1 and p1.p2.C2. This assumption is wrong. The declaration

```
import p1.*;
```

imports all types only from p1 package. It will not import the p1.p2.C2 class because the C2 class is not in the p1 package; rather it is in the p2 package, which is a sub-package of p1. The asterisk at the end of an import-on-demand declaration means all types only from the specified package. The asterisk does not mean sub-packages and types inside those sub-packages. Sometimes, developers attempt to use multiple asterisks in an import-on-demand declaration, thinking that it will import types from all sub-packages too.

```
import p1.*.*; // A compile-time error
```

This import-on-demand declaration results in a compile-time error because it uses multiple asterisks. It does not follow the syntax for an import-on-demand declaration. In an import-on-demand declaration, the declaration must end with a dot followed by one and only one asterisk.

If you want to import both classes C1 and C2, you need to use two import-on-demand declarations:

```
import p1.*;
import p1.p2.*;
```

You can rewrite the code for the ClassAccessTest class using an import-on-demand declaration.

```
// ClassAccessTest.java - Modified version uses import-on-demand
package com.jdojo.common;

// Import all types from the com.jdojo.cls package including the Human class
import com.jdojo.cls.*;
```

```
public class ClassAccessTest {
    public static void main(String[] args) {
        Human jack; // Use simple name of the Human class
    }
}
```

When the compiler tries to resolve the simple name Human in the previous code, it will use the import-on-demand declaration to see if a Human class exists in the com.jdojo.cls package. In fact, the asterisk in the import declaration will be replaced by Human and then the compiler checks if the com.jdojo.cls.Human class exists. Suppose you have two classes in the com.jdojo.cls package named Human and Table. The following code will compile with one import-on-demand declaration:

```
// ClassAccessTest.java - Modified version uses import-on-demand
package com.jdojo.common;

// Import all types from com.jdojo.cls package including Human and Table classes
import com.jdojo.cls.*;

public class ClassAccessTest {
    public static void main(String[] args) {
        Human jack; // Use simple name of the Human class
        Table t1;   // Use simple name of the Table class
    }
}
```

The one import-on-demand declaration in the previous code has the same effect as the following two single-type-import declarations:

```
import com.jdojo.cls.Human; // Import Human class
import com.jdojo.cls.Table; // Import Table class
```

Which type of import declaration is better to use in your Java program: single-type import or import-on-demand? It is simple to use the import-on-demand declaration. However, it is not readable. Let's look at the following code, which compiles fine. Assume that classes A and B are not in the com.jdojo.cls package.

```
// ImportOnDemandTest.java
package com.jdojo.cls;

import p1.*;
import p2.*;

public class ImportOnDemandTest {
    public static void main(String[] args) {
        A a; // Declare a variable of class A type
        B b; // Declare a variable of class B type
    }
}
```

Can you tell, by looking at this code, the fully qualified names of the classes A and B? Is class A in the package p1 or p2? It is impossible to tell just by looking at the code the package to which classes A and B belong because you have used import-on-demand declarations. Let's rewrite the previous code using two single-type-import declarations.

```
// ImportOnDemandTest.java
package com.jdojo.cls;

import p1.A;
import p2.B;

public class ImportOnDemandTest {
    public static void main(String[] args) {
        A a; // Declare a variable of class A type
        B b; // Declare a variable of class B type
    }
}
```

By looking at the import declarations, you can now tell that class A is in the package p1 and class B is in the package p2. A single-type import declaration makes it easy for readers to know which class is being imported from which package. It also makes it easy to know the number and name of the classes used from other packages in your program. This book uses single-type import declaration in all examples, except in examples where I discuss import-on-demand declarations.

Even though you are advised to use single-type-import declaration in your programs, you need to know some tricky uses and implications of using both single-type import and import-on-demand declarations in the same program. Subsequent sections discuss them in detail.

Import Declarations and Type Search Order

Import declarations are used to resolve simple names of types to their fully qualified names during compilation. The compiler uses predefined rules to resolve the simple names. Suppose the following statement appears in a Java program that uses a simple name A:

```
A var;
```

The Java compiler must resolve the simple name A to its fully qualified name during the compilation process. It searches for a type referenced in a program in the following order:

- The current compilation unit
- Single-type import declarations
- Types declared in the same package
- Import-on-demand declarations

This list of type search is not complete. If a type has nested types, the nested type is searched before looking in the current compilation unit. I will defer the discussion of nested types until inner classes are discussed in the second volume of this three-book series.

Let's discuss the rules for a type search using a few examples. Suppose you have a Java source file (a compilation unit) called B.java whose contents are as follows. Note that the file, B.java, contains declarations for two classes A and B.

```
// B.java
package p1;

class B {
    A var;
}
```

```
class A {
    // Code goes here
}
```

Class B refers to class A using the simple name when it declares an instance variable var of type A. When the B.java file is compiled, the compiler will look for a type with the simple name A in the current compilation unit (B.java file). It will find a class declaration whose simple name is A in the current compilation unit. The simple name A will be replaced with its fully qualified name p1.A. Note that both classes A and B are declared in the same compilation unit, and therefore they are in the same package, p1. The class B definition will be changed as follows by the compiler:

```
package p1;

class B {
    p1.A var; // A has been replaced by p1.A by the compiler
}
```

Suppose you want to use class A from package p2 in the previous example. That is, there is a class p2.A and you want to declare the instance variable var of type p2.A in class B instead of p1.A. Let's try to solve it by importing class p2.A using a single-type-import declaration, like so:

```
// B.java - Includes a new import declaration
package p1;

import p2.A;

class B {
    A var; // You want to use p2.A when you use A here
}

class A {
    // Code goes here
}
```

When you compile the modified B.java file, you will get the following compilation error:

```
"B.java": p1.A is already defined in this compilation unit at line 2, column 1
```

What is wrong with the modified source code? When you remove the single-type-import declaration from it, it compiles fine. It means it is the single-type import declaration that is causing the error. Before you resolve this error, you need to learn about a new rule about single-type import declarations. The rule is

> *It is a compile-time error to import more than one type with the same simple name using multiple single-type-import declarations.*

Suppose you have two classes, p1.A and p2.A. Note that both classes have the same simple name A placed in two different packages. According to this rule, if you want to use the two classes, p1.A and p2.A, in the same compilation unit, you cannot use two single-type-import declarations.

```
// Test.java
package pkg;

import p1.A;
import p2.A; // A compile-time error

class Test {
    A var1; // Which A to use p1.A or p2.A?
    A var2; // Which A to use p1.A or p2.A?
}
```

The reason behind this rule is that the compiler has no way of knowing which class (p1.A or p2.A) to use when you use simple name A in the code. Java might have solved this issue by using the first imported class or the last imported class, which would have been error prone. Java decided to nip the problem in the bud by giving you a compile-time error when you import two classes with the same simple names, so you cannot make silly mistakes like this and end up spending hours resolving them.

Let's go back to the problem of importing the p2.A class in a compilation unit, which already declares a class A. The following code produces a compile-time error:

```
// B.java - Includes a new import declaration
package p1;

import p2.A;

class B {
    A var1; // You want to use p2.A when you use A
}

class A {
    // Code goes here
}
```

This time, you have used only one single-type import declaration, not two. Why did you get an error? When you declare more than one class in the same compilation unit, most likely they are closely related and they would refer to each other. You need to think as if Java imports each of the classes declared in the same compilation unit using a single-type import declaration. You can think of the previous code being transformed by Java as shown:

```
// B.java - Includes a new import declaration
package p1;

import p1.A; // Think of it being added by Java
import p1.B; // Think of it being added by Java
import p2.A;

class B {
    A var; // We want to use p2.A when you use A
}

class A {
    // Code goes here
}
```

Can you now see the problem? The class A has been imported twice, once by Java and once by you, and this is the reason for the error. How do you refer to p2.A in your code anyway? It is simple. Use the fully qualified name p2.A whenever you want to use p2.A in your compilation unit.

```
// B.java - Uses fully qualified name p2.A in class B
package p1;

class B {
    p2.A var; // Use fully qualified name of A
}
class A {
    // Code goes here
}
```

■ **Tip**   It is a compile-time error to import a type using a single-type-import declaration into a compilation unit if a type with the same simple name exists in the same compilation unit.

Let's resolve the compile-time error with the code that needs to use classes from different packages with the same simple name. The code is as follows:

```
// Test.java
package pkg;

import p1.A;
import p2.A; // A compile-time error

class Test {
    A var1; // Which A to use p1.A or p2.A?
    A var2; // Which A to use p1.A or p2.A?
}
```

You can resolve the error using one of the following two methods. The first method is to remove both import declarations and use the fully qualified name of class A as follows:

```
// Test.java
package pkg;

class Test {
    p1.A var1; // Use p1.A
    p2.A var2; // Use p2.A
}
```

The second method is to use only one import declaration to import class A from one package, say p1, and use the fully qualified name of class A from the p2 package as follows:

```
// Test.java
package pkg;

import p1.A;
```

244

```
class Test {
    A var1;    // Refers to p1.A
    p2.A var2; // Uses the fully qualified name p2.A
}
```

▓ **Tip**   If you want to use multiple classes with the same simple name in a compilation unit, but from different packages, you can import a maximum of one class. For the rest of the classes, you must use the fully qualified name. You have the option of using the fully qualified name for all classes.

Let's discuss a few rules about using import-on-demand declarations. The compiler uses the import-on-demand declarations to resolve a simple name of a type after it has used all other means to resolve the simple name. It is valid to import a class with the same simple name using a single-type import declaration as well as an import-on-demand declaration. In such a case, the single-type import declaration is used. Suppose you have three classes: p1.A, p2.A, and p2.B. Suppose you have a compilation unit as follows:

```
// C.java
package p3;

import p1.A;
import p2.*;

class C {
    A var; // Will always use p1.A (not p2.A)
}
```

In this example, class A has been imported twice: once using simple type import declaration from package p1, and once using import-on-demand declaration from package p2. The simple name A is resolved to p1.A because a single-type import declaration always takes precedence over an import-on-demand declaration. Once the compiler finds a class using a single-type import declaration, it stops the search without looking for that class using any import-on-demand declarations.

Let's change the import declarations in the previous example to use import-on-demand declarations, as follows:

```
// C.java
package p3;

import p1.*;
import p2.*;

class  C {
    A var; // A compile-time error. Which A to use p1.A or p2.A?
}
```

Compiling class C generates the following error:

```
"C.java": reference to A is ambiguous, both class p2.A in p2 and class p1.A in p1 match at
line 8, column 5
```

245

The error message is loud and clear. When the compiler finds a class using an import-on-demand declaration, it continues searching for the class in all import-on-demand declarations. If it finds the class with the same simple name using multiple import-on-demand declarations, it generates an error. You can resolve this error in several ways:

- Use two single-type-import declarations.

- Use one single-type import and one import-on-demand declaration.

- Use fully qualified names for both classes.

The following list covers a few more rules about import declarations:

- Duplicate single-type import and import-on-demand declarations are ignored. The following code is valid:

```
// D.java
package p4;

import p1.A;
import p1.A; // Ignored. A duplicate import declaration.
import p2.*;
import p2.*; // Ignored. A duplicate import declaration.

class D {
    // Code goes here
}
```

- It is legal, though not needed, to import classes from the same package using single-type import declarations or import-on-demand declaration. The following code imports class F from the same package p5. Note that all classes declared in the same package are automatically imported for you. In such a case, the import declaration is ignored.

```
// E.java
package p5;

import p5.F; // Will be ignored

class E {
    // Code goes here
}

// F.java
package p5;

import p5.*; // Will be ignored

class F {
    // Code goes here
}
```

Automatic Import Declarations

You have been using the String class and the System class by their simple names and you never cared to import them in any of your programs. The fully qualified names of these classes are java.lang.String and java.lang.System. Java always imports all types declared in the java.lang package automatically. Think of the following import-on-demand declaration being added to your source code before compilation:

```
import java.lang.*;
```

This is the reason that you were able to use the simple names of String and System classes in your code without importing them. You can use any types from the java.lang package by their simple names in your programs.

It is not an error to use an import declaration to import types from the java.lang package. They will be simply ignored by the compiler. The following code will compile without errors:

```
package p1;

import java.lang.*;  // Will be ignored because it is automatically done for you

public class G {
    String anythingGoes; // Refers to java.lang.String
}
```

You need to be careful when using the simple name of a type, which is the same as a type that is defined in the java.lang package. Suppose you declare a p1.String class.

```
// String.java
package p1;

public class String {
    // Code goes here
}
```

Suppose you have a Test class in the same package, p1.

```
// Test.java
package p1;

public class Test {
    // Which String class will be used: p1.String or java.lang.String
    String myStr;
}
```

Which String class is referred in the Test class: p1.String or java.lang.String? It will refer to p1.String, not java.lang.String, because the package of the compilation unit (which is p1 in this case) is searched before any import declarations to resolve the simple names of types. The compiler finds the String class in package p1. It will not search the java.lang package for the String class. If you want to use the java.lang.String class in this example, you must use its fully qualified name, as shown:

```
// Test.java
package p1;

public class Test {
    java.lang.String s1; // Use java.lang.String
    p1.String s2;        // Use p1.String
    String s3;           // Will use p1.String
}
```

Static Import Declarations

A static import declaration does what its name suggests. It imports static members (static variables/methods) of a type into a compilation unit. You learned about static variables (or class variables) in the previous sections. I discuss static methods in the next section. A static import declaration comes in two flavors:

- Single-static import

- Static-import-on-demand

A single-static-import declaration imports one static member of a type. A static-import-on-demand declaration imports all static members of a type. The general syntax of static import declaration is as follows:

```
// Single-static-import declaration:
import static <package-name>.<type-name>.<static-member-name>;

//Static-import-on-demand declaration:
import static <package-name>.<type-name>.*;
```

You have been printing messages on the standard output using the System.out.println() method. System is a class in java.lang package that has a static variable named out. When you use System.out, you are referring to that static variable named out of the System class. You can use a static import declaration to import the out static variable from the System class as follows:

```
import static java.lang.System.out;
```

Your program now does not need to qualify the out variable with the System class name as System.out. Rather, it can use the name out to mean System.out in your program. The compiler will use the static import declaration to resolve the name out to System.out.

Listing 7-6 demonstrates how to use a static import declaration. It imports the out static variable of the System class. Note that the main() method uses the out.println() method, not System.out.println(). The compiler will replace the out.println() call with the System.out.println() call.

Listing 7-6. Using Static Import Declarations

```
// StaticImportTest.java
package com.jdojo.cls;

import static java.lang.System.out;
```

```java
public class StaticImportTest {
    public static void main(String[] args) {
        out.println("Hello static import!");
    }
}
```

```
Hello static import!
```

> ░ **Tip**   An import declaration imports a type name and it lets you use the type's simple name in your program. What an import declaration does with a type, a static import declaration does with a static member of a type. A static import declaration lets you use the name of a static member (static variable/method) of a type without qualifying it with the type name.

Let's look at another example of using static import declarations. The Math class in the java.lang package contains many utility constants and static methods. For example, it contains a class variable named PI, whose value is equal to 22/7 (the pi in mathematics). If you want to use any of the static variables or methods of the Math class, you need to qualify them with the class name Math. For example, you would refer to the PI static variable as Math.PI and the sqrt() method as Math.sqrt(). You can import all static members of the Math class using the following static-import-on-demand declaration:

```java
import static java.lang.Math.*;
```

Now you can use the name of the static member without qualifying them with the class name Math. Listing 7-7 demonstrates using the Math class by importing its static members.

Listing 7-7. Using Static Imports to Import Multiple Static Members of a Type

```java
// StaticImportTest2.java
package com.jdojo.cls;

import static java.lang.System.out;
import static java.lang.Math.*;

public class StaticImportTest2 {
    public static void main(String[] args) {
        double radius = 2.9;
        double area = PI * radius * radius;

        out.println("Value of PI is: " + PI);
        out.println("Radius of circle: " + radius);
        out.println("Area of circle: " + area);
        out.println("Square root of 2.0: " + sqrt(2.0));
    }
}
```

```
Value of PI is: 3.141592653589793
Radius of circle: 2.9
Area of circle: 26.420794216690158
Square root of 2.0: 1.4142135623730951
```

The following are a few important rules about static import declaration.

Static Import Rule #1

If two static members with the same simple name are imported, one using single-static-import declaration and other using static-import-on-demand declaration, the one imported using single-static-import declaration takes precedence. Suppose there are two classes, p1.C1 and p2.C2. Both classes have a static method named m1. The following code will use the p1.C1.m1() method because it is imported using the single-static-import declaration:

```java
// Test.java
package com.jdojo.cls;

import static p1.C1.m1; // Imports C1.m1() method
import static p2.C2.*;  // Imports C2.m1() method too

public class Test {
    public static void main(String[] args) {
        m1();   // C1.m1() will be called
    }
}
```

Static Import Rule #2

Using a single-static-import declaration to import two static members with the same simple name is not allowed. The following static import declarations generate a compile-time error because both of them import a static member with the same simple name m1:

```java
import static p1.C1.m1;
import static p1.C2.m1; // A compile-time error
```

Static Import Rule #3

If a static member is imported using a single-static-import declaration and there exists a static member in the same class with the same name, the static member in the class is used. The following is the code for two classes, p1.A and p2.Test:

```java
// A.java package p1;

public class A {
    public static void test() {
        System.out.println("p1.A.test()");
    }
}
```

```
// Test.java
package p2;

import static p1.A.test;

public class Test {
    public static void main(String[] args) {
        test(); // Will use p2.Test.test() method, not p1.A.test() method
    }

    public static void test() {
        System.out.println("p2.Test.test()");
    }
}
```

p2.Test.test()

The Test class imports the static method test() from class p1.A using a single-static-import declaration. The Test class also defines a static method test(). When you use the simple name, test, to call the test() method in the main() method, it refers to the p2.Test.test() method, not the one imported by the static import.

There is a hidden danger in using static import declarations in such cases. Suppose you did not have a test() static method in the p2.Test class. In the beginning, the test() method call will call the p1.A.test() method. Later, you add a test() method in the Test class. Now the test() method call will start calling p2.Test.test(), which will introduce a hard-to-find bug in your program.

▓ **Tip**   It may seem that static imports help you use simple names of static members to make the program simpler to write and read. Sometimes, static imports may introduce subtle bugs in your program, which may be hard to debug. You are advised not use static imports at all, or only in very rare circumstances.

Summary

Classes are the basic building blocks in object-oriented programming. A class represents a reference type in Java. Classes serve as templates to create objects. A class consists of four parts: fields, initializers, constructors, and methods. Fields represent the state of objects of the class. Initializers and constructors are used to initialize fields of the class. The new operator is used to create objects of a class. Methods represent the behavior of the objects of the class.

Fields and methods are known as members of the class. Constructors are not members of the class. A top-level class has an access level, which determines from what part of the program it is accessible. A top-level class can have either public- or package-level access. A public class can be accessed from anywhere in the same module. If the module of the class exports the class' package, the public class can also be accessible from inside other modules if those modules declare dependency on the class' module. Absence of an access-level modifiers on a top-level class gives the class package-level access, which makes the class accessible within its package.

Every class in Java defines a new reference type. Java has a special reference type called the null type. It has no name. Therefore, you cannot define a variable of the null reference type. The null reference type has only one value defined by Java, which is the `null` literal. It is simply `null`. The null reference type is assignment-compatible with all other reference types.

A class can have two types of fields. They are called instance variables and class variables, which are also known as non-static and static variables, respectively. Instance variables represent the state of an object of the class. A copy of all instance variables exists for each object of the class. Class variables represent the state of the class itself. Only one copy of class variables exists for a class. Fields of a class can be accessed using dot notation, which takes this form:

```
<qualifier>.<field-name>
```

For an instance variable, the qualifier is a reference of an instance of the class. For a class variable, the qualifier can be a reference of an instance of the class or the class name.

All fields of a class, static as well as non-static, are initialized to a default value. The default value of a field depends on its data type. A numeric field (`byte`, `short`, `char`, `int`, `long`, `float`, and `double`) is initialized to zero. A `boolean` field is initialized to `false`. A reference type field is initialized to `null`.

Import statements in a compilation unit are used to import types from other packages. They allow using the simple names of types from other packages. The compiler uses the import statements to resolve the simple names to fully qualified names. Static import statements are used to import static members of types from other packages.

EXERCISES

1. What is an instance variable of a class? What is another name for an instance variable?

2. What is a class variable of a class? What is another name used for a class variable?

3. What are the default values of different types of fields of a class?

4. Create a class named `Point` with two `int` instance variables named x and y. Both instance variables should be declared public. Do not initialize the two instance variables.

5. Add a `main()` method to the `Point` class that you created in the previous exercise. Create an object of the `Point` class and print the default values for the x and y instance variables. Set the values of x and y to 5 and 10, respectively, and print their values by reading them back in the program.

6. What will happen when the following snippet of code is run, assuming that `Point` is the class name that you created in the previous exercise?

```
Point p = null;
int x = p.x;
```

7. What is the output of the following code?

```
public class Employee {
    String name;
    boolean retired;
    double salary;

    public static void main(String[] args) {
        Employee emp = new Employee();
        System.out.println(emp.name);
        System.out.println(emp.retired);
        System.out.println(emp.salary);
    }
}
```

8. The `java.time` package contains a `LocalDate` class. The class contains a `now()` method that returns the current local date. The `CurrentDate` class uses the simple name of the class, `LocalDate`, in its main method. The code in its current form will not compile. Complete and run the following code by adding an import statement— first a single-type import statement and then an import-on-demand statement—to import the `LocalDate` class. When you run the `CurrentDate` class, it will print the current local date in ISO format, such as 2017-08-27.

```
// CurrentDate.java
package com.jdojo.cls.excercise;

/* Add an import statement here. */

public class CurrentDate {
    public static void main(String[] args) {
        LocalDate today = LocalDate.now();
        System.out.println(today);
    }
}
```

9. Consider the following code for a class named `StaticImport`. The code does not compile because it uses `out.println()` instead of the `System.out.println()` method in its `main()` method. Complete the code by adding a static import statement. The `System` class is in the `java.lang` package and `out` is a static variable in the `System` class.

```
// StaticImport.java
package com.jdojo.cls.excercise;

/* Add a static import statement here. */

public class StaticImport {
    public static void main(String[] args) {
        out.println("Hello static import");
    }
}
```

10. The following code for a class named `MathStaticImport` class does not compile. Add a static-import-on-demand statement to complete the code, so it compiles. The `java.lang.Math` class contains a static variable named `PI` and a static method named `sqrt()`.

```java
// MathStaticImport.java
package com.jdojo.cls.excercise;

/* Add a static-import-on-demand statement here. */

public class MathStaticImport {
    public static void main(String[] args) {
        double radius = 2.0;
        double perimeter = 2 * PI * radius;
        System.out.println("Value of PI is " + PI);
        System.out.println("Square Root of 2 is " + sqrt(2));
        System.out.println("Perimeter of a circle of radius 2.0 is "
                            + perimeter);
    }
}
```

CHAPTER 8

Methods

In this chapter, you will learn:

- What methods are and how to declare methods in a class

- The meaning of the pronouns this and super in a Java program

- What local variables are and rules for using them

- How to invoke methods of a class

- Different parameter-passing mechanisms in general, and then, the parameter-passing mechanisms in Java

- How to declare and use var-args parameters

Example classes in this chapter are in the com.jdojo.cls package, which is a member of the jdojo.cls module. You created the jdojo.cls module in *Chapter 7*.

What Is a Method?

A method in a class defines a behavior of the objects of that class or the behavior of the class itself. A method is a named block of code. The method can be invoked to execute its code. The code that invokes the method is called the caller of the method. Optionally, a method may accept input values from the caller and it may return a value to the caller. The list of input values is known as parameters. A method may have zero parameters. If a method has zero parameters, you say that method does not have any parameters or method does not take/accept any parameters. A method is always defined inside the body of a class or an interface. That is, you cannot have a method by itself. To keep the sample code simple, I show a method as an isolated block of code in this chapter. I show a method inside a class body when I discuss a complete example.

Declaring Methods of a Class

The general syntax for a method declaration is of the form:

```
[modifiers] <return-type> <method-name> (<parameters-list>) [throws-clause] {
    // Body of the method goes here
}
```

Here,

- `modifiers` is an optional list of modifiers for the method.

- `return-type` is the data type of the value returned by the method.

- `method-name` is the name of the method.

- `parameters-list` is the list of parameters that the method accepts. This is optional. Multiple parameters are separated by a comma. Parameters are always enclosed in an opening and closing parentheses. If a method takes no parameters an empty pair of parentheses is used.

- The list of parameters may optionally be followed by a `throws` clause that declares the types of exceptions that the method may throw.

- Finally, you specify the code for the method, also known as the body of the method, inside an opening brace and a closing brace.

Note that four parts in a method declaration are mandatory: the return type, method name, a pair of opening and closing parentheses, and a pair of opening and closing braces. Let's discuss each part in a method declaration in detail. I discuss modifiers in various sections of this chapter and subsequent chapters in this book. I discuss the `throws` clause in the chapter on exception handling. The following is an example of a method:

```
int add(int n1, int n2) {
    int sum = n1 + n2;
    return sum;
}
```

The method's name is add. It takes two parameters. Both parameters are of type `int`. Parameters are named n1 and n2. The method returns an `int` value, which is indicated in its return type. The body of the method computes the sum of two parameters and returns the sum. Figure 8-1 shows the different parts of the add method.

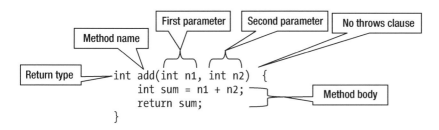

Figure 8-1. *Parts of the add method*

The return type of a method is the data type of the value that the method will return when it is invoked. It could be a primitive data type (for example, `int`, `double`, `boolean`, etc.) or a reference type (for example, `Human`, `String`, etc.). Sometimes, a method does not return a value to its caller. The keyword `void` is used as the return type if a method does not return any value to the caller. In the previous example, the add method returns the sum of two integers, which will be an integer. This is the reason that its return type is specified as `int`.

The method name must be a valid Java identifier. Conventionally, a Java method starts with a lowercase and subsequently a word cap is used. For example, getName, setName, getHumanCount, and createHuman are valid method names. AbCDeFg is also a valid method name; however, it just doesn't follow standard method naming conventions.

A method may take input values from its caller. A parameter is used to take an input value from the caller. A parameter consists of two parts: a data type and a variable name. In fact, a method parameter declaration is a variable declaration. Variables are used to hold the input values that are passed from the method's caller. A comma is used to separate two parameters of a method. In the previous example, the add method declares two parameters, n1 and n2. Both parameters are of the int data type. When the add method is called, the caller must pass two int values. The first value passed from the caller is stored in n1, and the second value in n2. The parameters n1 and n2 are also known as *formal parameters*.

A method has a signature, which uniquely identifies the method in a particular context. The signature of a method is the combination of the following four parts:

- Name of the method

- Number of parameters

- Types of parameters

- Order of parameters

Modifiers, return types, parameter names, and the throws clause are not part of the signature of a method. Table 8-1 lists some examples of method declarations and their signatures.

Table 8-1. *Examples of Method Declarations and Their Signatures*

Method Declaration	Method Signature
int add(int n1, int n2)	add(int, int)
int add(int n3, int n4)	add(int, int)
public int add(int n1, int n2)	add(int, int)
public int add(int n1, int n2) throws OutofRangeException	add(int, int)
void process(int n)	process(int)
double add(int n1, double d1)	add(int, double)
double add(double d1, int n1)	add(double, int)

Most often, you will have situations where you need to understand whether two methods have the same signature. It is very important to understand that the type and order of the method's parameters are part of its signature. For example, double add(int n1, double d1) and double add(double d1, int n1) have different signatures because the order of their parameters differs even though the number and types of parameters are the same.

▓ **Tip**   The signature of a method uniquely identifies the method within a class. It is not allowed to have more than one method in a class with the same signature.

Finally, the code for the method is specified in the method's body, which is enclosed in braces. Executing the code for a method is also called "calling a method" or "invoking a method." A method is invoked using its name with the values for its parameters, if any, within parentheses. To call the add method, you need to use the following statement:

```
add(10, 12);
```

This call to the add method passes 10 and 12 as the values for parameters n1 and n2, respectively. The two values, 10 and 12, that are used to call the add method are called *actual parameters*. Java copies the actual parameters to the formal parameters before it executes the code inside the body of the method. In the previous call to the add method, 10 will be copied in n1, and 12 will be copied in n2. You can refer to the formal parameter names as variables having actual parameter values inside the method's body. You can see n1 and n2 being treated as variables in the following statement in the add method:

```
int sum = n1 + n2;
```

A return statement is used to return a value from a method. It starts with the return keyword. If a method returns a value, the return keyword must be followed by an expression, which evaluates to the value being returned. If the method does not return a value, its return type is specified as void. If the method's return type is void, the method does not have to include a return statement. If a method with a void return type wants to include a return statement, the return keyword must not be followed by any expression; the return keyword is immediately followed by a semicolon to mark the end of the statement. Here are the two flavors of the return statement:

```
// If a method returns a value, <<an expression>> must evaluate to a data type,
// which is assignment compatible with the specified return type of the method
return <an expression>;
```

or

```
// If method's return type is void
return;
```

What does a return statement do? As its name suggests, it returns the control to the caller of the method. If it has an expression, it evaluates the expression and returns the value of the expression to the caller. If a return statement does not have an expression, it simply returns the control to its caller. A return statement is the last statement that is executed in a method's body. You can have multiple return statements in a method's body. However, at most, only one return statement may be executed for a particular method call.

The add method returns the sum of two of its parameters. How do you capture the returned value of a method? A method call itself is an expression whose data type is the return type of the method and it evaluates to the returned value from the method. For example, if you write a statement like this:

```
add(10, 12);
```

add(10, 12) is an expression and its data type is int. At runtime, it will be evaluated to an int value of 22, which is the value returned from the add method. To capture the value of a method call, you can use the method call expression anywhere you can use a value. For example, the following snippet of code assigns the value returned from the add method to a variable call sum:

```
int sum = add(10, 12); // sum variable will be assigned 22
```

Now turn your attention to a method, which does not return a value. You specify void as the return type for such a method. Consider the following method declaration for a method named printPoem:

```
void printPoem() {
    System.out.println("Strange fits of passion have I known:");
    System.out.println("And I will dare to tell,");
    System.out.println("But in the lover's ear alone,");
    System.out.println("What once to me befell.");
}
```

The printPoem method specifies void as its return type, which means that it does not return a value to its caller. It does not specify any parameters, which means it does not accept any input values from its caller. If you need to call the printPoem method, you need to write the following statement:

```
printPoem();
```

▓ **Note**   When I refer to a method in this book, I use the method name followed by a pair of opening and closing parentheses. For example, I refer to the add method as add() and printPoem method as printPoem(). Sometimes, I need to refer to the formal parameters of the method to make the meaning of the method clear. In those cases, I may just use the data type of the formal parameters, for example, add(int, int), to refer to the add(int n1, int n2) method. No matter what convention I use to refer to a method in the discussion, the context of its use will make the meaning clear.

Since the printPoem() method does not return any value, you cannot use a call to this method as part of any expression where a value is expected. For example, the following statement results in a compile-time error:

```
int x = printPoem(); // A compile-time error
```

When a method's return type is void, it is not necessary to use a return statement inside the method's body because you do not have a value to return from the method. Recall that a return statement does two things: evaluates its expression, if any, and returns the control to the caller by ending the execution in the method's body. Even if you do not return a value from a method, you can still use a return statement simply to end the execution of the method. Let's add a parameter to the printPoem method to allow the caller to pass the stanza number that it wants to print. The modified method declaration is as follows:

```
void printPoem(int stanzaNumber) {
    if (stanzaNumber < 1 || stanzaNumber > 2) {
        System.out.println("Cannot print stanza #" + stanzaNumber);
        return; // End the method call
    }

    if (stanzaNumber == 1) {
        System.out.println("Strange fits of passion have I known:");
        System.out.println("And I will dare to tell,");
        System.out.println("But in the lover's ear alone,");
        System.out.println("What once to me befell.");
    } else if (stanzaNumber == 2) {
```

259

```
        System.out.println("When she I loved looked every day");
        System.out.println("Fresh as a rose in June,");
        System.out.println("I to her cottage bent my way,");
        System.out.println("Beneath an evening-moon.");
    }
}
```

The modified `printPoem()` method knows how to print stanza #1 and #2. If its caller passes a stanza number outside this range, it prints a message and ends the method call. This is accomplished by using a `return` statement in the first `if` statement. You could have written the previous `printPoem()` method without writing any `return` statement as follows:

```
void printPoem(int stanzaNumber) {
    if (stanzaNumber == 1) {
        /* Print stanza #1 */
    } else if (stanzaNumber == 2) {
        /* Print stanza #2 */
    } else {
        System.out.println("Cannot print stanza #" + stanzaNumber);
    }
}
```

The compiler will force you to include a `return` statement in the body of a method that specifies a return type in its declaration. However, if the compiler determines that a method has specified a return type, but it always ends its execution abnormally, for example, by throwing an exception, you do not need to include a `return` statement in the method's body. For example, the following method declaration is valid. Do not worry about the `throw` and `throws` keywords at this time; I cover them later in this book.

```
int aMethod() throws Exception {
    throw new Exception("Do not call me...");
}
```

Local Variables

A variable declared inside a method, a constructor, or a block is called a local variable. I discuss constructors in Chapter 9. A local variable declared in a method exists only for the duration the method is being executed. Because a local variable exists only for a temporary duration, it cannot be used outside the method, the constructor, or the block in which it is declared. The formal parameters of a method are treated as local variables. They are initialized with the actual parameter values when the method is invoked, and before the method's body is executed. You need to observe the following rules about the usage of local variables.

Rule #1

Local variables are not initialized by default. Note that this rule is the opposite of the rule for instance/class variable's initialization. When an instance/class variable is declared, it is initialized with a default value. Consider the following partial definition of an `add()` method:

```
int add(int n1, int n2) {
    int sum;
    /* What is the value of sum? We do not know because it has not been initialized yet. */

    /* More code goes here... */
}
```

Rule #2

This rule is an offshoot of the first rule. A local variable cannot be accessed in the program until it is assigned a value. The following snippet of code will generate a compile-time error because it tries to print the value of the local variable, sum, before it is assigned a value. Note that Java runtime has to read (or access) the value of the sum variable to print it.

```
int add(int n1, int n2) {
    int sum;

    // A compile-time error. Cannot read sum because it is not assigned a value yet.
    System.out.println(sum);
}
```

The following snippet of code compiles fine because the local variable, sum, is initialized before it is read:

```
int add(int n1, int n2) {
    int sum = 0;
    System.out.println(sum); // Ok. Will print 0
}
```

Rule #3

A local variable can be declared anywhere in the body of a method. However, it must be declared before it is used. The implication of this rule is that you do not need to declare all local variables at the start of the method body. It is a good practice to declare a variable closer to its use.

Rule #4

A local variable hides the name of an instance variable and a class variable with the same name. Let's discuss this rule in detail. Every variable, irrespective of its type, has a scope. Sometimes the scope of a variable is also known as its visibility. The scope of a variable is the part of the program where the variable can be referred to with its simple name. The scope of a local variable declared in a method is the part of the method body that follows the variable declaration. The scope of a local variable declared in a block is the rest of the block that follows the variable declaration. The scope of the formal parameters of a method is the entire body of the method. It means that the name of the formal parameters of a method can be used throughout the body of that method. For example,

```
int sum(int n1, int n2) {
    // n1 and n2 can be used here
}
```

The scope of instance variables and class variables is the entire body of the class. For example, the instance variable n1 and the class variable n2 can be referred to with its simple name anywhere in the class NameHidingTest1, as shown:

```
class NameHidingTest1 {
    int n1 = 10;           // An instance variable
    static int n2 = 20;   // A class variable

    // m1 is a method
    void m1() {
        // n1 and n2 can be used here
    }

    int n3 = n1; // n1 can be used here
}
```

What happens when two variables, say one instance variable and one local variable, are in scope in the same part of a program? Consider the following code for the NameHidingTest2 class:

```
class NameHidingTest2 {
    // Declare an instance variable named n1
    int n1 = 10;

    // m1 is a method
    void m1() {
        // Declare a local variable named n1
        int n1 = 20;

        /* Both, instance variable n1 and local variable n1, are in scope here */

        // What value will be assigned to n2: 10 or 20?
        int n2 = n1;
    }

    /* Only instance variable n1 is in scope here */

    // n3 will be assigned 10 from the instance variable n1
    int n3 = n1;
}
```

When the m1() method is executed in the previous code, what value will be assigned to the variable n2? Note the class declares an instance variable with the name n1, and the method m1() also declares a local variable with the same name n1. The scope of the instance variable n1 is the entire class body that includes the body of the m1() method. The scope of the local variable n1 is the entire body of the m1() method. When this statement

```
int n2 = n1;
```

is executed inside the m1() method, two variables with the same name n1 are in scope: one has a value of 10 and another has a value of 20. Which n1 does the previous statement refer to: n1 the instance variable, or n1 as the local variable? When a local variable has the same name as the name of a class field, an instance/class variable, the local variable name hides the name of the class field. This is known as *name hiding*. In this case, the local variable name n1 hides the name of the instance variable n1 inside the m1() method. The previous statement will refer to the local variable n1, not the instance variable n1. Therefore, n2 will be assigned a value of 20.

■ **Tip**   A local variable with the same name as a class field hides the name of the class field. In other words, when a local variable as well as a class field with the same name are in the scope, the local variable takes precedence.

The following code for the class NameHidingTest3 clarifies the scenario when a local variable comes into scope:

```
public class NameHidingTest3 {
    // Declare an instance variable named n1
    int n1 = 10;

    public void m1() {
        /* Only the instance variable n1 is in scope here */

        // Assigns 10 to n2
        int n2 = n1;

        /* Only the instance variable n1 is in scope here. The local variable n2
           is also in scope here, which you are ignoring for our discussion for now.
        */

        // Declare a local variable named n1
        int n1 = 20;

        /* Both, instance variable n1 and local variable n1 are in scope here.
           We are ignoring n2 for now.
        */

        // Assigns 20 to n3
        int n3 = n1;
    }
}
```

The previous code assigns the value of the n1 variable to n2 inside the m1() method. You have not declared the local variable n1 at the time you assigned the value of n1 to n2. At this time, only the instance variable n1 is in scope. When you assign n1 to n3, at that time both instance variable n1 and local variable n1 are in scope. The values assigned to n2 and n3 depend on the name-hiding rule. When two variables with the same names are in scope, the local variable is used.

Does it mean that you cannot declare an instance/class variable and a local variable with the same name and use both at the same time? The answer is no. You can declare an instance/class variable and a local variable with the same name. The only thing you need to know is how to refer to the instance/class variable if its name is hidden by a local variable. You learn about referring to the hidden instance/class variables in the next section.

Instance Methods and Class Methods

In Chapter 7, you learned two types of class fields: instance variables and class variables. A class can have two types of methods: instance methods and class methods. Instance methods and class methods are also called non-static methods and static methods, respectively.

An instance method is used to implement behavior of the instances (also called objects) of the class. An instance method can only be invoked in the context of an instance of the class.

A class method is used to implement the behavior of the class itself. A class method always executes in the context of a class.

The static modifier is used to define a class method. The absence of the static modifier in a method declaration makes the method an instance method. The following are examples of declaring static and non-static methods:

```java
// A static or class method
static void aClassMethod() {
    // Method's body goes here
}

// A non-static or instance method
void anInstanceMethod() {
    // Method's body goes here
}
```

Recall that a separate copy of an instance variable exist for each instance of a class, whereas only one copy of a class variable exists, irrespective of the existence of the number of instances (possibly zero) of the class.

When a static method of a class is called, an instance of that class may not exist. Therefore, it is not allowed to refer to instance variables from inside a static method. Class variables exist as soon as the class definition is loaded into memory. The class definition is always loaded into memory before the first instance of a class is created. Note that it is not necessary to create an instance of a class to load its definition into memory. JVM guarantees that all class variables of a class exist before any instances of the class exist. Therefore, you can always refer to a class variable from inside an instance method.

▓ **Tip**   A class method (or static method) can refer to only class variables (or static variables) of the class. An instance method (non-static method) can refer to class variables as well as instance variables of the class.

Listing 8-1 demonstrates the types of class fields that are accessible inside instance and class methods.

Listing 8-1. Accessing Class Fields from Static and Non-Static Methods

```java
// MethodType.java
package com.jdojo.cls;

public class MethodType {
    static int m = 100; // A static variable
    int n = 200;        // An instance variable
```

```
    // Declare a static method
    static void printM() {
        /* You can refer to only static variable m in this method
           because you are inside a static method.
        */

        System.out.println("printM() - m = " + m);

        // Uncommenting the following statement results in a compile-time error.
        //System.out.println("printM() - n = " + n);
    }

    // Declare an instance method
    void printMN() {
        // You can refer to both static and instance variables m and n in this method.
        System.out.println("printMN() - m = " + m);
        System.out.println("printMN() - n = " + n);
    }
}
```

The MethodType class declares m as a static variable and n as a non-static variable. It declares printM() as a static method and printMN() as an instance method. Inside the printM() method, you can refer to only static variable m because a static method can refer to only static variables. If you uncomment the commented statement inside the printM() method, the code will not compile because a static method will attempt to access a non-static variable n. The printMN() method is a non-static method and it can access both static variable m and non-static variable n. Now you would like to invoke the printM() and printMN() methods of the MethodType class. The next section explains how to invoke a method.

Invoking a Method

Executing the code in the body of a method is called invoking (or calling) a method. Instance methods and class methods are invoked differently. An instance method is invoked on an instance of the class using dot notation. The syntax to invoke an instance method is as follows:

```
<instance-reference>.<instance-method-name>(<actual-parameters>)
```

Note that you must have a reference to an instance of a class before calling an instance method of that class. For example, you can write the following snippet of code to invoke the printMN() instance method of the MethodType class listed in Listing 8-1:

```
// Create an instance of MethodType class and store its reference in mt reference variable
MethodType mt = new MethodType();

// Invoke the printMN() instance method using the mt reference variable
mt.printMN();
```

To invoke a class method, you use the dot notation with the class name. The following snippet of code invokes the printM() class method of the MethodType class:

```
// Invoke the printM() class method
MethodType.printM();
```

265

Whatever belongs to a class also belongs to all instances of that class. You can also invoke a class method using a reference of an instance of that class.

```
MethodType mt = new MethodType();
mt.printM(); // Call the class method using an instance mt
```

Which is a better way to invoke a class method: using the class name or using an instance reference? Both ways do the same job. However, using the class name to invoke a class method is more intuitive than using an instance reference. This book uses a class name to invoke a class method, except for the purpose of demonstrating that you can also use an instance reference to invoke a class method. Listing 8-2 demonstrates how to invoke an instance method and a class method of a class. Note that the output shows the same result when you invoke the class method printM() using the class name or an instance reference.

Listing 8-2. Examples of Invoking Instance Methods and Class Methods of a Class

```
// MethodTypeTest.java
package com.jdojo.cls;

public class MethodTypeTest {
    public static void main(String[] args) {
        // Create an instance of the MethodType class
        MethodType mt = new MethodType();

        // Invoke the instance method
        System.out.println("Invoking instance method...");
        mt.printMN();

        // Invoke the class method using the class name
        System.out.println("Invoking class method using class name...");
        MethodType.printM();

        // Invoke the class method using the instance reference
        System.out.println("Invoking class method using an instance...");
        mt.printM();
    }
}
```

```
Invoking instance method...
printMN() - m = 100
printMN() - n = 200
Invoking class method using class name...
printM() - m = 100
Invoking class method using an instance...
printM() - m = 100
```

The Special main() Method

You learned about declaring a method in a class in the previous section. Let's discuss the main() method that you have been using to run your classes. The main() method declaration is as follows:

```
public static void main(String[] args) {
    // Method body goes here
}
```

Two modifiers, public and static, are used in the declaration of the main() method. The public modifier makes it accessible from anywhere in the application as long as the class in which it is declared is accessible. The static modifier makes it a class method, so it can be invoked using a class name. Its return type is void, which means it does not return a value to its caller. Its name is main and it accepts one parameter of type String array (String[]). Note that you have been using args as the name of its parameter. However, you can use any parameter name you wish. For example, you can declare the main method as public static void main(String[] myParameters), which is the same as declaring the main method as shown previously. Whatever parameter name you choose, you will need to use the same name in the body of the method if you need to refer to the parameter passed to this method.

What is special about the declaration of a main() method in a class? You run a Java application by passing a class name to the java command. For example, you would use the following command to run the MethodTypeTest class:

```
Java <other-options> --module jdojo.cls/com.jdojo.cls.MethodTypeTest
```

When the previous command is executed, the JVM (the java command essentially starts a JVM) finds and loads the MethodTypeTest class definition in memory. Then, it looks for a method declaration, which is declared as public and static, returns void, and has a method argument as String array. If it finds the main() method declaration, the JVM invokes the method. If it does not find the main() method, it does not know where to start the application and it throws an error stating that no main() method was found.

Why do you need to declare the main() method as static? The main() method serves as the entry point for a Java application. It is invoked by the JVM when you run a class. The JVM does not know how to create an instance of a class. It needs a standard way to start Java applications. Specifying all details about the main() method and making it static provides the JVM a standard way to start a Java application. By making the main() method static, the JVM can invoke it using the class name, which is passed on the command line.

What will happen if you do not declare the main() method as static? If you do not declare the main() method as static, it will be treated as an instance method. The code will compile fine. However, you will not be able to run the class, which has its main() method declared as an instance method.

Can you have more than one main() method in a class? The answer is yes. You can have multiple methods in a class, which can be named main as long as they do not have the same signature. The following declaration for the MultipleMainMethod class, which declares three main() methods, is valid. The first main() method, which is declared as public static void main(String[] args), may be used as the entry point to run an application. The other two main() methods have no special significance as far as the JVM is concerned.

```
// MultipleMainMethod.java
package com.jdojo.cls;

public class MultipleMainMethods {
    public static void main(String[] args) {
        /* May be used as the application entry point */
    }
```

```
    public static void main(String[] args, int a) {
        /* Another main() method */
    }

    public int main() {
        /* Another main() method */
        return 0;
    }
}
```

Is it required for each class in Java to have a `main()` method? The answer is no. It is required that you declare a `public static void main(String[] args)` method in a class if you want to run that class. If you have a Java application, you will need to have a `main()` method in at least one class so you can start you application by running that class. All other classes that are used in the application, but are not used to start the application, do not need to have a `main()` method.

Can you invoke the `main()` method in your code? Or, can it be invoked only by the JVM? The `main()` method is invoked by JVM when you run a class. Apart from that, you can treat the `main()` method as any other class method. Programmers have a general (and wrong) impression that the `main()` method can only be invoked by a JVM. However, that is not true. It is true that the `main()` method is generally (but not necessarily) invoked by a JVM to start a Java application. However, it does not have to be invoked (at least theoretically) only by a JVM. Here is an example that shows how the `main()` method can be invoked like any other class method. Listing 8-3 has the definition of a `MainTest1` class, which declares a `main()` method. Listing 8-4 has the definition of a `MainTest2` class, which declares a `main()` method.

Listing 8-3. A MainTest1 Class, Which Declares a main() Method

```
// MainTest1.java
package com.jdojo.cls;

public class MainTest1 {
    public static void main(String[] args) {
        System.out.println("Inside the MainTest1.main() method.");
    }
}
```

Listing 8-4. A MainTest2 Class, Which Declares a main() Method, Which in Turn Calls the main() Method of the MainTest1 Class

```
// MainTest2.java
package com.jdojo.cls;

public class MainTest2 {
    public static void main(String[] args) {
        System.out.println("Inside the MainTest2.main() method.");
        MainTest1.main(args);
    }
}
```

```
Inside the MainTest2.main() method.
Inside the MainTest1.main() method.
```

The main() method of the MainTest2 class prints a message and invokes the main() method of the MainTest1 class using the following code:

```
MainTest1.main(args);
```

Note that the main() method of the MainTest1 class accepts a String array as a parameter and the previous statement passes args as the actual value for that parameter.

The JVM will invoke the main() method of the MainTest2 class, which in turn invokes the main() method of the MainTest1 class. The output in Listing 8-4 confirms this. You can also let the JVM invoke the main() method of the MainTest1 class by running the MainTest1 class, which will produce the following output:

```
Inside the MainTest1.main() method.
```

▒ **Tip** The main() method in a class, which is declared as public static void main(String[] args), has a special meaning only when the class is run by the JVM; it serves as an entry point for the Java application. Otherwise, the main() method is treated the same as any other class methods.

What Is this?

Java has a keyword called this. It is a reference to the current instance of a class. It can be used only in the context of an instance. It can never be used in the context of a class because it means the current instance, and no instance exists in the context of a class. The keyword this is used in many contexts. I cover most of its uses in this chapter and in Chapter 9. Consider the following snippet of code that declares a class ThisTest1:

```
public class ThisTest1 {
    int varA = 555;
    int varB = varA;       // Assign value of varA to varB
    int varC = this.varA; // Assign value of varA to varC
}
```

The ThisTest1 class declares three instance variables: varA, varB, and varC. The instance variable varA is initialized to 555. The instance variable varB is initialized to the value of varA, which is 555. The instance variable varC is initialized to the value of varA, which is 555. Note the difference in the initialization expressions for varB and varC. I used unqualified varA when I initialized varB. I used this.varA when I initialized varC. However, the effect is the same. Both varB and varC are initialized with the value of varA. When I use this.varA, it means the value of varA for the current instance, which is 555. In this simple example, it was not necessary to use the keyword this. In the previous case, the unqualified varA refers to the varA for the current instance. However, there are some cases where you must use the keyword this. I discuss such cases shortly.

Since the use of the keyword this is illegal in the context of a class, you cannot use it when you initialize a class variable, like so:

```
// Would not compile
public class ThisTest2 {
    static int varU = 555;
    static int varV = varU;
    static int varW = this.varU; // A compile-time error
}
```

When you compile the code for the class ThisTest2, you receive the following error:

```
"ThisTest2.java": non-static variable this cannot be referenced from a static context at
line 4, column 21
```

The error is loud and clear that you cannot use the keyword this in a static context. Note that static and non-static words are synonymous with "class" and "instance" terms in Java. Static context is the same as class context and non-static context is the same as instance context. The previous code can be corrected by removing the qualifier this from the initialization expression for varW as follows:

```
public class CorrectThisTest2 {
    static int varU = 555;
    static int varV = varU;
    static int varW = varU; // Now it is fine
}
```

You can also qualify a class variable with a class name, as shown in the CorrectThisTest3 class:

```
public class CorrectThisTest3 {
    static int varU = 555;
    static int varV = varU;      '
    static int varW = CorrectThisTest3.varU;
}
```

■ **Tip**   Most of the time, you can use the simple name of instance and class variables within the class in which they are declared. You need to qualify an instance variable with the keyword this and a class variable with the class name only when the instance variable or the class variable is hidden by another variable with the same name.

Consider the following snippet of code for the ThisTest3 class:

```
public class ThisTest3 {
    int varU = 555;
    static int varV = varU; // A compile-time error
    static int varW = varU; // A compile-time error
}
```

When you compile the ThisTest3 class, you receive the following error:

```
"ThisTest3.java": non-static variable varU cannot be referenced from a static context at
line 3, column 21
"ThisTest3.java": non-static variable varU cannot be referenced from a static context at
line 4, column 21
```

The error is the same in kind, although differently phrased, compared to the error that you received for the ThisTest2 class. Last time, the complier complained about using the keyword this. This time, it complained about using the instance variable varU. Both the keyword this and the varU exist in the context of an instance. They do not exist in the context of a class. Whatever exists in the context of an instance cannot be used in the context of a class. However, whatever exists in the context of a class can always be used in the context of an instance. The instance variable declaration and initialization occurs in the context of an instance. In the ThisTest3 class, varU is an instance variable and it exists only in the context of an instance. The varV and varW in ThisTest3 class are class variables and they exist only in the context of a class. This is the reason that the compiler generated an error.

Consider the code for the ThisTest4 class, shown in Listing 8-5. It declares an instance variable, num, and an instance method, printNum(). In the printNum() instance method, it prints the value of the instance variable num. In its main() method, it creates an instance of the ThisTest4 class and invokes the printNum() method on it. The output of the ThisTest4 class shows the expected result.

Listing 8-5. An Example of Using the Simple Name of an Instance Variable in an Instance Method

```java
// ThisTest4.java
package com.jdojo.cls;

public class ThisTest4 {
    int num = 1982; // An instance variable

    public static void main(String[] args) {
        ThisTest4 tt4 = new ThisTest4();
        tt4.printNum();
    }

    void printNum() {
        System.out.println("Instance variable num: " + num);
    }
}
```

```
Instance variable num: 1982
```

Now modify the printNum() method of the ThisTest4 class so it accepts an int parameter and name the parameter num. Listing 8-6 has the modified code for the printNum() method as part of the ThisTest5 class.

Listing 8-6. Variables Name Hiding

```java
// ThisTest5.java
package com.jdojo.cls;

public class ThisTest5 {
    int num = 1982; // An instance variable

    public static void main(String[] args) {
        ThisTest5 tt5 = new ThisTest5();
        tt5.printNum(1969);
    }

    void printNum(int num) {
        System.out.println("Parameter num: " + num);
        System.out.println("Instance variable num: " + num);
    }
}
```

```
Parameter num: 1969
Instance variable num: 1969
```

The output of the ThisTest5 class indicates that the printNum() method is using its parameter num when you use the simple name num inside its body. This is an example of name hiding, where the local variable (method parameter is considered a local variable) num hides the name of the instance variable num inside the printNum() method's body. In the printNum() method, the simple name num refers to its parameter num, not the instance variable num. In this case, you must use the keyword this to qualify the num variable if you want to refer to the num instance variable inside the printNum() method.

Using this.num is the only way you can refer to the instance variable from inside the printNum() method, as long you keep the method's parameter name as num. Another way is to rename the parameter to something other than num, for example, numParam or newNum. Listing 8-7 shows how to use the keyword this to refer to the num instance variable inside the printNum() method.

Listing 8-7. Using the this Keyword to Refer to an Instance Variable Whose Name Is Hidden by a Local Variable

```java
// ThisTest6.java
package com.jdojo.cls;

public class ThisTest6 {
    int num = 1982; // An instance variable

    public static void main(String[] args) {
        ThisTest6 tt6 = new ThisTest6();
        tt6.printNum(1969);
    }

    void printNum(int num) {
        System.out.println("Parameter num: " + num);
        System.out.println("Instance variable num: " + this.num);
    }
}
```

```
Parameter num: 1969
Instance variable num: 1982
```

The output of ThisTest6 shows the expected result. If you do not want to use the keyword this, you can rename the parameter of the printNum() method, like so:

```
void printNum(int numParam) {
    System.out.println("Parameter num: " + numParam);
    System.out.println("Instance variable num: " + num);
}
```

Once you rename the parameter to something other than num, the num instance variable is no longer hidden inside the body of the printNum() method, and therefore you can refer to it using its simple name.

You can use the keyword this to refer to the instance variable num inside the printNum() method even if it is not hidden, as shown here. However, using the keyword this in the following case is a matter of choice, not a requirement.

```
void printNum(int numParam) {
    System.out.println("Parameter num: " + numParam);
    System.out.println("Instance variable num: " + this.num);
}
```

In the previous example, you saw that use of the keyword this is necessary to access instance variables when the instance variable name is hidden. You can avoid using the keyword this in such circumstances by renaming the variable that hides the instance variable name, or renaming the instance variable itself. Sometimes it is easier to keep the variable names the same, as they represent the same thing. This book uses the convention of using the same name for instance variables and local variables if they represent the same thing in the class. For example, the following code is very common:

```
public class Student {
    private int id; // An instance variable

    public void setId(int id) {
        this.id = id;
    }

    public int getId() {
        return this.id;
    }
}
```

The Student class declares an instance variable named id. In its setId() method, it also names the parameter id, and uses this.id to refer to the instance variable. It also uses this.id to refer to the instance variable id in its getId() method. Note that there is no name hiding occurring in the getId() method and you could use the simple name id, which means the instance variable id.

Table 8-2 lists the parts of a class, the context in which they occur, and the permitted use of the keyword this, the instance variable, and the class variable. I have not yet covered all parts of a class that are listed in this table. I cover them in this chapter and in Chapter 9.

Table 8-2. *The Context Type and Allowed Use of the Keyword this, an Instance Variable, and a Class Variable*

Part of a Class	Context	Can Use This Keyword?	Can Use Instance Variable?	Can Use Class Variable?
Instance variable initialization	Instance	Yes	Yes	Yes
Class variable initialization	Class	No	No	Yes
Instance initializer	Instance	Yes	Yes	Yes
Class initializer (Also called static initializer)	Class	No	No	Yes
Constructor	Instance	Yes	Yes	Yes
Instance method (Also called non-static method)	Instance	Yes	Yes	Yes
Class method (Also called static method)	Class	No	No	Yes

The keyword this is a final (a constant is called final in Java because Java uses the final keyword to declare a constant) reference to the current instance of the class in which it appears. Because it is final, you cannot change its value. Because this is a keyword, you cannot declare a variable named this. The following code will generate a compile-time error:

```
public class ThisError {
    void m1() {
        // An error. Cannot name a variable this
        int this = 10;

        // An error. Cannot assign a value to this because it is a constant.
        this = null;
    }
}
```

You can also use the keyword this to qualify an instance method name, although it is never required. The following snippet of code shows the m1() method invoking the m2() method using the keyword this. Note that both methods are instance methods and they could use the simple name to invoke each other.

```
public class ThisTestMethod {
    void m1() {
        // Invoke the m2() method
        this.m2(); // same as "m2();"
    }

    void m2() {
        // do something
    }
}
```

Access Levels for Class Members

In Chapter 7, I covered access levels for a class, which can be public or default (or package level). This section discusses access levels for class members: fields and methods. The access level for a class member determines what area of the program can access (use or refer to) it. One of the following four access level modifiers can be used for a class member:

- `public`
- `private`
- `protected`
- Default or package-level access

Three out of the four types of access levels for a class member are specified using one of the three keywords: `public`, `private`, or `protected`. The fourth type is called the default access level (or package-level access), and it is specified by using no access modifiers. That is, the absence of any of the three access level modifiers, `public`, `private`, or `protected`, specifies package-level access.

If a class member is declared as public using the `public` keyword, it can be accessed from anywhere, provided the class itself is accessible.

If a class member is declared as private using the `private` keyword, it can be accessed only within the body of the declaring class, and nowhere else.

If a class member is declared as protected using the `protected` keyword, it can be accessed from the same package or from descendants of the class, even if the descendants are in a different package. I discuss the protected access level in detail in Chapter 20.

If you do not use any access level modifier for a class member, it has package-level access. A class member with a package-level access can be accessed from the same package.

A class member belongs to the class defining the member. A class member is accessible based on these rules only if the class itself is accessible. If the class is inaccessible, its members are inaccessible irrespective of the access level of the members. Let us take an analogy. A kitchen belongs to a house. You can access the kitchen only if you can access the house. If the front door of the house is locked (the house is inaccessible), the kitchen is inaccessible even if the kitchen is labeled as public. Think of a class member as a kitchen in a house and the class as the house itself. In Java 8, a public class was accessible to all parts of the program, which has changed in Java 9 with the introduction of the module system. A public class may not be really public to everyone. A public class defined in a module may fall into one of the three categories:

- Public only within the defining module
- Public only to specific modules
- Public to everyone

If a class is defined public in a module, but the module does not export the package that contains the class, the class is public only within the module. No other modules can access the class. In this case, the public members of a public class are accessible anywhere in the module that contains the class, and nowhere else.

If a class is defined public in a module, but the module uses a *qualified export* to export the package that contains the class, the class will be accessible only to the modules specified in the qualified export. In this case, the public members of a public class are accessible to the module that contains the class and the specified modules to which the package of the class is exported.

If a class is defined public in a module, but the module exports the package of the class using an unqualified export, the class will be accessible to all modules that reads the module defining the class. In this case, the public members of a public class are accessible to all modules.

Access levels for a class member can be listed from the most restrictive to the least restrictive as private, package-level, protected, and public. Table 8-3 summarizes the four access levels for a class member, assuming that the class itself is accessible.

Table 8-3. *List of Access Levels for Class Members*

Access Level for Class Member	Accessibility
private	Only within the same class
package-level	In the same package
protected	Same package or descendant in any package
public	Everywhere

In this chapter, I restrict the discussion to accessing class members in the same module. I discuss the inter-module accessibility in Chapter 10. The following is a sample class that declares many class members with different access levels:

```
// AccessLevelSample.java
package com.jdojo.cls;

// Class AccessLevelSample has public access level
public class AccessLevelSample {
    private int num1;   // private access level
    int num2;           // package-level access
    protected int num3; // protected access level
    public int num4;    // public access level

    public static int count = 1; // public access level

    // The m1() method has private access level
    private void m1() {
        // Code goes here
    }

    // The m2() method has package-level access
    void m2() {
        // Code goes here
    }

    // The m3() method has protected access level
    protected void m3() {
        // Code goes here
    }

    // The m4() method has public access level
    public void m4() {
        // Code goes here
    }
```

```
    // The doSomething() method has private access level
    private static void doSomething() {
        // Code goes here
    }
}
```

Note that access levels can be specified for both instance and static members of a class. It is a convention to specify the access level modifier as the first modifier in the declaration. If you declare a static field for a class that is public, you should use the public modifier first, and then the static modifier, as a convention. For example, both of the following declarations for an instance variable num are valid:

```
// Declaration #1
public static int num; // Conventionally used
```

```
// Declaration #2
static public int num; // Technically correct, but conventionally not used.
```

Let's discuss a few examples of using access level modifiers for class members, and their effects. Consider the code for the AccessLevel class shown in Listing 8-8.

Listing 8-8. An AccessLevel Class with Class Members Having Different Access Levels

```
// AccessLevel.java
package com.jdojo.cls;

public class AccessLevel {
    private int v1 = 100;
    int v2 = 200;
    protected int v3 = 300;
    public int v4 = 400;

    private void m1() {
        System.out.println("Inside m1():");
        System.out.println("v1 = " + v1 + ", v2 = " + v2
                + ", v3 = " + v3 + ", v4 = " + v4);
    }

    void m2() {
        System.out.println("Inside m2():");
        System.out.println("v1 = " + v1 + ", v2 = " + v2
                + ", v3 = " + v3 + ", v4 = " + v4);
    }

    protected void m3() {
        System.out.println("Inside m3():");
        System.out.println("v1 = " + v1 + ", v2 = " + v2
                + ", v3 = " + v3 + ", v4 = " + v4);
    }
```

```
    public void m4() {
        System.out.println("Inside m4():");
        System.out.println("v1 = " + v1 + ", v2 = " + v2
                + ", v3 = " + v3 + ", v4 = " + v4);
    }
}
```

The class has four instance variables called v1, v2, v3, and v4 and four instance methods called m1(), m2(), m3(), and m4(). Four different access level modifiers have been used for instance variables and instance methods. I have chosen to use instance variables and methods in this example; the same access level rules apply to class variables and class methods. The code for the AccessLevel class compiles without any errors. Note that no matter what the access level for a class member is, it is always accessible inside the class in which it is declared. This can be verified by the fact that you have accessed (read their values) all instance variables, which have different access levels, inside all four methods. Consider the AccessLevelTest1 class shown in Listing 8-9.

Listing 8-9. A Test Class Located in the Same Package as the AccessLevel Class

```
// AccessLevelTest1.java
package com.jdojo.cls;

public class AccessLevelTest1 {
    public static void main(String[] args) {
        AccessLevel al = new AccessLevel();

        // int a = al.v1; /* A compile-time error */
        int b = al.v2;
        int c = al.v3;
        int d = al.v4;

        System.out.println("b = " + b + ", c = " + c + ", d = " + d);

        //al.m1(); /* A compile-time error */
        al.m2();
        al.m3();
        al.m4();

        // Modify the values of instance variables
        al.v2 = 20;
        al.v3 = 30;
        al.v4 = 40;

        System.out.println("\nAfter modifying v2, v3 and v4");

        al.m2();
        al.m3();
        al.m4();
    }
}
```

```
b = 200, c = 300, d = 400
Inside m2():
v1 = 100, v2 = 200, v3 = 300, v4 = 400
Inside m3():
v1 = 100, v2 = 200, v3 = 300, v4 = 400
Inside m4():
v1 = 100, v2 = 200, v3 = 300, v4 = 400

After modifying v2, v3 and v4
Inside m2():
v1 = 100, v2 = 20, v3 = 30, v4 = 40
Inside m3():
v1 = 100, v2 = 20, v3 = 30, v4 = 40
Inside m4():
v1 = 100, v2 = 20, v3 = 30, v4 = 40
```

The AccessLevel and AccessLevelTest1 classes are in the same package. The AccessLevelTest1 class can access all class members of the AccessLevel class, except the ones declared private. You cannot access the instance variable v1 and the instance method m1() of the AccessLevel class from the AccessLevelTest1 class because their access level is private. If you uncomment the two statements in the AccessLevelTest1 class, which attempts to access the private instance variable v1 and the private instance method m1() of the AccessLevel class, you will receive the following compile-time errors:

```
AccessLevelTest1.java:8: error: v1 has private access in AccessLevel
        int a = al.v1; /* A compile-time error */
                   ^
AccessLevelTest1.java:15: error: m1() has private access in AccessLevel
        al.m1(); /* A compile-time error */
           ^
2 errors
```

The AccessLevelTest1 class reads the values of the instance variables of the AccessLevel class, as well as modifies them. You must note one thing: even though you cannot access the private instance variable v1 and the private method m1() of the AccessLevel class from the AccessLevelTest1 class, you can print the value of the private instance variable v1 as shown in the output.

An access level modifier for a class member specifies who can access them directly. If a class member is not accessible directly, it might be accessible indirectly. In this example, the instance variable v1 and the instance method m1() are not directly accessible from outside the AccessLevel class; however, they may be indirectly accessible from outside. Indirect access to an inaccessible class member is usually given by providing another method, which is accessible from outside.

Suppose you want the outside world to read and modify the value of the otherwise inaccessible private instance variable v1. You need to add two public methods, getV1() and setV1(), to the AccessLevel class; these two methods will read and modify the value of the v1 instance variable. Your modified AccessLevel class would look as follows:

```
public class AccessLevel {
    private int v1;

    /* Other code goes here */
```

```
    public int getV1() {
        return this.v1;
    }

    public void setV1(int v1) {
        this.v1 = v1;
    }
}
```

Now, even if the private instance variable v1 is not directly accessible from outside, it is made indirectly accessible through the public methods getV1() and setV1(). Consider another test class, as shown in Listing 8-10.

Listing 8-10. A Test Class Located in a Different Package from the AccessLevel Class

```
// AccessLevelTest2.java
package com.jdojo.cls.p1;

import com.jdojo.cls.AccessLevel;

public class AccessLevelTest2 {
    public static void main(String[] args) {
        AccessLevel al = new AccessLevel();

        //int a = al.v1; /* A compile-time error */
        //int b = al.v2; /* A compile-time error */
        //int c = al.v3; /* A compile-time error */
        int d = al.v4;

        System.out.println("d = " + d);

        //al.m1(); /* A compile-time error */
        //al.m2(); /* A compile-time error */
        //al.m3(); /* A compile-time error */
        al.m4();

        /* Modify the values of instance variables */
        //al.v2 = 20;  /* A compile-time error */
        //al.v3 = 30;  /* A compile-time error */
        al.v4 = 40;

        System.out.println("After modifying v4...");
        //al.m2();   /* A compile-time error */
        //al.m3();   /* A compile-time error */
        al.m4();
    }
}
```

```
d = 400
Inside m4():
v1 = 100, v2 = 200, v3 = 300, v4 = 400
After modifying v4...
Inside m4():
v1 = 100, v2 = 200, v3 = 300, v4 = 40
```

Note the AccessLevelTest2 class in the com.jdojo.cls.p1 package, which is different from the com.jdojo.cls package in which the AccessLevel class exists. The code for the AccessLevelTest2 class is similar to the code for the AccessLevelTest1 class, except that most of the statements have been commented. Notice the use of an import statement to import the AccessLevel class from the com.jdojo.cls package so you can use its simple name inside the main() method. In the AccessLevelTest1 class, it was not necessary to import the AccessLevel class because they are in the same package. The AccessLevelTest2 class can access only the public members of the AccessLevel class because it is in a different package than the AccessLevel class. This is the reason that the uncommented statements access only the public instance variable v4 and the public method m4(). Note that even if only the v4 instance variable is accessible, you are able to print the values of v1, v2, and v3 as well, by accessing them indirectly through the public method m4().

Now consider a trickier situation. See Listing 8-11.

Listing 8-11. A Class with Package-Level Access Having a Public Instance Variable

```
// AccessLevel2.java
package com.jdojo.cls;

class AccessLevel2 {
    public static int v1 = 600;
}
```

Note that there is no access level modifier used for the AccessLevel2 class, which gives it a package-level access by default. That is, the AccessLevel2 class is accessible only within the com.jdojo.cls package. The AccessLeve2 class is simple. It declares only one member, which is the public static variable v1.

Consider the class AccessLevelTest3 shown in Listing 8-12, which is in a different package than the class AccessLevel2.

Listing 8-12. A Test Class That Attempts to Access a Public Member of a Class with a Package-level Access

```
// AccessLevelTest3.java
package com.jdojo.cls.p1;

import com.jdojo.cls.AccessLevel2; // A compile-time error

public class AccessLevelTest3 {
    public static void main(String[] args) {
        int a = AccessLevel2.v1; // A compile-time error
    }
}
```

The `AccessLeveTest3` class attempts to access the public static variable `v1` of the `AccessLevel2` class, which generates a compile-time error. Did I not say that a class member with public access level is accessible from anywhere? Yes. I did say that. Here is the catch—a public class member is accessible from anywhere if and only if the class itself is accessible. In the beginning of this section, I had given you an analogy of a house and a kitchen in the house. If you missed that analogy, let's have another.

Suppose you have some money in your pocket and you declare that your money is public. Therefore, anyone can have your money. However, you hide yourself so that no one can have access to you. How can anyone access your money unless you become accessible to him first? This is the case with the `AccessLevel2` class and its public static variable `v1`. Compare the `AccessLevel2` class with yourself, and its public static variable `v1` with your money. The `AccessLevel2` class has package-level access. Therefore, only the code within its package (`com.jdojo.cls`) can access its name. Its static variable `v1` has the access level of public, which means any code can access it from any package. The static variable `v1` belongs to the `AccessLevel2` class. Unless the `AccessLevel2` class itself is accessible, its static variable `v1` cannot be accessed, even though it has been declared public.

The `import` statement in Listing 8-12 will also generate a compile-time error for the reason that the `AccessLevel2` class is not accessible outside its package `com.jdojo.cls`.

▓ **Tip**   You must consider the access level of both the class and its member to determine whether a class member is accessible. The access level of a class member may make it accessible to a part of a program. However, that part of a program can access the class member only if the class itself, to which the member belongs, is also accessible.

Access Level: A Case Study

A class member can have one of the four access levels: `private`, `protected`, `public`, or package-level. Which access level should be used with a class member? The answer depends on the member type and its purpose. Let's discuss an example of a bank account. Suppose you create a class named `Account` to represent a bank account as follows:

```
// Account.java
package com.jdojo.cls;

public class Account {
    public double balance;
}
```

A bank account holds the balance in the account. This `Account` class does just that. In the real world, a bank account can hold many more pieces of information, for example, account number, account holder name, address, etc. Let's keep the `Account` class simple so you can focus on the discussion of access levels. It allows its every instance to hold a numeric value in its `balance` instance variable. If you want to create an instance of the `Account` class and manipulate its balance, it will look like this:

```
// Create an account object
Account ac = new Account();

// Change the balance to 1000.00
ac.balance = 1000.00;
```

```
// Change the balance to 550.29
ac.balance = 550.29;
```

This snippet of code can be executed anywhere in a Java application where the Account class is accessible because both the Account class and its balance instance variable are public. However, in the real world, no one would let his bank account be manipulated like this. For example, a bank may require you to have a minimum balance of zero in your account. With this implementation, nothing stops you from executing the following statement, which reduces the balance in an account to a negative number:

```
// Set a negative balance
ac.balance = -440.67;
```

In object-oriented programming, as a rule of thumb, the pieces of information that define the state of an object should be declared private. All instance variables of a class constitute the state of objects of that class. Therefore, they should be declared private. If code outside a class is needed to have access to a private instance variable, the access should be given indirectly, by providing a method. The method should have an appropriate access level, which will allow only intended client code to access it. Let's declare the balance instance variable as private. The modified code for the Account class is as follows:

```
// Account.java
package com.jdojo.cls;

public class Account {
    private double balance;
}
```

With the modified Account class, you can create an object of the Account class anywhere in a Java application if the Account class is accessible like so:

```
// Create an account object
Account ac = new Account();
```

However, you cannot access the balance instance variable of the Account object unless you write the code inside the Account class itself. The following code is valid only if the code is written inside the Account class because the private instance variable balance cannot be accessed from outside the Account class:

```
// Change the balance
ac.balance = 188.37;
```

The modified version of the Account class is not acceptable in this form because you can create an account, but you cannot read or manipulate its balance. The Account class must provide some interface for the outside world to access and manipulate its balance in a controlled way. For example, if you have money and want to share it with the outside world, you do not show the money to everyone and ask him to take it directly. Rather, anyone who wants your money needs to ask you (send you a message), and then you give him your money according to certain situations. In other words, money is your private possession and you let others access it in a controlled way by making them ask you for that money, instead of letting them just take money directly from your pocket. Similarly, you want others to view the balance of an account, credit money to an account, and debit money from an account. However, all these actions should happen through an Account object, rather than manipulating the balance of an account object directly.

Java lets you send a message to an object by using instance methods. An object can receive a message from the outside world and it can respond differently to the same message depending on its internal state. For example, when all your money is gone and someone asks you for money, you can respond by saying that you do not have any money. However, you responded to the same message (give me money) differently (by giving the money) when you had money.

Let's declare three public methods in the Account class that will serve as an interface to the outside world for those needing to access and manipulate the balance of an account.

- A getBalance() method will return the balance of an account.

- A credit() method will deposit a specified amount to an account.

- A debit() method will withdraw a specified amount from an account.

Both credit() and debit() methods will return 1 if the transaction is successful and -1 if the transaction fails.

Listing 8-13 has the code for the modified Account class.

Listing 8-13. A Modified Version of the Account Class with a Private Instance Variable and Public Methods

```java
// Account.java
package com.jdojo.cls;

public class Account {
    private double balance;

    public double getBalance() {
        // Return the balance of this account
        return this.balance;
    }

    public int credit(double amount) {
        // Make sure credit amount is not negative, NaN or infinity
        if (amount < 0.0 || Double.isNaN(amount) || Double.isInfinite(amount)) {
            System.out.println("Invalid credit amount: " + amount);
            return -1;
        }

        // Credit the amount
        System.out.println("Crediting amount: " + amount);
        this.balance = this.balance + amount;
        return 1;
    }

    public int debit(double amount) {
        // Make sure the debit amount is not negative, NaN or infinity */
        if (amount < 0.0 || Double.isNaN(amount) || Double.isInfinite(amount)) {
            System.out.println("Invalid debit amount: " + amount);
            return -1;
        }
```

```java
        // Make sure a minimum balance of zero is maintained
        if (this.balance < amount) {
            System.out.println("Insufficient funds. Debit attempted: " + amount);
            return -1;
        }

        // Debit the amount
        System.out.println("Debiting amount: " + amount);
        this.balance = this.balance - amount;
        return 1;
    }
}
```

The class contains a private instance variable. It contains public methods that let the outside world access and modify the private instance variable. The public methods are acting like protective covers for the private instance variable. They let the outside world read or modify the private instance variable in a controlled way. For example, you cannot credit a negative amount, and a minimum of zero balance must be maintained. Let's test the Account class. The test code is shown in Listing 8-14.

Listing 8-14. A Test Class to Test the Account Class Behavior

```java
// AccountTest.java
package com.jdojo.cls;

public class AccountTest {
    public static void main(String[] args) {
        Account ac = new Account();
        double balance = ac.getBalance();
        System.out.println("Balance = " + balance);

        // Credit and debit some amount
        ac.credit(234.78);
        ac.debit(100.12);

        balance = ac.getBalance();
        System.out.println("Balance = " + balance);

        // Attempt to credit and debit invalid amounts
        ac.credit(-234.90);
        ac.debit(Double.POSITIVE_INFINITY);

        balance = ac.getBalance();
        System.out.println("Balance = " + balance);

        // Attempt to debit more than the balance
        ac.debit(2000.00);

        balance = ac.getBalance();
        System.out.println("Balance = " + balance);
    }
}
```

```
Balance = 0.0
Crediting amount: 234.78
Debiting amount: 100.12
Balance = 134.66
Invalid credit amount: -234.9
Invalid debit amount: Infinity
Balance = 134.66
Insufficient funds. Debit attempted: 2000.0
Balance = 134.66
```

The AccountTest class creates an object of the Account class and attempts various operations on it using its public methods. The results are shown in the output, which indicates that this is an improved Account class that protects an account object from being manipulated incorrectly. You can also note that making the instance variables private and allowing access to them through public methods lets you enforce your business rules. If you expose the instance variables, you cannot enforce any business rules that control its valid values because anyone can modify it without any restrictions.

One important point to keep in mind when you design a class is its maintainability. Keeping all instance variables private and allowing access to them through public methods makes your code ready for future changes. Suppose you started with a zero minimum balance for an account. You have deployed the Account class in the production environment and it is being used in many places in the application. Now, you want to implement a new business rule that states that every account must have a minimum balance of 100. It is easy to make this change. Just change the code for the debit() method and you are done. You do not need to make any changes to the client code that is calling the debit() method of the Account class. Note that you need a little more work on the Account class to fully enforce the rule of a minimum balance of 100. When an account is created, the balance is zero by default. To enforce this new minimum balance rule at the time an account is created, you will need to know about constructors of a class. I discuss constructors in the next chapter.

Another option for the access level for the balance instance variable in the Account class is to give it a package-level access. Recall that a package-level access is given to a class member by using no access modifier in its declaration. If the balance instance variable has package-level access, it is a little better than giving it public access because it is not accessible from everywhere. However, it can be accessed and manipulated directly by the code inside the same package in which the Account class has been declared. By now, you understand that letting any code access the balance instance variable directly from outside the Account class is not acceptable. Additionally, if you declare the method of the Account class to have package-level access, it can be used only inside the same package in which the Account class has been declared. You want objects of the Account class to be manipulated from anywhere in the application using its methods. Therefore, you cannot declare the methods or the instance variable of the Account class to have package-level access. When do you declare a class and/or a class member to have package-level access? Typically, package-level access is used for a class and its members when the class has to serve as a helper class or internal implementation for other classes in a package.

When do you use a private access level for class members? You have already seen the benefits of using the private instance variables for the Account class. The private access level for instance variables provides data hiding, where the internal state of the object is protected from outside access. An instance method for a class defines a behavior for its objects. If a method is used only internally within a class, and no outside code has any business knowing about it, the method should have a private access level. Let's go back to your Account class. You have used the same logic to validate the amount passed to the credit() and debit() methods. You can move the code that validates the amount to a private method, isValidAmount(), which is used internally by the Account class. It checks if an amount being used for credit or debit is not a negative number, not a NaN, and not infinity. These three criteria for a number to be a valid number apply only to the Account class, and no other class needs to be using them. This is why you need to declare this method private. Declaring it private has another advantage. In the future, you may make a rule that you must credit or debit a minimum of 10 from any account. At that time, you could just change the private isValidAmount() method and you are done. If you had made this method public, it would affect all the client code, which was using it to validate an amount. You may not want to change the criteria for a valid amount globally. To keep the effect of a change localized in a class, when the business rules change, you must implement a method as private. You can implement this logic in your Account class as follows (only changed code is shown):

```
// Account.java
package com.jdojo.cls;

public class Account {
    /* Other code goes here */

    public int credit(double amount) {
        // Make sure credit amount is valid
        if (!this.isValidAmount(amount, "credit")) {
          return -1;
        }
        /* Other code goes here */
    }

    public int debit(double amount) {
        // Make sure debit amount is valid
        if (!this.isValidAmount(amount, "debit")) {
          return -1;
        }
        /* Other code goes here */
    }

    // Use a private method to validate credit/debit amount
    private boolean isValidAmount(double amount, String operation) {
        // Make sure amount is not negative, NaN or infinity
        if (amount < 0.0 || Double.isNaN(amount) || Double.isInfinite(amount)) {
          System.out.println("Invalid " + operation + " amount: " + amount);
          return false;
        }
        return true;
    }
}
```

Note that you might have implemented the credit() method (the debit() method as well) in a simpler way using the following logic:

```
if (amount >= 0) {
    this.balance = this.balance + amount;
    return 1;
} else {
    /* Print error here */
    return -1;
{
```

You could use the simpler logic to implement the credit() method, which checks if the amount is valid, instead of checking if the amount is invalid. I did not use this logic because I wanted to demonstrate in the same example how to use a private method. Sometimes one writes more code to drive home a point in a discussion.

Now you are left with the protected access level modifier. When do you declare a class member protected? A class member with the protected access level can be accessed in the same package and in the descendant class, even if the descendant class is not in the same package. I discuss how to create a descendant class and the use of the protected access level in Chapter 20.

What Is a Var-Args Method?

The term "var-args" is shorthand for "variable-length arguments". It lets you declare a method or constructor that accepts a variable number of arguments (or parameters). I use only the term "method" in this discussion. However, the discussion also applies to constructors.

The number of arguments a method accepts is called its *arity*. A method that accepts variable-length arguments is called a variable-arity method or var-args method. What does a var-args method look like? Let's discuss how a non-var-args method works before you look at a var-args method.

Consider the following code for a MathUtil class that declares a max() method. The method has two parameters. It computes and returns the maximum of its two arguments.

```
public class MathUtil {
    public static int max(int x, int y) {
        int max = x;

        if (y > max) {
            max = y;
        }

        return max;
    }
}
```

There is nothing extraordinary going on in the MathUtil class or its max() method. Suppose you want to compute the maximum of two integers, say 12 and 18, you would invoke the max() method as follows:

```
int max = MathUtil.max(12, 18);
```

When this statement is executed, 18 will be assigned to the variable max. Suppose you want to compute the maximum of three integers. You might come up with the following logic:

```
int max = MathUtil.max(MathUtil.max(70, 9), 30);
```

This logic works fine. It computes the maximum of two integers, and then computes the maximum of the two and the third integer. Suppose you want to compute maximum of ten integers. You might repeat this logic and that will work, although the code may not be readable. You need a better way of doing this.

Now try overloading the max() method, so it accepts three integer arguments. Here is the newer version of the MathUtil class, called MathUtil2:

```
public class MathUtil2 {
    public static int max(int x, int y) {
        int max = x;
```

```
        if (y > max) {
            max = y;
        }

        return max;
    }

    public static int max(int x, int y, int z) {
        int max = x;

        if (y > max) {
            max = y;
        }

        if (z > max) {
            max = z;
        }

        return max;
    }
}
```

You can compute the maximum of two and three integers as follows:

```
int max1 = MathUtil2.max(12, 18);
int max2 = MathUtil2.max(10, 8, 18);
```

Adding a max() method with three int arguments did solve the problem temporarily. The real problem still remains. You will have to add a max() method with all possible number of integer arguments. You would agree that no programmer wants to write a max() method where he will have to keep adding a newer versions.

Before the introduction of var-args methods in Java, when the number of arguments of a method was not known at design time, you would declare the method argument as an array of int, as shown here. I discuss arrays in detail in a later chapter.

```
public class MathUtil3 {
    public static int max(int[] num) {
        /* Must check for zero element in num here */

        int max = Integer.MIN_VALUE;
        for(int i = 0; i < num.length; i++) {
            if (num[i] > max) {
                max = num[i];
            }
        }

        return max;
    }
}
```

You can write the following snippet of code that will compute the maximum of two and three integers using the MathUtil3.max() method:

```
int[] num1 = new int[] {10, 1};
int max1 = MathUtil3.max(num1);

int[] num2 = new int[] {10, 8, 18} ;
int max2 = MathUtil3.max(num2);
```

You can pass an arbitrary number of integers to the MathUtil3.max() method. In a sense, you have a way to pass an arbitrary number of arguments to a method. What bothers programmers is the way the method needs to be called when its argument type is an array. You must create an array object and package the values of all its elements when you need to call the method with an array argument. The issue here is not the code inside the max(int[] num) method; rather, it is the client code that calls this method.

Var-args come to the rescue. Let's declare a max() method, which can accept any number of integer arguments including zero arguments. The beauty of a var-args method is in the simpler client code that calls the method. So, how do you declare a var-args method? All you need to do is to add an ellipsis (or triple-dot like ...) after the data type of the method's argument. The following snippet of code shows a max() method declaration with one variable-length argument, num, which is of the int data type. Note the placement of ellipsis after the data type int.

```
public static int max(int... num) {
    // Code goes here
}
```

Adding whitespace before and after ellipsis is optional. All of the following var-args method declarations are valid. They use different types of whitespace before and after the ellipsis.

```
public static int max(int... num)  // A space after
public static int max(int ... num) // A space before and after
public static int max(int...num)    // No space before and after
public static int max(int ...
num) // A space before and a newline after
```

A var-args method can have more than one argument. The following snippet of code shows that aMethod() accepts three arguments, one of which is a variable-length argument:

```
public static int aMethod(String str, double d1, int...num) {
    // Code goes here
}
```

There are two restrictions on a var-args method:

- A var-args method can have a maximum of one variable-length argument. The following declaration for the m1() method is invalid because it declares two variable-length arguments, n1 and n2:

```
// An invalid declaration
void m1(String str, int...n1, int...n2) {
    // Code goes here
}
```

- The variable-length argument of a var-args method must be the last argument in the argument list. The following declaration for the m2() method is invalid because the variable-length argument n1 is not declared as the last argument:

```
// An invalid declaration
void m2(int...n1, String str) {
    // Code goes here
}
```

You can fix the previous declaration by moving the argument n1 to the last, like so:

```
// A valid declaration
void m2(String str, int...n1) {
    // Code goes here
}
```

Let's rewrite the max() method to make it a var-args method, as shown:

```
public class MathUtil4 {
    public static int max(int...num) {
        int max = Integer.MIN_VALUE;

        for(int i = 0; i < num.length; i++) {
            if (num[i] > max) {
                max = num[i];
            }
        }

        return max;
    }
}
```

You almost always have a loop inside a var-args method that processes the list of arguments for the variable-length argument. The length property gives you the number of values that were passed for the variable-length argument. For example, num.length in the max() var-args method will give you the number of integers that were passed to the method. To get the nth value in the variable-length argument, you need to use varArgsName[n-1]. For example, num[0], num[1], and num[n-1] will contain the first, second, and n[th] value passed in for the num variable-length argument. If you just want to process all values passed in for a variable-length argument, you can use a simpler loop, a foreach loop. You can rewrite the code for the max() method using a foreach loop as follows:

```
public static int max2(int...num) {
    int max = Integer.MIN_VALUE;

    for(int currentNumber : num) {
        if (currentNumber > max) {
            max = currentNumber;
        }
    }

    return max;
}
```

The body of the MathUtil4.max() method is the same as if the num argument is declared as an int array. You are right in thinking so. The Java compiler implements a variable-length argument using an array. The previous declaration of the MathUtil4.max() method is changed by the compiler. The declaration part max(int…num) is changed to max(int[] num) when you compile the code. What benefit do you get using a variable-length argument? The benefit of using a variable-length argument in a method comes from the elegant way of calling the method. You can call the MathUtil4.max() method as follows:

```
int max1 = MathUtil4.max(12, 8);
int max2 = MathUtil4.max(10, 1, 30);
```

You can use zero or more arguments for a variable-length argument in a method. The following code is a valid call to the max() method:

```
int max = MathUtil4.max(); // Passing no argument is ok
```

What will be returned by calling the MathUtil4.max() method with no argument? If you look at the method's body, it will return Integer.MIN_VALUE, which is -2147483648. Practically, a call to the max() method without at least two arguments is not a valid call. You must check for invalid number of arguments when a method is a var-args method. You do not get a problem of invalid number of arguments for non-var-args methods because the compiler will force you to use the exact number of arguments. The following declaration of the max() method will force its caller to pass at least two integers:

```
// Arguments n1 and n2 are mandatory
public static int max(int n1, int n2, int... num) {
    // Code goes here
}
```

The compiler will treat the first two arguments, n1 and n2, as mandatory and the third argument, num, as optional. Now, you can pass two or more integers to the max() method. Listing 8-15 shows the final, complete code for the max() method.

Listing 8-15. A Utility Class to Compute the Maximum of Some Specified Integers Using a Var-Args Method

```
// MathUtil5.java
package com.jdojo.cls;

public class MathUtil5 {
    public static int max(int n1, int n2, int... num) {
        // Initialize max to the maximum of n1 and n2
        int max = (n1 > n2 ? n1 : n2);

        for(int i = 0; i < num.length; i++) {
            if (num[i] > max) {
                max = num[i];
            }
        }

        return max;
    }
```

```
    public static void main(String[] args) {
        System.out.println("max(7, 9) = " + MathUtil5.max(7, 9));
        System.out.println("max(70, 19, 30) = " + MathUtil5.max(70, 19, 30));
        System.out.println("max(-7, -1, 3) = " + MathUtil5.max(-70, -1, 3));
    }
}
```

```
max(7, 9) = 9
max(70, 19, 30) = 70
max(-7, -1, 3) = 3
```

You can pass any number of integers when you call the MathUtil5.max() method. All of the following statements are valid:

```
int max1 = MathUtil5.max(12, 8);        // Assigns 12 to max1
int max2 = MathUtil5.max(10, 1, 30);    // Assigns 30 to max2
int max3 = MathUtil5.max(11, 3, 7, 37); // Assigns 37 to max3
```

If you call the MathUtil5.max() method with no arguments or one argument, the compiler will generate an error.

```
int max1 = MathUtil5.max();   // A compile-time error
int max2 = MathUtil5.max(10); // A compile-time error
```

Overloading a Var-Args Method

The same overloading rules for methods also apply to var-args methods. You can overload a method with a variable-length argument as long as the parameters for the methods differ in type, order, or number. For example, the following is a valid example of an overloaded max() method:

```
public class MathUtil6 {
    public static int max(int x, int y) {
        // Code goes here
    }

    public static int max(int...num) {
        // Code goes here
    }
}
```

Consider the following snippet of code, which calls the overloaded method MathUtil6.max() with two arguments:

```
int max = MathUtil6.max(12, 13); // which max() will be called?
```

The MathUtil6 class has two max() methods. One method accepts two int parameters and another accepts a variable-length int parameter. In this case, Java will call the max(int x, int y). Java first attempts to find a method declaration using an exact match for the number of parameters. If it does not find an exact match, it looks for a match using variable-length parameters.

▒ **Tip**   If a var-args method is overloaded, Java uses the more specific version of the method instead of using a var-args method. Java uses var-args method as the last resort to resolve a method call.

Sometimes a call to an overloaded var-args method may cause confusion to the Java compiler. The overloading of the method itself may be valid. However, the call to it may cause an issue. Consider the following snippet of code for the `MathUtil7` class, which is a valid example of method overloading:

```
public class MathUtil7 {
    public static int max(int...num) {
        // Code goes here
    }

    public static int max(double...num) {
        // Code goes here
    }
}
```

Which version of the `max()` method will be called when the following statement is executed?

```
int max = MathUtil7.max(); // Which max() to call?
```

The previous statement will generate a compile-time error stating that the call to `MathUtil7.max()` is ambiguous. Java allows you to pass zero or more values for a variable-length argument. In the previous statement, both methods `max(int...num)` and `max(double...num)` qualify for the `MathUtil7.max()` call. The compiler cannot decide which one to call. You may find many other instances where a call to an overloaded var-args method results in an ambiguous method call and the compiler will generate an error. The error message will guide you to the offending code.

Var-Args Methods and the main() Method

Recall that if you want to run a class, you need to declare a `main()` method in it with a `String` array as its argument. The signature for the `main()` method must be `main(String[] args)`. A var-args method is implemented by the compiler using an array. If your method signature is `m1(Xxx…args)`, it is changed to `m1(Xxx[] args)` by the compiler. Now you can declare the `main()` method of your class using the older notation that uses a `String` array or using a newer notation that uses a var-args. The following declaration of `main()` method for the `Test` class is valid. You will be able to run the `Test` class using the `java` command.

```
public class Test {
    public static void main(String...args)  {
        System.out.println("Hello from varargs main()...");
    }
}
```

Parameter-Passing Mechanisms

This section discusses different ways of passing parameters to a method that are used in different programming languages. I do not discuss anything that is specific to Java in this section. The syntax or symbols used in this section may not be supported by Java. This section is important to programmers in understanding the memory states in the process of a method call. If you are an experienced programmer, you may skip this section. The next section discusses the parameter-passing mechanisms in Java.

The following are a few of the commonly used mechanisms to pass parameters to a method:

- Pass by value

- Pass by constant value

- Pass by reference

- Pass by reference value

- Pass by result

- Pass by result value

- Pass by name

- Pass by need

A variable has three components:a name, a memory address (or a location), and data. The name of a variable is a logical name that is used in a program to refer to its memory address. Data is stored at the memory address that is associated with the variable name. The data stored at the memory address is also known as the value of the variable. Suppose you have an int variable named id whose value is 785, which is stored at the memory address 131072. You may declare and initialize the id variable as follows:

```
int id = 785;
```

You can visualize the relationship between the variable name, its memory address, and the data stored at the memory address, as depicted in Figure 8-2.

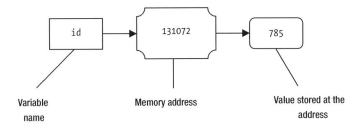

Figure 8-2. *Relationship between a variable name, its memory address, and data*

In Figure 8-2, you see that the actual data of the variable id is stored at the memory address. You can also store data at a memory address, which is not the actual value for the variable; rather it is the memory address of the location where the actual value is stored. In this case, the value stored at the first memory address is a reference to the actual data stored at some other memory address, and such a value is known as a reference or a pointer. If a variable stores the reference to some data, it is called a *reference variable*.

Contrast the phrases "a variable" and "a reference variable." A variable stores the actual data itself at its memory location. A reference variable stores the reference (or memory address) of the actual data. Figure 8-3 depicts the difference between a variable and a reference variable.

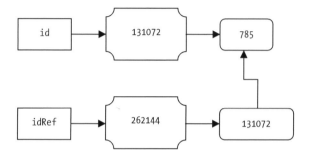

Figure 8-3. *Difference between a variable and a reference variable*

In Figure 8-3, `idRef` is a reference variable and `id` is a variable. Both variables are allocated memory separately. The actual value of 785 is stored at the memory location of `id` variable, which is 131072. However, the memory location (262144) of `idRef` stores the address of the `id` variable (or address or memory location, where 785 is stored). You can get to the value 785 in memory using either variable. The operation to get the actual data that a reference variable refers to is called *dereferencing*.

A method (also called a function or procedure in some programming languages) can optionally accept parameters from its caller. A method's parameters allow data sharing between the caller context and the method context. Many mechanisms are in practice to pass the parameters to a method. The following sections discuss some of the commonly used parameter-passing mechanisms.

Pass By Value

Pass by value is the simplest parameter-passing mechanism to understand. However, it is not necessarily the most efficient and the easiest to implement in all situations. When a method is called, the values of the actual parameters are copied to the formal parameters. When the method execution starts, two copies of the value exist in memory: one copy for the actual parameter and one copy for the formal parameter. Inside the method, the formal parameter operates on its own copy of the value. Any changes made to the value of the formal parameter do not affect the value of the actual parameter.

Figure 8-4 depicts the memory state when a method is called using the pass by value mechanism. It is to be emphasized that once the formal parameter gets its value, which is a copy of the actual parameter, the two parameters have nothing to do with each other. The formal parameter is discarded at the end of the method call. However, the actual parameter persists in memory after the method call ends. How long the actual parameter persists in memory depends on the context of the actual parameter.

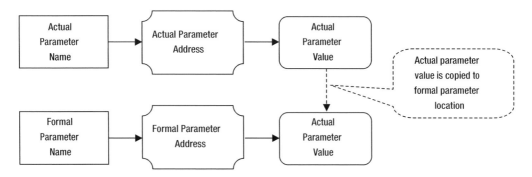

Figure 8-4. *Memory states for actual and formal parameters when a method is called*

Consider the following code for an `increment()` method, which accepts an `int` parameter and increments it by 2:

```
// Assume that num is passed by value
void increment(int num) {
    /* #2 */
    num = num + 2;
    /* #3 */
}
```

Suppose you call the `increment()` method with the following snippet of code:

```
int id = 57;
/* #1 */
increment(id);
/* #4 */
```

Four points of executions in the code are labeled as #1, #2, #3, and #4. Table 8-4 describes the memory states for the actual parameter and the formal parameter, before, after, and when the `increment()` method is invoked. Note that the formal parameter num no longer exists in memory at #4.

Table 8-4. *Description of Memory States for Actual and Formal Parameters When the increment() Method is Called and the Parameter is Passed by Value*

Point of Execution	Memory State of Actual Parameter id	Memory State of Formal Parameter num
#1	The id variable exists in memory and its value is 57.	The num variable does not exist at this point.
#2	The id variable exists in memory and its value is 57.	The formal parameter, num, has been created in memory. The value of the actual parameter id has been copied to the address associated with the num variable. At this point, num holds the value of 57.
#3	The id variable exists in memory and its value is 57.	At this point, num holds value of 59.
#4	The id variable exists in memory and its value is 57.	The formal parameter, num, does not exist in memory at this point because the method call is over.

All local variables, including formal parameters, are discarded when a method invocation is over. You can observe that incrementing the value of the formal parameter inside the increment() method was practically useless because it can never be communicated back to the caller environment. If you want to send back one value to the caller environment, you can use a return statement in the method body to do that. The following is the code for the smartIncrement() method, which returns the incremented value to the caller:

```
// Assume that num is passed by value
int smartIncrement(int num) {
    num = num + 2;
    return num;
}
```

You will need to use the following snippet of code to store the incremented value that is returned from the method in the id variable:

```
int id = 57;
id = smartIncrement(id);  // Store the returned value in id
/* At this point id has a value of 59 */
```

Note that pass by value lets you pass multiple values from the caller environment to the method using multiple parameters. However, it lets you send back only one value from the method. If you just consider the parameters in a method call, pass by value is a one-way communication. It lets you pass information from the caller to the method using parameters. However, it does not let you pass back information to the caller through the parameters. Sometimes you may want to send multiple values from a method to the caller's environment through the parameters. In those cases, you need to consider different ways to pass parameters to the method. The pass by value mechanism is of no help in such situations.

A method that is used to swap two values does not work when the parameters are passed by values. Consider the following code for a classical swap() method:

```
// Assume that x and y are passed by value
void swap(int x, int y) {
    int temp = x;
    x = y;
    y = temp;
}
```

You can call the previous swap() method using the following snippet of code:

```
int u = 75;
int v = 53;
swap(u, v);
/* At this point, u and v will be still 75 and 53, respectively */
```

By this time, you should be able to figure out why the values of u and v were not swapped when they were passed to the swap() method. When the swap() method was called, the values of u and v were copied to the locations of the x and y formal parameters, respectively. Inside the swap() method, the values of the formal parameters x and y were swapped and the values of actual parameters u and v were not touched at all. When the method call was over, the formal parameters x and y were discarded.

The advantages of using pass by value are as follows:

- It is easy to implement.

- If the data being copied is a simple value, it is faster.

- The actual parameters are protected from any side effects when they are passed to the method.

The disadvantages of using pass by value are as follows:

- If the actual parameter is a complex data, such as a large object, it may be difficult, if not impossible, to copy the data to another memory location.

- Copying a large amount of data takes memory space and time, which may slow down the method call.

Pass By Constant Value

Pass by constant value is essentially the same mechanism as *pass by value* with one difference that the formal parameters are treated as constants, and hence, they cannot be changed inside the method's body. The values of actual parameters are copied to the formal parameters as is done in *pass by value*. You can only read the value of formal parameters inside the method's body if they are passed by constant value.

Pass By Reference

It is important that you do not confuse the phrases "reference" and "pass by reference." A "reference" is a piece of information (typically a memory address) that is used to get to the actual data stored at some other location. "Pass by reference" is a mechanism to pass information from a caller's environment to a method using formal parameters.

In pass by reference, the memory address of the actual parameter is passed and the formal parameter is mapped (or associated) with the memory address of the actual parameter. This technique is also known as aliasing, where multiple variables are associated with the same memory location. The formal parameter name is an alias for the actual parameter name. When a person has two names, no matter which of the two names you use, you refer to the same person. Similarly, when a parameter is passed by reference, no matter which name you use in the code (the actual parameter name or the formal parameter name), you are referring to the same memory location and hence the same data.

In pass by reference, if the formal parameter is modified inside the method, the actual parameter sees the modification instantaneously. Figure 8-5 depicts the memory state for actual and formal parameters when a parameter to a method is passed by reference.

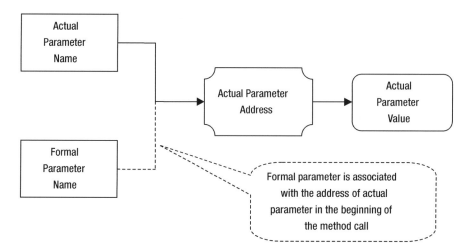

Figure 8-5. *Memory states of actual and formal parameters when the parameters are passed by reference*

Many books use the phrase "pass by reference." However, they do not mean the one we are discussing in this section. They really mean "pass by reference value," which I discuss in the next section. Note that in pass by reference, you do not allocate separate memory for the formal parameter. Rather, you just associate the formal parameter name to the same memory location of the actual parameter.

Let's do the increment() method call exercise again. This time, assume that the num parameter is passed by reference.

```
// Assume that num is passed by reference
void increment(int num) {
    /* #2 */
    num = num + 2;
    /* #3 */
}
```

You will call the increment() method with the following snippet of code:

```
int id = 57;
/* #1 */
increment(id);
/* #4 */
```

Table 8-5 describes the memory states for the actual parameter and formal parameter, before, after, and during the increment() method's invocation. Note that at #4, the formal parameter num no longer exists in memory and still the actual parameter id has the value of 59 after the method call is over.

Table 8-5. *Description of Memory States for Actual and Formal Parameters When the increment() Method Is Called and the Parameter Is Passed by Reference*

Point of Execution	Memory State of Actual Parameter id	Memory State of Formal Parameter num
#1	The id variable exists in memory and its value is 57.	The num variable does not exist at this point.
#2	The id variable exists in memory and its value is 57.	The formal parameter's name, num, has been associated with the memory address of actual parameter id. At this point, num refers to value of 57, which is exactly the same as what id refers to.
#3	The id variable exists in memory and its value is 59. Inside the method, you used the formal parameter named num to increment the value by 2. However, id and num are two names for the same memory location and therefore, the value of id is also 59.	At this point, num holds value of 59.
#4	The id variable exists in memory and its value is 59.	The formal parameter named num does not exist in memory at this point because the method call is over.

Pass by reference allows you to have two-way communication between the caller environment and the called method. You can pass multiple parameters by reference to a method and the method can modify all parameters. All modifications to formal parameters are reflected back to the caller's environment instantaneously. This lets you share multiple pieces of data between the two environments.

The classical swap() method example works when its parameters are passed by reference. Consider the following swap() method's definition:

```
// Assume that x and y are passed by reference
void swap(int x, int y) {
    int temp = x;
    x = y;
    y = temp;
}
```

You can call the previous swap() method using the following snippet of code:

```
int u = 75;
int v = 53;
swap(u, v);
/* At this point, u and v will be 53 and 75, respectively. */
```

Consider the following snippet of code for a method named getNumber():

```
// Assume that x and y are passed by reference
int getNumber(int x, int y) {
    int x = 3;
    int y = 5;
    int sum = x + y;
    return sum;
}
```

Suppose you call the getNumber() method as follows:

```
int w = 100;
int s = getNumber(w, w);
/* What is value of s at this point: 200, 8, 10 or something else? */
```

When the getNumber() method returns, what value will be stored in the variable s? Note that both parameters to the getNumber() method are passed by reference and you pass the same variable, w, for both parameters in your call. When the getNumber() method starts executing, the formal parameters x and y are aliases to the same actual parameter w. When you use w, x, or y, you are referring to the same data in memory. Before adding x and y, and storing the result in the sum local variable, the method sets the value of y to 5, which makes w, x, and y all have a value of 5. When x and y are added inside the method, both x and y refer to the value 5. The getNumber() method returns 10.

Consider another call to the getNumber() method as a part of an expression, as follows:

```
int a = 10;
int b = 19;
int c = getNumber(a, b) + a;
/* What is value of c at this point? */
```

It is little trickier to guess the value of c in the previous snippet of code. You need to consider the side effect of the getNumber() method call on the actual parameters. The getNumber() method will return 8, and it will also modify the value of a and b to 3 and 5, respectively. A value of 11 (8 + 3) will be assigned to c. Consider the following statement in which you have changed the order of the operands for the addition operator:

```
int a = 10;
int b = 19;
int d =  a + getNumber(a, b);
/* What is value of d at this point? */
```

The value of d will be 18 (10 + 8). The local value of 10 will be used for a. You need to consider the side effects on actual parameters by a method call if the parameters are passed by reference. You would have thought that expressions getNumber(a, b) + a and a + getNumber(a, b) would give the same results. However, when the parameters are passed by reference, the result may not be the same, as I have explained.

The advantages of using pass by reference are as follows:

- It is more efficient, compared to pass by value, as actual parameters values are not copied.

- It lets you share more than one piece of values between the caller and the called method environments.

The disadvantages of using pass by reference are as follows:

- It is potentially dangerous if the caller doesn't take into consideration the modification made to the actual parameters inside the called method.

- The program logic is not simple to follow because of the side effects on the actual parameters through formal parameters.

Pass By Reference Value

The mechanism of passing parameters to a method using a pass by reference value is different from that of pass by reference. However, both mechanisms have the same effect. In the pass by reference value, the reference of the actual parameter is copied to the formal parameter. The formal parameter uses a dereferencing mechanism to access the actual parameter's value. The modification made by the formal parameters inside the method is immediately visible to the actual parameters, as is the case in pass by reference. Figure 8-6 depicts the memory states for the actual and formal parameters when the pass by reference value mechanism is used.

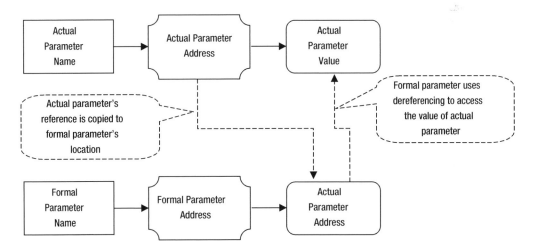

Figure 8-6. *Memory states for actual and formal parameters when a method call is made using pass by reference value mechanism*

There is an important difference between pass by reference and pass by reference values. In a pass by reference value, the reference of the actual parameter is copied to the formal parameter as part of the method call. However, you can change the formal parameter to refer to a different location in memory inside the method, which will not make the actual parameter refer to the new location in memory. Once you change the reference stored in the formal parameter, any changes made to the value stored at the new location will not change the value of the actual parameter.

The discussions and examples referring to the side effects and memory states for pass by reference also apply to the pass by reference value mechanism. Most of the programming languages simulate the pass by reference mechanism using pass by reference value.

Pass by Constant Reference Value

Pass by constant reference value is essentially the same as pass by reference value with one difference. The formal parameter is treated as a constant inside the method body. That is, the formal parameter holds the copy of the reference held by the actual parameter throughout the execution of the method. The formal parameter cannot be modified inside the method's body to hold reference of data other than what the actual parameter is referencing.

Pass by Result

You can think of pass by result as the opposite of pass by value. In pass by value, the value of the actual parameter is copied to the formal parameter. In pass by result, the value of the actual parameter is not copied to the formal parameter. The formal parameter is considered an uninitialized local variable when the method execution starts. During the method execution, the formal parameter is assigned a value. At the end of the method execution, the value of the formal parameter is copied back to the actual parameter.

Figure 8-7 depicts the memory state for the actual and formal parameters when the pass by result mechanism of parameter passing is used.

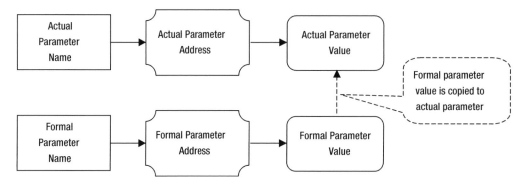

Figure 8-7. *Memory states for actual and formal parameters when the pass by result parameter-passing mechanism is used*

Sometimes the formal parameters are also known as OUT parameters when the pass by result mechanism is used. They are called OUT parameters because they are used to *copy out* a value from the method to the caller's environment. Likewise, formal parameters are sometimes known as IN parameters if they uses the pass by value mechanism because they are used to *copy in* the value of the actual parameter.

Pass by Value Result

Also known as pass by copy-restore, this is a combination of pass by value and pass by result (hence the name "pass by value result"). It is also known as the IN-OUT way of passing parameters. When a method is called, the value of the actual parameter is copied to the formal parameter. During the execution of the method, the formal parameter operates on its own local copy of data. When the method call is over, the value of the formal parameter is copied back to the actual parameter. This is the reason that it is also called pass by copy-restore. It copies the value of the actual parameter in the beginning of the method call and restores the value of formal parameter in the actual parameter at the end of the method call. Figure 8-8 depicts the memory state of actual and formal parameters when the pass by value result mechanism is used to pass parameters.

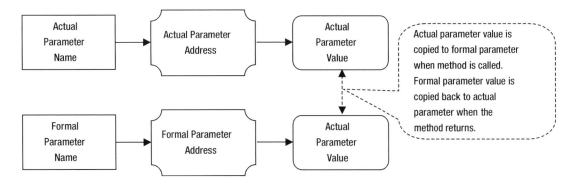

Figure 8-8. *Memory states for actual and formal parameters when the pass by result parameter-passing mechanism is used*

It achieves the effect of pass by reference in a different way. In pass by reference, any modification made to the formal parameter is visible to the actual parameter immediately. In a pass by value result, any modification to the formal parameter is visible to the actual parameter only when the method call returns. If the formal parameter, which uses a pass by value result, is modified multiple times inside a method, only the final modified value will be seen by the actual parameter.

A pass by value result is used to simulate a pass by reference in distributed applications. Suppose you make a remote method call, which executes on a different machine. The reference (memory address) of the actual parameter, which exists in one machine, will not make any sense in the machine on which the remote method is executed. In such cases, the client application sends a copy of the actual parameter to the remote machine. The value copied to the formal parameter is on the remote machine. The formal parameter operates on the copy. When the remote method call returns, the value of the formal parameter on the remote machine is copied back to the actual parameter on the client machine. This gives the client code the functionality of passing parameters by reference to remote methods that run on another machine.

Pass By Name

Typically, the actual parameter expression is evaluated before its value/reference is passed to a method. In pass by name, the actual parameter's expressions are not evaluated when a method is called. The formal parameter's name inside the body of the method is substituted textually with the expressions of their corresponding actual parameters. Actual parameters are evaluated each time they are encountered during the execution of the method and they are evaluated in the caller's context, not the method's context. If there is a name conflict between the local variables in the method and the actual parameter expression during substitution, the local variables are renamed to give every variable a unique name.

Pass by name is implemented using thunks. A *thunk* is a piece of code that computes and returns the value of an expression in a specific context. A thunk is generated for each actual parameter and its reference is passed to the method. At each use of a formal parameter, a call to thunk is made, which evaluates the actual parameter in the caller context.

The advantage of pass by name is that the actual parameters are never evaluated unless they are used in the method. This is also known as lazy evaluation. Contrast it with the pass by value mechanism, where actual parameters are always evaluated before they are copied to the formal parameter. This is called eager evaluation. The disadvantage of pass by name is that the actual parameters are evaluated every time the corresponding formal parameters are used inside the method's body. It is also harder to follow the logic of a method if it uses the pass by name formal parameter, which can also have side effects.

Consider the following declaration for a method squareDivide():

```
int squareDivide(int x, int y) {
    int z =  x * x/y * y;
    return z;
}
```

Consider the following snippet of code that calls the squareDivide() method:

```
squareDivide((4+4), (2+2));
```

You can visualize the execution of this call as if you have written the squareDivide() method as follows. Note that the actual argument expressions of (2+2) and (4+4) are evaluated multiple times inside the method's body.

```
int squareDivide() {
    int z = (4+4)*(4+4)/(2+2)*(2+2);
    return z;
}
```

Pass by Need

Pass by need is similar to pass by name with one difference. In pass by name, actual parameters are evaluated each time they are used in the method. In pass by need, the actual parameters are evaluated only once upon their first use. When a thunk for an actual parameter is called for the first time, it evaluates the actual parameter expression, caches the value and returns it. When the same thunk is called again, it simply returns the cached value, rather than re-evaluating the actual parameter expression again.

Parameter-Passing Mechanisms in Java

Java supports two kinds of data types: primitive data type and reference data type. A primitive data type is a simple data structure and it has only one value associated with it. A reference data type is a complex data structure and it represents an object. A variable of a primitive data type stores the value directly at its memory address. Suppose you have an int variable id. Further suppose it has been assigned a value of 754 and its memory address is 131072.

```
int id = 754;
```

Figure 8-9 shows the memory state of the id variable.

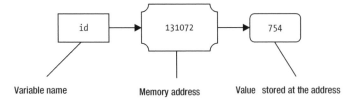

Figure 8-9. *The memory state for an id variable when its value is 754*

The value 754 is directly stored at the memory address 131072, which is associated with the id variable name. What happens if you execute the following statement, which assigns a new value of 351 to the id variable?

```
id = 351;
```

When a new value 351 is assigned to the id variable, the old value 754 is replaced with the new value at the memory address as shown in Figure 8-10.

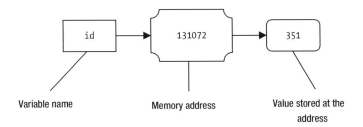

Figure 8-10. *The memory state for an id variable when a new value of 351 is assigned to it*

Things are different when you work with objects and reference variables. Consider the declaration of a Car class as shown in Listing 8-16. It has three instance variables—model, year, and price—which have been given initial values of "Unknown", 2000, and 0.0, respectively.

Listing 8-16. Car Class with Three Public Instance Variables

```
// Car.java
package com.jdojo.cls;

public class Car {
    public String model = "Unknown";
    public int year    = 2000;
    public double price = 0.0;
}
```

When you create an object of a reference type, the object is created on heap and it is stored at a specific memory address. Let's create an object of the Car class as follows:

```
new Car();
```

Figure 8-11 shows the memory state when the previous statement is executed to create a Car object. You probably assumed that the memory address where the object is stored is 262144. Notice that when an object is created, memory is allocated for all of its instance variables and they are initialized. In this case, model, year, and price of the new Car object have been initialized properly, as shown in the figure.

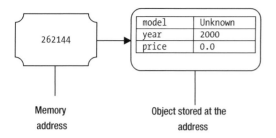

Figure 8-11. *Memory state when a Car object is created using the new Car() statement*

At this point, there is no way to refer to the newly created Car object from a Java program even though it exists in memory. The new operator (as used in new Car()) returns the memory address of the object it creates. In your case, it will return 262144. Recall that the memory address of the data (the Car object, in your case) is also called a reference of that data. From now onwards, you will say that the new operator in Java returns a reference to the object it creates instead of saying that it returns the memory address of the object. Both mean the same thing. However, Java uses the term "reference," which has a more generic meaning than "memory address." In order to access the newly created Car object, you must store its reference in a reference variable. Recall that a reference variable stores the reference to some data, which is stored somewhere else. All variables of reference types are reference variables in Java. A reference variable in Java can store a null reference, which means that it refers to nothing. Consider the following snippet of code that performs different things on reference variables:

```
Car myCar = null;      /* #1 */
myCar = new Car();     /* #2 */
Car xyCar = null;      /* #3 */
xyCar = myCar;         /* $4 */
```

When the statement labeled #1 is executed, memory is allocated for myCar reference variable, say at memory address 8192. The null value is a special value, typically a memory address of zero, which is stored at the memory address of the myCar variable. Figure 8-12 depicts the memory state for the myCar variable when it is assigned a null reference.

Figure 8-12. *Memory state for the myCar variable, when the "Car myCar = null" statement is executed*

The execution of statement labeled #2 is a two-step process. First, it executes the new Car() part of the statement to create a new Car object. Suppose the new Car object is allocated at memory address of 9216. The new Car() expression returns the reference of the new object, which is 9216. In the second step, the reference of the new object is stored in myCar reference variable. The memory state for the myCar reference variable and the new Car object after the statement labeled #2 is executed is shown in Figure 8-13. Note that the memory address of the new Car object (9216) and the value of the myCar reference variable match at this point. You do not need to worry about the numbers used in this example for memory addresses; I just made up some numbers to drive home the point of how the memory addresses are used internally. Java does not let you access the memory address of an object or a variable. Java lets you access/modify the state of objects through reference variables.

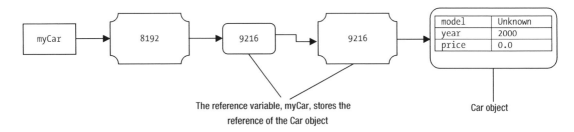

The reference variable, myCar, stores the
reference of the Car object

Car object

Figure 8-13. *Memory states for the myCar reference variable and the new Car object when the myCar = new Car() statement is executed*

The statement labeled #3 is similar to the statement labeled #1. The memory state for the xyCar reference variable is shown in Figure 8-14, assuming that 10240 is the memory address for the xyCar reference variable.

Figure 8-14. *Memory state of xyCar reference variable*

It is interesting to note the memory state when the statement labeled #4 is executed. The statement reads as follows:

```
xyCar = myCar;  /* #4 */
```

Recall that a variable name has two things associated with it: a memory address and a value stored at that memory address. The memory address (or location) is also known as its lvalue whereas the value stored at its memory address is also called rvalue. When a variable is used to the left of an assignment operator (xyCar in statement labeled #4), it refers to its memory address. When a variable is used to the right of assignment operator (myCar in statement labeled #4), it refers to its value (rvalue) stored at its memory address. The statement labeled #4 can be read as follows:

```
xyCar = myCar; /* #4 */
At lvalue of xyCar store rvalue of myCar;        /* #4 - another way */
At memory address of xyCar store value of myCar /* #4 - another way */
```

Therefore, when you execute the statement xyCar = myCar, it reads the value of myCar, which is 9216, and stores it at the memory address of xyCar. The reference variable myCar stores a reference to a Car object. An assignment like xyCar = myCar does not copy the object to which myCar refers. Rather, it copies the value stored in myCar (a reference to the Car object) to xyCar. When the assignment xyCar = myCar is complete, the reference variables of myCar and xyCar have reference to the same Car object in memory. At this point, only one Car object exists in memory. Figure 8-15 shows the memory state when statement labeled #4 is executed.

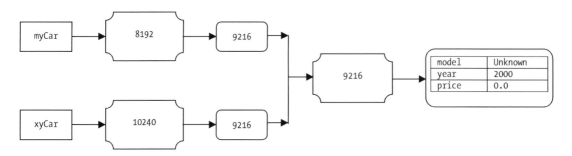

Figure 8-15. *Memory state showing myCar and xyCar referencing the same Car object in memory*

At this time, you can use reference variables myCar or xyCar to access the Car object in memory. The following snippet of code will access the same object in memory:

```
myCar.model = "Civic LX"; /* Use myCar to change model */
myCar.year  = 1999;       /* Use myCar to change year */
xyCar.price = 16000.00;   /* Use xyCar to change the price */
```

After executing the previous three statements, model, year, and price will be changed for the Car object and the memory state will look as shown in Figure 8-16.

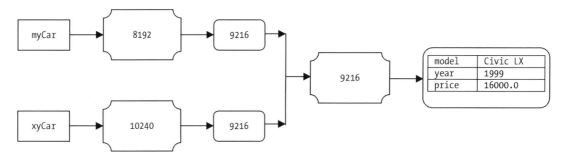

Figure 8-16. *Memory state showing myCar and xyCar referencing the same Car object in memory after myCar and xyCar have been used to change the state of the Car object*

At this point, two reference variables myCar and xyCar and one Car object exist in memory. Both reference variables are referencing the same Car object. Let's execute the following statement and label it as #5:

```
myCar = new Car(); /* #5 */
```

The previous statement will create a new Car object in memory with initial values for its instance variables and assign the reference of the new Car object to the myCar reference variable. The xyCar reference variable still references the Car object it was referencing before. Suppose the new Car object has been allocated at memory address 5120. The memory state for two reference variables myCar and xyCar and two Car objects are shown in Figure 8-17.

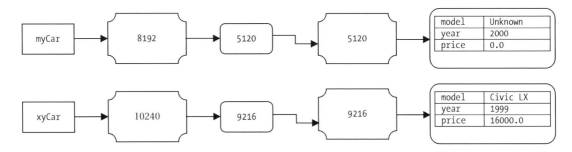

Figure 8-17. *Memory state of reference variables myCar and xyCar and two Car objects*

Let's make one more change and set the xyCar reference variable to null as shown:

```
xyCar = null; /* #6 */
```

Figure 8-18 shows the memory state after statement #6 is executed.

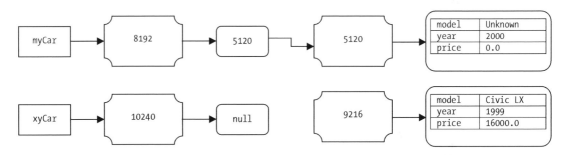

Figure 8-18. *Memory state of reference variables myCar and xyCar and two Car objects after xyCar has been assigned a null reference*

Now the xyCar reference variable stores a null reference and it no longer refers to any Car object. The Car object with the Civic LX model is not being referenced by any reference variable. You cannot access this Car object at all in your program because you do not have a reference to it. In Java terminology, the Car object with the Civic LX model is not reachable. When an object in memory is not reachable, it becomes eligible for garbage collection. Note that the Car object with the Civic LX model is not destroyed (or deallocated) immediately after xyCar is set to null. It stays in memory until the garbage collector runs and makes sure that it is not reachable. Refer to the chapter on garbage collection for more details on how an object's memory is deallocated.

I have covered enough background about variables types and how they work in Java. It is time to discuss the parameter-passing mechanism in Java. In brief, we can state

All parameters in Java are passed by value.

This brief statement causes a lot of confusion. Does it mean that when a parameter is a reference type, a copy of the object the actual parameter refers to is made and assigned to the formal parameter? It is important to elaborate on the phrase "All parameters in Java are passed by value" with examples. Even veteran Java programmers have problems understanding the parameter-passing mechanism in Java. To be more elaborate, Java supports the following four types of parameter-passing mechanisms:

- Pass by value

- Pass by constant value

- Pass by reference value

- Pass by constant reference value

Note that all four ways of passing parameters in Java includes the word "value." This is the reason that many books on Java summarize them as "Java passes all parameters by value." Refer to the previous section for more details for the previously mentioned four types of parameter-passing mechanisms.

The first two types, pass by value and pass by constant value, apply to parameters of primitive data types. The last two types, pass by reference value and pass by constant reference value, apply to the parameters of reference type.

When a formal parameter is of a primitive data type, the value of the actual parameter is copied to the formal parameter. Any changes made to the formal parameter's value inside the method's body will change only the copy of the formal parameter and not the value of the actual parameter. Now you can tell that swap() method to swap two primitive values will not work in Java.

Listing 8-17 demonstrates that swap() method cannot be written in Java because primitive type parameters are passed by value. The output shows that the x and y formal parameters of the swap() method receive the values of a and b. The values of x and y are swapped inside the method, which does not affect the values of actual parameters a and b at all.

Listing 8-17. An Incorrect Attempt to Write a swap() Method to Swap Values of Two Primitive Types in Java

```java
// BadSwapTest.java
package com.jdojo.cls;

public class BadSwapTest {
    public static void swap(int x, int y) {
        System.out.println("#2: x = " + x + ", y = " + y);

        int temp = x;
        x = y;
        y = temp;

        System.out.println("#3: x = " + x + ", y = " + y);
    }

    public static void main(String[] args) {
        int a = 19;
        int b = 37;

        System.out.println("#1: a = " + a + ", b = " + b);

        // Call the swap() method to swap values of a and b
        BadSwapTest.swap(a, b);
```

```
            System.out.println("#4: a = " + a + ", b = " + b);
    }
}
```

```
#1: a = 19, b = 37
#2: x = 19, y = 37
#3: x = 37, y = 19
#4: a = 19, b = 37
```

A primitive type parameter is passed by value. However, you can modify the value of the formal parameter inside the method without affecting the actual parameter value. Java also lets you use pass by constant value. In this case, the formal parameter cannot be modified inside the method. The formal parameter is initialized with the value of the actual parameter by making a copy of the actual parameter and then it is a constant value, which can only be read. You need to use the final keyword in the formal parameter declaration to indicate that you mean to pass the parameter by constant value. Any attempt to change the value of a parameter, which uses pass by constant value, results in a compile-time error. Listing 8-18 demonstrates how to use the pass by constant value mechanism to pass the parameter x to the test() method. Any attempt to change the value of the formal parameter x inside the test() method will result in a compile-time error. If you uncomment the "x = 10;" statement inside the test() method, you would get the following compiler error:

```
Error(10):  final parameter x may not be assigned
```

You have passed two parameters, x and y, to the test() method. The parameter y is passed by value, and hence it can be changed inside the method. This can be confirmed by looking at the output.

Listing 8-18. An Example of Pass by Constant Value

```java
// PassByConstantValueTest.java
package com.jdojo.cls;

public class PassByConstantValueTest {
    // x is passed by constant value and y is passed by value
    public static void test(final int x, int y) {
        System.out.println("#2: x = " + x + ", y = " + y);

        /* Uncommenting the following statement will generate a compile-time error */
        // x = 79; /* Cannot change x. It is passed by constant value */
        y = 223; // Ok to change y

        System.out.println("#3: x = " + x + ", y = " + y);
    }

    public static void main(String[] args) {
        int a = 19;
        int b = 37;
        System.out.println("#1: a = " + a + ", b = " + b);
        PassByConstantValueTest.test(a, b);
        System.out.println("#4: a = " + a + ", b = " + b);
    }
}
```

```
#1: a = 19, b = 37
#2: x = 19, y = 37
#3: x = 19, y = 223
#4: a = 19, b = 37
```

Let's discuss the parameter-passing mechanism for reference type parameters. Java lets you use the pass by reference value and pass by constant reference value mechanisms to pass reference type parameters to a method. When a parameter is passed by reference value, the reference stored in the actual parameter is copied to the formal parameter. When the method starts executing, both the actual parameter and the formal parameter refer to the same object in memory. If the actual parameter has a null reference, the formal parameter will contain the null reference. You can assign a reference to another object to the formal parameter inside the method's body. In this case, the formal parameter starts referencing the new object in memory and the actual parameter still references the object it was referencing before the method call. Listing 8-19 demonstrates the pass by reference mechanism in Java. It creates a Car object inside the main() method and stores the reference of the Car object in myCar reference variable.

```
// Create a Car object and assign its reference to myCar
Car myCar = new Car();
```

It modifies the model, year, and price of the newly created Car object using myCar reference variable.

```
// Change model, year and price of Car object using myCar
myCar.model = "Civic LX";
myCar.year  = 1999;
myCar.price = 16000.0;
```

The message labeled #1 in the output shows the state of the Car object. The myCar reference variable is passed to the test() method using the following call:

```
PassByReferenceValueTest.test(myCar);
```

Since the type of the formal parameter xyCar in the test() method is Car, which is a reference type, Java uses the pass by reference value mechanism to pass the value of the myCar actual parameter to the xyCar formal parameter. When the test(myCar) method is called, Java copies the reference of the Car object stored in the myCar reference variable to the xyCar reference variable. When the execution enters the test() method's body, myCar and xyCar reference the same object in memory. At this time, there is only one Car object in memory and not two. It is very important to understand that the test(myCar) method call did not make a copy of the Car object referenced by the myCar reference variable. Rather, it made a copy of the reference (memory address) of the Car object referenced by the myCar reference variable, which is the actual parameter, and copied that reference to the xyCar reference variable, which is the formal parameter. The fact that both myCar and xyCar reference the same object in memory is indicated by the message labeled #2 in the output, which is printed using the xyCar formal parameter inside the test() method.

Now you create a new Car object and assign its reference to the xyCar formal parameter inside the test() method.

```
// Let's make xyCar refer to a new Car object
xyCar = new Car();
```

At this point, there are two Car objects in memory. The xyCar formal parameter references the new Car object and not the one whose reference was passed to the method. Note that the actual parameter myCar still references the Car object that you created in the main() method. The fact that the xyCar formal parameter references the new Car object is indicated by the message labeled #3 in the output. When the test() method call returns, the main() method prints details of the Car object being referenced by the myCar reference variable. See Listing 8-19.

▓ **Tip**   When a reference type parameter is passed to a method in Java, the formal parameter can access the object the same way the actual parameter can access the object. The formal parameter can modify the object by directly changing the values of the instance variables or by calling methods on the object. Any modification made on the object through the formal parameter is immediately visible through the actual parameter because both hold the reference to the same object in memory. The formal parameter itself can be modified to reference another object (or the null reference) inside the method.

Listing 8-19. An Example of a Pass by Reference Value

```java
// PassByReferenceValueTest.java
package com.jdojo.cls;

public class PassByReferenceValueTest {
    public static void main(String[] args) {
        // Create a Car object and assign its reference to myCar
        Car myCar = new Car();

        // Change model, year and price of Car object using myCar
        myCar.model = "Civic LX";
        myCar.year = 1999;
        myCar.price = 16000.0;

        System.out.println("#1: model = " + myCar.model
                + ", year = " + myCar.year
                + ", price = " + myCar.price);

        PassByReferenceValueTest.test(myCar);

        System.out.println("#4: model = " + myCar.model
                + ", year = " + myCar.year
                + ", price = " + myCar.price);
    }

    public static void test(Car xyCar) {
        System.out.println("#2: model = " + xyCar.model
                + ", year = " + xyCar.year
                + ", price = " + xyCar.price);
```

```
        // Let's make xyCar refer to a new Car object
        xyCar = new Car();

        System.out.println("#3: model = " + xyCar.model
                + ", year = " + xyCar.year
                + ", price = " + xyCar.price);
    }
}
```

```
#1: model = Civic LX, year = 1999, price = 16000.0
#2: model = Civic LX, year = 1999, price = 16000.0
#3: model = Unknown, year = 2000, price = 0.0
#4: model = Civic LX, year = 1999, price = 16000.0
```

If you do not want the method to change the reference type formal parameter to reference a different object than the one referenced by the actual parameter, you can use the pass by constant reference value mechanism to pass that parameter. If you use the keyword final in the reference type formal parameter declaration, the parameter is passed by constant reference value and the formal parameter cannot be modified inside the method. The following declaration of the test() method declares the xyzCar formal parameter as final and it is passed by constant reference value. The method attempts to change the xyzCar formal parameter by assigning a null reference to it and then by assigning a reference to a new Car objects. Both of these assignment statements will generate a compiler error:

```
// xyzCar is passed by constant reference value because it is declared final
void test(final Car xyzCar) {
    // Can read the object referenced by xyzCar
    String model = xyzCar.model;

    // Can modify object referenced by xyzCar
    xyzCar.year = 2001;

    /* Cannot modify xyzCar. That is, xyzCar must reference the object what the actual
       parameter is referencing at the time this method is called. You cannot even set it to
       null reference.
    */
    xyzCar = null;      // A compile-time error. Cannot modify xyzCar
    xyzCar = new Car(); // A compile-time error. Cannot modify xyzCar
}
```

Let's discuss one more example on parameter-passing mechanism in Java. Consider the following code for the changeString() method:

```
public static void changeString(String s2) {
    /* #2 */
    s2 = s2 + " there";
    /* #3 */
}
```

Consider the following snippet of code that calls the changeString() method:

```
String s1 = "hi";
/* #1 */
changeString(s1);
/* #4 */
```

What will be the content of s1 at #4? String is a reference type in Java. At #1, s1 is referencing a String object whose content is "hi". When the changeString(s1) method is called, s1 is passed to s2 by reference value. At #2, s1 and s2 are referencing the same String object in memory whose content is "hi". When the

```
s2 = s2 + " there";
```

statement is executed, two things happens. First, s2 + " there" expression is evaluated, which creates a new String object in memory with content of "hi there" and returns its reference. The reference returned by the s2 + " there" expression is assigned to s2 formal parameter. At this time, there are two String objects in memory: one with the content of "hi" and another with the content of "hi there". At #3, the actual parameter s1 is referencing the String object with the content of "hi" and the formal parameter s2 is referencing the String object with content "hi there". When the changeString() method call is over, the formal parameter s2 is discarded. Note that the String object with content "hi there" still exists in memory after the changeString() method call is over. Only the formal parameter is discarded when a method call is over, not the object to which the formal parameter was referencing. At #4, the reference variable s1 still refers to the String object with content "hi". Listing 8-20 has the complete code that attempts to modify a formal parameter of String type.

▓ **Tip** A String object is immutable, meaning that its contents cannot be changed after it is created. If you need to change the contents of a String object, you must create a new String object with the new contents.

Listing 8-20. Another Example of Pass by Reference Value Parameter Passing in Java

```java
// PassByReferenceValueTest2.java
package com.jdojo.cls;

public class PassByReferenceValueTest2 {
    public static void changeString(String s2) {
        System.out.println("#2: s2 = " + s2);
        s2 = s2 + " there";
        System.out.println("#3: s2 = " + s2);
    }

    public static void main(String[] args) {
        String s1 = "hi";
        System.out.println("#1: s1 = " + s1);
        PassByReferenceValueTest2.changeString(s1);
        System.out.println("#4: s1 = " + s1);
    }
}
```

```
#1: s1 = hi
#2: s2 = hi
#3: s2 = hi there
#4: s1 = hi
```

Summary

A method in a class defines a behavior of the objects of that class or the behavior of the class itself. A method is a named block of code. The method can be invoked to execute its code. The code that invokes the method is called the caller of the method. Optionally, a method may accept input values from the caller and it may return a value to the caller. The list of input values is known as a method's parameters. Var-args parameters are used to define parameters for methods and constructors where they can take variable number of parameters. A method is always defined inside the body of a class or an interface.

Methods of a class can have one of the following four access levels: public, private, protected, and package-level. The presence of the keyword `public`, `private`, and `protected` in defining them gives them public, private, and protected access level, respectively. Absence of any of these keywords specifies the package-level access.

You can declare variables inside a method's body and such variables are called local variables. Unlike fields of a class, local variables are not initialized by default. Local variables must be initialized before their values can be read. An attempt to read a local variable's value before the local variable is initialized results in a compile-time error.

A class can have two types of methods: instance methods and class methods. Instance methods and class methods are also called non-static methods and static methods, respectively. An instance method is used to implement behavior of the instances (also called objects) of the class. An instance method can only be invoked in the context of an instance of the class. A class method is used to implement the behavior of the class itself. A class method always executes in the context of a class. The `static` modifier is used to define a class method. The absence of the `static` modifier in a method declaration makes the method an instance method.

Methods of a class can be accessed using dot notation, which is of the form:

```
<qualifier>.<method-name>(<method-actual-parameters>)
```

For an instance method, the qualifier is a reference of an instance of the class. For a class method, the qualifier can be a reference of an instance of the class or the class name.

You can call static methods of a class from a non-static method of the class; however, calling non-static methods from a static method is not allowed. Static methods of a class can access all static fields of the class whereas non-static methods can access both static and non-static fields of the class.

Java has a keyword called `this`. It is a reference to the current instance of a class. It can be used only in the context of an instance. It can never be used in the context of a class because it means the current instance, and no instance exists in the context of a class. The keyword `this` is used in many contexts such as non-static methods, constructors, instance initializers, and expressions to initialize instance variables.

Different mechanisms to pass parameters to methods and constructors exist. Java uses pass by value and pass by constant value mechanisms to pass parameters of primitive data types. Pass by reference value and pass by constant reference value are used to pass parameters of reference types in Java.

EXERCISES

1. What is a method in Java?

2. Describe the difference between a static method and a non-static method of a class.

3. Can a static method access instance variables of a class? If your answer is no, explain the reason.

4. What is the meaning of `void` when it is used as the return type of a method?

5. Create a class named `Point2D` with two `int` instance variables named x and y. Both instance variables should be declared private. Do not initialize the two instance variables. Add setters and getters for the two instance variables that will allow the users of the `Point` class to change and access their values. Declare the setters as `setX(int x)` and `setY(int y)` and getters as `getX()` and `getY()`.

6. Implement a method named `distance` in the `Point2D` class that you created in the previous exercise. The method accepts an instance of the `Point2D` class and returns the distance between the current point and the point represented by the parameter. The method should be declared as follows:

```
public class Point2D {
    /* Code from the previous exercise goes here. */

    public double distance(Point2D p) {
        /* Your code for this exercise goes here. */
    }
}
```

Hint: The distance between two points (x1, y1) and (x2, y2) is computed as

$\sqrt{(x1-x2)^2 + (y1-y2)^2}$. You can use `Math.sqrt(n)` method to compute the square root of a number n.

7. Enhance the `Point2D` method by adding a static factory method named `create()`. A factory method in a class is used to create objects of the class. The `create()` method should be declared as follows:

```
public class Point2D {
    /* Code from the previous exercise goes here. */

    public Point2D create(int x, int y) {
        /* Your code for this exercise goes here. */
    }
}
```

The x and y instance variables of the returned `Point2D` object from the `create()` method should be initialized to the x and y parameters of this method, respectively.

8. Create a class named MathUtil with a method name avg(). It computes and returns average of a list of numbers. The method must accept variable-arguments of double types with a minimum of two double values. Run the MathUtil class and verify that the output prints the correct results.

```
// MathUtil.java
package com.jdojo.cls.excercise;

public class MathUtil {
    public static void main(String[] args) {
        System.out.println("avg(10, 15) = " + avg(10, 15));
        System.out.println("avg(2, 3, 4) = " + avg(2, 3, 4));
        System.out.println("avg(20.5, 30.5, 40.5) = "
                            + avg(20.5, 30.5, 40.5));
        System.out.println("avg(-2.0, 0.0, 2.0) = "
                            + avg(-2.0, 0.0, 2.0));
    }

    public static double avg(/* Your parameters goes here. */) {
        /* Your code goes here. */
    }
}
```

9. The main() method of a class serves as an entry point of a Java application. It is declared as follows:

```
public static void main(String[] args) {
    // Your code goes here
}
```

Change this declaration of the main() method using a var-args.

10. What will be the output when the following PassByValueTest class is run?

```
// PassByValueTest.java
package com.jdojo.cls.excercise;

public class PassByValueTest {
    public static void main(String[] args) {
        int x = 100;
        System.out.println("x = " + x);
        change(x);
        System.out.println("x = " + x);

        Point2D p = new Point2D();
        p.setX(40);
        p.setY(60);
        System.out.println("p.x = " + p.getX()
                            + ", p.y = " + p.getY());
```

```
        changePointReference(p);
        System.out.println("p.x = " + p.getX()
                        + ", p.y = " + p.getY());

        changePoint(p);
        System.out.println("p.x = " + p.getX()
                        + ", p.y = " + p.getY());
    }

    public static void change(int x) {
        x = 200;
    }

    public static void changePointReference(Point2D p) {
        p = new Point2D();
    }

    public static void changePoint(Point2D p) {
        int newX = p.getX() / 2;
        int newY = p.getY() / 2;
        p.setX(newX);
        p.setY(newY);
    }
}
```

CHAPTER 9

Constructors

In this chapter, you will learn:

- What constructors are and how to use them
- Different types of initializers of a class
- Declaring final variables, classes, and methods
- What generic classes are and how to use them

What Is a Constructor?

A constructor is a named block of code that is used to initialize an object of a class immediately after the object is created. The structure of a constructor looks similar to a method. However, the similarity between the two stops right there, in their looks. They are two different constructs and they are used for different purposes.

Declaring a Constructor

The general syntax for a constructor declaration is as follows:

```
[modifiers] <constructor-name>(<parameters-list>) [throws-clause] {
    // Body of the constructor goes here
}
```

The declaration of a constructor starts with modifiers. A constructor can have its access modifier as `public`, `private`, `protected`, or package-level (no modifier). The constructor name is the same as the simple name of the class. The constructor name is followed by a pair of opening and closing parentheses, which may include parameters. Optionally, the closing parenthesis may be followed by a `throws` clause, which in turn is followed by a comma-separated list of exceptions. I discuss the use of the keyword `throws` in the chapter on exception handling. The body of the constructor, where you place your code, is enclosed in braces.

If you compare the syntax to declare a method with the syntax to declare a constructor, you will find that they are almost the same. It is suggested to keep the method declaration in mind when learning about constructor declaration because most of the characteristics are similar.

The following code shows an example of declaring a constructor for a class Test. Figure 9-1 shows the anatomy of the constructor.

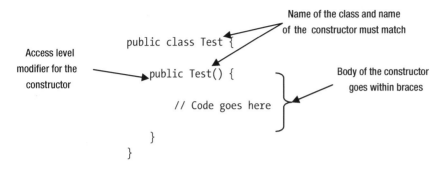

Figure 9-1. *Anatomy of the constructor for the Test class*

```
// Test.java
package com.jdojo.cls;

public class Test {
    public Test() {
        // Code goes here
    }
}
```

▓ **Tip**   The name of a constructor must match the simple name, not the fully qualified name, of the class.

Unlike a method, a constructor does not have a return type. You cannot even specify void as a return type for a constructor. Consider the following declaration of a class Test2:

```
public class Test2 {
    // Below is a method, not a constructor.
    public void Test2() {
        // Code goes here
    }
}
```

Does the class Test2 declare a constructor? The answer is no. The class Test2 does not declare a constructor. Rather, what you may be looking at is a method declaration, which has the same name as the simple name of the class. It is a method declaration because it specifies a return type of void. Note that a method name could also be the same as the class name, as is the case in this example.

Just the name itself does not make a method or constructor. If the name of a construct is the same as the simple name of the class, it could be a method or a constructor. If it specifies a return type, it is a method. If it does not specify a return type, it is a constructor.

When do you use a constructor? You use a constructor with the new operator to initialize an instance (or an object) of a class just after the new instance is created. Sometimes the phrases "create" and "initialize" are used interchangeably in the context of a constructor. However, you need to be clear about the difference in creating and initializing an object. The new operator creates an object and a constructor initializes that object.

The following statement uses a constructor of the Test class to initialize an object of the Test class:

```
Test t = new Test();
```

Figure 9-2 shows the anatomy of this statement. The new operator is followed by the call to the constructor. The new operator, along with the constructor call, for example "new Test()", is called an instance (or object) creation expression. An instance creation expression creates an object in memory, executes the code in the body of the specified constructor, and finally, returns the reference of the new object.

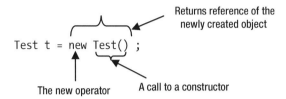

Figure 9-2. *Anatomy of a constructor call with the new operator*

I have covered enough theories for declaring a constructor. It is time to see a constructor in action. Listing 9-1 has the code for a Cat class.

Listing 9-1. A Cat Class with a Constructor

```java
// Cat.java
package com.jdojo.cls;

public class Cat {
    public Cat() {
        System.out.println("Meow...");
    }
}
```

The Cat class declares a constructor. Inside the constructor's body, it prints a message "Meow...". Listing 9-2 contains the code for a CatTest class, which creates two Cat objects in its main() method. Note that you always use an object creation expression to create a new object of the Cat class. It is up to you to store the reference of the new object in a reference variable. The first Cat object is created and its reference is not stored. The second Cat object is created and its reference is stored in a reference variable c.

Listing 9-2. A Test Class That Creates Two of the Cat Objects

```java
// CatTest.java
package com.jdojo.cls;

public class CatTest {
    public static void main(String[] args) {
        // Create a Cat object and ignore its reference
        new Cat();

        // Create another Cat object and store its reference in c
        Cat c = new Cat();
    }
}
```

```
Meow...
Meow...
```

Overloading a Constructor

A class can have more than one constructor. If a class has multiple constructors, they are called *overloaded* constructors. Since the name of the constructor must be the same as the simple name of the class, there is a need to differentiate one constructor from another. The rules for overloaded constructors are the same as for overloaded methods. If a class has multiple constructors, all of them must differ from the others in the number, order, or type of parameters. Listing 9-3 contains the code for a Dog class, which declares two constructors. One constructor accepts no parameters and another accepts a String parameter.

Listing 9-3. A Dog Class with Two Constructors, One with No Parameter and One with a String Parameter

```
// Dog.java
package com.jdojo.cls;

public class Dog {
    // Constructor #1
    public Dog() {
        System.out.println("A dog is created.");
    }

    // Constructor #2
    public Dog(String name) {
        System.out.println("A dog named " + name + " is created.");
    }
}
```

If a class declares multiple constructors, you can use any of them to create an object of that class. For example, the following two statements create two objects of the Dog class:

```
Dog dog1 = new Dog();
Dog dog2 = new Dog("Cupid");
```

The first statement uses the constructor with no parameters and the second one uses the constructor with a String parameter. If you use a constructor with parameters to create an object, the actual parameter's order, type, and number must match the formal parameter's order, type, and number. Listing 9-4 has the complete code that creates two Dog objects using different constructors.

Listing 9-4. Testing the Constructors of the Dog Class

```
// DogTest.java
package com.jdojo.cls;

public class DogTest {
    public static void main(String[] args) {
        Dog d1 = new Dog();         // Uses Constructor #1
        Dog d2 = new Dog ("Canis"); // Uses Constructor #2
    }
}
```

```
A dog is created.
A dog named Canis is created.
```

The output of running the DogTest class indicates that different constructors are called when two Dog objects are created in the main() method.

A constructor is called once per object creation expression. You can execute the code for one constructor only once in the process of an object creation. If the code for a constructor is executed N times, it means N number of objects of that class will be created and you must use N number of object creation expressions to do that. However, when an object creation expression calls a constructor, the called constructor may call another constructor from its body. I cover this scenario where one constructor calls another later in this section.

Writing Code for a Constructor

So far, you have been writing trivial code in constructors. What kind of code should you write in a constructor? The purpose of a constructor is to initialize the instance variables of the newly created object. Inside a constructor, you should restrict yourself only to write code that initializes instance variables of the object. An object is not fully created when a constructor is called. The object is still in the process of creation. If you write some processing logic in a constructor assuming that a full blown object exists in memory, sometimes you may get unexpected results. Let's create another class to represent a dog object. You will call this class SmartDog, as shown in Listing 9-5.

Listing 9-5. A SmartDog Class That Declares Two Constructors to Initialize Instance Variables Differently

```
// SmartDog.java
package com.jdojo.cls;

public class SmartDog {
    private String name;
    private double price;

    public SmartDog() {
        // Initialize the name to "Unknown" and the price to 0.0
        this.name = "Unknown";
        this.price = 0.0;

        System.out.println("Using SmartDog() constructor");
    }

    public SmartDog(String name, double price) {
        // Initialize name and price instance variables with the
        // values of the name and price parameters
        this.name = name;
        this.price = price;

        System.out.println("Using SmartDog(String, double) constructor");
    }

    public void bark() {
        System.out.println(name + " is barking...");
    }

    public void setName(String name) {
        this.name = name;
    }
```

```
    public String getName() {
        return this.name;
    }

    public void setPrice(double price) {
        this.price = price;
    }

    public double getPrice() {
        return this.price;
    }

    public void printDetails() {
        System.out.print("Name: " + this.name);
        if (price > 0.0) {
            System.out.println(", price: " + this.price);
        } else {
            System.out.println(", price: Free");
        }
    }
}
```

The SmartDog class looks a little bigger. However, its logic is very simple. The following are the main points in the SmartDog class that you need to understand:

- It declares two instance variables; they are name and price. The name instance variable stores the name of a smart dog. The price instance variable stores the price for which it can be sold.

- It declares two constructors. The first constructor has no parameters. It initializes the name and price instance variables to "Unknown" and 0.0, respectively. The second constructor accepts two parameters named name and price. It initializes the name and price instance variables to whatever values are passed for the two parameters. Note the use of the keyword this inside the constructors. The keyword this refers to the object for which the constructor's code is executing. The use of the keyword this is not necessary in the first constructor. However, you must use the keyword this to refer to instance variables in the second constructor because the names of the formal parameters hide the names of the instance variables.

- The two constructors initialize instance variables (or state of the object) in their bodies. They do not include any other processing logic.

- The instance method bark() prints a message on the standard output with the name of the smart dog who is barking.

- The setName() and getName() methods are used to set and get the name of the smart dog. The setPrice() and getPrice() methods are used to set and get the price of the smart dog.

- The printDetails() method prints the name and price of a smart dog. If the price for a smart dog is not set to a positive value, it prints the price as "Free".

Listing 9-6 has the code for a SmartDogTest class that demonstrates how the two constructors initialize the instance variables.

Listing 9-6. A Test Class to Demonstrate the Use of the SmartDog Class

```java
// SmartDogTest.java
package com.jdojo.cls;

public class SmartDogTest {
    public static void main(String[] args) {
        // Create two SmartDog objects
        SmartDog sd1 = new SmartDog();
        SmartDog sd2 = new SmartDog("Nova", 219.2);

        // Print details about the two dogs
        sd1.printDetails();
        sd2.printDetails();

        // Make them bark
        sd1.bark();
        sd2.bark();

        // Change the name and price of Unknown dog
        sd1.setName("Opal");
        sd1.setPrice(321.80);

        // Print details again
        sd1.printDetails();
        sd2.printDetails();

        // Make them bark one more time
        sd1.bark();
        sd2.bark();
    }
}
```

```
Using SmartDog() constructor
Using SmartDog(String, double) constructor
Name: Unknown, price: Free
Name: Nova, price: 219.2
Unknown is barking...
Nova is barking...
Name: Opal, price: 321.8
Name: Nova, price: 219.2
Opal is barking...
Nova is barking...
```

Calling a Constructor from Another Constructor

A constructor may call another constructor of the same class. Let's consider the following Test class. It declares two constructors; one accepts no parameters and one accepts an int parameter.

```
public class Test {
    Test() {
    }

    Test(int x) {
    }
}
```

Suppose you want to call the constructor with an int parameter from the constructor with no parameter. Your first attempt, which is wrong, would be as follows:

```
public class Test {
    Test() {
        // Call another constructor
        Test(103); // A compile-time error
    }

    Test(int x) {
    }
}
```

The previous code does not compile. Java has a special way to call a constructor from another constructor. You must use the keyword this, as if it is the name of the constructor, to call a constructor from another constructor. The following code calls the constructor with an int parameter from the constructor with no parameter using the statement, "this(103);". This is another use of the keyword this.

```
public class Test {
    Test() {
        // Call another constructor
        this(103); // OK. Note the use of the keyword this.
    }

    Test(int x) {
    }
}
```

There are two rules about calling a constructor from another constructor. The rules ensure that one constructor is executed only once during the process of an object creation of a class. These rules are as follows:

- The call to another constructor must be the first statement in the constructor.

- A constructor cannot call itself.

If a constructor calls another constructor, it must be the first executable statement in the constructor's body. This makes it easy for the compiler to check that a constructor has been called and it has been called only once. For example, the following code will generate a compile-time error because a call to the constructor with int parameter this(k) is the second statement inside the constructor's body, not the first statement.

```
public class Test {
    Test() {
        int k = 10; // First statement
        this(k);    // Second statement. A compile-time error
    }

    Test(int x) {
    }
}
```

An attempt to compile the code for this Test class will generate the following error message:

```
Error(4):  call to this must be first statement in constructor
```

A constructor cannot call itself because it will result in a recursive call. In the following code for the Test class, both constructors attempt to call themselves:

```
public class Test {
    Test() {
        this();
    }

    Test(int x ) {
        this(10);
    }
}
```

An attempt to compile this code will result in the following error. One error message is generated for each attempt to call the constructor itself.

```
Error(2):  recursive constructor invocation
Error(6):  recursive constructor invocation
```

Typically, you create overloaded constructors for a class when you have many ways to initialize an object of the class. Let's consider the SmartDog class shown in Listing 9-5. Two constructors give you two ways to initialize a new SmartDog object. The first one initializes the name and the price with default values. The second constructor lets you initialize name and price with the value supplied by the caller. Sometimes you may perform some logic to initialize the object inside a constructor. Letting you call another constructor from a constructor allows you to write such logic only once. You can use this feature for your SmartDog class, as shown:

```
// SmartDog.java
package com.jdojo.cls;

public class SmartDog {
    private String name;
    private double price;
```

```java
    public SmartDog() {
        // Call another constructor with "Unknown" and 0.0 as parameters
        this("Unknown", 0.0);

        System.out.println("Using SmartDog() constructor");
    }

    public SmartDog(String name, double price) {
        // Initialize name and price to specified name and price
        this.name = name;
        this.price = price;

        System.out.println("Using SmartDog(String, double) constructor");
    }

    /* Rest of code remains the same */
}
```

Note that you changed the code only inside the constructor that accepts no parameters. Instead of setting the default values for name and price in the first constructor, you called the second constructor with the default values as parameters from the first one.

Using a return Statement Inside a Constructor

A constructor cannot have a return type in its declaration. It means a constructor cannot return any value. Recall that a return statement is of two types: one with a return expression and one without a return expression. The return statement without a return expression simply returns the control to the caller without returning any value. You can use a return statement without a return expression inside a constructor body. When a return statement in a constructor is executed, the control returns to the caller, ignoring the rest of the constructor's code.

The following code shows an example of using a return statement in a constructor. If the parameter x is a negative number, the constructor simply executes a return statement to end the call to the constructor. Otherwise, it performs some logic.

```java
public class Test {
    public Test(int x) {
        if (x < 0) {
            return;
        }
        /* Perform some logic here */
    }
}
```

Access Level Modifier for a Constructor

Access level for a constructor determines the part of the program that can use that constructor in an object creation expression to create an object of that class. Similar to fields and methods, you can specify one of the four access levels for a constructor:

- public

- private

- protected

- <package-level>

The following code declares four constructors for the Test class. A comment for each constructor explains its access level.

```
// Class Test has public access level
public class Test {
    // Constructor #1 - package-level access
    Test() {
    }

    // Constructor #2 - public access level
    public Test(int x) {
    }

    // Constructor #3 - private access level
    private Test(int x, int y) {
    }

    // Constructor #4 - protected access level
    protected Test(int x, int y, int z){
    }
}
```

The effect of these access levels is the same as their effect on a method. A constructor with a public access level can be used in any part of the application provided the class itself is accessible. A constructor with private access level can be used only inside the same class in which it is declared. A constructor with protected access level can be used in any part of the program in the same package in which its class is declared and inside any descendant class in any package. A constructor with package-level access can be used inside the same package in which its class is declared.

You can specify public or package-level access level for a class. A class defines a new reference type, which you can use to declare a reference variable. The access level of a class determines in which part of the program the name of the class can be used. Usually, you use the name of a class in a cast or in a reference variable declaration as shown:

```
// Test class name is used to declare the reference variable t
Test t;

// Test class name is used to cast the reference variable xyz
Test t2 = (Test)xyz;
```

Let's discuss the different combinations of access levels for a class and its constructor, and its effects in a program. Consider the following code that declares a class T1 with `public` access level. It also has a constructor, which also has a `public` access level:

```
// T1.java
package com.jdojo.cls.p1;

public class T1 {
    public T1() {
    }
}
```

Because the class T1 has a `public` access level, you can declare a reference variable of type T1 anywhere in the same module. If this code is in a different module, assume that the module containing the class exports the class' package and the module having this code reads the first module:

```
// Code inside any package
T1 t;
```

Because the constructor for the class T1 has a `public` access level, you can use it in an object creation expression in any package.

```
// Code inside any package
new T1();
```

You can combine the previous two statements into one in the code in any package.

```
// Code inside any package
T1 t = new T1();
```

Let's consider the following code for the class T2, which has a `public` access level and has a constructor with a `private` access level:

```
// T2.java
package com.jdojo.cls.p1;

public class T2 {
    private T2() {
    }
}
```

Because class T2 has a `public` access level, you can use its name to declare a reference variable in any package in the same module. If the package is in a different module, assume that the module can read the package that contains the T2 class. The constructor for class T2 has a `private` access level. The implication of having a `private` constructor is that you cannot create an object of the T2 class outside the T2 class. Recall that a `private` method, field, or a constructor cannot be used outside the class in which it is declared. Therefore, the following code will not compile unless it appears inside the T2 class:

```
// Code outside the T2 class
new T2(); // A compile-time error
```

What is the use of the T2 class if you cannot create its object outside of the T2 class? Let's consider the possible situations where you can declare a constructor private, and still create and use objects of the class.

A constructor is used to create an object of a class. You may want to restrict the number of objects of a class. The only way you can restrict the number of objects of a class is by having full control over its constructors. If you declare all constructors of a class to have the private access level, you have full control over how the objects of that class will be created. Typically, you include one or more public static methods in that class, which create and/or return an object of that class. If you design a class so that only one object of the class may exist, it is called a *singleton pattern*. The following code is a version of the T2 class that is based on the singleton pattern.

```java
// T2.java
package com.jdojo.cls.p1;

public class T2 {
    private static T2 instance = new T2();

    private T2() {
    }

    public static T2 getInstance() {
        return T2.instance;
    }
    /* Other code goes here */
}
```

The T2 class declares a private static reference variable called instance, which holds the reference of an object of the T2 class. Note that the T2 class uses its own private constructor to create an object. Its public static getInstance() method returns the lone object of the class. More than one object of the T2 class cannot exist.

You can use the T2.getInstance() method to get the reference of an object of the T2 class. Internally, the T2 class does not create a new object every time you call the T2.getInstance() method. Rather, it returns the same object reference for all calls to this method.

```java
T2 t1 = T2.getInstance();
T2 t2 = T2.getInstance();
```

Sometimes you want a class to have only static members. It may not make sense to create an object of such a class. For example, the java.lang.Math class declares its constructor private. The Math class contains static variables and static methods to perform numeric operations. It does not make sense to create an object of the Math class.

You can also declare all constructors of a class private to prevent inheritance. Inheritance lets you define a class by extending the definition of another class. If you do not want anyone else to extend your class, one way to achieve this is to declare all constructors of your class private. Another way to prevent your class from being extended is to declare it final. I discuss inheritance in detail in Chapter 20.

Let's consider the class T3 whose constructor has protected access level as shown:

```java
// T3.java
package com.jdojo.cls.p1;

public class T3 {
    protected T3() {
    }
}
```

A constructor with protected access level can be used anywhere in the same package or inside a descendant class in any package. The class T3 is in the com.jdojo.cls.p1 package. You can write the following statement anywhere in com.jdojo.cls.p1 package, which creates an object of the T3 class:

```
// Valid anywhere in the com.jdojo.cls.p1 package
new T3();
```

I cover inheritance in detail later. However, to complete the discussion of a protected constructor, you will use inheritance in the following example. Things about inheritance will be clearer when I discuss it in Chapter 20. You inherit (or extend) a class using the keyword extends. The following code creates a T3Child class by inheriting it from the T3 class:

```
// T3Child.java
package com.jdojo.cls.p2;

import com.jdojo.cls.p1.T3;

public class T3Child extends T3 {
    public T3Child() {
        super(); // Ok. Calls T3() constructor, which is declared protected.
    }
}
```

The T3 class is called the parent class of the T3Child class. An object of a child class cannot be created until the object of its parent class is created. Note the use of the super() statement inside T3Child() constructor's body. The statement super() calls the protected constructor of the T3 class. The super keyword is used to call the parent class' constructor as you use the keyword this to call another constructor of the same class. You cannot call the protected constructor of T3 directly as this is outside the com.jdojo.cls.p1 package:

```
new T3();
```

Consider a T4 class with a constructor having package-level access. Recall that using no access level modifier gives package-level access.

```
// T4.java
package com.jdojo.cls.p1;

public class T4 {
    // T4() has package-level access
    T4() {
    }
}
```

You can use T4's constructor to create its object anywhere in the com.jdojo.cls.p1 package. Sometimes you need a class that works as a helper class for other classes in a package. Objects of these classes need to be created only within the package. You can specify package-level access for constructors of such helper classes.

Default Constructor

The primary goal of declaring a class is to create an object of its type. You need a constructor to create an object of a class. The necessity to have a constructor for a class is so obvious that the Java compiler adds a constructor to your class if you do not declare one. The constructor that is added by the compiler is called the *default constructor*. The default constructor does not have any parameters. Sometimes the default constructor is also called a *no-args constructor*. The access level of the default constructor is the same as the access level of the class.

The classes that you have been working with are called top-level classes. You can also declare a class within another class, which is called an *inner class*. A top-level class can have public or package-level access. However, an inner class can have public, private, protected, or package-level access. The Java compiler adds a default constructor for a top-level class as well as for a *nested class*. A default constructor for a top-level class can have either public or package-level access, depending on the access level of the class. However, a default constructor for an inner class can have access level of public, private, protected or package-level, depending on its class access level.

Table 9-1 shows a few examples of classes and the compiler adding a default constructor to them. When the compiler adds a default constructor, it also adds a statement called super() to call the no-args constructor of the parent class. Sometimes the call to the parent's no-args constructor inside the default constructor may cause your class not to compile. Refer to Chapter 20 for a complete discussion on this topic.

Table 9-1. *Examples of Classes for Which a Default Constructor Is Added by the Java Compiler*

Source Code for Your Class	Compiled Version of Your Class	Comments

`public class Test {`
`}`
	`public class Test {`
	`    public Test() {`
	`    }`
	`}`
		The compiler adds a default constructor with public level access.

`class Test {`
`}`
	`class Test {`
	`    Test() {`
	`    }`
	`}`
		The compiler adds a default construct with package-level access.

`public class Test {`
`    Test() {`
`    }`
`}`
	`public class Test {`
	`    Test() {`
	`    }`
	`}`
		The Test class already had a constructor. The compiler does not add any constructor.

`public class Test {`
`    public Test(int x) {`
`    }`
`}`
	`public class Test {`
	`    public Test(int x) {`
	`    }`
	`}`
		The Test class already had a constructor. The compiler does not add any constructor.

`public class Test {`
`    private class Inner {`
`    }`
`}`
	`public class Test {`
	`    public Test() {`
	`    }`
	`    private class Inner {`
	`        private Inner(){`
	`        }`
	`    }`
	`}`
		Test is a public top-level class and Inner is a private inner class. The compiler adds a public default constructor for the Test class and a private default constructor for the Inner class.

▧ **Tip**   It is good programming practice to add a constructor explicitly to all your classes rather than letting the compiler add a default constructor for your classes. The story of constructors is not over yet. You will revisit constructors in the chapter on inheritance.

A static Constructor

Constructors are used in the context of the creating a new object; hence, they are considered part of the object context, not the class context. You cannot declare a constructor static. The keyword this, which is a reference to the current object, is available inside the body of constructors, as it is available inside the body of all instance methods.

Instance Initialization Block

You have seen that a constructor is used to initialize an instance of a class. An instance initialization block, also called instance initializer, is also used to initialize objects of a class. Why does Java provide two constructs to perform the same thing?

Not all classes in Java can have a constructor. Are you surprised to learn that not all classes can have constructors? I did not mention this fact during the discussion on constructors. Briefly, I mentioned inner classes, which are different from top-level classes. I discuss one more type of class in volume II of this three-book series called an *anonymous class*. As the name suggests, an anonymous class does not have a name. Recall that a constructor is a named block of code whose name is the same as the simple name of the class. Because an anonymous class cannot have a name, it cannot have a constructor either. How will you initialize an object of an anonymous class? You can use an instance initializer to initialize an object of an anonymous class. The use of an instance initializer to initialize an object is not limited only to anonymous classes. Any type of class can use it to initialize its objects.

An instance initializer is simply a block of code inside the body of a class, but outside any methods or constructors. Recall that a block of code is a sequence of legal Java statements enclosed within braces. An instance initializer does not have a name. Its code is simply placed inside an opening brace and a closing brace. The following snippet of code shows how to declare an instance initializer for a Test class. Note that an instance initializer is executed in instance context and the keyword this is available inside the instance initializer.

```
public class Test {
    private int num;

    // An instance initializer
    {
        this.num = 101;

        /* Other code for the instance initializer goes here */
    }

    /* Other code for Test class goes here */
}
```

You can have multiple instance initializers for a class. All of them are executed automatically in textual order for every object you create. Code for all instance initializers is executed before any constructors. Listing 9-7 demonstrates the sequence in which the constructor and instance initializers are executed.

Listing 9-7. Example of Using an Instance Initializer

```
// InstanceInitializer.java
package com.jdojo.cls;

public class InstanceInitializer {
    {
        System.out.println("Inside instance initializer 1.");
    }

    {
        System.out.println("Inside instance initializer 2.");
    }

    public InstanceInitializer() {
        System.out.println("Inside no-args constructor.");
    }

    public static void main(String[] args) {
        InstanceInitializer ii = new InstanceInitializer();
    }
}

Inside instance initializer 1.
Inside instance initializer 2.
Inside no-args constructor.
```

■ **Tip** An instance initializer cannot have a `return` statement. It cannot throw checked exceptions unless all declared constructors list those checked exceptions in their `throws` clause; an exception to this rule is made in the case of an anonymous class because it does not have a constructor; an instance initializer of an anonymous class may throw checked exceptions.

static Initialization Block

A static initialization block is also known as a static initializer. It is similar to an instance initialization block. It is used to initialize a class. In other words, you can initialize class variables inside a static initializer block. An instance initializer is executed once per object, whereas a static initializer is executed only once for a class when the class definition is loaded into JVM. To differentiate it from an instance initializer, you need to use the `static` keyword at the beginning of its declaration. You can have multiple static initializers in a class. All static initializers are executed in textual order in which they appear and are executed before any instance initializers. Listing 9-8 demonstrates when a static initializer is executed.

Listing 9-8. An Example of Using a static Initializer in a Class

```java
// StaticInitializer.java
package com.jdojo.cls;

public class StaticInitializer {
    private static int num;

    // An instance initializer
    {
        System.out.println("Inside instance initializer.");
    }

    // A static initializer. Note the use of the keyword static below.
    static {
        num = 1245;
        System.out.println("Inside static initializer.");
    }

    // Constructor
    public StaticInitializer() {
        System.out.println("Inside constructor.");
    }

    public static void main(String[] args) {
        System.out.println("Inside main() #1. num: " + num);

        // Declare a reference variable of the class
        StaticInitializer si;

        System.out.println("Inside main() #2. num: " + num);

        // Create an object
        new StaticInitializer();

        System.out.println("Inside main() #3. num: " + num);

        // Create another object
        new StaticInitializer();
    }
}
```

```
Inside static initializer.
Inside main() #1. num: 1245
Inside main() #2. num: 1245
Inside instance initializer.
Inside constructor.
Inside main() #3. num: 1245
Inside instance initializer.
Inside constructor.
```

The output may be confusing at first. It shows that the `static` initializer has executed even before the first message is displayed in the `main()` method. You get the output when you run the `StaticInitializer` class using the following command:

```
c:\Java9Fundamentals>java --module-path dist --module jdojo.cls/com.jdojo.cls.StaticInitializer
```

The `java` command must load the definition of the `StaticInitializer` class before it can execute its `main()` method. When the definition of the `StaticInitializer` class is loaded into memory, at that time the class is initialized and its static initializer is executed. This is the reason that you see the message from the static initializer before you see the message from the `main()` method. Note that instance initializer is called twice because you create two objects of the `StaticInitializer` class.

▦ **Tip** A `static` initializer cannot throw checked exceptions and it cannot have a `return` statement.

The final Keyword

The `final` keyword is used in many contexts in a Java. It takes on different meanings in different contexts. However, as its name suggests, its primary meaning is the same in all contexts. Its primary meaning is as follows:

> *The construct with which the final keyword is associated does not allow modifying or replacing the original value or definition of the construct.*

If you remember the primary meaning of the `final` keyword, it will help you understand its specialized meaning in a specific context. The `final` keyword can be used in the following three contexts:

- A variable declaration

- A class declaration

- A method declaration

In this section, I discuss the use of the `final` keyword only in the context of a variable declaration. Chapter 20 discusses its use in the context of class and method declarations in detail. In this section, I briefly describe its meaning in all three contexts.

If a variable is declared `final`, it can be assigned a value only once. That is, the value of a `final` variable cannot be modified once it has been set. If a class is declared final, it cannot be extended (or subclassed). If a method is declared `final`, it cannot be redefined (overridden or hidden) in the subclasses of the class that contains the method.

Let's discuss the use of the `final` keyword in a variable declaration. In this discussion, a variable declaration means the declaration of a local variable, a formal parameter of a method/constructor, an instance variable, and a class variable. To declare a variable as `final`, you need to use the `final` keyword in the variable's declaration. The following snippet of code declares four `final` variables: YES, NO, MSG, and act:

```
final int YES = 1;
final int NO = 2;
final String MSG = "Good-bye";
final Account act = new Account();
```

You can set the value of a final variable only once. Attempting to set the value of a final variable the second time will generate a compile-time error.

```
final int x = 10;
int y = 101 + x; // Reading x is ok

// A compile-time error. Cannot change value of the final variable x once it is set
x = 17;
```

There are two ways to initialize a final variable:

- You can initialize it at the time of its declaration.

- You can defer its initialization until a later time.

How long you can defer the initialization of a final variable depends on the variable type. However, you must initialize the final variable before it is read the first time.

If you do not initialize a final variable at the time of its declaration, such a variable is known as a *blank final variable*. The following is an example of declaring a blank final variable.

```
// A blank final variable
final int multiplier;

/* Do something here... */

// Set the value of multiplier first time
multiplier = 3;

// Ok to read the multiplier variable
int value = 100 * multiplier;
```

Let's go through examples of each type of variable and see how to declare them final.

final Local Variables

You can declare a local variable final. If you declare a local variable as a blank final variable, you must initialize it before using. You will receive a compile-time error if you try to change the value of the final local variable the second time. The following snippet of code uses final and blank final local variables in a test() method. Comments in the code explain what you can do with the final variables in the code.

```
public static void test() {
    int x = 4;        // A variable
    final int y = 10; // A final variable. Cannot change y here onward
    final int z;      // A blank final variable

    // We can read x and y, and modify x
    x = x + y;

    /* We cannot read z here because it is not initialized yet */

    /* Initialize the blank final variable z */
    z = 87;
```

```
    /* Can read z now. Cannot change z here onwards */

    x = x + y + z;

    /* Perform other logic here... */
}
```

final Parameters

You can also declare a formal parameter final. A formal parameter is initialized automatically with the value of the actual parameter when the method or the constructor is invoked. Therefore, you cannot change the value of a final formal parameter inside the method's or the constructor's body. The following snippet of code shows the final formal parameter x for a test2() method:

```
public void test2(final int x) {
    // Can read x, but cannot change it
    int y = x + 11;

    /* Perform other logic here... */
}
```

final Instance Variables

You can declare an instance variable final and blank final. An instance variable is a part of an object's state. A final instance variable specifies part of the object's state that does not change after the object is created. A blank final instance variable must be initialized when an object is created. The following rules apply to initializing a blank final instance variable:

- It must be initialized in one of the instance initializers or all constructors. The following rules expand on this rule.

- If it is initialized in an instance initializer, it should not be initialized again in any other instance initializers or constructors.

- If it is not initialized in any of the instance initializers, the compiler makes sure it is initialized only once, when any of the constructors is invoked. This rule can be broken into two sub-rules. As a rule of thumb, a blank final instance variable must be initialized in all constructors. If you follow this rule, a blank final instance variable will be initialized multiple times if a constructor calls another constructor. To avoid multiple initialization of a blank final instance variable, it should not be initialized in a constructor if the first call in the constructor is a call to another constructor, which initializes the blank final instance variable.

These rules for initializing a blank final instance variable may seem complex. However, it is simple to understand if you remember only one rule—that a blank final instance variable must be initialized once and only once when any of the constructors of the class is invoked. All of the previously described rules are to ensure that this rule is followed.

Let's consider different scenarios of initializing final and blank final instance variables. We do not have anything to discuss about final instance variables where x is a final instance variable for the Test class:

```
public class Test {
    private final int x = 10;
}
```

The `final` instance variable x has been initialized at the time of its declaration and its value cannot be changed afterward. The following code shows a `Test2` class with a blank final instance variable named y:

```
public class Test2 {
    private final int y; // A blank final instance variable
}
```

Attempting to compile the `Test2` class generates an error because the blank final instance variable y is never initialized. Note that the compiler will add a default constructor for the `Test2` class, but it will not initialize y inside the constructor. The following code for the `Test2` class will compile because it initializes y in an instance initializer:

```
public class Test2 {
    private final int y;

    {
        y = 10; // Initialized in an instance initializer
    }
}
```

The following code will not compile because it initializes y more than once inside two instance initializers:

```
public class Test2 {
    private final int y;

    {
        y = 10; // Initialized y for the first time
    }

    {
        y = 10; // An error. Initializing y again
    }
}
```

This code may seem legal to you. However, it is not legal because two instance initializers are initializing y, even though both of them set y to the same value, 10. The rule is about number of times a blank final instance variable should be initialized, irrespective of the value being used for its initializations. Since all instance initializers are executed when an object of the `Test2` class is created, y will be initialized twice, which is not legal.

The following code for the class `Test2` with two constructors would compile:

```
public class Test2 {
    private final int y;

    public Test() {
        y = 10; // Initialize y
    }

    public Test(int z) {
        y = z; // Initialize y
    }
}
```

This code initializes the blank final instance variable y in both constructors. It may seem that y is being initialized twice—once in each constructor. Note that y is an instance variable and one copy of y exists for each object of the Test2 class. When an object of the Test2 class is created, it will use one of the two constructors, not both. Therefore, for each object of the Test2 class, y is initialized only once.

The following is the modified code for the Test2 class, which presents a tricky situation. Both constructors initialize the blank final instance variable y. The tricky part is that the no-args constructor calls another constructor.

```
public class Test2 {
    private final int y;

    public Test() {
        this(20); // Call another constructor
        y = 10;    // Initialize y
    }

    public Test(int z) {
        y = z; // Initialize y
    }
}
```

This code for the Test2 class does not compile. The compiler generates an error message, which reads as "*variable y might already have been assigned*". Let's consider creating an object of the Test2 class as follows:

```
Test2 t = new Test2(30);
```

There is no issue in creating an object of the Test2 class by invoking the one-arg constructor. The blank final instance variable y is initialized only once. Let's create an object of the Test2 class.

```
Test2 t2 = new Test2();
```

When the no-args constructor is used, it calls the one-arg constructor, which initializes y to 20. The no-args constructor initializes y again to 10, which is the second initialization for y. For this reason, the previous code for the Test2 class would not compile. You need to remove the initialization of y from the no-args constructor and the code would then compile. The following is the modified code for the Test2 class that would compile:

```
public class Test2 {
    private final int y;

    public Test() {
        this(20); // Another constructor will initialize y
    }

    public Test(int z) {
        y = z; // Initialize y
    }
}
```

final Class Variables

You can declare a class variable final and blank final. You must initialize a blank final class variable in one of the static initializers. If you have more than one static initializer for a class, you must initialize all the blank final class variables only once in one of the static initializers.

The following code for the Test3 class shows how to deal with a final class variable. It is customary to use all uppercase letters to name final class variables. It is also a way to define *constants* in Java programs. The Java class library has numerous examples where it defines public static final variables to use them as constants.

```
public class Test3 {
    public static final int YES = 1;
    public static final int NO = 2;
    public static final String MSG;

    static {
        MSG = "I am a blank final static variable";
    }
}
```

final Reference Variables

Any type of variables (primitive and reference) can be declared final. The primary meaning of the final keyword is the same in both cases. That is, the value stored in a final variable cannot be changed once it has been set. I cover the final reference variable in a little more detail in this section. A reference variable stores the reference of an object. A final reference variable means that once it references an object (or null), it cannot be modified to reference another object. Consider the following statement:

```
final Account act = new Account();
```

Here, act is a final reference variable of the Account type. It is initialized at the time of its declaration. At this time, act is referencing an object in memory.

Now, you cannot make the act variable reference another object in memory. The following statement generates a compile-time error:

```
act = new Account(); // A compile-time error. Cannot change act
```

A common misconception arises in this case. Mistakenly, programmers believe that the Account object that is referenced by the act reference variable cannot be changed. The declaration statement of the act reference variable as final has two things.

- An act as a reference variable, which is final.

- An Account object in memory whose reference is stored in the act variable.

It is the act reference variable that cannot be changed, not the Account object it is referencing. If the Account class allows you to change the state of its object, you can change the state using the act variable. The following are valid statements, which modify the balance instance variable of the Account object:

```
act.deposit(2001.00); // Modifies state of the Account object
act.debit(2.00);      // Modifies state of the Account object
```

If you do not want an object of a class to be modified after it is created, you need to include that logic in the class design. The class should not let any of its instance variables be modified after the object is created. Such objects are called *immutable objects*.

Compile-Time vs. Runtime final Variables

You use final variables to define constants. This is the reason that final variables are also called constants. If the value of a final variable can be computed by the compiler at compile-time, such a variable is a *compile-time constant*. If the value of a final variable cannot be computed by the compiler, it is a *runtime final variable*. The values of all blank final variables are not known until runtime. References are not computed until runtime. Therefore, all blank final variables and final reference variables are *runtime constants*.

Java performs an optimization when you use compile-time constants in an expression. It replaces the use of the compile-time constant with the actual value of the constant. Suppose you have a Constants class as follows, which declares a static final variable named MULTIPLIER:

```
public class Constants {
    public static final int MULTIPLIER = 12;
}
```

Consider the following statement:

```
int x = 100 * Constants.MULTIPLIER;
```

When you compile this statement, the compiler will replace Constants.MULTIPLIER with its value 12 and your statement is compiled as follows:

```
int x = 100 * 12;
```

Now, 100 * 12 is also a compile-time constant expression. The compiler will replace it with its value 1200 and your original statement will be compiled as follows:

```
int x = 1200;
```

There is one downside of this compiler optimization. If you change the value of the MULTIPLIER final variable in the Constants class, you must recompile all the classes that refer to the Constants.MULTIPLIER variable. Otherwise, they will continue using the old value of the MULTIPLIER constant that existed when they were compiled last time.

Generic Classes

Abstraction and polymorphism are at the heart of object-oriented programming. Defining a variable is an example of abstraction where the variable hides the actual values and the location where the values are stored. Defining a method hides the details of its implementation logic, which is another form of abstraction. Defining parameters for a method is part of polymorphism that allows the method to work on different types of values or objects.

Java has a feature called *generics* that allows for writing true polymorphic code in Java. Using generics, you can write code without knowing the type of the objects your code operates on. It lets you create generic classes, constructors, and methods.

A generic class is defined using formal type parameters. Formal type parameters are a list of comma-separated variable names placed in angle-brackets (<>) after the class name in the class declaration. The following snippet of code declares a generic class Wrapper that takes one formal type parameter:

```
public class Wrapper<T> {
    // Code for the Wrapper class goes here
}
```

The parameter has been given a name T. What is T at this point? The answer is that you do not know. All you know at this point is that T is a type variable, which could be any reference type in Java, such as String, Integer, Double, Human, Account, etc. The formal type parameter value is specified when the Wrapper class will be used. The classes that take formal type parameters are also known as *parameterized classes*.

You can declare a variable of the Wrapper<T> class by specifying the String type as the value for its formal type parameter as shown here. Here, String is the actual type parameter.

```
Wrapper<String> stringWrapper;
```

Java lets you use a generic class without specifying the formal type parameters. This is allowed for backward compatibility. You can also declare a variable of the Wrapper<T> class as shown:

```
Wrapper aRawWrapper;
```

When a generic class is used without specifying the actual type parameters, it is known as *raw type*. The previous declaration used the Wrapper<T> class as a raw type, as it did not specify the value for T.

░░ **Tip**   The actual type parameter for a generic class, if specified, must be a reference type, for example, String, Human, etc. Primitive types are not allowed as the actual type parameters for a generic class.

A class may take more than one formal type parameter. The following snippet of code declares a Mapper class that takes two formal parameters named T and R:

```
public class Mapper<T,R> {
    // Code for the Mapper class goes here
}
```

You can declare variable of the Mapper<T, R> class as follows:

```
Mapper<String,Integer> mapper;
```

Here, the actual type parameters are String and Integer.

It is customary, not a requirement, to give one-character names to the formal type parameters, for example, T, R, U, V, etc. Typically, T stands for "Type", R for "Return," etc. One-character names make the code more readable. However, nothing stops you from declaring a generic class as follows, which has four formal type parameters named MyType, YourType, Hello, and WhoCares.

```
public class Fun<MyType,YourType,Hello,WhoCares> {
    // Code for the Fun class goes here
}
```

Java will compile the Fun class, but readers of your code will complain for sure! The formal type parameters are available inside the class body to be used as types. Listing 9-9 declares a generic class Wrapper<T>.

Listing 9-9. Declaring a Generic Class Wrapper<T>

```java
// Wrapper.java
package com.jdojo.cls;

public class Wrapper<T> {
    private T obj;

    public Wrapper(T obj) {
        this.obj = obj;
    }

    public T get() {
        return obj;
    }

    public void set(T obj) {
        this.obj = obj;
    }
}
```

The Wrapper<T> class uses the formal type parameter to declare instance variable obj to declare a formal parameter for its constructor and set() method, and as a return type for the get() method.

You can create an object of the generic type by specifying the actual type parameter for the constructor as follows:

```java
Wrapper<String> w1 = new Wrapper<String>("Hello");
```

Most of the time, the compiler can infer the actual type parameter for the constructor. In those cases, you can omit the actual type parameter. In the following assignment statement, the compiler will infer the actual type parameter for the constructor as String:

```java
Wrapper<String> w1 = new Wrapper<>("Hello");
```

Once you have declared a variable of the generic class, you can think of the formal type parameter as the specified actual type parameter for all practical purposes. Now, you can think that, for w1, the get() method of the Wrapper<T> class returns a String.

```java
String s1 = w1.get();
```

The program in Listing 9-10 shows how to use the generic Wrapper<T> class.

Listing 9-10. Using a Generic Class in Your Code

```java
// WrapperTest.java
package com.jdojo.cls;
```

```java
public class WrapperTest {
    public static void main(String[] args) {
        Wrapper<String> w1 = new Wrapper<>("Hello");
        String s1 = w1.get();
        System.out.println("s1=" + s1);

        w1.set("Testing generics");
        String s2 = w1.get();
        System.out.println("s2=" + s2);

        w1.set(null);
        String s3 = w1.get();
        System.out.println("s3=" + s3);
    }
}
```

```
s1=Hello
s2=Testing generics
s3=null
```

This is just the tip of the iceberg when it comes to what generics offer in Java. To understand generics completely, you must cover other topics, such as inheritance, first. Generics are covered fully in a separate chapter in the second volume of this three-book series.

Summary

A constructor is a named block of code that is used to initialize an object of a class immediately after the object is created. The structure of a constructor looks similar to a method. However, they are two different constructs and they are used for different purposes. The name of a constructor is the same as the simple name of the class. Like methods, constructors may accept parameters. Unlike methods, constructors cannot specify a return type. A constructor is used with the new operator, which allocates memory for a new object and the constructor initializes the new object. A constructor does not return a value to its caller. You can use a return statement without an expression inside a constructor. The return statement ends the constructor call and returns the controls to the caller.

Constructors are not considered members of the class. Like fields and methods, constructors also have an access level: public, private, protected, and package-level. The presence of the keyword public, private, and protected in defining them gives them public, private, and protected access level, respectively. Absence of any of these keywords specifies the package-level access.

A class can have more than one constructor. If a class has multiple constructors, they are called overloaded constructors. Since the name of the constructor must be the same as the simple name of the class, there is a need to differentiate one constructor from another. All constrictors of a class must differ from the others in the number, order, or type of parameters.

A constructor may call another constructor of the same class using the keyword this as if it were a method name. If a constructor of a class calls another constructor of the same class, the following rules must be met:

- The call to another constructor must be the first statement in the constructor.

- A constructor cannot call itself.

If you do not add a constructor to your class, the Java compiler adds one. Such as constructor is called a *default constructor*. The default constructor has the same access level as its class and it takes no parameters.

A class can also have one or more instance initializers to initialize objects of the class. An instance initializer is simply a block of code inside the body of a class, but outside any methods or constructors. Recall that a block of code is a sequence of legal Java statements enclosed within braces. An instance initializer does not have a name. Its code is simply placed inside an opening brace and a closing brace. When an object of a class is created, all instance initializers of the class are executed in textual order. Typically, instance initializers are used to initialize an object of an anonymous class.

A class can have one or more static initializers, which are used to initialize a class, typically, class variables. An instance initializer is executed once per object, whereas a static initializer is executed only once for a class when the class definition is loaded into JVM. To differentiate it from an instance initializer, you need to use the static keyword in the beginning of its declaration. All static initializers of a class are executed in textual order in which they appear and are executed before any instance initializers.

You can define a class and its members final. If something is final, it means its definition or value, whatever it represents, cannot be modified. Final variables are used to define constants in Java. Compile-time constants are constants whose values are known when the program is compiled. Runtime constants are constants whose values are not known until the program is run.

A variable can be declared blank final, in which case the variable is declared final, but not assigned a value at the time of declaration. A blank final variable must be assigned a value before its value is read. A blank final instance variable must be initialized once in its instance initializers or constructors. You can declare a class variable as blank final. You must initialize a blank final class variable in one of the static initializers. If you have more than one static initializer for a class, you must initialize all the blank final class variables only once in one of the static initializers.

Java allows you to write true polymorphic code using generics in which code is written in terms of formal type parameters. A generic class is defined using formal type parameters. Formal type parameters are a list of comma-separated variable names placed in angle-brackets (<>) after the class name in the class declaration. Classes that take formal type parameters are also known as *parameterized classes*. The actual type parameters are specified when the parameterized classes are used.

EXERCISES

1. What is a constructor? What is the name of the operator that must be used along with a constructor to create an object of a class?

2. What is a default constructor? What is the access level of a default constructor?

3. How do you call a constructor of a class from another constructor of the same class? Describe any restrictions where such a call should be placed in the code.

4. What are static and instance initializers?

5. What are final variables and blank final variables?

6. What is the effect of declaring a method's parameter or a constructor's parameter final?

7. Consider the following code for a Cat class:

```java
// Cat.java
package com.jdojo.cls.excercise;

public class Cat {
}
```

When the Cat class is compiled, the compiler will add a default constructor to it. Rewrite the Cat class as if you are adding the default constructor instead of the compiler.

8. Consider the following code for a Mouse class:

```
// Mouse.java
package com.jdojo.cls.excercise;

class Mouse {
}
```

When the Mouse class is compiled, the compiler will add a default constructor to it. Rewrite the Mouse class as if you are adding the default constructor instead of the compiler.

9. Create a SmartPoint2D class with two int instance variables named x and y. The instance variables should be declared private and final. An instance of the SmartPoint2D class represents an immutable point in a 2D plane. That is, once an object of the SmartPoint2D class is created, the x and y values of that object cannot be changed. Add a public constructor to the class, which should accept the values for the two instance variables x and y and initialize them with the passed-in values.

10. Add getters for the x and y instance variables in the SmartPoint2D class that you created in the previous exercise.

11. Add a public static final variable named ORIGIN to the SmartPoint2D class. The ORIGIN variable is of the SmartPoint2D class and it is a SmartPoint2D with x = 0 and y = 0.

12. Implement a method named distance in the SmartPoint2D class that you created in the previous exercise. The method accepts an instance of the SmartPoint2D class and returns the distance between the current point and the point represented by the parameter. The method should be declared as follows:

```
public class SmartPoint2D {
    /* Code from the previous exercise goes here. */

    public double distance(SmartPoint2D p) {
        /* Your code for this exercise goes here. */
    }
}
```

Hint: The distance between two points (x1, y1) and (x2, y2) is computed as $\sqrt{(x1-x2)^2+(y1-y2)^2}$. You can use Math.sqrt(n) method to compute the square root of a number n.

13. Create a `Circle` class that has three private final instance variables named x, y, and radius. The x and y instance variables represent the x and y coordinates of the center of the circle; they are of `int` data type. The radius instance variable represents the radius of the circle; it is of the `double` data type. Add a constructor to the `Circle` class that accepts the values for its instance variables x, y, and radius. Add getters for the three instance variables.

14. Enhance the `Circle` class by adding four instance methods named `centerDistance`, `distance`, `overlaps`, and `touches`. All these methods accept a `Circle` as a parameter. The `centerDistance` method returns the distance (as a `double`) between the centers of the circle and another circle passed in as the parameter. The `distance` method returns the minimum distance (as a `double`) between the two circles. If two circles overlap, the `distance` method returns a negative number. The `overlaps` method returns `true` if two circles overlaps, `false` otherwise. The `touches` method returns `true` if two circles touches each other, `false` otherwise. The `distance` method must use the `centerDistance` method. The body of the `overlaps` and `touches` methods must contain only one statement that uses the `distance` method.

    Hint: The distance between two circles is the distance between their centers minus their radii. Two circles overlap if the distance between them is negative. Two circles touch if the distance between them is zero.

15. Enhance the `Circle` class by adding two methods named `perimeter` and `area` that compute and return the perimeter and area of the circle, respectively.

16. Add a second constructor to the `Circle` class that takes a `double` parameter, which is the radius of the circle. This constructor should call another existing constructor of the `Circle` class with three parameters passing zero as the values for x and y.

17. A double value can be NaN, positive infinity, and negative infinity. Enhance the constructor of the `Circle` class with three parameters, x, y, and radius, so it throws a `RuntimeException` when the value of the radius parameter is not a finite number or a negative number.

    Hint: The `java.lang.Double` class contains a static `isFinite(double n)` method, which returns `true` if the specified parameter n is a finite number, `false` otherwise. Use the following statement to throw a `RuntimeException`:

    ```
    throw new RuntimeException(
            "Radius must be a finite non-negative number.");
    ```

18. Consider the following `InitializerTest` class. How many static and instance initializers are in this class? What will be printed when this class is run?

    ```
    // InitializerTest.java
    package com.jdojo.cls.excercise;

    public class InitializerTest {
        private static int count;
    ```

```
    {
        System.out.println(count++);
    }

    {
        System.out.println(count++);
    }

    static {
        System.out.println(count);
    }

    public static void main(String[] args) {
        new InitializerTest();
        new InitializerTest();
    }
}
```

19. Describe why the following `FinalTest` class does not compile.

```
// FinalTest.java
package com.jdojo.cls.excercise;

public class FinalTest {
    public static int square(final int x) {
        x = x * x;
        return x;
    }
}
```

20. Describe why the following `BlankFinalTest` class does not compile.

```
// BlankFinalTest.java
package com.jdojo.cls.excercise;

public class BlankFinalTest {
    private final int x;
    private final int y;

    {
        y = 100;
    }

    public BlankFinalTest() {
        y = 100;
    }

    /* More code goes here */
}
```

CHAPTER 10

Modules

In this chapter, you will learn:

- What modules are

- How to declare modules

- What the implicit readability of a module means and how to declare it

- The difference between unqualified and qualified exports

- Declaring the runtime optional dependency of a module

- How to open an entire module or its selected packages for deep reflection

- Rules on splitting packages across modules

- Restrictions on module declarations

- Different types of modules: named, unnamed, explicit, automatic, normal, and open modules

- Knowing about modules at runtime

- How to disassemble a module's definition using the javap tool

The code for some examples in this chapter goes through several steps. The source code for this book contains the code used in the final step for those examples. If you want to see those examples in action at every step as you read through this chapter, you need to modify the source code a bit to keep it in sync with the step you are working on.

What Is a Module?

In simple terms, a module is a group of packages. A module may optionally contain resources such as images, property files, etc. For now, let's focus only on a module being a group of packages. A module specifies the accessibility for its packages to other modules and its dependence on other modules. The accessibility of a package in a module determines whether other modules can access the package. The dependence of a module determines the list of other modules that this module reads. Three terms—"depends on", "reads", and "requires"—are used interchangeably to indicate dependence of a module on another module. If module M depends on module N, the following three phrases mean the same: "Module M depends on module N", "Module M requires module N", or "Module M reads module N".

By default, a package in a module is accessible only within the same module. If a package in a module needs to be accessible outside its module, the module that contains the package needs to *export* the package. A module may export its packages to all other modules or only to a selected list of other modules.

© Kishori Sharan 2017
K. Sharan, *Beginning Java 9 Fundamentals*, https://doi.org/10.1007/978-1-4842-2902-6_10

If a module wants to access packages from another module, the first module must declare dependence on the second module and the second module must export packages in order for them to be accessible to the first module.

Declaring Modules

A module is declared in a compilation unit. I introduced the concept of the compilation unit in Chapter 3 in which a compilation unit contained type declarations (class and interface declarations). A compilation unit that contains a module declaration is different from a compilation unit that contains type declarations. Starting in Java 9, there are two types of compilation units:

- Ordinary compilation unit
- Modular compilation unit

An ordinary compilation unit consists of three parts: a package declaration, import declarations, and top-level type declaration. All parts in an ordinary compilation unit are optional. Refer to Chapter 3 for more detail on ordinary compilation units.

A modular compilation unit contains a module declaration. The module declaration may be preceded by optional import declarations. A modular compilation unit cannot have a package declaration. Import declarations in a modular compilation unit let you use the simple names of types and static members of types in the module declaration.

▒ **Tip**   A modular compilation unit is named `module-info` with an extension `.java` or `.jav`. All modular compilation units in this book's examples are named `module-info.java`.

The syntax to use a modular compilation unit is as follows:

```
[import-declarations]
<module-declaration>
```

Types used in import declarations may be from packages in the same module or other modules. Refer to Chapter 7 for more detail on how to use import declarations. The syntax for a module declaration is as follows:

```
[open] module <module-name> {
    <module-statement-1>;
    <module-statement-2>;
    ...
}
```

The `module` keyword is used to declare a module. A module declaration may optionally start with the open keyword to declare an open module. The `module` keyword is followed with a module name. A module name is a qualified Java identifier, which is a sequence of one or more Java identifiers separated by a dot.

The body of the module declaration is placed inside curly braces, which may have zero or more module statements. Module statements are also known as *module directives*. I use the term statement, not directive, in this book. There are five types of module statements:

- The exports statement

- The opens statement

- The requires statement

- The uses statement

- The provides statement

For one module to access types in another module, the first module makes the packages containing such types accessible and the second module reads the first module. All five types of module statements are used for these two purposes:

- Making types accessible

- Accessing those types

The exports, opens, and provides statements express availability of types in a module to other modules. The requires and uses statements in a module are used to express dependence of a module to read types that are made available using the exports, opens, and provides statements by other modules. The difference in these types of statements lies in the context in which the types are made available by a module and those types are used by other modules. The following is an example of a module declaration that contains all five types of module statements.

```
module jdojo.policy {
    exports com.jdojo.policy;

    requires java.sql;

    opens com.jdojo.policy.model;

    uses com.jdojo.common.Job;

    provides com.jdojo.common.Job with com.jdojo.policy.JobImpl;
}
```

The following terms are restricted keywords in Java 9: open, module, requires, transitive, exports, opens, to, uses, provides, and with. They are treated as keywords only when they appear in a modular compilation unit at specific positions. They are normal terms everywhere else. For example, the following module declaration is valid, even though the module name, which is module, is not very intuitive:

```
module module {
    exports com.jdojo.policy;
}
```

Here, the first "module" term is a restricted keyword and the second one is a normal term used as the name of the module.

The subsequent sections describe the exports and requires statements in detail. I explain the opens statement briefly in this chapter. I explain open modules and opens statement in detail in Chapter 3 and the uses and provides statements in detail in Chapter 14 in the second volume of this three-volume *Beginning Java 9* series.

Declaring Module Dependence

Up to Java SE 8, a public type in one package can be accessed by other packages without any restrictions. In other words, packages did not control the accessibility of the types they contained. The module system in Java SE 9 provides a fine-grained control over the accessibility of types contained in packages of a module.

Accessibility across modules is a two-way agreement between the used module and the using module. A module explicitly makes its public types available to other modules for use and the modules using those public types explicitly declare dependence on the first module. All non-exported packages of a module are private to the module and they cannot be accessed from outside the module.

Making public types in a package available to other modules is known as *exporting* that package and it is accomplished using an exports statement in the module's declaration. A module may export its packages to all other modules or to a selected list of modules. When a module exports its package to all other modules, it is called an *unqualified export*. The following is the syntax to export a package to all other modules:

```
exports <package>;
```

Here, <package> is the package in the current module. All other modules that read the current module can use the public types in this package. Consider the following declaration:

```
module jdojo.address {
    exports com.jdojo.address;
}
```

The jdojo.address module exports a package named com.jdojo.address to all other modules. All other packages in the jdojo.address module are accessible only within the jdojo.address module.

A module can also export a package selectively only to one or more named modules. Such exports are called *qualified exports* or *module-friendly exports*. The public types in a package in a qualified export are accessible only to the specified named modules. The following is the syntax for using a qualified export:

```
exports <package> to <friend-module> [, <friend-module>...] ;
```

Here, <package> is a package in the current module, which is exported only to friend modules listed in the to clause. The following is a module declaration for a jdojo.policy module that uses a qualified export:

```
module jdojo.policy {
    exports com.jdojo.policy to jdojo.claim, jdojo.payment;
}
```

The jdojo.policy module contains a package named com.jdojo.policy. The module uses a qualified export to export this package to only two modules named jdojo.claim and jdojo.payment.

▓ **Tip** Modules specified in the to clause of a qualified export do not need to be observable.

Which one is better to use—an unqualified export or a qualified export? An unqualified export should be used when you are sharing public types in a package to public, for example, when you are developing a module for public use. Once you distribute your module, you should not be changing the public APIs in the exported packages. Sometimes, bad APIs remain in a module forever because the module is in public use and changing/removing the APIs will impact a lot of users. Sometimes, you may need to share public types between modules where the modules are part of a library or framework; however, public types in those modules are not for public use. In such cases, you should use qualified exports, which will minimize the impact should you change the APIs involving those shared public types. The java.base module uses several qualified exports to export its packages to other JDK modules. You can describe the java.base module using the following command to list qualified exports:

```
C:\> java --describe-module java.base
```

```
java.base@9
exports java.io
exports java.lang
...
qualified exports jdk.internal.org.xml.sax to jdk.jfr
qualified exports sun.security.tools to jdk.jartool
...
contains sun.invoke
contains sun.invoke.util
contains sun.io
...
```

A requires statement is used to specify a module's dependence to another module. If a module reads another module, the first module needs to have a requires statement in its declaration. The general syntax for the requires statement is as follows:

```
requires [transitive] [static] <module>;
```

Here, <module> is the name of the module that the current module reads. Both transitive and static modifiers are optional. If the static modifier is present, the dependence on <module> is mandatory at compile-time, but optional at runtime. Without the static modifier, the read module is required at compiled-time and runtime. The presence of the transitive modifier implies that a module that reads the current module implicitly also reads <module>. I cover an example of using the transitive modifier in a requires statement shortly. The following is an example of using a requires statement.

```
module jdojo.claim {
    requires jdojo.policy;
}
```

Here, the jdojo.claim module uses a requires statement to indicate that it reads the jdojo.policy module. All public types from all exported packages in the jdojo.policy module are accessible inside the jdojo.claim module.

Every module implicitly reads the java.base module. The compiler adds a requires statement to read the java.base module to a module declaration if the declaration does not explicitly read the java.base module. The following two module declarations for a jdojo.common module are the same:

```
// Declaration #1
module jdojo.common {
    // The compiler will add a dependence to the java.base module
}
```

```
// Declaration #2
module jdojo.common {
    // Add a dependence to the java.base module explicitly
    requires java.base;
}
```

You can visualize dependence between two modules, as depicted in Figure 10-1, which depicts the dependence between two modules named jdojo.policy and jdojo.claim.

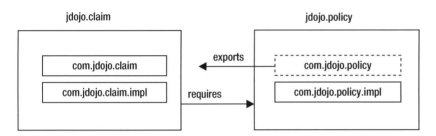

Figure 10-1. *Declaring dependency between modules*

The jdojo.policy module contains two packages named com.jdojo.policy and com.jdojo.policy. impl; it exports the com.jdojo.policy package, which I have shown in a dashed boundary to distinguish it from the com.jdojo.policy.impl package, which is not exported. The jdojo.claim module contains two packages—com.jdojo.claim and com.jdojo.claim.impl; it does not export any package and declares a dependence on the jdojo.policy module. The following two module declarations express this dependence in Java code:

```
module jdojo.policy {
    exports com.jdojo.policy;
}

module jdojo.claim {
    requires jdojo.policy;
}
```

▓ **Tip**   The dependence declarations in two modules, the used module and the using module, are asymmetric—the used module exports a *package* whereas the using module requires a *module*.

An Example of Module Dependence

In this section, I walk you through a complete example of using module dependence. Suppose you have two modules named jdojo.address and jdojo.person. The jdojo.address module contains a package named com.jdojo.address, which contains a class named Address. The jdojo.person module wants to use the Address class from the jdojo.address module. Figure 10-2 shows the module graph for the jdojo.person module.

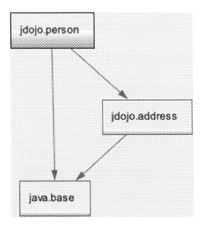

Figure 10-2. *The module graph for the jdojo.person module*

In NetBeans, you can create two modules named jdojo.address and jdojo.person. Listings 10-1 and 10-2 contain the module declaration and the code for the Address class.

Listing 10-1. The Module Declaration for the jdojo.address Module

```
// module-info.java
module jdojo.address {
    // Export the com.jdojo.address package
    exports com.jdojo.address;
}
```

Listing 10-2. The Address Class

```
// Address.java
package com.jdojo.address;

public class Address {
    private String line1 = "1111 Main Blvd.";
    private String city = "Jacksonville";
    private String state = "FL";
    private String zip = "32256";

    public Address() {
    }

    public Address(String line1, String city, String state, String zip) {
        this.line1 = line1;
        this.city = city;
        this.state = state;
        this.zip = zip;
    }
```

```java
    public String getLine1() {
        return line1;
    }

    public void setLine1(String line1) {
        this.line1 = line1;
    }

    public String getCity() {
        return city;
    }

    public void setCity(String city) {
        this.city = city;
    }

    public String getState() {
        return state;
    }

    public void setState(String state) {
        this.state = state;
    }

    public String getZip() {
        return zip;
    }

    public void setZip(String zip) {
        this.zip = zip;
    }

    @Override
    public String toString() {
        return "[Line1:" + line1 + ", State:" + state +
                ", City:" + city + ", ZIP:" + zip + "]";
    }
}
```

The Address class is a simple class with four fields and their getters and setters. I set the default values for these fields, so you don't have to type them in examples. I have added a toString() method to the Address class, which returns a string representation of the address object. I describe the use of the toString() method in detail in Chapter 11 and Chapter 20.

The jdojo.address module exports the com.jdojo.address package, so the Address class, which is public and in the exported com.jdojo.address package, can be used by other modules. You will be using the Address class in the jdojo.person module in this example. Listings 10-3 and 10-4 contain the module declaration for the jdojo.person module and the code for the Person class.

Listing 10-3. The Module Declaration for the jdojo.person Module

```java
// module-info.java
module jdojo.person {
    // Read the jdojo.address module
    requires jdojo.address;

    // Export the com.jdojo.person package
    exports com.jdojo.person;
}
```

Listing 10-4. A Person Class

```java
// Person.java
package com.jdojo.person;

import com.jdojo.address.Address;

public class Person {
    private long personId;
    private String firstName;
    private String lastName;
    private Address address = new Address();

    public Person(long personId, String firstName, String lastName) {
        this.personId = personId;
        this.firstName = firstName;
        this.lastName = lastName;
    }

    public long getPersonId() {
        return personId;
    }

    public void setPersonId(long personId) {
        this.personId = personId;
    }

    public String getFirstName() {
        return firstName;
    }

    public void setFirstName(String firstName) {
        this.firstName = firstName;
    }

    public String getLastName() {
        return lastName;
    }
}
```

```
    public void setLastName(String lastName) {
        this.lastName = lastName;
    }

    public Address getAddress() {
        return address;
    }

    public void setAddress(Address address) {
        this.address = address;
    }

    @Override
    public String toString() {
        return "[Person Id:" + personId + ", First Name:" + firstName +
                ", Last Name:" + lastName + ", Address:" + address + "]";
    }
}
```

The Person class is in the `jdojo.person` module and it uses a field of the `Address` type, which is in the `jdojo.address` module. This means that the `jdojo.person` module reeds the `jdojo.address` module. This is indicated by the `requires` statement in `jdojo.person module` declaration:

```
// Read the jdojo.address module
requires jdojo.address;
```

The declaration of the `jdojo.person module` includes a `requires` statement without a `static` modifier, implying that the `jdojo.address module` is required at compile-time as well as at runtime. When you compile the `jdojo.person module`, you must include the `jdojo.address module` in the module path. In the supplied source code, these two modules are part of a single NetBeans modular project and you do not need to perform an additional step to modify the module path.

If you create the two modules using two separate NetBeans projects, you need to include the project for the `jdojo.address` module in the module path of the `jdojo.person` module. Right-click the `jdojo.person` project in NetBeans and select Properties. In the Categories list, select Libraries. Select the Compile tab and click the + sign on the Modulepath row. Select the Add Project... from the menu, as shown in Figure 10-3, and select the `jdojo.address` NetBeans project from the file system. If you have a compiled `jdojo.address` module in a modular JAR or a directory, you can use the Add JAR/Folder menu option.

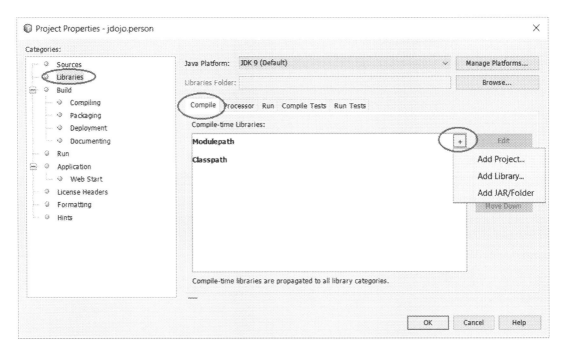

Figure 10-3. *Setting the module path for a project in NetBeans*

The jdojo.person module also exports the com.jdojo.person package, so the public types in this package, for example, the Person class, may be used by other modules. Listing 10-5 contains the code for a Main class, which is in the jdojo.person module.

Listing 10-5. A Main Class to Test the jdojo.person Module

```java
// Main.java
package com.jdojo.person;

import com.jdojo.address.Address;

public class Main {
    public static void main(String[] args) {
        Person john = new Person(1001, "John", "Jacobs");

        String fName = john.getFirstName();
        String lName = john.getLastName();
        Address addr = john.getAddress();

        System.out.printf("%s %s%n", fName, lName);
        System.out.printf("%s%n", addr.getLine1());
        System.out.printf("%s, %s %s%n", addr.getCity(),
                        addr.getState(), addr.getZip());
    }
}
```

```
John Jacobs
1111 Main Blvd.
Jacksonville, FL 32256
```

When you run this class, the output shows that you are able to use the `Address` class from the `jdojo.address` module. We are done with this example that shows how to use the `exports` and `requires` module statements. If you have any trouble running this example, refer the next section, which lists a few possible errors and their solutions.

At this point, you can also run this example using a command prompt. You will need to include the compiled exploded directories or the modular JARs for the `jdojo.person` and `jdojo.address` modules to the module path. The following command uses the modular JARs from the `dist` directory:

```
C:\Java9Fundamentals>java --module-path dist\jdojo.person.jar;dist\jdojo.address.jar
--module jdojo.person/com.jdojo.person.Main
```

```
John Jacobs
1111 Main Blvd.
Jacksonville, FL 32256
```

The supplied source code for this book contains all modular JARs in the `Java9Fundamentals\dist` directory. In this command, I selectively included the modular JARs for the `jdojo.person` and `jdojo.address` modules to show you that all other modules are not being used when you run the `com.jdojo.person.Main` class. You can simplify this command by adding only the `dist` directory to the module path, as follows, and the Java runtime will use the needed two modules as before:

```
C:\Java9Fundamentals>java --module-path dist --module jdojo.person/com.jdojo.person.Main
```

```
John Jacobs
1111 Main Blvd.
Jacksonville, FL 32256
```

Troubleshooting

If you are using the JDK 9 for the first time, a numbers of things can go wrong when you are working through this example. The following are a few scenarios with error messages and the corresponding solutions.

Empty Package Error

The error is:

```
error: package is empty or does not exist: com.jdojo.address
    exports com.jdojo.address;
                  ^
1 error
```

You get this error when you compile the module declaration for the `jdojo.address` module without including the source code for the `Address` class. The module exports the `com.jdojo.address` package. You must have at least one type defined in the exported package.

Module Not Found Error

The error is:

```
error: module not found: jdojo.address
    requires jdojo.address;
                   ^
1 error
```

You get this error when you compile the module declaration for the jdojo.person module without including the jdojo.address module in the module path. The jdojo.person module reads the jdojo.address module, so the former must be able to find the latter on the module path at compile-time as well as at runtime. If you are using a command prompt, use the --module-path option to specify the module path for the jdojo.address module. If you are using NetBeans, refer to the previous section on how to configure the module path for the jdojo.person module.

Package Does Not Exist Error

The error is:

```
error: package com.jdojo.address does not exist
import com.jdojo.address.Address;
                       ^
error: cannot find symbol
    private Address address = new Address();
            ^
  symbol:   class Address
  location: class Person
```

You get this error when you compile the Person and Main classes in the jdojo.person module without adding a requires statement in the module declaration. The error message states that the compiler is not able to find the com.jdojo.address.Address class. The solution is to add a requires jdojo.address statement to the module declaration for the jdojo.person module and add the jdojo.address module to the module path while compiling and running the jdojo.person module.

Module Resolution Exception

The partial error is:

```
Error occurred during initialization of VM
java.lang.module.ResolutionException: Module jdojo.person not found
...
```

You may get this error for the following reasons when you attempt to run the example using a command prompt:

- The module path is not specified correctly.

- The module path is correct, but no compiled code in the specified directories or modular JARs are found on the module path.

Suppose you use the following command to run the example:

```
C:\Java9Fundamentals>java --module-path dist --module jdojo.person/com.jdojo.person.Main
```

Make sure that the following modular JARs exist:

- `C:\Java9Fundamentals\dist\jdojo.person.jar`
- `C:\Java9Fundamentals\dist\jdojo.address.jar`

If these modular JARs do not exist, build the `Java9Fundamentals` project in NetBeans. If you are running the example using the modules code from the exploded directories using the following command, make sure to compile the projects in NetBeans:

```
C:\Java9Fundamentals>java --module-path build\modules\jdojo.person;build\modules\jdojo.
address
--module jdojo.person/com.jdojo.person.Main
```

Implicit Dependence

If a module can read another module without the first module including in its declaration a `requires` statement to read the second module, it is said that the first module implicitly reads the second module. Every module implicitly reads the `java.base` module. An implicit read is not limited to the `java.base` module. A module can also implicitly read another module, other than the `java.base` module. Before I show you how to add an implicit readability to a module, I will build an example to show you why we need this feature.

In the previous section, you created two modules named `jdojo.address` and `jdojo.person`, where the second module reads the first module using the following declaration:

```
module jdojo.person {
    requires com.jdojo.address;
    ...
}
```

The `Person` class in the `jdojo.person` module refers to the `Address` class in `jdojo.address` module. Let's create another module named `jdojo.person.test`, which reads the `jdojo.person` module. The module declaration is shown in Listing 10-6.

Listing 10-6. The Module Declaration for the com.jdojo.person.test Module

```
// module-info.java
module jdojo.person.test {
    requires jdojo.person;
}
```

The module graph for the `jdojo.person.test` module is shown in Figure 10-4. Notice that the `jdojo.person.test` module does not read the `jdojo.address` module, so the public types in the `com.jdojo.address` package exported by the `jdojo.address` module are not accessible in the `jdojo.person.test` module.

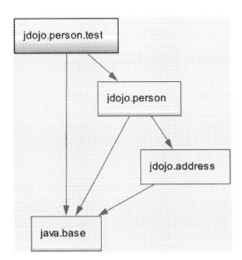

Figure 10-4. *The module graph of the jdojo.person.test module*

Listing 10-7 contains the code for a Main class in the jdojo.person.test module.

Listing 10-7. A Main Class to Test the jdojo.person.test Module

```java
// Main.java
package com.jdojo.person.test;

import com.jdojo.person.Person;

public class Main {
    public static void main(String[] args) {
        Person john = new Person(1001, "John", "Jacobs");

        // Get John's city and print it
        String city = john.getAddress().getCity();
        System.out.printf("John lives in %s%n", city);
    }
}
```

The code in the main() method is very simple—it creates a Person object and reads the value of the city in a person's address:

```java
Person john = new Person(1001, "John", "Jacobs");
String city = john.getAddress().getCity();
```

Compiling the code for the jdojo.person.test module generates the following error:

```
C:\Java9Fundamentals\src\jdojo.person.test\classes\com\jdojo\person\test\Main.java:11:
error: Address.getCity() in package com.jdojo.address is not accessible
        String city = john.getAddress().getCity();
  (package com.jdojo.address is declared in module jdojo.address, but module jdojo.person.
test does not read it)
1 error
```

The compiler message is not very clear. It is stating that the Address class is not accessible to the jdojo.person.test module. Recall that the Address class is in the jdojo.address module, which the jdojo.person.test module does not read. Looking at the code, it seems obvious that the code should compile. You have access to the Person class, which uses the Address class; so you should be able to use the Address class. Here, the call to the john.getAddress() method returns an object of the Address type, which you do not have access to. The module system is simply doing its job in enforcing the encapsulation defined by the jdojo.address module. If a module wants to use the Address class, explicitly or implicitly, it must read the jdojo.address module. How do you fix it? The simple answer would be for the jdojo.person.test module to read the jdojo.address module by changing the declaration to the one shown in Listing 10-8.

Listing 10-8. The Modified Module Declaration for the jdojo.person.test Module

```
// module-info.java
module jdojo.person.test {
    requires jdojo.person;
    requires jdojo.address;
}
```

Figure 10-5 shows the modified module graph for the jdojo.person.test module.

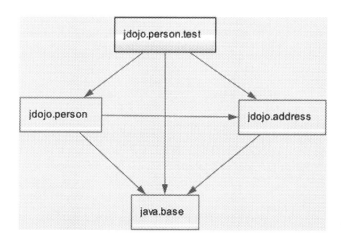

Figure 10-5. *The modified module graph for the jdojo.person.test module*

Compile and run the Main class in the jdojo.person.test module and it will print the following:

```
John lives in Jacksonville
```

You solved the problem by adding a requires statement in the jdojo.person.test module's declaration. However, it is very likely that other modules that read the jdojo.person module will need to work with addresses and they will need to add the same requires statement. If the jdojo.person module exposes types in its public API from more than one other module, the modules reading the jdojo.person module will need to add a requires statement for each such module. It will be simply cumbersome for all those modules to add an extra requires statement.

There is another use case that may create this kind of scenario. Suppose there are only two modules—jdojo.person.test and jdojo.person—where the former reads the latter and the latter exports all packages whose public types are used by the former. The com.jdojo.address package is in the jdojo.person module and the jdojo.person.test module compiled fine. Later, the jdojo.person module is refactored into two modules—jdojo.person and jdojo.address. Now, the jdojo.person.test module stops working because some the public types that were in the jdojo.person modules are now moved to the jdojo.address module, which is not read by the jdojo.person.test module.

The JDK 9 designers realized this problem and provided a simple way to solve this. In this case, all you need to do is change the declaration for the jdojo.person module to add a transitive modifier in the requires statement to read the jdojo.address module. Listing 10-9 contains the modified declaration for the jdojo.person module.

Listing 10-9. The Modified Module Declaration for the jdojo.person Module That Uses a Transitive Export

```
// module-info.java
module jdojo.person {
    // Read the jdojo.address module
    requires transitive jdojo.address;

    // Export the com.jdojo.person package
    exports com.jdojo.person;
}
```

Now, you can remove this statement

```
requires jdojo.address;
```

from the declaration of the jdojo.person.test module. You need to keep the jdojo.address project on the module path to compile and run the jdojo.person.test module project, because the jdojo.address module is still needed to use the Address type in this module. Recompile the jdojo.person module. Recompile and run the main class in the jdojo.person.test module to get the desired output.

▒ **Tip** When a module M uses public types from module N and those public types are part of the public API of module M, consider using a `requires transitive` N in module M. Suppose you have a module P that exports packages and another module Q that reads module P. If you refactor module P to split it into multiple modules, say S and T, consider adding `requires transitive` S and `requires transitive` T statements to P's module declaration to ensure that all modules reading P (module Q in this case) continue to work without any changes.

When a requires statement contains the transitive modifier, the module that depends on the current module implicitly reads the module specified in the requires statement. Referring to Listing 10-9, any module that reads the jdojo.person module implicitly reads the jdojo.address module. Essentially, an implicit read makes the module declaration simpler to read and refactoring a module into multiple modules easier, but harder to reason about because, by just looking at a module declaration, you cannot tell about all its dependencies. Figure 10-6 shows the final module graph for the jdojo.person.test module.

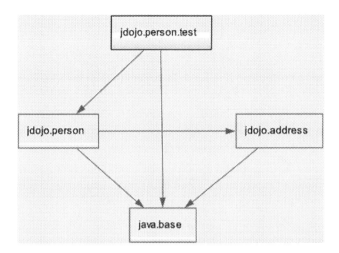

Figure 10-6. *The module graph for the jdojo.person.test module*

When modules are resolved, the module graph is augmented by adding a read edge for each transitive dependency. In this example, a read edge will be added from the jdojo.person.test module to the jdojo.address module, as shown by a dashed arrow in Figure 10-7. I show the edge connecting the jdojo.person.test module to the jdojo.address module in a dashed line to indicate that it is added after the module graph is resolved.

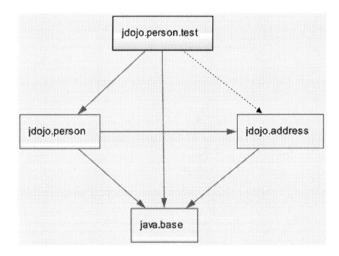

Figure 10-7. *The module graph for the jdojo.person.test module after augmenting it with implicit read edges*

Optional Dependence

The module system verifies the module dependences at compile-time and runtime. There are times when you want to make a module dependence mandatory at compile-time, but optional at runtime.

You may develop a library that performs better if a specific module is available at runtime. Otherwise, it falls back to another module that makes it perform less than optimal. However, the library is compiled against the optional module and it makes sure that the code dependent on the optional module is not executed if the optional module is not available.

Another example would be a module that exports an annotation bundle. The Java runtime already ignores non-existent annotation types. However, module dependence is verified at startup and if the module is missing at runtime, the application won't start. Therefore, it is essential to declare the module dependence on the module containing the annotation bundle as optional.

You can declare an optional dependency by using the `static` keyword in a `requires` statement:

```
requires static <optional-module>;
```

The following module declaration contains an optional dependence on the `jdojo.annotation` module:

```
module jdojo.claim {
    requires static jdojo.anotation;
}
```

It is allowed to have both `transitive` and `static` modifiers in a `requires` statement:

```
module jdojo.claim {
    requires transitive static jdojo.anotation;
}
```

Opening Modules and Packages

Reflection is a vast topic. If this is your first encounter with Java, you may have difficulty in understanding this section. You can revisit this section when you gain more experience in Java or just read it without worrying about following everything that is explained. I cover reflection in detail in Chapter 3 of the second volume of this series.

Reflection is a way to work with Java types without knowing about them at compile-time. You have used types such as the `Person` class in this chapter. To create a `Person` and call its `getFirstName()` method, you write code as shown:

```
import com.jdojo.person.Person;
...

Person john = new Person(1001, "John", "Jacobs");
String firstName = john.getFirstName();
```

In this case, the Java compiler makes sure that there is a class named `Person` in the `com.jdojo.person` package. The compiler also makes sure that this code has access to the `Person` class, its constructor, and its `getFirstName()` method. If the `Person` class does not exist, you cannot compile this code. When you run this code, the Java runtime again verifies the existence of the `Person` and the access need for this code to use it. Using reflection, you can rewrite this code without knowing about the existence of the `Person` class. Your code and the compiler will have no knowledge of the `Person` class, yet you will be able to achieve the same. For this to happen, this code will need only runtime access to the `Person` class. There are two types of access in Java:

- Compile-time access

- Runtime access

The compiler verifies the compile-time access during compilation. Compile-time access must follow the Java language access rules, for example, code outside a class cannot access the private members of the class.

The Java runtime verifies the runtime access to types and their members. At runtime, code may access types and their members in two ways:

- The first way is to run compiled code that was written in terms of the types being accessed. In this case, the runtime reinforces the accessibility rules of the Java language as it does during compilation.

- The second way is to use reflection to access types and their members at runtime. In this case, the compiler has no knowledge of the types and their members your code would access at runtime. Accessing types and their members using reflection is called using *reflective access*. Unlike normal access, reflective access allows access to all types (not just public types) and all members of those types (even private members).

Reflective access is good as well as bad. It is good because it lets you develop libraries that will work on all types that are not known. There are several great frameworks such as Spring and Hibernate, which depend heavily on deep reflective access to members of types defined in application libraries. Reflective access is bad because it breaks encapsulation—it can access types and members of those types, which are otherwise inaccessible using normal access rules. Accessing otherwise inaccessible types and their members using reflection is sometimes referred to as *deep reflection*.

For over 20 years, Java has allowed reflective access. Designers of the module system in Java 9 faced a big challenge in designing the deep reflective access to the modular code. Allowing deep reflection on the types of an exported package violates the *strong encapsulation* theme of the module system. It makes everything accessible to the outside code even if the module developer did not want to expose some part of the module. On the other hand, not allowing deep reflection will devoid the Java community of some great widely used frameworks and it will also break many existing applications that rely on deep reflection. Many existing applications will simply not migrate to JDK 9 because of this limitation.

After a few iterations of design and experiments, the module system designers came up with a middle ground—you can have your cake and it eat too! The current design allows you have a module with strong encapsulation, deep reflective access, and partly both. Here are the rules:

- An exported package will allow access to only public types and their public/protected members at compile-time and runtime. If you do not export a package, all types in that package are inaccessible to other modules. This provides strong encapsulation.

- You can open a module to allow deep reflection on all types in all packages in that module at runtime. Such a module is called an *open module*.

- You can have a normal module—a module that is not open for deep reflection—with specific packages opened for deep reflection at runtime. All other packages, which are not open, are strongly encapsulated. Packages in a module that allow for deep reflection are known as *open packages*.

- Sometimes, you may want to access types in a package at compile-time to write code in terms of the types in that package and, at the same time, you want deep reflective access to those types at runtime. You can export and open the same package to achieve this.

Open Modules

An open module is declared using the open modifier before the `module` keyword:

```
open module jdojo.model {
    // Module statements go here
}
```

Here, the `jdojo.model` module is an open module. Other modules can use deep reflection on all types on all packages in this module. You can have `exports`, `requires`, `uses`, and `provides` statements in the declaration of an open module. You cannot have `opens` statements inside an open module. An `opens` statement is used to open a specific package for deep reflection. Because an open module opens all packages for deep reflection, an `opens` statement is not allowed inside an open module.

Opening Packages

Opening a package means granting normal runtime access to other modules on public types in that package and allowing other modules to use deep reflection on the types in that package. You can open a package to all other modules or to a specific list of modules. The syntax for the `opens` statement to open a package to all other modules is as follows:

```
opens <package>;
```

Here, `<package>` is available for deep reflection to all other modules. You can also open a package to specific modules using a qualified `opens` statement:

```
opens <package> to <module1>, module2>...;
```

Here, `<package>` is open for deep reflection only to `<module1>`, `<module2>`, etc. The following is an example of using the `opens` statement in a module declaration:

```
module jdojo.model {
    // Export the com.jdojo.util package to all modules
    exports com.jdojo.util;

    // Open the com.jdojo.util package to all modules
    opens com.jdojo.util;

    // Open the com.jdojo.model.policy package only to the hibernate.core module
    opens com.jdojo.model.policy to hibernate.core;
}
```

The jdojo.model module exports the com.jdojo.util package, which means all public types and their public members are accessible at compile-time and for normal reflection at runtime. The second statement opens the same package for deep reflection at runtime. In summary, all public types and their public members of the com.jdojo.util package are accessible at compile-time and the package allows deep reflection at runtime. The third statement opens the com.jdojo.model.policy package only to the hibernate.core module for deep reflection, which means that no other modules can access any types of this package at compile-time and the hibernate.core module can access all types and their members using deep reflection at runtime.

▓ **Tip**   A module that performs deep reflection on open packages of another module does not need to read the module containing the open packages. However, adding a dependence on a module with open packages is allowed and strongly encouraged—if you know the module name—so the module system can verify the dependence at compile-time and at runtime.

When a module M opens its package P for deep reflection to another module N, it is possible that the module N grants the deep reflective access that it has on package P to another module Q. The module N will need to do it programmatically using the module API. Delegating reflective access to another module avoids opening the entire module to all other modules and, at the same time, it creates additional work on the part of the module that is granted the reflective access. I show an example of this in Chapter 15 of the second volume of this series. Refer to Chapter 3 of the second volume of this series for examples on using open modules and open packages in a module.

Splitting Packages Across Modules

Splitting packages into multiple modules is not *allowed*. That is, the same package cannot be defined in multiple modules. If types in the same package are in multiple modules, those modules should be combined into one module or you need to rename packages. Sometimes, you can compile these modules successfully and receive a runtime error; other times, you receive a compile-time error. Splitting packages is not disallowed unconditionally as I mentioned in the beginning. You need to know the simple rule behind such errors.

If two modules named M and N define the same package named P, there must not exist a module Q such that the package P in both M and N modules is accessible to Q. In other words, the same package in multiple modules must not be readable to a module at the same time. Otherwise, an error occurs. If a module is using a type T in package P that is found in two modules, the module system cannot make a decision about using P.T from one of the two modules. It generates an error and wants you to fix the problem. Consider the following snippet of code:

```
// Test.java
package java.util;

public class Test {
}
```

The java.base module in the JDK contains a java.util package, which is available to all modules. If you compile the Test class in JDK 9 as part of a module or by itself, you will receive the following error:

```
error: package exists in another module: java.base
package java.util;
^
1 error
```

If you have this class in a module named M, the compile-time error is stating that the java.util package is readable by the module M in this module as well as in the java.base module. You must change the package for this Test class from java.util to something else, say, com.jdojo.util, which does not exist in any observable modules.

Restrictions in Module Declarations

There are several restrictions in declaring modules. If you violate them, you will get errors at compile-time or at startup:

- A module graph cannot contain circular dependences. That is, two modules cannot read each other. If they do, they should be one module, not two. Note that it is possible to have circular dependences at runtime by adding readability edges programmatically or using the command-line options.

- Module declarations do not support module versions. You will need to add module's version as the class file attribute using the jar tool or some other tools such as javac.

- The module system does not have a concept of sub-modules. That is, jdojo.person and jdojo.person.client are two separate modules; the first one is not a sub-module of the second one.

Types of Modules

Java has been around for over 20 years and applications, old as well as new, will keep using libraries that have not been modularized or will never be modularized. If JDK 9 forced everyone to modularize their applications, the JDK 9, probably, will not be adopted by most. The JDK 9 designers kept the backward compatibility in mind. You can adopt JDK 9 by modularizing your application at your own pace or by deciding not to modularize at all—by just running your existing application in JDK 9. In most cases, your application that worked in JDK 8 or earlier will continue to work in JDK 9 without any changes. To ease migration, JDK 9 defines four types of modules:

- Normal modules

- Open modules

- Automatic modules

- Unnamed modules

In fact, you will come across six terms describing six different types of modules, which are, for a beginner to JDK 9, confusing at best. The other two types of modules are used to convey broader categories of these four types of modules. Figure 10-8 shows a pictorial view of all types of modules.

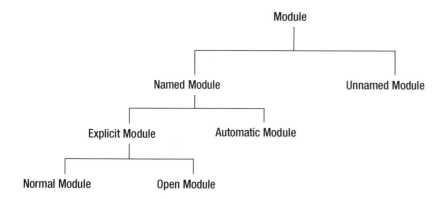

Figure 10-8. *Types of modules*

Before I describe the main types of modules, I give you brief definitions of the module types shown in Figure 10-8.

- A module is a collection of code and data.

- Based on whether a module has a name or not, a module can be a *named module* or an *unnamed module*. There are no further categories of unnamed modules.

- When a module has a name, the name can be given explicitly in a module declaration or the name can be generated automatically (or implicitly). If the name is given explicitly in a module declaration, it is called an *explicit module*. If the name is generated by the module system by reading the JAR file name on the module path, it is called an *automatic module*.

- If you declare a module without using the open modifier, it is called a *normal module*.

- If you declare a module using the open modifier, it is called an *open module*.

Based on these definitions, an open module is also an explicit module and a named module. An automatic module is a named module as it has a name, which is automatically generated, but it is not an explicit module because it is implicitly declared by the module system at compile-time and runtime. The following subsections describe these module types.

▓ **Tip**   If the Java platform was initially designed with the module system, you would have only one module type—a normal module! All other module types exist for backward compatibility and smooth migration and adoption of JDK 9.

Normal Modules

A module that is declared explicitly using a module declaration without using an open modifier is always given a name and it is called a *normal module* or simply a *module*. So far, you have been working mostly with normal modules. I have been referring to normal modules as modules and I continue using this term in this sense unless I need to make a distinction between the four types of modules. By default, all types in a normal module are encapsulated. An example of a normal module is as follows:

```
module a.normal.module {
    // Module statements go here
}
```

Open Modules

If a module declaration contains the open modifier, the module is known as an open module. An example of an open module is as follows:

```
open module an.open.module {
    // Module statements go here
}
```

Automatic Modules

For backward compatibility, the class path mechanism to look up types still works in JDK 9. You have options to place your JARs on the class path, module path, and a combination of both. Note that you can place modular JARs as well as JARs on both the module path and the class path.

When you place a JAR on the module path, the JAR is treated as a module, which is called an *automatic* module. The name *automatic* module is derived from the fact that the module is automatically defined out of a JAR—you do not explicitly declare the module by adding a module-info.class file. An automatic module has a name. What is the name of an automatic module? What modules does it read and what packages does it export? I will answer these questions shortly.

Automatic modules exist solely for the purpose of migrating existing Java application to JDK 9. They let you use the existing JARs as modules by placing them on the module path. However, they are unreliable because when the author of the JARs convert them to modular JARs, he may choose to give them different module names than are automatically derived. Exported packages in automatic modules may also change when the author converts the JARs to modular JARs. Keep these risks in mind when you use automatic modules in your application.

To safeguard against the module name change for automatic modules, the author may suggest a module name before he converts his JAR to a modular JAR. You can use the suggested module name in the MANIFEST. MF file of the JAR to specify it as an automatic module name. You can specify an automatic module name as the value for the attribute "Automatic-Module-Name" in the main section of the MANIFEST.MF file in the JAR.

An automatic module is also a named module. Suppose that you want to use a JAR com.jdojo.intro-1.0 as an automatic module. Its name and version are derived from the name of the JAR file using the following rules:

- If the JAR file has the attribute "Automatic-Module-Name" in its main section in its MANIFEST.MF file, the attribute's value is the module name. The module name is otherwise derived from the name of the JAR file using the following steps.

- The .jar extension of the JAR file is removed. This step removes the .jar extension and the following steps uses com.jdojo.intro-1.0 to derive the name of the module and its version.

- If the name ends with a hyphen followed by at least one digit, which is optionally followed by a dot, the module name is derived from the part of the name that precedes the last hyphen. The part that follows the hyphen is assigned as the version of the module if it can be parsed as a valid version; otherwise, this part is ignored. In our example, the module name will be derived from `com.jdojo.intro`. The version will be derived as 1.0.

- For module name, all trailing digits and dots are removed. In our case, the remaining part for the module name, `com.jdojo.intro`, does not contain any trailing digits and dots. So, this step does not change anything.

- Every non-alphanumeric character in the name part is replaced with a dot and, in the resulting string, two consecutive dots are replaced by one dot, and all leading and trailing dots are removed. In our example, we do not have any non-alphanumeric characters in the name part, so the module name is `com.jdojo.intro`.

Applying these rules in sequence gives you a module name and a module version. In the end of this section, I show you how to know the name of an automatic module by having the JAR file. Table 10-1 lists a few JAR names and derived automatic module names for them. Note that the table does not show the extension `.jar` in the JAR file names and it is assumed that the no "Automatic-Module-Name" attribute has been specified in the main section in the `MANIFEST.MF` file of the JAR.

Table 10-1. *Examples of Deriving Names of Automatic Modules from a JAR File Name*

JAR Name	Module Name	Module Version
`com.jdojo.intro-1.0`	`com.jdojo.intro`	`1.0`
`junit-4.10.jar`	`junit`	`4.10`
`jdojo-logging1.5.0`	N/A	
`spring-core-4.0.1.RELEASE`	`spring.core`	`4.0.1.RELEASE`
`jdojo-trans-api_1.5_spec-1.0.0`	N/A	N/A
_	N/A	N/A

Let's look at three odd cases in the table where you will receive an error if you place the JARs on the module path. The first JAR name is `jdojo-logging1.5.0`. Applying all the rules, the derived module name is `jdojo.logging1.5.0`, which is an invalid module name. Recall that a module name is a qualified Java identifier. That is, every part in a module name must be a valid Java identifier. In this case, the two parts of the name, "5" and "0", are not valid Java identifiers. Using this JAR on module path will generate an error unless you specify a valid module name using the "Automatic-Module-Name" attribute in the manifest file.

The second JAR name that gives error is `jdojo-trans-api_1.5_spec-1.0.0`. Let's apply the rules to derive the automatic module name:

- It finds the last hyphen after which you have only digits and dots and splits the JAR name into two parts: `jdojo-trans-api_1.5_spec` and `1.0.0`. The first part is used to derive the module name. The second part is the module version.

- The name part does not contain any trailing digits and dots. So, the next rule is applied that converts all non-alphanumeric characters to a dot. The resulting string is `jdojo.trans.api.1.5.spec`. Now, "1" and "5" are two parts in the module name, which are not valid Java identifiers. So, the derived module name is invalid and this is the reason you get an error when you add this JAR file on the module path.

The third JAR name, which is the last entry in the table, is an underscore (_). That is, the JAR file is named _.jar. If you apply the rules, the underscore is replaced by a dot and that dot will be removed, leaving the derived name an empty string, which is not a valid module name. The _.jar file on the module path will cause the following exception:

```
java.lang.module.ResolutionException: Unable to derive module descriptor for: _.jar
```

You can use the jar command with the --describe-module option to know the name of the automatic module that will be derived from a JAR. The general syntax is as follows:

```
jar --describe-module --file <your-JAR-file-path>
```

The following command prints the automatic module name for the JAR named jdojo.person-2.2.jar, assuming that the JAR exists in the C:\bj9f directory:

```
c:\bj9f\jars>jar --describe-module --file jdojo.util-2.2.jar
```

```
No module descriptor found. Derived automatic module.

jdojo.util@2.2 automatic
requires java.base mandated
contains com.jdojo.person
```

The first line in the output indicates that the jdojo.person-2.2.jar is a JAR, not a modular JAR. If it were a modular JAR, the module name would be read from the module-info.class file. The first line indicates that no module descriptor was found. The second line prints jdojo.util as the module name and 2.2 as the module version. In the end of the second line, the word automatic is printed to indicate that this module name was derived as an automatic module name. The third and fourth lines in the output prints the dependence and package information of the automatic module.

You can use the jar command to update the manifest entries. I show you how to add the "Automatic-Module-Name" attribute to a JAR. I use the jdojo.person-2.2.jar in this example. You need to create a text file and add the manifest attribute. Listing 10-10 shows the contents of a manifest file named manifest.txt. The file contains two lines. The first line specifies an attribute named "Automatic-Module-Name" and its value is jdojo.misc. The second line is an empty line that you do not see. Make sure to have an empty line in this file. Otherwise, the next command will not work.

Listing 10-10. Contents of a manifest.txt File

```
Automatic-Module-Name: jdojo.misc
```

The following command will update the manifest file in the jdojo.util-2.2.jar file, assuming that both the JAR file and the manifest.txt file are placed in the same directory, C:\bj9f:

```
c:\bj9f\jars>jar --update --manifest manifest.txt --file jdojo.util-2.2.jar
```

If you describe the `jdojo.util-2.2.jar` file to see the derived automatic module name, the module name will be read from the "Automatic-Module-Name" attribute of its manifest file. Let's rerun the previous command to describe the module:

```
c:\bj9f\jars>jar --describe-module --file jdojo.util-2.2.jar
No module descriptor found. Derived automatic module.

jdojo.misc@2.2 automatic
requires java.base mandated
contains com.jdojo.person
```

Once you know the name of an automatic module, other explicit modules can read it using `requires` statements. The following module declaration reads the automatic module named `jdojo.misc` that comes from the `jdojo.util-2.2.jar` on the module path, assuming that the automatic module name is derived from the JAR file name:

```
module jdojo.lib {
    requires jdojo.util;
    //...
}
```

An automatic module, to be used effectively, must export packages and read other modules. Let's look at the rules on this:

- An automatic module reads all other modules. It is important to note that readability from an automatic module to all other modules is added after the module graph is resolved.

- All packages in an automatic module are exported and opened.

The two rules are based on the fact that there is no practical way to tell which other modules an automatic module depends on and which packages of the automatic module other modules will need to compile or for deep reflection.

An automatic module reading all other modules may create cyclic dependency, which is allowed after the module graph has been resolved. Recall that cyclic dependency between modules is not allowed during the module graph resolution. That is, you cannot have cyclic dependency in your module declarations.

Automatic modules do not have a module declaration, so they cannot declare dependence on other modules. Explicit modules may declare dependence on other automatic modules. Consider a case where an explicit module M reads an automatic module P and the module P uses a type T in another automatic module Q. When you launch the application using the main class from module M, the module graph will consist of only M and P—excluding the `java.base` module in this discussion for brevity. The resolution process will start with the module M and will see that it reads another module P. The resolution process has no practical way to tell that the module P reads the module Q. You will be able to compile both modules P and Q by placing them on the class path. However, when you run this application, you will receive a `ClassNotFoundException`. The exception occurs when the module P tries to access a type from the module Q. To solve this problem, the module Q must be included in the module graph by adding it as a root module using the `--add-modules` command-line option and specifying Q as the value for this option.

Unnamed Modules

You can place JARs and modular JARs on the class path. When a type is being loaded and its package is not found in any known modules, the module system attempts to load the type from the class path. If the type is found on the class path, it is loaded by a class loader and becomes a member of a module called *unnamed module* of that class loader. Every class loader defines an unnamed module whose members are all types it loads from the class path. An unnamed module does not have a name, so an explicit module cannot declare a dependency on it using a `requires` statement. If you have an explicit module that needs to use the types in an unnamed module, you must use the JAR for the unnamed module as an automatic module by placing the JAR on the module path.

It is a common mistake to try to access types in an unnamed module from explicit modules at compile-time. This is simply not possible because an unnamed module does not have a name and an explicit module needs a module name to read another module at compile-time. Automatic modules act as bridge between explicit modules and unnamed modules, as shown in Figure 10-9. Explicit modules can access automatic modules using `requires` statements and the automatic modules can access unnamed modules.

Figure 10-9. *An automatic module acting as a bridge between an explicit module and an unnamed module*

An unnamed module does not have a name. This does not mean that an unnamed module's name is the empty string, "unnamed", or null. The following declaration for a module, which attempts to declare dependence on an unnamed module, is invalid:

```
module some.module {
    requires "";        // A compile-time error
    requires "unnamed"; // A compile-time error
    requires unnamed;   // A compile-time error, unless a named module named unnamed exists
    requires null;      // A compile-time error
}
```

An unnamed module reads other modules, and exports and opens all its packages to other modules using the following rules:

- An unnamed module reads every other module. Therefore, an unnamed module can access public types in all exported packages in all modules, including the platform modules. This rule makes it possible for applications using the class path that compiled and ran in Java SE 8 to continue to compile and run in Java SE 9, provided they use only standard, non-deprecated Java SE APIs.

- An unnamed module opens all its packages to all other modules. Therefore, it is possible that an explicit module can access types in unnamed modules using reflection at runtime.

- An unnamed module exports all its packages. An explicit module cannot read an unnamed module at compile-time. After the module graph is resolved, all automatic modules are made to read unnamed modules.

▓ **Tip**   It is possible for an unnamed module to contain a package that is also exported by a named module. In such a case, the package in the unnamed module is ignored.

383

Aggregator Modules

You can create a module that contains no code of its own. It collects and re-exports the contents of other modules. Such a module is called an *aggregator module*. Suppose there are several modules that depend on five modules. You can create an aggregator module for those five modules, and now, your modules can depend only one module—the aggregator module. An aggregator module is not a separate type of module than I have explained in previous sections. It is a named module. It got a special name, "aggregator," because it does not have contents of its own. Rather, it combines the contents of several other modules into one module under a different name.

An aggregator module contains only one class file and that is module-info.class. The module declaration for an aggregator module consists of all requires transitive <module> statements. The following is an example of an aggregator module declaration. The aggregator module is named jdojo.all and it aggregates three modules: jdojo.policy, jdojo.claim, and jdojo.payment.

```
module jdojo.all {
    requires transitive jdojo.policy;
    requires transitive jdojo.claim;
    requires transitive jdojo.payment;
}
```

Aggregator modules exist for convenience. Java 9 contains several aggregator modules such as java.se and java.se.ee. The java.se module gathers parts of the Java SE that do not overlap with Java EE. The java.se.ee module gathers all of the modules that comprise the Java SE, including modules that overlap with the Java EE.

Knowing about Modules at Runtime

Java SE 9 provides a set of classes and interfaces to work with modules programmatically. They are collectively known as the *Module API*. The Module API lets you query module information and modify it. I cover it in detail in Chapter 15 of the second volume of this series. In this section, I give a quick preview of the Module API.

Each type loaded in the JVM is represented by an instance of the java.lang.Class<T> class. That is, an instance of the Class<T> class represents type T at runtime. You can get the reference of a type using the getClass() method of the object of that class. Assuming that a Person class exists, the following snippet of code gets the reference of the Person class:

```
Person p = new Person();
Class<Person> cls = p.getClass();
```

You can also get the reference of a class using a class literal. A class literal is the name of a class with a .class. For example, you can get the reference of the Person class using the class literal, Person.class. You can rewrite the previous snippet of code as follows:

```
Class<Person> cls = Person.class;
```

At runtime, each type is loaded as a member of a module. If the type is loaded from the class path, it is a member of an unnamed module of the class loader that loads the type. If the type is loaded from the module path, it is a member of a named module. An instance of the java.lang.Module class represents a module at runtime. The Class class contains a getModule() method that returns a Module representing the module of the type. The following snippet of code gets the reference of the Module object of which the Person class is a member:

```
Class<Person> cls = Person.class;
Module m = cls.getModule();
```

The Module class contains several methods that let you query the module's declared state that existed at compile-time and actual state at runtime. Note that a module state can be changed from how it was declared in the source code. Other classes and interfaces in the Module API are in the java.lang.module package. For example, an instance of the ModuleDescriptor class, which is in the java.lang.module package, represents the module descriptor as it was declared in the source file for explicit modules and as it was synthesized for automatic modules. You can use the getDescriptor() method of the Module class to an instance of the ModuleDescriptor class. An unnamed module does not have a module descriptor, so the getDescriptor() method returns null for an unnamed module. You can use the getName() method of the Module class to get the name of the module; the method returns null for an unnamed module.

Listing 10-11 contains the declaration for a jdojo.mod module. Listing 10-12Listing 10- contains the code for a ModuleInfo class, which prints the module information of which it is a member.

Listing 10-11. The Module Declaration for the jdojo.mod Module

```
// module-info.java
module jdojo.mod {
    exports com.jdojo.mod;
}
```

Listing 10-12. A ModuleInfo Class

```
// ModuleInfo.java
package com.jdojo.mod;

import java.lang.module.ModuleDescriptor;

public class ModuleInfo {
    public static void main(String[] args) {
        // Get the class reference
        Class<ModuleInfo> cls = ModuleInfo.class;

        // Get the module reference
        Module m = cls.getModule();

        if (m.isNamed()) {
            // It is a named module

            // Get the module name
            String name = m.getName();

            // Get the module descriptor
            ModuleDescriptor md = m.getDescriptor();
```

```
            // Print the module details
            System.out.println("Module Name: " + name);
            System.out.println("Module is open: " + md.isOpen());
            System.out.println("Module is automatic: " + md.isAutomatic());

        } else {
            // It is an unnamed module
            System.out.println("Unnamed module.");
        }
    }
}
```

The following command runs the ModuleInfo class by placing the modular JAR for the jdojo.mod module on the module path. The output clearly shows the correct module information:

```
C:\Java9Fundamentals>java --module-path dist\jdojo.mod.jar --module jdojo.mod/com.jdojo.mod.
ModuleInfo
```

```
Module Name: jdojo.mod
Module is open: false
Module is automatic: false
```

The following command runs the ModuleInfo class by placing the modular JAR for the jdojo.mod module on the class path. This time, the class is loaded from the class path and it becomes a member of the unnamed module of the class loader that loads it.

```
C:\Java9Fundamentals>java --class-path dist\jdojo.mod.jar com.jdojo.mod.ModuleInfo
```

```
Unnamed module.
```

Migration Path to JDK 9

If you are learning Java 9 for the first time, you may skip this section. You can revisit when you have to migrate existing Java applications to use JDK 9.

When you are to migrate your application to JDK 9, you should keep two benefits in mind that are provided by the module system: strong encapsulation and reliable configuration. Your goal is to have an application that consists of solely normal modules with an exception of a few open modules. It may seem that someone can give you a clear list of steps you need to perform to migrate your existing applications to JDK 9. However, that is not possible, given the variety of applications, their interdependence of other code, and different configurations needs. All I can do is lay out a few generic guidelines that may help you through the migration and that is what I am going to do in this section.

Before JDK 9, a non-trivial Java application consisted of several JARs residing in three layers:

- Application JARs in the application layer developed by application developers

- Library JARs in the library layer provided by third parties

- Java runtime JARs in the JVM layer

JDK 9 has already modularized the Java runtime JARs by converting them to modules. That is, the Java runtime consists of modules and only modules.

The library layer consists of mainly third-party JARs placed on the class path. If you want to migrate your application to JDK 9, you may not get a modular version of the third-party JARs. You also do not have control on how the third-party JARs will be converted into modules by their vendors. You can place the library JARs onto the module path and treat them as automatic modules.

You have a choice to fully modularize your application code. The following are the choices you have for the module type selection, starting from the least desirable to the most desirable:

- Unnamed modules

- Automatic modules

- Open modules

- Normal module

The first step in migration is to check if your application runs in JDK 9 by placing all JARs—application JARs and libraries JARs—onto the class path, without any modification to your code. All types from the JARs on the class path will be part of unnamed modules. Your application in this state uses JDK 9 without any strong encapsulation and reliable configuration.

Once your application runs as-is in JDK 9, you can start converting the application code into automatic modules. All packages in an automatic module are open for deep reflective access and exported for ordinary compile-time and runtime access to their public types. In this sense, it is no better than unnamed modules; it does not provide you with strong encapsulation. However, automatic modules provide you reliable configuration because other explicit modules can declare dependence on automatic modules.

You have another choice of converting your application code into open modules that offers a modest degree of stronger encapsulation: In open modules, all packages are open for deep reflective access, but you can specify which packages, if any, are exported for ordinary compile-time and runtime access. Explicit modules can also declare dependence on open modules, thus giving you a benefit of reliable configuration.

A normal module offers the strongest encapsulation, which lets you choose which packages, if any, are open, exported, or both. Explicit modules can also declare dependence on open modules, thus giving you a benefit of reliable configuration.

Table 10-2 contains the list of modules types with the degree of strong encapsulation and reliable configuration they offer.

Table 10-2. *Module Types and Varying Degrees of Strong Encapsulation and Reliable Configuration They Offer*

Module Type	Strong Encapsulation	Reliable Configuration
Unnamed	No	No
Automatic	No	Modest
Open	Modest	Yes
Normal	Strongest	Strongest

Disassembling Module Definitions

In this section, I explain the javap tool that ships with the JDK, which can be used to disassemble class files. This tool is very useful in learning the module system, especially in decompiling the module's descriptors.

I use the code from the bj9f directory in the supplied source code. I assume that you have extracted it in the C:\bj9f directory. If it is different, replace this path with yours in the following examples.

In Chapter 3, you had two copies of the module-info.class file for the jdojo.intro module: one in the mod\jdojo.intro directory and another in the modular JAR in the lib\com.jdojo.intro.jar file. When you packaged the module's code into a JAR, you had specified a version and a main class for the module. Where did these pieces of information go? They were added to the module-info.class file as class attributes. Therefore, the contents of the two module-info.class files are not the same. How do you prove it? Start by printing the module declaration in both module-info.class files. You can use the javap tool, which is located in the JDK_HOME\bin directory, to disassemble code in any class file. You can specify a file name, a URL, or a class name to be disassembled. The following commands print the module declarations:

```
C:\bj9f>javap mod\jdojo.intro\module-info.class
```

```
Compiled from "module-info.java"
module jdojo.intro {
  requires java.base;
}
```

```
C:\bj9f>javap jar:file:lib/com.jdojo.intro.jar!/module-info.class
```

```
Compiled from "module-info.java"
module jdojo.intro {
  requires java.base;
}
```

The first command uses a file name and the second command uses a URL using the jar scheme. Both commands use relative paths. You can use absolute paths if you wish.

The outputs indicate that both module-info.class files contain the same module declaration. You need to print the class information using the –verbose option (or the –v option) to see the class attributes. The following command prints the module-info.class file information from the mod directory and it shows that the module version and main class name do not exist. A partial output is shown.

```
C:\bj9f>javap -verbose mod\jdojo.intro\module-info.class
```

```
Classfile /C:/bj9f/mod/jdojo.intro/module-info.class
  Last modified Jul 23, 2017; size 154 bytes
  MD5 checksum 2e4a3e6b8b8b03c92fdede9a5784b1d7
  Compiled from "module-info.java"
module jdojo.intro
...
```

The following command prints the module-info.class file information from the lib\com.jdojo.intro.jar file and it shows that the module version and main class name do exist. A partial output is shown. The relevant lines in the output have been shown in a boldface font.

```
C:\bj9f>javap -verbose jar:file:lib/com.jdojo.intro.jar!/module-info.class
```

```
Classfile jar:file:lib/com.jdojo.intro.jar!/module-info.class
  Last modified Jul 24, 2017; size 263 bytes
  MD5 checksum 60f5f169a580f02fa8085fd36e50c0e5
  Compiled from "module-info.java"
module jdojo.intro@1.0
...
   #8 = Utf8                ModuleMainClass
   #9 = Utf8                com/jdojo/intro/Welcome
  #10 = Class               #9                // com/jdojo/intro/Welcome
...
  #14 = Utf8                1.0
  ...
ModulePackages:
  #7                                          // com.jdojo.intro
ModuleMainClass: #10                          // com.jdojo.intro.Welcome
Module:
  #13,0                                       // "jdojo.intro"
  #14                                         // 1.0
  ...
```

You can also disassemble the code for a class in a module. You need to specify the module path, the module name, and the fully qualified name of the class. The following command prints the code for the com.jdojo.intro.Welcome class from its modular JAR:

```
C:\bj9f>javap --module-path lib --module jdojo.intro com.jdojo.intro.Welcome
```

```
Compiled from "Welcome.java"
public class com.jdojo.intro.Welcome {
  public com.jdojo.intro.Welcome();
  public static void main(java.lang.String[]);
}
```

You can also print the class information for system classes. The following command prints the class information for the java.lang.Object class from the java.base module. Note that you do not need to specify the module path when you print system class information.

```
C:\bj9f>javap --module java.base java.lang.Object
```

```
Compiled from "Object.java"
public class java.lang.Object {
  public java.lang.Object();
  public final native java.lang.Class<?> getClass();
  public native int hashCode();
  public boolean equals(java.lang.Object);
  ...
}
```

How would you print the module declaration for a system module such as java.base or java.sql? Recall that system modules are packaged in a special file format called JIMAGE, not as modular JARs. JDK 9 introduced a new URL scheme called jrt (jrt is short for Java runtime) to refer to the contents of the Java runtime image (or system modules). The syntax for using the jrt scheme is:

```
jrt:/<module>/<path-to-a-file>
```

The following command prints the module declaration for the system module named java.sql:

```
C:\bj9f>javap jrt:/java.sql/module-info.class
```

```
Compiled from "module-info.java"
module java.sql@9 {
  requires transitive java.logging;
  requires transitive java.xml;
  requires java.base;
  exports javax.transaction.xa;
  exports javax.sql;
  exports java.sql;
  uses java.sql.Driver;
}
```

The following command prints the module declaration for the java.se, which is an aggregator module:

```
C:\bj9f>javap jrt:/java.se/module-info.class
```

```
Compiled from "module-info.java"
module java.se@9 {
  requires transitive java.naming;
  requires transitive java.instrument;
  requires transitive java.compiler;
  requires transitive java.sql.rowset;
  requires transitive java.logging;
  requires transitive java.management.rmi;
  requires transitive java.desktop;
  requires transitive java.rmi;
  requires transitive java.datatransfer;
  requires transitive java.prefs;
  requires transitive java.xml.crypto;
  requires transitive java.sql;
  requires transitive java.xml;
  requires transitive java.security.sasl;
  requires transitive java.scripting;
  requires transitive java.management;
  requires java.base;
  requires transitive java.security.jgss;
}
```

You can also use the jrt scheme to refer to a system class. The following command prints the class information for the java.lang.Object class in the java.base module:

```
C:\Java9Revealed>javap jrt:/java.base/java/lang/Object.class
```

```
Compiled from "Object.java"
public class java.lang.Object {
  public java.lang.Object();
  public final native java.lang.Class<?> getClass();
  public native int hashCode();
  public boolean equals(java.lang.Object);
  ...
}
```

Summary

In simple terms, a module is a group of packages. A module may optionally contain resources such as images, property files, etc. If a module needs to use public types contained in another module, the second module needs to export the package containing the types and the first module needs to read the second module.

A module exports its packages using the exports statement. A module can export its packages only to a set of named modules or to all other modules. Public types in exports packages are available to other modules at compile-time and runtime. An exported package does not allow deep reflection on non-public members of public types.

If a module wants to allow other modules to access all types of members—public and non-public—using reflection, the module must either be declared as an open module or the module can open packages selectively using the opens statement. A module accessing types from open packages does not need to read the module containing those open packages.

A module declares a dependence on another module using the requires statement. Such a dependence can be declared transitive using the transitive modifier. If module M declares a transitive dependence on module N, any module declaring a dependence on module M declares an implicit dependence on module N.

A dependence can be declared mandatory at compile-time, but optional at runtime using the static modifier in the requires statement. A dependency can be optional at runtime and transitive at the same time.

Based on how a module is declared and whether it has a name, there are several types of modules. Based on whether a module has a name or not, a module can be a *named module* or an *unnamed module*. When a module has a name, the name can be given explicitly in a module declaration or the name can be generated automatically (or implicitly). If the name is given explicitly in a module declaration, it is called an *explicit module*. If the name is specified in the "Automatic-Module-Name" attribute in the JAR's manifest or is generated by the module system by reading the JAR file name on the module path, it is called an *automatic module*. If you declare a module without using the open modifier, it is called a *normal module*. If you declare a module using the open modifier, it is called an *open module*. Based on these definitions, an open module is also an explicit module and a named module. An automatic module is a named module as it has a name, which is automatically generated, but it is not an explicit module because it is implicitly declared by the module system at compile-time and runtime.

When you place a JAR (not a modular JAR) on the module path, the JAR represents an automatic module whose name is specified in the "Automatic-Module-Name" attribute of the JAR's manifest or is derived from the JAR file name. An automatic module reads all other modules and all its packages are exported and opened.

In JDK 9, a class loader can load a class from a module or from the class path. Every class loader maintains a module called unnamed module that contains all types that it loads from the class path. An unnamed module reads every other module. It exports and opens all its packages to all other modules. An unnamed module does not have a name, so an explicit module cannot declare a compile-time dependence on an unnamed module. If an explicit module needs to access types in an unnamed module, the former can use an automatic module as a bridge or use reflection.

You can create a module that contains no code of its own. It collects and re-exports the contents of other modules. Such a module is called an *aggregator module*. An aggregator module contains only one class file and that is `module-info.class`. The module declaration for an aggregator module consists of all `requires transitive <module>` statements.

Splitting packages into multiple modules is not *allowed*. That is, the same package cannot be defined in multiple modules. If two modules named M and N define the same package named P, there must not exist a module Q such that the package P in both M and N modules is accessible to Q. In other words, the same package in multiple modules must not be readable to a module at the same time. Otherwise, an error occurs.

Java 9 provides a set of classes and interfaces to work with modules at runtime. They are collectively known as the Module API. The Module API lets you query module information and modify it at runtime. A module is represented as an instance of the `java.lang.Module` class at runtime. You can get the reference of the module of a type using the `getModule()` method of the `java.lang.Class<T>` class.

You can use the `javap` tool print the module declaration or attributes. Use the `-verbose` (or `-v`) option of the tool to print the class attributes of the module descriptor. JDK 9 stores the runtime image in a special format. JDK 9 introduced a new file scheme called `jrt` that you can use to access the contents of the runtime image. Its syntax is `jrt:/<module>/<path-to-a-file>`.

EXERCISES

1. What is a module?

2. What keyword do you use to declare a module?

3. What are the rules to specify a module name? Which of the following module names are valid?

    ```
    jdojo.dashboard
    $jdojo.$dashboard
    jdojo.policy.1.0
    java9Fundamentals
    ```

4. List all restricted keywords that are treated as keywords only when used in specific positions in a module declaration.

5. What module statement do you use to export a package to all other modules or to a set of named modules?

6. Consider the following declaration for a module named jdojo.core:

```
module jdojo.core {
    exports com.jdojo.core to jdojo.ext, jdojo.util;
}
```

Explain the effect of the exports statement in this module declaration. Do these two modules, jdojo.ext and jdojo.util, have to exist when the jdojo.core module is compiled?

7. What module statement do you use to express dependence of a module to another module? What is a transitive dependence and what are the benefits of using a transitive dependence?

8. Consider the following declaration for a module named jdojo.ext:

```
module jdojo.ext {
    requires jdojo.core;
}
```

What are the two modules the jdojo.ext reads?

9. How do you express dependence of a module on another module that is mandatory at compile-time, but optional at runtime?

10. What is an open module? When do you use an open module?

11. What is the difference between an open module and opening the packages of a module selectively? Why can't you use the opens statement inside an open module?

12. Consider the following declaration for a module named jdojo.misc:

```
module jdojo.misc {
    opens com.jdojo.misc;
    exports com.jdojo.misc;
}
```

Is this module declaration valid? If it is valid, explain the effects of opening and exporting the same package of the module.

13. Can you have two modules that contain the same package? Describe the exact rule that prohibits two modules having the same package.

14. What is an automatic module? Describe two ways that the name of an automatic module can be specified or derived.

15. What is an unnamed module? If you place a modular JAR on the class path, will all types from the modular JAR be members of an unnamed module?

16. What is an aggregator module? Name an aggregator module in the JDK 9.

17. What is the fully qualified class name of the class that represents a module at runtime?

18. How do you get the reference of the module that a class belongs to at runtime?

19. Consider the following snippet of code assuming that a Person class exists:

```
Person john = new Person();
String moduleName = john./* Complete the code */;
System.out.println("Module name of Person class is " + moduleName);
```

Complete this snippet of code by replacing the comment in the second line with your code. This snippet of code is supposed to print the name of the module the Person class is a member of or null if it is a member of an unnamed module.

20. What option do you use with the jar and java tools to describe a module?

21. If you are given a module-info.class file that contains the compiled code for a module declaration, how will you get the source code of the module? In other words, what tool do you use to disassemble a class file, which can also be a module-info.class file?

22. JDK modules are stored in an internal format called JIMAGE. What is the name of the new scheme that JDK 9 introduced to access the class files and resources of a JDK module?

23. Use the javap command to print the declaration of the java.sql module, which is a JDK module.

CHAPTER 11

Object and Objects Classes

In this chapter, you will learn:

- About the hierarchical class structure in Java

- About the Object class being the superclass of all other classes

- How to use methods of the Object class with detailed examples

- How to reimplement methods of the Object class in your class

- How to check two objects for equality

- The difference between immutable and mutable objects

- How to use the utility methods of the Objects class to deal with null values gracefully

All classes in this chapter are a member of a jdojo.object module, as declared in Listing 11-1.

Listing 11-1. The Declaration of a jdojo.object Module

```
// module-info.java
module jdojo.object {
    exports com.jdojo.object;
}
```

The Object Class

Java has an Object class in the java.lang package, which is a member of the java.base module. All Java classes, those that are included in the Java class libraries and those that you create, extend the Object class directly or indirectly. All Java classes are a subclass of the Object class and the Object class is the superclass of all classes. Note that the Object class itself does not have a superclass.

Classes in Java are arranged in a tree-like hierarchical structure, where the Object class is at the root (or top). I discuss class hierarchy in detail in Chapter 20, which covers inheritance. I discuss some details of the Object class in this chapter.

There are two important rules about the Object class. I do not explain the reasons behind these rules here. The reasons why you could do these things with the Object class will be clear after you read Chapter 20.

Rule #1

A reference variable of the Object class can hold a reference of an object of any class. As any reference variable can store a null reference, so can a reference variable of the Object type. Consider the following declaration of a reference variable obj of the Object type:

```
Object obj;
```

You can assign a reference of any object in Java to obj. All of the following statements are valid:

```
// Can assign the null reference
obj = null;

// Can assign a reference of an object of the Object class
obj = new Object();

// Can assign a reference of an object of the Account class
Account act = new Account();
obj = act;

// Can assign a reference of object of any class. Assume that the AnyClass class exists
obj = new AnyClass();
```

The opposite of this rule is not true. You cannot assign a reference of an object of the Object class to a reference variable of any other type. The following statement is not valid:

```
Account act = new Object(); // A compile-time error
```

Sometimes, you may store the reference of an object of a specific type, say an Account type, in a reference variable of the Object type, and later you would like to assign the same reference back to a reference variable of the Account type. You can do so by using a cast as shown:

```
Object obj2 = new Account(); Account act = (Account)obj2; // Must use a cast
```

Sometimes you may not be sure that a reference variable of the Object class holds a reference to an object of a specific type. In those situations, you need to use the instanceof operator to test. The left operand of the instanceof operator is a reference variable and its right operand is a class name—to be specific, a type name, which includes class and interface. If its left operand is a reference of its right operand type, it returns true. Otherwise, it returns false. Refer to Chapter 20 for a more detailed discussion of the instanceof operator.

```
Object obj;
Cat c;

/* Do something here and store a reference in obj... */

if (obj instanceof Cat) {
    // If we get here, obj holds a reference of a Cat for sure
    c = (Cat)obj;
}
```

You need to use this rule when you have a method that takes an Object as a parameter. You can pass a reference of any object for the parameter of the Object class. Consider the following snippet of code that shows a method declaration:

```
public void m1(Object obj) {
  // Code goes here
}
```

You can call m1() in a number of different ways:

```
m1(null);            // Pass null reference
m1(new Object());    // Pass a reference of an object of the Object class
m1(new AnyClass()); // Pass a reference of an object of the AnyClass class
```

Rule #2

The Object class contains nine methods, which are available to be used in all classes in Java. We can put the methods into two categories.

- Methods in the first category have been implemented in the Object class. You are supposed to use them as they have been implemented. You cannot reimplement (the technical term for reimplement is *override*) these methods in any class you create. Their implementation is final. Methods that fall into this category are getClass(), notify(), notifyAll(), and wait().

- Methods in the second category have a default implementation in the Object class. You can customize their implementation by reimplementing them in your classes. Methods that fall into this category are toString(), equals(), hashCode(), clone(), and finalize().

A Java programmer must understand the proper use of all of the methods in the Object class. I discuss them in detail, except for the notify(), notifyAll(), and wait() methods. These methods are used in thread synchronization. They are discussed in Chapter 6 of the second volume of this series. Table 11-1 lists all methods in the Object class with a brief description. The "Yes" in the "Implemented" column indicates that the Object class has implementation for the method, which can be used without writing any code. The "No" in this column means that you need to implement the method before using it. The "Yes" in the "Customizable" column indicates that you can reimplement the method in your class to customize it. The "No" in this column indicates that the Object class has implemented the method and its implementation is final.

Table 11-1. *Methods in the Object Class*

Method	Implemented	Customizable	Description
public String toString()	Yes	Yes	Returns a string representation of an object. Typically, it is used for debugging purposes.
public boolean equals(Object obj)	Yes	Yes	Used to compare two objects for equality.
public int hashCode()	Yes	Yes	Returns a hash code (an integer) value of an object.
protected Object clone() throws CloneNotSupportedException	No	Yes	Used to make a copy of an object.
protected void finalize() throws Throwable	No	Yes	Called by the garbage collector before an object is destroyed. It has been deprecated in Java SE 9.
public final Class getClass()	Yes	No	Returns a reference to the Class object of the object.
public final void notify()	Yes	No	Notifies one thread in the wait queue of the object.
public final void notifyAll()	Yes	No	Notifies all threads in the wait queue of the object.
public final void wait() throws InterruptedException public final void wait(long timeout) throws InterruptedException public final void wait(long timeout, int nanos) throws InterruptedException	Yes	No	Makes a thread wait in the wait queue of the object with or without a timeout.

To reimplement a method of the Object class, you need to declare the method the same way as it has been declared in the Object class, and then write your own code in its body. There are more rules to reimplement a method. I cover all rules in Chapter 20. You can reimplement the toString() method of the Object class in your class, say Test, as shown:

```
public class Test {
    /* Reimplement the toString() method of the Object class */
    public String toString() {
        return "Here is a string";
    }
}
```

I discuss six methods of the Object class in detail in the sections to follow.

What Is the Class of an Object?

Every object in Java belongs to a class. You define a class in source code, which is compiled into a binary format (a class file with the .class extension). Before a class is used at runtime, its binary representation is loaded into JVM. Loading the binary representation of a class into the JVM is handled by an object called a class loader. Typically, multiple class loaders are used in a Java application to load different types of classes. A class loader is an instance of the class java.lang.ClassLoader. Java lets you create your own class loaders by extending the ClassLoader class. Typically, you do not need to create your own class loaders. The Java runtime will use its built-in class loaders to load your classes.

A class loader reads the binary format of the class definition into the JVM. The binary class format may be loaded from any accessible location, for example, a local file system, a network, a database, etc. Then, it creates an object of the java.lang.Class<T> class, which represents the binary representation of type T in JVM. Note the uppercase C in the class name java.lang.Class. The binary format of a class definition may be loaded multiple times in the JVM by different class loaders. A class inside a JVM is identified by the combination of its fully qualified name and its class loader. Typically, the binary definition of a class is loaded only once in a JVM.

▓ **Tip**   You can think of an object of the Class<T> class as a runtime descriptor of the source code of a class. Your source code for a class is represented by an object of the Class class at runtime. In fact, all types in Java—classes, interfaces, and primitive types—are represented by an instance of the Class class at runtime.

The getClass() method of the Object class returns the reference of the Class object. Since the getClass() method is declared and implemented in the Object class, you can use this method on a reference variable of any type. The following snippet of code shows how to get the reference of the Class object for a Cat object:

```
Cat c = new Cat();
Class catClass = c.getClass();
```

The Class class is generic and its formal type parameter is the name of the class that is represented by its object. You can rewrite this statement using generics, like so:

```
Class<Cat> catClass = c.getClass();
```

By default, the class definition is loaded only once, and there is only one Class object per Java class. We are not considering those cases where you have written code to load the same class more than once. If you use the getClass() method on different objects of the same class, you will get the reference of the same Class object. Consider the following snippet of code:

```
Cat c2 = new Cat();
Cat c3 = new Cat();

Class catClass2 = c2.getClass();
Class catClass3 = c3.getClass();
```

Here, c2 and c3 are two objects of the same Cat class. Therefore, c2.getClass() and c3.getClass() return the reference of the same Class object, which represents the Cat class in the JVM. The expression catClass2 == catClass3 will evaluate to true.

The Class class has many useful methods. I discuss most of its methods in Chapter 3 of the second volume of this series. You can use its getName() method to get the fully qualified name of the class. You can use its getSimpleName() to get the simple name of the class. For example,

```
String fullName = catClass.getName();
String simpleName = catClass.getSimpleName();
```

░ **Tip** Not all classes in an application are loaded into JVM when the application starts. A class is loaded and a corresponding Class object is created when the application uses the class for the first time.

Computing the Hash Code of an Object

A hash code is an integer value that is computed for a piece of information using an algorithm. A hash code is also known as a hash sum, a hash value, or simply a hash. The algorithm to compute an integer from a piece of information is called a hash function. The definition of a hash code involves three things:

- A piece of information
- An algorithm
- An integer value

You have a piece of information. You apply an algorithm to it to produce an integer value. The integer value that you get is the hash code for the piece of information you have. If you change the piece of information or the algorithm, the computed hash code may or may not change. Figure 11-1 depicts the process of computing a hash code.

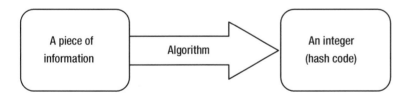

Figure 11-1. *Process of computing a hash code*

Computing a hash code is a one-way process. Getting the original piece of information from a hash code is not an easy task and it is not the goal of the hash code computation either.

The piece of information that could be used to generate a hash code could be an arbitrary sequence of bytes, characters, numbers, or a combination of them. For example, you may want to compute the hash code for a string "Hello".

What does a hash function look like? A hash function may be as simple as the following function, which returns the integer zero for all input data:

```
int myHashFunction(<your input data>) {
    return 0;   // Always return zero
}
```

This hash function fits the definition of a hash function, although it is not a practically good one. Writing a good hash function is not an easy task. You need to consider a number of things about the input data before you can write a good hash function.

Why would you need a hash code? It is needed for efficient retrieval of data associated with it when the data is stored in a hash based collection (or container). Before data is stored in a container, its hash code is computed, and then it is stored at a location (also called a *bucket*), which is based on its hash code. When you want to retrieve the data, its hash code is used to find its location in the container, making the retrieval of the information faster. It is worth noting that an efficient retrieval of data using a hash code is based on the distribution of the hash code values over a range. If the hash codes that are generated are not uniformly distributed, the retrieval of data may not be efficient. In the worst case, the retrieval of data may be as bad as a linear search through all elements stored in the container. If you use a hash function, all elements in the container will be stored in the same bucket, which will require searching through all elements. Using a good hash function so that it gives you uniformly distributed hash codes is critical in implementing an efficient hash based container for fast data retrieval.

What is the use of hash codes in Java? Java uses hash codes for the same reason described—to efficiently retrieve data from hash based collections. If the objects of your class are not used as keys in a hash based collection, for example, in a HashSet, HashMap, etc., you need not worry about hash codes for your objects.

You can compute a hash code for an object in Java. In the case of an object, the pieces of information that will be used to compute the hash code are the pieces of information that make up the state of the object. Java designers considered the hash code for an object so important that they provided a default implementation to compute the hash code for an object in the Object class.

The Object class contains a hashCode() method that returns an int, which is the hash code of the object. The default implementation of this method computes the hash code of an object by converting the memory address of the object into an integer. Since the hashCode() method is defined in the Object class, it is available in all classes in Java. However, you are free to override the implementation in your class. Here are the rules that you must follow when you override the hashCode() method in your class. Suppose there are two object references, x and y.

- If x.equals(y) returns true, x.hashCode() must return an integer, which is equal to y.hashCode(). That is, if two objects are equal using the equals() method, they must have the same hash codes.

- If x.hashCode() is equal to y.hashCode(), it is not necessary that x.equals(y) returns true. That is, if two objects have the same hash codes using the hashCode() method, they do not have to be equal using the equals() method.

- If the hashCode() method is called on the same object multiple times in the same execution of a Java application, the method must return the same integer value. The hashCode() and equals() methods are closely tied. If your class overrides any of these two methods, it must override both for the objects of your class to work correctly in hash-based collections. Another rule is that you should use only those instance variables to compute the hash code for an object, which are also used in the equals() method to check for equality.

If your class is mutable, you should not be using objects of your class as keys in hash-based collections. If the object has been used as a key changes after their use, you will not be able to locate the object in the collection because locating an object in a hash based collection is based on its hash code. In such cases, you will have stranded objects in the collection.

How should you implement a hashCode() method for a class? Here are some guidelines to write the logic for the hashCode() method for your class, which is reasonable for most purposes:

1. Start with a prime number, say 37.

    ```
    int hash = 37;
    ```

2. Compute the hash code value for each instance variable of primitive data types separately using the following logic. Note that you need to use only those instance variables in the hash code computation, which are also part of the equals() method logic. Let's store the result of this step in an int variable code. Let's assume that value is the name of the instance variable.

    For byte, short, int, and char data types, use their integer value as

    ```
    code = (int)value;
    ```

    For long data type, use the XOR for two halves of 64-bit as

    ```
    code = (int)(value ^ (value >>> 32));
    ```

    For float data type, convert its floating-point values to an equivalent integer value using

    ```
    code = Float.floatToIntBits(value);
    ```

    For double data type, convert its floating-point value to long using the doubleToLongBits() method of the Double class and then convert the long value to an int value using the procedure described previously for the long data type.

    ```
    long longBits = Double.doubleToLongBits(value);
    code = (int)(longBits ^ (longBits >>> 32));
    ```

    For the boolean data type, use 1 for true and 0 for false.

    ```
    code = (value ? 1 : 0);
    ```

3. For a reference instance variable, use 0 if it is null. Otherwise, call its hashCode() method to get its hash code. Suppose ref is the name of the reference variable.

    ```
    code = (ref == null ? 0: ref.hashCode());
    ```

4. Compute the hash code using the following formula. Using 59 in the formula is an arbitrary decision. Any other prime number, say 47, will work fine.

    ```
    hash = hash * 59 + code;
    ```

5. Repeat the previous three steps for all instance variables you want to include in your hashCode() computation.

6. Finally, return the value contained in the hash variable from your hashCode() method.

This method is one of the many ways, not the only way, to compute the hash code of an object in Java. Consult a good textbook on computing hash codes if you need a stronger hash function. All primitive wrapper classes and the String class override the hashCode() method to provide reasonably good implementations of hash functions.

▦ **Tip** Java 7 added a utility class java.lang.Objects. It contains a hash() method that computes the hash code for any number of values of any type. From Java 7, you are advised to use the Objects.hash() method to compute the hash code of an object. Refer to "The Objects Class" section later in this chapter for more details.

Listing 11-2 contains the code for a Book class. It shows one of the possible implementations of the hashCode() method. Notice the use of the @Override annotation in the declaration of the hashCode() method. It is an annotation that you should use when you reimplement a method of the superclass in your class. I use this annotation on all reimplemented methods in all classes. Annotations are covered in Chapter 1 of the second volume of this series.

Listing 11-2. A Book Class That Reimplements the hashCode() Method

```java
// Book.java
package com.jdojo.object;

public class Book {
    private String title;
    private String author;
    private int pageCount;
    private boolean hardCover;
    private double price;

    /* Other code goes here */

    /* Must implement the equals() method too. */

    @Override
    public int hashCode() {
        int hash = 37;
        int code = 0;

        // Use title
        code = (title == null ? 0 : title.hashCode());
        hash = hash * 59 + code;

        // Use author
        code = (author == null ? 0 : author.hashCode());
        hash = hash * 59 + code;

        // Use pageCount
        code = pageCount;
        hash = hash * 59 + code;
```

```
        // Use hardCover
        code = (hardCover ? 1 : 0);
        hash = hash * 59 + code;

        // Use price
        long priceBits = Double.doubleToLongBits(price);
        code = (int) (priceBits ^ (priceBits >>> 32));
        hash = hash * 59 + code;

        return hash;
    }
}
```

The Book class has five instance variables: title, author, pageCount, hardcover, and price. The implementation uses all five instance variables to compute the hash code for a Book object. You must also implement the equals() method for the Book class, which must use all the five instance variables to check if two Book objects are equal. You need to make sure that the equals() method and the hashCode() method use the same set of instance variables in their logic. Suppose you add one more instance variable to the Book class. Let's call it ISBN. Because ISBN identifies a book uniquely, you might use only the ISBN instance variable to compute its hash code and to compare for equality with another Book object. In this case, it will be sufficient to use only one instance variable to compute the hash code and check for equality.

There are some misconceptions about the hash code of an object in Java. Developers think that the hash code uniquely identifies an object and it must be a positive integer. However, they are not true. The hash code does not identify an object uniquely. Two distinct objects may have the same hash codes. A hash code does not have to be only a positive number. It could be any integer value, positive or negative. There is also confusion about the usage of hash codes. They are used solely for the purpose of efficient retrieval of data from a hash based collection. If your objects are not used as keys in hash based collections and you do not override the equals() method in your class, you do not need to worry about reimplementing the hashCode() method in your class at all. Most likely, it will be overriding the equals() method that will prompt you to override the hashCode() method for your class. If you do not override and provide correct implementation of the hashCode() and equals() methods in your class at the same time, the objects of your class would not behave properly in hash based collections. The Java compiler or the Java runtime will never give you any warnings or errors about the incorrect implementations of these two methods in your class.

Comparing Objects for Equality

Every object in the universe is different from all other objects, and every object in a Java program is different from all other objects. All objects have a unique identity. The memory address at which an object is allocated can be treated as its identity, which will make it always unique. Two objects are the same if they have the same identity (or reference in Java terminology). Consider the following snippet of code:

```
Object obj1;
Object obj2;

/* Do something... */
if (obj1 == obj2) {
    /* obj1 and obj2 are the same object based on identity */
} else {
    /* obj1 and obj2 are different objects based on identity */
}
```

This code uses identity comparison to test for equality of obj1 and obj2. It compares the references of two objects to test whether they are equal.

Sometimes you want to treat two objects as equal if they have the same state based on some or all of their instance variables. If you want to compare two objects of your class for equality based on criteria other than their references (identities), your class needs to reimplement the equals() method of the Object class. The default implementation of the equals() method in the Object class compares the references of the object being passed as the parameter and the object on which the method is called. If the two references are equal, it returns true. Otherwise, it returns false. In other words, the equals() method in the Object class performs identity based comparison for equality. The implementation of the method is as follows. Recall that the keyword this inside an instance method of a class refers to the reference of the object on which the method is called.

```
public boolean equals(Object obj) {
    return (this == obj);
}
```

Consider the following snippet of code. It compares some Point objects using the equality operator (==), which always compares the references of its two operands. It also uses the equals() method of the Object class to compare the same two references. The output shows that the result is the same. Note that your Point class does not contain an equals() method. When you call the equals() method on a Point object, the equals() method's implementation of the Object class is used.

```
Point pt1 = new Point(10, 10);
Point pt2 = new Point(10, 10);
Point pt3 = new Point(12, 19);
Point pt4 = pt1;

System.out.println("pt1 == pt1: " + (pt1 == pt1));
System.out.println("pt1.equals(pt1): " + pt1.equals(pt1));

System.out.println("pt1 == pt2: " + (pt1 == pt2));
System.out.println("pt1.equals(pt2): " + pt1.equals(pt2));

System.out.println("pt1 == pt3: " + (pt1 == pt3));
System.out.println("pt1.equals(pt3): " + pt1.equals(pt3));

System.out.println("pt1 == pt4: " + (pt1 == pt4));
System.out.println("pt1.equals(pt4): " + pt1.equals(pt4));
```

```
pt1 == pt1: true
pt1.equals(pt1): true
pt1 == pt2: false
pt1.equals(pt2): false
pt1 == pt3: false
pt1.equals(pt3): false
pt1 == pt4: true
pt1.equals(pt4): true
```

In practice, two points are considered the same if they have the same (x, y) coordinates. If you want to implement this rule of equality for your Point class, you must reimplement the equals() method, as shown in Listing 11-3.

Listing 11-3. A SmartPoint Class That Reimplements equals() and hashCode() Methods

```java
// SmartPoint.java
package com.jdojo.object;

public class SmartPoint {
    private int x;
    private int y;

    public SmartPoint(int x, int y) {
        this.x = x;
        this.y = y;
    }

    /* Reimplement the equals() method */
    @Override
    public boolean equals(Object otherObject) {
        // Are the same?
        if (this == otherObject) {
            return true;
        }

        // Is otherObject a null reference?
        if (otherObject == null) {
            return false;
        }

        // Do they belong to the same class?
        if (this.getClass() != otherObject.getClass()) {
            return false;
        }

        // Get the reference of otherObject in a SmartPoint variable
        SmartPoint otherPoint = (SmartPoint)otherObject;

        // Do they have the same x and y co-ordinates
        boolean isSamePoint = (this.x == otherPoint.x && this.y == otherPoint.y);

        return isSamePoint;
    }

    /* Reimplement hashCode() method of the Object class,
       which is a requirement when you reimplement equals() method
    */
    @Override
    public int hashCode() {
        return (this.x + this.y);
    }
}
```

406

You call your new class SmartPoint. Java advises to reimplement hashCode() and equals() methods together if any one of them is reimplemented in your class. The Java compiler would not complain if you reimplement the equals() method and not the hashCode() method. However, you will get unpredictable results when you use the objects of your class in hash based collections.

The only requirement for a hashCode() method is that if the m.equals(n) method returns true, m.hashCode() must return the same value as n.hashCode(). Because your equals() method uses (x, y) coordinates to test for equality, you return the sum of the x and y coordinates from the hashCode() method, which fulfills the technical requirement. Practically, you need to use a better hashing algorithm to compute the hash value.

You have written a few lines of code in the equals() method of the SmartPoint class. Let's go through the logic one by one. First, you need to check if the object passed is the same as the object on which the method is called. If the two objects are the same, you consider them equal by retuning true. This is accomplished by the following code:

```
// Are they the same?
if (this == otherObject) {
    return true;
}
```

If the parameter being passed is null, the two objects cannot be the same. Note that the object on which the method is called can never be null because you cannot call a method on a null reference. Java runtime will throw a runtime exception when an attempt is made to call a method on a null reference. The following code makes sure that you are comparing two non-null objects:

```
// Is otherObject a null reference?
if (otherObject == null) {
    return false;
}
```

The parameter type of the method is Object. This means that any type of object reference can be passed. For example, you can use apple.equals(orange), where apple and orange are references to an Apple object and an Orange object, respectively. In your case, you want to compare only a SmartPoint object to another SmartPoint object. To make sure that the objects being compared are of the same class, you need the following code. If someone calls the method with a parameter that is not a SmartPoint object, it returns false.

```
// Do they have the same class?
if (this.getClass() != otherObject.getClass()) {
    return false;
}
```

At this point, you are sure that someone is trying to compare two non-null SmartPoint objects that have different identities (references). Now you would like to compare the (x, y) coordinates of two objects. To access the x and y instance variables of the otherObject formal parameter, you must cast it to a SmartPoint object. The following statement does it:

```
// Get the reference of otherObject in a SmartPoint variable
SmartPoint otherPoint = (SmartPoint)otherObject;
```

At this point, it is just the matter of comparing the values of x and y instance variables of the two SmartPoint objects. If they are the same, you consider two objects equal by returning true. Otherwise, two objects are not equal and you return false. This is accomplished by the following code:

```
// Do they have the same x and y co-ordinates
boolean isSamePoint = (this.x == otherPoint.x && this.y == otherPoint.y);
return isSamePoint;
```

It is time to test your reimplementation of the equals() method in the SmartPoint class. Listing 11-4 is your test class. You can observe in the output that you have two ways of comparing two SmartPoint objects for equality. The equality operator (==) compares them based on identity and the equals() method compares them based on values of the (x, y) coordinates. Note that if (x, y) coordinates are the same for two SmartPoint objects, the equals() method returns true.

Listing 11-4. A Test Class to Demonstrate the Difference Between Identity and State Comparisons

```
// SmartPointTest.java
package com.jdojo.object;

public class SmartPointTest {
    public static void main(String[] args)  {
        SmartPoint pt1 = new SmartPoint(10, 10);
        SmartPoint pt2 = new SmartPoint(10, 10);
        SmartPoint pt3 = new SmartPoint(12, 19);
        SmartPoint pt4 = pt1;

        System.out.println("pt1 == pt1: " + (pt1 == pt1));
        System.out.println("pt1.equals(pt1): " + pt1.equals(pt1));

        System.out.println("pt1 == pt2: " + (pt1 == pt2));
        System.out.println("pt1.equals(pt2): " + pt1.equals(pt2));

        System.out.println("pt1 == pt3: " + (pt1 == pt3));
        System.out.println("pt1.equals(pt3): " + pt1.equals(pt3));

        System.out.println("pt1 == pt4: " + (pt1 == pt4));
        System.out.println("pt1.equals(pt4): " + pt1.equals(pt4));
    }
}
```

```
pt1 == pt1: true
pt1.equals(pt1): true
pt1 == pt2: false
pt1.equals(pt2): true
pt1 == pt3: false
pt1.equals(pt3): false
pt1 == pt4: true
pt1.equals(pt4): true
```

There are some specifications for implementing the equals() method in your class, so your class will work correctly when used with other areas (e.g., hash-based collections) of Java. It is the responsibility of the class designer to enforce these specifications. If your class does not conform to these specifications, the Java compiler or Java runtime will not generate any errors. Rather, objects of your class will behave incorrectly. For example, you will add your object to a collection, but you may not be able to retrieve it. Here are specifications for the equals() method's implementation. Assume that x, y, and z are non-null references of three objects.

- *Reflexivity*: It should be reflexive. The expression x.equals(x) should return true. That is, an object must be equal to itself.

- *Symmetry*: It should be symmetric. If x.equals(y) returns true, y.equals(x) must return true. That is, if x is equal to y, y must be equal to x.

- *Transitivity*: It should be transitive. If x.equals(y) returns true and y.equals(z) returns true, x.equals(z) must return true. That is, if x is equal to y and y is equal to z, x must be equal to z.

- *Consistency*: It should be consistent. If x.equals(y) returns true, it should keep returning true until the state of x or y is modified. If x.equals(y) returns false, it should keep returning false until the state of x or y is modified.

- *Comparison with null reference*: An object of any class should not be equal to a null reference. The expression x.equals(null) should always return false.

- *Relationship with hashCode() method*: If x.equals(y) returns true, x.hashCode() must return the same value as y.hashCode(). That is, if two objects are equal according to the equals() method, they must have the same hash code values returned from their hashCode() methods. However, the opposite may not be true. If two objects have the same hash codes, that does not imply that they must be equal according to the equals() method. That is, if x.hashCode() is equal to y.hashCode(), that does not imply that x.equals(y) will return true.

Your SmartPoint class satisfies all six rules for equals() and hashCode() methods. It was fairly easy to implement the equals() method for the SmartPoint class. It has two primitive type instance variables and you used both of them in comparison for equality.

There are no rules as to how many of instance variables should be used to compare for equality of two objects of a class. It all depends on the use of the class. For example, if you have an Account class, the account number itself may be sufficient in your case to compare for the equality of two Account objects. However, make sure you use the same instance variables in the equals() method to compare for equality and in the hashCode() method to compute hash code value. If your class has reference instance variables, you may call their equals() methods from inside the equals() method of your class. Listing 11-5 shows how to use a reference instance variable comparison inside the equals() method.

Listing 11-5. Overriding the equals() and hashCode() Methods in a Class

```java
// SmartCat.java
package com.jdojo.object;

public class SmartCat {
    private String name;

    public SmartCat(String name) {
        this.name = name;
    }
```

```java
        /* Reimplement the equals() method */
        @Override
        public boolean equals(Object otherObject) {
            // Are they the same?
            if (this == otherObject) {
                return true;
            }

            // Is otherObject a null reference?
            if (otherObject == null) {
                return false;
            }

            // Do they belong to the same class?
            if (this.getClass() != otherObject.getClass()) {
                return false;
            }

            // Get the reference of otherObject is a SmartCat variable
            SmartCat otherCat = (SmartCat)otherObject;

            // Do they have the same names
            boolean isSameName = (this.name == null ? otherCat.name == null
                            : this.name.equals(otherCat.name) );

            return isSameName;
        }

        /* Reimplement the hashCode() method, which is a requirement
           when you reimplement equals() method
        */
        @Override
        public int hashCode() {
            return (this.name == null ? 0 : this.name.hashCode());
        }
    }
}
```

The SmartCat class has a name instance variable, which is of the type String. The String class has its own version of the equals() method implementation that compares two strings character by character. The equals() method of the SmartCat class calls the equals() method on the name instance variables to check if two names are equal. Similarly, it makes use of the hashCode() method's implementation in the String class in its hashCode() method.

String Representation of an Object

An object is represented by its state, which is the combination of values of all its instance variables at a point in time. Sometimes it is helpful, usually in debugging, to represent an object in a string form. What should be in the string that represents an object? The string representation of an object should contain enough information about the state of the object in a readable format. The toString() method of the Object class lets you write your own logic to represent the object of your class as a string. The Object class provides a default implementation of the toString() method. It returns a string in the following format:

```
<fully-qualified-class-name>@<hash-code-of-object-in-hexadecimal-format>
```

Consider the following snippet of code and its output. You may get a different output.

```
// Create two objects
Object obj = new Object();
IntHolder intHolder = new IntHolder(234);

// Get string representation of objects
String objStr = obj.toString();
String intHolderStr = intHolder.toString();

// Print the string representations
System.out.println(objStr);
System.out.println(intHolderStr);
```

```
java.lang.Object@360be0
com.jdojo.object.IntHolder@45a877
```

Note that the IntHolder class does not have a toString() method. Still, you were able to call the toString() method using the intHolder reference variable because all methods in the Object class are available in all classes automatically.

You may notice that the string representation that is returned from the toString() method for the IntHolder object is not so useful. It does not give you any clues about the state of the IntHolder object. Let's reimplement the toString() method in the IntHolder class. You will call the new class SmartIntHolder. What should your toString() method return? An object of the SmartIntHolder class represents an integer value. It would be fine just to return the stored integer value as a string. You can convert an integer value, say 123, into a String object using the valueOf() static method of the String class as follows:

```
String str = String.valueOf(123); // str contains "123" as a string
```

Listing 11-6 contains the complete code for the SmartIntHolder class.

Listing 11-6. .Reimplementing toString() Method of the Object Class in the SmartIntHolder Class

```
// SmartIntHolder.java
package com.jdojo.object;

public class SmartIntHolder {
    private int value;

    public SmartIntHolder(int value) {
        this.value = value;
    }
```

```
    public void setValue(int value) {
        this.value = value;
    }

    public int getValue() {
        return value;
    }

    /* Reimplement toString() method of the Object class */
    @Override
    public String toString() {
        // Return the stored value as a string
        String str = String.valueOf(this.value);
        return str;
    }
}
```

The following snippet of code shows you how to use the toString() method of the SmartIntHolder class:

```
// Create an object of the SmartIntHolder class
SmartIntHolder intHolder = new SmartIntHolder(234);
String intHolderStr = intHolder.toString();
System.out.println(intHolderStr);

// Change the value in SmartIntHolder object
intHolder.setValue(8967);
intHolderStr = intHolder.toString();
System.out.println(intHolderStr);
```

```
234
8967
```

There is no special technical requirement for reimplementing the toString() method in your class. You need to make sure it is declared public, its return type is String, and it does not take any parameters. The returned string should be human readable text to give an idea about the state of the object at the time the method is called. It is recommended to reimplement the toString() method of the Object class in every class you create.

Suppose you have a Point class to represent a 2D point, as shown in Listing 11-7. A Point holds the x and y coordinates of a point. An implementation of the toString() method in the Point class may return a string of the form (x, y), where x and y are the coordinates of the point.

Listing 11-7. A Point Class Whose Object Represents a 2D Point

```
// Point.java
package com.jdojo.object;

public class Point {
    private int x;
    private int y;
```

```
    public Point(int x, int y) {
        this.x = x;
        this.y = y;
    }

    /* Reimplement toString() method of the Object class */
    @Override
    public String toString() {
        String str = "(" + x + ", " + y + ")";
        return str;
    }
}
```

The toString() method of a class is very important, and Java provides you with easy ways to use it. Java calls the toString() method of an object automatically for you in situations when it needs a string representation of the object. Two such situations that are worth mentioning:

- A string concatenation expression involving a reference of an object

- A call to the System.out.print() and System.out.println() methods with an object reference as a parameter

When you concatenate a string and an object like this:

```
String str = "Hello" + new Point(10, 20);
```

Java calls the toString() method on the Point object and concatenates the returned value to the "Hello" string. This statement will assign a "Hello(10, 20)" string to the str variable. This statement is the same as the following one:

```
String str = "Hello" + new Point(10, 20).toString();
```

You use the string concatenation operator (+) to concatenate data of different types. First, Java gets the string representations of all data before concatenating them. Calling the toString() method of an object automatically for you in a concatenation expression helps you save some typing. If the object reference that is used in concatenation is a null reference, Java uses a "null" string as the string representation.

The following snippet of code makes the call to the toString() method on object references clear. You may observe that the result is the same when you use the object's reference by itself or you call its toString() method in a string concatenation expression. Similarly, when you use System.out.println(pt), Java automatically calls the toString() method on the pt reference variable.

```
Point pt = new Point(10, 12);

// str1 and str2 will have the same contents
String str1 = "Test " + pt;
String str2 = "Test " + pt.toString();

System.out.println(pt);
System.out.println(pt.toString());
System.out.println(str1);
System.out.println(str2);
```

```
(10, 12)
(10, 12)
Test (10, 12)
Test (10, 12)
```

The following snippet of code shows the effect of using a null reference in a string concatenation expression and in the System.out.println() method call. Note that you cannot use pt.toString() when pt is holding a null reference. The call to any method on a null reference will generate a runtime exception.

```
// Set pt to null
Point pt = null;
String str3 = "Test " + pt;
System.out.println(pt);
System.out.println(str3);
//System.out.println(pt.toString()); /* Will generate a runtime exception */
```

```
null
Test null
```

Cloning Objects

Java does not provide an automatic mechanism to clone (make a copy) an object. Recall that when you assign a reference variable to another reference variable, only the reference of the object is copied, not the content of the object. Cloning an object means copying the content of the object bit by bit. If you want objects of your class to be cloned, you must reimplement the clone() method in your class. Once you reimplement the clone() method, you should be able to clone objects of your class by calling the clone() method. The declaration of the clone() method in the Object class is as follows:

```
protected Object clone() throws CloneNotSupportedException
```

You need to observe a few things about the declaration of the clone() method.

- It is declared protected. Therefore, you will not be able to call it from the client code. The following code is not valid:

  ```
  Object obj = new Object();
  Object clone = obj.clone(); // Error. Cannot access protected clone()
                              // method
  ```

- This means you need to declare the clone() method public in your class if you want the client code to clone objects of your class.

- Its return type is Object. It means you will need to cast the returned value of the clone() method. Suppose MyClass is cloneable. Your cloning code will look like this:

  ```
  MyClass mc = new MyClass();
  MyClass clone = (MyClass)mc.clone(); // Need to use a cast
  ```

You do not need to know any internal details about an object to clone it. The clone() method in the Object class has all the code that is needed to clone an object. All you need to do is call it from the clone() method of your class. It will make a bitwise copy of the original object and return the reference of the copy.

The clone() method in the Object class throws a CloneNotSupportedException. It means when you call the clone() method of the Object class, you need to place the call in a try-catch block, or rethrow the exception. You will learn more about the try-catch block in Chapter 13. You have the option not to throw a CloneNotSupportedException from the clone() method of your class. The following snippet of code is placed inside the clone() method of your class, which calls the clone() method of the Object class using the super keyword:

```
YourClass obj = null;
try {
    // Call clone() method of the Object class using super.clone()
    obj = (YourClass)super.clone();
} catch (CloneNotSupportedException e) {
    e. printStackTrace();
}

return obj;
```

One important thing that you must do is add an implements Cloneable clause in your class declaration. Cloneable is an interface declared in the java.lang package. You will learn about interfaces in Chapter 21. For now, just add this clause in your class declaration. Otherwise, you will get a runtime error when you call the clone() method on the objects of your class. Your class declaration must look like this:

```
public class MyClass implements Cloneable {
    // Code for your class goes here
}
```

Listing 11-8 contains the complete code for a DoubleHolder class. It overrides the clone() method of the Object class. The comments in the clone() method explain what the code is doing. The clone() method of the DoubleHolder class does not have a throws clause like the clone() method of the Object class has. When you override a method, you have an option to drop the throws clause that is declared in the superclass.

Listing 11-8. A DoubleHolder Class with Cloning Capability

```
// DoubleHolder.java
package com.jdojo.object;

public class DoubleHolder implements Cloneable {
    private double value;

    public DoubleHolder(double value) {
        this.value = value;
    }

    public void setValue(double value) {
        this.value = value;
    }
```

```java
    public double getValue() {
        return this.value;
    }

    @Override
    public Object clone() {
        DoubleHolder copy = null;
        try {
            // Call the clone() method of the Object class, which will do a
            // bit-by-bit copy and return the reference of the clone
            copy = (DoubleHolder) super.clone();
        } catch (CloneNotSupportedException e) {
            // If anything goes wrong during cloning, print the error details
            e.printStackTrace();
        }
        return copy;
    }
}
```

Once your class implements the clone() method correctly, cloning an object of your class is as simple as calling its clone() method. The following snippet of code shows how to clone an object of the DoubleHolder class. Note that you must cast the returned reference from the dh.clone() method call to the DoubleHolder type.

```java
DoubleHolder dh = new DoubleHolder(100.00);
DoubleHolder dhClone = (DoubleHolder) dh.clone();
```

At this point, there are two separate objects of the DoubleHolder class. The dh variable references the original object and dhClone variable references the clone of the original object. The original as well as the cloned object hold the same value of 100.00. However, they have separate copies of the value. If you change the value in the original object, for example, dh.setValue(200), the value in the cloned object remains unchanged. Listing 11-9 shows how to use the clone() method to clone an object of the DoubleHolder class. The output proves that once you clone an object, there are two separate objects in memory.

Listing 11-9. A Test Class to Demonstrate Object Cloning

```java
// CloningTest.java
package com.jdojo.object;

public class CloningTest {
    public static void main(String[] args)  {
        DoubleHolder dh = new DoubleHolder(100.00);

        // Clone dh
        DoubleHolder dhClone = (DoubleHolder)dh.clone();

        // Print the values in original and clone
        System.out.println("Original:" + dh.getValue());
        System.out.println("Clone:" + dhClone.getValue());
```

```
        // Change the value in original and clone
        dh.setValue(200.00);
        dhClone.setValue(400.00);

        // Print the values in original and clone again
        System.out.println("Original:" + dh.getValue());
        System.out.println("Clone :" + dhClone.getValue());
    }
}
```

```
Original:100.0
Clone:100.0
Original:200.0
Clone:400.0
```

From Java 5, you need not specify the return type of the clone() method in your class as the Object type. You can specify your class as the return type in the clone() method declaration. This will not force the client code to use a cast when it calls the clone() method of your class. The following snippet of code shows the changed code for the DoubleHolder class, which will compile only in Java 5 or later. It declares DoubleHolder as the return type of the clone() method and uses a cast in the return statement.

```
// DoubleHolder.java
package com.jdojo.object;

public class DoubleHolder implements Cloneable {
    /* The same code goes here as before... */

    public DoubleHolder clone() {
        Object copy = null;

        /* The same code goes here as before... */

        return (DoubleHolder)copy;
    }
}
```

With the previous declaration for the clone() method, you can write code to clone an object as follows. Note that no cast is needed anymore.

```
DoubleHolder dh = new DoubleHolder(100.00);
DoubleHolder dhClone = dh.clone();// Clone dh. No cast is needed
```

An object may be composed of another object. In such cases, two objects exist in memory separately—a contained object and a container object. The container object stores the reference of the contained object. When you clone the container object, the reference of the contained object is cloned. After cloning is performed, there are two copies of the container object; both of them have references to the same contained object. This is called a *shallow* cloning because references are copied, not the objects. The clone() method of the Object class makes only shallow cloning, unless you code it otherwise. Figure 11-2 shows the memory state of a compound object, where an object contains a reference of another object. Figure 11-3 shows the memory state when the compound object is cloned using a shallow cloning. You may notice that in shallow cloning, the contained object is shared by the original compound object and the cloned compound object.

417

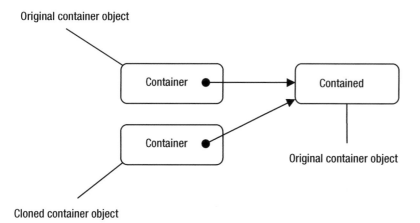

Figure 11-2. *A compound object. The container object stores a reference of another object (contained object).*

Figure 11-3. *Memory state after the container object is cloned using shallow cloning*

When the contained objects are copied rather than their references during cloning of a compound object, it is called deep cloning. You must clone all the objects referenced by all reference variables of an object to get a deep cloning. A compound object may have multiple levels of chaining of contained objects. For example, the container object may have a reference of another contained object, which in turn has a reference of another contained object and so on. Whether you will be able to perform a deep cloning of a compound object depends on many factors. If you have a reference of a contained object, it may not support cloning and in that case, you have to be content with shallow cloning. You may have a reference of a contained object, which itself is a compound object. However, the contained object supports only shallow cloning, and in that case again, you will have to be content with shallow cloning. Let's look at examples of shallow and deep cloning.

If the reference instance variables of an object store references to immutable objects, you do not need to clone them. That is, if the contained objects of a compound object are immutable, you do not need to clone the contained objects. In this case, shallow copy of the immutable contained objects is fine. Recall that immutable objects cannot be modified after they are created. An immutable object's references can be shared by the multiple objects without any side effects. This is one of the benefits of having immutable objects. If a compound object contains some references to mutable objects and some to immutable objects, you must clone the referenced mutable objects to have a deep copy. Listing 11-10 has code for a ShallowClone class.

Listing 11-10. A ShallowClone Class That Supports Shallow Cloning

```
// ShallowClone.java
package com.jdojo.object;

public class ShallowClone implements Cloneable {
    private DoubleHolder holder = new DoubleHolder(0.0);
```

```java
    public ShallowClone(double value) {
        this.holder.setValue(value);
    }

    public void setValue(double value) {
        this.holder.setValue(value);
    }

    public double getValue() {
        return this.holder.getValue();
    }

    @Override
    public Object clone() {
        ShallowClone copy = null;
        try {
            copy = (ShallowClone) super.clone();
        } catch (CloneNotSupportedException e) {
            e.printStackTrace();
        }
        return copy;
    }
}
```

An object of the ShallowClone class is composed of an object of the DoubleHolder class. The code in the clone() method of the ShallowClone class is the same as for the clone() method of the DoubleHolder class. The difference lies in the type of instance variables that are used for the two classes. The DoubleHolder class has an instance variable of primitive type double, whereas the ShallowClone class has an instance variable of the reference type DoubleHolder. When the ShallowClone class calls the clone() method of the Object class (using super.clone()), it receives a shallow copy of itself. That is, it shares the DoubleHolder object used in its instance variable with its clone.

Listing 11-11 has test cases to test an object of the ShallowClone class and its clone. The output shows that after you make a clone, changing the value through the original object also changes the value in the cloned object. This is so because the ShallowClone object stores the value in another object of the DoubleHolder class, which is shared by both the cloned and the original objects.

Listing 11-11. A Test Class to Demonstrate the Shallow Copy Mechanism

```java
// ShallowCloneTest.java
package com.jdojo.object;

public class ShallowCloneTest {
    public static void main(String[] args) {
        ShallowClone sc = new ShallowClone(100.00);
        ShallowClone scClone = (ShallowClone) sc.clone();

        // Print the value in original and clone
        System.out.println("Original: " + sc.getValue());
        System.out.println("Clone: " + scClone.getValue());
```

```
        // Change the value in original and it will change the value
        // for clone too because we have done shallow cloning
        sc.setValue(200.00);

        // Print the value in original and clone
        System.out.println("Original: " + sc.getValue());
        System.out.println("Clone: " + scClone.getValue());
    }
}
```

```
Original: 100.0
Clone: 100.0
Original: 200.0
Clone: 200.0
```

In a deep cloning, you need to clone all objects referenced by all reference instance variables of an object. You must perform a shallow cloning before you can perform a deep cloning. The shallow cloning is performed by calling the clone() method of the Object class. Then you need to write code to clone all reference instance variables. Listing 11-12 shows code for a DeepClone class, which performs a deep cloning.

Listing 11-12. A DeepClone Class That Performs Deep Cloning

```java
// DeepClone.java
package com.jdojo.object;

public class DeepClone implements Cloneable {
    private DoubleHolder holder = new DoubleHolder(0.0);

    public DeepClone(double value) {
        this.holder.setValue(value);
    }

    public void setValue(double value) {
        this.holder.setValue(value);
    }

    public double getValue() {
        return this.holder.getValue();
    }

    @Override
    public Object clone() {
        DeepClone copy = null;
        try {
            copy = (DeepClone) super.clone();
```

```
            // Need to clone the holder reference variable too
            copy.holder = (DoubleHolder) this.holder.clone();
        } catch (CloneNotSupportedException e) {
            e.printStackTrace();
        }

        return copy;
    }
}
```

If you compare the code in the clone() method of the ShallowClone and DeepClone classes, you will find that, for deep cloning, you had to write only one extra line of code:

```
// Need to clone the holder reference variable too
copy.holder = (DoubleHolder)this.holder.clone();
```

What will happen if the DoubleHolder class is not cleanable? In that case, you would not be able to write this statement to clone the holder instance variable. You could have cloned the holder instance variable as follows:

```
// Need to clone the holder reference variable too
copy.holder = new DoubleHolder(this.holder.getValue());
```

The goal is to clone the holder instance variable and it does not have to be done by calling its clone() method. Listing 11-13 shows how your DeepClone class works. Compare its output with the output of the ShallowCloneTest class to see the difference.

Listing 11-13. A Test Class to Test Deep Cloning of Objects

```
// DeepCloneTest.java
package com.jdojo.object;

public class DeepCloneTest {
    public static void main(String[] args) {
        DeepClone sc = new DeepClone(100.00);
        DeepClone scClone = (DeepClone) sc.clone();

        // Print the value in original and clone
        System.out.println("Original: " + sc.getValue());
        System.out.println("Clone: " + scClone.getValue());

        // Change the value in original and it will not change the value
        // for clone because we have done deep cloning
        sc.setValue(200.00);

        // Print the value in original and clone
        System.out.println("Original: " + sc.getValue());
        System.out.println("Clone: " + scClone.getValue());
    }
}
```

```
Original: 100.0
Clone: 100.0
Original: 200.0
Clone: 100.0
```

▓ **Tip**   Using the `clone()` method of the `Object` class is not the only way to make a clone of an object. You can use other methods to clone an object. You may provide a copy constructor, which accepts an object of the same class and creates a clone of that object. You may provide a factory method in your class, which may accept an object and return its clone. Another way to clone an object is to serialize it and then deserialized it. Serializing and deserializing objects is covered in Chapter 7 of the second volume of this series.

Finalizing an Object

Sometimes an object uses resources that need to be released when the object is destroyed. Java provides you with a way to perform resource release or some other type of cleanup, when an object is about to be destroyed. In Java, you create objects, but you cannot destroy objects. The JVM runs a low priority special task called *garbage collector* to destroy all objects that are no longer referenced. The garbage collector gives you a chance to execute your cleanup code before an object is destroyed. The `Object` class has a `finalize()` method, which is declared as follows:

```
protected void finalize() throws Throwable { }
```

The `finalize()` method in the `Object` class does not do anything. You need to override the method in your class. The `finalize()` method of your class will be called by the garbage collector before an object of your class is destroyed. Listing 11-14 contains code for the `Finalize` class. It overrides the `finalize()` method of the `Object` class and prints a message on the standard output. You can perform any cleanup logic in this method. The code in the `finalize()` method is also called *finalizer*.

Listing 11-14. A Finalize Class That Overrides the finalize() Method of the Object Class

```java
// Finalize.java
package com.jdojo.object;

public class Finalize {
    private int x;

    public Finalize(int x) {
        this.x = x;
    }

    @Override
    public void finalize() {
        System.out.println("Finalizing " + this.x);

        /* Perform any cleanup work here... */
    }
}
```

The garbage collector calls the finalizer for each object only once. Running a finalizer for an object does not necessarily mean that the object will be destroyed immediately after the finalizer finishes. A finalizer is run when the garbage collector determines that no references to the object exist. However, an object may pass its own reference to some other part of the program when its finalizer is run. This is the reason that the garbage collector checks one more time after it runs an object's finalizer to make sure that no references exist for that object and then it destroys (de-allocates memory) the object. The order in which finalizers are run and the time at which they are run are not specified. It is not even guaranteed that a finalizer will run at all. This makes it undependable for a programmer to write cleanup logic in the finalize() method. There are better ways to perform cleanup logic, for example, using a try-finally block. It is suggested not to depend on the finalize() method in your Java program to clean up resources uses by an object.

▓ **Tip**   The finalize() method in the Object class has been deprecated since Java 9 because using the finalize() method to clean up resources is inherently problematic. There are several better alternatives to clean up resources, for example, using try-with-resources and try-finally blocks. I discuss these techniques in Chapter 13 of this volume and Chapter 11 of the second volume of this series. I have covered the finalize() method in this chapter just for the purpose of completeness.

Listing 11-15 contains code to test the finalizers for your Finalize class. You may get different output when you run this program.

Listing 11-15. A Test Class to Test Finalizers

```
// FinalizeTest.java
package com.jdojo.object;

public class FinalizeTest {
    public static void main(String[] args) {
        // Create many objects, say 2000000 objects.
        for(int i = 0; i < 2000000; i++) {
            new Finalize(i);
        }
    }
}
```

```
Finalizing 977620
Finalizing 977625
Finalizing 977627
```

The program creates 2000000 objects of the Finalize class without storing their references. It is important that you do not store the references of the objects you create. As long as you hold the reference of an object, it will not be destroyed and its finalizer will not be run. You can see from the output that only three objects got a chance to run their finalizers before the program finished. You may get no output at all or a different output. If you do not get any output, you can try by increasing the number of objects to create. The garbage collector will destroy objects when it feels it is running low in memory. You may need to create more objects to trigger garbage collection, which in turn will run finalizers of your objects.

Immutable Objects

An object whose state cannot be changed after it is created is called an immutable object. A class whose objects are immutable is called an immutable class. If an object's state can be changed (or mutated) after it has been created, it is called a mutable object, and its class is called a mutable class.

Before I go into details of creating and using immutable objects, let's define the word "immutability". Instance variables of an object define the state of an object. There are two views of an object's state: internal and external. The internal state of the object is defined by the actual values of its instance variables at a point in time. The external state of the object is defined by the values that the users (or clients) of the object see at a point in time. When we state that an object is immutable, we must be specific about which state of the object we mean to be immutable: internal state, external state, or both.

Typically, when we use the phrase "an immutable object" in Java, we mean external immutability. In external immutability, an object may change its internal state after its creation. However, the change in its internal state is not visible to external users. The users do not see any changes in its state after its creation. In internal immutability, the state of an object does not change after it is created. If an object is internally immutable, it is also externally immutable. I discuss examples of both.

Immutable objects have several advantages over mutable objects. An immutable object can be shared by different areas of a program without worrying about its state changes. Testing an immutable class is easy. An immutable object is inherently thread-safe. You do not have to synchronize access to your immutable object from multiple threads since its state does not change. Refer to Chapter 6 of the second volume of this series for more details on thread synchronization. An immutable object does not have to be copied and passed to another area of the program in the same Java application because its state does not change. You can just pass its reference and that serves as a copy. Its reference can be used to access its content. Avoiding copying is a big performance advantage as it saves both time and space.

Let's start with a mutable class whose object's state can be modified after it is created. Listing 11-16 contains the code for an IntHolder class.

Listing 11-16. An Example of a Mutable Class Whose Object's State Can Be Changed After Creation

```java
// IntHolder.java
package com.jdojo.object;

public class IntHolder {
    private int value;

    public IntHolder(int value) {
        this.value = value;
    }

    public void setValue(int value) {
        this.value = value;
    }

    public int getValue() {
        return value;
    }
}
```

The value instance variable defines the state of an IntHolder object. You create an object of the IntHolder class as shown:

```
IntHolder holder = new IntHolder(101);
int v = holder.getValue(); // Stores 101 in v
```

At this time, the value instance variable holds 101, which defines its state. You can get and set the instance variable using the getter and setter.

```
// Change the value
holder.setValue(505);
int w = holder.getValue(); // Stores 505 in w
```

At this point, the value instance variable has changed from 101 to 505. That is, the state of the object has changed. The change in state was facilitated by the setValue() method. Objects of the IntHolder class are examples of mutable objects.

Let's make the IntHolder class immutable. All you need to do is remove the setValue() method from it to make it an immutable class. Let's call your immutable version of the IntHolder class as IntWrapper, as shown in Listing 11-17.

Listing 11-17. An Example of an Immutable Class

```java
// IntWrapper.java
package com.jdojo.object;

public class IntWrapper {
    private final int value;

    public IntWrapper(int value) {
        this.value = value;
    }

    public int getValue() {
        return value;
    }
}
```

This is how you create an object of the IntWrapper class:

```
IntWrapper wrapper = new IntWrapper(101);
```

At this point, the wrapper object holds 101 and there is no way to change it. Therefore, the IntWrapper class is an immutable class and its objects are immutable objects. You might have noticed that two changes were made to the IntHolder class to convert it to the IntWrapper class. The setValue() method was removed and the value instance variable was made final. In this case, it was not necessary to make the value instance variable final. The use of the final keyword makes your intention clear to the reader of the class and it protects the value instance variable from being changed inadvertently. It is good practice (use it as a rule of thumb) to declare all instance variables that define the immutable state of an object final so the Java compiler will enforce the immutability during compilation. The objects of IntWrapper class are immutable internally as well as externally. There is no way to change its state once it is created.

Let's create a variant of the IntWrapper class, which will be externally immutable but internally mutable. Let's call it IntWrapper2. It is listed in Listing 11-18.

Listing 11-18. An Example of an Externally Immutable and Internally Mutable Class

```java
// IntWrapper2.java
package com.jdojo.object;

public class IntWrapper2 {
    private final int value;
    private int halfValue = Integer.MAX_VALUE;

    public IntWrapper2(int value) {
        this.value = value;
    }

    public int getValue() {
        return value;
    }

    public int getHalfValue() {
        // Compute half value if it is not already computed
        if (this.halfValue == Integer.MAX_VALUE) {
            // Cache the half value for future use
            this.halfValue = this.value / 2;
        }

        return this.halfValue;
    }
}
```

IntWrapper2 adds another instance variable called halfValue, which will hold the half value of the value that is passed to the constructor. It is a trivial example. However, it serves the purpose to explain what you mean by externally and internally immutable objects. Suppose (just for the sake of this discussion) that computing half of an integer is a very costly process and you do not want to compute it in the constructor of the IntWrapper2 class, especially if not everybody asks for it. The halfValue instance variable is initialized to the maximum integer value, which works as a flag that it is not computed yet. You have added a getHalfValue() method, which checks if you have already computed the half value. For the first time, it will compute the half value and cache it in the halfValue instance variable. From the second time onward, it will simply return the cached value.

The question is, "Is an IntWrapper2 object immutable?" The answer is yes and no. It is internally mutable. However, it is externally immutable. Once it is created, its client will see the same return value from the getValue() and getHalfValue() methods. However, its state (halfValue to be specific) changes once in its lifetime when the getHalfValue() method is called for the first time. However, this change is not visible to the users of the object. This method returns the same value on all subsequent calls. Objects like IntWrapper2 are called immutable objects. Recall that typically an immutable object means externally immutable.

The String class in the Java class library is an example of an immutable class. It uses the caching technique discussed for the IntWrapper2 class. The String class computes hash code for its content when its hashCode() method is called for the first time and caches the value. Thus, a String object changes its state internally, but not for its client. You will not come across the phrase, "A String object in Java is externally immutable and internally mutable." Rather, you will come across the phrase, "A String object in Java is immutable." You should understand that it means String objects are at least externally immutable.

Listing 11-19 shows a tricky situation where an attempt has been made to create an immutable class. The IntHolderWrapper class has no method that can directly lets you modify the value stored in its valueHolder instance variable. It seems to be an immutable class.

Listing 11-19. An Unsuccessful Attempt to Create an Immutable Class

```
// IntHolderWrapper.java
package com.jdojo.object;

public class IntHolderWrapper {
    private final IntHolder valueHolder;

    public IntHolderWrapper(int value) {
        this.valueHolder = new IntHolder(value);
    }

    public IntHolder getIntHolder() {
        return this.valueHolder;
    }

    public int getValue() {
        return this.valueHolder.getValue();
    }
}
```

Listing 11-20 contains a test class to test the immutability of the IntHolderWrapper class.

Listing 11-20. A Test Class to Test Immutability of the IntHolderWrapper Class

```
// BadImmutableTest.java
package com.jdojo.object;

public class BadImmutableTest {
    public static void main(String[] args) {
        IntHolderWrapper ihw = new IntHolderWrapper(101);

        int value = ihw.getValue();
        System.out.println("#1 value = " + value);

        IntHolder holder = ihw.getIntHolder();
        holder.setValue(207);

        value = ihw.getValue();
        System.out.println("#2 value = " + value);
    }
}
```

```
#1 value = 101
#2 value = 207
```

The output shows that the IntHolderWrapper class is mutable. Two calls to its getValue() method return different values. The culprit is its getIntHolder() method. It returns the valueHolder instance variable, which is a reference variable. Note that the valueHolder instance variable represents an object of the IntHolder class, which makes up the state of an IntHolderWrapper object. If the object that the valueHolder reference variable references is changed, the state of IntHolderWrapper is changed, too. Since the IntHolder object is mutable, you should not return its reference to the client from the getIntHolder() method. The following two statements change the state of the object from the client code:

```
IntHolder holder = ihw.getIntHolder(); /* Got hold of instance variable */
holder.setValue(207); /* Change the state by changing the instance variable's state */
```

Note that the designer of the IntHolderWrapper class missed the point when he returned the valueHolder reference, that even though there is no direct way to change the state of the IntHolderWrapper class, it can be changed indirectly.

How do you correct the problem? The solution is easy. In the getIntHolder() method, make a copy of the valueHolder object and return the reference of the copy instead of the instance variable itself. This way, if the client changes the value, it will be changed only in the client's copy, not in the copy held by IntHolderWrapper object. Listing 11-21 contains the correct immutable version of the IntHolderWrapper class, which you call IntHolderWrapper2.

Listing 11-21. A Modified, Immutable Version of the IntHolderWrapper Class

```java
// IntHolderWrapper2.java
package com.jdojo.object;

public class IntHolderWrapper2 {
    private final IntHolder valueHolder;

    public IntHolderWrapper2(int value) {
        this.valueHolder = new IntHolder(value);
    }

    public IntHolder getIntHolder() {
        // Make a copy of valueHolder
        int v = this.valueHolder.getValue();
        IntHolder copy = new IntHolder(v);

        // Return the copy instead of the original
        return copy;
    }

    public int getValue() {
        return this.valueHolder.getValue();
    }
}
```

Creating an immutable class is a little trickier than it seems. I have covered some of the cases in this section. Here is another case where you need to be careful. Suppose you have designed an immutable class that has a reference type instance variable. Suppose it accepts the initial value of its reference type instance variable in one of its constructors. If the instance variable's class is a mutable class, you must make a copy of the parameter passed to its constructor and store the copy in the instance variable. The client code that passes the object's reference in the constructor may change the state of this object through the same reference later. Listing 11-22 shows how to implement the second constructor for the IntHolderWrapper3 class correctly. It has the incorrect version of the implementation for the second constructor commented.

Listing 11-22. Using a Copy Constructor to Correctly Implement an Immutable Class

```java
// IntHolderWrapper3.java
package com.jdojo.object;

public class IntHolderWrapper3 {
    private final IntHolder valueHolder;

    public IntHolderWrapper3(int value) {
        this.valueHolder = new IntHolder(value);
    }

    public IntHolderWrapper3(IntHolder holder) {
        // Must make a copy of holder parameter
        this.valueHolder = new IntHolder(holder.getValue());

        /* Following implementation is incorrect. Client code will be able to change the
            state of the object using holder reference later */
        //this.valueHolder = holder; /* do not use it */
    }

    /* Rest of the code goes here... */
}
```

The Objects Class

The JDK contains a utility class named Objects in the java.util package for working with objects. It consists of all static methods. Most methods of the Objects class deal with null values gracefully. Java 9 added a few more utility methods to the class. Methods in the Objects class fit into the following categories depending on the kind of operation they perform:

- Bounds checks

- Comparing objects

- Computing hash code

- Checking for null

- Validating arguments

- Obtaining string representation of objects

Bounds Checks

Methods in this category are used to check if an index or a sub-range is within the bounds of a range. Typically, you use these methods on arrays before performing an operation that involves the array bounds. An array in Java is a collection of the same type of elements. Each element in an array has an index that is used to access them. Array indexes are zero-based. The first element has an index of 0, the second 1, the third 2, etc. Suppose you have an array of five elements and someone asks you to give him four elements of the array starting at index 3. This request is invalid because the array index ranges from 0 to 4 and the requested elements are from index 3 to 6. The Objects class contains the following three methods to perform bounds checks—all of which were added in Java 9:

- int checkFromIndexSize(int fromIndex, int size, int length)

- int checkFromToIndex(int fromIndex, int toIndex, int length)

- int checkIndex(int index, int length)

All these methods throw an IndexOutOfBoundsException if the check for an index or a sub-range is not within the bounds of 0 to length, where length is one of the arguments to the methods.

The checkFromIndexSize(int fromIndex, int size, int length) method checks if the sub-range from fromIndex (inclusive) to fromIndex + size (exclusive) is within the bounds of range from 0 (inclusive) to length (exclusive).

The checkFromToIndex(int fromIndex, int toIndex, int length) method checks if the sub-range from fromIndex (inclusive) to toIndex (exclusive) is within the bounds of range from 0 (inclusive) to length (exclusive).

The checkIndex(int index, int length) method checks if the index is within the bounds of the range from 0 (inclusive) to length (exclusive).

Comparing Objects

Methods in this category are used to compare objects for sorting purposes or for equality. There are three methods in this category:

- <T> int compare(T a, T b, Comparator<? super T> c)

- boolean deepEquals(Object a, Object b)

- boolean equals(Object a, Object b)

The compare() method is used to compare two objects for sorting purposes. It returns 0 if both arguments are identical. Otherwise, it returns the value of c.compare(a, b). It returns 0 if both arguments are null.

The deepEquals() method is used to check if two objects are deeply equal. It returns true if both arguments are deeply equal. Otherwise, it returns false. It returns true if both arguments are null.

The equals() method compares two objects for equality. It returns true if both arguments are equal. Otherwise, it returns false. It returns true if both arguments are null. It returns false if only one argument is null.

Computing Hash Code

Methods in this category are used to compute hash codes for one or more objects. There are two methods in this category:

- int hash(Object... values)
- int hashCode(Object obj)

The hash() method generates a hash code for all specified objects in its arguments. It can be used to compute the hash code for an object that contains multiple instance fields. Listing 11-23 contains another version of the Book class. This time, the hashCode() method uses the Objects.hash() method to compute the hash code of a Book object. Compare the code for the Book class in Listing 11-2 with the code for the Book2 class in Listing 11-23. Notice how easy it is to compute the hash code of an object using the Objects.hash() method.

Listing 11-23. Using the Objects.hash() Method to Compute the Hash Code of an Object

```java
// Book2.java
package com.jdojo.object;

import java.util.Objects;

public class Book2 {
    private String title;
    private String author;
    private int pageCount;
    private boolean hardCover;
    private double price;

    /* Other code goes here */

    /* Must implement the equals() method too. */

    @Override
    public int hashCode() {
        return Objects.hash(title, author, pageCount, hardCover, price);
    }
}
```

If a single object reference is passed to the Objects.hash() method, the returned hash code is not equal to the hash code returned from the object's hashCode() method. In other words, if book is an object reference, book.hashCode() is not equal to Objects.hash(book).

The Objects.hashCode(Object obj) method returns the hash code value of the specified object. If the argument is null, it returns 0.

Checking for Null

Methods in this category are used to check if an object is null or not. There are two methods in this category:

- boolean isNull(Object obj)
- boolean nonNull(Object obj)

The isNull() method returns true if the specified object is null. Otherwise, it returns false. You can also check whether an object is null using the comparison operator ==, for example, obj == null returns true if obj is null. The isNull() method was added in Java 8. It exists to be used as a method reference like (Objects::isNull) in lambda expressions. Lambda expressions are covered in Chapter 5 of the second volume of this series.

The nonNull() method performs the check opposite of what the isNull() method does. It was added in Java 8 to be used in lambda expressions as a method reference like (Objects::nonNull).

Validating Arguments

Methods in this category are used to validate requires arguments of constructor and methods. What you could achieve writing a few lines of code with if statements, you can achieve the same in one line of code using these methods. There are five methods in this category:

- \<T> T requireNonNull(T obj)
- \<T> T requireNonNull(T obj, String message)
- \<T> T requireNonNull(T obj, Supplier<String> messageSupplier)
- \<T> T requireNonNullElse(T obj, T defaultObj)
- \<T> T requireNonNullElseGet(T obj, Supplier<? extends T> supplier)

The requireNonNull(T obj) method checks if the argument is not null. If the argument is null, it throws a NullPointerException. This method is designed for validating arguments of methods and constructors. Notice the formal type parameter \<T> in the method's declaration. It is a generic method. Any type of object can be passed as an argument to this method. Its return type is the same as the type of the passed object. The method is overloaded. The second version of the method lets you specify the message for the NullPointerException that is thrown when the argument is null. The third version of the method takes a Supplier<String> as the second argument. It defers the creation of the message until the null check is performed. If the argument is null, the get() method of the Supplier<String> object is called to get the error message that is used in NullPointerException. Using a supplier delays the construction of the error message and it also gives you more options such as adding the timestamp in your error message.

Java 9 added the requireNonNullElse() and requireNonNullElseGet() methods to the Objects class. The requireNonNullElse() method returns the first argument if it is not null; otherwise, it returns the second argument if the second argument is not null. If both arguments are null, it throws a NullPointerException. The requireNonNullElseGet() method returns the first argument if it is not null; otherwise, it returns the not null value returned from the get() method of the supplier. If the first argument is null, and supplier is null or the supplier returns null, it throws a NullPointerException.

Obtaining String Representation of Objects

Methods in this category are used to obtain a string representation of an object. There are two methods in this category:

- String toString(Object o)

- String toString(Object o, String nullDefault)

The toString() method returns a "null" string if the argument is null. For a non-null argument, it returns the value returned by calling the toString() method on the argument. The second version of the method lets you specify the default retuned string when the argument is null.

Using the Objects Class

Listing 11-24 demonstrates how to use some of the methods of the Objects class. The program uses a lambda expression to create a Supplier<String> object. Lambda expressions are discussed in Chapter 5 in the second volume of this book. I used it here to give you a complete example.

Listing 11-24. A Test Class to Demonstrate the Use of the Methods of the Objects Class

```java
// ObjectsTest.java
package com.jdojo.object;

import java.time.Instant;
import java.util.Objects;
import java.util.function.Supplier;

public class ObjectsTest {
    public static void main(String[] args) {
        // Compute hash code for two integers, a char, and a string
        int hash = Objects.hash(10, 8900, '\u20b9', "Hello");
        System.out.println("Hash Code is " + hash);

        // Test for equality
        boolean isEqual = Objects.equals(null, null);
        System.out.println("null is equal to null: " + isEqual);

        isEqual = Objects.equals(null, "XYZ");
        System.out.println("null is equal to XYZ: " + isEqual);

        // toString() method test
        System.out.println("toString(null) is " + Objects.toString(null));
        System.out.println("toString(null, \"XXX\") is " + Objects.toString(null, "XXX"));

        // Testing requireNonNull(T obj, String message)
        try {
            printName("Doug Dyer");
            printName(null);
        } catch (NullPointerException e) {
            System.out.println(e.getMessage());
        }
```

```
        // requireNonNull(T obj, Supplier<String> messageSupplier)
        try {
            // Using a lambda expression to create a Supplier<String> object.
            // The Supplier returns a timestamped message.
            Supplier<String> messageSupplier =
                    () -> "Name is required. Error generated on " + Instant.now();
            printNameWithSupplier("Babalu", messageSupplier);
            printNameWithSupplier(null, messageSupplier);
        } catch (NullPointerException e) {
            System.out.println(e.getMessage());
        }

        //<T> T requireNonNullElse(T obj, T defaultObj)
        printNameWithDefault("Kishori Sharan");

        // Default name "John Doe" will be used
        printNameWithDefault(null);
    }

    public static void printName(String name) {
        // Test name for not null. Generate a NullPointerException if it is null.
        Objects.requireNonNull(name, "Name is required.");

        // Print the name if the above statement did not throw an exception
        System.out.println("Name is " + name);
    }

    public static void printNameWithSupplier(String name, Supplier<String> messageSupplier)
    {
        // Test name for not null. Generate a NullPointerException if it is null.
        Objects.requireNonNull(name, messageSupplier);

        // Print the name if the above statement did not throw an exception
        System.out.println("Name is " + name);
    }

    public static void printNameWithDefault(String name) {
        // Test name for not null. Generate a NullPointerException if it is null.
        Objects.requireNonNullElse(name, "John Doe");

        // Print the name if the above statement did not throw an exception
        System.out.println("Name is " + name);
    }
}
```

```
Hash Code is 79643668
null is equal to null: true
null is equal to XYZ: false
toString(null) is null
toString(null, "XXX") is XXX
Name is Doug Dyer
Name is required.
Name is Babalu
Name is required. Error generated on 2017-07-29T02:44:25.974523900Z
Name is Kishori Sharan
Name is null
```

Summary

Classes in Java are arranged in a tree-like hierarchy. Classes in the tree have a superclass-subclass relationship. The Object class is at the root of the class hierarchy. It is the superclass of all classes in Java. The Object class is in the java.lang package, which in turn is in the java.base module. The Object class contains methods that are automatically available in all classes. Some methods have been implemented and some have an empty implementation. Classes can also reimplement some methods in the Object class. A reference variable of the Object class can store the reference of any reference type in Java.

Every type loaded into the JVM is represented by an instance of the Class<T> class. The getClass() method of the Object class returns the reference of the Class<T> object of the type of the object on which this method is called.

A hash code is an integer value that is computed for a piece of information using an algorithm. A hash code is also known as a hash sum, a hash value, or simply a hash. The algorithm to compute an integer from a piece of information is called a hash function. The Object class contains a hashCode() method that returns an int, which is the hash code of the object. The default implementation of this method computes the hash code of an object by converting the memory address of the object into an integer. Since the hashCode() method is defined in the Object class, it is available in all classes in Java. However, you are free to override the implementation in your class.

Every object in the universe is different from all other objects, and every object in a Java program is different from all other objects. All objects have a unique identity. The memory address at which an object is allocated can be treated as its identity, which will make it always unique. Two objects are the same if they have the same identity (or reference in Java terminology). The equality operator (==) in Java compares the references of two objects to test whether they are equal. Sometimes you want to treat two objects as equal if they have the same state based on some or all of their instance variables. If you want to compare two objects of your class for equality based on criteria other than their references (identities), your class needs to reimplement the equals() method of the Object class. The default implementation of the equals() method in the Object class compares the references of the object being passed as the parameter and the object on which the method is called.

Sometimes it is helpful, usually when debugging, to represent an object in a string form, which should contain enough information about the state of the object in a readable format. The toString() method of the Object class lets you write your own logic to represent the object of your class as a string. The Object class provides a default implementation of the toString() method. It returns a string containing the full qualified class name of the object and the hash code of the object in hexadecimal format.

Cloning an object means copying the content of the object bit by bit. Java does not provide an automatic mechanism to clone (make a copy) an object. If you want objects of your class to be cloned, you must reimplement the clone() method of the Object class in your class. Once you reimplement the clone() method, you should be able to clone objects of your class by calling the clone() method.

Sometimes an object uses resources that need to be released when the object is destroyed. The garbage collector gives you a chance to execute your cleanup code before an object is destroyed by calling the finalize() method of your object. The method is declared in the Object class and its default implementation does not do anything. The code in the finalize() method is also called *finalizer*. You need to reimplement the finalize() method in your class and write the logic to release resources. The finalize() method is problematic and it has been deprecated in Java 9. Many other techniques are available to release resources held by an object.

Java 7 added a utility class Objects in the java.util package. Java 8 and Java 9 added a few more methods to this class. Methods in the Objects class fit into the following categories depending on the kind of operation they perform: bounds checks for an index or sub-range inside a range, comparing objects, computing hash code, checking for null, validating constructor and method arguments, and obtaining string representation of objects. Most of the methods in this class exist to deal with null values gracefully.

EXERCISES

1. What is the fully qualified name of the class that is the superclass of all classes in Java?

2. What is the superclass of the java.lang.Object class?

3. Name three methods that are available in the Object class and describe their usage in brief.

4. What is a hash code? When is it used in Java? What method in the Object class is used to return the hash code of an object?

5. How is the comparison of two objects performed using the == operator?

6. What method of the Object class must be overridden in your class if you want to compare objects of your class for equality based on their state, not their references?

7. What is the default implementation of the equals() method in the Object class?

8. Is the following statement true in Java?

   If two objects are equal according to the equals(Object) method, then calling the hashCode method on each of the two objects must produce the same integer result.

9. If your class overrides the equals() method of the Object class, which other method of the Object class should also be overridden by your class?

10. What is the cloning of objects in Java? What are shallow and deep cloning?

11. What method of the Object class do you need to override in your class to allow cloning of objects of your class? Create a Phone class with two fields as shown:

```
// Phone.java
package com.jdojo.object.excercise;

public class Phone {
    private String areaCode;
    private String number;
}
```

Implement the clone() method in the Phone class, so the Phone objects can be cloned correctly. Both instance variables in the class are required.

12. What method of the Object class do you need to override to provide a string representation of objects of your class? Enhance the Phone class by implementing the toString() method.

13. What is the use of the finalize() method in a class? Should you use the finalize() method to clean up resources held by objects of your class?

14. What is an immutable object and an immutable class? What are the benefits of using immutable objects? Name one immutable class in Java that you use very often.

15. Use the methods of the Objects class to implement the hashCode() method and other methods of the Phone class. For example, use the requireNonNull() method of the Objects class inside the constructors and methods of the Phone class to validate arguments' values.

16. Write the missing pieces of the following snippet of code that will print the simple name and the fully qualified name of the Phone class:

```
Phone p = new Phone();
Class cls = /* your code goes here */;
String simpleName = cls./* your code goes here */;
String fullyQualifedName = cls./* your code goes here */;
System.out.println("Simple class name: " + simpleName);
System.out.println("Fully qualified name: " + fullyQualifedName);
```

CHAPTER 12

Wrapper Classes

In this chapter, you will learn:

- About the wrapper classes in Java and how to use them

- How to get primitive values from strings

- How primitive values are automatically boxed into wrapper objects when needed

- How wrapper objects are automatically unboxed into primitive values when needed

All classes in this chapter are a member of a jdojo.wrapper module, as declared in Listing 12-1.

Listing 12-1. The Declaration of a jdojo.wrapper Module

```
// module-info.java
module jdojo.wrapper {
    exports com.jdojo.wrapper;
}
```

Wrapper Classes

In previous chapters, you learned that primitive and reference types are not assignment compatible. You cannot even compare a primitive value with an object reference. Some parts of the Java library work only with objects; for example, collections in Java work only with objects. You cannot create a list of primitive values, such as 1, 3, 8, and 10. You need to wrap the primitive values into objects before you can store them in a list or set.

The assignment incompatibility between primitive values and reference values has existed in Java since its first release. The Java library provided eight classes in the java.lang package to represent each of the eight primitive types. These classes are called *wrapper classes,* as they wrap a primitive value in an object. Table 12-1 lists the primitive types and their corresponding wrapper classes. Notice the names of the wrapper classes. Following the Java convention for naming classes, they start with an uppercase letter.

Table 12-1. *List of Primitive Types and Their Corresponding Wrapper Classes*

Primitive Type	Wrapper Class
byte	Byte
short	Short
int	Integer
long	Long
float	Float
double	Double
char	Character
boolean	Boolean

All wrapper classes are immutable. They provide three ways to create their objects:

- Using constructors.

- Using the valueOf() factory methods.

- Using parseXxx() method, where Xxx is the name of the wrapper class. It is not available in the Character class.

▓ **Tip** All constructors in all wrapper classes have been deprecated since Java SE 9, as they were rarely needed to create wrapper objects. You should use other ways, such as the valueOf() and parseXxx() methods, to create their objects instead.

Each wrapper class, except Character, provides at least two constructors: one takes a value of the corresponding primitive type and another takes a String. The Character class provides only one constructor that takes a char. The following snippet of code creates objects of a few wrapper classes using their constructors:

```
// Creates an Integer object from an int
Integer intObj1 = new Integer(100);

// Creates an Integer object from a String
Integer intObj2 = new Integer("1969");

// Creates a Double object from a double
Double doubleObj1 = new Double(10.45);

// Creates a Double object from a String
Double doubleObj2 = new Double("234.60");

// Creates a Character object from a char
Character charObj1 = new Character('A');
```

```
// Creates a Boolean object from a boolean
Boolean booleanObj1 = new Boolean(true);

// Creates Boolean objects from Strings
Boolean booleanTrue = new Boolean("true");
Boolean booleanFalse = new Boolean("false");
```

The preferred way to create objects of wrapper classes is to use their valueOf() static methods. The following snippet of code creates objects of a few wrapper classes using their valueOf() methods:

```
Integer intObj1 = Integer.valueOf(100);
Integer intObj2 = Integer.valueOf("1969");
Double doubleObj1 = Double.valueOf(10.45);
Double doubleObj2 = Double.valueOf("234.60");
Character charObj1 = Character.valueOf('A');
```

Use of the valueOf() method to create objects for integer numeric values (byte, short, int, and long) results in better memory usage, as this method caches some objects for reuse. The wrapper classes for these primitive types cache wrapper objects for primitive values between -128 and 127. For example, if you call Integer.valueOf(25) multiple times, the reference of the same Integer object from the cache is returned. However, when you call new Integer(25) multiple times, a new Integer object is created for each call. Listing 12-2 demonstrates the difference in using constructors and valueOf() methods for the Integer wrapper class.

Listing 12-2. The Difference Between Using Constructors and the valueOf() Method to Create Integer Objects

```
// CachedWrapperObjects.java
package com.jdojo.wrapper;

public class CachedWrapperObjects {
    public static void main(String[] args) {
        System.out.println("Using the constructor:");

        // Create two Integer objects using constructors
        Integer iv1 = new Integer(25);
        Integer iv2 = new Integer(25);
        System.out.println("iv1 = " + iv1 + ", iv2 = " + iv2);

        // Compare iv1 and iv2 references
        System.out.println("iv1 == iv2: " + (iv1 == iv2));

        // Let's see if they are equal in values
        System.out.println("iv1.equals(iv2): " + iv1.equals(iv2));

        System.out.println("\nUsing the valueOf() method:");

        // Create two Integer objects using the valueOf()
        Integer iv3 = Integer.valueOf(25);
        Integer iv4 = Integer.valueOf(25);
        System.out.println("iv3 = " + iv3 + ", iv4 = " + iv4);
```

441

```
        // Compare iv3 and iv4 references
        System.out.println("iv3 == iv4: " + (iv3 == iv4));

        // Let's see if they are equal in values
        System.out.println("iv3.equals(iv4): " + iv3.equals(iv4));
    }
}
```

```
Using the constructor:
iv1 = 25, iv2 = 25
iv1 == iv2: false
iv1.equals(iv2): true

Using the valueOf() method:
iv3 = 25, iv4 = 25
iv3 == iv4: true
iv3.equals(iv4): true
```

Notice that iv1 and iv2 are references to two different objects, as iv1 == iv2 returns false. However, iv3 and iv4 are references to the same object, as iv3 == iv4 returns true. Of course, iv1, iv2, iv3, and iv4 represent the same primitive value of 25, as indicated by the returned value from the equals() method. Typically, programs use smaller integer literals. If you are wrapping bigger integers, the valueOf() method creates a new object every time it is called.

▓ **Tip**   The new operator always creates a new object. If you do not need new objects of the primitive values, use the valueOf() factory method of the wrapper class instead of using the constructors. The equals() methods in the wrapper classes have been reimplemented to compare the wrapped primitive values in wrapper objects, not their references.

Numeric Wrapper Classes

Byte, Short, Integer, Long, Float, and Double classes are numeric wrapper classes. They are all inherited from the Number class. The Number class is declared abstract. You cannot create an object of the Number class. However, you can declare reference variables of the Number class. You can assign an object reference of any of the six numeric wrapper classes to a reference of the Number class.

The Number class contains six methods. They are named xxxValue(), where xxx is the name of one of the six primitive data types (byte, short, int, long, float, and double). The return type of the methods is the same as xxx. That is, the byteValue() method returns a byte, the intValue() method returns an int, etc. The following snippet of code shows how to retrieve different primitive type values from a numeric wrapper object:

```
// Creates an Integer object
Integer intObj = Integer.valueOf(100);

// Gets byte from Integer
byte b = intObj.byteValue();
```

```
// Gets double from Integer
double dd = intObj.doubleValue();
System.out.println("intObj = " + intObj);
System.out.println("byte from intObj = " + b);
System.out.println("double from intObj = " + dd);

// Creates a Double object
Double doubleObj = Double.valueOf("329.78");

// Gets different types of primitive values from Double
double d = doubleObj.doubleValue();
float f = doubleObj.floatValue();
int i = doubleObj.intValue();
long l = doubleObj.longValue();

System.out.println("doubleObj = " + doubleObj);
System.out.println("double from doubleObj = " + d);
System.out.println("float from doubleObj = " + f);
System.out.println("int from doubleObj = " + i);
System.out.println("long from doubleObj = " + l);
```

```
intObj = 100
byte from intObj = 100
double from intObj = 100.0
doubleObj = 329.78
double from doubleObj = 329.78
float from doubleObj = 329.78
int from doubleObj = 329
long from doubleObj = 329
```

Java 8 added some methods like sum(), max(), and min() in some of the numeric wrapper classes such as Integer, Long, Float, and Double. For example, Integer.sum(10, 20) simply returns the result of 10 + 20. At first, you might think, "Did the wrapper class designers not have any useful things to do instead of adding these trivial methods? Did we forget using the addition operator + to add two numbers, so we will use the Integer.sum(10, 20)?" Your assumption is wrong. These methods have been added for a greater purpose. They are not intended to be used as Integer.sum(10, 20). Their references are used in lambda expressions working with collections. I cover them in the lambda expression discussion in Chapter 5 of the second volume of this series.

Your program may receive numbers as strings. You may want to obtain primitive values or wrapper objects from those strings. Sometimes the integer values in a string may be encoded in different bases (also called radix), for example, decimal, binary, hexadecimal, etc. Wrapper classes help in working with strings containing primitive values.

- Use the valueOf() methods to convert strings into wrapper objects.

- Use the parseXxx() methods to convert strings into primitive values

The Byte, Short, Integer, Long, Float, and Double classes contain parseByte(), parseShort(), parseInt(), parseLong(), parseFloat() and parseDouble() methods to parse strings into primitive values, respectively.

The following snippet of code converts a string containing an integer in binary format into an Integer object and an int value:

```
String str = "01111111";
int radix = 2;

// Creates an Integer object from the string
Integer intObject = Integer.valueOf(str, radix);

// Extracts the int value from the string
int intValue = Integer.parseInt(str, 2);

System.out.println("str = " + str);
System.out.println("intObject = " + intObject);
System.out.println("intValue = " + intValue);
```

```
str = 01111111
intObject = 127
intValue = 127
```

Java 9 added a few methods in the Integer and Long classes to parse a string whose contents are not all integers. The following is a list of such methods in the Integer class. Method names in the Long class end with Long and return long. All these methods throw a NumberFormatException.

- int parseInt(CharSequence s, int beginIndex, int endIndex, int radix)
- int parseUnsignedInt(CharSequence s, int beginIndex, int endIndex, int radix)
- int parseUnsignedInt(String s)
- int parseUnsignedInt(String s, int radix)

The new version of the parseInt() method parses the CharSequence argument (such as a String) as a signed int in the specified radix, beginning at the specified beginIndex and extending to endIndex - 1. The following snippet of code shows you how to use the new parseInt() method to extract year, month, and day values as integers from a date in a string, which is in the yyyy-mm-dd format.

```
String dateStr = "2017-07-29";
int year = Integer.parseInt(dateStr, 0, 4, 10);
int month = Integer.parseInt(dateStr, 5, 7, 10);
int day = Integer.parseInt(dateStr, 8, 10, 10);

System.out.println("Year = " + year);
System.out.println("Month = " + month);
System.out.println("Day = " + day);
```

```
Year = 2017
Month = 7
Day = 29
```

The three versions of the parseInt() method parse strings as signed integers, whereas the three versions of the parseUnsignedInt() method parse digits in a string as an unsigned integer in the specified radix.

All numeric wrapper classes contain several useful constants. Their MIN_VALUE and MAX_VALUE constants represent the minimum and maximum values that can be represented by their corresponding primitive type. For example, the Byte.MIN_VALUE constant is -128 and the Byte.MAX_VALUE constant is 127, which are the minimum and maximum values that can be stored in a byte. They also have a SIZE constant that represents the size in bits that a variable of the corresponding primitive type occupies. For example, Byte.SIZE is 8 and Integer.SIZE is 32.

Typically, you receive strings from external sources, for example, a file. If strings cannot be converted to numbers, wrapper classes will throw a NumberFormatException. It is common to place the string parsing logic inside a try-catch block and handle the exceptions.

The following snippet of code attempts to parse two strings into double values. The first string contains a valid double and the second one contains an invalid double. A NumberFormatException is thrown when the parseDouble() method is called to parse the second string.

```
String str1 = "123.89";
try {
    double value1 = Double.parseDouble(str1);
    System.out.println("value1 = " + value1);
} catch (NumberFormatException e) {
    System.out.println("Error in parsing " + str1);
}

String str2 = "78H.90"; // An invalid double
try {
    double value2 = Double.parseDouble(str2);
    System.out.println("value2 = " + value2);
} catch (NumberFormatException e) {
    System.out.println("Error in parsing " + str2);
}
```

```
value1 = 123.89
Error in parsing 78H.90
```

░ **Note**   The java.math package contains the BigDecimal and BigInteger classes. They are used to hold big decimal and integer numbers, which do not fit into the primitive types double and long. These classes are mutable and they are typically not called wrapper classes. Use them if you perform computations on big numbers and you do not want to lose intermediate values that exceed the standard primitive type range.

The Character Wrapper Class

An object of the Character class wraps a char value. The class contains several constants and methods that are useful while working with characters. For example, it contains isLetter() and isDigit() methods to check if a character is a letter and a digit. The toUpperCase() and toLowerCase() methods convert a character to uppercase and lowercase. It is worth exploring the API documentation for this class.

The class provides a constructor and a factory valueOf() method to create objects from a char. Use the factory method for better performance. The charValue() method returns the char that the object wraps. The following snippet of code shows how to create Character objects and how to use some of their methods:

```
// Using the constructor
Character c1 = new Character('A');

// Using the factory method - preferred
Character c2 = Character.valueOf('2');
Character c3 = Character.valueOf('ñ');

// Getting the wrapped char values
char cc1 = c1.charValue();
char cc2 = c2.charValue();
char cc3 = c3.charValue();

System.out.println("c1 = " + c1);
System.out.println("c2 = " + c2);
System.out.println("c3 = " + c3);

// Using some Character class methods on c1
System.out.println("isLowerCase c1  = " + Character.isLowerCase(cc1));
System.out.println("isDigit c1  = " + Character.isDigit(cc1));
System.out.println("isLetter c1  = " + Character.isLetter(cc1));
System.out.println("Lowercase of c1  = " + Character.toLowerCase(cc1));

// Using some Character class methods on c2
System.out.println("isLowerCase c2  = " + Character.isLowerCase(cc2));
System.out.println("isDigit c2  = " + Character.isDigit(cc2));
System.out.println("isLetter c2  = " + Character.isLetter(cc2));
System.out.println("Lowercase of c2  = " + Character.toLowerCase(cc2));

System.out.println("Uppercase of c3  = " + Character.toUpperCase(cc3));
```

```
c1 = A
c2 = 2
c3 = ñ
isLowerCase c1  = false
isDigit c1  = false
isLetter c1  = true
Lowercase of c1  = a
isLowerCase c2  = false
isDigit c2  = true
isLetter c2  = false
Lowercase of c2  = 2
Uppercase of c3  = Ñ
```

The Boolean Wrapper Class

An object of the Boolean class wraps a boolean. Boolean.TRUE and Boolean.FALSE are two constants of the Boolean type that represent boolean true and false values. You can create a Boolean object using the constructors or the valueOf() factory method. When parsing a string, this class treats "true" (ignoring the case of all characters) as the true and any other strings as the false. Use the valueOf() method of this class to create a Boolean object as much as possible because it returns the Boolean.TRUE or Boolean.FALSE constant instead of creating new objects. The following snippet of code shows how to use the Boolean class. The variable name in each statement indicates the type of boolean value (true or false) represented in the Boolean object.

```
// Using constructors
Boolean b11True = new Boolean(true);
Boolean b21True = new Boolean("true");
Boolean b31True = new Boolean("tRuE");
Boolean b41False = new Boolean("false");
Boolean b51False = new Boolean("how is this"); // false

// Using the factory methods
Boolean b12True = Boolean.valueOf(true);
Boolean b22True = Boolean.valueOf("true");
Boolean b32True = Boolean.valueOf("tRuE");
Boolean b42False = Boolean.valueOf("false");
Boolean b52False = Boolean.valueOf("how is this"); // false

// Getting a boolean value from a Boolean object
boolean bbTrue = b12True.booleanValue();

// Parsing strings to boolean values
boolean bTrue = Boolean.parseBoolean("true");
boolean bFalse = Boolean.parseBoolean("This string evaluates to false");

// Using constants
Boolean bcTrue   = Boolean.TRUE;
Boolean bcFalse = Boolean.FALSE;

// Printing some Boolean objects
System.out.println("bcTrue = " + bcTrue);
System.out.println("bcFalse = " + bcFalse);
```

```
bcTrue = true
bcFalse = false
```

Unsigned Numeric Operations

Java does not support unsigned primitive integer data types. The byte, short, int, and long are signed data types. For a signed data type, half of the range of values is used for storing positive numbers and half for negative numbers, as one bit is used to store the sign of the value. For example, a byte takes 8 bits; its range is -128 to 127. If you were to store only positive numbers in a byte, its range would have been 0 to 255.

Java 8 added a few static methods in wrapper classes that support operations treating the bits in the signed values as if they are unsigned integers. The Byte class contains two static methods:

- `int toUnsignedInt(byte x)`

- `long toUnsignedLong(byte x)`

The methods convert the specified byte argument into an `int` and a `long` as if the byte stores an unsigned value. If the specified byte argument is zero or a positive number, the converted `int` and `long` values will be the same as the argument value. If the argument is a negative number, the converted number will be $2^8 + x$. For example, for an input of 10, the returned value will be 10, and for an input of -10, the returned value will be $2^8 + (-10)$, which is 246. Negative numbers are stored in 2's complement form. The value -10 will be stored as 11110110. The most significant bit 1 indicates that it is a negative number. The 2's complement of the first seven bits (1110110) would be 001010, which is 10 in decimal. If you consider the actual bits, 11110110, in a byte as an unsigned integer, its value is 246 (128 + 64 + 32 + 16 + 0 + 4 + 2 + 0). The following snippet of code shows how to get the value stored in a byte as an unsigned integer:

```
byte b = -10;
int x = Byte.toUnsignedInt(b);
System.out.println("Signed value in byte = " + b);
System.out.println("Unsigned value in byte = " + x);
```

```
Signed value in byte = -10
Unsigned value in byte = 246
```

The Short class contains the same two methods as the Byte class, except they take a `short` as an argument and convert it to an `int` and a `long`. Java 9 added a new static method, `compareUnsigned(short x, short y)`, to the Short class, which compares two short values numerically treating the values as unsigned. It returns 0 if x is equal to y; a value less than 0 if x is less than y as unsigned values; and a value greater than 0 if x is greater than y as unsigned values.

The Integer class contains the following static methods to support unsigned operations and conversions:

- `int compareUnsigned(int x, int y)`

- `int divideUnsigned(int dividend, int divisor)`

- `int parseUnsignedInt(String s)`

- `int parseUnsignedInt(String s, int radix)`

- `int remainderUnsigned(int dividend, int divisor)`

- `long toUnsignedLong(int x)`

- `String toUnsignedString(int i)`

- `String toUnsignedString(int i, int radix)`

Notice that the Integer class does not contain `addUnsigned()`, `subtractUnsigned()`, and `multiplyUnsigned()` methods as the three operation are bitwise identical on two signed and two unsigned operands. The following snippet of code shows the division operation on two `int` variables as if their bits represent unsigned values:

```
// Two negative ints
int x = -10;
int y = -2;
```

```
// Performs signed division
System.out.println("Signed x = " + x);
System.out.println("Signed y = " + y);
System.out.println("Signed x/y = " + (x/y));

// Performs unsigned division by treating x and y holding unsigned values
long ux = Integer.toUnsignedLong(x);
long uy = Integer.toUnsignedLong(y);
int uQuotient = Integer.divideUnsigned(x, y);
System.out.println("Unsigned x = " + ux);
System.out.println("Unsigned y = " + uy);
System.out.println("Unsigned x/y = " + uQuotient);
```

```
Signed x = -10
Signed y = -2
Signed x/y = 5
Unsigned x = 4294967286
Unsigned y = 4294967294
Unsigned x/y = 0
```

The Long class contains methods to perform unsigned operations. The methods are similar to the ones in the Integer class. Note that you cannot convert the value stored in a long to an unsigned value as you would need a bigger storage than provided by the long data type to do so, but long is the biggest integer data type provided by Java. This is the reason that the Byte and Short classes have toUsignedInt() and toUnSignedLong() methods, as int and long are bigger than byte and short. In fact, to store the value of a signed data type X as an unsigned value in a signed data type Y, the size of the data type Y needs to be at least twice as big as that of X. Following this storage requirement, there is a toUnsignedLong() method in the Integer class, but no such method exists in the Long class.

Autoboxing and Unboxing

Autoboxing and unboxing are used to automatically convert values between primitive data types and their corresponding wrapper classes. They are implemented completely in the compiler. Before we define autoboxing/unboxing, let's discuss an example. The example is trivial, but it serves the purpose of demonstrating the pain you had to go through before autoboxing was added in Java 5, when you were working with conversion between primitive types to their wrapper objects and vice versa.

Suppose you have a method that accepts two int values, adds them, and returns an int value. You might say, "What is the big deal about this method?" It should be as simple as the following:

```
// Only method code is shown
public static int add(int a, int b) {
    return a + b;
}
```

The method can be used as follows:

```
int a = 200;
int b = 300;
int result = add(a, b); // result will get a value of 500
```

And you are right that there is no big deal about this method at all. Let's add a bit of a twist to the logic. Think about the same method working with Integer objects instead of int values. Here is the code for the same method:

```
public static Integer add(Integer a, Integer b) {
    int aValue = a.intValue();
    int bValue = b.intValue();
    int resultValue = aValue + bValue;
    Integer result = new Integer(resultValue);

    return result;
}
```

Did you notice the complexity that is involved when you changed the same method to use Integer objects? You had to perform three things to add two int values in the Integer objects.

- Unwrap the methods arguments, a and b, from Integer objects to int values using their intValue() method.

  ```
  int aValue = a.intValue();
  int bValue = b.intValue();
  ```

- Perform an addition of two int values.

  ```
  int resultValue = aValue + bValue;
  ```

- Wrap the result into a new Integer object and return the result.

  ```
  Integer result = Integer.valueOf(resultValue);
  return result;
  ```

Listing 12-3 has the complete code to demonstrate the use of the add() method.

Listing 12-3. Adding Two int Values Using Integer Objects

```
// MathUtil.java
package com.jdojo.wrapper;

public class MathUtil {
    public static Integer add(Integer a, Integer b) {
        int aValue = a.intValue();
        int bValue = b.intValue();
        int resultValue = aValue + bValue;
        Integer result = Integer.valueOf(resultValue);
        return result;
    }

    public static void main(String[] args) {
        int iValue = 200;
        int jValue = 300;
        int kValue;
        /* will hold result as int */
```

```
        // Box iValue and jValue into Integer objects
        Integer i = Integer.valueOf(iValue);
        Integer j = Integer.valueOf(jValue);

        // Store returned value of the add() method in an Integer object k
        Integer k = MathUtil.add(i, j);

        // Unbox Integer object's int value into kValue int variable
        kValue = k.intValue();

        // Display the result using int variables
        System.out.println(iValue + " + " + jValue + " = " + kValue);
    }
}
```

```
200 + 300 = 500
```

Note the amount of code needed just to add two int values. Wrapping/unwrapping an int value to an Integer and vice versa is a pain for Java developers. Java designers realized it (though too late) and they automated this wrapping and unwrapping process for you.

The automatic wrapping from a primitive data type (byte, short, int, long, float, double, char, and boolean) to its corresponding wrapper object (Byte, Integer, Long, Float, Double, Character, and Boolean) is called *autoboxing*. The reverse, unwrapping from wrapper object to its corresponding primitive data type value, is called *unboxing*. With autoboxing/unboxing, the following code is valid:

```
Integer n = 200; // Boxing
int a = n;       // Unboxing
```

The compiler will replace the previous statement with the following:

```
Integer n = Integer.valueOf(200);
int a = n.intValue();
```

The code in the main() method of the MathUtil class listed in Listing 12-3 can be rewritten as follows. The boxing and unboxing are done for you automatically.

```
int iValue = 200;
int jValue = 300;
int kValue = MathUtil.add(iValue, jValue);
System.out.println(iValue + " + " + jValue + " = " + kValue);
```

⬛ **Tip**   Autoboxing/unboxing is performed when you compile the code. The JVM is completely unaware of the boxing and unboxing performed by the compiler.

Beware of Null Values

Autoboxing/unboxing saves you from writing additional lines of code. It also makes your code look neater. However, it does come with some surprises. One of the surprises is getting a NullPointerException where you would not expect it to happen. Primitive types cannot have a null value assigned to them, whereas reference types can have a null value. The boxing and unboxing happens between primitive types and reference types. Look at the following snippet of code:

```
Integer n = null; // n can be assigned a null value
int a = n;        // will throw NullPointerException at run time
```

In this snippet of code, suppose you do not control the assignment of null to n. You might get a null Integer object as a result of a method call, for example, int a = getSomeValue(), where getSomeValue() returns an Integer object. A NullPointerException in such places may be a surprise for you. However, it will happen, because int a = n is converted to int a = n.intValue() and n is null in this case. This surprise is the part of the advantage you get from autoboxing/unboxing and you need to be aware of it.

Overloaded Methods and Autoboxing/Unboxing

You have a few surprises when you call an overloaded method and want to rely on the autoboxing/unboxing feature. Suppose you have two methods in a class.

```
public void test(Integer iObject) {
    System.out.println("Integer=" + iObject);
}

public void test(int iValue) {
    System.out.println("int=" + iValue);
}
```

Suppose you make two calls to the test() method.

```
test(101);
test(new Integer(101));
```

Which of the following will be the output?

```
int=101
Integer=101
```

or

```
Integer=101
int=101
```

The rule for a method invocation that uses autoboxing/unboxing follows a two-step process.

1. If the actual argument being passed is a primitive type (as in test(10)):

   a. Try to find a method with the primitive type argument. If there is no exact match, try widening the primitive type to find a match.

   b. If the previous step fails, box the primitive type and try to find a match.

2. If the actual argument being passed is a reference type (as in test(new Integer(101)):

   a. Try to find a method with the reference type argument. If there is a match, call that method. In this case, a match does not have to be exact. It should follow the subtype and supertype assignment rule.

   b. If the previous step fails, unbox the reference type to the corresponding primitive type and try to find an exact match, or widen the primitive type and find a match.

If you apply these rules to the previous snippet of code, it will print this:

```
int=101
Integer=101
```

Suppose you have the following two test() methods:

```
public void test(Integer iObject) {
    System.out.println("Integer=" + iObject);
}

public void test(long iValue) {
    System.out.println("long=" + iValue);
}
```

What will be printed if you use the following code?

```
test(101);
test(new Integer(101));
```

It will print this:

```
long=101
Integer=101
```

The first call of test(101) will try to find an exact match for an int argument. It does not find a method test(int), so it widens the int data type, finds a match test(long), and calls this method. Suppose you have two test() methods as follows:

```
public void test(Long lObject) {
    System.out.println("Long=" + lObject);
}
```

```
public void test(long lValue) {
    System.out.println("long=" + lValue);
}
```

What will be printed if you execute the following code?

```
test(101);
test(new Integer(101));
```

It will print this:

```
long=101
long=101
```

Are you surprised by looking at this output? Apply the rules that I have listed and you will find that this output followed those rules. The call to test(101) is clear because it widens 101 from int to long and executes the test(long) method. To call test(new Integer(101)), it looks for a method test(Integer) and it does not find one. That is, an Integer is never widened to Long. Therefore, it unboxes the Integer to int and looks for test(int) method, which it does not find. Now, it widens the int and finds test(long) and executes it.

Consider the following three test() methods. I added a test(Number nObject) method in the previous list of methods:

```
public void test(Long lObject) {
    System.out.println("Long=" + lObject);
}

public void test(Number nObject) {
    System.out.println("Number=" + nObject);
}

public void test(long lValue) {
    System.out.println("long=" + lValue);
}
```

What will be printed if you execute the following code?

```
test(101);
test(new Integer(101));
```

It will print the following:

```
long=101
Number=101
```

Are you surprised again by looking at the output? Apply the rules that I have listed. The call to test(101) is clear. To call test(new Integer(101)), it looks for a method test(Integer) and it does not find one. It tries to widen the Integer argument to a Number or an Object per rule 2(a) in the list of rules.

Recall that all numeric wrapper classes are inherited from the Number class. So, an Integer can be assigned to a Number type variable. It finds a match in the second test(Number nObject) method and executes it.

I have one more surprise for you. Consider the following two test() methods:

```
public void test(Long lObject) {
    System.out.println("Long=" + lObject);
}

public void test(Object obj) {
    System.out.println("Object=" + obj);
}
```

What will be printed when you execute the following code?

```
test(101);
test(new Integer(101));
```

This time, you will get the following output:

```
Object=101
Object=101
```

Does it make sense? Not really. Here is the explanation. When it calls test(101), it has to box int to an Integer, because there is no match for test(int), even after widening the int value. So, test(101) becomes test(Integer.valueOf(101)). Now it does not find any test(Integer) either. Note that Integer is a reference type and it inherits the Number class, which in turn inherits the Object class. Therefore, an Integer is always an Object, and Java allows you to assign an object of subtype (Integer) to a variable of supertype (Object). This is the reason that the test(Object) is called in this case. The second call, test(new Integer(101)), works the same way. It tries for the test(Integer) method. When it does not find it, the next match for it is test(Object) based on the subtype and supertype assignment rule for reference types.

Comparison Operators and Autoboxing/Unboxing

This section discusses the comparison operations ==, >, >=, <, and <=. Only == (logical equality operator) can be used with both reference types and primitive types. The other operators must be used only with primitive types.

Let's look at the easy ones (>, >=, <, and <=) first. If a numeric wrapper object is used with these comparison operators, it must be unboxed and the corresponding primitive type must be used in the comparison. Consider the following snippet of code:

```
Integer a = 100;
Integer b = 100;
System.out.println("a : " + a);
System.out.println("b : " + b);
System.out.println("a > b: " + (a > b));
System.out.println("a >= b: " + (a >= b));
System.out.println("a < b: " + (a < b));
System.out.println("a <= b: " + (a <= b));
```

```
a : 100
b : 100
a > b: false
a >= b: true
a < b: false
a <= b: true
```

There is no surprise in this output. If you mix the two types, reference and primitive, with these comparison operators, you still get the same results. First, the reference type is unboxed and a comparison with the two primitive types takes place. For example,

```
if (101 > new Integer(100)) {
    // Do something
}
```

is converted to

```
if(101 <= (new Integer(100)).intValue()) {
    // Do something
}
```

Now, let's discuss the == operator and the autoboxing rules. If both operands are primitive types, they are compared as primitive types using a value comparison. If both operands are reference types, their references are compared. In these two cases, no autoboxing/unboxing takes place. When one operand is a reference type and another is a primitive type, the reference type is unboxed to a primitive type and a value comparison takes place. Let's see examples of each type.

Consider the following snippet of code. It is an example of using both primitive type operands for the == operator.

```
int a = 100;
int b = 100;
int c = 505;
System.out.println(a == b); // will print true
System.out.println(a == c); // will print false
```

Consider the following snippet of code:

```
Integer aa = new Integer(100);
Integer bb = new Integer(100);
Integer cc = new Integer(505);
System.out.println(aa == bb); // will print false
System.out.println(aa == cc); // will print false
```

In this snippet of code, no autoboxing/unboxing takes place. Here, aa == bb and aa == cc compare the references of aa, bb, and cc, not their values. Every object created with the new operator has a unique reference. Now, here's a surprise: consider the following snippet of code. This time you are relying on autoboxing.

```
Integer aaa = 100; // Boxing - Integer.valueOf(100)
Integer bbb = 100; // Boxing - Integer.valueOf(100)
Integer ccc = 505; // Boxing - Integer.valueOf(505)
```

```
Integer ddd = 505; // Boxing - Integer.valueOf(505)
System.out.println(aaa == bbb); // will print true
System.out.println(aaa == ccc); // will print false
System.out.println(ccc == ddd); // will print false
```

You used aaa, bbb, ccc, and ddd as reference types. How is aaa == bbb true whereas ccc == ddd false? All right. This time, there is no surprise coming from the autoboxing feature. Rather, it is coming from the Integer.valueOf() method. For all values between -128 and 127, the Integer class caches Integer object references. The cache is used when you call its valueOf() method. For example, if you call Integer.valueOf(100) twice, you get the reference of the same Integer object from the cache that represents the int value of 100. However, if you call Integer.valueOf(n), where n is outside the range –128 to 127, a new object is created for every call. This is the reason that aaa and bbb have the same reference from the cache, whereas ccc and ddd have different references. Byte, Short, Character, and Long classes also cache object references for values in the range –128 to 127.

Collections and Autoboxing/Unboxing

Autoboxing/unboxing helps you work with collections. Collections work only with reference types. You cannot use primitive types in collections. If you want to store primitive types in a collection, you must wrap the primitive value before storing it, and unwrap it after retrieving it. Suppose you have a List and you want to store integers in it. This is how you do it:

```
List list = new ArrayList();
list.add(new Integer(101));
Integer a = (Integer)list.get(0);
int aValue = a.intValue();
```

You are back to square one. The add() and get() methods of the List interface work with Object type, and you had to resort to wrapping and unwrapping the primitive types again. The autoboxing/unboxing may help you in wrapping the primitive type to a reference type, and this code may be rewritten as follows:

```
List list = new ArrayList();
list.add(101);                      // Autoboxing will work here
Integer a = (Integer)list.get(0);
int aValue = a.intValue();
/*int aValue = list.get(0); */    // autounboxing won't compile
```

Because the return type of the get() method is Object, the last statement in this snippet of code would not work. Note that unboxing happens from a primitive wrapper type (such as Integer) to its corresponding primitive type (such as int). If you try to assign an Object reference type to an int primitive type, the autounboxing does not happen. In fact, your code would not even compile, because Object to int conversion is not allowed.

Try the following code:

```
List<Integer> list = new ArrayList<>();
list.add(101); // autoboxing will work
int aValue = list.get(0); // autounboxing will work, too
```

All collection classes are generic. They declare formal type parameters. Specifying the Integer type in angle brackets (<Integer>) while creating the List object tells the compiler that the List will hold an object of only Integer type. This gives the compiler freedom to wrap and unwrap your primitive int values while you work with the List object. Refer to Chapter 4 on generics in the second volume of this series for more details.

Summary

For each primitive data type, Java provides a class to represent values of the primitive data type as objects. Java does not support unsigned primitive numeric data types and unsigned numeric operations. Java 8 added limited support for unsigned operations on primitive data types by adding some methods in the wrapper classes. Java 9 added a few methods in the Integer and Long classes to parse a string as an unsigned integer. Java 9 also added a method in the Short class to compare two short values as unsigned short values.

Java does not allow mixing of primitive type and reference type values in the same expression. It is inconvenient to convert the primitive values to their wrapper objects and vice versa. Java 5 added support for automatically converting the primitive values to wrapper objects and vice versa depending on the context. This feature is called autoboxing/unboxing. For example, it allows assigning an integer 25 to a reference of the Integer object; the compiler automatically boxes the integer 25 in a wrapper object using the expression Integer.valueOf(25).

QUESTIONS AND EXERCISES

1. What are wrapper classes in Java? Name the wrapper classes for the following primitive types: byte, int, long, and char.

2. Using the wrapper class Integer, print the maximum and minimum values of the int data type.

3. What is the name of the superclass of the numeric wrapper classes?

4. Suppose you have a string "1969". Complete the following snippet of code to store the integer value in the string into an int variable and an Integer object.

```
String str = "1969";
int value = /* Your code goes here */;
Integer object = /* Your code goes here */;
```

5. You have a string "7B1", which contains an integer in hexadecimal format. Use the Integer class to parse and store its value in an int variable.

6. Will the following snippet of code compile? If it will, describe the rules/reasons.

```
Integer x = 19;
```

7. You have an integer value of 1969 and you want to print its value in hexadecimal format. Complete the following snippet of code that achieves this:

```
int x = 1969;
String str = Integer./* your code goes here */;
System.out.println("1969 in hex is " + str);
```

8. Why does the following statement not compile

    ```
    Double x = 1969;
    ```

    and the following statement does?

    ```
    double y = 1969;
    ```

    Make sure you understand the reasons behind these statements being invalid and
    valid. Describe how the following statement compiles.

    ```
    Number x = 1969;
    ```

9. What will be the output of the following snippet of code? Explain your answer.

    ```
    Number x = 1969;
    System.out.println(x.getClass().getSimpleName());
    ```

10. What will be the output when the following snippet of code is run?

    ```
    Double x = 128.5;
    System.out.println(x.intValue());
    System.out.println(x.byteValue());
    ```

CHAPTER 13

Exception Handling

In this chapter, you will learn:

- About error handling in Java using exceptions
- How to use `try-catch` blocks to handle exceptions
- How to use `finally` blocks to clean up resources
- The difference between checked and unchecked exceptions
- How to create a new exception type and use it in your program
- How to use auto-closeable resources using a `try-catch-resources` block
- How to access the stack frames of a thread
- How to get the class name of the caller of a method

All classes in this chapter are a member of a `jdojo.exception` module, as declared in Listing 13-1.

Listing 13-1. The Declaration of a jdojo.exception Module

```
// module-info.java
module jdojo.exception {
    exports com.jdojo.wrapper;
}
```

What Is an Exception?

An *exception* is a condition that may arise during the execution of a Java program when a normal path of execution is not defined. For example, a Java program may encounter a numeric expression that attempts to divide an integer by zero. Such a condition may occur during the execution of the following snippet of code:

```
int x = 10, y = 0, z;
z = x / y; // Divide-by-zero
```

The statement z = x / y attempts to divide x by y. Because y is zero, the result of x / y is not defined in Java. Note that dividing a floating-point number by zero, for example 9.5 / 0.0, is defined and it is infinity. In generic terms, the abnormal condition, such as dividing an integer by zero, can be phrased as follows:

An error occurs when a Java program attempts to divide an integer by zero.

The Java programming language describes the previous error condition differently. In Java, it is said:

An exception is thrown when a Java program attempts to divide an integer by zero.

Practically, both statements mean the same thing. They mean that an abnormal condition in a program has occurred. What happens after the abnormal condition occurs in a program? You need to handle such an abnormal condition. One of the ways to handle it is to check for all possibilities that may lead to an abnormal condition, before performing the action. You may rewrite the previous code as follows:

```java
int x = 10, y = 0, z;
if (y == 0) {
    // Report the abnormal/error condition here
} else {
    // Perform division here
    z = x / y;
}
```

You may observe that this snippet of code does two things: it handles the error condition and performs the intended action. It mixes the code for performing error handling and the action. One line of code (z = x / y) has bloated to at least five lines of code. This is a simple example. You may not fully realize the real problem when the error handling code is mixed with the actual code performing actions.

To make this problem clear, consider another example. Suppose you want to write Java code that will update an employee's salary. An employee's records are stored in a database. The pseudocode might look as follows:

```
Connect to the database
Fetch the employee record
Update the employee salary
Commit the changes
```

The actual code would perform these four actions. Any of the four actions may result in an error. For example, you may not be able to connect to the database because the database is down; you may not be able to commit the changes because of some validations failed. You need to perform error checking after an action is performed and before the subsequent action is started. The pseudocode with error checking may look as follows:

```
// Connect to the database
if (connected to the database successfully) {
    // Fetch the employee record
    if (employee record fetched) {
        // Update the employee salary
        if (update is successful) {
```

```
    // Commit the changes
    if (commit was successful ) {
        // Employee salary was saved successfully
    } else {
        // An error. Save failed
    }
    } else {
        //An error. Salary could not be updated
    }
} else {
    // An error. Employee record does not exist
}
} else {
    // An error. Could not connect to the database
}
```

Notice that when you added error handling to your four lines of pseudocode, the code bloated to over twenty lines. The worst thing about this code is that the code that performs the action has been cluttered with error-handling code. It has also introduced many nested if-else statements resulting in spaghetti code.

In the last two examples, you saw that the way of handling errors that uses if-else statements is not elegant and maintainable. Java has a better way to handle errors: by separating the code that performs actions from the code that handles errors. In Java, we use the phrase "exception" instead of "error" to indicate an abnormal condition in a program; the phrase "exception handling" is used instead of the phrase "error handling." In general, we say that an error occurs and you handle it. In Java, we say that an exception is thrown and you catch it. This is the reason that *exception handling* is also called *catching an exception*. The code that handles the exception is known as an *exception handler*. You could rewrite the previous pseudocode using Java syntax (not full-fledged Java code, though) as follows:

```
try {
    // Connect to the database
    // Fetch employee record
    // Update employee salary
    // Commit the changes
} catch(DbConnectionException e1){
    // Handle DB Connection exception here
} catch(EmpNotFoundException e2){
    // Handle employee not found exception here
} catch(UpdateFailedException e3){
    // Handle update failed exception here
} catch(CommitFailedException e4){
    // Handle commit failed exception here
}
```

You do not need to understand the previous pseudocode fully. I discuss the details shortly. You need to observe the structure of the code, which allows for separation of the code that performs actions from the code that handles exceptions. The code that performs the actions is placed inside a try block and the code that handles the exception is placed inside a catch block. You will observe that this code is much better in terms of elegance and maintainability compared to the previous attempt in which you had to write many if-else statements to achieve the same effect.

■ **Tip**   In Java, an exception is thrown and caught. Catching an exception is the same as handling the exception. The code that performs the action may throw an exception and the code that handles the exception catches the thrown exception. This style of exception handling allows you to separate the code that performs actions from the code that handles the exceptions that may arise while performing the actions.

An Exception Is an Object

How does the exception handling part of the code know about the exception that occurs in another part of the code? When an exception occurs, Java creates an object with all pieces of information about the exception (e.g., type of exception, line number in the code where the exception occurred, etc.) and passes it to the appropriate exception handler. The term "exception" is used to mean one of two things—the exceptional condition and the Java object to represent the exceptional condition. The meaning of the term will be clear from the context. When we talk about throwing an exception, we are talking about three things.

- Occurrence of an exceptional condition

- Creation of a Java object to represent the exceptional condition

- Throwing (or passing) the exception object to the exception handler

The throwing of an exception is the same as passing an object reference to a method. Here, you may imagine the exception handler as a method that accepts a reference of an exception object. The exception handler catches the exception object and takes appropriate action. You can think of catching an exception by the exception handler as a method call without the return, where the exception object's reference is the actual parameter to the method. Java also lets you create your own object that represents an exception and then throw it.

■ **Tip**   An exception in Java is an object that encapsulates the details of an error in the program.

Using a try-catch Block

Before I discuss the `try-catch` block, let's write a Java program that attempts to divide an integer by zero, as shown in Listing 13-2.

Listing 13-2. A Java Program Attempting to Divide an Integer by Zero

```java
// DivideByZero.java
package com.jdojo.exception;

public class DivideByZero {
    public static void main(String[] args) {
        int x = 10, y = 0, z;
        z = x / y;
        System.out.println("z = " + z);
    }
}
```

```
Exception in thread "main" java.lang.ArithmeticException: / by zero
    at com.jdojo.exception.DivideByZero.main(DivideByZero.java:7)
```

Were you expecting this output from Listing 13-2? It indicates an exception has occurred when you ran the DivideByZero class. The output contains four pieces of information:

- It includes the name of the thread in which the exception occurred. The name of the thread is "main". You can learn about threads and the name of a thread in detail in Chapter 6 of the second volume of this series.

- It includes the type of the exception that has occurred. The type of an exception is indicated by the name of the class of the exception object. In this case, java.lang. ArithmeticException is the name of the class of the exception. The Java runtime creates an object of this class and passes its reference to the exception handler.

- It includes a message that describes the exceptional condition in the code that caused the error. In this case, the message is "/ by zero" (read "divide by zero").

- It includes the location where the exception occurred. The second line in the output indicates that the exception has occurred inside the main() method of the com.jdojo.exception.DivideByZero class. The source code is contained in the DivideByZero.java file. The line number in the source code that caused the exception is 7.

You may notice that in just two lines of output the Java runtime has printed enough pieces of information to help you track down the error in your code.

When z = x / y at line 7 is executed, the Java runtime detects the exceptional condition, which is an attempt to divide an integer by zero. It creates a new object of the class ArithmeticException with all relevant pieces of information about the exception, and then throws (or passes) this object to an exception handler. Who caught (or handled) the exception in this case? You did not specify any exception handler in the code. In fact, you do not even know how to specify an exception handler at this point. Because you did not specify an exception handler in this case, the Java runtime handled the exception for you. Does the Java runtime handle all exceptions that are thrown in a Java program? The answer is yes. The Java runtime handles all exceptions in a Java program. However, it handles an exception only when you do not handle it yourself.

If an exception occurs and the Java runtime does not find a programmer-defined exception handler to handle it, such an exception is called an *uncaught exception*. All uncaught exceptions are handled by the Java runtime. Because an uncaught exception is always handled by the Java runtime, why should you even worry about providing any exception handler in your program? This is an interesting point. Why do you need to worry about doing something that would be done by the Java runtime for you? If you are too lazy to clean up your own mess (handling your own error condition), there is bad news for you. You should not expect too much from the Java runtime. You may not like the way the runtime handles exceptions for you. It catches the uncaught exception, prints the error stack on the standard error, and halts your Java application. In other words, if you let the Java runtime handle all your exceptions, your program stops executing at the point where the exception occurs. Is this what you want to do? The answer is no. Sometimes, after you handle the exception, you may want to proceed with executing the rest of your program rather than halting the program. When you ran the DivideByZero class, the expression x / y in the statement z = x / y resulted in an exception. Java did not finish executing the statement z = x / y. Sometimes this situation is phrased as "The statement z = x / y completed abnormally." The runtime handled the exception, but it stopped executing the whole program. This is the reason that you do not see the output of the following statement in your program:

```
System.out.println("z = " + z);
```

465

Now you know that letting the runtime handle your exception is not always a good idea. If you want to handle exceptions yourself, you need to place your code in a try block. A try block looks like the following:

```
try {
    // Code for the try block goes here
}
```

A try block starts with the keyword try, followed by an opening brace and a closing brace. The code for the try block is placed inside the opening and the closing braces.

A try block cannot be used just by itself. It must be followed by one or more catch blocks, or one finally block, or a combination of both. To handle an exception that might be thrown by the code inside a try block, you need to use a catch block. One catch block can be used to handle multiple types of exceptions. For now, I'll focus on handling only one type of exception in a catch block; I'll cover how to handle multiple exceptions in a catch block in a separate section. The syntax for a catch block is similar to the syntax for a method:

```
catch (ExceptionClassName parameterName) {
    // Exception handling code goes here
}
```

Note that a catch block's declaration is exactly like a method declaration. It starts with the keyword catch, followed by a pair of parentheses. Within the parentheses, you declare a parameter, as you do in a method. The parameter type is the name of the exception class that it is supposed to catch. The parameterName is a user-given name. Parentheses are followed by an opening brace and a closing brace. The exception handling code is placed within the braces. When an exception is thrown, the reference of the exception object is copied to the parameterName. You can use the parameterName to get information from the exception object. It behaves exactly like a formal parameter of a method.

You can associate one or more catch blocks to a try block. The general syntax for a try-catch block is as follows. The following snippet of code shows a try block, which has three catch blocks associated with it. You can associate as many catch blocks to a try block as you want.

```
try {
    // Your code that may throw an exception goes here
} catch (ExceptionClass1 e1){
    // Handle exception of ExceptionClass1 type
} catch (ExceptionClass2 e2){
    // Handle exception of ExceptionClass2 type
} catch (ExceptionClass3 e3){
    // Handle exception of ExceptionClass3 type
}
```

Let's use a try-catch block to handle the possible divide by zero exception in your code. Listing 13-3 shows the complete code.

Listing 13-3. Handling an Exception Using a try-catch Block

```
// DivideByZeroWithTryCatch.java
package com.jdojo.exception;

public class DivideByZeroWithTryCatch {
    public static void main(String[] args) {
        int x = 10, y = 0, z;
```

```java
    try {
        z = x / y;
        System.out.println("z = " + z);
    } catch (ArithmeticException e) {
        // Get the description of the exception
        String msg = e.getMessage();

        // Print a custom error message
        System.out.println("An error has occurred. The error is: " + msg);
    }

    System.out.println("At the end of the program.");
  }
}
```

```
An exception has occurred. The error is: / by zero
At the end of the program.
```

The output of Listing 13-3 is nicer than that of Listing 13-2. It tells you exactly what happened when the program was executed. Notice that the program did not terminate when the exception occurred because you handled the exception. The program executed the last statement that printed the "At the end of the program" message.

Transfer of Control

You need to understand very precisely the flow of control when an exception is thrown in a try block. First, the Java runtime creates an object of the appropriate class to represent the exception that has occurred. The first catch block following the try block is checked. If the exception object can be assigned to the parameter for the catch block, the parameter of the catch block is assigned the reference of the exception object, and the control is transferred to the body of the catch block. When the catch block finishes executing its body, the control is transferred to the point following the try-catch block. It is very important to note that after executing the catch block the control is not transferred back to the try block. Rather, it is transferred to the code that follows the try-catch block. If a try block has many catch blocks associated with it, a maximum of one catch block is executed. Figure 13-1 shows the transfer of control in a typical Java program when an exception occurs in a try block.

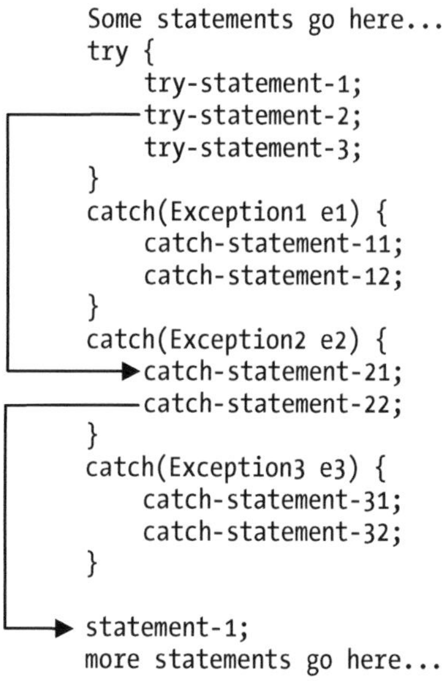

```
    Some statements go here...
    try {
        try-statement-1;
        try-statement-2;
        try-statement-3;
    }
    catch(Exception1 e1) {
        catch-statement-11;
        catch-statement-12;
    }
    catch(Exception2 e2) {
        catch-statement-21;
        catch-statement-22;
    }
    catch(Exception3 e3) {
        catch-statement-31;
        catch-statement-32;
    }

    statement-1;
    more statements go here...
```

Figure 13-1. *Transfer of control when an exception occurs in a try block*

You assume that when try-statement-2 is executed, it throws an exception of type Exception2. When the exception is thrown, the control is transferred to the second catch block, and catch-statement-21 and catch-statement-22 are executed. After catch-statement-22 is executed, control is transferred outside the try-catch block, and statement-1 starts executing. It is very important to understand that try-statement-3 is never executed when try-statement-2 throws an exception. Among three catch blocks, a maximum of one will be executed when a statement inside the try block throws an exception.

Exception Class Hierarchy

The Java class library contains many exception classes. Figure 13-2 shows a few exception classes. Note that the Object class does not belong to the family of exception classes. It is shown in the figure as an ancestor of the Throwable class in the inheritance hierarchy.

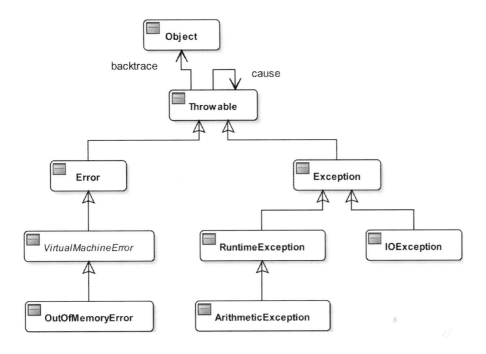

Figure 13-2. *A few classes in the exception class hierarchy*

The exception class hierarchy starts at the java.lang.Throwable class. Recall that the Object class is the superclass for all classes in Java. It is also the superclass of the Throwable class. This is the reason that the figure shows the Object class at the top of the class hierarchy. It is to be emphasized that the Java exception class family starts at the Throwable class, not at the Object class.

When an exception is thrown, it must be an object of the Throwable class or any of its subclasses. The parameter of the catch block must be of type Throwable or one of its subclasses, such as Exception, ArithmeticException, IOException, etc. The following catch blocks are not valid catch blocks because their parameters are not a Throwable or a subclass of Throwable:

```
// A compile-time error. The Object class is not a throwable class.
catch(Object e1) {
}
```

```
// A compile-time error. The String class is not a throwable class.
catch(String e1) {
}
```

The following catch blocks are valid because they specify throwable types as a parameter, which are the Throwable class or its subclasses:

```
// Throwable is a valid exception class
catch(Throwable t) {
}

// Exception is a valid exception class because it is a subclass of Throwable
catch(Exception e) {
}

// IOException class is a valid exception class because it is a subclass of Throwable
catch(IOException t) {

}

// ArithmeticException is a valid exception class because it is a subclass of Throwable
catch(ArithmeticException t) {
}
```

You can also create your own exception classes by inheriting your classes from one of the exception classes. Figure 13-2 shows only a few of the hundreds of exception classes that are available in the Java class library. I discuss how to inherit a class from another class in Chapter 20.

Arranging Multiple catch Blocks

A reference variable of the Object class can refer to any type of object. Assuming AnyClass is a class, the following is a valid statement:

```
Object obj = new AnyClass();
```

The rule behind the previous assignment is that the reference of an object of a class can be assigned to a reference variable of its own type or its superclass. Because the Object class is the superclass (direct or indirect) of all classes in Java, it is valid to assign a reference of any object to a reference variable of the Object class. This assignment rule is not limited to just a reference variable of the Object class. It is applicable to any object. It is stated as follows:

> *A reference variable of class T can refer to an object of class S if S is the same as T or S is a subclass of T. The following statements are always valid in Java assuming S is a subclass of T:*

```
T t1 = new T();
T t2 = new S();
```

This rule implies that any object's reference can be stored in a reference variable of the Object type. You can apply this rule to the exception class hierarchy. Because the Throwable class is the superclass of all exception classes, a reference variable of the Throwable class can refer to an object of any exception class. All of the following statements are valid:

```
Throwable e1 = new Exception();
Throwable e2 = new IOException();
Throwable e3 = new RuntimeException();
Throwable e4 = new ArithmeticException();
```

With this rule of assignment in mind, consider the following try-catch block:

```
try {
    statement1;
    statement2; // Exception of class MyException is thrown here
    statement3;
} catch (Exception1 e1) {
    // Handle Exception1
} catch(Exception2 e2) {
    // Handle Exception2
}
```

When the previous snippet of code is executed, statement2 throws an exception of the MyException type. Suppose the runtime creates an object of MyException as follows:

```
new MyException();
```

Now the runtime selects the appropriate catch block, which can catch the exception object. It starts looking for the appropriate catch clock sequentially, starting from the first catch block that is associated with the try block. The process to check if a catch block can handle an exception is very simple. Take the parameter type and parameter name of the catch block and place them to the left of an assignment operator and place the exception object that is thrown to the right. If the statement thus formed is a valid Java statement, that catch block will handle the exception. Otherwise, the runtime will repeat this check with the next catch block. To check if the first catch block can handle the MyException in the previous snippet of code, Java will form the following statement:

```
// Catch parameter declaration = thrown exception object reference
Exception1 e1 = new MyException();
```

The previous statement is a valid Java statement only if the MyException class is a subclass of the Exception1 class, or MyException and Exception1 are the same class. If the previous statement is valid, the runtime will assign the reference of the MyException object to e1, and then execute the code inside the first catch block. If the previous statement is not a valid statement, the runtime will apply the same check for the second catch block by using the following statement:

```
// Catch parameter declaration = thrown exception object reference
Exception2 e2 = new MyException();
```

If the previous statement is valid, the MyException object is assigned to e2 and the body of the catch block is executed. If the previous statement is not valid, the runtime did not find a matching catch block for the exception thrown in the try block, and then a different execution path is chosen, which I discuss shortly.

Typically, you add a catch block after a try block for every type of exception that can be thrown from the try block. Suppose there is a try block and it can throw three kinds of exceptions, which are represented by three classes—Exception1, Exception2, and Exception3. Suppose Exception1 is the superclass of Exception2, and Exception2 is the superclass of Exception3. The class hierarchy for the three exception classes is shown in Figure 13-3.

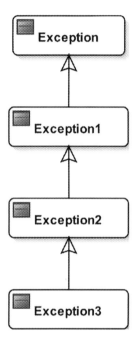

Figure 13-3. *The class hierarchy for Exception1, Exception2, and Exception3 exception classes*

Consider the following try-catch block:

```
try {
    // Exception1, Exception2 or Exception 3 could be thrown here
} catch (Exception1 e1) {
    // Handle Exception1
} catch (Exception2 e2) {
    // Handle Exception2
} catch (Exception3 e3) {
    // Handle Exception3
}
```

If you try to apply the steps to find an appropriate catch block, the previous snippet of code would always execute the first catch block, irrespective of the type of exception thrown (Exception1, Exception2, or Exception3) from the try block. This is because Exception1 is the direct/indirect superclass of Exception2 and Exception3. The previous snippet of code shows a logical mistake made by the developer.

The Java compiler is designed to handle this kind of logical mistake that you might make and it generates a compile-time error. To fix the error, you need to reverse the sequence of these three catch blocks. You must apply the following rule for arranging multiple catch blocks for a try block:

Multiple catch blocks for a try block must be arranged from the most specific exception type to the most generic exception type. Otherwise, a compile-time error occurs. The first catch block should handle the most specific exception type and the last the most generic exception type.

The following snippet of code uses a valid sequence of multiple catch blocks. The ArithmeticException class is a subclass of the RuntimeException class. If both of these exceptions are handled in catch blocks for the same try block, the most specific type, which is ArithmeticException, must appear before the most generic type, which is RuntimeException.

```
try {
    // Do something, which might throw Exception
} catch(ArithmeticException e1) {
    // Handle ArithmeticException first
} catch(RuntimeException e2) {
    // Handle RuntimeException after ArithmeticException
}
```

A Multi-catch Block

You can use a multi-catch block to handle multiple types of exceptions in a single catch block. You can specify multiple exceptions types in a multi-catch block. Multiple exceptions are separated by a vertical bar (|). The following is the syntax:

```
try {
    // May throw ExceptionA, ExceptionB, or ExceptionC
} catch (ExceptionA | ExceptionB | ExceptionC  e) {
    // Handle ExceptionA, ExceptionB, and ExceptionC
}
```

In a multi-catch block, it is not allowed to have alternative exceptions that are related by subclassing. That is, ExceptionA, ExceptionB, and ExceptionC cannot be related by being subclass or superclass of each other. For example, the following multi-catch block is not allowed, because ExceptionA and ExceptionB are subclasses of Throwable. In fact, all exception classes are a direct or indirect subclass of Throwable.

```
try {
    // May throw ExceptionA, ExceptionB, or ExceptionC
} catch (ExceptionA | ExceptionB | Throwable  e) {
    // Handle Exceptions here
}
```

The previous snippet of code will generate the following compile-time error:

```
error: Alternatives in a multi-catch statement cannot be related by subclassing
        } catch(ExceptionA | ExceptionB | Throwable e) {
                                          ^
  Alternative ExceptionA is a subclass of alternative Throwable
1 error
```

Checked and Unchecked Exceptions

Before I start discussing checked and unchecked exceptions, let's look at a Java program that reads a character from the standard input. You have been using the System.out.println() method to print messages on the standard output, which is typically the console. You can use the System.in.read() method to read a byte from the standard input, which is typically the keyboard. It returns the value of the byte as an int between 0 and 255. It returns –1 if the end of input is reached. Listing 13-4 contains the code for a ReadInput class whose readChar() method reads a byte from the standard input and returns the byte as a character. It assumes that the language you are using has all alphabets whose Unicode values are between 0 and 255. The readChar() method has the main code. To read a character from the standard input, you need to use the ReadInput.readChar() method.

Listing 13-4. Reading Input from Standard Input

```java
// ReadInput.java
package com.jdojo.exception;

public class ReadInput {
    public static char readChar() {
        char c = '\u0000';
        int input = System.in.read();
        if (input != -1) {
            c = (char)input;
        }

        return c;
    }
}
```

Compile the ReadInput class. Oops! The compiler generated the following error:

```
"ReadInput.java": unreported exception java.io.IOException; must be caught or declared to be
thrown at line 7, column 31
```

The error is pointing to line 7 in the source code:

```
int input = System.in.read();
```

There is something missing in this statement. The error also tells you that there is an uncaught exception, which must be caught or declared. You know about catching an exception using a try-catch block. However, you probably do not understand how to declare an exception. You will learn about declaring an exception in the next section.

The System.in.read() method invocation may throw a java.io.IOException. The error is telling you to place this method call in a try-catch block, so you can handle the exception. If you do not catch this exception, you need to include in the declaration of the readChar() method that it might throw a java.io.IOException. You learned in the previous sections that the runtime handles all uncaught exceptions. So why can't the Java runtime handle java.io.IOException in this case? Here comes the concept of checked and unchecked exceptions. You need to learn about checked and unchecked exceptions to fully understand this error. Three kinds of exceptional conditions may occur in a Java program:

- In the first category are exceptions that have a higher potential to occur, and you can handle them. For example, when you read from a file, it is more likely that an I/O error may occur. It is better to handle these kinds of exceptions in your program. Classes in the exception class hierarchy (refer to Figure 13-2), which are subclasses of the Exception class, including the Exception class itself and excluding RuntimeException and all its subclasses, fall into this category. If a method or constructor may throw an exception that falls in this category, you must take an appropriate action to handle that exception in your code that calls the method or constructor. What is that "appropriate action" that you need to take to handle these kinds of exceptions? You may take one of the following two actions:

  - You can place the code that can throw the exception in a try-catch block. One of the catch blocks must be capable of handling the type of exception that may be thrown.

  - You can specify in the calling method/constructor declaration that it may throw an exception. You accomplish this by using a throws clause in the method/constructor declaration.

- In the second category are the exceptions that may occur during the course of the execution of a Java program, and there is little you can do to handle it. For example, you will receive a java.lang.OutOfMemeoryError exception when the runtime is out of memory. You cannot do anything to recover from an out of memory error. It is better for you to let the application crash, and then look at ways to manage the memory more efficiently in your program. Classes in the exception class hierarchy (refer to Figure 13-2), which are subclasses of the Error class, and the Error class itself, fall into this category of exception. If a piece of code may throw an exception that falls in this category, the compiler does not insist on taking an action on your part. If an exception of this kind is thrown at runtime, the runtime will handle it for you by displaying a detailed error message and halting the application.

- In the third category are exceptions that may occur at runtime, and you may be able to recover from the exceptional condition if you handle them yourself. There are numerous exceptions in this category. However, if you feel that it is more likely that an exception of this kind may be thrown, you should handle it in your code. If you attempt to handle them by using try-catch blocks, your code tends to get cluttered. Classes in the exception class hierarchy (refer to Figure 13-2), which are subclasses of the RuntimeException class, and the RuntimeException class itself, fall into this category of exception. If a piece of code may throw an exception that falls in this category, the compiler does not insist on taking an action on your part. If an exception of this kind is thrown at runtime, the runtime will handle it for you by displaying a detailed error message and halting the program.

Exceptions in the first category are known as checked exceptions. The `Throwable` class also falls under checked exceptions. The `Throwable` class, the `Exception` class, and subclasses of the `Exception` class, excluding the `RuntimeException` class and its subclasses, are called checked exceptions. They are called checked exceptions because the compiler checks that they are handled in the code.

All exceptions that are not checked exceptions are called unchecked exceptions. The `Error` class, all subclasses of the `Error` class, the `RuntimeException` class, and all its subclasses are unchecked exceptions. They are called unchecked exceptions because the compiler does not check if they are handled in the code. However, you are free to handle them. The program structure for handling a checked or an unchecked exception is the same. The difference between them is in the way the compiler forces (or does not force) you to handle them in the code.

Let's fix the compile-time error for the `ReadInput` class. Now you know that `java.io.IOException` is a checked exception and the compiler will force you to handle it. You will handle it by using a `try-catch` block. Listing 13-5 shows the code for the `ReadInput` class. This time, you have handled the `IOException` in its `readChar()` method and the code will compile fine.

Listing 13-5. A ReadInput Class Whose readChar() Method Reads One Character from the Standard Input

```java
// ReadInput.java
package com.jdojo.exception;

import java.io.IOException;

public class ReadInput {
    public static char readChar() {
        char c = '\u0000';
        int input = 0;
        try {
            input = System.in.read();
            if (input != -1) {
                c = (char)input;
            }
        } catch (IOException e) {
            System.out.print("IOException occurred while reading input.");
        }

        return c;
    }
}
```

How do you use the `ReadInput` class? You can use it the same way you use other classes in Java. You need to call the `ReadInput.readChar()` static method if you want to capture the first character entered by the user. Listing 13-6 contains the code that shows how to use the `ReadInput` class. It prompts the user to enter some text. The first character of the entered text is shown on the standard output.

Listing 13-6. A Program to Test the ReadInput Class

```java
// ReadInputTest.java
package com.jdojo.exception;

public class ReadInputTest {
    public static void main(String[] args) {
        System.out.print("Enter some text and press Enter key: ");
```

```
        char c = ReadInput.readChar();
        System.out.println("First character you entered is: " + c);
    }
}
```

```
Enter some text and press Enter key: Hello
First character you entered is: H
```

Checked Exception: Catch or Declare

If a piece of code may throw a checked exception, you must do one of the following:

- Handle the checked exception by placing the piece of code inside a try-catch block.

- Specify in your method/constructor declaration that it throws the checked exception.

The call to the System.in.read() method in the readChar() method of the ReadInput class (see Listing 13-5) throws a checked exception of the IOException type. You applied the first option in this case and handled the IOException by placing the call to the System.in.read() method in a try-catch block.

Let's assume that you are writing a method m1() for a class that has three statements. Suppose three statements may throw checked exceptions of types Exception1, Exception2, and Exception3, respectively. The code for the method may look as follows:

```
// Will not compile
public void m1() {
    statement-1; // May throw Exception1
    statement-2; // May throw Exception2
    statement-3; // May throw Exception3
}
```

You cannot compile the code for the m1() method in this form. You must either handle the exception using a try-catch block or include in its declaration that it may throw the three checked exceptions. If you want to handle the checked exceptions in the m1() method's body, your code may look as follows:

```
public void m1() {
    try {
        statement-1; // May throw Exception1
        statement-2; // May throw Exception2
        statement-3; // May throw Exception3
    } catch(Exception1 e1) {
        // Handle Exception1 here
    } catch(Exception2 e2) {
        // Handle Exception2 here
    } catch(Exception3 e3) {
        // Handle Exception3 here
    }
}
```

The previous code assumes that when one of the three exceptions is thrown, you do not want to execute the remaining statements.

If you want to use different logic, you might need more than one try-catch block. For example, if your logic states that you must attempt to execute all three statements, even if the previous statement throws an exception, your code would look as follows:

```
public void m1() {
    try {
        statement-1; // May throw Exception1
    } catch(Exception1 e1) {
        // Handle Exception1 here
    }

    try {
        statement-2; // May throw Exception2
    } catch(Exception2 e2) {
        // Handle Exception2 here
    }

    try {
        statement-3; // May throw Exception3
    } catch(Exception3 e3) {
        // Handle Exception3 here
    }
}
```

The second way to get rid of the compile-time error is to specify in the m1() method's declaration that it throws three checked exceptions. This is accomplished by using a throws clause in the m1() method's declaration. The general syntax for specifying a throws clause is as follows:

```
[modifiers] <return-type> <method-name>([paramaters]) [throws <list-of-exceptions>] {
    // Method body goes here
}
```

The keyword throws is used to specify a throws clause. The throws clause is placed after the closing parenthesis of the method's parameters list. The throws keyword is followed by a comma-separated list of exception types. Recall that an exception type is nothing but the name of a Java class, which is in the exception class hierarchy. You can specify a throws clause in the declaration of the m1() method as follows:

```
public void m1() throws Exception1, Exception2, Exception3 {
    statement-1; // May throw Exception1
    statement-2; // May throw Exception2
    statement-3; // May throw Exception3
}
```

You can also mix the two options in the same method when a piece of code throws more than one checked exception. You can handle some of them using a try-catch block and declare some using a throws clause in method's declaration. The following code handles Exception2 using a try-catch block and uses a throws clause to declare exceptions Exception1 and Exception3:

```
public void m1() throws Exception1, Exception3 {
    statement-1; // May throw Exception1

    try {
        statement-2; // May throw Exception2
    } catch(Exception2 e){
        // Handle Exception2 here
    }

    statement-3; // May throw Exception3
}
```

Let's get back to the ReadInput class example. Listing 13-3 fixed the compile-time error by adding a try-catch block. Let's now use the second option: include a throws clause in the readChar() method's declaration. Listing 13-7 contains another version of the ReadInput class, which is called ReadInput2.

Listing 13-7. Using a throws Clause in a Method's Declaration

```
// ReadInput2.java
package com.jdojo.exception;

import java.io.IOException;

public class ReadInput2 {
    public static char readChar() throws IOException {
        char c = '\u0000';
        int input = 0;
        input = System.in.read();
        if (input != -1) {
            c = (char) input;
        }

        return c;
    }
}
```

Listing 13-8 contains the code for a ReadInput2Test class that tests the readChar() method of the ReadInput2 class.

Listing 13-8. Using a throws Clause in a Method's Declaration

```
// ReadInput2Test.java
package com.jdojo.exception;

public class ReadInput2Test {
    public static void main(String[] args) {
        System.out.print("Enter some text and then press Enter key: ");
        char c = ReadInput2.readChar();
        System.out.print("The first character you entered is: " + c);
    }
}
```

Now, compile the ReadInput2Test class. Oops! Compiling the ReadInput2Test class generates the following error:

```
Error(6,11): unreported exception: class java.io.IOException; must be caught or declared to
be thrown
```

The compiler error may not be very clear to you at this point. The readChar() method of the ReadInput2 class declares that it may throw an IOException. The IOException is a checked exception. Therefore, the following piece of code in the main() method of ReadInput2Test may throw a checked IOException:

```
char c = ReadInput2.readChar();
```

Recall the rules about handling the checked exceptions, which I mentioned at the beginning of this section. If a piece of code may throw a checked exception, you must use one of the two options: place that piece of code inside a try-catch block to handle the exception, or specify the checked exception using a throws clause in the method's or constructor's declaration. Now, you must apply one of these two options for the ReadInput2.readChar() method's call in the main() method. Listing 13-9 uses the first option and places the call to ReadInput2.readChar() method inside a try-catch block. Note that you have placed three statements inside the try block, which is not necessary. You needed to place inside the try block only the code that may throw the checked exception.

Listing 13-9. A Program to Test the ReadInput2.readChar() Method

```java
// ReadInput2Test2.java
package com.jdojo.exception;

import java.io.IOException;

public class ReadInput2Test2 {
    public static void main(String[] args) {
        char c = '\u0000';
        try {
            System.out.print("Enter some text and then press Enter key:");
            c = ReadInput2.readChar();
            System.out.println("The first character you entered is: " + c);
        } catch (IOException e) {
            System.out.println("Error occurred while reading input.");
        }
    }
}
```

You can also use the second option to fix the compiler error. Listing 13-10 contains the code using the second option.

Listing 13-10. A Program to Test the ReadInput2.readChar() Method

```java
// ReadInput2Test3.java
package com.jdojo.exception;

import java.io.IOException;

public class ReadInput2Test3 {
    public static void main(String[] args) throws IOException {
```

```
        System.out.print("Enter some text and then press Enter key: ");
        char c = ReadInput2.readChar();
        System.out.println("The first character you entered is: " + c);
    }
}
```

The program includes a throws clause with an IOException for the main() method. Can you run the ReadInput2Test3 class as you have been running other classes using the java command? Yes. You can run the ReadInput2Test3 class the same way you run other classes in Java. The requirement to run a class is that it should include a main() method, which is declared as public static void main(String[] args). The requirement does not specify anything about a throws clause. A main() method, which is used to run a class as a starting point, may or may not contain a throws clause.

Suppose you run the ReadInput2Test3 class and the call to the System.in.read() method in the readChar() method of the ReadInput2 class throws an IOException. How will the IOException be handled and who will handle it? When an exception is thrown in a method body, the runtime checks if the code throwing the exception is inside a try-catch block. If the exception throwing code is inside a try-catch block, the Java runtime looks for the catch block that can handle the exception. If it does not find a catch block that can handle the exception, or the method call is not inside a try-catch block, the exception is propagated up the method call stack. That is, the exception is passed to the caller of the method. In your case, the exception is not handled in the readChar() method of the ReadInput2 class. Its caller is the piece of code in the main() method of the ReadInput2Test2 class. In this case, the same exception is thrown at the point where the ReadInput2.readChar() method call is made inside the ReadInput2Test2.main() method. The runtime applies the same checks to handle the exception. If you run the ReadInput2Test2 class and an IOException is thrown, the runtime finds that the call to ReadInput2.readChar() is inside a try-catch block, which can handle the IOException. Therefore, it will transfer the control to the catch block, which handles the exception, and the program continues in the main() method of the ReadInput2Test2 class. It is very important to understand that the control does not go back to the ReadInput2.readChar() method after it throws an exception and the exception is handled inside the ReadInput2Test2.main() method.

When you run the ReadInput2Test3 class, the call to the ReadInput2.readChar() method is not inside a try-catch block. In this case, the Java runtime will have to propagate the exception up the method call stack. The main() method is the beginning of the method call stack for a Java application. This is the method where all Java applications start. If the main() method throws an exception, the runtime handles it. Recall that if the runtime handles an exception for you, it prints the call stack details on the standard error and exits the application.

Recall that a catch block with an exception type can handle an exception of the same type, or any of its subclass type. For example, a catch block with Throwable exception type is capable of handling all types of exceptions in Java, because the Throwable class is the superclass of all exception classes. This concept is also applicable to the throws clause. If a method throws a checked exception of Exception1 type, you can mention Exception1 type in its throws clause or any of the superclasses of Exception1. The reasoning behind this rule is that if the caller of the method handles an exception that is the superclass of Exception1, the same handler can also handle Exception1.

▪ **Tip** The Java compiler forces you to handle a checked exception either by using a `try-catch` block or by using a `throws` clause in the method or constructor declaration. If a method throws an exception, it should be handled somewhere in the call stack. That is, if a method throws an exception, its caller can handle it, or its caller's caller can handle, and so on. If an exception is not handled by any callers in the call stack, it is known as an uncaught exception (or an unhandled exception). An uncaught exception is finally handled by the Java runtime, which prints the exception stack trace on the standard error and exits the Java application. A different behavior may be specified for uncaught exceptions in a thread. Refer to Chapter 6 on threads in the second volume of this series. for more details on how to specify an exception handler for a thread.

The compiler is very particular about checked exceptions being handled by programmers. If the code in a try block cannot throw a checked exception and its associated catch blocks catch checked exceptions, the compiler will generate an error. Consider the code in Listing 13-11, which uses a try-catch block. The catch block specifies an IOException, which is a checked exception. However, the corresponding try block does not throw an IOException.

Listing 13-11. Catching a Checked Exception That is Never Thrown in the try Block

```
// CatchNonExistentException.java
package com.jdojo.exception;

import java.io.IOException;

// Will not compile
public class CatchNonExistentException {
    public static void main(String[] args) {
        int x = 10, y = 0, z = 0;
        try {
            z = x / y;
        } catch(IOException e) {
            // Handle the exception
        }
    }
}
```

When you compile the code for the CatchNonExistentException class, you would get the following compiler error:

```
Error(12): exception java.io.IOException is never thrown in body of corresponding try
statement
```

The error message is self-explanatory. It states that IOException is never thrown in the try block. Therefore, the catch block must not catch it. One way to fix this error is to remove the try-catch block altogether. Listing 13-12 shows another interesting way (but not a good way) to mention a generic catch block.

Listing 13-12. Catching a Checked Exception That is Never Thrown in the try Block

```java
// CatchNonExistentException2.java
package com.jdojo.exception;

// Will compile fine
public class CatchNonExistentException2 {
    public static void main(String[] args) {
        int x = 10, y = 0, z = 0;
        try {
            z = x / y;
        } catch(Exception e) {
            // Handle the exception
        }
    }
}
```

Exception is also a checked exception type in Java as is IOException. If a catch block should not catch a checked exception unless it is thrown in the corresponding try block, how does the code for CatchNonExistentException2 compile fine? Should it not generate the same compile-time error? At first thought, you are right. It should fail compilation for the same reason the CatchNonExistentException class failed. There are two checked exceptions classes that are exceptions to this rule. Those two exception classes are Exception and Throwable. The Exception class is the superclass of IOException and other exceptions, which are checked exceptions. It is also the superclass of RuntimeException and all subclasses of RuntimeException, which are unchecked exceptions. Recall the rule that a superclass exception type can also handle a subclass exception type. Therefore, you can use the Exception class to handle checked exceptions as well as unchecked exceptions. The rule of checking catch blocks for un-thrown exceptions applies only to checked exceptions. Exception and Throwable classes in a catch block can handle checked as well as unchecked exceptions because they are superclasses of both types. This is the reason that the compiler will let you use these two checked exception types in a catch block, even though the associated try block does not throw any checked exceptions.

■ **Tip**　All rules about the compiler check for exceptions being handled or thrown are applicable only to checked exceptions. Java does not force you to handle the unchecked exceptions in your code. However, you are free to handle them as you feel appropriate to do so.

Checked Exceptions and Initializers

You cannot throw a checked exception from a static initializer. If a piece of code in a static initializer throws a checked exception, it must be handled using a try-catch block inside the initializer itself. The static initializer is called only once for a class, and the programmer does not have a specific point in code to catch it. This is the reason that a static initializer must handle all possible checked exceptions that it may throw.

```
public class Test {
    static {
        // Must use try-catch blocks to handle all checked exceptions
    }
}
```

The rule is different for instance initializers. An instance initializer is called as part of a constructor invocation for the class. It may throw checked exceptions. However, all those checked exceptions must be included in the throws clause of all constructors for that class. This way, the compiler can make sure all checked exceptions are taken care of by programmers when any of the constructors are called. The following code for the Test class assumes that the instance initializer throws a checked exception of a CException type. The compiler will force you to add a throws clause with CException to all constructors of Test.

```
public class Test {
    // Instance initializer
    {
        // Throws a checked exception of type CException
    }

    // All constructors must specify that they throw CException
    // because the instance initializer throws CException
    public Test() throws CException {
        // Code goes here
    }

    public Test(int x) throws CException {
        // Code goes here
    }

    // Rest of the code goes here
}
```

You must handle the CException when you create an object of the Test class using any of its constructors, as follows:

```
Test t = null;
try {
    t = new Test();
} catch (CException e) {
    // Handle the exception here
}
```

If you do not handle the CException using a try-catch block, you must use a throws clause to specify that the method or constructor that uses the constructor of the Test class may throw CException.

If an instance initializer throws a checked exception, you must declare a constructor for your class. The compiler will add a default constructor to your class if you do not add one. However, the compiler will not add a throws clause to the default constructor, which will break the previous rule. The following code will not compile:

```
public class Test123 {
    {
        // May throw CException, which is a checked exception.
    }
}
```

When the Test123 class is compiled, the compiler adds a default constructor, and the class Test123 will look as follows:

```
public class Test123 {
    {
        // May throw CException, which is a checked exception.
    }

    public Test123() {
        // An empty body. The compiler did not add a throws clause.
    }
}
```

Note that the default constructor, which was added by the compiler, does not contain a throws clause to include CException, which is thrown by the instance initializer. This is the reason that the Test123 class will not compile. To make the Test123 class compile, you must add at least one constructor explicitly and use a throws clause to specify that it may throw CException.

Throwing an Exception

A Java exception is not something that is always thrown by the runtime. You can also throw an exception in your code using a throw statement. The syntax for a throw statement is

```
throw <a-throwable-object-reference>;
```

Here, throw is a keyword, which is followed by a reference to a throwable object. A throwable object is an instance of a class, which is a subclass of the Throwable class, or the Throwable class itself. The following is an example of a throw statement, which throws an IOException:

```
// Create an object of IOException
IOException e1 = new IOException("File not found");

// Throw the IOException
throw e1;
```

Recall that the new operator returns the reference of the new object. You can also create a throwable object and throw it in one statement.

```
// Throw an IOException
throw new IOException("File not found");
```

The same rules for handling exceptions apply when you throw an exception in your code. If you throw a checked exception, you must handle it by placing the code in a try-catch block, or by using a throws clause in the method or constructor declaration that contains the throw statement. These rules do not apply if you throw an unchecked exception.

Creating an Exception Class

You can also create your own exception classes. They must extend (or inherit from) an existing exception class. I cover how to extend a class in detail in Chapter 20 on inheritance. This section explains the necessary syntax to extend a class. The keyword extends is used to extend a class as shown:

```
[modifiers] class <class-name> extends <superclass-name> {
    // Body for <class-name> goes here
}
```

Here, <class-name> is your exception class name and <superclass-name>> is an existing exception class name, which is extended by your class.

Suppose you want to create a MyException class, which extends the java.lang.Exception class. The syntax would be as follows:

```
public class MyException extends Exception {
    // Body for MyException class goes here
}
```

How does the body of an exception class look? An exception class is like any other classes in Java. Typically, you do not add any methods to your exception class. Many useful methods that can be used to query an exception object's state are declared in the Throwable class and you can use them without re-declaring them. Typically, you include four constructors to your exception class. All constructors will call the corresponding constructor of its superclass using the super keyword. Listing 13-13 shows the code for a MyException class with four constructors.

Listing 13-13. A MyException Class That Extends the Exception Class

```
// MyException.java
package com.jdojo.exception;

public class MyException extends Exception {
    public MyException() {
        super();
    }

    public MyException(String message) {
        super(message);
    }
```

```
    public MyException(String message, Throwable cause) {
        super(message, cause);
    }

    public MyException(Throwable cause) {
        super(cause);
    }
}
```

The first constructor creates an exception with null as its detailed message. The second constructor creates an exception with a detailed message. The third and fourth constructors let you create an exception by wrapping another exception with/without a detailed message.

You can throw an exception of type MyException as follows:

```
throw new MyException("Your message goes here");
```

You can use the MyException class in a throws clause in a method/constructor declaration or as a parameter type in a catch block. The following snippet of code shows that:

```
import com.jdojo.exception.MyException;
...
public void m1() throws MyException {
    // Code for m1() body goes here
}

try {
    // Code for the try block goes here
} catch(MyException e) {
    // Code for the catch block goes here
}
```

Table 13-1 shows some of the commonly used methods of the Throwable class. Note that the Throwable class is the superclass of all exception classes in Java. All of the methods shown in this table are available in all exception classes.

Table 13-1. *A Partial List of Methods of the Throwable Class*

Method	Description
Throwable getCause()	This method was added in Java 1.4. It returns the cause of the exception. If the cause of the exception is not set, it returns null.
String getMessage()	It returns the detailed message of the exception.
StackTraceElement[] getStackTrace()	This method was added in Java 1.4. It returns an array of stack trace elements. Each element in the array represents one stack frame. The first element of the array represents the top of the stack and the last element of the array represents the bottom of the stack. The top of the stack is the method/constructor where the exception object is created. The object of StackTraceElement class holds information such as class name, method name, file name, line number, etc.
Throwable initCause(Throwable cause)	This method was added in Java 1.4. There are two ways to set an exception as the cause of an exception. One way is to use the constructor, which accepts the cause as a parameter. Another way is to use this method.
void printStackTrace()	It prints the stack trace on the standard error stream. The output prints the description of the exception object itself as the first line and then the description of each stack frame. Printing stack trace for an exception is very useful for the debugging purpose.
void printStackTrace(PrintStream s)	It prints the stack trace to the specified PrintStream object.
void printStackTrace(PrintWriter s)	It prints the stack trace to the specified PrintWriter object.
String toString()	It returns a short description of the exception object. The description of an exception object contains the name of the exception class and the detailed message.

Listing 13-14 demonstrates the use of the printStackTrace() method for an exception class. The main() method calls the m1() method, which in turn calls the m2() method. The stack frame for this call starts with the main() method, which will be at the bottom of the stack. The top of the stack contains the m2() method. The output shows that the printStackTrace() method prints the stack information from top to bottom. Each stack frame contains the name of the class, the method name, the source file name, and the line number. The first line of the printStackTrace() method prints the class name of the exception object with a detailed message.

Listing 13-14. Printing the Stack Trace of an Exception

```
// StackTraceTest.java
package com.jdojo.exception;

public class StackTraceTest {
    public static void main(String[] args) {
        try {
            m1();
        } catch (MyException e) {
```

```
        e.printStackTrace(); // Print the stack trace
    }
}

public static void m1() throws MyException {
    m2();
}

public static void m2() throws MyException {
    throw new MyException("Some error has occurred.");
}
}
```

```
com.jdojo.exception.MyException: Some error has occurred.
        at jdojo.exception/com.jdojo.exception.StackTraceTest.m2(StackTraceTest.java:18)
        at jdojo.exception/com.jdojo.exception.StackTraceTest.m1(StackTraceTest.java:14)
        at jdojo.exception/com.jdojo.exception.StackTraceTest.main(StackTraceTest.java:7)
```

Listing 13-14 demonstrates how to print the stack trace of an exception on the standard error. Sometimes you may need to save the stack trace in a file or in a database. You may need to get the stack trace information as a string in a variable. Another version of the printStackTrace() method lets you do this. Listing 13-15 shows how to use the printStackTrace(PrintWriter s) method to print the stack trace of an exception object to a String object. The program is the same as Listing 13-14 with one difference. It stores the stack trace in a string and then prints that string on the standard output. The method getStackTrace() writes the stack trace to a string and returns that string. Refer to the Chapter 7 of the second volume of this series for more information on how to use the StringWriter and PrintWriter classes.

Listing 13-15. Writing Stack Trace of an Exception to a String

```java
// StackTraceAsStringTest.java
package com.jdojo.exception;

import java.io.StringWriter;
import java.io.PrintWriter;

public class StackTraceAsStringTest {
    public static void main(String[] args) {
        try {
            m1();
        } catch (MyException e) {
            String str = getStackTrace(e);

            // Print the stack trace to the standard output
            System.out.println(str);
        }
    }
```

```
    public static void m1() throws MyException {
        m2();
    }

    public static void m2() throws MyException {
        throw new MyException("Some error has occurred.");
    }

    public static String getStackTrace(Throwable e) {
        StringWriter strWriter = new StringWriter();
        PrintWriter printWriter = new PrintWriter(strWriter);
        e.printStackTrace(printWriter);

        // Get the stack trace as a string
        String str = strWriter.toString();

        return str;
    }
}
```

```
com.jdojo.exception.MyException: Some error has occurred.
    at jdojo.exception/com.jdojo.exception.StackTraceAsStringTest.
    m2(StackTraceAsStringTest.java:24)
    at jdojo.exception/com.jdojo.exception.StackTraceAsStringTest.
    m1(StackTraceAsStringTest.java:20)
    at jdojo.exception/com.jdojo.exception.StackTraceAsStringTest.
    main(StackTraceAsStringTest.java:10)
```

The finally Block

You have seen how to associate one or more catch blocks to a try block. A try block can also have zero or one finally block. A finally block is never used by itself. It is always used with a try block. The syntax for using a finally block is

```
finally {
    // Code for finally block goes here
}
```

A finally block starts with the keyword finally, which is followed by an opening brace and a closing brace. The code for a finally block is placed inside the braces.

There are two possible combinations of try, catch, and finally blocks: try-catch-finally or try-finally. A try block may be followed by zero or more catch blocks. A try block can have a maximum of one finally block. A try block must have a catch block, a finally block, or both. The syntax for a try-catch-finally block is

```
try {
    // Code for try block goes here
} catch(Exception1 e1) {
    // Code for catch block goes here
} finally {
    // Code for finally block goes here
}
```

The syntax for a try-finally block is

```
try {
    // Code for try block goes here
} finally {
    // Code for finally block goes here
}
```

When you use a try-catch-finally block, your intention is to execute the following logic:

Try executing the code in the try block. If the code in the try block throws any exception, execute the matching catch block. Finally, execute the code in the finally block no matter how the code in the try and catch blocks finish executing.

When you use a try-finally block, your intention is to execute the following logic:

Try executing the code in the try block. When the code in the try block finishes, execute the code in the finally block.

░ **Tip**   A finally block is guaranteed to be executed no matter what happens in the associated try and/or catch block. There are two exceptions to this rule: the finally block may not be executed if the thread that is executing the try or catch block dies, or a Java application may exit, for example, by calling System.exit() method inside the try or catch block.

Why do you need to use a finally block? Sometimes you want to execute two sets of statements, say set-1 and set-2. The condition is that set-2 should be executed no matter how the statements in set-1 finish executing. For example, statements in set-1 may throw an exception or may complete normally. You may be able to write the logic, which will execute set-2 after set-1 is executed, without using a finally block. However, the code may not be as clean. You may end up repeating the same code multiple places and writing spaghetti if-else statements. For example, set-1 may use constructs, which make the control jump from one point of the program to another. It may use constructs like break, continue, return, throw, etc. If set-1 has many points of exit, you will need to repeat the call to set-2 before exiting at many places. It is difficult and ugly to write logic that will execute set-1 and set-2. The finally block makes it easy to write this logic. All you need to do is place set-1 code in a try block and the set-2 code in a finally block. Optionally, you can also use catch blocks to handle exceptions that may be thrown from set-1. You can write Java code to execute set-1 and set-2 as follows:

```
try {
    // Execute all statements in set-1
} catch(MyException e1) {
    // Handle any exceptions here that may be thrown by set-1
} finally {
    // Execute statements in set-2
}
```

If you structure your code to execute set-1 and set-2 this way, you get cleaner code with guaranteed execution of set-2 after set-1 is executed.

Typically, you use a finally block to write cleanup code. For example, you may obtain some resources in your program that must be released when you are done with them. A try-finally block lets you implement this logic. Your code structure would look as follows:

```
try {
    // Obtain and use some resources here
} finally {
    // Release the resources that were obtained in the try block
}
```

You write try-finally blocks frequently when you write programs that perform database transactions and file input/output. You obtain and use a database connection in the try block and release the connection in the finally block. When you work with a database-related program, you must release the database connection, which you obtained at the beginning, no matter what happens to the transaction. It is similar to executing statements in set-1 and set-2, as described previously. Listing 13-16 demonstrates the use of a finally block in four different situations.

Listing 13-16. Using a finally Block

```
// FinallyTest.java
package com.jdojo.exception;

public class FinallyTest {
    public static void main(String[] args) {
        int x = 10, y = 0, z;
        try {
            System.out.println("Before dividing x by y.");
            z = x / y;
            System.out.println("After dividing x by y.");
        } catch (ArithmeticException e) {
            System.out.println("Inside catch block - 1.");
        } finally {
            System.out.println("Inside finally block - 1.");
        }

        System.out.println("------------------------------");

        try {
```

```
                System.out.println("Before setting z to 2449.");
                z = 2449;
                System.out.println("After setting z to 2449.");
            } catch (Exception e) {
                System.out.println("Inside catch block - 2.");
            } finally {
                System.out.println("Inside finally block - 2.");
            }

            System.out.println("------------------------------");

            try {
                System.out.println("Inside try block - 3.");
            } finally {
                System.out.println("Inside finally block - 3.");
            }

            System.out.println("------------------------------");

            try {
                System.out.println("Before executing System.exit().");
                System.exit(0);
                System.out.println("After executing System.exit().");
            } finally {
                // This finally block will not be executed
                // because application exits in try block
                System.out.println("Inside finally block - 4.");
            }
        }
}
```

```
Before dividing x by y.
Inside catch block - 1.
Inside finally block - 1.
------------------------------
Before setting z to 2449.
After setting z to 2449.
Inside finally block - 2.
------------------------------
Inside try block - 3.
Inside finally block - 3.
------------------------------
Before executing System.exit().
```

The first try-catch-finally block attempts to perform a divide-by-zero operation on an integer. The expression x / y throws an ArithmeticException and control is transferred to the catch block. The finally block is executed after the catch block finishes. Note that the second message in the try block is not printed because once an exception is thrown, the control jumps to the nearest matching catch block and the control never goes back to the try block again.

The second `try-catch-finally` block is an example where the `try` block finishes normally (without throwing an exception). After the `try` block finishes, the `finally` block is executed.

The third `try-finally` block is simple. The `try` block finishes normally, and then the `finally` block is executed.

The fourth `try-finally` block demonstrates an exceptional case when a `finally` block is not executed. The `try` block exits the application by executing the `System.exit()` method. The application stops executing when the `System.exit()` method is called without executing the associated `finally` block.

Rethrowing an Exception

An exception that is caught can be rethrown. You may want to rethrow an exception for different reasons. One of the reasons could be to take an action after catching it, but before propagating it up the call stack. For example, you may want to log the details about the exception and then rethrow it to the client. Another reason is to hide the exception type/location from the client. You are not hiding the exceptional condition itself from the client. Rather, you are hiding the type of the exceptional condition. You may want to hide the actual exception type from clients for two reasons:

- The client may not be ready to handle the exception that is thrown.

- The exception that is thrown does not make sense to the client.

Rethrowing an exception is as simple as using a `throw` statement. The following code snippet catches the exception, prints its stack trace, and rethrows the same exception. When the same exception object is rethrown, it preserves the details of the original exception.

```
try {
    // Code that might throw MyException
} catch(MyException e) {
    e.printStackTrace(); // Print the stack trace

    // Rethrow the same exception
    throw e;
}
```

When an exception is thrown from a `catch` block, another `catch` block in the same group is not searched to handle that exception. If you want to handle the exception thrown from a `catch` block, you need to enclose the code that throws the exception inside another `try-catch` block. Another way to handle it is to enclose the whole `try-catch` block inside another `try-catch` block. The following snippet of code shows the two ways of arranging nested `try-catch` to handle `Exception1` and `Exception2`. The actual arrangement of nested `try-catch` depends on the situation at hand. If you do not enclose the code that may throw an exception inside a `try` block or the `try` block does not have a matching associated `catch` block that can catch the exception, the runtime will propagate the exception up the call stack provided the method is defined with a `throws` clause.

```
// #1 - Arranging nested try-catch
try {
    // May throw Exception1
} catch(Exception1 e1) {
    // Handle Exception1 here
    try {
        // May throw Exception2
    } catch(Exception2 e2) {
```

```
        // Handle Exception2 here
    }
}

/* #2 - Arranging nested try-catch */
try {       try {       // May throw Exception1
    }     catch(Exception1 e1) {
        // Handle Exception1 here

        // May throw Exception2
    }
} catch(Exception2 e2) {
    // Handle Exception2 here
}
```

The following snippet of code shows how to catch an exception of one type and rethrow an exception of another type:

```
try {
    // Code that might throw a MyException
} catch(MyException e) {
    e.printStackTrace(); // Print the stack trace

    // Rethrow a RuntimeException
    throw new RuntimeException(e.getMessage());
}
```

The catch block catches the MyException, prints its stack trace, and rethrows a RuntimeException. In the process, it loses the details of the original exception that was thrown. When the RuntimeException is created, it packages the information of stack frames from the point where it was created. The client gets the information about the rethrown RuntimeException from the point it was created, not about the original MyException. In the previous code, you have hidden both the type and the location of the original exception from the client.

You can also rethrow another type of exception and use the original exception as the cause of the rethrown exception. It is as if the new exception is a wrapper for the original exception. You can set the cause of an exception using one of the constructors of the new exception type that accepts a cause as a parameter. You can also use the initCause() method to set the cause of the exception. The following snippet of code rethrows a RuntimeException setting MyException as its cause:

```
try {
    // Code that might throw a MyException
} catch(MyException e) {
    e.printStackTrace(); // Print the stack trace

    // Rethrow a RuntimeException using the original exception as its cause
    throw new RuntimeException(e.getMessage(), e);
}
```

You also have the option just to hide the location of the exception from the client when you rethrow an exception. The fillInStackTrace() method of the Throwable class fills in the stack trace information in an exception object from the point where this method is called. You need to call this method on the exception you catch and want to rethrow to hide the location of the original exception. The following snippet of code shows how to rethrow an exception by hiding the location of the original exception:

```
try {
    // Code that might throw MyException
} catch(MyException e) {
    // Re-package the stack frames in the exception object
    e.fillInStackTrace();

    // Rethrow the same exception
    throw e;
}
```

Listing 13-17 demonstrates how to rethrow an exception by hiding the location of the original exception. The MyException is thrown inside the m2() method. The m1() method catches the exception, refills the stack trace, and rethrows it. The main() method receives the exception as if the exception were thrown inside m1(), not inside m2().

Listing 13-17. Rethrowing an Exception to Hide the Location of the Original Exception

```java
// RethrowTest.java
package com.jdojo.exception;

public class RethrowTest {

    public static void main(String[] args) {
        try {
            m1();
        } catch (MyException e) {
            // Print the stack trace
            e.printStackTrace();
        }
    }

    public static void m1() throws MyException {
        try {
            m2();
        } catch (MyException e) {
            e.fillInStackTrace();
            throw e;
        }
    }

    public static void m2() throws MyException {
        throw new MyException("An error has occurred.");
    }
}
```

```
om.jdojo.exception.MyException: An error has occurred.
    at jdojo.exception/com.jdojo.exception.RethrowTest.m1(RethrowTest.java:19)
    at jdojo.exception/com.jdojo.exception.RethrowTest.main(RethrowTest.java:8)
```

Analysis of Rethrown Exceptions

Java 7 improved the mechanism of rethrowing exceptions. Consider the following snippet of code for a method declaration:

```
public void test() throws Exception {
    try {
        // May throw Exception1, or Exception2
    } catch (Exception e) {
        // Rethrow the caught exception
        throw e;
    }
}
```

The try block may throw Exception1 or Exception2. The catch block specifies Exception as its parameter and it rethrows the exception it catches. Prior to Java 7, the compiler sees the catch block throwing an exception of Exception type and it insisted that, in the throws clause, the test() method must specify that it threw an exception of the Exception type or the supertype of the Exception type.

Because the try block can throw exceptions of only Exception1 and Exception2 types, the catch block will rethrow an exception that is always of these two types. Java 7 performs this analysis when an exception is rethrown. It lets you specify the throws clause of the test() method accordingly. Starting Java 7, you can specify more specific exception types, Exception1 and Exception2, in the test() method's throws clause, as follows:

```
public void test() throws Exception1, Exception2 {
    try {
        // May throw Exception1, Exception2 or Exception3
    } catch (Exception e) {
        // Rethrow the caught exception
        throw e;
    }
}
```

Throwing Too Many Exceptions

There is no limit on the number of exception types that a method/constructor can list in its throws clause. However, it is better to keep the number low. The client that uses a method has to deal with all the exceptions that the method may throw in one way or another. It is also important to keep in mind that a method should not throw a new type of exception once it has been designed, implemented, and released to public. If a method starts throwing a new type of exception after its public release, all client code that calls this method must change. It indicates poor design if a method throws too many exceptions or a new exception is added after its public release. You can avoid these issues with your method by catching all lower-level exceptions inside your method and rethrowing a higher-level exception. The exception that you throw may contain the lower-level exception as its cause. Consider the following snippet of code for a method m1() that throws three exceptions (Exception1, Exception2, and Exception3):

```
public void m1() throws Exception1, Exception2, Exception3 {
    // Code for m1() method goes here
}
```

You can redesign the m1() method to throw only one exception, say MyException, as follows:

```
public void m1() throws MyException {
    try {
        // Code for m1() method goes here
    } catch(Exception1 e){
        throw new MyException("Msg1", e);
    } catch(Exception2 e){
        throw new MyException("Msg2", e);
    } catch(Exception3 e){
        throw new MyException("Msg3", e);
    }
}
```

The redesigned method throws only one exception, which is of type MyException. The detailed message for the exception is specific to the lower-level exception that is thrown and caught inside the method. The lower-level exception is also propagated to the client as the cause of the higher-level exception. If the m1() method needs to throw a new exception in the future, you can still fit the new exception in the old design. You need to add a catch block to catch the new exception and rethrow MyException. This design keeps the throws clause of the m1() method stable. It also allows for more exception types to be included in its body in the future.

■ **Tip**   Do not throw a generic exception from your method, such as Throwable, Exception, Error, RuntimeException, etc. Do not specify a generic exception type in a catch block. The purpose of exception throwing or handling is to know exactly the error condition that occurred and take appropriate action. It helps you understand the cause of an error by giving specific error messages to users. Generating a specific error message is possible only when you handle exceptions using specific exception types.

Accessing the Stack of a Thread

The stack is an area of memory that is used to store temporary data. It uses last-in, first-out (LIFO) style to add and remove data. A stack resembles a stack in everyday life, such as a stack of books. The bottom of the stack has the first book that was placed on it. The top of the stack has the last book that was placed on it. When a book has to be removed from the stack, the last book that was placed on the stack will be removed first. This is the reason a stack is also called last-in, first-out memory. Figure 13-4 shows the arrangement of a stack.

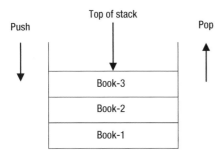

Figure 13-4. *Memory arrangement in a stack*

The figure shows three books placed on a stack. Book-1 was placed first, Book-2 second, and Book-3 third. Book-3, which is added last onto the stack, represents the top of the stack. Book-1, which is added first onto the stack, represents the bottom of the stack. Adding an element to a stack is called a *push* operation and removing an element from a stack is called a *pop* operation. Initially, a stack is empty and the first operation is the push operation. When a stack is being discarded, it must perform an equal number of push and pop operations so it is empty again.

Each thread in Java is allocated a stack to store its temporary data. A thread stores the state of a method invocation onto its stack. The state of a Java method comprises the parameters' values, local variables, any intermediate computed values, and the method's return value, if any. A Java stack consists of stack frames. Each frame stores the state of one method invocation. A new frame is pushed onto a thread's stack for a method invocation. The frame is popped from a thread's stack when the method completes.

Suppose a thread starts at the m1() method. The m1() method calls the m2() method, which in turn calls the m3() method. Figure 13-5 shows the frames on the stack of a thread when methods m1(), m2(), and m3() are called. Note that the figures show the frames when the method m3() is called from the method m2(), which in turn is called from the method m1().

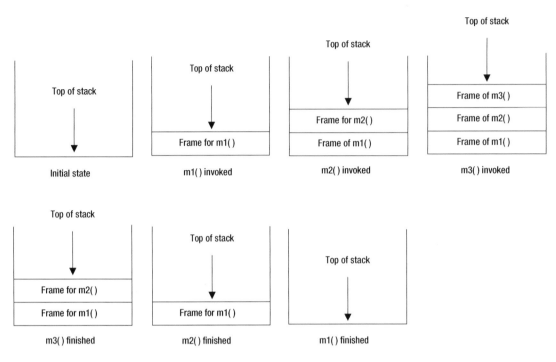

Figure 13-5. *State of the stack of a thread when methods m1(), m2(), and m3() are called*

You can get some pieces of information about the stack of a thread at a specific point in time. Note that the state of a thread's stack is always changing as the program executes. Therefore, you get a snapshot of the stack of a thread as it existed at the time you requested it. An object of the java.lang.StackTraceElement class represents a stack frame. You can query four pieces of information about a stack frame: class name, file name, method name, and line number. To get the stack information, you need to call the getStackTrace() method of a Throwable object. It returns an array of StackTraceElement objects. The first element of the array represents the top stack frame. The last element of the array represents the bottom stack frame. When you create an object of the Throwable class (or any exception class in Java), it captures the stack of the thread that is executing.

░ **Tip**   Java 9 has introduced a Stack Walking API that I cover in detail in Chapter 18 of the second volume of this series. Traversing stack trace and getting the reference of the caller class inside a method is much easier using the new Stack Walking API.

Listing 13-18 demonstrates how to get to the stack frames of a thread. A Throwable object captures the stack of the thread at the point it is created. If you have a Throwable object and want to capture the snapshot of the stack of a thread at a different point where the Throwable object was created, you can call the fillInStackTrace() method of the Throwable class. It captures the current state of stack for the current thread at the point you call this method.

Listing 13-18. A Sample Program That Prints the Details of the Stack Frames of a Thread

```java
// StackFrameTest.java
package com.jdojo.exception;

public class StackFrameTest {
    public static void main(String[] args) {
        m1();
    }

    public static void m1() {
        m2();
    }

    public static void m2() {
        m3();
    }

    public static void m3() {
        // Create a Throwable object that will hold the stack state
        // at this point for the thread that executes the following statement
        Throwable t = new Throwable();

        // Get the stack trace elements
        StackTraceElement[] frames = t.getStackTrace();

        // Print details about the stack frames
        printStackDetails(frames);
    }

    public static void printStackDetails(StackTraceElement[] frames) {
        System.out.println("Frame count: " + frames.length);

        for (int i = 0; i < frames.length; i++) {
            // Get frame details
            int frameIndex = i; // i = 0 means top frame
            String fileName = frames[i].getFileName();
            String className = frames[i].getClassName();
            String methodName = frames[i].getMethodName();
            int lineNumber = frames[i].getLineNumber();

            // Print frame details
            System.out.println("Frame Index: " + frameIndex);
            System.out.println("File Name: " + fileName);
            System.out.println("Class Name: " + className);
            System.out.println("Method Name: " + methodName);
            System.out.println("Line Number: " + lineNumber);
            System.out.println("--------------------------");
        }
    }
}
```

```
Frame count: 4
Frame Index: 0
File Name: StackFrameTest.java
Class Name: com.jdojo.exception.StackFrameTest
Method Name: m3
Line Number: 21
-----------------------------------------------
Frame Index: 1
File Name: StackFrameTest.java
Class Name: com.jdojo.exception.StackFrameTest
Method Name: m2
Line Number: 15
-----------------------------------------------
Frame Index: 2
File Name: StackFrameTest.java
Class Name: com.jdojo.exception.StackFrameTest
Method Name: m1
Line Number: 11
-----------------------------------------------
Frame Index: 3
File Name: StackFrameTest.java
Class Name: com.jdojo.exception.StackFrameTest
Method Name: main
Line Number: 7
-----------------------------------------------
```

Now that you have access to the stack frames of a thread, you may want to know what you can do with this information. The information about a thread's stack lets you know the location in the program where the code is executing. Typically, you log this information for debugging purposes. If you compare the output of the printStackTrace() method with the output of Listing 13-18, you would observe that they are similar, except that they print the same information in different formats.

The try-with-resources Block

When you worked with a resource, such as a file, a SQL statement, etc., you had to use a finally block and write a few lines of boilerplate code to close the resource. The typical code to work with a resource looked as follows:

```
AnyResource aRes;
try {
    aRes = create the resource...;
    // Work with the resource here
} finally {
    // Let us try to close the resource
    try {
        if (aRes != null) {
            aRes.close(); // Close the resource
```

```
        }
    } catch(Exception e) {
        e.printStackTrace();
    }
}
```

With a `try-with-resources` block, the previous code can be written as follows:

```
try (AnyResource aRes = create the resource...) {
    // Work with the resource here. The resource will be closed automatically.
}
```

Wow! You could write the same logic in just three lines of code using a `try-with-resources` block, when it used to take 14 lines of code. The `try-with-resources` block automatically closes the resources when the program exits the block. A `try-with-resource` block may have one or more `catch` blocks and/or a `finally` block.

On the surface, the `try-with-resources` block is as simple as it seems in the previous example. However, it comes with some subtleties that I need to discuss in detail.

You can specify multiple resources in a `try-with-resources` block. Two resources must be separated by a semicolon. The last resource must not be followed by a semicolon. The following snippet of code shows some usage of a `try-with-resources` block to use one and multiple resources:

```
try (AnyResource aRes1 = getResource1()) {
    // Use aRes1 here
}
```

```
try (AnyResource aRes1 = getResource1(); AnyResource aRes2 = getResource2()) {
    // Use aRes1 and aRes2 here
}
```

The resources that you specify in a `try-with-resources` are implicitly final. You can declare the resources final, even though it is redundant to do so.

```
try (final AnyResource aRes1 = getResource1()) {
    // Use aRes1 here
}
```

A resource that you specify in a `try-with-resources` must be of the type `java.lang.AutoCloseable`. The `AutoCloseable` interface has a `close()` method. When the program exits the `try-with-resources` block, the `close()` method of all the resources is called automatically. In the case of multiple resources, the `close()` method is called in the reverse order in which the resources are specified.

Consider a `MyResource` class as shown in Listing 13-19. It implements the `AutoCloseable` interface and provides implementation for the `close()` method. If the `exceptionOnClose` instance variable is set to `true`, its `close()` method throws a `RuntimeException`. Its `use()` method throws a `RuntimeException` if the `level` is zero or less. Now use the `MyResource` class to demonstrate various rules in using the `try-with-resources` block.

Listing 13-19. An AutoCloseable Resource Class

```java
// MyResource.java
package com.jdojo.exception;

public class MyResource implements AutoCloseable {
    private int level;
    private boolean exceptionOnClose;

    public MyResource(int level, boolean exceptionOnClose) {
        this.level = level;
        this.exceptionOnClose = exceptionOnClose;
        System.out.println("Creating MyResource. Level = " + level);
    }

    public void use() {
        if (level <= 0) {
            throw new RuntimeException("Low in level.");
        }

        System.out.println("Using MyResource level " + this.level);
        level--;
    }

    @Override
    public void close() {
        if (exceptionOnClose) {
            throw new RuntimeException("Error in closing");
        }
        System.out.println("Closing MyResource...");
    }
}
```

Listing 13-20 shows a simple case of using a MyResource object in a try-with-resources block. The output demonstrates that the try-with-resources block automatically calls the close() method of the MyResource object.

Listing 13-20. A Simple Use of MyResource Object in a try-with-resources Block

```java
// SimpleTryWithResource.java
package com.jdojo.exception;

public class SimpleTryWithResource {
    public static void main(String[] args) {
        // Create and use a resource of MyResource type.
        // Its close() method will be called automatically
        try (MyResource mr = new MyResource(2, false)) {
            mr.use();
            mr.use();
        }
    }
}
```

```
Creating MyResource. Level = 2
Using MyResource level 2
Using MyResource level 1
Closing MyResource...
```

When a resource is being closed automatically, an exception may be thrown. If a try-with-resources block completes without throwing an exception and the call to the close() method throws the exception, the runtime reports the exception thrown from the close() method. If a try-with-resources block throws an exception and the call to the close() method also throws an exception, the runtime suppresses the exception thrown from the close() method and reports the exception thrown from the try-with-resources block. The following snippet of code demonstrates this rule:

```
// Create a resource of MyResource type with two levels, which can throw exception on
// closing and use it thrice so that its use() method throws an exception
try (MyResource mr = new MyResource (2, true) ) {
    mr.use();
    mr.use();
    mr.use(); // Will throw a RuntimeException
} catch(Exception e) {
    System.out.println(e.getMessage());
}
```

```
Creating MyResource. Level = 2
Using MyResource level 2
Using MyResource level 1
Low in level.
```

The third call to the use() method throws an exception. In the previous snippet of code, the automatic close() method call will throw a RuntimeException because you pass true as the second argument when you create the resource. The output shows that the catch block received the RuntimeException that was thrown from the use() method, not from the close() method.

You can retrieve the suppressed exceptions by using the getSuppressed() method of the Throwable class. The method was added in Java 7. It returns an array of Throwable objects. Each object in the array represents a suppressed exception. The following snippet of code demonstrates the use of the getSuppressed() method to retrieve the suppressed exceptions:

```
try (MyResource mr = new MyResource (2, true) ) {
    mr.use();
    mr.use();
    mr.use(); // Throws an exception
} catch(Exception e) {
    System.out.println(e.getMessage());

    // Display messages of suppressed exceptions
    System.out.println("Suppressed exception messages are...");
    for(Throwable t : e.getSuppressed()) {
        System.out.println(t.getMessage());
    }
}
```

```
Creating MyResource. Level = 2
Using MyResource level 2
Using MyResource level 1
Low in level.
Suppressed exception messages are...
Error in closing
```

■ **Tip** Before Java 9, the variable referencing the resource used in a try-with-resources block had to be declared in the same try-with-resources block. This restriction has been lifted in Java 9, which allows an effectively final resource variable to be used in a try-with-resources block.

Until Java 9, the try-with-resources block had a limitation that you must declare the variable referencing the resource in the same try-with-resources block. If you received a resource reference as an argument in a method, you would not be able to write your logic like this:

```
void useIt(MyResource res) {
    // A compile-time error in JDK 7 and 8
    try(res) {
        // Work with res here
    }
}
```

To circumvent this restriction, you had to declare another variable of the resource type and initialize it with your argument value. The following snippet of code shows this approach. It declares a new reference variable called res1 on which the close() method will be called when the try-with-resources block exits:

```
void useIt(MyResource res) {
    try(MyResource res1 = res) {
        // Work with res1 here
    }
}
```

JDK 9 removed this restriction that you must declare fresh variables for resources that you want to manage using a try-with-resource block. Now, you can use a *final* or *effectively final* variable that references a resource to be managed by a try-with-resources block. A variable is final if it is explicitly declared using the final keyword:

```
// res is explicitly final
final MyResource res = new MyResource(2, false);
```

A variable is effectively final if its value is never changed after it is initialized. In the following snippet of code, the res variable is effectively final even though it is not declared final. It is initialized and is never changed again.

```
void doSomething() {
    // res is effectively final
    MyResource res = new MyResource(2, false);

    res.use();
}
```

In JDK 9, you can write something like this:

```
MyResource res = new MyResource(2, false);
try (res) {
    // Work with res here
}
```

If you have multiple resources that you want to manage using a try-with-resources block, you can do it like this:

```
MyResource res1 = new MyResource(2, false);
MyResource res2 = new MyResource(3, false);

try (res1; res2) {
    // Use res1 and res2 here
}
```

You can mix JDK 8 and JDK 9 approaches in the same try-with-resources block. The following snippet of code uses two pre-declared effectively final variables and one freshly declared variable in a try-with-resources block:

```
MyResource res1 = new MyResource(2, false);
MyResource res2 = new MyResource(3, false);

try (res1; res2; MyResource res3 = new MyResource(5, false)) {
    // Use res1, res2, and res3 here
}
```

Since JDK 7, variables declared inside a try-with-resource block are implicitly final. The following snippet of code explicitly declares such a variable final:

```
MyResource res1 = new MyResource(2, false);
MyResource res2 = new MyResource(2, false);

// Declare res3 explicitly final
try (res1; res2; final MyResource res3 = new MyResource(2, false)) {
    // Use res1, res2, and res3 here
}
```

Listing 13-21 contains the code for a ResourceTest class that shows you how to use the new feature of Java 9 that lets you manage resources using try-with-resources blocks using final or effectively final variables that reference those resources.

Listing 13-21. A ResourceTest Class to Demonstrate the Use of try-catch Blocks in JDK 9

```java
// ResourceTest.java
package com.jdojo.exception;

public class ResourceTest {
    public static void main(String[] args) {
        MyResource r1 = new MyResource(1, false);
        MyResource r2 = new MyResource(2, false);

        try (r1; r2) {
            r1.use();
            r2.use();
            r2.use();
        }

        useResource(new MyResource(3, false));
    }

    public static void useResource(MyResource res) {
        try (res; MyResource res4 = new MyResource(4, false)) {
            res.use();
            res4.use();
        }
    }
}
```

```
Creating MyResource. Level = 1
Creating MyResource. Level = 2
Using MyResource level 1
Using MyResource level 2
Using MyResource level 1
Closing MyResource...
Closing MyResource...
Creating MyResource. Level = 3
Creating MyResource. Level = 4
Using MyResource level 3
Using MyResource level 4
Closing MyResource...
Closing MyResource...
```

Summary

An exception is the occurrence of an abnormal condition in a Java program where a normal path of execution is not defined. Java lets you separate the code that performs the actions from the code that handles exceptions that may occur when the actions are performed.

Use a try-catch block to place your action-performing code in the try block and exception-handling code in the catch block. A try block may also have a finally block, which is typically used to clean up resources used in the try block. You can have a combination of try-catch, try-catch-finally, or try-finally blocks.

The try-with-resources block comes in handy to close resources automatically. You can use AutoCloseable resources in a try-with-resources block. When the block exits, the close() method of those resources are called automatically. Before Java 9, the variable referencing the resource used in a try-with-resources block must be declared in the same try-with-resources block. This restriction has been lifted in Java 9, which allows an effectively final resource variable to be used in a try-with-resources block.

There are two types of exceptions: checked exceptions and unchecked exceptions. The compiler makes sure that all checked exceptions are handled in the program or the program declares them in a throws clause. Handling or declaring unchecked exceptions is optional.

EXERCISES

1. What is an exception in Java? Name the two types of exceptions that Java supports.

2. What is the superclass of all exception classes in Java?

3. What type of statement/block would you use to place your code if a piece of code may throw an exception?

4. How many exceptions can you catch in one catch block?

5. Can you throw an exception from inside a catch block?

6. Name two constructs in Java that you may use to clean up resources after their use.

7. What are checked and unchecked exceptions in Java? Is java.lang.ArithmeticException a checked exception? Is java.io.IOException a checked exception?

8. What keyword do you use to in a method's declaration to declare that the method throws an exception?

9. What keyword do you use to throw an exception?

10. Will the following statement compile?

    ```
    throw null;
    ```

    If this statement compiles, what will happen when it is executed?

11. Can you throw a runtime exception from a method without specifying the exception in the throws clause of the method's declaration?

12. Will the following method declaration compile? If no, describe the reason.

```
public void test() {
    throw new RuntimeException("An error has occurred.");
    System.out.println("Everything is cool!");
}
```

13. Complete the following snippet of code, so the error message associated with the exception is printed on the standard output.

```
try {
    int x = 100 / 0;
} catch (ArithmeticException e) {
    String errorMessage = e./* You code goes here */;
    System.out.println(errorMessage);
}
```

14. What method of the Throwable class do you use to print the stack trace of the exception object?

15. Describe the reason why the following try-catch block does not compile.

```
try {
    // The following statement throws NumberFormatException
    int luckNumber = Integer.parseInt("Hello");
} catch (Exception e) {
    // Handle the exception here
} catch (NumberFormatException e) {
    // Handle the exception here
}
```

16. Consider the following code inside a method, assuming that MyResource is a class that implements the AutoCloseable interface. The code does not compile. Describe the reason why the code does not compile and fix it, so it compiles.

```
MyResource res = new MyResource(1, false);
try (res) {
    res.use();
}
res = null;
```

CHAPTER 14

Assertions

In this chapter, you will learn:

- What an assertion is in Java
- How to use assertions in Java programs
- How to enable and disable assertions
- How to check the status of an assertion

All classes in this chapter are members of a jdojo.assertion module, as declared in Listing 14-1.

Listing 14-1. The Declaration of a jdojo.assertion Module

```
// module-info.java
module jdojo.assertion {
    exports com.jdojo.assertion;
}
```

What Is an Assertion?

The literal meaning of assertion is to state something in a strong, confident, and forceful way. When you assert "something," you believe that "something" to be true. Note that asserting "something" does not make that "something" always true. It simply means that chances are very high (or you are very confident) that "something" is true. Sometimes you may be wrong and that "something" may be false, even if you assert it to be true.

The meaning of an assertion in Java is similar to its literal meaning. It is a statement in a Java program. It lets programmers assert a condition to be true at a specific point in the program. Consider the following snippet of code, which has two statements with one comment in between:

```
int x = 10 + 15;
/* We assert that value of x is 25 at this point */
int z = x + 12;
```

The first statement uses two hard-coded integer values, 10 and 15, and assigns their sum to the variable x. You can assert that the value of variable x is 25 after the first statement is executed. Note the use of comments to make the assertion in this case. What is the probability that the value of x will be other than 25 in this code? You may think that the probability of x having a value other than 25 is zero. It means your assertion will be true all the time. So, what was the point in adding a comment, which asserts that the value of x is 25, when it is obvious by just looking at the code? In programming, what seems obvious at one time may not be obvious at other times.

Consider the following snippet of code assuming that a getPrice() method exists:

```
int quantity = 15;
double unitPrice = getPrice();
/* We assert that unitPrice is greater than 0.0 at this point */
double totalPrice = quantity * unitPrice;
```

In this code, you have made an assertion that the value of the variable unitPrice will be greater than 0.0 after the second statement is executed. What is the probability that the value of unitPrice will be greater than 0.0 after the second statement is executed? It is difficult to answer this question by just looking at the code. However, you assume, for the code to work correctly, that your assertion "the value of unitPrice is greater than 0.0" must be true. Otherwise, your code will indicate a serious bug in the getPrice() method. It may be obvious for a customer that the price for an item will be always greater than zero. However, it is not so obvious to a programmer, because he has to depend on the correct implementation of the getPrice() method. If the getPrice() method has a bug, the programmer's assertion will be false. If the programmer's assertion is false, he needs to know about the failure of his assertion, and he needs to fix the bug. If his assertion was false, he would not want to proceed with the price computations. He would want to halt the price computation as soon as his assertion fails. You have used a comment to state your assertion. A comment is not executable code. Even if the value of unitPrice is not greater than zero, your comment is not going to report this error condition or halt the program. You need to use the assertion facility in such cases to receive a detailed error message and halt the program.

You can make an assertion in Java using an assert statement. The syntax for an assert statement comes in two forms:

- assert booleanAssertionExpression;

- assert booleanAssertionExpression : errorMessageExpression;

An assert statement starts with the assert keyword, which is followed by a boolean assertion expression that is the condition that a programmer believes to be true. If the assertion expression evaluates to true, no action is taken. If the assertion expression evaluates to false, the runtime throws a java.lang. AssertionError.

The second form of the assert statement syntax allows you to specify a custom error message expression when the assertion error is thrown. The assertion condition and the custom message are separated by a colon. The errorMessageExpression does not have to be a string. It could an expression that may evaluate to any data type, except the void data type. The runtime will convert the result of the error message expression to string. You can rewrite the code shown previously to take advantage of the assert statement, like so:

```
int x = 10 + 15;
assert x == 25; // Uses the first form of the assert statement
int z = x + 12;
```

Here you replaced the comment with an assert statement. All you need to specify is the condition you assert to be true. You used the first form of the assert statement. You did not use any custom message when your assertion fails. When the assertion fails, the Java runtime provides you with all details such as line number, source code, file name, etc. about the error.

In most cases, the first form of the `assert` statement is sufficient. If you think some values from the program at the time of the error may help you diagnose the problem better, you should use the second form of the `assert` statement. Suppose you want to print the value of x when the assertion fails. You can use the following snippet of code:

```
int x = 10 + 15;
assert x == 25: "x = " + x; // Uses the second form of the assert statement
int z = x + 12;
```

If you want just the value of x and nothing else, you can use the following snippet of code:

```
int x = 10 + 15;
assert x == 25: x; // Uses the second form of the assert statement
int z = x + 12;
```

Note that the `errorMessageExpression` in the second form of `assert` statement could be of any data type, excluding void. This snippet of code provides x as the value of `errorMessageExpression`, which evaluates to an `int`. The runtime will use the string representation of the value of x when it throws an `AssertionError`.

At this point, you may be tempted to test the `assert` statement. Let's discuss some more details before you compile and run Java classes with `assert` statements. However, you will use Java code with an `assert` statement, as shown in Listing 14-2.

Listing 14-2. A Simple Test Class to Test the assert Statement

```
// AssertTest.java
package com.jdojo.assertion;

public class AssertTest {
    public static void main(String[] args) {
        int x = 10 + 15;
        assert x == 100 :  "x = " + x; // should throw an AssertionError
    }
}
```

The code for the `AssertTest` class is simple. It assigns a value of 25 to the variable x and asserts that the value of x should be 100. When you run the `AssertTest` class, you expect that it would always throw an `AssertionError`.

Testing Assertions

It is time to see the `assert` statement in action. Try to run the `AssertTest` class in NetBeans or using the following command on a command prompt:

```
C:\Java9Fundamentals>java --module-path dist --module jdojo.assertion/com.jdojo.assertion.
AssertTest
```

This command finishes without any output. Did you not expect an error message on the standard output? Is your assertion x == 100 not false? The value of x is 25, not 100. You need to perform one more step before you can see the assert statement in action. Try the following command to run the AssertTest class:

```
C:\Java9Fundamentals>java -ea --module-path dist --module jdojo.assertion/com.jdojo.
assertion.AssertTest
```

```
Exception in thread "main" java.lang.AssertionError: x = 25
        at jdojo.assertion/com.jdojo.assertion.AssertTest.main(AssertTest.java:7)
```

You can also enable assertions in a NetBeans project. Right-click the project name in NetBeans and specify -ea as the VM Option under the Run Categories, as shown in Figure 14-1. Once assertion is enabled, running the AssertTest class in NetBeans will generate the same error.

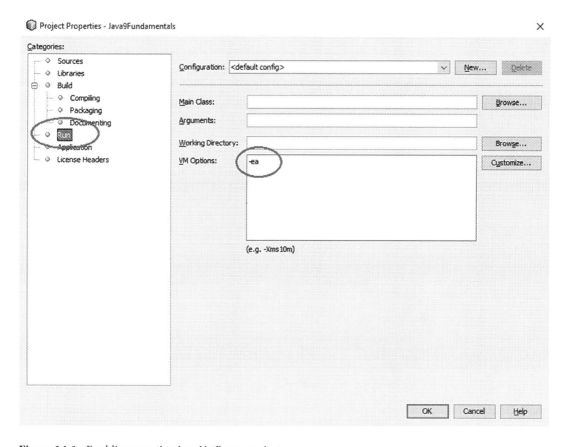

Figure 14-1. *Enabling assertion in a NetBeans project*

An `AssertionError` was generated with `"x = 25"` as the error message when you ran the `AssertTest` class. This is what happens when an assertion fails in your code. The Java runtime throws an `AssertionError`. Because you used the second form of the `assert` statement in your code, the error message also contains your custom assertion message, which prints the value of x. Note that the assertion error, by default, contains the line number and the source code file name where the assertion fails. This error message states that the assertion failed at line 7 in the `AssertFile.java` source file.

So, what is the magic behind using the –ea switch with the `java` command? By default, `assert` statements are not executed by the Java runtime. In other words, the assertion is disabled by default. You must enable the assertion when you run your class, so your `assert` statements are executed. The –ea switch enables the assertion at runtime. This is the reason that you received the expected error message when you used the –ea switch to run the `AssertTest` class. I discuss enabling/disabling assertion in detail in the next section.

Enabling/Disabling Assertions

The goal in using assertions is to detect logic errors in programs. Typically, assertions should be enabled in development and test environments. Assertions help programmers find the location and type of problems in code quickly. Once an application is tested, it is very unlikely that the assertions will fail. Java designers kept in mind the performance penalty that you may incur by using assertions in production environment. This is the reason that assertions are disabled at runtime by default. Although it is not desirable to enable assertions in a production environment, you have options to do so.

Java provides command-line options (or switches) to enable assertions at runtime at various levels. For example, you have options to enable assertions in all user-defined classes, all system classes, all classes in a package and its sub-packages, just for one class, etc. Table 14-1 lists all switches that you can use on the command line to enable/disable assertions at runtime. Each switch has a long form and a short form.

Table 14-1. *Command-Line Switches to Enable/Disable Assertions at Runtime*

Command-Line Switch	Description
`-enableassertions, -ea`	Used to enable assertions at runtime for system classes as well as user-defined classes. You can pass an argument to this switch to control the level at which assertions are enabled.
`-disableassertions, -da`	Used to disable assertions at runtime for system classes as well as user-defined classes. You can pass an argument to this switch to control the level at which assertions are disabled.
`-enablesystemassertions, -esa`	Used to enable assertions in all system classes. You cannot pass any arguments to this switch.
`-disablesystemassertions, -dsa`	Used to disable assertions in all system classes. You cannot pass any arguments to this switch.

Two switches, -ea and –da, let you control the enabling and disabling of assertions at various levels. You can pass an argument to these switches to control the level at which assertions should be enabled or disabled. Note that you cannot pass any arguments to –esa and –dsa switches. They enable and disable assertions in all system classes. If you pass an argument to the –ea or –da switch, the switch and the argument must be separated by a colon, as shown next. Table 14-2 lists the possible arguments that can be used with these switches.

- `-ea:<argument>`

- `-da:<argument>`

Table 14-2. *List of Arguments That Can Be Passed to –ea and –da Switches*

Argument for –ea and –da Switches	Description
`(no argument)`	Enables or disables assertions in all user-defined classes. Note that to enable/disable assertions in all system classes, you need to use the –esa and –dsa switches, respectively, with no argument.
`packageName...`	Note the three dots after the `packageName`. It enables/disables assertions in the specified `packageName` and any of its subpackages. It can also be used to enable/disable assertions in system packages.
`...`	This argument value is three dots. It enables/disables assertions in the unnamed package in the current working directory.
`className`	Enables/disables assertions in the specified `className`. It can also be used to enable/disable assertions in system classes.

The following are examples of using assertion switches with different arguments. All examples assume that you are enabling assertions when you are running the `com.jdojo.assertion.AssertTest` class. The examples show you only how to enable assertions. By default, all assertions are disabled.

```
/* Enable assertions in all system classes */
C:\Java9Fundamentals>java -esa --module-path dist --module jdojo.assertion/com.jdojo.
assertion.AssertTest

/* Enable assertions in all user-defined classes */
C:\Java9Fundamentals>java -ea --module-path dist --module jdojo.assertion/com.jdojo.
assertion.AssertTest

/* Enable assertions in com.jdojo package and its sub-packages */
C:\Java9Fundamentals>java -ea:com.jdojo... --module-path dist --module jdojo.assertion/com.
jdojo.assertion.AssertTest

C:\Java9Fundamentals>java -ea:... --module-path dist --module jdojo.assertion/com.jdojo.
assertion.AssertTest

/* Enable assertions in com.jdojo.assertion.AssertTest class */
C:\Java9Fundamentals>java -ea:com.jdojo.assertion.AssertTest --module-path dist --module
jdojo.assertion/com.jdojo.assertion.AssertTest
```

You can use multiple –ea or –da switches in one command to achieve finer granularity in enabling/disabling assertions. All switches are processed from left to right in the order they are specified.

```
/* Enable assertions in the p1 package and all its sub-packages, and disable assertion for
 * the p1.p2.MyClass class
 */
C:\Java9Fundamentals>java -ea:p1... -da:p1.p2.MyClass --module-path dist --module jdojo.
assertion/com.jdojo.assertion.AssertTest
```

■ **Tip**   Assertions for a class are enabled or disabled when a class is loaded. The assertion status for a class cannot be changed after it is set. There is one exception to this rule. If an `assert` statement is executed before a class has been initialized, the Java runtime executes it as if assertions are enabled. This situation arises when two classes refer to each other in their `static` initializers by calling the constructors or the methods of another class.

Using Assertions

Confusion may arise as to when to use assertions in a program. An assertion is implemented in Java by adding a new class, `java.lang.AssertionError`, into the existing exception class hierarchy. Sometimes programmers mistake an assertion as another exception. This may be true when you just look at the class hierarchy and you may say that it is just another class in the existing exception class hierarchy. However, the similarity between exceptions and assertions stops right there in the class hierarchy. The main difference lies in the reason behind their usage. An exception is used to handle a user's error and business rules implementation. If it is possible to recover from exceptional conditions, you want to recover from them and proceed with the application. An assertion is used to detect programming errors made by programmers. You do not want to recover from a programming error and proceed with the application. Assertions are used to verify that what a programmer assumes about his program at a specific point in his code is true. You should never use an assertion to handle a user's error or to validate data, because assertions are not meant to be enabled in the production environment.

Assertions should not be used to validate data arguments for public methods. The following snippet of code is for a `credit()` method of a `BankAccount` class, which uses assertion to validate the amount being credited:

```java
// An incorrect implementation
public void credit(double amount) {
    assert amount > 0.0 : "Invalid credit amount: " + amount;
    // Other code goes here
}
```

The code for the `credit()` method depends on enabling an assertion to validate the amount of credit to an account. Most likely, the assertion will be disabled in the production environment, which will allow a credit of even a negative number. Such validations for a public method's arguments should be performed using exceptions, as shown:

```java
// A correct implementation
public void credit(double amount) {
    if (amount <=  0.0) {
        throw new IllegalArgumentException("Invalid credit amount:" + amount);
    }
    // Other code goes here
}
```

You can use assertions to validate a method's arguments for a non-public method. A non-public method cannot be called by clients directly. If a method's parameters for a non-public method are incorrect, it indicates that the programmer's errors and use of assertions is appropriate.

You should not use an assertion that has side effects, such as an assertion that modifies the state of an object. Consider the following snippet of code in a method assuming that reComputeState() alters the state of the object of the class:

```
assert reComputeState();
```

When this assert statement is executed, it will alter the state of the object. The subsequent interaction with the object depends on its altered state. If the assertions are disabled, this code will not execute and the object will not behave properly.

You can use assertions to implement class invariants. Class invariants are conditions that always hold true about the values that determine the state of an object of a class. Class invariants may not be true for brief moments when an object is transitioning from one state to another. Suppose you have a BankAccount class with four instance variables: name, dob, startDate, and balance. The following class invariants must be true for a BankAccount object:

- The name on the account must not be null.

- The dob on the account must not be null and must not be a date in the future.

- The startDate on the account must not be null.

- The startDate on the account must not be before dob.

- The balance on the account must be greater than zero.

You can pack all these condition checks into one method, say the validAccount() method.

```
private boolean validAccount() {
    boolean valid = false;

    // Check for class invariants here. Return true if it is true. Otherwise, return false.

    return valid;
}
```

You can use the following assertion in methods and constructors to make sure that the class invariants are enforced. You assume that the toString() method of the BankAccount class returns enough pieces of information to help programmers debug the error.

```
assert validAccount(); this.tostring();
```

You can use this assert statement in the beginning of every method and before you return from the method. You do not need to check for class invariants inside a method if it does not modify the object's state. You should use it only at the end in a constructor because class invariants will not hold when the constructor starts executing.

Checking for Assertion Status

How do you know in your program if assertions are enabled? It is easy to check for the assertion status using an assert statement. Consider the following snippet of code:

```
boolean enabled = false;
assert enabled = true;
/* Check the value of enabled here */
```

This code uses the first form of the `assert` statement. Note that it uses the assignment operator (=), not the equality comparison operator (==) in the expression, `enabled = true`. The expression will assign true to the enabled variable and it will evaluate to `true`. Note that the enabled variable has been initialized to `false`. If assertion is enabled, the `enabled` variable will have a value of `true` after the `assert` statement is executed. If assertion is disabled, the variable `enabled` will have a value of `false`. Therefore, checking for the value of the `enabled` variable after the `assert` statement will give you a clue whether assertions are enabled for your class. Listing 14-3 shows the complete code for checking if assertions are enabled for the `AssertionStatusTest` class. Note that assertion can be enabled or disabled on a class basis, too. If assertions are enabled for a specific class, it does not guarantee that it is also enabled for all other classes.

Listing 14-3. A Program to Check Whether Assertion Is Enabled

```java
// AssertionStatusTest.java
package com.jdojo.assertion;

public class AssertionStatusTest {
    public static void main(String[] args)  {
        boolean enabled = false;
        assert enabled = true;
        if (enabled) {
            System.out.println("Assertion is enabled.");
        } else {
            System.out.println("Assertion is disabled.");
        }
    }
}
```

Summary

Assertions are a feature of the Java programming language that let you assert in your program for some conditions to hold. The keyword `assert` is used to write an assert statement. Assertions are used for detecting logical errors in a program and they are typically enabled in development and testing environments. Assertions can be enabled and disabled for packages and classes. They should not be used to validate user's inputs or business rules. Assertions do not replace exceptions. Rather they complement each other.

QUESTIONS AND EXERCISES

1. What is an assertion in Java? What statement do you use to add assertions to your programs?

2. Describe two forms of the `assert` statement.

3. Is assertion enabled by default? If your answer is no, how do you enable it?

4. In which of the following environment(s) are you supposed to enable assertion: development, test, and production?

5. What are the command-line options that you use to enable and disable assertions in all system classes?

6. Complete the `assert` statement in the following snippet of code assuming that x must be greater than 10.

```
int x = getValue();
assert /* Your code goes here */ : 'x must be greater than 10.";
```

7. You are writing code for a public method and you want to validate method's arguments. Will you use assertion or exception to achieve it? Describe your response.

CHAPTER 15

Strings

In this chapter, you will learn:

- What a `String` object is

- How to create `String` objects

- How to use `String` literals

- How to manipulate `Strings`

- How to use `Strings` in a `switch` statement

- How to use `StringBuilder` and `StringBuffer` objects to work with mutable strings

All classes in this chapter are members of a `jdojo.string` module, as declared in Listing 15-1.

Listing 15-1. The Declaration of a jdojo.string Module

```
// module-info.java
module jdojo.string {
    exports com.jdojo.string;
}
```

What Is a String?

A sequence of zero or more characters is known as a string. In Java programs, a string is represented by an object of the `java.lang.String` class. The `String` class is immutable. That is, the contents of a `String` object cannot be modified after it has been created. The `String` class has two companion classes, `java.lang.StringBuilder` and `java.lang.StringBuffer`. The companion classes are mutable. You should use them when the contents of your string can be modified.

Prior to Java 9, the implementation of the `String` class stored characters in a `char` array, using two bytes for each character in the string. Most `String` objects contain only Latin-1 characters requiring only one byte to store one character in the string. So, in most cases, half of the space in the `char` arrays of such `String` objects is not used. Java 9 has changed the internal implementation of the `String` class to use a byte array to store the contents of the `String` object; it also stores an encoding flag to indicate if each character in the `String` takes one byte or two bytes. This change in Java 9 is an implementation change. This was done to have efficient use of the memory used by `String` objects. As a developer, you do not need to know anything new to use strings in your programs. No public interface was changed for the `String` class in Java 9.

String Literals

A string literal consists of a sequence of zero or more characters enclosed in double quotes. All string literals are objects of the String class. Examples of string literals are

```
String s1 = "";                    // An empty string
String s2 = "Hello";               // String literal consisting of 5 characters
String s3 = "Just a string literal";  // String literal consisting of 21 characters
```

Multiple string literals can be used to compose a single string literal.

```
// Composed of two string literals "Hello" and "Hi". It represents one string literal
"HelloHi"
String s4 = "Hello" + "Hi";
```

A string literal cannot be broken into two lines.

```
// Cannot break a string literal in multiple lines. A compile-time error
String wronStr = "He
                 llo";
```

If you want to break "Hello" in two lines, you must break it using the string concatenation operator (+), as shown:

```
String s5 = "He" +
            "llo";
```

or

```
String s6 = "He"
            + "llo";
```

Another example of a multi-line string literal is shown here. The entire text represents a string literal.

```
String s7 = "This is a big string literal" +
" and it will continue in several lines." +

" It is also valid to insert multiple new lines as we did here. " +
"Adding more than one line in between two string literals " +
"is a feature of Java Language syntax, " +
" not of string literal.";
```

Escape Sequence Characters in String Literals

A string literal is composed of characters. It is valid to use all escape sequence characters to form a string literal. For example, to include a line feed character and a carriage return character in a string literal, you use \n and \r, as shown:

```
"\n"      // String literal with a line feed
"\r"      // String literal with a carriage return
```

```
"\n\r"     // String literal with a line feed and a carriage return
"First line.\nSecond line." // An embedded line feed
"Tab\tSeparated\twords"     // An embedded tab escape character
"Double quote \" is here"   // Embedded double quote in string literal
```

Unicode Escapes in String Literals

A character can also be represented as a Unicode escape in the form \uxxxx, where an x is a hexadecimal digit (0-9 or A-F). In a string literal, the character 'A', the first uppercase English letter, can also be written as '\u0041', for example, Apple and \u0041pple are treated the same in Java. Line feed and carriage return escape characters can also be represented in Unicode escape characters as '\u000A' and '\u000D', respectively. You cannot use Unicode escapes to embed a line feed and a carriage return character in string literals. In other words, you cannot replace '\n' with '\u000A' and '\r' with '\u000D' in a string literal. Why? The reason is that Unicode escapes are processed at the very beginning of the compilation process, resulting in the conversion of '\u000A' and '\u000D' into a real line feed and a carriage return, respectively. This violates the rule that a string literal cannot be continued in two lines. For example, in the early stages of compilation, "Hel\u000Alo" is translated into the following, which is an invalid string literal and generates a compile-time error:

```
"Hel
lo"
```

▓ **Tip**   It is a compile-time error to use Unicode escapes \u000A and \u000D in a string literal to represent a line feed and a carriage return, respectively. You must use the escape sequences of \n and \r instead.

What Is a CharSequence?

A CharSequence is an interface in the java.lang package. I discuss interfaces in Chapter 21. For now, you can think of a CharSequence as an object that represents a readable sequence of characters. String, StringBuffer, and StringBuilder, to name a few, are instances of CharSequence. They provide read-only methods to read some properties and the content of the sequence of characters represented by them. In the API documentation for the String class, you will see arguments of many methods declared as CharSequence. You can always pass a String, a StringBuilder, or a StringBuffer where a CharSequence is required.

Creating String Objects

The String class contains many constructors that can be used to create a String object. The default constructor lets you create a String object with an empty string as its contents. For example, the following statement creates an empty String object and assigns its reference to the emptyStr variable:

```
String emptyStr = new String();
```

The String class contains another constructor, which takes another String object as an argument.

```
String str1 = new String();
String str2 = new String(str1); // Passing a String as an argument
```

Now `str1` represents the same sequence of characters as `str2`. At this point, both `str1` and `str2` represent an empty string. You can also pass a string literal to this constructor.

```
String str3 = new String("");
String str4 = new String("Have fun!");
```

After these two statements are executed, `str3` will refer to a `String` object, which has an empty string (a sequence of zero characters) as its contents, and `str4` will refer to a `String` object, which has `"Have fun!"` as its contents.

Length of a String

The `String` class contains a `length()` method that returns the number of characters in the `String` object. Note that the `length()` method returns the number of characters in the string, not the number of bytes used by the string. The return type of the method `length()` is `int`. Listing 15-2 demonstrates how to compute the length of a string. The length of an empty string is zero.

Listing 15-2. Knowing the Length of a String

```
// StringLength.java
package com.jdojo.string;

public class StringLength {
    public static void main (String[] args) {
        // Create two string objects
        String str1 = new String() ;
        String str2 = new String("Hello") ;

        // Get the length of str1 and str2
        int len1 = str1.length();
        int len2 = str2.length();

        // Display the length of str1 and str2
        System.out.println("Length of \"" + str1 + "\" = " + len1);
        System.out.println("Length of \"" + str2 + "\" = " + len2);
    }
}
```

```
Length of "" = 0
Length of "Hello" = 5
```

String Literals Are String Objects

All string literals are objects of the `String` class. The compiler replaces all string literals with a reference to a `String` object. Consider the following statement:

```
String str1 = "Hello";
```

When this statement is compiled, the compiler encounters the string literal "Hello", and it creates a String object with "Hello" as its content. For all practical purposes, a string literal is the same as a String object. Wherever you can use the reference of a String object, you can also use a String literal. All methods of the String class can be used with String literals directly. For example, to compute the length of String literals, you can write

```
int len1 =  "".length();      // len1 is equal to 0
int len2 =  "Hello".length(); // len2 is equal to 5
```

String Objects Are Immutable

String objects are immutable. That is, you cannot modify the content of a String object. This leads to an advantage that strings can be shared without worrying about them being modified. For example, if you need two objects of the String class with the identical content (the same sequence of characters), you can create one String object and you can use its reference at both places. Sometimes the immutability of strings in Java is misunderstood, typically by beginners. Consider the following piece of code:

```
String str;
str = new String("Just a string");
str = new String("Another string");
```

Here, str is a reference variable that can refer to any String object. In other words, str can be changed and it is mutable. However, the String object, which str refers to, is always immutable. This scenario is depicted in Figures 15-1 and 15-2.

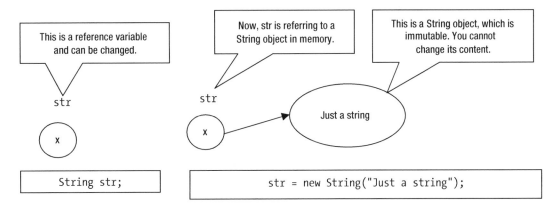

Figure 15-1. *A String reference variable and a String object*

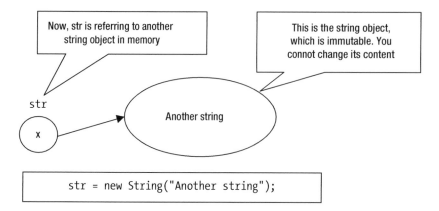

Figure 15-2. *Assigning a different String object reference to a string variable*

If you do not want str to refer to any other String object after it has been initialized, you can declare it final, like so:

```
final String str = new String("str cannot refer to other object");
str = new String("Let us try"); // A compile-time error. str is final
```

▒ **Tip**   It is the String object in memory that is immutable, not the reference variable of the String type. If you want a reference variable to refer to the same String object in memory all the time, you must declare the reference variable final.

Comparing Strings

You may want to compare the sequence of characters represented by two String objects. The String class overrides the equals() method of the Object class and provides its own implementation, which compares two strings for equality based on their contents. For example, you can compare two strings for equality, as shown:

```
String str1 = new String("Hello");
String str2 = new String("Hi");
String str3 = new String("Hello");

boolean b1, b2;

b1 = str1.equals(str2); // false will be assigned to b1
b2 = str1.equals(str3); // true will be assigned to b2
```

You can also compare string literals with string literals or string objects, as shown:

```
b1 = str1.equals("Hello");   // true will be assigned to b1
b2 = "Hello".equals(str1);   // true will be assigned to b2
b1 = "Hello".equals("Hi");   // false will be assigned to b1
```

Recall that the == operator always compares the references of two objects in memory. For example, str1 == str2 and str1 == str3 will return false, because str1, str2, and str3 are references of three different String objects in memory. Note that the new operator always returns a new object reference.

Sometimes you want to compare strings for sorting purposes. You may want to sort strings based on Unicode values of their characters or in the order they appear in the dictionary. The compareTo() method in the String class and the compare() method of the java.text.Collator class let you compare strings for sorting purposes.

If you want to compare two strings based on the Unicode values of their characters, use the compareTo() method of the String class, whose declaration is as follows:

```
public int compareTo(String anotherString)
```

It returns an integer, which can be 0 (zero), a positive integer, or a negative integer. It compares the Unicode values of the corresponding characters of two strings. If any two characters differ in their Unicode values, the method returns the difference between the Unicode values of those two characters. For example, "a".compareTo("b") will return –1. The Unicode value is 97 for 'a' and 98 for 'b'. It returns the difference 97 – 98, which is –1. The following are examples of string comparisons:

```
"abc".compareTo("abc") will return 0
"abc".compareTo("xyz") will return -23 (value of 'a' - 'x')
"xyz".compareTo("abc") will return 23 (value of 'x' - 'a')
```

It is very important to note that the compareTo() method compares two strings based on the Unicode values of their characters. The comparison may not be the same as the dictionary order comparison. This is fine for English and some other languages in which the Unicode values for characters are in the same order as the dictionary order of characters. This method should not be used to compare two strings in languages where the dictionary order of characters may not be the same as their Unicode values. To perform language-based string comparisons, you should use the compare() method of the java.text.Collator class instead. Refer the "Locale-Insensitive String Comparison" section in this chapter to learn how to use the java.text.Collator class. Listing 15-3 demonstrates the string comparisons.

Listing 15-3. Comparing Strings

```java
// StringComparison.java
package com.jdojo.string;

public class StringComparison {
    public static void main(String[] args) {
        String apple = new String("Apple");
        String orange = new String("Orange");

        System.out.println(apple.equals(orange));
        System.out.println(apple.equals(apple));
        System.out.println(apple == apple);
        System.out.println(apple == orange);
        System.out.println(apple.compareTo(apple));
        System.out.println(apple.compareTo(orange));
    }
}
```

```
false
true
true
false
0
-14
```

String Pool

Java maintains a pool of all string literals in order to minimize the memory usage and for better performance. It creates a `String` object in the string pool for every string literal it finds in a program. When it encounters a string literal, it looks for a string object in the string pool with the identical content. If it does not find a match in the string pool, it creates a new `String` object with that content and adds it to the string pool. Finally, it replaces the string literal with the reference of the newly created `String` object in pool. If it finds a match in the string pool, it replaces the string literal with the reference of the `String` object found in the pool. Let's discuss this scenario with an example. Consider the following statement:

```
String str1 = new String("Hello");
```

When Java encounters the string literal `"Hello"`, it tries to find a match in the string pool. If there is no `String` object with the content `"Hello"` in the string pool, a new `String` object with `"Hello"` content is created and added to the string pool. The string literal `"Hello"` will be replaced by the reference of that new `String` object in the string pool. Because you are using the new operator, Java will create another string object on the heap. Therefore, two `String` objects will be created in this case. Consider the following code:

```
String str1 = new String("Hello");
String str2 = new String("Hello");
```

How many `String` objects will be created by this code? Suppose when the first statement is executed, `"Hello"` was not in the string pool. Therefore, the first statement will create two `String` objects. When the second statement is executed, the string literal `"Hello"` will be found in the string pool. This time, `"Hello"` will be replaced by the reference of the already existing object in the pool. However, Java will create a new `String` object because you are using the new operator in the second statement. The previous two statements will create three `String` objects assuming that `"Hello"` was not there in the string pool. If `"Hello"` was already in the string pool when these statements started executing, only two `String` objects will be created. Consider the following statements:

```
String str1 = new String("Hello");
String str2 = new String("Hello");
String str3 = "Hello";
String str4 = "Hello";
```

What will be the value returned by `str1 == str2`? It will be `false` because the new operator always creates a new object in memory and returns the reference of that new object.

What will be the value returned by `str2 == str3`? It will be `false` again. This needs a little explanation. Note that the new operator always creates a new object. Therefore, `str2` has a reference to a new object in memory. Because `"Hello"` has already been encountered while executing the first statement, it exists in the string pool and `str3` refers to the `String` object with content `"Hello"` in the string pool. Therefore, `str2` and `str3` refer to two different objects and `str2 == str3` returns `false`.

What will be the value returned by str3 == str4? It will be true. Note that "Hello" has already been added to the string pool when the first statement was executed. The third statement will assign a reference of a String object from the string pool to str3. The fourth statement will assign the same object reference from the string pool to str4. In other words, str3 and str4 are referring to the same String object in the string pool. The == operator compares the two references; therefore, str3 == str4 returns true. Consider another example:

```
String s1 = "Have" + "Fun";
String s2 = "HaveFun";
```

Will s1 == s2 return true? Yes, it will return true. When a String object is created in a compile-time constant expression, it is also added to the string pool. Since "Have" + "Fun" is a compile-time constant expression, the resulting string, "HaveFun", will be added to the string pool. Therefore, s1 and s2 will refer to the same object in the string pool.

All compile-time constant string literals are added to the string pool. Consider the following examples to clarify this rule:

```
final String constStr = "Constant";  // constStr is a constant
String varStr = "Variable";          // varStr is not a constant

// "Constant is pooled" will be added to the string pool
String s1 = constStr + " is pooled";

// Concatenated string will not be added to the string pool
String s2 = varStr + " is not pooled";
```

After executing this snippet of code, "Constant is pooled" == s1 will return true, whereas "Variable is not pooled" == s2 will return false.

░ **Tip**   All string literals and string literals resulting from compile-time constant expressions are added to the string pool.

You can add a String object to the string pool using its intern() method. The intern() method returns the reference of the object from the string pool if it finds a match. Otherwise, it adds a new String object to the string pool and returns the reference of the new object. For example, in the previous snippet of code, s2 refers to a String object, which has the content "Variable is not pooled". You can add this String object to the string pool by writing

```
// Will add the content of s2 to the string pool and return the reference
// of the string object from the pool
s2 = s2.intern();
```

Now "Variable is not pooled" == s2 will return true because you have already called the intern() method on s2 and its content has been pooled.

▓ **Tip**   The String class maintains a pool of strings internally. All string literals are added to the pool automatically. You can add your own strings to the pool by invoking the intern() method on the String objects. You cannot access the pool directly. There is no way to remove string objects from the pool, except by exiting and restarting the app.

String Operations

This section describes some of the frequently used operations on String objects.

Getting the Character at an Index

You can use the charAt() method to get a character at a particular index from a String object. The index starts at zero. Table 15-1 shows indexes of all characters in the string "HELLO".

Table 15-1. *Indexes of All Characters in the String "HELLO"*

Index ->	0	1	2	3	4
Character ->	H	E	L	L	O

Note that the index of the first character H is 0 (zero), the second character E is 1, and so on. The index of the last character O is 4, which is equal to the length of the string "Hello" minus 1.

The following snippet of code will print the index value and the character at each index in a string of "HELLO":

```
String str = "HELLO";

// Get the length of string
int len = str.length();

// Loop through all characters and print their indexes
for (int i = 0; i < len; i++) {
    System.out.println(str.charAt(i) + " is at index " + i);
}
```

```
H is at index 0
E is at index 1
L is at index 2
L is at index 3
O is at index 4
```

Testing Strings for Equality

If you want to compare two strings for equality and ignore their cases, you can use the equalsIgnoreCase() method. If you want to perform a case-sensitive comparison for equality, you need to use the equals() method instead, as previously described.

```
String str1 = "Hello";
String str2 = "HELLO";

if (str1.equalsIgnoreCase(str2)) {
    System.out.println ("Ignoring case str1 and str2 are equal");
} else {
    System.out.println("Ignoring case str1 and str2 are not equal");
}

if (str1.equals(str2)) {
    System.out.println("str1 and str2 are equal");
} else {
    System.out.println("str1 and str2 are not equal");
}
```

```
Ignoring case str1 and str2 are equal
str1 and str2 are not equal
```

Testing a String to be Empty

Sometimes you need to test whether a String object is empty. The length of an empty string is zero. There are three ways to check for an empty string:

- Use the isEmpty() method.

- Use the equals() method.

- Get the length of the String and check if it is zero.

The following snippet of code shows how to use all three methods:

```
String str1 = "Hello";
String str2 = "";

// Using the isEmpty() method
boolean empty1 = str1.isEmpty(); // Assigns false to empty1
boolean empty2 = str2.isEmpty(); // Assigns true to empty1

// Using the equals() method
boolean empty3 = "".equals(str1); // Assigns false to empty3
boolean empty4 = "".equals(str2); // Assigns true to empty4

// Comparing length of the string with 0
boolean empty5 = str1.length() == 0; // Assigns false to empty5
boolean empty6 = str2.length() == 0; // Assigns true to empty6
```

Which of these methods is the best? The first method may seem more readable as the method name suggests what is intended. However, the second method is preferred as it handles the comparison with null gracefully. The first and third methods throw a NullPointerException if the string is null. The second method returns false when the string is null, for example, "".equals(null) returns false.

Changing the Case

To convert the content of a string to lower- and uppercase, you can use the toLowerCase() and the toUpperCase() methods, respectively. For example, "Hello".toUpperCase() will return the string "HELLO", whereas "Hello".toLowerCase() will return the string "hello".

Recall that String objects are immutable. When you use the toLowerCase() or toUpperCase() method on a String object, the content of the original object is not modified. Rather, Java creates a new String object with the identical content as the original String object and with the cases of the original characters changed. The following snippet of code creates three String objects:

```
String str1 = new String("Hello"); // str1 contains "Hello"
String str2 = str1.toUpperCase();  // str2 contains "HELLO"
String str3 = str1.toLowerCase();  // str3 contains "hello"
```

Searching for a String

You can get the index of a character or a string within another string using the indexOf() and lastIndexOf() methods. For example:

```
String str = "Apple";

int index = str.indexOf('p');      // index will have a value of 1
index = str.indexOf("pl");         // index will have a value of 2
index = str.lastIndexOf('p');      // index will have a value of 2
index = str.lastIndexOf("pl");     // index will have a value of 2
index = str.indexOf("k");          // index will have a value of -1
```

The indexOf() method starts searching for the character or the string from the start of the string and returns the index of the first match. The lastIndexOf() method matches the character or the string from the end and returns the index of the first match. If the character or string is not found in the string, these methods return –1.

Representing Values as Strings

The String class has an overloaded valueOf() static method. It can be used to get the string representation of the values of any primitive data type or any object. For example:

```
String s1 = String.valueOf('C');    // s1 has "C"
String s2 = String.valueOf("10");   // s2 has "10"
String s3 = String.valueOf(true);   // s3 has "true"
String s4 = String.valueOf(1969);   // s4 has "1969"
```

Getting a Substring

You can use the substring() method to get a part of a string. This method is overloaded as follows:

- `String substring(int beginIndex)`

- `String substring(int beginIndex, int endIndex)`

The first version returns a string that begins at the character at index beginIndex and extends to the end of this string. The second version returns a string that begins at the character at index beginIndex and extends to the character at index endIndex - 1. Both methods throw a IndexOutOfBoundsException if the specified indexes are outside the range of the string. The following are examples of using these methods:

```
String s1 = "Hello".substring(1);    // s1 has "ello"
String s2 = "Hello".substring(1, 4); // s2 has "ell"
```

Trimming a String

You can use the trim() method to remove all leading and trailing whitespace and control characters from a string. In fact, the trim() method removes all leading and trailing characters from the string, which have Unicode values less than \u0020 (decimal 32). For example:

- `"    hello    ".trim()` will return "hello"

- `"hello     ".trim()` will return "hello"

- `"\n    \r \t   hello\n\n\n\r\r"` will return "hello"

Note that the trim() method removes only leading and trailing whitespace. It does not remove any whitespace or control characters if they appear in the middle of the string. For example:

- `" he\nllo    ".trim()` will return "he\nllo" because \n is inside the string.

- `"h ello".trim()` will return "h ello" because the space is inside the string.

Replacing Part of a String

The String class contains the following methods that let you create a new string by replacing part of the old string with a different character or string:

- `String replace(char oldChar, char newChar)`

- `String replace(CharSequence target, CharSequence replacement)`

- `String replaceAll(String regex, String replacement)`

- `String replaceFirst(String regex, String replacement)`

The replace(char oldChar, char newChar) method returns a new String object by replacing all occurrences of oldChar with newChar. Here is an example:

```
// Both 'o's in "tooth" will be replaced by two 'e'. str will contain "teeth"
String str = "tooth".replace('o', 'e');
```

The replace(CharSequence target, CharSequence replacement) method works with CharSequence. It returns a new String object by replacing all occurrences of target with replacement. Here is an example:

```
// "oo" in "tooth" will be replaced by "ee". str will contain "teeth"
String str = "tooth".replace("oo", "ee");
```

The replaceAll(String regex, String replacement) method uses a regular expression in regex to find matches. It returns a new String object by replacing each match with replacement. A regular expression to match a digit is \d. I cover regular expressions in Chapter 18. Here is an example:

```
// Replace all digits with an *. str contains "Born on Sept **, ****"
String str = "Born on Sept 19, 1969".replaceAll("\\d", "*");
```

The replaceFirst(String regex, String replacement) method works the same as the replaceAll() method, except that it replaces only the first match with replacement. Here is an example:

```
// Replace the first digit with an *. str contains "Born on Sept *9, 1969"
String str = "Born on Sept 19, 1969".replaceFirst("\\d", "*");
```

Matching the Start and End of a String

The startsWith() method checks if the string starts with the specified argument, whereas endsWith() checks if the string ends with the specified string argument. Both methods return a boolean value. Here are examples of using these methods:

```
String str = "This is a Java program";

// Test str if it starts with "This"
if (str.startsWith("This")){
    System.out.println("String starts with This");
} else {
    System.out.println("String does not start with This");
}

// Test str if it ends with "program"
if (str.endsWith("program")) {
    System.out.println("String ends with program");
} else {
    System.out.println("String does not end with program");
}
```

```
String starts with This
String ends with program
```

Splitting and Joining Strings

It is often useful to split a string around a specified delimiter and join multiple strings into one string using a specified delimiter.

Use the split() method to split a string into multiple strings. Splitting is performed using a delimiter. The split() method returns an array of String. You will learn about arrays in Chapter 19. However, you will use it in this section just to complete the operations of strings.

▓ **Note**   The split() method takes a regular expression that defines a pattern as a delimiter.

```
String str = "AL,FL,NY,CA,GA";

// Split str using a comma as the delimiter
String[] parts = str.split(",");

// Print the the string and its parts
System.out.println(str);

for(String part : parts) {
    System.out.println(part);
}
```

```
AL,FL,NY,CA,GA
AL
FL
NY
CA
GA
```

Java 8 added a static join() method to the String class that joins multiple strings into one string. It is overloaded.

- String join(CharSequence delimiter, CharSequence… elements)

- String join(CharSequence delimiter, Iterable<? extends CharSequence> elements)

The first version takes a delimiter and a sequence of strings to be joined. The second argument is a var-args, so you can also pass an array to this method.

The second version takes a delimiter and an Iterable, for example, a List or Set. The following snippet of code uses the first version to join a few strings:

```
// Join some strings using a comma as the delimiter
String str = String.join(",", "AL", "FL", "NY", "CA", "GA");
System.out.println(str);
```

```
AL,FL,NY,CA,GA
```

Strings in a switch Statement

I discussed the switch statement in Chapter 6. You can also use strings in a switch statement. The switch expression uses a String type. If the switch expression is null, a NullPointerException is thrown. The case labels must be String literals. You cannot use String variables in the case labels. The following is an example of using a String in a switch statement, which will print "Turn on" on the standard output:

```
String status = "on";
switch(status) {
    case "on":
        System.out.println("Turn on"); // Will execute this
        break;
    case "off":
        System.out.println("Turn off");
        break;
    default:
        System.out.println("Unknown command");
        break;
}
```

The switch statement for strings compares the switch expression with case labels as if the equals() method of the String class has been invoked. In the previous example, status.equals("on") will be invoked to test if the first case block should be executed. Note that the equals() method of the String class performs a case-sensitive string comparison. It means that the switch statement that uses strings is case-sensitive.

The following switch statement will print "Unknown command" on the standard output, because the switch expression "ON" in uppercase will not match the first case label "on" in lowercase.

```
String status = "ON";
switch(status) {
    case "on":
        System.out.println("Turn on");
        break;
    case "off":
        System.out.println("Turn off");
        break;
    default:
        System.out.println("Unknown command"); // Will execute this
        break;
}
```

As a good programming practice, you need to do the following two things before executing a switch statement with strings:

- Check if the switch expression for the switch statement is null. If it is null, do not execute the switch statement.

- If you want to perform a case-insensitive comparison in a switch statement, you need to convert the switch expression to lowercase or uppercase and use lowercase or uppercase in the case labels accordingly.

You can rewrite the previous switch statement example, as shown in Listing 15-4, which takes care of the two suggestions.

Listing 15-4. Using Strings in a switch Statement

```java
// StringInSwitch.java
package com.jdojo.string;

public class StringInSwitch {
    public static void main(String[] args) {
        operate("on");
        operate("off");
        operate("ON");
        operate("Nothing");
        operate("OFF");
        operate(null);
    }

    public static void operate(String status) {
        // Check for null
        if (status == null) {
            System.out.println("status cannot be null.");
            return;
        }

        // Convert to lowercase
        status = status.toLowerCase();

        switch (status) {
            case "on":
                System.out.println("Turn on");
                break;
            case "off":
                System.out.println("Turn off");
                break;
            default:
                System.out.println("Unknown command");
                break;
        }
    }
}
```

```
Turn on
Turn off
Turn on
Unknown command
Turn off
status cannot be null.
```

Testing a String for Palindrome

If you are an experienced programmer, you may skip this section. This is meant to serve as a simple exercise for beginners.

A palindrome is a word, a verse, a sentence, or a number that reads the same in forward and backward directions. For example, "Able was I ere I saw Elba" and 1991 are examples of palindromes. Let's write a method that will accept a string as an argument and test if that string is a palindrome. The method will return true if the string is a palindrome. Otherwise, it will return false. You will use some methods of the String class that you learned in the previous sections. The following is the description of the steps to be performed inside the method.

Assume that the number of characters in the input string is n. You need to compare the character at indexes 0 and (n-1), 1 and (n -2), 2 and (n - 3), and so on. Note that if you continue the comparison, in the end, you will compare the character at the index (n-1) with the character at index 0, which you have already compared in the beginning. You need to compare the characters only halfway through. If all comparisons for equality return true, the string is a palindrome.

The number of characters in a string may be odd or even. Comparing characters only halfway works in both cases. The middle of a string varies depending on whether the length of the string is odd or even. For example, the middle of the string "FIRST" is the character R. What is the middle character in the string "SECOND"? You can say there is no middle character in it, as its length is even. For this purpose, it is interesting to note that if the number of characters in the string is odd, you do not need to compare the middle character with any other character.

You need to continue the character comparison up to half of the string's length if the number of characters in the string is even, and up to half of the string's *length minus one* if the number of characters is odd. You can get the numbers of comparisons to be done in both the cases by dividing the length of the string by 2. Note that the length of a string is an integer and if you divide an integer by 2, the integer division will discard the fraction part, if any, which will take care of cases with an odd number of characters. Listing 15-5 contains the complete code.

Listing 15-5. Testing a String for a Palindrome

```java
// Palindrome.java
package com.jdojo.string;

import java.util.Objects;

public class Palindrome {
    public static void main(String[] args) {
        String str1 = "hello";
        boolean b1 = Palindrome.isPalindrome(str1);
        System.out.println(str1 + " is a palindrome: " + b1);

        String str2 = "noon";
        boolean b2 = Palindrome.isPalindrome(str2);
        System.out.println(str2 + " is a palindrome: " + b2);
    }

    public static boolean isPalindrome(String inputString) {
        Objects.requireNonNull(inputString, "String cannot be null.");

        // Get the length of string
        int len = inputString.length();
```

```java
        // In case of an empty string and one character strings, we do not need to
        // do any comparisons. They are always palindromes.
        if (len <= 1) {
            return true;
        }

        // Convert the string into uppercase, so we can make the comparisons case insensitive
        String newStr = inputString.toUpperCase();

        // Initialize the result variable to true
        boolean result = true;

        // Get the number of comparisons to be done
        int counter = len / 2;

        // Do the comparison
        for (int i = 0; i < counter; i++) {
            if (newStr.charAt(i) != newStr.charAt(len - 1 - i)) {
                // It is not a palindrome
                result = false;

                // Exit the loop
                break;
            }
        }

        return result;
    }
}
```

```
hello is a palindrome: false
noon is a palindrome: true
```

StringBuilder and StringBuffer

StringBuilder and StringBuffer are companion classes for the String class. Unlike a String, they represent a mutable sequence of characters. That is, you can change the content of StringBuilder and StringBuffer without creating a new object. You might wonder why two classes exist to represent the same thing—a mutable sequence of characters. The StringBuffer class has been part of the Java library since the beginning, whereas the StringBuilder class was added in Java 5. The difference between the two lies in thread safety. StringBuffer is thread-safe and StringBuilder is not thread-safe. Most of the time, you do not need thread safety and using StringBuffer in those cases has a performance penalty. This is the reason that StringBuilder was added later. Both classes have the same methods, except that all methods in StringBuffer are synchronized. I will discuss only StringBuilder in this section. Using StringBuffer in your code would be just a matter of changing the class name.

▓ **Tip** Use `StringBuilder` when no thread safety is needed, for example, manipulating a sequence of characters in a local variable in a method or constructor. Otherwise, use `StringBuffer`. Thread safety and synchronization are described in Chapter 6 of the second volume of this series.

You can use objects of the `StringBuilder` class, instead of the `String` class, in situations where content of a string changes frequently. Recall that because of the immutability of the `String` class, string manipulations using a `String` object result in many new `String` objects, which in turn degrade the performance. A `StringBuilder` object can be thought of as a modifiable string. It has many methods to modify its contents. The `StringBuilder` class contains four constructors:

- `StringBuilder()`
- `StringBuilder(CharSequence seq)`
- `StringBuilder(int capacity)`
- `StringBuilder(String str)`

The no-args constructor creates an empty `StringBuilder` with a default capacity of 16.

The second constructor takes a `CharSequence` object as an argument. It creates a `StringBuilder` object, whose content is the same as the specified `CharSequence`.

The third constructor takes an `int` as argument; it creates an empty `StringBuilder` object whose initial capacity is the same as the specified argument. The capacity of a `StringBuilder` is the number of characters it can hold without allocating more space. The capacity is adjusted automatically when additional space is needed.

The fourth constructor takes a `String` and creates a `StringBuilder` that has the same content as the specified `String`. The following are some examples of creating `StringBuilder` objects:

```
// Create an empty StringBuilder with a default initial capacity of 16 characters
StringBuilder sb1 = new StringBuilder();

// Create a StringBuilder from of a string
StringBuilder sb2 = new StringBuilder("Here is the content");

// Create an empty StringBuilder with 200 characters as the initial capacity
StringBuilder sb3 = new StringBuilder(200);
```

The `append()` method lets you add text to the end of the `StringBuilder`. It is overloaded. It takes many types of arguments. Refer to the API documentation for the class for the complete list of all overloaded `append()` methods. It has other methods, for example `insert()` and `delete()`, that let you modify its content, too.

The `StringBuilder` class has two properties: `length` and `capacity`. At a given point in time, their values may not be the same. Its length refers to the length of its content whereas its capacity refers to the maximum number of characters it can hold without needing new memory to be allocated. Its length can be, at most, equal to its capacity at any time. The `length()` and `capacity()` methods return its length and capacity, respectively. For example:

```
StringBuilder sb = new StringBuilder(200);  // Capacity:200, length:0
sb.append("Hello");                         // Capacity:200, length:5
int len = sb.length();                      // len is assigned 5
int capacity = sb.capacity();               // capacity is assigned 200
```

Capacity of a StringBuilder is controlled by the runtime, whereas its length is controlled by the content you place in it. The runtime adjusts the capacity as its content is modified.

You can get the content of a StringBuilder as a String by using its toString() method.

```
// Create a String object
String s1 = new String("Hello");

// Create a StringBuilder from of the String object s1
StringBuilder sb = new StringBuilder(s1);

// Append " Java" to the StringBuilder's content
sb.append(" Java"); // Now, sb contains "Hello Java"

// Get a String from the StringBuilder
String s2 = sb.toString(); // s2 contains "Hello Java"
```

Unlike String, StringBuilder has a setLength() method, which takes its new length as an argument. If the new length is greater than the existing length, the extra positions are filled with null characters (a null character is \u0000). If the new length is less than the existing length, its content is truncated to fit in the new length.

```
// Length is 5
StringBuilder sb = new StringBuilder("Hello");

// Now the length is 7 with last two characters as null character '\u0000'
sb.setLength(7);

// Now the length is 2 and the content is "He"
sb.setLength(2);
```

The StringBuilder class has a reverse() method, which replaces its contents with the same sequence of characters, but in reverse order. Listing 15-6 illustrates some of the methods of the StringBuilder class.

Listing 15-6. Using a StringBuilder Object

```
// StringBuilderTest.java
package com.jdojo.string;

public class StringBuilderTest {
    public static void main(String[] args) {
        // Create an empty StringNuffer
        StringBuilder sb = new StringBuilder();
        printDetails(sb);

        // Append "blessings"
        sb.append("blessings");
        printDetails(sb);

        // Insert "Good " in the beginning
        sb.insert(0, "Good ");
        printDetails(sb);
```

```
        // Delete the first o
        sb.deleteCharAt(1);
        printDetails(sb);

        // Append " be with you"
        sb.append(" be with you");
        printDetails(sb);

        // Set the length to 3
        sb.setLength(3);
        printDetails(sb);

        // Reverse the content
        sb.reverse();
        printDetails(sb);
    }

    public static void printDetails(StringBuilder sb) {
        System.out.println("Content: \"" + sb + "\"");
        System.out.println("Length: " + sb.length());
        System.out.println("Capacity: " + sb.capacity());

        // Print an empty line to separate results
        System.out.println();
    }
}
```

```
Content: ""
Length: 0
Capacity: 16

Content: "blessings"
Length: 9
Capacity: 16

Content: "Good blessings"
Length: 14
Capacity: 16

Content: "God blessings"
Length: 13
Capacity: 16

Content: "God blessings be with you"
Length: 25
Capacity: 34

Content: "God"
Length: 3
Capacity: 34
```

```
Content: "doG"
Length: 3
Capacity: 34
```

String Concatenation Operator (+)

There are three ways to concatenate strings:

- Using the concat(String str) method of the String class
- Using the + string concatenation operator
- Using a StringBuilder or a StringBuffer

The concat() method takes a String as argument, which means you can use it to concatenate strings only. If you want to concatenate values of different data types into a string, use the concatenation operator. For example:

```
// Assigns "hi there" to s1
String s1 = "hi ".concat(" there");

// Assign "XY12.56" to s2
String s2 = "X" + "Y" + 12.56;

// Assign "XY12.56" to s3
String s3 = new StringBuilder().append("X").append("Y").append(12.56).toString();
```

Language-Sensitive String Comparison

The String class compares strings based on the Unicode values of their characters. Sometimes you may want to compare strings based on the dictionary order instead.

Use the compare() method of the java.text.Collator class to perform language-sensitive (dictionary order) string comparisons. The method takes two strings to be compared as arguments. It returns 0 if two strings are the same, 1 if the first string comes after the second, and -1 if the first string comes before the second. Listing 15-7 illustrates the use of the Collator class.

Listing 15-7. Language-Sensitive String Comparisons

```
// CollatorStringComparison.java
package com.jdojo.string;

import java.text.Collator;
import java.util.Locale;

public class CollatorStringComparison {
    public static void main(String[] args) {
        // Create a Locale object for US
        Locale USLocale = new Locale("en", "US");
```

```
        // Get a Collator instance for US
        Collator c = Collator.getInstance(USLocale);
        String str1 = "cat";
        String str2 = "Dog";

        int diff = c.compare(str1, str2);

        System.out.print("Comparing using Collator class: ");
        print(diff, str1, str2);

        System.out.print("Comparing using String class: ");
        diff = str1.compareTo(str2);
        print(diff, str1, str2);
    }

    public static void print(int diff, String str1, String str2) {
        if (diff > 0) {
            System.out.println(str1 + " comes after " + str2);
        } else if (diff < 0) {
            System.out.println(str1 + " comes before " + str2);
        } else {
            System.out.println(str1 + " and " + str2 + " are the same.");
        }
    }
}
```

```
Comparing using Collator class: cat comes before Dog
Comparing using String class: cat comes after Dog
```

The program also shows the comparison of the same two strings using the String class. Note that the word "cat" comes before the word "Dog" in the dictionary order. The Collator class uses their dictionary orders to compare them. However, the String class compares the Unicode value of the first character of "cat", which is 99, and the first character of "Dog", which is 68. Based on these two values, the String class determines that "Dog" comes before "cat". The output confirms the two different ways of comparing strings.

Summary

In this chapter, you learned about the String, StringBuilder, and StringBuffer classes. A String represents an immutable sequence of characters, whereas StringBuilder and StringBuffer represent a mutable sequence of characters. StringBuilder and StringBuffer work the same way, except the latter is thread-safe and the former is not.

The String class provides several methods to operate on its content. Whenever you obtain a part of the content from a String, a new String object is created. The String class compares two strings based on the Unicode values of their characters. Use the java.text.Collator class to compare strings in dictionary order. From Java 7 and on, you can use strings in a switch statement.

QUESTIONS AND EXERCISES

1. What is a string in Java? Can you change the contents of a `String` object after it is created?

2. What is a string literal?

3. What is the difference between the `String` class and the `StringBuilder` class?

4. What is the difference between the `StringBuffer` class and the `StringBuilder` class?

5. Write the output when the following snippet of code is executed.

```
String s1 = "Hello";
String s2 = "\"Hello\"";
System.out.println("s1 = " + s1);
System.out.println("s2 = " + s2);
```

6. Write the output when the following snippet of code is executed.

```
String s1 = "Who\nknows";
System.out.println("s1 = " + s1);
```

7. Write the output when the following snippet of code is executed.

```
String s1 = "Having fun with strings";
int len = s1.length();
char c = s1.charAt(4);
```

8. Write the output when the following snippet of code is executed.

```
String s1 = "Fun";
String s2 = new String("Fun");
System.out.println(s1 == s2);
System.out.println(s1.equals(s2));
System.out.println("Fun" == "Fun");
```

9. Write the output when the following snippet of code is executed.

```
StringBuilder sb = new StringBuilder(200);
sb.append("Hello").append(false);
System.out.println("length = " + sb.length());
System.out.println("capacity = " + sb.capacity());
System.out.println(sb.toString());
```

10. Write the output when the following snippet of code is executed.

```
String s1 = 10 + 20 + " = what";
String s2 = 10 + String.valueOf(20) + " = what";
System.out.println(s1);
System.out.println(s2);
```

11. Complete the code for a method named `equalsContents()`, as declared here. The method should return `true` if both arguments have the same contents after removing leading and trailing whitespace and ignoring cases. If both arguments are null, it should return `true`. Otherwise, it should return `false`.

```
public static boolean equalsContents(String s1, String s2) {
    /* your code goes here*/
}
```

12. Complete the following code so that the year, month, and day are printed as 1969, 09, and 19.

```
String date = "1969-09-19";
String year = date./*your code goes here*/;
String month = date./*your code goes here*/;
String day = date./*your code goes here*/;
System.out.println("year = " + year);
System.out.println("month = " + month);
System.out.println("day = " + day);
```

13. Complete the following snippet of code so it prints the expected output, which is shown after the snippet.

```
String s1 = "noon and spoon";
String s2 = s1./*Your code goes here*/;
System.out.println(s1);
System.out.println(s2);
```

Expected output is as follows:

```
noon and spoon
nun and spun
```

14. Complete the following snippet of code so it prints the expected output, which is shown after the snippet.

```
String s1 = "noon and spoon";
String s2 = s1./*Your code goes here*/;
System.out.println(s1);
System.out.println(s2);
```

Expected output is as follows:

```
noon and spoon
nn and spn
```

15. Complete the code for a `reverse(String str)` method. It takes a string and returns the reverse of that string. Do not use the `StringBuilder` or `StringBuffer` classes.

```
public static String reverse(String str) {
    /* Your code goes here */
}
```

16. What is the value of the expression `"abc".compareTo("abc")`?

CHAPTER 16

Dates and Times

In this chapter, you will learn:

- What the new Date-Time API is

- About the design principles behind the Date-Time API

- About the evolution of timekeeping, time zones, and Daylight Savings Time

- About the ISO-8601 standard for date, time, and datetime keeping

- How to represent date, time, and datetime using the Date-Time API classes and how to query, adjust, format, and parse them

- How to use the legacy Date-Time API

- How to interoperate between the legacy and new Date-Time APIs

The Date-Time API was introduced in Java 8 and has been enhanced in Java 9 with a lot of new methods in several interfaces and classes. This chapter covers a comprehensive coverage of the Date-Time API with enhancements to the API in Java 9. The API consists of `java.time.*` packages, which are in the `java.base` module. All example programs in this chapter are a member of a `jdojo.datetime` module, as declared in Listing 16-1.

Listing 16-1. The Declaration of a jdojo.datetime Module

```java
// module-info.java
module jdojo.datetime {
    exports com.jdojo.datetime;
}
```

The Date-Time API

Java 8 introduced a new Date-Time API to work with date and time. In this chapter, I refer to the date- and time-related classes available before Java 8 as the legacy Date-Time API. The legacy Date-Time API includes classes like `Date`, `Calendar`, `GregorianCalendar`, etc. They are in the `java.util` and `java.sql` packages. The Date class has existed since the inception of JDK; others were added in JDK 1.1.

Why did we need a new Date-Time API? The simple answer is that the designers of the legacy Date-Time API did not get it right in two attempts. To list a few, some of the issues with the legacy Date-Time API are as follows:

- A date always had two components: a date and a time. If you needed just a date without any time information, you had no choice. Developers used to set the time to midnight in a date object to represent a date-only date, which was incorrect for several reasons. The same argument is valid for storing only time.

- A datetime was simply stored as the number of milliseconds elapsed since January 1, 1970 midnight UTC.

- Manipulating dates was as complex as you can think; the year field in a Date object was stored as an offset from 1900; months ran from 0 to 11, not from 1 to 12, as humans are used to conceptualizing them.

- Legacy datetime classes were mutable and, therefore, not thread-safe.

Is the third time the charm? Here is a third attempt to provide a correct, powerful, and extensible Date-Time API. At least, so we say at the time of this writing! The new API is not a free ride, however. It has a steep learning curve if you want to use its full potential. It consists of about 80 classes. Do not worry about the big number of classes. They have been carefully designed and named. Once you understand the thoughts behind its design, it's relatively easy to figure out the name of a class and the methods that you need to use in a particular situation. As a developer, you need to understand about 15 classes to use the new Date-Time API effectively in your daily programming.

Design Principles

Before you start learning the details of the new Date-Time API, you will need to understand a few basic concepts about dates and times. The new Date-Time API is based on ISO-8601 datetime standards. A Java datetime framework named Joda-Time inspired the new API. If you have used Joda-Time before, you will be able to learn the new Date-Time API quickly. You can find the details of the Joda-Time project at http://joda-time.sourceforge.net.

The new API makes a distinction between how dates and times are used by machines and humans. Machines deal with time as continual ticks as a single incrementing number measured in seconds, milliseconds, etc. Humans use a calendar system to deal with time in terms of year, month, day, hour, minute, and second. The Date-Time API has a separate set of classes to deal with machine-based time and calendar-based human time. It lets you convert machine-based time to human-based time and vice versa.

The legacy Date-Time API has been around for over 15 years. It is very likely that you will encounter legacy datetime classes while working with existing applications. The legacy datetime classes have been retrofitted to work seamlessly with the new classes. When you write new code, use the new Date-Time API classes. When you receive objects of legacy classes as input, convert the legacy objects into new datetime objects, and use the new Date-Time API.

The new Date-Time API consists of mostly immutable classes. Because the new API is extensible, you are advised to create immutable classes, whenever possible, to extend the API. An operation on a datetime object creates a new datetime object. This pattern makes it easy to chain method calls.

Classes in the Date-Time API do not provide public constructors. They provide allow you to create their objects by providing static factory methods named of(), ofXxx(), and from(). The new API uses a well-defined naming convention for naming methods. Each class in the API has several methods. Knowing the method-naming convention lets you find the right method for your purpose easily. I discuss the method-naming convention shortly in a separate section.

A Quick Example

Let's look at an example of working with dates and times using the new Date-Time API. An instance of the LocalDate class represents a local date without a time; an instance of the LocalTime class represents a local time without a date; an instance of the LocalDateTime class represents a local date and time; an instance of the ZonedDateTime class represents date and time with a time zone.

A LocalDate and a LocalTime are also called *partials,* as they do not represent an instant on the timeline; they are not aware of changes in Daylight Savings Time. A ZonedDateTime represents a point in time in a given time zone that can be converted to an instant on the timeline; it is aware of Daylight Savings Time. For example, adding four hours to a LocalTime of 1 AM will give you another LocalTime of 5 AM irrespective of the date and location. However, if you add four hours to a ZonedDateTime representing 1 AM on March 9, 2014 in the Chicago/America time zone, it will give you 6 AM time on March 9, 2014 in the same time zone, as the clock is moved forward by one hour at 2 AM on that day because of Daylight Savings Time. Airline applications use instances of the ZonedDateTime class to store departure time and arrival time of flights.

In the Date-Time API, classes representing date, time, and datetime have a now() method that returns the current date, time, or datetime, respectively. The following snippet of code creates datetime objects representing a date, a time, and a combination of them with and without a time zone:

```
LocalDate dateOnly = LocalDate.now();
LocalTime timeOnly = LocalTime.now();
LocalDateTime dateTime = LocalDateTime.now();
ZonedDateTime dateTimeWithZone = ZonedDateTime.now();
```

A LocalDate is not time zone-aware. It will be interpreted differently in different time zones at the same moment of time. A LocalDate object is used for storing a date value when the time and time zone are not important to give a meaning to the date value, such as a birth date, the publication date of a book, etc.

You can specify the components of a datetime object using the static factory method of(). The following snippet of code creates a LocalDate by specifying the year, month, and day components of a date:

```
// Create a LocalDate representing January 12, 1968
LocalDate myBirthDate = LocalDate.of(1968, JANUARY, 12);
```

▒ **Tip** A LocalDate stores a date-only value without a time and time zone. When you obtain a LocalDate using the static method now(), the system default time zone is used to get the date value.

Listing 16-2 shows how to get the current date, time, datetime, and datetime with the time zone. It also shows how to construct a date from year, month of year, and day of month. You may get a different output, as it prints the current values for date and time.

Listing 16-2. Obtaining Current Date, Time, and Datetime, and Constructing a Date

```
// CurrentDateTime.java
package com.jdojo.datetime;

import java.time.LocalDate;
import java.time.LocalTime;
import java.time.LocalDateTime;
import java.time.ZonedDateTime;
import static java.time.Month.JANUARY;
```

551

```java
public class CurrentDateTime {
    public static void main(String[] args) {
        // Get current date, time, and datetime
        LocalDate dateOnly = LocalDate.now();
        LocalTime timeOnly = LocalTime.now();
        LocalDateTime dateTime = LocalDateTime.now();
        ZonedDateTime dateTimeWithZone = ZonedDateTime.now();

        System.out.println("Current Date: " + dateOnly);
        System.out.println("Current Time: " + timeOnly);
        System.out.println("Current Date and Time: " + dateTime);
        System.out.println("Current Date, Time, and Zone: " + dateTimeWithZone);

        // Construct a birth date and time from datetime components
        LocalDate myBirthDate = LocalDate.of(1968, JANUARY, 12);
        LocalTime myBirthTime = LocalTime.of(7, 30);
        System.out.println("My Birth Date: " + myBirthDate);
        System.out.println("My Birth Time: " + myBirthTime);
    }
}
```

```
Current Date: 2017-08-04
Current Time: 08:48:29.402753900
Current Date and Time: 2017-08-04T08:48:29.402753900
Current Date, Time, and Zone: 2017-08-04T08:48:29.403754200-05:00[America/Chicago]
My Birth Date: 1968-01-12
My Birth Time: 07:30
```

The program uses four classes to get a local date, a time, a datetime, and a datetime with a time zone. In the legacy Date-Time API, you could have gotten a similar result using only the Calendar class.

The Date-Time API is comprehensive. It spans about 80 classes and about 1,000 methods. It lets you represent and manipulate dates and times using different scales and different calendar systems. Several local standards and one universal standard (ISO-8601) have been in use for timekeeping. To take full advantage of the Date-Time API, you need to understand the history of timekeeping. The next few sections give you a brief overview of different ways to measure time using calendar systems and ISO-8601 date and time standards. If you have a good understanding of these topics, you may skip these sections and continue from the "Exploring the New Date-Time API" section.

Evolution of Timekeeping

A scale is used to measure the quantity of physical things such as length of a string in meters, weight of a person in pounds, volume of water in liters, etc. Here, meters, pounds, and liters are units of measurement on a particular scale.

How do we measure time? Time is not a physical thing. To measure time, we link it to a periodic physical phenomenon, for example, swinging of a pendulum, rotation of earth on its axis, revolution of earth around the sun, oscillations of an electromagnetic signal associated with a quantum transition between two energy levels in an atom, etc. Thus, a time scale is an arrangement of events to define the duration of time.

In ancient times, events such as sunrise and sunset, which are generated because of the rotation of Earth on its axis, were used as a time scale; the unit of the time scale was day. Duration between two consecutive sunrises counted as one day.

As the human civilization progressed, devices for timekeeping were developed. Some of those were

- A sundial based on the position of the sun

- A mechanical clock based on periodic movement of a pendulum

- Finally, an atomic clock based on the properties of the caesium-133 atom

A clock is a timekeeping device that consists of two components: a frequency standard and a counter. The frequency standard in a clock is a component to obtain equally spaced periodic events to measure the length of a desired time interval. The counter (also called an accumulator or adder) counts the number of occurrences of the periodic event. For example, in a pendulum clock, the occurrence of a complete cycle of a pendulum indicates a time interval of one second, gears count the number of seconds, and the face of the clock displays the time. Even in ancient times, there was the concept of two-part clocks for timekeeping. The rotation of Earth provided the first component of the clock in terms of the periodic events of sunrise and sunset; a calendar provided the second component of the clock to count days, months, and years.

Based on Earth's rotation on its axis, several time scales, known as Universal Time (UT), have been used. Earth motion, around its axis and the sun, is irregular. Because of the irregularities in Earth motion, the length of the day from day to day and the number of the fractional days in a year from year to year vary. A solar day (also called an apparent or true solar day) is the length of time measured by observing two consecutive passing of the sun at local noon. If you use a perfect clock to observe the sun at a local meridian at noon every day, you would find that, throughout the year, position of the sun in the sky varies about four degrees (about 16 minutes in time) East-West of the local meridian. This implies that, on a particular day during a year, there could be up to 16 minutes difference between the time when it is noon shown by the clock and when the sun passes the local meridian. The difference between the clock time and the sun time, which arises because of the tilt of the earth rotation axis relative to its orbital plane and its elliptical orbit around the sun, is known as the equation of time. The time that is measured using the solar day is called apparent solar time.

The time obtained by applying corrections to the solar time to account for the equation of time is known as Universal Time Zero (UT0) or mean solar time. The midnight at prime meridian (zero degree longitude), which passes through Greenwich, England, is defined as 00 hours for UT0. The second is defined as 1/86400 of a mean solar day.

The wobbling of Earth relative to its axis of rotation is known as polar motion. UT0 corrected for polar motion yields another time scale, which is called UT1. Earth's rotational speed is not uniform. UT1 corrected for the seasonal variation in the rotational speed of Earth yields another time scale, which is called UT2.

The irregular spin rate of the Earth led to another time scale, known as Ephemeris Time (ET). ET was based on the period of one revolution of Earth around the sun and motion of other celestial bodies. On ET scale, the ephemeris second was defined as the fraction 1/31556925.9747 of the tropical year for 1900 January 0 at 12 hours ephemeris time. ET was replaced by Terrestrial Dynamical Time (TDT) and Barycentric Dynamical Time (TDB) in early 1980s.

The International Atomic Time (also known as TAI, for the French name Temps Atomique International) scale is an atomic time scale. The atomic second, the unit of time in the TAI scale, is defined as the duration of 9192631770 periods of the radiation corresponding to the transition between the two hyperfine levels of the ground state of the cesium-133 atom. In 1967, the definition of the atomic second became the definition of the International System of Units (SI) second. The International Bureau of Weights and Measures (BIPM) is the official timekeeper of atomic time. There are 65 laboratories with over 230 atomic clocks contributing to the TAI scale. Each clock contributing to TAI is assigned a weighting factor based on its performance. The weighted average of all the contributing atomic clocks gives TAI.

Why do we use many atomic clocks to measure TAI? One clock may fail and stop measuring time. Even atomic clocks are affected by environmental changes. To avoid such failures and inaccuracies, several atomic clocks are used to track TAI.

On January 1, 1972, Coordinated Universal Time (UTC) was adopted as the official time scale for the world for all civil purposes. UTC and atomic clocks run at the same rate. As BIPM counts the seconds on TAI scale, astronomers continue to measure time using the rotation of earth on its axis. Astronomical time is compared to UTC, and if they differ by more than 0.9 seconds, a leap second is added or subtracted to UTC to keep the time scales UT0 and UTC as close as possible. International Earth Rotation Service (IERS) makes the decision to introduce a leap second to UTC.

At any time, UTC differs from TAI by an integral number of seconds. The relation between UTC and TAI may be given as follows:

```
UTC = TAI - (algebraic sum of leap seconds)
```

As of July 1, 2012, 35 leap seconds have been added to UTC. So far, no leap second has been subtracted from UTC. Therefore, on July 1, 2012 and until another leap second is introduced, UTC and TAI are related as follows:

```
UTC = TAI - 35
```

You might think, because we have been adding leap seconds to UTC, UTC should be ahead of TAI. That is not true. Adding a leap second to UTC makes that hour on UTC scale 61 seconds long instead of 60 seconds. TAI is a continuous time scale; it keeps ticking all the time. When UTC completes the 61st second of the hour, TAI has moved to the first second in the next hour. Thus, UTC lags TAI when a leap second is added to it. Similar logic, but in reverse order, applies when a leap second is subtracted from UTC. If, at any time in the future, the leap seconds added to and subtracted from UTC become equal, UTC and TAI will read the same time.

UTC represents the time of day at the prime meridian (zero degree longitude) on Earth, which passes through Greenwich, England. UTC is based on a 24-hour clock with the day starting at 00 hours midnight. UTC is also known as Zulu time. The ISO-8601 standard uses the letter Z as the UTC of day designator; for example, the UTC of day 19 minutes and 23 seconds past 15 hours is written as 15:19:23Z.

You're not done with UTC yet! I discuss two more versions of UTC: Simplified UTC and UTC with Smoothed Leap Seconds (UTC-SLS).

Humans are used to understanding a solar day in terms of a 24-hour period: each hour consisting of 60 minutes and each minute consisting of 60 seconds. A solar day consists of 86400 seconds. On the UTC scale, a solar day may also consist of 86399 or 86401 seconds because of a leap second. For easier understanding for the common user, most computer systems ignore the leap seconds on the UTC scale. The UTC scale that ignores the leap seconds is called a simplified-UTC scale.

▓ **Tip** To meet the expectations of most users, the new Java Date-Time API uses simplified UTC, where leap seconds are ignored, making all days have the same number of 86400 seconds.

When the leap second is added or subtracted in UTC, it creates a gap or overlap of one second in the time scale at the end of the day. UTC-SLS is a proposed standard for handling a UTC leap second. Instead of introducing a leap second at the end of a day, UTC-SLS proposes to perform a smooth adjustment of 1 second over last 1000 seconds of the day by changing the rate of the clock by 0.1%. On a day when a leap second is added to UTC, UTC-SLS will make the last 1000 seconds of that day 1001 milliseconds long; thus, reducing the rate of the UTC-SLS clock from 23:43:21 to 24:00:00 by 0.1%. On a day when a leap second is added to UTC, UTC-SLS will make the last 1000 seconds of that day as 999 milliseconds long; thus, increasing the rate of the UTC-SLS clock from 23:43:19 to 24:00:00 by 0.1%.

Finally, there are proposals to have universal and monotonous civil time by getting rid of the leap seconds from UTC. Some have also proposed to replace the UTC leap seconds by leap hours!

Time Zones and Daylight Savings Time

When it was midnight of April 20, 2012 UTC, what local time was it in New Delhi, India and Chicago, USA? It was 5:30 in the morning of April 20, 2012 in New Delhi, India, and 7:00 in the evening of April 19, 2012 in Chicago, USA. How do we determine local time at a place? Wouldn't it be nice to have only one time for the entire world? If it is midnight UTC, it is midnight everywhere in the world. Maybe this would have been a good idea in the past as human minds are capable of getting used to new ideas over time through practice. Local time in a region is set such that a day starts at 00 hours, which is midnight. Therefore, 00 hours is midnight in New Delhi as well as Chicago.

Geographically, the world may be divided into 24 longitudinal bands, each covering a 15-degree range of longitude starting at the prime meridian; each band represents a one-hour time zone. The area covered by a time zone will observe the same time.

Humans are divided more politically than geographically. In this world, our political differences always override the geographical similarity! Sometimes an imaginary border separating two countries or states makes people observe different times on each side of the border.

In practice, time zones have been divided based on political regions: countries and regions within countries. Local time in each time zone is an offset from UTC. The offset, the difference in UTC and local time in a time zone, is called a zone offset. The regions east of the prime meridian use a positive zone offset. A negative zone offset is used for regions west to the prime meridian. The zone offset is expressed in hours and minutes such as +5:30 hours, -10:00 hours, etc. For example, India uses a zone offset of +5:30 hours; therefore, you can add 5 hours and 30 minutes to UTC to get Indian local time. You may think that the value for a zone offset is fixed for a time zone. Alas, we, the civilized and advanced humans, were so simple in timekeeping!

Some countries have more than one time zone. For example, USA has five time zones: Alaska, Pacific, Mountain, Central, and Eastern; India has only one time zone. In USA, when the local time in Mobile, Alabama (Central time zone) is 7:00 AM, it is 5:00 AM local time in Los Angeles, California (Pacific time zone). Every part of India, because of only one time zone, observes the same time.

The zone offset for some time zones vary in a year. For example, in Chicago, USA (called Central time zone), the zone offset is -5:00 hours in summer and -6:00 hours in winter. Most countries use a fixed zone offset. For example, India uses a +5:30 hours fixed zone offset. The rules for a time zone, governing the time when the zone offset changes, and by how much it changes, are decided by government. These rules are known as time zone rules.

The zone offset ranges between +14:00 hours to -12:00 hours. If there are only 24 hours in a day, how do we have +14 as a zone offset? The range, +14 to -12, makes it a 26 hours day! Note that some countries consist of several small islands situated far apart on two sides of the International Date Line making them a day apart. This posed problems in official communication among the islands of these countries as they observed only four common weekdays. They extended the zone offset beyond 12:00, thus moving the International Date Line for their country, to keep the whole country on one side of the International Date Line. Examples of countries using +13:00 and +14:00 hours of zone offsets are Kiribati (pronounced "kirbas"), Samoa, and Tokelau.

Daylight Savings Time is used to make better use of the daylight in the evening by moving the clocks forward (usually by one hour) in spring. Clocks are set back by the same amount of time in fall. The period of the year during which DST is observed is called summer; the other part of the year is called winter. Not all countries observe DST. The government of a country decides whether the country (or only some locations within a country) observes DST; if it does, government decides the dates and times to move the clocks forward and backward. For example, zones observing DST in the United States of America moved the clocks one hour forward at 2:00 AM local time on March 11, 2012, thus creating a gap of one hour. Note that on March 11, 2012, the local time between 2:00 AM and 3:00 AM did not exist in those zones in the USA. In fall, when clocks are moved back, a time overlap of the equal amount is created. India and Thailand are two among several countries that do not observe DST. DST changes the zone offset of the DST observing locations from UTC twice a year.

Calendar Systems

Humans use calendars to work with time. The time units used in calendars are year, month, day, hour, minute, and second. In this sense, a calendar is a system of tracking time, past and future, for humans in a meaningful way for social, political, legal, religious, etc. purposes.

Typically, a calendar system does not keep track of the time of day; it works in terms of day, month, and year. Broadly speaking, in a calendar, a day is based on the rotation of earth on its axis, month on the revolution of the moon around Earth, and year on the revolution of Earth around the sun. Sometimes, a calendar system is based on week, which is based on a non-astronomical cycle.

Throughout the history of humankind, different civilizations have been known to use different calendar systems. Most of the ancient calendar systems have been based on astronomical cycles generated by solar motion, lunar motion, or both, thus giving rise to three types of calendric systems: solar, lunar, and lunisolar calendars.

A solar calendar is designed to align with a tropical year (also called a solar year), which is the mean interval between the vernal equinox. An equinox occurs twice a year when the center of the sun is in the same plane as the equator of earth. The term "equinox" means equal night; on an equinox, day and night are almost of the same length. A vernal equinox occurs during spring around March 21; an autumnal equinox occurs during autumn around September 22. The Gregorian calendar, which is the most used calendar worldwide for civil purposes, is an example of a solar calendar.

A lunar calendar is based on lunar phase cycle. It is not aligned to a tropical year. In a year, it drifts by 11 to 12 days from a tropical year. A lunar calendar takes about 33 years to catch up with a tropical year, to drift again for another 33 years. A lunar month, which is also called a synodic month, is the interval of time between new moons that is equal to 29 days, 12 hours, 44 minutes, and 2.8 seconds. The Islamic calendar is an example of a lunar calendar.

A lunisolar calendar computes months based on lunar phase cycle like a lunar calendar. However, it intercalates, in a 2-year or 3-year period, a month to keep itself aligned with a tropical year. The Buddhist, Hindu lunisolar, Chinese, Hebrew calendars are some examples of lunisolar calendars.

The Julian Calendar

The Julian calendar is a solar calendar introduced in the year -45 by Julius Caesar. It was widely used by the European civilization until year +1582 when the Gregorian calendar was introduced.

An ordinary year consists of 365 days. Every four years, a day is intercalated between February 28 and March 1, which is designated as February 29, to make the year 366 days, which is called a leap year. The year 0 (1 B. C.) is considered a leap year. The average length of a Julian calendar year is 365.25 days that is close to the length of a tropical year known in those days.

A year consists of 12 months. Months are fixed in lengths. Table 16-1 lists the order, name, and number of days in months in the Julian calendar.

Table 16-1. *Order, Name, and Number of Days in Months in the Julian (and Gregorian) Calendar*

Order	Month Name	Number of Days
1	January	31
2	February	28 (29 in a leap year)
3	March	31
4	April	30
5	May	31
6	June	30
7	July	31
8	August	31
9	September	30
10	October	31
11	November	30
12	December	31

The Gregorian Calendar

The Gregorian calendar is the most widely used calendar in the world for civil purposes. It follows the rules of the Julian calendar for number of months in a year and number of days in months. However, it changed the rule for computing a leap year: a year is a leap year if it is exactly divisible by 4. A year exactly divisible by 100 is not a leap year unless it is also divisible by 400.

For example, 4, 8, 12, 400, and 800 are known as leap years, and 1, 2, 3, 5, 300, and 100 are known as common years. Year 0 (1 B. C.) is considered a leap year. With a new definition of a leap year, the average length of a year in the Gregorian calendar is 365.2425 days, which is very close to the length of a tropical year. The Gregorian calendar repeats every 400 years. If you save your paper calendar for year 2014, your nth great-grandchildren will be able to reuse it in year 2414!

The Gregorian calendar was introduced on Friday, October 15, 1582. The day before the Gregorian calendar started, it was Thursday, October 4, 1582 according to the existing Julian calendar. Note that the introduction of the Gregorian calendar left the cycle of weekdays unaffected; however, it left a discontinuity of 10 days between the two calendars that is called the cutover. Dates before the cutover are Julian dates, dates after the cutover are Gregorian dates, and dates during the cutover do not exist.

The Gregorian calendar did not exist before October 15, 1582. How do we assign dates to the events before the start of the Gregorian calendar? The Gregorian calendar applied to the dates when it was not in effect is called a proleptic Gregorian calendar. Therefore, October 14, 1582 exists in a proleptic Gregorian calendar, which is the same as October 4, 1582 in the Julian calendar.

Why was the first day of the Gregorian calendar Friday, October 15, 1582, and not Friday, October 5, 1582? According to Doggett, *Calendars* (n.d.), in the Julian calendar, the date of Easter, a Christian festival, was computed based on an assumption that March 21 is the date for vernal equinox. Later, it was realized that vernal equinox had been drifting from March 21; hence, the date of Easter drifts from the seasonal springtime. To keep the date of Easter synchronized with springtime, the adjustment of 10 days was made in the start date of the Gregorian calendar, so the vernal equinox in year 1583 and later occurs approximately on March 21.

≡ **Tip** The main difference between the Julian and Gregorian calendar is the rule for determining a leap year. The mean length of a year in the Gregorian calendar is closer to the length of the tropical year than that of in the Julian calendar.

ISO-8601 Standards for Datetime

The new Date-Time API has extensive support for ISO-8601 standards. This section is intended to present a brief and limited overview of the datetime components and their textual representations included in the ISO-8601 standards. A datetime in ISO 8601 consists of three components: date, time, and zone offset that are combined in the following format:

```
[date]T[time][zone offset]
```

A date component consists of three calendar fields: year, month, and day. Two fields in a date are separated by a hyphen.

```
year-month-day
```

For example, 2012-04-30 represents the 30th day in April of year 2012.

Sometimes humans deal with dates that may not contain complete information to identify a specific day in a calendar. For example, December 25 makes sense as a Christmas day without specifying the year part of the date. To identify a specific Christmas day in a calendar, we must also specify the year. A date with some missing parts is known as a partial. 2012, 2012-05, -----05-29, etc. are examples of partials. ISO-8601 allows omitting parts in a date only from the right end. That is, it allows omitting day, or month and day. The Date-Time API allows three types of partials: year, year-month, and month-day.

Date and time components are separated by a character T. A time component consists of fields: hour, minute, and second. A colon separates two fields in a time component. A time is represented in this format:

```
hour:minute:second
```

ISO-8601 uses a 24-hour timekeeping system. The hour element can be between 00 and 24. The hour 24 is used to denote the end of a calendar day. The value for the minute element ranges from 00 to 59. The second element may range from 00 to 60. The value 60 for the second element indicates a positive leap second. For example, 15:20:56 represents a local time of 20 minutes and 56 seconds past 15 hours after midnight. When reduced accuracy is allowed, second, or second and minute elements may be omitted from a time. For example, 15:19 and 07 denote 19 minutes past 15 hours, and 07 hours from midnight, respectively.

Midnight is the start of a calendar day. It is represented by 00:00:00 or 00:00. The start of a calendar day coincides with the end of the previous calendar day. Therefore, midnight of a calendar day may also be represented by 24:00:00 or 24:00.

When a date, time, or datetime is specified without a zone offset, it is considered a local date, time, or datetime, respectively. Examples of a local date, time, and datetime are 2012-05-01, 13:52:05, and 2012-05-01T13:52:05, respectively.

Using a zone offset, you can represent a time component relative to UTC of day. The zone offset represents a fixed difference between a local time and UTC. It starts with a plus or minus sign (+ or -) followed by hour and minute elements, which are separated by a colon. Some examples of zone offset are +05:30, -06:00, +10:00, +5:30, etc. The character Z is used as a zone offset designator to denote the UTC time of day. For example, 10:20:40Z represents the UTC of day 20 minutes and 40 seconds past 10 in the morning; 12:20:40+2:00 represents a local time of day 20 minutes and 40 seconds past 12 in the afternoon, which is 2 hours ahead of UTC. Both times, 10:20:40Z and 12:20:40+2:00, represent the same point in time.

▒ **Tip**   ISO-8601 specifies standards for using a fixed zone offset from the UTC component in time representation. Recall that a zone offset may vary for time zones that observe Daylight Savings Time. In addition to ISO-8601 standards, the Date-Time API supports a variable zone offset as well.

An example of a datetime having all three components fully specified is the following:

```
2012-05-01T16:30:00-06:00
```

This datetime represents May 1, 2012 30 minutes past 16 hours from midnight that is 6 hours behind UTC.

ISO-8601 includes standards for several other date- and time-related concepts such as instant, duration, period, time interval, etc. The Date-Time API provides classes whose objects directly represent most, but not all, ISO date and time concepts.

The toString() methods of all date and time classes in the Date-Time API return a textual representation of date and time in ISO formats. The API includes classes to let you format a date and time in non-ISO formats.

The ISO standards include formats for specifying an amount of time known as duration. ISO-8601 defines duration as a non-negative quantity. However, the Date-Time API also allows a negative quantity treated as duration. The ISO format for representing duration is as follows:

```
PnnYnnMnnDTnnHnnMnnS
```

In this format, P is a duration designator; nn denotes a number; Y, M, D, H, M, and S denote year, month, day, hour, month, and second, respectively; and T is a time designator that is present only if the duration involves hour, minute, and second. The following are examples of textual representations of some durations. Inline comments describe the duration.

```
P12Y       // A duration of 12 years
PT15:30    // A duration of 15 hours and 30 minutes
PT20S      // A duration of 20 seconds
P4Y2MT30M  // A duration of 4 years 2 months and 30 minutes
```

▒ **Tip**   The Date-Time API provides Duration and Period classes to deal with an amount of time. A Duration represents an amount of time on the machine-scale timeline. A Period represents an amount of time on human-scale timeline.

Exploring the New Date-Time API

At first, exploring the Date-Time API is intimidating as it contains many classes with numerous methods. Learning the naming convention of methods will help understand the API tremendously. The Date-Time API has been designed carefully to keep the names of classes and their methods consistent and intuitive. Methods starting with the same prefix do the similar work. For example, an of() method in a class is used as a static factory method to create an object of that class.

All classes, interfaces, and enums for the Date-Time API are in the java.time package and four of its subpackages, as listed in Table 16-2.

Table 16-2. *Packages and Subpackages of the Date-Time API*

Package	Description
java.time	Contains frequently used classes. The LocalDate, LocalTime, LocalDateTime, ZonedDateTime, Period, Duration, and Instant classes are in this package. Classes in this package are based on ISO standards.
java.time.chrono	Contains classes supporting non-ISO calendar systems, for example, Hijrah calendar, Thai Buddhist calendar, etc.
java.time.format	Contains classes for formatting and parsing dates and times.
java.time.temporal	Contains classes for accessing components of dates and times. It also contains classes that acts like datetime adjusters.
java.time.zone	Contains classes supporting time zones and zone rules.

The following sections explain the prefixes used in method names in the Date-Time API with their meanings and examples.

The ofXxx() Methods

Classes in the Date-Time API do not provide public constructors to create their objects. They let you create objects through static factory methods named ofXxx(). The following snippet of code shows how to create objects of the LocalDate class:

```
LocalDate ld1 = LocalDate.of(2012, 5, 2);          // 2012-05-02
LocalDate ld2 = LocalDate.of(2012, Month.JULY, 4); // 2012-07-04
LocalDate ld3 = LocalDate.ofEpochDay(2002);        // 1975-06-26
LocalDate ld4 = LocalDate.ofYearDay(2014, 40);     // 2014-02-09
```

The from() Methods

A from() method is a static factory method, similar to an of() method, that is used to derive a datetime object from the specified argument. Unlike an of() method, a from() method requires data conversion on the specified argument.

To understand what a from() method does, think of it named as deriveFrom() method. Using a from() method, you derive a new datetime object from the specified argument. The following snippet of code shows how to derive a LocalDate from a LocalDateTime:

```
LocalDateTime ldt = LocalDateTime.of(2012, 5, 2, 15, 30); // 2012-05-02T15:30
LocalDate ld = LocalDate.from(ldt);                        // 2012-05-02
```

The withXxx() Methods

Most classes in the Date-Time API are immutable. They do not have setXxx() methods. If you want to change a field of a datetime object, for example, the year value in a date, you need to look for a method with a prefix like withXxx. A withXxx() method returns a copy of the object with the specified field changed.

Assume that you have a LocalDate object and you want to change its year. You need to use the withYear(int newYear) method of the LocalDate class. The following snippet of code shows how to obtain a LocalDate from another LocalDate with the year changed:

```
LocalDate ld1 = LocalDate.of(2012, Month.MAY, 2); // 2012-05-02
LocalDate ld2 = ld1.withYear(2014);               // 2014-05-02
```

You can obtain a new LocalDate from an existing LocalDate by changing multiple fields by chaining the withXxx() method calls. The following snippet of code creates a new LocalDate from an existing LocalDate by changing the year and month:

```
LocalDate ld3 = LocalDate.of(2012, 5, 2); // 2012-05-02
LocalDate ld4 = ld3.withYear(2014)
                   .withMonth(7);         // 2014-07-02
```

The getXxx() Methods

A getXxx() method returns the specified element of the object. For example, the getYear() method in the LocalDate class returns the year part of the date. The following snippet of code shows how to get year, month, and day from a LocalDate object:

```
LocalDate ld = LocalDate.of(2012, 5, 2);
int year = ld.getYear();          // 2012
Month month = ld.getMonth();      // Month.MAY
int day = ld.getDayOfMonth();     // 2
```

The toXxx() Methods

A toXxx() method converts an object to a related Xxx type. For example, the toLocalDate() method in the LocalDateTime class returns a LocalDate object with the date in the original LocalDateTime object. Here are some examples of using toXxx() methods.

```
LocalDate ld = LocalDate.of(2017, 8, 29); // 2017-08-29

// Convert the date to epoch days. The epoch days is the number of days from
// 1970-01-01 to a date. A date before 1970-01-01 returns a negative integer.
long epochDays = ld.toEpochDay(); // 17407

// Convert a LocalDateTime to a LocalTime using the toLocalTime() method
LocalDateTime ldt = LocalDateTime.of(2017, 8, 29, 16, 30);
LocalTime lt = ldt.toLocalTime(); // 16:30
```

The atXxx() Methods

An atXxx() method lets you build a new datetime object from an existing datetime object by supplying some additional pieces of information. Contrast the use of an atXxx() method with that of a withXxx() method; the former lets you create a new type of object by providing additional information whereas the latter lets you create a copy of an object by changing its fields.

Suppose you have the date 2012-05-02. If you want to create a new date of 2012-07-02 (with month changed to 7), you would use a withXxx() method. If you want to create a datetime of 2012-05-02T15:30 (by adding time 15:30), you would use an atXxx() method. Some examples of using atXxx() methods are shown here.

```
LocalDate ld = LocalDate.of(2012, 5, 2);  // 2012-05-02
LocalDateTime ldt1 = ld.atStartOfDay();    // 2012-05-02T00:00
LocalDateTime ldt2 = ld.atTime(15, 30);    // 2012-05-02T15:30
```

The atXxx() methods supports the builder pattern. The following snippet of code shows how to use a builder pattern to build a local date:

```
// Use a builder pattern to build a date 2012-05-22
LocalDate d1 = Year.of(2012).atMonth(5).atDay(22);

// Use an of() factory method to build a date 2012-05-22
LocalDate d2 = LocalDate.of(2012, 5, 22);
```

The plusXxx() and minusXxx() Methods

A plusXxx() method returns a copy of an object by adding a specified value. For example, the plusDays(long days) method in the LocalDate class returns a copy of the LocalDate object by adding the specified number of days.

A minusXxx() method returns a copy of an object by subtracting a specified value. For example, the minusDays(long days) method in the LocalDate class returns a copy of the LocalDate object by subtracting the specified number of days.

```
LocalDate ld = LocalDate.of(2012, 5, 2); // 2012-05-02
LocalDate ld1 = ld.plusDays(5);     // 2012-05-07
LocalDate ld2 = ld.plusMonths(3);   // 2012-08-02
LocalDate ld3 = ld.plusWeeks(3);    // 2012-05-23
LocalDate ld4 = ld.minusMonths(7);  // 2011-10-02
LocalDate ld5 = ld.minusWeeks(3);   // 2012-04-11
```

The multipliedBy(), dividedBy(), and negated() Methods

Multiplication, division, and negation do not make sense on dates and times. They are applicable to the datetime types that denote an amount of time such as Duration and Period. Durations and periods can be added and subtracted. The Date-Time API supports negative durations and periods.

```
Duration d = Duration.ofSeconds(200); // PT3M20S (3 minutes and 20 seconds)
Duration d1 = d.multipliedBy(2);      // PT6M40S (6 minutes and 40 seconds)
Duration d2 = d.negated();            // PT-3M-20S (-3 minutes and -20 seconds)
```

Instants and Durations

A timeline (or a time axis) is a mathematical representation of the passage of time in terms of instantaneous events along a unique axis. A machine-scale timeline represents the passage of time as a single incrementing number, as shown in Figure 16-1.

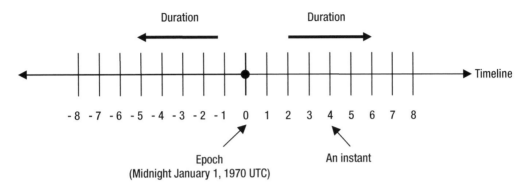

Figure 16-1. *A timeline representing the passage of machine-scale time*

An instant is a point representing a unique moment in time on a timeline. An epoch is an instant on a timeline that is used as a reference point (or the origin) to measure other instants.

An object of the Instant class represents an instant on the timeline. It uses a timeline to represent simplified UTC to a nanosecond precision. That is, the time interval (or duration) between two consecutive instants on the timeline is one nanosecond. The timeline uses 1970-01-01T00:00:00Z as the epoch. Instants after the epoch have positive values; instants before the epoch have negative values. The instant at the epoch is assigned a zero value.

There are different ways you can create an instance of the Instant class. Using its now() method, you can get the current instant using the system default clock.

```
// Get the current instant
Instant i1 = Instant.now();
```

You can obtain an instance of the Instant class using an amount of time in different units from the epoch. The following snippet of code creates an Instant object to represent 19 seconds from the epoch, which represents 1970-01-01T00:00:19Z:

```
// An instant: 19 seconds from the epoch
Instant i2 = Instant.ofEpochSecond(19);
```

An object of the Duration class represents an amount of time between two instants on the timeline. The Duration class supports a directed duration. That is, it allows a positive as well as negative duration. Figure 16-1 shows durations with arrows to signify that they are directed durations.

You can create an instance of the Duration class using one of its ofXxx() static factory methods.

```
// A duration of 2 days
Duration d1 = Duration.ofDays(2);
```

```
// A duration of 25 minutes
Duration d2 = Duration.ofMinutes(25);
```

⬛ **Tip** The `toString()` method of the Instant class returns a textual representation of the `Instant` in the ISO-8601 format `yyyy-MM-ddTHH:mm:ss.SSSSSSSSSZ`. The `toString()` method of the `Duration` class returns a textual representation of the duration in `PTnHnMnS` format, where n is the number of hours, minutes, or seconds.

What can you do with instants and durations? Typically, they are used for recording timestamps and elapsed time between two events. Two instants can be compared to know whether one occurs before or after the other. You can add (and subtract) a duration to an instant to obtain another instant. Adding two durations results in another duration. Classes in the Date-Time API are `Serializable`. You can use `Instant` to store timestamps in databases.

Instant and Duration classes store second and nanosecond-of-second parts of their values separately. The Duration class has `getSeconds()` and `getNano()` methods, whereas the `Instant` class has `getEpochSecond()` and `getNano()` methods to get the two values. The following is an example of getting second and nanosecond of an `Instant`:

```
// Get the current instant
Instant i1 = Instant.now();

// Get seconds and nanoseconds
long seconds = i1.getEpochSecond();
int nanoSeconds = i1.getNano();

System.out.println("Current Instant: " + i1);
System.out.println("Seconds: " + seconds);
System.out.println("Nanoseconds: " + nanoSeconds);
```

```
(You may get a different output.)
Current Instant: 2017-08-04T19:12:44.859580900Z
Seconds: 1501873964
Nanoseconds: 859580900
```

Listing 16-3 demonstrates use of some operations that can be performed on instants and durations.

Listing 16-3. Using Instant and Duration Classes

```
// InstantDurationTest.java
package com.jdojo.datetime;

import java.time.Duration;
import java.time.Instant;

public class InstantDurationTest {
    public static void main(String[] args) {
        Instant i1 = Instant.ofEpochSecond(20);
        Instant i2 = Instant.ofEpochSecond(55);
        System.out.println("i1:" + i1);
        System.out.println("i2:" + i2);
```

```
        Duration d1 = Duration.ofSeconds(55);
        Duration d2 = Duration.ofSeconds(-17);
        System.out.println("d1:" + d1);
        System.out.println("d2:" + d2);

        // Compare instants
        System.out.println("i1.isBefore(i2):" + i1.isBefore(i2));
        System.out.println("i1.isAfter(i2):" + i1.isAfter(i2));

        // Add and subtract durations to instants
        Instant i3 = i1.plus(d1);
        Instant i4 = i2.minus(d2);
        System.out.println("i1.plus(d1):" + i3);
        System.out.println("i2.minus(d2):" + i4);

        // Add two durations
        Duration d3 = d1.plus(d2);
        System.out.println("d1.plus(d2):" + d3);
    }
}
```

```
i1:1970-01-01T00:00:20Z
i2:1970-01-01T00:00:55Z
d1:PT55S
d2:PT-17S
i1.isBefore(i2):true
i1.isAfter(i2):false
i1.plus(d1):1970-01-01T00:01:15Z
i2.minus(d2):1970-01-01T00:01:12Z
d1.plus(d2):PT38S
```

Java 9 added several useful methods to the Duration class that can be put into the following three categories:

- Methods to divide a duration by another duration

- Methods to get a duration in terms of a specific time unit and methods to get a specific part of a duration such as days, hours, seconds, etc.

- Methods to truncate a duration to a specific time unit

I present examples of using these new methods in Java 9 in the following sections. In the examples, I use a duration of 23 days, 3 hours, 45 minutes, and 30 seconds. The following snippet of code creates this as a Duration object and stores its reference in a variable named compTime:

```
// Create a duration of 23 days, 3 hours, 45 minutes, and 30 seconds
Duration compTime = Duration.ofDays(23)
                            .plusHours(3)
                            .plusMinutes(45)
                            .plusSeconds(30);
System.out.println("Duration: " + compTime);
```

```
Duration: PT555H45M30S
```

After the days are converted to hours by multiplying them by 24, as the output shows, this duration represents 555 hours, 45 minutes, and 30 seconds.

Dividing a Duration by Another Duration

There is only one method in this category:

```
long dividedBy(Duration divisor)
```

The dividedBy() method lets you divide a duration by another duration. It returns the number of times the specific divisor occurs within the duration on which the method is called. To know how many whole weeks are in this duration, you call the dividedBy() method using 7 days as the duration. The following snippet of code shows you how to compute number of whole days, weeks, and hours in a duration:

```
long wholeDays = compTime.dividedBy(Duration.ofDays(1));
long wholeWeeks = compTime.dividedBy(Duration.ofDays(7));
long wholeHours = compTime.dividedBy(Duration.ofHours(7));

System.out.println("Number of whole days: " + wholeDays);
System.out.println("Number of whole weeks: " + wholeWeeks);
System.out.println("Number of whole hours: " + wholeHours);
```

```
Number of whole days: 23
Number of whole weeks: 3
Number of whole hours: 79
```

Converting and Retrieving Duration Parts

There are several methods added to the Duration class in this category:

- long toDaysPart()
- int toHoursPart()
- int toMillisPart()
- int toMinutesPart()
- int toNanosPart()
- long toSeconds()
- int toSecondsPart()

The Duration class contains two sets of methods. They are named toXxx() and toXxxPart(), where Xxx may be Days, Hours, Minutes, Seconds, Millis, and Nanos. In this list, you may notice that toDaysPart() is included, but toDays() is missing. If you see methods in one set missing for some Xxx, it means those methods already existed in JDK 8. For example, the toDays() method has been in the Duration class since JDK 8.

Methods named toXxx() convert the duration to the Xxx time unit and return the whole part. Methods named toXxxPart() break down the duration in parts as days:hours:minutes:seconds:millis:nanos and return the Xxx part from it. In this example, toDays() will convert the duration to days and return the whole part, which will be 23. The toDaysPart() will break down the duration to 23Days:3Hours:45Minutes:30Seconds:0Millis:0Nanos and return the first part, which is 23. Let's apply the same rules to toHours() and toHoursPart() methods. The toHours() method will convert the duration to hours and return the whole number of hours, which will be 555. The toHoursPart() method will break the duration into parts as it did for the toDaysPart() method and return the hours part, which is 3. The following snippet of code shows you a few examples:

```
System.out.println("toDays(): " + compTime.toDays());
System.out.println("toDaysPart(): " + compTime.toDaysPart());
System.out.println("toHours(): " + compTime.toHours());
System.out.println("toHoursPart(): " + compTime.toHoursPart());
System.out.println("toMinutes(): " + compTime.toMinutes());
System.out.println("toMinutesPart(): " + compTime.toMinutesPart());
```

```
Duration: PT555H45M30S
toDays(): 23
toDaysPart(): 23
toHours(): 555
toHoursPart(): 3
toMinutes(): 33345
toMinutesPart(): 45
```

Truncating Duration

There is only one method added to the Duration class in this category:

```
Duration truncatedTo(TemporalUnit unit)
```

The truncatedTo() method returns a copy of the duration with conceptual time units smaller than the specified unit truncated. The temporal unit specified must be DAYS or smaller. Specifying a temporal unit greater than DAYS such as WEEKS and YEARS throws a runtime exception.

▓ **Tip** A truncatedTo(TemporalUnit unit) method already existed in the LocalTime and Instant classes in Java 8.

The following snippet of code shows you how to use this method:

```
System.out.println("Truncated to DAYS: " + compTime.truncatedTo(ChronoUnit.DAYS));
System.out.println("Truncated to HOURS: " + compTime.truncatedTo(ChronoUnit.HOURS));
System.out.println("Truncated to MINUTES: " + compTime.truncatedTo(ChronoUnit.MINUTES));
```

```
Truncated to DAYS: PT552H
Truncated to HOURS: PT555H
Truncated to MINUTES: PT555H45M
```

The duration is 23Days:3Hours:45Minutes:30Seconds:0Millis:0Nanos. When you truncate this to DAYS, all parts smaller than days are dropped and it returns 23 days, which is the same as 552, hours as shown in the output. When you truncate to HOURS, it drops all parts smaller than hours and returns 555 hours. Truncating it to MINUTES keeps parts up to minutes and drops all smaller parts such as seconds and milliseconds.

Human-Scale Time

In the previous section, I discussed the use of Instant and Duration classes whose instances are more suited to dealing with machine-scale time. Humans deal with time in terms of fields such as year, month, day, hour, minute, and second. Recall the following format for specifying date and time in ISO-8601 format:

```
[date]T[time][zone offset]
```

The Date-Time API provides several classes, listed in Table 16-3, to represent all fields and their combinations of human-scale time. A Yes or No in the component column for a class indicates whether an instance of the class stores that component or not. I discuss all of these classes in detail shortly.

Table 16-3. *Human-Scale Date and Time Classes and Their Components*

Class Name	Date	Time	Zone Offset	Zone Rule
LocalDate	Yes	No	No	No
LocalTime	No	Yes	No	No
LocalDateTime	Yes	Yes	No	No
OffsetTime	No	Yes	Yes	No
OffsetDateTime	Yes	Yes	Yes	No
ZonedDateTime	Yes	Yes	Yes	Yes
ZoneOffset	No	No	Yes	No
ZoneId	No	No	Yes	Yes

The ZoneOffset Class

An instance of the ZoneOffset class represents a fixed zone offset from UTC time zone, for example, +05:30, -06:00, etc. It is a period of time that a time zone differs from the UTC. A ZoneOffset is not aware of the changes in zone offset because of the observed Daylight Savings Time. The ZoneOffset class declares three constants:

- UTC
- MAX
- MIN

UTC is the time zone offset constant for UTC. MAX and MIN are the maximum and minimum supported zone offsets.

▓ **Tip**   Z, not +00:00 or -00:00, is used as the zone offset designator for the UTC time zone.

The ZoneOffset class provides methods to create its instances using a combination of hour, minute, and second. Listing 16-4 demonstrates how to create instances of the ZoneOffset class.

Listing 16-4. Creating Instances of the ZoneOffset Class

```java
// ZoneOffsetTest.java
package com.jdojo.datetime;
import java.time.ZoneOffset;

public class ZoneOffsetTest {
    public static void main(String[] args) {
        // Create zone offset using hour, minute, and second
        ZoneOffset zos1 = ZoneOffset.ofHours(-6);
        ZoneOffset zos2 = ZoneOffset.ofHoursMinutes(5, 30);
        ZoneOffset zos3 = ZoneOffset.ofHoursMinutesSeconds(8, 30, 45);
        System.out.println(zos1);
        System.out.println(zos2);
        System.out.println(zos3);

        // Create zone offset using offset ID as a string
        ZoneOffset zos4 = ZoneOffset.of("+05:00");
        ZoneOffset zos5 = ZoneOffset.of("Z"); // Same as ZoneOffset.UTC
        System.out.println(zos4);
        System.out.println(zos5);

        // Print the values for zone offset constants
        System.out.println("ZoneOffset.UTC: "  + ZoneOffset.UTC);
        System.out.println("ZoneOffset.MIN: "  + ZoneOffset.MIN);
        System.out.println("ZoneOffset.MAX: "  + ZoneOffset.MAX);
    }
}
```

```
-06:00
+05:30
+08:30:45
+05:00
Z
ZoneOffset.UTC: Z
ZoneOffset.MIN: -18:00
ZoneOffset.MAX: +18:00
```

According to ISO-8601 standards, a zone offset may include hours and minutes, or hours only. The new Date-Time API also allows seconds in a zone offset. You can use the compareTo() method of the ZoneOffset class to compare a zone offset to another zone offset. Zone offsets are compared in descending order that is the order in which they occur in the time of the day, for example, a zone offset of +5:30 occurs before a zone offset of +5:00. ISO-8601 standards support zone offsets between -12:00 to +14:00. However, to avoid any problems in the future if the zone offset gets extended, the Date-Time API supports zone offsets between -18:00 to +18:00.

The ZoneId Class

An instance of the ZoneId class represents a combination of a zone offset and the rules for changing the zone offset for observed Daylight Savings Time. Not all time zones observe Daylight Savings Time. To simplify your understanding about the ZoneId, you can think of it as follows:

```
ZoneId = ZoneOffset + ZoneRules
```

■ **Tip**   A ZoneOffset represents a fixed zone offset from UTC time zone, whereas a ZoneId represents a variable zone offset. The variation, the time in the year when the zone offset is changed, and the amount of change, are all controlled by the time zone rules. The ZoneOffset class inherits from the ZoneId class.

A time zone has a unique textual ID, which can be specified in three formats:

- In this format, the zone ID is specified in terms of zone offset, which can be in one of the following formats: +h, +hh, +hh:mm, -hh:mm, +hhmm, -hhmm, +hh:mm:ss, -hh:mm:ss, +hhmmss, and -hhmmss, where h, m, and s denote a single digit of hours, minutes, and seconds, respectively. Z is used for UTC. An example of a zone offset is +06:00.

- In this format, the zone ID is prefixed with UTC, GMT, or UT and followed by a zone offset, for example, UTC+06:00.

- In this format, the zone ID is specified by using a region, for example, America/Chicago.

Using the first two forms of zone IDs, you create a ZoneId with a fixed zone offset. You can create a ZoneId using the of() factory method.

```
ZoneId usChicago = ZoneId.of("America/Chicago");
ZoneId bdDhaka = ZoneId.of("Asia/Dhaka");
ZoneId fixedZoneId = ZoneId.of("+06:00");
```

The ZoneId class provides access to all known time zone IDs. Its getAvailableZoneIds() static method returns a Set<String> containing all available zone IDs. Listing 16-5 shows how to print all zone IDs. A partial list of zone IDs is shown in the output.

Listing 16-5. Printing All Available Zone IDs

```java
// PrintAllZoneIds.java
package com.jdojo.datetime;

import java.time.ZoneId;
import java.util.Set;

public class PrintAllZoneIds {
    public static void main(String[] args) {
        Set<String> zoneIds = ZoneId.getAvailableZoneIds();
        for (String zoneId: zoneIds) {
            System.out.println(zoneId);
        }
    }
}
```

```
Asia/Aden
Africa/Cairo
Pacific/Honolulu
America/Chicago
Europe/Athens
...
```

A ZoneId object gives you access to zone rules for the time zone represented by the ZoneId. You can use the getRules() method of the ZoneId class to get an instance of the ZoneRules class to work with rules such as transitions for Daylight Savings Time, the zone offset for a specified datetime, the amount of daylight savings, etc. Typically, you will not use zone rules directly in your code. As a developer, you would use a ZoneId to create a ZonedDateTime, which is discussed shortly. The program in Listing 16-6 shows how to query the ZoneRules object to get information about the time offset and time changes for a ZoneId. The list of time transitions is very big and it is shown partially in the output.

Listing 16-6. Knowing the Time Change Rules (the ZoneRules) for a ZoneId

```java
// ZoneRulesTest.java
package com.jdojo.datetime;

import java.time.LocalDateTime;
import java.time.ZoneId;
import java.time.ZoneOffset;
import java.time.zone.ZoneOffsetTransition;
import java.time.zone.ZoneRules;
import java.util.List;

public class ZoneRulesTest {
    public static void main(String[] args) {
        LocalDateTime now = LocalDateTime.now();
        System.out.println("Current Date Time: " + now);

        ZoneId fixedZoneId = ZoneId.of("+06:00");
        ZoneId bdDhaka = ZoneId.of("Asia/Dhaka");
        ZoneId usChicago = ZoneId.of("America/Chicago");

        // Print some zone rules for ZoneIds
        printDetails(fixedZoneId, now);
        printDetails(bdDhaka, now);
        printDetails(usChicago, now);
    }

    public static void printDetails(ZoneId zoneId, LocalDateTime now) {
        System.out.println("Zone ID: " + zoneId.getId());

        ZoneRules rules = zoneId.getRules();
        boolean isFixedOffset = rules.isFixedOffset();
        System.out.println("isFixedOffset(): " + isFixedOffset);
```

```
        ZoneOffset offset = rules.getOffset(now);
        System.out.println("Zone offset: " + offset);

        List<ZoneOffsetTransition> transitions = rules.getTransitions();
        System.out.println(transitions);
    }
}
```

```
Current Date Time: 2017-08-04T14:33:30.352524400
Zone ID: +06:00
isFixedOffset(): true
Zone offset: +06:00
[]
Zone ID: Asia/Dhaka
isFixedOffset(): false
Zone offset: +06:00
[Transition[Overlap at 1890-01-01T00:00+06:01:40 to +05:53:20], ..., Transition[Overlap at
2010-01-01T00:00+07:00 to +06:00]]
Zone ID: America/Chicago
isFixedOffset(): false
Zone offset: -05:00
[Transition[Overlap at 1883-11-18T12:09:24-05:50:36 to -06:00], ..., Transition[Overlap at
2008-11-02T02:00-05:00 to -06:00]]
```

Several organizations and groups provide a set of time zone rules as a database that contains the code and data for all time zones in the world. Each provider is given a unique group ID. One of the standard rules providers is a TZ database that is identified by TZDB group ID. Refer to `www.twinsun.com/tz/tz-link.htm` for more details on the TZ database.

As the rules for a time zone change over time, a group provides multiple versions of rules data for different regions. Typically, a region represents a time zone where the time zone rules are the same. Each group has its own naming scheme for the versions and regions.

TZDB stores region names in a `[area]/[city]` format. Examples of some region names are Africa/Tunis, America/Chicago, Asia/Kolkata, Asia/Tokyo, Europe/Istanbul, Europe/London, and Europe/Moscow.

The Date-Time API uses the TZDB as the default time zone rules provider. If you are using a region-based zone ID from the TZDB, use the region name as the zone id. The region name should be prefixed with the group ID of the provider in the form of "group~region" if a group other than TZDB is used for zone rules. For example, if you are using International Air Transport Association (IATA) provider, use "IATA~CHI" for the Chicago region. Refer to the `ZoneRulesProvider` class in the `java.time.zone` package for more details on how to register your own zone rules provider.

Useful Datetime-Related Enums

Before I discuss classes that represent different combinations of date and time, it is worth discussing some enums representing constants for date and time components:

- `Month`
- `DayOfWeek`
- `ChronoField`
- `ChronoUnit`

Most of the time, you will use the constants in these enums directly as arguments to methods or receive them as return values from methods. Some enums include methods to compute useful date time values using the constant itself as input.

Representing Months

The Month enum has 12 constants to represents the 12 months of the year. The constant names are JANUARY, FEBRUARY, MARCH, APRIL, MAY, JUNE, JULY, AUGUST, SEPTEMBER, OCTOBER, NOVEMBER, and DECEMBER. Months are numbered sequentially from 1 to 12, January being 1 and December being 12. The Month enum provides some useful methods such as of() to get an instance of Month from an int value, from() to get the Month from any date object, getValue() to get the int value of the Month, etc.

For better readability, use an enum constant, if and when available in the Date-Time API, instead of an integer value. For example, for the month of July, use Month.JULY in your code, not integer 7. Sometimes the API provides two versions of a method: one takes the Month enum argument and another the int value of the month. An example of such methods is the static factory method of() method in the LocalDate class:

- static LocalDate of(int year, int month, int dayOfMonth)

- static LocalDate of(int year, Month month, int dayOfMonth)

Listing 16-7 demonstrates some uses of the Month enum.

Listing 16-7. Using the Month enum

```java
// MonthTest.java
package com.jdojo.datetime;

import java.time.LocalDate;
import java.time.Month;

public class MonthTest {
    public static void main(String[] args) {
        // Use Month.JULY as a method argument
        LocalDate ld1 = LocalDate.of(2012, Month.JULY, 1);

        // Derive a Month from a local date
        Month m1 = Month.from(ld1);

        // Create a Month from an int value 2
        Month m2 = Month.of(2);

        // Get the next month from m2
        Month m3 = m2.plus(1);

        // Get the Month from a local date
        Month m4 = ld1.getMonth();

        // Convert an enum constant to an int
        int m5 = m2.getValue();

        System.out.format("%s, %s, %s, %s, %d%n", m1, m2, m3, m4, m5);
    }
}
```

JULY, FEBRUARY, MARCH, JULY, 2

Representing the Day of the Week

The DayOfWeek enum has seven constants to represent seven days of the week. The constants are MONDAY, TUESDAY, WEDNESDAY, THURSDAY, FRIDAY, SATURDAY, and SUNDAY. Its getValue() method returns an int value: 1 for Monday, 2 for Tuesday, and so on, which follows ISO-8601 standards. The DayOfWeek enum is in the java.time package. Here are some examples of using the DayOfWeek enum and its methods.

```
LocalDate ld = LocalDate.of(2012, 5, 10);

// Extract the day-of-week from a LocalDate
DayOfWeek dw1 = DayOfWeek.from(ld); // THURSDAY

// Get the int value of the day-of-week
int dw11 = dw1.getValue(); // 4

// Use the method of the LocalDate class to get day-of-week
DayOfWeek dw12 = ld.getDayOfWeek(); // THURSDAY

// Obtain a DayOfWeek instance using an int value
DayOfWeek dw2 = DayOfWeek.of(7); // SUNDAY

// Add one day to the day-of-week to get the next day
DayOfWeek dw3 = dw2.plus(1); // MONDAY

// Get the day-of-week two days ago
DayOfWeek dw4 = dw2.minus(2); // FRIDAY
```

Representing DateTime Fields

Most fields in datetime can be represented as a numeric value, for example, year, month, day, hour, etc. An instance of the TemporalField interface represents a field of datetime, for example, year, month-of-year, minutes-of-hour, etc. The ChronoField enum implements the TemporalField interface and provides several constants to represent datetime fields. The ChronoField enum contains a long list of constants. Some of them are as follows: AMPM_OF_DAY, CLOCK_HOUR_OF_AMPM, CLOCK_HOUR_OF_DAY, DAY_OF_MONTH, DAY_OF_WEEK, DAY_OF_YEAR, ERA, HOUR_OF_AMPM, HOUR_OF_DAY, INSTANT_SECONDS, MINUTE_OF_HOUR, MONTH_OF_YEAR, SECOND_OF_MINUTE, YEAR, and YEAR_OF_ERA.

Typically, you use a TemporalField to get the value of the field from a datetime. All datetime classes have a get() method that returns an int value for the specified TemporalField. If the value for a field is too long for an int, use the companion getLong() method to get the value in a long.

Not all datetime classes support all type of fields. For example, a LocalDate does not support the MINUTE_OF_HOUR field. Use the isSupported() method of the datetime classes to check whether they support a specific type of field. Use the isSupportedBy() method of ChronoField to check if a field is supported by a datetime class.

Constants for some datetime fields that are specific to the ISO-8601 calendar system are declared in the IsoFields class. For example, IsoFields.DAY_OF_QUARTER represents ISO-8601 based day-of-quarter.

The following snippet of code demonstrates how to use a ChronoField to extract a field value from a datetime and whether the datetime supported the field:

```
import java.time.LocalDate;
import java.time.LocalDateTime;
import java.time.temporal.ChronoField;
...
LocalDateTime now = LocalDateTime.now();
System.out.println("Current Date Time: " + now);
System.out.println("Year: " + now.get(ChronoField.YEAR));
System.out.println("Month: " + now.get(ChronoField.MONTH_OF_YEAR));
System.out.println("Day: " + now.get(ChronoField.DAY_OF_MONTH));
System.out.println("Hour-of-day: " + now.get(ChronoField.HOUR_OF_DAY));
System.out.println("Hour-of-AMPM: " + now.get(ChronoField.HOUR_OF_AMPM));
System.out.println("AMPM-of-day: " + now.get(ChronoField.AMPM_OF_DAY));

LocalDate today = LocalDate.now();
System.out.println("Current Date : " + today);
System.out.println("LocalDate supports year: " + today.isSupported(ChronoField.YEAR));
System.out.println("LocalDate supports hour-of-day: " + today.isSupported(ChronoField.
                   HOUR_OF_DAY));
System.out.println("Year is supported by LocalDate: " + ChronoField.YEAR.isSupportedBy(today));
System.out.println("Hour-of-day is supported by LocalDate: " + ChronoField.HOUR_OF_DAY.
                   isSupportedBy(today));
```

```
Current Date Time: 2017-08-04T14:41:38.922063700
Year: 2017
Month: 8
Day: 4
Hour-of-day: 14
Hour-of-AMPM: 2
AMPM-of-day: 1
Current Date : 2017-08-04
LocalDate supports year: true
LocalDate supports hour-of-day: false
Year is supported by LocalDate: true
Hour-of-day is supported by LocalDate: false
```

The value for the AMPM_OF_DAY field can be 0 or 1; 0 indicates AM and 1 indicates PM.

Representing the Units of Datetime Fields

Time is measured in units such as years, months, days, hours, minutes, seconds, weeks, etc. An instance of the TemporalUnit interface in the java.time.temporal package represents a unit of time. The ChronoUnit in the same package contains the following constants to represent units of time: CENTURIES, DAYS, DECADES, ERAS, FOREVER, HALF_DAYS, HOURS, MICROS, MILLENNIA, MILLIS, MINUTES, MONTHS, NANOS, SECONDS, WEEKS, and YEARS.

The ChronoUnit enum implements the TemporalUnit interface. Therefore, all constants in the enum are an instance of the TemporalUnit.

░ **Tip**   Constants for some datetime units that are specific to the ISO-8601 calendar system are declared in the IsoFields class. For example, IsoFields.QUARTER_YEARS and IsoFields.WEEK_BASED_YEARS represent ISO-8601 based a quarter-year (3 months) and a week-based year (52 or 53 weeks), respectively. The ISO-8601 standard considers a seven day period as a week; a week starts on a Monday; the first calendar week of the year is the one that includes the first Thursday of the year; the first week of a year may start in the previous year and the last week of a year may end in the succeeding year. This may result in 53 weeks in a year. For example, the first week of 2009 started on December 29, 2008 and the last week on December 29, 2009, making 2009 a 53 week year.

Datetime classes provide two methods, minus() and plus(). They take an amount of time and the unit of time to return a new datetime by subtracting and adding the specified time. Convenience methods such as minusDays(), minusHours(), plusDays(), plusHours(), etc. are also provided by the applicable classes to subtract and add time. The following snippet of code illustrates the use of the ChronoUnit enum constants with these methods:

```
import java.time.LocalDateTime;
import java.time.temporal.ChronoUnit;
...
LocalDateTime now = LocalDateTime.now();

// Get the date time 4 days ago
LocalDateTime ldt2 = now.minus(4, ChronoUnit.DAYS);

// Use the minusDays() method to get the same result
LocalDateTime ldt3 = now.minusDays(4);

// Get date and time 4 hours later
LocalDateTime ldt4 = now.plus(4, ChronoUnit.HOURS);

// Use the plusHours() method to get the same result
LocalDateTime ldt5 = now.plusHours(4);

System.out.println("Current Datetime: " + now);
System.out.println("4 days ago: " + ldt2);
System.out.println("4 days ago: " + ldt3);
System.out.println("4 hours after: " + ldt4);
System.out.println("4 hours after: " + ldt5);
```

```
Current Datetime: 2017-08-04T14:44:10.511389400
4 days ago: 2017-07-31T14:44:10.511389400
4 days ago: 2017-07-31T14:44:10.511389400
4 hours after: 2017-08-04T18:44:10.511389400
4 hours after: 2017-08-04T18:44:10.511389400
```

Local Date, Time, and Datetime

An instance of the LocalDate class represents a date without a time or time zone. Several methods in the class let you convert a LocalDate to other datetime objects and manipulate its fields (year, month, and day) to obtain another LocalDate. The following snippet of code creates some LocalDate objects:

```
// Get the current local date
LocalDate ldt1 = LocalDate.now();

// Create a local date May 10, 2012
LocalDate ldt2 = LocalDate.of(2012, Month.MAY, 10);

// Create a local date, which is 10 days after the epoch date 1970-01-01
LocalDate ldt3 = LocalDate.ofEpochDay(10); // 1970-01-11
```

The LocalDate class contains two constants, MAX and MIN, that are the maximum and minimum supported LocalDate, respectively. The value for LocalDate.MAX is +999999999-12-31 and LocalDate.MIN is -999999999-01-01.

An instance of the LocalTime class represents a time without a date or time zone. Time is represented to a nanosecond precision. It contains MIN, MAX, MIDNIGHT, and NOON constants that represent time constants of 00:00, 23:59:59.999999999, 00:00, and 12:00, respectively. Several methods in this class let you create, manipulate, and compare times in different ways. The following snippet of code creates some LocalTime objects:

```
// Get the current local time
LocalTime lt1 = LocalTime.now();

// Create a local time 07:30
LocalTime lt2 = LocalTime.of(7, 30);

// Create a local time 07:30:50
LocalTime lt3 = LocalTime.of(7, 30, 50);

// Create a local time 07:30:50.000005678
LocalTime lt4 = LocalTime.of(7, 30, 50, 5678);
```

An instance of the LocalDateTime class represents a date and a time without a time zone. It provides several methods to create, manipulate, and compare datetimes. You can think of a LocalDateTime as a combination of LocalDate and LocalTime.

```
LocalDateTime = LocalDate + LocalTime
```

The following snippet of code creates some `LocalDateTime` objects:

```
// Get the current local datetime
LocalDateTime ldt1 = LocalDateTime.now();

// A local datetime 2012-05-10T16:14:32
LocalDateTime ldt2 = LocalDateTime.of(2012, Month.MAY, 10, 16, 14, 32);

// Construct a local datetime from a local date and a local time
LocalDate ld1 = LocalDate.of(2012, 5, 10);
LocalTime lt1 = LocalTime.of(16, 18, 41);
LocalDateTime ldt3 = LocalDateTime.of(ld1, lt1); // 2012-05-10T16:18:41
```

Refer to the online API documentation for these classes for a complete list of methods. Make sure to read the "Exploring the New Date-Time API" section in this chapter before exploring the online API documentation. You will find over 60 methods just in one class, `LocalDateTime`. Without knowing the pattern behind those method names, looking at the API documentation for these classes will be overwhelming. Remember that you can achieve the same results using different methods in the API.

Listing 16-8 demonstrates some ways to create and perform operations on a local date, time, and datetime.

Listing 16-8. Using a Local Date, Time, and Datetime

```
// LocalDateTimeTest.java
package com.jdojo.datetime;

import java.time.LocalDate;
import java.time.LocalDateTime;
import java.time.LocalTime;
import java.time.Month;

public class LocalDateTimeTest {
    public static void main(String[] args) {
        // Create a local date and time
        LocalDate ld = LocalDate.of(2012, Month.MAY, 11);
        LocalTime lt = LocalTime.of(8, 52, 23);
        System.out.println("ld: " + ld);
        System.out.println("ld.isLeapYear(): " + ld.isLeapYear());
        System.out.println("lt: " + lt);

        // Create a local datetime from the local date and time
        LocalDateTime ldt = LocalDateTime.of(ld, lt);
        System.out.println("ldt: " + ldt);

        // Add 2 months and 25 minutes to the local datetime
        LocalDateTime ldt2 = ldt.plusMonths(2).plusMinutes(25) ;
        System.out.println("ldt2: " + ldt2);

        // Derive the local date and time from the localdatetime
        LocalDate ld2 = LocalDate.from(ldt2);
        LocalTime lt2 = LocalTime.from(ldt2);
```

```
        System.out.println("ld2: " + ld2);
        System.out.println("lt2: " + lt2);
    }
}
```

```
ld: 2012-05-11
ld.isLeapYear(): true
lt: 08:52:23
ldt: 2012-05-11T08:52:23
ldt2: 2012-07-11T09:17:23
ld2: 2012-07-11
lt2: 09:17:23
```

You can add years, months, and days to a LocalDate. What would be the result if you add one month to 2014-01-31? If the Date-Time API simply adds the month to the month field, the result would be 2014-02-31, which is an invalid date. After adding the month, the result is checked if it is a valid date. If it is not a valid date, the day of month is adjusted to the last day of the month. In this case, the result would be 2014-02-28.

```
LocalDate ld1 = LocalDate.of(2014, Month.JANUARY, 31);
LocalDate ld2 = ld1.plusMonths(1);
System.out.println(ld1);
System.out.println(ld2);
```

```
2014-01-31
2014-02-28
```

If you add days to a LocalDate, the month and year fields are adjusted to keep the result a valid date.

```
LocalDate ld1 = LocalDate.of(2014, Month.JANUARY, 31);
LocalDate ld2 = ld1.plusDays(30);
LocalDate ld3 = ld1.plusDays(555);
System.out.println(ld1);
System.out.println(ld2);
System.out.println(ld3);
```

```
2014-01-31
2014-03-02
2015-08-09
```

How will you get all dates in a specific year that fall on Sunday? How will you get all dates in next five years that fall on the 13th of the month and fall on Friday? These kinds of computations were possible in Java 8 using a sequential loop to generate all such dates and check for specific conditions for each date. Java 9 made such computations very easy by providing a datesUntil() method in the LocalDate class. The method is overloaded:

- Stream<LocalDate> datesUntil(LocalDate endExclusive)

- Stream<LocalDate> datesUntil(LocalDate endExclusive, Period step)

These methods produce a sequential ordered stream of LocalDates. I cover the streams in Chapter 13 of the second volume of this series. The first element in the stream is the LocalDate on which the method is called. The datesUntil(LocalDate endExclusive) method increments the elements in the stream one day at a time. The datesUntil(LocalDate endExclusive, Period step) method increments dates by the specified step. The specified end date is exclusive. There are several useful computations that you can do on the returned streams. The following snippet of code counts the number of Sundays in 2017. Note that the code uses January 1, 2018 as the last date, which is exclusive, and that will make the stream return all dates in 2017.

```
long sundaysIn2017 = LocalDate.of(2017, 1, 1)
                        .datesUntil(LocalDate.of(2018, 1, 1))
                        .filter(ld -> ld.getDayOfWeek() == DayOfWeek.SUNDAY)
                        .count();
System.out.println("Number of Sundays in 2017: " + sundaysIn2017);
```

```
Number of Sundays in 2017: 53
```

The following snippet of code prints all dates between January 1, 2017 (inclusive) to January 1, 2022 (exclusive) that are Fridays and fall on the 13th of the month:

```
System.out.println("Fridays that fall on 13th of the month between 2017 - 2021: ");
LocalDate.of(2017, 1, 1)
        .datesUntil(LocalDate.of(2022, 1, 1))
        .filter(ld -> ld.getDayOfMonth() == 13 && ld.getDayOfWeek() == DayOfWeek.FRIDAY)
        .forEach(System.out::println);
```

```
Fridays that fall on 13th of the month between 2017 - 2021 (inclusive):
2017-01-13
2017-10-13
2018-04-13
2018-07-13
2019-09-13
2019-12-13
2020-03-13
2020-11-13
2021-08-13
```

The following snippet of code prints the last day of each month in 2017:

```
System.out.println("Last Day of months in 2017:");
LocalDate.of(2017, 1, 31)
        .datesUntil(LocalDate.of(2018, 1, 1), Period.ofMonths(1))
        .map(ld -> ld.format(DateTimeFormatter.ofPattern("EEE MMM dd, yyyy")))
        .forEach(System.out::println);
```

```
Last Day of months in 2017:
Tue Jan 31, 2017
Tue Feb 28, 2017
Fri Mar 31, 2017
```

```
Sun Apr 30, 2017
Wed May 31, 2017
Fri Jun 30, 2017
Mon Jul 31, 2017
Thu Aug 31, 2017
Sat Sep 30, 2017
Tue Oct 31, 2017
Thu Nov 30, 2017
Sun Dec 31, 2017
```

How do you convert an Instant to a LocalDate, a LocalTime, and a LocalDateTime? In Java 8, the LocalDateTime class contained a static method named ofInstant(Instant instant, ZoneId zone) that let you convert an Instant to a LocalDateTime by supplying a ZoneId. However, there were no such methods in the LocalDate and LocalTime classes. Java 9 bridged this gap by providing an ofInstant() method in these two classes. The following snippet of code shows you how to convert an Instant to a LocalDate and a LocalTime in Java 8 as well as Java 9:

```java
/* In JDK 8 */
// Get an Instant
Instant now = Instant.now();

// Get the system default time zone
ZoneId zone = ZoneId.systemDefault();

// Convert the Instant to a ZonedDateTime
ZonedDateTime zdt = now.atZone(zone);

// Get the LocalDate from the ZonedDateTime
LocalDate ld1 = zdt.toLocalDate();

// Get the LocalTime from the ZonedDateTime
LocalTime lt1 = zdt.toLocalTime();

System.out.println("In Java 8");
System.out.println("Instant: " + now);
System.out.println("Local Date: " + ld1);
System.out.println("Local Time: " + lt1);

/* In JDK 9 */

// Get a LocalDate from the Instant
LocalDate ld2 = LocalDate.ofInstant(now, zone);

// Get the LocalTime from the Instant
LocalTime lt2 = LocalTime.ofInstant(now, zone);

System.out.println("\nIn Java 9");
System.out.println("Instant: " + now);
System.out.println("Local Date: " + ld2);
System.out.println("Local Time: " + lt2);
```

How do you compute number of days, hours, etc. between two dates and times? The Date-Time API has different ways to compute the period between two dates and times. I defer the discussion on such computations until the section called "Period Between Two Dates and Times".

Offset Time and Datetime

An instance of the OffsetTime and OffsetDateTime classes represents a time and a datetime, respectively, with a fixed zone offset from UTC. An offset time and datetime have no knowledge of a time zone. Examples of an offset time and an offset datetime in the ISO-8601 format are 10:50:11+5:30 and 2012-05-11T10:50:11+5:30, respectively.

▓ **Tip**   There is no OffsetDate class. It was part of the initial design. Later, it was dropped.

The relationships between local and offset dates and times can be represented follows:

```
OffsetTime = LocalTime + ZoneOffset
OffsetDateTime = LocalDateTime + ZoneOffset
```

Working with an offset time and datetime is similar to working with their local counterparts, except that you have to use a zone offset. You can always extract a LocalXxx from an OffsetXxx. An OffsetDateTime stores an instant on the timeline, and hence, conversion between OffsetDateTime and Instant is supported.

Listing 16-9 shows examples of creating offset time and datetime. When you get the current offset time and datetime using the now() method, the system default time zone is used to obtain the zone offset value. You will get a different output for current time and datetime.

Listing 16-9. Using Offset Dates, Times, and Datetimes

```java
// OffsetDateTimeTest.java
package com.jdojo.datetime;

import java.time.Instant;
import java.time.LocalDate;
import java.time.LocalTime;
import java.time.OffsetDateTime;
import java.time.OffsetTime;
import java.time.ZoneId;
import java.time.ZoneOffset;

public class OffsetDateTimeTest {
    public static void main(String[] args) {
        // Get the current offset time
        OffsetTime ot1 = OffsetTime.now();
        System.out.println("Current offset time: " + ot1);

        // Create a zone offset +05:30
        ZoneOffset offset = ZoneOffset.ofHoursMinutes(5, 30);
```

```
            // Create an offset time
            OffsetTime ot2 = OffsetTime.of(16, 40, 28, 0, offset);
            System.out.println("An offset time: " + ot2);

            // Get the current offset datetime
            OffsetDateTime odt1 = OffsetDateTime.now();
            System.out.println("Current offset datetime: " + odt1);

            // Create an offset datetime
            OffsetDateTime odt2 = OffsetDateTime.of(2012, 5, 11,
                                                    18, 10, 30, 0,
                                                    offset);
            System.out.println("An offset datetime: " + odt2);

            // Get the local date and time from the offset datetime
            LocalDate ld1 = odt1.toLocalDate();
            LocalTime lt1 = odt1.toLocalTime();
            System.out.println("Current Local Date: " + ld1);
            System.out.println("Current Local Time: " + lt1);

            // Get the instant from the offset datetime
            Instant i1 = odt1.toInstant();
            System.out.println("Current Instant: " + i1);

            // Create an offset datetime from the instant
            ZoneId usChicago = ZoneId.of("America/Chicago");
            OffsetDateTime odt3 = OffsetDateTime.ofInstant(i1, usChicago);
            System.out.println("Offset datetime from instant: " + odt3);
    }
}
```

```
Current offset time: 20:31:21.678068400-05:00
An offset time: 16:40:28+05:30
Current offset datetime: 2017-08-04T20:31:21.709320400-05:00
An offset datetime: 2012-05-11T18:10:30+05:30
Current Local Date: 2017-08-04
Current Local Time: 20:31:21.709320400
Current Instant: 2017-08-05T01:31:21.709320400Z
Offset datetime from instant: 2017-08-04T20:31:21.709320400-05:00
```

Zoned Datetime

An instance of the ZonedDateTime class represents a datetime with time zone rules. The time zone rules include a zone offset and rules for its variation because of Daylight Savings Time. There are no ZonedDate and ZonedTime; they do not make sense. The relationships between a ZonedDateTime and a LocalDateTime can be represented as follows:

```
ZonedDateTime = LocalDateTime + ZoneId
```

The following is an example of creating a ZonedDateTime from a LocalDateTime:

```
ZoneId usCentral = ZoneId.of("America/Chicago");
LocalDateTime ldt = LocalDateTime.of(2012, Month.MAY, 11, 7, 30);
ZonedDateTime zdt = ZonedDateTime.of(ldt, usCentral);
System.out.println(zdt);
```

```
2012-05-11T07:30-05:00[America/Chicago]
```

Not all combinations of a LocalDateTime and a ZoneId result in a valid ZonedDateTime. There may be a gap or overlap on the local timeline in a time zone because of the Daylight Savings Time change. For example, in the America/Chicago time zone on March 10, 2013 at 02:00, the clock was moved an hour forward, thus leaving a gap of one hour on the local timeline; the time between 02:00 and 02:59 did not exist. In the same America/Chicago time zone on November 3, 2013 at 02:00, the clock was moved an hour backward, thus creating an overlap of one hour on the local timeline; the time between 01:00 and 01:59 existed twice. The Date-Time API has well-defined rules to handle such gaps and overlaps.

- If the local datetime falls in the middle of the gap, the time is moved forward by the same amount as the gap. For example, if you want to construct a zoned datetime for the time zone America/Chicago for March 10, 2013 at 02:30:00, you will get March 10, 2013 at 3:30:00. The time is moved forward by an hour, which is equal to the gap of an hour.

- If the local datetime falls in the middle of the overlap, the time is valid. In the gap, two zone offsets exist: one the earlier offset that existed before moving the clock backward and one the later offset that exists after moving the clock backward. By default, for the time in the gap, the zone offset that existed earlier is used. The ZonedDateTime class contains withEarlierOffsetAtOverlap() and withLaterOffsetAtOverlap(), which let you select the desired zone offset if the time falls in the overlap.

The following snippet of code demonstrates the results of ZonedDateTime with the time falling in the gap and overlap:

```
ZoneId usChicago = ZoneId.of("America/Chicago");

// 2013-03-10T02:30 did not exist in America/Chicago time zone
LocalDateTime ldt = LocalDateTime.of(2013, Month.MARCH, 10, 2, 30);
ZonedDateTime zdt = ZonedDateTime.of(ldt, usChicago);
System.out.println(zdt);

// 2013-10-03T01:30 existed twice in America/Chicago time zone
LocalDateTime ldt2 = LocalDateTime.of(2013, Month.NOVEMBER, 3, 1, 30);
ZonedDateTime zdt2 = ZonedDateTime.of(ldt2, usChicago);
System.out.println(zdt2);

// Try using the two rules for overlaps: one will use the earlier
// offset -05:00 (the default) and another the later offset -06:00
System.out.println(zdt2.withEarlierOffsetAtOverlap());
System.out.println(zdt2.withLaterOffsetAtOverlap());
```

```
2013-03-10T03:30-05:00[America/Chicago]
2013-11-03T01:30-05:00[America/Chicago]
2013-11-03T01:30-05:00[America/Chicago]
2013-11-03T01:30-06:00[America/Chicago]
```

The ZonedDateTime class contains a static factory method ofLocal(LocalDateTime localDateTime, ZoneId zone, ZoneOffset preferredOffset). You can use this method to create a ZonedDateTime by specifying the preferred zone offset in case there are two zone offsets available for the local time in the specified zone. If the specified referred zone offset is invalid, the earlier zone offset for the overlap is used. The following snippet of code demonstrates the use of this method. When I provide an invalid preferred offset -07:00, the earlier offset -05:00 is used.

```
ZoneId usChicago = ZoneId.of("America/Chicago");
ZoneOffset offset5 = ZoneOffset.of("-05:00");
ZoneOffset offset6 = ZoneOffset.of("-06:00");
ZoneOffset offset7 = ZoneOffset.of("-07:00");

// At 2013-10-03T01:30, -05:00 and -06:00 offsets were valid for
// the time zone America/Chicago
LocalDateTime ldt = LocalDateTime.of(2013, Month.NOVEMBER, 3, 1, 30);
ZonedDateTime zdt5 = ZonedDateTime.ofLocal(ldt, usChicago, offset5);
ZonedDateTime zdt6 = ZonedDateTime.ofLocal(ldt, usChicago, offset6);
ZonedDateTime zdt7 = ZonedDateTime.ofLocal(ldt, usChicago, offset7);
System.out.println("With offset " + offset5 + ": " + zdt5);
System.out.println("With offset " + offset6 + ": " + zdt6);
System.out.println("With offset " + offset7 + ": " + zdt7);
```

```
With offset -05:00: 2013-11-03T01:30-05:00[America/Chicago]
With offset -06:00: 2013-11-03T01:30-06:00[America/Chicago]
With offset -07:00: 2013-11-03T01:30-05:00[America/Chicago]
```

The ZonedDateTime class contains several methods to convert it to local and offset date, time and datetime representations, compare its instances, and obtain its new instances by changing some of its fields. Listing 16-10 shows how to work with zoned datetimes. You will get a different output for the current date and time.

Listing 16-10. Using the ZonedDateTime Class

```
// ZonedDateTimeTest.java
package com.jdojo.datetime;

import java.time.Instant;
import java.time.LocalDateTime;
import java.time.Month;
import java.time.OffsetDateTime;
import java.time.ZoneId;
import java.time.ZoneOffset;
import java.time.ZonedDateTime;
```

585

```java
public class ZonedDateTimeTest {
    public static void main(String[] args) {
        // Get the current zoned datetime for the system default time zone
        ZonedDateTime zdt1 = ZonedDateTime.now();
        System.out.println("Current zoned datetime:" + zdt1);

        // Create a local datetime
        LocalDateTime ldt = LocalDateTime.of(2012, Month.MARCH, 11, 7, 30);

        // Create some zoned datetimes
        ZoneId usCentralZone = ZoneId.of("America/Chicago");
        ZonedDateTime zdt2 = ZonedDateTime.of(ldt, usCentralZone);
        System.out.println(zdt2);

        // Get zone offset and zone id
        ZoneOffset offset = zdt2.getOffset();
        ZoneId zone = zdt2.getZone();
        System.out.println("Offset:" + offset + ", Zone:" + zone);

        // Subtract 10 hours. Zone-offset changes from -05:00 to -06:00
        ZonedDateTime zdt3 = zdt2.minusHours(10);
        System.out.println(zdt3);

        // Create a datetime in Asia/Kolkata time zone
        ZoneId indiaKolkataZone = ZoneId.of("Asia/Kolkata");
        ZonedDateTime zdt4 = ZonedDateTime.of(ldt, indiaKolkataZone);
        System.out.println(zdt4);

        // Perform some conversions on zoned date time
        LocalDateTime ldt2 = zdt4.toLocalDateTime();
        OffsetDateTime odt = zdt4.toOffsetDateTime();
        Instant i1 = zdt4.toInstant();
        System.out.println("To local datetime: " + ldt2);
        System.out.println("To offset datetime: " + odt);
        System.out.println("To instant: " + i1);
    }
}
```

```
Current zoned datetime:2017-08-04T20:34:59.674634400-05:00[America/Chicago]
2012-03-11T07:30-05:00[America/Chicago]
Offset:-05:00, Zone:America/Chicago
2012-03-10T20:30-06:00[America/Chicago]
2012-03-11T07:30+05:30[Asia/Kolkata]
To local datetime: 2012-03-11T07:30
To offset datetime: 2012-03-11T07:30+05:30
To instant: 2012-03-11T02:00:00Z
```

Same Instant, Different Times

Sometimes you want to convert a date-time in a time zone to a date-time in another time zone. It is similar to asking the date and time in India when it is May 14, 2012 16:30 in Chicago. You can get this in several ways. You can use the toInstant() method of the ZonedDateTime class to get the instant from the first zoned datetime and use the ofInstant() method to create the second zoned datetime. You can also use the withZoneSameInstant(ZoneId newZoneId) method of the ZonedDateTime class, as shown in Listing 16-11, to achieve the same result.

Listing 16-11. Converting a Datetime in a Time Zone to Another Time Zone

```
// DateTimeZoneConversion.java
package com.jdojo.datetime;

import java.time.LocalDateTime;
import java.time.Month;
import java.time.ZoneId;
import java.time.ZonedDateTime;

public class DateTimeZoneConversion {
    public static void main(String[] args) {
        LocalDateTime ldt = LocalDateTime.of(2012, Month.MAY, 14, 16, 30);

        ZoneId usCentral = ZoneId.of("America/Chicago");
        ZonedDateTime zdt = ZonedDateTime.of(ldt, usCentral);
        System.out.println("In US Central Time Zone:" + zdt);

        ZoneId asiaKolkata = ZoneId.of("Asia/Kolkata");
        ZonedDateTime zdt2 = zdt.withZoneSameInstant(asiaKolkata);
        System.out.println("In Asia/Kolkata Time Zone:" + zdt2);

        ZonedDateTime zdt3 = zdt.withZoneSameInstant(ZoneId.of("Z"));
        System.out.println("In UTC Time Zone:" + zdt3);
    }
}
```

```
In US Central Time Zone:2012-05-14T16:30-05:00[America/Chicago]
In Asia/Kolkata Time Zone:2012-05-15T03:00+05:30[Asia/Kolkata]
In UTC Time Zone:2012-05-14T21:30Z
```

Clocks

The Clock class is an abstraction for the real-world clock. It provides access to the current instant, date, and time in a time zone. You can obtain a clock for the system default time zone.

```
Clock clock = Clock.systemDefaultZone();
```

You can also get a clock for a specified time zone.

```
// Get a clock for Asia/Kolkata time zone
ZoneId asiaKolkata = ZoneId.of("Asia/Kolkata");
Clock clock2 = Clock.system(asiaKolkata);
```

To get the current instant, date, and time from a clock, you can use the now(Clock c) method of the datetime related classes.

```
// Get the system default clock
Clock clock = Clock.systemDefaultZone();

// Get the current instant of the clock
Instant instant1 = clock.instant();

// Get the current instant using the clock and the Instant class
Instant instant2 = Instant.now(clock);

// Get the local date using the clock
LocalDate ld = LocalDate.now(clock);

// Get the zoned datetime using the clock
ZonedDateTime zdt = ZonedDateTime.now(clock);
```

The now() method without arguments in all date, time, and datetime classes uses the system default clock for the default time zone. The following two statements use the same clock:

```
LocalTime lt1 = LocalTime.now();
LocalTime lt2 = LocalTime.now(Clock.systemDefaultZone());
```

The systemUTC() method of the Clock class returns a clock for the UTC time zone. You can also obtain a fixed clock that always returns the same time. A fixed clock is useful in testing when you want your test cases to use the same current time and not depend on the current time of the system clock. You can use the fixed(Instant fixedInstant, ZoneId zone) static method of the Clock class to get a clock with a fixed instant in a specified time zone. The Clock class also lets you obtain a clock that gives the time at a fixed offset from another clock.

A clock is always aware of its time zone. You can obtain the system default time zone using the Clock class as follows:

```
ZoneId defaultZone = Clock.systemDefaultZone().getZone();
```

▓ **Tip**   The default implementation of the Clock class ignores the leap seconds. You can also extend the Clock class to implement your own clock.

The Clock class contains many static factory methods that let you create a clock that ticks at a specified interval. Those methods are as follows:

- static Clock tick(Clock baseClock, Duration tickDuration)
- static Clock tickMillis(ZoneId zone)

- `static Clock tickMinutes(ZoneId zone)`

- `static Clock tickSeconds(ZoneId zone)`

The `tick()` method lets you specify the granularity of the tick in the form of a `Duration`. The clock returned by this method uses the clock specified as the first argument. The returned clock makes the specified clock tick in the specified duration as the second argument. The following snippet of code gets a clock for the system default time zone that ticks every 1 millisecond:

```
Clock clock = Clock.tick(Clock.systemDefaultZone(), Duration.ofMillis(1));
```

Other `tickXxx()` methods return the best available clock for the specified time zone that ticks at Xxx interval. For example, the clock returns by the `tickSeconds()` method tick every second.

▓ **Tip** The `tickMillis()` method was added to the `Clock` class in Java 9.

Periods

A period is an amount of time defined in terms of calendar fields years, months, and days. A duration is also an amount of time measured in terms of seconds and nanoseconds. Negative periods are supported.

What is the difference between a period and a duration? A duration represents an exact number of nanoseconds, whereas a period represents an inexact amount of time. A period is for humans what a duration is for machines.

Some examples of periods are 1 day, 2 months, 5 days, 3 months and 2 days, etc. When someone mentions a 2 month period, you do not know the exact amount of nanoseconds in that 2 months. A 2 month period may mean different number of days (and hence different nanoseconds) depending on when that period starts. For example, a 2 month period from midnight January 1 may represent 59 or 60 days depending on whether the year is a leap year or not. Similarly, a period of 1 day may represent 23, 24, or 25 hours depending on the day whether that day observes the start/end of the Daylight Savings Time or not.

An instance of the `Period` class represents a period. Use one of the following static factory methods to create a Period:

- `static Period of(int years, int months, int days)`

- `static Period ofDays(int days)`

- `static Period ofMonths(int months)`

- `static Period ofWeeks(int weeks)`

- `static Period ofYears(int years)`

The following snippet of code creates some instances of the `Period` class:

```
Period p1 = Period.of(2, 3, 5);    // 2 years, 3 months, and 5 days
Period p2 = Period.ofDays(25);     // 25 days
Period p3 = Period.ofMonths(-3);   // -3 months
Period p4 = Period.ofWeeks(3);     // 3 weeks (21 days)
System.out.println(p1);
System.out.println(p2);
System.out.println(p3);
System.out.println(p4);
```

```
P2Y3M5D
P25D
P-3M
P21D
```

You can perform additions, subtractions, multiplications, and negation on a period. The division operation performs an integer division, for example, 7 divided by 3 is 2. The following snippet of code shows some of the operations and their results on periods:

```
Period p1 = Period.ofDays(15);   // P15D
Period p2 = p1.plusDays(12);     // P27D
Period p3 = p1.minusDays(12);    // P3D
Period p4 = p1.negated();        // P-15D
Period p5 = p1.multipliedBy(3);  // P45D
```

Use the plus() and minus() methods of the Period class to add one period to another and to subtract one period from another. Use the normalized() method of the Period class to normalize the years and months. The method ensures that the month value stays within 0 to 11. For example, a period of "2 years and 15 months" will be normalized to "3 years and 3 months."

```
Period p1 = Period.of(2, 3, 5);
Period p2 = Period.of(1, 15, 28);

System.out.println("p1: " + p1);
System.out.println("p2: " + p2);
System.out.println("p1.plus(p2): " + p1.plus(p2));
System.out.println("p1.plus(p2).normalized(): " + p1.plus(p2).normalized());
System.out.println("p1.minus(p2): " + p1.minus(p2));
```

```
p1: P2Y3M5D
p2: P1Y15M28D
p1.plus(p2): P3Y18M33D
p1.plus(p2).normalized(): P4Y6M33D
p1.minus(p2): P1Y-12M-23D
```

There is a big difference in the way the Date-Time API treats computations based on periods and durations. Computations including periods behave the way humans would expect. For example, when you add a period of one day to a ZonedDateTime, the date component changes to the next day, keeping the time the same, irrespective of how many hours the day had (23, 24, or 25 hours). However, when you add a duration of a day, it will always add 24 hours. Let's walk through an example to clarify this.

On 2012-03-11T02:00, the clocks in the US Central time zone were moved forward by one hour, making 2012-03-11 a 23-hour day. Suppose you give a person a datetime of 2012-03-10T07:30 in the US Central time zone. If you ask him what would be the datetime after a day, his answer would be 2012-03-11T07:30. His answer is natural because, for humans, adding one day to the current datetime gives the next day with the same time. Let's ask the same question of a machine. Ask the machine to add 24 hours, which is considered the same as 1 day, to 2012-03-10T07:30. The machine's response would be 2012-03-11T08:30 because it will add exactly 24 hours to the initial datetime, knowing that the hour between 02:00 and 03:00 did not exist. Listing 16-12 demonstrates this discussion using a Java program.

Listing 16-12. Difference in Adding a Period and Duration to a Datetime

```java
// PeriodTest.java
package com.jdojo.datetime;

import java.time.Duration;
import java.time.LocalDateTime;
import java.time.Month;
import java.time.Period;
import java.time.ZoneId;
import java.time.ZonedDateTime;

public class PeriodTest {
    public static void main(String[] args) {
        ZoneId usCentral = ZoneId.of("America/Chicago");
        LocalDateTime ldt = LocalDateTime.of(2012, Month.MARCH, 10, 7, 30);
        ZonedDateTime zdt1 = ZonedDateTime.of(ldt, usCentral);
        Period p1 = Period.ofDays(1);
        Duration d1 = Duration.ofHours(24);

        // Add a period of 1 day and a duration of 24 hours
        ZonedDateTime zdt2 = zdt1.plus(p1);
        ZonedDateTime zdt3 = zdt1.plus(d1);

        System.out.println("Start Datetime: " + zdt1);
        System.out.println("After 1 Day period: " + zdt2);
        System.out.println("After 24 Hours duration: " + zdt3);
    }
}
```

```
Start Datetime: 2012-03-10T07:30-06:00[America/Chicago]
After 1 Day period: 2012-03-11T07:30-05:00[America/Chicago]
After 24 Hours duration: 2012-03-11T08:30-05:00[America/Chicago]
```

Period Between Two Dates and Times

It is a common requirement to compute the amount of time elapsed between two dates, times, and datetimes. For example, you may need to compute the number of days between two local dates or the number of hours between two local datetimes. The Date-Time API provides methods to compute the elapsed period between two dates and times. There are two ways to get the amount of time between two dates and times.

- Use the between() method on one of the constants in the ChronoUnit enum.

- Use the until() method on one of the datetime-related classes, for example, LocalDate, LocalTime, LocalDateTime, ZonedDateTime, etc.

The ChronoUnit enum has a between() method, which takes two datetime objects and returns a long. The method returns the amount of time elapsed from the first argument to the second argument. If the second argument occurs before the first one, it returns a negative amount. The returned amount is the complete number of units between two dates and times. For example, if you call HOURS.between(lt1, lt2),

591

where lt1 and lt2 are 07:00 and 09:30 respectively, it will return 2, not 2.5. However, if you call MINUTES. between(lt1, lt2), it will return 150.

The until() method takes two parameters. The first parameter is the end date or time. The second parameter is the time unit in which to compute the elapsed time. The program in Listing 16-13 shows how to use both methods to compute the amount of time between two dates and times.

Listing 16-13. Computing the Amount of Time Elapsed Between Two Dates and Times

```java
// TimeBetween.java
package com.jdojo.datetime;

import java.time.LocalDate;
import java.time.LocalTime;
import java.time.Month;
import static java.time.temporal.ChronoUnit.DAYS;
import static java.time.temporal.ChronoUnit.HOURS;
import static java.time.temporal.ChronoUnit.MINUTES;

public class TimeBetween {
    public static void main(String[] args) {
        LocalDate ld1 = LocalDate.of(2014, Month.JANUARY, 7);
        LocalDate ld2 = LocalDate.of(2014, Month.MAY, 18);
        long days = DAYS.between(ld1, ld2);

        LocalTime lt1 = LocalTime.of(7, 0);
        LocalTime lt2 = LocalTime.of(9, 30);
        long hours = HOURS.between(lt1, lt2);
        long minutes = MINUTES.between(lt1, lt2);

        System.out.println("Using between (days): " + days);
        System.out.println("Using between (hours): " + hours);
        System.out.println("Using between (minutes): " + minutes);

        // Using the until() method
        long days2 = ld1.until(ld2, DAYS);
        long hours2 = lt1.until(lt2, HOURS);
        long minutes2 = lt1.until(lt2, MINUTES);

        System.out.println("Using until (days): " + days2);
        System.out.println("Using until (hours): " + hours2);
        System.out.println("Using until (minutes): " + minutes2);
    }
}
```

```
Using between (days): 131
Using between (hours): 2
Using between (minutes): 150
Using until (days): 131
Using until (hours): 2
Using until (minutes): 150
```

It is not always possible to compute the amount of time elapsed between two dates and times. For example, you cannot tell the number of hours between a LocalDate and a LocalDateTime as the LocalDate does not store a time component. If such parameters are passed to the methods, a runtime exception is thrown. The rule is that the specified end date/time should be convertible to the start date/time.

Partials

A partial is a date, time, or datetime that does not fully specify an instant on a timeline, but still makes sense to humans. With some more information, a partial may match multiple instants on the timeline. For example, December 25 is not a complete date that can be determined uniquely on a timeline; however, it makes sense when we talk about Christmas. Similarly, January 1 makes sense as New Year's Day.

You must have a date, time, and time zone to identify an instant uniquely on the timeline. If you have some, but not all, of the three pieces of information, you have a partial. You cannot obtain an Instant from a partial without supplying some more pieces of information. I already discussed some partials in previous sections.

LocalDate, LocalTime, LocalDateTime, and OffsetTime are examples of partials. OffsetDateTime and ZonedDateTime are not partials; they have information to identify an instant on the timeline uniquely. I discuss three more partials in this section:

- Year

- YearMonth

- MonthDay

The names of these partials easily describe them. A Year represents a year, for example, 2012, 2013, etc. A YearMonth represents a valid combination of a year and a month, for example, 2012-05, 2013-09, etc. A MonthDay represents a valid combination of a month and a day of month, for example, - -12-15. Listing 16-14 shows some of the operations you can perform on these partials.

Listing 16-14. Using Year, YearMonth, and MonthDay Partials

```
// Partials.java
package com.jdojo.datetime;

import java.time.Month;
import java.time.MonthDay;
import java.time.Year;
import java.time.YearMonth;

public class Partials {
    public static void main(String[] args) {
        // Use Year
        Year y1 = Year.of(2012);     // 2012
        Year y2 = y1.minusYears(1); // 2011
        Year y3 = y1.plusYears(1);  // 2013
        Year y4 = Year.now();        // current year
        if (y1.isLeap()) {
            System.out.println(y1 + " is a leap year.");
        } else {
            System.out.println(y1 + " is not a leap year.");
        }
```

```
        // Use YearMonth
        YearMonth ym1 = YearMonth.of(2012, Month.MAY); // 2012-05

        // Get the number of days in the month
        int monthLen = ym1.lengthOfMonth(); // 31
        System.out.println("Days in month in " + ym1 + ": " + monthLen);

        // Get the number of days in the year
        int yearLen = ym1.lengthOfYear(); // 366
        System.out.println("Days in year in " + ym1 + ": " + yearLen);

        // Use MonthDay
        MonthDay md1 = MonthDay.of(Month.DECEMBER, 25);
        MonthDay md2 = MonthDay.of(Month.FEBRUARY, 29);
        if (md2.isValidYear(2009)) {
            System.out.println(md2 + " occurred in 2009");
        } else {
            System.out.println(md2 + " did not occur in 2009");
        }
    }
}
```

```
2012 is a leap year.
Days in month in 2012-05: 31
Days in year in 2012-05: 366
--02-29 did not occur in 2009
```

Finally, Listing 16-15 contains an example of combining two partials to get another partial. It's the complete program to compute Christmas days for five years starting from the year in which the program is run. You may get a different output.

Listing 16-15. Combining a Year and MonthDay to get a LocalDate

```
// ChristmasDay.java
package com.jdojo.datetime;

import java.time.LocalDate;
import java.time.Month;
import java.time.MonthDay;
import java.time.Year;
import java.time.format.TextStyle;
import java.util.Locale;

public class ChristmasDay {
    public static void main(String[] args) {
        MonthDay dec25 = MonthDay.of(Month.DECEMBER, 25);
        Year year = Year.now();

        // Construct and print Christmas days in next five years
        for (int i = 0; i < 5; i++) {
            LocalDate ld = year.plusYears(i).atMonthDay(dec25);
```

```
            int yr = ld.getYear();
            String weekDay = ld.getDayOfWeek()
                              .getDisplayName(TextStyle.FULL, Locale.getDefault());
            System.out.format("Christmas in %d is on %s.%n", yr, weekDay);
        }
    }
}
```

```
Christmas in 2017 is on Monday.
Christmas in 2018 is on Tuesday.
Christmas in 2019 is on Wednesday.
Christmas in 2020 is on Friday.
Christmas in 2021 is on Saturday.
```

The program creates a MonthDay partial for December 25 and keeps combining a year to it to get a LocalDate. You can rewrite the program in Listing 16-15 using the LocalDate class as shown here. It shows the versatility of the Date-Time API, which allows you do achieve the same result in different ways.

```
LocalDate ld = LocalDate.of(Year.now().getValue(), Month.DECEMBER, 25);
for (int i = 0; i < 5; i++) {
    LocalDate newDate = ld.withYear(ld.getYear() + i);
    int yr = newDate.getYear();
    String weekDay = newDate.getDayOfWeek()
                        .getDisplayName(TextStyle.FULL, Locale.getDefault());
    System.out.format("Christmas in %d is on %s.%n", yr, weekDay);
}
```

Adjusting Dates

Sometimes you want to adjust a date and time to have a particular characteristic, for example, the first Monday of the month, the next Tuesday, etc. You can perform adjustments to a date and time using an instance of the TemporalAdjuster interface. The interface has one method, adjustInto(), that takes a Temporal and returns a Temporal. The Date-Time API provides several commonly used datetime adjusters. If they do not suit your needs, you can roll out your own adjusters. I discuss examples of both.

A TemporalAdjusters class is provided. It consists of all static methods that return different types of predefined date adjusters. The datetime-related classes contain a with(TemporalAdjuster adjuster) method. You need to pass the returned object from one of the methods of the TemporalAdjusters class to the with() method. The with() method will return a copy of the original datetime object by adjusting its components using the logic in the adjuster. The following snippet of code computes the first Monday after January 1, 2014:

```
import java.time.DayOfWeek;
import java.time.LocalDate;
import java.time.Month;
import java.time.temporal.TemporalAdjusters;
...
LocalDate ld1 = LocalDate.of(2014, Month.JANUARY, 1);
LocalDate ld2 = ld1.with(TemporalAdjusters.next(DayOfWeek.MONDAY));
```

```
System.out.println(ld1);
System.out.println(ld2);
```

```
2014-01-01
2014-01-06
```

The method names are self-explanatory, as you can see in Table 16-4.

Table 16-4. *Useful Methods in the TemporalAdjusters Class*

Method	Description
next(DayOfWeek dayOfWeek)	Returns an adjuster that adjusts the date to be the first specified day of week after the date being adjusted.
nextOrSame(DayOfWeek dayOfWeek)	Returns an adjuster that adjusts the date to be the first specified day of week after the date being adjusted. If the date being adjusted is already on the specified day of week, it returns the same date.
previous(DayOfWeek dayOfWeek)	Returns an adjuster that adjusts the date to be the first specified day of week before the date being adjusted.
previousOrSame(DayOfWeek dayOfWeek)	Returns an adjuster that adjusts the date to be the first specified day of week before the date being adjusted. If the date being adjusted is already on the specified day of week, it returns the same date.
firstInMonth(DayOfWeek dayOfWeek), lastInMonth(DayOfWeek dayOfWeek)	Each returns an adjuster that adjusts the date to be the first/last (respectively) specified day of week in the month represented by the date being adjusted.
dayOfWeekInMonth(int ordinal, DayOfWeek dayOfWeek)	Returns an adjuster that adjusts the date to be the specified ordinal day of week in the month represented by the date being adjusted. It is suitable for computing dates like the third Monday in January 2014.
firstDayOfMonth() lastDayOfMonth()	Each returns an adjuster that adjusts the date to be the first/last day of the month represented by the date being adjusted.
firstDayOfYear() lastDayOfYear()	Each returns an adjuster that adjusts the date to be the first/last day of the year represented by the date being adjusted.
firstDayOfNextMonth()	Returns an adjuster that adjusts the date to be the first day of the next month represented by the date being adjusted.
firstDayOfNextYear()	Returns an adjuster that adjusts the date to be the first day of the next year represented by the date being adjusted.
ofDateAdjuster(UnaryOperator <LocalDate> dateBasedAdjuster)	A convenience method for developers to write their own LocalDate-based adjusters.

The TemporalAdjuster class provides a dayOfWeekInMonth() method. This method returns a date adjuster that adjusts a date to the specified ordinal day of week, for example, the first Sunday of month, the third Friday of month, etc. The specified ordinal value may be between 1 and 5. If the ordinal is 5 and the month does not have a fifth specified dayOfWeek, it returns the first specified dayOfWeek from the next month. The following snippet of code requests the date adjuster the fifth Sunday in May 2012. The date adjuster returns the first Sunday in June 2012 because May 2012 does not have a fifth Sunday.

```
LocalDate ld1 = LocalDate.of(2012, Month.MAY, 22);
LocalDate ld2 = ld1.with(TemporalAdjusters.dayOfWeekInMonth(5, DayOfWeek.SUNDAY));
System.out.println(ld1);
System.out.println(ld2);
```

```
2012-05-22
2012-06-03
```

You can use a date adjuster with other methods to perform a complex adjustment. You can obtain the date for the second Friday of month after 3 months and 14 days from today, as follows:

```
LocalDate date = LocalDate.now()
                        .plusMonths(3)
                        .plusDays(14)
                        .with(DateAdjusters.dayOfWeekInMonth(2, DayOfWeek.FRIDAY));
```

You can use the ofDateAdjuster() method to create your own date adjuster for a LocalDate. The following snippet of code creates a date adjuster and uses it. The adjuster adds 3 months and 2 days to the date being adjusted. Note that I have used a lambda expression to create the adjuster, which I have not discussed yet.

```
// Create an adjuster that returns a date after 3 months and 2 days
TemporalAdjuster adjuster =
    TemporalAdjusters.ofDateAdjuster((LocalDate date) -> date.plusMonths(3).plusDays(2));

// Use the adjuster
LocalDate today = LocalDate.now();
LocalDate dayAfter3Mon2Day = today.with(adjuster);
System.out.println("Today: " + today);
System.out.println("After 3 months and 2 days: " + dayAfter3Mon2Day);
```

```
Today: 2017-08-04
After 3 months and 2 days: 2017-11-06
```

Listing 16-16 demonstrates how to adjust dates.

Listing 16-16. Adjusting Dates and Times

```
// AdjustDates.java
package com.jdojo.datetime;

import java.time.DayOfWeek;
import java.time.LocalDate;
```

```java
import java.time.temporal.TemporalAdjuster;
import java.time.temporal.TemporalAdjusters;

public class AdjustDates {
    public static void main(String[] args) {
        LocalDate today = LocalDate.now();
        System.out.println("Today: " + today);

        // Use a DateAdjuster to adjust today's date to the next Monday
        LocalDate nextMonday = today.with(TemporalAdjusters.next(DayOfWeek.MONDAY));
        System.out.println("Next Monday: " + nextMonday);

        // Use a DateAdjuster to adjust today's date to the last day of month
        LocalDate lastDayOfMonth = today.with(TemporalAdjusters.lastDayOfMonth());
        System.out.println("Last day of month: " + lastDayOfMonth);

        // Create an adjuster that returns a date after 3 months and 2 days
        TemporalAdjuster adjuster = TemporalAdjusters.ofDateAdjuster(
                (LocalDate date) -> date.plusMonths(3).plusDays(2));
        LocalDate dayAfter3Mon2Day = today.with(adjuster);
        System.out.println("Date after adding 3 months and 2 days: " + dayAfter3Mon2Day);
    }
}
```

```
Today: 2017-08-04
Next Monday: 2017-08-07
Last day of month: 2017-08-31
Date after adding 3 months and 2 days: 2017-11-06
```

Let's create a custom date adjuster. If the date being adjusted is on weekends or Friday 13, it returns the next Monday. Otherwise, it returns the original date. That is, the adjuster will return only weekdays, except Friday 13. Listing 16-17 contains the complete code for the adjuster. The adjuster has been defined as a constant in the class. Using the adjuster is as easy as passing the CustomAdjusters.WEEKDAYS_WITH_NO_ FRIDAY_13 constant to the with() method of the datetime classes that can supply a LocalDate.

```java
LocalDate ld = LocalDate.of(2013, Month.DECEMBER, 13); // Friday
LocalDate ldAdjusted = ld.with(CustomAdjusters.WEEKDAYS_WITH_NO_FRIDAY_13); // Next Monday
```

Listing 16-17. *Creating a Custom Date Adjuster*

```java
// CustomAdjusters.java
package com.jdojo.datetime;

import java.time.DayOfWeek;
import static java.time.DayOfWeek.FRIDAY;
import static java.time.DayOfWeek.MONDAY;
import static java.time.DayOfWeek.SATURDAY;
import static java.time.DayOfWeek.SUNDAY;
import java.time.LocalDate;
import java.time.temporal.TemporalAdjuster;
import java.time.temporal.TemporalAdjusters;
```

```java
public class CustomAdjusters {
    public final static TemporalAdjuster WEEKDAYS_WITH_NO_FRIDAY_13
            = TemporalAdjusters.ofDateAdjuster(CustomAdjusters::getWeekDayNoFriday13);

    // No public constructor as it is a utility class
    private CustomAdjusters() {
    }

    private static LocalDate getWeekDayNoFriday13(LocalDate date) {
        // Initialize the new date with the original one
        LocalDate newDate = date;

        DayOfWeek day = date.getDayOfWeek();
        if (day == SATURDAY || day == SUNDAY || (day == FRIDAY && date.getDayOfMonth() == 13)) {
            // Return next Monday
            newDate = date.with(TemporalAdjusters.next(MONDAY));
        }
        return newDate;
    }
}
```

Listing 16-18 demonstrates how to use the custom date adjuster. December 12, 2013 was on Thursday. You use the adjuster to adjust December 12, 13, and 14 in 2013. December 12, 2013 is returned without any adjustments. The other two dates are adjusted to next Monday, which is December 16, 2013. Note that the adjuster can be used on any datetime object that can supply a LocalDate. The program uses it to adjust a ZonedDateTime.

Listing 16-18. Using the Custom Date Adjuster

```java
// CustomAdjusterTest.java
package com.jdojo.datetime;

import java.time.LocalDate;
import java.time.LocalTime;
import java.time.Month;
import java.time.ZoneId;
import java.time.ZonedDateTime;

public class CustomAdjusterTest {
    public static void main(String[] args) {
        LocalDate ld1 = LocalDate.of(2013, Month.DECEMBER, 12); // Thursday
        LocalDate ld2 = LocalDate.of(2013, Month.DECEMBER, 13); // Friday
        LocalDate ld3 = LocalDate.of(2013, Month.DECEMBER, 14); // Saturday

        LocalDate ld1Adjusted = ld1.with(CustomAdjusters.WEEKDAYS_WITH_NO_FRIDAY_13);
        System.out.println(ld1 + " adjusted to " + ld1Adjusted);
```

```
        LocalDate ld2Adjusted = ld2.with(CustomAdjusters.WEEKDAYS_WITH_NO_FRIDAY_13);
        System.out.println(ld2 + " adjusted to " + ld2Adjusted);

        LocalDate ld3Adjusted = ld3.with(CustomAdjusters.WEEKDAYS_WITH_NO_FRIDAY_13);
        System.out.println(ld3 + " adjusted to " + ld3Adjusted);

        // Use it to adjust a ZonedDateTime
        ZonedDateTime zdt
                = ZonedDateTime.of(ld2, LocalTime.of(8, 45), ZoneId.of("America/Chicago"));
        ZonedDateTime zdtAdjusted = zdt.with(CustomAdjusters.WEEKDAYS_WITH_NO_FRIDAY_13);
        System.out.println(zdt + " adjusted to " + zdtAdjusted);
    }
}
```

```
013-12-12 adjusted to 2013-12-12
2013-12-13 adjusted to 2013-12-16
2013-12-14 adjusted to 2013-12-16
2013-12-13T08:45-06:00[America/Chicago] adjusted to 2013-12-16T08:45-06:00[America/
Chicago]
```

Querying Datetime Objects

All datetime classes support queries. A query is a request for information. Note that you can obtain the components of a datetime object, for example, the year from a LocalDate, using the get(TemporalField field) method of the datetime object. Use a query to request information that is not available as components. For example, you can query a LocalDate whether it is a Friday 13. The result of a query can be of any type.

An instance of the TemporalQuery<R> interface represents a query. All datetime classes contain a query() method, which takes a TemporalQuery as a parameter and returns a result.

TemporalQueries is a utility class that contains several predefined queries as its static methods, as shown in Table 16-5. If a datetime object does not have the information sought in the query, the query returns null. For example, the query for a LocalDate from a LocalTime object returns null. Chronology is an interface that is used to identify and manipulate dates in a calendar system.

Table 16-5. *Utility Methods in the TemporalQueries Class*

Method	Return Type	Description
chronology()	TemporalQuery<Chronology>	A query to get the chronology.
localDate()	TemporalQuery<LocalDate>	A query to get the LocalDate.
localTime()	TemporalQuery<LocalTime>	A query to get the LocalTime.
offset()	TemporalQuery<ZoneOffset>	A query to get the ZoneOffset.
precision()	TemporalQuery<TemporalUnit>	A query to get the smallest supported unit.
zone()	TemporalQuery<ZoneId>	A query to get the ZoneId. If the ZoneId is not available it queries for ZoneOffset. It returns null if both are not available, for example, a LocalDate has neither.
zoneId()	TemporalQuery<ZoneId>	A query to get the ZoneId. If ZoneId is not available, it returns null.

The program in Listing 16-19 shows how to use predefined queries. It uses queries to get the precision and LocalDate from a LocalDate, a LocalTime, and a ZonedDateTime. The program uses the current date, so you may get a different output.

Listing 16-19. Querying Datetime Objects

```
// QueryTest.java
package com.jdojo.datetime;

import java.time.LocalDate;
import java.time.LocalTime;
import java.time.ZonedDateTime;
import java.time.temporal.TemporalQueries;
import java.time.temporal.TemporalQuery;
import java.time.temporal.TemporalUnit;

public class QueryTest {
    public static void main(String[] args) {
        // Get references of the precision and local date queries
        TemporalQuery<TemporalUnit> precisionQuery = TemporalQueries.precision();
        TemporalQuery<LocalDate> localDateQuery = TemporalQueries.localDate();

        // Query a LocalDate
        LocalDate ld = LocalDate.now();
        TemporalUnit precision = ld.query(precisionQuery);
        LocalDate queryDate = ld.query(localDateQuery);
        System.out.println("Precision of LocalDate: " + precision);
        System.out.println("LocalDate of LocalDate: " + queryDate);

        // Query a LocalTime
        LocalTime lt = LocalTime.now();
        precision = lt.query(precisionQuery);
        queryDate = lt.query(localDateQuery);
```

```
            System.out.println("Precision of LocalTime: " + precision);
            System.out.println("LocalDate of LocalTime: " + queryDate);

            // Query a ZonedDateTime
            ZonedDateTime zdt = ZonedDateTime.now();
            precision = zdt.query(precisionQuery);
            queryDate = zdt.query(localDateQuery);
            System.out.println("Precision of ZonedDateTime: " + precision);
            System.out.println("LocalDate of ZonedDateTime: " + queryDate);
        }
}
```

```
Precision of LocalDate: Days
LocalDate of LocalDate: 2017-08-04
Precision of LocalTime: Nanos
LocalDate of LocalTime: null
Precision of ZonedDateTime: Nanos
LocalDate of ZonedDateTime: 2017-08-04
```

Creating and using a custom query is easy. You can create a custom query in two ways.

- Create a class that implements the TemporalQuery interface and use instances of the class as a query.

- Use any method reference as a query. The method should take a TemporalAccessor and return an object. The return type of the method defines the result type for the query.

Listing 16-20 contains the code for a Friday13Query class. The class implements the TemporalQuery interface. The queryFrom() method is part of the interface implementation. The method returns true if the datetime object contains a date that falls on Friday 13. Otherwise, it returns false. The query returns false if the datetime object does not contain a day of month and day of week information, for example a LocalTime object. The class defines a constant IS_FRIDAY_13 that can be used as a query.

Listing 16-20. A Class Implementing the TemporalQuery Interface

```
// Friday13Query.java
package com.jdojo.datetime;

import java.time.DayOfWeek;
import java.time.temporal.TemporalAccessor;
import java.time.temporal.TemporalQuery;
import static java.time.temporal.ChronoField.DAY_OF_MONTH;
import static java.time.temporal.ChronoField.DAY_OF_WEEK;
import static java.time.DayOfWeek.FRIDAY;

public class Friday13Query implements TemporalQuery<Boolean> {
    public final static Friday13Query IS_FRIDAY_13 = new Friday13Query();

    // Prevent outside code from creating objects of this class
    private Friday13Query() {
    }
```

```
    @Override
    public Boolean queryFrom(TemporalAccessor temporal) {
        if (temporal.isSupported(DAY_OF_MONTH) && temporal.isSupported(DAY_OF_WEEK)) {
            int dayOfMonth = temporal.get(DAY_OF_MONTH);
            int weekDay = temporal.get(DAY_OF_WEEK);
            DayOfWeek dayOfWeek = DayOfWeek.of(weekDay);
            if (dayOfMonth == 13 && dayOfWeek == FRIDAY) {
                return Boolean.TRUE;
            }
        }
        return Boolean.FALSE;
    }
}
```

The following snippet of code uses the Friday13Query with three datetime objects. The first LocalDate falls on Friday 13, and as you can see in the output, the query returns true.

```
LocalDate ld1 = LocalDate.of(2013, 12, 13);
Boolean isFriday13 = ld1.query(Friday13Query.IS_FRIDAY_13);
System.out.println("Date: " + ld1 + ", isFriday13: " + isFriday13);

LocalDate ld2 = LocalDate.of(2014, 1, 10);
isFriday13 = ld2.query(Friday13Query.IS_FRIDAY_13);
System.out.println("Date: " + ld2 + ", isFriday13: " + isFriday13);

LocalTime lt = LocalTime.of(7, 30, 45);
isFriday13 = lt.query(Friday13Query.IS_FRIDAY_13);
System.out.println("Time: " + lt + ", isFriday13: " + isFriday13);
```

```
Date: 2013-12-13, isFriday13: true
Date: 2014-01-10, isFriday13: false
Time: 07:30:45, isFriday13: false
```

Listing 16-21 contains the code for a CustomQueries class. The class contains a static method isFriday13(). The method reference for isFriday13() method can be used as a query.

Listing 16-21. A CustomQueries Class with a IsFriday13 Method That Can Be Used a Query

```
// CustomQueries.java
package com.jdojo.datetime;

import java.time.DayOfWeek;
import static java.time.DayOfWeek.FRIDAY;
import static java.time.temporal.ChronoField.DAY_OF_MONTH;
import static java.time.temporal.ChronoField.DAY_OF_WEEK;
import java.time.temporal.TemporalAccessor;

public class CustomQueries {
    public static Boolean isFriday13(TemporalAccessor temporal) {
        if (temporal.isSupported(DAY_OF_MONTH) && temporal.isSupported(DAY_OF_WEEK)) {
            int dayOfMonth = temporal.get(DAY_OF_MONTH);
```

```
            int weekDay = temporal.get(DAY_OF_WEEK);
            DayOfWeek dayOfWeek = DayOfWeek.of(weekDay);
            if (dayOfMonth == 13 && dayOfWeek == FRIDAY) {
                return Boolean.TRUE;
            }
        }
    }
    return Boolean.FALSE;
    }
}
```

The following snippet of code uses the method reference of the isFriday13() method in the CustomQueries class as a query. The code uses the same datetime objects as in the previous example and you get the same result.

```
LocalDate ld1 = LocalDate.of(2013, 12, 13);
Boolean isFriday13 = ld1.query(CustomQueries::isFriday13);
System.out.println("Date: " + ld1 + ", isFriday13: " + isFriday13);

LocalDate ld2 = LocalDate.of(2014, 1, 10);
isFriday13 = ld2.query(CustomQueries::isFriday13);
System.out.println("Date: " + ld2 + ", isFriday13: " + isFriday13);

LocalTime lt = LocalTime.of(7, 30, 45);
isFriday13 = lt.query(CustomQueries::isFriday13);
System.out.println("Time: " + lt + ", isFriday13: " + isFriday13);
```

```
Date: 2013-12-13, isFriday13: true
Date: 2014-01-10, isFriday13: false
Time: 07:30:45, isFriday13: false
```

It is typical of the Date-Time API to provide multiple choices to perform the same task. Let's consider a task of getting the LocalTime from a ZonedDateTime. The program in Listing 16-22 shows five ways of achieving this.

Listing 16-22. Multiple Ways of Getting the LocalTime from a ZonedDateTime

```
// LocalTimeFromZonedDateTime.java
package com.jdojo.datetime;

import java.time.LocalTime;
import java.time.ZonedDateTime;
import java.time.temporal.TemporalQueries;

public class LocalTimeFromZonedDateTime {
    public static void main(String[] args) {
        ZonedDateTime zdt = ZonedDateTime.now();

        // Use the toLocalTime() method of the ZonedDateTime class (preferred)
        LocalTime lt1 = zdt.toLocalTime();
```

```
        // Use the from() method of the LocalTime class
        LocalTime lt2 = LocalTime.from(zdt);

        // Use the localTime() query
        LocalTime lt3 = zdt.query(TemporalQueries.localTime());

        // Use the LocalTime::from method as a query
        LocalTime lt4 = zdt.query(LocalTime::from);

        // Get all time components and construct a LocalTime
        int hours = zdt.getHour();
        int minutes = zdt.getMinute();
        int seconds = zdt.getSecond();
        int nanos = zdt.getNano();
        LocalTime lt5 = LocalTime.of(hours, minutes, seconds, nanos);

        // Print all LocalTimes
        System.out.println("zdt: " + zdt);
        System.out.println("lt1: " + lt1);
        System.out.println("lt2: " + lt2);
        System.out.println("lt3: " + lt3);
        System.out.println("lt4: " + lt4);
        System.out.println("lt5: " + lt5);
    }
}
```

```
zdt: 2017-08-04T21:11:42.547440400-05:00[America/Chicago]
lt1: 21:11:42.547440400
lt2: 21:11:42.547440400
lt3: 21:11:42.547440400
lt4: 21:11:42.547440400
lt5: 21:11:42.547440400
```

Which method is the correct way? Most of the time, all methods will execute the same logic. However, some methods are more readable than others. In this case, the code calling the toLocalTime() method of the ZonedDateTime class should be used as it is straightforward and most readable. At least, you should not extract the time components from the ZonedDateTime to construct the LocalTime, as shown in the fifth method in the example.

Non-ISO Calendar Systems

The date classes such as LocalDate use the ISO calendar system, which is the Gregorian calendar. The Date-Time API also lets you use other calendars such as Thai Buddhist calendar, Hijrah calendar, Minguo calendar, and Japanese calendar. The non-ISO calendar-related classes are in the java.time.chrono package.

There is an XxxChronology and XxxDate class for each of the available non-ISO calendar system. The XxxChronology class represents the Xxx calendar system whereas XxxDate class represents a date in the Xxx calendar system. Each XxxChronology class contains an INSTANCE constant that represents a singleton instance of that class. For example, HijrahChronology and HijrahDate are classes that you will be using to work with the Hijrah calendar system. The following snippet of code shows two ways to get the current date in the Thai Buddhist calendar. You may get a different output.

```
import java.time.chrono.ThaiBuddhistChronology;
import java.time.chrono.ThaiBuddhistDate;
...
ThaiBuddhistChronology thaiBuddhistChrono = ThaiBuddhistChronology.INSTANCE;
ThaiBuddhistDate now = thaiBuddhistChrono.dateNow();
ThaiBuddhistDate now2 = ThaiBuddhistDate.now();
System.out.println("Current Date in Thai Buddhist: " + now);
System.out.println("Current Date in Thai Buddhist: " + now2);
```

```
Current Date in Thai Buddhist: ThaiBuddhist BE 2560-08-04
Current Date in Thai Buddhist: ThaiBuddhist BE 2560-08-04
```

You can also convert dates in one calendar system to another. ISO dates to non-ISO dates conversion is also allowed. Converting dates from one calendar system to another is just a matter of calling the from() static method of the target date class and passing the source date object as its parameter. Listing 16-23 shows how to convert ISO date to Thai Buddhist date and vice versa. You may get a different output.

Listing 16-23. Using the Thai Buddhist and ISO Calendars

```
// InterCalendarDates.java
package com.jdojo.datetime;

import java.time.LocalDate;
import java.time.chrono.ThaiBuddhistDate;

public class InterCalendarDates {
    public static void main(String[] args) {
        ThaiBuddhistDate thaiBuddhistNow = ThaiBuddhistDate.now();
        LocalDate isoNow = LocalDate.now();
        System.out.println("Thai Buddhist Current Date: " + thaiBuddhistNow);
        System.out.println("ISO Current Date: " + isoNow);

        // Convert Thai Buddhist date to ISO date and vice versa
        ThaiBuddhistDate thaiBuddhistNow2 = ThaiBuddhistDate.from(isoNow);
        LocalDate isoNow2 = LocalDate.from(thaiBuddhistNow);
        System.out.println("Thai Buddhist Current Date from ISO: " + thaiBuddhistNow2);
        System.out.println("ISO Current Date from Thai Buddhist: " + isoNow2);
    }
}
```

```
Thai Buddhist Current Date: ThaiBuddhist BE 2560-08-04
ISO Current Date: 2017-08-04
Thai Buddhist Current Date from ISO: ThaiBuddhist BE 2560-08-04
ISO Current Date from Thai Buddhist: 2017-08-04
```

Formatting Dates and Times

An object of the DateTimeFormatter class lets you format and parse a datetime object. By formatting, I mean representing a datetime object in a user-defined textual form, for example, representing a LocalDate May 24, 2012 as "05/24/2012." Sometimes formatting is also referred as printing, because formatting features also let you print (or output) a textual representation of a datetime object to an Appendable object such as a StringBuilder.

Parsing is the reverse of formatting. It lets you construct a datetime object from a textual representation of a datetime. Creating a LocalDate object from the text "05/24/2012" to represent May 24, 2012 is an example of parsing.

Different ways of formatting and parsing datetimes exist. Learning how to format datetimes may be difficult, if you do not learn it the right way. The most important point to keep in mind is that formatting and parsing are always performed by an object of the DateTimeFormatter class. The difference lies in how you create that object. The DateTimeFormatter class does not provide any public constructors. You must obtain its object indirectly. In the beginning, the confusion lies in how to get its object. Use one of the following two methods of the DateTimeFormatter class to format a date, time, or datetime:

- String format(TemporalAccessor temporal)

- void formatTo(TemporalAccessor temporal, Appendable appendable)

The format() method takes a date, time, or datetime object and returns a textual representation of the object based on the rules of the formatter. The formatTo() method lets you write the textual representation of the object to an Appendable, for example, a file, a StringBuilder, etc.

To format a datetime object, a formatter needs two pieces of information: a format pattern and a locale. Sometimes one or both pieces of information are defaulted for you; sometimes, you provide them.

You can perform formatting in several ways. They all use, directly or indirectly, a DateTimeFormatter object.

- Using pre-defined standard datetime formatters

- Using the format() method of the datetime classes

- Using user-defined patterns

- Using the DateTimeFormatterBuilder class

Using Predefined Formatters

Predefined formatters are defined as constants in the DateTimeFormatter class. They are listed in in Table 16-6. Most of the formatters use ISO datetime formats; some formatters use a slightly modified version of ISO formats.

Table 16-6. *Predefined Datetime Formatters*

Formatter	Description	Example
BASIC_ISO_DATE	An ISO date formatter to format and parse a date without using a separator between two date components.	20140109, 20140109-0600
ISO_DATE, ISO_TIME, ISO_DATE_TIME	Date, time, and datetime formatters to format and parse dates, times, and datetimes using the ISO separators.	2014-01-09, 2014-01-09-06:00, 15:38:32.927, 15:38:32.943-06:00, 2014-01-09T15:20:07.747-06:00, 2014-01-09T15:20:07.825-06:00[America/Chicago]
ISO_INSTANT	An instant formatter to format and parse an instant (or a datetime object representing an instant such as a ZonedDateTime) in UTC format.	2014-01-09T21:23:56.870Z
ISO_LOCAL_DATE, ISO_LOCAL_TIME, ISO_LOCAL_DATE_TIME	Date, time, and datetime formatters to format or parse dates, times, and datetimes without an offset.	2014-01-09, 15:30:14.352, 2014-01-09T15:29:11.384
ISO_OFFSET_DATE, ISO_OFFSET_TIME, ISO_OFFSET_DATE_TIME	Date, time, and datetime formatters to format and parse dates, times, and datetimes with an offset using ISO format.	2014-01-09-06:00, 15:34:29.851-06:00, 2014-01-09T15:33:07.07-06:0
ISO_ZONED_DATE_TIME	A datetime formatter to format and parse a datetime with a zone id, if available.	2014-01-09T15:45:49.112-06:00, 2014-01-09T15:45:49.128-06:00[America/Chicago]
ISO_ORDINAL_DATE	A date formatter to format and parse a date with year and day-of-year.	2014-009
ISO_WEEK_DATE	A date formatter to format and parse week-based dates. The format is year-week_of_year-day_of_week. For example, 2014-W02-4 means the fourth day of the second week in 2014.	2014-W02-4, 2014-W02-4-06:00
RFC_1123_DATE_TIME	A datetime formatter to format and parse datetimes for e-mails using the RFC1123 specification.	Thu, 9 Jan 2014 15:50:44 -05:00

Using the predefined formatters is easy: just pass the date/time object to the format(). The following snippet of code uses ISO_DATE formatter to format a LocalDate, an OffsetDateTime, and ZonedDateTime. You may get a different output as it formats and prints the current date.

```
import java.time.LocalDate;
import java.time.OffsetDateTime;
import java.time.ZonedDateTime;
import static java.time.format.DateTimeFormatter.ISO_DATE;
...
// Format dates using the ISO_DATE formatter
String ldStr = ISO_DATE.format(LocalDate.now());
```

```
String odtStr = ISO_DATE.format(OffsetDateTime.now());
String zdtStr = ISO_DATE.format(ZonedDateTime.now());

System.out.println("Local Date: " + ldStr);
System.out.println("Offset Datetime: " + odtStr);
System.out.println("Zoned Datetime: " + zdtStr);
```

```
Local Date: 2017-08-04
Offset Datetime: 2017-08-04-05:00
Zoned Datetime: 2017-08-04-05:00
```

Pay attention to the names of the predefined formatters. The datetime object being formatted must contain the components as suggested by their names. For example, the ISO_DATE formatter expects the presence of the date components, and hence, it should be not used to format time-only objects such as a LocalTime. Similarly, the ISO_TIME formatter should be used to format a LocalDate.

```
// A runtime error as a LocalTime does not contain date components
String ltStr = ISO_DATE.format(LocalTime.now());
```

Using the format() Method of Datetime Classes

You can format a datetime object using its format() method. The format() method takes an object of the DateTimeFormatter class. The following snippet of code uses this approach. The ISO_DATE formatter is used.

```
import java.time.LocalDate;
import java.time.OffsetDateTime;
import java.time.ZonedDateTime;
import static java.time.format.DateTimeFormatter.ISO_DATE;
...
LocalDate ld = LocalDate.now();
String ldStr = ld.format(ISO_DATE);
System.out.println("Local Date: " + ldStr);

OffsetDateTime odt = OffsetDateTime.now();
String odtStr = odt.format(ISO_DATE);
System.out.println("Offset Datetime: " + odtStr);

ZonedDateTime zdt = ZonedDateTime.now();
String zdtStr = zdt.format(ISO_DATE);
System.out.println("Zoned Datetime: " + zdtStr);
```

```
Local Date: 2017-08-04
Offset Datetime: 2017-08-04-05:00
Zoned Datetime: 2017-08-04-05:00
```

Using User-Defined Patterns

One of the most commonly used methods in the DateTimeFormatter class is the ofPattern() method, which returns a DateTimeFormatter object with the specified format pattern and locale.

- static DateTimeFormatter ofPattern(String pattern)

- static DateTimeFormatter ofPattern(String pattern, Locale locale)

The following snippet obtains two formatters to format a date in "Month day, Year" format. The first formatter formats the datetime in the default locale and the second one in the German locale.

```
// Get a formatter for the default locale
DateTimeFormatter fmt1 = DateTimeFormatter.ofPattern("MMMM dd, yyyy");

// Get a formatter for the German locale
DateTimeFormatter fmt2 = DateTimeFormatter.ofPattern("MMMM dd, yyyy", Locale.GERMAN);
```

Sometimes you have a DateTimeFormatter object for a pattern and a locale. You want to use the same pattern to format a datetime in another locale. The DateTimeFormatter class has a withLocale() method that returns a DateTimeFormatter object for the specified locale that uses the same pattern. In the previous snippet of code, you could have replaced the second statement with the following one:

```
// Get a formatter for the German locale using the same pattern as fmt1
DateTimeFormatter fmt2 = fmt1.withLocale(Locale.GERMAN);
```

▓ **Tip** Use the getLocale() method of the DateTimeFormatter class to know the locale that it will use to format datetimes.

Datetime formatting is performed based on a pattern. A formatting pattern is a sequence of characters that have special meanings. For example, MMMM in a pattern uses the fully spelled name of a month, such as January, February, etc.; MMM uses the short form of a month name, such as Jan, Feb, etc.; MM uses two digits month number, such as 01, 02, etc.; M uses one or two digits month number, such as 1, 2, 10, 11, etc.

In a format pattern, some characters have special meanings and some are used literally. Characters with special meanings will be interpreted by the formatter and they will be replaced with datetime components. A formatter outputs the literal characters as they appear in the pattern. All letters, A to Z and a to z, are reserved as pattern letters, although not all are used. If you want to include a literal string in a pattern, you need to enclose it in single quotes. To output a single quote, you need to use two consecutive single quotes.

A datetime formatter outputs any non-letter characters, other than [,] and a single quote, directly. However, it is recommended that you enclose them in single quotes. Suppose you have a local date of May 29, 2012. Both patterns of "1997 MMMM dd, yyyy" and "'1997' MMMM dd, yyyy" will output 1997 May 29, 2012; however, the latter, which uses single quotes around the literal 1997, is recommended.

Table 16-7 lists the symbols used in patterns and their meanings. All examples in the table use "2012-07-29T07:30:12.789-05:00[America/Chicago]" as the input datetime.

Table 16-7. *Datetime Formatting Symbols and Descriptions with Examples*

Symbol	Description	Examples	
		Pattern	**Output**
G	Era	G	AD
		GGGG	Anno Domini
		GGGGG	A
u	Year It can be a positive or negative number. After an era start date, it is a positive number. Before an era start date, it is a negative number. For example, the year value for 2014 AD is 2014 and the year value for 2014 BC is -2014.	u/uuu/uuuu	2012
		uu	12
		uuuuu	02012
y	Year of era It counts the year forward or backward from the era start date. It is always a positive number. For example, the year value for 2014 AD is 2014 and the year value for 2014 BC is 2015. In Common Era, year 0 is 1 BC.	y/yyy/yyyy	2012
		yy	12
		yyyyy	02012
D	Day of year (1 -366)	D	150
M/L	Month of year	M	5
		MM	05
		MMM	Jul
		MMMM	July
d	Day of month	d	5, 29
		dd	05, 29
g	Modified Julian day (Added in Java 9)	g	57796
		ggg	57796
		gggggg	057796
Q/q	Quarter of year	Q	3
		QQ	03
		QQQ	Q3
		QQQQ	3rd quarter
Y	Week-based year	Y	2012
		YY	12
		YYY/YYYY	2012
w	Week of week-based year	w	31
W	Week of month	W	5
E	Day of week	E	7
		EE	07
		EEE	Sun
		EEEE	Sunday

(continued)

Table 16-7. (*continued*)

Symbol	Description	Examples	
		Pattern	**Output**
F	Day of week in month	F	1
a	AM/PM of day	a	AM
h	Clock hour of AM/PM (1-12)	h	7
K	Hour of AM/PM (0-11)	K	7
k	Clock hour of AM/PM (1-24)	k	7
H	Hour of day (0-23)	H	7
		HH	07
m	Minute of hour	mm	30
s	Second of minute	ss	12
S	Fraction of second	SSSSSSSSS	000000789
A	Millisecond of day	A	27012000
n	Nanosecond of second	n	789
N	Nanosecond of day	N	27012000000789
V	Time zone ID	VV	America/Chicago
v	Generic non-location zone name (Added in Java 9)	v	CT
		vvvv	Central Time
z	Time zone name	z	CDT
Z	Zone offset. When the zone offset is zero, it outputs +0000 or +00:00, depending on whether you use Z, ZZ, or ZZZ.	Z	-0500
		ZZ	-0500
		ZZZ	-05:00
		ZZZZ	GMT-05:00
O	Localized zone offset	O	GMT-5
X	Zone offset. Unlike the symbol Z, it prints Z for the zone offset Zero. X outputs only the hour if minutes and seconds are zero such as +09; XX outputs the hour and minute, without a colon, such as +0830; XXX outputs the hour and minute with a colon such as +08:30; XXXX outputs the hour, minute, and optional second, without a colon, such as +083045; and XXXXX outputs the hour, minute, and optional second with a colon, such as +08:30:45.	X	+0530
		XX	+0530
		XXX	+05:30
		XXXX	+053045
		XXXXX	+05:30:45
x	Same as X, except that it prints +00 for the zone offset zero, not Z.	xx	-0500

(*continued*)

Table 16-7. (*continued*)

Symbol	Description	Examples	
		Pattern	**Output**
p	Pad next It pads the output of the pattern following it with spaces. For example, if mm outputs 30, pppmm will output ' 30' and ppppmm will output ' 30'. The number of ps determines the width of the output	pppmm	' 30' (Single quotes have been shown to display the padding with a space.)
'	Escape for text Text within single quotes is output directly. To output a single quote, use two consecutive single quotes.	'Hello' 'Hello' MMMM	Hello Hello July
' '	A single quote	'''Hello''' MMMM	'Hello' July
[ ]	An optional section Refer to the discussion for an example.		
#, {, }	These are reserved for future use.		

You can have optional sections in a pattern string. The symbols [and] denote the start and the end of an optional section, respectively. A pattern enclosed within an optional section is output only if information is available for all its elements. Otherwise, an optional section is skipped. An optional section may be nested inside another optional section. Listing 16-24 shows how to use an optional section in a pattern. The optional section contains time information. When you format a date, the optional section is skipped.

Listing 16-24. Using an Optional Section in a Datetime Formatting Pattern

```java
// OptionalSectionTest.java
package com.jdojo.datetime;

import java.time.LocalDate;
import java.time.LocalDateTime;
import java.time.LocalTime;
import java.time.Month;
import java.time.format.DateTimeFormatter;

public class OptionalSectionTest {
    public static void main(String[] args) {
        // A pattern with an optional section
        String pattern = "MM/dd/yyyy[ 'at' HH:mm:ss]";
        DateTimeFormatter fmt = DateTimeFormatter.ofPattern(pattern);

        LocalDate ld = LocalDate.of(2012, Month.MAY, 30);
        LocalTime lt = LocalTime.of(17, 30, 12);
        LocalDateTime ldt = LocalDateTime.of(ld,lt);
```

```
        // Format a date. Optional section will be skipped because a
        // date does not have time (HH, mm, and ss) information.
        String str1 = fmt.format(ld);
        System.out.println(str1);

        // Format a datetime. Optional section will be output.
        String str2 = fmt.format(ldt);
        System.out.println(str2);
    }
}
```

```
05/30/2012
05/30/2012 at 17:30:12
```

Listing 16-25 shows how to use different patterns to format dates and times.

Listing 16-25. Using Patterns to Format Dates and Times

```
// FormattingDateTime.java
package com.jdojo.datetime;

import java.time.LocalDate;
import java.time.LocalTime;
import java.time.Month;
import java.time.ZoneId;
import java.time.ZonedDateTime;
import java.time.format.DateTimeFormatter;
import java.time.temporal.Temporal;
import java.util.Locale;

public class FormattingDateTime {
    public static void main(String[] args) {
        LocalDate ld = LocalDate.of(2012, Month.APRIL, 30);
        System.out.println("Formatting date: " + ld);
        format(ld, "M/d/yyyy");
        format(ld, "MM/dd/yyyy");
        format(ld, "MMM dd, yyyy");
        format(ld, "MMMM dd, yyyy");
        format(ld, "EEEE, MMMM dd, yyyy");
        format(ld, "'Month' q 'in' QQQ");
        format(ld, "[MM-dd-yyyy][' at' HH:mm:ss]");

        LocalTime lt = LocalTime.of(16, 30, 5, 78899);
        System.out.println("\nFormatting time:" + lt);
        format(lt, "HH:mm:ss");
        format(lt, "KK:mm:ss a");
        format(lt, "[MM-dd-yyyy][' at' HH:mm:ss]");

        ZoneId usCentral = ZoneId.of("America/Chicago");
        ZonedDateTime zdt = ZonedDateTime.of(ld, lt, usCentral);
        System.out.println("\nFormatting zoned datetime:" + zdt);
```

```
            format(zdt, "MM/dd/yyyy HH:mm:ssXXX");
            format(zdt, "MM/dd/yyyy VV");
            format(zdt, "[MM-dd-yyyy][' at' HH:mm:ss]");
    }

    public static void format(Temporal co, String pattern) {
        DateTimeFormatter fmt = DateTimeFormatter.ofPattern(pattern, Locale.US);
        String str = fmt.format(co);
        System.out.println(pattern + ": " + str);
    }
}
```

```
Formatting date: 2012-04-30
M/d/yyyy: 4/30/2012
MM/dd/yyyy: 04/30/2012
MMM dd, yyyy: Apr 30, 2012
MMMM dd, yyyy: April 30, 2012
EEEE, MMMM dd, yyyy: Monday, April 30, 2012
'Month' q 'in' QQQ: Month 2 in Q2
[MM-dd-yyyy][' at' HH:mm:ss]: 04-30-2012

Formatting time:16:30:05.000078899
HH:mm:ss: 16:30:05
KK:mm:ss a: 04:30:05 PM
[MM-dd-yyyy][' at' HH:mm:ss]:  at 16:30:05

Formatting zoned datetime:2012-04-30T16:30:05.000078899-05:00[America/Chicago]
MM/dd/yyyy HH:mm:ssXXX: 04/30/2012 16:30:05-05:00
MM/dd/yyyy VV: 04/30/2012 America/Chicago
[MM-dd-yyyy][' at' HH:mm:ss]: 04-30-2012 at 16:30:05
```

Using Locale Specific Formats

The DateTimeFormatter class has several methods that return a DateTimeFormatter with a predefined formatting pattern suitable for humans to read. Use the following methods to obtain a reference to such formatters:

- DateTimeFormatter ofLocalizedDate(FormatStyle dateStyle)

- DateTimeFormatter ofLocalizedDateTime(FormatStyle dateTimeStyle)

- DateTimeFormatter ofLocalizedDateTime(FormatStyle dateStyle, FormatStyle timeStyle)

- DateTimeFormatter ofLocalizedTime(FormatStyle timeStyle)

These methods accept an argument of FormatStyle enum type, which has four constants: SHORT, MEDIUM, LONG, and FULL. These constants are used to output formatted date and time with a varying degree of detail. The details in the output are locale-specific. The methods use the system default locale. For a different locale, use the withLocal() method to obtain a new DateTimeFormatter with the specified locale.

Listing 16-26 shows how to use some predefined locale-specific formats. It formats dates and times in US (default), German, and Indian locales.

Listing 16-26. Using Predefined Format Patterns

```java
// LocalizedFormats.java
package com.jdojo.datetime;

import java.time.LocalDate;
import java.time.LocalDateTime;
import java.time.LocalTime;
import java.time.Month;
import java.time.format.DateTimeFormatter;
import static java.time.format.FormatStyle.FULL;
import static java.time.format.FormatStyle.LONG;
import static java.time.format.FormatStyle.MEDIUM;
import static java.time.format.FormatStyle.SHORT;

import java.util.Locale;

public class LocalizedFormats {
    public static void main(String[] args) {
        LocalDate ld = LocalDate.of(2012, Month.APRIL, 19);
        LocalTime lt = LocalTime.of(16, 30, 20);
        LocalDateTime ldt = LocalDateTime.of(ld, lt);

        DateTimeFormatter fmt = DateTimeFormatter.ofLocalizedDate(SHORT);
        System.out.println("Formatter Default Locale: " + fmt.getLocale());
        System.out.println("Short Date: " + fmt.format(ld));

        fmt = DateTimeFormatter.ofLocalizedDate(MEDIUM);
        System.out.println("Medium Date: " + fmt.format(ld));

        fmt = DateTimeFormatter.ofLocalizedDate(LONG);
        System.out.println("Long Date: " + fmt.format(ld));

        fmt = DateTimeFormatter.ofLocalizedDate(FULL);
        System.out.println("Full Date: " + fmt.format(ld));

        fmt = DateTimeFormatter.ofLocalizedTime(SHORT);
        System.out.println("Short Time: " + fmt.format(lt));

        fmt = DateTimeFormatter.ofLocalizedDateTime(SHORT);
        System.out.println("Short Datetime: " + fmt.format(ldt));

        fmt = DateTimeFormatter.ofLocalizedDateTime(MEDIUM);
        System.out.println("Medium Datetime: " + fmt.format(ldt));

        // Use German locale to format the datetime in medius style
        fmt = DateTimeFormatter.ofLocalizedDateTime(MEDIUM)
                            .withLocale(Locale.GERMAN);
        System.out.println("German Medium Datetime: " + fmt.format(ldt));
```

```
        // Use Indian(English) locale to format datetime in short style
        fmt = DateTimeFormatter.ofLocalizedDateTime(SHORT)
                            .withLocale(new Locale("en", "IN"));
        System.out.println("Indian(en) Short Datetime: " + fmt.format(ldt));

        // Use Indian(English) locale to format datetime in medium style
        fmt = DateTimeFormatter.ofLocalizedDateTime(MEDIUM)
                            .withLocale(new Locale("en","IN"));
        System.out.println("Indian(en) Medium Datetime: " + fmt.format(ldt));

    }
}
```

```
Formatter Default Locale: en_US
Short Date: 4/19/12
Medium Date: Apr 19, 2012
Long Date: April 19, 2012
Full Date: Thursday, April 19, 2012
Short Time: 4:30 PM
Short Datetime: 4/19/12, 4:30 PM
Medium Datetime: Apr 19, 2012, 4:30:20 PM
German Medium Datetime: 19.04.2012, 16:30:20
Indian(en) Short Datetime: 19/04/12, 4:30 PM
Indian(en) Medium Datetime: 19-Apr-2012, 4:30:20 PM
```

Using the DateTimeFormatterBuilder Class

Internally, all datetime formatters are obtained using DateTimeFormatterBuilder. Typically, you will not need to use this class. The previously discussed methods are sufficient in almost all use cases. The class has a no-args constructor and many appendXxx() methods. You create an instance of the class and call those appendXxx() methods to build the desired formatter. Finally, call the toFomatter() method to get a DateTimeFormatter object. The following snippet of code builds a DateTimeFormatter object to format a date in the format like "Christmas in YEAR is on WEEK_DAY":

```
import java.time.LocalDate;
import java.time.format.DateTimeFormatter;
import java.time.format.DateTimeFormatterBuilder;
import static java.time.format.TextStyle.FULL_STANDALONE;
import static java.time.temporal.ChronoField.DAY_OF_WEEK;
import static java.time.temporal.ChronoField.YEAR;
...
DateTimeFormatter formatter = new DateTimeFormatterBuilder()
                                .appendLiteral("Christmas in ")
                                .appendValue(YEAR)
                                .appendLiteral(" is on ")
                                .appendText(DAY_OF_WEEK, FULL_STANDALONE)
                                .toFormatter();
```

```
LocalDate ld = LocalDate.of(2020, 12, 25);
String str = ld.format(formatter);
System.out.println(str);
```

```
Christmas in 2020 is on Friday
```

You can create the same formatter using a pattern, which is a lot easier to write and read than the previous code using the DateTimeFormatterBuilder.

```
LocalDate ld = LocalDate.of(2020, 12, 25);
String pattern = "'Christmas in' yyyy 'is on' EEEE";
DateTimeFormatter formatter = DateTimeFormatter.ofPattern(pattern);
String str = ld.format(formatter);
System.out.println(str);
```

```
Christmas in 2020 is on Friday
```

Parsing Dates and Times

Parsing is the process of creating a date, time, or datetime object from a string. Like formatting, parsing is also handled by a DateTimeFormatter. Refer to the previous section, "Formatting Dates and Times," for details on how to get an instance of the DateTimeFormatter class. The same symbols used for formatting are also used as parsing symbols. There are two ways to parse a string into a datetime object:

- Using the parse() method of the datetime class
- Using the parse() method of the DateTimeFormatter class

░ **Tip**   A DateTimeParseException is thrown if the text cannot be parsed. It is a runtime exception. The class contains two methods to provide the error details. The getErrorIndex() method returns the index in the text where the error occurred. The getParsedString() method returns the text being parsed. It is good practice to handle this exception while parsing a datetime.

Each datetime class has two overloaded versions of the parse() static method. The return type of the parse() method is the same as the defining datetime class. The following are the two versions of the parse() method in LocalDate class:

- `static LocalDate parse(CharSequence text)`
- `static LocalDate parse(CharSequence text, DateTimeFormatter formatter)`

The first version of the parse() method takes the textual representation of the datetime object in ISO format. For example, for a LocalDate, the text should be in the yyyy-mm-dd format. The second version lets you specify a DateTimeFormatter. The following snippet of code parses two strings into two LocalDate objects:

```
// Parse a LocalDate in ISO format
LocalDate ld1 = LocalDate.parse("2014-01-10");

// Parse a LocalDate in MM/dd/yyyy format
DateTimeFormatter formatter = DateTimeFormatter.ofPattern("MM/dd/yyyy");
LocalDate ld2 = LocalDate.parse("01/10/2014", formatter);

System.out.println("ld1: " + ld1);
System.out.println("ld2: " + ld2);
```

```
ld1: 2014-01-10
ld2: 2014-01-10
```

The DateTimeFormatter class contains several parse() methods to facilitate parsing of strings into datetime objects. The DateTimeFormatter class does not know the type of datetime object that can be formed from the strings. Therefore, most of them return a TemporalAccessor object that you can query to get the datetime components. You can pass the TemporalAccessor object to the from() method of the datetime class to get the specific datetime object. The following snippet of code shows how to parse a string in MM/dd/yyyy format using a DateTimeFormatter object to construct a LocalDate:

```
import java.time.LocalDate;
import java.time.format.DateTimeFormatter;
import java.time.temporal.TemporalAccessor;
...
DateTimeFormatter formatter = DateTimeFormatter.ofPattern("MM/dd/yyyy");
TemporalAccessor ta = formatter.parse("01/10/2014");
LocalDate ld = LocalDate.from(ta);
System.out.println(ld);
```

```
2014-01-10
```

Another version of the parse() method takes a TemporalQuery that can be used to parse the string directly into a specific datetime object. The following snippet of code uses this version of the parse() method. The second parameter is the method reference of the from() method of the LocalDate class. You can think of the following snippet of code as shorthand of the previous code:

```
DateTimeFormatter formatter = DateTimeFormatter.ofPattern("MM/dd/yyyy");
LocalDate ld = formatter.parse("01/10/2014", LocalDate::from);

System.out.println(ld);
```

```
2014-01-10
```

The DateTimeFormatter class contains a parseBest() method. Using this method needs little explanation. Suppose you receive a string as an argument to a method. The argument may contain varying pieces of information for date and time. In such a case, you want to parse the string using the most pieces of information. Consider the following pattern:

```
yyyy-MM-dd['T'HH:mm:ss[Z]]
```

This pattern has two optional sections. A text with this pattern may be fully parsed to an OffsetDateTime, and partially parsed to a LocalDateTime and a LocalDate. You can create a parser for this pattern as follows:

```
DateTimeFormatter formatter = DateTimeFormatter.ofPattern("yyyy-MM-dd['T'HH:mm:ss[Z]]");
```

The following snippet of code specifies OffsetDateTime, LocalDateTime, and LocalDate as the preferred parsed result types:

```
String text = ...
TemporalAccessor ta =
    formatter.parseBest(text, OffsetDateTime::from, LocalDateTime::from, LocalDate::from);
```

The method will try to parse the text as the specified types in order and return the first successful result. Typically, a call to the parseBest() method is followed by a series of if-else statements with an instanceof operator to check what type of object was returned. Listing 16-27 shows how to use the parseBest() method. Notice that the fourth text is in invalid format and parsing it throws an exception.

Listing 16-27. Using the parseBest() Method of the DateTimeFormatter Class

```java
// ParseBestTest.java
package com.jdojo.datetime;

import java.time.LocalDate;
import java.time.LocalDateTime;
import java.time.OffsetDateTime;
import java.time.format.DateTimeFormatter;
import java.time.format.DateTimeParseException;
import java.time.temporal.TemporalAccessor;

public class ParseBestTest {
    public static void main(String[] args) {
        DateTimeFormatter parser
                = DateTimeFormatter.ofPattern("yyyy-MM-dd['T'HH:mm:ss[Z]]");
        parseStr(parser, "2012-05-31");
        parseStr(parser, "2012-05-31T16:30:12");
        parseStr(parser, "2012-05-31T16:30:12-0500");
        parseStr(parser, "2012-05-31Hello");
    }

    public static void parseStr(DateTimeFormatter formatter, String text) {
        try {
            TemporalAccessor ta = formatter.parseBest(text,
                    OffsetDateTime::from,
                    LocalDateTime::from,
```

```
                    LocalDate::from);
            if (ta instanceof OffsetDateTime) {
                OffsetDateTime odt = OffsetDateTime.from(ta);
                System.out.println("OffsetDateTime: " + odt);
            } else if (ta instanceof LocalDateTime) {
                LocalDateTime ldt = LocalDateTime.from(ta);
                System.out.println("LocalDateTime: " + ldt);
            } else if (ta instanceof LocalDate) {
                LocalDate ld = LocalDate.from(ta);
                System.out.println("LocalDate: " + ld);
            } else {
                System.out.println("Parsing returned: " + ta);
            }
        } catch (DateTimeParseException e) {
            System.out.println(e.getMessage());
        }
    }
}
```

```
LocalDate: 2012-05-31
LocalDateTime: 2012-05-31T16:30:12
OffsetDateTime: 2012-05-31T16:30:12-05:00
Text '2012-05-31Hello' could not be parsed, unparsed text found at index 10
```

Legacy Datetime Classes

I refer to the datetime-related classes that were available before Java 8 as *legacy datetime classes*. The main legacy classes are Date, Calendar, and GregorianCalendar. They are in the java.util package. Refer to the section called "Interopability with Legacy Datetime Classes," for how to convert Date and Calendar objects to datetime objects of the new Date-Time API and vice versa.

The Date Class

An object of the Date class represents an instant in time. A Date object stores the number of milliseconds elapsed since the epoch, midnight January 1, 1970 UTC.

▓ **Tip**   The Date class in the legacy Date-Time API is similar to the Instant class in the new Date-Time API. They have the precision of milliseconds and nanoseconds, respectively.

Most of the constructors and methods of the Date class have been deprecated since JDK 1.1. The default constructor of the Date class is used to create a Date object with the current system datetime. Listing 16-28 illustrates the use of the Date class. You may get a different output because it prints the current date and time.

Listing 16-28. Using the Date Class

```java
// CurrentLegacyDate.java
package com.jdojo.datetime;

import java.util.Date;

public class CurrentLegacyDate {
    public static void main (String[] args) {
        // Create a new Date object
        Date currentDate = new Date();
        System.out.println("Current date: " + currentDate);

        // Get the milliseconds value of the current date
        long millis = currentDate.getTime();
        System.out.println("Current datetime in millis: " + millis);
    }
}
```

```
Current date: Sat Jan 11 11:19:55 CST 2014
Current datetime in millis: 1389460795979
```

A Date object works with a 1900-based year. When you call the setYear() method of this object to set the year as 2017, you will need to pass 117 (2017 - 1900 = 117). Its getYear() method returns 117 for the year 2017. Months in this class range from 0 to 11 where January is 0, February is 2... and December is 11.

The Calendar Class

Calendar is an abstract class. An abstract class cannot be instantiated. I discuss abstract classes in detail in Chapter 20 on inheritance. The GregorianCalendar class is a concrete class, which inherits the Calendar class.

The Calendar class declares some final static fields to represent date fields. For example, Calendar. JANUARY can be used to specify the January month in a date. The GregorianCalendar class has a default constructor, which creates an object to represent the current datetime. You can also create a GregorianCalendar object to represent a specific date using its other constructors. It also lets you obtain the current date in a particular time zone.

```java
// Get the current date in the system default time zone
GregorianCalendar currentDate = new GregorianCalendar();

// Get GregorianCalendar object representing March 26, 2003 06:30:45 AM
GregorianCalendar someDate = new GregorianCalendar(2003, Calendar.MARCH, 26, 6, 30, 45);

// Get Indian time zone, which is GMT+05:30
TimeZone indianTZ = TimeZone.getTimeZone("GMT+05:30");

// Get current date in India
GregorianCalendar indianDate = new GregorianCalendar(indianTZ);
```

```
// Get Moscow time zone, which is GMT+03:00
TimeZone moscowTZ = TimeZone.getTimeZone("GMT+03:00");

// Get current date in Moscow
GregorianCalendar moscowDate = new GregorianCalendar(moscowTZ);
```

▓ **Tip**   A `Date` contains a datetime. A `GregorianCalendar` contains a datetime with a time zone.

The month part of a date ranges from 0 to 11. That is, January is 0, February is 1, and so on. It is easier to use the constants declared for months and the other date fields in the `Calendar` class rather than using their integer values. For example, you should use `Calendar.JANUARY` constant to represent the January month in your program instead of a 0. You can get the value of a field in a datetime using the `get()` method by passing the requested field as an argument.

```
// Create a GregorianCalendar object
GregorianCalendar gc = new GregorianCalendar();

// year will contain the current year value
int year = gc.get(Calendar.YEAR);

// month will contain the current month value
int month = gc.get(Calendar.MONTH);

// day will contain day of month of the current date
int day = gc.get(Calendar.DAY_OF_MONTH);

// hour will contain hour value
int hour = gc.get(Calendar.HOUR);

// minute will contain minute value
int minute = gc.get(Calendar.MINUTE);

// second will contain second values
int second = gc.get(Calendar.SECOND);
```

You can set the date interpretation to be lenient or not lenient by using the `setLenient()` method of the `GregorianCalendar` class. By default, it is lenient. If the date interpretation is lenient, a date such as March 35, 2003 is interpreted as April 5, 2003. If date interpretation is not lenient, such a date will result in an error. You can also compare two dates, whether one date occurs before or after another, by using `before()` and `after()` methods. There are two methods, `add()` and `roll()`, which need explanation. They are described in the following sections.

The add() Method

The `add()` method is used to add an amount to a particular field in a date. The amount being added may be negative or positive. Suppose you have the date of December 1, 2003 stored in a `GregorianCalendar` object. You want to add 5 to the month field. The value for the month field will be 16, which is out of range (0 – 11). In such a case, the larger date field (here, year is larger than month) will be adjusted to accommodate the overflow. The date, after adding 5 to the month field, will be May 1, 2004. The following snippet of code illustrates this concept:

```
GregorianCalendar gc = new GregorianCalendar(2003, Calendar.DECEMBER, 1);
gc.add(Calendar.MONTH, 5); // Now gc represents May 1, 2004
```

This method may result in adjusting smaller fields, too. Suppose you have the date of January 30, 2003 stored in a GregorianCalendar object. You add 1 to the month field. The new month field does not overflow. However, the resulting date, February 30, 2003, is not a valid date. The day of month must be between 1 and 28 in the month of February 2003. In this case, the day of month field is automatically adjusted. It is set to the nearest possible valid value, which is 28. The resulting date will be February 28, 2003.

The roll() Method

The roll() method works the same as the add() method, except it does not change the larger field when the field being changed overflows. It may adjust the smaller fields to make the date a valid date. It is an overloaded method.

- void roll(int field, int amount)

- void roll(int field, boolean up)

The second version rolls up/down the specified field by a single unit of time, whereas the first version rolls the specified field by the specified amount. Therefore, gc.roll(Calendar.MONTH, 1) is the same as gc.roll(Calendar.MONTH, true) and gc.roll(Calendar.MONTH, -1) is the same as gc.roll(Calendar. MONTH, false). Listing 16-29 illustrates the use of some of the methods of the GregorianCalendar class. You may get a different output.

Listing 16-29. Using the GregorianCalendar Class

```java
// GregorianDate .java
package com.jdojo.datetime;

import java.util.Calendar;
import java.util.Date;
import java.util.GregorianCalendar;

public class GregorianDate {
    public static void main(String[] args) {
        GregorianCalendar gc = new GregorianCalendar();
        System.out.println("Current Date: " + getStr(gc));

        // Add 1 year
        gc.add(Calendar.YEAR, 1);
        System.out.println("After adding a year: " + getStr(gc));

        // Add 15 days
        gc.add(Calendar.DATE, 15);
        System.out.println("After adding 15 days: " + getStr(gc));

        long millis = gc.getTimeInMillis();
        Date dt = gc.getTime();
```

```
        System.out.println("Time in millis: " + millis);
        System.out.println("Time as Date: " + dt);
    }

    public static String getStr(GregorianCalendar gc) {
        int day = gc.get(Calendar.DAY_OF_MONTH);
        int month = gc.get(Calendar.MONTH);
        int year = gc.get(Calendar.YEAR);
        int hour = gc.get(Calendar.HOUR);
        int minute = gc.get(Calendar.MINUTE);
        int second = gc.get(Calendar.SECOND);

        String str = day + "/" + (month + 1) + "/" + year + " "
                + hour + ":" + minute + ":" + second;
        return str;
    }
}
```

```
Current Date: 4/8/2017 9:53:49
After adding a year: 4/8/2018 9:53:49
After adding 15 days: 19/8/2018 9:53:49
Time in millis: 1534733629830
Time as Date: Sun Aug 19 21:53:49 CDT 2018
```

Interoperability with Legacy Datetime Classes

The legacy datetime classes had been around for over 18 years when the new Date-Time API became available. The new Date-Time API is not going to replace them overnight. As a Java developer, you will be tasked to maintain applications that use the legacy classes. For this reason, interoperability between the legacy classes and the new Date-Time API was also provided. New methods have been added to the legacy classes to convert their objects to the new datetime objects and vice versa. Interoperability of the following legacy classes is discussed in this section:

- java.util.Date
- java.util.Calendar
- java.util.GregorianCalendar
- java.util.TimeZone
- java.sql.Date
- java.sql.Time
- java.sql.Timestamp
- java.nio.file.attribute.FileTime

Table 16-8 contains the list of legacy datetime classes and their new Date-Time counterparts. All legacy classes, except the Calendar class, provides two-way conversion. The toXxx() methods are instance methods. They return an object of the new datetime class. The other methods are static methods, which accept an object of the new datetime class and return an object of the legacy class. For example, the from()

method in the java.util.Date class is a static method, which takes an Instant argument and returns a java.util.Date. The toInstant() method is an instance method and converts a java.util.Date into an Instant.

Table 16-8. *Conversion Between New Datetime and Legacy Datetime Classes*

Legacy Class	New Methods in Legacy Class	Equivalent New Datetime Class
java.util.Date	from(), toInstant()	Instant
Calendar	toInstant()	None
GregorianCalendar	from(), toZonedDateTime()	ZonedDateTime
TimeZone	getTimeZone(), toZoneId()	ZoneId
java.sql.Date	valueOf(), toLocalDate()	LocalDate
Time	valueOf(), toLocalTime()	LocalTime
Timestamp	from(), toInstant()	Instant
	valueOf(), toLocalDateTime()	LocalDateTime
FileTime	from(), toInstant()	Instant

Listing 16-30 shows how to convert a Date to an Instant and vice versa. You may get a different output.

Listing 16-30. Converting a Date to an Instant and Vice Versa

```
// DateAndInstant.java
package com.jdojo.datetime;

import java.util.Date;
import java.time.Instant;

public class DateAndInstant {
    public static void main(String[] args) {
        // Get the current date
        Date dt = new Date();
        System.out.println("Date: " + dt);

        // Convert the Date to an Instant
        Instant in = dt.toInstant();
        System.out.println("Instant: " + in);

        // Convert the Instant back to a Date
        Date dt2 = Date.from(in);
        System.out.println("Date: " + dt2);
    }
}
```

```
Date: Fri Aug 04 22:05:14 CDT 2017
Instant: 2017-08-05T03:05:14.786Z
Date: Fri Aug 04 22:05:14 CDT 2017
```

Typically, the legacy code uses GregorianCalendar to store date, time, and datetime. You can convert it to a ZonedDateTime, which can be converted to any other classes in the new Date-Time API. The Calendar class provides a toInstant() method to convert its instance to an Instant. The Calendar class is abstract. Typically, you would have an instance of its concrete subclass class, for example, GregorianCalendar. Therefore, converting an Instant to a GregorianCalendar is a two-step process:

- Convert the Instant to a ZonedDateTime.

- Use the from() static method of the GregorianCalendar class to get a GregorianCalendar.

The program in Listing 16-31 shows how to convert a GregorianCalendar to a ZonedDateTime and vice versa. The program also shows how to get a LocalDate, LocalTime, etc. from a GregorianCalendar. You may get a different output because the output depends on the system's default time zone.

Listing 16-31. Converting a GregorianCalendar to New Datetime Types and Vice Versa

```java
// GregorianCalendarAndNewDateTime.java
package com.jdojo.datetime;

import java.time.LocalDate;
import java.time.LocalDateTime;
import java.time.LocalTime;
import java.time.OffsetDateTime;
import java.time.OffsetTime;
import java.time.ZoneId;
import java.time.ZonedDateTime;

import java.util.GregorianCalendar;
import java.util.TimeZone;

public class GregorianCalendarAndNewDateTime {
    public static void main(String[] args) {
        // Create a GC for the default time zone
        GregorianCalendar gc = new GregorianCalendar(2014, 1, 11, 15, 45, 50);
        System.out.println("Gregorian Calendar: " + gc.getTime());

        // Convert the GC to a LocalDate
        LocalDate ld = gc.toZonedDateTime().toLocalDate();
        System.out.println("Local Date: " + ld);

        // Convert the GC to a LocalTime
        LocalTime lt = gc.toZonedDateTime().toLocalTime();
        System.out.println("Local Time: " + lt);

        // Convert the GC to a LocalDateTime
        LocalDateTime ldt = gc.toZonedDateTime().toLocalDateTime();
        System.out.println("Local DateTime: " + ldt);

        // Convert the GC to an OffsetDate
        OffsetDateTime od = gc.toZonedDateTime().toOffsetDateTime();
        System.out.println("Offset Date: " + od);
```

```
        // Convert the GC to an OffsetTime
        OffsetTime ot = gc.toZonedDateTime().toOffsetDateTime().toOffsetTime();
        System.out.println("Offset Time: " + ot);

        // Convert the GC to an ZonedDateTime
        ZonedDateTime zdt = gc.toZonedDateTime();
        System.out.println("Zoned DateTime: " + zdt);

        // Convert the ZonedDateTime to a GC. In GC month starts at 0
        // and in new API at 1
        ZoneId zoneId = zdt.getZone();
        TimeZone timeZone = TimeZone.getTimeZone(zoneId);
        System.out.println("Zone ID: " + zoneId);
        System.out.println("Time Zone ID: " + timeZone.getID());

        GregorianCalendar gc2 = GregorianCalendar.from(zdt);
        System.out.println("Gregorian Calendar: " + gc2.getTime());
    }
}
```

```
Gregorian Calendar: Tue Feb 11 15:45:50 CST 2014
Local Date: 2014-02-11
Local Time: 15:45:50
Local DateTime: 2014-02-11T15:45:50
Offset Date: 2014-02-11T15:45:50-06:00
Offset Time: 15:45:50-06:00
Zoned DateTime: 2014-02-11T15:45:50-06:00[America/Chicago]
Zone ID: America/Chicago
Time Zone ID: America/Chicago
Gregorian Calendar: Tue Feb 11 15:45:50 CST 2014
```

How do you convert a Date to a LocalDate? A Date represents an instant in time, so first you need to convert the Date into a ZoneDateTime using a ZoneId and then get a LocalDate from the ZonedDateTime. The following snippet of code converts the current date into a Date to a LocalDate in Java8:

```
Date dt = new Date();
LocalDate ld = dt.toInstant()
                .atZone(ZoneId.systemDefault())
                .toLocalDate();
System.out.println("Date: " + dt);
System.out.println("LocalDate: " + ld);
```

```
Date: Sat Aug 05 11:01:02 CDT 2017
LocalDate: 2017-08-05
```

This kind of conversion is frequently needed. Java 9 added an ofInstant() method to the LocalDate class to make this kind of conversion easier. The method is declared as follows:

```
static LocalDate ofInstant(Instant instant, ZoneId zone)
```

The following snippet of code performs the same conversion using Java 9:

```
Date dt = new Date();
LocalDate ld = LocalDate.ofInstant(dt.toInstant(), ZoneId.systemDefault());
System.out.println("Date: " + dt);
System.out.println("LocalDate: " + ld);
```

```
Date: Sat Aug 05 11:01:02 CDT 2017
LocalDate: 2017-08-05
```

Summary

Through the `java.time` packages, Java 8 provided a comprehensive Date-Time API to work with date, time, and datetime. By default, most of the classes are based on the ISO-8601 standards. The main classes are

- `Instant`
- `LocalDate`
- `LocalTime`
- `LocalDateTime`
- `OffsetTime`
- `OffsetDateTime`
- `ZonedDateTime`

The `Instant` class represents an instant on the timeline and it is suitable for machines, for example, as timestamps for event. The `LocalDate`, `LocalTime`, and `LocalDateTime` classes represent human readable date, time, and datetime without a time zone. The `OffsetTime` and `OffsetDateTime` classes represent a time and datetime with a zone offset from UTC. The `ZoneDateTime` class represents a datetime for a time zone with zone rules, which will adjust the time according to the Daylight Savings Time changes in the time zone.

The Date-Time API provides classes for representing an amount of time used with machines and humans. The `Duration` class represents an amount of time for machines whereas the `Period` class represents an amount of time as perceived by humans. The Date-Time API provides extensive support for formatting and parsing date and times through the `java.time.format.DateTimeFormatter` class. The Date-Time API supports non-ISO calendar systems through the `java.time.chrono` package. Built-in supports for Hijrah, Japanese, Minguo, and Thai Buddhist calendars are provided. The API is extensible and supports building your own calendar systems.

EXERCISES

1. What class would you use to store a date without the time and time zone parts in it?

2. What class would you use to store a date and time that is aware of the Daylight Savings Time?

3. What is the difference between a `ZoneId` and `ZoneOffset`?

4. What is the difference between a `ZonedDateTime` and an `OffsetDateTime`?

5. Write the code to convert the `Instant` representing the current time in the system default time zone to a `LocalDate`.

6. Write a program that prints all years from 2001 to 2099 in which the last day of the year (December 31) falls on Monday.

7. Write the code that converts a `java.util.Date` to a `LocalDate` in the system default time zone.

8. Complete the following snippet of code, so it prints "`Friday January 12, 1968`". It is supposed to format the date 1968-01-12 and print it.

```
LocalDate bday = LocalDate.of(1968, Month.JANUARY, 12);
String pattern = /* Your code goes here */;
DateTimeFormatter fmt = DateTimeFormatter.ofPattern(pattern);
        String formattedBDay = fmt.format(bday);
        System.out.println(formattedBDay);
```

9. Complete the following snippet of code that prints the number of days between 1968-01-12 and 1969-09-19. It should print `616`.

```
LocalDate ld1 = LocalDate.of(1968, Month.JANUARY, 12);
LocalDate ld2 = LocalDate.of(1969, Month.SEPTEMBER, 19);
long daysBetween = /* Your code goes here */;
System.out.println(daysBetween);
```

10. Complete the code in the `printFirstDayOfMonth()` method. The method takes a `LocalDate` as an argument and prints the first day of the month in which the date occurs. Suppose the `LocalDate` passed in to this method is 2017-08-05; it will print "`First day of AUGUST, 2017 is on SATURDAY`".

```
public static void printFirstDayOfMonth(LocalDate ld) {
    LocalDate newDate = ld.with(/* Your Code goes here */);
    System.out.printf("First day of %s, %d is on %s%n",
        ld.getMonth(), ld.getYear(), newDate.getDayOfWeek());
}
```

CHAPTER 17

Formatting Data

In this chapter, you will learn:

- How to format and parse dates and numbers
- How to use the `printf`-style formatting
- How to create a class that uses a custom formatter

Java provides a rich set of APIs for formatting data. The data may include simple values such as numbers or objects such as strings, dates, and other types of objects. This chapter covers formatting options in Java for different types of values. All example programs in this chapter are a member of a `jdojo.format` module, as declared in Listing 17-1.

Listing 17-1. The Declaration of a jdojo.format Module

```
// module-info.java
module jdojo.format {
    exports com.jdojo.format;
}
```

Formatting Dates

Java 8 provided new a Date-Time API to work with dates and times, and to format and parse them. The Date-Time API was covered in Chapter 16. If you are writing new code that is related to dates and times, you are advised to use the new Date-Time API. This section is provided in case you need to work with legacy code that uses old ways of formatting dates and time that existed before Java 8.

In this section, I discuss how to format dates. I also discuss how to parse a string to create a date object. You can format dates in predefined formats or in formats of your choice. The Java library provides two classes to format dates:

- `java.text.DateFormat`
- `java.text.SimpleDateFormat`

The next two sections show you how to format dates in predefined and custom formats.

Using Predefined Date Formats

Use the DateFormat class to format dates using a predefined format. It is an abstract class. The class is abstract, so you cannot create an instance of this class using the new operator. You can call one of its getXxxInstance() methods, where Xxx can be Date, DateTime, or Time, to get the formatter object, or just getInstance(). The formatted text depends on two things: style and locale. Use the format() method of the DateFormat class to format a date and time. The style of formatting determines how much date/time information is included in the formatted text, whereas the locale determines how all pieces of information are assembled. The DateFormat class defines five styles as constants:

- DateFormat.DEFAULT

- DateFormat.SHORT

- DateFormat.MEDIUM

- DateFormat.LONG

- DateFormat.FULL

The DEFAULT format is the same as MEDIUM, unless you use getInstance() where the default is SHORT. Table 17-1 shows the same date formatted in different styles for a US locale.

Table 17-1. *Predefined Date Format Styles and Formatted Text for Locale as United States*

Style	Formatted Date
DEFAULT	Mar 27, 2003
SHORT	3/27/03
MEDIUM	Mar 27, 2003
LONG	March 27, 2003
FULL	Thursday, March 27, 2003

The java.util.Locale class contains constants for some common locales. For example, you can use Locale.FRANCE for a locale with language "fr" and country code "FR". Alternatively, you can create a Locale object for France like so:

```
Locale french FranceLocale = new Locale("fr", "FR") ;
```

To create a Locale, you need to use a two-letter lowercase language code and a two-letter uppercase country code if the Locale class does not declare a constant for that country. Language codes and country codes have been listed in ISO-639 code and ISO-3166 code. Some more examples of creating locales are as follows:

```
Locale hindiIndiaLocale = new Locale("hi", "IN");
Locale bengaliIndiaLocale = new Locale("bn", "IN");
Locale thaiThailandLocale = new Locale("th", "TH");
```

▦ **Tip**   Use the Locale.getDefault() method to get the default Locale for your system.

The following snippet of code prints the current date formatted in long format for the US locale:

```
Date today = new Date();
DateFormat formatter = DateFormat.getDateInstance(DateFormat.LONG, Locale.US);
String formattedDate = formatter.format(today);
System.out.println(formattedDate);
```

August 6, 2017

The program listed in Listing 17-2 displays dates in short and medium formats for locales as default (which is US for the JVM running this example), France, and Germany. The program prints the current date. It will print different formats of the same date when you run this program. You may get a different output because the program prints the current date.

Listing 17-2. Using the Predefined Date Formats

```
// PredefinedDateFormats.java
package com.jdojo.format;

import java.text.DateFormat;
import java.util.Date;
import java.util.Locale;

public class PredefinedDateFormats {
    public static void main(String[] args) {
        // Get the current date
        Date today = new Date();

        // Print date in the default locale format
        Locale defaultLocale = Locale.getDefault();
        printLocaleDetails(defaultLocale);
        printDate(defaultLocale, today);

        // Print date in French (France) format
        printLocaleDetails(Locale.FRANCE);
        printDate(Locale.FRANCE, today);

        // Print date in German (Germany) format. You could also use Locale.GERMANY
        // instead of new Locale ("de", "DE").
        Locale germanLocale = new Locale("de", "DE");
        printLocaleDetails(germanLocale);
        printDate(germanLocale, today);
    }

    public static void printLocaleDetails(Locale locale) {
        String languageCode = locale.getLanguage();
        String languageName = locale.getDisplayLanguage();
        String countryCode = locale.getCountry();
        String countryName = locale.getDisplayCountry();
```

633

```
        // Print the locale info
        System.out.println("Language: " + languageName + "("
                + languageCode + "); "
                + "Country: " + countryName
                + "(" + countryCode + ")");
    }

    public static void printDate(Locale locale, Date date) {
        // Format and print the date in SHORT style
        DateFormat formatter = DateFormat.getDateInstance(DateFormat.SHORT, locale);
        String formattedDate = formatter.format(date);
        System.out.println("SHORT: " + formattedDate);

        // Format and print the date in MEDIUM style
        formatter = DateFormat.getDateInstance(DateFormat.MEDIUM, locale);
        formattedDate = formatter.format(date);
        System.out.println("MEDIUM: " + formattedDate);

        // Print a blank line at the end
        System.out.println();
    }
}
```

```
Language: English(en); Country: United States(US)
SHORT: 1/24/14
MEDIUM: Jan 24, 2014

Language: French(fr); Country: France(FR)
SHORT: 24/01/14
MEDIUM: 24 janv. 2014

Language: German(de); Country: Germany(DE)
SHORT: 24.01.14
MEDIUM: 24.01.2014
```

Using Custom Date Formats

If you want to use custom date formats, use the SimpleDateFormat class. Formatting using the SimpleDateFormat class is locale-sensitive. Its default constructor creates a formatter with the default locale and default date format for that locale. You can create a formatter using other constructors where you can specify your own date format and locale. Once you have an object of the SimpleDateFormat class, you can call its format() method to format the date. If you want to change the date format for subsequent formatting, you can use the applyPattern() method by passing the new date format (or pattern) as an argument. The following snippet of code shows you how to format a date using the SimpleDateFormat class:

```
// Create a formatter with a pattern dd/MM/yyyy.
SimpleDateFormat simpleFormatter = new SimpleDateFormat("dd/MM/yyyy");

// Get the current date
Date today = new Date();

// Format the current date
String formattedDate = simpleFormatter.format(today);

// Print the date
System.out.println("Today is (dd/MM/yyyy): " + formattedDate);

// Change the date format. Now month will be spelled fully.
simpleFormatter.applyPattern("MMMM dd, yyyy");

// Format the current date
formattedDate = simpleFormatter.format(today);

// Print the date
System.out.println("Today is (MMMM dd, yyyy): " + formattedDate);
```

```
Today is (dd/MM/yyyy): 06/08/2017
Today is (MMMM dd, yyyy): August 06, 2017
```

Note that the output will be different when you run this code on your computer. It will print the current date in this format using the default locale. The previous output is in the US locale.

Letters that are used to create patterns to format dates and times are listed with their meanings in Table 17-2. The examples are shown as if the date to display is July 10, 1996 at 12:30:55 in the afternoon.

Table 17-2. *List of Formatting Symbols for Formatting Date and Time*

Letter	Date or Time Component	Presentation	Examples
G	Era designator	Text	AD
y	Year	Year	2003; 03
Y	Week-based year	Year	2003; 03
M	Month in year	Month	March; Mar; 03
w	Week in year	Number	27
W	Week in month	Number	2
D	Day in year	Number	189
d	Day in month	Number	10
F	Day of week in month	Number	2
E	Day in week	Text	Tuesday; Tue
a	AM/PM marker	Text	PM
H	Hour in day (0-23)	Number	0
k	Hour in day (1-24)	Number	24
K	Hour in AM/PM (0-11)	Number	0
h	Hour in AM/PM (1-12)	Number	12
m	Minute in hour	Number	30
s	Second in minute	Number	55
S	Millisecond	Number	978
z	Time zone	General time zone	Pacific Standard Time; PST; GMT-08:00
Z	Time zone	RFC 822 time zone	-0800

You can embed literals inside formatted dates. Suppose you have your birth date (September 19, 1969) stored in a date object and now you want to print it as "I was born on the Day 19 of the month September in 1969". Some parts in the message come from the birth date and others are literals, which are intended to appear in the message as they are. You cannot use letters, such as a-z and A-Z, as literals inside a date pattern. You need to place them inside single quotes to treat them as literals, not part of the formatting pattern. First, you need a Date object to represent September 19, 1969. The Date class' constructor, which takes year, month, and day, has been deprecated. Let's start with the GregorianCalendar class and use its getTime() method to get a Date object. The following snippet of code prints this message:

```
// Create a GregorianCalendar object with September 19, 1969 as date
GregorianCalendar gc = new GregorianCalendar(1969, Calendar.SEPTEMBER,19);

// Get a Date object
Date birthDate = gc.getTime();

// Create the pattern. You must place literals inside single quotes
String pattern = "'I was born on the day' dd 'of the month' MMMM 'in' yyyy";
```

```
// Create a SimpleDateFormat with the pattern
SimpleDateFormat simpleFormatter = new SimpleDateFormat(pattern);

// Format and print the date
System.out.println(simpleFormatter.format(birthDate));
```

```
I was born on the Day 19 of the month September in 1969
```

Parsing Dates

In the previous sections, you have converted date objects into formatted text. Let's look at converting text into Date objects. This is accomplished by using the parse() method of the SimpleDateFormat class. The signature of the parse() method is as follows:

```
Date parse(String text, ParsePosition startPos)
```

The method takes two arguments. The first argument is the text from which you want to extract the date. The second one is the starting position of the character in the text from where you want to start parsing. The text can have date part embedded in it. For example, you can extract two dates from text such as "First date is 01/01/1995 and second one is 12/12/2001". Because the parser does not know where the date begins in the text, you need to tell it using the ParsePosition object. It simply keeps track of the parsing position. There is only one constructor for the ParsePosition class and it takes an int, which is the position where parsing starts. After the parse() method is successful, the index for the ParsePosition object is set to the index of the last character of the date text used plus one. Note that the method does not use all the text passed as its first argument. It uses only the text as necessary to create a date object.

Let's start with a simple example. Suppose you have a string of "09/19/1969", which represents the date September 19, 1969. You want to get a Date object out of this string. The following snippet of code illustrates the steps:

```
// Our text to be parsed
String text = "09/19/1969";

// Create a pattern for the date text "09/19/1969"
String pattern = "MM/dd/yyyy";

// Create a SimpleDateFormat object to represent this pattern
SimpleDateFormat simpleFormatter = new SimpleDateFormat(pattern);

// Since the date part in text "09/19/1969" start at index zero,
// we create a ParsePosition object with value zero
ParsePosition startPos = new ParsePosition(0);

// Parse the text
Date parsedDate = simpleFormatter.parse(text, startPos);

// Here, parsedDate will have September 19, 1969 as date and startPos current index
// will be set to 10, which you can get calling startPos.getIndex() method.
```

Let's parse more complex text. If the text in the previous example were "09/19/1969 Junk", you would have gotten the same result, because after reading 1969, the parser will not look at any more characters in the text. Suppose you have text "XX01/01/1999XX12/31/2000XX". There are two dates embedded in the text. How would you parse these two dates? Text for the first date starts at index 2 (the first two Xs have indices 0 and 1). Once parsing is done for the first date text, the ParsePosition object will point to the third X in the text. You just need to increment its index by 2 to point to the first character of the second date text. The following snippet of code illustrates the steps:

```
// Our text to be parsed
String text = "XX01/01/1999XX12/31/2000XX";

// Create a pattern for our date text "09/19/1969"
String pattern = "MM/dd/yyyy";

// Create a SimpleDateFormat object to represent this pattern
SimpleDateFormat simpleFormatter = new SimpleDateFormat(pattern);

// Set the start index at 2
ParsePosition startPos = new ParsePosition(2);

// Parse the text to get the first date (January 1, 1999)
Date firstDate = simpleFormatter.parse(text, startPos);

// Now, startPos has its index set after the last character of the first date parsed.
// To set its index to the next date increment its index by 2.
int currentIndex = startPos.getIndex();
startPos.setIndex(currentIndex + 2);

// Parse the text to get the second date (December 31, 2000)
Date secondDate = simpleFormatter.parse(text, startPos);
```

It is left to the readers as an exercise to write a program that will extract the date in a Date object from the text "I was born on the day 19 of the month September in 1969". The date extracted should be September 19, 1969. (Hint: You already have the pattern for this text in one of the previous examples, when you worked on formatting date objects.)

Here's one more example of parsing text that contains date and time. Suppose you have the text "2003-04-03 09:10:40.325", which represents a timestamp in the format year-month-day hour:minute:second. millisecond. You want to get the time parts of the timestamp. Listing 17-3 shows how to get time parts from this text.

Listing 17-3. Parsing a Timestamp to Get Its Time Parts

```
// ParseTimeStamp.java
package com.jdojo.format;

import java.util.Date;
import java.util.Calendar;
import java.text.ParsePosition;
import java.text.SimpleDateFormat;
```

```
public class ParseTimeStamp {
    public static void main(String[] args){
        String input = "2003-04-03 09:10:40.325";

        // Prepare the pattern
        String pattern = "yyyy-MM-dd HH:mm:ss.SSS" ;

        SimpleDateFormat sdf = new SimpleDateFormat(pattern);

        // Parse the text into a Date object
        Date dt = sdf.parse(input, new ParsePosition(0));
        System.out.println(dt);

        // Get the Calendar instance
        Calendar cal = Calendar.getInstance();

        // Set the time
        cal.setTime(dt);

        // Print time parts
        System.out.println("Hour:" + cal.get(Calendar.HOUR));
        System.out.println("Minute:" + cal.get(Calendar.MINUTE));
        System.out.println("Second:" + cal.get(Calendar.SECOND));
        System.out.println("Millisecond:" + cal.get(Calendar.MILLISECOND));

    }
}
```

```
Thu Apr 03 09:10:40 CST 2003
Hour:9
Minute:10
Second:40
Millisecond:325
```

Formatting Numbers

In this section, I discuss how to format numbers. I also discuss how to parse a string to create a Number object. The following two classes can be used to format and parse numbers:

- java.text.NumberFormat
- java.text.DecimalFormat

The NumberFormat class is used to format numbers in a particular locale's predefined format. The DecimalFormat class is used to format numbers in a format of your choice in a particular locale.

Using Predefined Number Formats

You can use a getXxxInstance() method of the NumberFormat class to get the instance of a formatter object, where Xxx can be replaced by Number, Currency, Integer, or Percent, or just getInstance(). These methods are overloaded. If you call them without any argument, they return a formatter object for the default locale. Call the format() method, passing the number as an argument to get the formatted number as a string. The following snippet of code shows you how to get different types of number formatter for different locales. It also shows you how to use a currency formatter for US locale to format a salary.

```
// Get a number formatter for default locale
NumberFormat defaultFormatter = NumberFormat.getNumberInstance();

// Get a number formatter for French (France) locale
NumberFormat frenchFormatter = NumberFormat.getNumberInstance(Locale.FRENCH);

// Get a currency formatter for US
NumberFormat usCurrencyFormatter = NumberFormat.getCurrencyInstance(Locale.US);

double salary = 12590.90;
String str = usCurrencyFormatter.format(salary);
System.out.println("Salary in US currency: " + str);
```

```
Salary in US currency: $12,590.90
```

Listing 17-4 illustrates how to format numbers in default format for the current locale (the United States is the default locale for this example) and Indian locale.

Listing 17-4. Formatting Numbers Using Default Formats

```java
// DefaultNumberFormatters.java
package com.jdojo.format;

import java.util.Locale;
import java.text.NumberFormat;

public class DefaultNumberFormatters {
    public static void main(String[] args){
        double value = 1566789.785 ;

        // Default locale
        printFormatted(Locale.getDefault(), value);

        // Indian locale
        // (Rupee is the Indian currency. Short form is Rs.)
        Locale indianLocale = new Locale("en", "IN");
        printFormatted(indianLocale, value);
    }
```

```
    public static void printFormatted(Locale locale, double value) {
        // Get number and currency formatter
        NumberFormat nf = NumberFormat.getInstance(locale);
        NumberFormat cf = NumberFormat.getCurrencyInstance(locale);

        System.out.println("Formatting value: " + value + " for locale: " + locale);
        System.out.println("Number: "   + nf.format(value));
        System.out.println("Currency: " + cf.format(value));
    }
}
```

```
Formatting value: 1566789.785 for locale: en_US
Number: 1,566,789.785
Currency: $1,566,789.78
Formatting value: 1566789.785 for locale: en_IN
Number: 1,566,789.785
Currency: Rs. 1,566,789.78
```

Using Custom Number Formats

To perform more advanced formatting, you can use the DecimalFormat class. It allows you to supply your own format pattern. Once you create an object of the DecimalFormat class, you can change the format pattern using its applyPattern() method. You can specify different patterns for positive and negative numbers. The two patterns are separated by a semicolon.

The DecimalFormat class uses round-to-even rounding mode while formatting numbers. For example, if you have specified only two digits after the decimal point in your number format, 12.745 will be rounded to 12.74, because 5 is in the middle and 4 is even; 12.735 will also be rounded to 12.74 because 5 is in the middle and the nearest event number at the second position would be 4; and 12.746 will be rounded to 12.75. Listing 17-5 illustrates the use of the DecimalFormat class.

Listing 17-5. Formatting Numbers

```java
// DecimalFormatter.java
package com.jdojo.format;

import java.text.DecimalFormat;

public class DecimalFormatter {
    private static DecimalFormat formatter = new DecimalFormat();

    public static void main(String[] args) {
        formatNumber("##.##", 12.745);
        formatNumber("##.##", 12.746);
        formatNumber("0000.0000", 12.735);
        formatNumber("#.##", -12.735);
```

```
        // Positive and negative number format
        formatNumber("#.##;(#.##)", 12.735);
        formatNumber("#.##;(#.##)", -12.735);
    }

    public static void formatNumber(String pattern, double value) {
        // Apply the pattern
        formatter.applyPattern(pattern);

        // Format the number
        String formattedNumber = formatter.format(value);

        System.out.println("Number: " + value + ", Pattern: "
                + pattern + ", Formatted Number: "
                + formattedNumber);
    }
}
```

```
Number: 12.745, Pattern: ##.##, Formatted Number: 12.74
Number: 12.746, Pattern: ##.##, Formatted Number: 12.75
Number: 12.735, Pattern: 0000.0000, Formatted Number: 0012.7350
Number: -12.735, Pattern: #.##, Formatted Number: -12.73
Number: 12.735, Pattern: #.##;(#.##), Formatted Number: 12.73
Number: -12.735, Pattern: #.##;(#.##), Formatted Number: (12.73)
```

Parsing Numbers

You can also parse a string to a number using the parse() method of the DecimalFormat class. The parse()
method returns an object of the java.lang.Number class. You can use xxxValue() methods to get the
primitive value, where xxx can be byte, double, float, int, long, and short.

Listing 17-6 illustrates the use of the DecimalFormat class to parse a number. Note that you can also use
the parseDouble() method of the java.lang.Double class to parse a string into a double value. However,
the string has to be in the default number format. The advantage of using the parse() method of the
DecimalFormat class is that the string can be in any format.

Listing 17-6. Parsing Numbers

```
// ParseNumber.java
package com.jdojo.format;

import java.text.DecimalFormat;
import java.text.ParsePosition;

public class ParseNumber {
    public static void main(String[] args) {
        // Parse a string to decimal number
        String str = "XY4,123.983";
        String pattern = "#,###.###";
        DecimalFormat formatter = new DecimalFormat(pattern);
```

```
        // Create a ParsePosition object to specify the first digit of number
        // in the string. It is 4 in "XY4,123.983" with the index 2.
        ParsePosition pos = new ParsePosition(2);

        Number numberObject = formatter.parse(str, pos);

        double value = numberObject.doubleValue();
        System.out.println("Parsed Value is " + value);
    }
}
```

Parsed Value is 4123.983

printf-Style Formatting

In this section, I discuss how to format objects and values using printf-style formatting similar to that supported by the printf() function in C. First I cover the general ideas of the printf-style formatting support in Java and then cover the details of formatting all types of values.

The Big Picture

The java.util.Formatter class supports printf-style formatting, which is similar to the formatting supported by the printf() function in the C programming language. If you are familiar with C, C++, and C#, it should be easier for you to understand the discussion in this section. In this section, you will use formatting strings such as "%1$s", "%1$4d", etc. in your code without a full explanation of their meanings. You may not be able to understand them fully; you should ignore them for now. Just focus on the output and try to get the bigger picture of what the Formatter class is intended to accomplish, rather than trying to understand the details. I discuss the details in the next section. Let's start with a simple example shown in Listing 17-7. You may get a slightly different output.

Listing 17-7. Using C's printf-Style Formatting in Java

```
// PrintfTest.java
package com.jdojo.format;

import java.util.Date;

public class PrintfTest {
    public static void main(String[] args) {
        // Formatting strings
        System.out.printf("%1$s, %2$s, and %3$s %n", "Fu", "Hu", "Lo");
        System.out.printf("%3$s, %2$s, and %1$s %n", "Fu", "Hu", "Lo");

        // Formatting numbers
        System.out.printf("%1$4d, %2$4d, %3$4d %n", 1, 10, 100);
        System.out.printf("%1$4d, %2$4d, %3$4d %n", 10, 100, 1000);
        System.out.printf("%1$-4d, %2$-4d, %3$-4d %n", 1, 10, 100);
        System.out.printf("%1$-4d, %2$-4d, %3$-4d %n", 10, 100, 1000);
```

```
        // Formatting date and time
        Date dt = new Date();
        System.out.printf("Today is %tD %n", dt);
        System.out.printf("Today is %tF %n", dt);
        System.out.printf("Today is %tc %n", dt);
    }
}
```

```
Fu, Hu, and Lo
Lo, Hu, and Fu
   1,   10,  100
  10,  100, 1000
1    , 10  , 100
10   , 100, 1000
Today is 08/06/17
Today is 2017-08-06
Today is Sun Aug 06 10:29:03 CDT 2017
```

You have been using the `System.out.println()` and `System.out.print()` methods to print text on the standard output. In fact, `System.out` is an instance of the `java.io.PrintStream` class, which has `println()` and `print()` instance methods. The `PrintStream` class contains two more methods, `format()` and `printf()`, which can be used to write a formatted output to a `PrintStream` instance. Both methods work the same. Listing 17-5 uses `System.out.printf()` method to print the formatted text to the standard output.

The `String` class contains a `format()` static method, which returns a formatted string. The formatting behavior of the `format()`/`printf()` method of the `PrintStream` class and the `format()` static method of the `String` class is the same. The only difference between them is that the `format()` and `printf()` method in the `PrintStream` class writes the formatted output to an output stream, whereas the `format()` method of the `String` class returns the formatted output as a `String`.

The `format()` and `printf()` method of the `PrintStream` class and the `format()` method of the `String` class are convenience methods. They exist to make text formatting easier. However, the `Formatter` class does the real work. Let's discuss the `Formatter` class in detail. You will use these convenience methods in the examples. A `Formatter` is used to format text. The formatted text can be written to the following destinations:

- An `Appendable` (e.g., `StringBuffer`, `StringBuilder`, `Writer`, etc.)
- A `File`
- An `OutputStream`
- A `PrintStream`

The following snippet of code accomplishes the same thing as the code in Listing 17-7. This time, you use a `Formatter` object to format the data. When you call the `format()` method of the `Formatter` object, the formatted text is stored in the `StringBuilder` object, which you pass to the constructor of the `Formatter` object. When you are done with formatting all text, you call the `toString()` method of the `StringBuilder` to get the entire formatted text.

```
// Create an Appendable data storage for our formatted output
StringBuilder sb = new StringBuilder();

// Create a Formatter that will store its output to the StringBuffer
Formatter fm = new Formatter(sb);
```

```
// Formatting strings
fm.format("%1$s, %2$s, and %3$s %n", "Fu", "Hu", "Lo");
fm.format("%3$s, %2$s, and %1$s %n", "Fu", "Hu", "Lo");

// Formatting numbers
fm.format("%1$4d, %2$4d, %3$4d %n", 1, 10, 100);
fm.format("%1$4d, %2$4d, %3$4d %n", 10, 100, 1000);
fm.format("%1$-4d, %2$-4d, %3$-4d %n", 1, 10, 100);
fm.format("%1$-4d, %2$-4d, %3$-4d %n", 10, 100, 1000);

// Formatting date and time
Date dt = new Date();
fm.format("Today is %tD %n", dt);
fm.format("Today is %tF %n", dt);
fm.format("Today is %tc %n", dt);

// Display the entire formatted string
System.out.println(sb.toString());
```

If you want to write all formatted text to a file, you can do so using the following snippet of code. You will need to handle the FileNotFoundException, which may be thrown from the constructor of the Formatter class if the specified file does not exist. When you are done with the Formatter object, you will need to call its close() method to close the output file. Notice the use of a try-with-resources block in the sample code, so the formatter is closed automatically.

```
import java.io.File;
import java.io.FileNotFoundException;
import java.util.Formatter;
...
// Create a Formatter that will write the output to the file C:\kishori\xyz.txt
try (Formatter fm = new Formatter(new File("C:\\kishori\\xyz.txt"))) {
    // Formatting strings
    fm.format("%1$s, %2$s, and %3$s %n", "Fu", "Hu", "Lo");
    fm.format("%3$s, %2$s, and %1$s %n", "Fu", "Hu", "Lo");
} catch (FileNotFoundException e) {
    e.printStackTrace();
}
```

The format() method of the Formatter class is overloaded. Its declarations are as follows.

- Formatter format(String format, Object... args)

- Formatter format(Locale l, String format, Object... args)

The first version of the format() method uses the default locale for formatting. The second version allows you to specify a locale. The format()/printf() method of the PrintStream class and the format() method of the String class provide the same two versions of the format() method, which accept the same types of arguments. This discussion of the format() method of the Formatter class equally applies to these convenience methods in the PrintStream and String classes.

The Formatter class uses the locale-specific formatting whenever it is applicable. For example, if you want to format a decimal number, say 12.89, the number is formatted as 12,89 (notice a comma between 12 and 89) in France whereas it is formatted as 12.89 (notice a dot between 12 and 89) in the United States. The locale argument of the format() method is used to format text in a locale-specific format. The following snippet of code demonstrates the effects of locale-specific formatting. Note the difference in the formatted output for US and France for the same input values.

```
System.out.printf(Locale.US, "In US: %1$.2f %n", 12.89);
System.out.printf(Locale.FRANCE, "In France: %1$.2f %n", 12.89);

Date dt = new Date();
System.out.printf(Locale.US, "In US: %tA %n", dt);
System.out.printf(Locale.FRANCE, "In France: %tA %n", dt);
```

```
In US: 12.89
In France: 12,89
In US: Friday
In France: vendredi
```

The Details

Formatting data using a `Formatter` requires two types of inputs:

- A format string

- A list of values

The format string is the template that defines how the output will look. It contains zero or more occurrences of fixed texts and zero or more embedded format specifiers. No formatting is applied to the fixed text. A format specifier serves two purposes. It acts as a placeholder for the formatted data inside the format string and it specifies how the data should be formatted.

Let's consider the following example. Suppose you want to print text with the birth date of a person. The following is an example of such a text:

```
January 16, 1970 is John's birth day.
```

░ **Note** All outputs in this section are in the US locale unless specified otherwise.

The previous text contains fixed text and formatted text. The fixed text should appear in the output literally. The formatted text will depend on the inputs. You can convert the previous text into a template as shown:

```
<month> <day>, <year> is <name>'s birth day.
```

You have replaced the text that may vary with placeholders that are enclosed in angle brackets, for example, <month>, <day>, etc. You will need four input values (month, day, year, and name) to use the previous template to get a formatted text. For example, if you supply the values for <month>, <day>, <year>, and <name> as "January", "16", "1970", and "John", respectively, the template will produce

```
January 16, 1970 is John's birth day.
```

In this example, you have just replaced the placeholders in your template with their actual values. You did not perform any formatting for the actual values. The formatting that is provided by the Formatter class works in a similar fashion. What we called a placeholder in this example is called a *format specifier*. What we called a template in this example is called a *format string*.

A format specifier always starts with a percent sign (%). You can convert your template into a format string, which can be used with the Formatter class as follows:

```
%1$tB %1$td, %1$tY is %2$s's birth day.
```

In this format string, "%1$tB", "%1$td", "%1$tY", and %2$s" are four format specifiers, whereas " ", ", ", "is ", and "'s birth day." are fixed text.

The following snippet of code uses this format string to print formatted text. Note that dob and "John" are the input values for the format string. In this case, the input value dob is an instance of the LocalDate class that contains the birth date.

```
LocalDate dob = LocalDate.of(1970, Month.JANUARY, 16);
System.out.printf("%1$tB %1$td, %1$tY is %2$s's birth day.", dob, "John");
```

```
January 16, 1970 is John's birth day.
```

The general syntax for a format specifier is as follows:

```
%<argument-index$><flags><width><.precision><conversion>
```

Except the % and <conversion> parts, all other parts are optional. Note that there is no space between any two parts of a format specifier. The % (percent sign) denotes the start of a format specifier inside a format string. If you want to specify % as the part of a fixed text inside a format string, you need to use two consecutive % as %%.

The <argument-index$> denotes the index of the argument that the format specifier refers to. It consists of an integer in base-10 format followed by a $ (dollar sign). The first argument is referred to as 1$, the second as 2$, and so on. You can refer to the same argument multiple times in different format specifiers inside the same format string.

The <flags> denotes the format of the output. It is a set of characters. The valid values for <flags> depend on the data type of the argument that the format specifier refers to.

The <width> denotes the minimum number of characters that need to be written to the output.

Typically, the <.precision> denotes the maximum number of characters to be written to the output. However, its exact meaning varies depending on the value for <conversion>. It is a decimal number. It starts with a dot (.).

The <conversion> denotes how the output should be formatted. Its value depends on the data type of the argument, which the format specifier refers to. It is mandatory.

There are two special format specifiers: %% and %n. The %% format specifier outputs % (a percent sign) and %n outputs a platform-specific newline character. The following snippet of code demonstrates the use of these two special format specifiers:

```
System.out.printf("Interest rate is 10%%.%nJohn%nDonna");
```

```
Interest rate is 10%.
John
Donna
```

You have not supplied any arguments to the printf() method in the code because these two special format specifiers do not work on any arguments. Note the two newlines in the output that are generated by the two %n format specifiers in the format string.

Referencing an Argument Inside a Format Specifier

I have not covered the conversion part of the format specifier yet. For the discussion in this section, I use s as the conversion character for the format specifiers. The s conversion formats its argument as a string. In its simplest form, you can use %s as a format specifier. Let's consider the following snippet of code and its output:

```
System.out.printf("%s, %s, and %s", "Ken", "Lola", "Matt");
```

```
Ken, Lola, and Matt
```

A format specifier in a format string can refer to an argument in three ways:

- Ordinary indexing

- Explicit indexing

- Relative indexing

Ordinary Indexing

When a format specifier does not specify an argument-index value (as in %s), it is called ordinary indexing. In ordinary indexing, the argument-index is determined by the index of the format specifier in the format string. The first format specifier without an argument-index has the index of 1, the second has the index of 2, and so on. The format specifier with the index 1 refers to the first argument; the format specifier with the index 2 refers to the second argument; and so on. Figure 17-1 shows the indices of the format specifiers and the arguments.

Figure 17-1. *Indexes of format specifiers in a format string and indexes of the arguments*

Figure 17-1 shows how indices are mapped in the previous example. The first %s format specified refers to the first argument, "Ken". The second %s format specified refers to the second argument, "Lola". And, the third %s format specified refers to the third argument, "Matt".

If the number of arguments is more than the number of format specifiers in the format string, the extra arguments are ignored. Consider the following snippet of code and its output. It has three format specifiers (three %s) and four arguments. The fourth argument, "Lo", is an extra argument, which is ignored.

```
System.out.printf("%s, %s, and %s", "Ken", "Lola", "Matt", "Lo");
```

```
Ken, Lola, and Matt
```

A java.util.MissingFormatArgumentException is thrown if a format specifier references a non-existent argument. The following snippet of code will throw this exception because the number of arguments is one less than the number of format specifiers. There are three format specifiers, but only two arguments.

```
// Compiles fine, but throws a runtime exception
System.out.printf("%s, %s, and %s", "Ken", "Lola");
```

Note that the last argument to the format() method of the Formatter class is a var-args argument. You can also pass an array to a var-args argument. The following snippet of code is valid even though it uses three format specifiers and only one argument of array type. The array type argument contains three values for the three format specifiers.

```
String[] names = {"Ken", "Matt", "Lola"};
System.out.printf("%s, %s, and %s", names);
```

```
Ken, Matt, and Lola
```

The following snippet of code is also valid because it passes four values in the array type argument but has only three format specifiers:

```
String[] names = {"Ken", "Matt", "Lola", "Lo"};
System.out.printf("%s, %s, and %s", names);
```

```
Ken, Matt, and Lola
```

The following snippet of code is not valid because it uses an array type argument that has only two elements and there are three format specifiers. A MissingFormatArgumentException will be thrown when the following snippet of code is run.

```
String[] names = {"Ken", "Matt"};
System.out.printf("%s, %s, and %s", names); // Throws an exception
```

Explicit Indexing

When a format specifier specifies an argument index explicitly, it is called explicit indexing. Note that an argument index is specified just after the % sign in a format specifier. It is an integer in the decimal format and it ends with $ (a dollar sign). Consider the following snippet of code and its output. It uses three format specifiers: %1$s, %2$s, and %3$s, which use explicit indexing.

```
System.out.printf("%1$s, %2$s, and %3$s", "Ken", "Lola", "Matt");
```

```
Ken, Lola, and Matt
```

When a format specifier uses explicit indexing, it can refer to an argument at any index in the argument list using the index of the argument. Consider the following snippet of code:

```
System.out.printf("%3$s, %1$s, and %2$s", "Lola", "Matt", "Ken");
```

```
Ken, Lola, and Matt
```

This snippet of code has the same output as the snippet of code before it. However, in this case, the values in the argument list are not in the same order. The first format specifier, %3$s, refers to the third argument, "Ken"; the second format specifier, %1$s, refers to the first argument, "Lola"; and the third format specifier, %2$s, refers to the second argument, "Matt".

It is allowed to reference the same argument multiple times using explicit indexing. It is also allowed not to reference some arguments inside the format string. In the following snippet of code, the first argument of "Lola" is not referenced and the third argument of "Ken" is referenced twice:

```
System.out.printf("%3$s, %2$s, and %3$s", "Lola", "Matt", "Ken");
```

```
Ken, Matt, and Ken
```

Relative Indexing

There is a third way to refer to an argument inside a format specifier, which is called relative indexing. In relative indexing, a format specifier uses the same argument that was used by the previous format specifier. Relative indexing does not use an argument-index value. Rather, it uses the < character as a flag in the format specifier. Since in relative indexing, a format specifier uses the same argument that is used by the previous format specifier, it cannot be used with the first format specifier because there is no previous format specifier for the first format specifier. Consider the following snippet of code and its output, which uses relative indexing:

```
System.out.printf("%1$s, %<s, %<s, %2$s, and %<s", "Ken", "Matt");
```

```
Ken, Ken, Ken, Matt, and Matt
```

This snippet of code uses five format specifiers: %1$s, %<s, %<s, %2$s, and %<s. It uses two arguments: "Ken" and "Matt". Note that it is possible to have less number of arguments than the number of format specifiers if some format specifiers use relative indexing. The first format specifier of %1$s uses explicit indexing to reference the first argument, "Ken". The second format specifier of %<s uses relative indexing (notice the < flag) and, therefore, it will use the same argument, which was used by the previous format specifier, 1$s. This way, both the first and the second format specifiers use the first argument, "Ken". This is confirmed by the output that displays "Ken" as the first two names. The third format specifier of %<s also uses relative indexing. It will use the same argument as used by the previous format specifier (the second format specifier). Since the second format specifier used the first argument, "Ken", the third one will also use the same argument. This is confirmed in the output that shows "Ken" as the third name. The fourth %2$s format specifier uses explicit indexing to use the second argument of "Matt". The fifth and last format specifier of %<s uses relative indexing and it will use the same argument that is used by its previous format specifier (the fourth format specifier). Since the fourth format specifier uses the second argument, "Matt", the fifth format specifier will also use the second argument of "Matt". This is confirmed in the output that displays "Matt" as the fifth name.

The following statement will throw a MissingFormatArgumentException because it uses relative indexing for the first format specifier:

```
System.out.printf("%<s, %<s, %<s, %2$s, and %<s", "Ken", "Matt");
```

It is possible to mix all three types of indexing to reference arguments inside different format specifiers in the same format string. Consider the following statement and its output:

```
System.out.printf("%1$s, %s, %<s, %s, and %<s", "Ken", "Matt");
```

```
Ken, Ken, Ken, Matt, and Matt
```

The first format specifier uses the explicit indexing to use the first argument of "Ken". The second and the fourth format specifiers (both %s) use ordinary indexing. The third and the fifth format specifiers (both %<s) use relative indexing. It is clear from the rule of relative indexing that the third and fifth format specifiers will use the same arguments as used by the second and the fourth format specifiers, respectively. Which arguments will be used by the second and the fourth format specifiers? The answer is simple. When you have some format specifiers that use ordinary indexing and some explicit indexing, just for the purpose of understanding this rule, ignore the format specifiers that use explicit indexing and number the format specifiers that use ordinary indexing as 1, 2, and so on. Using this rule, you can think of the previous statement the same as the following one:

```
System.out.printf("%1$s, %1$s, %<s, %2$s, and %<s", "Ken", "Matt");
```

Notice that you have replaced the first occurrence of %s with %1$s and the second occurrence with %2$s as if they are using explicit indexing. This explains the output generated by the previous statement.

Using Flags in a Format Specifier

Flags act as modifiers. They modify the formatted output. Table 17-3 lists all flags that can be used in a format specifier.

Table 17-3. *List of Valid Flags, Their Descriptions, and Examples of Their Usage*

Flag	Description	Examples		
		Format String	**Argument**	**Formatted Text**
-	The result is left justified. Note that the result is right justified when you do not use the - flag in a format specifier.	"'%6s'"	"Ken"	' Ken'
		"'%-6s'"	"Ken"	'Ken '
#	The argument is formatted in alternate form depending on the conversion part of the format specifier. The example shows the same decimal number, 6270185, being formatted to a hexadecimal format. When the # flag is used, the hexadecimal number is prefixed with 0x.	"%x"	6270185	5face9
		"%#x"	6270185	0x5face9
+	The result contains a + sign for positive values. It applies only to numeric values.	"%d"	105	105
		"%+d"	105	+105
' '	The result contains a leading space for positive values. It applies only to numeric values.	"'%d'"	105	'105'
		"'% d'"	105	' 105'
0	The result is zero padded. It applies only to numeric values.	"'%6d'"	105	' 105'
		"'%06d'"	105	'000105'
,	The result contains a locale-specific grouping separator. It applied only to numeric values. For example, a comma is used as a thousand-separator in US locale, whereas a space is used in France locale.	"%,d"	89105	89,105 (US Locale)
		"%,d"	89105	89 105 (France locale)
(	The result is enclosed in parentheses for a negative number. It applies only to numeric values.	"%d"	-1969	-1969
		"%(d"	-1969	(1969)
<	It causes the argument for the previous format specifier to be reused. It is mostly used in formatting dates and times.	"%s and %<s"	"Ken"	Ken and Ken

The valid use of a flag depends on the context of its use. Depending on the value being formatted, it is allowed to use multiple flags in a format specifier. For example, the format specifier %1$,0(12d uses three flags: ,, 0, and (. If -122899 is used as the argument by this format specifier, it will output (000122,899). The effects of using each flag are discussed in detail when I discuss formatting for different data types in the sections to follow.

Conversion Characters

Different conversion characters are used to format values of different data types. For example, s is used to format a value as a string. The valid values for other parts in a format specifier are also determined by the conversion character and the data type of the argument that the format specifier references. Formatting types based on data types can be broadly classified into in four categories:

- General formatting
- Character formatting
- Numeric formatting
- Date/time formatting

Many of the conversion characters have uppercase variants. For example, S is the uppercase variant of s. The uppercase variant converts the formatted output to uppercase as if the output.toUpperCase() method was called, where output is the reference to the formatted output string. The following statement and its output demonstrate the effect of using the uppercase variant S. Note that s produces "Ken" and S produces "KEN" for the same input value "Ken".

```
System.out.printf("%s and %<S", "Ken");
```

```
Ken and KEN
```

General Formatting

The general formatting can be used to format values of any data types. Table 17-4 has the list of conversions that are available under the general formatting category.

Table 17-4. *List of Conversion Characters for General Formatting*

Conversion	Uppercase Variant	Description
b	B	It produces true or false based on the value of the argument. It produces false for a null argument and for a boolean argument whose value is false. Otherwise, it produces true.
h	H	It produces a string that is the hash code value in hexadecimal format of the argument. If the argument is null, it produces "null".
s	S	It produces a string representation of the argument. If the argument is null, it produces a "null" string. If the argument implements the Formattable interface, it invokes the formatTo() method on the argument and the returned value is the result. If the argument does not implement the Formattable interface, toString() method is invoked on the argument to get the result.

The general syntax for a format specifier for general formatting is as follows:

```
%<argument_index$><flags><width><.precision><conversion>
```

The width denotes the minimum number of characters to be written to the output. If the length of the string representation of the argument is less than the width value, the result will be padded with spaces. The space padding is performed to the left of the argument value. If a - flag is used, space padding is performed to the right. The value of width alone does not decide the content of the result. The values of width and precision together decide the final content of the result.

The precision denotes the maximum number of characters to be written to the output. The precision is applied to the argument before the width is applied. You need to understand the consequences of applying the precision before the width. If the precision is less than the length of the argument, the argument is truncated to the precision, and space padding is performed to match the length of the output to the value of the width. Consider the following snippet of code:

```
System.out.printf("'%4.1s'", "Ken");
```

```
'   K'
```

The argument is "Ken" and the format specifier is %4.1s, where 4 is the width and 1 is the precision. First, the precision is applied that will truncate the value "Ken" to K. Now, the width is applied, which states that a minimum of four characters should be written to the output. However, after the precision is applied, you have only one character left. Therefore, K will be left padded with three spaces to match the width value of four.

Consider the following snippet of code:

```
System.out.printf("'%1.4s'", "Ken");
```

```
'Ken'
```

The argument value is "Ken" and the format specifier is %1.4s where 1 is the width and 4 is the precision. Because the precision value of 4 is greater than the length of the argument, which is 3, there is no effect of the precision. Because the width value of 1 is less than the width of the result after precision is applied, there is no effect of the width value on the output.

The following are a few examples of using boolean, string, and hash code formatting conversions. Note that the hash code formatting conversion (h and H) outputs the hash code value of the argument in a hexadecimal format. These examples also demonstrate the effect of using the uppercase variants of the conversions.

```
// Boolean conversion
System.out.printf("'%b', '%5b', '%.3b'%n", true, false, true);
System.out.printf("'%b', '%5b', '%.3b'%n", "Ken", "Matt", "Lola");
System.out.printf("'%B', '%5B', '%.3B'%n", "Ken", "Matt", "Lola");
System.out.printf("%b %n", 1969);
System.out.printf("%b %n", new Object());
```

```
'true', 'false', 'tru'
'true', ' true', 'tru'
'TRUE', ' TRUE', 'TRU'
true
true
```

```
// String conversion
System.out.printf("'%s', '%5s', '%.3s'%n", "Ken", "Matt", "Lola");
System.out.printf("'%S', '%5S', '%.3S'%n", "Ken", "Matt", "Lola");

// Use '-' flag to left-justify the result. You must use width when you specify the '-' flag
System.out.printf("'%S', '%-5S', '%.3S'%n", "Ken", "Matt", "Lola");
System.out.printf("%s %n", 1969);
System.out.printf("%s %n", true);
System.out.printf("%s %n", new Object());
```

```
'Ken', ' Matt', 'Lol'
'KEN', ' MATT', 'LOL'
'KEN', 'MATT ', 'LOL'
1969
true
java.lang.Object@de6f34
```

```
// Hash Code conversion
System.out.printf("'%h', '%5h', '%.3h'%n", "Ken", "Matt", "Lola");
System.out.printf("'%H', '%5H', '%.3H'%n", "Ken", "Matt", "Lola");
System.out.printf("%h %n", 1969);
System.out.printf("%h %n", true);
System.out.printf("%h %n", new Object());
```

```
'12634', '247b34', '243'
'12634', '247B34', '243'
7b1
4cf
156ee8e
```

If you pass a value of a primitive type as an argument to the format() method of the Formatter class (or the printf() method of the PrintStream class), the primitive type value is converted to a reference type using an appropriate type of wrapper class using the autoboxing rules. For example, this statement

```
System.out.println("%s", 1969);
```

is converted to

```
System.out.println("%s", new Integer(1969));
```

Writing a Custom Formatter

The Formatter class supports custom formatting through s and S conversions. If the argument implements java.util.Formattable interface, the s conversion calls the formatTo() method on the argument to get the formatted result. The formatTo() method is passed the reference of a Formatter object, flags, width, and precision values that are used in the format specifier. You can apply any custom logic inside the formatTo() method of the class to format the objects of your class. Listing 17-8 contains the code for a FormattablePerson class, which implements the Formattable interface.

Listing 17-8. Implementing a Custom Formatter Using the Formattable Interface

```java
// FormattablePerson.java
package com.jdojo.format;

import java.util.Formattable;
import java.util.Formatter;
import java.util.FormattableFlags;

public class FormattablePerson implements Formattable {
    private String firstName = "Unknown";
    private String lastName = "Unknown";

    public FormattablePerson(String firstName, String lastName) {
        this.firstName = firstName;
        this.lastName = lastName;
    }

    /* Other code goes here... */

    @Override
    public void formatTo(Formatter formatter, int flags, int width, int precision) {
        String str = this.firstName + " " + this.lastName;

        int alternateFlagValue = FormattableFlags.ALTERNATE & flags;
        if (alternateFlagValue == FormattableFlags.ALTERNATE) {
            str = this.lastName + ", " + this.firstName;
        }

        // Check if uppercase variant of the conversion is being used
        int upperFlagValue = FormattableFlags.UPPERCASE & flags;
        if (upperFlagValue == FormattableFlags.UPPERCASE) {
            str = str.toUpperCase();
        }

        // Call the format() method of formatter argument,
        // so our result is stored in it and the caller will get it
        formatter.format(str);
    }
}
```

Your Formattable person has a first name and a last name. The logic inside the formatTo() method is intentionally kept simple. You check for alternate flag #. If this flag is used in the format specifier, you format the person name in the LastName, FirstName format. If the alternate flag is not used, you format the person name in the FirstName LastName format. You also support uppercase variant S to s conversion. If S conversion is used, you format the person name in uppercase. Your logic does not use other values of the flags, width, and precision. The flags are passed in as an int value as bitmask. To check if a flag was passed, you will need to use the bitwise & operator. The operands to be used in the bitwise & operator are defined by constants in the java.util.FormattableFlags class. For example, to check if the format specifier uses a left-justify - flag, you need to use the following logic:

```
int leftJustifiedFlagValue = FormattableFlags.LEFT_JUSTIFY & flags;

if (leftJustifiedFlagValue == FormattableFlags.LEFT_JUSTIFY) {
    // Left-justified flag '-' is used
} else {
    // Left-justified flag '-' is not used
}
```

You can use your FormattablePerson objects with format specifiers using string conversion s and S as shown here:

```
FormattablePerson fp = new FormattablePerson("Ken", "Smith");
System.out.printf("%s %n", fp );
System.out.printf("%#s %n", fp );
System.out.printf("%S %n", fp );
System.out.printf("%#S %n", fp );
```

```
Ken Smith
Smith, Ken
KEN SMITH
SMITH, KEN
```

Character Formatting

Character formatting may be applied to the values of char primitive data type or Character objects. It can also be applied to the values of byte, Byte, short, Short, int, or Integer types if their values are valid Unicode code points. You can test if an integer value represents a valid Unicode code point by using the isValidCodePoint(int value) static method of the Character class.

The conversion character for character formatting is c. Its uppercase variant is C. The flag # and the precision are not supported for character formatting. The flag - and width have the same meaning as in the context of the general formatting. The following snippet of code demonstrates the use of character formatting:

```
System.out.printf("%c %n", 'a');
System.out.printf("%C %n", 'a');
System.out.printf("%C %n", 98);
System.out.printf("'%5C' %n", 100);
System.out.printf("'%-5C' %n", 100);
```

657

```
a
A
B
'    D'
'D    '
```

Numeric Formatting

Numeric formatting can be broadly classified into two categories:

- Integral number formatting
- Floating-point number formatting

A lot of locale-specific formatting is automatically applied when a numeric value is formatted. For example, the numeric digits that are used for number formatting are always locale-specific. If the formatted number contains a decimal separator or group separators, they are always replaced with locale-specific decimal separator or group separators, respectively. The following snippet of code shows the same number 1234567890 formatted differently for three different locales—US, Indian, and Thailand:

```
Locale englishUS = new Locale ("en", "US");
Locale hindiIndia = new Locale ("hi", "IN");
Locale thaiThailand = new Locale ("th", "TH", "TH");
System.out.printf(englishUS, "%d %n", 1234567890);
System.out.printf(hindiIndia, "%d %n", 1234567890);
System.out.printf(thaiThailand, "%d %n", 1234567890);
```

1234567890

౧౨౩౪౫౬౭౮౯౦

ဝဿ၀ဆ၆ဂ၀ဝၚ၀

Integral Number Formatting

The integral number formatting deals with formatting whole numbers. It can be applied to format values of byte, Byte, short, Short, int, Integer, long, Long, and BigInteger. Table 17-5 contains the list of conversions that are available under integral number formatting category.

Table 17-5. *List of Conversions Applicable to byte, Byte, short, Short, int, Integer, long, Long, and BigInteger Data Types*

Conversion	Uppercase Variant	Description
d		It formats the argument in locale-specific decimal integer (base-10). The # flag cannot be used with this conversion.
o		It formats the argument as a base-8 integer without any localization. If the # flag is used with this conversion, the output always begins with a 0 (a zero). The (, +, ' ', and , flags cannot be used with this conversion.
x	X	It formats the argument as a base-16 integer without any localization. If the # flag is used with this conversion, the output always begins with a 0x. When the uppercase variant X is used with the # flag, the output always begins with 0X. The (, +, ' ', and , flags cannot be used with this conversion with an argument of byte, Byte, short, Short, int, Integer, long, and Long data types. The , flag cannot be used with this conversion with an argument of BigInteger data type.

The general syntax for a format specifier for integral number formatting is as follows:

```
%<argument_index$><flags><width><conversion>
```

Note that precision part in a format specifier is not applicable to integral number formatting. The following snippet of code demonstrates the use of the d conversion with various flags to format integers:

```
System.out.printf("'%d' %n", 1969);
System.out.printf("'%6d' %n", 1969);
System.out.printf("'%-6d' %n", 1969);
System.out.printf("'%06d' %n", 1969);
System.out.printf("'%(d' %n", 1969);
System.out.printf("'%(d' %n", -1969);
System.out.printf("'% d' %n", 1969);
System.out.printf("'% d' %n", -1969);
System.out.printf("'%+d' %n", 1969);
System.out.printf("'%+d' %n", -1969);
```

```
'1969'
'  1969'
'1969  '
'001969'
'1969'
'(1969)'
' 1969'
'-1969'
'+1969'
'-1969'
```

When conversions o and x are used with a negative argument of byte, Byte, short, Short, int, Integer, long, and Long data types, the argument value is first converted to an unsigned number by adding a number 2N to it, where N is the number of bits used to represent the value of the data type of the argument. For example, if the argument data type is byte, which takes 8 bits to store the value, the argument value of –X will be converted to a positive value of –X + 256 by adding 256 to it. The result contains the base-8 or base-16 equivalent of the value –X + 256. The conversions o and x do not transform the negative argument value to an unsigned value for a BigInteger argument type. Consider the following snippet of code and the output:

```
byte b1 = 9;
byte b2 = -9;
System.out.printf("%o %n", b1);
System.out.printf("%o %n", b2);
```

```
11
367
```

The conversion o outputs the base-8 integer 11 for a positive decimal integer 9. However, when a negative decimal integer -9 is used with the o conversion, -9 is converted to a positive number -9 + 256 (=247). The final output contains 367, which is the base-8 equivalent of the decimal 247.

The following snippet of code shows some more examples of o and x conversions for int and BigInteger argument types:

```
System.out.printf("%o %n", 1969);
System.out.printf("%o %n", -1969);
System.out.printf("%o %n", new BigInteger("1969"));
System.out.printf("%o %n", new BigInteger("-1969"));

System.out.printf("%x %n", 1969);
System.out.printf("%x %n", -1969);
System.out.printf("%x %n", new BigInteger("1969"));
System.out.printf("%x %n", new BigInteger("-1969"));

System.out.printf("%#o %n", 1969);
System.out.printf("%#x %n", 1969);
System.out.printf("%#o %n", new BigInteger("1969"));
System.out.printf("%#x %n", new BigInteger("1969"));
```

```
3661
37777774117
3661
-3661
7b1
fffff84f
7b1
-7b1
03661
0x7b1
03661
0x7b1
```

Floating-Point Number Formatting

Floating-point number formatting deals with formatting numbers, which have a whole part and a fraction part. It can be applied to format values of the float, Float, double, Double, and BigDecimal data types. Table 17-6 contains the list of conversions used for formatting floating-point number formatting.

Table 17-6. *List of Conversions Applicable to float, Float, double, Double, and BigDecimal Data Types*

Conversion	Uppercase Variant	Description
e	E	It formats the argument in a locale-specific computerized scientific notation, for example, 1.969919e+03. The output contains one digit followed by a decimal separator, which is followed by the exponent part. For example, 1969.919 will be formatted as 1.969919e+03 if the precision is 6. Precision is the number of digits after the decimal separator. The group separator flag , cannot be used with this conversion.
g	G	It formats the argument in a locale-specific general scientific notation. Depending on the value of the argument, it acts as e conversion or f conversion. It applies rounding to the value of the argument depending on the value of the precision. If the value after rounding is greater than or equal to 10^{-4} but less than $10^{precision}$, it formats the value as if f conversion is used. If the value after rounding is less than 10^{-4} or greater than or equal to $10^{precision}$, it formats the value as if e conversion is used. Note that the total number of significant digits in the result is equal to the value of the precision. By default, a precision of 6 is used.
f		It formats the argument in a locale-specific decimal format. Precision is the number of digits after the decimal separator. The value is rounded depending on the specified value of the precision.
a	A	It formats the argument in hexadecimal exponential form. It is not applicable to the argument of a BigDecimal type.

The general syntax for a format specifier for floating-point number formatting is as follows:

```
%<argument_index$><flags><width><.precision><conversion>
```

The precision has different meanings. The meanings depend on the conversion character. By default, the value of precision is 6. For e and f conversions, the precision is the number of digits after the decimal separator. For the g conversion, the precision is the total number of digits in the resulting magnitude after rounding. Precision is not applicable to the a conversion.

The following snippet of code shows how to format floating-point numbers with the default precision, which is 6:

```
System.out.printf("%e %n", 10.2);
System.out.printf("%f %n", 10.2);
System.out.printf("%g %n", 10.2);
```

```
System.out.printf("%e %n", 0.000002079);
System.out.printf("%f %n", 0.000002079);
System.out.printf("%g %n", 0.000002079);

System.out.printf("%a %n", 0.000002079);
```

```
1.020000e+01
10.200000
10.2000
2.079000e-06
0.000002
2.07900e-06
'1.97e+03'
0x1.1709e564a6d14p-19
```

The following snippet of code shows the effects of using width and precision in floating-point number formatting:

```
System.out.printf("%.2e %n", 1969.27);
System.out.printf("%.2f %n", 1969.27);
System.out.printf("%.2g %n", 1969.27);

System.out.printf("'%8.2e' %n", 1969.27);
System.out.printf("'%8.2f' %n", 1969.27);
System.out.printf("'%8.2g' %n", 1969.27);

System.out.printf("'%10.2e' %n", 1969.27);
System.out.printf("'%10.2f' %n", 1969.27);
System.out.printf("'%10.2g' %n", 1969.27);

System.out.printf("'%-10.2e' %n", 1969.27);
System.out.printf("'%-10.2f' %n", 1969.27);
System.out.printf("'%-10.2g' %n", 1969.27);

System.out.printf("'%010.2e' %n", 1969.27);
System.out.printf("'%010.2f' %n", 1969.27);
System.out.printf("'%010.2g' %n", 1969.27);
```

```
1.97e+03
1969.27
2.0e+03
'1.97e+03'
' 1969.27'
' 2.0e+03'
'  1.97e+03'
'   1969.27'
'   2.0e+03'
'1.97e+03  '
```

```
'1969.27   '
'2.0e+03   '
'001.97e+03'
'0001969.27'
'0002.0e+03'
```

If the argument value for a floating-point conversion is NaN or Infinity, the output contains the strings "NaN" and "Infinity", respectively. The following snippet of code shows the formatting of floating-point numbers when their values are NaN or infinities:

```
System.out.printf("%.2e %n", Double.NaN);
System.out.printf("%.2f %n", Double.POSITIVE_INFINITY);
System.out.printf("%.2g %n", Double.NEGATIVE_INFINITY);
System.out.printf("%(f %n", Double.POSITIVE_INFINITY);
System.out.printf("%(f %n", Double.NEGATIVE_INFINITY);
```

```
NaN
Infinity
-Infinity
Infinity
(Infinity)
```

Formatting Dates and Times

Date/time formatting deals with formatting date, time, and date/time. It can be applied to format values of the long, Long, java.util.Calandar, java.util.Date, and java.time.temporal.TemporalAccessor types. The value in a long/Long type argument is interpreted as the milliseconds passed since January 1, 1970 midnight UTC.

■ **Note** TemporalAccessor is an interface added in Java 8. It is part of the new Date-Time API. All classes in the API that specify some kind of date, time, or both are TemporalAccessor. LocalDate, LocalTime, LocalDateTime, and ZonedDateTime are some examples of TemporalAccessor. Refer to Chapter 16 for more information on using the new Date-Time API.

The t conversion character is used to format date/time values. It has an uppercase variant T. The general syntax for a format specifier for date/time formatting is as follows:

```
%<argument_index$><flags><width><conversion>
```

Note that precision part in a format specifier is not applicable to date/time formatting. For date/time formatting, the conversion is a two-character sequence. The first character in the conversion is always t or T. The second character is called the conversion suffix, which determines the format of the date/time argument. Tables 17-7 through 17-9 list all the conversion suffixes that can be used with t/T data/time conversion character.

Table 17-7. *List of Suffix Characters for Time Formatting*

Conversion Suffix	Description
H	A two-digit hour of the day for the 24-hour clock. The valid values are 00 to 23.00 is used for midnight.
I	A two-digit hour of the day for the 12-hour clock. The valid values are 01 to 12. The 01 value corresponds to one o'clock in the morning or afternoon.
k	It behaves the same as the H suffix except that it does not add a leading zero to the output. Valid values are 0 to 23.
l	It behaves the same as I suffix except that it does not add a leading zero. Valid values are 1 to 12.
M	A two-digit minute within an hour. Valid values are 00 to 59.
S	A two-digit second within a minute. Valid values are 00 to 60. The value 60 is a special value that is required to support leap seconds.
L	A three-digit millisecond within a second. Valid values are 000 to 999.
N	A nine-digit nanosecond within a second. The valid values are 000000000 to 999999999. The precision of the nanosecond value is dependent on the precision that is supported by the operating system.
p	It outputs a locale-specific morning or afternoon marker in lowercase. For example, for US locale, it will output "am" or "pm". If you want the output in uppercase (e.g., "AM" and "PM" for US locale), you need to use the uppercase variant T as the conversion character.
z	It outputs the numeric time zone offset from GMT (e.g., +0530).
Z	It is a string abbreviation of the time zone (e.g., CST, EST, IST, etc.).
s	It outputs seconds since the beginning of the epoch starting at January 1, 1970 midnight UTC.
Q	It outputs milliseconds since the beginning of the epoch starting at January 1, 1970 midnight UTC.

Table 17-8. *List of Suffix Characters for Date Formatting*

Conversion Suffix	Description
B	Locale-specific full name of the month, such as "January", "February", etc. for US locale.
b	Locale-specific abbreviated month name, such as "Jan", "Feb", etc. for US locale.
h	Same as b.
A	Locale-specific full name of the day of the week, such as "Sunday", "Monday", etc. for US locale.
a	Locale-specific short name of the day of the week, such as "Sun", "Mon", etc. for US locale.
C	It divides the four-digit year by 100 and formats the result as two digits. It adds a leading zero if the resulting number is one digit. It ignores the fraction part from the result of the division by 100. Valid values are 00 to 99. For example, if the four-digit year is 2011, it will output 20; if the four-digit year is 12, it will output 00.
Y	At least a four-digit year. It adds leading zeros if the year contains less than four digits. For example, if the year is 789, it will output 0789; if the year is 2011, it will output 2011; if the year is 20189, it will output 20189.
y	The last two digits of the year. It adds a leading zero if necessary. For example, if the year is 9, it will output 09; if the year is 123, it will output 23; if the year is 2011, it will output 11.
j	A three-digit day of the year. Valid values are 000 to 366.
m	A two-digit month. Valid values are 01 to 13. The special value of 13 is required to support the lunar calendar.
d	A two-digit day of the month. Valid values are 01 to 31.
e	Day of the month. Valid values are 1 to 31. It behaves the same as 'd' except that it does not add a leading zero to the output.

Table 17-9. *List of Suffix Characters for Date/Time Formatting*

Conversion Suffix	Description
R	It formats time in 24-hour clock format as hour:minute. Its effects are the same as using %tH:%tM as a format specifier. Examples are 11:23, 01:35, 21:30, etc.
T	It formats time in 24-hour clock format as hour:minute:second. Its effect is the same as using %tH:%tM:%tS as a format specifier. Examples are 11:23:10, 01:35:01, 21:30:34, etc.
r	It formats time in 12-hour clock format as hour:minute:second morning/afternoon marker. Its effect is the same as using %tI:%tM:%tS %Tp as a format specifier. The morning/afternoon marker may be locale-specific. 09:23:45 AM, 09:30:00 PM, etc. are examples of the US locale.
D	It formats the date as %tm/%td/%ty, such as 01/19/11.
F	It formats the date as %tY-%tm-%td, such as 2011-01-19.
c	It formats the date and time as %ta %tb %td %tT %tZ %tY, such as Wed Jan 19 11:52:06 CST 2011.

The data/time conversion applies localization wherever it is applicable. The following snippet of code formats the same date and time, January 25, 2014 11:48:16 AM, in US, Indian, and Thai locales. Note the use of the < flag in the format specifier. It lets you use the argument that holds the date and time value in multiple format specifiers.

```
Locale englishUS = Locale.US;
Locale hindiIndia = new Locale ("hi", "IN");
Locale thaiThailand = new Locale ("th", "TH", "TH");

// Construct a LocalDateTime
LocalDateTime ldt = LocalDateTime.of(2014, Month.JANUARY, 25, 11, 48, 16);

System.out.printf(englishUS, "In US: %tB %<te, %<tY %<tT %<Tp%n", ldt);
System.out.printf(hindiIndia, "In India: %tB %<te, %<tY %<tT %<Tp%n", ldt);
System.out.printf(thaiThailand, "In Thailand: %tB %<te, %<tY %<tT %<Tp%n", ldt);
```

```
In US: January 25, 2014 11:48:16 AM
```

```
In India: जनवरी २५, २०१४ ११:४८:१६ पूर्वाह्न
```

```
In Thailand: มกราคม ๒๕, ๒๐๑๔ ๑๑:๔๘:๑๖ ก่อนเที่ยง
```

The following snippet of code formats the current date and time in the default locale (US in this case). You will get different output when you run the code. It uses a ZonedDateTime argument that holds the current date/time with time zone.

```
ZonedDateTime currentTime = ZonedDateTime.now();

System.out.printf("%tA %<tB %<te, %<tY %n", currentTime);
System.out.printf("%TA %<TB %<te, %<tY %n", currentTime);
System.out.printf("%tD %n", currentTime);
System.out.printf("%tF %n", currentTime);
System.out.printf("%tc %n", currentTime);
System.out.printf("%Tc %n", currentTime);
```

```
Saturday January 25, 2014
SATURDAY JANUARY 25, 2014
01/25/14
2014-01-25
Sat Jan 25 00:47:26 CST 2014
SAT JAN 25 00:47:26 CST 2014
```

Note the effect of using the uppercase variant T as the conversion character. It formats the argument in uppercase letters. The definition of uppercase depends on the locale that is used. If the locale does not have different uppercase and lowercase letters, the output will be the same when you use T or t as the conversion character.

Summary

The DateFormat class is used to format dates and times using predefined formats, whereas the SimpleDateFormat class is used to format dates and times in custom formats.

The NumberFormat class is used to format numbers in a particular locale's predefined format. The DecimalFormat class is used to format a number in a format of your choice in a particular locale.

You can use printf-style formatting using the java.util.Formatter class to format strings, numbers, and date/time. It lets you send the formatted output to a StringBuilder, a StringBuffer, a File, an OutputStream, a PrintStream, etc. You have been using the System.out.format() and System.out.printf() methods to send the formatted output to the standard output. Use the static String.format() method to get a formatted string. Use a Formatter to send the formatted output to the destination of your choice. You can implement the Formattable interface to apply a custom formatting to the objects of the class.

QUESTIONS AND EXERCISES

1. What class would you use to format a date in a java.util.Date object using a predefined locale-specific format?

2. What class would you use to format a date in a java.util.Date object using a custom format?

3. What class would you use to parse a date in a String object to get a java.util. Date object?

4. What class would you use to format a number in a predefined locale-specific format?

5. What class would you use to format a number in a custom format?

6. What class would you use to parse a double in a string to get a number?

7. Assuming the current date returned by the new Date() expression in the following snippet of code as January 12, 1968, what will be the output of the following snippet of code?

```
import java.text.SimpleDateFormat;
import java.util.Date;
...
SimpleDateFormat sdf = new SimpleDateFormat("dd/MM/yyyy");
String currDate = sdf.format(new Date());
System.out.println(currDate);
```

8. What method would you use to print a formatted output to the standard output—System.out.println() or System.out.printf()?

9. What are the format specifiers for outputting a Boolean value, a character, an integer, a floating-point number, and a string?

10. The following statements throws a `MissingFormatArgumentException`. Describe the reasons behind the exception and how you will fix it.

    ```
    System.out.printf("%d %f", 1969);
    System.out.printf("%d %f", 1969, 2017);
    ```

11. Write the output of the following statement.

    ```
    System.out.printf("%s %s%n", "Ken", "Lu");
    System.out.printf("%s %<s%n", "Ken", "Lu");
    System.out.printf("%s %<s %2s%n", "Ken", "Lu");
    ```

12. Write the output for the following snippet of code.

    ```
    System.out.println(new DecimalFormat("##.##").format(12.675));
    System.out.printf("%.2f%n", 12.675);
    System.out.printf("%1.2f%n", 12.675);
    System.out.printf("%2.2f%n", 12.675);
    System.out.printf("%2.1f%n", 12.675);
    ```

13. Complete the following snippet of code that will output "My birthday is on FRIDAY SEPTEMBER 19, 1969". Note that you have to output the names of the week day and month in uppercase.

    ```
    LocalDate bDay = LocalDate.of(1969, 9, 19);
    String format = /* Your code goes here*/;
    System.out.printf(format, bDay);
    ```

14. Write the output of the following snippet of code.

    ```
    System.out.printf("%d%n", 16);
    System.out.printf("%x%n", 10);
    System.out.printf("%c%n", 'a');
    System.out.printf("'%5C' %n", 'a');
    System.out.printf("'%-5C' %n", 'a');
    ```

15. Write the output of the following snippet of code.

    ```
    System.out.printf("%s %<s %s %1$s %s%n", "Li", "Hu", "Xi");
    ```

CHAPTER 18

Regular Expressions

In this chapter, you will learn:

- How to create regular expressions

- How to use convenience methods in the `String` class to perform regular expression-based find-and-replace

- How to use the `Pattern` class to compile regular expressions

- How to use the `Matcher` class to match a regular expression against an input string

- How to use groups in regular expressions

- How to perform advanced find-and-replace using the `Matcher` class

All example programs in this chapter are a member of a `jdojo.regex` module, as declared in Listing 18-1.

Listing 18-1. The Declaration of a jdojo.regex Module

```
// module-info.java
module jdojo.regex {
    exports com.jdojo.regex;
}
```

What Is a Regular Expression?

A *regular expression* is a way to describe a pattern in a sequence of characters. The pattern may be used to validate the sequence of characters, to search through the sequence of characters, to replace the sequence of characters matching the pattern with other sequence of characters, etc.

Let's start with an example. Suppose you have a string, which may be an e-mail address. How would you make sure that the string is in a valid e-mail address format? At this point, you are not interested in the existence of the e-mail address. You just want to validate its format.

You would like to validate the string against some rules. For example, it must contain an @ sign, which is preceded by at least one character and followed by a domain name. Optionally, you may specify that the text preceding the @ sign must contain only letters, digits, underscores, and hyphens. The domain name must contain a dot. You may want to add some more validations. If you just want to check for a @ character in a string, you can do it by calling `email.indexOf('@')`, where `email` is the reference of the string holding the e-mail address. If you want to make sure that there is only one @ character in the e-mail string, you need to add more logic. In such cases, you may end up with 20 to 50, or even more, lines of code depending on the number of validations you want to perform.

This is where regular expressions come in handy. It will make your e-mail address validation easy. You can accomplish it in just one line of code. Doesn't that sound too good to be true? Just a little while ago, you were told that you might end up with 50 lines of code. Now you are told that you could accomplish the same in just one line of code. This is true. It can be done in one line of code. Before I go into the details of how to do this, let's list the steps needed to accomplish this task.

- To validate these kinds of strings, you need to recognize the pattern you are looking for. For example, in the simplest form of e-mail address validation, the string should consist of some text (at least one character) plus an @ sign followed by some text for domain name. Let's ignore any other details for now.

- You need a way to express the recognized pattern. A regular expression is used to describe such a pattern.

- You need a program that can match the pattern against the input string. Such a program is also known as a regular expression engine.

Suppose you want to test whether a string is of the form X@X, where X is any character. Strings "a@a", "b@f", "3@h" are in this form. You can observe a pattern here. The pattern is "A character followed by @, which is followed by another character." How do you express this pattern in Java?

The string ".@." will represent your regular expression in this case. In ".@.", the dots have a special meaning. They represent any character. All characters that have special meanings inside a regular expression are called metacharacters. I discuss metacharacters in the next section. The String class contains a matches() method. It takes a regular expression as an argument and returns true if the whole string matches the regular expression. Otherwise, it returns false. The signature of this method is

```
boolean matches(String regex)
```

Listing 18-2 contains the complete code to illustrate the use of the matches() method of the String class.

Listing 18-2. Matching a String Against a Pattern

```
// RegexMatch.java
package com.jdojo.regex;

public class RegexMatch {
    public static void main(String[] args) {
        // Prepare a regular expression to represent a pattern
        String regex = ".@.";

        // Try matching many strings against the regular expression
        RegexMatch.matchIt("a@k", regex);
        RegexMatch.matchIt("webmaster@jdojo.com", regex);
        RegexMatch.matchIt("r@j", regex);
        RegexMatch.matchIt("a%N", regex);
        RegexMatch.matchIt(".@.", regex);
    }

    public static void matchIt(String str, String regex) {
        // Test for pattern match
        boolean matched = str.matches(regex);
        System.out.printf("%s matched %s = %b%n", str, regex, matched);
    }
}
```

```
a@k matched .@. = true
webmaster@jdojo.com matched .@. = false
r@j matched .@. = true
a%N matched .@. = false
.@. matched .@. = true
```

Some important points to note are the following:

- The regular expression ".@." did not match "webmaster@jdojo.com", because a dot means only one character and the String.matches() method matches the pattern in the regular expression against the entire string. Note that the string "webmaster@jdojo.com" has the pattern represented by .@.; that is, a character followed by @ and another character. However, the pattern matches part of the string, not the entire string. The "r@j" part of "webmaster@jdojo.com" matches that pattern. I present some examples where you will match the pattern anywhere in the string rather than match the entire string.

- If you want to match a dot character in a string, you need to escape the dot in the regular expression. The regular expression ".\\.." will match any string of three characters in which the middle character is a dot character. For example, The method call "a.b".matches(".\\..") will return true; the method call "...".matches(".\\..") will return true; the method calls "abc".matches(".\\..") and "aa.ca".matches(".\\..") will return false.

You can also replace the matching string with another string. The String class has two methods to do the match replacement:

- String replaceAll(String regex, String replacementString)

- String replaceFirst(String regex, String replacementString)

The replaceAll() method replaces strings, which match the pattern represented by the specified regex, with the specified replacementString. It returns the new string after replacement. Some examples of using the replaceAll() method are as follows:

```
String regex = ".@.";

// newStr will contain "webmaste***dojo.com" String newStr = "webmaster@jdojo.com".
replaceAll(regex,"***");

// newStr will contain "***"
newStr = "A@B".replaceAll(regex,"***");

// newStr will contain "***and***"
newStr = "A@BandH@G".replaceAll(regex,"***");

// newStr will contain "B%T" (same as the original string)
newStr = "B%T".replaceAll(regex,"***");
```

The `replaceFirst()` method replaces the first occurrence of the match with the `replacementString`. It returns the new string after replacement. Some examples of using the `replaceFirst()` method are as follows:

```
String regex = ".@.";

// newStr will contain "webmaste***dojo.com"
String newStr = "webmaster@jdojo.com".replaceFirst(regex, "***");

// newStr will contain "***"
newStr = "A@B".replaceFirst(regex, "***");

// newStr will contain "***andH@G"
newStr = "A@BandH@G".replaceFirst(regex, "***");

// newStr will contain "B%T" (same as the original string)
newStr = "B%T".replaceFirst(regex, "***");
```

Metacharacters

Metacharacters are characters with special meanings. They are used in regular expressions. Sometimes metacharacters do not have any special meanings and they are treated as ordinary characters. They are treated as ordinary characters or metacharacters depending on the context in which they are used. The metacharacters supported by the regular expressions in Java are as follows:

- ((a left parenthesis)
-) (a right parenthesis)
- [(a left bracket)
-] (a right bracket)
- { (a left brace)
- { (a right brace)
- \ (a backslash)
- ^ (a caret)
- $ (a dollar sign)
- | (a vertical bar)
- ? (a question mark)
- * (an asterisk)
- + (an addition sign)
- . (a dot or period)
- < (a less-than sign)
- > (a greater-than sign)

- • - (a hyphen)
- • = (an equal to sign)
- • ! (an exclamation mark)

Character Classes

The metacharacters [and] (left and right brackets) are used to specify a character class inside a regular expression. A character class is a set of characters. The regular expression engine will attempt to match one character from the set. Note that a character class has no relation with a class construct or class files in Java. The character class "[ABC]" will match characters A, B, or C. For example, the strings "A@V", "B@V", and "C@V" will match the regular expression "[ABC]@.". However, the string "H@V" will not match the regular expression "[ABC]@." because @ is not preceded by A, B, or C. As another example, the strings "man" or "men" will match the regular expression "m[ae]n".

When I use the word "match," I mean that the pattern exists in a string. I do not mean that the whole string matches the pattern. For example, "WEB@JDOJO.COM" matches the pattern "[ABC]@.", because @ is preceded by B. The string "A@BAND@YEA@U" matches the pattern "[ABC]@." twice even though the string contains three @ signs. The second @ is not part of a match, because it is preceded by D and not A, B, or C.

You can also specify a range of characters using a character class. The range is expressed using a hyphen (-) character. For example, "[A-Z]" in a regular expression represents any uppercase English letters; "[0-9]" represents any digit between 0 and 9. If you use ^ in the beginning of a character class, it means complement (meaning not). For example, "[^ABC]" means any character except A, B, and C. The character class "[^A-Z]" represents any character except uppercase English letters. If you use ^ anywhere in a character class except in the beginning, it loses its special meaning (i.e., the special meaning of complement) and it matches just a ^ character. For example, "[ABC^]" will match A, B, C, or ^.

You can also include two or more ranges in one character class. For example, "[a-zA-Z]" matches any character a through z and A through Z. "[a-zA-Z0-9]" matches any character a through z (uppercase and lowercase), and any digit 0 through 9. Some examples of character classes are listed in Table 18-1.

Table 18-1. *Examples of Character Classes*

Character Classes	Meaning	Category
[abc]	Character a, b, or c	Simple character class
[^xyz]	A character except x, y, and z	Complement or negation
[a-p]	Characters a through p	Range
[a-cx-z]	Characters a through c, or x through z, which would include a, b, c, x, y, or z	Union
[0-9&&[4-8]]	Intersection of two ranges (4, 5, 6, 7, or 8)	Intersection
[a-z&&[^aeiou]]	All lowercase letters minus vowels. In other words, a lowercase letter, which is not a vowel. That is, all lowercase consonants.	Subtraction

Predefined Character Classes

Some frequently used predefined character classes are listed in Table 18-2.

Table 18-2. *List of the Predefined Regular Expression Character Classes*

Predefined Character Classes	Meaning
. (a dot)	Any character (may or may not match line terminators). Refer to the section "Line terminators" in the API documentation of the `java.util.regex.Pattern` class for more details.
\d	A digit. Same as [0-9].
\D	A non-digit. Same as [^0-9].
\s	A whitespace character. Same as [\t\n\x0B\f\r]. The list includes a space, a tab, a new line, a vertical tab, a form feed, and a carriage return characters.
\S	A non-whitespace character. Same as [^\s].
\w	A word character. Same as [a-zA-Z_0-9]. The list includes lowercase letters, uppercase letter, underscore, and decimal digits.
\W	A non-word character. Same as [^\w].

If you allow all uppercase and lowercase letters, underscore and digits in your e-mail address validations, the regular expression to validate e-mail addresses of only three characters would be "\w@\w". Now you are one step ahead in your e-mail address validation process. Instead of allowing only A, B, or C in the first part of e-mail (as expressed by regular expression [ABC]@.), now you are allowing any word character as the first part as well as second part.

More Powers to Regular Expressions

Until now, you have seen only three methods of the `String` class using the regular expressions. The package `java.util.regex` contains three classes to support the full version of regular expressions. Those classes are as follows:

- `Pattern`
- `Matcher`
- `PatternSyntaxException`

A `Pattern` holds the compiled form of a regular expression. The compiled form of a regular expression is its specialized in-memory representation to facilitate faster string matching.

A `Matcher` associates the string to be matched with a `Pattern` and it performs the actual match.

A `PatternSyntaxException` represents an error in a malformed regular expression.

Compiling Regular Expressions

A `Pattern` holds the compiled form of a regular expression. It is immutable. It can be shared. It has no `public` constructor. The class contains a static `compile()` method, which returns a `Pattern` object. The `compile()` method is overloaded:

- `static Pattern compile(String regex)`
- `static Pattern compile(String regex, int flags)`

The following snippet of code compiles a regular expression into a `Pattern` object:

```
// Prepare a regular expression
String regex = "[a-z]@.";

// Compile the regular expression into a Pattern object
Pattern p = Pattern.compile(regex);
```

The second version of the `compile()` method lets you specify flags that modify the way the pattern is matched. The `flags` parameter is a bit mask. The flags are defines as `int` constants in the `Pattern` class, as listed in Table 18-3.

Table 18-3. *List of Flags Defined in the Pattern Class*

Flag	Description
Pattern.CANON_EQ	Enables canonical equivalence. If this flag is set, two characters match only if their full canonical decompositions match.
Pattern.CASE_INSENSITIVE	Enables case-insensitive matching. This flag sets the case-insensitive matching only for US-ASCII charset. For case-insensitive matching of Unicode charset, the UNICODE_CASE flag should also be set in conjunction with this flag.
Pattern.COMMENTS	Permits whitespace and comments in pattern. When this flag is set, whitespace is ignored and embedded comments starting with # are ignored until the end of a line.
Pattern.DOTALL	Enables *dotall* mode. By default, the expression . (a dot) does not match line terminators. When this flag is set, the expression matches any character, including a line terminator.
Pattern.LITERAL	Enables literal parsing of the pattern. When this flag is set, the characters in the regular expression are treated literally. That is, metacharacters and escape sequences have no special meanings. CASE_INSENSTIVE and UNICODE_CASE flags retain their effects when used with this flag.
Pattern.MULTILINE	Enables multiline mode. By default, the expressions ^ and $ match the beginning and the end of the entire input sequence. When this flag is set, they match just after and just before a line terminator or the end of the input sequence, respectively.
Pattern.UNICODE_CASE	Enables Unicode-aware case folding. When this flag is set in conjunction with the CASE_INSENSITIVE flag, the case-insensitive matching is performed according to the Unicode standard.
Pattern.UNICODE_CHARACTER_CLASS	Enables the Unicode version of predefined character classes and POSIX character classes. Setting this flag also has the effect of setting the UNICODE_CASE flag. When this flag is set, the (US-ASCII only) Predefined character classes and POSIX character classes are in conformance with Unicode Technical Standard #18: Unicode Regular Expression Annex C: Compatibility Properties.
Pattern.UNIX_LINES	Enables UNIX lines mode. When this flag is set, only the \n character is recognized as a line terminator.

The following snippet of code compiles a regular expression setting the CASE_INSENSTIVE and DOTALL flags, so the matching will be case-insensitive for US-ASCII charset and the expression . (a dot) will match a line terminator. For example, "A@\n" will be matched by the following pattern:

```
// Prepare a regular expression
String regex = "[a-z]@.";

// Compile the regular expression into a Pattern object with
// the CASE_INSENSITIVE and DOTALL flags
Pattern p = Pattern.compile(regex, Pattern.CASE_INSENSITIVE | Pattern.DOTALL);
```

Creating a Matcher

An instance of the Matcher class is used to perform a match on a sequence of characters by interpreting the compiled pattern held in a Pattern object. It has no public constructor. The matcher() method of the Pattern class is used to get an instance of the Matcher class. The method takes the string to be matched by the pattern as an argument. The following snippet of code shows how to get a Matcher:

```
// Create a Pattern object and compile it into a Pattern
String regex = "[a-z]@.";
Pattern p = Pattern.compile(regex);

// String to perform the match
String str = "abc@yahoo.com,123@cnn.com,ksharan@jdojo.com";

// Get a matcher object using Pattern object p for str
Matcher m = p.matcher(str);
```

At this point, the Matcher object, m, has associated the pattern represented in the Pattern object p with the sequence of characters in str. It is ready to start the match operation. Typically, a Matcher object is used to find a match in the sequence of characters. The match may succeed or fail. If the match succeeds, you may be interested in knowing the start and end positions of the match and the matched text. You can query a Matcher object to get all these pieces of information.

Matching the Pattern

You need to use the following methods of the Matcher to perform the match on the input:

- The find() method
- The start() method
- The end() method
- The group() method

The find() method is used to find a match for the pattern in the input. If the find succeeds, it returns true. Otherwise, it returns false. The first call to this method starts the search for the pattern at the beginning of the input. If the previous call to this method was successful, the next call to this method starts the search after the previous match. Typically, a call to the find() method is used in a while-loop to find all the matches. It is an overloaded method. Another version of the find() method takes an integer argument, which is the offset to start the find for a match.

The start() method returns the start index of the previous match. Typically, it is used after a successful find() method call.

The end() method returns the index of the last character in the matched string plus one. Therefore, after a successful invocation of the find() method, the difference between the values returned by the end() and start() methods will give you the length of the matched string. Using the substring() method of the String class, you can get the matched string as follows:

```
// Continued from previous fragment of code
if (m.find()) {
    // str is the string we are looking into
    String foundStr = str.substring(m.start(), m.end());

    System.out.println("Found string is:" + foundStr);
}
```

The group() method returns the found string by the previous successful find() method call. Recall that you can also get the previous matched string using the substring() method of the String class by using the start and end of the match. Therefore, the previous snippet of code can be replaced with the following code:

```
if (m.find()) {
    String foundStr = m.group();
    System.out.println("Found text is:" + foundStr);
}
```

Listing 18-3 illustrates the use of these methods. The validations for the method's arguments have been omitted for clarity. The program attempts to find the "[abc]@." pattern in different strings.

Listing 18-3. Using Pattern and Matcher Classes

```
// PatternMatcher.java
package com.jdojo.regex;

import java.util.regex.Pattern;
import java.util.regex.Matcher;

public class PatternMatcher {
    public static void main(String[] args) {
        String regex = "[abc]@.";

        String source = "cric@jdojo.com is a valid email address";
        PatternMatcher.findPattern(regex, source);

        source = "kelly@jdojo.com is invalid";
        PatternMatcher.findPattern(regex, source);

        source = "a@band@yea@u";
        PatternMatcher.findPattern(regex, source);

        source = "There is an @ sign here";
        PatternMatcher.findPattern(regex, source);
    }
```

```java
public static void findPattern(String regex, String source) {
    // Compile regex into a Pattern object
    Pattern p = Pattern.compile(regex);

    // Get a Matcher object
    Matcher m = p.matcher(source);

    // Print regex and source text
    System.out.println("\nRegex: " + regex);
    System.out.println("Text: " + source);

    // Perform find
    boolean found = false;
    while (m.find()) {
        System.out.printf("Matched Text: %s, Start: %s, End: %s%n",
                m.group(), m.start(), m.end());

        // We found at least one match. Set the found flag to true
        found = true;
    }

    if (!found) {
        // We did not find any match
        System.out.println("No match found");
    }
}
}
```

```
Regex: [abc]@.
Text: cric@jdojo.com is a valid email address
Matched Text: c@j, Start: 3, End: 6

Regex: [abc]@.
Text: kelly@jdojo.com is invalid
No match found

Regex: [abc]@.
Text: a@band@yea@u
Matched Text: a@b, Start: 0, End: 3
Matched Text: a@u, Start: 9, End: 12

Regex: [abc]@.
Text: There is an @ sign here
No match found
```

Querying a Match

In the previous section, I showed you how to query a Matcher for the state (or details) of a match. The methods to get such states were start(), end(), group(), and groupCount(). The match state can also be represented as an instance of MatchResult, which is an interface. You can use the following methods of MatchResult to get the match state:

- int end()

- int end(int group)

- String group()

- String group(int group)

- int groupCount()

- int start()

- int start(int group)

How do you get an instance of MatchResult? Call the toMatchResult() method of a Matcher get to a copy of the match state:

```
Matcher m = /* get a matcher here */

while (m.find()) {
    MatchResult result = m.toMatchResult();

    // Use result here...
}
```

Why would you use a MatchResult to get the match state instead of methods on the Matcher? There are two reasons:

- The toMatchResult() of the Matcher returns a copy of the match state, which means any subsequent change in the match state of the Matcher will not affect the MatchResult. During matching, you can collect all match states into instances of MatchResult and analyze them later in your program.

- A MatchResult is immutable. If you have processors to process matches, you can safely pass MatchResult instances to those processors. Passing the Matcher is not safe because the processor may accidently modify the Matcher, which will affect your program in an unintentional way.

There are a few methods in the Matcher class that work with MatchResult. I cover them later in this chapter. For now, just remember that a MatchResult contains a copy of the details of a match.

Beware of Backslashes

Beware of using backslashes in regular expressions. The character class \w (that is, a backslash followed by a w) represents a word character. Recall that a backslash character is also used as a part of an escape character. Therefore, \w must be written as \\w as a string literal. You can also use a backslash to nullify the special meaning of metacharacters. For example, a [marks the beginning of a character class. What would be the regular expression that will match a digit enclosed in brackets, for example, [1], [5], etc.? Note that the regular expression [0-9] will match any digit. The digit may or may not be enclosed in a bracket. You may think about using [[0-9]]. It will not give you any error; however, it will not do the job either. You can also embed a character class within another. For example, you can write [a-z[0-9]], which is the same as [a-z0-9]. In this case, the first [in [[0-9]] should be treated as an ordinary character, not as a metacharacter. You must use a backslash as \[[0-9]\]. To write this regular expression as a string literal, you need to use two backslashes as "\\[[0-9]\\]]" when you enclose it in double quotes.

Quantifiers in Regular Expressions

You can also specify the number of times a character in a regular expression may match the sequence of characters. If you want to match all two digit integers, your regular expression would be \d\d, which is the same as [0-9][0-9]. What would be the regular expression to match any integer? You cannot write the regular expression to match any integer with the knowledge you have gained so far. You need to be able to express a pattern "one digit or more" using a regular expression. Here comes the concept of quantifiers. Quantifiers and their meanings are listed in Table 18-4.

Table 18-4. *Quantifiers and Their Meanings*

Quantifier	Meaning
*	Zero or more times
+	One or more times
?	Once or not at all
{m}	Exactly m times
{m, }	At least m times
{m, n}	At least m times but not more than n times

It is important to note that quantifiers must follow a character or character class for which it specifies the quantity. The regular expression to match any integer would be \d+, which says that match one or more number of digits. Is this solution for matching integer correct? No, it is not. Suppose your text is "This is text123 which contains 10 and 120". If you run your pattern \d+ against this string, it will match against 123, 10, and 120. Note that 123 is not used as an integer; rather it is a part of word text123. If you are looking for integers inside text, certainly 123 in text123 does not qualify as an integer. You want to match all integers that form a word in the text.

Necessity is the mother of invention. Now you need to specify that the match should be performed only on word boundaries, not inside text having embedded integers. This is necessary to exclude integer 123 from your previous result. The next section discusses the use of metacharacters to match boundaries.

With the knowledge you have gained in this section, let's improve your e-mail address validation. Inside an e-mail address, there must be one and only one @ sign. To specify one and only one character, you use that character one time in the regular expression although you can use {1} as the quantifier. For example, X{1} and X means the same inside a regular expression. You are fine on this account. However, your solution until now supports only one character before and after the @ sign. In reality, there can be more than one character before and after the @ sign in an e-mail address. You can specify the pattern to validate an e-mail address as \w+@\w+, which means: one or more word characters, an @ sign, and one or more word characters.

Matching Boundaries

Until now, you did not care about the location of the pattern match in the text. Sometimes, you may be interested in knowing if the match occurred at the beginning of a line. You may be interested in finding and replacing a particular match only if the match was found in a word, not as part of any word. For example, you may want to replace the word apple inside a string with the word orange. Suppose your string is "I have an apple and five pineapples". Certainly, you do not want to replace all occurrences of apple with orange in this string. If you do, your new string would be "I have an orange and five pineoranges". In fact, you want the new string to be "I have an orange and five pineapples". You want to match the word apple as a standalone word, not the part of any other word.

Table 18-5 lists all boundary matchers that can be used in a regular expression.

Table 18-5. *List of Boundary Matchers Inside Regular Expressions*

Boundary Matcher	Meaning
^	The beginning of a line
$	The end of a line
\b	A word boundary
\B	A non-word boundary
\A	The beginning of the input
\G	The end of previous match
\Z	The end of the input but for the final terminator, if any
\z	The end of the input

In Java, a word character is defined by [a-zA-Z_0-9]. A word boundary is a zero-width match that can match the following:

- Between a word character and a non-word character

- Start of the string and a word character

- A word character and the end of the string

A non-word boundary is also a zero-width match and it is the opposite of the word boundary. It matches the following:

- The empty string

- Between two word characters

- Between two non-word characters

- Between a non-word character and the start or end of the string

The regular expression to match the word apple would be \bapple\b, which means the following: a word boundary, the word apple, and a word boundary. Listing 18-4 demonstrates how to match a word boundary using a regular expression.

Listing 18-4. Matching a Word Boundary

```java
// MatchBoundary.java
package com.jdojo.regex;

public class MatchBoundary {
    public static void main(String[] args) {
        // Prepare regular expression. Use \\b to get \b inside the string literal.
        String regex = "\\bapple\\b";
        String replacementStr = "orange";
        String inputStr = "I have an apple and five pineapples";
        String newStr = inputStr.replaceAll(regex, replacementStr);

        System.out.printf("Regular Expression: %s%n", regex);
        System.out.printf("Input String: %s%n", inputStr);
        System.out.printf("Replacement String: %s%n", replacementStr);
        System.out.printf("New String: %s%n", newStr);
    }
}
```

```
Regular Expression: \bapple\b
Input String: I have an apple and five pineapples
Replacement String: orange
New String: I have an orange and five pineapples
```

There are two boundary matchers: ^ (beginning of a line) and \A (beginning of the input). Input string may consist of multiple lines. In that case, \A will match the beginning of the entire input string, whereas ^ will match the beginning of each line in the input. For example, regular expression "^The" will match the input string, which is in the beginning of any line.

Groups and Back Referencing

You can treat multiple characters as a unit by using them as a group. A group is created inside a regular expression by enclosing one or more characters inside parentheses. (ab), ab(z), ab(ab)(xyz), (the((is) (is))) are examples of groups. Each group in a regular expression has a group number. The group number starts at 1. The Matcher class has a method groupCount() that returns the number of groups in the pattern associated with the Matcher instance. There is a special group called group 0 (zero). It refers to the entire regular expression. The group 0 is not reported by the groupCount() method.

How is each group numbered? Each left parenthesis inside a regular expression marks the start of a new group. Table 18-6 lists some examples of group numbering in a regular expression. Note that I have also listed group 0 for all regular expressions although it is not reported by the groupCount() method of the Matcher class. The last example in the list shows that the group 0 is present, even if there are no explicit groups present in the regular expression.

Table 18-6. *Examples of Groups in Regular Expressions*

Regular Expression: AB(XY)

Number of groups reported by `Matcher` class's `groupCount()` method: 1

Group Number	Group Text
0	AB(XY)
1	(XY)

Regular Expression: (AB)(XY)

Number of groups reported by `Matcher` class's `groupCount()` method: 2

Group Number	Group Text
0	(AB)(XY)
1	(AB)
2	(XY)

Regular Expression: ((A)((X)(Y)))

Number of groups reported by `Matcher` class's `groupCount()` method: 5

Group Number	Group Text
0	((A)((X)(Y)))
1	((A)((X)(Y)))
2	(A)
3	((X)(Y))
4	(X)
5	(Y)

Regular Expression: ABXY

Number of groups reported by `Matcher` class's `groupCount()` method: 0

Group Number	Group Text
0	ABXY

You can also back reference group numbers in a regular expression. Suppose you want to match text that starts with "ab" followed by "xy", which is followed by "ab". You can write a regular expression as "abxyab". You can also achieve the same result by forming a group that contains "ab" and back referencing it as "(ab)xy\1". Here, "\1" refers to group 1, which is "(ab)" in this case. You can use "\2" to refer to group 2, "\3" to refer to group 3, and so on. How will regular expression "(ab)xy\12" be interpreted? You have used "\12" as the group back reference. The regular expression engine is smart enough to detect that it contains only one group in "(ab)xy\12". It uses "\1" as back reference to group 1, which is "(ab)" and 2 as an ordinary character. Therefore, the regular expression "(ab)xy\12" is the same as "abxyab2". If a regular expression has 12 or more groups, \12 in the regular expression will refer to the 12th group.

You can also fetch part of a matched text by using a group number in the regular expression. The `group()` method in the `Matcher` class is overloaded. You have already seen the `group()` method, which takes no arguments. Another version of the method takes a group number as an argument and returns the matched text by that group. Suppose you have phone numbers embedded in the input text. All phone numbers occur as a word and are ten digits long. The first three digits are the area code. The regular expression `\b\d{10}\b` will match all phone numbers in the input text. However, to get the first three digits (the area code), you will have to write extra code. If you form a regular expression using groups, you can get the area code using the group number. The regular expression placing the first three digits of a phone number in a group would be \b(\d{3})\d{7}\b. If m is the reference to a Matcher object associated with this pattern, m.group(1) will return the first three digits of the phone number after a successful match. You can also use m.group(0) to get the entire matched text. Listing 18-5 illustrates the use of groups in regular expressions to get the area code part of phone numbers. Note that 2339829 does not match the pattern because it has only 7 digits whereas the pattern used looks for only 10-digit phone numbers.

Listing 18-5. Using Groups in Regular Expressions

```java
// PhoneMatcher.java
package com.jdojo.regex;

import java.util.regex.Pattern;
import java.util.regex.Matcher;

public class PhoneMatcher {
    public static void main(String[] args) {
        // Prepare a regular expression: A group of 3 digits followed by 7 digits.
        String regex = "\\b(\\d{3})\\d{7}\\b";

        // Compile the regular expression
        Pattern p = Pattern.compile(regex);

        String source = "3342449027, 2339829, and 6152534734";

        // Get the Matcher object
        Matcher m = p.matcher(source);

        // Start matching and display the found area codes
        while (m.find()) {
            String phone = m.group();
            String areaCode = m.group(1);
            System.out.printf("Phone: %s, Area Code: %s%n", phone, areaCode);
        }
    }
}
```

```
Phone: 3342449027, Area Code: 334
Phone: 6152534734, Area Code: 615
```

Groups are also used to format or replace the matched string with another string. Suppose you want to format all 10-digit phone numbers as (xxx) xxx-xxxx, where an x denotes a digit. As you can see, the phone number is in three groups: the first three digits, the next three digits, and the last four digits. You need to form a regular expression using three groups so you can refer to the three matched groups by their group numbers. The regular expression would be \b(\d{3})(\d{3})(\d{4})\b. The \b in the beginning and in the end denotes that you are interested in matching ten digits only at word boundaries. The following snippet of code illustrates how you can display formatted phone numbers:

```
// Prepare the regular expression
String regex = "\\b(\\d{3})(\\d{3})(\\d{4})\\b";

// Compile the regular expression
Pattern p = Pattern.compile(regex);

String source = "3342449027, 2339829, and 6152534734";

// Get Matcher object
Matcher m = p.matcher(source);

// Start match and display formatted phone numbers
while (m.find()) {
    System.out.printf("Phone: %s, Formatted Phone: (%s) %s-%s%n",
            m.group(), m.group(1), m.group(2), m.group(3));
}
```

```
Phone: 3342449027, Formatted Phone: (334) 244-9027
Phone: 6152534734, Formatted Phone: (615) 253-4734
```

You can also replace all 10-digit phone numbers in the input text by formatted phone numbers. You have already learned how to replace the matched text with another text using the replaceAll() method of the String class. The Matcher class also has a replaceAll() method, which accomplishes the same thing. The problem you are facing in replacing the phone numbers by the formatted phone numbers is getting the matched parts of the matched phone numbers. In this case, the replacement text also contains the matched text. You do not know what text matches the pattern in advance. Groups come to your rescue. $n, where n is a group number, inside replacement text refers to the matched text for group n. For example, $1 refers to the first matched group. The replacement text to replace the phone numbers with the formatted phone numbers will be ($1) $2-$3. Listing 18-6 illustrates the technique of referencing groups in replacement text.

Listing 18-6. Back Referencing a Group in Replacement Text

```
// MatchAndReplace.java
package com.jdojo.regex;

import java.util.regex.Matcher;
import java.util.regex.Pattern;

public class MatchAndReplace {
    public static void main(String[] args) {
        // Prepare the regular expression
        String regex = "\\b(\\d{3})(\\d{3})(\\d{4})\\b";
        String replacementText = "($1) $2-$3";
        String source = "3342449027, 2339829, and 6152534734";

        // Compile the regular expression
        Pattern p = Pattern.compile(regex);
```

```
        // Get Matcher object
        Matcher m = p.matcher(source);

        // Replace the phone numbers by formatted phone numbers
        String formattedSource = m.replaceAll(replacementText);

        System.out.printf("Text: %s%n", source );
        System.out.printf("Formatted Text: %s%n", formattedSource );
    }
}
```

```
Text: 3342449027, 2339829, and 6152534734
Formatted Text: (334) 244-9027, 2339829, and (615) 253-4734
```

You can also achieve the same result by using the String class. You do not need to use the Pattern and Matcher classes at all. The following snippet of code illustrates the same concept, using the String class instead. The String class uses Pattern and Matcher class internally to get the result.

```
// Prepare the regular expression
String regex = "\\b(\\d{3})(\\d{3})(\\d{4})\\b";
String replacementText = "($1) $2-$3";
String source = "3342449027, 2339829, and 6152534734";

// Use replaceAll() method of the String class
String formattedSource = source.replaceAll(regex, replacementText)
```

The Matcher class contains the following replaceAll() and replaceFirst() methods:

- String replaceAll(String replacement)

- String replaceAll(Function<MatchResult,String> replacer)

- String replaceFirst(String replacement)

- String replaceFirst(Function<MatchResult,String> replacer)

▓ **Tip**   The replaceAll(Function<MatchResult,String> replacer) and replaceFirst(Function<Match Result,String> replacer) methods were added to the Matcher class in Java 9.

The replaceAll(String) and replaceFirst(String) methods work the same as the methods with the same name in the String class as I have explained them in this section. The other versions take a Function<MatchResult,String> as an argument. The Function takes a MatchResult and returns a replacement string. These methods give you a chance to use your logic inside the Function to get the replacement string. All the four methods first reset the matcher before performing the find and replace. Function<T,R> is an interface in the java.util.function package. I discuss the Function interface in Chapter 5 of the second volume of this series.

Suppose you want to find 10-digit phone numbers in an input string and you want to mask all phone numbers with the area code 334. For example, if a phone number is 3342449027, you want to replace it with (***) ***-****. You can do so using the new replaceAll() method in the Matcher class. Listing 18-7 contains the complete program.

Listing 18-7. Using Logic to Mask or Format Phone Number Depending on the Area Code

```java
// MaskAndFormat.java
package com.jdojo.regex;

import java.util.regex.MatchResult;
import java.util.regex.Matcher;
import java.util.regex.Pattern;

public class MaskAndFormat {
    public static void main(String[] args) {
        // Prepare the regular expression
        String regex = "\\b(\\d{3})(\\d{3})(\\d{4})\\b";
        String source = "3342449027, 2339829, and 6152534734";

        // Compile the regular expression
        Pattern p = Pattern.compile(regex);

        // Get Matcher object
        Matcher m = p.matcher(source);

        // Replace the phone numbers by formatted phone numbers
        String formattedSource = m.replaceAll(MaskAndFormat::mask);

        System.out.printf("Text: %s%n", source );
        System.out.printf("Formatted Text: %s%n", formattedSource );
    }

    private static String mask(MatchResult result) {
        String replacementText = "($1) $2-$3";

        String areaCode = result.group(1);
        if("334".equals(areaCode)) {
            replacementText = "(***) ***-****";
        }

        return replacementText;
    }
}
```

```
Text: 3342449027, 2339829, and 6152534734
Formatted Text: (***) ***-****, 2339829, and (615) 253-4734
```

Note use of the following statement in the main() method:

```java
String formattedSource = m.replaceAll(MaskAndFormat::mask);
```

The argument to the replaceAll() method is MaskAndFormat::mask, which is a method reference to the mask() static method of the MaskAndFormat class. When a match is found, the MatchResult is passed to the mask() method and returned string from the method is used as replacement text. Notice how you have masked the phone number with the area code 334 inside the mask() method. All other area codes uses the same replacement text as was used in the previous example.

Using Named Groups

Using group numbers in a big regular expression is cumbersome. Java also supports named groups. You can do everything with the group name as you were able to do using the group numbers in the previous section:

- You can name a group.

- You can back reference groups using their names.

- You can reference group names in replacement text.

- You can get the matched text using the group names.

As before, you need to use a pair of parentheses to create a group. The start parenthesis is followed by a ? and a group name placed in angle brackets. The format to define a named group is as follows:

```
(?<groupName>pattern)
```

The group name must consist of only letters and digits: a through z, A through Z, and 0 through 9. The group name must start with a letter. The following is an example of a regular expression that uses three named groups. The group names are areaCode, prefix, and lineNumber. The regular expression is to match a 10-digit phone number.

```
\b(?<areaCode>\d{3})(?<prefix>\d{3})(?<lineNumber>\d{4})\b
```

You can use \k<groupName> to back reference the group named groupName. The area code and prefix parts in a phone number use the same pattern. You can rewrite the previous regular expression that back reference the areaCode group as the following:

```
\b(?<areaCode>\d{3})\k<areaCode>(?<lineNumber>\d{4})\b
```

You can reference a named group in replacement text as ${groupName}. The following snippet of code shows a regular expression with three named groups and replacement text referencing those three groups using their names:

```
String regex = "\\b(?<areaCode>\\d{3})(?<prefix>\\d{3})(?<lineNumber>\\d{4})\\b";
String replacementText = "(${areaCode}) ${prefix}-${lineNumber}";
```

When you name a group, the group still gets a group number, as discussed in the previous section. You can still refer to a group by its group number even though it has a name. The previous snippet code is rewritten as follows in which the third group, which has been named lineNumber, is referenced using its group number as $3 in the replacement text:

```
String regex = "\\b(?<areaCode>\\d{3})(?<prefix>\\d{3})(?<lineNumber>\\d{4})\\b";
String replacementText = "(${areaCode}) ${prefix}-$3";
```

After a successful match, you can use the group(String groupName) method of the Matcher class to get the matched text for the group.

Listing 18-8 shows how to use group names in a regular expression and how to use the names in replacement text.

Listing 18-8. Using Named Groups in Regular Expressions

```java
// NamedGroups.java
package com.jdojo.regex;

import java.util.regex.Matcher;
import java.util.regex.Pattern;

public class NamedGroups {
    public static void main(String[] args) {
        // Prepare the regular expression
        String regex =
            "\\b(?<areaCode>\\d{3})(?<prefix>\\d{3})(?<lineNumber>\\d{4})\\b";

        // Reference first two groups by names and the third one as its number
        String replacementText = "(${areaCode}) ${prefix}-$3";

        String source = "3342449027, 2339829, and 6152534734";

        // Compile the regular expression
        Pattern p = Pattern.compile(regex);

        // Get Matcher object
        Matcher m = p.matcher(source);

        // Replace the phone numbers by formatted phone numbers
        String formattedSource = m.replaceAll(replacementText);

        System.out.printf("Text: %s%n", source);
        System.out.printf("Formatted Text: %s%n", formattedSource);
    }
}
```

```
Text: 3342449027, 2339829, and 6152534734
Formatted Text: (334) 244-9027, 2339829, and (615) 253-4734
```

After a successful match using the find() method of the Matcher class, you can use its start() and end() methods to know the match boundary for groups. These methods are overloaded:

- int start()
- int start(int groupNumber)
- int start(String groupName)
- int end()
- int end(int groupNumber)
- int end(String groupName)

The methods that take no arguments return the start and end of the previous match. Other two sets of methods return the start and end of a group in the previous match. The following snippet of code uses the previous example of matching 10-digit phone number in a string. It prints the start of each group for each successful match.

```
// Prepare the regular expression
String regex = "\\b(?<areaCode>\\d{3})(?<prefix>\\d{3})(?<lineNumber>\\d{4})\\b";

String source = "3342449027, 2339829, and 6152534734";
System.out.println("Source Text: " + source);

// Compile the regular expression
Pattern p = Pattern.compile(regex);

// Get Matcher object
Matcher m = p.matcher(source);

while(m.find()) {
    String matchedText = m.group();
    int start1 = m.start("areaCode");
    int start2 = m.start("prefix");
    int start3 = m.start("lineNumber");

    System.out.printf("Matched Text: %s", matchedText);
    System.out.printf(". Area code start: %d", start1);
    System.out.printf(", Prefix start: %d", start2);
    System.out.printf(", Line Number start: %d%n", start3);
}
```

```
Source Text: 3342449027, 2339829, and 6152534734
Matched Text: 3342449027. Area code start: 0, Prefix start: 3, Line Number start: 6
Matched Text: 6152534734. Area code start: 25, Prefix start: 28, Line Number start: 31
```

Resetting the Matcher

If you have finished matching a pattern against input text and you want to restart matching from the beginning of the input text again, you need to use the reset() method of the Matcher class. After a call to the reset() method, the next call to match a pattern will start from the beginning of the input text. The reset() method is overloaded. Another version allows you to associate a different input text with the pattern. These two versions of reset() methods allow you to reuse any existing instance of the Matcher class if your pattern remains the same. This enhances the performance of your program by avoiding the need to recreate a new Matcher object to perform matches against the same pattern.

Final Words on E-Mail Validations

You now have learned the major parts of regular expressions. You are ready to complete your e-mail address validation example. Your e-mail addresses will be validated against the following rules:

- All e-mail addresses will be of the form name@domain.

- The name part must start with an alphanumeric character (a-z, A-Z, 0-9).

- The name part must have at least one character.

- The name part may have any alphanumeric character (a-z, A-Z, 0-9), underscore, hyphen, or dot.

- The domain part must contain at least one dot.

- The dot in domain part must be preceded and followed by at least one alphanumeric character.

- You should also be able to refer to the name and the domain parts using group numbers. This validation states that you place name and domain part as groups inside the regular expression.

The following regular expression will match an e-mail address according to these rules. Group 1 is the name part, whereas group 2 is the domain part.

```
([a-zA-Z0-9]+[\\w\\-.]*)@([a-zA-Z0-9]+\\.[a-zA-Z0-9\\-.]+)
```

The more validations you add, the more complex the regular expression. Readers are encouraged to add some more validations for e-mail addresses and modify the previous regular expression accordingly. This regular expression allows two consecutive dots in the domain part. How would you prevent that?

Find-and-Replace Using Regular Expressions

Find-and-replace is a very powerful technique supported by regular expressions. Sometimes you may be required to find a pattern and replace it depending upon the text it matches; that is, the replacement text is decided based on some conditions. The Java regular expression designers visualized this need and they have included two methods in the Matcher class that let you accomplish this task:

- Matcher appendReplacement(StringBuffer sb, String replacement)

- Matcher appendReplacement(StringBuilder sb, String replacement)

- StringBuffer appendTail(StringBuffer sb)

- StringBuffer appendTail(StringBuilder sb)

▒ **Tip**   The versions of the appendReplacement() and appendTail() methods that work with a StringBuilder were added in Java 9.

Consider the following text:

```
"A train carrying 125 men and women was traveling at the speed of 100 miles per hour. The
train fare was 75 dollars per person."
```

You want to find all numbers in the text (e.g., 125, 100, and 75) and replace them as follows:

- "100" by "a hundred"

- "> 100" by "more than a hundred"

- "< 100" by "less than a hundred"

After replacement, this text should read as follows:

```
"A train carrying more than a hundred men and women was traveling at the speed of a hundred
miles per hour. The train fare was less than a hundred dollars per person."
```

To accomplish this task, you need to find all numbers embedded in the text, compare the found number with 100, and decide on the replacement text. Such a situation also arises when you find and replace text using a text editor. The text editor highlights the word you were searching for, you enter a new word, and text editor does the replacement for you. You can also create a find/replace program as found in text editors using these two methods. Typically, these methods are used in conjunction with the find() method of the Matcher class. The steps that are performed to accomplish find and replace texts using these two methods are outlined here.

1. Create a Pattern object.

2. Create a Matcher object.

3. Create a StringBuffer/StringBuilder object to hold the result.

4. Use the find() method in a loop to match the pattern.

5. Call the appendReplacement() and appendTail() methods depending on the position of the found match.

Let's create a Pattern by compiling the regular expression. Since you want to find all numbers, your regular expression would be \b\d+\b. Note the first and last \b. They specify that you are interested in numbers only on word boundaries.

```
String regex = "\\b\\d+\\b"; Pattern p = Pattern.compile(regex);
```

Create a Matcher by associating the pattern with the text.

```
String text = "A train carrying 125 men and women was traveling" +
              " at the speed of 100 miles per hour. The train" +
              " fare was 75 dollars per person.";
Matcher m = p.matcher(text);
```

Create a StringBuilder to hold the new text:

```
StringBuilder sb = new StringBuilder();
```

Start using the `find()` method on the `Matcher` object to find a match. When you invoke the `find()` method for the first time, the number 125 will match the pattern. At this point, you would like to prepare the replacement text depending on the matched text as:

```
String replacementText = "";

// Get the matched text. Recall that group() method returns the whole matched text
String matchedText = m.group();

// Convert the text into integer for comparison
int num = Integer.parseInt(matchedText);

// Prepare the replacement text
if (num == 100) {
    replacementText = "a hundred";
} else if (num < 100) {
    replacementText = "less than a hundred";
} else {
    replacementText = "more than a hundred";
}
```

Now, you will call the `appendReplacement()` method on the `Matcher` object, passing an empty `StringBuilder` and `replacementText` as arguments. In this case, `replacementText` has a string "more than hundred" because the `find()` method call matched the number 125.

```
m.appendReplacement(sb, replacementText);
```

It is interesting to know what the `appendReplacement()` method call does. It checks if there was a previous match. Because this is the first call to the `find()` method, there is no previous match. For the first match, it appends the text starting from the beginning of the input text until the character before the matching text. In your case, the following text is appended to the `StringBuilder`. At this point, the text in the `StringBuilder` is

```
"A train carrying "
```

Now the `appendReplacement()` method appends the text in the `replacementText` argument to the `StringBuilder`. This will change the `StringBuilder` contents to:

```
"A train carrying more than a hundred"
```

The `appendReplacement()` method does one more thing. It sets the append position, which is an internal state of the `Matcher` object, to the character position just after the first matching text. In your case, the append position will be set to the character following 125, which is the position of the space character that follows 125. This finishes the first find and replace step.

You will call the `find()` method of the `Matcher` object again. It will find the pattern, that is, another number, which is 100. You will compute the value of the replacement text using the same procedure as you did after the first match. This time, the `replacementText` will contain the string "a hundred". You call `appendReplacement()` method as follows:

```
m.appendReplacement(sb, replacementText);
```

Again, it checks if there was a previous match. Since this was the second call to the find() method, it will find a previous match and it will use the append position saved by the last appendReplacement() call as the starting position. The last character to be appended will be the character just before the second match. It will also set the append position to the character position following the number 100. At this point, the StringBuilder contains the following text:

"A train carrying more than a hundred men and women was traveling at the speed of a hundred"

When you call the find() method for the third time, it will find the number 75 and the StringBuilder content will be as follows after the replacement. The append position will be set to the character position following the number 75.

"A train carrying more than a hundred men and women was traveling at the speed of a hundred miles per hour. The train fare was less than a hundred"

If you call the find() method again, it will not find any match. However, the StringBuilder does not contain the text following the last match, which is "dollars per person." To append the text following the last match, you need to call the appendTail() method. It appends the text to the StringBuilder starting at append position until the end of the input string. The call to this method

m.appendTail(sb);

will modify the StringBuilder to this:

"A train carrying more than a hundred men and women was traveling at the speed of a hundred miles per hour. The train fare was less than a hundred dollars per person."

What will the content of the StringBuilder be if you would have called the appendTail() method just after the second call to the appendReplacement() method? The complete program is shown in Listing 18-9.

Listing 18-9. Find-and-Replace Using Regular Expressions and appendReplacement() and appendTail() Methods

```java
// AdvancedFindReplace.java
package com.jdojo.regex;

import java.util.regex.Pattern;
import java.util.regex.Matcher;

public class AdvancedFindReplace {
    public static void main(String[] args) {
        String regex = "\\b\\d+\\b";
        StringBuilder sb = new StringBuilder();

        String text = "A train carrying 125 men and women was traveling at"
                + " the speed of 100 miles per hour. "
                + "The train fare was 75 dollars per person.";

        Pattern p = Pattern.compile(regex);
        Matcher m = p.matcher(text);
```

```
    while (m.find()) {
        String matchedText = m.group();

        // Convert the text into an integer for comparing
        int num = Integer.parseInt(matchedText);

        // Prepare the replacement text
        String replacementText;
        if (num == 100) {
            replacementText = "a hundred";
        } else if (num < 100) {
            replacementText = "less than a hundred";
        } else {
            replacementText = "more than a hundred";
        }

        m.appendReplacement(sb, replacementText);
    }

    // Append the tail
    m.appendTail(sb);

    // Display the old and new text
    System.out.printf("Old Text: %s%n", text);
    System.out.printf("New Text: %s%n", sb.toString());
    }
}
```

```
Old Text: A train carrying 125 men and women was traveling at the speed of 100 miles per
hour. The train fare was 75 dollars per person.
New Text: A train carrying more than a hundred men and women was traveling at the speed of
a hundred miles per hour. The train fare was less than a hundred dollars per person.
```

Streams of Matched Results

Java 9 added a new method to the Matcher class that returns a stream of MatchResult:

```
Stream<MatchResult> results()
```

The Streams API is a vast topic. It lets you apply filter-map-reduce operations to a stream of data. I cover the Streams API in Chapter 13 of the second volume of this series. I present an example of using the results() method to complete the discussion of the Matcher class. If you have difficulty undemanding the examples in this section, revisit this section after you read about the Streams API.

The results() method returns match results in a stream whose elements are of the MatchResult type. You can query the MatchResult to get the match details. The results() method does not reset the matcher. If you want to reuse the matcher, don't forget to call its reset() method to reset it to a desired position. Operations such as counting number of matches, getting a list of matches, and finding distinct area codes becomes easy when you use the results() methods. Listing 18-10 shows a few interesting uses of this method. It searches for 10-digit or 7-digit phone numbers in an input string. It gets the list of all formatted matched phone numbers. In the second example, it prints a set of distinct area codes in matched results.

695

Listing 18-10. Using the results() Method of the Matcher Class

```java
// DistinctAreaCode.java
package com.jdojo.regex;

import java.util.List;
import java.util.Set;
import java.util.regex.Matcher;
import java.util.regex.Pattern;
import static java.util.stream.Collectors.toList;
import static java.util.stream.Collectors.toSet;

public class DistinctAreaCode {
    public static void main(String[] args) {
        // A regex to match 7-digit or 10-digit phone numbers
        String regex = "\\b(\\d{3})?(\\d{3})(\\d{4})\\b";

        // An input string
        String source = "1, 3342229999, 2330001, 6159996666, 123, 3340909090";
        System.out.println("Input: " + source);

        // Create a matcher
        Matcher matcher = Pattern.compile(regex)
                .matcher(source);

        // Collect formatted phone numbers into a list
        List<String> phones = matcher.results()
                .map(mr -> (mr.group(1) == null ? "" : "(" + mr.group(1) + ") ")
                        + mr.group(2) + "-" + mr.group(3))
                .collect(toList());
        System.out.println("Phones: " + phones);

        // Reset the matcher, so we can reuse it from start
        matcher.reset();

        // Get distinct area codes
        Set<String> areaCodes = matcher.results()
                .filter(mr -> mr.group(1) != null)
                .map(mr -> mr.group(1))
                .collect(toSet());
        System.out.println("Distinct Area Codes: " + areaCodes);
    }
}
```

```
Input: 1, 3342229999, 2330001, 6159996666, 123, 3340909090
Phones: [(334) 222-9999, 233-0001, (615) 999-6666, (334) 090-9090]
Distinct Area Codes: [334, 615]
```

In the `main()` method, the following regular expression will match 7 or 10-digit phone numbers:

```
// A regex to match 7-digit or 10-digit phone numbers
String regex = "\\b(\\d{3})?(\\d{3})(\\d{4})\\b";
```

You want to format a 10-digit phone number as (xxx) xxx-xxxx and a 7-digit phone number as xxx-xxxx. Finally, you want to collect all formatted phone numbers into a List<String>. The following statement performs this:

```
// Collect formatted phone numbers into a list
List<String> phones = matcher.results()
                  .map(mr -> (mr.group(1) == null ? "" : "(" + mr.group(1) + ") ")
                         + mr.group(2) + "-" + mr.group(3))
                  .collect(toList());
```

Note the use of the `map()` method that takes a `MatchResult` and returns a formatted phone number as a `String`. When a match is a 7-digit phone number, the group 1 will be `null`. Now, you want to reuse the matcher to find distinct area codes in 10-digit phone numbers. You must reset the matcher, so the next match starts at the beginning of the input string:

```
// Reset the matcher, so we can reuse it from start
matcher.reset();
```

The first group in the `MatchResult` contains the area code. You need to filter out 7-digit phone numbers and collect the value of group 1 in a `Set<String>` to get a distinct set of area codes. The following statement does this:

```
// Get distinct area codes
Set<String> areaCodes = matcher.results()
                        .filter(mr -> mr.group(1) != null)
                        .map(mr -> mr.group(1))
                        .collect(toSet());
```

Summary

A regular expression is a sequence of characters used as a pattern to match some text. Java provides comprehensive support for using regular expressions through the `Pattern` and `Matcher` classes in the `java.util.regex` package. Several convenience methods for using regular expression exist in the `String` class.

A `Pattern` object represents a compiled regular expression. A `Matcher` object is used to associate a `Pattern` with an input text to be searched for the pattern. The `find()` method of the `Matcher` class is used to find a match for the pattern in the input text. Regular expressions allow you to use groups. Groups are automatically numbered from 1 to N. The first group from left is number 1. A special group 0 exists that contains the entire regular expression. Starting with Java 7, you can also name groups. You can refer to the groups by numbers or their names.

Java 9 added a few useful methods to the `Matcher` class. The `replaceAll()` and `replaceFirst()` methods have been overloaded; now they take a `Function<MatchResult,String>` as a replacer for the matched results, allowing you to use any logic to generate the replacement text for a match. The new `results()` method returns a `Stream<MatchResult>`, allowing you to stream operations to the matched results.

QUESTIONS AND EXERCISES

1. What is a regular expression?

2. What is a metacharacter? How do you use a metacharacter as an ordinary character in a regular expression?

3. What class do you use to compile a pattern?

4. What class do you use to match a compiled pattern?

5. What does the regular expression "[aieou]" mean? Will it match the string "Hello"?

6. Write a regular expression that will match any word that starts with a consonant in lowercase, followed by one or more vowels in lowercase, and then followed by a consonant in lowercase. For example, it should match cat, dog, cool, cot, doom, deem, etc., but not cola, Cat, fish, Cold, etc.

7. What will be the output of the following snippet of code:

```
String source = "I saw the rat running.";
String regex = "r..";
Pattern p = Pattern.compile(regex);
Matcher m = p.matcher(source);
while(m.find()) {
    System.out.println(m.group());
}
```

8. Complete the following snippet of code that will match two words—cat and cot in the input. When the code is run, it should print cat and cot on two separate lines.'

```
String source = "cat camera can pen cow cab cot";
String regex = /* Your code goes here */;
Pattern p = Pattern.compile(regex);
Matcher m = /* Your code goes here */;
while(m.find()) {
    System.out.println(m.group());
}
```

9. Complete the following snippet of code that will replace all three-letter words that start with c with their uppercase equivalents. The code should print "CAT camera CAN pen COW CAB COT".

```
String source = "cat camera can pen cow cab cot";
String regex = "/* You code goes here*/";
Pattern p = Pattern.compile(regex);
Matcher m = p.matcher(source);
String str = m.replaceAll(mr -> mr.group().toUpperCase());
System.out.println(str);
```

10. Write the output of the following snippet of code:

```
String source = "ABXXXABB";
String regex = "AB*";
Pattern p = Pattern.compile(regex);
Matcher m = p.matcher(source);
String str = m.replaceAll("Hello");
System.out.println(str);
```

11. Write the output of the following snippet of code:

```
String source = "ABXXXABB";
String regex = "AB?";
Pattern p = Pattern.compile(regex);
Matcher m = p.matcher(source);
String str = m.replaceAll("Hello");
System.out.println(str);
```

12. Write the output of the following snippet of code:

```
String source = "ABXXXABB";
String regex = "AB+";
Pattern p = Pattern.compile(regex);
Matcher m = p.matcher(source);
String str = m.replaceAll("Hello");
System.out.println(str);
```

13. Describe the intent of the following snippet of code and write the output:

```
String source = "I have 25 cents and 400 books.";
String regex = "\\b(\\d+)\\b";
Pattern p = Pattern.compile(regex);
Matcher m = p.matcher(source);
int sum = m.results()
            .mapToInt(mr -> Integer.parseInt(mr.group()))
            .sum();
System.out.println(sum);
```

14. How many groups are present in the following regular expression:

```
String regex = "\\b((\\d{3})(\\d{3})(\\d{4}))|((\\d{3})(\\d{4}))\\b";
```

15. Complete the following snippet of code that prints 7-digit and 10-digit phone numbers in xxx-xxxx and (xxx) xxx-xxxx formats. The output should be `"(334) 233-0908, 233-7656, 234, (617) 908-6547, unknown"`.

```
String source = "3342330908, 2337656, 234, 6179086547, unknown";
String regex = "/* Your code goes here*/";
Pattern p = Pattern.compile(regex);
Matcher m = p.matcher(source);
StringBuilder sb = new StringBuilder();
while(m.find()) {
    String replacement =
        m.group(1) != null ? /* Your code goes here*/;
    m.appendReplacement(sb, replacement);
}

m.appendTail(sb);
System.out.println(sb.toString());
```

16. Complete the following snippet of code that will print each word in the source string on a separate line:

```
String source = "bug dug jug mug tug";
String regex = "/*your code goes here*/";
Pattern p = Pattern.compile(regex);
Matcher m = p.matcher(source);
while(m.find()) {
    System.out.println(m.group());
}
```

17. The following snippet of code attempts to count and print the number of questions marks (?) in the input string. Complete the following snippet of code, so the output is 3:

```
String source = "What? How? I do not know. Why?";
String regex = "/* Your code goes here */";
Pattern p = Pattern.compile(regex);
Matcher m = p.matcher(source);
long questionMarkCount = m.results().count();
System.out.println(questionMarkCount);
```

CHAPTER 19

Arrays

In this chapter, you will learn:

- How to declare variable variables of array types

- How to create arrays

- How to access elements of an array

- How to use a for loop and a for-each loop to iterate through elements of an array

- How to copy elements of one array to another array

- How to copy primitive and reference types arrays

- How to use multi-dimensional arrays

- How to use an ArrayList when a variable-length array is needed

- How to convert elements of an ArrayList to an array and vice versa

- How to perform array-related operations such as sorting elements of an array, comparing two arrays, performing binary search in an array, filling an array with a value, getting a string representation of an array, etc.

All example programs in this chapter are a member of a jdojo.array module, as declared in Listing 19-1.

Listing 19-1. The Declaration of a jdojo.array Module

```
// module-info.java
module jdojo.array {
    exports com.jdojo.array;
}
```

What Is an Array?

An array is a fixed-length data structure that is used to hold more than one value of the same data type. Let's consider an example, which will explain why we need arrays. Suppose you have been asked to declare variables to hold employee IDs of three employees. The employee IDs will be integers. The variable declarations to hold three integer values will look like this:

```
int empId1, empId2, empId3;
```

What do you do if the number of employees increases to five? You may modify your variable declarations to look like this:

```
int empId1, empId2, empId3, empId4, empId5;
```

What do you do if the number of employees increases to 1,000? You definitely would not want to declare 1,000 int variables like empId1, empId2...empId1000. Even if you do that, the resulting code would be unmanageable and clumsy. Arrays come to your rescue in such situations. Using an array, you can declare a variable of a type, which can hold as many values of that type as you want. In fact, Java has a restriction on the number of values an array can hold. An array can hold a maximum of 2,147,483,647 values, which is the maximum value of the int data type.

What makes a variable an array? Placing [ ] (empty brackets) after the data type or after the variable name in a variable declaration makes the variable an array. For example,

```
int empId;
```

is a simple variable declaration. Here, int is the data type and empId is the variable name. This declaration means that the empId variable can hold one integer value. Placing [ ] after the data type in the previous declaration as in

```
int[] empId;
```

makes empId an array variable. The previous declaration is read as "empId is an array of int." You can also make the empId variable an array by placing the [ ] after the variable name, like so:

```
int empId[];
```

Both of these declarations are valid. This book uses the first convention to declare an array. I started our discussion with an example of variable declaration to hold three employee IDs. Until now, you have prepared the ground to hold more than one value in one variable. That is, your empId variable declared as an array of int is capable of holding more than one int value. How many values can your empId array variable hold? The answer is you do not know yet. You cannot specify the number of values an array can hold at the time you declare the array. The subsequent sections explain how to specify the number of values an array can hold. You can declare an array of primitive type as well as reference type. The following are more examples of array declarations:

```
// salary can hold multiple float values
float[] salary;

// name can hold multiple references to String objects
String[] name;

// emp can hold multiple references to Employee objects
Employee[] emp;
```

▓ **Tip** An array is a fixed-length data structure to store data items of the same type. All elements of an array are stored contiguously in memory.

Arrays Are Objects

An array in Java is an object. Every object in Java belongs to a class; so does every array object. You can create an array object using the new operator. You have used the new operator with a constructor to create an object of a class. The name of a constructor is the same as the name of the class. What is the name of the class of an array object? The answer to this question is not so obvious. I answer this question later in this chapter.

For now, let's concentrate on how to create an array object of a particular type. The general syntax for array creation expression is as follows:

```
new <array-data-type>[<array-length>];
```

The array object creation expression starts with the new operator, followed by the data type of the values you want to store in the array, followed by an integer enclosed in [ ] (brackets), which is the number of elements in the array. For example, you can now create an array to store five int values as follows:

```
new int[5];
```

In this expression, 5 is the *length of the array* (also called the dimension of the array). The word "dimension" is also used in another context. You can have an array of dimension one, two, three, or more. An array with more than one dimension is called a multi-dimensional array. I cover the multi-dimensional array later in this chapter. In this book, I refer to 5 in the previous expression as the length of the array, not as the dimension of the array.

Note that the previous expression creates an array object in memory, which allocates memory to store five integers. The new operator returns the reference of the new object in memory. If you want to use this object later in your code, you must store that reference in an object reference variable. The reference variable type must match the type of object reference returned by the new operator. In the previous case, the new operator will return an object reference of int array type. You have already seen how to declare a reference variable of int array type. It is declared as follows:

```
int[] empId;
```

To store the array object reference in empId, you can write this:

```
empId = new int[5];
```

You can also combine the declaration of an array and its creation in one statement, as follows:

```
int[] empId = new int[5];
```

How would you create an array to store 252 employee IDs? You can do this as follows:

```
int[] empId = new int[252];
```

You can also use an expression to specify the length of an array while creating the array.

```
int total = 23;
int[] array1 = new int[total];     // array1 has 23 elements
int[] array2 = new int[total * 3]; // array2 has 69 elements
```

Because all arrays are objects, their references can be assigned to a reference variable of the Object type. For example,

```
int[] empId = new int[5]; // Create an array object
Object obj = empId;       // A valid assignment
```

However, if you have the reference of an array in a reference variable of the Object type, you need to cast it to the appropriate array type before you can assign it to an array reference variable or access elements by index. Remember that every array is an object. However, not every object is necessarily an array.

```
// Assume that obj is a reference of the Object type that holds a reference of int[]
int[] tempIds = (int[]) obj;
```

Accessing Array Elements

Once you create an array object using the new operator, you can refer to each individual element of the array using an element's index enclosed in brackets. The index for the first element is 0, the second element 1, the third element 2, and so on. This is called zero-based indexing. The index for the last element of an array is the length of the array minus 1. If you have an array of length 5, the indexes of the array elements would be 0, 1, 2, 3, and 4. Consider the following statement:

```
int[] empId = new int[5];
```

The length of the empId array is 5; its elements can be referred to as empId[0], empId[1], empId[2], empId[3], and empId[4].

It is a runtime error to refer to a non-existing element of an array. For example, using empId[5] in your code will throw an exception, because empId has a length of 5 and empId[5] refers to the sixth element, which is non-existent. You can assign values to elements of an array as follows:

```
empId[0] = 10;  // Assign 10 to the first element of empId
empId[1] = 20;  // Assign 20 to the second element of empId
empId[2] = 30;  // Assign 30 to the third element of empId
empId[3] = 40;  // Assign 40 to the fourth element of empId
empId[4] = 50;  // Assign 50 to the fifth element of empId
```

Table 19-1 shows the details of an array. It shows the indexes, values, and references of the elements of the array after the statements are executed.

Table 19-1. *Array Elements in Memory for the empId Array*

Element's Index	0	1	2	3	4
Element's Value	10	20	30	40	50
Element's Reference	empId[0]	empId[1]	empId[2]	empId[3]	empId[4]

The following statement assigns the value of the third element of the empId array to an int variable temp:

```
int temp = empId[2]; // Assigns 30 to temp
```

Length of an Array

An array object has a `public` `final` instance variable named `length`, which contains the number of elements in the array.

```
int[] empId = new int[5];   // Create an array of length 5
int len = empId.length;     // 5 will be assigned to len
```

Note that `length` is the property of the array object you create. Until you create the array object, you cannot use its `length` property. The following code fragment illustrates this:

```
// salary is a reference variable, which can refer to an array of int.
// At this point, it contains null. That is, it is not referencing a valid object.
int[] salary = null;

// A runtime error. salary is not referring to any array object yet.
int len = salary.length;

// Create an int array of length 1000 and assign its reference to salary
salary = new int[1000];

// Correct. len2 has a value 1000
int len2 = salary.length;
```

Typically, elements of arrays are accessed using loops. If you want to do any processing with all of the elements of an array, you execute a loop starting from index 0 (zero) to length minus 1. For example, to assign the values 10, 20, 30, 40, and 50 to the elements of the empId array of length 5, you would execute a `for` loop as shown:

```
for (int i = 0 ; i < empId.length; i++) {
    empId[i] = (i + 1) * 10;
}
```

It is important to note that while executing the loop, the loop condition must check for array index/subscript for being less than the length of array as in "`i < empId.length`" because the array index starts with 0, not 1. Another common mistake made by programmers while processing an array using a `for` loop is to start the loop counter at 1 as opposed to 0. What will happen if you change the initialization part of the `for` loop in the previous code from `int i = 0` to `int i = 1`? It would not give you any errors. However, the first element, `empId[0]`, would not be processed and would not be assigned the value of 10.

You cannot change the length of an array after it is created. You may be tempted to modify the `length` property.

```
int[] roll = new int[5]; // Create an array of 5 elements

// A compile-time error. The length property of an array is final. You cannot modify it.
roll.length = 10;
```

You can have a zero-length array. Such an array is called an empty array.

```
// Create an array of length zero
int[] emptyArray = new int[0];

// Will assign zero to len
int len = emptyArray.length;
```

░ **Tip** Arrays use zero-based indexing. That is, the first element of an array has an index of zero. Arrays are created dynamically at runtime. The length of an array cannot be modified after the array has been created. If you need to modify the length of an array, you must create a new array and copy the elements from the old array to the new array. An array can have its length as zero.

Initializing Array Elements

Recall from Chapter 7 that, unlike class member variables (instance and static variables), local variables are not initialized by default. You cannot access a local variable unless it has been assigned a value. The same rule applies to the blank final variables. The compiler uses *Rules of Definite Assignment* to make sure that all variables have been initialized before their values are used in a program.

Array elements are always initialized irrespective of the scope in which the array is created. Array elements of primitive data type are initialized to the default value for their data types. For example, the numeric array elements are initialized to zero, boolean elements to false, and char elements to '\u0000'. Array elements of reference type are initialized to null. The following snippet of code illustrates the array initialization:

```
// intArray[0], intArray[1] and intArray[2] are initialized to zero by default.
int[] intArray = new int[3];

// bArray[0] and bArray[1] are initialized to false.
boolean[] bArray = new boolean[2];

// An example of a reference type array. strArray[0] and strArray[1] are
// initialized to null.
String[] strArray = new String[2];

// Another example of a reference type array.
// All 100 elements of the person array are initialized to null.
Person[] person = new Person[100];
```

Listing 19-2 illustrates the array initialization for an instance variable and some local variables.

Listing 19-2. Default Initialization of Array Elements

```
// ArrayInit.java
package com.jdojo.array;

public class ArrayInit {
    private final boolean[] bArray = new boolean[3];  // An instance variable
```

```
    public ArrayInit() {
        // Display the initial value for elements of the instance variable bArray
        for (int i = 0; i < bArray.length; i++) {
            System.out.println("bArray[" + i + "]:" + bArray[i]);
        }
    }

    public static void main(String[] args) {
        System.out.println("int array initialization:");

        int[] empId = new int[3];  // A local array variable
        for (int i = 0; i < empId.length; i++) {
            System.out.println("empId[" + i + "]:" + empId[i]);
        }

        System.out.println("\nboolean array initialization:");

        // Initial value for bArray elements are displayed inside the constructor
        new ArrayInit();

        System.out.println("\nReference type array initialization:");

        String[] name = new String[3];  // A local array variable
        for (int i = 0; i < name.length; i++) {
            System.out.println("name[" + i + "]:" + name[i]);
        }
    }
}
```

```
int array initialization:
empId[0]:0
empId[1]:0
empId[2]:0

boolean array initialization:
bArray[0]:false
bArray[1]:false
bArray[2]:false

Reference type array initialization:
name[0]:null
name[1]:null
name[2]:null
```

Beware of Reference Type Arrays

Array elements of a primitive type contain values of that primitive type, whereas array elements of a reference type contain the reference to objects. Suppose you have an int array of

```
int[] empId = new int[5];
```

Here, empId[0], empId[1]...empId[4] contain an int value. Suppose you have an array of String, like so:

```
String[] name = new String[5];
```

Here, name[0], name[1]...name[4] may contain a reference to a String object. Note that the String objects, the elements of the name array, have not been created yet. As discussed in the previous section, all elements of the name array contain null at this point. You need to create the String objects and assign their references to the elements of the array one by one, as shown:

```
name[0] = "John";
name[1] = "Donna";
name[2] = "Wally";
name[3] = "Reddy";
name[4] = "Buddy";
```

It is a common mistake to refer to the elements of an array of reference type just after creating the array and before assigning a valid object reference to each element. The following code illustrates this common mistake:

```
// Create an array of String
String[] name = new String[5];

// A runtime error as name[0] is null
int len = name[0].length();

// Assign a valid string object to all elements of the array
name[0] = "John";
name[1] = "Donna";
name[2] = "Wally";
name[3] = "Reddy";
name[4] = "Buddy";

// Now you can get the length of the first element
int len2 = name[0].length(); // Correct. len2 has value 4
```

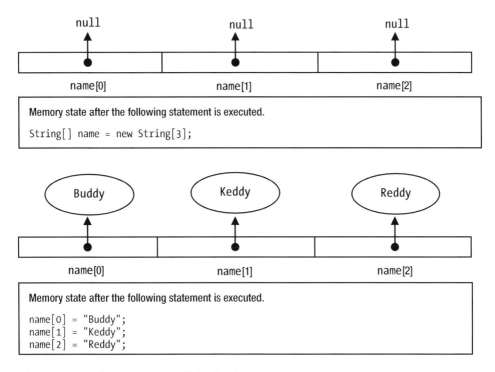

Figure 19-1. *Reference type array initialization*

The concept of initialization of the String reference type array is depicted in Figure 19-1. This concept applies to all reference types.

All elements of an array are stored contiguously in memory. In case of a reference type array, the array elements store the references of the objects. Those references in the elements are stored contiguously, not the objects they are referring to. The objects are stored on the heap and their locations are, typically, not contiguous.

Explicit Array Initialization

You can initialize elements of an array explicitly when you declare the array or when you create the array object using the new operator. The initial values for elements are separated by a comma and enclosed in braces ({}).

```
// Initialize the array at the time of declaration
int[] empId = {1, 2, 3, 4, 5};
```

This code creates an array of int of length 5, and initializes its elements to 1, 2, 3, 4, and 5. Note that you do not specify the length of an array when you specify the array initialization list at the time of the array declaration. The length of the array is the same as the number of values specified in the array initialization list. Here, the length of the empId array will be 5, because you passed five values in the initialization list {1, 2, 3, 4, 5}. A comma may follow the last value in an initialization list.

```
int[] empId = {1, 2, 3, 4, 5, }; // A comma after the last value 5 is valid.
```

Alternatively, you can initialize the elements of an array as shown:

```
int[] empId = new int[]{1, 2, 3, 4, 5};
```

Note that you cannot specify the length of an array if you specify the array initialization list. The length of the array is the same as the number of values specified in the initialization list. It is valid to create an empty array by using an empty initialization list.

```
int[] emptyNumList = { };
```

For a reference type array, you can specify the list of objects in the initialization list. The following snippet of code illustrates array initialization for String and Account types. Assume that the Account class exists and it has a constructor, which takes an account number as an argument.

```
// Create a String array with two Strings "Sara" and "Truman"
String[] names = {new String("Sara"), new String("Truman")};

// You can also use String literals
String[] names = {"Sara", "Truman"};

// Create an Account array with two Account objects
Account[] ac = new Account[]{new Account(1), new Account(2)};
```

░ **Tip**   When you use an initialization list to initialize the elements of an array, you cannot specify the length of the array. The length of the array is set to the number of values in the initialization list.

Limitations of Using Arrays

An array in Java cannot be expanded or shrunk after it is created. Suppose you have an array of 100 elements, and later, you need to keep only 15 elements. You cannot get rid of the remaining 85 elements. If you need 135 elements, you cannot append 35 more elements to it. You can deal with the first limitation (memory cannot be freed for unused array elements) if you have enough memory available to your application. However, there is no way out if you need to add more elements to an existing array. The only solution is to create another array of the desired length, and copy the array elements from the original array to the new array. You can copy array elements from one array to another in two ways:

- Using a loop

- Using the static arraycopy() method of the java.lang.System class

- Using the copyOf() method of the java.util.Arrays class

Suppose you have an int array of the length originalLength and you want to modify its length to newLength. You can apply the first method of copying arrays as shown in the following snippet of code:

```
int originalLength = 100;
int newLength = 15;
int[] ids = new int[originalLength];
```

```
// Do some processing here...

// Create a temporary array of new length
int[] tempIds = new int[newLength];

// While copying array elements we have to check if the new length
// is less than or greater than original length
int elementsToCopy = originalLength > newLength ? newLength : originalLength;

// Copy the elements from the original array to the new array
for (int i = 0; i < elementsToCopy; i++){
    tempIds[i] = ids[i];
}

// Finally assign the reference of new array to ids
ids = tempIds;
```

Another way to copy elements of an array to another array is by using the arraycopy() method of the System class. The signature of the arraycopy() method is as follows:

```
public static void arraycopy(Object sourceArray, int sourceStartPosition,
                             Object destinationArray,
                             int destinationStartPosition,
                             int lengthToBeCopied)
```

Here,

- sourceArray is the reference to the source array.

- sourceStartPosition is the starting index in the source array from where the copying of elements will start.

- destinationArray is the reference to the destination array.

- destinationStartPosition is the start index in the destination array from where new elements from source array will be copied.

- lengthToBeCopied is the number of elements to be copied from the source array to the destination array.

You can replace the previous for loop with the following code:

```
// Now copy array elements using the arraycopy() method
System.arraycopy (ids, 0, tempIds, 0, elementsToCopy);
```

You can also use the copyOf() static method of the Arrays class. The following show some of copyOf() method's declarations:

- boolean[] copyOf(boolean[] original, int newLength)

- byte[] copyOf(byte[] original, int newLength)

- char[] copyOf(char[] original, int newLength)

- double[] copyOf(double[] original, int newLength)

- `float[] copyOf(float[] original, int newLength)`

- `int[] copyOf(int[] original, int newLength)`

- `short[] copyOf(long[] original, int newLength)`

- `<T> T[] copyOf(T[] original, int newLength)`

The first argument to the copyOf() method is the source array. The second argument, newLength, is the number of elements in the new array. If newLength is less than the length of the source array, the returned array will be a truncated copy of the source array. If newLength is greater than the length of the source array, the returned array will contain all elements from the original array and the extra elements will be having default values set based on the data type of the array. If newLength is equal to the length of the source array, the returned array contain the same number of elements as the source array.

▓ **Tip**   The Arrays class contains a copyOfRange() method that lets you copy a range of elements from an array to another array. Its declaration for the int array is `int[] copyOfRange(int[] original, int from, int to)`. The method is overloaded for all data types. Here, from and to are the initial index (inclusive) and final index (exclusive) of the elements in the source array to be copied. These indexes must be within the range of the source array, which means the length of the destination array can be, at maximum, equal to the source array.

The objects of the two classes, java.util.ArrayList and java.util.Vector, can be used in place of an array, where the length of the array needs to be modified. You can think of the objects of these two classes as variable length arrays. The next section discusses these two classes in detail.

Listing 19-3 demonstrates how to copy an array using a for loop, the System.arraycopy() method, the Arrays.copyOf() method, and the Arrays.copyOfRange() method.

Listing 19-3. Copying an Array Using a for Loop and the System.arraycopy() Method

```
// ArrayCopyTest.java
package com.jdojo.array;

import java.util.Arrays;

public class ArrayCopyTest {
    public static void main(String[] args) {
        // Have an array with 5 elements
        int[] data = {1, 2, 3, 4, 5};

        // Expand the data array to 7 elements
        int[] eData = expandArray(data, 7);

        // Truncate the data array to 3 elements
        int[] tData = expandArray(data, 3);

        System.out.println("Using for-loop...");
        printArrays(data, eData, tData);

        /* Using System.arraycopy() method */
        // Copy data array to new arrays
        eData = new int[7];
        tData = new int[3];
```

```
        System.arraycopy(data, 0, eData, 0, 5);
        System.arraycopy(data, 0, tData, 0, 3);

        System.out.println("\nUsing System.arraycopy() method...");
        printArrays(data, eData, tData);

        /* Using Arrays.copyOf() method  */
        // Copy data array to new arrays
        eData = Arrays.copyOf(data, 7);
        tData = Arrays.copyOf(data, 3);
        System.out.println("\nUsing Arrays.copyOf() method...");
        printArrays(data, eData, tData);

        /* Using Arrays.copyOfRange() method */
        // Copy data array to new arrays
        int[] copy1 = Arrays.copyOfRange(data, 0, 3);
        int[] copy2 = Arrays.copyOfRange(data, 2, 4);
        System.out.println("\nUsing Arrays.copyOfRange() method...");
        System.out.println("Original Array: " + Arrays.toString(data));
        System.out.println("Copy1 (0, 3): " + Arrays.toString(copy1));
        System.out.println("Copy2 (2, 4): " + Arrays.toString(copy2));
    }

    // Uses a for-loop to copy an array
    public static int[] expandArray(int[] oldArray, int newLength) {
        int originalLength = oldArray.length;
        int[] newArray = new int[newLength];
        int elementsToCopy = originalLength > newLength ? newLength : originalLength;

        for (int i = 0; i < elementsToCopy; i++) {
            newArray[i] = oldArray[i];
        }

        return newArray;
    }

    private static void printArrays(int[] original, int[] expanded, int[] truncated) {
        System.out.println("Original Array: " + Arrays.toString(original));
        System.out.println("Expanded Array: " + Arrays.toString(expanded));
        System.out.println("Truncated Array: " + Arrays.toString(truncated));
    }
}
```

```
Using for-loop...
Original Array: [1, 2, 3, 4, 5]
Expanded Array: [1, 2, 3, 4, 5, 0, 0]
Truncated Array: [1, 2, 3]

Using System.arraycopy() method...
Original Array: [1, 2, 3, 4, 5]
Expanded Array: [1, 2, 3, 4, 5, 0, 0]
Truncated Array: [1, 2, 3]
```

713

```
Using Arrays.copyOf() method...
Original Array: [1, 2, 3, 4, 5]
Expanded Array: [1, 2, 3, 4, 5, 0, 0]
Truncated Array: [1, 2, 3]

Using Arrays.copyOfRange() method...
Original Array: [1, 2, 3, 4, 5]
Copy1 (0, 3): [1, 2, 3]
Copy2 (2, 4): [3, 4]
```

The Arrays class is in the java.util package. It contains many convenience methods to deal with arrays. For example, it contains methods for converting an array to a string format, sorting an array, etc. You used the Arrays.toString() static method to get the contents of an array in the string format. The method is overloaded; you can use it to get the content of any type of array in string format. In this example, you used a for loop and the System.arraycopy() method to copy arrays. Notice that using the arraycopy() method is much more powerful than that of a for loop. For example, the arraycopy() method is designed to handle copying of the elements of an array from one region to another region in the same array. It takes care of any overlap in the source and the destination regions within the array. For a reference type array, you can change the type of the returned array using the following version of the copyOfRange() method:

```
<T,U> T[] copyOfRange(U[] original, int from, int to, Class<? extends T[]> newType)
```

The method takes a U type array and returns an array of the T type.

Simulating Variable-Length Arrays

You know that Java does not provide variable-length arrays. However, Java libraries provide some classes whose objects can be used as variable-length arrays. These classes provide methods to obtain an array representation of their elements. ArrayList and Vector are two classes in the java.util package that can be used whenever variable-length arrays are needed.

ArrayList and Vector classes work the same way, except that the methods in the Vector class are synchronized, whereas methods in ArrayList are not. If your object list is accessed and modified by multiple threads simultaneously, use the Vector class, which will be slower but thread safe. Otherwise, you should use the ArrayList class. For the rest of the discussion, I refer to ArrayList only. However, the discussion applies to Vector as well.

The big difference between arrays and the ArrayList class is that the latter works with only objects, not with primitive data types. The ArrayList class is a generic class and it takes the type of its elements as the type parameter. If you want to work with primitive values, you need to declare an ArrayList of one of the wrapper classes. For example, use ArrayList<Integer> to work with int elements and all your int values will be boxed into Integer objects automatically for you. The following code fragment illustrates the use of the ArrayList class:

```
import java.util.ArrayList;
...

// Create an ArrayList of Integer
ArrayList<Integer> ids = new ArrayList<>();

// Get the size of array list
int total = ids.size();    // total will be zero at this point
```

```
// Print the details of array list
System.out.println("ArrayList size is " + total);
System.out.println("ArrayList elements are " + ids);

// Add three ids 10, 20, 30 to the  array list.
ids.add(new Integer(10)); // Adding an Integer object.
ids.add(20);              // Adding an int. Autoboxing is at play.
ids.add(30);              // Adding an int. Autoboxing is at play.

// Get the size of the array list
total = ids.size(); // total will be 3

// Print the details of array list
System.out.println("ArrayList size is " + total);
System.out.println("ArrayList elements are " + ids);

// Clear all elements from array list
ids.clear();

// Get the size of the array list
total = ids.size(); // total will be 0

// Print the details of array list
System.out.println("ArrayList size is " + total);
System.out.println("ArrayList elements are " + ids);
```

```
ArrayList size is 0
ArrayList elements are []
ArrayList size is 3
ArrayList elements are [10, 20, 30]
ArrayList size is 0
ArrayList elements are []
```

Note one important observation from this output. You can print the list of all elements in an ArrayList just by passing its reference to the System.out.println() method. The toString() method of the ArrayList class returns a string that is a comma-separated string representation of its elements enclosed in brackets ([]).

Like arrays, ArrayList uses zero-based indexing. That is, the first element of ArrayList has an index of zero. You can get the element stored at any index by using the get(int index) method.

```
// Get the element at the index 0 (the first element)
Integer firstId = ids.get(0);

// Get the element at the index 1 (the second element)
int secondId = ids.get(1); // Autounboxing is at play
```

You can check if the ArrayList contains an object using its contains() method.

```
Integer id20 = 20;
Integer id50 = 50;
```

```
// Add three objects to the arraylist
ids.add(10);
ids.add(20);
ids.add(30);

// Check if the array list contains id20 and id50
boolean found20 = ids.contains(id20); // found20 will be true
boolean found50 = ids.contains(id50); // found50 will be false
```

You can iterate through the elements of an ArrayList in one of the two ways: using a loop or using an iterator. In this chapter, I discuss how to iterate through elements of an ArrayList using a for loop. Refer to Chapter 15 in the second volume of this series to learn how to iterate through elements of an ArrayList (or any type of collection) using an iterator. The following snippet of code shows how to use a for loop to iterate through the elements of an ArrayList:

```
// Get the size of the ArrayList
int total = ids.size();

// Iterate through all elements
for (int i = 0; i < total; i++) {
    int temp = ids.get(i);
    // Do some processing...
}
```

If you want to iterate through all elements of the ArrayList without caring for their indexes, you can use the for-each loop as shown:

```
// Iterate through all elements
for (int temp : ids) {
    // Do some processing with temp...
}
```

Listing 19-4 illustrates the use of a for loop and a for-each loop to iterate through elements of an ArrayList. It also shows you how to remove an element from an ArrayList using the remove() method.

Listing 19-4. Iterating Through Elements of an ArrayList

```
// NameIterator.java
package com.jdojo.array;

import java.util.ArrayList;

public class NameIterator {
    public static void main(String[] args) {
        // Create an ArrayList of String
        ArrayList<String> nameList = new ArrayList<>();

        // Add some names
        nameList.add("Chris");
        nameList.add("Laynie");
        nameList.add("Jessica");
```

```
        // Get the count of names in the list
        int count = nameList.size();

        // Let us print the name list using a for loop
        System.out.println("List of names...");
        for(int i = 0; i < count; i++) {
            String name = nameList.get(i);
            System.out.println(name);
        }

        // Let us remove Jessica from the list
        nameList.remove("Jessica");

        // Get the count of names in the list again
        count = nameList.size();

        // Let us print the name list again using a for-each loop
        System.out.println("\nAfter removing Jessica...");
        for(String name : nameList) {
            System.out.println(name);
        }
    }
}
```

```
List of names...
Chris
Laynie
Jessica

After removing Jessica...
Chris
Laynie
```

Passing an Array as a Parameter

You can pass an array as a parameter to a method or a constructor. The type of array you pass to the method must be assignment-compatible to the formal parameter type. The syntax for an array type parameter declaration for a method is the same as for the other data types. That is, parameter declaration should start with the array type, followed by whitespace and the argument name, as shown:

```
[modifiers] <return-type> <methodName>([<array-type> argumentName, ...])
```

The following are some examples of method declarations with array arguments:

```
// The processSalary() method has two parameters:
// 1. id is an array of int
// 2. salary is an array of double
public static void processSalary(int[] id, double[] salary) {
    // Code goes here...
}
```

```
// The setAka() method has two parameters:
// 1. id is int (It is simply int type, not array of int)
// 2. aka is an array of String
public static void setAka(int id, String[] aka) {
    // Code goes here...
}

// The printStates() method has one parameter:
// 1. stateNames is an array of String
public static void printStates(String[] stateNames) {
    // Code goes here...
}
```

The following snippet of code for a method mimics the toString() method of ArrayList. It accepts an int array and returns the comma-separated values enclosed in brackets ([ ]).

```
public static String arrayToString(int[] source) {
    if (source == null) {
        return null;
    }

    // Use StringBuilder to improve performance
    StringBuilder result = new StringBuilder("[");

    for (int i = 0; i < source.length; i++) {
        if (i == source.length - 1) {
            result.append(source[i]);
        } else {
            result.append(source[i] + ",");
        }
    }

    result.append("]");
    return result.toString();
}
```

This method may be called as follows:

```
int[] ids = {10, 15, 19};
String str = arrayToString(ids);  // Pass ids int array to arrayToString() method
```

Because an array is an object, the array reference is passed to the method. The method, which receives an array parameter, can modify the elements of the array. Listing 19-5 illustrates how a method can change the elements of its array parameter; this example also shows how to implement the swap() method to swap two integers using an array.

Listing 19-5. Passing an Array as a Method Parameter

```java
// Swap.java
package com.jdojo.array;

public class Swap {
    public static void main(String[] args) {
        int[] num = {17, 80};

        System.out.println("Before swap");
        System.out.println("#1: " + num[0]);
        System.out.println("#2: " + num[1]);

        // Call the swap() method passing the num array
        swap(num);

        System.out.println("After swap");
        System.out.println("#1: " + num[0]);
        System.out.println("#2: " + num[1]);
    }

    // The swap() method accepts an int array as an argument and swaps the values
    // if array contains two values.
    public static void swap (int[] source) {
        if (source != null && source.length == 2) {
            // Swap the first and the second elements
            int temp = source[0];
            source[0] = source[1];
            source[1] = temp;
        }
    }
}
```

```
Before swap
#1: 17
#2: 80
After swap
#1: 80
#2: 17
```

Recall, in Chapter 8, that we were not able to implement a method for swapping two integers using the method's parameters of primitive types. It was so, because, for primitive types, the actual parameters are copied to the formal parameter. Here, you were able to swap two integers inside the swap() method, because you used an array as the parameter. The array's reference is passed to the method, not the copy of the elements of the array.

There is a risk when an array is passed to a method. The method may modify the array elements, which, sometimes, may not be desired or intended. In such a case, you should pass a copy of the array to the method, not the original array; so if the method modifies the array, your original array is not affected.

You can make a quick copy of your array using array's clone() method. The phrase "quick copy" warrants special attention. For primitive types, the cloned array will have a true copy of the original array. A new array of the same length is created and the value of each element in the original array is copied to the corresponding element of the cloned array. However, for reference types, the reference of the object stored in each element of the original array is copied to the corresponding element of the cloned array. This is known as a shallow copy, whereas the former type, where the object (or the value) is copied, is known as a deep copy. In the case of a shallow copy, elements of both arrays, the original and the cloned, refer to the same object in memory. You can modify the objects using their references stored in the original array as well as the cloned array. In this case, even if you pass a copy of the original array to a method, the state of objects referenced in your original array can be modified inside the method. The solution to this problem is to make a deep copy of your original array to pass it to the method. The following snippet of code illustrates the cloning of an int array and a String array. Note that the return type of the clone() method is Object and you need to cast the returned value to an appropriate array type.

```
// Create an array of 3 integers 1, 2, and 3
int[] ids = {1, 2, 3};

// Declare an array of int named clonedIds.
int[] clonedIds;

// The clonedIds array has the same values as the ids array.
clonedIds = (int[]) ids.clone();

// Create an array of 3 strings.
String[] names  = {"Lisa", "Pat", "Kathy"};

// Declare an array of String named clonedNames.
String[] clonedNames;

// The clonedNames array has the reference of the same three strings as the names array.
String[] clonedNames = (String[]) names.clone();
```

The cloning process for primitive array ids and reference array names in the previous snippet of code is depicted in Figures 19-2 through 19-5.

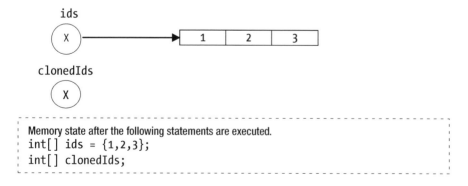

Figure 19-2. The ids array is populated and the clonedIds array is declared

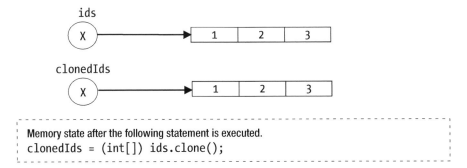

Figure 19-3. The ids array is cloned in the clonedIds array

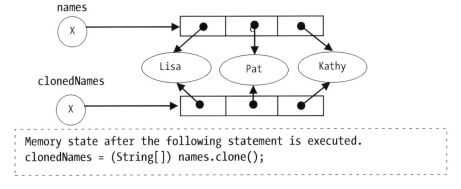

Figure 19-4. The names array is populated and the clonedNames array is declared

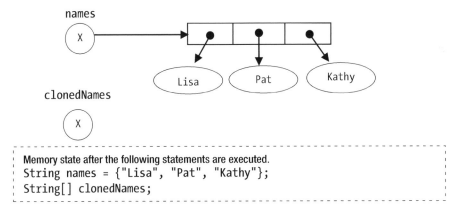

Figure 19-5. The names array is cloned in the clonedNames array

Notice that when the names array is cloned, the clonedNames array elements refer to the same String objects in memory. When you mention a method of modifying an array parameter passed to it, you may mean one or all of the following three things:

- Array parameter reference

- Elements of the array parameter

- The object referred by the array parameter elements

Array Parameter Reference

Because an array is an object, a copy of its reference is passed to a method. If the method changes the array parameter, the actual parameter is not affected. Listing 19-6 illustrates this. The main() method passes array to the tryArrayChange() method, which in turn assigns a different array reference to the parameter. The output shows that the array in the main() method remains unaffected.

Listing 19-6. Modifying an Array Parameter Inside a Method

```java
// ModifyArrayParam.java
package com.jdojo.array;

import java.util.Arrays;

public class ModifyArrayParam {
    public static void main(String[] args) {
        int[] origNum = {101, 307, 78};
        System.out.println("Before method call: " + Arrays.toString(origNum));

        // Pass the array to the method
        tryArrayChange(origNum);

        System.out.println("After method call: " + Arrays.toString(origNum));
    }

    public static void tryArrayChange(int[] num) {
        System.out.println("Inside method-1: " + Arrays.toString(num));

        // Create and store a new int array in num
        num = new int[]{10, 20};

        System.out.println("Inside method-2: " + Arrays.toString(num));
    }
}
```

```
Before method call: [101, 307, 78]
Inside method-1: [101, 307, 78]
Inside method-2: [10, 20]
After method call: [101, 307, 78]
```

If you do not want your method to change the array reference inside the method body, you must declare the method parameter as final, like so:

```
public static void tryArrayChange(final int[] num) {
    // An error. num is final and cannot be changed
    num = new int[]{10, 20};
}
```

Elements of the Array Parameter

The values stored in the elements of an array parameter can always be changed inside a method. Listing 19-7 illustrates this.

Listing 19-7. Modifying Elements of an Array Parameter Inside a Method

```
// ModifyArrayElements.java
package com.jdojo.array;

import java.util.Arrays;

public class ModifyArrayElements {
    public static void main(String[] args) {
        int[] origNum = {10, 89, 7};
        String[] origNames = {"Mike", "John"};
        System.out.println("Before method call, origNum: " + Arrays.toString(origNum));
        System.out.println("Before method call, origNames: " + Arrays.toString(origNames));

        // Call methods passing the arrays
        tryElementChange(origNum);
        tryElementChange(origNames);

        System.out.println("After method call, origNum: " + Arrays.toString(origNum));
        System.out.println("After method call, origNames: " + Arrays.toString(origNames));
    }

    public static void tryElementChange(int[] num) {
        // If the array has at least one element, store 1116 in its first element.
        if (num != null && num.length > 0) {
            num[0] = 1116;
        }
    }

    public static void tryElementChange(String[] names) {
        // If the array has at least one element, store "Twinkle" in its first element
        if (names != null && names.length > 0) {
            names[0] = "Twinkle";
        }
    }
}
```

```
Before method call, origNum: [10, 89, 7]
Before method call, origNames: [Mike, John]
After method call, origNum: [1116, 89, 7]
After method call, origNames: [Twinkle, John]
```

Notice that first element of the arrays changed after the method calls. You can change the elements of an array parameter inside a method, even if the array parameter is declared final.

The Object Referred by the Array Parameter Elements

This section applies to array parameters of only the reference type. If the array's reference type is mutable, you can change the state of the object stored in the array elements. In the previous section, I discussed replacing the reference stored in an array element by a new object reference. This section discusses changing the state of the object referred to by the elements of the array. Consider an Item class, as shown in Listing 19-8.

Listing 19-8. An Item Class

```java
// Item.java
package com.jdojo.array;

public class Item {
    private double price;
    private final String name;

    public Item (String name, double price) {
        this.name = name;
        this.price = price;
    }

    public double getPrice() {
        return this.price;
    }

    public void setPrice(double price ) {
        this.price = price;
    }

    @Override
    public String toString() {
        return "[" + this.name + ", " + this.price + "]";
    }
}
```

Listing 19-9 illustrates this. The main() method creates an array of Item. The array is passed to the tryStateChange() method, which changes the price of the first element in the array to 10.38. The output shows that the price is changed for the original element in the array created in the main() method.

Listing 19-9. Modifying the States of Array Elements of an Array Parameter Inside a Method

```java
// ModifyArrayElementState.java
package com.jdojo.array;

public class ModifyArrayElementState {
    public static void main(String[] args) {
        Item[] myItems = {new Item("Pen", 25.11), new Item("Pencil", 0.10)};
        System.out.println("Before method call #1:" + myItems[0]);
        System.out.println("Before method call #2:" + myItems[1]);

        // Call the method passing the array of Item
        tryStateChange(myItems);

        System.out.println("After method call #1:" + myItems[0]);
        System.out.println("After method call #2:" + myItems[1]);
    }

    public static void tryStateChange(Item[] allItems) {
        if (allItems != null && allItems.length > 0) {
            // Change the price of the first item to 10.38
            allItems[0].setPrice(10.38);
        }
    }
}
```

```
Before method call #1:[Pen, 25.11]
Before method call #2:[Pencil, 0.1]
After method call #1:[Pen, 10.38]
After method call #2:[Pencil, 0.1]
```

⬛ **Tip** The clone() method can be used to make a clone of an array. For a reference array, the clone() method performs a shallow copy. An array should be passed to a method and returned from a method with caution. If a method may modify its array parameter and you do not want your actual array parameter to get affected by that method call, you must pass a deep copy of your array to that method.

If you store the state of an object in an array instance variable, you should think carefully before returning the reference of that array from any methods of your class. The caller of that method will get the handle of the array instance variable and will be able to change the state of the objects of that class outside the class. This situation is illustrated in the following example:

```java
public class MagicNumber {
    // Magic numbers are not supposed to be changed. They can be looked up though.
    private int[] magicNumbers = {5, 11, 21, 51, 101};

    // Other code goes here...
```

```
    public int[] getMagicNumbers () {
        /* Never do the following. If you do this, callers of this
           method will be able to change the magic numbers.
        */
        // return this.magicNumbers;

        /* Do the following instead. In case of reference arrays, make a deep copy, and
           return that copy. For primitive arrays you can use the clone() method.
        */
        return (int[]) magicNumbers.clone();
    }
}
```

You can also create an array and pass it to a method without storing the array reference in a variable. Suppose there is a method named setNumbers(int[] nums), which takes an int array as a parameter. You can call this method as shown:

```
setNumbers(new int[]{10, 20, 30});
```

Note that you must use the new operator in this case. The following method call will not work:

```
// A compile-time error. The array initialization list is supported only
// in an array declaration statement
setNumbers({10, 20, 30});
```

Command-Line Arguments

A Java application can be launched from a command prompt (a command prompt in Windows and a shell prompt in UNIX). It can also be launched from within a Java development environment tool, such as NetBeans, Eclipse, JDeveloper, etc. A Java application is run at the command line like so:

```
java --module-path <module-path> --module <module-name/<class-name>
java --module-path <module-path> --module <module-name/<class-name> <list-of-command-line
arguments>
```

Each argument in the argument list is separated by a space. For example, the following command runs the com.jdojo.array.Test class and passes three names as the command-line arguments:

```
C:\Java9Fundamentals>java --module-path build\modules\jdojo.array --module jdojo.array/com.
jdojo.array.Test Cat Dog Rat
```

What happens to these three command-line arguments when the Test class is run? The operating system passes the list of the arguments to the JVM. Sometimes the operating system may expand the list of arguments by interpreting their meanings and may pass a modified arguments list to the JVM. The JVM parses the argument lists using a space as a separator. It creates an array of String whose length is the same as the number of arguments in the list. It populates the String array with the items in the arguments list sequentially. Finally, the JVM passes this String array to the main() method of the Test class that you are running. This is the time when you use the String array argument passed to the main() method. If there is no command-line argument, the JVM creates a String array of zero length and passes it to the main() method. If you want to pass space-separated words as one argument, you can enclose them in double quotes. You can also avoid the operating system interpretation of special characters by enclosing them in double quotes. Let's create a class called CommandLine, as shown in Listing 19-10.

Listing 19-10. Processing Command-line Arguments Inside the main() Method

```java
// CommandLine.java
package com.jdojo.array;

public class CommandLine {
    public static void main(String[] args) {
        // args contains all command-line arguments
        System.out.println("Total Arguments: " + args.length);

        // Display all arguments
        for (int i = 0; i < args.length; i++) {
            System.out.println("Argument #" + (i + 1) + ": " + args[i]);
        }
    }
}
```

The following are a few examples of passing command-line arguments to the CommandLine class:

```
C:\Java9Fundamentals>java --module-path build\modules\jdojo.array --module jdojo.array/com.
jdojo.array.CommandLine
```

```
Total Arguments: 0
```

```
C:\Java9Fundamentals>java --module-path build\modules\jdojo.array --module jdojo.array/com.
jdojo.array.CommandLine Cat Dog Rat
```

```
Total Arguments: 3
Argument #1: Cat
Argument #2: Dog
Argument #3: Rat
```

```
C:\Java9Fundamentals>java --module-path build\modules\jdojo.array --module jdojo.array/com.
jdojo.array.CommandLine "Cat Dog Rat"
```

```
Total Arguments: 1
Argument #1: Cat Dog Rat
```

```
C:\Java9Fundamentals>java --module-path build\modules\jdojo.array --module jdojo.array/com.
jdojo.array.CommandLine 29 Dogs
```

```
Total Arguments: 2
Argument #1: 29
Argument #2: Dogs
```

What is the use of command-line arguments? They let you change the behavior of your program without re-compiling it. For example, you may want to sort the contents of a file in ascending or descending order. You may pass command-line arguments, which will specify the sorting order. If there is no sorting order specified on the command line, you may assume ascending order by default. If you call the sorting class com.jdojo.array.SortFile, you may run it in the following ways.

```
// To sort employee.txt file in ascending order
C:\Java9Fundamentals>java --module-path build\modules\jdojo.array --module jdojo.array/com.jdojo.array.SortFile names.txt asc

// To sort department.txt file in descending order
C:\Java9Fundamentals>java --module-path build\modules\jdojo.array --module jdojo.array/com.jdojo.array.SortFile names.txt desc

// To sort salary.txt in ascending order
C:\Java9Fundamentals>java --module-path build\modules\jdojo.array --module jdojo.array/com.jdojo.array.SortFile names.txt
```

Depending on the second element, if any, of the String array passed to the main() method of the SortFile class, you may sort the file differently.

Note that all command-line arguments are passed to the main() method as a String. If you pass a numeric argument, you need to convert the string argument to a number. To illustrate this numeric argument conversion, let's develop a mini calculator class, which takes an expression as command-line argument and prints the result. The mini calculator supports only four basic operations: add, subtract, multiply, and divide; see Listing 19-11.

Listing 19-11. A Mini Command-line Calculator

```java
// Calc.java
package com.jdojo.array;

import java.util.Arrays;

public class Calc {
    public static void main(String[] args) {
        // Print the list of commandline argument
        System.out.println(Arrays.toString(args));

        // Make sure we received three arguments and the
        // the second argument has only one character to indicate operation.
        if (!(args.length == 3 && args[1].length() == 1)) {
            printUsage();
            return;     // Stop the program here
        }

        // Parse the two number operands. Place the parsing code inside a try-catch,
        // so we will handle the error in case both operands are not numbers.
        double n1;
        double n2;
```

```
        try {
            n1 = Double.parseDouble(args[0]);
            n2 = Double.parseDouble(args[2]);
        } catch (NumberFormatException e) {
            System.out.println("Both operands must be a number");
            printUsage();
            return;    // Stop the program here
        }

        String operation = args[1];
        double result = compute(n1, n2, operation);

        // Print the result
        System.out.println(args[0] + args[1] + args[2] + " = " + result);
    }

    public static double compute(double n1, double n2, String operation) {
        // Initialize the result with not-a-number
        double result = Double.NaN;
        switch (operation) {
            case "+":
                result = n1 + n2;
                break;
            case "-":
                result = n1 - n2;
                break;
            case "*":
                result = n1 * n2;
                break;
            case "/":
                result = n1 / n2;
                break;
            default:
                System.out.println("Invalid operation:" + operation);
        }

        return result;
    }

    public static void printUsage() {
        System.out.println("Usage: java com.jdojo.array.Calc expr");
        System.out.println("Where expr could be:");
        System.out.println("n1 + n1");
        System.out.println("n1 - n2");
        System.out.println("n1 * n2");
        System.out.println("n1 / n2");
        System.out.println("n1 and n2 are two numbers");
    }
}
```

The following are a few ways to use the Calc class to perform basic arithmetic operations:

```
C:\Java9Fundamentals>java --module-path build\modules\jdojo.array --module jdojo.array/com.
jdojo.array.Calc 3 + 7
```

```
[3, +, 7]
3+7 = 10.0
```

```
C:\Java9Fundamentals>java --module-path build\modules\jdojo.array --module jdojo.array/com.
jdojo.array.Calc 78.9 * 98.5
```

```
[78.9, *, 98.5]
78.9*98.5 = 7771.650000000001
```

You may get an error when you try to use * (asterisk) as an operation to multiply two numbers. The operating system may interpret it as all files names in the current directory. To avoid such errors, you can enclose the operator in double quotes or the escape character provided by the operating system as follows:

```
C:\Java9Fundamentals>java --module-path build\modules\jdojo.array --module jdojo.array/com.
jdojo.array.Calc 78.9 "*" 98.5
```

▓ **Tip**   If your program uses command-line arguments, it is not a 100% Java program. This is because the program does not fit in the category of "write once, run everywhere." Some operating systems do not have a command prompt, and therefore, you may not be able to use the command-line argument feature. Additionally, an operating system may interpret the metacharacters in the command-line arguments differently.

Multi-Dimensional Arrays

If a data element in a list is identified using more than one dimension, you can use a multi-dimensional array to represent the list. For example, a data element in a table is identified by two dimensions, row and column. You can store a tabular data in a two dimensional array. You can declare a multi-dimensional array by using a pair of brackets ([ ]) for each dimension in the array declaration. For example, you can declare a two dimensional array of int as shown:

```
int[][] table;
```

Here, table is a reference variable that can hold a reference to a two-dimensional array of int. At the time of declaration, memory is allocated only for the reference variable table, not for any array elements. The memory state after this code is executed is depicted in Figure 19-6.

table

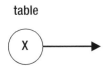

Figure 19-6. *Memory state after the declaration of a two-dimensional array*

A two-dimensional array of int with three rows and two columns can be created as shown:

```
table = new int[3][2];
```

The memory state after execution of this code is depicted in Figure 19-7. All elements have been shown to have a value of zero, because all elements of a numeric array are initialized to zero by default. The rules for default initialization of array elements of a multi-dimensional array are the same as that of a single dimensional array, as discussed previously in this chapter.

table

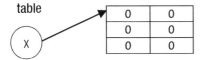

Figure 19-7. *Memory state after the creation of a two-dimensional array*

The indexes of each dimension in a multi-dimensional array are zero-based. Each element of the table array can be accessed as table[rowNumber][columnNumber]. The row number and the column number always starts at zero. For example, you can assign a value to the first row and the second column in the table array as shown:

```
table[0][1] = 32;
```

You can assign a value 71 to the third row and the first column like so:

```
table[2][0] = 71;
```

The memory state after the two assignments is depicted in Figure 19-8.

table

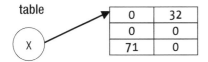

Figure 19-8. *Memory state after two assignments to the two-dimensional array elements*

Java does not support a multi-dimensional array in a true sense. Rather, it supports an array of arrays. Using an array of arrays, you can implement the same functionality as provided by multi-dimensional arrays. When you create a two-dimensional array, the elements of the first array are of an array type, which can refer to a single dimensional array. The size of each single-dimensional array need not be the same. Considering the array of arrays concept for the table two-dimensional array, you can depict the memory state after array creation and assignments of two values as shown in Figure 19-9.

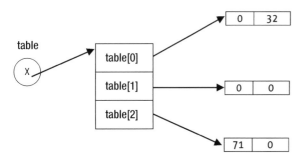

Figure 19-9. *An array of arrays*

The name of the two-dimensional array, table, refers to an array of three elements. Each element of the array is a one-dimensional array of int. The data type of table[0], table[1] and table[2] is an int array. The length of table[0], table[1], and table[2] is each 2.

You must specify the dimension of at least the first level array at the time you create a multi-dimensional array. For example, when you create a two-dimensional array, you must specify at least the first dimension, which is the number of rows. You can achieve the same results as the previous code fragment as follows:

```
table = new int[3][];
```

This statement creates only first level of array. Only table[0], table[1] and table[2] exist at this time. They are referring to null. At this time, table.length has a value of 3. Since table[0], table[1] and table[2] are referring to null, you cannot access their length attribute. That is, you have created three rows in a table, but you do not know how many columns each row will contain. Since table[0], table[1] and table[2] are arrays of int, you can assign them values as follows:

```
table[0] = new int[2]; // Create 2 columns for row 1
table[1] = new int[2]; // Create 2 columns for row 2
table[2] = new int[2]; // Create 2 columns for row 3
```

You have completed the creation of the two-dimensional array, which has three rows and each row has two columns. You can assign the values to some cells as follows:

```
table[0][1] = 32;
table[2][0] = 71;
```

It is also possible to create a two-dimensional array with different number of columns for each row. Such an array is called a *ragged* array. Listing 19-12 illustrates working with a ragged array.

Listing 19-12. An Example of a Ragged Array

```java
// RaggedArray.java
package com.jdojo.array;

public class RaggedArray {
    public static void main(String[] args) {
        // Create a two-dimensional array of 3 rows
        int[][] raggedArr = new int[3][];

        // Add 2 columns to the first row
        raggedArr[0] = new int[2];

        // Add 1 column to the second row
        raggedArr[1] = new int[1];

        // Add 3 columns to the third row
        raggedArr[2] = new int[3];

        // Assign values to all elements of raggedArr
        raggedArr[0][0] = 1;
        raggedArr[0][1] = 2;
        raggedArr[1][0] = 3;
        raggedArr[2][0] = 4;
        raggedArr[2][1] = 5;
        raggedArr[2][2] = 6;

        // Print all elements. One row at one line
        System.out.println(raggedArr[0][0] + "\t" + raggedArr[0][1]);
        System.out.println(raggedArr[1][0]);
        System.out.println(raggedArr[2][0] + "\t" + raggedArr[2][1] + "\t" +
                           raggedArr[2][2]);
    }
}
```

```
1    2
3
4    5        6
```

▓ **Tip**   Java supports an array of arrays, which can be used to achieve functionalities provided by a multi-dimensional array. Multi-dimensional arrays are widely used in scientific and engineering applications. If you are using arrays in your business application program that have more than two dimensions, you may need to reconsider the choice of multi-dimensional arrays as the choice for your data structure.

Accessing Elements of a Multi-Dimensional Array

Typically, a multi-dimensional array is populated using nested for loops. The number of for loops used to populate a multi-dimensional array equals the number of dimensions in the array. For example, two for loops are used to populate a two-dimensional array. Typically, a loop is used to access the elements of a multi-dimensional array. Listing 19-13 illustrates how to populate and access elements of a two-dimensional array.

Listing 19-13. Accessing Elements of a Multi-dimensional Array

```java
// MDAccess.java
package com.jdojo.array;

public class MDAccess {
    public static void main(String[] args){
        int[][] ra = new int[3][];
        ra[0] = new int[2];
        ra[1] = new int[1];
        ra[2] = new int[3];

        // Populate the ragged array using for loops
        for(int i = 0; i < ra.length; i++) {
            for(int j = 0; j < ra[i].length; j++){
                ra[i][j] = i + j;
            }
        }

        // Print the array using for loops
        for(int i = 0; i < ra.length; i++) {
            for (int j = 0; j < ra[i].length; j++){
                System.out.print(ra[i][j] + "\t");
            }

            // Add a new line after each row is printed
            System.out.println();
        }
    }
}
```

```
0    1
1
2    3        4
```

Initializing Multi-Dimensional Arrays

You may initialize the elements of a multi-dimensional array by supplying the list of values at the time of its declaration or at the time of creation. You cannot specify the length of any dimension if you initialize the array with a list of values. The number of initial values for each dimension will determine the length of each dimension in the array. Since many dimensions are involved in a multi-dimensional array, the list of values for a level is enclosed in braces. For a two-dimensional array, the list of values for each row is enclosed in a pair of braces, like so:

```
int[][] arr = {{10, 20, 30}, {11, 22}, {222, 333, 444, 555}};
```

This statement creates a two-dimensional array with three rows. The first row contains three columns with values 10, 20, and 30. The second row contains two columns with values 11 and 22. The third row contains four columns with values 222, 333, 444, and 555. A zero-row and zero-column two-dimensional array can be created as shown:

```
int[][] empty2D = { };
```

Initialization of a multi-dimensional array of reference type follows the same rule. You can initialize a two-dimensional String array like so:

```
String[][] acronymList = {{"JMF", "Java Media Framework"},
                          {"JSP", "Java Server Pages"},
                          {"JMS", "Java Message Service"}};
```

You can initialize the elements of a multi-dimensional array at the time you create it, like so:

```
int[][] arr = new int[][]{{1, 2}, {3,4,5}};
```

Enhanced for Loop for Arrays

Java has an enhanced for loop that lets you loop through elements of an array in a cleaner way. The enhanced for loop is also known as a for-each loop. The syntax is as follows:

```
for(DataType e : array) {
    // Loop body goes here...

    // e contains one element of the array at a time
}
```

The for-each loop uses the same for keyword used by the basic for loop. Its body is executed as many times as the number of elements in the array. DataType e is a variable declaration, where e is the variable name and DataType is its data type. The data type of the variable e should be assignment-compatible with the type of the array. The variable declaration is followed by a colon (:), which is followed by the reference of the array that you want to loop through. The for-each loop assigns the value of an element of the array to the variable e, which you can use inside the body of the loop. The following snippet of code uses a for-each loop to print all elements of an int array:

```
int[] numList = {1, 2, 3};

for(int num : numList) {
    System.out.println(num);
}
```

```
1
2
3
```

You can accomplish the same feat using the basic `for` loop, as follows:

```java
int[] numList = {1, 2, 3};

for(int i = 0; i < numList.length; i++) {
    int num = numList[i];
    System.out.println(num);
}
```

```
1
2
3
```

Note that the `for-each` loop provides a way to loop through elements of an array, which is cleaner than the basic `for` loop. However, it is not a replacement for the basic `for` loop because you cannot use it in all circumstances. For example, you cannot access the index of the array element and you cannot modify the value of the element inside the loop as you do not have the index of the element.

Array Declaration Syntax

You can declare an array by placing a pair of brackets ([ ]) after the data type of the array or after the name of the array reference variable. For example, the following declaration

```java
int[] empIds;
int[][] points2D;
int[][][] points3D;
Person[] persons;
```

is equivalent to

```java
int empIds[];
int points2D[][];
int points3D[][][];
Person persons[];
```

Java also allows you to mix two syntaxes. In the same array declaration, you can place some brackets after the data type and some after the variable name. For example, you can declare a two-dimensional array of `int` as follows:

```java
int[] points2D[];
```

You can declare a two-dimensional and a three-dimensional array of int in one declaration statement as follows:

```
int[] points2D[], points3D[][];
```

or

```
int[][] points2D, points3D[];
```

Runtime Array Bounds Checks

At runtime, Java checks array bounds for every access to an array element. If the array bounds are exceeded, an java.lang.ArrayIndexOutOfBoundsException is thrown. The only requirement for array index values at compile-time is that they must be integers. The Java compiler does not check if the value of an array index is less than zero or beyond its length. This check must be performed at runtime, before every access to an array element is allowed. Runtime array bounds checks slow down the program execution for two reasons:

- The first reason is the cost of bound checks itself. To check the array bounds, the length of the array must be loaded in memory and two comparisons (one for less than zero and one for greater than or equal to its length) must be performed.

- The second reason is that an exception must be thrown when the array bounds are exceeded. Java must do some housekeeping and get ready to throw an exception if the array bounds are exceeded.

Listing 19-14 illustrates the exception thrown if the array bounds are exceeded. The program creates an array of int named test, which has a length of 3. The program cannot access the fourth element (test[3] as it does not exist. An ArrayIndexOutOfBoundsException is thrown when such an attempt is made.

Listing 19-14. Array Bounds Checks

```
// ArrayBounds.java
package  com.jdojo.array;

public class ArrayBounds {
    public static void main(String[] args) {
        int[] test = new int[3];

        System.out.println("Assigning 12 to the first element");
        test[0] = 12;  // OK. Index 0 is between 0 and 2.

        System.out.println("Assigning 79 to the fourth element");

        // Index 3 is not between 0 and 2. At runtime, an exception is thrown.
        test[3] = 79;

        System.out.println("We will not get here");
    }
}
```

```
Assigning 12 to the first element
Assigning 79 to the fourth element
Exception in thread "main" java.lang.ArrayIndexOutOfBoundsException: 3
        at com.jdojo.array.ArrayBounds.main(ArrayBounds.java:14)
```

It is good practice to check for array length before accessing its elements. The fact that array bounds violation throws an exception may be misused as shown in the following snippet of code, which prints values stored in an array:

```
/* Do not use this code, even if it works.*/
// Create an array
int[] arr = new int[10];

// Populate the array here...

// Print the array. Wrong way
try {
    // Start an infinite loop. When we are done with all elements an exception is
    // thrown and we will be in catch block and hence out of the loop.
    int counter = 0;
    while (true) {
        System.out.println(arr[counter++]);
    }
} catch (ArrayIndexOutOfBoundsException e) {
    // We are done with printing array elements
}

// Do some processing here...
```

The previous snippet of code uses an infinite while loop to print values of the elements of an array and relies on the exception throwing mechanism to check for array bounds. The right way is to use a for loop and check for array index value using the length property of the array.

What Is the Class of an Array Object?

Arrays are objects. Because every object has a class, you must have a class for every array. All methods of the Object class can be used on arrays. Because the getClass() method of the Object class gives the reference of the class for any object in Java, you will use this method to get the class name for all arrays. Listing 19-15 illustrates how to get the class name of an array.

Listing 19-15. Knowing the Class of an Array

```
// ArrayClass.java
package com.jdojo.array;

public class ArrayClass {
    public static void main (String[] args){
        int[] iArr = new int[2];
        int[][] iiArr = new int[2][2];
        int[][][] iiiArr = new int[2][2][2];

        String[] sArr  = {"A", "B"} ;
        String[][] ssArr = {{"AA"}, {"BB"}} ;
        String[][][] sssArr = {} ; // A 3D empty array of string

        // Print the class name for all arrays
        System.out.println("int[]: " + getClassName(iArr));
        System.out.println("int[][]: " + getClassName(iiArr));
        System.out.println("int[][][]: " + getClassName(iiiArr));
        System.out.println("String[]: " + getClassName(sArr));
        System.out.println("String[][]: " + getClassName(ssArr));
        System.out.println("String[][][]: " + getClassName(sssArr));
    }

    // Any Java object can be passed to getClassName() method.
    // Since every array is an object, we can also pass an array to this method.
    public static String getClassName(Object obj) {
        // Get the reference of its class
        Class<?> c = obj.getClass();

        // Get the name of the class
        String className = c.getName();
        return className;
    }
}
```

```
int[]: [I
int[][]: [[I
int[][][]: [[[I
String[]: [Ljava.lang.String;
String[][]: [[Ljava.lang.String;
String[][][]: [[[Ljava.lang.String;
```

The class name of an array starts with left bracket(s) ([ ). The number of left brackets is equal to the dimension of the array. For an int array, the left bracket(s) is followed by a character I. For a reference type array, the left bracket(s) is followed by a character L, followed by the name of the class name, which is followed by a semicolon. The class names for one-dimensional primitive arrays and a reference type are shown in Table 19-2.

Table 19-2. *Class Name of Arrays*

Array Type	Class Name
byte[]	[B
short[]	[S
int[]	[I
long[]	[J
char[]	[C
float[]	[F
double[]	[D
boolean[]	[Z
com.jdojo.array.Person[]	[Lcom.jdojo.array.Person;

The class names of arrays are not available at compile-time for declaring or creating them. You must use the syntax described in this chapter to create an array. That is, you cannot write the following to create an int array:

```
[I myIntArray;
```

Rather, you must write the following to create an int array:

```
int[] myIntArray;
```

Array Assignment Compatibility

The data type of each element of an array is the same as the data type of the array. For example, each element of an int[] array is an int; each element of a String[] array is a String. The value assigned to an element of an array must be assignment-compatible to its data type. For example, it is allowed to assign a byte value to an element of an int array, because byte is assignment-compatible to int. However, it is not allowed to assign a float value to an element of an int array, because float is not assignment-compatible to int.

```
int[] sequence = new int[10];
sequence[0] = 10;    // OK. Assigning an int 10 to an int
sequence[1] = 19.4f; // A compile-time error. Assigning a float to an int
```

The same rule must be followed when dealing with a reference type array. If there is a reference type array of type T, its elements can be assigned an object reference of type S, if and only if, S is assignment-compatible to T. The subclass object reference is always assignment-compatible to the superclass of all classes in Java, you can use an array of Object class to store objects of any class. For example,

```
Object[] genericArray = new Object[4];

genericArray[0] = new String("Hello");  // OK
genericArray[1] = new Person("Daniel"); // OK. Assuming Person class exists
genericArray[2] = new Account(189);     // OK. Assuming Account class exist
genericArray[3] = null;                 // Ok. null can be assigned to any reference type
```

You need to perform a cast at the time you read back the object from the array, as shown:

```
/* The compiler will flag an error for the following statement. genericArray is of Object
   type and an Object reference cannot be assigned to a String reference variable. Even
   though genericArray[0] contains a String object reference, we need to cast it to String
   as we do in next statement.
*/
String s = genericArray[0]; // A compile-time error

String str = (String) genericArray[0]; // OK
Person p = (Person) genericArray[1];    // OK
Account a = (Account) genericArray[2]; // OK
```

If you try to cast the array element to a type, whose actual type is not assignment-compatible to the new type, a java.lang.ClassCastException is thrown. For example, the following statement will throw a ClassCastException at runtime:

```
String str = (String) genericArray[1]; // Person cannot be cast to String
```

You cannot store an object reference of the superclass in an array of the subclass. The following snippet of code illustrates this:

```
String[] names = new String[3];
names[0] = new Object(); // A compile-time error. Object is superclass of String
names[1] = new Person(); // A compile-time error. Person is not subclass of String
names[2] = null;         // OK.
```

Finally, an array reference can be assigned to another array reference of another type if the former type is assignment-compatible to the latter type.

```
Object[] obj = new Object[3];
String[] str = new String[2];
Account[] a = new Account[5];

obj = str;          // OK
str = (String[]) obj; // OK because obj has String array reference

obj = a;

// A ClassCastException will be thrown. obj has the reference of an Account array and
// an Account cannot be converted to a String
str = (String[]) obj;

a = (Account[]) obj; // OK
```

Converting an ArrayList/Vector to an Array

An ArrayList can be used when the number of elements in the list is not precisely known. Once the number of elements in the list is fixed, you may want to convert an ArrayList to an array. You may do this for one of the following reasons:

- The program semantics may require you to use an array, not an ArrayList. For example, you may need to pass an array to a method, but you have data stored in an ArrayList.

- You may want to store user inputs in an array. However, you do not know the number of values the user will input. In such a case, you can store values in an ArrayList while accepting input from the user. At the end, you can convert the ArrayList to an array.

- Accessing array elements is faster than accessing ArrayList elements. If you have an ArrayList and you want to access the elements multiple times, you may want to convert the ArrayList to an array for better performance.

The ArrayList class has an overloaded method named toArray():

- Object[] toArray()

- \<T> T[] toArray(T[] a)

The first method returns the elements of ArrayList as an array of Object. The second method takes an array of any type as argument. All ArrayList elements are copied to the passed array if there is enough space and the same array is returned. If there is not enough space in the passed array, a new array is created. The type of new array is the same as the passed array. The length of the new array is equal to the size of ArrayList. Listing 19-16 shows how to convert an ArrayList to an array.

Listing 19-16. An ArrayList to an Array Conversion

```
// ArrayListToArray.java
package com.jdojo.array;

import java.util.ArrayList;
import java.util.Arrays;

public class ArrayListToArray {
    public static void main(String[] args) {
        ArrayList<String> al = new ArrayList<>();
        al.add("cat");
        al.add("dog");
        al.add("rat");

        // Print the content of the ArrayList
        System.out.println("ArrayList: " + al);

        // Create an array of the same length as the ArrayList
        String[] s1 = new String[al.size()];

        // Copy the ArrayList elements to the array
        String[] s2 = al.toArray(s1);
```

```
            // s1 has enough space to copy all ArrayList elements.
            // al.toArray(s1) returns s1 itself
            System.out.println("s1 == s2: " + (s1 == s2));
            System.out.println("s1: " + Arrays.toString(s1));
            System.out.println("s2: " + Arrays.toString(s2));

            // Create an array of string with 1 element.
            s1 = new String[1];
            s1[0] = "hello"; // Store hello in first element

            // Copy ArrayList to the array s1
            s2 = al.toArray(s1);

            /* Since s1 doesn't have sufficient space to copy all ArrayList elements,
               al.toArray(s1) creates a new String array with 3 elements in it. All
               elements of arraylist are copied to new array. Finally, the new array is
               returned. Here, s1 == s2 is false. s1 will be untouched by the method call.
             */
            System.out.println("s1 == s2: " + (s1 == s2));
            System.out.println("s1: " + Arrays.toString(s1));
            System.out.println("s2: " + Arrays.toString(s2));
    }
}
```

```
ArrayList: [cat, dog, rat]
s1 == s2: true
s1: [cat, dog, rat]
s2: [cat, dog, rat]
s1 == s2: false
s1: [hello]
s2: [cat, dog, rat]
```

Performing Array Operations

There are several routine array operations such as sorting, searching, comparing, and copying that you need to perform in everyday programming. The java.util.Arrays class is a utility class that contains over 150 static convenience methods to perform such types of array operations. Before you roll out your own code to perform array operations, refer to the Arrays class API documentation and you might find a method to achieve the same.

Do not get intimidated by the large number of methods in this class. It does not support over 150 types of array operations. The reason for the large number of methods in the Arrays class is to support the same operations on arrays of all primitive types and reference types. Most methods have at least nine overloaded versions—one for each of the eight primitive type arrays and one for the reference type array. Sometimes, operations can be performed on the entire array or on a range of elements that doubles the number of minimum methods for one array operation to at least 18. It is not possible to go through each and every method and provide examples. That will take over 100 pages of this book. I put all methods into different categories based on the type of operations they perform and provide a few examples. Table 19-3 lists such categories and the names of the methods that perform array operations in those categories.

Table 19-3. *Methods in the Arrays Class and Their Categories with Description*

Category	Method Name	Description
Conversion	asList()	Returns a *fixed-size* list backed by the specified array. There is only one version of this method.
	stream()	Returns a sequential stream of an array for all elements or a range of elements.
	toString()	Returns a string representation of the contents of the specified array.
	deepToString()	Returns a string representation of the "deep contents" of an array. Suitable for using for a multi-dimensional array.
Searching	binarySearch()	Allows you to search a sorted array using the binary search algorithm. The array must be sorted before passed to this method; otherwise, the result is undefined. Search is allowed in the entire array or in a range of elements within the array.
Comparing	compare()	Compares two arrays lexicographically. It returns 0 if the first and second array are equal and contain the same elements in the same order; a value less than 0 if the first array is lexicographically less than the second array; and a value greater than 0 if the first array is lexicographically greater than the second array. The method was added in Java 9.
	compareUnsigned()	Works the same as the compare() method, numerically treating elements as unsigned. The method was added in Java 9.
	deepEquals()	Returns true if the two specified arrays are deeply equal to one another.
	equals()	Returns true if the two specified arrays of ints are equal to one another. You can compare entire arrays or a range of elements in them for equality. The method was added in Java 9.
	mismatch()	Finds and returns the index of the first mismatch between two arrays, otherwise return -1 if no mismatch is found. The entire contents of two arrays of their range of elements can be compared for a mismatch. The method was added in Java 9.
Copying	copyOf()	Copies an array to another array. The length of the new array is specified. The new array may be smaller of bigger than the source array. If it is bigger, additional elements are filled with the default value of the data type of the array.
	copyOfRange()	Copies a range of elements from one array to another.
Filling	fill()	Allows you to assign the same value to all elements or to a range of elements in an array.
	setAll()	Allows you to assign a value to all elements or to a range of elements in an array. The values are generated by a generator function.
Computing Hash Code	deepHashCode()	Returns a hash code based on the "deep contents" of an array. For a multi-dimensional array, contents in all dimensions are included in computing the hash code.

(continued)

Table 19-3. (*continued*)

Category	Method Name	Description
	hashCode()	Returns a hash code based on the contents of the specified array.
Parallel Update	parallelPrefix()	Cumulates, in parallel, each element of an array in place, using the supplied function.
	parallelSetAll()	Sets all elements of the specified array, in parallel, using a generator function to compute each element.
Sorting	parallelSort()	Sorts all elements or a range of elements in an array using parallel sort.
	sort()	Sorts all elements or a range of elements in an array.
Obtaining Spliterator	spliterator()	Returns a Spliterator including all or a range of elements in an array.

The following sections show you how to use some of these methods. You will need to import several classes and interfaces from the java.util package to run the example snippets of code. The following import will do the job:

```
import java.util.*;
```

Converting Arrays to Another Type

In this category, methods in the Arrays class lets you obtain a List, a Stream, and a String from an array. The asList(T... a) method takes a var-args argument of type T and returns a List<T>. The following are a few examples:

```
// Create a String array
String[] animals = {"rat", "dog", "cat"};

// Convert the array to a List
List<String> animalList = Arrays.asList(animals);
System.out.println("As a List: " + animalList);

// Convert the array to a String
String str = Arrays.toString(animals);
System.out.println("As a String: " + str);

// Get a sorted Stream of the array and print its elements
System.out.println("Sorted Stream of Animals: ");
Arrays.stream(animals)
     .sorted()
     .forEach(System.out::println);
```

```
As a List: [rat, dog, cat]
As a String: [rat, dog, cat]
Sorted Stream of Animals:
cat
dog
rat
```

Searching an Array

Use the binarySearch() method to search for a key in an array. The array must be sorted. The method returns the index of the search key if it is contained in the array. Otherwise, it returns a negative number, which is equal to

```
(-(insertion point) - 1)
```

Here, insertion point is defined as the index at which the key would be inserted into the array. This guarantees that the returned value is a negative integer if the key is not present in the array. The following is an example:

```java
// Create an array to work with
int[] num = {2, 4, 3, 1};
System.out.println("Original Array: " + Arrays.toString(num));

// Sort the array before using the binary search
Arrays.sort(num);
System.out.println("Array After Sorting: " + Arrays.toString(num));

int index = Arrays.binarySearch(num, 3);
System.out.println("Found index of 3: " + index);

index = Arrays.binarySearch(num, 200);
System.out.println("Found index of 200: " + index);
```

Comparing Arrays

The equals() method lets you compare two arrays for equality. Two arrays are considered equal if the number of elements in the arrays or slices is the same, and all corresponding pairs of elements in the arrays or slices are equal.

The compare() and compareUnsigned() methods compare elements in arrays or arrays' slices lexicographically. The compareUnsigned() method treats the integer values as unsigned. A null array is lexicographically less than a non-null array. Two null arrays are equal.

The mismatch() method compares two arrays or array's slices. The method returns the index of the first mismatch. If there is no mismatch, it returns -1. If either array is null, it throws a NullPointerException. Listing 19-17 contains a complete program that compares two arrays and their slices. The program uses int arrays for comparisons.

Listing 19-17. Comparing Arrays and Array's Slices Using the Arrays Class Methods

```java
// ArrayComparison.java
package com.jdojo.array;

import java.util.Arrays;

public class ArrayComparison {
    public static void main(String[] args) {
        int[] a1 = {1, 2, 3, 4, 5};
        int[] a2 = {1, 2, 7, 4, 5};
        int[] a3 = {1, 2, 3, 4, 5};

        // Print original arrays
        System.out.println("Three arrays:");
        System.out.println("a1: " + Arrays.toString(a1));
        System.out.println("a2: " + Arrays.toString(a2));
        System.out.println("a3: " + Arrays.toString(a3));

        // Compare arrays for equality
        System.out.println("\nComparing arrays using equals() method:");
        System.out.println("Arrays.equals(a1, a2): " + Arrays.equals(a1, a2));
        System.out.println("Arrays.equals(a1, a3): " + Arrays.equals(a1, a3));
        System.out.println("Arrays.equals(a1, 0, 2, a2, 0, 2): "
                + Arrays.equals(a1, 0, 2, a2, 0, 2));

        // Compare arrays lexicographically
        System.out.println("\nComparing arrays using compare() method:");
        System.out.println("Arrays.compare(a1, a2): " + Arrays.compare(a1, a2));
        System.out.println("Arrays.compare(a2, a1): " + Arrays.compare(a2, a1));
        System.out.println("Arrays.compare(a1, a3): " + Arrays.compare(a1, a3));
        System.out.println("Arrays.compare(a1, 0, 2, a2, 0, 2): "
                + Arrays.compare(a1, 0, 2, a2, 0, 2));

        // Find the mismatched index in arrays
        System.out.println("\nFinding mismatch using the mismatch() method:");
        System.out.println("Arrays.mismatch(a1, a2): " + Arrays.mismatch(a1, a2));
        System.out.println("Arrays.mismatch(a1, a3): " + Arrays.mismatch(a1, a3));
        System.out.println("Arrays.mismatch(a1, 0, 5, a2, 0, 1): "
                + Arrays.mismatch(a1, 0, 5, a2, 0, 1));
    }
}
```

```
Three arrays:
a1: [1, 2, 3, 4, 5]
a2: [1, 2, 7, 4, 5]
a3: [1, 2, 3, 4, 5]

Comparing arrays using equals() method:
Arrays.equals(a1, a2): false
Arrays.equals(a1, a3): true
Arrays.equals(a1, 0, 2, a2, 0, 2): true
```

```
Comparing arrays using compare() method:
Arrays.compare(a1, a2): -1
Arrays.compare(a2, a1): 1
Arrays.compare(a1, a3): 0
Arrays.compare(a1, 0, 2, a2, 0, 2): 0

Finding mismatch using the mismatch() method:
Arrays.mismatch(a1, a2): 2
Arrays.mismatch(a1, a3): -1
Arrays.mismatch(a1, 0, 5, a2, 0, 1): 1
```

Copying Arrays

The copyOf() method lets you copy elements of the original array by specifying a new length for the new array. If the length of the new array is greater than the length of the original array, the additional elements are assigned a default value according to the type of the array. The copyOfRange() method lets you copy a slice of an array to another array. Here is an example:

```
// Create an array to work with
int[] num = {2, 4, 3, 1};
System.out.println("Original Array: " + Arrays.toString(num));

// Copy of the truncated num to 2 elements
int[] numCopy1 = Arrays.copyOf(num, 2);
System.out.println("Truncated Copy: " + Arrays.toString(numCopy1));

// Copy of the extended num to 6 elements
int[] numCopy2 = Arrays.copyOf(num, 6);
System.out.println("Extended Copy: " + Arrays.toString(numCopy2));

// Copy of the range index 2 (inclusive) to 4 (exclusive)
int[] numCopy3 = Arrays.copyOfRange(num, 2, 4);
System.out.println("Range Copy: " + Arrays.toString(numCopy3));
```

```
Original Array: [2, 4, 3, 1]
Truncated Copy: [2, 4]
Extended Copy: [2, 4, 3, 1, 0, 0]
Range Copy: [3, 1]
```

Filling Arrays

You can use the fill() method to lets you fill all elements or a range of elements of an array with the same value. The setAll() method lets you set values for all elements in an array using a function. The function is passed the index of the array and it returns the value for the element at that index. Here are examples of using both methods:

```
// Create an array to work with
int[] num = {2, 4, 3, 1};
System.out.println("Original Array: " + Arrays.toString(num));
```

```
// Fill elements of the array with 10
Arrays.fill(num, 10);
System.out.println("Array filled with 10: " + Arrays.toString(num));

// Fill elements of the array with a value (index + 1) * 10
Arrays.setAll(num, index -> (index + 1) * 10);
System.out.println("Array filled with a function: " + Arrays.toString(num));
```

```
Original Array: [2, 4, 3, 1]
Array filled with 10: [10, 10, 10, 10]
Array filled with a function: [10, 20, 30, 40]
```

Computing Hash Code

Use the hashCode() method to compute the hash code for an array based on its elements' values. If the passed in array is null, the method returns 0. For any two arrays a1 and a2 such that Arrays.equals (a1, a2), it is also the case that Arrays.hashCode(a1) == Arrays.hashCode(a2). Here is an example:

```
// Create an array to work with
int[] num = {2, 4, 3, 1};
System.out.println("Array: " + Arrays.toString(num));

// Compute the hash code of the array
int hashCode = Arrays.hashCode(num);
System.out.println("Hash Code: " + hashCode);
```

```
Array: [2, 4, 3, 1]
Hash Code: 987041
```

Performing Parallel Accumulation

```
int[] num = {2, 4, 3, 1};
System.out.println("Before: " + Arrays.toString(num));
Arrays.parallelPrefix(num, (n1, n2) -> n1 * n2);
System.out.println("After: " + Arrays.toString(num));
```

```
Before: [2, 4, 3, 1]
After: [2, 8, 24, 24]
```

Sorting Arrays

Use the sort() and parallelSort() methods to sort elements of an array. The former is suitable for smaller arrays and the latter for bigger arrays. Here are a few examples:

```
// Create an array to work with
int[] num1 = {2, 4, 3, 1};
System.out.println("Original Array: " + Arrays.toString(num1));

// Sort the array
Arrays.sort(num1);
System.out.println("Using sort(): " + Arrays.toString(num1));

// Create an array to work with
int[] num2 = {2, 4, 3, 1};
System.out.println("Original Array: " + Arrays.toString(num2));

// Sort the array
Arrays.parallelSort(num2);
System.out.println("Using parallelSort(): " + Arrays.toString(num2));
```

```
Original Array: [2, 4, 3, 1]
Using sort(): [1, 2, 3, 4]
Original Array: [2, 4, 3, 1]
Using parallelSort(): [1, 2, 3, 4]
```

Summary

An array is a data structure to store multiple data values of the same type. All array elements are allocated contiguous space in memory. Array elements are accessed using their indexes. Arrays use zero-based indexing. The first element has an index of zero. Every array has a property named length, which contains the number of elements in the array. An array can have a length of zero.

Arrays in Java are objects. Java supports fixed-length arrays. That is, once an array is created, its length cannot be changed. Use an ArrayList if you need a variable-length array. The ArrayList class provides a toArray() method to convert its elements to an array. Java supports multi-dimensional arrays in the form of ragged arrays that are arrays of arrays. You can clone an array using the clone() method. The method performs a shallow cloning for reference arrays.

The Arrays class in the java.util package contains several static convenience methods that let you perform many different types of operations on an array like searching, sorting, comparing, filling, etc.

EXERCISES

1. What is an array? Name the property of an array that gives you the number of elements in the array.

2. What is the index of the first element of an array?

3. Write the code to initialize an `int` array in two ways. The array contains elements 10, 20, and 30.

4. You have to store values in an array, but you do not know the number of elements in advance. How will you code this situation, so you get all elements in an array in the end?

5. Complete the following snippet of code that prints the class name of an array object:

```
String[] names = {"Corky", "Bryce", "Paul", "Tony"};
String className = names./* Your code goes here */;
System.out.println("Class Name: " + className);
```

6. Consider the following declaration of a method named `test()` that takes an `int[]` array as an argument:

```
public static void test(int[] num) {
    if(num.length > 0) {
        num[0] = 100;
    }
    num = new int[]{1000, 2000};
 }
```

Write the output when the following code is executed:

```
int[] num = {2, 4, 3, 1};
System.out.println("num[0] = " + num[0]);
test(num);
System.out.println("num[0] = " + num[0]);
```

7. Which of the following statements declares a two-dimensional `int` array:

```
int[][] y;
int z[][];
int[] x[];
int[] x = {2, 2};
```

8. Declare a two-dimensional array of three rows and three columns named `table`. Demonstrate how you will initialize all elements of the array with a value 10 during declaration and using a `for` loop.

9. Consider the following declaration for an array:

```
int[] x = {10, 20, 30, 40};
```

Write a `for` loop and a `for-each` loop to print each element's value in the array on a single line on the standard output.

10. Consider the following declaration for an array:

```
int[] x = {10, 20, 30, 40};
System.out.println(x[5]);
```

What will happen when this snippet of code is executed?

11. What method of the `Arrays` class will you use to sort a large array: `sort()` or `parallelSort()`?

12. Name the method in the `Arrays` class that converts an array to its string representation.

13. The `Arrays` class contains a `binarySearch()` method that lets you search a value in the array, What condition must the array meet before you should use the `binarySearch()` method?

14. Write and explain the output of the following snippet of code:

```
int[][] table1 = {{1, 2, 3}, {10, 20, 30}};
int[][] table2 = {{1, 2, 3}, {10, 20, 30}};

boolean equal1 = Arrays.equals(table1, table2);
boolean equal2 = Arrays.deepEquals(table1, table2);

System.out.println(equal1);
System.out.println(equal2);
```

15. Consider the following snippet of code that is meant to copy the contents of a two-dimensional array named `table1` to another two-dimensional array named `table2`. Help the author of this code to complete the missing logic. You need to write two lines of code.

```
int[][] table1 = {{1, 2, 3}, {10, 20, 30}};
int[][] table2 = new int[table1.length][];

// Complete missing logic
for(int i = 0; i < table1.length; i++) {
    /* Your one line code goes here */
    for(int j = 0; j < table1[i].length; j++) {
        /* Your one line code goes here */
    }
}

boolean equal = Arrays.deepEquals(table1, table2);
System.out.println(equal);
System.out.println(Arrays.deepToString(table1));
System.out.println(Arrays.deepToString(table2));
```

This snippet of code is supposed to have the following output:

```
true
[[1, 2, 3], [10, 20, 30]]
[[1, 2, 3], [10, 20, 30]]
```

CHAPTER 20

Inheritance

In this chapter, you will learn:

- What inheritance is

- How to inherit a class from another class

- The difference between early binding and late binding

- What method overriding is and how to override methods

- What field hiding and method hiding are and how to use them

- What abstract classes are and where to use them

- How to declare `final` classes and methods

- The difference between "is-a," "has-a," and "part-of" relationships

All example programs in this chapter are a member of a `jdojo.inheritance` module, as declared in Listing 20-1.

Listing 20-1. The Declaration of a jdojo.inheritance Module

```
// module-info.java
module jdojo.inheritance {
    exports com.jdojo.inheritance;
}
```

What Is Inheritance?

Sometimes you may need the same functionality at multiple places in your application. There are different ways to write code to achieve this. One way is to copy the same code in all places where you need the same functionality. If you follow this logic, you need to make changes at all places when the functionality changes. Consider an example where you need the same functionality at three different places. Suppose you have an application that deals with three kinds of objects: planets, employees, and managers. Further, suppose that all three kinds of objects have a name. You create three classes: `Planet`, `Employee`, and `Manager` to represent the three kinds of objects. Each class has an instance variable called `name` and two methods called `getName()` and `setName()`. If you think about the code in three classes to maintain the name of their objects, you would find that they are the same. You might have written code for one class and copied it to other two classes. You may realize the problem in maintaining this kind of code when the same code is copied multiple places. If you need to handle the name differently later, you will need to make changes in three places. Inheritance is the feature of object-oriented programming that helps in such circumstances to avoid copying the same code at multiple places, thus facilitating code reuse. Inheritance also lets you customize the code without changing the existing code. Inheritance offers much more than just the code reuse and customization.

Inheritance is one of the cornerstones of object-oriented programming languages. It lets you create a new class by reusing code from an existing class. The new class is called a subclass and the existing class is called the superclass. A superclass contains the code that is reused and customized by the subclass. It is said that the subclass inherits from the superclass. A superclass is also known as a base class or a parent class. A subclass is also known as a derived class or a child class. Technically, it may be possible to inherit a class from any existing class. However, practically it is not always a good idea to do so. Inheritance in software development works much the same way as inheritance in normal human life. You inherit something from your parents; your parents inherit something from their parents, and so on. If you look at inheritance in human lives, there exists a relationship between humans for inheritance to occur. Similarly, there exists a relationship between objects of the superclass and the subclass. The relationship that must exist between the superclass and the subclass in order for inheritance to be effective is called an "is-a" relationship. You need to ask yourself a simple question before you should inherit class Q from class P: "Is an object of class Q also an object of class P?" In other words, "Does an object of class Q behave like an object of class P". If the answer is yes, class Q may inherit from class P. Consider three classes Planet, Employee, and Manager. Let's ask the same question using these three classes one-by-one.

- Is a planet an employee? That is, does an "is-a" relationship exist between a planet and an employee? The answer is no. Is an employee a planet? The answer is no.

- Is a planet a manager? The answer is no. Is a manager a planet? The answer is no.

- Is an employee a manager? The answer is maybe. An employee may be a manager, a clerk, a programmer, or any other type of employee. However, an employee is not necessarily always a manager. Is a manager an employee? The answer is yes.

You asked six questions using the three classes. You got "yes" as the answer in only one case. This is the only case that is fit for using inheritance. The Manager class should inherit from the Employee class.

Inheriting Classes

How does a class inherit from another class? It is very simple to inherit a class from another class. You need to use the keyword extends followed by the superclass name in the class declaration of your subclass. The general syntax is as follows:

```
[modifiers] class <subclass-name> extends <superclass-name> {
    // Code for the subclass goes here
}
```

For example, the following code declares a class Q, which inherits from class P, assuming that class P already exists:

```
public class Q extends P {
    // Code for class Q goes here
}
```

You can use either the simple name or the fully qualified name of the superclass in a class declaration. If the subclass and the superclass do not reside in the same package, you may need to import the superclass name to use its simple name in the extends clause. Suppose the fully qualified names of class P and Q are pkg1.P and pkg2.Q, respectively. The previous declaration may be rewritten in one of the following two ways: using simple name of the superclass or using the fully qualified name of the superclass.

```
// #1 - Use the simple name of P in the extends clause and use an import statement.
package pkg2;

import pkg1.P;

public class Q extends P {
    // Code for class Q goes here
}

// #2 - Use the fully qualified name of P. No need to use an import statement.
package pkg2;

public class Q extends pkg1.P {
    // Code for class Q goes here
}
```

Let's look at the simplest example of inheritance in Java. Let's start with an Employee class, as shown in Listing 20-2.

Listing 20-2. An Employee Class

```
// Employee.java
package com.jdojo.inheritance;

public class Employee {
    private String name = "Unknown";

    public void setName(String name) {
        this.name = name;
    }

    public String getName() {
        return name;
    }
}
```

Employee is a simple class with a private instance variable, name, and two public methods, setName() and getName(). The instance variable is used to store the name for an employee and the two methods are used to get and set the name instance variable. Note that there is no special code in the Employee class. It is one of the simplest classes you can write in Java. It is easy to write and understand the following snippet of code that uses the Employee class:

```
Employee emp = new Employee();
emp.setName("John Jacobs");
String empName = emp.getName();
System.out.println("Employee Name: " + empName);
```

```
Employee Name: John Jacobs
```

Listing 20-3 contains the code for a Manager class, which inherits from the Employee class. Note the use of the keyword extends to indicate that the Employee class is the superclass and the Manager class is the subclass. The Manager class does not contain any code, except its declaration. That is all you need in the Manager class for now.

Listing 20-3. A Manager Class

```java
// Manager.java
package com.jdojo.inheritance;

public class Manager extends Employee {
    // No code is needed for now
}
```

Let's test the Manager class. Listing 20-4 contains the test program.

Listing 20-4. Testing the Manager Class

```java
// SimplestInheritanceTest.java
package com.jdojo.inheritance;

public class SimplestInheritanceTest {
    public static void main(String[] args) {
        // Create an object of the Manager class
        Manager mgr = new Manager();

        // Set the manager name
        mgr.setName("Leslie Zanders");

        // Get the manager name
        String mgrName = mgr.getName();

        // Print the manager name
        System.out.println("Manager Name: " + mgrName);
    }
}
```

```
Manager Name: Leslie Zanders
```

Even if you did not write any code for the Manager class, it works the same as the Employee class, because it inherits from the Employee class. You create a manager object by using the Manager class's constructor:

```java
Manager mgr = new Manager();
```

After the Manager object is created, the code looks similar to the one you used for dealing with an Employee object. You used the setName() and getName() methods with the Manager object.

```java
mgr.setName("Leslie Zanders");
String mgrName = mgr.getName();
```

Note that the Manager class does not declare the setName() and getName() methods. Neither does it declare the name instance variable. However, it appears that all of them have been declared inside the Manager class, because it uses the "extends Employee" clause in its declaration. When a class inherits from another class, it inherits its superclass members (instance variables, methods, etc.). There are many rules that govern inheritance. I discuss those rules in detail, one by one later in this chapter.

The Object Class Is the Default Superclass

If a class does not specify a superclass using the keyword extends in its class declaration, it inherits from the java.lang.Object class. For example, the following two class declarations for class P are the same:

```
// #1 - "extends Object" is implicitly added for class P
public class P {
    // Code for class P goes here
}

// #2 - "extends Object" is explicitly added for class P
public class P extends Object {
    // Code for class P goes here
}
```

In the previous chapters, you did not use the extends clause to declare your classes. They were implicitly inherited from the Object class. This is the reason that objects of those classes were able to use the methods of the Object class. Consider the following snippet of code:

```
Employee emp = new Employee();
int hc = emp.hashCode();
String str = emp.toString();
```

The Employee class does not specify its superclass using an extends clause. This means that it inherits from the Object class. The Object class declares the hashCode() and toString() methods. Because the Employee class is implicitly a subclass of the Object class, it can use these methods as if they have been included in its own declaration. You have been using inheritance from the very first Java program you wrote, although you were not aware of it. This section has demonstrated the power of inheritance that comes as code reuse. You will see other benefits of inheritance later in this chapter.

Inheritance and Hierarchical Relationship

I touched upon this point in the previous section that inheritance should be used only if an "is-a" relationship exists between the subclass and the superclass. A subclass can have its own subclasses, which in turn can have their own subclasses, and so on. All classes in an inheritance chain form a tree-like structure, which is known as an inheritance hierarchy or a class hierarchy. All classes above a class in the inheritance hierarchy are called ancestors for that class. All classes below a class in the inheritance hierarchy are called descendants of that class.

Java allows single inheritance for a class. That is, a class can have only one superclass (or parent). However, a class can be the superclass for multiple classes. All classes in Java have a superclass except the Object class. The Object class sits at the top of the inheritance hierarchies. Figure 20-1 shows a sample inheritance hierarchy for the Employee class and its descendants using a UML (Unified Modeling Language) diagram. In a UML diagram, a superclass and a subclass are connected using an arrow pointing from the subclass to the superclass.

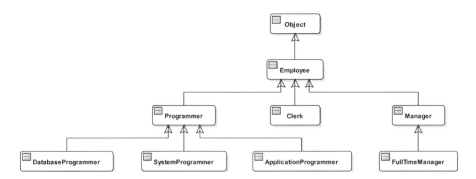

Figure 20-1. *A sample inheritance class hierarchy*

Sometimes, the term "immediate superclass" is used to mean the ancestor class, which is one level up in the inheritance hierarchy whereas the term "superclass" is used to mean an ancestor class at any level. This book uses the term "superclass" to mean ancestor of a class, which is one level up in the inheritance hierarchy. For example, `Programmer` is the superclass of `SystemProgrammer`, whereas `Employee` and `Object` are ancestors of `SystemProgrammer`. Sometimes, the term "immediate subclass" is used to mean a descendant class, which is one level down in the inheritance hierarchy, whereas the term "subclass" is used to mean a descendant class at any level. This book uses the term "subclass" to mean a descendant of a class, which is one level down in the inheritance hierarchy. For example, `Employee` is a subclass of Object, whereas `Clerk`, `Programmer`, and `Manager` are subclasses of `Employee`. `Clerk`, `Programmer`, `ApplicationProgrammer`, `SystemProgrammer`, `DatabaseProgrammer`, `Manager`, `FullTimeManager`, and `PartTimeManager` are all descendants of `Employee`. If a class is a descendant of another class, it is also a descendant of the ancestor of that class. For example, all descendants of the `Employee` class are also descendants of the `Object` class. All descendants of the `Manager` class are also descendants of the `Employee` class and the `Object` class.

What Is Inherited by a Subclass?

A subclass does not inherit everything from its superclass. However, a subclass may use, directly or indirectly, everything from its superclass. Let's discuss the distinction between "a subclass *inheriting* something from its superclass" and "a subclass *using* something from its superclass".

Let's take a real world example. Suppose your parent (a superclass) has money in a bank account. The money belongs to your parent. You (a subclass) need some money. If you inherit the money, you would just use the money at will as if the money is yours. If you can just use the money, you cannot get to the parent's money directly. Rather, you need to ask your parents for money and they will give it to you. In both cases, you used your parent's money. In the case of inheritance, the money appears to be owned by you. That is, you have direct access to it. In the second case, your parent's money was available to you for use without you having direct access to it. In the latter case, you had to go through your parents to use their money.

A subclass inherits non-private *members* of its superclass. I discuss this rule in detail shortly. Note that constructors and initializers (static and instance) are not members of a class, and therefore, they are not inherited. Members of a class are all members that are declared inside the body of the class and members that it inherits from the superclass. This definition of members of a class has a trickle-down effect.

Suppose there are three classes: A, B, and C. The class A inherits from the `Object` class. The class B inherits from the class A, and the class C inherits from the class B. Suppose that class A declares a private member m1 and a non-private member m2. The members of class A are m1, m2, and all inherited members from the `Object` class. Note that m1 and m2 members of class A are declared members, whereas others are inherited members. Members of class B will be any members that are declared in class B and all non-private members of class A. The member m1 is declared private in class A, so it is not inherited by class B. The same logic applies to the members of class C. Non-private members of the Object class trickle down to class A, B, and C through the inheritance hierarchy. The non-private members of class A trickle down to class B, which in turn trickle down to class C, through the inheritance hierarchy.

▒ **Tip** A superclass and its subclasses may be in different modules. A subclass in module P can inherit from a superclass in module Q only if the subclass has been declared public and module Q exports the package containing the superclass to at least module P. Refer to Chapter 10 for more on accessing classes across module boundaries.

There are four access modifiers: private, public, protected, and package-level. The absence of the private, public, and protected access modifier is considered as the default or package-level access. The access level modifier of a class member determines two things:

- Who can access (or use) that class member directly

- Whether a subclass inherits that class member or not

Access modifiers are also used with non-members (e.g., constructors) of a class. In such cases, an access modifier role is only one: "who can access that non-member?"

If a class member is declared private, it is accessible only inside the class that declares it. A private class member is not inherited by subclasses of that class.

A public class member is accessible from everywhere, provided the class itself is accessible. A subclass inherits all public members of its superclass.

If a class member is declared protected, it is accessible in the package in which it is declared. A protected class member is always accessible inside the body of a subclass whether the subclass is in the same package as the class or in a different package. A protected class member is inherited by a subclass. The protected access modifier is used with a class member when you want subclasses to access and inherit the class member. Note that a protected class member can be accessed both through the package in which it is declared and subclasses. If you want to provide access to a class member only from inside its package, you should use a package-level access modifier, not a protected access modifier.

If a class member is declared package-level, it is accessible only inside the package in which the class is declared. A package-level class member is inherited only if the superclass and subclass are in the same package. If the superclass and the subclass are in different packages, the subclass does not inherit package-level members from its superclass.

▒ **Tip** The access modifiers build on each other where you start with no access to the outside world (private), and add to it, first package (default), then subclasses (protected), and then the world (public).

Let's look at your example of inheritance in Listing 20-2 and Listing 20-3. The Employee class has three members: a name field, a getName() method, and a setName() method. The name field has been declared private and hence it is not accessible inside the Manager class because it is not inherited. The getName() and setName() methods have been declared public and they are accessible from anywhere including the Manager class. They are inherited from the Employee class by the Manager class, though since they are public, the fact they are inherited doesn't matter.

Upcasting and Downcasting

An "is-a" relationship in the real world translates into inheritance class hierarchy in software. A class is a type in Java. When you express the "is-a" relationship using inheritance, you create a subclass, which is a more specific type of the superclass. For example, a Manager is a specific type of Employee. An Employee is a specific type of Object. As you move up in the inheritance hierarchy, you move from a specific type to a more general type. How does inheritance affect the client code? In this context, the client code is any code that uses the classes in a class hierarchy. Inheritance guarantees that whatever behavior is present in a class will also be present in its subclass. A method in a class represents a behavior of the objects of that class. This means that whatever behavior a client code expects to be present in a class will also be present in the class's subclass. This leads to the conclusion that if client code works with a class, it will also work with the class's subclass, because a subclass guarantees at least the same behaviors as its superclass. For example, the Manager class provides at least the same behaviors as provided by its superclass Employee. Consider the following snippet of code:

```
Employee emp;
emp = new Employee();
emp.setName("Richard Castillo");
String name = emp.getName();
```

This snippet of code compiles without any errors. When the compiler comes across emp. setName("Richard Castillo") and emp.getName() calls, it checks the declared type of the emp variable. It finds that the declared type of the emp variable is Employee. It makes sure that the Employee class has setName() and getName() methods that conform to the call being made. It finds that the Employee class does have a setName() method that takes a String as a parameter. It finds that the Employee class does have a getName() method that takes no parameters and returns a String. After verifying these two facts, the compiler is fine with the emp.setName() and emp.getName() method calls.

With the point in mind that a subclass guarantees at least the same behavior (methods) as its superclass, consider the following snippet of code:

```
Employee emp;
emp = new Manager(); // A Manager object assigned to an Employee variable
emp.setName("Richard Castillo");
String name = emp.getName();
```

The compiler will compile this snippet of code too, even though you have changed the code this time to assign the emp variable an object of the Manager class. It will pass the setName() and getName() method calls on the same basis as described in the previous case. It also passes the assignment statement:

```
emp = new Manager();
```

The compile-time type of the new Manager() expression is the Manager type. The compile-time type (or declared type) of the emp variable is Employee type. Since the Manager class inherits from the Employee class, an object of the Manager class "is-a" object of the Employee class. Simply, you say that a manager is always an employee. Such an assignment (from subclass to superclass) is called *upcasting* and it is always allowed in Java. It is also called a widening conversion because an object of the Manager class (more specific type) is assigned to a reference variable of the Employee type (a more generic type). All of the following assignments are allowed and they are all examples of upcasting:

```
Object obj;
Employee emp;
Manager mgr;
PartTimeManager ptm;
```

```
// An employee is always an object
obj = emp;

// A manager is always an employee
emp = mgr;

// A part-time manager is always a manager
mgr = ptm;

// A part-time manager is always an employee
emp = ptm;

// A part-time manager is always an object
obj = ptm;
```

Use a simple rule to check if an assignment is a case of upcasting. Look at the compile-time type (declared type) of the expression on the right side of the assignment operator (e.g., b in a = b). If the compile-time type of the right-hand operand is a subclass of the compile-time of the left-hand operand, it is a case of upcasting, and the assignment is safe and allowed. Upcasting is a direct technical translation of the fact that an object of a subclass "is-a" object of the superclass, too.

⬛ **Tip**   Inheritance armed with upcasting and late binding is the basis for inclusion polymorphism in Java. Refer to Chapter 1 for more on inclusion polymorphism.

Upcasting is a very powerful feature of inheritance. It lets you write polymorphic code that works with classes that exist and classes that will be added in the future. It lets you code your application logic in terms of a superclass that will always work with all subclasses (existing subclasses or subclasses to be added in the future). It lets you write generic code without worrying about a specific type (class) with which the code will be used at runtime. Listing 20-5 is a simple utility class to test your upcasting rule. It has a printName() static method that accepts an argument of the Employee type. The method uses the getName() method of the Employee class to get the name of the employee object and print the name on the standard output.

Listing 20-5. A Utility Class That Uses Employee Type Parameter in Its printName() Method

```java
// EmpUtil.java
package com.jdojo.inheritance;

public class EmpUtil {
    public static void printName(Employee emp){
        // Get the name of employee
        String name = emp.getName();

        // Print employee name
        System.out.println(name);
    }
}
```

Listing 20-6 contains a program to test the upcasting rule using the EmpUtil class.

Listing 20-6. A Test Class to Test the Upcasting Rule

```java
// UpcastTest.java
package com.jdojo.inheritance;

public class UpcastTest {
    public static void main(String[] args) {
        Employee emp = new Employee();
        emp.setName("Ken Wood");

        Manager mgr = new Manager();
        mgr.setName("Ken Furr"); // Inheritance of setName() at work

        // Print names
        EmpUtil.printName(emp);
        EmpUtil.printName(mgr); // Upcasting at work
    }
}
```

```
Ken Wood
Ken Furr
```

The main() method creates two objects (emp and mgr): one of the Employee class and one of the Manager class. It sets names for both objects. Finally, it calls the printName() method of the EmpUtil class to print the names of both objects. The first call to EmpUtil.printName(emp) is fine, because the printName() method accepts an Employee object and you have passed an Employee object (emp). The second call, EmpUtil.printName(mgr), is fine because of the upcasting rule. The printName(Employee emp) accepts an Employee object and you were able to pass a Manager object (mgr) instead, because a manager is always an employee and upcasting rules allows the assignment of a subclass object to a variable of superclass type.

Assigning a superclass reference to a subclass variable is called *downcasting* (or narrowing conversion). Downcasting is the opposite of upcasting. In upcasting, the assignment moves up the class hierarchy whereas in downcasting the assignment moves down the class hierarchy. The Java compiler cannot make sure at compile-time that downcasting is legal. Consider the following snippet of code:

```java
Employee emp;
Manager mgr = new Manager();
emp = mgr; // OK. Upcasting
mgr = emp; // A compile-time error. Downcasting
```

The assignment emp = mgr is allowed because of upcasting. However, the assignment mgr = emp is not allowed because it is a case of downcasting where a variable of superclass (Employee) is being assigned to a variable of subclass (Manager). The compiler is right in assuming that every manager is an employee (upcasting). However, not every employee is a manager (downcasting). In the previous snippet of code, you would like the downcasting to work because you know for sure that the emp variable holds a reference to a Manager. Java imposes an additional rule in order for your downcast to succeed at compile-time. You need to give additional assurance to the compiler that you have considered the assignment of a superclass reference to a subclass reference variable and you would like the compiler to pass it. You give this assurance by adding a typecast (or simply a cast) to the assignment, as shown:

```java
mgr = (Manager) emp; // OK using a typecast. Downcast at work
```

This downcasting with a typecast succeeds at compile-time. However, the Java runtime will perform an additional verification. The job of the compiler is just to make sure that the declared type of mgr variable, which is Manager, is assignment-compatible with the typecast being used, which is Manager. The compiler cannot check what type of object emp variable will actually refer to at runtime. The Java runtime verifies the correctness of the typecast (Manager) emp in the previous statement.

The type of the object to which the emp variable refers at runtime is also called its runtime type. The runtime compares the runtime type of the emp variable and the Manager type (the Manager type is used in the typecast). If the runtime type of emp variable is assignment-compatible with the type used in typecast, the typecast succeeds at runtime. Otherwise, runtime throws a java.lang.ClassCastException.

Consider the following snippet of code assuming that you have a subclass of the Manager class, which is called PartTimeManager.

```
Employee emp;
Manager mgr = new Manager();
PartTimeManager ptm = new PartTimeManager();

emp = mgr;                     // Upcasting. OK
ptm = (PartTimeManager) emp; // Downcasting. OK at compile-time. A runtime error.
```

The last assignment, which uses downcasting, succeeds at compile-time because the declared type of the ptm variable and the typecast type are the same. The runtime type of emp is Manager, because the emp = mgr statement assigns a Manager object's reference to it. When the runtime attempts to execute the "(PartTimeManager) emp" part of the downcasting, it finds that the runtime type of emp, which is Manager, is not assignment-compatible with the typecast type, which is PartTimeManager. This is the reason that the runtime will throw a ClassCastException.

You can think of a statement that involves a downcasting as having two parts for the verification purpose. Suppose the statement is a2 = (K) b2. The compiler's job is to verify that the declared type of a2 is assignment-compatible with type K. The runtime's job is to verify that the runtime type of b2 is assignment-compatible with type K. If any of the two checks fails, you get an error at compile-time or runtime depending of which check fails. Figure 20-2 depicts this scenario.

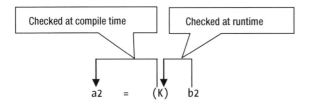

Figure 20-2. *Runtime and compile-time checks made for downcasting*

▓ **Tip** The Object class is at the top of every class hierarchy in Java. This allows you to assign a reference of any class type to a variable of the Object type. The following type of assignment is always allowed:

```
Object obj = new AnyJavaClass(); // Upcasting
```

Whether downcasting from an Object type to another class type will succeed depends on the downcasting rule, as discussed in this section.

The instanceof Operator

How can you be sure that a downcasting will always succeed at runtime? Java has an instanceof operator, which helps you determine whether a reference variable has a reference to an object of a class or a subclass of the class at runtime. It takes two operands and evaluates to a boolean value true or false. Its syntax is as follows:

```
<reference-variable> instanceof <type-name>
```

If <reference-variable> refers to an object of the type <type-name> or any of its descendants, instanceof returns true. Otherwise, it returns false. If <reference-variable> is null, instanceof always returns false.

You should use the instanceof operator before downcasting to check if the reference variable you are trying to downcast is of the type you expected it to be. For example, if you want to check if a variable of Employee type refers to a Manager object at runtime, you would write the following:

```
Manager mgr = new Manager();
Employee emp = mgr;

if (emp instanceof Manager) {
    // The following downcast will always succeed
    mgr = (Manager) emp;
} else {
    // emp is not a Manager type
}
```

The instanceof operator goes through two types of checks: compile-time check and runtime check. The compiler checks if it is ever possible for the left-hand operand to refer to an object of the right-hand operand. This check may not be obvious to you at this point. The purpose of using the instanceof operator is to compare the runtime type of a reference variable to a type. In short, it compares two types. Does it ever make sense to compare a mango with an employee? You would say no. The compiler adds checks for this kind of illogical comparison using the instanceof operator. It makes sure that it is possible for the left-hand operand of the instanceof operator to hold a reference to an object of the right-hand operand type. If it is not possible, the compiler generates an error. It is easy to find out whether the compiler will generate an error for using the instanceof operator or not. Consider the following snippet of code:

```
Manager mgr = null;

if (mgr instanceof Clerk) { //  A compile-time error
}
```

The variable mgr can hold a reference to Manager type or its descendant type. However, it can never hold a reference to the Clerk type. The Clerk type is not in the same inheritance-chain as the Manager class, although it is in the same inheritance tree. For the same reason, the following use of the instanceof operator will generate a compile-time error because the String class is not in the inheritance-chain of the Employee class.

```
String str = "test";

if (str instanceof Employee) { // A compile-time error
}
```

Sometimes you may end up writing code that uses the `instanceof` operator to test for multiple conditions at one place, as follows:

```
Employee emp;

// Some logic goes here...

if (emp instanceof Employee) {
    // Code to deal with an employee
} else if (emp instanceof Manager) {
    // Code to deal with a manager
} else if (emp instanceof Clerk) {
    // Code to deal with a clerk
}
```

You should avoid writing this kind of code. If you add a new subclass of `Employee`, you will need to add the logic for the new subclass to this code. Usually, this kind of code indicates a design flaw. Always ask yourself the question, "Will this code keep working when I add a new class to the existing class hierarchy?" If the answer is yes, you are fine. Otherwise, reconsider the design.

The `equals()` method is the one place in which you will often end up using the `instanceof` operator. It is defined in the `Object` class and the method is inherited by all classes. It takes an `Object` as an argument. It returns `true` if the argument and the object on which this method is called are considered equal. Otherwise, it returns `false`. Objects of each class may be compared for equality differently. For example, two employees may be considered equal if they work for the same company and in the same department and have same employee id. What happens if a `Manager` object is passed to the `equals()` method of the `Employee` class? Since a manager is also an employee, it should compare the two for equality. Listing 20-7 contains a possible implementation of the `equals()` method for the `Employee` class.

Listing 20-7. Implementing the equals() Method for the Employee Class

```
// Employee.java
package com.jdojo.inheritance;

public class Employee {
    private String name = "Unknown";

    public void setName(String name) {
        this.name = name;
    }

    public String getName() {
        return name;
    }
```

```
    public boolean equals(Object obj) {
        boolean isEqual = false;

        // We compare objects of the Employee class with the objects of
        // Employee class or its descendants
        if (obj instanceof Employee) {
            // If two have the same name, consider them equal.
            Employee e = (Employee) obj;
            String n = e.getName();
            isEqual = n.equals(this.name);
        }

        return isEqual;
    }
}
```

After you have added the equals() method to the Employee class, you can write code like the following, which compares two objects of the Employee type for equality based on their names:

```
Employee emp = new Employee();
emp.setName("John Jacobs");

Manager mgr = new Manager();
mgr.setName("John Jacobs");

System.out.println(mgr.equals(emp));          // prints true
System.out.println(emp.equals(mgr));          // prints true
System.out.println(emp.equals("John Jacobs")); // prints false
```

In the third comparison, you compare an Employee object with a String object, which returns false. Comparing an Employee and a Manager object returns true because they related by subclassing and have the same name.

Binding

Classes have methods and fields; we write code to access them as follows. Assume that myMethod() and xyz are members of the MyClass class, which is the declared type of the myObject reference variable.

```
MyClass myobject = get an object reference;
myObject.myMethod();   // Which myMethod() to call?
int a = myObject.xyz;  // Which xyz to access?
```

Binding is the process of identifying the accessed method's code (myMethod() in this case) or the field (xyz in this case), which will be used when the code executes. In other words, binding is a process of making a decision, which method's code or field will be accessed, when the code executes. There are two stages where the binding can happen: compile-time and runtime. When the binding occurs at compile-time, it is known as *early binding*. Early binding is also known as *static binding* or *compile-time binding*. When the binding occurs at runtime, it is known as *late binding*. Late binding is also known as *dynamic binding* or *runtime binding*.

Early Binding

Early binding is simple to understand compared to late binding. In early binding, the decision about which method code and field will be accessed is made by the compiler at compile-time. For a method call, the compiler decides which method from which class will be executed when the code having the method call is executed. For a field access, the compiler decides which field from which class will be accessed when the code having the field access is executed. Early binding is used for the following types of methods and fields of a class:

- All types of fields: static and non-static

- Static methods

- Non-static final methods

In early binding, a method or a field is accessed based on the declared type (or compile-time type) of the variable (or expression) accessing the method or the field. For example, if early binding is used for an a2.m1() method call, if a2 has been declared of type A, the m1() method in class A will be called when a2.m1() is executed.

Let's look at a detailed example that demonstrates the early binding rules. Consider the two classes shown in Listings 20-8 and 20-9.

Listing 20-8. An EarlyBindingSuper Class That Has a Static Field, an Instance Field, and a Static Method

```java
// EarlyBindingSuper.java
package com.jdojo.inheritance;

public class EarlyBindingSuper {
    // An instance variable
    public String str = "EarlyBindingSuper";

    // A static variable
    public static int count = 100;

    public static void print() {
        System.out.println("Inside EarlyBindingSuper.print()");
    }
}
```

Listing 20-9. An EarlyBindingSub Class, Which Inherits from EarlyBindingSuper Class and Has a Static Field, an Instance Field, and a Static Method, Which Are of the Same Type as in Its Superclass

```java
// EarlyBindingSub.java
package com.jdojo.inheritance;

public class EarlyBindingSub extends EarlyBindingSuper{
    // An instance variable
    public String str = "EarlyBindingSub";

    // A static variable
    public static int count = 200;

    public static void print() {
        System.out.println("Inside EarlyBindingSub.print()");
    }
}
```

The EarlyBindingSuper class declares two fields: str and count. The str field is declared non-static and count is declared static. The print() method is declared static.

The EarlyBindingSub class inherits from the EarlyBindingSuper class and it declares the same types of fields and methods, which have the same names. Fields are set to different values and the method prints a different message in the EarlyBindingSub class, so you can know which one is accessed when you execute your code. The EarlyBindingTest class in Listing 20-10 demonstrates the result of the early binding.

Listing 20-10. A Test Class to Demonstrate Early Binding for Fields and Methods

```
// EarlyBindingTest.java
package com.jdojo.inheritance;

public class EarlyBindingTest {
    public static void main(String[] args) {
        EarlyBindingSuper ebSuper = new EarlyBindingSuper();
        EarlyBindingSub ebSub = new EarlyBindingSub();

        // Will access EarlyBindingSuper.str
        System.out.println(ebSuper.str);

        // Will access EarlyBindingSuper.count
        System.out.println(ebSuper.count);

        // Will access EarlyBindingSuper.print()
        ebSuper.print();

        System.out.println("-----------------------------");

        // Will access EarlyBindingSub.str
        System.out.println(ebSub.str);

        // Will access EarlyBindingSub.count
        System.out.println(ebSub.count);

        // Will access EarlyBindingSub.print()
        ebSub.print();

        System.out.println("-----------------------------");

        // Will access EarlyBindingSuper.str
        System.out.println(((EarlyBindingSuper) ebSub).str);

        // Will access EarlyBindingSuper.count
        System.out.println(((EarlyBindingSuper) ebSub).count);

        // Will access EarlyBindingSuper.print()
        ((EarlyBindingSuper) ebSub).print();

        System.out.println("-----------------------------");

        // Assign the ebSub to ebSuper
        ebSuper = ebSub; // Upcasting
```

```
        /* Now access methods and fields using ebSuper variable, which is
           referring to a EarlyBindingSub object
         */
        // Will access EarlyBindingSuper.str
        System.out.println(ebSuper.str);

        // Will access EarlyBindingSuper.count
        System.out.println(ebSuper.count);

        // Will access EarlyBindingSuper.print()
        ebSuper.print();
        System.out.println("----------------------------");
    }
}
```

```
EarlyBindingSuper
100
Inside EarlyBindingSuper.print()
----------------------------
EarlyBindingSub
200
Inside EarlyBindingSub.print()
----------------------------
EarlyBindingSuper
100
Inside EarlyBindingSuper.print()
----------------------------
EarlyBindingSuper
100
Inside EarlyBindingSuper.print()
----------------------------
```

The main() method creates an object of each type EarlyBindingSuper and EarlyBindingSub:

```
EarlyBindingSuper ebSuper = new EarlyBindingSuper();
EarlyBindingSub ebSub = new EarlyBindingSub();
```

According to early binding rules, the statements ebSuper.str, ebSuper.count, and ebSuper.print() will always access the str and count fields, and the print() method of the EarlyBindingSuper class because you have declared ebSuper of the EarlyBindingSuper type. This decision is made by the compiler because str and count are fields and for fields, Java always uses early binding. The print() method is a static method and Java always uses early binding for static methods. The same rule applies when you access these members using ebSub variable.

The output of the following statements may not be obvious.

```
// Will access EarlyBindingSuper.str
System.out.println(((EarlyBindingSuper)ebSub).str);

// Will access EarlyBindingSuper.count
System.out.println(((EarlyBindingSuper)ebSub).count);
```

```
// Will access EarlyBindingSuper.print()
((EarlyBindingSuper)ebSub).print();
```

These three statements use an expression to access fields and methods. When you write ebSub.
str, you access str field using the ebSub variable directly. It is clear that ebSub variable is of type
EarlyBindingSub and therefore, ebSub.str will access str field of the EarlyBindingSub class. When
you use typecast, the compile-time type of the expression changes. For example, the compile-time type
of ebSub is EarlyBindingSub. However, the compile-time type of the expression, (EarlyBindingSuper)
ebSub, is EarlyBindingSuper. This is the reason that all of the previous three statements will access fields
and methods from the EarlyBindingSuper class, not from the EarlyBindingSub class even though they
all use the ebSub variable, which is of the EarlyBindingSub type. The output of Listing 20-10 validates this
explanation discussion about the early binding rules.

▨ **Tip**   You can also access static fields and methods of a class using the name of the class, for example,
EarlyBindingSub.str. The early binding rules still apply and the compiler will bind the access to those fields
and methods to the class whose name is used to access them. Using the class name to access static members
of the class should be preferred for readability.

Late Binding

Binding for all non-static, non-final methods follows the rules of late binding. That is, if your code accesses
a non-static method, which is not declared final, the decision as to which version of the method is called is
made at runtime. The version of the method that will be called depends on the runtime type of the object on
which the method call is made, not on its compile-time type. Consider the following snippet of code, which
creates an object of the Manager class and assigns the reference to a variable emp of the Employee class. The
emp variable accesses the setName() method.

```
Employee emp = new Manager();
emp.setName("John Jacobs");
```

The compiler performs only one check for the emp.setName() method call in this code. It makes sure
that the declared type of the emp variable, which is Employee, has a method called setName(String s). The
compiler detects that the setName(String s) method in the Employee class is an instance method, which
is not final. For an instance method call, the compiler does not perform binding. It will leave this work for
the runtime. The method call, emp.setName("John Jacobs"), is an example of late binding. At runtime, the
JVM decides which setName(String s) method should be called. The JVM gets the runtime type of the emp
variable. The runtime type of the emp variable is Manager when the emp.setName("John Jacobs") statement
is looked at in this code. The JVM traverses up the class hierarchy starting from the runtime type (that is,
Manager) of the emp variable looking for the definition of a setName(String s) method. First, it looks at the
Manager class and it finds that the Manager class does not declare a setName(String s) method. The JVM
now moves one level up the class hierarchy, which is the Employee class. It finds that the Employee class
declares a setName(String s) method. Once the JVM finds a match, it binds the call to that method and
stops the search. Recall that the Object class is always at the top of all class hierarchies in Java. The JVM
continues its search for a method definition up to the Object class. If it does not find a match in the Object
class, it throws a runtime exception.

Let's look at an example that will demonstrate the late binding process. Listings 20-11 20-12 have code for LateBindingSuper and LateBindingSub classes, respectively. The LateBindingSub class inherits from the LateBindingSuper class. It defines the same instance method print() as defined in the LateBindingSuper class. The print() method in both classes prints different messages so that you can see which method is being called.

Listing 20-11. A LateBindingSuper Class, Which Has an Instance Method Named print()

```
// LateBindingSuper.java
package com.jdojo.inheritance;

public class LateBindingSuper {
    public void print() {
        System.out.println("Inside LateBindingSuper.print()");
    }
}
```

Listing 20-12. A LateBindingSub Class, Which Has an Instance Method Named print()

```
// LateBindingSub.java
package com.jdojo.inheritance;

public class LateBindingSub extends LateBindingSuper {
    @Override
    public void print() {
        System.out.println("Inside LateBindingSub.print()");
    }
}
```

Listing 20-13 demonstrates the result of late binding.

Listing 20-13. A Test Class to Demonstrate Early Binding for Fields and Methods

```
// LateBindingTest.java
package com.jdojo.inheritance;

public class LateBindingTest {
    public static void main(String[] args) {
        LateBindingSuper lbSuper = new LateBindingSuper();
        LateBindingSub lbSub = new LateBindingSub();

        // Will access LateBindingSuper.print()
        lbSuper.print(); // #1

        // Will access LateBindingSub.print()
        lbSub.print();   // #2

        // Will access LateBindingSub.print()
        ((LateBindingSuper) lbSub).print(); // #3

        // Assign the lbSub to lbSuper
        lbSuper = lbSub; // Upcasting
```

773

```
        // Will access LateBindingSub.print() because lbSuper
        // is referring to a LateBindingSub object
        lbSuper.print(); // #4
    }
}
```

```
Inside LateBindingSuper.print()
Inside LateBindingSub.print()
Inside LateBindingSub.print()
Inside LateBindingSub.print()
```

The main() method creates an object of each type LateBindingSuper and LateBindingSub:

```
LateBindingSuper lbSuper = new LateBindingSuper();
LateBindingSub lbSub = new LateBindingSub();
```

The calls to the print() method are labeled #1, #2, #3 and #4, so we may refer to them in our discussion.

Both variables, lbSuper and lbSub, are used to access the print() instance method. The runtime decides which version of the print() method is called. When you use lbSuper.print(), which print() method is called depends on the object to which lbSuper variable is referring to at that point in time. Recall that a reference variable of a class type may also refer to an object of any of its descendant. The lbSuper variable may refer to an object of LateBindingSuper or LateBindingSub.

When the statement #1, lbSuper.print(), is ready to execute, the runtime will need to find the code for the print() method. The runtime looks for the runtime type of the lbSuper variable and it finds that the lbSuper variable is referring to an object of LateBindingSuper type. It looks for a print() method in the LateBindingSuper class and finds it. Therefore, the runtime binds the print() method call in the statement labeled #1 to the print() method of the LateBindingSuper class. This is confirmed by the first line in the output.

The logic for binding the print() method in statement #2 is the same as for the statement labeled #1, but the class this time is LateBindingSub.

Statement #3 is tricky. When you use a typecast such as (LateBindingSuper) lbSub, the object to which lbSub refers to at runtime does not change. Using a typecast, all you say is that you want to use the object to which lbSub variable refers as an object of the LateBindingSuper type. However, the object itself never changes. You can verify this by using the following code, which gets the class name of an object:

```
// Both s1 and s2 have "com.jdojo.inheritance.LateBindingSub" class name LateBindingSub
lbSub = new LateBindingSub();
String s1 = lbSub.getClass().getName();
String s2 = ((LateBindingSuper)lbSub).getClass().getName();
```

When statement #3 is ready to execute, at that time the expression with the typecast still refers to an object of LateBindingSub type, and therefore, the print() method of the LateBindingSub class will be called. This is confirmed by the third line in the output.

Consider two lines of code to discuss statement #4:

```
lbSuper = lbSub; // Upcasting
lbSuper.print(); // #4
```

The first source line assigns lbSub to lbSuper. The effect of this line is that lbSuper variable starts referring to an object of LateBindingSub object. When statement #4 is ready to execute, the runtime needs to find the code for the print() method. The runtime finds that the runtime type of the lbSuper variable is the LateBindingSub class. It looks for the print() method in the LateBindingSub class and finds it right there. Therefore, statement #4 executes the print() method in the LateBindingSub class. This is confirmed by the fourth line in the output.

▓ **Tip**   Late binding incurs a small performance overhead compared to early binding because the method calls are resolved at runtime. However, many techniques (e.g., virtual method table) can be used by the programming languages to implement late binding, so the performance hit is minimal or negligible. The benefit of late binding overshadows the little performance hit. It lets you implement inclusion polymorphism. When you write code like a2.print(), the a2 variable exhibits polymorphic behavior with respect to the print() method. The same code, a2.print(), may call the print() method of the class of the a2 variable or any of its descendant classes depending on what type of object a2 is referring to at runtime. Inheritance and late binding lets you write polymorphic code, which is written in terms of superclass type and works for all subclass types as well.

Method Overriding

Redefining an instance method in a class, which is inherited from the superclass, is called method overriding. Consider the following declarations of class A and class B:

```
public class A {
    public void print() {
        System.out.println("A");
    }
}
```

```
public class B extends A {
    @Override
    public void print() {
        System.out.println("B");
    }
}
```

Class B is a subclass of class A. Class B inherits the print() method from its superclass and redefines it. It is said that the print() method in class B overrides the print() method of class A. It is like class B telling class A, "Thanks for being my superclass and letting me inherit your print() method. However, I need to work differently. I am going to redefine it my way, without affecting your print() method in any way. You can keep using your print() method." If a class overrides a method, it affects the overriding class and its subclasses. Consider the following declaration of class C:

```
public class C extends B {
    // C inherits B.print()
}
```

Class C does not declare any methods. What method does class C inherit: A.print() or B.print(), or both? It inherits the print() method from class B. A class always inherits what is available from its immediate superclass (declared in superclass or inherited by its super superclass). If a class D inherits from class C, it will inherit print() method of class B through class C.

```
public class D extends C {
    // D inherits B.print() through C
}
```

Consider two more classes E and F, which inherit from D and E, respectively. Class E overrides the print() method of class B, which it inherited from class D.

```
public class E extends D {
    @Override
    public void print() {
        System.out.println("E");
    }
}
```

```
public class F extends E {
    // F inherits E.print() through E
}
```

What will be the output of the following snippet of code?

```
A a = new A();
a.print();      // will print A
a = new B();
a.print();      // will print B
a = new C();
a.print();      // will print B
a = new D();
a.print();      // will print B
a = new E();
a.print();      // will print E
a = new F();
a.print();      // will print E
```

The comments in the code tell you what will be printed. Can you figure out why you get this output? There are three things at work. First, you can assign an object of a descendant of class A to a variable of class A type. This is the reason that you have called a.print() in all statements. Second, the print() method has been overridden by some of the descendants of class A in the class hierarchy. Third, late binding performs the magic of calling the appropriate print() method depending on the class of the object to which the variable is referring to at runtime. Consider the following definitions of two classes S and T:

```
public class S {
    public void print() {
        System.out.println("S");
    }
}
```

```
public class T extends S {
    public void print(String msg) {
        System.out.println(msg);
    }
}
```

Does the print() method in class T override the print() method in its superclass S? The answer is no. The print() method in class T does not override the print() method in class S. This is called method overloading. Class T will now have two print() methods: one inherited from its superclass S, which takes no arguments and one declared in it, which takes a String argument. However, both methods of class T have the same name print. This is the reason that it is called method overloading because the same method name is used more than once in the same class.

Here are the rules when a class is said to override a method, which it inherits from its superclass.

Method Overriding Rule #1

The method must be an instance method. Overriding does not apply to static methods.

Method Overriding Rule #2

The overriding method must have the same name as the overridden method.

Method Overriding Rule #3

The overriding method must have the same number of parameters of the same type in the same order as the overridden method. Java 5 has changed this rule slightly when the methods use generic types as their parameters. When the method's parameters use generic type, you need to consider the erasure of the generic type parameter, not the generic type itself when comparing with other methods to check if one overrides another. I revisit this rule in later to discuss it in detail with examples. For now, consider a method as overriding another method if they have the same number of parameters of the same type in the same order. Note that the name of the parameter does not matter. For example, void print(String str) and void print(String msg) are considered the same method. The different names of the parameters, str and msg, do not make them different methods.

Method Overriding Rule #4

Before Java 5, the return type of the overriding and the overridden methods must be the same. In Java 5, this rule remains the same for return types of primitive data types. However, it has changed for return types of reference data types. If the return type of the overridden method is a reference type, the return type of the overriding method must be assignment-compatible with the return type of the overridden method. Suppose a class has a method definition of R1 m1(), which is overridden by a method definition R2 m1(). This method overriding is allowed only if an instance of R2 can be assigned to a variable of R1 type without any typecast. Consider the following snippet of code that defines three classes—P, Q, and R:

```
public class P {
    public Employee getEmp() {
        // Code goes here
    }
}
```

```
public class Q extends P {
    public Employee getEmp() {
        // code goes here
    }
}

public class R extends P {
    public Manager getEmp() {
        // code goes here
    }
}
```

Class P defines a getEmp() method that returns an object of Employee type. The getEmp() method of Class Q overrides the getEmp() method of its superclass P because it has the same name, number of parameters (zero in this case) of the same type in the same order, and the same return type, Employee. The getEmp() method of class R also overrides the getEmp() method of class P even though its return type Manager is different from the return type of the overridden method, which is Employee. The getEmp() method of class R overrides its superclass getEmp() method because an instance of Manager type can always be assigned to a variable of Employee type without any typecast.

Method Overriding Rule #5

The access level of the overriding method must be at least the same or more relaxed than that of the overridden method. The three access levels are public, protected and package-level that allow for inheritance. Recall that private members are not inherited and hence cannot be overridden. The order of access level from the most relaxed to the strictest is public, protected, and package-level. If the overridden method has public access level, the overriding method must have the public access level because public is the most relaxed access level. If the overridden method has protected access level, the overriding method may have public or protected access level. If the overridden method has package-level access, the overriding method may have public, protected, or package-level access. Table 20-1 summarizes this rule. I discuss why this rule exists shortly.

Table 20-1. *Allowed Access Levels for an Overriding Method*

Overridden Method Access Level	Allowed Overriding Method Access Level
public	public
protected	public, protected
package-level	public, protected, package-level

Method Overriding Rule #6

A method may include a list of checked exceptions in its throws clause. Although it is allowed to include an unchecked exception in the throws clause of a method, it is not required. In this section, I am discussing only checked exceptions. The overriding method cannot add a new exception to the list of exceptions in the overridden method. It may remove one or all exceptions or it may replace an exception with another exception, which is one of the descendants of the exception listed in the overridden method. Consider the following class definitions:

```
public class G {
    public void m1() throws CheckedException1, CheckedException2 {
        // Code goes here
    }
}
```

If a class overrides m1() method of class G, it must not add any new checked exception to it. The following code will not compile, because it has added a new checked exception CheckException3 in the overridden method m1():

```
public class H extends G {
    public void m1() throws CheckedException1, CheckedException2, CheckedException3 {
        // Code goes here
    }
}
```

The following class declarations override the m1() method in class G and they are all valid. In class I, the method m1() removes both exceptions. In class J, it removes one exception and keeps one. In class K, it keeps one and replaces the other one with a descendant type assuming that the CheckedException22 is a descendant class of CheckedException2.

```
public class I extends G {
    // m1() removes all exceptions
    public void m1() {
        // Code goes here
    }
}
```

```
public class J extends G {
    // m1() removes one exception and keeps another
    public void m1() throws CheckedException1 {
        // Code goes here
    }
}
```

```
public class J extends G {
    // m1() removes one, keep one, and replaces one with a subclass
    public void m1() throws CheckedException1, CheckedException22 {
        // Code goes here
    }
}
```

The rules about the return type and the list of exceptions of an overriding method may not be obvious. I discuss the reasons behind these rules. There is a reason behind these rules, which is "A variable of a class type can hold the reference to an object of any of its descendants." When you write code using the superclass type, that code must also work without any modification with objects of subclass types. Consider the following definition of class P assuming the EmpNotFoundException is a checked exception class:

```
public class P {
    public Employee getEmp(int empId) throws EmpNotFoundException {
        // code goes here
    }
}
```

You can write the following snippet of code:

```
P p = // get an object reference of P or its descendant;

try {
    Employee emp = p.getEmp(10);
} catch (EmpNotFoundException e) {
    // Handle the exception here
}
```

There are two points that need to be considered in this snippet of code. First, the variable p, which is of type P, can point to an object of type P or to an object of any descendant of class P. Second, when the p.getEmp(10) method is called, the compiler verifies that the declared type of variable p (P class) has a getEmp() method, which accepts one parameter of type int, returns an Employee type object and throws EmpNotFoundException. These pieces of information are verified by the compiler with class P. The assumption made (and verified, too) by the compiler about the getEmp() method should never be invalidated at runtime. Otherwise, it will result in a chaos—code compiles, but might not run.

Consider one of the possible cases of overriding the getEmp() method, as shown:

```
public class Q extends P {
    public Manager getEmp(int empId) {
        // code goes here
    }
}
```

If the variable p is assigned an object of class Q, the code

```
Employee emp = p.getEmp(10);
```

inside the try-catch block is still valid. In this case, the variable p will refer to an object of class Q whose getEmp() method returns a Manager object and does not throw any exception. Returning a Manager object from the getEmp() method is fine because you can assign a Manager object to the emp variable, which is a case of upcasting. Not throwing an exception from the getEmp() method is also fine because the code was ready to handle the exception (by using a try-catch block) in case the exception was thrown.

What is the reason behind the access level rules for overriding methods? Note that when a variable p accesses the getEmp() method, the compiler verifies that the code, where p.getEmp() is used, has access to the getEmp() method of class P. If the subclasses of P reduces the access level, the same code, p.getEmp(), may not work at runtime, because the code executing the statement may not have access to the getEmp() method in the descendant of class P.

Consider the following definition of class Q2, which inherits from class P. It overrides the getEmp() method and replaces the EmpNoFoundException with another checked exception named BadEmpIdException.

```
// Won't compile
public class Q2 extends P {
    public Manager getEmp(int empId) throws BadEmpIdException {
        // code goes here
    }
}
```

Suppose the code, which was written in terms of P type, gets a reference of a Q2 object as follows:

```
P p = new Q2();

try {
    Employee emp = p.getEmp(10);
} catch(EmpNotFoundException e) {
    // Handle exception here
}
```

Note that the try-catch block is not prepared to handle the BadEmpIdException, which the method getEmp() of the Q2 class may throw. This is why the declaration of class Q2 would not compile.

To summarize the rules of overriding, let's break down the parts of a method declaration as follows:

- Name of the method

- Number of parameters

- Type of parameters

- Order of parameters

- Return type of parameters

- Access level

- List of checked exceptions in the throws clause

The first four parts must always be the same in the overriding and the overridden methods. Before Java 5, the return type must be the same in the overriding and the overridden methods. From Java 5, if the return type is a reference type, overriding a method's return type could also be a subtype (any descendant) of the return type of the overridden method. Access level and list of exceptions in the overridden method may be thought of as its constraints. An overriding method may relax (or even remove) the constraints of the overridden method. However, an overriding method can never have more restrictive constraints than that of the overridden method.

The rules of overriding a method are complex. It may take you a long time to master them. All rules are directly supported by the compiler. If you make a mistake in the source code while overriding a method, the compiler will generate a nice (not always) error message that will give you a clue about your mistake. There is a golden rule about method overriding that helps you avoid mistakes: "Whatever code is written using the superclass type must also work with the subclass type."

░ **Tip**   If you want to override a method in your class, you should annotate the method with an @Override annotation. For a method annotated with @Override, the compiler verifies that the method really overrides a method in the superclass; otherwise, it generates a compile-time error.

Accessing Overridden Method

Sometimes you may need to access the overridden method from a subclass. A subclass can use the keyword super as a qualifier to call the overridden method of the superclass. Note that the Object class has no superclass. It is illegal to use the keyword super in the Object class. As a programmer, you will never need to write code for the Object class anyway, as it is part of the Java class library. Consider the code for the AOSuper class in Listing 20-14. It has a print() method, which prints a message on the standard output.

Listing 20-14. An AOSuper Class

```
// AOSuper.java
package com.jdojo.inheritance;

public class AOSuper {
    public void print() {
        System.out.println("Inside AOSuper.print()");
    }
}
```

The code in Listing 20-15 contains the declaration for an AOSub class, which inherits from the AOSuper class.

Listing 20-15. An AOSub Class, Which Inherits from the AOSuper Class

```
// AOSub.java
package com.jdojo.inheritance;

public class AOSub extends AOSuper {
    @Override
    public void print() {
        // Call print() method of AOSuper class
        super.print();

        // Print a message
        System.out.println("Inside AOSub.print()");
    }
```

```
    public void callOverridenPrint() {
        // Call print() method of AOSuper class
        super.print();
    }
}
```

The AOSub class overrides the print() method of the AOSuper class. Note the super.print() method call inside the print() method and the callOverridenPrint() methods of the AOSub class. It will call the print() method of AOSuper class. The output of Listing 20-16 shows that a method call with a super qualifier calls the overridden method in the superclass.

Listing 20-16. A Test Class to Test a Method Call with the super Qualifier

```
// AOTest.java
package com.jdojo.inheritance;

public class AOTest {
    public static void main(String[] args) {
        AOSub aoSub = new AOSub();
        aoSub.print();
        aoSub.callOverridenPrint();
    }
}
```

```
Inside AOSuper.print()
Inside AOSub.print()
Inside AOSuper.print()
```

There is no way to directly call an instance method of the superclass of the superclass. You can call the overridden method of the superclass (only the immediate ancestor) using the keyword super. Suppose there are three classes: A, B, and C, where class B inherits from class A, and class C inherits from class B. There is no way to call methods of class A from inside class C. If class C needs to call a method of class A, you need to provide a method in class B that will call method of class A. Class C will call the method of class B, which in turn will call the method of class A.

▓ **Tip**   When a method call is made using the keyword super, Java uses early binding, even though the method is an instance method. Another instance when Java uses early binding for an instance method call is a private method call because a private method cannot be invoked from outside its defining class. A private method cannot be overridden either. The keyword super refers to the instance fields, methods, or constructors of the immediate ancestor of the class in which it appears.

Method Overloading

Having more than one method with the same name in the same class is called method overloading. Methods with the same name in a class could be declared methods, inherited methods, or a combination of both. Overloaded methods must have different number of parameters, different types of parameters, or both. The return type, access level and `throws` clause of a method play no role in making it an overloaded method. The `m1()` method of the `OME1` class is an example of an overloaded method.

```
public class OME1 {
    public void m1(int a) {
        // Code goes here
    }

    public void m1(int a, int b) {
        // Code goes here
    }

    public int m1(String a) {
        // Code goes here
    }

    public int m1(String a, int b) throws CheckedException1 {
        // Code goes here
    }
}
```

The following is an example of an incorrect attempt to overload the `m2()` method in class `OME2`:

```
// Won't compile
public class OME2 {
    public void m2(int p1) {
        // Code goes here
    }

    public void m2(int p2) {
        // Code goes here
    }
}
```

Using different names for parameters (`p1` and `p2`) does not make the `m2()` method overloaded. The code for the `OME2` class would not compile because it has a duplicate declaration for the `m2()` method. Both methods have the same number and type of parameters, which makes it not overloaded.

The order of the parameters may play a role in making a method overloaded. The `m3()` method of the `OME3` class is overloaded because parameter types are different. Both methods have one parameter of type `int` and another of type `double`. However, they are in a different order.

```
public class OME3 {
    public void m3(int p1, double p2) {
        // Code goes here
    }
```

```
    public void m3(double p1, int p2) {
        // Code goes here
    }
}
```

Use a simple rule to check if two methods can be termed as an overloaded method. List the name of the methods and the type of their parameters from left to right separated by a comma. You can use any other separator. If the two methods of a class having the same name give you different lists, they are overloaded. Otherwise, they are not overloaded. If you make such lists for m1(), m2(), and m3() methods in class OME1, OME2, and OME3 classes, you will come up with the following results:

```
// Method list for m1 in class OME1 - Overloaded
m1,int
m1,int,int
m1,String
m1,String,int

// Method list for m2 in class OME2 - Not Overloaded
m2,int
m2,int

// Method list for m3 in class OME3 - Overloaded
m3,int,double
m3,double,int
```

You should realize that the results for the m2() method in class OME2 are the same for both versions and hence OME2.m2() is not overloaded. Table 20-2 lists some important differences between method overriding and method overloading.

Table 20-2. *Some Important Differences Between Method Overriding and Method Overloading*

Method Overriding	Method Overloading
Overriding involves inheritance and at least two classes.	Overloading has nothing to do with inheritance. Overloading involves only one class.
It occurs when a class defines a method with the same name and the same number of parameters of the same type in the same order as defined by its superclass.	It occurs when a class defines more than one method with the same name. All methods with the same name must differ at least in one respect from others— the number of parameters, their types or orders, etc.
The return type of the overriding method must be assignment-substitutable with the return type of the overridden method.	Return types of overloaded methods do not play a role in overloading.
The overriding method cannot have an additional throws clause than the overridden method. It can have the same or a less restrictive list of exceptions as the overridden method.	Throws clauses of overloaded methods do not play a role in overloading.
Overriding applies only to instance (non-static) methods.	Any method (static or non-static) can be overloaded.

Method overloading is another kind of polymorphism where the same method name has different meanings. Method overloading is bound at compile-time as opposed to method overriding that is bound at runtime. The compiler resolves only the version of the overloaded methods that will be called. It determines which version of the overloaded method will be called matching the actual parameters with the formal parameters of the overloaded methods. If the overloaded method is an instance method, which code will be executed is still determined at runtime using late binding.

For an overloaded method call, the compiler chooses the most specific method. If it does not find an exact match, it will try to look for a more generic version by converting the actual parameter type to a more generic type using the rules of automatic type widening. Listing 20-17 demonstrates how the compiler chooses an overloaded method.

Listing 20-17. A Test Program That Demonstrates How the Compiler Chooses the Most Specific Method from Several Versions of an Overloaded Method

```
// OverloadingTest.java
package com.jdojo.inheritance;

public class OverloadingTest {
    public static void main(String[] args) {
        OverloadingTest ot = new OverloadingTest();

        int i = 10;
        int j = 15;
        double d1 = 10.4;
        double d2 = 2.5;
        float f1 = 2.3F;
        float f2 = 4.5F;
        short s1 = 2;
        short s2 = 6;

        ot.add(i, j);
        ot.add(d1, j);
        ot.add(i, s1);
        ot.add(s1, s2);
        ot.add(f1, f2);
        ot.add(f1, s2);

        Employee emp = new Employee();
        Manager mgr = new Manager();
        ot.test(emp);
        ot.test(mgr);

        emp = mgr;
        ot.test(emp);
    }

    public double add(int a, int b) {
        System.out.println("Inside add(int a, int b)");
        double s = a + b;
        return s;
    }
```

```
    public double add(double a, double b) {
        System.out.println("Inside add(double a, double b)");
        double s = a + b;
        return s;
    }

    public void test(Employee e) {
        System.out.println("Inside test(Employee e)");
    }

    public void test(Manager e) {
        System.out.println("Inside test(Manager m)");
    }
}
```

```
Inside add(int a, int b)
Inside add(double a, double b)
Inside add(int a, int b)
Inside add(int a, int b)
Inside add(double a, double b)
Inside add(double a, double b)
Inside test(Employee e)
Inside test(Manager m)
Inside test(Employee e)
```

The compiler knows only the compile-time type (the declared type) of the actual and the formal parameters. Look at the ot.add(f1, s2) method call. The types of actual parameters are float and short. There is no add(float, short) method in the OverloadingTest class. The compiler tries to widen the type of the first argument to a double type and it finds a match based on the first parameter add(double, double). Still, the second parameter type does not match; the actual type is short and the formal type is double. Java allows automatic widening from short to double. The compiler converts the short type to the double type and binds add(f1, s2) call to the add(double, double) method. When ot.test(mgr) is called, the compiler looks for an exact match and, in this case, it finds one, test(Manager m), and binds the call to this version of the test() method. Suppose the test(Manager m) method is not present in the OverloadingTest class. The compiler will bind ot.test(mgr) call to test(Employee e) method because a Manager type can be widened (using upcasting) to Employee type automatically.

Sometimes, overloaded methods and automatic type widening may confuse the compiler resulting in a compile-time error. Consider Listings 20-18 and 20-19 for an Adder class with an overloaded add() method and how to test it.

Listing 20-18. The Adder Class, Which Has an Overloaded add() Method

```
// Adder.java
package com.jdojo.inheritance;

public class Adder {
    public double add(int a, double b) {
        return a + b;
    }
```

```
    public double add(double a, int b) {
        return a + b;
    }
}
```

Listing 20-19. Testing add() Method of the Adder Class

```java
// AdderTest.java
package com.jdojo.inheritance;

public class AdderTest {
    public static void main(String[] args) {
        Adder a = new Adder();

        // A compile-time error
        double d = a.add(2, 3);
    }
}
```

An attempt to compile the AdderTest class generates the following error:

```
"AdderTest.java": reference to add is ambiguous, both method add(int,double) in com.jdojo.
inheritance.Adder and method add(double,int) in com.jdojo.inheritance.Adder match at line 7,
column 18
```

The error message states that compiler is not able to decide which one of the two add() methods in the Adder class to call for the a.add(3, 7) method invocation. The compiler is confused in deciding if it should widen the int type of 3 to make it double type 3.0 and call the add(double, int) or if it should widen the int type of 7 to make it double type 7.0 and call the add(int, double). In situations like this, you need to help the compiler by using a typecast, as follows:

```java
double d1 = a.add((double)2, 3); // OK. Will use add(double, int)
double d2 = a.add(2, (double)3); // OK. Will use add(int, double)
```

Inheritance and Constructors

An object has two things: state and behavior. Instance variables in a class represent the state of its objects. Instance methods represent the behavior of its objects. Each object of a class maintains its own state. When you create an object of a class, memory is allocated for all instance variables declared in the class and all instance variables declared in its ancestors at all levels. Your Employee class declares a name instance variable. When you create an object of the Employee class, the memory is allocated for its name instance variable. When an object of the Manager class is created, memory is allocated for the name field that is present in its superclass Employee. After all, a manager has a similar state as that of an employee. A manager behaves similar to an employee. Let's look at an example. Consider two classes, U and V, as shown:

```java
public class U {
    private int id;
    protected String name;
}
```

```
public class V extends U {
    protected double salary;
    protected String address;
}
```

Figure 20-3 depicts the memory allocation when objects of class U and V are created. When an object of class U is created, memory is allocated only for the instance variables that are declared in class U. When an object of class V is created, memory is allocated for all instance variables in class U and class V.

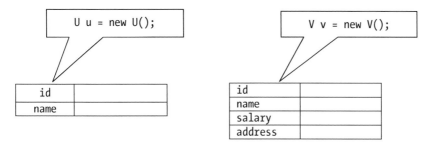

Figure 20-3. *Memory allocation for an object includes all instance variable of the class and all its ancestors*

Let's get to the main topic of discussion for this section, which is constructors. Constructors are not members of a class and they are not inherited by subclasses. They are used to initialize instance variables. When you create an object of a class, the object contains instance variables from the class and all of its ancestors. To initialize the instance variables of ancestor classes, the constructors of ancestor classes must be called. Consider the following two classes, CSuper and CSub, as shown in Listings 20-20 and 20-21. The CTest class in Listing 20-22 is used to create an object of the CSub class.

Listing 20-20. A CSuper Class with a No-Args Constructor

```
// CSuper.java
package com.jdojo.inheritance;

public class CSuper {
    public CSuper() {
        System.out.println("Inside CSuper() constructor.");
    }
}
```

Listing 20-21. A CSub Class, Which Inherits from the CSuper Class and Has a No-Args Constructor

```
// CSub.java
package com.jdojo.inheritance;

public class CSub extends CSuper {
    public CSub() {
        System.out.println("Inside CSub() constructor.");
    }
}
```

Listing 20-22. A Test Class, Which Demonstrates That Constructors for All Ancestors Are Called When an Object of a Class Is Created Starting at the Top of the Class Hierarchy and Going Down

```java
// CTest.java
package com.jdojo.inheritance;

public class CTest {
    public static void main(String[] args) {
        CSub cs = new CSub();
    }
}
```

```
Inside CSuper() constructor.
Inside CSub() constructor.
```

The output of the CTest class shows that the constructor of the CSuper class is called first, and then the constructor of the CSub class. In fact, the constructor of the Object class is called before the constructor of the CSuper class. You cannot print the fact the constructor of the Object class is called because the Object class is not your class, and therefore you cannot modify it. The question is, "How does the constructor of the CSuper class get called?" The answer to this question is based on the rule that when an object of a class is created, memory is allocated for all instance variables including instance variables in all its ancestor classes. Instance variables for all classes must be initialized by calling their constructors. The compiler helps you to enforce this rule to a great extent. The compiler injects the call to the immediate ancestor's no-args constructor as the first statement in every constructor you add to your class. The keyword super is used in many contexts. It also refers to the immediate ancestor of a class. If it is followed by parentheses, it refers to the constructor of the superclass. If a superclass constructor accepts parameters, you can pass a list of parameters within parentheses similar to a method call. The following are examples of calling the constructor of a superclass:

```java
// Call no-args constructor of superclass
super();
```

```java
// Call superclass constructor with a String argument
super("Hello");
```

```java
// Call superclass constructor with two double arguments
super(10.5, 89.2);
```

You can call constructor of the superclass explicitly or let the compiler inject the call to the no-args constructor for you. When you compile the CSuper and CSub class, the compiler modifies their constructors' code, which looks as shown in Listings 20-23 and 20-24.

Listing 20-23. Compiler Injection of a super() Call to Call the Immediate Ancestor's No-Args Constructor

```java
// CSuper.java
package com.jdojo.inheritance;

public class CSuper {
    public CSuper() {
        super();  // Injected by the compiler
        System.out.println("Inside CSuper() constructor.");
    }
}
```

Listing 20-24. Compiler Injection of a super() Call to Call the Immediate Ancestor's No-Args Constructor

```java
// CSub.java
package com.jdojo.inheritance;

public class CSub extends CSuper {
    public CSub() {
        super();  // Injected by the compiler
        System.out.println("Inside CSub() constructor.");
    }
}
```

░ **Tip**   The keyword super refers to the immediate ancestor of a class. You can call superclass constructors using the super keyword only as the first statement inside a constructor.

You can also call the no-args constructor or any other constructors of the superclass explicitly as the first statement inside constructors of your class. The compiler injects the no-args constructor call only if you have not added one explicitly. Let's try to improve your Employee and Manager classes. Let's add a constructor to the Employee class that accepts the name of the employee as a parameter. You will call the new class Employee2, as shown in Listing 20-25.

Listing 20-25. Employee2 Class, Which Is a Modified Version of the Original Employee Class and Has a Constructor That Accepts a String Argument

```java
// Employee2.java
package com.jdojo.inheritance;

public class Employee2 {
    private String name = "Unknown";

    public Employee2(String name) {
        this.name = name;
    }

    public void setName(String name) {
        this.name = name;
    }

    public String getName() {
        return name;
    }
}
```

Let's call your new Manager class Manager2, which inherits from the Employee2 class.

```
// Manager2.java
package com.jdojo.inheritance;

// Won't compile
public class Manager2 extends Employee2 {
    // No code for now
}
```

The previous code for the Manager2 class does not compile. It generates the following compile-time error:

```
Error(4,23): constructor Employee2() not found in class com.jdojo.inheritance.Employee2
```

You have not added any constructor for the Manager2 class. Therefore, the compiler will add a no-args constructor for it. It will also try to inject a super() call as the first statement inside the no-args constructor, which will call the no-args constructor of the Employee2 class. However, the Employee2 class does not have a no-args constructor. This is the reason that you get the previous error. The code for the Manager2 class looks as follows, after it is modified by the compiler. You may notice that that the super() call is invalid, because the Employee2 class does not have a no-args constructor.

```
// Code for Manager2 class after compiler injects a no-args constructor with a call to
super()
package com.jdojo.inheritance;

// Won't compile
public class Manager2 extends Employee2 {
    // Injected by the compiler
    public Manager2() {
        // Injected by the compiler
        // Calls the nonexistent no-args constructor of Employee2 class
        super();
    }
}
```

So, how do you fix the Manager2 class? There are many ways to fix it. Some of the ways you can fix the Manager2 class are as follows.

You can add a no-args constructor to the Employee2 class, like so:

```
public class Employee2 {
    // A no-args constructor
    public Employee2() {
    }

    /* All other code for class remains the same */
}
```

After adding a no-args constructor to the Employee2 class, the code for the Manager2 class will compile fine.

You can add a no-args constructor to the Manager2 class and explicitly call the constructor of the Employee2 class with a String argument, as follows:

```
public class Manager2 extends Employee2 {
    public Manager2() {
        // Call constructor of Employee2 class explicitly
        super("Unknown");
    }
}
```

You can add a constructor to the Manager2 class, which takes a String argument and pass the argument value to the Employee2 class constructor. This way, you can create a Manager2 by passing the name of the Manager2 as a parameter to its constructor.

```
public class Manager2 extends Employee2 {
    public Manager2(String name) {
        // Call constructor of Employee2 class explicitly
        super(name);
    }
}
```

Normally, the third option is used where you would provide a way to create an object of the Manager2 class with manager's name. Note that Manager2 class does not have access to the name instance variable of the Employee2 class. Still, you can initialize the name instance variable in the Employee2 class from the Manager2 class using the super keyword and invoking the constructor of the Employee2 class. Listing 20-26 has the complete code for the Manager2 class that will compile. Listing 20-27 has code to test the Manager2 class and its output shows that it works as expected.

▓ **Tip**   Every class must call the constructor of its superclass from its constructors directly or indirectly. If the superclass does not have a no-args constructor, you must call any other constructors of the superclass explicitly, as was done in Listing 20-26.

Listing 20-26. A Manager2 Class That Has a Constructor That Accepts a String Argument and Calls the Constructor of the Employee2 Class Explicitly

```
// Manager2.java
package com.jdojo.inheritance;

public class Manager2 extends Employee2 {
    public Manager2(String name) {
        super(name);
    }
}
```

Listing 20-27. A Test Class to Test the Manager2 Class

```
// Manager2Test.java
package com.jdojo.inheritance;

public class Manager2Test {
    public static void main(String[] args) {
        Manager2 mgr = new Manager2("John Jacobs");
        String name = mgr.getName();
        System.out.println("Manager name: " + name);
    }
}
```

```
Manager name: John Jacobs
```

I need to discuss a few more rules about using the constructors of the superclass from the subclass. Consider the following definition of classes X and Y, which are in two different packages:

```
// X.java
package com.jdojo.inheritance.pkg1;

public class X {
    // X() has package-level access
    X() {
    }
}
```

```
// Y.java
package com.jdojo.inheritance.pkg2;

import com.jdojo.inheritance.pkg1.X;

public class Y extends X {
    public Y() {
    }
}
```

The code for class Y would not compile. It generates a compile-time error as follows:

```
Error(7):  X() is not public in com.jdojo.inheritance.pkg1.X; cannot be accessed from
outside package
```

The error states that the no-args constructor in class X has a package-level access. Therefore, it cannot be accessed from class Y, which is in a different package. You received this error because the compiler will modify class Y definition as follows:

```
// Compiler modified version of class Y
// Y.java
package com.jdojo.inheritance.pkg2;

import com.jdojo.inheritance.pkg1.X;
```

```
public class Y extends X {
    public Y() {
        // Injected by the compiler to call X() constructor
        super();
    }
}
```

The no-args constructor of class X has a package-level access. Therefore, it can only be accessed from the com.jdojo.inheritance.pkg1 package. How do you fix class Y? It is tricky to suggest a solution in such a case. The solution depends on the design that is used behind the creation of class X and class Y. However, for the class Y to compile, you must create a constructor for the class X, which has a public or protected access, so it can be accessed from class Y.

Here is another rule for using constructors along with inheritance. The superclass constructor must be called explicitly or implicitly from inside the constructor of a class using the super keyword. However, the access to a superclass constructor from a class is controlled by the access level of the constructor of the superclass. Sometimes, consequences of the access level of the constructors of a class could be that it cannot be accessed at all. Consider the following definition of the class called NoSubclassingAllowed:

```
public class NoSubclassingAllowed {
    private NoSubclassingAllowed() {
    }

    // Other code goes here
}
```

The NoSubclassingAllowed class has explicitly declared a private constructor. A private constructor cannot be accessed from anywhere including subclasses. For a subclass to exist, the subclass must be able to call at least one of the constructors of its superclass. This concludes that the NoSubclassingAllowed class cannot be inherited by any other classes. This is one of the ways to disable inheritance for a class. The following code will not compile, which tries to subclass the NoSubclassingAllowed class, which has no accessible constructors:

```
// Won't compile.
public class LetUsTryInVain extends NoSubclassingAllowed {
}
```

One thing you may notice is that no one can create an object of the NoSubclassingAllowed class because its constructor is not accessible from outside. Classes like this provide methods that create its object and return it to the caller. This is also a way to control and encapsulate object creation of a class.

Recall from Chapter 9 that you can call a constructor of a class from another constructor of the same class using the this keyword and the call must be the first statement in the constructor's body. When you look at the rule to call another constructor of the same class and constructor of the superclass, you would find that both state that the call must be the first statement inside the body of the constructor. The result of these two rules is that from one constructor either you can use this() to call another constructer of the same class or super() to call a constructor of the superclass, but not both. This rule also ensures that the constructor of the superclass is always called once and only once.

Method Hiding

A class also inherits all non-private `static` methods from its superclass. Redefining an inherited `static` method in a class is known as method hiding. The redefined `static` method in a subclass is said to hide the `static` method of its superclass. Recall that redefining a non-static method in a class is called method overriding. Listing 20-28 contains code for a MHidingSuper class, which has a `static print()` method. Listing 20-29 has the code for a MHidingSub class that inherits from the MHidingSuper class. It redefines the `print()` method, which hides the `print()` method in the MHidingSuper class. The `print()` method in MHidingSub is an example of method hiding.

Listing 20-28. A MHidingSuper Class That Has a Static Method

```
// MHidingSuper.java
package com.jdojo.inheritance;

public class MHidingSuper {
    public static void print() {
        System.out.println("Inside MHidingSuper.print()");
    }
}
```

Listing 20-29. A MHidingSub Class That Hides the print() of its Superclass

```
// MHidingSub.java
package com.jdojo.inheritance;

public class MHidingSub extends MHidingSuper {
    public static void print() {
        System.out.println("Inside MHidingSub.print()");
    }
}
```

All rules about the redefined method (name, access level, return types, and exception) for method hiding are the same as for method overriding. Refer to the "Method Overriding" section for more detailed discussion on these rules. One rule that is different for method hiding is the binding rule. Early binding is used for static methods. Based on the compile-time type of the expression, the compiler determines what code will be executed at runtime for a `static` method call. Note that you can use the class name as well as a reference variable to invoke a `static` method. There is no ambiguity about method binding, when you use a class name to invoke a `static` method. The compiler binds the `static` method that is defined (or redefined) in the class. If a class does not define (or redefine) the `static` method, the compiler binds the method that the class inherits from its superclass. If the compiler does not find a defined/redefined/inherited method in the class, it generates an error. Listing 20-30 contains the code that demonstrates the early binding rules for method hiding for static methods of a class.

Listing 20-30. A Test Class to Demonstrate Method Hiding

```
// MHidingTest.java
package com.jdojo.inheritance;

public class MHidingTest {
    public static void main(String[] args) {
        MHidingSuper mhSuper = new MHidingSub();
        MHidingSub mhSub = new MHidingSub();
```

```
        System.out.println("#1");

        // #1
        MHidingSuper.print();
        mhSuper.print();

        System.out.println("#2");

        // #2
        MHidingSub.print();
        mhSub.print();
        ((MHidingSuper) mhSub).print();

        System.out.println("#3");

        // #3
        mhSuper = mhSub;
        mhSuper.print();
        ((MHidingSub) mhSuper).print();
    }
}
```

```
#1
Inside MHidingSuper.print()
Inside MHidingSuper.print()
#2
Inside MHidingSub.print()
Inside MHidingSub.print()
Inside MHidingSuper.print()
#3
Inside MHidingSuper.print()
Inside MHidingSub.print()
```

The test code has three sections labeled #1, #2, and #3. Let's discuss how early binding is performed by the compiler in each section.

```
// #1
MHidingSuper.print();
mhSuper.print();
```

The first call, MHidingSuper.print(), is made using a class name. The compiler binds this call to execute the print() method of the MHidingSuper class. The second call, mhSuper.print(), is made using the reference variable mhSuper. The compile-time type (or declared type) of the mhSuper variable is MHidingSuper. Therefore, the compiler binds this call to execute the print() method of the MHidingSuper class.

```
// #2
MHidingSub.print();
mhSub.print();
((MHidingSuper)mhSub).print();
```

The first two calls in section #2 are similar to the two calls in section #1. They are bound to the print() method of the MHidingSub class. The third call, ((MHidingSuper) mhSub).print(), needs a little explanation. The compile-time type of the mhSub variable is MHidingSub. When you use a typecast (MHidingSuper) on the mhSub variable, the compile-time type of the expression, (MHidingSuper) mhSub, becomes MHidingSuper. When you call the print() method on this expression, the compiler binds it to its compile-time type, which is MHidingSuper. Therefore, the third method call in section #2 is bound to the print() method of the MHidingSuper class.

```
// #3
mhSuper = mhSub;
mhSuper.print();
((MHidingSub)mhSuper).print();
```

The first statement in section #3 assigns a reference of MHidingSub object to the mhSuper reference variable. After the first statement is executed, the mhSuper variable is referring to an object of the MHidingSub class. When the first call to the print() method is made, the compiler looks at the compile-time type (or declared type) of mhSuper variable, which is MHidingSuper. Therefore, the compiler binds the call mhSuper.print() to the print() method of the MHidingSuper class. The second call to the print() method is bound to the print() method of the MHidingSub class because the typecast (MHidingSub) makes the type of the entire expression as MHidingSub.

░ **Tip** A static method of a class cannot hide an instance method of its superclass. If you want to invoke a hidden method of the superclass from inside a class, you need to qualify the hidden method call with the superclass name. For example, if you want to call the print() method of the MHidingSuper class from inside the MHidingSub class, you need to use MHidingSuper.print(). Inside the MHidingSub class, the call to the print() method, without using the class name or a variable, refers to the hiding method print() of the MHidingSub class.

Field Hiding

A field declaration (static or non-static) in a class hides the inherited field with the same name in its superclass. The type of the field and its access level are not considered in the case of field hiding. Field hiding occurs solely based on the field name. Early binding is used for field access. That is, the compiler-time type of the class is used to bind the field access. Consider the following declaration of two classes G and H:

```
public class G {
    protected int x = 200;
    protected String y = "Hello";
    protected double z = 10.5;
}

public class H extends G {
    protected int x = 400;        // Hides x in class G
    protected String y = "Bye";   // Hides y in class G
    protected String z = "OK";    // Hides z in class G
}
```

The field declarations x, y, and z in class H hide the inherited fields x, y, and z in class G. It is to be emphasized that the same field name in a class alone hides a field of its superclass. Data types of the hidden and the hiding fields are immaterial. For example, the data type of z in class G is double, whereas data type of z in class H is String. Still, the field z in class H hides the field z in class G. The simple names of fields x, y, and z in class H refer to the hiding fields, not inherited fields. Therefore, if you use the simple name x in class H, it refers to the field x declared in class H, not in class G. If you want to refer to the field x in class G from inside class H, you need to use the keyword super, for example, super.x.

In Listing 20-31, the FHidingSuper class declares fields, num and name. In Listing 20-32, the FHidingSub class inherits from the FHidingSuper class and it inherits the num and name fields from it. The print() method of the FHidingSub class prints the values of the num and name fields. The print() method uses simple names of num and name fields and they refer to the inherited fields from the FHidingSuper class. When you run the FHidingTest class in Listing 20-33, the output shows that the FHidingSub class really inherits num and name fields from its superclass.

Listing 20-31. FHidingSuper Class with Two Protected Instance Fields

```
// FHidingSuper.java
package com.jdojo.inheritance;

public class FHidingSuper {
    protected int num = 100;
    protected String name = "John Jacobs";
}
```

Listing 20-32. FHidingSub Class, Which Inherits from the FHidingSuper Class and Inherits Fields num and name

```
// FHidingSub.java
package com.jdojo.inheritance;

public class FHidingSub extends FHidingSuper {
    public void print() {
        System.out.println("num: " + num);
        System.out.println("name: " + name);
    }
}
```

Listing 20-33. A Test Class to Demonstrate field's Inheritances

```
// FHidingTest.java
package com.jdojo.inheritance;

public class FHidingTest {
    public static void main(String[] args) {
        FHidingSub fhSub = new FHidingSub();
        fhSub.print();
    }
}
```

```
num: 100
name: John Jacobs
```

Consider the definition of class FHidingSub2, as shown in Listing 20-34.

Listing 20-34. A FHidingSub2 Class That Inherits from FHidingSuper and Declares Two Variables with the Same Name as Declared in Its Superclass

```java
// FHidingSub2.java
package com.jdojo.inheritance;

public class FHidingSub2 extends FHidingSuper {
    // Hides num field in FHidingSuper class
    private int num = 200;

    // Hides name field in FHidingSuper class
    private String name = "Wally Inman";

    public void print() {
        System.out.println("num: " + num);
        System.out.println("name: " + name);
    }
}
```

The FHidingSub2 class inherits from the FHidingSuper class. It declares two fields, num and name, which have the same names as the two fields declared in its superclass. This is a case of field hiding. The num and name fields in FHidingSub2 hide the num and name fields that are inherited from the FHidingSuper class. When the num and name fields are used by their simple names inside the FHidingSub2 class, they refer to the fields declared in the FHidingSub2 class, not to the inherited fields from the FHidingSuper class. This is verified by running the FHidingTest2 class, as shown in Listing 20-35.

Listing 20-35. A Test Class to Demonstrate Field Hiding

```java
// FHidingTest2.java
package com.jdojo.inheritance;

public class FHidingTest2 {
    public static void main(String[] args) {
        FHidingSub2 fhSub2 = new FHidingSub2();
        fhSub2.print();
    }
}
```

```
num: 200
name: Wally Inman
```

The FHidingSub2 class has four fields, two inherited (num and name) and two declared (num and name). If you want to refer to the inherited fields from the superclass, you need to qualify the field names with the keyword super. For example, super.num and super.name inside FHidingSub2 refers to the num and name fields in FHidingSuper class.

The print() method of the FHidingSub3 class in Listing 20-36 uses the keyword super to access hidden fields of the superclass and uses the simple names of the fields to access fields from its own class. The output of Listing 20-37 verifies this.

Listing 20-36. A FHidingSub3 Class That Demonstrates How to Access Hidden Fields of Superclass Using the super Keyword

```java
// FHidingSub3.java
package com.jdojo.inheritance;

public class FHidingSub3 extends FHidingSuper {
    // Hides the num field in FHidingSuper class
    private int num = 200;

    // Hides the name field in FHidingSuper class
    private String name = "Wally Inman";

    public void print() {
        // FHidingSub3.num
        System.out.println("num: " + num);

        // FHidingSuper.num
        System.out.println("super.num: " + super.num);

        // FHidingSub3.name
        System.out.println("name: " + name);

        // FHidingSuper.name
        System.out.println("super.name: " + super.name);
    }
}
```

Listing 20-37. A Test Class That Accesses Hidden Fields

```java
// FHidingTest3.java
package com.jdojo.inheritance;

public class FHidingTest3 {
    public static void main(String[] args) {
        FHidingSub3 fhSub3 = new FHidingSub3();
        fhSub3.print();
    }
}
```

```
num: 200
super.num: 100
name: Wally Inman
super.name: John Jacobs
```

Recall that when an object is created, the Java runtime allocates memory for all instance variables in the class of the object and all of its ancestors. When you create an object of the FHidingSub2 or FHidingSub3 class, memory will be allocated for the four instance variables, as shown in Figure 20-4.

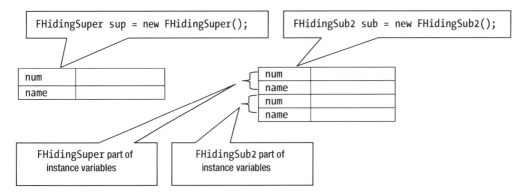

Figure 20-4. *Memory layout for objects of FHidingSuper and FHidingSub2 classes*

Here's a summary of the field hiding rules:

- Field hiding occurs when a class declares a variable with the same name as an inherited variable from its superclass.

- Field hiding occurs only based on the name of the field. Access level, data type, and the type of field (static or non-static) are not considered for field hiding. For example, a static field can hide an instance field. A field of int type can hide a field of String type, etc. A private field in a class can hide a protected field in its superclass. A public field in a class can hide a protected field in its superclass.

- A class should use the keyword super to access the hidden fields of the superclass. The class can use the simple names to access the redefined fields in its body.

Disabling Inheritance

You can disable subclassing for a class by declaring the class final. You have seen the use of the final keyword before for declaring constants. The same final keyword is used in a class declaration. A final class cannot be subclassed. The following snippet of code declares a final class named Security:

```
public final class Security {
    // Code goes here
}
```

The following declaration of class CrackedSecurity will not compile:

```
// Won't compile. Cannot inherit from Security
public final class CrackedSecurity extends Security {
    // Code goes here
}
```

You can also declare a method as final. A final method cannot be overridden or hidden by a subclass. Since a final method cannot be overridden or hidden, a call to a final method may be inlined by a code optimizer for better performance.

```java
public class A {
    public final void m1() {
        // Code goes here
    }

    public void m2() {
        // Code goes here
    }
}

public class B extends A {
    // Cannot override A.m1() here because it is final in class A

    // OK to override m2() because it is not final in class A
    public void m2() {
        // Code goes here
    }
}
```

You will find many classes and methods in the Java class libraries that are declared final. Most notably, the String class is final. Why would you declare a class or a method as final? In other words, why would you want to prevent subclassing of a class or overriding/hiding of a method? The main reasons for doing this are security, correctness, and performance. If your class is important for security reasons, you do not want someone to inherit from your class and mess with the security that your class is supposed to implement. Sometimes, you declare a class/method final to preserve the correctness of the program. A final method may result in better performance at runtime because a code optimizer is free to inline the final method calls.

Abstract Classes and Methods

Sometimes you may create a class just to represent a concept rather than to represent objects. Suppose you want to develop classes to represent different shapes. A shape is just an idea or a concept. It does not exist in reality. Suppose someone asks you to draw a shape. Your immediate response would be, "What shape do you want me to draw?" If someone asks you to draw a circle or a rectangle, it makes sense to you. Java lets you create a class whose objects cannot be created. Its purpose is just to represent an idea, which is common to objects of other classes. Such a class is called an *abstract* class. The term "concrete class" is used to denote a class that is not abstract and whose objects can be created. So far, all your classes have been concrete classes.

You need to use the abstract keyword in the class declaration to declare an abstract class. For example, the following code declares a Shape class abstract:

```java
public abstract class Shape {
    // No code for now
}
```

Because the Shape class has been declared abstract, you cannot create its object even though it has a public constructor (the default one added by the compiler). You can declare a variable of an abstract class as you do for a concrete class. The following code snippet shows some valid and invalid uses of Shape class:

```java
Shape s;      // OK
new Shape(); // A compile-time error. Cannot create a Shape object
```

If you look at the definition of the Shape class, it looks the same as any other concrete classes, except the use of the abstract keyword in the declaration. A class has instance variables and instance methods to define the state and behavior of its objects. By declaring a class abstract, you indicate that the class has some incomplete method definitions (behaviors) for its objects and it must be considered incomplete for object creation purposes.

What is an incomplete method in a class? A method which has a declaration, but no body, is an incomplete method. Missing body of a method does not mean an empty body. It means no body. The braces that follow the method's declaration indicate the body of the method. In the case of an incomplete method, the braces are replaced with a semicolon. If a method is incomplete, you must indicate it by using the abstract keyword in the method's declaration. Your Shape class does not know how to draw a shape until you mention a specific shape. However, one thing is for sure—you should be able to draw a shape no matter what kind of shape it is. In this case, you know the behavior name (draw), but you do not know how to implement it. Therefore, draw is a good candidate to be declared as an abstract method (or incomplete method) in the Shape class. The Shape class looks as follows, with an abstract draw() method:

```
public abstract class Shape {
    public Shape() {
    }

    public abstract void draw();
}
```

When you declare a class abstract, it does not necessarily mean that it has at least one abstract method. An abstract class may have all concrete methods. It may have all abstract methods. It may have some concrete and some abstract methods. If you have an abstract class, it means that an object of that class cannot exist. However, if a class has an abstract method (either declared or inherited), it must be declared abstract. Declaring a class as abstract is like placing an "under construction" sign in front of a building. If an "under construction" sign is placed in front of a building, it is not supposed to be used (not supposed to be created in case of a class). It does not matter whether the building is complete or not. An "under construction" sign is enough to indicate that it cannot be used. However, if some parts of the building are incomplete (like a class having abstract methods), you must place an "under construction" sign in front of it (must declare the class abstract) to avoid any mishap, in case someone attempts to use it.

░ **Tip**　You cannot create objects of an abstract class. If a class has an abstract method, declared or inherited, the class must be declared abstract. If a class does not have any abstract methods, you can still declare the class abstract. An abstract method is declared the same way as any other method, except that its body is indicated by a semicolon.

Listing 20-38 has the complete code for this Shape class.

Listing 20-38. An Abstract Shape Class with One Instance Variable, Two Constructors, and One Abstract Method

```
// Shape.java
package com.jdojo.inheritance;

public abstract class Shape {
    private String name;
```

```java
    public Shape() {
        this.name = "Unknown shape";
    }

    public Shape(String name) {
        this.name = name;
    }

    public String getName() {
        return this.name;
    }

    public void setName(String name) {
        this.name = name;
    }

    // Abstract methods
    public abstract void draw();

    public abstract double getArea();

    public abstract double getPerimeter();
}
```

Each shape will have a name. The name instance variable stores the name of the shape. The getName()
and setName() methods let you read and change the name of the shape, respectively. Two constructors
let you set the name of the shape or leave the name as the default name "Unknown shape". A shape does
not know how to draw, so it has declared its draw() method abstract. A shape also does not know how to
compute its area and perimeter, so it has declared getArea() and getPerimeter() methods abstract.

An abstract class guarantees the use of inheritance, at least theoretically. Otherwise, an abstract class
by itself is useless. For example, until someone supplies the implementations for the abstract methods of the
Shape class, its other parts (instance variables, concrete methods, and constructors) are of no use. You create
subclasses of an abstract class, which override the abstract methods providing implementations for them.
Listing 20-39 has code for a Rectangle class, which inherits from the Shape class.

Listing 20-39. A Rectangle Class, Which Inherits from the Shape Class

```java
// Rectangle.java
package com.jdojo.inheritance;

public class Rectangle extends Shape {
    private final double width;
    private final double height;

    public Rectangle(double width, double height) {
        // Set the shape name as "Rectangle"
        super("Rectangle");
        this.width = width;
        this.height = height;
    }
```

```java
    // Provide an implementation for inherited abstract draw() method
    @Override
    public void draw() {
        System.out.println("Drawing a rectangle...");
    }

    // Provide an implementation for inherited abstract getArea() method
    @Override
    public double getArea() {
        return width * height;
    }

    // Provide an implementation for inherited abstract getPerimeter() method
    @Override
    public double getPerimeter() {
        return 2.0 * (width + height);
    }
}
```

Note that you have not declared the Rectangle class abstract, which means that it is a concrete class and its objects can be created. An abstract method is also inherited by a subclass like any other methods. Since the Rectangle class is not declared abstract, it must override all three abstract methods of its superclass and provide implementations for them. If the Rectangle class does not override all abstract methods of its superclass and provides implementation for them, it is considered incomplete and must be declared abstract. Your Rectangle class overrides the draw(), getArea(), and getPerimeter() methods of the Shape class and provides implementation (body within braces) for them. The instance variables width and height are used to keep track of the width and height of the rectangle. Inside the constructor, you call the constructor of the Shape class using the super keyword, super("Rectangle"), to set its name. Listing 20-40 has code for a Circle class, which inherits from the Shape class. It also overrides three abstract methods of the Shape class and provides implementations for them.

Listing 20-40. A Circle Class, Which Inherits from Shape Class

```java
// Circle.java
package com.jdojo.inheritance;

public class Circle extends Shape {
    private final double radius;

    public Circle(double radius) {
        super("Circle");
        this.radius = radius;
    }

    // Provide an implementation for inherited abstract draw() method
    @Override
    public void draw() {
        System.out.println("Drawing a circle...");
    }
```

```
    // Provide an implementation for inherited abstract getArea() method
    @Override
    public double getArea() {
        return Math.PI * radius * radius;
    }

    // Provide an implementation for inherited abstract getPerimeter() method
    @Override
    public double getPerimeter() {
        return 2.0 * Math.PI * radius;
    }
}
```

It is time to use your abstract Shape class along with its concrete subclasses Rectangle and Circle. Note that the only restriction that is applied to an abstract class, when it is used in code, is that you cannot create its objects. Apart from this restriction, you can use it the same way you can use a concrete class. For example, you can declare a variable of an abstract class type; you can call methods of the abstract class using that variable, etc. How do you call a method on a Shape variable, if you cannot create an object of the Shape class? This is a good point. Consider the following snippet of code:

```
// Upcasting at work
Shape s = new Rectangle(2.0, 5.0);

// Late binding at work. s.getArea() will call the getArea() method of the Rectangle class.
double area = s.getArea();
```

If you look at the previous code, it makes sense. The first statement creates a Rectangle and assigns its reference to a variable of the Shape class, which is a simple case of upcasting. In the second statement, you are calling the getArea() method using the s variable. The compiler only verifies the existence of the getArea() method in the Shape class, which is the declared type of the s variables. The compiler does not care whether the getArea() method in the Shape class is incomplete (abstract) or not. It does not care if the getArea() method is abstract in the Shape class because it is an instance method and it knows that late binding at runtime will decide which code for the getArea() method will be executed. All it cares about is the existence of a method declaration of the getArea() method. At runtime, the late binding process finds that the variable s is referring to a Rectangle and it calls the getArea() method of the Rectangle class. Is it not unlike having one's cake and eating it too—can you have an abstract class (incomplete class) and use it too? If you look at the previous two lines of code, you would find that these magical two statements involve so many concepts of object-oriented programming: abstract class, abstract method, upcasting, method overriding, late binding, and runtime polymorphism. All of these features are involved in the previous two statements, thereby giving you the ability to write generic and polymorphic code. Consider a ShapeUtil class, as shown in Listing 20-41.

Listing 20-41. A ShapeUtil Class Having Utility Methods to Draw Any Shapes and Print Details About Them

```java
// ShapeUtil.java
package com.jdojo.inheritance;

public class ShapeUtil {
    public static void drawShapes(Shape[] list) {
        for (Shape s : list) {
            // Draw the shape, no matter what it is
            s.draw(); // Late binding
        }
    }

    public static void printShapeDetails(Shape[] list) {
        for (Shape s : list) {
            // Gather details about the shape
            String name = s.getName();              // Late Binding
            double area = s.getArea();               // Late binding
            double perimeter = s.getPerimeter(); // Late binding

            // Print details
            System.out.println("Name: " + name);
            System.out.println("Area: " + area);
            System.out.println("Perimeter: " + perimeter);
        }
    }
}
```

The ShapeUtil class contains two static methods: drawShapes() and printShapeDetails(). Both accept an array of Shape objects as a parameter. The drawShapes() method draws all the shapes by calling the draw() method of each element in the array passed to it. The printShapeDetails() method prints details, name, area, and perimeter of the shapes passed to it. The beauty of the code in the ShapeUtil class is that it never refers to any subclasses of the Shape class. It has no knowledge about the Rectangle or Circle class at all. It does not even care if a Rectangle class or a Circle class exists, although the code will work with Rectangles, Circles, and objects of any descendants of the Shape class. You may argue that you could have written the same code even if you did not declare the Shape class as abstract. So, what is the big deal about declaring the Shape class as abstract? You are getting two advantages by declaring the Shape class as abstract:

- If you did not declare the Shape class abstract, you were forced to provide implementations for the three abstract methods in the class. Since the Shape class does not know what shape object it will take the form of, it is not appropriate for it to provide implementations for these methods. For now, let's assume that you can handle this issue by providing an empty body for the draw() method and returning zero (or maybe a negative number) from the getArea() and getPerimeter() methods in the Shape class. Let's move to the next advantage, which is more compelling.

- You are forced to declare the Shape class as abstract because you had declared three abstract methods in it. The greatest advantage of declaring an abstract method in a class is to force its subclasses to override and provide implementation for it. The abstract methods in the Shape class forced the Rectangle and Circle subclasses to override them and provide implementations for them. Was that not what you wanted?

Listing 20-42 contain the code that tests the ShapeUtil class along with the Shape, Rectangle, and Circle classes. It creates an array of Shape objects. It populates one element of the array with a Rectangle and another with a Circle. It passes the array to the drawShapes() and printShapeDetails() methods of the ShapeUtil class, which draws the shapes and prints their details according to the type of objects placed in the array.

Listing 20-42. A Test Class to Test Shape, Rectangle, Circle, and the ShapeUtil Class

```
// ShapeUtilTest.java
package com.jdojo.inheritance;

public class ShapeUtilTest {
    public static void main(String[] args) {
        // Create some shapes, draw, and print their details
        Shape[] shapeList = new Shape[2];
        shapeList[0] = new Rectangle(2.0, 4.0);  // Upcasting
        shapeList[1] = new Circle(5.0);          // Upcasting

        // Draw all shapes
        ShapeUtil.drawShapes(shapeList);

        // Print details of all shapes
        ShapeUtil.printShapeDetails(shapeList);
    }
}
```

```
Drawing a rectangle...
Drawing a circle...
Name: Rectangle
Area: 8.0
Perimeter: 12.0
Name: Circle
Area: 78.53981633974483
Perimeter: 31.41592653589793
```

You have finished discussing the main rules of declaring classes and methods abstract. However, there are many other rules that govern the use of abstract classes and methods in a Java program. Most of those rules (if not all) are listed here. All rules point to only one basic rule: "Abstract class should be subclassed to be useful and the subclass should override and provide implementation for the abstract methods."

- A class may be declared abstract even if it does not have an abstract method.

- A class must be declared abstract if it declares or inherits an abstract method. If the class overrides and provides implementations for all inherited abstract methods and does not declare any abstract methods, it does not have to be declared abstract. Although it could be declared abstract.

- You cannot create an object of an abstract class. However, you can declare a variable of the abstract class type and call methods using it.

- An abstract class cannot be declared `final`. Recall that a `final` class cannot be subclassed, which conflicts with the requirement of an `abstract` class that it must be subclassed to be useful in a true sense.

- An abstract class should not declare all constructors `private`. Otherwise, the abstract class cannot be subclassed. Note that constructors of all ancestor classes (including an `abstract` class) are always invoked when an object of a class is created. When you create an object of a `Rectangle` class, constructors for the `Object` class and the `Shape` class are also invoked. If you declare all constructors of an `abstract` class `private`, you cannot create a subclass for your `abstract` class, which makes it the same as declaring an abstract `final` class.

- An abstract method cannot be declared `static`. Note that an `abstract` method must be overridden and implemented by a subclass. A `static` method cannot be overridden. However, it can be hidden.

- An abstract method cannot be declared `private`. Recall that a `private` method is not inherited and hence it cannot be overridden. The requirement for an `abstract` method is that a subclass must be able to override and provide implementation for it.

- An abstract method cannot be declared `native`, `strictfp`, or `synchronized`. These keywords refer to implementation details of a method. The `native` keyword denotes that a method is implemented in native code as opposed to Java code. The `strictfp` keyword denotes that the code inside a method uses FP-strict rules for floating-point computations. Refer to http://en.wikipedia.org/wiki/Strictfp for more details on the `strictfp` keyword and its usage. The `synchronized` keyword denotes that the object on which the method is invoked must be locked by the thread before it can execute method's code. Since an `abstract` method does not have an implementation, the keywords that imply an implementation cannot be used for an abstract method.

- An abstract method in a class can override an `abstract` method in its superclass without providing an implementation. The subclass `abstract` method may refine the return type or exception list of the overridden `abstract` method. Consider the following code. Class B overrides the abstract `m1()` method of class A and it does not provide its implementation. It only removes one exception from the `throws` clause. Class C overrides the `m1()` method of class B and provides implementation for it. Note that the change in return type or exception list, as shown in the `m1()` method for class B and class C, must follow the rules of method overriding.

```
public abstract class A {
    public abstract void m1() throws CE1, CE2;
}

public abstract class B extends A {
    public abstract void m1() throws CE1;
}

public class C extends B {
    public void m1() {
        // Code goes here
    }
}
```

- A concrete instance method may be overridden by an abstract instance method. This can be done to force the subclasses to provide implementation for that method. All classes in Java inherit equals(), hashCode(), and toString() methods of the Object class. Suppose you have a class CA and you want all its subclasses to override and provide implementation for the equals(), hashCode(), and toString() methods of the Object class. You need to override these three methods in class CA and declare them abstract, like so:

```java
public abstract class CA {
    public abstract int hashCode();
    public abstract boolean equals(Object obj);
    public abstract String toString();
    // Other code goes here
}
```

- In this case, concrete methods of the Object class have been overridden by abstract methods in the CA class. All concrete subclasses of CA are forced to override and provide implementations for the equals(), hashCode(), and toString() methods.

Method Overriding and Generic Method Signatures

Java 5 introduced the concept of generic types. If you are using a version of Java prior to Java 5, this section does not apply. Java 5 lets you declare generic methods. When the code with generics types is compiled, the generic types are transformed into raw types. The process that is used to transform the generic type parameters information is known as *type erasure*. Consider the GenericSuper class in Listing 20-43. It has a generic type parameter T. It has two methods, m1() and m2(). Its m1() method uses the generic type T as its parameter type. Its m2() method defines a new generic type to use it as its parameter type.

Listing 20-43. A Sample Class That Uses Generic Type Parameters

```java
// GenericSuper.java
package com.jdojo.inheritance;

public class GenericSuper<T> {
    public void m1(T a) {
        // Code goes here
    }

    public <P extends Employee> void m2(P a) {
        // Code goes here
    }
}
```

When the GenericSuper class is compiled, the erasure transforms the code during compilation and the resulting code looks like Listing 20-44.

Listing 20-44. The GenericSuper Class Transformed Code During Compilation After Erasure Is Used

```java
// GenericSuper.java
package com.jdojo.inheritance;

public class GenericSuper {
    public void m1(Object a) {
        // Code goes here
    }

    public void m2(Employee a) {
        // Code goes here
    }
}
```

The GenericSub class in Listing 20-45 inherits the GenericSuper class.

Listing 20-45. A GenericSub Class Inherits from the GenericSuper Class and Overrides m1() and m2() Methods

```java
// GenericSub.java
package com.jdojo.inheritance;

public class GenericSub extends GenericSuper {
    @Override
    public void m1(Object a) {
        // Code goes here
    }

    @Override
    public void m2(Employee a) {
        // Code goes here
    }
}
```

In the GenericSub class, the m1() and m2() methods override the corresponding methods in the GenericSuper class. If you compare the methods m1() and m2() between Listing 20-43 and Listing 20-45 for overriding rules, you would think that they do not have the same signature because the code in Listing 20-43 uses generics. The rules for checking for override equivalent method signature is that if a method uses generic parameters, you need to compare its erasure, not the generic version of its declaration. When you compare erasure of m1() and m2() method's declaration in the GenericSuper class (in Listing 20-44) with m1() and m2() methods declarations in Listing 20-45, you would find that m1() and m2() methods are overridden in the GenericSub class.

Typo Danger in Method Overriding

Sometimes it is easy to get it wrong when you try to override a method in a class. It may seem that you have overridden a method when it is not overridden. Consider the following two classes, C1 and C2:

```java
// C1.java
package com.jdojo.inheritance;

public class C1 {
    public void m1(double num) {
        System.out.println("Inside C1.m1(): " + num);
    }
}
```

```java
// C2.java
package com.jdojo.inheritance;

public class C2 extends C1 {
    public void m1(int num) {
        System.out.println("Inside C2.m1(): " + num);
    }
}
```

The intent was that the m1() method in class C2 overrides the m1() method of class C1. However, this is not true. It is a case of method overloading, not method overriding. The m1() method in C2 is overloaded; m1(double num) is inherited from class C1 and m1(int num) is declared in C2. Things becomes more difficult when you start running your program and you do not get the desired results. Consider the following code snippet;

```java
C1 c = new C2();
c.m1(10); // Which method is called - C1.m() or C2.m2()?
```

What should be printed when you execute the previous code? It prints the following:

```
Inside C1.m1(): 10.0
```

Are you surprised to see the output of the previous snippet of code? Let's discuss in detail what happens when the previous snippet of code is compiled and executed. When the compiler comes across the second statement, c.m1(10), it does the following thing: it finds out the compile-time type of the reference variable c, which is C1.

It looks for a method named m1 in C1. The argument value 10 passed to the method m1() is an int. The compiler looks for a method named m1 (inherited or declared) in C1, which takes an int parameter. It finds that class C1 has a method m1(double num), which accepts a double parameter. It tries type-widening conversion and finds that m1(double num) method in class C1 can be used for the c.m1(10) method call. At this time, the compiler binds the method signature for the call. Note that the compiler binds the method signature, not the method code. The method code is bound at runtime because m1() is an instance method. The compiler does not decide which m1() method's code will be executed for c.m1(10). Keep in mind that the compiler's decision is solely based on its knowledge about class C1. When c.m1(10) is compiled, the compiler does not know (or care) about the existence of any other class, for example, C2. You can see what code is generated for the c.m1(10) method call by the Java compiler. You need to use the javap command line utility with a -c option to disassemble the compiled code as follows. You need to pass the fully qualified name of the class to the javap command.

```
javap -c <fully-qualified-class-name>
```

For the previous code snippet that contains the c.m1(10) call, javap will print instructions that are generated by the compiler. I show only one instruction:

```
12:   invokevirtual   #14; // Method com/jdojo/inheritance /C1.m1:(D)V
```

The invokevirtual instruction is used to denote a call to an instance method that will use late binding. The #14 (it may be different for you) indicates the method table entry number, which is the entry for the C1.m1(D)V method. The syntax may be a little cryptic for you. The character D denotes double, which is the parameter type and V denotes void, which is the return type of the method m1().

At runtime, when the JVM attempts to run c.m1(10), it uses the late binding mechanism to find the method code that it will execute. Note that the JVM will search for m1(D)V method signature, which is the compiler syntax for void m1(double). It starts the search by looking at the runtime type of c, which is class C2. Class C2 does not have a method named m1, which accepts a parameter of type double. The search moves up in the class hierarchy to class C1. The JVM finds the method in class C1 and it executes it. This is the reason that you got the output that indicates that m1(double num) in the class C1 is called for c.m1(10).

Such mistakes are very difficult to hunt down. You avoid such mistakes by using the @Override annotation. You have already using this annotation. For more information about annotations, refer to Chapter 1 in the second volume of this series. The annotation has compiler support. The compiler will make sure a method that is annotated with the @Override annotation really overrides a method in its superclass. Otherwise, it will generate an error. Using the @Override annotation is easy. Just add it to the method declaration anywhere before the method's return type. The following code for class C2 uses @Override annotation for the m1() method:

```java
public class C2 extends C1 {
    @Override
    public void m1(int num) {
        System.out.println("Inside C2.m1(): " + num);
    }
}
```

When you compile the previous code for class C2, the compiler will generate an error stating that the method m1() in class C2 does not override any method in its superclass. Using the @Override annotation with a method that is supposed to override a superclass method saves you a lot of debugging time. Note that the @Override annotation does not change the way method overriding works. It is used as an indicator to the compiler that it needs to make sure the method really overrides the method of its superclass.

Is-a, has-a, and part-of Relationships

A software application, which is designed based on object-oriented paradigm, consists of interacting objects. Objects of one class may be related to objects of another class in some ways. Is-a, has-a, and part-of are the three most commonly used relationships that exist between objects of two classes. I have already discussed that an is-a relationship is modeled using inheritance between two classes. For example, the relationship "A part-time manager *is-a* manager" is modeled by inheriting the PartTimeManager class from the Manager class.

Sometimes an object of a class contains an object of another class, which indicates a whole-part relationship. This relationship is called *aggregation*. It is also known as *has-a* relationship. The example of has-a relationship is "A person has an address." As a whole-part relationship, the person represents the whole and the address represents the part. Java does not have any special feature that lets you indicate a has-a relationship in your code. In Java code, aggregation is implemented by using an instance variable in the whole, which is of the type part. In this example, the Person class will have an instance variable of type Address, as follows. Note that an object of the Address class is created outside of a Person class and passed in to the Person class constructor.

```
public class Address {
    // Code goes here
}

public class Person {
    // Person has-a Address
    private Address addr;

    public Person(Address addr) {
        this.addr = addr;
    }

    // Other code goes here
}
```

Composition is a special case of aggregation in which the whole controls the life cycle of the part. It is also known as *part-of* relationship. Sometimes, has-a and part-of relationships are used interchangeably. The main difference between aggregation and composition is that in composition the whole controls the creation/destruction of the part. In composition, the part cannot exist by itself. Rather, the part is created and destroyed as a part of the whole. Consider the relationship "A CPU is part-of a computer." You can also rephrase the relationship as "A computer has a CPU." Does the existence of a CPU outside a computer make sense? The answer is no. It is true that a computer and a CPU represent a whole-part relationship. However, there are some more constraints to this whole-part relationship and that is, "The existence of a CPU makes sense only inside a computer." You can implement composition in Java code by declaring an instance variable of a type part and creating the part object as part of creation of the whole as shown here. A CPU is created when a Computer is created. The CPU is destroyed when the computer is destroyed.

```
public class CPU {
    // Code goes here
}

public class Computer {
    // CPU part-of Computer
    private CPU cpu = new CPU();

    // Other code goes here
}
```

Java has a special class type called inner class, which can also be used to represent composition. An object of an inner class can exist only within an object of its enclosing class. The enclosing class would be the whole and the inner class would be the part. You can represent the part-of relationship between CPU and computer using an inner class, as follows:

```
public class Computer {
    private CPU cpu = new CPU();

    // CPU is an inner class of Computer
    private class CPU {
        // Code goes here
    }

    // Other code goes here for Computer class
}
```

Compare this implementation of composition between a computer and a CPU with the previous one. When you use an inner class, an object of the CPU class cannot exist without an object of the Computer class. This restriction may be problematic when the object of the same class, say CPU, is part of another object in a composition relationship.

Composition also denotes owner-owned relationship. A computer is an owner and a CPU is owned by the computer. The owned object cannot exist without the owner object. Typically, but not necessarily, the owned object is destroyed when the owner object is destroyed. Sometimes, when the owner object is being destroyed, it passes the reference of the owned object to another owner. In such cases, the owned object survives the death of its current owner. The point to note is that the owned object always has an owner.

Sometimes programmers get confused between the choice of using inheritance and composition and they use inheritance instead of composition. You can find this kind of mistake in the Java class library where the java.util.Stack class is inherited from the java.util.Vector class. A Vector is a list of objects. A Stack is also a list of objects, but is not simply a list of object as Vector is. A Stack is supposed to allow you to add an object to its top and remove an object from its top. However, a Vector allows you to add/remove an object at any position. Since the Stack class inherits from the Vector class, it also inherits methods that will let you add/remove an object at any position, which are simply wrong operations for a stack. The Stack class should have used composition to use a Vector object as its internal representation rather than inheriting from it. The following code snippet shows the correct use of a "has-a" relationship between the Stack and Vector classes:

```
public class Stack {
    // Stack has-a Vector
    private Vector items = new Vector();

    // Other code goes here
}
```

▓ **Tip** Whenever you are in doubt in choosing between composition and inheritance, give preference to composition. Both let you share the code. However, inheritance forces your class to be in a specific class hierarchy. Inheritance also creates a subtype, whereas composition is used to create a new type.

No Multiple Inheritance of Classes

Typically, a class signifies implementation. Java does not support multiple inheritance of implementation. That is, a class in Java cannot have more than one superclass. Inheritance lets a class inherit implementation and/or interface from its superclass. In the case of implementation inheritance, the superclass provides implementation for functionality that its subclass inherits and reuses. For example, the Employee class has implemented the getName() and setName() methods, which are inherited by the Manager class. In the case of interface inheritance, the superclass provides specification for functionality that its subclass inherits and implements. Note that declaring abstract methods in Java defines a specification whereas declaring a concrete (non-abstract) method defines an implementation. For example, the Shape class has specification for a draw() method, which is inherited by its subclasses (e.g., Rectangle and Circle). It does not provide any implementation for the draw() method. All concrete subclasses of the Shape class must provide implementation for its draw() method.

Multiple inheritance is defined as having a class inherit from more than one superclass. It poses some problems when a class inherits an implementation from multiple superclasses. Suppose there are two classes, Singer and Employee, and both provide implementation for processing salary (say, a pay() method). Further, suppose you inherit a class SingerEmployee, which inherits from the Singer and Employee classes. The new class, SingerEmployee, inherits the pay() method from two different superclasses, which have different implementations. When the pay() method is invoked on a SingerEmployee, which pay() method should be used—from the Employee class or from the Singer class?

Multiple inheritance makes programmer's job as well as language designer's job complex. Java supports multiple inheritance of interfaces (or types), not implementations. It has a construct, called interface, which is different from a class. An interface can inherit from multiple interfaces. A class can implement multiple interfaces. Java's approach to support only multiple inheritance of types avoids problems for programmers as well as its designers. Multiple types inheritance is easier to understand and design than the multiple implementations inheritance.

Summary

Inheritance lets you define a class based on the definition of another class. Inheritance is one of the techniques to implement inclusion polymorphism. It promotes code reuse. It lets you write code in terms of a class that works for the class and all its subclasses. The subclass inherits members of its superclass based on some rules. Constructors are not members of a class and they are not inherited by subclasses.

The keyword extends is used to inherit a class from another class. If a class declaration does not contain the keyword extends, the class implicitly inherits from the Object class. Inheritance creates a tree-like class hierarchy—the Object class being at the top of all class hierarchies. The Object class itself does not have a superclass.

Java supports two types of binding: early binding and late binding. In early binding, the compiler determines the fields and methods that will be accessed, based on the compile-time type of the references accessing the fields and methods. Java uses early binding for accessing all types of fields and static methods. In late binding, the runtime type of the reference variable determines the method that is executed. Inheritance, along with late binding, makes it possible to use runtime polymorphism in Java. Java uses late binding for accessing instance methods.

A variable of a superclass can always be assigned a reference of its subclasses. This is called upcasting. When a variable of a subclass is type cast and assigned to a variable of the superclass, it is called downcasting. For a downcasting to succeed at runtime, the variable of the superclass must contain a reference of the subclass or one of the subclasses of the subclass. The instanceof operator is used to test whether a reference variable is an instance of a specific class.

You can declare abstract classes and methods. The keyword abstract is used to declare abstract classes and methods. Abstract classes cannot be instantiated. If a class contains an abstract method, the class must be declared abstract. A class can be declared abstract even if it contains no abstract methods. Abstract methods are supposed to be overridden and provided an implementation by subclasses.

A subclass may access the constructors, methods, and fields of its superclass using the keyword super. The call to access the constructor of the superclass must be the first statement in the constructor of the subclass.

Redefining the static methods of a superclass inside a subclass is called method hiding. A field with the same name as a field in the superclass hides the field in the superclass and it is called field hiding. The hidden methods may be accessed from the subclass using the superclass name as the qualifier for the method. You can use the keyword super to access the hidden fields from the subclass.

Classes and methods may be declared final. A final class cannot be subclassed. A final method cannot be overridden. Declaring all constructors of a class private also stops subclassing for that class.

EXERCISES

1. What keyword do you use in a class declaration to inherit your class from another class?

2. What are the names of the superclass and subclass in the following class declaration?

    ```
    public class Letter extends Document
    ```

3. Write the fully qualified name of the superclass of class A, which is declared as follows:

    ```
    public class A {
    }
    ```

4. How many superclasses can a class have in Java?

5. What keyword do you use to call the constructor of the superclass? Write the statement that calls the superclass constructor, which takes a string as an argument. The argument value is "Hello".

6. What types of members of a superclass are inherited by a subclass: public, private, protected, and package-level?

7. Name the annotation that you should use when you override a method in your class, so the compiler can verify your intent of overriding the method.

8. How do you call an overridden instance method of a superclass from a subclass? Consider the following snippet of code:

    ```
    public class A {
        public void print() {
            System.out.println("A");
        }
    }
    ```

```
public class B extends A {
    @Override
    public void print() {
        /* Your one line code goes here */
        System.out.println("B");
    }

    public static void main(String[] args) {
        new B().print();
    }
}
```

Complete the code inside the `print()` method of class B, so when you run class B, it should print the following. You are to call the `print()` method of class A:

A
B

9. Write the reasons why the following class declaration does not compile.

```
public abstract final class A {
    // Code goes here
}
```

10. Write the reasons why the following declarations of class B and class C do not compile.

```
public class A {
    public A(int x) {
    }
}

public class B extends A {
}

public class C extends A {
    public C() {
    }
}
```

11. What is the difference between method overloading and method overriding?

12. Consider the following declarations for class A and class B. What will be printed when class B is run? Is the declaration of method `m1()` in class B a case of method overriding or method overloading? Explain your answer.

```
public class A {
    public void m1(int x) {
        System.out.println("A.m1(): " + x);
    }
}
```

```java
public class B extends A {
    public void m1(Integer x) {
        System.out.println("B.m1(): " + x);
    }

    public static void main(String[] args) {
        B b = new B();
        b.m1(100);
    }
}
```

13. Consider the following two class declarations:

```java
public class A {
}
```

```java
public class B extends A {
}
```

One of the following statements does not compile. Describe the reason behind the compile-time error and fix it. Identify examples of upcasting and downcasting in the following statements.

```java
A a = new B();
B b = new B();
a = b;
b = a;
```

14. What is the difference between early binding and late binding? Which type of binding is solely decided by the compiler?

15. Write the output when the following class B is run. This exercise is to test your knowledge of early binding and late binding.

```java
public class A {
    public void m1() {
        System.out.println("A.m1()");
    }

    public static void m2() {
        System.out.println("A.m2()");
    }
}
```

```java
public class B extends A {
    @Override
    public void m1() {
        System.out.println("B.m1()");
    }

    public static void m2() {
        System.out.println("B.m2()");
    }
```

```
        public static void main(String[] args) {
            A a = new B();
            a.m1();
            a.m2();
            ((B)a).m2();
            A.m2();
            B.m2();
        }
    }
```

16. Name the operator that you are supposed to use before downcasting a reference, so the downcasting always succeeds.

17. Write the output of the following snippet of code:

```
public class A {
}

public class B extends A {
}

A a = new B();
System.out.println("a instanceof A: " + (a instanceof A));
System.out.println("a instanceof B: " + (a instanceof B));
System.out.println("a instanceof Object: " + (a instanceof Object));
System.out.println("null instanceof A: " + (null instanceof A));
System.out.println("null instanceof B: " + (null instanceof B));
```

18. Explain why the following declaration for class B does not compile.

```
public abstract class A {
    public abstract void print();
}

public class B extends A {
}
```

19. Explain why the following declaration for class B does not compile.

```
public class A {
    private A() {
        System.out.println("Hello");
    }
}

public class B extends A {
}
```

20. Write the output when the following class B is run. This exercise is to test your knowledge of field hiding, method overriding, and use of the `super` keyword to call the method of the superclass.

```
public class A {
    protected int x = 100;

    public A() {
        System.out.println("x = " + x);
    }

    public void print() {
        System.out.println("x = " + x);
    }
}

public class B extends A {
    private final int x = 200;
    public B() {
        System.out.println("x = " + x);
    }

    @Override
    public void print() {
        super.print();
        System.out.println("x = " + x);
    }

    public static void main(String[] args) {
        A a = new B();
        a.print();
    }
}
```

CHAPTER 21

Interfaces

In this chapter, you will learn:

- What interfaces are

- How to declare interfaces

- How to declare abstract, default, and static methods in interfaces

- How to fully and partially implement interfaces in a class

- How to evolve interfaces after they are published

- How to inherit an interface from other interfaces

- Using the `instanceof` operator with interfaces

- What marker interfaces are

- How interfaces can be used to implement polymorphism

- How dynamic binding applies to method calls on interface type variables

All example programs in this chapter are a member of a `jdojo.interfaces` module, as declared in Listing 21-1.

Listing 21-1. The Declaration of a jdojo.interfaces Module

```
// module-info.java
module jdojo.interfaces {
    exports com.jdojo.interfaces;
}
```

What Is an Interface?

The *interface* is a very important concept in Java. The knowledge of a Java developer is incomplete unless he understands the role of interfaces. It is better understood by examples than by a formal definition. Let's discuss a simple example that will set the stage for the detailed discussion about the need for interfaces, before I provide its formal definition.

A Java application consists of interacting objects. An object interacts with other objects by sending messages. The ability of an object to receive messages is implemented by providing methods in the object's class. Suppose there is a class called Person, which provides a walk() method. The walk() method gives the ability to receive a "walk" message to every object of the Person class. Let's define the Person class as follows:

```java
public class Person {
    private String name;

    public Person(String name) {
        this.name = name;
    }

    public void walk() {
        System.out.println(name + " (a person) is walking.");
    }
}
```

An object of the Person class will have a name that will be set in its constructor. When it receives a "walk" message, that is, when its walk() method is called, it prints a message on the standard output.

Let's create a utility class named Walkables, which is used to send a specific message to a collection of objects. Let's assume that you want to add a letThemWalk() static method to the Walkables class, which accepts an array of Person objects. It sends a "walk" message to all the elements in the array. You can define your Walkables class as follows. The method does what its name suggests; that is, it lets everyone walk!

```java
public class Walkables {
    public static void letThemWalk(Person[] list) {
        for (Person person : list) {
            person.walk();
        }
    }
}
```

The following snippet of code can be used to test the Person and Walkables classes:

```java
public class WalkablesTest {
    public static void main(String[] args) {
        Person[] persons = new Person[3];
        persons[0] = new Person("Jack");
        persons[1] = new Person("Jeff");
        persons[2] = new Person("John");

        // Let everyone walk
        Walkables.letThemWalk(persons);
    }
}
```

```
Jack (a person) is walking.
Jeff (a person) is walking.
John (a person) is walking.
```

So far, you don't see any problem with the design of the Person and Walkables classes, right? They perform the actions they were designed to perform. The design of the Person class guarantees that its objects will respond to a "walk" message. By declaring the Person array as the parameter type for the letThemWalk() method in the Walkables class, the compiler makes sure that the call to persons[i].walk() is valid, because a Person object is guaranteed to respond to the "walk" message.

Let's expand this project by adding a new class called Duck, which represents a duck in the real world. We all know that a duck can also walk. A duck can do many other things that a person can or cannot do. However, for the purpose of our discussion, we'll focus on only the walking ability of ducks. You can define your Duck class as follows:

```java
public class Duck {
    private String name;

    public Duck(String name) {
        this.name = name;
    }

    public void walk() {
        System.out.println(name + " (a duck) is walking.");
    }
}
```

You may notice that there is a similarity between the Person class and the Duck. An object of both classes can respond to a "walk" message as both of them provide a walk() method. However, the similarity between the two classes ends right there. They are not linked in any other ways at all, except for the fact that both of them have the Object class as their common ancestor. The introduction of the Duck class has expanded the walking ability of objects in your application. Before there were ducks, only people could walk. After you add the Duck class, ducks can walk as well.

Now, you want to let ducks walk using your Walkables class. Can your Walkables class let the ducks walk? No. It cannot let the ducks walk unless you make some changes. The ability of a Duck to walk does not pose any problem for the existing Walkables class. The problem at this point is that the letThemWalk() method has declared its parameter type as an array of Person. A Duck is not a Person. You cannot write code shown here. A Duck object cannot be assigned to a reference variable of the type Person. The following snippet of code will not compile:

```java
Person[] list = new Person[3];
list[0] = new Person("Jack");
list[1] = new Duck("Jeff"); // A compile-time error
list[2] = new Person("John");
Walkables.letThemWalk(list);
```

How do you solve this problem so your Walkables class will let a person and a duck walk together? There are three ways to solve this problem with your existing knowledge of the Java programming language. Note that we are not talking about interfaces at this point. You will solve this problem efficiently and correctly using interfaces at the end of this section. Let's just forget about the title of this chapter for now, so you can appreciate the important role that an interface plays in Java programming. The three ways to solve this problem are as follows:

- Change the parameter type of the letThemWalk() method of the Walkables class from an array of Person to an array of Object. Use reflection to invoke the walk() method on all elements of the passed-in array. Do not worry about the term "reflection" at this point. This is covered in Chapter 3 book of the second volume of this series.

- Define a new static method called letDucksWalk(Duck[] ducks) in the Walkables class. Call this method when you want ducks to walk.

- Inherit the Person and Duck classes from a common ancestor class, say Animal class, and add a walk() method in the Animal class. Change the parameter type of the letThemWalk() method of the Walkables class from an array of Person to an array of Animal.

Let's look at the three solutions in detail.

Proposed Solution #1

You can implement the first solution by adding the two methods to the Walkables class, as shown:

```
// Walkables.java
import java.lang.reflect.Method;

public class Walkables {
    public static void letThemWalk(Object[] list) {
        for (Object obj : list) {
            // Get the walk method reference
            Method walkMethod = getWalkMethod(obj);

            if (walkMethod != null) {
                try {
                    // Invoke the walk() method
                    walkMethod.invoke(obj);
                } catch (Exception e) {
                    e.printStackTrace();
                }
            }
        }
    }

    public static Method getWalkMethod(Object obj) {
        Class<?> c = obj.getClass();
        try {
            Method walkMethod = c.getMethod("walk");
            return walkMethod;
        } catch (NoSuchMethodException e) {
            // walk() method does not exist
        }
        return null;
    }
}
```

The getWalkMethod() method looks for a walk() method in the specified object's class. If it finds a walk() method, it returns the reference of the method. Otherwise, it returns null. You have changed the parameter type of the letThemWalk() method from an array of Person to an array of Object. You can use the following snippet of code to test the modified Walkables class:

```
Object[] list = new Object[4];
list[0] = new Person("Jack");
list[1] = new Duck("Jeff");
list[2] = new Person("John");
list[3] = new Object(); // Does not have a walk() method

// Let everyone walk
Walkables.letThemWalk(list);
```

```
Jack (a person) is walking.
Jeff (a duck) is walking.
John (a person) is walking.
```

The output shows that your solution works. It lets persons and ducks walk together. At the same time, it does not force an object to walk if that object does not know how to walk. You passed four objects to the letThemWalk() method and no attempt was made to invoke the walk() method on the fourth element of the array because the Object class does not have a walk() method.

Let's reject this solution for the very simple reason that you used reflection to invoke the walk() method on all objects passed in and you relied on the fact that all objects that know how to walk will have a method named "walk." This solution is easily and silently broken if you change the method name, say in the Person class, from walk() to walkMe(). Your program will keep working without any errors, but when you call the letThemWalk() method with a Person object, its changed walkMe() method will not be invoked.

Proposed Solution #2

Let's look at the second proposed solution. You propose to add a new method letDucksWalk() to your Walkables class, as shown:

```
public class Walkables {
    public static void letThemWalk(Person[] list) {
        for (Person person : list) {
            person.walk();
        }
    }

    public static void letDucksWalk(Duck[] list) {
        for (Duck duck : list) {
            duck.walk();
        }
    }
}
```

This solves the problem in the sense that it will let all ducks walk. However, it is not an ideal solution either. It still will not let persons and ducks walk together. Another problem with this solution is extensibility. It is not an extensible solution. If you look at the two methods, letThemWalk() and letDucksWalk(), you will find that except for the parameter types, Person and Duck, they have the same logic. What happens if you add a new class called Cat whose objects can walk too? This solution would force you to add another method, letCatsWalk(Cat[] cats), to the Walkables class. Therefore, you should reject this solution because it is not extensible.

Proposed Solution #3

Let's look at the third proposed solution. It proposes to inherit the Person class and the Duck class from a common ancestor class, say, Animal, which has a walk() method. It will also make you change the parameter of the letThemWalk() method in the Walkables class from a Person array to an Animal array. This solution is very close to the one you are looking for, and it may be considered a good solution in some situations. However, you reject this solution for the following two reasons:

- This solution forces you to have a common ancestor in your class hierarchy. For example, all classes whose objects know how to walk must have the same ancestor (direct or indirect). Suppose you create a new class called Dog whose object can walk. Under this proposed solution the Dog class must be inherited from the Animal class, so you can use the letThemWalk() method to let a Dog walk. Sometimes you want to add the walking ability to objects of a class, which is already inherited from another class. In such cases, it is not possible to change the superclass of the existing classes to the Animal class.

- Suppose you go forward with this solution. You add a new class called Fish, which inherits the Animal class. An object of the Fish class does not know how to walk. Because the Fish class is inherited from the Animal class, it will also inherit the walk() method, which is the ability to walk. Definitely, you will need to override the walk() method inside the Fish class. Now the question arises, how should the Fish class implement the walk() method? Should it respond by stating "I am a fish and I do not know how to walk."? Should it throw an exception stating "It is illegal to ask a fish to walk."?

You can see that the third solution seems to be a very close solution. However, it is not an ideal one. It also proves a point that inheritance is a good thing to use in Java programs, but it does not always provide an ideal solution.

An Ideal Solution

You are looking for a solution that provides two things:

- A single method, letThemWalk(), in the Walkables class, should be able to send a "walk" message (that is, invoke the walk() method) on all objects that are passed to it as its parameter. This method should work with all types of objects that can walk (which you have now or you will have in future).

- If you want to add the ability to walk to objects of an existing class, you should not be forced to change the superclass of the class.

Interfaces in Java provide a perfect solution in this scenario. Before we start discussing interfaces in detail, let's complete the solution to the problem presented in this section. First, you need to define an interface. For now, just think of an interface as a programming construct.

An interface is declared using the keyword `interface`, which can have `abstract` method declarations. Note that an `abstract` method does not have a body. Each interface should be given a name. Your interface is named `Walkable`. It contains one method called `walk()`. The complete code for your `Walkable` interface is shown in Listing 21-2.

Listing 21-2. The Declaration for a Walkable Interface

```
// Walkable.java
package com.jdojo.interfaces;

public interface Walkable {
    void walk();
}
```

All classes whose objects can walk should implement the `Walkable` interface. A class can implement one or more interfaces using the keyword `implements` in its declaration. By implementing an interface, a class guarantees that it will provide an implementation for all `abstract` methods declared in the interface or the class will declare itself `abstract`. For now, let's ignore the second part and assume that the class implements all `abstract` methods of the interfaces it implements. If a class implements the `Walkable` interface, it must provide implementation for the `walk()` method.

Objects of the `Person` and `Duck` classes need the ability to walk. You need to implement the `Walkable` interface to these classes. Listing 21-3 and Listing 21-4 have the complete revised code for these classes.

Listing 21-3. The Revised Person Class, Which Implements the Walkable Interface

```
// Person.java
package com.jdojo.interfaces;

public class Person implements Walkable {
    private String name;

    public Person(String name) {
        this.name = name;
    }

    public void walk() {
        System.out.println(name + " (a person) is walking.");
    }
}
```

Listing 21-4. The Revised Duck Class, Which Implements the Walkable Interface

```
// Duck.java
package com.jdojo.interfaces;

public class Duck implements Walkable {
    private String name;

    public Duck(String name) {
        this.name = name;
    }
```

```
    public void walk() {
        System.out.println(name + " (a duck) is walking.");
    }
}
```

Note that the declarations of the revised classes have a minor difference from their original declarations. Both of them have a new implements Walkable clause added to their declarations. Since both of them implement the Walkable interface, they must provide the implementation for the walk() method as declared in the Walkable interface. You did not have to define a fresh walk() method as you had it implemented from the very beginning. If these classes did not have a walk() method, you had to add it to them at this stage.

Before you revise the code for your Walkables class, let's look at other things that you can do with the Walkable interface. Like a class, an interface defines a new reference type. When you define a class, it defines a new reference type and it lets you declare variable of that type. Similarly, when you define a new interface (e.g., Walkable), you can define a reference variable of the new interface type. The variable scope could be local, instance, static, or a method parameter. The following declaration is valid:

```
// w is a reference variable of type Walkable
Walkable w;
```

You cannot create an object of an interface type. The following code is invalid:

```
// A compile-time error
new Walkable();
```

You can create an object of only a class type. However, an interface type variable can refer to any object whose class implements that interface. Because the Person and Duck classes implement the Walkable interface, a reference variable of the Walkable type can refer to an object of these classes.

```
Walkable w1 = new Person("Jack"); // OK
Walkable w2 = new Duck("Jeff");   // OK

// A compile-time error as the Object class does not implement the Walkable interface
Walkable w3 = new Object();
```

What can you do with the reference variable of an interface type? You can access any members of the interface using its reference type variable. Since your Walkable interface has only one member, which is the walk() method, you can write code as shown:

```
// Let the person walk
w1.walk();
```

```
// Let the duck walk
w2.walk();
```

When you invoke the walk() method on w1, it invokes the walk() method of the Person object because w1 is referring to a Person object. When you invoke the walk() method on w2, it invokes the walk() method of the Duck object because w2 is referring to a Duck object. When you call a method using a reference variable of an interface type, it calls the method on the object to which it is referring. With this knowledge about an interface, let's revise the code for your Walkables class. Listing 21-5 contains the revised code. Note that in the revised code for the letThemWalk() method, all you had to do is to change the parameter type from Person to Walkable. Everything else remains the same.

Listing 21-5. The Revised Walkables Class

```java
// Walkables.java
package com.jdojo.interfaces;

public class Walkables {
    public static void letThemWalk(Walkable[] list) {
        for (Walkable w : list) {
            w.walk();
        }
    }
}
```

Listing 21-6 shows how to test your revised classes with the Walkable interface. It creates an array of the Walkable type. Declaring an array of an interface type is allowed because an array provides a shortcut to create many variables of the same type. This time, you can pass objects of the Person class as well as the Duck class in one array of the Walkable type to the letThemWalk() method of the Walkables class, which lets everyone walk together, as shown in the output.

Listing 21-6. A Test Class to Test the Revised Person, Duck, and Walkables Classes

```java
// WalkablesTest.java
package com.jdojo.interfaces;

public class WalkablesTest {
    public static void main(String[] args) {
        Walkable[] w = new Walkable[3];
        w[0] = new Person("Jack");
        w[1] = new Duck("Jeff");
        w[2] = new Person("John");

        // Let everyone walk
        Walkables.letThemWalk(w);
    }
}
```

```
Jack (a person) is walking.
Jeff (a duck) is walking.
John (a person) is walking.
```

How will your existing code change if you want to create a new class called Cat whose objects should have the ability to walk? You will be surprised to see that you do not need to change anything in your existing code. The Cat class should implement the Walkable interface and that is all. Listing 21-7 contains the code for the Cat class.

Listing 21-7. A Cat Class

```
// Cat.java
package com.jdojo.interfaces;

public class Cat implements Walkable {
    private String name;

    public Cat(String name) {
        this.name = name;
    }

    public void walk() {
        System.out.println(name + " (a cat) is walking.");
    }
}
```

You can use the following snippet of code to test the new Cat class with the existing code. Looking at the output, you have made persons, ducks, and cats walk together by using the Walkable interface! This is one of the uses of an interface in Java: it lets you put unrelated classes under one umbrella.

```
Walkable[] w = new Walkable[4];
w[0] = new Person("Jack");
w[1] = new Duck("Jeff");
w[2] = new Person("John");
w[3] = new Cat("Jace");

// Let everyone walk
Walkables.letThemWalk(w);
```

```
Jack (a person) is walking.
Jeff (a duck) is walking.
John (a person) is walking.
Jace (a cat) is walking.
```

You have achieved the objective of making different kinds of objects walk together using the interface construct. So, what is an interface anyway?

An interface in Java defines a reference type to specify an abstract concept. It is implemented by classes that provide an implementation of the concept. Prior to Java 8, an interface could contain only abstract methods, so it represented a pure abstract concept. Java 8 allows an interface to have static and default methods that can also contain implementation. Interfaces let you define a relationship between unrelated classes through the abstract concept. In your example, the Walkable interface represented a concept that enabled you to treat the two unrelated classes of Person and Duck the same way because both implemented the same concept (of walking).

It is time to go over details of how to create and use interfaces in a Java program. As I discuss the technical details of interfaces, I also go over proper uses and common misuses of interfaces.

Declaring an Interface

An interface can be declared as a top-level interface, a nested interface, or an annotation type. I discuss nested interfaces later in this chapter. Annotation type interfaces are discussed in Chapter 1 of the second volume of this series. I use the term *interface* to mean a top-level interface. The general (incomplete) syntax for declaring an interface is as follows:

```
[modifiers] interface <interface-name> {
    <constant-declaration>
    <method-declaration>
    <nested-type-declaration>
}
```

An interface declaration starts with an optional list of modifiers. Like a class, an interface can have a public or package-level scope. The keyword public is used to indicate that the interface has a public scope. A public interface can be referred to from anywhere in the application. Referring to an interface across modules depends on module's accessibility rules, as discussed in Chapter 10. Absence of a scope-modifier indicates that the interface has a package-level scope. An interface with a package-level scope can be referred to only within the members of its package.

The keyword interface is used to declare an interface. The keyword is followed by the name of the interface. The name of an interface is a valid Java identifier. An interface body follows its name, which is placed inside braces. Members of an interface are declared inside the body. In a special case, the body of an interface can be empty. The following is the simplest interface declaration:

```
package com.jdojo.interfaces;

interface Updatable {
    // The interface body is empty
}
```

This code declares an interface named Updatable, which has a package-level scope. It can be used only inside the com.jdojo.interfaces package because it has a package-level scope. It does not contain any member declarations.

Like a class, an interface has a simple name and a fully qualified name. The identifier that follows the keyword interface is its simple name. The fully qualified name of an interface is formed by using its package name and the simple name separated by a dot. In the previous example, Updatable is the simple name and com.jdojo.interfaces.Updatable is the fully qualified name. The rules of using simple and fully qualified name of an interface are the same as that of a class.

The following code declares an interface named ReadOnly. It has a public scope. That is, the definition of the ReadOnly interface is available anywhere in the same module or other module depending on module's accessibility rules.

```
package com.jdojo.interfaces;

public interface ReadOnly {
    // The interface body is empty
}
```

An interface declaration is implicitly abstract. You can declare Updatable and ReadOnly interfaces as follows, without changing their meanings. In other words, an interface declaration is always abstract whether you declare it abstract explicitly or not.

```
abstract interface Updatable {
    // The interface body is empty
}

public abstract interface ReadOnly {
    // The interface body is empty
}
```

▓ **Note** Interfaces in Java are implicitly `abstract`. Using the keyword `abstract` in their declarations is obsolete and it should not be used in new programs. The previous examples are only for illustration purposes.

Declaring Interface Members

An interface can have three types of members:

- Constant fields

- Abstract, static, and default methods

- Static types (nested interfaces and classes)

Note that an interface declaration is much like a class declaration, except that an interface cannot have mutable instance and class variables. Unlike a class, an interface cannot be instantiated. All members of an interface are implicitly public.

▓ **Tip** Up to Java 8, all types of members in an interface were implicitly public. Java 9 allows you to have private methods in an interface, which I discuss later in this chapter.

Constant Fields Declarations

You can declare constant fields in an interface, as shown in Listing 21-8. It declares an interface named Choices, which has declarations of two `int` fields: YES and NO.

Listing 21-8. Declaring Fields in an Interface

```
// Choices.java
package com.jdojo.interfaces;

public interface Choices {
    public static final int YES = 1;
    public static final int NO = 2;
}
```

All fields in an interface are implicitly public, static, and final. Although the interface declaration syntax permits the use of these keywords in a field declaration, their use is redundant. It is recommended not to use these keywords when declaring fields in an interface. The Choices interface can be declared as follows without changing its meaning:

```
public interface Choices {
    int YES = 1;
    int NO = 2;
}
```

You can access the fields in an interface using the dot notation in the form of the following:

```
<interface-name>.<field-name>
```

You can use Choices.YES and Choices.NO to access the values of YES and NO fields in the Choices interface. Listing 21-9 demonstrates how to use the dot notation to access fields of an interface.

Listing 21-9. Accessing Fields of an Interface

```
// ChoicesTest.java
package com.jdojo.interfaces;

public class ChoicesTest {
    public static void main(String[] args) {
        System.out.println("Choices.YES = " + Choices.YES);
        System.out.println("Choices.NO = " + Choices.NO);
    }
}
```

```
Choices.YES = 1
Choices.NO = 2
```

Fields in an interface are always final whether the keyword final is used in its declaration or not. This implies that you must initialize a field at the time of declaration. You can initialize a field with a compile-time or runtime constant expression. Since a final field (constant field) is assigned a value only once, you cannot set the value of the field of an interface, except in its declaration. The following snippet of code generates a compile-time error:

```
Choices.YES = 5; // A compile-time error
```

The following snippet of code shows some valid and invalid field declarations for an interface:

```
/* All fields declarations are valid in the ValidFields interface */
public interface ValidFields {
    int X = 10;

    // You can use one field to initialize another if the referenced
    // field is declared before the one that references it.
    int Y = X;
    double N = X + 10.5;
```

```
    boolean YES = true;
    boolean NO = false;

    // Assuming Test is a class that exists
    Test TEST = new Test();
}

/* Examples of invalid field declarations. */
public interface InvalidFields {
    int X;       // Invalid. X is not initialized
    int Y = Z;   // Invalid. Forward referencing of Z is not allowed.
    int Z = 10;  // Valid by itself.
    Test TEST;   // Invalid. TEST is not initialized, assuming a Test class exists
}
```

▓ **Tip**   It is a convention to use all uppercase letters in the name of a field in an interface to indicate that they are constants. However, Java does not impose any restrictions on naming the fields of an interface as long as they follow the naming rules for identifiers. Fields of an interface are always `public`. However, the accessibility of `public` fields from outside the declaring package depends on the scope of the interface. For example, if an interface is declared to have a package-level scope, its fields are not accessible outside the package, because the interface itself is not accessible outside the package, even though its fields are `public`.

You are advised not to declare an interface to only have constant fields in it. The proper (and most commonly used) use of an interface is to declare a set of methods to define APIs. If you want to group constants in one construct, use a class, not an interface. If you are using Java 5 or a higher version, consider using an enum to declare your constants. Using an enum provides type safety and compile-time checks for your constants.

Methods Declarations

You can declare three types of methods in an interface:

- Abstract methods

- Static methods

- Default methods

Prior to Java 8, you could declare only abstract methods in interfaces. The modifiers `static` and `default` are used to declare static and default methods, respectively. The lack of `static` and `default` modifiers makes a method abstract. The following is an example of an interface with all three types of methods:

```
interface AnInterface {
    // An abstract method
    int m1();
```

```
    // A static method
    static int m2() {
        // The method implementation goes here
    }

    // A default method
    default int m3() {
        // The method implementation goes here
    }
}
```

The following sections discuss each method type declaration in detail.

Abstract Methods Declarations

The main purpose of declaring an interface is to create an abstract specification (or concept) by declaring zero or more abstract methods. All method declarations in an interface are implicitly abstract and public unless they are declared static or default. Like in a class, an abstract method in an interface does not have an implementation. The body of the abstract method is always represented by a semicolon, not by a pair of braces. The following snippet of code declares an interface named Player:

```
public interface Player {
    public abstract void play();
    public abstract void stop();
    public abstract void forward();
    public abstract void rewind();
}
```

The Player interface has four methods: play(), stop(), forward(), and rewind(). The Player interface is a specification for an audio/video player. A real player, for example, a DVD player, will provide the concrete implementation of the specification by implementing all four methods of the Player interface.

Use of the abstract and public keywords in a method declaration in an interface is redundant, even though allowed by the compiler, because a method in an interface is implicitly abstract and public. The previous declaration of the Player interface can be rewritten as follows without changing its meaning:

```
public interface Player {
    void play();
    void stop();
    void forward();
    void rewind();
}
```

Abstract method declarations in an interface may include parameters, a return type, and a throws clause. The following snippet of code declares an ATM interface. It declares four methods. If the account information is wrong, the login() method throws an AccountNotFoundException. The withdraw() method throws an InsufficientBalanceException when the user attempts to withdraw an amount, which will reduce the balance to an amount lower than the required minimum balance amount.

```
public interface ATM {
    boolean login(int account) throws AccountNotFoundException;
    boolean deposit(double amount);
    boolean withdraw(double amount) throws InsufficientBalanceException;
    double getBalance();
}
```

Abstract methods of an interface are inherited by classes that implement the interface, and classes override them to provide an implementation. This implies that an abstract method in an interface cannot be declared final as the final keyword in a method declaration indicates that the method is final and it cannot be overridden. However, a class may declare the overridden method of an interface final indicating that the subclasses cannot override the method.

Static Methods Declarations

Let's refer to the code for the Walkables class shown in Listing 21-5. It is a utility class that contains a static method called letThemWalk(). Creating such a utility class for providing static methods for working with an interface was common prior to Java 8. You will find a number of interface/utility-class pairs in the Java library, for example, Collection/Collections, Path/Paths, Channel/Channels, Executor/Executors, etc. Following this convention, you named your interface/utility-class pair as Walkable/Walkables. Java designers realized the necessity of the extra utility classes along with interfaces. From Java 8, you can have static methods in interfaces. A static method's declaration contains the static modifier. They are implicitly public. You can redefine the Walkable interface, as shown in Listing 21-10, to include the letThemWalk() method and get rid of the Walkables class altogether.

Listing 21-10. The Revised Walkable Interface with an Additional Static Convenience Method

```
// Walkable.java
package com.jdojo.interfaces;

public interface Walkable {
    // An abstract method
    void walk();

    // A static convenience method
    public static void letThemWalk(Walkable[] list) {
        for (Walkable w : list) {
            w.walk();
        }
    }
}
```

You can use the static methods of an interface using the dot notation.

```
<interface-name>.<static-method>
```

The following snippet of code calls the Walkable.letThemWalk() method:

```
Walkable[] w = new Walkable[4];
w[0] = new Person("Jack");
w[1] = new Duck("Jeff");
```

```
w[2] = new Person("John");
w[3] = new Cat("Jace");

// Let everyone walk
Walkable.letThemWalk(w);
```

```
Jack (a person) is walking.
Jeff (a duck) is walking.
John (a person) is walking.
Jace (a cat) is walking.
```

Unlike static methods in a class, static methods in an interface are not inherited by implementing classes or subinterfaces. An interface that inherits from another interface is called a subinterface. There is only one way to call the static methods of an interface: by using the interface name. A static method m() of an interface I must be called using I.m(). You can use the unqualified name m() of the method to call it only within the body of the interface or when you import the method using a static import statement.

Default Methods Declarations

A default method in an interface is declared with the modifier default. A default method provides a default implementation of the method for the classes that implements the interface, but does not override the default method.

The default methods were introduced in Java 8. Prior to Java 8, interfaces could have only abstract methods. Why were default methods added in Java 8? The short answer is that they were added so the existing interfaces may evolve. At this point, the answer may be hard to understand. Let's look at an example to clear this up.

Suppose, prior to Java 8, you wanted to create a specification for movable objects to describe their locations in a 2D plane. Let's create the specification by creating an interface named Movable, as shown in Listing 21-11.

Listing 21-11. A Movable Interface

```
// Movable.java
package com.jdojo.interfaces;

public interface Movable {
    void setX(double x);
    void setY(double y);
    double getX();
    double getY();
}
```

The interface declares four abstract methods. The setX() and setY() methods let Movable change the location using the absolute positioning. The getX() and getY() methods return the current location in terms of the x and y coordinates.

Consider the Pen class in Listing 21-12. It implements the Movable interface, and as part of the specification, it provides implementation for the four methods of the interface. The class contains two instance variables, called x and y, to track the location of the pen.

Listing 21-12. A Pen Class That Implements the Movable Interface

```java
// Pen.java
package com.jdojo.interfaces;

public class Pen implements Movable {
    private double x;
    private double y;

    public Pen() {
        // By default, the pen is at (0.0, 0.0)
    }

    public Pen(double x, double y) {
        this.x = x;
        this.y = y;
    }

    @Override
    public void setX(double x) {
        this.x = x;
    }

    @Override
    public void setY(double y) {
        this.y = y;
    }

    @Override
    public double getX() {
        return x;
    }

    @Override
    public double getY() {
        return y;
    }

    @Override
    public String toString() {
        return "Pen(" + x + ", " + y + ")";
    }
}
```

The following snippet of code uses the Movable interface and the Pen class:

```java
// Create a Pen and assign its reference to a Movable variable
Movable p1 = new Pen();
System.out.println(p1);
```

```
// Move the Pen
p1.setX(10.0);
p1.setY(5.0);
System.out.println(p1);
```

```
Pen(0.0, 0.0)
Pen(10.0, 5.0)
```

So far, there is nothing extraordinary going on with the Movable interface and the Pen class. Suppose the Movable interface is part of a library that you have developed. You have distributed the library to your customers. Customers have implemented the Movable interface in their classes.

Now comes a twist in the story. Some customers have requested that the Movable interface include specifications for changing the location using relative coordinates. They want you to add a move() method to the Movable interface as follows. The requested part is shown in boldface.

```
public interface Movable {
    void setX(double x);
    void setY(double y);
    double getX();
    double getY();
    void move(double deltaX, double deltaY);
}
```

You are a nice business person; you always want a happy customer. You oblige the customer. You make the changes and redistribute the new version of your library. After a few hours, you get calls from several angry customers. They are angry because the new version of the library broke their existing code. Let's analyze what went wrong.

Prior to Java 8, all methods in an interface were implicitly abstract. Therefore, the new method move() is an abstract method. All classes that are implementing the Movable interface must provide the implementation for the new method. Note that customers already have several classes, for example, the Pen class, which implement the Movable interface. All those classes will not compile anymore unless the new method is added to those classes. The moral of the story is that, prior to Java 8, it was not possible to add methods to an interface after it was distributed to the public, without breaking the existing code.

Java libraries have published hundreds of interfaces, which were used thousands of times by customers worldwide. Java designers were in a dire need of a way to evolve the existing interfaces without breaking the existing code. They explored several solutions. Default methods were the accepted solution to evolve interfaces. A default method can be added to an existing interface. It provides a default implementation for the method. All classes implementing the interface will inherit the default implementation, thus not breaking them. Classes may choose to override the default implementation.

A default method is declared using the keyword default. A default method cannot be declared abstract or static. It must provide an implementation. Otherwise, a compile-time error occurs. Listing 21-13 shows the revised code for the Movable interface. It contains a default method called move() that is defined in terms of the existing four methods.

Listing 21-13. The Movable Interface with a Default Method

```java
// Movable.java
package com.jdojo.interfaces;

public interface Movable {
    void setX(double x);
    void setY(double y);
    double getX();
    double getY();

    // A default method
    default void move(double deltaX, double deltaY) {
        double newX = getX() + deltaX;
        double newY = getY() + deltaY;
        setX(newX);
        setY(newY);
    }
}
```

Any existing classes, including the Pen class, that implement the Movable interface will continue to compile and work as before. The new move() method with its default implementation is available for all those classes. Listing 21-14 shows the old and new methods of the Movable interface with the Pen class.

Listing 21-14. Testing the New Movable Interface with the Existing Pen Class

```java
// MovableTest.java
package com.jdojo.interfaces;

public class MovableTest {
    public static void main(String[] args) {
        // Create a Pen and assign its reference to a Movable variable
        Movable p1 = new Pen();
        System.out.println(p1);

        // Move the Pen using absolute coordinates
        p1.setX(10.0);
        p1.setY(5.0);
        System.out.println(p1);

        // Move the Pen using relative coordinates
        p1.move(5.0, 2.0);
        System.out.println(p1);
    }
}
```

```
Pen(0.0, 0.0)
Pen(10.0, 5.0)
Pen(15.0, 7.0)
```

Another common use of default methods is to declare optional methods in an interface. Consider a Named interface, as shown in Listing 21-15.

Listing 21-15. A Named Interface Using Default Methods to Provide Optional Methods

```
// Named.java
package com.jdojo.interfaces;

public interface Named {
    void setName(String name);

    default String getName() {
        return "John Doe";
    }

    default void setNickname(String nickname) {
        throw new UnsupportedOperationException("setNickname");
    }

    default String getNickname() {
        throw new UnsupportedOperationException("getNickname");
    }
}
```

The interface provides specification for getting and setting the official name and nickname. Not everything has a nickname. The interface provides methods to get and set the nickname as default methods making them optional. If a class implements the Named interface, it can override the setNickname() and getNickname() methods to provide implementation, if the class supports a nickname. Otherwise, the class does not have to do anything for these methods. They simply throw a runtime exception to indicate that they are not supported. The interface declares the getName() method as default and provides a sensible default implementation for it by return "John Doe" as the default name. The classes implementing the Named interface are expected to override the getName() method to return the real name.

This has just touched the tip of the iceberg in terms of the benefits and power that default methods have brought to the Java language. It has given a new life to the existing Java APIs. In Java 8, default methods have been added to several interfaces in the Java library to provide more expressiveness and functionality for the existing APIs.

What are the similarities and differences between a concrete method in a class and a default method in an interface?

- Both provide an implementation.

- Both have access to the keyword this in the same way. That is, the keyword this is the reference of the object on which the method is called.

- The major difference lies in the access to the state of the object. A concrete method in a class can access the instance variables of the class. However, a default method does not have access to the instance of variables of the class implementing the interface. The default method has access to the other members of the interface, for example other methods, constants, and type members. For example, the default method in the Movable interface is written using the other member methods getX(), getY(), setX(), and setY().

843

- Needless to say, both types of methods can use their parameters.

- Both methods can have a throws clause.

We are not done with default methods yet. I discuss their roles in inheritance shortly.

Private Methods in an Interface

JDK 8 introduced static and default methods to interfaces. If you had to perform the same logic multiple times in these methods, you had no choice but to repeat the logic or move the logic to another class to hide the implementation. Consider the interface named Alphabet, as shown in Listing 21-16.

Listing 21-16. An Interface Named Alphabet Having Two Default Methods Sharing Logic

```
// Alphabet.java
package com.jdojo.interfaces;

public interface Alphabet {
    default boolean isAtOddPos(char c) {
        if (!Character.isLetter(c)) {
            throw new RuntimeException("Not a letter: " + c);
        }

        char uc = Character.toUpperCase(c);
        int pos = uc - 64;

        return pos % 2 == 1;
    }

    default boolean isAtEvenPos(char c) {
        if (!Character.isLetter(c)) {
            throw new RuntimeException("Not a letter: " + c);
        }

        char uc = Character.toUpperCase(c);
        int pos = uc - 64;

        return pos % 2 == 0;
    }
}
```

The isAtOddpos() and isAtEvenPos() methods check if the specified character is at odd or even position alphabetically, assuming we are dealing with only English alphabets. The logic assumes that A and a are at position 1, B and b are at position 2, etc. Notice that the logic in two methods differ only in the return statements. The entire body of these methods is identical, except for the last statements. We need to refactor this logic. Moving the common logic to another method and calling the new method from both methods would be the ideal case. However, you don't want to do this in JDK 8 because interfaces support only public methods. Doing so will make the third method public, which will expose it to the outside world, which you don't want to do.

JDK 9 comes to the rescue. It lets you declare private methods in interfaces. Listing 21-17 shows the refactored version of the Alphabet interface using a private method that contains the common logic used by the two methods. This time, I named the interface AlphabetJdk9 just to make sure I can include both versions in the source code. The two existing methods become one-liners.

Listing 21-17. An Interface Named AlphabetJdk9 That Uses a Private Method

```java
// AlphabetJdk9.java
package com.jdojo.misc;

// AlphabetJdk9.java
package com.jdojo.interfaces;

public interface AlphabetJdk9 {
    default boolean isAtOddPos(char c) {
        return getPos(c) % 2 == 1;
    }

    default boolean isAtEvenPos(char c) {
        return getPos(c) % 2 == 0;
    }

    private int getPos(char c) {
        if (!Character.isLetter(c)) {
            throw new RuntimeException("Not a letter: " + c);
        }

        char uc = Character.toUpperCase(c);
        int pos = uc - 64;

        return pos;
    }
}
```

Before JDK 9, all methods in an interface were implicitly public. Remember these simple rules that apply to all programs in Java:

- A private method is not inherited and, therefore, cannot be overridden.

- A final method cannot be overridden.

- An abstract method is inherited and is meant to be overridden.

- A default method is an instance method and provides a default implementation. It is meant to be overridden.

With the introduction of private methods in JDK 9, you need to follow a few rules while declaring methods in an interface. All combinations of modifiers—abstract, public, private, static, and final—are not supported because they do not make sense. Table 21-1 lists a combination of modifiers, supported and not supported, in method declarations of interfaces in JDK 9. Note that the final modifier is not allowed in method declarations for interfaces. According to this list, you can have a private method in an interface that is either a non-abstract, non-default instance method, or a static method.

Table 21-1. *Supported Modifiers in Method Declarations in Interfaces*

Modifiers	Supported?	Description
public static	Yes	Supported since JDK 8.
public abstract	Yes	Supported since JDK 1.
public default	Yes	Supported since JDK 8.
private static	Yes	Supported since JDK 9.
private	Yes	Supported since JDK 9. This is a non-abstract instance method.
private abstract	No	This combination does not make sense. A private method is not inherited, so it cannot be overridden, whereas an abstract method must be overridden to be useful.
private default	No	This combination does not make sense. A private method is not inherited, so it cannot be overridden, whereas a default method is meant to be overridden, if needed.

Nested Type Declarations

A nested type declaration in an interface defines a new reference type. You can declare a class, interface, enum, and annotation as nested types. I have not discussed enum and annotation yet, so I restrict the discussion to nested interfaces and classes in this section. An interface/class declared inside an interface is called a nested interface/class.

An interface and a class define new reference types, so do a nested interface and a nested class. Sometimes a type makes more sense as a nested type. Suppose you have an ATM interface and you want to define another interface called ATMCard. The ATMCard interface can be defined as a top-level interface or a nested interface of ATM. Since an ATM card is used with an ATM, it might make more sense to define ATMCard as a nested interface of the ATM interface. Since you are defining ATMCard as a nested interface of ATM, you can also drop the "ATM" from its name and you can name it just Card, as shown:

```
public interface ATM {
    boolean login(int account) throws AccountNotFoundException;
    boolean deposit(double amount);
    boolean withdraw(double amount) throws InsufficientFundsException;
    double getBalance();

    // Card is a nested interface. You can omit the keywords public and static.
    public static interface Card {
        String getNumber();
        String getSecurityCode();
        LocalDate getExpirationDate();
        String getCardHolderName();
    }
}
```

A nested interface is always accessed through its enclosing interface. In the previous snippet of code, ATM is a top-level interface (or simply an interface) and Card is a nested interface. The ATM interface is also called an enclosing interface for the Card interface. The fully qualified name of the ATM and Card interfaces are com.jdojo.interfaces.ATM and com.jdojo.interfaces.ATM.Card, respectively. All nested types are

implicitly public and static. The previous snippet of code used the keywords public and static to declare
the ATMCard interface, which is redundant.

You can also declare a nested class inside an interface. You may not understand the use of a nested class
described in this section until you know how to implement an interface, which is described in the next section.
The following discussion is included here to complete the discussion about the nested types of an interface.
You may revisit this section after reading about how to implement an interface in the next few sections.

It is not common to declare a nested class inside an interface. However, you should not be surprised
if you find an interface that declares a nested class as its member. What advantage does it offer to have a
nested class inside an interface? There is only one advantage of doing this and it is a better organization of
related entities: interfaces and classes. Suppose you want to develop a Job interface that will let the user
submit a job to a job scheduler. The following is the code for the Job interface:

```
public interface Job {
    public void runJob();
}
```

Suppose each department must submit a job every day, even if they do not have something to run. It
suggests that sometimes you need an empty job or a job with nothing real to do. The developer of the Job
interface may provide a constant, which represents a trivial implementation of the Job interface as listed in
Listing 21-18. It has a nested class called EmptyJob, which implements the enclosing Job interface.

Listing 21-18. The Job Interface with a Nested Class and a Constant Field

```
// Job.java
package com.jdojo.interfaces;

public interface Job {
    // A nested class
    class EmptyJob implements Job {
        private EmptyJob() {
            // Do not allow outside to create its object
        }

        @Override
        public void runJob() {
            System.out.println("Nothing serious to run...");
        }
    }

    // A constant field
    Job EMPTY_JOB = new EmptyJob();

    // An abstract method
    void runJob();
}
```

If a department does not have a meaningful job to submit, it can use Job.EMPTY_JOB constant as a
job. The fully qualified name of the EmptyJob class is com.jdojo.interfaces.Job.EmptyJob. Note that the
enclosing interface Job provides an additional namespace for the EmptyJob class. Inside the Job interface,
the EmptyJob class can be referred to by its simple name of EmptyJob. However, outside the Job interface,
it must be referred to as Job.EmptyJob. You may notice that a trivial job object is represented by the Job.
EMPTY_JOB constant. You have made the constructor for the EmptyJob nested class private, so no one outside

the interface can create its object. Listing 21-19 shows how to use the class. Typically, in such cases, you would make the constructor of the Job.EmptyJob class private so its object cannot be created outside the Job interface because the EMPTY_JOB constant already provides an object of this class.

Listing 21-19. A Test Program to Test the Job Interface and Its Nested EmptyJob Class

```java
// JobTest.java
package com.jdojo.interfaces;

public class JobTest {
    public static void main(String[] args) {
        submitJob(Job.EMPTY_JOB);
    }

    public static void submitJob(Job job) {
        job.runJob();
    }
}
```

Nothing serious to run...

An Interface Defines a New Type

An interface defines a new reference type. You can use an interface type anywhere you can use a reference type. For example, you can use an interface type to declare a variable (instance, static, or local) or to declare a parameter type in a method, as a return type of a method, etc.

Consider the following interface declaration named Swimmable, which declares a method swim(), as shown in Listing 21-20. The SwimmableTest class in Listing 21-21 shows how to use the Swimmable interface as a reference data type.

Listing 21-20. The Declaration for a Swimmable Interface

```java
// Swimmable.java
package com.jdojo.interfaces;

public interface Swimmable {
    void swim();
}
```

Listing 21-21. A Test Class That Demonstrates the Use of an Interface Type as a Variable Type

```java
// SwimmableTest.java
package com.jdojo.interfaces;

public class SwimmableTest {
    // Interface type to define instance variable
    private Swimmable iSwimmable;
```

```
    // Interface type to define parameter type for a constructor
    public SwimmableTest(Swimmable aSwimmable) {
        this.iSwimmable = aSwimmable;
    }

    // Interface type to define return type of a method
    public Swimmable getSwimmable() {
        return this.iSwimmable;
    }

    // Interface type to define parameter type for a method
    public void setSwimmable(Swimmable newSwimmable) {
        this.iSwimmable = newSwimmable;
    }

    public void letItSwim() {
        // Interface type to declare a local variable
        Swimmable localSwimmable = this.iSwimmable;

        // An interface variable can be used to invoke any method
        // declared in the interface and the Object class
        localSwimmable.swim();
    }
}
```

The SwimmableTest class uses the new type defined by the Swimmable interface in a number of ways. The purpose of the class is just to demonstrate the use of an interface as a new type. It uses the Swimmable interface as a type to declare the following:

- An instance variable named iSwimmable.

- A parameter named aSwimmable for its constructor.

- The return type of its getSwimmable() method.

- A parameter named newSwimmable for its setSwimmable() method.

- A local variable named localSwimmable inside its letItSwim() method. Inside the method, you could have invoked swim() method directly on the instance variable, iSwimmable. I used a local variable just to demonstrate that an interface type can be used anywhere a type can be used.

At this point, two questions about interfaces need to be answered.

- What object in memory does a variable of an interface type refer to?

- What can you do with a variable of an interface type?

Because an interface defines a reference type, what object in memory does a variable of an interface type refer to? Let's expand on this question with an example. You have a Swimmable interface and you can declare a reference variable of type Swimmable as follows:

```
Swimmable sw;
```

What is the value of the variable sw at this point? A variable of a reference data type refers to an object in memory. To be precise, let's rephrase the question as "What object in memory does sw refer to?" You cannot answer this question completely at this point. The partial and unexplained answer is that a variable of an interface type refers to an object in memory whose class implements that interface. The answer will be clearer when I discuss implementing an interface in the next section. You cannot create an object of an interface type. An interface is implicitly abstract and it does not have a constructor. That is, you cannot use an interface type with the new operator to create an object. The following code would not compile:

```
Swimmable sw2 = new Swimmable(); // A compile-time error
```

In this statement, the use of the new operator causes the compile-time error, not the Swimmable sw2 part. The Swimmable sw2 part is a variable declaration, which is valid.

However, one thing is certain: a variable of an interface type can refer to an object in memory. This scenario is depicted in Figure 21-1.

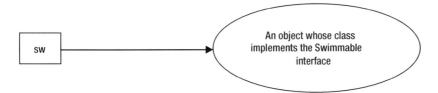

Figure 21-1. *A Swimmable type variable (sw) referring to an object in memory*

Let's answer the second question. What can you do with the variable of an interface type? All rules for a reference type variable equally apply to a variable of an interface type. A few important things that you can do with a variable of a reference type are as follows:

- You can assign a reference of an object in memory including a null reference value.

  ```
  Swimmable sw2 = null;
  ```

- You can access any constant fields declared in an interface using a variable of the interface type or directly using the interface name. It is preferred to access the constants of an interface using the interface name. Consider the Choices interface with two constants called YES and NO. You can access the value of the two constants using the simple name of the interface as Choices.YES, Choices.NO, and using the interface reference variable sw2.YES, and sw2.NO.

- You can use a variable of an interface type to invoke any methods declared in the interface. For example, a variable of the Swimmable type can invoke the swim() method as follows:

  ```
  Swimmable sw3 = get an object instance of the Swimmable type...
  sw3.swim();
  ```

- A variable of an interface type can invoke any method of the Object class. This rule is not very obvious. However, if you think carefully, it is a very simple and important rule. A variable of an interface type can refer to an object in memory. No matter what object in memory it refers to, the object will always be of a class type. All classes in Java must have the Object class as their direct/indirect parent. As a result, all objects in Java have access to all methods of the Object class. Therefore, it is logical to allow an interface type variable to access all methods of the Object class. The following snippet of code calls the hashCode(), getClass(), and toString() methods of the Object class using a Swimmable type variable:

```
Swimmable sw4 = get a Swimmable type object...
int hc = sw4.hashCode();
Class c = sw4.getClass();
String str = sw4.toString();
```

- Another important rule to remember is that an instance or static variable of an interface type is initialized to null by default. As is the case with all types of local variables, a local variable of an interface type is not initialized by default. You must explicitly assign it a value before you can use it.

Implementing an Interface

An interface defines a specification for objects about the ways they will communicate with other objects. A specification is a contract or agreement for an object's behavior. It is very important that you understand the difference between the two terms *specification* (or *contract*) and *implementation*. A specification is a set of statements and implementation is the realization of those statements.

Let's take a real-world example. The statement "Jack will give ten dollars to John on June 8, 2014." is a specification. When Jack gives ten dollars to John on June 8, 2014, the specification is executed. You can restate it as when Jack gives ten dollars to John on June 8, 2014, the specification is implemented. Sometimes, while discussing interface, a specification is also referred to as a contract, a protocol, an agreement, a plan, or a draft. No matter which term you use to refer to a specification, it is always abstract. The implementation of a specification could be partial or complete. Jack may give seven dollars to John on June 8, 2014, and, in that case, the specification has not been implemented completely.

An interface specifies a protocol that an object guarantees to offer when it interacts with other objects. It specifies the protocol in terms of abstract and default methods. A specification is implemented at some time by someone, and so is the case with an interface. An interface is implemented by a class. When a class implements an interface, the class provides implementations for all abstract methods of the interface. A class may provide a partial implementation of the abstract methods of the interface, and in that case, the class must declare itself abstract.

A class that implements an interface uses an implements clause to specify the name of the interface. An implements clause consists of the keyword implements, followed by a comma-separated list of interface types. A class can implement multiple interfaces. Let's focus on a class implementing only one interface for now. The general syntax for a class declaration that implements an interface looks as follows:

```
[modifiers] class <class-Name> implements <comma-separated-list-of-interfaces> {
    // Class body goes here
}
```

Suppose there is a Fish class.

```
public class Fish {
    // Code for Fish class goes here
}
```

Now, you want to implement the Swimmable interface in the Fish class. The following code shows the Fish class and declares that it implements the Swimmable interface:

```
public class Fish implements Swimmable {
    // Code for the Fish class goes here
}
```

The text in boldface font shows the changed code. This code for the Fish class will not compile. A class inherits all abstract and default methods from the interfaces it implements. Therefore, the Fish class inherits the abstract swim() method from the Swimmable interface. A class must be declared abstract if it contains (inherited or declared) abstract methods. You have not declared the Fish class abstract. This is the reason the previous declaration will not compile. In the following code, the Fish class overrides the swim() method to provide an implementation:

```
public class Fish implements Swimmable {
    //  Override and implement the swim() method
    @Override
    public void swim() {
        // Code for swim method goes here
    }

    // More code for the Fish class goes here
}
```

The class that implements an interface must override to implement all abstract methods declared in the interface. Otherwise, the class must be declared abstract. Note that default methods of an interface are also inherited by the implementing classes. The implementing classes may choose (but are not required) to override the default methods. The static methods in an interface are not inherited by the implementing classes.

A class implementing interfaces can have other methods that are not inherited from the implemented interfaces. Other methods can have the same name and different number and/or types of parameters than the one declared in the implemented interfaces.

In this case, the only requirement for the Fish class is that it must have a swim() method, which accepts no parameters and returns void as declared in the Swimmable interface. The following code defines two swim() methods in the Fish class. The first one with no parameters implements the swim() method of the Swimmable interface. The second one, swim(double distanceInYards), has nothing to do with the Swimmable interface implementation by the Fish class.

```
public class Fish implements Swimmable {
    // Override the swim() method in the Swimmable interface
    @Override
    public void swim() {
        // More code goes here
    }
```

```
    // A valid method for the Fish class. This method declaration has nothing to do
    // with the Swimmable interface's swim() method
    public void swim(double distanceInYards) {
        // More code goes here
    }
}
```

Listing 21-22 shows the complete code for the Fish class. A Fish object will have a name, which is supplied in its constructor. It implements the swim() method of Swimmable interface to print a message on the standard output.

Listing 21-22. Code for the Fish Class That Implements the Swimmable Interface

```
// Fish.java
package com.jdojo.interfaces;

public class Fish implements Swimmable {
    private String name;

    public Fish(String name) {
        this.name = name;
    }

    @Override
    public void swim() {
        System.out.println(name + " (a fish) is swimming.");
    }
}
```

How do you create an object of a class that implements an interface? You create an object of a class the same way (by using the new operator with its constructor) whether it implements an interface or not. You can create an object of the Fish class as follows:

```
// Create an object of the Fish class
Fish fifi = new Fish("Fifi");
```

When you execute the statement new Fish("Fifi"), it creates an object in memory and that object's type is Fish (the type defined by its class). When a class implements an interface, its object has one more type, which is the type defined by the implemented interface. In your case, the object created by executing has two types: Fish and Swimmable. In fact it has a third type, too, which is the Object type by virtue of the Fish class inheriting the Object class, which happened by default. Since an object of the Fish class has two types, Fish and Swimmable, you can assign the reference of a Fish object to a variable of the Fish type as well as to a variable of the Swimmable type. The following code summarizes this:

```
Fish guppi = new Fish("Guppi");
Swimmable hilda = new Fish("Hilda");
```

The variable guppi is of the Fish type. It is referring to the Guppi fish object. There is no surprise in the first assignment; a Fish object being assigned to a variable of the Fish type. The second assignment is also valid because the Fish class implements the Swimmable interface and every object of the Fish class is also of the Swimmable type. At this point hilda is a variable of the Swimmable type. It is referring to the Hilda fish object. The following assignment is always valid:

```
// A Fish is always Swimmable
hilda = guppi;
```

However, the other way is not valid. Assigning a variable of the Swimmable type to a variable of the Fish type generates a compile-time error.

```
// A Swimmable is not always a Fish
guppi = hilda; // A compile-time error
```

Why does the previous assignment generate a compile-time error? The reason is very simple. An object of the Fish class is always Swimmable because the Fish class implements the Swimmable interface. Since a variable of the Fish type can only refer to a Fish object, which is always Swimmable, the assignment hilda = guppi is always valid. However, a variable of the Swimmable type can refer to any object whose class implements the Swimmable interface, not necessarily only to a Fish object. For example, consider a class Turtle, which implements the Swimmable interface.

```
public class Turtle implements Swimmable {
    @Override
    public void swim() {
        System.out.println("A turtle can swim too!");
    }
}
```

You can assign an object of the Turtle class to the hilda variable.

```
hilda = new Turtle(); // OK. A Turtle is always Swimmable
```

If the assignment guppi = hilda is allowed at this point, a Fish variable guppi will be referring to a Turtle object! This would be a disaster. The Java runtime would throw an exception, even if the compiler had allowed this assignment. This kind of assignment is not allowed for the following reason:

A Fish is always Swimmable. However, not every Swimmable is a Fish.

Suppose you know (programmatically) for sure that a variable of the Swimmable type contains reference to a Fish object. If you want to assign the Swimmable type variable to a variable of the Fish type, you can do so by using a type cast, as shown:

```
// The compiler will pass it. The runtime may throw a ClassCastException.
guppi = (Fish)hilda;
```

The compiler will not complain about this statement. It assumes that you have made sure that the hilda variable is referring to a Fish object and the cast, (Fish) hilda, will succeed at runtime. If, by any chance, the hilda variable is not referring to a Fish object, the Java runtime will throw a ClassCastException. For example, the following snippet of code will pass the compiler check, but will throw a ClassCastException:

```
Fish fred = new Fish("Fred");
Swimmable turti = new Turtle();

// OK for the compiler, but not OK for the runtime. turti is a Turtle, not a Fish at
// runtime. fred can refer to only a Fish, not a Turtle
fred = (Fish) turti;
```

Listing 21-23 shows the short but complete code that lets you test the Fish class and the Swimmable interface.

Listing 21-23. Demonstrating That a Variable of an Interface Can Store the Reference of the Object of the Class Implementing the Interface

```
// FishTest.java
package com.jdojo.interfaces;

public class FishTest {
    public static void main(String[] args) {
        Swimmable finny = new Fish("Finny");
        finny.swim();
    }
}
```

```
Finny (a fish) is swimming.
```

Implementing Interface Methods

When a class fully implements an interface, it provides an implementation for all abstract methods of the interfaces by overriding those methods. A method declaration in an interface includes constraints (or rules) for the methods. For example, a method may declare a throws clause in its declaration. The throws clause in the method declaration is a constraint for the method. If the throws clause declares some checked exceptions, the caller of that method must be ready to handle them. Methods in an interface are implicitly public. This defines another constraint on the methods, which states that all methods of an interface are accessible publicly, with an assumption that the interface itself is accessible publicly. Consider a Banker interface, defined as follows:

```
public interface Banker {
    double withdraw(double amount) throws InsufficientFundsException;
    void deposit(double amount) throws FundLimitExceededException;
}
```

The Banker interface declares two methods called withdraw() and deposit(). Consider the following implementation of the Banker interface in the MinimumBalanceBank class. The overridden methods in this class have the same constraints as defined in the Banker interface. Both methods are declared public and both of them throw the same exception as declared in their declarations in the Banker interface.

```
public class MinimumBalanceBank implements Banker {
    public double withdraw(double amount) throws InsufficientFundsException {
        // Code for this method goes here
    }

    public void deposit(double amount) throws FundLimitExceededException {
        // Code for this method goes here
    }
}
```

Consider the following implementation of the Banker interface in the NoLimitBank class. The NoLimitBank has rules that a customer can have unlimited overdraft (wish it happened in reality) and there is no upper limit on the balance. NoLimitBank dropped the throws clause when it overrode the withdraw() and deposit() methods of the Banker interface.

```
public class NoLimitBank implements Banker {
    public double withdraw(double amount) {
        // Code for this method goes here
    }

    public void deposit(double amount) {
        // Code for this method goes here
    }
}
```

The code for NoLimitBank is valid, even though its two methods that overrode the Banker interface methods have dropped the throws clause. Dropping constraints (exceptions in this case) is allowed when a class overrides an interface method. An exception in the throws clause imposes a restriction that the caller must handle the exception. If you use the Banker type to write the code, here is how you will call the withdraw() method:

```
Banker b = get a Banker type object...;
try {
    double amount = b.withdraw(1000.90);
    // More code goes here
} catch (InsufficientFundsException e) {
    // Handle the exception here
}
```

At compile-time, when the b.withdraw() method is called, the compiler forces you to handle the exception thrown from the withdraw() method because it knows the type of the variable b is Banker and the Banker type's withdraw() method throws an InsufficientFundsException. If you assign an object of NoLimitBank to the variable b in the previous code, no exception will be thrown from the withdraw() method of the NoLimitBank class when b.withdraw() is called, even though the call to withdraw() method is inside a try-catch block. The compiler cannot check the runtime type of variable b. Its safety check is based on the compile-time types of the variable b. It would never be a problem if the runtime throws a fewer number of exceptions or no exceptions than expected in the code. Consider the following implementation of the Banker interface by the UnstablePredictableBank class:

```
// The following code will not compile
public class UnstablePredictableBank implements Banker {
    public double withdraw(double amount) throws InsufficientFundsException,
            ArbitraryException {
        // Code for this method goes here
    }

    public void deposit(double amount) throws FundLimitExceededException {
        // Code for this method goes here
    }
}
```

This time, the withdraw() method adds a new exception, ArbitraryException, which adds a new constraint to the overridden method. Adding constraints to an overridden method is never allowed. Consider the following snippet of code:

```
Banker b = new UnstablePredictableBank();
try {
    double amount = b.withdraw(1000.90);
    // More code goes here
} catch (InsufficientFundsException e) {
    // Handle exception here
}
```

The compiler does not know that, at runtime, the variable b, which is of type Banker, will refer to an object of the UnstablePredictableBank type. Therefore, the compiler will force you to handle only the InsufficientFundsException when you call b.withdraw(). What happens when ArbitraryException is thrown from the withdraw() method at runtime? Your code is not ready to handle it. This is the reason that you cannot add new exceptions to a method declaration in a class, which overrides a method in its implementing interface.

If a class overrides a method of the implemented interface, that method must be declared public. Recall that all methods in an interface are implicitly public, and public is the least restricting scope modifier for a method. Declaring a method in the class that overrides an interface method as private, protected, or package-level is like restricting the scope of the overridden method (like placing more constraints). The following snippet of code will not compile because the withdraw() and deposit() methods are not declared public:

```
// Code would not compile
public class UnstablePredictableBank implements Banker{
    // withdraw() method must be public
    private double withdraw(double amount) throws InsufficientFundsException {
        // Code for this method goes here
    }

    // deposit() method must be public
    protected void deposit(double amount) throws FundLimitExceededException {
        // Code for this method goes here
    }
}
```

Use a general rule of thumb to check if adding or dropping a constraint is allowed in a class method, which overrides an interface's method. Write code using an interface type variable that is assigned to an object of the class that implements the interface. If the code makes sense to you (of course, it has to make sense to the compiler too), it is allowed. Otherwise, it is not allowed. Suppose J is an interface, which declares a method m1(), Suppose the class C implements the interface J and it modifies the declaration of the method m1(). If the following code makes sense and compiles, the modification in the m1() declaration inside the class C is fine.

```
J obj = new C(); // Or any object of any subclass of C
obj.m1();
```

Another rule of thumb is to see if the overriding method in the class is relaxing the restrictions declared in the interface for the same method. If an overriding method relaxes the constraints of the overridden method, it is fine. Otherwise, the compiler will generate an error.

Implementing Multiple Interfaces

A class can implement multiple interfaces. All interfaces that a class implements are listed after the keyword implements in the class declaration. Interface names are separated by a comma. By implementing multiple interfaces, the class agrees to provide the implementation for all abstract methods in all interfaces. Suppose there are two interfaces called Adder and Subtractor, declared as follows:

```
public interface Adder {
    int add(int n1, int n2);
}

public interface Subtractor {
    int subtract(int n1, int n2);
}
```

If an ArithOps class implements the two interfaces, its declaration would look as shown:

```
public class ArithOps implements Adder, Subtractor {
    // Override the add() method of the Adder interface
    @Override
    public int add(int n1, n2) {
        return n1 + n2;
    }

    // Override the subtract() method of the Subtractor interface
    @Override
    public int subtract(int n1, int n2) {
        return n1 - n2;
    }

    // Other code for the class goes here
}
```

There is no limit on the maximum number of interfaces implemented by a class. When a class implements an interface, its objects get an additional type. If a class implements multiple interfaces, its objects get as many new types as the number of implemented interfaces. Consider the object of the ArithOps class, which can be created by executing new ArithOps(). The object of the ArithOps class gets two additional types, which are Adder and Subtractor. The following snippet of code shows the result of the object of the ArithOps class getting two new types. You can treat an object of ArithOps as ArithOps type, Adder type, or Subtractor type. Of course, every object in Java can always be treated as an Object type.

```
ArithOps a = new ArithOps();
Adder b = new ArithOps();
Subtractor c = new ArithOps();
b = a;
c = a;
```

Let's look at a more concrete and complete example. You already have two interfaces, Walkable and Swimmable. If a class implements the Walkable interface, it must provide the implementation for the walk() method. If you want an object of a class to be treated as the Walkable type, the class would implement the Walkable interface. The same argument goes for the Swimmable interface. If a class implements both interfaces, Walkable and Swimmable, its objects can be treated as a Walkable type as well as a Swimmable type. The only thing that the class must do is to provide implementation for both the walk() and swim() methods. Let's create a Turtle class, which implements both of these interfaces. A Turtle object will have ability to walk as well as swim.

Listing 21-24 contains the code for the Turtle class. A turtle can bite too. You have added this behavior to the Turtle objects by adding a bite() method to the Turtle class. Note that adding the bite() method to the Turtle class has nothing to do with implementations of the two interfaces. A class, which implements interfaces, can have any number of additional methods of its own.

Listing 21-24. A Turtle Class, Which Implements the Walkable and Swimmable Interfaces

```
// Turtle.java
package com.jdojo.interfaces;

public class Turtle implements Walkable, Swimmable {
    private String name;

    public Turtle(String name) {
        this.name = name;
    }

    // Adding a bite() method to the Turtle class
    public void bite() {
        System.out.println(name + " (a turtle) is biting.");
    }

    // Implementation for the walk() method of the Walkable interface
    @Override
    public void walk() {
        System.out.println(name + " (a turtle) is walking.");
    }
```

```
    // Implementation for the swim() method of the Swimmable interface
    @Override
    public void swim() {
        System.out.println(name + " (a turtle) is swimming.");
    }
}
```

Listing 21-25 shows using a Turtle object as a Turtle type, Walkable type, and Swimmable type.

Listing 21-25. Using the Turtle Class

```
// TurtleTest.java
package com.jdojo.interfaces;

public class TurtleTest {
    public static void main(String[] args) {
        Turtle turti = new Turtle("Turti");

        // Using Turtle type as Turtle, Walkable and Swimmable
        letItBite(turti);
        letItWalk(turti);
        letItSwim(turti);
    }

    public static void letItBite(Turtle t) {
        t.bite();
    }

    public static void letItWalk(Walkable w) {
        w.walk();
    }

    public static void letItSwim(Swimmable s) {
        s.swim();;
    }
}
```

```
Turti (a turtle) is biting.
Turti (a turtle) is walking.
Turti (a turtle) is swimming.
```

Note that a Turtle type variable can access all three methods—bite(), walk(), and swim()—like so:

```
Turtle t = new Turtle("Turti");
t.bite();
t.walk();
t.swim();
```

When you use a Turtle object as the Walkable type, you can access only the walk() method. When you use a Turtle object as the Swimmable type, you can access only the swim() method. The following snippet of code demonstrates this rule:

```
Turtle t = new Turtle("Trach");
Walkable w = t;
w.walk(); // OK. Using w, you can access only the walk() method of Turtle object

Swimmable s = t;
s.swim(); // OK. Using s you can access only the swim() method
```

Implementing an Interface Partially

A class agrees to provide an implementation for all abstract methods of the interfaces it implements. However, a class does not have to provide implementations for all methods. In other words, a class can provide partial implementations of the implemented interfaces. Recall that an interface is implicitly abstract (means incomplete). If a class does not provide a full implementation of interfaces, it must be declared abstract (means incomplete). Otherwise, the compiler will refuse to compile the class. Consider an interface named IABC that has three methods—m1(), m2(), and m3().

```
package com.jdojo.interfaces;

public interface IABC {
    void m1();
    void m2();
    void m3();
}
```

Suppose a class named ABCImpl implements the IABC interface and it does not provide implementations for all three methods.

```
package com.jdojo.interfaces;

// A compile-time error
public class ABCImpl implements IABC {
    // Provides implementation for only one method of the IABC interface
    @Override
    public void m1() {
        // Code for the method goes here
    }
}
```

The previous code for the ABCImpl class would not compile. It agrees to provide implementations for all three methods of the IABC interface. However, the body of the class does not keep the promise. It provides an implementation for only for one method, m1(). Because the class ABCImpl did not provide implementations for the other two methods of the IABC interface, the ABCImpl class is incomplete, which must be declared abstract to indicate its incompleteness. If you attempt to compile the ABCImpl class, the compiler will generate the following errors:

```
Error(3,14): class com.jdojo.interfaces.ABCImpl should be declared abstract; it does not
define method m2() of interface com.jdojo.interfaces.IABC
Error(3,14): class com.jdojo.interfaces.ABCImpl should be declared abstract; it does not
define method m3() of interface com.jdojo.interfaces.IABC
```

The compiler error is loud and clear. It states that the ABCImpl class must be declared abstract because it did not implement the m2() and m3() methods of the IABC interface. The following snippet of code fixes the compiler error by declaring the class abstract:

```
package com.jdojo.interfaces;

public abstract class ABCImpl implements IABC {
    @Override
    public void m1() {
        // Code for the method goes here
    }
}
```

The implication of declaring a class as abstract is that it cannot be instantiated. The following code will generate a compile-time error:

```
new ABCImpl(); // A compile-time error. ABCImpl is abstract
```

The only way to use the ABCImpl class is to inherit another class from it and provide the missing implementations for the m2() and m3() methods of the IABC interface. The following is the declaration for a new class DEFImpl, which inherits from the ABCImpl class:

```
package com.jdojo.interfaces;

public class DEFImpl extends ABCImpl {
    // Other code goes here

    @Override
    public void m2() {
        // Code for the method goes here
    }

    @Override
    public void m3() {
        // Code for the method goes here
    }
}
```

The DEFImpl class provides implementations for the m2() and m3() methods of the ABCImpl class. Note that the DEFImpl class inherits the m1(), m2(), and m3() methods from its superclass ABCImpl and m3(). The compiler does not force you to declare the DEFImpl class as an abstract class anymore. You can still declare the DEFImpl class abstract, if you want to.

You can create an object of the DEFImpl class because it is not abstract. What are the types of an object of the DEFImpl class? It has four types: DEFImpl, ABCImpl, Object, and IABC. An object of the DEFImpl class is also of the ABCImpl type because DEFImpl inherits from ABCImpl. An object of the ABCImpl class is also of type IABC because ABCImpl implements IABC interface. Since a DEFImpl is an ABCImpl, and an ABCImpl is an IABC, it is logical that a DEFImpl is also an IABC. This rule has been demonstrated by the following snippet of code. An object of the DEFImpl class has been assigned to variables of DEFImpl, Object, ABCImpl, and IABC types.

```
DEFImpl d = new DEFImpl();
Object obj = d;
ABCImpl a = d;
IABC ia = d;
```

The Supertype-Subtype Relationship

Implementing an interface to a class establishes a supertype-subtype relationship. The class becomes a subtype of all the interfaces it implements and all interfaces become a supertype of the class. The rule of substitution applies in this supertype-subtype relationship. The rule of substitution is that a subtype can replace its supertype everywhere. Consider the following class declaration for a class C, which implements three interfaces J, K, and L:

```
public class C implements J, K, L {
    // Code for class C goes here
}
```

The previous code establishes supertype-subtype relationship between three the interfaces J, K, and L, and the class C. Recall that an interface declaration defines a new type. Suppose that you have already declared three interfaces: J, K, and L. The three interface declarations define three types: type J, type K, and type L. The declaration of the class C defines a fourth type: type C. What is the relationship between the four types, J, K, L, and C? Class C is a subtype of types J, K, and L; type J is a supertype of type C; type K is a supertype of type C; and, type L is a supertype of type C. The implication of this supertype-subtype relationship is that wherever a value of type J, K, or L is required, you can safely substitute a value of type C. The following snippet code demonstrates this rule:

```
C cObject = new C();

// cObject is of type C. It can always be used where J, K or L type is expected.
J jobject = cObject; // OK
K kobject = cObject; // OK
L lobject = cObject; // OK
```

Interface Inheritance

An interface can inherit from another interface. Unlike a class, an interface can inherit from multiple interfaces. Consider the Singer, Writer, and Player interfaces shown in Listings 21-26 through 21-28.

Listing 21-26. A Singer Interface

```
// Singer.java
package com.jdojo.interfaces;

public interface Singer {
    void sing();
    void setRate(double rate);
    double getRate();
}
```

Listing 21-27. A Writer Interface

```
// Writer.java
package com.jdojo.interfaces;

public interface Writer {
    void write();
    void setRate(double rate);
    double getRate();
}
```

Listing 21-28. A Player Interface

```
// Player.java
package com.jdojo.interfaces;

public interface Player {
    void play();
    void setRate(double rate);

    default double getRate() {
        return 300.0;
    }
}
```

All three types of professionals (singers, writers, and players) perform their jobs and they are paid. The three interfaces contain two types of methods. One type of method signifies the job they do, for example, sing(), write(), and play(). Another type of method signifies their minimum hourly rates. The Singer and Writer interfaces have declared the setRate() and getRate() methods abstract, letting the implementing classes to specify their implementation. The Player interface declares the setRate() method abstract and provides a default implementation for the getRate() method.

Like a class inheriting from another class, an interface uses the keyword extends to inherit from other interfaces. The keyword extends is followed by a comma-separated list of inherited interface names. The inherited interfaces are known as superinterfaces and the interface inheriting them is known as subinterface. An interface inherits the following members of its superinterfaces:

- Abstract and default methods

- Constant fields

- Nested types

░ **Tip**   An interface does not inherit static methods from its superinterfaces.

An interface may override the inherited abstract and default methods that it inherits from its superinterfaces. If the interface contains constant fields and nested types with the same names as the inherited constant fields and nested types from the superinterfaces, the constant fields and nested types in the interface are said to hide the respective names of their inherited counterparts.

Suppose you want to create an interface to represent charity singers who do not charge for singing. A charity singer is also a singer. You will create an interface named CharitySinger that inherits from the Singer interface, as shown:

```
public interface CharitySinger extends Singer {
}
```

At this point, the CharitySinger interface inherits the three abstract methods from the Singer interface. Any class implementing the CharitySinger interface will need to implement those three methods. Because charity singers do not charge for singing, the CharitySinger interface may override the setRate() and getRate() methods and provide a default implementation using the default methods shown in Listing 21-29.

Listing 21-29.   A CharitySinger Interface

```
// CharitySinger.java
package com.jdojo.interfaces;

public interface CharitySinger extends Singer {
    @Override
    default void setRate(double rate) {
        // A no-op method
    }

    @Override
    default double getRate() {
        return 0.0;
    }
}
```

The setRate() method is a no-op. The getRate() method returns zero. The class that implements the CharitySinger interface will need to implement the sing() method and provide an implementation for it. The class will inherit the default methods setRate() and getRate().

It is possible that the same person is a singer as well as a writer. You can create an interface named SingerWriter, which inherits from the two interfaces Singer and Writer, as shown in Listing 21-30.

Listing 21-30. A SingerWriter Interface That Inherits from Singer and Writer Interfaces

```java
// SingerWriter.java
package com.jdojo.interfaces;

public interface SingerWriter extends Singer, Writer {
    // No code
}
```

How many methods does the SingerWriter interface have? It inherits three abstract methods from the Singer interface and three abstract methods from the Writer interface. It inherits methods setRate() and getRate() twice—once from the Singer interface and once from the Writer interface. These methods have the same declarations in both superinterfaces and they are abstract. This does not cause a problem, as both methods are abstract. The class that implements the SingerWriter interface will need to provide implementation for both methods only once.

Listing 21-31 shows the code for a Melodist class that implements the SingerWriter interface. Note that it overrides the setRate() and getRate() methods only once.

Listing 21-31. A Melodist Class That Implements the SingerWriter Interface

```java
// Melodist.java
package com.jdojo.interfaces;

public class Melodist implements SingerWriter {
    private String name;
    private double rate = 500.00;

    public Melodist(String name) {
        this.name = name;
    }

    @Override
    public void sing() {
        System.out.println(name + " is singing.");
    }

    @Override
    public void setRate(double rate) {
        this.rate = rate;
    }

    @Override
    public double getRate() {
        return rate;
    }
```

```
    @Override
    public void write() {
        System.out.println(name + " is writing");
    }
}
```

The following snippet of code shows how to use the Melodist class:

```
SingerWriter purcell = new Melodist("Henry Purcell");
purcell.setRate(700.00);
purcell.write();
purcell.sing();
```

```
Henry Purcell is writing
Henry Purcell is singing.
```

A person may sing as well as play games. Let's create a SingerPlayer interface to represent this kind of person. Let's inherit the interface from the Singer and Player interfaces as shown:

```
public interface SingerPlayer extends Singer, Player {
    // No code for now
}
```

Trying to compile the SingerPlayer interface results in the following error:

```
SingerPlayer.java:4: error: interface SingerPlayer inherits abstract and default for
getRate() from types Player and Singer
```

The error resulted from the conflict in the two inherited versions of the getRate() method. The Singer interface declares the getRate() method abstract and the Player interface declares it default. This causes a conflict. The compiler cannot decide which method to inherit. This kind of conflict may arise when multiple versions of the same default method are inherited from different superinterfaces. Consider the following declaration of the CharitySingerPlayer interface:

```
public interface CharitySingerPlayer extends CharitySinger, Player {
}
```

Trying to compile the CharitySingerPlayer interface results in the following error:

```
CharitySingerPlayer.java:4: error: interface CharitySingerPlayer inherits unrelated defaults for
getRate() from types CharitySinger and Player
CharitySingerPlayer.java:4: error: interface CharitySingerPlayer inherits abstract and
default for setRate(double) from types CharitySinger and Player
```

This time, the error is because of two reasons:

- The interface inherits two default getRate() methods, one from the CharitySinger interface and one from the Player interface.

- The interface inherits a default setRate() method from the CharitySinger interface and an abstract setRate() method from the Player interface.

This type of conflict was not possible before Java 8 as the default methods were not available. The compiler does not know which method to inherit when it encounters a combination of abstract-default or default-default method. To resolve such conflicts, the interface needs to override the method in the interface. There are several ways to resolve the conflict—all involve overriding the conflicting method in the interface.

- You can override the conflicting method with an abstract method.

- You can override the conflicting method with a default method and provide a new implementation.

- You can override the conflicting method with a default method and call one of the methods of the superinterfaces.

Let's resolve the conflict in the SingerPlayer interface. Listing 21-32 contains a declaration for the interface that overrides the getRate() method with an abstract getRate() method. Any class implementing the SingerPlayer interface will have to provide an implementation for the getRate() method.

Listing 21-32. Overriding the Conflicting Method with an Abstract Method

```
// SingerPlayer.java
package com.jdojo.interfaces;

public interface SingerPlayer extends Singer, Player {
    // Override the getRate() method with an abstract method
    @Override
    double getRate();
}
```

The declaration in Listing 21-33 for the SingerPlayer interface resolves the conflict by overriding the getRate() method with a default getRate() method, which simply returns a value 700.00. Any class implementing this SingerPlayer interface will inherit the default implementation of the getRate() method.

Listing 21-33. Overriding the Conflicting Method with a Default Method

```
// SingerPlayer.java
package com.jdojo.interfaces;

public interface SingerPlayer extends Singer, Player {
    // Override the getRate() method with a default method
    @Override
    default double getRate() {
        return 700.00;
    }
}
```

Sometimes an interface may want to access the overriden default methods of its superinterfaces. Java 8 introduced a new syntax for calling the overridden default methods of direct superinterfaces from an interface. The new syntax uses the keyword super as shown:

```
<superinterface-name>.super.<superinterface-default-method(arg1, arg2...)>
```

▓ **Tip** Using the keyword `super`, only the default methods of the direct superinterfaces can be accessed. Accessing default methods of the superinterfaces of superinterfaces are not supported by the syntax. You cannot access the abstract methods of the superinterfaces using this syntax.

Listing 21-34 contains the declaration for the `SingerPlayer` interface that resolves the conflict by overriding the getRate() method with a default getRate() method. The method calls the getRate() method of the Player interface using the Player.super.getRate() call, multiplies the value by 3.5, and returns it. It simply implements a rule that a SingerPlayer is paid minimum 3.5 times what a Player is paid. Any class implementing the SingerPlayer interface will inherit the default implementation of the getRate() method.

Listing 21-34. Overriding the Conflicting Method with a Default Method That Calls the Method in the Superinterface

```
// SingerPlayer.java
package com.jdojo.interfaces;

public interface SingerPlayer extends Singer, Player{
    // Override the getRate() method with a default method that calls the
    // Player superinterface getRate() method
    @Override
    default double getRate() {
        double playerRate = Player.super.getRate();
        double singerPlayerRate = playerRate * 3.5;
        return singerPlayerRate;
    }
}
```

Listing 21-35 contains the code for the CharitySingerPlayer interface. It overrides the setRate() method with an abstract method and the getRate() method with a default method. The getRate() method calls the default getRate() method of the Player interface

Listing 21-35. Overriding the Conflicting Methods in the CharitySinger Interface

```
// CharitySingerPlayer.java
package com.jdojo.interfaces;

public interface CharitySingerPlayer extends CharitySinger, Player {
    // Override the setRate() method with an abstract method
    @Override
    void setRate(double rate);

    // Override the getRate() method with a default method that calls the
    // Player superinterface getRate() method
    @Override
    default double getRate() {
        return Player.super.getRate();
    }
}
```

The Superinterface-Subinterface Relationship

Interface inheritance establishes a *superinterface-subinterface* (also called *supertype-subtype*) relationship. When the interface CharitySinger inherits from the Singer interface, the Singer interface is known as the superinterface of the CharitySinger interface, and the CharitySinger interface is known as the subinterface of the Singer interface. An interface can have multiple superinterfaces and an interface can be a subinterface for multiple interfaces. A reference of a subinterface can be assigned to a variable of the superinterface. Consider the following snippet of code to demonstrate the use of superinterface-subinterface relationship. Comments in the code explain why an assignment will succeed or fail.

```
public interface Shape {
    // Code goes here
}

public interface Line extends Shape {
    // Code goes here
}

public interface Circle extends Shape {
    // Code goes here
}
```

The following is sample code that you can write using these interfaces with comments explaining what the code is supposed to do:

```
Shape shape = get an object reference of a Shape...;
Line line = get an object reference of a Line...;
Circle circle = get an object reference of a Circle...;

/* More code goes here... */

shape = line;   // Always fine. A Line is always a Shape.
shape = circle; // Always fine. A Circle is always a Shape.

// A compile-time error. A Shape is not always a Line. A Shape may be a Circle.
// Must use a cast to compile.
line = shape;

// OK with the compiler. The shape variable must refer to a Line at runtime.
// Otherwise, the runtime will throw a ClassCastException.
line =(Line) shape;
```

Inheriting Conflicting Implementations

Before Java 8, it was not possible for a class to inherit multiple implementations (non-abstract methods) from multiple supertypes. Introduction of default methods made it possible for a class to inherit conflicting implementations from its superclass and superinterfaces. When a class inherits a method with the same signature from multiple paths (superclass and superinterfaces), Java uses the three simple rules in order to resolve the conflict.

- *The superclass always wins*: If a class inherits a method (abstract or concrete) from its superclass and a method with the same signature from one of its superinterfaces, the superclass wins. That is, the class inherits the method of the superclass and the methods in the superinterfaces are ignored. This rule treats a default method in an interface as a fallback if the same method is not available in the class through the class hierarchy.

- *The most specific superinterface wins*: This rule is used if the first rule did not resolve the conflict. If the inherited default method comes from multiple superinterfaces, the method from the most specific superinterface is inherited by the class.

- *The class must override the conflicting method*: This rule is used if the previous two rules did not resolve the conflict. In this case, the developer must override the conflicting method in the class.

Let's discuss different scenarios where these three rules will apply.

The Superclass Always Wins

This rule is simple to apply. If a class inherits or declares a method, the methods with the same signature in the superinterfaces will be ignored.

Example #1

Consider the following two classes, Employee and Manager.

```
public abstract class Employee {
    private double rate;

    public abstract void setRate(double rate);

    public double getRate() {
        return rate;
    }
}

public abstract class Manager extends Employee implements CharitySinger {
    // Code goes here
}
```

The Manager class inherits from the Employee class. The following five methods are available to the Manager class for inheritance:

- The abstract CharitySinger.sing() method

- The default CharitySinger.setRate() method

- The default CharitySinger.getRate() method

- The abstract Employee.setRate() method

- The concrete Employee.getRate() method

There is no conflict for the sing() method. Therefore, the Manager class inherits the sing() method from the CharitySinger interface. There are two choices for the setRate() and getRate() methods. The two methods are available in the superclass. Therefore, the Manager class inherits the setRate() and getRate() methods from the Employee class.

Example #2

The "superclass always wins" rule implies that the methods declared in the Object class cannot be overridden with a default method in an interface. The following declaration for the Runner interface will not compile:

```
// Won't compile
public interface Runner {
    void run();

    // Not allowed
    @Override
    default String toString() {
        return "WhoCares";
    }
}
```

Before I give the reasons behind this rule, let's assume that the Runner interface compiles. Suppose a Thinker class implements the Runner interface as shown:

```
public class Thinker implements Runner {
    @Override
    public void run() {
        System.out.println();
    }

    // Which method is inherited - Object.toString() or Runner.toString()?
}
```

The Thinker class has two choices for inheriting the toString() method: one from the superclass Object and one from the superinterface Runner. Remember that the superclass always wins, and therefore, the Thinker class inherits the toString() method from the Object class, not the Runner interface. This argument is true for all methods in the Object class and all classes. Because such default methods in an interface will never be used by any class, it is not allowed for interfaces to override the methods of the Object class with a default method.

Example #3

Default methods in interfaces cannot be declared final for two reasons:

- Default methods are intended to be overridden in classes.
- If a default method is added in an existing interface, all implementing classes should continue to work if they contained a method with the same signature.

Consider a Sizeable interface and a Bag class that implement the interface.

```
public interface Sizeable {
    int size();
}

public class Bag implements Sizeable {
    private int size;

    @Override
    public int size() {
        return size;
    }

    public boolean isEmpty() {
        return (size == 0);
    }

    // More code goes here
}
```

The Bag class overrides the size() method of the Sizeable interface. The class contains an additional concrete method called isEmpty(). There is no problem at this point. Now, the designer of the Sizeable interface decides to add a default isEmpty() method to the interface that will look as follows:

```
public interface Sizeable {
    int size();

    // A new default method. Cannot declare it final
    default boolean isEmpty() {
        return (size() == 0);
    }
}
```

After the new default isEmpty() method is added to the Sizeable interface, the Bag class will continue to work. The class simply overrides the default isEmpty() method of the Sizeable interface. If it were allowed to declare the default isEmpty() method final, it would have resulted in an error as a final method is not allowed to be overridden. The rule not to allow a final default method ensures backward-compatibility. The existing classes will continue to work if the class contains a method and a default method with the same signature is added in the interfaces the class implements.

The Most Specific Superinterface Wins

This rule tries to resolve the inheritance of a conflicting method with the same signature from multiple interfaces. If the same method (abstract or default) is inherited from multiple superinterfaces through different paths, the most specific path is used. Suppose I1 is an interface with a method m(). I2 is a subinterface of I1 and I2 overrides the method m(). If a class Test implements both interfaces I1 and I2, it has two choices of inheriting the m() method—I1.m() and I2.m(). In this case, I2.m() is considered most specific as it overrides I1.m(). The rules can be summarized as follows:

- Make a list of all choices of the method with the same signature that are available from different superinterfaces.

- Remove all methods from the list that have been overridden by others in the list.

- If you are left with only one choice, that is the method the class will inherit.

Consider the following Employee class. It implements the Singer and Player interfaces.

```
public class Employee implements Singer, SingerPlayer {
    // Code goes here
}
```

There are no conflicts in inheriting the play() methods, which is inherited from the Player interface. There is no conflict in inheriting the sing() method, as both superinterfaces lead to the same sing() method that is in the Singer interface. Which setRate() method is inherited by the Employee class? You have the following choices:

- Singer.setRate()

- SingerPlayer.setRate()

Both choices lead to an abstract setRate() method. Therefore, there is no conflict. However, the Player.setRate() method is most specific in this case, as it overrides the Singer.setRate() method. Which getRate() method is inherited by the Employee class? You have the following choices:

- Singer.getRate()

- SingerPlayer.getRate()

The Singer.getRate() method has been overridden by the Player.getRate() method. Therefore, Singer.getRate() is removed as a choice, which leaves you only one choice, Player.getRate(). Therefore, the Employee class inherits the default getRate() method from the Player interface.

The Class Must Override the Conflicting Method

If the previous two rules were not able to resolve the conflicting method's inheritance, the class must override the method and choose what it wants to do inside the method. It may implement the method in a completely new way or it may choose to call one of the methods in the superinterfaces. You can call the default method of one of the superinterfaces of a class using the following syntax:

```
<superinterface-name>.super.<superinterface-default-method(arg1, arg2...)>
```

If you want to call one of the methods in the superclass of a class, you can use the following syntax:

```
<class-name>.super.<superclass-method(arg1, arg2...)>
```

Consider the following declaration for a MultiTalented class, which inherits from the Singer and Player interfaces:

```
// Won't compile
public abstract class MultiTalented implements Singer, Player {
}
```

874

This class declaration will not compile. The class inherits the sing(), play(), and setRate() methods without any conflicts. There are two choices to inherit the getRate() method:

- The abstract Singer.getRate() method

- The default Player.getRate() method

None of the two versions of the getRate() method are more specific than others. In this case, the MultiTalented class must override the getRate() method to resolve the conflict. The following code for the MultiTalented class will compile:

```
public abstract class MultiTalented implements Singer, Player {
    // A MultiTalented is paid the rate of a Player plus 200.00
    @Override
    public double getRate() {
        // Get the default rate for a Player from the Player interafce
        double playerRate = Player.super.getRate();
        double rate = playerRate + 200.00;
        return rate;
    }
}
```

The class overrides the getRate() method to resolve the conflict. The method calls the default getRate() method of the Player interface and performs other logic. The class is still declared abstract, as it does not implement abstract methods from the Singer and Player interfaces.

The instanceof Operator

You can use the instanceof operator to evaluate if a reference type variable refers to an object of a specific class or its class implements a specific interface. It is a two-operand operator and it evaluates to a boolean value. The general syntax of the instanceof operator is as follows:

```
<reference-variable> instanceof <reference-type>
```

Consider the following snippet of code that defines two interfaces (Generous and Munificent) and four classes (Giver, GenerousGiver, MunificentGiver, and StingyGiver).

```
public interface Generous {
    void give();
}

public interface Munificent extends Generous {
    void giveALot();
}

public class Giver {
}

public class GenerousGiver extends Giver implements Generous {
    @Override
    public void give() {
    }
}
```

```
public class MunificentGiver extends Giver implements Munificent {
    @Override
    public void give() {
    }

    @Override
    public void giveALot() {
    }
}

public final class StingyGiver extends Giver {
    public void giveALittle() {
    }
}
```

Figure 21-2 shows a class diagram of these interfaces and classes.

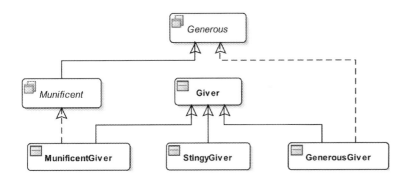

Figure 21-2. *A class diagram showing the relationship between interfaces and classes: Generous, Munificent, Object, Giver, GenerousGiver, MunificentGiver, and StingyGiver*

Every expression in Java has two types, a compile-time type and a runtime type. The compile-time type is also known as the static type or the declared type. The runtime type is also known as the dynamic type or the actual type. The compile-time type of an expression is known at compile-time. The runtime type of an expression is known when the expression is actually executed. Consider the following statement:

```
Munificent john = new MunificentGiver();
```

This code involves one variable declaration, Munificent john, and one expression, new MunificentGiver(). The compile-time type of the variable john is Munificent. The compile-time type of the expression new MunificentGiver() is MunificentGiver. At runtime, the variable john will have a reference to an object of the MunificentGiver class and its runtime type will be MunificentGiver. The runtime type for the expression new MunificentGiver() will be the same as its compile-time type, which is MunificentGiver.

The `instanceof` operator performs compile-time check as well as runtime check. At compile-time, it checks if it is possible for its left-hand operand to point to an instance of its right-hand operand type. It is allowed for the left-hand operand to point to the `null` reference. If it is possible for the left-hand operand to have a reference of its right-hand operand type, the code passes the compiler check. For example, the following code would compile and print `true` at runtime:

```
Munificent john = new MunificentGiver();
if (john instanceof Munificent) {
    System.out.println("true");
} else {
    System.out.println("false");
}
```

Looking at the compile-time type of john, which is `Munificent`, the compiler is assured that john will refer to either `null` or to an object whose class implements the `Munificent` interface. Therefore, the compiler will not complain about the `john instanceof Munificent` expression.

Consider the following snippet of code, which compiles and prints `false`:

```
Giver donna = new Giver();
if (donna instanceof Munificent) {
    System.out.println("true");
} else {
    System.out.println("false");
}
```

The compile-time type of the variable donna is `Giver`. At runtime, it also points to an object of the `Giver` type. That is, its runtime type is `Giver`. When the compiler attempts to compile the `donna instanceof Munificent` expression, it asks a question: "Is it possible that the variable donna whose compile-time type is Giver may point to an object of a class that implements the `Munificent` interface?" The answer is yes. Are you getting confused by the answer? The compiler does not look at the whole statement `Giver donna = new Giver();` in the previous snippet of code when it evaluates the `instanceof` operator. It just looks at the compile-time type of variable donna, which is `Giver`. The `Giver` class itself does not implement the `Munificent` interface. However, any subclass of the `Giver` class might implement the `Munificent` interface and the variable donna may refer to the object of any such classes. For example, it is possible to write code as shown:

```
Giver donna = new MunificentGiver();
```

In this case, the compile-time type of the variable donna remains the `Giver` type. However, at runtime, it will refer to an object whose class implements the `Munificent` interface. The job of the compiler is just to make sure about a "possibility" that may be `true` or `false` at runtime. When the variable donna refers to an object of the `Giver` class, the `donna instanceof Munificent` expression will return `false` at runtime, because the `Giver` class does not implement the `Munificent` interface. When the variable donna refers to an object of the `MunificentGiver` class, the `donna instanceof Munificent` expression will return `true` at runtime because the `MunificentGiver` class implements the `Munificent` interface.

The following snippet of code will compile and print `false`:

```
Giver kim = new StingyGiver();
if (kim instanceof Munificent) {
    System.out.println("true");
} else {
    System.out.println("false");
}
```

Consider a variation of the previous code as follows:

```
StingyGiver jim = new StingyGiver();
if (jim instanceof Munificent) { // A compile-time error
    System.out.println("true");
} else {
    System.out.println("false");
}
```

This time, the compiler will refuse to compile the code. Let's apply the logic and try to figure out what is wrong with the code. The compiler will generate an error about the jim instanceof Munificent expression. It is saying that it knows for sure that there is no possibility at runtime that the variable jim can refer to an object whose class implements the Munificent interface. How can the compiler be so sure about this possibility? It is easy. You have declared the StingyGiver class as final, which means it cannot be subclassed. This implies that the variable jim whose compile-time type is StingyGiver can only refer to an object whose class is StingyGiver. The compiler also knows that the StingyGiver class and none of its ancestor classes implement the Munificent interface. With all this reasoning, the compiler determines that you have a logical error in your program and you need to fix it.

If the instanceof operator returns true at runtime, it means that its left-hand operand can be safely cast to the type represented by its right-hand operand. Typically, your logic will be as follows when you need to use the instanceof operator:

```
ABC a = null;
DEF d = null;
if (x instanceof ABC) {
    // Safe to cast x to ABC type
    a = (ABC) x;
} else if (x instanceof DEF) {
    // Safe to cast x to DEF type
    d = (DEF) x;
}
```

If the left-hand operand of the instanceof operator is null or a reference variable, which points to null at runtime, it returns false. The following snippet of code will also print false:

```
Giver ken = null;
if (ken instanceof Munificent) {
    System.out.println("true");
} else {
    System.out.println("false");
}
```

You can conclude that if v instanceof XYZ returns true, you can assume the following two things safely:

- v is not null. That is, v is pointing to a valid object in memory.

- The cast (XYZ) v will always succeed. That is, the following code is guaranteed to work at runtime without a ClassCastException:

  ```
  XYZ x = (XYZ) v;
  ```

Marker Interfaces

You can declare an interface with no members. Note that an interface can have members in two ways: by declaring its own members or by inheriting members from its superinterfaces. When an interface has no members (declared or inherited), it is known as a *marker* interface. A marker interface is also called a *tag* interface.

What is the use of a marker interface? Why would any class implement a marker interface? As the name suggests, a marker interface is used to mark the class with a special meaning that can be used in a particular context. The meaning added to a class by a marker interface depends on the context. The developer of the marker interface has to document the meaning of the interface and the consumer of the interface will make use of its intended meaning. For example, let's declare a marker interface called Funny, as follows. The meaning of this Funny interface is up to the developer who uses it.

```
public interface Funny {
    // No code goes here
}
```

Every interface defines a new type, so does a marker interface. Therefore, you can declare a variable of type Funny.

```
Funny simon = an object of a class that implements the Funny interface;
```

What can you access using the variable simon, which is of type Funny? You cannot access anything using the simon variable, except all methods of the Object class. You could do that without implementing the Funny interface to your class, too. Typically, a marker interface is used with the instanceof operator to check if a reference type variable refers to an object, whose class implements the marker interface. For example, you may write code like this:

```
Object obj = any java object;
...
if (obj instanceof Funny) {
    // obj is an object whose class implements the Funny interface. Display a message on the
    // standard output that we are using a Funny object. Or, do something that is intended
    // by the developer of the Funny interface
    System.out.println("Using a Funny object");
}
```

The Java API has many marker interfaces. java.lang.Cloneable, java.io.Serializable, and java.rmi.Remote are a few of the marker interfaces in the Java class library. If a class implements the Cloneable interface, it means that the developer of that class intended to allow the cloning of the objects of that class. You need to take additional steps of overriding the clone() method of the Object class in your class, so the clone() method can be called on objects of your class because the clone() method has been declared protected in the Object class. Even though your class overrides the clone() method, the object of your class cannot be cloned until your class implements the Cloneable marker interface. You can see that implementing Cloneable interface associates a meaning to the class that its object can be cloned. When the clone() method of the Object class is invoked, Java performs a check if the object's class implements the Cloneable interface. If the object's class does not implement the Cloneable interface, it throws an exception at runtime.

Java 5 introduced a specialized form of interface known as *annotations*. It can be used to associate a meaning to any element, for example, a class, a method, a variable, a package, etc., of a Java program. I cover annotations in Chapter 1 of the second volume of this series.

Functional Interfaces

An interface with just one abstract method is known as a *functional* interface. The static and default methods are not counted to designate an interface a functional interface. No additional steps, other than what I have already discussed, are needed to declare an interface as functional. I discuss more about functional interfaces in Chapter 5 of the second volume of this series. The Walkable and Swimmable interfaces are examples of functional interfaces because they contain only one abstract method. The Singer interface is an example of a non-functional interface because it contains more than one abstract method. You can annotate a functional interface with the @FunctionalInterface annotation and the compiler will verify the annotated interface really contains only one abstract method; otherwise, the interface declaration will not compile. The following is an example of a functional interface annotated with the @FunctionalInterface annotation:

```
@FunctionalInterface
public interface Runner {
    public void run();
}
```

Comparing Objects

When you have a group of objects, sometimes you may want to order them based on some criteria. The java.lang.Comparable and java.util.Comparator are two commonly used interfaces for the purpose of ordering objects. I discuss both interfaces in this section.

Using the Comparable Interface

A class implements the Comparable interface if objects of the class need to be compared for sorting purposes. For example, you may want to compare two objects of a Person class when sorting a collection of persons in an array or a list. The criteria you use to compare the two objects depend on the context. For example, when you need to display many persons, you may want to display them sorted by their last names, person IDs, addresses, or telephone numbers.

The ordering on the objects of a class that is imposed by the Comparable interface is also called the class's natural ordering. The Comparable interface contains an abstract compareTo() method that takes one parameter. The method returns zero if the two objects being compared are considered equal; it returns a negative integer if the object is less than the specified parameter; it returns a positive integer if the object is greater than the specified parameter. The Comparable interface is a generic interface declared as follows:

```
public interface Comparable<T> {
    public int compareTo(T o);
}
```

The String class and wrapper classes (Integer, Double, Float, etc.) implement the Comparable interface. The String class's compareTo() method sorts strings lexicographically. All wrapper classes for the numeric primitive types compare the two objects numerically.

It is typical to compare objects of the same type. The following class declaration for the class A implements the Comparable<A> interface using A as its generic type, which states that the class A supports only comparing objects of its own type:

```
public class A implement Comparable<A> {
    public int compareTo(A a) {
        // Code goes here
    }
}
```

Listing 21-36 contains the code for a ComparablePerson class that implements the Comparable<ComparablePerson> interface. In the compareTo() method, first you compare the two objects based on their last names. If the last names are the same, you compare their first names. You have used the compareTo() method of the String class to compare the last and first names of two comparable persons. Note that the compareTo() method does not handle null values.

Listing 21-36. A ComparablePerson Class That Implements the Comparable Interface

```
// ComparablePerson.java
package com.jdojo.interfaces;

public class ComparablePerson implements Comparable<ComparablePerson> {
    private String firstName;
    private String lastName;

    public ComparablePerson(String firstName, String lastName) {
        this.firstName = firstName;
        this.lastName = lastName;
    }

    public String getFirstName() {
        return firstName;
    }

    public void setFirstName(String firstName) {
        this.firstName = firstName;
    }

    public String getLastName() {
        return lastName;
    }

    public void setLastName(String lastName) {
        this.lastName = lastName;
    }
```

```
    // Compares two persons based on their last names. If last names are
    // the same, use first names
    @Override
    public int compareTo(ComparablePerson anotherPerson) {
        int diff = getLastName().compareTo(anotherPerson.getLastName());
        if (diff == 0) {
            diff = getFirstName().compareTo(anotherPerson.getFirstName());
        }
        return diff;
    }

    @Override
    public String toString() {
        return getLastName() + ", " + getFirstName();
    }
}
```

Listing 21-37 contains the code that tests the ComparablePerson class by sorting their objects in an array. The output shows that objects of the ComparablePerson class are sorted by last name and first name.

Listing 21-37. A Test Class to Test the ComparablePerson Class and the Comparable Interface

```
// ComparablePersonTest.java
package com.jdojo.interfaces;

import java.util.Arrays;

public class ComparablePersonTest {
    public static void main(String[] args) {
        ComparablePerson[] persons = new ComparablePerson[] {
                new ComparablePerson("John", "Jacobs"),
                new ComparablePerson("Jeff", "Jacobs"),
                new ComparablePerson("Wally", "Inman")};

        System.out.println("Before sorting...");
        print(persons);

        // Sort the persons list
        Arrays.sort(persons);

        System.out.println("\nAfter sorting...");
        print(persons);
    }

    public static void print(ComparablePerson[] persons) {
        for(ComparablePerson person: persons){
            System.out.println(person);
        }
    }
}
```

```
Before sorting...
Jacobs, John
Jacobs, Jeff
Inman, Wally

After sorting...
Inman, Wally
Jacobs, Jeff
Jacobs, John
```

Using the Comparator Interface

The Comparable interface, which I explained in the previous section, imposes a specified ordering on objects of a class. Sometimes you may want to specify a different ordering for objects of the class from the ordering specified in the class by the Comparable interface. Sometimes you may want to specify a particular ordering for the objects of a class that does not implement the Comparable interface. For example, you may want to specify ordering on objects of the ComparablePerson class based on the first name and the last name, as opposed to the ordering specified by its compareTo() method of the Comparable interface, which is the last name and the first name. The Comparator interface lets you specify a custom ordering on objects of any class. Typically, the Java API dealing with a collection of objects requires a Comparator object to specify a custom ordering. The Comparator interface is a generic interface:

```
public interface Comparator<T> {
    int compare(T o1, T o2);
    boolean equals(Object obj);

    // Default and static methods are not shown here
}
```

The Comparator interface has been overhauled in Java 8. Several static and default methods have been added to the interface. I discuss some of the new methods in this chapter and some later in Chapter 5 of the second volume of this series when I discuss lambda expressions.

Typically, you do not need to implement the equals() method of the Comparator interface. Every class in Java inherits the equals() method from the Object class and that is fine in most cases. The compare() method takes two parameters and it returns an integer. It returns a negative integer, zero, or a positive integer if the first argument is less than, equal to, or greater than the second argument, respectively. Listings 21-38 and 21-39 contain two implementations of the Comparator interface: one compares two ComparablePerson objects based on their first names and another based on their last names.

Listing 21-38. A Comparator Comparing ComparablePersons Based on Their First Names

```
// FirstNameComparator.java
package com.jdojo.interfaces;

import java.util.Comparator;
```

```
public class FirstNameComparator implements Comparator<ComparablePerson> {
    @Override
    public int compare(ComparablePerson p1, ComparablePerson p2) {
        String firstName1 = p1.getFirstName();
        String firstName2 = p2.getFirstName();
        int diff = firstName1.compareTo(firstName2);
        return diff;
    }
}
```

Listing 21-39. A Comparator Comparing ComparablePersons Based on Their Last Names

```
// LastNameComparator.java
package com.jdojo.interfaces;

import java.util.Comparator;

public class LastNameComparator implements Comparator<ComparablePerson> {
    @Override
    public int compare(ComparablePerson p1, ComparablePerson p2) {
        String lastName1 = p1.getLastName();
        String lastName2 = p2.getFirstName();
        int diff = lastName1.compareTo(lastName2);
        return diff;
    }
}
```

Using a Comparator is easy. Create its object and pass it to the methods that take a collection of objects and a comparator to compare them. For example, to sort an array of ComparablePerson objects, pass the array and a FirstNameComparator to the static sort() method of the Arrays class.

```
ComparablePerson[] persons = create and populate the array...

// Sort the persons array based on first name
Comparator fnComparator = new FirstNameComparator();
Arrays.sort(persons, fnComparator);
```

You can use a similar logic to sort the array based on the last name:

```
// Sort the persons array based on last name
Comparator lnComparator = new LastNameComparator();
Arrays.sort(persons, lnComparator);
```

Prior to Java 8, if you wanted to sort the array based on the first name and then the last name, you needed to create another implementation of the Comparator interface. Thanks to Java 8's introducing default methods to interfaces, you do not need to create a new implementation of the Comparator interface. The Comparator class contains a thenComparing() default method declared as follows:

```
default Comparator<T> thenComparing(Comparator<? super T> other)
```

The method takes a Comparator as an argument and returns a new Comparator. The new Comparator is used for ordering if the two objects being compared are equal using the original Comparator. The following snippet of code combines the first name and last Comparators to create a new Comparator:

```
// Sort using first name, then last name
Comparator firstLastComparator = fnComparator.thenComparing(lnComparator);
Arrays.sort(persons, firstLastComparator);
```

░ **Tip**   You can chain the call to the thenComparing() method to create a Comparator that imposes ordering on several nested levels.

There is another useful addition to the Comparator interface in Java 8: a default method named reversed(). The method returns a new Comparator that imposes the reverse ordering of the original Comparator. If you want to sort the array based on first name, then last name in descending order, you can do so as follows:

```
// Sort using first name, then last name in reversed order
Comparator firstLastReverseComparator = firstLastComparator.reversed();
Arrays.sort(persons, firstLastReverseComparator);
```

Comparators do not handle null values well. Typically, they throw a NullPointerException. Java 8 added the following two useful, null-friendly, convenience static methods to the Comparator interface:

- static <T> Comparator<T> nullsFirst(Comparator<? super T> comparator)

- static <T> Comparator<T> nullsLast(Comparator<? super T> comparator)

These methods take a Comparator and return a null-friendly Comparator that places the null values first or last. You can use these methods as follows:

```
// Sort using first name, then last name, placing null values first
Comparator nullFirstComparator = Comparator.nullsFirst(firstLastComparator);
Arrays.sort(persons, nullFirstComparator);
```

Listing 21-40 uses an object of this class to sort objects of the ComparablePerson class. As the output indicates, this time you can sort a list of comparable persons based on their first names and last names. If you want to sort a list of objects of the ComparablePerson in any other order, you need to use an object of the Comparator interface that imposes the desired order.

Listing 21-40. A Test Class That Uses a Comparator Object to Sort ComparablePerson Objects

```
// ComparablePersonTest2.java
package com.jdojo.interfaces;

import java.util.Arrays;
import java.util.Comparator;

public class ComparablePersonTest2 {
    public static void main(String[] args) {
        ComparablePerson[] persons = new ComparablePerson[]{
            new ComparablePerson("John", "Jacobs"),
```

```
                new ComparablePerson("Jeff", "Jacobs"),
                new ComparablePerson("Wally", "Inman")};

        System.out.println("Original array...");
        print(persons);

        // Sort using first name
        Comparator<ComparablePerson> fnComparator = new FirstNameComparator();
        Arrays.sort(persons, fnComparator);
        System.out.println("\nAfter sorting on first name...");
        print(persons);

        // Sort using last name
        Comparator<ComparablePerson> lnComparator = new LastNameComparator();
        Arrays.sort(persons, lnComparator);
        System.out.println("\nAfter sorting on last name...");
        print(persons);

        // Sort using first name, then last name
        Comparator<ComparablePerson> firstLastComparator
                = fnComparator.thenComparing(lnComparator);
        Arrays.sort(persons, firstLastComparator);
        System.out.println("\nAfter sorting on first, then last name...");
        print(persons);

        // Sort using first name, then last name in reversed order
        Comparator<ComparablePerson> firstLastReverseComparator
                = firstLastComparator.reversed();
        Arrays.sort(persons, firstLastReverseComparator);
        System.out.println("\nAfter sorting on first, then last name in reversed...");
        print(persons);

        // Sort using first name, then last name using null first
        Comparator<ComparablePerson> nullFirstComparator
                = Comparator.nullsFirst(firstLastComparator);
        ComparablePerson[] personsWithNulls = new ComparablePerson[]{
            new ComparablePerson("John", "Jacobs"),
            null,
            new ComparablePerson("Jeff", "Jacobs"),
            new ComparablePerson("Wally", "Inman"),
            null};

        Arrays.sort(personsWithNulls, nullFirstComparator);
        System.out.println("\nAfter sorting on first, then last name "
                + "using null first...");
        print(personsWithNulls);
    }
```

```
    public static void print(ComparablePerson[] persons) {
        for (ComparablePerson person : persons) {
            System.out.println(person);
        }
    }
}
```

```
Original array...
Jacobs, John
Jacobs, Jeff
Inman, Wally

After sorting on first name...
Jacobs, Jeff
Jacobs, John
Inman, Wally

After sorting on last name...
Inman, Wally
Jacobs, John
Jacobs, Jeff

After sorting on first, then last name...
Jacobs, Jeff
Jacobs, John
Inman, Wally

After sorting on first, then last name in reversed...
Inman, Wally
Jacobs, John
Jacobs, Jeff

After sorting on first, then last name using null first...
null
null
Jacobs, Jeff
Jacobs, John
Inman, Wally
```

Polymorphism—One Object, Many Views

Polymorphism refers to the ability of an object to take on many forms. I use the term "view" instead of the term "form." The term "view" gives better understanding of polymorphism in the context of interfaces. Let's rephrase the definition of polymorphism: It is an ability of an object to provide its different views. Interfaces let you create a polymorphic object. Consider the Turtle class declaration shown in Listing 21-24. It implements the Swimmable and Walkable interfaces. You create a Turtle object, as shown:

```
Turtle turti = new Turtle("Turti");
```

Because the Turtle class implements the Walkable and Swimmable interfaces, you can treat the turti object as a Walkable or a Swimmable.

```
Walkable turtiWalkable = turti;
Swimmable turtiSwimmable = turti;
```

Since every class in Java is inherited from the Object class, you can also treat the turti object as an Object:

```
Object turiObject = turti;
```

Figure 21-3 shows four different views of the same Turtle object. Note that there is only one object, which is of the Turtle class. When you look at a house from different directions (top, front, back, left, right, etc.), you get different views of the same house. Nevertheless, there is only one house. When you are looking at a house from its front, you do not get to see its other views, for example, the back view or the left view. Like a house, a Java object can exhibit different views of itself, which is called polymorphism.

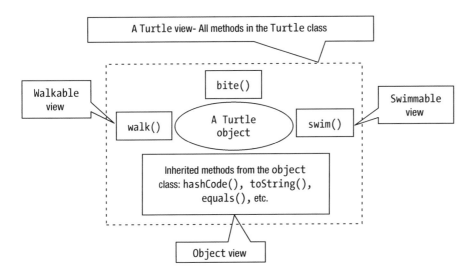

Figure 21-3. *Polymorphism: one object, many views. Four different views of a Turtle object*

What defines a particular view of a Java object and how do you get that view of the object? A view is something that is available for an outsider (in technical terms, for clients or users of the class). The set of methods (accessible to clients) defined in a type (a class or an interface) defines a view of an object of that type. For example, the Walkable type defines one method: walk(). If you get a Walkable view of an object, it means that you have access to only the walk() method of that object. Similarly, if you have a Swimmable view of an object, you can access only the swim() method of that object. How about having a Turtle view of a Turtle object? The Turtle class defines three methods: bite(), walk(), and swim(). It also inherits methods from the Object class. Therefore, if you have a Turtle view of an object, you can access all methods that are available in the Turtle class (directly declared or inherited from its superclass and superinterfaces). Every class in Java is inherited, directly or indirectly, from the Object class. By virtue of this, every object in Java has at least two views: one view defined by the set of methods that are available (declared or inherited) in the object's class and another view defined by the set of methods defined in the Object class. When you are using the Object view of an object, you can access methods of only the Object class.

You get different views of an object by accessing it using reference variables of different types. For example, to get the Walkable view of a Turtle object, you do any of the following things:

```
Turtle t = new Turtle("Turti");
Walkable w2 = t;           // w2 gives Walkable view of the Turtle object
Walkable w3 = new Turtle(); // w3 gives Walkable view of the Turtle object
```

With this knowledge of a Java object that can support different views, let's look at the use of the instanceof operator. It is used to test if an object supports a specific view or not. Consider the following snippet of code:

```
Object anObject = get any object reference...;
if(anObject instanceof Walkable) {
    // anObject has a Walkable view
    Walkable w = (Walkable) anObject;

    // Now access the Walkable view of the object using w
} else {
    // anObject does not have a Walkable view
}
```

The anObject variable refers to an object. The instanceof operator is used to test if the object to which anObject variable refers to supports a Walkable view. Note that just defining a walk() method in a class does not define a Walkable view for the objects of that class. The class must implement the Walkable interface and implement the walk() method in order for its object to have a Walkable view. A view of an object is synonymous with its type. Recall that implementing an interface to a class gives the objects of that class an additional type (that is, an additional view). How many views an object of a class has? An object of a class can have the following views:

- A view that is defined by its class type

- Views that are defined by all superclasses (direct or indirect) of its class

- Views that are defined by all interfaces implemented by their classes or superclasses (direct or indirect)

Dynamic Binding and Interfaces

Java uses dynamic binding (also known as runtime binding or late binding) when a method is invoked using a variable of an interface type. Consider the following snippet of code:

```
Walkable john = a Walkable object reference...
john.walk();
```

The variable john has two types: a compile-time type and a runtime type. Its compile-time type is its declared type, which is Walkable. The compiler knows about the compile-time type of a variable. When the code john.walk() is compiled, the compiler has to verify that this call is valid according to all pieces of information that are available at compile-time. The compiler adds instruction similar to the following for the john.walk() method invocation:

```
invokeinterface #5,  1; //InterfaceMethod com/jdojo/interfaces/Walkable.walk:()V
```

The previous instruction states that the `john.walk()` method invocation is being made on a variable of an interface type `Walkable`. The object to which the variable `john` refers at runtime is its runtime type. The compiler does not know about the runtime type of the variable john. The variable john may refer to an object of a `Person` class, a `Turtle` class, a `Duck` class, or any other class that implements the `Walkable` interface. The compiler does not state which implementation of the `walk()` method should be used when `john.walk()` is executed. The runtime decides the implementation of the `walk()` method to invoke as follows:

1. It gets the information about the class of the object to which the variable john refers to. For example, consider the following snippet of code:

   ```
   Walkable john = new Person("John"); // john refers to a Person object
   john.walk();
   ```

   Here, the class type of the object to which the variable john refers to at runtime is Person.

2. It looks for the `walk()` method implementation in the class that is determined in the previous step. If the `walk()` method implementation is not found in that class, the runtime looks for the `walk()` method's implementation in the ancestor class recursively.

3. If the `walk()` method's implementation is found in the previous step, it is executed as soon as it is found. That is, if the `walk()` method's implementation is found in the class of the object to which the variable john refers, the runtime executes that method implementation and it does not look for the method any further in its ancestor class.

4. If the `walk()` method's implementation is not found in the class hierarchy, the inheritance hierarchy of the superinterfaces implemented by the class is searched. If a `walk()` method is found using the most specific rules of finding methods in interfaces described previously, that method is invoked if it is a default method. If multiple default `walk()` methods are found, an `IncompatibleClassChangeError` is thrown. If an abstract `walk()` method is found, an `AbstractMethodError` is thrown.

5. If the `walk()` method's implementation is still not found, a `NoSuchMethodError` is thrown. If all classes are consistently compiled, you should not get this error.

Summary

An interface is a specification that is meant to be implemented by classes. An interface may contain members that are static constants, abstract methods, default methods, static methods, and nested types. An interface cannot have instance variables. An interface cannot be instantiated.

An interface with no members is known as a marker interface. An interface with only one abstract method is known as a functional interface.

A class implements interfaces. The keyword `implements` is used in a class declaration to implement interfaces. The class implementing an interface inherits all members from the interface, except the static methods. If the class inherits abstract methods from the implemented interfaces, it needs to override them and provide an implementation or the class should declare itself abstract. The class implementing interfaces are subtypes of the implemented interfaces and the implemented interfaces are supertypes of the class. If a class inherits the same methods from multiple supertypes (superclasses or superinterfaces) with the same signature; in such a case, the method from the superclass takes precedence; if all methods are inherited from superinterfaces, the most specific method is used; if there are still multiple candidates, the class must override the method to resolve the conflict.

An interface may inherit from other interfaces. The keyword extends is used in the interface declaration to specify all inherited interfaces. The interfaces from which the interface is inherited are known as superinterfaces and the interface itself is known as a subinterface. A subinterface inherits all members of its superinterfaces, except their static methods. A conflict may arise if an interface inherits a method combination default-default or default-abstract with the same signature from multiple superinterfaces. The conflict is resolved in two steps—the most specific candidate is used; if there are multiple most specific candidates, the interface must override the conflicting method.

Before Java 8, it was not possible, without breaking the existing code, to change interfaces after they are published. From Java 8, you can add default and static methods to existing interfaces. Until Java 9, all methods in an interfaces were implicitly public and you were not allowed to have private methods. Java 9 allows you have private methods in an interface.

Dynamic binding is used when an abstract or default method is called using a variable of an interface type. Static binding is used when the static methods of an interface are called. Note that the static methods of an interface can be called using only one syntax:

```
InterfaceName.staticMethodName(arg1, arg2...)
```

EXERCISES

1. What are interfaces in Java? What is a marker interface? What is a functional interface?

2. What keyword do you use to implement an interface to class?

3. How many interfaces can a class implement?

4. What keyword do you use in an interface declaration to inherit the interface from other interfaces?

5. Can you declare instance variables in an interface?

6. Which version of Java SE allows you have to have private methods in an interface?

7. What kinds of methods in an interface can be declared private? Can you have an abstract private method in an interface? If no, explain your answer.

8. What interface do you implement in a class to implement natural sorting for the objects of the class? What interface do you use to implement custom sorting for the objects of the class?

9. Describe the reason that the following interface declaration does not compile and suggest a fix.

```
public interface Choices {
    int YES;
    int NO = 1;
    private int CANCEL = 2;
}
```

10. What is wrong with the following interface declaration?

```
public interface ScheduledJob {
    public void run() {
        System.out.println("Running the job...");
    }
}
```

11. Consider the following declaration of an interface named Greeting.

```
interface Greeting {
    void sayHello();
}
```

Create a class named Greeter that implements the Greeting interface in such a way that when the following snippet of code is executed, it prints "Hello" on the standard output.

```
Greeting g = new Greeter();
g.sayHello();
```

12. The following interface declaration does not compile. Describe the reason and suggest a fix.

```
public final interface Colorable {
    public void color();
}
```

13. Is the following interface declaration valid? What is the special name for an interface like the Sensitive interface?

```
public interface Sensitive {
    // No code goes here
}
```

14. Will the following interface declaration compile? If no, give the reason.

```
@FunctionalInterface
public interface Runner {
    public void run();
}
```

15. Is the following declaration for the Printer interface a valid functional interface declaration? Describe your reasons for how it fits or does not fit the definition of a functional interface.

```
@FunctionalInterface
public interface Printer {
    public void print();
```

```
        public default void sayHello() {
            System.out.println("Hello");
        }
    }
```

16. Consider the following declarations.

```
public interface Greeting {
    default void greet() {
        System.out.println("Hello");
    }
}

public class EnglishGreeting implements Greeting {
}

public class HispanicGreeting implements Greeting {
    @Override
    public void greet() {
        System.out.println("Ola");
    }
}
```

What will the output be when the following snippet of code is executed?

```
Greeting usGreeting = new EnglishGreeting();
Greeting mxGreeting = new HispanicGreeting();
usGreeting.greet();
mxGreeting.greet();
```

17. Consider the following partial declaration of an Item class.

```
public class Item implements Comparable<Item> {
    private String name;
    private double price;
    /* Your code goes here */
}
```

Complete the Item class by adding the needed constructor to allow for initial value for the name and price of the item. Also add getters and setters for the two instance variable. Add the required method, so the class implements the Comparable<Item> interface. The natural order for sorting items is by their names.

18. Create a custom comparator class—a class that implements the Comparator<Item> interface. The comparator class will sort the objects of the Item class by price and then by name.

19. Consider the following declarations for the Greeting interface and the Greeter class:

```
public interface Greeting {
    default void greet() {
        System.out.println("Namaste");
    }
}

public class Greeter implements Greeting {
    @Override
    public void greet() {
        /* Calls the greet() method of the Greeting interface here */

        System.out.println("Hello");
    }
}
```

Complete the code in the greet() method of the Greeter class by adding one statement as the first statement in the method. The statement should call the greet() method of the Greeting interface. When the following snippet of code is executed, it should print "Namaste" and "Hello"—each word in a separate line.

```
Greeting g = new Greeter();
g.greet();
```

The expected output is as follows:

```
Namaste
Hello
```

CHAPTER 22

Enum Types

In this chapter, you will learn:

- What enum types are

- How to declare enum types and enum constants

- How to use enums in `switch` statements

- How to associate data and methods to enum constants

- How to declare nested enums

- How to implement interfaces to an enum type

- How to perform a reverse lookup for enum constants

- How to use `EnumSet` to work with ranges of enum constants

All example programs in this chapter are a member of a `jdojo.enums` module, as declared in Listing 22-1.

Listing 22-1. The Declaration of a jdojo.enums Module

```
// module-info.java
module jdojo.enums {
    exports com.jdojo.enums;
}
```

What Is an Enum Type?

An enum (also known as enumeration and enumerated data type) lets you create an ordered list of constants as a type. Before we discuss what an enum is and why we need it, let's consider a problem and solve it using Java features that were available before enum, which was introduced in Java 5. Suppose you are working on a defect tracking application in which you need to represent the severity of a defect. The application lets you specify the severity of a defect as low, medium, high, and urgent. A typical way to represent the four types of severity before Java 5 was to declare four `int` constants in a class, say `Severity`, as shown in Listing 22-2.

© Kishori Sharan 2017
K. Sharan, *Beginning Java 9 Fundamentals*, https://doi.org/10.1007/978-1-4842-2902-6_22

Listing 22-2. A Severity Class with a Few Constants

```java
// Severity.java
package com.jdojo.enums;

public class Severity {
    public static final int LOW = 0;
    public static final int MEDIUM = 1;
    public static final int HIGH = 2;
    public static final int URGENT = 3;
}
```

Suppose you want to write a utility class named DefectUtil that has a method to compute the projected turnaround days for a defect based on its severity. The code for the DefectUtil class may look as shown in Listing 22-3.

Listing 22-3. A DefectUtil Class

```java
// DefectUtil.java
package com.jdojo.enums;

public class DefectUtil {
    public static int getProjectedTurnaroundDays(int severity) {
        int days = 0;

        switch (severity) {
            case Severity.LOW:
                days = 30;
                break;
            case Severity.MEDIUM:
                days = 15;
                break;
            case Severity.HIGH:
                days = 7;
                break;
            case Severity.URGENT:
                days = 1;
                break;
        }

        return days;
    }

    // Other code for the DefectUtil class goes here
}
```

The following are a few problems with this approach in handling the severity of a defect:

- Since a severity is represented as an integer constant, you can pass any integer value to the getProjectedTurnaroundDays() method, not just 0, 1, 2, and 3, which are the valid values for the severity type. You may want to add a check inside this method so only valid severity values can be passed to it. Otherwise, the method may throw an exception. However, that does not solve the problem forever. You will need to update the code that checks for valid severity values whenever you add new severity types.

- If you change the value for a severity constant, you must recompile the code that uses it to reflect the changes. When you compile the DefectUtil class, Severity.LOW is replaced with 0, Severity.MEDIUM is replaced with 1, and so on. If you change the value for the constant LOW in the Severity class to 10, you must recompile the DefectUtil class to reflect this change. Otherwise, the DefectUtil class will still keep using the value 1.

- When you save the value of the severity on disk, its corresponding integer value will be saved, for example, 0, 1, 2, etc., not the string values LOW, MEDIUM, HIGH, etc. You must maintain a separate map to convert from an integer value to its corresponding string representation for all severity types.

- When you print the severity value of a defect, it will print an integer, for example, 0, 1, 2, etc. An integer value for a severity does not mean anything to end users.

- Severity types of defects have a specific order. For example, a LOW severity defect is given less priority than a MEDIUM severity defect. Since severity is being represented by an arbitrary number, you must write code using hard-coded values to maintain the order of the constants defined in the Severity class. Suppose you add another severity type of VERY_HIGH, which has less priority than URGENT and more priority than HIGH. Now you must change the code that handles ordering of severity type because you have added one in the middle of the existing severity types.

- There is no automatic way (except by hard coding) that will let you list all severity types.

You would agree that representing the severity types using integer constants is difficult to maintain. That was the only easily implemented solution available before Java 5 to define enumerated constants. You could have solved this problem effectively before Java 5. However, the amount of code you had to write was disproportionate to the problem. The enum type in Java 5 solves this problem in a simple and effective way.

According to the Merriam-Webster online dictionary, the term "enumerate" means "to specify one after another." This is exactly what the enum type lets you do. It lets you specify constants in a specific order. The constants defined in an enum type are instances of that enum type. You define an enum type using the keyword enum. Its simplest general syntax is

```
[access-modifier] enum <enum-type-name> {
    // List of comma separated names of enum constants
}
```

The access modifier for an enum is the same as the access modifier for a class: public, private, protected, or package-level. The enum type name is a valid Java identifier. The body of the enum type is placed within braces following its name. The body of the enum type can have a list of comma-separated constants and other elements that are similar to the elements you have in a class, for example, instance variables, methods, etc. Most of the time, the enum body includes only constants. The following code declares an enum type called Gender, which declares two constants—MALE and FEMALE:

```
public enum Gender {
    MALE, FEMALE; // The semi-colon is optional in this case
}
```

░ **Tip**   It is a convention to name the enum constants in uppercase. The semicolon after the last enum constant is optional if there is no code that follows the list of constants.

Listing 22-4 declares a public enum type called Severity with four enum constants: LOW, MEDIUM, HIGH, and URGENT.

Listing 22-4. Declaration of a Severity Enum

```
// Severity.java
package com.jdojo.enums;

public enum Severity {
    LOW, MEDIUM, HIGH, URGENT;
}
```

A public enum type can be accessed from anywhere in the application. Accessibility rules across modules for enum types are the same as for other types, which I discussed in Chapter 10.

Just like a public class, you need to save the code in Listing 22-4 in a file named Severity.java. When you compile the code, the compiler will create a Severity.class file. Note that except for the use of the enum keyword and the body part, everything for the Severity enum type looks the same as if it were a class declaration. In fact, Java implements an enum type as a class. The compiler does a lot of work for an enum type and generates code for it that is essentially a class. You need to place an enum type in a package as you have been placing all classes in a package. You can use an import statement to import an enum type, as you import a class type, into a compilation unit.

You declare a variable of an enum type the same way you declare a variable of a class type:

```
// Declare defectSeverity variable of the Severity enum type
Severity defectSeverity;
```

You can assign null to an enum type variable, like so:

```
Severity defectSeverity = null;
```

What other values can you assign to an enum type variable? An enum type defines two things:

- The enum constants, which are the only valid values for its type
- The order for those constants

The Severity enum type defines four enum constants. Therefore, a variable of the Severity enum type can have only one of the four values—LOW, MEDIUM, HIGH, and URGENT–or null. You can use dot notation to refer to the enum constants by using the enum type name as the qualifier. The following snippet of code assigns values to a variable of Severity enum type:

```
Severity low = Severity.LOW;
Severity medium = Severity.MEDIUM;
Severity high = Severity.HIGH;
Severity urgent = Severity.URGENT;
```

You cannot instantiate an enum type. The following code that attempts to instantiate the Severity enum type results in a compile-time error:

```
Severity badAttempt = new Severity(); // A compile-time error
```

▓ **Tip** An enum type acts as a type as well as a factory. It declares a new type and a list of valid instances of that type as its constants.

An enum type also assigns an order number (or position number), called an *ordinal*, to all of its constants. The ordinal starts with zero and it is incremented by one as you move from first to last in the list of constants. The first enum constant is assigned the ordinal value of zero, the second of 1, the third of 2, and so on. The ordinal values assigned to constants declared in Severity enum type are 0 to LOW, 1 to MEDIUM, 2 to HIGH, and 3 to URGENT. If you change the order of the constants in the enum type body or add new ones, their ordinal values will change accordingly.

Each enum constant has a name. The name of an enum constant is the same as the identifier specified for the constant in its declaration. For example, the name for the LOW constant in the Severity enum type is "LOW".

You can read the name and the ordinal of an enum constant using the name() and ordinal() methods, respectively. Each enum type has a static method named values() that returns an array of constants in the order they are declared in its body. The program in Listing 22-5 prints the name and ordinal of all enum constants declared in the Severity enum type.

Listing 22-5. Listing Name and Ordinal of Enum Type Constants

```
// ListEnumConstants.java
package com.jdojo.enums;

public class ListEnumConstants {
    public static void main(String[] args) {
        for(Severity s : Severity.values()) {
            String name = s.name();
            int ordinal = s.ordinal();
            System.out.println(name + "(" + ordinal + ")");
        }
    }
}
```

```
LOW(0)
MEDIUM(1)
HIGH(2)
URGENT(3)
```

The Superclass of an Enum Type

An enum type is similar to a Java class type. In fact, the compiler creates a class when an enum type is compiled. You can treat an enum type as a class type for all practical purposes. However, there are some rules that apply only to the enum. An enum type can also have constructors, fields, and methods. Did I not say that an enum type cannot be instantiated? (In other words, new Severity() is invalid.) Why do you need constructors for an enum type if it cannot be instantiated?

Here is the reason why you need constructors for an enum type. An enum type is instantiated only in the code generated by the compiler. All enum constants are objects of the same enum type. These instances are created and named the same as the enum constants in the code generated by the compiler. The compiler is playing the tricks. The compiler generates code for an enum type similar to the one shown next. The following sample code is just to give you an idea what goes on behind the scenes. The actual code generated by the compiler may be different from the one shown. For example, the code for the valueOf() method gives you a sense that it compares the name with enum constant names and returns the matching constant instance. In reality, the compiler generates code for a valueOf() method that makes a call to the valueOf() method in the Enum superclass.

```
// Transformed code for Severity enum type declaration
package com.jdojo.enums;

public final class Severity extends Enum {
    public static final Severity LOW;
    public static final Severity MEDIUM;
    public static final Severity HIGH;
    public static final Severity URGENT;

    // Create constants when class is loaded
    static {
        LOW    = new Severity("LOW", 0);
        MEDIUM = new Severity("MEDIUM", 1);
        HIGH   = new Severity("HIGH", 2);
        URGENT = new Severity("URGENT", 3);
    }

    // The private constructor to prevent direct instantiation
    private Severity(String name, int ordinal) {
        super(name, ordinal);
    }

    public static Severity[] values() {
        return new Severity[] { LOW, MEDIUM, HIGH, URGENT };
    }

    public static Severity valueOf(String name) {
        if (LOW.name().equals(name)) {
            return LOW;
        }

        if (MEDIUM.name().equals(name)) {
            return MEDIUM;
        }

        if (HIGH.name().equals(name)) {
            return HIGH;
        }
```

```
        if (URGENT.name().equals(name)) {
            return URGENT;
        }

        throw new IllegalArgumentException("Invalid enum constant " + name);
    }
}
```

By looking at the transformed code for the Severity enum declaration, the following points can be made:

- Every enum type implicitly extends the java.lang.Enum class. This means that all methods defined in the Enum class can be used with all enum types. Table 22-1 lists the methods that are defined in the Enum class.

- An enum type is implicitly final. In some situations (discussed later), the compiler cannot declare it as final as it has done in the sample code for the Severity class.

- The compiler adds two static methods, values() and valueOf(), to every enum type. The values() method returns the array of enum constants in the same order they are declared in the enum type. You have seen the use of the values() method in Listing 22-5. The valueOf() method is used to get the instance of an enum type using the constant name as a string. For example, Severity.valueOf("LOW") will return the Severity.LOW constant. The valueOf() method facilitates reverse lookup—from a string value to an enum type value.

- The Enum class implements the java.lang.Comparable and java.io.Serializable interfaces. This means instances of every enum type can be compared and serialized. The Enum class makes sure that during the deserialization process no other instances of an enum type are created than the ones declared as the enum constants. You can use the compareTo() method to determine if one enum constant is declared before or after another enum constant. Note that you can also determine the order of two enum constants by comparing their ordinals. The compareTo() method does the same, with one more check, that the enum constants being compared must be of the same enum type. The following code snippet shows how to compare two enum constants:

```
Severity s1 = Severity.LOW;
Severity s2 = Severity.HIGH;

// s1.compareTo(s2) returns s1.ordinal() - s2.ordinal()
int diff = s1.compareTo(s2);
if (diff > 0) {
    System.out.println(s1 + " occurs after " + s2);
} else {
    System.out.println(s1 + " occurs before " + s2);
}
```

Table 22-1. *List of Methods in the Enum Class That Are Available in All Enum Types*

Method Name	Description
`public final String name()`	Returns the name of the enum constant exactly as declared in the enum type declaration.
`public final int ordinal()`	Returns the order (or position) of the enum constant as declared in the enum type declaration.
`public final boolean equals(Object other)`	Returns `true` if the specified object is equal to the enum constant. Otherwise, it returns `false`. Note that an enum type cannot be instantiated directly and it has a fixed number of instances, which are equal to the number of enum constants it declares. It implies that the `==` operator and the `equals()` method return the same result, when they are used on two enum constants.
`public final int hashCode()`	Returns the hash code value for an enum constant.
`public final int compareTo(E o)`	Compares the order of this enum constant with the order of the specified enum constant. It returns the difference in ordinal value of this enum constant and the specified enum constant. Note that to compare two enum constants, they must be of the same enum type. Otherwise, a runtime exception is thrown.
`public final Class<E> getDeclaringClass()`	Returns the `Class` object for the class that declares the enum constant. Two enum constants are considered to be of the same enum type if this method returns the same class object for both. Note that the `Class` object returned by the `getClass()` method, which every enum type inherits from the `Object` class, might not be the same as the class object returned by this method. When an enum constant has a body, the actual class of the object for that enum constant is not the same as the declaring class; actually, it is one of the subclasses of the declaring class.
`public String toString()`	By default, it returns the name of the enum constant, which is the same as the return value of the `name()` method. Note that this method is not declared final and hence you can override it to return a more meaningful string representation for each enum constant.
`public static <T extends Enum<T>> T valueOf(Class<T> enumType, String name)`	Returns an enum constant of the specified enum type and name. For example, you can use the following code to get the `LOW` enum constant value of the `Severity` enum type in your code: `Severity lowSeverity = Enum.valueOf(Severity.class, "LOW")`
`protected final Object clone() throws CloneNotSupportedException`	The Enum class redefines the `clone()` method. It declares the method final, so it cannot be overridden by any enum type. The method always throws an exception. This is done intentionally to prevent cloning of enum constants. This makes sure that only one set of enum constants exists for each enum type.
`protected final void finalize()`	The Enum class is declared final so that it cannot be overridden by any enum type. It provides an empty body. Since you cannot create an instance of an enum type, except its constants, it makes no sense to have a `finalize()` method for your enum type.

Using Enum Types in switch Statements

You can use enum types in switch statements. When the switch expression is of an enum type, all case labels must be unqualified enum constants of the same enum type. The switch statement deduces the enum type name from the type of its expression. You may include a default label.

Listing 22-6 contains a revised version of the DefectUtil class using a switch statement. Now you do not need to handle the exceptional case of receiving a null value in the severity parameter inside the getProjectedTurnaroundDays() method. If the enum expression of the switch statement evaluates to null, it throws a NullPointerException.

Listing 22-6. A Revised Version of the DefectUtil Class Using the Severity Enum

```
// DefectUtil.java
package com.jdojo.enums;

public class DefectUtil {
    public static int getProjectedTurnaroundDays(Severity severity) {
        int days = 0;
        switch (severity) {
            // Must use the unqualified name LOW, not Severity.LOW
            case LOW:
                days = 30;
                break;
            case MEDIUM:
                days = 15;
                break;
            case HIGH:
                days = 7;
                break;
            case URGENT:
                days = 1;
                break;
        }

        return days;
    }
}
```

Associating Data and Methods to Enum Constants

Generally, you declare an enum type just to have some enum constants, as you have done in the Severity enum type. Since an enum type is actually a class type, you can declare pretty much everything inside an enum type body that you can declare inside a class body. Let's associate one data element, projected turnaround days, with each of your Severity enum constants. You will name your enhanced Severity enum type SmartSeverity. Listing 22-7 contains the code for the SmartSeverity enum type, which is very different from the code for the Severity enum type.

Listing 22-7. A SmartSeverity enum Type Declaration That Uses Fields, Constructors, and Methods

```java
// SmartSeverity.java
package com.jdojo.enums;

public enum SmartSeverity {
    LOW(30), MEDIUM(15), HIGH(7), URGENT(1);

    // Declare an instance variable
    private int projectedTurnaroundDays;

    // Declare a private constructor
    private SmartSeverity(int projectedTurnaroundDays) {
        this.projectedTurnaroundDays = projectedTurnaroundDays;
    }

    // Declare a public method to get the turnaround days
    public int getProjectedTurnaroundDays() {
        return projectedTurnaroundDays;
    }
}
```

Let's discuss the new things that are in the SmartSeverity enum type.

- It declares an instance variable called projectedTurnaroundDays, which will store the value of the projected turnaround days for each enum constant.

  ```java
  // Declare an instance variable
  private int projectedTurnaroundDays;
  ```

- It defines a private constructor, which accepts an int parameter. It stores the value of its parameter in the instance variable. You can add multiple constructors to an enum type. If you do not add a constructor, a no-args constructor is added. You cannot add a public or protected constructor to an enum type. All constructors in an enum type declaration go through parameter and code transformations by the compiler and their access levels are changed to private. Many things are added or changed in the constructor of an enum type by the compiler. As a programmer, you do not need to know the details of the changes the compiler makes.

  ```java
  // Declare a private constructor
  private SmartSeverity(int projectedTurnaroundDays) {
      this.projectedTurnaroundDays = projectedTurnaroundDays;
  }
  ```

- It declares a public method getProjectedTurnaroundDays(), which returns the value of the projected turnaround days for an enum constant (or the instance of the enum type).

- The enum constant declarations have changed to LOW(30), MEDIUM(15), HIGH(7), URGENT(1); This change is not obvious. Now every enum constant name is followed by an integer value in parentheses, for example, LOW(30). This syntax is shorthand for calling the constructor with an int parameter type. When an enum constant is created, the value inside the parentheses will be passed to the constructor that you have added. By simply using the name of the enum constant (for example, LOW in the constant declaration), you invoke a default no-args constructor.

The program in Listing 22-8 tests the SmartSeverity enum type. It prints the names of the constants, their ordinals, and their projected turnaround days. Note that the logic to compute the projected turnaround days is encapsulated inside the declaration of the enum type itself. The SmartSeverity enum type combines the code for the Severity enum type and the getProjectedTurnaroundDays() method in the DefectUtil class. You do not have to write a switch statement anymore to get the projected turnaround days. Each enum constant knows about its projected turnaround days.

Listing 22-8. A Test Class to Test the SmartSeverity Enum Type

```
// SmartSeverityTest.java
package com.jdojo.enums;

public class SmartSeverityTest {
    public static void main(String[] args) {
        for (SmartSeverity s : SmartSeverity.values()) {
            String name = s.name();
            int ordinal = s.ordinal();
            int days = s.getProjectedTurnaroundDays();
            System.out.println("name=" + name + ", ordinal=" + ordinal
                    + ", days=" + days);
        }
    }
}
```

```
name=LOW, ordinal=0, days=30
name=MEDIUM, ordinal=1, days=15
name=HIGH, ordinal=2, days=7
name=URGENT, ordinal=3, days=1
```

Associating a Body to an Enum Constant

SmartSeverity is an example of adding data and methods to an enum type. The code in the getProjectedTurnaroundDays() method is the same for all enum constants. You can also associate a different body to each enum constant. The body can have fields and methods. The body for an enum constant is placed inside braces following its name. If the enum constant accepts arguments, its body follows its argument list. The syntax for associating a body to an enum constant is as follows:

```
[access-modifier] enum <enum-type-name> {
    CONST1 {
        // Body for CONST1 goes here
    },
    CONST2 {
        // Body for CONST2 goes here
    },
    CONST3(arguments-list) {
        // Body of CONST3 goes here
    };

    // Other code goes here
}
```

It is a little different game when you add a body to an enum constant. The compiler creates an anonymous class, which inherits from the enum type. It moves the body of the enum constant to the body of that anonymous class. Anonymous classes are covered in Chapter 2 of the second volume of this series. I use it briefly to complete the discussion of the enum type. For now, you can think of it just as a different way of declaring a class and, at the same time, creating objects of that class.

Consider an ETemp enum type, as shown:

```
public enum ETemp {
    C1 {
        // Body of constant C1
        public int getValue() {
            return 100;
        }
    },
    C2,
    C3;
}
```

The body of the ETemp enum type declares three constants: C1, C2, and C3. You have added a body to the C1 constant. The compiler will transform the code for ETemp into something like the following code:

```
public enum ETemp {
    public static final ETemp C1 = new ETemp() {
        // Body of constant C1
        public int getValue() {
            return 100;
        }
    };
    public static final ETemp C2 = new ETemp();
    public static final ETemp C3 = new ETemp();

    // Other code goes here
}
```

Note that the constant C1 is declared of type ETemp and assigned an object using an anonymous class. The ETemp enum type has no knowledge of the getValue() method defined in the anonymous class. Therefore, it is useless for all practical purposes because you cannot call the method as ETemp. C1.getValue().

To let the client code use the getValue() method, you must declare a getValue() method for the ETemp enum type. If you want all constants of ETemp to override and provide implementation for this method, you need to declare it as abstract. If you want it to be overridden by some, but not all, constants, you need to declare it non-abstract and provide a default implementation for it. The following code declares a getValue() method for the ETemp enum type, which returns 0.

```
public enum ETemp {
    C1 {
        // Body of constant C1
        public int getValue() {
            return 100;
        }
    },
```

```
    C2,
    C3;

    // Provide the default implementation for the getValue() method
    public int getValue() {
        return 0;
    }
}
```

The C1 constant has its body, which overrides the getValue() method and returns 100. Note that the constants C2 and C3 do not have to have a body; they do not need to override the getValue() method. Now, you can use the getValue() method on the ETemp enum type.

The following code rewrites the previous version of ETemp and declares the getValue() method abstract. An abstract method for an enum type forces you to provide a body for all constants and override that method. Now all constants have a body. The body of each constant overrides and provides implementation for the getValue() method.

```
public enum ETemp {
    C1 {
        // Body of constant C1
        public int getValue() {
            return 100;
        }
    },
    C2 {
        // Body of constant C2
        public int getValue() {
            return 0;
        }
    },
    C3 {
        // Body of constant C3
        public int getValue() {
            return 0;
        }
    };

    // Make the getValue() method abstract
    public abstract int getValue();
}
```

Let's enhance your SmartSeverity enum type. You are running out of good names for your enum type. You will name the new one SuperSmartSeverity. Listing 22-9 has the code.

Listing 22-9. Using a Body for Enum Constants

```
// SuperSmartSeverity.java
package com.jdojo.enums;

public enum SuperSmartSeverity {
    LOW("Low Priority", 30) {
        @Override
```

```java
        public double getProjectedCost() {
            return 1000.0;
        }
    },
    MEDIUM("Medium Priority", 15) {
        @Override
        public double getProjectedCost() {
            return 2000.0;
        }
    },
    HIGH("High Priority", 7) {
        @Override
        public double getProjectedCost() {
            return 3000.0;
        }
    },
    URGENT("Urgent Priority", 1) {
        @Override
        public double getProjectedCost() {
            return 5000.0;
        }
    };

    // Declare instance variables
    private final String description;
    private final int projectedTurnaroundDays;

    // Declare a private constructor
    private SuperSmartSeverity(String description,
            int projectedTurnaroundDays) {
        this.description = description;
        this.projectedTurnaroundDays = projectedTurnaroundDays;
    }

    // Declare a public method to get the turn around days
    public int getProjectedTurnaroundDays() {
        return projectedTurnaroundDays;
    }

    // Override the toString() method in the Enum class to return description
    @Override
    public String toString() {
        return this.description;
    }

    // Provide getProjectedCost() abstract method, so all constants
    // override and provide implementation for it in their body
    public abstract double getProjectedCost();
}
```

The following are new features in the SuperSmartSeverity enum type:

- It has added an abstract method getProjectedCost() to return the projected cost of each type of severity.

- It has a body for each constant that provides implementation for the getProjectedCost() method. Note that declaring an abstract method in an enum type forces you to provide a body for all its constants.

- It has added another parameter to the constructor, which is a nicer name for the severity type.

- It has overridden the toString() method in the Enum class. The toString() method in the Enum class returns the name of the constant. Your toString() method returns a brief and more intuitive name for each constant.

▦ **Tip**   Typically, you do not need to write this kind of complex code for an enum type. Java enum is very powerful. It has features for you to utilize, if you need them.

The code in Listing 22-10 demonstrates the use of the new features added to the SuperSmartSeverity enum type.

Listing 22-10. A Test Class to Test the SuperSmartSeverity Enum Type

```
// SuperSmartSeverityTest.java
package com.jdojo.enums;

public class SuperSmartSeverityTest {
    public static void main(String[] args) {
        for (SuperSmartSeverity s : SuperSmartSeverity.values()) {
            String name = s.name();
            String desc = s.toString();
            int ordinal = s.ordinal();
            int projectedTurnaroundDays = s.getProjectedTurnaroundDays();
            double projectedCost = s.getProjectedCost();
            System.out.println("name=" + name
                    + ", description=" + desc
                    + ", ordinal=" + ordinal
                    + ", turnaround days="
                    + projectedTurnaroundDays
                    + ", projected cost=" + projectedCost);
        }
    }
}
```

```
name=LOW, description=Low Priority, ordinal=0, turnaround days=30, projected cost=1000.0
name=MEDIUM, description=Medium Priority, ordinal=1, turnaround days=15, projected cost=2000.0
name=HIGH, description=High Priority, ordinal=2, turnaround days=7, projected cost=3000.0
name=URGENT, description=Urgent Priority, ordinal=3, turnaround days=1, projected cost=5000.0
```

Comparing Two Enum Constants

You can compare two enum constants in three ways:

- Using the compareTo() method of the Enum class
- Using the equals() method of the Enum class
- Using the == operator

The compareTo() method of the Enum class lets you compare two enum constants of the same enum type. It returns the difference in ordinal for the two enum constants. If both enum constants are the same, it returns zero. The following snippet of code will print -3 because the difference of the ordinals for LOW(ordinal=0) and URGENT(ordinal=3) is -3. A negative value means the constant being compared occurs before the one being compared against.

```
Severity s1 = Severity.LOW;
Severity s2 = Severity.URGENT;
int diff = s1.compareTo(s2);
System.out.println(diff);
```

```
-3
```

Suppose you have another enum called BasicColor, as shown in Listing 22-11.

Listing 22-11. A BasicColor Enum

```
// BasicColor.java
package com.jdojo.enums;

public enum BasicColor {
    RED, GREEN, BLUE;
}
```

The following snippet of code will not compile because it tries to compare the two enum constants, which belong to different enum types:

```
int diff = BasicColor.RED.compareTo(Severity.URGENT); // A compile-time error
```

You can use the equals() method of the Enum class to compare two enum constants for equality. An enum constant is equal only to itself. Note that the equals() method can be invoked on two enum constants of different types. If the two enum constants are from different enum types, the method returns false.

```
Severity s1 = Severity.LOW;
Severity s2 = Severity.URGENT;
BasicColor c = BasicColor.BLUE;
System.out.println(s1.equals(s1));
System.out.println(s1.equals(s2));
System.out.println(s1.equals(c));
```

```
true
false
false
```

You can also use the equality operator (==) to compare two enum constants for equality. Both operands to the == operator must be of the same enum type. Otherwise, you get a compile-time error.

```
Severity s1 = Severity.LOW;
Severity s2 = Severity.URGENT;
BasicColor c = BasicColor.BLUE;
System.out.println(s1 == s1);
System.out.println(s1 == s2);

// A compile-time error. Cannot compare Severity and BasicColor enum types
//System.out.println(s1 == c);
```

```
true
false
```

Nested Enum Types

You can have a nested enum type declaration. You can declare a nested enum type inside a class, an interface, or another enum type. Nested enum types are implicitly static. You can also declare a nested enum type static explicitly in its declaration. Since an enum type is always static, whether you declare it or not, you cannot declare a local enum type (e.g., inside a method's body). You can use any of the access modifiers (public, private, protected, or package) levels for a nested enum type. Listing 22-12 shows the code that declares a nested public enum type named Gender inside a Person class.

Listing 22-12. A Gender Enum Type as a Nested Enum Type Inside a Person Class

```
// Person.java
package com.jdojo.enums;

public class Person {
    public enum Gender {MALE, FEMALE}
}
```

The Person.Gender enum type can be accessed from anywhere in the same module because it has been declared public. Accessing it in other modules depends on module accessibility rules. You need to import the enum type to use its simple name in other packages, as shown in the following code:

```
// Test.java
package com.jdojo.enums.pkg1;

import com.jdojo.enums.Person.Gender;

public class Test {
    public static void main(String[] args) {
```

```
        Gender m = Gender.MALE;
        Gender f = Gender.FEMALE;
        System.out.println(m);
        System.out.println(f);
    }
}
```

MALE
FEMALE

You can also use the simple name of an enum constant by importing the enum constants using static imports. The following code snippet uses MALE and FEMALE, which are simple names of constants of the Person.Gender enum type. Note that the first import statement is needed to import the Gender type itself to use its simple name in the code.

```
// Test.java
package com.jdojo.enums.pkg1;

import com.jdojo.enums.Person.Gender;
import static com.jdojo.enums.Person.Gender.*;

public class Test {
    public static void main(String[] args) {
        Gender m = MALE;
        Gender f = FEMALE;
        System.out.println(m);
        System.out.println(f);
    }
}
```

MALE
FEMALE

You can also nest an enum type inside another enum type or an interface. The following are valid enum type declarations:

```
public enum OuterEnum {
    C1, C2, C3;

    public enum NestedEnum {
        C4, C5, C6;
    }
}

public interface MyInterface {
    int operation1();
    int operation2();
```

```
    public enum AnotherNestedEnum {
        CC1, CC2, CC3;
    }
}
```

Implementing an Interface to an Enum Type

An enum type may implement interfaces. The rules for an enum type implementing an interface are
the same as the rules for a class implementing an interface. An enum type is never inherited by another
enum type. Therefore, you cannot declare an enum type as abstract. This also implies that if an enum type
implements an interface, it must also provide implementation for all abstract methods in that interface. The
program in Listing 22-13 declares a Command interface.

Listing 22-13. A Command Interface

```
// Command.java
package com.jdojo.enums;

public interface Command {
    void execute();
}
```

The program in Listing 22-14 declares an enum type called CommandList that implements the Command
interface. Each enum constant implements the execute() method of the Command interface. Alternatively,
you can implement the execute() method in the enum type body and omit the implementations from some
or all enum constants. Listing 22-15 demonstrates using the enum constants in the CommandList enum type
as Command type.

Listing 22-14. A CommandList Enum Type Implementing the Command Interface

```
// CommandList.java
package com.jdojo.enums;

public enum CommandList implements Command {
    RUN {
        @Override
        public void execute() {
            System.out.println("Running...");
        }
    },
    JUMP {
        @Override
        public void execute() {
            System.out.println("Jumping...");
        }
    };

    // Force all constants to implement the execute() method.
    @Override
    public abstract void execute();
}
```

Listing 22-15. Using the CommandList Enum Constants as Command Types

```java
// CommandTest.java
package com.jdojo.enums;

public class CommandTest {
    public static void main(String... args) {
        // Execute all commands in the command list
        for(Command cmd : CommandList.values()) {
            cmd.execute();
        }
    }
}
```

```
Running...
Jumping...
```

Reverse Lookup for Enum Constants

You can get the reference of an enum constant if you know its name or position in the list. This is known as *reverse lookup* based on the name or ordinal of an enum constant. You can use the valueOf() method, which is added by the compiler to an enum type, to perform reverse lookup based on a name. You can use the array returned by the values() method, which is added by the compiler to an enum type, to perform reverse lookup by ordinal. The order of the values in the array that is returned by values() method is the same as the order in which the enum constants are declared. The ordinal of enum constants starts at zero. This implies that the ordinal value of an enum constant can be used as an index in the array that is returned by the values() method. The following snippet of code demonstrates how to reverse look up enum constants:

```java
Severity low1 = Severity.valueOf("LOW"); // A reverse lookup using a name
Severity low2 = Severity.values()[0];    // A reverse lookup using an ordinal
System.out.println(low1);
System.out.println(low2);
System.out.println(low1 == low2);
```

```
LOW
LOW
true
```

The reverse lookup for enum constants is case-sensitive. If you use an invalid constant name with the valueOf() method, an IllegalArgumentException is thrown. For example, Severity.valueOf("low") will throw an IllegalArgumentException stating that no enum constant called "low" exists in the Severity enum.

Range of Enum Constants

The Java API provides a java.util.EnumSet collection class to work with ranges of enum constants of an enum type. The implementation of the EnumSet class is very efficient. Suppose you have an enum type called Day, as shown in Listing 22-16.

Listing 22-16. A Day Enum Type

```java
// Day.java
package com.jdojo.enums;

public enum Day {
    MONDAY, TUESDAY, WEDNESDAY, THURSDAY, FRIDAY, SATURDAY, SUNDAY;
}
```

You can work with a range of days using the EnumSet class; for example, you can get all days between MONDAY and FRIDAY. An EnumSet can contain enum constants only from one enum type. Listing 22-17 demonstrates how to use the EnumSet class to work with the range for enum constants.

Listing 22-17. A Test Class to Demonstrate How to Use the EnumSet Class

```java
// EnumSetTest.java
package com.jdojo.enums;

import java.util.EnumSet;

public class EnumSetTest {
    public static void main(String[] args) {
        // Get all constants of the Day enum
        EnumSet<Day> allDays = EnumSet.allOf(Day.class);
        print(allDays, "All days: ");

        // Get all constants from MONDAY to FRIDAY of the Day enum
        EnumSet<Day> weekDays = EnumSet.range(Day.MONDAY, Day.FRIDAY);
        print(weekDays, "Weekdays: ");

        // Get all constants that are not from MONDAY to FRIDAY of the Day enum.
        // Essentially, we will get days representing weekends.
        EnumSet<Day> weekends = EnumSet.complementOf(weekDays);
        print(weekends, "Weekends: ");
    }

    public static void print(EnumSet<Day> days, String msg) {
        System.out.print(msg);
        for (Day d : days) {
            System.out.print(d + " ");
        }
        System.out.println();
    }
}
```

```
All days: MONDAY TUESDAY WEDNESDAY THURSDAY FRIDAY SATURDAY SUNDAY
Weekdays: MONDAY TUESDAY WEDNESDAY THURSDAY FRIDAY
Weekends: SATURDAY SUNDAY
```

Summary

Like a class and an interface, an enum defines a new reference type in Java. An enum type consists of a pre-defined, ordered set of values, which are known as the elements or constants of the enum type. Constants of the enum type have a name and an ordinal. You can obtain the reference of an enum constant using its name and ordinal, and vice versa. Typically, an enum type is used to define type-safe constants.

An enum type has several things that a class has. It has constructors, instance variables, and methods. However, the constructors of an enum type are implicitly private. An enum type can also implement interfaces just as a class can.

You can declare a variable of the enum type. The variable can be assigned null or one of the constants of the enum type. Every enum type is implicitly inherited from the java.lang.Enum class. An enum type can implement interfaces. An enum type can be used in the switch statement. Java provides an efficient implementation of an EnumSet class to work with a range of enum constants of a specific enum type.

QUESTIONS AND EXERCISES

1. What are enum types in Java?

2. What is the superclass of all enums in Java?

3. Can an enum in Java extend another enum?

4. Can an enum in Java implement one or more interfaces?

5. Is the following enum declaration valid? If yes, how many enum constants does it declare?

```
public enum Gender {
    MALE, FEMALE,
}
```

6. Consider the following declaration for an enum named Day.

```
public enum Day {
    MONDAY, TUESDAY, WEDNESDAY, THURSDAY, FRIDAY, SATURDAY, SUNDAY;
}
```

Given a string "FRIDAY", how will you look up the Day.FRIDAY enum constant?

7. Consider the following declaration for an enum named Day.

```
public enum Day {
    MONDAY, TUESDAY, WEDNESDAY, THURSDAY, FRIDAY, SATURDAY, SUNDAY;
}
```

How will you look up the ordinal for Day.SUNDAY?

8. Consider the following declaration for an enum named Day.

```
public enum Day {
    MONDAY, TUESDAY, WEDNESDAY, THURSDAY, FRIDAY, SATURDAY, SUNDAY;
}
```

Complete the following snippet of code that will print the ordinal of TUESDAY from the Day enum. It should print 1.

```
String dayName = "TUESDAY";
int ordinal = /* Complete this statement. */;
System.out.println(ordinal);
```

9. Consider the following declaration for an enum named Day.

```
public enum Day {
    MONDAY, TUESDAY, WEDNESDAY, THURSDAY, FRIDAY, SATURDAY, SUNDAY;
}
```

Use a for-each loop to print the name of each day with its ordinal, like MONDAY(0), TUESDAY(1), etc.

10. Write the output for the following snippet of code.

```
public enum Day {
    MONDAY, TUESDAY, WEDNESDAY, THURSDAY, FRIDAY, SATURDAY, SUNDAY;
}

EnumSet<Day> es = EnumSet.range(Day.TUESDAY, Day.FRIDAY);
for(Day d : es) {
    System.out.printf("%s(%d)%n", d.name(), d.ordinal());
}
```

11. Write the output for the following snippet of code.

```
public enum Day {
    MONDAY, TUESDAY, WEDNESDAY, THURSDAY, FRIDAY, SATURDAY, SUNDAY;
}

EnumSet<Day> es =
    EnumSet.complementOf(EnumSet.range(Day.TUESDAY, Day.FRIDAY));
for(Day d : es) {
    System.out.printf("%s(%d)%n", d.name(), d.ordinal());
}
```

12. Consider the following declaration for an enum named Country.

```
public enum Country {
    BHUTAN("Bhutan", "BT"),
    BRAZIL("Brazil", "BR"),
    FIJI("Fiji", "FJ"),
    INDIA("India", "IN"),
    SPAIN("Spain", "ES");

    private final String fullName;
    private final String isoName;
```

```
        private Country(String fullName, String isoName) {
            this.fullName = fullName;
            this.isoName = isoName;
        }

        public String fullName() {
            return this.fullName;
        }

        public String isoName() {
            return this.isoName;
        }

        @Override
        public String toString() {
            return this.fullName;
        }
    }
```

Write the output when the following snippet of code is executed:

```
for(Country c : Country.values()) {
    System.out.printf("%s[%d, %s, %s]%n",
            c.name(), c.ordinal(), c, c.isoName());
}
```

13. Consider the following declaration for a Gender enum:

```
public enum Gender {
    MALE, FEMALE
}
```

Modify the code for the Gender enum, so that the output of the following snippet of code is as shown in the expected output section that follows the code. You are supposed to change the code for the Gender enum, not the following snippet of code.

```
for(Gender c : Gender.values()) {
    System.out.printf("%s%n", c);
}
```

Expected output:

```
Male
female
```

14. Suppose Color is an enum. Is the following declaration of a MyFavColor enum valid? If not, explain your answer.

```
public enum MyFavColor extends Color {
    WHITE, BLACK
}
```

15. What will the output be when the following snippet of code is run?

```
public enum Day {
    MONDAY, TUESDAY, WEDNESDAY, THURSDAY, FRIDAY, SATURDAY, SUNDAY;
}

Day[] days = {Day.FRIDAY, Day.MONDAY, Day.WEDNESDAY};
System.out.println(Arrays.toString(days));
Arrays.sort(days);
System.out.println(Arrays.toString(days));
```

16. What will the output of the following snippet of code be?

```
public enum Gender {
    MALE, FEMALE
}

System.out.println(Gender.MALE == Gender.MALE);
System.out.println(Gender.MALE.equals(Gender.MALE));
```

CHAPTER 23

Java Shell

In this chapter, you will learn:

- What the Java shell is

- What the JShell tool and the JShell API are

- How to configure the JShell tool

- How to use the JShell tool to evaluate snippets of Java code

- How to use the JShell API to evaluate snippets of Java code

All example programs in this chapter are a member of a jdojo.jshell module, as declared in Listing 23-1.

Listing 23-1. The Declaration of a jdojo.jshell Module

```
// module-info.java
module jdojo.jshell {
    exports com.jdojo.jshell;

    requires jdk.jshell;
}
```

Before you begin reading this chapter, let me clarify the usage of the following three phrases that are used frequently in this chapter:

- The JShell command-line tool or the JShell tool

- jshell

- The JShell API

In this chapter, the main topic of discussion is JShell, which can be used as a command-line tool and as a Java API. "The JShell command-line tool" refers to the capability of JShell being used as a command-line tool. The JShell command-line tool is named jshell (all lowercase), which is installed as a jshell.exe file in the JDK_HOME\bin directory, when you install JDK 9 on Windows. "The JShell API" refers to the capability of JShell as a Java API.

© Kishori Sharan 2017
K. Sharan, *Beginning Java 9 Fundamentals*, https://doi.org/10.1007/978-1-4842-2902-6_23

What Is the Java Shell?

The Java shell, which is called JShell in JDK 9, is a command-line tool that provides an interactive way to access the Java programming language. It lets you evaluate snippets of Java code instead of forcing you to write an entire Java program. It is a REPL (Read-Eval-Print loop) for Java. JShell is also an API that you can use to develop an application to provide the same functionality as the JShell command-line tool.

Read-**E**val-**P**rint loop (REPL) is a command-line tool (also known as interactive language shell) that lets users evaluate snippets of code quickly without having to write a complete program. The name REPL comes from the three primitive functions in Lisp—read, eval, and print—used in a loop. The read function reads the user input and parses into a data structure; the eval function evaluates the parsed user input to yield a result; the print function prints the result. After the result is printed, the tool is ready to accept user input again, hence triggering a read-eval-print loop. The term REPL is used for an interactive tool that lets you interact with a programming language. Figure 23-1 shows a conceptual diagram for a REPL. A UNIX shell or a Windows command prompt acts like a REPL that reads an operating system command, executes it, prints the output, and waits to read another command.

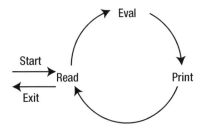

Figure 23-1. *A conceptual diagram for a read-eval-print loop*

Why was JShell included in JDK 9? One of the main reasons to include it in JDK 9 was the feedback from academia that Java has a steep learning curve. Other programming languages such as Lisp, Python, Ruby, Groovy, and Clojure have been supporting REPL for a long time. Just to write a "Hello, world!" program in Java, you have to resort to an Edit-Compile-Execute loop (ECEL) that involves writing a full program, compiling it, and execute it. If you need to make a change, you must repeat these steps. Apart from some other housekeeping work such as defining the directory structure, compiling, and executing the program, the following is the minimum you have to write to print a "Hello, world!" message using the modular Java program in JDK 9:

```
// module-info.java
module HelloWorld {
}


// HelloWorld.java
package com.jdojo.intro;

public class HelloWorld {
    public static void main(String[] args) {
        System.out.println("Hello, world!");
    }
}
```

This program, when executed, prints a message on the console: "Hello, world!". Writing a full program to evaluate a simple expression such as this is overkill. This was the main reason academia was moving away from teaching Java as the initial programming language to students. Java designers listened to the feedback from teaching communities and introduced the JShell tool in JDK 9. To achieve the same as this program, you need to write only one line of code on a `jshell` command prompt:

```
jshell> System.out.println("Hello, world!")
Hello, world!

jshell>
```

The first line is the code you enter on the `jshell` command prompt; the second line is the output. After printing the output, the `jshell` prompt returns and you can enter another Java expression to evaluate.

▓ **Tip** JShell is not a new language or a new compiler. It is a tool and an API used to access the Java programming language interactively. For beginners, it provides a way to explore the Java programming language quickly. For experienced developers, it provides a quick way to see results of a code snippet without having to compile and run an entire program. It also provides a way to quickly develop a prototype using an incremental approach. You add a snippet of code, get immediate feedback, and add another snippet of code until your prototype is complete.

JDK 9 ships with a JShell command-line tool and the `JShell` API. All features supported by the tool are also supported by the API. That is, you can run snippets of code using the tool or programmatically using the API. You should be able to distinguish between the two using the context in this discussion. Most of the chapter is devoted to explaining the tool. At the end, I include a section describing the API with an example.

The JShell Architecture

The Java compiler does not recognize snippets such as method declarations or variable declarations by themselves. Only classes and `import` statements can be top-level constructs, which can exist by themselves. Other types of snippets have to be part of a class. JShell lets you execute snippets of Java code and lets you evolve them.

The guiding principle for the current JShell architecture is to use the existing Java language support and other Java technologies in the JDK to keep it compatible with the current and future versions of the language. As the Java language evolves over time, so will its support in JShell with little or no modification to the JShell implementation. Figure 23-2 shows the high-level architecture of JShell.

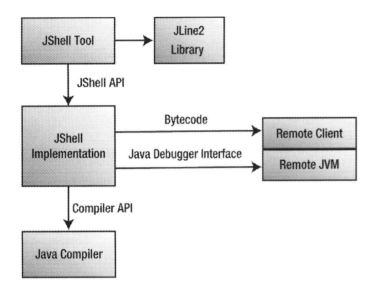

Figure 23-2. *The JShell architecture*

The JShell tool uses version 2 of JLine, which is a Java library for handling console input. The standard JDK compiler does not know how to parse and compile snippets of Java code. Therefore, the JShell implementation has its own parser that parses snippets and determines the type of snippets, for example, a method declaration, a variable declaration, etc. Once the snippet type is determined, the snippet is wrapped in a synthetic class using the following rules:

- Import statements are used "as-is". That is, all `import` statements are placed "as-is" at the top of the synthetic class.

- Variables, methods, and class declarations become static members of a synthetic class.

- Expressions and statements are wrapped in a synthetic method of a synthetic class.

All synthetic classes belong to a package called REPL. Once snippets are wrapped, the wrapped source code is analyzed and compiled by standard Java compiler using the Compiler API. The compiler takes the wrapped source code in string format as input and compiles it into bytecode, which is stored in memory. The generated bytecode is sent over a socket to a remote process running a JVM for loading and execution. Sometimes, existing snippets loaded into the remote JVM need to be replaced by the JShell tool, which it accomplishes using the Java Debugger API.

Starting the JShell Tool

JDK 9 ships with a JShell tool, which is located in the `JDK_HOME\bin` directory. The tool is named `jshell`. If you installed JDK 9 in the `C:\java9` directory on Windows, you will have an executable file named `C:\java9\bin\jshell.exe`, which is the JShell tool. To start the JShell tool, you need to open a command prompt and enter the `jshell` command:

```
C:\Java9Fundamentals>jshell
|  Welcome to JShell -- Version 9
|  For an introduction type: /help intro

jshell>
```

Entering the jshell command on the command prompt may give you an error:

```
C:\Java9Fundamentals>jshell
'jshell' is not recognized as an internal or external command,
operable program or batch file.

C:\Java9Fundamentals>
```

This error indicates that the JDK_HOME\bin directory is not included in the PATH environment variable on your computer. I installed JDK 9 in the C:\java9 directory, so the JDK_HOME is C:\java9 for me. To fix this error, you either include the C:\java9\bin directory in the PATH environment variable or use the full path of the jshell command, which would be C:\java9\bin\jshell for me. The following sequence of commands show you how to set the PATH environment variable on Windows and run the JShell tool:

```
C:\Java9Fundamentals>SET PATH=C:\java9\bin;%PATH%
C:\Java9Fundamentals>jshell
|  Welcome to JShell -- Version 9
|  For an introduction type: /help intro

jshell>
```

The following command shows you how to use the full path of the jshell command to launch the tool:

```
C:\Java9Fundamentals>C:\java9\bin\jshell
|  Welcome to JShell -- Version 9
|  For an introduction type: /help intro

jshell>
```

When jshell is launched successfully, it prints a welcome message with its version information. It also prints the command, which is /help intro. You can use this command to print a short introduction to the tool itself:

```
jshell> /help intro
|
|  intro
|
|  The jshell tool allows you to execute Java code, getting immediate results.
|  You can enter a Java definition (variable, method, class, etc), like:  int x = 8
|  or a Java expression, like:  x + x
|  or a Java statement or import.
|  These little chunks of Java code are called 'snippets'.
|
|  There are also jshell commands that allow you to understand and
|  control what you are doing, like:  /list
|
|  For a list of commands: /help

jshell>
```

If you need help on the tool, you can enter the command /help on jshell to print a list of commands with their short descriptions:

```
jshell> /help
<The output is not shown here.>

jshell>
```

▓ **Tip** NetBeans has integrated supported for the JShell tool. You can open the JShell prompt from within the NetBeans IDE by choosing the Tools ➤ Open Java Platform Shell menu. NetBeans JShell prompt offers you all the features of the jshell command-line tool and a lot more—all using UI options. For example, NetBeans lets you save all your code snippets as a class using its Save to Class toolbar option. It also lets you auto-complete your code as it does in a normal Java editor.

You can use several command-line options with the jshell command to pass values to the tool itself. For example, you can pass values to the compiler used to parse and compile snippets and to the remote JVM used to execute/evaluate snippet. Run the jshell program with a --help option to see a list of all available standard options. Run it with a --help-extra or -X option to see a list of all available non-standard options. For example, using these options, you can set class path and module path for the JShell tool. I explain these options later in this chapter.

You can also customize the startup scripts for the jshell tool using the command-line --start option. You can use DEFAULT and PRINTING as arguments to this option. The DEFAULT argument starts jshell with several import statements, so you do not need to import commonly used classes while you use jshell. The following two commands launch the jshell the same way:

- jshell

- jshell --start DEFAULT

You can use System.out.println() method to print messages to the standard output. You can launch jshell using the --start option with a PRINTING argument, which will include all versions of the System.out.print(), System.out.println(), and System.out.printf() methods as print(), println(), and printf() top-level methods. This will allow you to use print(), println(), and printf() methods on jshell instead of their longer versions, System.out.print(), System.out.println(), and System.out.printf().

```
C:\Java9Fundamentals>jshell --start PRINTING
|  Welcome to JShell -- Version 9
|  For an introduction type: /help intro

jshell> println("hello")
hello

jshell>
```

You can repeat the --start option when you launch jshell to include the default import statements and the printing methods:

```
C:\Java9Fundamentals>jshell --start DEFAULT --start PRINTING
|  Welcome to JShell -- Version 9
|  For an introduction type: /help intro

jshell>
```

Exiting the JShell Tool

To exit jshell, enter /exit on the jshell prompt and press Enter. The command prints a goodbye message, exits the tool, and returns you to the command prompt:

```
C:\Java9Fundamentals>jshell
|  Welcome to JShell -- Version 9
|  For an introduction type: /help intro

jshell> /exit
|  Goodbye

C:\Java9Fundamentals>
```

The JShell tool is forgiving in a number of ways. If you use a keyword in a Java construct that is not supported, it simply ignores it. You can use partial commands. If the partial command you entered can be auto-completed to a unique command name, the tool would work as if you entered the full command. For example, /edit and /exit are two commands starting with /e. If you enter /ex instead of /exit, jshell will interpret it as an /exit command for you.

```
jshell> /ex
|  Goodbye

C:\Java9Fundamentals>
```

If you enter /e, you will receive an error because there are multiple possible commands starting with /e:

```
jshell> /e
|  Command: '/e' is ambiguous: /edit, /exit, /env
|  Type /help for help.

jshell>
```

What Are Snippets and Commands?

You can use the JShell tool to:

- Evaluate snippets of Java code, which are simply called *snippets* in JShell terminology.

- Execute commands, which are used to query the JShell state and set the JShell environment.

To distinguish commands from snippets, all commands start with a slash (/). You have already seen a few of them in previous sections such as /exit and /help. Commands are used to interact with the tool itself, such as to customize its output, print help, exit the tool, and print the history of commands and snippets. I explain more commands later. If you are interested in learning all the available commands, use the /help command.

Using the JShell tool, you write a fragment of Java code at a time and evaluate it. Those fragments of code are known as *snippets*. Snippets must follow the syntax specified in the Java Language Specification. Snippets can be:

- Import declarations

- Class declarations

- Interface declarations

- Method declarations

- Field declarations

- Statements

- Expressions

░ **Tip** You can use all Java language constructs in JShell, except for package declarations. All snippets in a JShell occur in an internal package named REPL and inside an internal synthetic class.

The JShell tool knows when you are done entering a snippet. When you press Enter, the tool will either execute the snippet if it is complete or take you to the next line and wait for you to complete the snippet. If a line begins with ...>, it means the snippet is not complete and you need to enter more text to complete the snippet. The default prompt for more input, which is ...>, can be customized. Here are a few examples:

```
C:\Java9Fundamentals>jshell
|  Welcome to JShell -- Version 9
|  For an introduction type: /help intro

jshell> 2 + 2
$1 ==> 4

jshell> 2 +
   ...> 2
$2 ==> 4

jshell> 2
$3 ==> 2

jshell>
```

When you enter 2 + 2 and press Enter, jshell considers it as a complete snippet (an expression). It evaluates the expression and prints feedback that the expression was evaluated to 4 and the result was assigned to a variable named $1. The variable named $1 was automatically generated by the tool. I explain variables generated by tools in more detail later. When you enter 2 + and press Enter, jshell prompts you to enter more input because 2 + is not a complete snippet in Java. When you enter 2 on the second line, the snippet is complete; jshell evaluates the snippet and prints feedback. When you enter 2 and press Enter, jshell evaluates the snippet because 2 is a complete expression by itself.

Evaluating Expressions

You can execute any valid Java expression in jshell. The following examples evaluate two expressions that add and multiply numbers:

```
jshell> 2 + 2
$1 ==> 4

jshell> 9.0 * 6
$2 ==> 54.0
```

When you evaluate an expression, jshell prints feedback if the expression evaluates to a value. In these cases, 2 + 2 evaluates to 4 and 9.0 * 6 evaluates to 54.0. The value of an expression is assigned to a variable. The feedback contains the name of the variable and the value of the expressions. In the first case, the feedback $1 ==> 4 means that the expression 2 + 2 evaluated to 4 and the result was assigned to a variable named $1. Similarly, the expression 9.0 * 6 was evaluated to 54.0 and the value was assigned to a variable named $2. You can use these variable names in other expressions. You can print their values by simply entering their names:

```
jshell> $1
$1 ==> 4

jshell> $2
$2 ==> 54.0

jshell> System.out.println($1)
4

jshell> System.out.println($2)
54.0
```

■ **Tip** In jshell, you do not need to terminate a statement with a semicolon as you must do in a Java program. The tool will insert the missing semicolons for you.

In Java, every variable has a data type. In these examples, what are the data types of the variables named $1 and $2? In Java, 2 + 2 evaluates to an int and 9.0 * 6 evaluates to a double. Therefore, the data types for the $1 and $2 variables should be int and double, respectively. How do you verify this? Let's first do it the hard way. You can cast $1 and $2 to an Object and invoke the getClass() method on them, which should give you Integer and Double. Note that primitive values of int and double types are boxed to Integer and Double reference types in these examples when you cast them as an Object:

```
jshell> 2 + 2
$1 ==> 4

jshell> 9.0 * 6
$2 ==> 54.0

jshell> ((Object)$1).getClass()
$3 ==> class java.lang.Integer
```

929

```
jshell> ((Object)$2).getClass()
$4 ==> class java.lang.Double

jshell>
```

There is an easier way to determine the data type of variables created by jshell—you just tell jshell to give you verbose feedback and it will print the data type of the variables it creates and much more! The following commands set the feedback mode to verbose and evaluate the same expressions:

```
jshell> /set feedback verbose
|  Feedback mode: verbose

jshell> 2 + 2
$1 ==> 4
|  created scratch variable $1 : int

jshell> 9.0 * 6
$2 ==> 54.0
|  created scratch variable $2 : double

jshell>
```

Notice that jshell printed the data types of the variables named $1 and $2 as int and double, respectively. It will be helpful for beginners to execute the following command using a -retain option, so the verbose feedback mode *persists* across the jshell sessions:

```
jshell> /set feedback -retain verbose
```

You can also use the /vars command to list all variables defined in jshell:

```
jshell> /vars
|    int $1 = 4
|    double $2 = 54.0

jshell>
```

If you want to use the normal feedback mode again, use the following command:

```
jshell> /set feedback -retain normal
|  Feedback mode: normal

Jshell>
```

You are not limited to evaluating simple expressions such as 2 + 2. You can evaluate any Java expression. The following example evaluates string concatenation expressions and uses methods of the String class. It also shows you how to use for loops:

```
jshell> "Hello " + "world! " + 2017
$1 ==> "Hello world! 2017"

jshell> $1.length()
$2 ==> 17
```

```
jshell> $1.toUpperCase()
$3 ==> "HELLO WORLD! 2017"

jshell> $1.split(" ")
$4 ==> String[3] { "Hello", "world!", "2017" }

jshell> for(String s : $4) {
   ...>      System.out.println(s);
   ...> }
Hello
world!
2017

Jshell>
```

Listing Snippets

Whatever you enter in jshell ends up being part of a snippet. Every snippet is assigned a unique snippet ID, which you can use to refer to the snippet later, for example, to drop the snippet. The /list command lists all snippets. It has the following forms:

- /list
- /list -all
- /list -start
- /list <snippet-name>
- /list <snippet-id>

The /list command without an argument/option prints all user-entered, active snippets, which may also have been opened from a file using the /open command.

Use the -all option to list all snippets—active, inactive, erroneous, and startup.

Use the -start option to list only the startup snippets. The startup snippets are cached and the -start option prints the cached snippets. It prints startup snippets even if you have dropped them in the current session.

Some of the snippet types have a name (e.g., variable/method declarations) and all snippets have an ID. Using the name or ID of a snippet with the /list command prints the snippet identified by that name or ID. The /list command prints a list of snippets in the following format:

```
<snippet-id> : <snippet-source-code>
<snippet-id> : <snippet-source-code>
<snippet-id> : <snippet-source-code>
...
```

The JShell tool generates unique snippet IDs. They are s1, s2, s3... for startup snippets, 1, 2, 3..., and so on for valid snippets, and e1, e2, e3... for erroneous snippets. The following jshell session shows you how to list snippets using the /list command. The examples use the /drop command to drop snippets using a snippet name as well as a snippet ID.

```
C:\Java9Fundamentals>jshell
|  Welcome to JShell -- Version 9
|  For an introduction type: /help intro
```

```
jshell> /list

jshell> 2 + 2
$1 ==> 4

jshell> /list

   1 : 2 + 2

jshell> int x = 100
x ==> 100

jshell> /list

   1 : 2 + 2
   2 : int x = 100;

jshell> /list -all

   s1 : import java.io.*;
   s2 : import java.math.*;
   s3 : import java.net.*;
   s4 : import java.nio.file.*;
   s5 : import java.util.*;
   s6 : import java.util.concurrent.*;
   s7 : import java.util.function.*;
   s8 : import java.util.prefs.*;
   s9 : import java.util.regex.*;
  s10 : import java.util.stream.*;
    1 : 2 + 2
    2 : int x = 100;

jshell> /list -start

   s1 : import java.io.*;
   s2 : import java.math.*;
   s3 : import java.net.*;
   s4 : import java.nio.file.*;
   s5 : import java.util.*;
   s6 : import java.util.concurrent.*;
   s7 : import java.util.function.*;
   s8 : import java.util.prefs.*;
   s9 : import java.util.regex.*;
  s10 : import java.util.stream.*;

jshell> string str = "String type is misspelled as string"
|  Error:
|  cannot find symbol
|    symbol:   class string
|  string str = "String type is misspelled as string";
|  ^----^
```

```
jshell> /list

   1 : 2 + 2
   2 : int x = 100;

jshell> /list -all

  s1 : import java.io.*;
  s2 : import java.math.*;
  s3 : import java.net.*;
  s4 : import java.nio.file.*;
  s5 : import java.util.*;
  s6 : import java.util.concurrent.*;
  s7 : import java.util.function.*;
  s8 : import java.util.prefs.*;
  s9 : import java.util.regex.*;
 s10 : import java.util.stream.*;
   1 : 2 + 2
   2 : int x = 100;
  e1 : string str = "String type is misspelled as string";

jshell> /drop 1
|  dropped variable $1

jshell> /list

   2 : int x = 100;

jshell> /drop x
|  dropped variable x

jshell> /list

jshell> /list -all

  s1 : import java.io.*;
  s2 : import java.math.*;
  s3 : import java.net.*;
  s4 : import java.nio.file.*;
  s5 : import java.util.*;
  s6 : import java.util.concurrent.*;
  s7 : import java.util.function.*;
  s8 : import java.util.prefs.*;
  s9 : import java.util.regex.*;
 s10 : import java.util.stream.*;
   1 : 2 + 2
   2 : int x = 100;
  e1 : string str = "String type is misspelled as string";

jshell> /exit
|  Goodbye
```

933

The names of variables, methods, and classes become the snippet names. Note that Java allows you to have a variable, a method, and a class with the same name because they occur in their own namespaces. You can use the names of these entities to list them using the /list command:

```
C:\Java9Fundamentals>jshell
|  Welcome to JShell -- Version 9
|  For an introduction type: /help intro

jshell> /list x
|  No such snippet: x

jshell> int x = 100
x ==> 100

jshell> /list x

   1 : int x = 100;

jshell> void x() {}
|  created method x()

jshell> /list x

   1 : int x = 100;
   2 : void x() {}

jshell> void x(int n) {}
|  created method x(int)

jshell> /list x
   1 : int x = 100;
   2 : void x() {}
   3 : void x(int n) {}

jshell> class x {}
|  created class x

jshell> /list x

   1 : int x = 100;
   2 : void x() {}
   3 : void x(int n) {}
   4 : class x {}

jshell> /exit
|  Goodbye
```

Editing Snippets

The JShell tool offers several ways to edit snippets and commands. You can use navigation keys listed in Table 23-1 to navigate on the command line while entering snippets and commands in jshell. You can use keys listed in Table 23-2 to edit text entered on a line in jshell.

Table 23-1. *Navigation Keys While Editing in the JShell Tool*

Key	Description
Enter	Enters the current line
Left arrow	Moves one character backward
Right arrow	Moves one character forward
Ctrl+A	Moves to the beginning of the line
Ctrl+E	Moves to the end of the line
Meta+B (or Alt+B)	Moves a word backward
Meta+F (or Alt+F)	Moves a word forward

Table 23-2. *Keys to Modify Text on the JShell Tool*

Key	Description
Delete	Deletes character under the cursor
Backspace	Deletes character before the cursor
Ctrl+K	Deletes the text from the cursor to the end of the line
Meta+D (or Alt+D)	Deletes the text from the cursor to the end of the word
Ctrl+W	Deletes the text from the cursor to the previous whitespace
Ctrl+Y	Pastes (or yanks) the most recently deleted text into the line
Meta+Y (or Alt+Y)	After Ctrl+Y, this key combination cycles through previously deleted text

It is hard to edit multi-line snippets in jshell, even though you have access to a rich set of edit key combinations. The tool designer realized this problem and provided a built-in snippet editor. You can configure the tool to use the platform-specific snippet editor of your choice. Refer to the section entitled "Setting the Snippet Editor" for more information on how to set up your own editor.

You need to use the /edit command to start editing a snippet. The command takes three forms:

- /edit <snippet-name>
- /edit <snippet-id>
- /edit

You can use the snippet name or snippet ID to edit a specific snippet. The /edit command without an argument opens all active snippets in an editor for editing. By default, the /edit command opens a built-in editor called JShell Edit Pad, and it is shown in Figure 23-3.

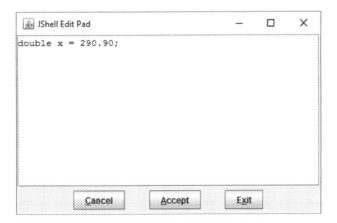

Figure 23-3. *The built-in JShell editor called the JShell Edit Pad*

The JShell Edit Pad is written in Swing and it shows a JFrame with a JTextArea and three JButtons. If you edit snippets, make sure to click the Accept button before exiting the window so that the editing takes effect. If you cancel out or exit the editor without accepting the changes, your edits will be lost.

If you know the name of a variable, a method, or a class, you can edit it using its name. The following jshell session creates a variable, the methods, and a class with the same name x and uses the /edit x command to edit them all at once:

```
C:\Java9Fundamentals>jshell
|   Welcome to JShell -- Version 9
|   For an introduction type: /help intro

jshell> int x = 100
x ==> 100

jshell> void x(){}
|   created method x()

jshell> void x (int n) {}
|   created method x(int)

jshell> class x{}
|   created class x
jshell> 2 + 2
$5 ==> 4

jshell> /edit x
```

The /edit x command opens all snippets with the name x in a JShell Edit Pad, as shown in Figure 23-4. You can edit these snippets, accept the changes, and exit the editing, to continue with the jshell session.

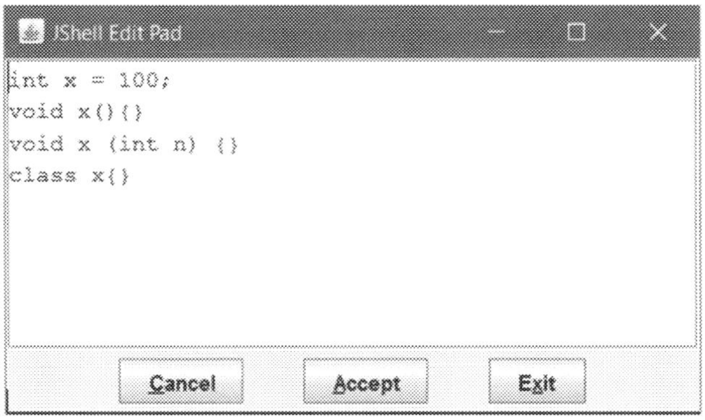

Figure 23-4. *Editing snippets by name*

Rerunning Previous Snippets

In a command-line tool like jshell, you'll often want to rerun previous snippets. You can use the Up/Down arrows to navigate through the snippet/command history and then press the Enter key when you are on a previous snippet/command. You can also use one of the three commands to rerun previous snippets (not commands):

- /!
- /<snippet-id>
- /-<n>

The /! command reruns the last snippet. The /<snippet-id> command reruns the snippet identified by <snippet-id>. The /-<n> command reruns the nth last snippet. For example, /-1 reruns the last snippet, /-2 reruns the second last snippet, and so on. The /! and /-1 commands have the same effect—they both rerun the last snippet.

Declaring Variables

You can declare variables in jshell as you do in Java programs. A variable declaration may occur at the top-level, inside a method, or as a field declaration within a class. The static and final modifiers are not allowed in top-level variable declarations. If you use them, they will be ignored with a warning. The static modifier specifies a class context and the final modifier restricts you from changing the variable's value. You are not allowed to use these modifiers because the tool allows you to declare free-standing variables that you would like to experiment with by changing their values over time. The following examples show you how to declare variables:

```
jshell> int x
x ==> 0

jshell> int y = 90
y ==> 90

jshell> side = 90
|  Error:
```

```
|    cannot find symbol
|      symbol:    variable side
|    side = 90
|    ^--^

jshell> static double radius = 2.67
|    Warning:
|    Modifier 'static'  not permitted in top-level declarations, ignored
|    static double radius = 2.67;
|    ^----^
radius ==> 2.67

jshell> String str = new String("Hello")
str ==> "Hello"

jshell>
```

Using an undeclared variable in top-level expressions generates an error. Notice the use of an undeclared variable named side in the previous example, which generated an error. I show you later that you can use an undeclared variable inside a method's body.

It is also possible to change the data type of a variable. You can declare a variable named x as an int and re-declare it later as a double or a String. The following examples show this feature:

```
jshell> int x = 10;
x ==> 10

jshell> int y = x + 2;
y ==> 12

jshell> double x = 2.71
x ==> 2.71

jshell> y
y ==> 12

jshell> String x = "Hello"
x ==> "Hello"

jshell> y
y ==> 12

jshell>
```

Notice that the value of the variable named y did not change or was not reevaluated when the data type or the value of x changed.

You can also drop a variable using the /drop command, which takes the variable name as an argument. The following command will drop the variable named x:

```
jshell> /drop x
```

You can list all variables in jshell using the /vars command. It will list user-declared variables and the variables automatically declared by jshell, which happens while jshell evaluates result-bearing expressions. The command has the following forms:

- /vars
- /vars <variable-name>
- /vars <variable-snippet-id>
- /vars -start
- /vars -all

The command without an argument lists all active variables in the current session. If you use a snippet name or ID, it lists the variable declaration with that snippet name or ID. If you use it with the -start option, it lists all variables added to the startup script. If you use it with the -all option, it lists all variables including failed, overwritten, dropped, and startup. The following examples show you how to use the /vars command:

```
C:\Java9Fundamentals>jshell
|  Welcome to JShell -- Version 9
|  For an introduction type: /help intro

jshell> /vars

jshell> 2 + 2
$1 ==> 4

jshell> /vars
|    int $1 = 4

jshell> int x = 20;
x ==> 20

jshell> /vars
|    int $1 = 4
|    int x = 20

jshell> String str = "Hello";
str ==> "Hello"

jshell> /vars
|    int $1 = 4
|    int x = 20
|    String str = "Hello"

jshell> double x = 90.99;
x ==> 90.99

jshell> /vars
|    int $1 = 4
|    String str = "Hello"
|    double x = 90.99
```

```
jshell> /drop x
|  dropped variable x

jshell> /vars
|    int $1 = 4
|    String str = "Hello"

jshell>
```

Import Statements

You can use import statements in jshell. Recall that, in a Java program, all types in the java.lang package are imported by default. To use types from other packages, you need to add appropriate import statements in your compilation unit. I start with an example. I try to create three objects: a String, a List<Integer>, and a ZonedDateTime. Note that the String class is in the java.lang package; the List and Integer classes are in the java.util and java.lang packages, respectively; and the ZonedDateTime class is in the java.time package.

```
jshell> String str = new String("Hello")
str ==> "Hello"

jshell> List<Integer> nums = List.of(1, 2, 3, 4, 5)
nums ==> [1, 2, 3, 4, 5]

jshell> ZonedDateTime now = ZonedDateTime.now()
|  Error:
|  cannot find symbol
|    symbol:   class ZonedDateTime
|  ZonedDateTime now = ZonedDateTime.now();
|  ^-----------^
|  Error:
|  cannot find symbol
|    symbol:   variable ZonedDateTime
|  ZonedDateTime now = ZonedDateTime.now();
|                      ^-----------^
|

jshell>
```

The examples generate an error if you try to use the ZonedDateTime class from the java.time package. We were also expecting a similar error when we try to create a List because it is in the java.util package, which is not imported in a Java program by default.

The sole purpose of the JShell tool is to make developers' lives easier when evaluating snippets. To achieve this goal, the tool imports all types from a few packages by default. What are those default packages whose types are imported? You can print a list of all active imports in jshell using the /imports command:

```
jshell> /imports
|    import java.io.*
|    import java.math.*
|    import java.net.*
|    import java.nio.file.*
```

```
|    import java.util.*
|    import java.util.concurrent.*
|    import java.util.function.*
|    import java.util.prefs.*
|    import java.util.regex.*
|    import java.util.stream.*

jshell>
```

Notice the default import statement that imports all types from the java.util package. This is the reason that you can use List without importing it. You can also add your own imports to jshell. The following example shows you how to import the ZonedDateTime class and use it. You will get different output when jshell prints the value of the current date with the time zone.

```
jshell> /imports
|    import java.util.*
|    import java.io.*
|    import java.math.*
|    import java.net.*
|    import java.util.concurrent.*
|    import java.util.prefs.*
|    import java.util.regex.*

jshell> import java.time.*

jshell> /imports
|    import java.io.*
|    import java.math.*
|    import java.net.*
|    import java.nio.file.*
|    import java.util.*
|    import java.util.concurrent.*
|    import java.util.function.*
|    import java.util.prefs.*
|    import java.util.regex.*
|    import java.util.stream.*
|    import java.time.*

jshell> ZonedDateTime now = ZonedDateTime.now()
now ==> 2017-08-19T13:01:33.060708200-05:00[America/Chicago]

jshell>
```

Note that any imports you add to the jshell session will be lost when you exit the session. You can also drop import statements—the default imports and the ones you added. You need to know the snippet ID to drop a snippet. The IDs for startup snippets are s1, s2, s3, etc. and for user-defined snippets, they are 1, 2, 3, etc. The following examples show you how to add and drop import statements in jshell:

```
C:\Java9Fundamentals>jshell
|  Welcome to JShell -- Version 9
|  For an introduction type: /help intro
```

```
jshell> import java.time.*

jshell> List<Integer> list = List.of(1, 2, 3, 4, 5)
list ==> [1, 2, 3, 4, 5]

jshell> ZonedDateTime now = ZonedDateTime.now()
now ==> 2017-02-19T21:08:08.802099-06:00[America/Chicago]

jshell> /list -all

   s1 : import java.io.*;
   s2 : import java.math.*;
   s3 : import java.net.*;
   s4 : import java.nio.file.*;
   s5 : import java.util.*;
   s6 : import java.util.concurrent.*;
   s7 : import java.util.function.*;
   s8 : import java.util.prefs.*;
   s9 : import java.util.regex.*;
  s10 : import java.util.stream.*;
    1 : import java.time.*;
    2 : List<Integer> list = List.of(1, 2, 3, 4, 5);
    3 : ZonedDateTime now = ZonedDateTime.now();

jshell> /drop s5

jshell> /drop 1

jshell> /list -all

   s1 : import java.io.*;
   s2 : import java.math.*;
   s3 : import java.net.*;
   s4 : import java.nio.file.*;
   s5 : import java.util.*;
   s6 : import java.util.concurrent.*;
   s7 : import java.util.function.*;
   s8 : import java.util.prefs.*;
   s9 : import java.util.regex.*;
  s10 : import java.util.stream.*;
    1 : import java.time.*;
    2 : List<Integer> list = List.of(1, 2, 3, 4, 5);
    3 : ZonedDateTime now = ZonedDateTime.now();

jshell> /imports
|    import java.io.*
|    import java.math.*
|    import java.net.*
|    import java.nio.file.*
|    import java.util.concurrent.*
|    import java.util.function.*
|    import java.util.prefs.*
```

```
|    import java.util.regex.*
|    import java.util.stream.*

jshell> List<Integer> list2 = List.of(1, 2, 3, 4, 5)
|  Error:
|  cannot find symbol
|    symbol:   class List
|  List<Integer> list2 = List.of(1, 2, 3, 4, 5);
|  ^--^
|  Error:
|  cannot find symbol
|    symbol:   variable List
|  List<Integer> list2 = List.of(1, 2, 3, 4, 5);
|                        ^--^

jshell> import java.util.*
|    update replaced variable list, reset to null

jshell> List<Integer> list2 = List.of(1, 2, 3, 4, 5)
list2 ==> [1, 2, 3, 4, 5]

jshell> /list -all

  s1 : import java.io.*;
  s2 : import java.math.*;
  s3 : import java.net.*;
  s4 : import java.nio.file.*;
  s5 : import java.util.*;
  s6 : import java.util.concurrent.*;
  s7 : import java.util.function.*;
  s8 : import java.util.prefs.*;
  s9 : import java.util.regex.*;
 s10 : import java.util.stream.*;
   1 : import java.time.*;
   2 : List<Integer> list = List.of(1, 2, 3, 4, 5);
   3 : ZonedDateTime now = ZonedDateTime.now();
  e1 : List<Integer> list2 = List.of(1, 2, 3, 4, 5);
   4 : import java.util.*;
   5 : List<Integer> list2 = List.of(1, 2, 3, 4, 5);

jshell> /imports
|    import java.io.*
|    import java.math.*
|    import java.net.*
|    import java.nio.file.*
|    import java.util.concurrent.*
|    import java.util.function.*
|    import java.util.prefs.*
|    import java.util.regex.*
|    import java.util.stream.*
|    import java.util.*

jshell>
```

Method Declarations

You can declare and call methods in jshell. You can declare top-level methods, which are methods that are entered in jshell directly and are not inside any class. You can also declare classes (see the next section) with methods. In this section, I show you how to declare and call top-level methods. You can also call methods of existing classes. The following example declares a method named square() and calls it:

```
jshell> long square(int n) {
   ...>    return n * n;
   ...> }
|  created method square(int)

jshell> square(10)
$2 ==> 100

jshell> long n2 = square(37)
n2 ==> 1369

jshell>
```

Forward references are allowed inside a method's body. That is, you can refer to methods or variables, which are not declared yet, inside a method's body. The method being declared cannot be called until all missing references are defined.

```
jshell> long multiply(int n) {
   ...>      return multiplier * n;
   ...> }
|  created method multiply(int), however, it cannot be invoked until variable multiplier is
declared

jshell> multiply(10)
|  attempted to call method multiply(int) which cannot be invoked until variable multiplier
is declared

jshell> int multiplier = 2
multiplier ==> 2

jshell> multiply(10)
$6 ==> 20

jshell> void printCube(int n) {
   ...>      System.out.printf("Cube of %d is %d.%n", n, cube(n));
   ...> }
|  created method printCube(int), however, it cannot be invoked until method cube(int) is
declared

jshell> long cube(int n) {
   ...>      return n * n * n;
   ...> }
|  created method cube(int)
```

```
jshell> printCube(10)
Cube of 10 is 1000.

jshell>
```

This example declares a method named multiply(int n). It multiplies the argument with a variable named multiplier, which has not been declared yet. Notice the feedback after you declare this method. The feedback clearly states that you cannot call the multiply() method until you declare the multiplier variable. Calling the method generates an error. Later, the multiplier variable is declared and the multiply() method is called successfully.

░ **Tip**   You can also declare a recursive method using a forward reference.

Type Declarations

You can declare all types such as classes, interfaces, enums, and annotations in jshell as you do in Java. The following jshell session creates a class named Counter, creates its object, and calls its methods:

```
jshell> class Counter {
   ...>     private int counter;
   ...>     public synchronized int next() {
   ...>         return ++counter;
   ...>     }
   ...>
   ...>     public int current() {
   ...>         return counter;
   ...>     }
   ...> }
|  created class Counter

jshell> Counter c = new Counter();
c ==> Counter@25bbe1b6

jshell> c.current()
$3 ==> 0

jshell> c.next()
$4 ==> 1

jshell> c.next()
$5 ==> 2

jshell> c.current()
$6 ==> 2

jshell>
```

You can use the /types command to print a list of all declared types in jshell. The command has the following forms:

- /types
- /types <type-name>
- /types <snippet-id>
- /types -start
- /types -all

The command without an argument lists the current active jshell classes, interfaces, enums, and annotations. Commands with a type name and a snippet ID arguments the list types with the specified name and specified snippet ID, respectively. The command with the -start option lists the automatically added startup types. The command with the -all option lists all types, including failed, overwritten, dropped, and startup. The following jshell is a continuation of the previous example session; it shows how to print all active types defined in a jshell session:

```
jshell> /types
|    class Counter

jshell>
```

The Counter class is small. You may quickly realize that it is not easy to enter the source code for bigger classes on a command line. You may want to use your favorite Java source code editor such as NetBeans to write the source code and quickly test your classes in jshell. You can open a source code file as a source input in jshell using the /open command. The syntax is as follows:

```
/open <file-path>
```

You can find the source code for the Counter class in the bj9f/src/jdojo.jshell/Counter.java file. The following jshell session shows you how to open the saved Counter.java file in jshell. It is assumed that you have saved the source code for this book in C:\ on Windows. If you are using another operating system, just follow the file-path naming convention for your operating system and your directory structure to use the following example.

```
jshell> /open C:\bj9f\src\jdojo.jshell\Counter.java
jshell> Counter c = new Counter()
c ==> Counter@25bbe1b6

jshell> c.current()
$3 ==> 0

jshell> c.next()
$4 ==> 1

jshell> c.next()
$5 ==> 2

jshell> c.current()
$6 ==> 2

jshell>
```

Note that the source code for the Counter class does not contain a package declaration because jshell does not allow you to declare a class (or any type) in a package. All types that you declare in jshell are considered static types of an internal synthetic class. However, you may want to test your own class that is in a package. You can use an already compiled class, which is in a package, in jshell. You will usually need it when you are using libraries to develop your application and you want to experiment with your application logic by writing snippets against library classes. You will need to set the class path using the /env command, so your classes may be found.

A Person class in the com.jdojo.jshell package is included in the book's source code. The class declaration is shown in Listing 23-2.

Listing 23-2. The Source Code for a Person Class

```java
// Person.java
package com.jdojo.jshell;

public class Person {
    private String name;

    public Person() {
        this.name = "Unknown";
    }

    public Person(String name) {
        this.name = name;
    }

    public String getName() {
        return name;
    }

    public void setName(String name) {
        this.name = name;
    }
}
```

The following jshell session sets the class path on Windows assuming the source code for this book was stored in C:\. Use the syntax for the class path string for your operating system and the source code location on your computer if they are different from the assumed.

```
jshell> /env -class-path C:\Java9Fundamentals\build\modules\jdojo.jshell
|   Setting new options and restoring state.

jshell> Person guy = new Person("Martin Guy Crawford")
|   Error:
|   cannot find symbol
|     symbol:   class Person
|   Person guy = new Person("Martin Guy Crawford");
|   ^----^
|   Error:
|   cannot find symbol
|     symbol:   class Person
|   Person guy = new Person("Martin Guy Crawford");
|                     ^----^
```

947

Do you know the reason for this error? We used the simple name of the class, `Person`, without importing it and `jshell` was not able to locate the class. We need to import the `Person` class or use its fully qualified name. The following is a continuation of this `jshell` session that fixes this error:

```
jshell> import com.jdojo.jshell.Person
jshell> Person guy = new Person("Martin Guy Crawford")
guy ==> com.jdojo.jshell.Person@192b07fd

jshell> guy.getName()
$9 ==> "Martin Guy Crawford"

jshell> guy.setName("Forrest Butts")

jshell> guy.getName()
$11 ==> "Forrest Butts"

jshell>
```

Setting the Execution Environment

In the previous section, you learned how to set the class path using the `/env` command. The command can be used to set many other components of the execution context such as the module path. You can also use it to resolve modules, so you can use types in modules on `jshell`. Its complete syntax is as follows:

```
/env [-class-path <path>] [-module-path <path>] [-add-modules <modules>]
[-add-exports <m/p=n>]
```

The `/env` command without arguments prints values for the current execution context. The `-class-path` option sets the class path. The `-module-path` option sets the module path. The `-add-modules` option adds modules to the default set of root modules, so they can be resolved. The `-add-exports` option exports non-exported packages from a module to a set of modules. These options have the same meanings as they have when used with the `javac` and `java` commands.

▓ **Tip**   On the command line, these options must start with two dashes, for example, `--module-path`. In `jshell`, they can start with one dash or two dashes. For example, both `-module-path` and `--module-path` are allowed in `jshell`.

When you set the execution context, the current session is reset and all previously executed snippets in the current session are replayed in quiet mode. That is, the replayed snippets are not shown. However, errors during the replay will be shown.

You can set the execution context using the `/env`, `/reset`, and `/reload` commands. Each of these command has different effects. The meaning of the context options such as `-class-path` and `-module-path` are the same. You can list all options that can be used to set the execution context using the command `/help context`.

Let's walk through an example of using the module-related settings using the /env command. You created a jdojo.intro module in Chapter 3. The module contains a package named com.jdojo.intro, but it does not export the package. Now, you want to call the static main(String[] args) method of the Welcome class in the non-exported package. Here are the steps you need to perform in jshell:

1. Set the module path, so the module will be found.

2. Resolve the module by adding it to the default set of root modules. You can do this using the -add-modules option with the /env command.

3. Export the package using the -add-exports command. The snippets entered in jshell are executed in an unnamed module, so you will need to export the package to all unnamed modules using the ALL-UNNAMED keyword. If you do not supply target modules in the -add-exports option, ALL-UNNAMED is assumed and the package is exported to all unnamed modules.

4. Optionally, import the com.jdojo.intro.Welcome class if you want to use its simple name in snippets.

5. Now, you will be able to call the Welcome.main() method from jshell.

The following jshell session shows you how to perform these steps. It is assumed that you are launching the jshell session with C:\Java9Fundamentals as the current directory and the C:\Java9Fundamentals\build\modules\jdojo.intro directory contains the compiled code for the jdojo.intro module. If your directory structure and the current directory are different, substitute the directory paths used in the session with yours.

```
C:\Java9Fundamentals>jshell
|  Welcome to JShell -- Version 9
|  For an introduction type: /help intro

jshell> /env -module-path build\modules\jdojo.intro
|  Setting new options and restoring state.

jshell> /env -add-modules jdojo.intro
|  Setting new options and restoring state.

jshell> /env -add-exports jdojo.intro/com.jdojo.intro=ALL-UNNAMED
|  Setting new options and restoring state.

jshell> import com.jdojo.intro.Welcome

jshell> Welcome.main(null)
Welcome to Java 9!

jshell> /env
|      --add-modules jdojo.intro
|      --module-path build\modules\jdojo.intro
|      --add-exports jdojo.intro/com.jdojo.intro=ALL-UNNAMED

jshell>
```

No Checked Exceptions

In a Java program, if you call a method that throws checked exceptions, you must handle those exceptions using a `try-catch` block or by adding a `throws` clause. The JShell tool is supposed to be a quick and easy way to evaluate snippets, so you do not need to handle checked exceptions in your snippets. If a snippet throws a checked exception when it's executed, `jshell` will print the stack trace and continue.

```
jshell> FileReader fr = new FileReader("secrets.txt")
|    java.io.FileNotFoundException thrown: secrets.txt (The system cannot find the file specified)
|        at FileInputStream.open0 (Native Method)
|        at FileInputStream.open (FileInputStream.java:196)
|        at FileInputStream.<init> (FileInputStream.java:139)
|        at FileInputStream.<init> (FileInputStream.java:94)
|        at FileReader.<init> (FileReader.java:58)
|        at (#1:1)

jshell>
```

This snippet threw a `FileNotFoundException` because a file named `secrets.txt` does not exist in the current directory. If the file existed, you were able to create a `FileReader` without having to use a `try-catch` block. Note that if you try to use this snippet inside a method, the normal Java syntax rule applies and your method declaration will not compile:

```
jshell> void readSecrets() {
   ...> FileReader fr = new FileReader("secrets.txt");
   ...> // More code goes here
   ...> }
|  Error:
|  unreported exception java.io.FileNotFoundException; must be caught or declared to be thrown
|  FileReader fr = new FileReader("secrets.txt");
|                  ^--------------------------^

jshell>
```

Auto-Completion

The JShell tool has an auto-completion feature that you can invoke by entering partial text and pressing the Tab key. This feature is available when you are entering a command or a snippet. The tool will detect the context and help you auto-complete the command. When there are multiple possibilities, it shows all possibilities and you will need to enter one of them manually. When it finds a unique possibility, it will complete the text. To see the full description of auto-complete shortcuts, use the `/help shortcuts` command. There are three auto-complete key combinations:

- Tab
- Shift+Tab+V
- Shift+Tab+I

Press the Tab key in the middle of an expression and jshell will complete the expression or show you possible options. Pressing Shift+Tab+V lets you convert an expression into a variable declaration. The V in the shortcut stands for variable. Pressing Shift+Tab+I lets you import types for unresolvable identifiers, I discuss examples of these shortcuts in details.

The following is an example of the tool finding multiple possibilities. You need to enter /e and press Tab. <Tab> in the command indicates that you need to press Tab:

```
jshell> /e <Tab>
/edit     /env     /exit

<press tab again to see synopsis>

jshell> /e <Tab>
/edit
edit a source entry referenced by name or id

/env
view or change the evaluation context

/exit
exit jshell

<press tab again to see full documentation>

jshell>
```

The tool detected that you were trying to enter a command because your text started with a slash (/). There are three commands (/edit, /env, and /exit) that start with /e, and they are printed for you. Now you will need to complete the command yourself by entering the rest of the command. In case of commands, if you enter just enough text to make the command name unique and press Enter, the tool will execute that command. In this case, you can enter /ed, /en, or /ex and press Enter to execute the /edit, /env, or /exit command, respectively. If you are shown multiple options after you press Tab, you can press Tab again to see description of all options. Pressing Tab the third time shows you full documentation of all options. If you try this to auto-complete Java expression, you can view the entire Javadoc for Java entities such as a class' method.

You can enter a slash (/) and press Tab to see a list of all available jshell commands:

```
jshell> /
/!           /?           /drop        /edit        /env         /exit        /help        /history
/imports     /list        /methods     /open        /reload      /reset       /save        /set
/types       /vars

<press tab again to see synopsis>
```

The following snippet creates a String variable named str with an initial value of "GoodBye":

```
jshell> String str = "GoodBye"
str ==> "GoodBye"
```

Continuing with this jshell session, enter str. and press Tab:

```
jshell> str.<Tab>
charAt(                chars()              codePointAt(         codePointBefore(
codePointCount(        codePoints()         compareTo(           compareToIgnoreCase(
concat(                contains(            contentEquals(       endsWith(
equals(                equalsIgnoreCase(    getBytes(            getChars(
getClass()             hashCode()           indexOf(             intern()
isEmpty()              lastIndexOf(         length()             matches(
notify()               notifyAll()          offsetByCodePoints(  regionMatches(
replace(               replaceAll(          replaceFirst(        split(
startsWith(            subSequence(         substring(           toCharArray()
toLowerCase(           toString()           toUpperCase(         trim()
wait(

jshell> str.
```

This snippet printed all method names for the String class that you can invoke on the variable str. Notice that a few method names end with () and others end with only (. This is not a bug. If a method takes no arguments, its name is following with a (). If a method takes arguments, its name is followed with a (.

Continuing with this example, enter str.sub and press Tab:

```
jshell> str.sub <Tab>
subSequence(   substring(
```

This time, the tool found two methods in the String class that start with sub. You can enter the entire method call, str.substring(0, 4), and press Enter to evaluate the snippet:

```
jshell> str.substring(0, 4)
$2 ==> "Good"
```

Alternatively, you can let the tool auto-complete the method name by entering str.subs. When you enter str.subs and press Tab, the tool completes the method name, inserts a (, and waits for you to enter the arguments for the method:

```
jshell> str.substring(
substring(

jshell> str.substring(
```

Now you can enter the method's argument and press Enter to evaluate the expression:

```
jshell> str.substring(0, 4)
$3 ==> "Good"

jshell>
```

When a method takes arguments, most likely you would like to see those arguments' types. You can see the method's synopsis by pressing Tab after you enter the entire method/constructor name and an opening parenthesis. In the previous example, if you enter str.substring(and press Tab, the tool will print the synopsis for the substring() method:

```
jshell> str.substring(
Signatures:
String String.substring(int beginIndex)
String String.substring(int beginIndex, int endIndex)

<press tab again to see documentation>

jshell> str.substring(
```

Notice the output. It says if you press Tab again, it will show you the Javadoc for the `substring()` method. In the following prompt, I pressed Tab again to print the Javadoc. If more of the Javadoc needs to be displayed, press the Tab again.

At times, you enter an expression and want to assign the value of the expression to a variable of the appropriate type. Sometimes you know the type and sometimes you don't. The `JShell` tool will help you auto-complete the assignment part after you enter the complete expression. Enter the complete expression and then press Shift+Tab. Now, press V, which will auto-complete the expression assignment by adding the appropriate variable type and placing the cursor to the position where you can enter the variable name. The sequence of key presses is as follows:

1. Press Shift.

2. Keep holding down Shift and press Tab.

3. Release Tab.

4. Release Shift.

5. Press V.

Let's walk through these steps. Enter the expression `2 + 2` into `jshell`:

```
jshell> 2 + 2
```

Now, press the sequence of keys as listed previously. `jshell` auto-completes the assignment expression and waits for you to enter the variable name:

```
jshell> int  = 2 + 2
```

The cursor is placed just before the = symbol. Enter x as the variable name and press Enter:

```
jshell> int x = 2 + 2
x ==> 4

jshell>
```

Let's use the Shift+Tab+I shortcut to import a missing import for an unresolved identifier. You need to press the key combination in the following order:

1. Press Shift.

2. Keep holding down Shift and press Tab.

3. Release Tab.

4. Release Shift.

5.   Press I.

6.   jshell will print the possible import statements with option numbered 0, 1, 2, 3, etc. jshell waits for you to enter an option.

7.   Enter the option number and jshell will execute the import statement.

Suppose you want to use the LocalDate class from the java.time package. The following jshell session will show you how to import java.time.LocalDate class using the shortcut keys. You need to press the Shift+Tab+I shortcut just after entering LocalDate on jshell:

```
jshell> LocalDate
0: Do nothing
1: import: java.time.LocalDate
Choice:
Imported: java.time.LocalDate

jshell> LocalDate.now()
$1 ==> 2017-08-19
```

Snippets and Commands History

JShell maintains a history of all commands and snippets that you enter in all sessions. You can navigate through the history using the Up and Down arrow keys. You can also use the /history command to print the history of all you typed in the current session:

```
jshell> 2 + 2
$1 ==> 4

jshell> System.out.println("Hello")
Hello

jshell> /history

2 + 2
System.out.println("Hello")
/history

jshell>
```

At this point, pressing the Up arrow once shows /history, pressing it twice shows System.out.println("Hello"), and pressing it three times shows 2 + 2. Pressing the Up arrow a fourth time will show you the last entered command/snippet from the previous jshell session. If you want to execute a previously entered snippet/command, use the Up arrow until the desired command/snippet is shown, and then press Enter to execute it. Pressing the Down arrow navigates you to the next command or snippet in the list. Suppose you press the Up arrow five times to navigate to the fifth last snippet/command. Now pressing the Down arrow will navigate you to the fourth last snippet/command. When you are at the first and the last snippet/commands, pressing the Up arrow or the Down arrow does nothing.

Reading JShell Stack Trace

Snippets entered on jshell are part of a synthetic class. Java does not let you declare a top-level method. A method declaration must be part of a type. When an exception is thrown in a Java program, the stack trace prints the type names and the line numbers. In jshell, an exception may be thrown from a snippet. Printing the synthetic class name and line numbers in such cases will be misleading and will make no sense to developers. The format for the location of the code in snippets in the stack trace is in this form:

```
at <snippet-name> (#<snippet-id>:<line-number-in-snippet>)
```

Note that some snippets may not have a name. For example, entering a snippet 2 + 2 will not give it a name. Some snippets have name such as a snippet declaring a variable is assigned the same name as the variable's name; the same goes with a method and a type declaration. Sometimes, you may have two snippets with the same name, for example, by declaring a variable and a method/type with the same name. jshell assigns a unique snippet ID to all snippets. You can find the ID of a snippet using the /list -all command.

The following jshell session declares a divide() method and prints the exception stack trace with a runtime ArithmeticException exception that is thrown when an integer is divided by zero:

```
jshell> int divide(int x, int y) {
   ...> return x/y;
   ...> }
|  created method divide(int,int)

jshell> divide(10, 2)
$2 ==> 5

jshell> divide(10, 0)
|  java.lang.ArithmeticException thrown: / by zero
|        at divide (#1:2)
|        at (#3:1)

jshell> /list -all

   s1 : import java.io.*;
   s2 : import java.math.*;
   s3 : import java.net.*;
   s4 : import java.nio.file.*;
   s5 : import java.util.*;
   s6 : import java.util.concurrent.*;
   s7 : import java.util.function.*;
   s8 : import java.util.prefs.*;
   s9 : import java.util.regex.*;
  s10 : import java.util.stream.*;
    1 : int divide(int x, int y) {
        return x/y;
        }
    2 : divide(10, 2)
    3 : divide(10, 0)

jshell>
```

Let's try to read the stack trace. The last line, at (#3:1), is stating that the exception was caused at line 1 of snippet number 3. Notice in the output of the /list -all command that the snippet number 3 is the expression divide(10, 0) that caused the exception. The second line, at divide (#1:2), is indicating that the second level in the stack trace is at line 2 of the snippet named divide whose snippet ID is 1 and the line number is 2.

Reusing JShell Sessions

You can enter many snippets and commands in a jshell session and may want to reuse them in other sessions. You can use the /save command to save commands and snippets to a file and use the /open command to load the previously saved commands and snippets. The syntax for the /save command is as follows:

```
/save <option> <file-path>
```

Here, <option> can be one of the options: -all, -history, and -start. <file-path> is the file path where the snippets/commands will be saved.

The /save command with no option saves all active snippets in the current sessions. Note that it does not save any commands or failed snippets.

The /save command with the -all option saves all snippets for the current session to the specified file, including failed and startup snippets. Note that it does not save any commands.

The /save command with the -history option saves everything that you typed in jshell since it was launched.

The /save command with the -start option saves the default startup definitions to the specified file.

You can reload the snippets from a file using the /open command. The command takes the file name as an argument.

The following jshell session declares a class named Counter, creates its object, and invokes methods on the object. Finally, it saves all active snippets to a file named jshell.jsh. Note that the file extension .jsh is customary for jshell files. You can use any other extension you want.

```
C:\Java9Fundamentals>jshell
|  Welcome to JShell -- Version 9
|  For an introduction type: /help intro

jshell> class Counter {
   ...>     private int count;
   ...>     public synchronized int next() {
   ...>       return ++count;
   ...>     }
   ...>     public int current() {
   ...>       return count;
   ...>     }
   ...> }
|  created class Counter

jshell> Counter counter = new Counter()
counter ==> Counter@25bbe1b6

jshell> counter.current()
$3 ==> 0
```

```
jshell> counter.next()
$4 ==> 1

jshell> counter.next()
$5 ==> 2

jshell> counter.current()
$6 ==> 2

jshell> /save jshell.jsh

jshell> /exit
|  Goodbye
```

At this point, you should have a file named jshell.jsh in your current directory with the contents shown in Listing 23-3.

Listing 23-3. Contents of the jshell.jsh File

```
class Counter {
   private int count;
   public synchronized int next() {
     return ++count;
   }
   public int current() {
     return count;
   }
}
Counter counter = new Counter();
counter.current()
counter.next()
counter.next()
counter.current()
```

The following jshell session opens the jshell.jsh file, which will replay all the snippets that were saved in the previous session. After opening the file, you can start calling methods on the counter variable.

```
C:\Java9Fundamentals>jshell
|  Welcome to JShell -- Version 9
|  For an introduction type: /help intro

jshell> /open jshell.jsh

jshell> counter.current()
$7 ==> 2

jshell> counter.next()
$8 ==> 3

jshell>
```

Resetting the JShell State

You can reset the JShell's execution state using the /reset command. Executing this command has the following effects:

- All snippets you enter in the current session are lost, so be careful before you execute this command.

- The startup snippets are re-executed.

- The execution state of the tool is restarted.

- The jshell configurations that were set using the /set command are retained.

- The execution environment set using the /env command is retained.

The following jshell session declares a variable, resets the session, and attempts to print the variable's value. Note that, on resetting a session, all declared variables are lost, so the variable previously declared is not found:

```
jshell> int x = 987
x ==> 987

jshell> /reset
|  Resetting state.

jshell> x
|  Error:
|  cannot find symbol
|    symbol:   variable x
|  x
|  ^

jshell>
```

Reloading the JShell State

Suppose you used many snippets in a jshell session and exited the session. Now you want to go back and replay those snippets. One way to do it is to start a new jshell session and re-enter those snippets. Re-entering several snippets in jshell is a hassle. There is an easy way to achieve this—by using the /reload command. The /reload command resets the jshell state and replays all valid snippets and /drop commands in the same sequence they were entered before. You can use the -restore and -quiet options to customize its behavior.

The /reload command without any options resets the jshell state and replays the valid history from one of the following prior actions/events, whichever occurred last:

- Beginning of the current session

- When the last /reset command was executed

- When the last /reload command was executed

You can use the `-restore` option with the `/reload` command. It resets and replays the history between the following two actions/events, whichever are the last two:

- The launch of jshell
- Execution of the /reset command
- Execution of the /reload command

The effect of executing the `/reload` command with the `-restore` option is a little tricky to understand. Its primary purpose is to restore the previous execution state. If you execute this command in the beginning of every jshell session, starting from the second session, your session will contain all snippets you had ever executed in jshell sessions! This is a powerful feature. That is, you can evaluate snippets, close jshell, restart jshell, and execute the /reload -restore command as your first command, and you never lose any snippets that you previously entered. Sometimes, you will execute the /reset command twice in a session and want to restore the state that existed between those two resets. You can achieve this result by using this command.

The following jshell sessions create a variable in each session and restore the previous session by executing the `/reload  -restore` command in the beginning of each session. The example shows that the fourth session uses the variable named x1 that was declared in the first session.

```
C:\Java9Fundamentals>jshell
|  Welcome to JShell -- Version 9
|  For an introduction type: /help intro

jshell> int x1 = 10
x1 ==> 10

jshell> /exit
|  Goodbye

C:\Java9Fundamentals>jshell
|  Welcome to JShell -- Version 9
|  For an introduction type: /help intro

jshell> /reload -restore
|  Restarting and restoring from previous state.
-: int x1 = 10;

jshell> int x2 = 20
x2 ==> 20

jshell> /exit
|  Goodbye

C:\Java9Fundamentals>jshell
|  Welcome to JShell -- Version 9
|  For an introduction type: /help intro

jshell> /reload -restore
|  Restarting and restoring from previous state.
-: int x1 = 10;
-: int x2 = 20;
```

```
jshell> int x3 = 30
x3 ==> 30

jshell> /exit
|  Goodbye

C:\Java9Fundamentals>jshell
|  Welcome to JShell -- Version 9
|  For an introduction type: /help intro

jshell> /reload -restore
|  Restarting and restoring from previous state.
-: int x1 = 10;
-: int x2 = 20;
-: int x3 = 30;

jshell> System.out.println("x1 is " + x1)
x1 is 10

jshell>
```

The /reload command displays the history that it replays. You can use the -quiet option to suppress the replay display. You can use this option with or without the -restore option. The -quiet option does not suppress the error messages that may be generated while replaying the history. The following example uses two jshell sessions. The first session declares a variable named x1. The second session uses the -quiet option with the /reload command. Note that, this time, you did not see the replay display that the variable x1 is reloaded in the second session because you used the -quiet option.

```
C:\Java9Fundamentals>jshell
|  Welcome to JShell -- Version 9
|  For an introduction type: /help intro

jshell> int x1 = 10
x1 ==> 10

jshell> /exit
|  Goodbye

C:\Java9Fundamentals>jshell
|  Welcome to JShell -- Version 9
|  For an introduction type: /help intro

jshell> /reload -restore -quiet
|  Restarting and restoring from previous state.

jshell> x1
x1 ==> 10

jshell>
```

Configuring JShell

Using the /set command, you can customize the jshell session, ranging from startup snippets and commands to setting a platform-specific snippet editor. In this section, I explain those customizations in detail.

Setting the Snippet Editor

The JShell tool comes with a default snippet editor. In jshell, you can use the /edit command to edit all snippets or a specific snippet. The /edit command opens the snippet in an editor. The snippet editor is a platform-specific program such as notepad.exe on Windows that will be invoked to edit snippets. You can use the /set command with editor as an argument to set or delete an editor setting. The valid forms of the command are as follows:

- /set editor [-retain] [-wait] <command>
- /set editor [-retain] -default
- /set editor [-retain] -delete

If you use the -retain option, the setting will persist across jshell sessions.

If you specify a command, the command must be platform-specific. That is, you need to specify a Windows command on Windows, a UNIX command on UNIX, and so on. The command may contain flags. The JShell tool will save the snippets to be edited in a temporary file and will append the name of the temporary file to the command. You cannot work with jshell while an editor is open. If your editor exits immediately, you should specify the -wait option, which will make jshell wait until the editor is closed. The following command sets Notepad as an editor on Windows:

```
jshell> /set editor -retain notepad.exe
```

The -default option sets the snippet editor to the default editor. The -delete option deletes the current editor setting. If the -retain option is used with the -delete option, the retained editor setting is deleted:

```
jshell> /set editor -retain -delete
|  Editor set to: -default

jshell>
```

The editor set in one of the following environment variables—JSHELLEDITOR, VISUAL, or EDITOR—takes precedence over the default editor. These environment variables are looked up for an editor in order. If none of these environment variables is set, the default editor is used. The intent behind all these rules is to have an editor all the time and then use the default editor as a fallback. The /set editor command without any arguments and options prints information about the current editor setting.

The following jshell session sets Notepad as an editor on Windows. Note that this example will not work on platforms other than Windows, where you need to specify your platform-specific program as an editor.

```
C:\Java9Fundamentals>jshell
|  Welcome to JShell -- Version 9
|  For an introduction type: /help intro
```

```
jshell> /set editor
|   /set editor -default

jshell> /set editor -retain notepad.exe
|   Editor set to: notepad.exe
|   Editor setting retained: notepad.exe

jshell> /exit
|   Goodbye

C:\Java9Fundamentals>jshell
|   Welcome to JShell -- Version 9
|   For an introduction type: /help intro

jshell> /set editor
|   /set editor -retain notepad.exe

jshell> 2 + 2
$1 ==> 4

jshell> /edit

jshell> /set editor -retain -delete
|   Editor set to: -default

jshell> /exit
|   Goodbye

C:\Java9Fundamentals>SET JSHELLEDITOR=notepad.exe

C:\Java9Fundamentals>jshell
|   Welcome to JShell -- Version 9
|   For an introduction type: /help intro

jshell> /set editor
|   /set editor notepad.exe

jshell>
```

Setting Feedback Mode

When you execute a snippet or a command, jshell prints feedback. The amount and format of the feedback depends on the *feedback mode*. You can use one of the four predefined feedback modes or a custom feedback mode:

- silent
- concise
- normal
- verbose

The silent mode gives you no feedback at all and the verbose mode gives you the most feedback. The concise mode gives you the same feedback as the normal mode, but in a compact format. The default feedback mode is normal.

Table 23-3 shows the details of each built-in feedback mode. The Prompt column contains the prompt where \n indicates a new line. Other columns shows where a feedback is shown or not and, if it is shown, what the format of the feedback is. Declaration, Update, and Command columns show whether the feedbacks are shown for declarations, updates to existing snippets, and command, respectively. The "Snippet with a Value" column shows the format of the feedback when a result-bearing snippet is entered.

Table 23-3. *Features for Built-In Feedback Modes*

Mode	Prompt	Declaration	Update	Command	Snippet with a Value
silent	->	No	No	No	No
concise	jshell>	No	No	No	name ==> value (for expressions only)
normal	\njshell>	Yes	No	Yes	name ==> value
verbose	\njshell>	Yes	Yes	Yes	name ==> value (with description)

The command to set the feedback mode is as follows:

```
/set feedback [-retain] <mode>
```

Here, <mode> is one of the four feedback modes. Use the -retain option if you want to persist the feedback mode across the jshell sessions.

You can also launch jshell in a specific feedback mode:

```
jshell --feedback <mode>
```

The following command starts jshell in verbose feedback mode:

```
C:\Java9Fundamentals>jshell --feedback verbose
```

The following examples show you how to set different feedback modes:

```
C:\Java9Fundamentals>jshell
|  Welcome to JShell -- Version 9
|  For an introduction type: /help intro

jshell> 2 + 2
$1 ==> 4

jshell> /set feedback verbose
|  Feedback mode: verbose

jshell> 2 + 2
$2 ==> 4
|  created scratch variable $2 : int
```

```
jshell> /set feedback concise
jshell> 2 + 2
$3 ==> 4
jshell> /set feedback silent
-> 2 + 2
-> System.out.println("Hello")
Hello
-> /set feedback verbose
|  Feedback mode: verbose

jshell> 2 + 2
$6 ==> 4
|  created scratch variable $6 : int
```

The feedback mode set in jshell is temporary. It is set only for the current session. To persist the feedback mode across jshell sessions, use the /set command with feedback as an argument and -retain as an option:

```
jshell> /set feedback -retain
```

This command will persist the current feedback mode. When you start jshell again, it will configure the feedback mode that was set before you executed this command. It is still possible to change the feedback mode temporarily in a session. If you want to set a new feedback mode permanently, you need to use the /set feedback <mode> command and execute the command again to persist the new setting.

It is also possible to set a new feedback mode and, at the same time, persist it for future sessions by using the -retain option. The following command will set the feedback mode to verbose and retain it in future sessions:

```
jshell> /set feedback -retain verbose
```

To determine the current feedback mode, execute the /set command with the feedback argument. It prints the command used to set the current feedback mode in the first line followed by all available feedback modes, as shown:

```
jshell> /set feedback
|  /set feedback normal
|
|  Available feedback modes:
|     concise
|     normal
|     silent
|     verbose

jshell>
```

■ **Tip**   When learning jshell, it is recommended you start it in verbose feedback mode, so you get a lot of details about the state of execution of your commands and snippets. This will help you learn the tool faster.

Creating Custom feedback Modes

The four preconfigured feedback modes are good to work with jshell. They provide you different levels of granularity to customize your jshell. You can have your own custom feedback mode. I doubt you will ever need a custom feedback mode, but the feature is there, if you need it. Creating a custom feedback mode is a little more involved. You have to write several customization steps. Most likely, you will want to customize a few items in a predefined feedback mode. You can create a custom feedback mode from scratch or by copying one from an existing feedback mode and customizing it selectively. The syntax to create a custom feedback mode is as follows:

```
/set mode <mode> [<old-mode>] [-command|-quiet|-delete]
```

Here, <mode> is the name of the custom feedback mode; for example, kverbose. <old-mode> is the name of an existing feedback mode whose settings will be copied to the new mode. Using the -command option displays information about the mode when it is set, whereas using the -quiet option does not display any information when the mode is set. The -delete option is used to delete the mode.

The following command creates a new feedback mode called kverbose by copying all settings from the predefined verbose feedback mode:

```
/set mode kverbose verbose -command
```

The following command will persist the new feedback mode for future use:

```
/set mode kverbose -retain
```

You need to use the -delete option to delete a custom feedback mode. You cannot delete a predefined feedback mode. If you persisted the custom feedback mode, you can use the -retain option to delete it from current and all future sessions. The following command will delete the kverbose feedback mode:

```
/set mode kverbose -delete -retain
```

At this point, there is no difference between the predefined verbose mode and the custom kverbose mode. After you create a feedback mode, you need to customize three settings:

- Prompts

- Output truncation limits

- Output format

▓ **Tip** Once you are done defining a custom feedback mode, you need to use the /set feedback <new-mode> command to start using it.

You can set two types of prompts for feedback mode—the main prompt and the continuation prompt. The main prompt is displayed when jshell is ready to read a new snippet/command. The continuation prompt is displayed at the beginning of a line when you are entering a multi-line snippet. The syntax for setting prompts is as follows:

```
/set prompt <mode> "<prompt>" "<continuation-prompt>"
```

Here, `<prompt>` is the main prompt and `<continuation-prompt>` is the continuation prompt. The following command sets the prompts for the kverbose mode:

```
/set prompt kverbose "\njshell-kverbose> " "more... "
```

You can set the maximum number of characters displayed for each type of action/event for a feedback mode using the following command:

```
/set truncation <mode> <length> <selectors>
```

Here, `<mode>` is the feedback mode for which you set the truncation limit; `<length>` is the maximum number of characters displayed for the specified selectors. `<selectors>` is a comma-separated list of selectors that determines the context to which the truncation limit applies. Selectors are predefined keywords that represent specific contexts, for example, `vardecl` is a selector that represents a variable declaration without initialization. Use the following command for more information about setting the truncation limits and selectors:

```
/help /set truncation
```

The following commands set the truncation limit to 80 characters for everything and to five characters for a variable value or expression:

```
/set truncation kverbose 80
/set truncation kverbose 5 expression,varvalue
```

Note that the most specific selector determines the actual truncation limit to be used. The following settings use two selectors—one for all types of snippets (80 characters) and one for expressions and variable values (5 characters). For an expression, the second setting is the most specific setting. In this case, if you have a variable whose value is more than five characters, it will be truncated to five characters when displayed.

Setting the output format is a complex job. You will need to set the format for all types of output you are expecting based on the actions/events. I do not go through defining all types of output formats. Use the following command for more information about setting the output formats:

```
/help /set format
```

The syntax for setting the output format is as follows:

```
/set format <mode> <field> "<format>" <selectors>
```

Here, `<mode>` is the name of the feedback mode for which you are setting the output format; `<field>` is the context-specific format to define; "`<format>`" is used for displaying the output. `<format>` can contain names of predefined fields in braces—for example, {name}, {type}, {value}, etc., which will be replaced with actual values based on the context. `<selectors>` are selectors that determine the context in which this format will be used.

The following command sets a display format for feedback when an expression is added, modified, or replaced for entered snippets. The entire command is entered in one line.

```
/set format kverbose display "{result}{pre}created a temporary variable named {name} of type
{type} and initialized it with {value}{post}" expression-added,modified,replaced-primary
```

The following jshell session creates a new feedback mode called kverbose by copying all settings from the predefined verbose feedback mode. It customizes the prompts, truncation limits, and output formats. It uses the verbose and kverbose feedback modes to compare jshell behavior. Note that all commands in the following examples need to be entered in one line even though they sometimes appear on multiple lines in the book.

```
C:\Java9Fundamentals>jshell
|  Welcome to JShell -- Version 9
|  For an introduction type: /help intro

jshell> /set feedback
|  /set feedback -retain normal
|
|  Available feedback modes:
|     concise
|     normal
|     silent
|     verbose

jshell> /set mode kverbose verbose -command
|  Created new feedback mode: kverbose

jshell> /set mode kverbose -retain

jshell> /set prompt kverbose "\njshell-kverbose> " "more... "

jshell> /set truncation kverbose 5 expression,varvalue

jshell> /set format kverbose display "{result}{pre}created a temporary variable named {name}
of type {type} and initialized it with {value}{post}" expression-added,modified,replaced-
primary

jshell> /set feedback kverbose
|  Feedback mode: kverbose

jshell-kverbose> 2 +
more... 2
$2 ==> 4
|  created a temporary variable named $2 of type int and initialized it with 4

jshell-kverbose> 111111 + 222222
$3 ==> 33333
|  created a temporary variable named $3 of type int and initialized it with 33333

jshell-kverbose> /set feedback verbose
|  Feedback mode: verbose

jshell> 2 +
   ...> 2
$4 ==> 4
|  created scratch variable $4 : int
```

```
jshell> 111111 + 222222
$5 ==> 333333
|  created scratch variable $5 : int

jshell> /exit
|  Goodbye

C:\Java9Fundamentals>jshell
|  Welcome to JShell -- Version 9
|  For an introduction type: /help intro

jshell> /set feedback
|  /set feedback -retain normal
|
|  Retained feedback modes:
|     kverbose
|  Available feedback modes:
|     concise
|     kverbose
|     normal
|     silent
|     verbose

jshell>
```

In this jshell sessions, you set the truncation limits for expressions and variable values to five characters for the kverbose feedback mode. This is why in the kverbose feedback mode, the value of the expression 111111 + 222222 is printed as 33333, not as 333333. This not a bug. This was caused by your setting.

Note that the command /set feedback shows the command used to set the current feedback mode and a list of available feedback modes, which lists your new feedback mode named kverbose.

When you are creating a custom feedback mode, it will be helpful to know all the settings for the existing feedback modes. You can print a list of all settings for all the feedback modes using the following command:

```
/set mode
```

You can also print a list of all settings for a specific feedback mode by passing the mode name as an argument to the command. The following command prints a list of all settings for the silent feedback mode. The first line in the output is the command used to create silent mode.

```
jshell> /set mode silent
|   /set mode silent -quiet
|   /set prompt silent "-> " ">> "
|   /set format silent display ""
|   /set format silent err "%6$s"
|   /set format silent errorline "    {err}%n"
|   /set format silent errorpost "%n"
|   /set format silent errorpre "|   "
|   /set format silent errors "%5$s"
|   /set format silent name "%1$s"
|   /set format silent post "%n"
```

```
|  /set format silent pre "|   "
|  /set format silent type "%2$s"
|  /set format silent unresolved "%4$s"
|  /set format silent value "%3$s"
|  /set truncation silent 80
|  /set truncation silent 1000 expression,varvalue
```

Setting Up Startup Snippets

You can use the /set command with a start argument to set up your startup snippets and commands. Startup snippets and commands are automatically executed when you launch jshell. You have seen the default startup snippets that import types from a few commonly used packages. Typically, you would set the class path and module path using an /env command and import statements to your startup script.

You can print a list of default startup snippets using the /list -start command. Note that this command prints the default startup snippets, not the current startup snippets. Remember you can also drop startup snippets. Default startup snippets include what you get when you start jshell. Current startup snippets include the default startup snippets minus those you have dropped in the current jshell session. You can use one of the following forms of the /set command to set startup snippets/commands:

- /set start [-retain] <file>

- /set start [-retain] -default

- /set start [-retain] -none

Using the -retain option is optional. If it is used, the setting persists across jshell sessions.

The first form is used to set startup snippets/commands from a file. When a /reset or a /reload command is executed in the current session, the file's contents will be used as startup snippets/commands. Once you set the startup code from a file, jshell caches the file's contents for future use. Modifying the file's contents does not affect the startup code until you set the startup snippets/commands again.

The second form is used to set the startup snippets/commands to the built-in default.

The third form is used to set an empty startup. That is, there will be no snippets/commands executed at startup.

The /set start command without any options or files shows the current startup setting. If the startup was set from a file, it shows the file name, the startup snippets, and the time at which the startup snippets were set.

Consider the following scenario. The Java9Fundamentals/build/modules/jdojo.jshell directory in the book's source code contains a com.jdojo.jshell.Person class. Let's test this class in jshell and use the types from the java.time package. To do this, your startup settings will look like the contents shown in Listing 23-4.

Listing 23-4. Contents of a File Named startup.jsh

```
/env -class-path C:\Java9Fundamentals\build\modules\jdojo.jshell
import java.io.*
import java.math.*
import java.net.*
import java.nio.file.*
import java.util.*
import java.util.concurrent.*
import java.util.function.*
import java.util.prefs.*
```

```
import java.util.regex.*
import java.util.stream.*
import java.time.*;
import com.jdojo.jshell.*;
void printf(String format, Object... args) { System.out.printf(format, args); }
```

Save the settings in a file named startup.jsh in your current directory. If you save it in any other directory, you can use an absolute path for this file while working with this example. Note that the first command is a /env -class-path command for Windows assuming that you stored the source code in the C:\ directory. Change the class path value according to your platform and the location of the book's source code on your computer.

Note the last snippet in the startup.jsh file. It defines a top-level function named printf() that is a wrapper for the System.out.printf() method. The printf() function was included in the initial builds of the JShell tool by default. Later, it was removed. If you want to use a short method name, such as printf(), instead of System.out.printf() to print messages on the standard output, you can include this snippet in your startup script. If you want to use println() and printf() top-level methods in jshell by default, you need to start jshell as following:

```
C:\Java9Fundamentals>jshell --start DEFAULT --start PRINTING
```

The DEFAULT argument will include all default import statements and the PRINTING argument will include all versions of the print(), println(), and printf() methods. After you launch jshell using this command, execute the /list -start command to see all startup imports and methods added by the two --start options used in the command.

The following jshell sessions show you how to set the startup settings from a file and its usage in subsequence sessions:

```
C:\Java9Fundamentals>jshell
|  Welcome to JShell -- Version 9
|  For an introduction type: /help intro

jshell> /set start
|  /set start -default

jshell> /set start -retain startup.jsh

jshell> Person p;
|  created variable p, however, it cannot be referenced until class Person is declared

jshell> /reset
|  Resetting state.

jshell> Person p;
p ==> null

jshell> /exit
|  Goodbye

C:\Java9Fundamentals>jshell
|  Welcome to JShell -- Version 9
|  For an introduction type: /help intro
```

```
jshell> /set start
|   /set start -retain startup.jsh
|   ---- startup.jsh @ Aug 20, 2017, 9:58:11 AM ----
|   /env -class-path C:\Java9Fundamentals\build\modules\jdojo.jshell
|   import java.io.*
|   import java.math.*
|   import java.net.*
|   import java.nio.file.*
|   import java.util.*
|   import java.util.concurrent.*
|   import java.util.function.*
|   import java.util.prefs.*
|   import java.util.regex.*
|   import java.util.stream.*
|   import java.time.*;
|   import com.jdojo.jshell.*;
|   void printf(String format, Object... args) { System.out.printf(format, args); }

jshell> Person p;
p ==> null

jshell> LocalDate.now()
$15 ==> 2017-08-20

jshell> printf("2 + 2 = %d%n", 2 + 2)
2 + 2 = 4

jshell>
```

░░ **Tip**   Setting the startup snippets/commands does not take effect until you relaunch jshell, execute a /reset, or execute a /reload command. Do not include a /reset or a /reload command in your startup file. It will cause an infinite loop when your startup file loads.

There are three predefined scripts whose names are as follows:

- DEFAULT
- PRINTING
- JAVASE

The DEFAULT script contains commonly used import statements as you have seen them in the "Import Statements" section. The PRINTING script defines top-level JShell methods that redirect to the print(), println(), and printf() methods in PrintStream as shown in this section. The JAVASE script imports all Java SE packages, which is big and takes a few seconds to complete. The following commands show you how to save these scripts as the startup script:

```
C:\Java9Fundamentals>jshell
|   Welcome to JShell -- Version 9
|   For an introduction type: /help intro
```

```
jshell> println("Hello")
|  Error:
|  cannot find symbol
|    symbol:   method println(java.lang.String)
|  println("Hello")
|  ^-----^

jshell> /set start -retain DEFAULT PRINTING

jshell> /exit
|  Goodbye

C:\Java9Fundamentals>jshell
|  Welcome to JShell -- Version 9
|  For an introduction type: /help intro

jshell> println("Hello")
Hello

jshell>
```

Notice that using the `println()` method for the first time resulted in an error. After saving the `PRINTING` script as the startup script and restarting the tool, the method works.

Using JShell Documentation

The JShell tool ships with extensive documentation. Because it is a command-line tool, it is little harder to read the documentation on a command line. You can use the /help or /? command to display a list of commands and their brief descriptions.

```
jshell> /help
|  Type a Java language expression, statement, or declaration.
|  Or type one of the following commands:

|  /list [<name or id>|-all|-start]  -- list the source you have typed
|  /edit <name or id>  -- edit a source entry referenced by name or id
|  /drop <name or id>  -- delete a source entry referenced by name or id
|  ...
```

You can use a specific command as an argument to the /help command to get information about the command. The following command prints information about the /help command itself:

```
jshell> /help /help
|
|  /help
|
|  Display information about jshell.
|  /help
|       List the jshell commands and help subjects.
|
```

```
|   /help <command>
|        Display information about the specified command. The slash must be included.
|        Only the first few letters of the command are needed -- if more than one
|        each will be displayed.  Example:  /help /li
|
|   /help <subject>
|        Display information about the specified help subject. Example: /help intro
```

The following commands will display information about the /list and /set commands. Outputs are not shown because they are long:

```
jshell> /help /list
|...

jshell> /help /set
|...
```

Sometimes, a command is used to work with multiple topics, for example, the /set command can be used to set the feedback mode, a snippet editor, startup scripts, etc. If you want to print information about a specific topic of a command, you can use the /help command in the following format:

```
/help /<command> <topic-name>
```

The following command prints information about setting the feedback mode:

```
jshell> /help /set feedback
```

The following command prints information about creating a custom feedback mode:

```
jshell> /help /set mode
```

Use the /help command with a subject as an argument to print information about the subject. Currently, there are three predefined subjects: intro, shortcuts, and context. The following command will print an introduction to the JShell tool:

```
jshell> /help intro
```

The following command will print a list of shortcuts and their descriptions that you can use in the JShell tool:

```
jshell> /help shortcuts
```

The following command will print a list of options used to set the execution context. These options are used with the /env, /reset, and /reload commands.

```
jshell> /help context
```

The JShell API

The JShell API gives you programmatic access to the snippet evaluation engine. As a developer, you may not use this API. It is meant to be used by tools such as the NetBeans IDE that includes a UI equivalent of the JShell command-line tool to let developers evaluate snippets of code from inside the IDE instead of opening a command prompt to do the same. In this section, I briefly introduce the JShell API and show its use with a simple example.

The JShell API is in the `jdk.jshell` module and the `jdk.jshell` package. If you are using the JShell API, your module will need to read the `jdk.jshell` module. The JShell API is simple. It consists mainly of three abstract classes and one interface:

- `JShell`
- `Snippet`
- `SnippetEvent`
- `SourceCodeAnalysis`

An instance of the `JShell` class represents a snippet evaluation engine. This is the main class in the JShell API. A `JShell` instance maintains the state of all snippets as they are executed.

A snippet is represented by an instance of the `Snippet` class. A `JShell` instance generates snippet events as it executes snippets.

A snippet event is represented by an instance of the `SnippetEvent` interface. A snippet event contains the current and previous statuses of snippets, the value of the snippet for a result-bearing snippet, the source code of the snippet that caused the event, an `Exception` object if an exception occurred during the snippet execution, etc.

An instance of the `SourceCodeAnalysis` class provides source code analysis and suggestion features for a snippet. It answers questions like the following:

- Is it a complete snippet?
- Can this snippet be completed by appending a semicolon?

A `SourceCodeAnalysis` instance also provides a list of suggestions, for example, for Tab completion and accessing the documentation. This class is meant to be used by a tool providing the JShell functionality. I do not discuss it any further. Refer to the Javadoc of this class if you are interested in exploring it further.

Figure 23-5 shows the use case diagram for the different components of the JShell API. In subsequent sections, I explain these classes and their uses. I show you a complete example in the last section.

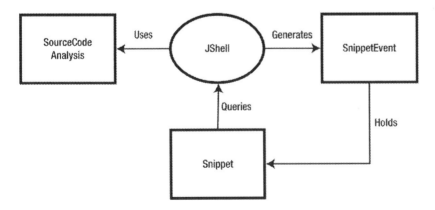

Figure 23-5. *A use case diagram for the components of the JShell API*

Creating a JShell

The JShell class is abstract. It provides two ways to create its instances:

- Using its static create() method

- Using a static builder class named JShell.Builder

The create() method returns a preconfigured JShell instance. The following snippet of code shows how to create a JShell using the create() method:

```
// Create a JShell instance
JShell shell = JShell.create()
```

The JShell.Builder class lets you configure the JShell instance by letting you specify a snippet ID generator, a temporary variable name generator, a print stream for printing the output, an input stream to read snippets, and an error output stream to log errors. You can obtain an instance of the JShell.Builder class using the builder() static method of the JShell class. The following snippet of code shows how to use the JShell.Builder class to create a JShell, where myXXXStream in the code are references to your stream objects:

```
// Create a JShell instance
JShell shell = JShell.builder()
                    .in(myInputStream)
                    .out(myOutputStream)
                    .err(myErrorStream)
                    .build();
```

Once you have a JShell instance, you can start evaluating snippets using its eval(String snippet) method. You can drop a snippet using its drop(PersistentSnippet snippet) method. You can append a path to the class path using its addToClasspath(String path) method. These three methods change the state of the JShell instance.

▓ **Tip**   When you are done using a JShell instance, you need to call its close() method to free resources. The JShell class implements the AutoCloseable interface, and therefore, using a try-with-resources block to work with a JShell instance is the best way to ensure that it is closed when it is no longer in use. A JShell instance is mutable and not thread-safe.

You can register snippet event handlers and JShell shutdown event handlers using the onSnippetEvent (Consumer<SnippetEvent> listener) and onShutdown(Consumer<JShell> listener) methods of the JShell class. A snippet event is fired when the status of a snippet changes because it is evaluated the first time or its status is updated because of evaluation of another snippet.

The sourceCodeAnalysis() method in the JShell class returns an instance of the SourceCodeAnalysis class, which you can use for code-assist functionality.

Other methods in the JShell class are used to query the state. For example, the snippets(), types(), methods(), and variables() methods return a list of all snippets, all snippets with active type declarations, snippets with active method declarations, and snippets with active variable declarations, respectively.

The eval() method is the most frequently used method in the JShell class. It evaluates/executes the specified snippet and returns a List<SnippetEvent>. You can query the snippet events in the list for the state of execution. The following is a snippet of code that uses the eval() method:

```
// Create a snippet
String snippet = "int x = 100;";

// Evaluate the snippet
List<SnippetEvent> events = shell.eval(snippet);

// Process the results
events.forEach((SnippetEvent se) -> {
    /* Handle the snippet event here */
});
```

Working with Snippets

An instance of the Snippet class represents a snippet. The class does not provide a way to create its objects. You supply snippets to a JShell as strings and you receive instances of the Snippet class as part of the snippet events. Snippet events also provide you with the previous and current statuses of a snippet. If you have a Snippet object, you can query its current status using the status(Snippet s) method of the JShell class, which returns a Snippet.Status.

■ **Tip**　The Snippet class is immutable and thread-safe.

There are several types of snippets in Java, for example, a variable declaration, a variable declaration with initialization, a method declaration, a type declaration, etc. The Snippet class is an abstract class and there is a subclass to represent each specific type of snippet. Figure 23-6 shows the class diagram for the Snippet class and its descendants.

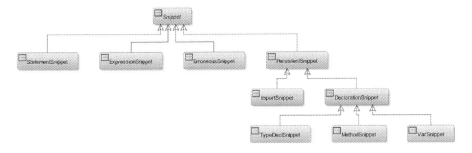

Figure 23-6. *A class diagram for the Snippet class and its descendants*

The name of the subclasses of the Snippet class are intuitive. For example, an instance of the PersistentSnippet represents a snippet that is stored in a JShell and can be reused such as a class declaration or a method declaration. The Snippet class contains the following methods:

- String id()

- String source()

- Snippet.Kind kind()

- Snippet.SubKind subKind()

The id() method returns a unique ID of the snippet and the source() method returns its source code. The kind() and subKind() methods return the type and sub-type of a snippet.

The type of a snippet is one of the constants of the Snippet.Kind enum, for example, IMPORT, TYPE_DECL, METHOD, VAR, etc. The sub-type of a snippet provides more specific information about its type, for example, if a snippet is a type declaration, its sub-type will tell you if it is a class, interface, enum, or annotation declaration. The sub-type of a snippet is one of the constants of the Snippet.SubKind enum such as CLASS_SUBKIND, ENUM_SUBKIND, etc. The Snippet.Kind enum contains an isPersistent property whose value is true if the snippet of this kind is persistent and false otherwise.

Subclasses of the Snippet class add more methods to return specific information about the specific type of snippet. For example, the VarSnippet class contains a typeName() method, which returns the data type of the variable. The MethodSnippet class contains the parameterTypes() and signature() methods, which return parameter types and the full signature of the method as a string.

A snippet does not contain its status. A JShell executes and holds the status of a Snippet. Note that executing a snippet may affect the status of other snippets. For example, a snippet declaring a variable may change the status of a snippet declaring a method from valid to invalid or vice versa if the method was referencing the variable. If you need the current status of a snippet, use the status(Snippet s) method of the JShell class, which returns one of the following constants of the Snippet.Status enum:

- DROPPED: The snippet is inactive because it was dropped using the drop() method of the JShell class.

- NONEXISTENT: The snippet is inactive because it does not yet exist.

- OVERWRITTEN: The snippet is inactive because it has been replaced by a new snippet.

- RECOVERABLE_DEFINED: The snippet is a declaration snippet containing unresolved references. The declaration has a valid signature and it is visible to other snippets. It can be recovered and used when other snippets change its status to VALID.

- RECOVERABLE_NOT_DEFINED: The snippet is a declaration snippet containing unresolved references. The snippet has an invalid signature and it is not visible to other snippets. It can be used later when its status changes to VALID.

- REJECTED: The snippet is inactive because it failed compilation on initial evaluation and it is not capable of becoming valid with further changes to the JShell state.

- VALID: The snippet is valid in the context of the current JShell state.

Handling Snippet Events

A JShell instance generates snippet events as part of snippet evaluation or execution. You can handle snippet events by registering event handlers using the onSnippetEvent() method of the JShell class or by using the return value of the eval() method of the JShell class, which is a List<SnippetEvent>. The following snippet of code shows you how to process snippet events using the return value of the eval() method:

```
try (JShell shell = JShell.create()) {
    // Create a snippet
    String snippet = "int x = 100;";

    shell.eval(snippet)
        .forEach((SnippetEvent se) -> {
            Snippet s = se.snippet();
            System.out.printf("Snippet: %s%n", s.source());
            System.out.printf("Kind: %s%n", s.kind());
            System.out.printf("Sub-Kind: %s%n", s.subKind());
            System.out.printf("Previous Status: %s%n", se.previousStatus());
            System.out.printf("Current Status: %s%n", se.status());
            System.out.printf("Value: %s%n", se.value());
        });
}
```

An Example

Let's look at the JShell API in action. Listing 23-5 contains the complete code for a class named JShellApiTest, which is a member of the jdojo.jshell module.

Listing 23-5. A JShellApiTest Class to Test the JShell API

```
// JShellApiTest.java
package com.jdojo.jshell;

import jdk.jshell.JShell;
import jdk.jshell.Snippet;
import jdk.jshell.SnippetEvent;

public class JShellApiTest {
    public static void main(String[] args) {
        // Create an array of snippets to evaluate/execute
        // them sequentially
        String[] snippets = {"int x = 100;",
            "double x = 190.89;",
            "long multiply(int value) {return value * multiplier;}",
            "int multiplier = 2;",
            "multiply(200)",
            "mul(99)"
        };
```

```java
        try (JShell shell = JShell.create()) {
            // Register a snippet event handler
            shell.onSnippetEvent(JShellApiTest::snippetEventHandler);

            // Evaluate all snippets
            for (String snippet : snippets) {
                shell.eval(snippet);
                System.out.println("------------------------");
            }
        }
    }

    public static void snippetEventHandler(SnippetEvent se) {
        // Print the details of this snippet event
        Snippet snippet = se.snippet();
        System.out.printf("Snippet: %s%n", snippet.source());

        // Print the cause of this snippet event
        Snippet causeSnippet = se.causeSnippet();
        if (causeSnippet != null) {
            System.out.printf("Cause Snippet: %s%n", causeSnippet.source());
        }

        System.out.printf("Kind: %s%n", snippet.kind());
        System.out.printf("Sub-Kind: %s%n", snippet.subKind());
        System.out.printf("Previous Status: %s%n", se.previousStatus());
        System.out.printf("Current Status: %s%n", se.status());
        System.out.printf("Value: %s%n", se.value());

        Exception e = se.exception();
        if (e != null) {
            System.out.printf("Exception: %s%n", se.exception().getMessage());
        }
    }
}
```

```
Snippet: int x = 100;
Kind: VAR
Sub-Kind: VAR_DECLARATION_WITH_INITIALIZER_SUBKIND
Previous Status: NONEXISTENT
Current Status: VALID
Value: 100
----------------------------------------------------------------
Snippet: double x = 190.89;
Kind: VAR
Sub-Kind: VAR_DECLARATION_WITH_INITIALIZER_SUBKIND
Previous Status: VALID
Current Status: VALID
Value: 190.89
Snippet: int x = 100;
Cause Snippet: double x = 190.89;
```

```
Kind: VAR
Sub-Kind: VAR_DECLARATION_WITH_INITIALIZER_SUBKIND
Previous Status: VALID
Current Status: OVERWRITTEN
Value: null
-----------------------------------------------------------------
Snippet: long multiply(int value) {return value * multiplier;}
Kind: METHOD
Sub-Kind: METHOD_SUBKIND
Previous Status: NONEXISTENT
Current Status: RECOVERABLE_DEFINED
Value: null
-----------------------------------------------------------------
Snippet: int multiplier = 2;
Kind: VAR
Sub-Kind: VAR_DECLARATION_WITH_INITIALIZER_SUBKIND
Previous Status: NONEXISTENT
Current Status: VALID
Value: 2
Snippet: long multiply(int value) {return value * multiplier;}
Cause Snippet: int multiplier = 2;
Kind: METHOD
Sub-Kind: METHOD_SUBKIND
Previous Status: RECOVERABLE_DEFINED
Current Status: VALID
Value: null
-----------------------------------------------------------------
Snippet: multiply(200)
Kind: VAR
Sub-Kind: TEMP_VAR_EXPRESSION_SUBKIND
Previous Status: NONEXISTENT
Current Status: VALID
Value: 400
-----------------------------------------------------------------
Snippet: mul(99)
Kind: ERRONEOUS
Sub-Kind: UNKNOWN_SUBKIND
Previous Status: NONEXISTENT
Current Status: REJECTED
Value: null
-----------------------------------------------------------------
```

The main() method creates the following six snippets and stores them in a String array:

- "int x = 100;"

- "double x = 190.89;"

- "long multiply(int value) {return value * multiplier;}"

- "int multiplier = 2;"

- "multiply(200)"

- "mul(99)"

A try-with-resources block is used to create a JShell instance. The snippetEventHandler() method is registered as a snippet event handler. The method prints details about the snippets such as its source code, the source code of the snippet that caused the update in the snippet status, the snippet's previous and current status, its value, etc. Finally, a for-each loop is used to iterate through all the snippets and the eval() method is called to execute them.

Let's walk through the state of the JShell engine when each of these snippets is executed:

- When snippet #1 is executed, the snippet did not exist, so it transitions from a NONEXISTENT to a VALID status. It is a variable declaration snippet and it evaluates to 100.

- When snippet #2 is executed, it already existed. Note that it declares the same variable named x with a different data type. Its previous status was VALID and its current status is VALID too. The execution of this snippet changes the status of snippet #1, whose status changes from VALID to OVERWRITTEN, because you cannot have two variables with the same name.

- Snippet #3 declares a method named multiply(), which uses an undeclared variable named multiplier in its body, so its status changes from NONEXISTENT to RECOVERABLE_DEFINED. The method is defined, which means that it can be referenced but cannot be invoked until a variable named multiplier of appropriate type is defined.

- Snippet #4 defines a variable named multiplier, which makes snippet #3 valid.

- Snippet #5 evaluates an expression that calls the multiply() method. The expression is valid and it evaluates to 400.

- Snippet #6 evaluates an expression that calls a mul() method, which you have never defined. The snippet is erroneous and is rejected.

Typically, you will not use JShell API and the JShell tool together. However, let's use them together just for fun. The JShell API is just another API in Java and it can also be used inside the JShell tool. The following jshell session instantiates a JShell, registers a snippet event handler, and evaluates two snippets.

```
C:\Java9Fundamentals>jshell
|  Welcome to JShell -- Version 9
|  For an introduction type: /help intro

jshell> /set feedback silent
-> import jdk.jshell.*
-> JShell shell = JShell.create()
-> shell.onSnippetEvent(se -> {
>>   System.out.printf("Snippet: %s%n", se.snippet().source());
>>   System.out.printf("Previous Status: %s%n", se.previousStatus());
>>   System.out.printf("Current Status: %s%n", se.status());
>>   System.out.printf("Value: %s%n", se.value());
>> });
-> shell.eval("int x = 100;");
Snippet: int x = 100;
Previous Status: NONEXISTENT
Current Status: VALID
Value: 100
-> shell.eval("double x = 100.89;");
Snippet: double x = 100.89;
```

```
Previous Status: VALID
Current Status: VALID
Value: 100.89
Snippet: int x = 100;
Previous Status: VALID
Current Status: OVERWRITTEN
Value: null
-> shell.close()
-> /exit

C:\Java9Fundamentals>
```

Summary

The Java shell, which is called JShell in JDK 9, is a command-line tool that provides an interactive way to access the Java programming language. It lets you evaluate snippets of Java code instead of forcing you to write an entire Java program. It is a REPL for Java. JShell is also an API that provides programmatic access to the REPL functionality for the Java code for other tools such as IDEs.

You can start the JShell command-line tool by running the jshell program that is copied to the JDK_HOME\bin directory when you install JDK 9. The tool supports executing snippets and commands. Snippets are pieces of Java code. As snippets are evaluated/executed, JShell maintains its state. It also keeps track of the status of all entered snippets. You can use commands to query the JShell state and configure the jshell environment. To distinguish commands from snippets, all the commands start with a slash (/).

JShell contains several features that make developers more productive and provide a better user experience, such as auto-completion of code and displaying the Javadoc inside the tool. It attempts to use the already existing functionalities in the JDK such as the Compiler API to parse, analyze, and compile snippets, and the Java Debugger API to replace existing snippets with new ones in the JVM. Its design makes it possible to use new constructs in the Java languages without any changes or with a few changes to the JShell tool itself.

EXERCISES

1. What is Java shell?

2. What command do you use to start the JShell command-line tool?

3. What command do you use to exit the JShell command-line tool?

4. What command do you use to print help in the JShell tool?

5. How does the JShell tool differentiate between snippets and commands?

6. Why can't you have a package declaration in your snippet that you enter in jshell?

7. What command do you use to list all active snippets, all snippets, and all startup snippets?

8. What command do you use to set the module path and the class path in the JShell tool?

9. How do you run the previous snippet in jshell?

10. What happens when a checked exception is thrown when you execute a snippet in jshell?

11. What key do you use for auto-completing code on the JShell tool?

12. What key combination do you use to auto-convert an expression into a variable declaration of the appropriate type?

13. What key combination do you use to auto-import an unresolved type in a snippet?

14. What are the four built-in feedback modes in JShell tool? Which feedback mode are you supposed to use when learning the JShell tool? Can you customize the built-in feedback mode?

15. Write the command that sets the feedback mode to `verbose` for the current and all future sessions.

16. What is the effect of executing the `/reset` command?

17. What is the effect of executing the `/reload` command?

18. What commands do you use to save snippets in a `jshell` session to a file and load snippets from a file to a `jshell` session?

19. Describe the role of the `JShell`, `Snippet`, and `SnippetEvent` classes in the JShell API.

20. How do you create an instance of the `JShell` class?

21. How do you get an instance of the `Snippet` class in your program?

22. How do you start the JShell tool so that you can use the `println()` function to print a message instead of using the `System.out.println()`. Show the command to make this setting permanent in the JShell tool.

APPENDIX A

■ ■ ■

Character Encodings

A character is the basic unit of a writing system, for example, a letter of the English alphabet, and an ideograph of an ideographic writing system such as Chinese and Japanese ideographs. In the written form, a character is identified by its shape, also known as *glyph*. The identification of a character with its shape is not precise. It depends on many factors, for example, a hyphen is identified as a minus sign in a mathematical expression; some Greek and Latin letters have the same shapes, but they are considered different characters in two written scripts. Computers understand only numbers, more precisely, only bits 0 and 1. Therefore, it was necessary to convert, with the advent of computers, the characters into codes (or bit combinations) inside the computer's memory, so that the text (sequence of characters) could be stored and reproduced. However, different computers may represent different characters with the same bit combinations, which may lead to misinterpretation of text stored by one computer system and reproduced by another. Therefore, for correct exchange of information between two computer systems, it is necessary that one computer system understand unambiguously the coded form of the characters represented in bit combinations produced by another computer system and vice versa. Before we begin our discussion of some widely used character encodings, it is necessary to understand some commonly used terms.

- An *abstract character* is a unit of textual information, for example, the Latin capital letter A ('A').

- A *character repertoire* is defined as the set of characters to be encoded. A character repertoire can be fixed or open. In a fixed character repertoire, once the set of characters to be encoded is decided, it is never changed. ASCII and POSIX portable character repertoires are examples of fixed character repertoires. In an open character repertoire, a new character may be added any time. Unicode and Windows Western European repertoires are examples of open character repertoires. The Euro currency sign and Indian Rupee sign were added to Unicode because it is an open repertoire.

- A *coded character set* is defined as a mapping from a set of non-negative integers (also known as code positions, code points, code values, character numbers, and code space) to a set of abstract characters. The integer that maps to a character is called the *code point* for that character and the character is called an *encoded character*. A coded character set is also called a character encoding, coded character repertoire, character set definition, or code page. Figure A-1 depicts two different coded character sets; both of them have the same character repertoire, which is the set of three characters (A, B, and C) and the same code points, which is the set of three non-negative integers (1, 2, and 3).

© Kishori Sharan 2017
K. Sharan, *Beginning Java 9 Fundamentals*, https://doi.org/10.1007/978-1-4842-2902-6

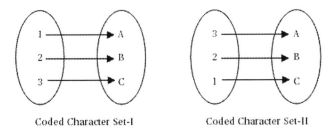

Figure A-1. *Two coded character sets having the same character repertoire and code points*

To define a coded character set, you need to specify three things:

- A set of code points
- A set of characters
- A mapping between the set of code points and the set of characters

The number of bits used to represent a character determines how many distinct characters can be represented in a coded character set. Some widely used coded character sets are outlined in the following sections.

ASCII

ASCII, the American Standard Code for Information Interchange, is a 7-bit coded character set. ASCII has 2^7 (=128) code points and so it represents 128 distinct characters whose numeric values range from 0 (binary 0000000) to 127 (binary 1111111). The characters NUL and DELETE are represented by code points 0000000 and 1111111, respectively. There are historical reasons to assign these code points to NUL and DELETE characters. It was common to use punched paper tapes to store data for processing by the time ASCII was developed. A 1 bit was used to represent a hole on the paper tape, whereas a 0 bit represented the absence of a hole. Since a row of seven 0 bits would be indistinguishable from blank tape, the coding 0000000 would have to represent a NUL character, that is, the absence of any effect. Since holes, once punched, could not be erased but an erroneous character could always be converted into 111111, this bit pattern was adopted as the DELETE character.

ASCII uses the first 32 bit combinations (or code points) to represent control characters. This range includes the NUL character, but not the DELETE character. Therefore, it leaves 95 bit combinations for printing characters.

```
128(All characters) - 32(Control Characters) - 1(DELETE) = 95(Printing characters)
```

All printing characters are arranged in the order that could be used for sorting purposes. The SPACE character is normally sorted before any other printing character. Therefore, the SPACE character is allocated the first position among the printing characters. The code point for the SPACE character in ASCII is 32, or 1100000. The code point range of 48 to 57 represents 0 to 9 digits, 65 to 90 represents 26 uppercase letters A to Z, and 97 to 122 represents 26 lowercase letters a to z. Modern computers use an 8-bit combination, also known as a *byte*, as the smallest unit for storage. Therefore, on modern computers, a 7-bit ASCII character uses 8 bits (or 1 byte) of memory, of which the most significant bit is always set to 0; for example, SPACE is stored as 01100000 and DELETE is stored as 0111111. Table A-1 contains the list of characters in the ASCII character set.

Table A-1. *ASCII Character Set*

Decimal	Hexadecimal	Binary	Character	Official Name
0	0	0	NUL	NULL
1	1	1	SOH	Start of heading
2	2	10	STX	Start of text
3	3	11	ETX	End of text
4	4	100	EOT	End of transmission
5	5	101	ENQ	Enquiry
6	6	110	ACK	Acknowledge
7	7	111	BEL	Bell
8	8	1000	BS	Backspace
9	9	1001	TAB	Horizontal tab
10	0A	1010	LF	Line feed (new line)
11	0B	1011	VT	Vertical tab
12	0C	1100	FF	Form feed (new page)
13	0D	1101	CR	Carriage return
14	0E	1110	SO	Shift out
15	0F	1111	SI	Shift in
16	10	10000	DLE	Data link escape
17	11	10001	DC1	Device control 1
18	12	10010	DC2	Device control 2
19	13	10011	DC3	Device control 3
20	14	10100	DC4	Device control 4
21	15	10101	NAK	Negative acknowledge
22	16	10110	SYN	Synchronous idle
23	17	10111	ETB	End of transmission block
24	18	11000	CAN	Cancel
25	19	11001	EM	End of medium
26	1A	11010	SUB	Substitute
27	1B	11011	ESC	Escape
28	1C	11100	FS	File separator
29	1D	11101	GS	Group separator
30	1E	11110	RS	Record separator
31	1F	11111	US	Unit separator
32	20	100000	SP	Space
33	21	100001	!	Exclamation mark

(continued)

Table A-1. (*continued*)

Decimal	Hexadecimal	Binary	Character	Official Name
34	22	100010	"	Quotation mark
35	23	100011	#	Number sign
36	24	100100	$	Dollar sign
37	25	100101	%	Percent sign
38	26	100110	&	Ampersand
39	27	100111	'	Apostrophe
40	28	101000	(	Left parenthesis
41	29	101001	)	Right parenthesis
42	2A	101010	*	Asterisk
43	2B	101011	+	Plus sign
44	2C	101100	,	Comma
45	2D	101101	-	Hyphen/minus
46	2E	101110	.	Full stop/period
47	2F	101111	/	Solidus/slash
48	30	110000	0	Digit zero
49	31	110001	1	Digit one
50	32	110010	2	Digit two
51	33	110011	3	Digit three
52	34	110100	4	Digit four
53	35	110101	5	Digit five
54	36	110110	6	Digit six
55	37	110111	7	Digit seven
56	38	111000	8	Digit eight
57	39	111001	9	Digit nine
58	3A	111010	:	Colon
59	3B	111011	;	Semicolon
60	3C	111100	<	Less-than sign
61	3D	111101	=	Equals sign
62	3E	111110	>	Greater-than sign
63	3F	111111	?	Question mark
64	40	1000000	@	Commercial at
65	41	1000001	A	Latin capital letter A
66	42	1000010	B	Latin capital letter B

(*continued*)

Table A-1. (*continued*)

Decimal	Hexadecimal	Binary	Character	Official Name
67	43	1000011	C	Latin capital letter C
68	44	1000100	D	Latin capital letter D
69	45	1000101	E	Latin capital letter E
70	46	1000110	F	Latin capital letter F
71	47	1000111	G	Latin capital letter G
72	48	1001000	H	Latin capital letter H
73	49	1001001	I	Latin capital letter I
74	4A	1001010	J	Latin capital letter J
75	4B	1001011	K	Latin capital letter K
76	4C	1001100	L	Latin capital letter L
77	4D	1001101	M	Latin capital letter M
78	4E	1001110	N	Latin capital letter N
79	4F	1001111	O	Latin capital letter O
80	50	1010000	P	Latin capital letter P
81	51	1010001	Q	Latin capital letter Q
82	52	1010010	R	Latin capital letter R
83	53	1010011	S	Latin capital letter S
84	54	1010100	T	Latin capital letter T
85	55	1010101	U	Latin capital letter U
86	56	1010110	V	Latin capital letter V
87	57	1010111	W	Latin capital letter W
88	58	1011000	X	Latin capital letter X
89	59	1011001	Y	Latin capital letter Y
90	5A	1011010	Z	Latin capital letter Z
91	5B	1011011	[	Left square bracket/opening square bracket
92	5C	1011100	\	Reverse solidus/backslash
93	5D	1011101	]	Right square bracket/closing square bracket
94	5E	1011110	^	Circumflex accent
95	5F	1011111	_	Low line/spacing underscore
96	60	1100000	`	Grave accent
97	61	1100001	A	Latin small letter A
98	62	1100010	B	Latin small letter B
99	63	1100011	C	Latin small letter C

(*continued*)

Table A-1. (*continued*)

Decimal	Hexadecimal	Binary	Character	Official Name
100	64	1100100	D	Latin small letter D
101	65	1100101	E	Latin small letter E
102	66	1100110	F	Latin small letter F
103	67	1100111	G	Latin small letter G
104	68	1101000	H	Latin small letter H
105	69	1101001	I	Latin small letter I
106	6A	1101010	J	Latin small letter J
107	6B	1101011	K	Latin small letter K
108	6C	1101100	L	Latin small letter L
109	6D	1101101	M	Latin small letter M
110	6E	1101110	N	Latin small letter N
111	6F	1101111	O	Latin small letter O
112	70	1110000	P	Latin small letter P
113	71	1110001	Q	Latin small letter Q
114	72	1110010	R	Latin small letter R
115	73	1110011	S	Latin small letter S
116	74	1110100	T	Latin small letter T
117	75	1110101	U	Latin small letter U
118	76	1110110	V	Latin small letter V
119	77	1110111	W	Latin small letter W
120	78	1111000	X	Latin small letter X
121	79	1111001	Y	Latin small letter Y
122	7A	1111010	Z	Latin small letter Z
123	7B	1111011	{	Left curly bracket/opening curly bracket
124	7C	1111100	|	Vertical line/vertical bar
125	7D	1111101	}	Right curly bracket/closing curly bracket
126	7E	1111110	~	Tilde
127	7F	1111111	DEL	DELETE

8-Bit Character Sets

The ASCII character set worked fine for the English language. Representing the alphabets from other languages, for example, French and German, led to the development of an 8-bit character set. An 8-bit character set defines 2^8 (or 256) character positions whose numeric values range from 0 to 255. The bit combination for an 8-bit character set ranges from 00000000 to 11111111. The 8-bit character set is divided into two parts. The first part represents characters, which are the same as in the ASCII character set. The second part introduces 128 new characters. The first 32 positions in the second part are reserved for control characters. Therefore, there are two control character areas in an 8-bit character set: 0-31 and 128-159. Since the SPACE and DELETE characters are already defined in the first part, an 8-bit character set can accommodate 192 printing characters (95 + 97), including SPACE. ISO Latin-1 is one example of an 8-bit character set.

Even an 8-bit character set is not large enough to accommodate most of the alphabets of all languages in the world. This lead to the development of a bigger (may be the biggest) character set, which is known as the Universal Character Set (UCS).

Universal Multiple-Octet Coded Character Set (UCS)

The Universal Multiple-Octet Coded Character Set, simply known as UCS, is intended to provide a single coded character set for the encoding of written forms of all the languages of the world and of a wide range of additional symbols that may be used in conjunction with such languages. It is intended not only to cover languages in current use, but also languages of the past and such additions as may be required in the future. The UCS uses a 4-octet (1 octet is 8 bits) structure to represent a character. However, the most significant bit of the most significant octet is constrained to be 0, which permits its use for private internal purposes in a data processing system. The remaining 31 bits allow us to represent more than two thousand million characters. The four octets are named as follows:

- The Group-Octet, or G
- The Plane-Octet, or P
- The Row-Octet, or R
- The Cell-Octet, or C

G is the most significant octet and C is the least significant octet. So, the whole code range for UCS is viewed as a four-dimensional structure composed of

- 128 groups
- 256 planes in each group
- 256 rows in each plane
- 256 cells in each row

Two hexadecimal digits (0-9, A-F) specify the values of any octet. The values of G are restricted to the range 00-7F. The plane with G=00 and P=00 is known as the Basic Multilingual Plane (BMP). The row of BMP with R=00 represents the same set of characters as 8-bit ISO Latin-I. Therefore, the first 128 characters of ASCII, ISO Latin-1, and BMP with R=00 match. Characters 129th to 256th of ISO Latin-I and that of BMP with R=00 match. This makes UCS compatible with the existing 7-bit ASCII and 8-bit ISO Latin-I. Further, BMP has been divided into five zones.

- *A-zone:* It is used for alphabetic and symbolic scripts together with various symbols. The code position available for A-zone ranges from 0000-4DFF. The code positions 0000-001F and 0080-009F are reserved for control characters. The code position 007F is reserved for the DELETE character. Thus, it has 19903 code positions available for graphics characters.
- *I-zone:* It is used for Chinese/Japanese/Korean (CJK) unified ideographs. Its range is 4E00-9FFF, so 20992 code positions are available in this zone.
- *O-zone:* It is used for Korean Hangul syllabic scripts and for other scripts. Its range is A000-D7FF, so 14336 code positions are available in this zone.

- *S-zone:* It is reserved for use with transformation format UTF-16. The transformation format UTF-16 is described shortly. Its range is D800-DFFF, so 2048 code positions are available in this zone.

- *R-zone:* It is known as the restricted zone. It can be used only in special circumstances. One of the uses of this zone is for specific user-defined characters. However, in this case an agreement is necessary between the sender and the recipient to communicate successfully. Its range is E000-FFFD, so 8190 code positions are available in this zone.

UCS is closely related to another popular character set called Unicode, which has been prepared by the Unicode Consortium. Unicode uses a 2-octet (16 bits) coding structure and hence it can accommodate 2^{16} (= 65536) distinct characters. The Unicode can be considered as the 16-bit coding of the BMP of UCS. These two character sets, Unicode and UCS, were developed and are maintained by two different organizations. However, they cooperate to keep Unicode and UCS compatible. If a computer system uses the Unicode character set to store some text, each character in the text has to be allocated 16 bits even if all characters in the text are from the ASCII character set. Note that the first 128 characters of Unicode match with that of ASCII, and a character in ASCII can be represented only in 8-bits. So, to use 16 bits to represent all characters in Unicode is wasteful of computer memory. An alternative would be to use 8 bits for all characters from ASCII and 16 bits for characters outside the range of ASCII. However, this method of using different bits to represent different characters from Unicode has to be consistent and uniform, resulting in no ambiguity when data is stored or interchanged between different computer systems. This issue led to the development of the character encoding methods. Currently, there are four character-encoding methods specified in ISO/IEC 10646-1.

- UCS-2
- UCS-4
- UTF-16
- UTF-8

UCS-2

This is a 2-octet BMP form of encoding, which allows the use of two octets to represent a character from the BMP. This is a fixed-length encoding method. That is, each character from BMP is represented by exactly two octets.

UCS-4

This encoding method is also called the 4-octet canonical form of encoding, which uses four octets for every character in UCS. This is also a fixed-length encoding method.

UTF-16 (UCS Transformation Format 16)

Once characters outside the BMP are used, the UCS-2 encoding method cannot be applied to represent them. In this case, the encoding must switch over to use UCS-4, which will just double the use of resources, such as memory, network bandwidth, etc. The transformation format UTF-16 has been designed to avoid such a waste of memory and other resources, which would have resulted in using the UCS-4 encoding method. The UTF-16 is a variable-length encoding method. In the UTF-16 encoding method, UCS-2 is used for all characters within BMP and UCS-4 is used for encoding the characters outside BMP.

UTF-8 (UCS Transformation Format 8)

This is a variable-length encoding method, which may use 1 to 6 octets to represent a character from UCS. All ASCII characters are encoded using one octet. In the UTF-8 format of character encoding, characters are represented using one or more octets, as shown in Table A-2.

Table A-2. *List of Legal UTF-8 Sequences*

Number of Octets	Bit Patterns Used	UCS Code
1	Octet 1: 0xxxxxxx	00000000-0000007F
2	Octet 1: 110xxxxx Octet 2: 10xxxxxx	00000080-000007FF
3	Octet 1: 1110xxxx Octet 2: 10xxxxxx Octet 3: 10xxxxxx	00000800-0000FFFF
4	Octet 1: 11110xxx Octet 2: 10xxxxxx Octet 3: 10xxxxxx Octet 4: 10xxxxxx	00010000-001FFFFF
5	Octet 1: 111110xx Octet 2: 10xxxxxx Octet 3: 10xxxxxx Octet 4: 10xxxxxx Octet 5: 10xxxxxx	00200000-03FFFFFF
6	Octet 1: 1111110x Octet 2: 10xxxxxx Octet 3: 10xxxxxx Octet 4: 10xxxxxx Octet 5: 10xxxxxx Octet 6: 10xxxxxx	04000000-7FFFFFFF

The "x" in the table indicates either a 0 or a 1. Note that, in UTF-8 format, an octet that starts with a 0 bit indicates that it is representing an ASCII character. An octet starting with 110-bit combinations indicates that it is the first octet of the 2-octet representation of a character, and so on. Also note that, when an octet is part of a multi-octet character representation, the octet other than the first one starts with a 10-bit pattern. Security checks can be easily implemented for UTF-8 encoded data. UTF-8 octet sequences, which do not conform to the octet sequences shown in the table, are considered invalid.

Java and Character Encodings

Java stores and manipulates all characters and strings as Unicode characters. In serialization and byte codes, Java uses the UTF-8 encoding of the Unicode character set. All implementations of Java virtual machine are required to support the character encoding methods, as shown in Table A-3.

Table A-3. *List of the Supported Character Encodings by a JVM*

Character Encoding	Description
ASCII	7-bit ASCII (also known as ISO646-US, the basic Latin block of the Unicode character set).
ISO-8859-1	ISO Latin Alphabet No. 1 (also known as ISO-LATIN-1).
UTF-8	8-bit Unicode Transformation Format.
UTF-16BE	16-bit Unicode Transformation Format, big-endian byte order. Big-endian is discussed in Chapter 3.
UTF-16LE	16-bit Unicode Transformation Format, little-endian byte order. Little-endian is discussed in Chapter 3.
UTF-16	16-bit Unicode Transformation Format, byte-order specified by a mandatory initial byte-order mark (either order accepted on input; big-endian used on output).

Java supports UTF-8 format with the following two significant modifications:

- Java uses 16 bits to represent a NUL character in a class file, whereas standard UTF-8 uses only 8 bits. This compromise has been made to make it easier for other languages to parse a Java class file where a NUL character is not allowed within a string. However, in some cases, Java uses standard UTF-8 format to represent the NUL character.

- Java recognizes only 1-octet, 2-octet, and 3-octet UTF-8 formats, whereas standard UTF-8 format may use 1-octet, 2-octet, 3-octet, 4-octet, 5-octet, and 6-octet sequences. This is because Java supports the Unicode character set and all characters from Unicode can be represented in 1-, 2- or 3-octet formats of UTF-8.

When you compile the Java source code, by default, the Java compiler assumes that the source code file has been written using the platform's default encoding (also known as local code page or native encoding). The platform's default character encoding is Latin-1 on Windows and Solaris, and MacRoman on Mac. Note that Windows does not use true Latin-1 character encoding. It uses a variation of Latin-1 that includes fewer control characters and more printing characters. You can specify a file-encoding name (or code page name) to control how the compiler interprets characters beyond the ASCII character set. At the time of compiling your Java source code, you can pass the character-encoding name used in your source code file to Java compiler. The following command tells the Java compiler (javac) that the Java source code Test.java has been written using a traditional Chinese encoding named Big5. Now, the Java compiler will convert all characters encoded in Big5 to Unicode.

```
javac -encoding Big5 Test.java
```

The JDK includes the `native2ascii` tool, which can be used to convert files that contain other character encoding into files containing Latin-1 and/or Unicode-encoded characters. The general syntax of using `native2ascii` tool is

```
native2ascii option inputfile outputfile
```

For example, the following command converts all characters in Source.java file into Unicode-encoded characters and places the output in the Destination.java file assuming that the Source.java file has been written using the platform's default encoding:

```
native2ascii Source.java Destination.java
```

The following command converts all characters in the Source.java file into Unicode-encoded characters and places the output in the Destination.java file. It is assumed that the Source.java file has been written using Chinese Big5 encoding.

```
native2ascii -encoding Big5 Source.java Destination.java
```

The following command performs the reverse operation, that is, it converts the Source.java file with Latin-1 and/or Unicode-encoded characters to the Destination.java file with native-encoded characters:

```
native2ascii -reverse Source.java Destination.java
```

The `native2ascii` tool uses the standard output for the output if the `outputfile` name is omitted. It uses standard input for the input if the `inputfile` name is omitted too.

APPENDIX B

■ ■ ■

Documentation Comments

The Java programming language lets you include comments in the source code that can be used to prepare documentation for the application. Such comments are known as documentation comments or Javadoc comments. JDK provides a javadoc command-line tool to extract the documentation comments from the source codes and generate documentation in HTML format. The javadoc tool is located in the bin directory of the JDK_HOME directory. For example, if you have installed the JDK in C:\java9 directory, the javadoc tool will be located in the C:\java9\bin directory. Execute the javadoc tool with --help and --help-extra to see all available options.

Although a documentation comment can appear anywhere in Java source code, the javadoc tool uses only those documentation comments to generate the HTML pages that appear just before the declaration of classes, nested classes, interfaces, enums, annotations, constructors, methods, and fields. Note that the tool does not generate documentation for the documentation comments that are written for anonymous classes, package declarations, and import declarations. You need to write the documentation comments in a separate special file for a package, which will be used by the tool to generate documentation for that package.

■ **Tip**   Java SE 9 introduced a new construct called a *module*. The javadoc tool supports documentation comments in module declarations.

A documentation comment starts with the /** characters and ends with the */ characters. The leading asterisks (*) on each line of the documentation comment are ignored. The following is an example of a documentation comment that is written for the Calc class declaration:

```
// Calc.java
package com.jdojo.utility;

/**
 * A utility class to perform basic calculations on numbers. All
 * methods in this class are <code>static</code>. It provides methods
 * to perform addition, subtraction, multiplication, and division.
 *
 * @author Kishori Sharan
 */
public final class Calc {
    // Code for Calc class goes here
}
```

K. Sharan, *Beginning Java 9 Fundamentals*, https://doi.org/10.1007/978-1-4842-2902-6

It is important to note that the documentation comment must appear just before the declaration of the program element for which it is intended. Otherwise, it will be ignored by the javadoc tool or shown for the wrong element. The following two documentation comments are not the same:

```
/* Example #1 */
/**
 * This documentation comment is intended for the class declaration Xyz. However, it will be
 * ignored by the javadoc tool, because there is a package declaration between this
 * documentation comment and the Xyz class declaration. Note that a documentation comment
for a
 * package declaration is written differently and it is not written in the source code.
 */
package com.jdojo.utility;

public class Xyz {
    /* Code for Xyz class goes here */
}

/* Example #2 */
package com.jdojo.utility;

/**
 * This documentation comment is intended for the class declaration Xyz. It will be used by
the
 * javadoc tool, because it appears just before the Xyz class declaration.
 */
public class Xyz {
    /* Code for Xyz class goes here */
}
```

Writing Documentation Comments

You can write three types of comments in Java source code:

- Single-line comments
- Multi-line comments
- Documentation comments

The first two types of comments are free-form comments and they are meant for the developers to read. The third type of the comment is meant to be processed by the javadoc tool to generate HTML documents for the source code.

The textual part of the documentation comment may include HTML tags, and those tags will be interpreted as HTML in the generated HTML document. For example, to display the text "Hello" in boldface font as part of the documentation comment, you can write <b>Hello<b> as shown:

```
/**
 * You can include HTML tags in documentation comments. This will display <b>Hello</b> in
 * boldface font.
 */
```

▓ **Tip**   In Java SE 9, the `javadoc` tool supports HTML5 in documentation comments.

Apart from HTML tags, you can also use some special tags. A tag in a documentation comment is a special type of keyword that is interpreted and processed by the `javadoc` tool. Two types of tags can be used:

- Block tags

- Inline tags

A block tag is of the following form:

```
@tagName tagText
```

A block tag starts with an @ character, which is followed by the tag name. The tag text follows the tag name. The following is an example of a block tag, which uses the @author block tag and `Kishori Sharan` as the tag text:

```
@author Kishori Sharan
```

A block tag must appear at the beginning of a line in a documentation comment. Note that the asterisks, whitespace, and the /** characters are ignored by the `javadoc` tool if they appear at the beginning of a line. When I state that a block tag must appear at the beginning of a line, I mean the beginning of a line after ignoring these characters. The following is an example of using the @author and @since block tags. The @author tag lets you specify an author name and the @since tag allows you to specify the version since the API was introduced.

```
/**
 * A utility class to perform basic calculations on numbers. All methods in this class are
 * <code>static</code>. It provides methods to perform addition, subtraction, multiplication,
 * and division.
 *
 * @author Kishori Sharan
 * @since Version 1.0
 */
public final class Calc {
    // More code goes here
}
```

If a line in a documentation comment starts with an @ character, it will be interpreted as the start of a block tag. If you want to start a line with an @ character without getting it interpreted as the start of a block tag, you need to use the HTML entity &#064 instead of the @ character. However, an @ character may appear as part of the text inside a line, provided the prior character isn't a {, which is explained more next.

The associated text with a block tag may appear in multiple lines, which includes all text that follows the tag name until another block tag or the end of the documentation comment is encountered.

An inline tag can appear anywhere in the documentation comment where text can appear. It is of the form:

```
{@tagName tagText}
```

An inline tag is enclosed inside braces ({ and }). The following is an example of a documentation comment that uses a {@code text} inline tag to display the text n1 + n2 in code font:

```
/**
 * An example of inline tag. It computes {@code n1 + n2}.
 */
```

▓ **Tip**   When you are writing a documentation comment, make sure that the first sentence of the description selection of the comment is a summary sentence. The comment for a package, a class, and a member is split into two sections: a summary section and a detail section. The first sentence of the comment is displayed in the summary section and the entire comment is displayed in the detail section in the documentation.

List of Block and Inline Tags

Not all tags can be used for the documentation comment in all contexts. Table B-1 contains the list contexts and the tags that can be used in those contexts. JDK 9 has added several tags to support documentation comments on a module's declaration and to enhance the generated Javadoc. I discuss them in in subsequent sections.

Table B-1. *List of Block and Inline Tags, and the Contexts in Which They Can Be Used*

Context	Available Tags
Overview	@author, @see, @since, @serialField, @version, {@code}, {@docRoot}, {@index}, {@link}, {@linkplain}, {@literal}
Module Declaration	@author, @deprecated, @provides, @see, @since, @serialField, @uses, @version, {@code}, {@docRoot}, {@index}, {@link}, {@linkplain}, {@literal}
Package Declaration	@author, @see, @since, @serialField, @version, {@code}, {@docRoot}, {@index}, {@link}, {@linkplain}, {@literal}
Type Declaration	@author, @deprecated, @hidden, @param, @see, @since, @serialField, @version, {@code}, {@docRoot}, {@index}, {@link}, {@linkplain}, {@literal}
Constructor and Method Declaration	@deprecated, @exception, @hidden, @param, @return, @see, @since, @serialData, @throws, @version, {@code}, {@docRoot}, {@index}, {@inheritDoc}, {@link}, {@linkplain}, {@literal}
Field Declaration	@deprecated, @hidden, @see, @since, @serial, @serialField, {@code}, {@docRoot}, {@index}, {@link}, {@linkplain}, {@literal}, {@value}

The Overview context in the table may not be obvious, because there is no such construct as "overview" in the Java programming language. The javadoc tool lets you add documentation comments for the entire application in one place, which is called an overview comment. The overview comment is displayed on the overview page that is generated by the tool. I discuss an example of how to include an overview comment in the generated documentation later. The following sections describe the tags in brief.

@author <author-name(s)>

The @author tag adds the author name or names under the Author section in the documentation.
A documentation comment may contain multiple @author tags. If you have multiple author names, you can
use only one @author tag to specify all author names or you can use a separate @author tag to specify each
author name. If you use multiple @author tags, all author names will be concatenated using a locale-specific
separator and placed under one Author entry. Table B-2 shows the effects of using one and multiple @author
tags. Note that the table shows only the Author entry from the generated text.

Table B-2. *The Effects of Using One and Multiple @author Tags in Documentation Comments*

Documentation Comment	Generated Author Entry
```/** * A dummy class. * * @author Kishori Sharan */```	**Author**: Kishori Sharan
```/** * A dummy class. * * @author Kishori Sharan * @author Greg Langham * @author John Jacobs */```	**Author**: Kishori Sharan, Greg Langham, John Jacobs

@deprecated <explanation-text>

The @deprecated tag is used to generate documentation for program elements that should no longer be
used, although they may function correctly. The explanation text for this tag should explain why the program
element should not be used. If there is a replacement for the deprecated program element, the explanation
text should contain a link to or explanation about the replacement. The following documentation comment
uses the @deprecated tag for the Dummy class. It provides a link to Dummy2 class, which is the replacement
class.

```
/**
 * A dummy class.
 *
 * @deprecated As of version 1.1. Use {@link com.jdojo.utility.Dummy2 Dummy2} instead.
 */
public class Dummy {
}
```

@exception <class-name> <description>

The @exception tag is a synonym for the @throws tag. Refer to the description of the @throws tag for details.

@param <parameter-name> <description>

The @param is applicable only to classes, methods, and constructors. It generates a Parameters section with the specified parameter-name and the description. If the parameter is a type parameter, the specified parameter-name should be enclosed in angle brackets (<>). The following is an example of using the @param tags to document the parameters of a method:

```
/**
 * Returns the result of multiplication of <code>n1</code> and
 * <code>n2</code>. It may return incorrect result if the value of
 * the multiplication of <code>n1</code> and <code>n2</code> exceeds
 * the range of the <code>int</code> data type.
 *
 * @param n1 The multiplicand
 * @param n2 The multiplier
 * @return Returns the result of multiplication of <code>n1</code> and <code>n2</code>
 */
public static int multiply(int n1, int n2) {
    return n1 * n2;
}
```

The following is an example of using the @param tags to document the type parameters of a class:

```
/**
 * Wraps an object of any type.
 *
 * @param <T> Type of the object wrapped in the Wrapper
 */
public class Wrapper<T> {
    // Code for the Wrapper class goes here
}
```

@return <description>

It is valid only for methods. It adds a Returns section with the specified description. The specified description should contain the return type and the description of value that is returned from the method. Refer to the example of the @param tag to see how to use @return tag in a documentation comment.

@see <reference>

It adds a See Also section with a link or text that points to the specified reference. A documentation comment can have multiple @see tags. All @see tags will be displayed under one See Also section for a documentation comment. You can specify the reference in one of the three following forms:

```
@see "text"
@see <a href="URL">label</a>
@see package.Classname#member label
```

In the first form, the reference is specified as text that is enclosed in double quotes. The javadoc tool adds the specified text in the See Also section, without any link.

In the second form, the reference is specified using an HTML anchor tag (<a> tag). The javadoc tool generates a hyperlink that points to the specified URL. If specified, the specified label is displayed as the link text.

In the third form, the reference is specified to a class, an interface, a field, a constructor, or a method. Note that if you are referencing a field, a constructor, or a method, its name is preceded by a hash sign (#), not a dot. The javadoc tool generates a link to the reference that has the specified label as the visible text. The label is optional. If label is omitted, the tool uses a suitable text for the link that is derived from the first argument to the @see tag. The reference to the program element could use the fully qualified name or a partial name. The tool uses the same rules as the Java compiler to resolve the partial name of a program element.

The following is an example of how to use different forms of the @see tag. It assumes that Calc class is in the same package as the Dummy class and the Calc class contains the add() and multiply() methods.

```
package com.jdojo.utility;

/**
 * A dummy class.
 *
 * @see "Online Java Tutorial"
 * @see <a href="http://www.oracle.com">Oracle Website</a>
 * @see com.jdojo.utility.Calc Calculator
 * @see com.jdojo.utility.Calc#add(int, int) Add Method
 * @see com.jdojo.utility.Calc#multiply(int, int)
 */
public class Dummy {
}
```

The generated See Also section for the Dummy class would look as shown:

See Also:
```
"Online Java Tutorial" Oracle Website, Calculator, Add Method,
        Calc.multiply(int, int)
```

@serial <field-description or include/exclude>

The javadoc tool generates a Serialized Form page that contains all pieces of information about serialized forms of all serialized classes. The tool creates a See Also section for serialized classes that contains a link to the Serialized Form page. A class needs to implement java.io.Serializable or java.io.Externalizable interface to be added to the Serialized Form page.

The @serial tag is used to add a description for default serializable fields of a class. The specified description will be added to the Serialized Form page for the field. The following is an example of using the @serial tag for a field:

```
/**
 * A dummy class.
 */
public class Dummy implements java.io.Serializable {
    /**
     * @serial The description for value field goes here
     */
    private int value;
}
```

You may include or exclude a package or a class from appearing on the Serialized Form page by using the include or exclude argument with the @serial tag. If the @serial tag is used at both package and class levels, the class-level tag takes precedence. By default, a serializable class that is public or protected is included in the Serialized Form page. The following documentation comment excludes the Dummy class from the Serialized Form page:

```
/**
 * A dummy class. It will not appear on the serialized Form page.
 *
 * @serial exclude
 */
public class Dummy implements java.io.Serializable {
    /**
     * @serial The description for value field goes here
     */
    private int value;
}
```

@serialData <data-description>

A class that implement java.io.Externalizable interface needs to implement the readExternal() and writeExternal() methods. A serializable class may also implement the writeObject(), readObject(), writeReplace(), and readResolve() methods to customize the serialization of the objects of the class. The @serialData tag may be used with the documentation comments of any of these six methods. The data description text should describe the types and the order of the data in the serialized form.

@serialField <field-name> <field-type> <field-description>

A serializable class can include a serialPersistentFields field that is an array of ObjectStreamField. The @serialField tag describes each component of that array. The description of the elements will appear in the Serialized Form page. The following documentation comment uses @serialField tags to document the name and the height components of the ObjectStreamField:

```
package com.jdojo.utility;

import java.io.ObjectStreamField;
import java.io.Serializable;

/**
 * A class to represent a person
 */
public class Person implements Serializable {
    private String name;
    private String gender;
    private double height;
```

```
    /**
     * @serialField name String The name of the person
     * @serialField height double The height of the person in feet
     */
    private static final ObjectStreamField[] serialPersistentFields
            = {new ObjectStreamField("name", String.class),
                new ObjectStreamField("height", double.class)
                };
}
```

@since <description>

The @since tag adds a Since section to the documentation. The specified description indicates the release of the software that added the program element being documented. The following documentation comment shows how to use the @since tag:

```
/**
 * A dummy class.
 *
 * @since 1.0
 */
public class Dummy {
}
```

@throws <class-name> <description>

The @throws tag is a synonym for the @exception tag. It adds a Throws section to the documentation. It is used to describe an exception that may be thrown from a constructor or a method. Multiple @throws tags can be used in a documentation comment. If a method throws a checked exception and there is no @throws tag, the javadoc tool will add one without a description to make sure that all checked exceptions are documented. The following documentation comment for the divide() method shows how to use the @throws tag. If you do not provide the fully qualified name of the class, the javadoc tool will use the same search order as used by the Java compiler to resolve the partial class name.

```
/**
 * Returns the result of integer division of <code>n1</code> by
 * <code>n2</code>.
 *
 * @param n1 The dividend
 * @param n2 The divisor
 * @return Returns the result of <code>n1 / n2</code>
 * @throws ArithmeticException If <code>n2</code> is zero.
 */
public static int divide(int n1, int n2) throws ArithmeticException {
    return n1 / n2;
}
```

@version <version-text>

The `@version` tag adds a `Version` section to the generated documentation. The version text should contain the current version of the program element. The `@since` tag is used to specify the version of the software when a program element was added, whereas the `@version` tag is used to specify the current version. The following documentation comment shows how to use the `@version` tag:

```
/**
 * A dummy class.
 *
 * @since 1.0
 * @version 1.6
 */
public class Dummy {
}
```

{@code <text>}

It displays the specified text in code font without interpreting the text as HTML markup or nested documentation comments tag. It is equivalent to the following:

```
<code>{@literal <text>}</code>
```

{@docRoot}

It resolves to the relative path of the root directory of the generated documents. It is used in the URL part of links. Suppose you have a file called `myfiles/copyright.html` that is located under the root directory of the generated documents. If you want to include a link to the `copyright.html` file in your documentation comment, you can do the following:

```
/**
 * A dummy class.  Please read
 * the <a href="{@docRoot}/myfiles/copyright.html">Copyright</a> page.
 */
public class Dummy {
}
```

{@inheritDoc}

It copies the documentation of a method from the nearest inheritable class or the implementable interface. Note that for this tag to copy the documentation, the method in which this tag appears must override a method in its parent class or implement a method of the implemented interfaces.

This tag may be used only inside the main description in the documentation comment for a method or inside the text argument of `@return`, `@param`, and `@throws` tags for a method. If it appears inside the main description, it copies the main description of the overridden method. If it appears in other tag's text, it copies the tag's text from the overridden method.

If a method overrides a method in the parent class or implements a method of an interface, the `javadoc` tool automatically copies the documentation for the main description, `@return`, `@param`, and `@throws` if the main description of these tags is missing in the overriding method.

The following documentation comment demonstrates the use of the {@ inheritDoc} tag. It is used inside the documentation comment for the getId() method of the SmartPerson class. It is used inside the main description as well as the text section of the @return tag. Note that the @param tag is missing from the getId() method of the SmartPerson class. The javadoc tool will automatically copy the documentation for the @param tag from the getId() method of the Person class.

```
/**
 * A class to represent a person
 */
public class Person {
    /**
     * Returns the person id.
     * @param x The value to add to the id
     * @return The person id.
     */
    public int getId(int x) {
        return x + 10;
    }
}

/**
 * A class to represent a smart person
 */
public class SmartPerson extends Person {
    /**
     * {@inheritDoc}
     * @return {@inheritDoc}
     */
    public int getId(int x) {
        return 20 + x;
    }
}
```

The generated documentation for the getId() method of the SmartPerson class is as follows:

```
getId
public int getId(int x)
    Returns the person id.

    Overrides:
    getId in class Person

    Parameters:
    x - The value to add to the id

    Returns:
    The person id.
```

{@link <package.class#member> <label>}

It inserts an inline link with the specified label as the text for the link. This tag generates a link that is similar to the link generated by one of the forms of the @see tag. The main difference between the two are that this tag is an inline tag, whereas the @see tag is a block tag. The following documentation comment shows how to use this tag. The use of the following tag will create a link with the text add, which will point to the documentation of the add() method of the Calc class.

```
/**
 * A dummy class.  Please see
 * {@link com.jdojo.utility.Calc#add(int, int) add} method of the
 * Calc class to learn how to add two integers.
 *
 */
public class Dummy {
}
```

{@linkplain <package.class#member> <label>}

It works similarly to the {@link} tag, except that it displays the label for the link in plain text, whereas the {@link} displays the label for the link in code font. Refer to the description of the {@link} tag for more details.

{@literal <text>}

It displays the specified text without interpreting it as HTML markup or a nested documentation comment tag. Note that HTML tags are enclosed in angle brackets (<>). If you want to use angle brackets in documentation comments, you need to use the HTML entities < and >. If you do not want to use HTML entities, you can use this tag with your raw text. For example, it is valid to write {@literal x < y} anywhere in the documentation comment rather than writing x < y.

{@value <package.class#field>}

It is used to copy the value of a static and final field (a constant field). If it is used without the argument, it copies the value of the constant field at its location. The following documentation comments show how to use {@value} tag. In the documentation comment for the MULTIPLIER field, it uses the {@value} tag without an argument, which will insert the value of the MULTIPLIER field. In the documentation comment for the DIVISOR field, it uses both forms of the {@value} tag, one with an argument and one without an argument. The argument, #MULTIPLIER, refers to the MULTIPLIER field of the same class.

```
/**
 * A dummy class.
 */
public class Dummy {
    /**
     * The MULTIPLIER is {@value}
     */
    public static final int MULTIPLIER = 2000;
```

```
    /**
     * The value of MULTIPLIER is {@value #MULTIPLIER}.
     * The value of DIVISOR is {@value}.
     */
    public final static int DIVISOR = 1000;
}
```

The following is the generated documentation comment that shows the effects of using the {@value} tag:

MULTIPLIER
```
public static final int MULTIPLIER
```

The MULTIPLIER is 2000

DIVISOR
```
public static final int DIVISOR
```

The value of MULTIPLIER is 2000. The value of DIVISOR is 1000.

@hidden

JDK 9 introduced the @hidden block tag. It hides a program element from the generated API documentation. There are ways to hide program elements from the generated Javadoc; for example, all private members of a type are not part of the Javadoc unless you specify the option with the javadoc tool to include them. Use the @hidden tag to hide program elements, which is otherwise not possible to be excluded using any other options. Typically, I create a Test class in each module to test my logic when I work on a chapter. I can hide the Test class from appearing in the Javadoc using the @hidden tag as shown:

```
// Test.java
package com.jdojo.utility;

/**
 * @hidden
 */
public class Test {
    public static void main(String[] args) {
        // Code goes here
    }
}
```

{@index <keyword> <description>}

JDK 9 introduced the @index inline tag. It can be used to tell the javadoc tool to index a keyword. It can appear in Javadoc as follows:

```
{@index <keyword> <description>}
```

Here, `<keyword>` is the keyword to be indexed and `<description>` is the keyword's description. If the keyword is a phrase consisting of multiple words, enclose it in double quotes. The following Javadoc tag is an example of using the @index tag with a keyword, jdojo:

```
{@index jdojo Info site (www.jdojo.com) for the Java 9 Revealed book!}.
```

@provides <service-type> <description>

JDK 9 introduced the @provides block tag. You can use it only in a module's declaration. It documents an implementation of a service provided by the module. The description may specify how to obtain an instance of this service provider and other details of the provider. The following declaration of a module shows an example.

```
/**
 * @provides com.jdojo.prime.PrimeChecker Provides a generic implementation for the
PrimeChecker
 *                                        service.
 */
module jdojo.prime.generic {
    requires com.jdojo.prime;

    provides com.jdojo.prime.PrimeChecker with com.jdojo.generic.GenericPrimeChecker;
}
```

@uses <service-type> <description>

JDK 9 introduced the @uses block tag. You can use it only in a module's declaration. It documents that a service may be used by this module. The description may specify the details of the provider. The following declaration of a module shows an example.

```
/**
 * @uses com.jdojo.prime.PrimeChecker Loads the PrimeChecker services
 */
module jdojo.prime {
    exports com.jdojo.prime;

    uses com.jdojo.prime.PrimeChecker;
}
```

Documenting Packages

A package declaration appears multiple times in an application. There needs to be a simpler and separate way to document a package. You can document a package by placing either of the following two files, but not both, in the package directory along with the source files (`.java` files):

- `package-info.java`
- `package.html`

▓ **Tip**   If both `package-info.java` and `package.html` files are available, the `package-info.java` file is used.

When you run the `javadoc` tool, it automatically uses the documentation in one of these two files as the documentation for your package. The first sentence of the package documentation should be a summary statement about the package. The first sentence of the package documentation is displayed in the package summary description.

com/jdojo/utility/package-info.java file

It contains the package declaration with documentation comments for a package. In a `package-info.java` file, a package is documented the same way as any other program elements are documented. The content of the `package-info.java` file for the `com.jdojo.utility` package is as follows:

```
/**
 * Contains utility classes. More description for
 * com.jdojo.utility package goes here.
 * @since 1.1
 * @version 2.0
 */
package com.jdojo.utility;
```

com/jdojo/utility/package.html file

It is a regular HTML file with HTML tags. The HTML contents within the <body> and </body> tags are used as the package documentation. It does not contain a package declaration. It does not use the /** and */ characters as the start and end of the documentation comment. However, you can use documentation tags that are valid for the package. The content of the `package.html` file for `com.jdojo.utility` package is as shown:

```
<html>
    <body>
        Contains utility classes. More description for
        com.jdojo.utility package goes here.
        @since 1.1
        @version 2.0
    </body>
</html>
```

Overview Documentation

The overview documentation is used to write documentation for the entire application in a separate HTML file. There is no rule for naming the overview documentation file. Generally, it is named as `overview.html`. The comment is placed inside the `<body>` and `</body>` tags in the HTML file. You need to pass the path of this file to the `javadoc` tool using the `-overview` command-line option. The following is a sample overview comment contained in an HTML file:

```
<html>
<body>
    API documentation for the dummy application. More overview text goes here.
    @author Kishori Sharan
    @version 2.0
</body>
</html>
```

Including Unprocessed Files in Documentation

Sometimes you may want to include some files with your Java documentation, which you reference inside the documentation comments. For example, you may want to display graphics or source code. The `javadoc` tool lets you include files, which it copies to the generated documentation directory without processing them. You need to create a directory called `doc-files` under any package directory that contains `.java` source files and copy your extra files in that directory. The `javadoc` tool will copy all your files to the destination directory without processing them.

Skipping Source Files Processing

Sometimes you may have some Java source files that you do not want the `javadoc` tool to process. For example, you may have some test files for which you do not want to generate documentation. The `javadoc` tool looks at the file name before it decides to process the content of the file. If the file name is not a valid Java identifier, it skips that file. If you have a `.java` source file, which the `javadoc` tool should skip, you need to name that file such that the name is not a valid Java identifier. For example, you may include a hyphen (`-`) in the file name to skip it. Note that this strategy of skipping source file processing is needed when you are using the `javadoc` tool to generate documentation by passing it wildcards (`*`) or package name. If you supply the `javadoc` tool the list of source files to process, you do not need to use this strategy.

An Example of Documentation Comments

Listing B-1 contains the declaration of `com.jdojo` module with documentation comments. Listing B-2 contains the source code for a `Calc` class. It is a trivial class. Its purpose is only to demonstrate how to write documentation comments. It uses many of the tags I discussed earlier. Note the use of the `@index` tag in the documentation comment for the `Calc` class, which will make the term `jdojo` searchable in the generated Javadoc. The term `jdojo` is also searchable because it is part of many modules and packages.

Listing B-1. The Declaration of a jdojo.utility Module

```java
// module-info.java
/**
 * A utility module that shows you how to use documentation comments.
 *
 * @author Kishori SHaran
 * @since 2.0
 */
module jdojo.utility {
    exports com.jdojo.utility;
}
```

Listing B-2. Calc Class Source Code with Documentation Comment

```java
// Calc.java
package com.jdojo.utility;

/**
 * A utility class to perform basic calculations on numbers.
 * All methods in this class are <code>static</code>. It
 * provides methods to perform addition, subtraction,
 * multiplication and division.
 *
 * {@index jdojo Visit www.jdojo.com for more info on Beginning Java 9 Fundamentals book!}
 *
 * @author Kishori Sharan
 * @since Version 1.0
 */
public final class Calc {
    /**
     * Stop someone from instantiating this class. This class is not
     * meant for instantiation as all its methods are
     * <code>static</code>.
     */
    private Calc() {
    }

    /**
     * Performs addition on two numbers. It returns the result of
     * <code> n1 + n2 </code>as an <code>int</code>. If the result
     * of <code>n1 + n2</code> exceeds the range of the
     * <code>int</code> data type, it will not return the correct
     * result. For bigger numbers, use {@link #add(long, long)}.
     *
     * @param n1 The first number
     * @param n2 The second number
     * @return Returns the value of <code>n1 + n2</code>
     */
```

```java
public static int add(int n1, int n2) {
    return n1 + n2;
}

/**
 * Performs addition on two numbers. It returns the result of
 * <code>n1 + n2</code> as a <code>long</code>.
 *
 * @param n1 The first number
 * @param n2 The second number
 * @return Returns the value of <code>n1 + n2</code>
 */
public static long add(long n1, long n2) {
    return n1 + n2;
}

/**
 * Returns the result of <code>n1 - n2</code>.
 *
 * @param n1 The first number
 * @param n2 The second number
 * @return Returns the result of <code>n1 - n2</code>
 */
public static int subtract(int n1, int n2) {
    return n1 - n2;
}

/**
 * Returns the result of multiplication of <code>n1</code> and
 * <code>n2</code>. It may return incorrect result if the value of
 * the multiplication of <code>n1</code> and <code>n2</code>
 * exceeds the range of the <code>int</code> data type.
 *
 * @param n1 The multiplicand
 * @param n2 The multiplier
 * @return Returns the result of multiplication of
 *         <code>n1</code> and <code>n2</code>
 */
public static int multiply(int n1, int n2) {
    return n1 * n2;
}

/**
 * Returns the result of integer division of <code>n1</code> by
 * <code>n2</code>.
 *
 * @param n1 The dividend
 * @param n2 The divisor
 * @return Returns the result of <code>n1 / n2</code>
 * @throws ArithmeticException If <code>n2</code> is zero.
 */
```

```
    public static int divide(int n1, int n2) throws ArithmeticException {
        return n1 / n2;
    }
}
```

Running the javadoc Tool

You need to run the javadoc command-line tool to generate HTML pages for your documentation comments in the source files (.java files). In JDK 9, the javadoc tool has been enhanced to work with modules. It is easier to generate the Javadoc for multiple modules, if you place the source code for all your modules into one directory, which contains a subdirectory named after each module. In the source code supplied with this book, I created a directory Java9Fundamentals/docsrc, which contains the source code for the jdojo.utility and jdojo.jshell modules. The contents of the docsrc subdirectory is as follows. For these examples of running the javadoc tool, I assume that the following files contain documentation comments:

- Java9Fundamentals/docsrc/jdojo.jshell/com/jdojo/jshell/JShellApiTest.java
- Java9Fundamentals/docsrc/jdojo.jshell/com/jdojo/jshell/Person.java
- Java9Fundamentals/docsrc/jdojo.jshell/module-info.java
- Java9Fundamentals/docsrc/jdojo.utility/com/jdojo/utility/Calc.java
- Java9Fundamentals/docsrc/jdojo.utility/com/jdojo/utility/package-info.java
- Java9Fundamentals/docsrc/jdojo.utility/module-info.java
- Java9Fundamentals/docsrc/overview.html

The overview.html file is the overview documentation file for the documentation. There is a package-info.java file for the com.jdojo.utility package. Calc.java is a Java source file. The module-info.java file contains the module declaration for the jdojo.utility module. If you copied the source code for this book in C:\Java9Fundamentals, the C:\Java9Fundamentals\docsrc directory contains the .java source files for the two modules. The syntax to run the javadoc tool is as follows:

```
javadoc [options] [@args-file-paths]
```

[options] is zero or more command-line options for the javadoc tool. Options are used to customize the output. For example, the -d option lets you specify the output directory where the javadoc tool will store all generated output files and the --module option lets you specify the names of the modules whose documentation you want to generate.

The <@args-file-paths> lets you include arguments for the tool in files. Sometimes the comment text for the javadoc tool becomes too big. Some command prompts have limitations on how many characters can be entered as part of a command. In those circumstances, you can place the command-line arguments in one or more arguments files and supply those argument file paths as the arguments to the javadoc tool. Note that the arguments file path is preceded by the @ sign. The javadoc tool does not support -J options and wildcards (*) in an argument file.

▓ **Tip**   The javadoc tool provides many options to customize the generated output files. To list all options, you can run it using the --help option. You can use a -J-version option to print the version of the javadoc tool.

The following command will generate Javadoc for you:

```
C:\Java9Fundamentals>javadoc -d docs -html5 -author -version --module-source-path docsrc
--module jdojo.utility,jdojo.jshell -overview docsrc\overview.html
```

Here are the details of each part in the command:

- The current directory is C:\Java9Fundamentals.

- The -d docs option specifies that the generated Javadoc should be copied to the C:\Java9Fundamentals\docs directory.

- The -html5 option specifies that the generated output should be in HTML 5. This option was added in Java 9.

- By default, the javadoc tool does not generate documentation for the @author and @version tags. The -author and -version options instruct the tool to include the text for the @author and @version tags in the generated documentation, respectively.

- The --module-source-path docsrc option specifies that the source for modules is in the C:\Java9Fundamentals\docsrc directory.

- The --module jdojo.utility,jdojo.jshell option indicates that you want to generate Javadoc for the two modules—jdojo.utility and jdojo.jshell. If you want to generate Javadoc for more modules, place their source code in the docsrc directory and include their names in this list.

- The -overview docsrc\overview.html option specifies the location of the HTML file that contains the overview comment for the application for which you are generating the Javadoc.

You can use one or more argument files to store all the arguments to the javadoc tool. Note that -J options and wildcards (*) are not supported in argument files. You must use the command line to enter these two types of arguments. Suppose the following is the contents of a file named args.txt, which is placed in the C:\Java9Fundamentals directory:

```
-d docs
-html5
-author
-version
--module-source-path docsrc
--module jdojo.utility,jdojo.jshell
-overview docsrc\overview.html
```

You can run the javadoc tool that will use arguments from the args.txt file, as shown here. All relative paths in the argument file are resolved with respect to the current directory.

```
C:\Java9Fundamentals>javadoc @args.txt
```

You can split the arguments for the javadoc into multiple files. You can pass multiple argument files to the javadoc tool by separating them by a space, as shown here. Options can be distributed among multiple argument files in any order. You can use a relative path (e.g., args.txt) or the absolute path (e.g., C:\ Java9Fundamentals\args.txt) of the argument file to the javadoc tool.

```
C:\projects>javadoc @args1.txt @args2.txt @args3.txt
```

The NetBeans IDE lets you generate Javadoc for your project. On the Properties dialog box for your project, choose Build --> Documenting to get the Javadoc properties sheet, where you can specify all options for the javadoc tool. To generate the Javadoc, select Generate Javadoc from the right-click menu options for your project or from the Run menu.

Generated Documentation Files

The javadoc tool generates many HTML files. All generated files can be classified into three categories:

- Files for modules, classes, interfaces, enums, annotations, packages, and overviews

- Files to cross-reference some pieces of information from one HTML page to another, such as an index page, a class hierarchy page for each package, a use page for each package, etc.

- Support files

The tool generates one HTML file per class/interface/enum/annotation. The files are placed in directories that mimic the package hierarchies of classes, interfaces, enums, and annotations. The file names are the same as the program elements for which they contain the documentation. A package-summary.html file is included in every package directory that contains package documentation. An overview-summary. html file is generated for all packages to serve as overview documentation. Separate pages are generated for modules.

The generated HTML pages include the class hierarchy pages, a deprecated API page, constants values pages, serialized forms pages, etc. These files have self-explanatory names and they contain a hyphen in their names. Support files include any image files, a help-doc.html file to describe the generated documentation files, etc.

Viewing Generated HTML Documentation

You can view the documentation generated by the javadoc tool in an HTML page using HTML frames or with no frames. The javadoc tool generates an index.html file, which is placed at the root in the output directory. You need to open the index.html file in a browser, for example, Microsoft Internet Explorer, Google Chrome, Mozilla Firefox, Safari, etc., to view the documentation using HTML frames. You can click the FRAMES and NO FRAMES links at any time to switch between HTML frames and no frames view of the documentation. The HTML frames are organized as shown in Figure B-1.

Figure B-1. *Arrangement of the HTML frames that are generated by the javadoc tool*

Figure B-2 shows the `index.html` page opened in Frames mode for the Javadoc that you created. It shows the Javadoc for the `Calc` class in the `com.jdojo.utility` package.

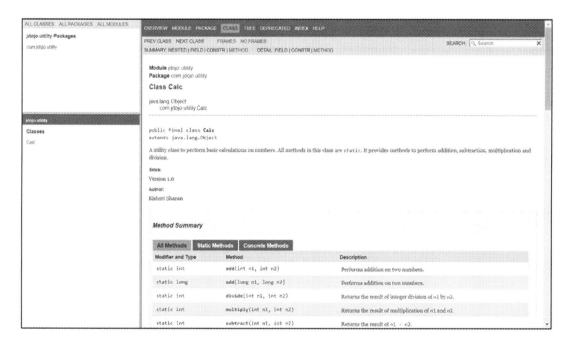

Figure B-2. *The generated HTML page for the Calc class*

In Frames mode, the `index.html` page contains three frames:

- A `Modules/Packages` frame at top-left
- A `Classes` frame at bottom-left
- A `Details` frame at right

The top-left frame contains the list of all classes, all packages, and all modules. The navigation bar contains links to switch between these views in the top-left frame. If the documentation that you generate contains only one package, this frame is not generated. That is, you must generate documentation for at least two packages in order for the `javadoc` tool to generate the `Modules/Packages` frame. In the upper-left frame, you can view all packages or all modules. When you click on a module, the upper-left frame displays all packages in that module. The navigation bar in the bottom-left frame display a link with the selected module or package as the text. When you click this link, the Details frame displays the documentation for the module or the package.

The bottom-left frame contains the list of classes, interfaces, enums, exceptions, and annotations in a package that is selected from the Module/Packages frame. The frame on the right side displays the details of the selection from the left frames.

Searching Javadoc

Consider this scenario. You are looking for logic to implement something in Java and you find a piece of code on the Internet, which uses a class, but does not show the import statement importing that class. You have access to the Javadoc for Java SE and you want to know little more about the class. How do you get the package name of the class, which is needed to get to the documentation of the class? You search the Internet again. This time, search for the class name, which might get you a link to the Javadoc for the class. Alternatively, you can copy and paste the piece of code in a Java IDE such as NetBeans and Eclipse, and the IDE will help you generate the import statements to give you the package name of the class. Don't worry about this inconvenience of searching for the package name of a class in Java 9.

There is another addition to the Details frame in the Javadoc generated by the javadoc tool. All pages in this frame display a Search box on the top-right (see Figure B-2). The search box lets you search the Javadoc. The javadoc tool prepares an index of terms that can be searched. To know what is searchable, you need to know the terms that are indexed:

- You can search for declared names of modules, packages, types, and members. The type of formal parameters of constructors and methods are indexed, but not the names of those parameters. So, you can search on the type of formal parameter. If you enter "(String, int, int)" in the search box, it will find you the list of constructors and methods that take three formal parameters of String, int, and int. If you enter "util" as a search term, it will show you a list of all packages, types, and members that contain the term "util" in their names.

- You can search for all keywords and phrases specified with an @index inline tag.

Everything else that is not listed in this list is not searchable using the Javadoc search box. The search box displays the found results as a list when you enter the search term. The results list is divided into categories such as Modules, Packages, Types, Members, and SearchTags. The SearchTags category contains results found from the indexed keywords that are specified using @index tags.

░ **Tip**   The Javadoc search does not support regular expressions. The entered search keyword is searched for its occurrence anywhere in the indexed terms.

Figure B-3 shows using the Javadoc search box with the list of results. I generated the Javadoc for the com.jdojo.utility module and used it to search for jdojo, as shown on the left of the figure. I used the Javadoc for Java SE 9 to search for the term, Module, as shown on the right of the figure.

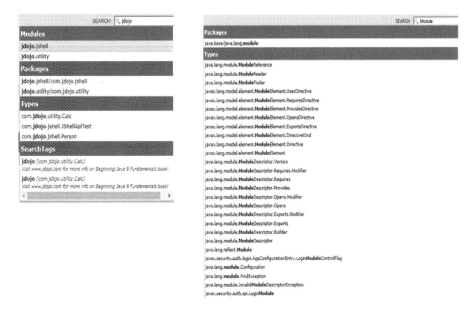

Figure B-3. *The Javadoc search box with keywords and searched results*

You can use the Up and Down arrow keys to navigate through the search results. You can view the details of the search results in one of the following two ways:

- Click on a search result to open the Javadoc for that topic.

- When a search result is highlighted using the Up/Down arrows, press Enter to open the details about that topic.

▓ **Tip** You can use the -noindex option with the javadoc tool to disable the Javadoc search. No index will be generated and no search box will be available in the generated Javadoc.

A Javadoc search is performed locally using client-side JavaScript. There is no computation or search logic implemented in the server. If you have disabled JavaScript in your browser, you will not be able to use the Javadoc search feature.

Summary

Java allows writing comments in source code that can be used to generate documentation. The documentation comment starts with /** and ends with */. The javadoc tool, which is included in the JDK, is used to extract and generate the documentation comments from source code. The tool generates documentation in HTML format. The tool contains support for many custom tags with special meaning. It also lets you use HTML tags inside the documentation.

Apart from HTML tags, you can also use some special tags. A tag in a documentation comment is a special type of keywords that is interpreted and processed by the javadoc tool. Two types of tags can be used: block tags and inline tags.

A block tag starts with an @ character, which is followed by the tag name. The tag text follows the tag name. A block tag must appear at the beginning of a line in a documentation comment. Note that the asterisks, whitespace, and the /** characters are ignored by the javadoc tool if they appear at the beginning of a line.

An inline tag can appear anywhere in the documentation comment where text can appear. An inline tag is enclosed in braces.

JDK 9 introduced the following new Javadoc tags: @hidden, @provides, @uses, and {@index}. The @hidden tag hides a program element in the generated Javadoc. The @provides and @uses tags are used only on module declarations to document the services provided and used by modules. The {@index} tag is used to specify a searchable keyword in the Javadoc.

JDK 9 adds a Search box at the top-right of each page. You can search for program element names and the keywords specified with the {@index} tag. If you do not want the Search box to appear in the generated Javadoc, use the -noindex option with the javadoc tool. JDK 9 has also added several new options for the javadoc tool to work with modules.

Index

D